ARCTIC OCEAN

SIBERIA

RUSSIAN EMPIRE

SWEDEN

FINLAND

NY. POLAND
AUSTRIA-
HUNGARY
SERVIA RUMAN
MONT BULG
NIS GREECE
TURKEY
IPOLI
EGYPT
UDAN
ABYSSINIA
CONGO
STATE
PORT.
W.
AFRICA
GER.
S.W.
Af.
RHODESIA
BR.
BECH.
LAND
ORANGE TR.
FREE ST. VAAL
CAPE
COLONY

PERSIA
AFGHANISTAN
ARABIA
MUSCAT
OMAN
ADEN
BR. EAST
AFRICA
GER.
EAST
AFRICA
PORT. E. AFRICA

MONGOLIA

MANCHURIA

CHINESE
EMPIRE

KOREA

JAPANESE
EMPIRE

TIBET

BHUTAN
NEPAL
INDIA
BURMA
FR. INDO-CHINA
SIAM
MALAYA

PHILIPPINE
IS.

PACIFIC

OCEAN

MADAGASCAR

SUMATRA
BORNEO
DUTCH EAST INDIES
NEW GUINEA
Dutch German
British

INDIAN

OCEAN

COMMONWEALTH OF
AUSTRALIA

TASMANIA

NEW
ZEALAND

*A History of the World*
*in the Twentieth Century*

# A HISTORY

# OF THE WORLD

# IN THE TWENTIETH

# CENTURY

*D. C. Watt*

*Frank Spencer*

*Neville Brown*

SCOTT, FORESMAN AND COMPANY

First published in Great Britain in 1967.
Published in the United States in 1968.

Part I copyright © 1967 by D. C. Watt

Part II copyright © 1967 by Frank Spencer

Part III copyright © 1967 by Neville Brown

Printed in the United States of America.

# CONTENTS

6

**PART TWO**
1918-1945
Frank Spencer

8

11

12

13

# LIST OF MAPS

# PREFACE

In writing this book, we have attempted to compose a history of the world seen as a whole. That is to say, we have started with the assumption that in this century most of the barriers and divisions which made different areas of the world into selfcontained compartments, whose histories could be studied in isolation since the events which they recorded were not influenced by any causes from outside each individual area, most of these barriers, we say, have disappeared. In this century the chain of causation in each area can as well originate outside as within it. The divisions are down, the old compartments unreal. In Wendell Wilkie's phrase, it is one world.

For the historian this assumption, if defensible, is at first an unwelcome one. The study of history has become more specialized because of the increasing range of source materials and the growing variety of languages needed to study them, not to speak of their sheer volume. For example the records of the German Foreign Ministry for the years 1880–1936 which were captured by the Allies in 1945 comprised some 400 tons of documents. And this is only one source for today's diplomatic historians. To command the source materials of a single major area of the world even within the last sixty-seven years takes a considerable part of a historian's career. And it is only through such specialization, or so it is believed, that the historian learns his craft.

For this reason much of what has come to pass as world history is not written as such. Rather it appears as a series of short histories of its major component areas, a chapter on France, a chapter on Russia, a chapter on India, a chapter on China.

In contrast, what we have attempted to do is to weave together the histories of the separate states and areas so as to make one history of them. Inevitably this has imposed certain limitations on the scope of our study. Our history concentrates on the political events of the world since 1900. That is, it concerns itself mainly with the political and power relationships between the recognized component political units of the twentieth century world. Events in the sphere of economics, technology, ideas, demography are of importance to this study only in so far as they affect or have affected the course of political developments.

Secondly, our history inevitably focuses more on the international aspects of world history, since it is in the relations between states that the stuff of a world history must soon be found. This restriction has proved less hampering than might have been thought, since in this century no state, no political unit, is an island to itself. Inevitably, however, some things will have been omitted. Thus out of necessity some details of purely parochial interest must fail to appear on so broad a canvas, even though we have preferred the attention to detail of a Peter Breughel rather than the broad impressions of a Turner or a Cézanne.

17

Lastly, this book is written in the belief, which is not purely confined to its authors, that nationalism has too long made slaves of the historical profession. The historian now has to try to single out not those events which are peculiar to each political unit, but those common to them: to concentrate not on the unique but the common characteristics. Other more senior historians have pointed the way. It is our hope that this book will encourage others to follow. Although economics, war and technology have made us one world, men still believe that history has made them uniquely different from others. Such beliefs will continue to keep the world divided. If men wish to believe in their uniqueness, that is their affair and their blindness but it is no business of the historian to organize his work so as to lend them support. True history cannot serve the partisans of a creed, a nation, an ideology or a race.

The authors would like to express their thanks to Dr Frank O. Marzari, now of the University of British Columbia for his help in the preparation of the statistical tables, to Mr R. Urwin, who compiled the index, and to Mr A. Spark, who drew the maps.

D. C. Watt<br>
Frank Spencer<br>
Neville Brown

# PART ONE
## 1899-1918
## D. C. WATT

# SECTION ONE    THE WORLD ON THE EVE OF THE TWENTIETH CENTURY: EUROPE AT ITS ZENITH

## Chapter I
## EUROPE AND THE EXTERNAL WORLD

*Introduction*

A MARTIAN visiting our world in 1900 could have been forgiven for regarding it as completely dominated by Europe. Six European powers, Britain, France, Germany, Austria-Hungary, Italy and Russia bestrode the globe. Their fleets policed the oceans. Their soldiers, explorers, traders and missionaries were busy bringing under Europe's sway the last areas of Asia and Africa. The last great non-European empires, Ottoman Turkey and Manchu China, were falling apart under the impact of those Europeans they had so long regarded as infidels and barbarians. Japan in the Far East and the United States in the western hemisphere counted as powers in their own parts of the world. But elsewhere only a few isolated statelets, like Abyssinia in Africa or Siam in South-East Asia, retained their independence; and they owed their survival only to the agreement of the great powers of Europe that to recognize their independence was a better course than to fight over their possession.

Our Martian visitor might, it is true, have balked a little at counting Russia as truly European. And, traversing the Pacific, he might well have been equally hesitant at counting Japan and the United States as parts of the European system. But a closer look would have shown him that all three were firmly tied into the European system by the web of capital investment and trade which financed and furthered the massive economic expansion through which they were passing. In Japan he would have recognized a state which had embraced European political models as firmly as it had adopted European weapons and money. And both in America and Russia he would have found the ruling *élites* thoroughly Europeanized, often educated at European universities, such as Oxford, the Sorbonne, Heidelberg or Uppsala, and regular visitors to Paris, London and the spas of Central Europe. In the salons of St Petersburg he would have been addressed in the language of Paris. In New York he would have been more conscious of the influence of London. But in both countries he would have easily recognized opposed wings of the great central spread of European culture and power. Moreover when he returned to London and Paris he would have discovered that each of the two countries, Russia and America, were in turn beginning to contribute their share towards the enrichment of Europe's culture. Within ten years of his visit, in fact, Dostoevski, Pushkin and Tolstoy, Chekov, Borodin and Moussorgsky, Diaghilev, Pavlova and Chaliapin were to be the toast of Europe. And from the United States, American painters and writers, Whistler, Henry James, Ezra Pound and T. S. Eliot, would be adding their contributions to the great panoply of English art and literature.

On his return sixty-six years later, he would find a very different scene. The heartland of the culture and power of 1900, the continent of Europe, he would find divided between two great and hostile coalitions. America and Russia, in 1900 only wings of the great central spread of European power and culture, have each developed their own culture and ideologies and have grown into super-powers dominating the Europe they have divided between them. In Europe itself he would find the inhabitants torn between the pulls of a movement for European unity and those of the two super-powers in much the same way as his Russian and American contacts in 1900 had been torn between their own emergent cultures and those of Europe. Of the great powers of 1900, the Habsburg Empire has disappeared entirely. Germany is divided by concrete, cement and barbed wire and part of its oldest territories in the east have been recolonized by Russians and Poles. Only Britain and France preserve any claims to great power status and any role beyond the confines of Europe. But how much that role has changed since 1900.

The most far-reaching changes in the sixty-six years since his last visit would only strike the visitor from Mars when he left Europe for Asia and Africa. From the Mediterranean to the Zambesi, he would find in Africa independent African states where he had previously seen European colonies. Even southwards of the Zambesi, always supposing he passed the racial standards of the Rhodesian and South African governments, he would find that the ruling groups, though of European extraction, were largely or entirely composed of persons born in Africa. As he moved from Africa to Asia, he would find still greater changes. The Indian sub-continent no longer lies subject to British rule. Instead it lies divided between Pakistan and India, both recognized as being among the powers. Farther east the former Chinese empire has recovered its strength and fallen subject to a new crusading expansionist creed—while losing none of its old contempt for, and isolation from, the rest of the world. China's rate of expansion into her borderlands, so our Martian will learn, has already led to armed clashes with India and caused the United States to commit a large section of its armed forces to intervention in South-East Asia. Japan is tied, albeit reluctantly, to the American security system, and all the central and northern Pacific lies under the shadow of American power. And wherever he goes in Asia or Africa, the Martian will find the attitudes of those with whom he speaks dominated by the values and vocabulary of anti-colonialism as the non-European world slowly recovers its balance and the tide of European dominion, at its full in 1900, ebbs finally away.

If he should enquire as to the causes of these changes, the visitor from Mars will hear of two intensely destructive wars, which devastated Europe's heart and spread death and destruction across much of the rest of the world. He will discover that the daemonic forces which led the European powers so rapidly to dominate the rest of the world drove them also into near-suicidal conflict with one another. And he will perhaps marvel that no one could be found, within so creative and dynamic a culture, capable of controlling its destructive impulses and diverting them to more fruitful purposes.

## The World and European Expansion to 1900

European expansion overseas had begun slowly enough in the fifteenth century, with Henry the Navigator's caravels inching their way in successive expeditions down the coast of Africa; until finally, within two years of one another, Vasco da Gama had burst into the Indian Ocean, and Columbus, taking ship westwards for Cathay, instead had re-discovered America. The next fifty years had seen a spasmodic outburst of Spanish and Portuguese power which divided the Americas, settled colonies on the coasts of India, Africa and the East Indies, and captured for their coffers the specie of the Peruvian empire and the riches of the Indian spice trade. They had been followed at a slower pace by the Dutch, the British and the French. Meanwhile new powers had arisen in Central Europe with the disintegration of the Holy Roman Empire, the rise of Prussia, the withdrawal of the Ottoman Empire under Austrian pressure from the plains of Hungary and Croatia, the decay and partition of the Polish state and the rise of Russia. And with this ferment in Europe, Britain had become residual legatee to the bulk of the overseas empires of France and the Netherlands. In 1776 she had seen her own earliest overseas colonies seek the road to independence and in the first decades of the nineteenth century she had aided and abetted the Latin American revolt against Spain.

But all of this was in slow motion compared with the speed with which the new powers of Europe had moved in the three decades before 1900. In 1870 a map of Africa would have shown a continent sprinkled only with the coastal stations of Spain, Portugal, France and Britain. In the north only Algeria acknowledged European rule, that of France. In the south, the British colonies of the Cape and Natal were expanding slowly in the wake of the retreating republics of the Boers, quondam Dutch settlers, trekking northwards to get away from the alien rule of Britain. The northern Mediterranean coast was lined with states nominally in tributary relationship with the Sultan of the Ottoman Empire, but in fact virtually independent, Morocco, Tunis, Tripoli, Egypt. Inland from the Red Sea

23

lay the Amharic kingdom of Abyssinia, chastised by a British expedition in the 1860s but otherwise independent. Further south lay the Arab sultanate of Zanzibar, founded by the Arabs of Muscat and Oman in the early years of the nineteenth century, now independent, its ruler passing under the magnetic influence of the great British consul, Sir John Kirk. Otherwise the continent was *terra incognita*, the only European presence that of missionaries (the first mission stations were established in the Nyasa highlands in the 1850s) and of explorers.

By 1900 the picture had completely changed. Britain occupied Egypt and the whole Nile valley of the Sudan. Italian colonies lay at Eritrea and on the Somali coast, dividing the horn of Africa with Britain and France. Zanzibar and the mainland up to and beyond the Great Lakes were British. Below this the German colony of Tanganyika bordered on to the expanded Portuguese colony of Mozambique. Below this again, Natal and British South Africa swung around the embattled Boer states. To the west lay the long tongue of British Bechuanaland, and beyond this to the north lay the two Rhodesias and Nyasaland. West again lay German South-West Africa, to its north Portuguese Angola, and then a chain of French and British colonies alternating with the occasional Spanish station, and the German colony of the Cameroons. Central Africa north of the Rhodesias lay under the personal rule of Leopold of the Belgians, whose ruthless and, on the whole, inefficient exploitation of the Congo was soon to lead to a European outcry. North of that lay the great hinterland of West Africa, which the French were in the midst of bringing under their sway. On the Mediterranean coast only Morocco and Tripoli still remained outside European rule. Elsewhere in Africa only Abyssinia was to survive, after the Italian armies had been defeated at Adowa in 1896. The only other independent state in all Africa was that of Liberia, founded by philanthropic Americans as a home for American Negroes some sixty-plus years before.

As with Africa so with the Far East and the vast expanses of the Pacific. In 1900 Russian troops occupied Manchuria. A mixed force of western troops had marched under German command (the German contingent did not arrive there in time) to relieve the foreign legations at Peking besieged by the populist rebels against the west, the Boxers. Germany occupied Kiaou-Chou, Britain Wei-Hei-Wei and Hong Kong. The Germans claimed the Shantung peninsula as their sphere of interest, Britain took the great valley of the Yantgse-Kiang, the French that of the Si-Kiang towards the Indo-Chinese border. Indo-China was French, the Philippines American, the Malay archipelago largely Dutch, all but the large island of Singapore, which with Malaya itself was British. India, Burma, Ceylon came under the British government of India. In Asia only Japan remained free. Within two years she was to become Britain's ally. Two years later she was to perform the inconceivable and attack and defeat Russia (as in 1896 she had defeated China), the first major defeat of a European great power at the hands of an Asiatic state since the siege of Vienna.

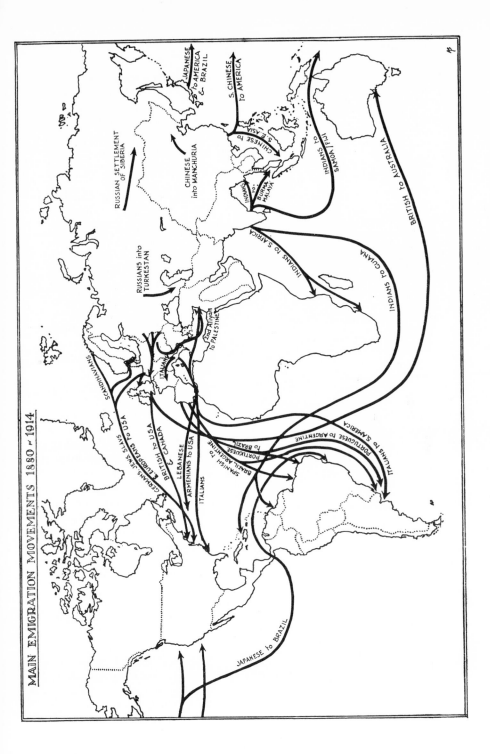

MAIN EMIGRATION MOVEMENTS 1880 – 1914

RUSSIAN SETTLEMENT OF SIBERIA

CHINESE into MANCHURIA

RUSSIANS into TURKESTAN

JAPANESE to AMERICA & BRAZIL

S. CHINESE to AMERICA

CHINESE to S.E. ASIA

INDIANS to BURMA MALAYA

INDIANS to SAMOA, FIJI

INDIANS to S. AFRICA

INDIANS to GUIANA

BRITISH to AUSTRALIA

2nd Aliyah to PALESTINE

SCANDINAVIANS

GERMANS, JEWS, SLAVS To USA

EUROPEANS to USA

BRITISH to CANADA

LEBANESE

ARMENIANS to USA

ITALIANS

ITALIANS

SPANISH to ARGENTINE

PORTUGUESE to BRAZIL

PORTUGUESE to ARGENTINE Brazil

ITALIANS to S.AMERICA

JAPANESE to BRAZIL

In the Pacific the picture was the same. Japan's fleet was modern and efficient and soon to win a great naval victory. Elsewhere everything was for the Europeans or the Americans. The isles of the Hawaiian cluster had passed finally under American rule in 1898. International crisis had flared briefly over Samoa before its partition in 1900 between Germany and the United States. The islands of the central and southern Pacific, for years the prey of the guano trader and the 'black-birder', the slave-raider of the Pacific, had passed with few exceptions under German, French or British rule. In the south, Australia and New Zealand were on the last stages of the road to self-government. In the Far South, Antarctica remained an imminent lure to explorers, the South Pole as yet undiscovered.

One section of the world remained for the powers of Europe to partition, the Near and Middle East, the Islamic world from the Golden Horn to Kabul, from the Red Sea to the Black. Egypt was occupied by the British. Morocco and Tripoli were still nominally tributary to the Ottoman Sultan. Palestine, Syria, the Lebanon, Mesopotamia were provinces of the Ottoman Empire, which also claimed sovereignty over the Islamic holy land of the Hedjaz, and the adjoining Yemen; claimed, too, sway over the rest of the Arabian peninsula including Nejd, home of the Saud family, and the waterless but strategically important sheikhdom of Kuwait. The sheikhdoms of the Gulf lived in enforced peace with one another under the benign and protecting eye of the government of British India. On the northern side of the Gulf the ancient kingdom of Persia lay between the naval pressure of Britain and the land pressure of Russia in the north, seething with discontent and seeking German aid as a balance. Oil was suspected but had not yet been struck in commercial quantities. Britain's interest was everywhere. France entered as the traditional protector of the Catholic Arabs, her claims vindicated by the Crimean War. American missionaries were active working through colleges in Beirut and Istanbul. Otherwise the area was given to Islam. By 1920 it would be all under European dominion, virtual or actual, save only Persia, the Nejd and the Anatolian heartland of Turkey. One other state remained, an agreed buffer between British India and Russia, the state of Afghanistan which British India had three times tried to subjugate but each time in vain, an area of feudal near-anarchy, its Amir a pensionary of India.

## The Bases of Western Strength

The superiority which the great powers of Europe displayed over the states and political systems of the rest of the world rested essentially on two items. First, in population resources they were superior to any non-European power except China with its three hundred odd millions. The rough population tables of 1900 show that apart from British India and the

Tsarist Empire, the population statistics of the great powers lie in a solid lump at the top of the table ranging from Italy's 31 million at the bottom, Britain and France at 37·9 and 38·9 million each, Austria-Hungary at 45·2 million, Germany at 56 million, to the United States at 62 million at the top. Second, and more important, the European powers commanded a series of techniques for the mobilization of their natural resources different both in degree and kind from those employed by their victims.

The first of these techniques was the use of mechanical power, generated mostly by coal (though oil was coming to supersede it in places where motive power was important), to extract and process the raw materials of iron and steel. The second was a command of technological innovation, which in the period between 1880 and 1913 was running at one of the highest rates of development in history. The third was the evolution of systems of administration, management and public finance capable of mobilizing the wealth of individual states for the purposes of state in a manner inconceivable to the older empires of Rome or China. Hand in hand with this went a system of financial institutions like the joint-stock companies, the banks and the investment houses which produced both private and collective wealth by allowing investors to take far greater risks than was ever possible during the days of the mercantile powers of medieval Arabia, India or China.

The technological superiority enjoyed by the European powers expressed itself most markedly in the control they exercised over international transport and communications. The growth of cables, news agencies and, in the decade after 1900, long-distance wireless stations, meant that their owners came naturally to control the flow and dissemination of information and intelligence, and to enjoy an immediacy of command denied to their opponents and bitterly contested among themselves. Their mobility enabled them to magnify their strength and to mobilize its potential in a way impossible to conceive in the earlier empires, so making the concept of the *levée en masse*, the nation in arms, realizable in a way undreamt of by the Jacobin originators of the idea. For, ultimately, the superiority of the European great powers lay on the battlefield. The revolution through which they had passed had as one of its essential elements a revolution in the technology of war.

This last great outburst of European expansionism was accompanied by a series of economic and social developments which are easy to describe, but whose causal interconnections are still controversial and difficult to explain. To begin with there was a very considerable increase in population, usually accounted for by a rapid fall in the overall death rate in the 1880s in various countries (the birth rate remaining more or less standard). Thus the total population of Europe, excluding Russia, rose by some 80 millions between 1880 and 1913, the most rapid expansion being in Britain (12 million) and in Germany (22 million), Italy (7 million) and Austria-Hungary (12 million). Between 1900 and 1913 the population of Germany was actually increasing by a million a year.

This growth in population was accompanied by an even more striking increase in industrial production. In a civilization founded on coal as the source of energy for mechanical power European production rose from 238 million tons in 1880 to 563 million tons in 1913; between 1900 and 1913 the rise in production was 163 million tons alone. Steel production rose with equal speed from a mere $9\frac{1}{2}$ million tons in 1880 to 42 million in 1913. Similar figures can be adduced in all the other major heavy industries, Only in agriculture did Europe remain depressed.

Almost all of this growth in manufacturing capacity and power took place in three countries, Britain, France and the new German Empire. Together they accounted for about 70% of Europe's total manufacturing capacity. In the key fields of coal, steel and machinery production, the figures were 93%, 78% and 80% respectively. Their domestic markets were large enough to provide an adequate framework for their own industries. Together they dominated the world market for manufactured products, commanding about 60% of world exports. In fact, France's share alone was larger than that of America, while Britain's and Germany's were each two to three times as large.

Of the three European powers, the fastest growing was Germany, which between 1895 and 1905 overtook Britain in most fields except textiles. In 1900 Germany was in fact entering on a period of growth which was to lead to a virtual doubling of her steel, iron and coal manufacturing capacity over the next ten years.

To these fantastic rates of growth in population and economic and industrial power one must add Europe's superiority in the technology of war. The long-range rifle, the Maxim machine-gun, quick-firing artillery with high explosive and shrapnel, gave European troops an immense superiority of fire over their non-European opponents. As Hilaire Belloc wrote of such engagements

> *Whatever happens, we have got*
> *The Maxim gun, and they have not.*

The defence was being greatly strengthened with the advent of land-mines and barbed wire, first invented in the 1850s to enclose the great American desert.

But there was more to modern European warfare than superiority in weapons technology. Discipline was something that Europe had evolved with the professional armies of the eighteenth century, as they had the rudiments of army staff organization. In the mid-nineteenth century the Prussian army had adapted the railways to its purposes, making out of them an instrument of speed in the mobilization and concentration of military strength which had brought Prussia two immensely rapid victories in 1866 and 1870 and made Germany the premier power in Europe. They had also evolved the concept of war economics, the harnessing of modern industrial methods and productivity for war. But the idea of mobilizing the economy of a country for war demanded more than military staff work and the ability to organize railway time-tables. It called for effective central administrative systems in government and for the mobilization of the nation's financial strength.

The administrative apparatus of two of the three greatest European powers, France and Germany, had in fact been directly evolved out of the need to make the state a more efficient machine for waging war. The French administrative system had its origin in the aggressive absolutism of Louis XIV, as modernized and harnessed to the idea of the national will by Napoleon. Its equivalent in Germany developed first under the militant absolutism of the first four Hohenzollern monarchs of Prussia, to be profoundly modernized under the impact of defeat at Napoleon's hands at Jena in 1806. Common elements to both were a national system of state finance and public accounting, national conscription in which every citizen served two to three years with the active forces and a further twenty-five to twenty-eight years with the reserves. Common, too, was the idea of universal compulsory public education to produce an educated citizenry, and a bureaucracy selected and recruited by competitive examination from the best products of the national educational system.

The effect was to produce in each country a military strength that could be immediately mobilized for national purposes and which proved much greater than that controlled by any non-western political unit. The only major weakness in each country lay in its financial machinery, which rested mainly on indirect taxation of the customs, tariff and excise type. Easy to administer, these forms of taxation provided a regular income adequate to the normal purposes of the state. However, they lacked devices by which reserves of financial strength could be quickly tapped in times of national emergency other than those provided by public loans.

In contrast to the continental bureaucracies which were designed to cope with the problems of war, the British administrative machinery was largely concerned with economic growth, industrialization and the social services. Like France and Germany, Britain had a professional civil service recruited by open competition from the educated *élites* of the nation. Britain's educational system was a curious *mélange* of state, religious and independent schools with a much smaller university system at its head than that of Germany, even though a system of free scholarships and the like ensured that reserves of talent among the lower levels of society did not go totally untapped. Its private sector of education, far more highly developed than that of the continental powers, was geared to the task of producing a governing class not only for Britain but also for the colonial and Indian empires, one in which the virtues of character and initiative were as highly valued as those of intellect alone.

By contrast with the continental powers Britain relied on professional military and naval forces designed mainly for overseas operations. For home defence a militia, formerly conscript, but voluntary since the mid-nineteenth century, and other volunteer forces sufficed. Not until 1907 was the militia incorporated into the Army Reserve and the other volunteer forces reorganized into the Territorial Army. In matters of military organization the South African War of 1899–1901 was to show that Britain lacked any kind of military staff capable of dealing with the problems of large-scale warfare. Her first line of defence remained the Royal Navy, in 1900 more than twice as strong as that of any potential rival, and still dominant over every part of the seven seas.

Britain's great strength *vis-à-vis* her continental rivals lay in her financial machinery which had evolved in part in response to the needs of financing coalition warfare against the dominant powers of the continent during the eighteenth century. The problems of administering a standing public debt had long been solved in Britain, and British systems of public accounting and political regulation of government expenditure were equal to those of France on which they had originally been modelled. British resistance to indirect taxation as an impediment to trade had led in 1842 to the revival of the idea of a direct tax on incomes, originally introduced during the Napoleonic wars. The British government drew its other revenues from excise and customs duties on luxury goods, and from a tax on inherited wealth introduced in 1894. The inheritance duties and the graduated income tax together gave Britain an immense reservoir of taxable wealth, hardly tapped at all in 1900, but available for times of national emergency.

If this ability to mobilize for the purposes of state their full material and human resources had given the powers of Europe the necessary margin of strength against the much more numerous populations of the older non-European empires, the most important advantage enjoyed by them had come much earlier. This was the control of the oceans which gave them access to every part of the world except the centre of the Eurasian land-mass. The last major challenges to European naval power had been defeated in the sixteenth century with the Portuguese victories in the Indian Ocean over the sea powers of the Indian littoral, and the Spanish-Venetian defeat of Ottoman sea power at Lepanto in 1571. From that date the only threats to the ships of the west had come from the Barbary pirates, whose strongholds had finally been cleaned up in the early nineteenth century with the French occupation of the Algerian coast. Similar piracy, though on a smaller scale, had led the British to intervene in the Persian Gulf in the mid-nineteenth century. Thereafter the general adoption of steam propulsion and coal-fired boilers had made piracy virtually impossible, except under the guise of state action, since the steamship needed elaborate bases and frequent coaling. The armoured warship of the 1900s could only be produced by the steel and engineering techniques of the major industrial powers, by the yards of Britain, France, Germany, Italy, the United States, Russia or Japan. The steamship made western commerce normally independent of wind and tide; though the disaster which struck the S.S. *Titanic* in 1912 was to show that nature could still set limits on men's pride.

From the conquest of the oceans, western man stood in 1900 on the edge of controlled flight in heavier-than-air-vehicles. Men had been ballooning since the eighteenth century. The first successful airship, driven by steam, had been demonstrated in Paris in 1812. In 1884, also in Paris, an airship had flown with electric motors. The first rigid airship was demonstrated in Germany in 1897, and the first of the famous Zeppelins made its maiden flight in July 1900 on Lake Constance. In ten years they were to be running passenger services. Moreover the initial steps necessary for the development of the aeroplane were also being taken. Otto Lilienthal made the first successful glider flight in 1891. The box-kite followed in 1893, the kite balloon in 1896. The glider and the box-kite had solved the aerodynamic problems and the advance of technology in the nineteenth century had given men the ability to power the aeroplane. On December 17th, 1903, at Kitty Hawk, North Carolina, the Wright brothers of the United States flew their first heavier-than-air vehicle. In the next five years, monoplanes and biplanes multiplied in England, France, Germany and Italy. In 1909 M. Blériot flew across the English Channel, and Britain's isolation from attack was about to end.

Mobility by air followed mobility on land. The steam engine and the railway locomotive had already carried western power and ideas everywhere. But from the 1880s onwards, with German engineers taking the lead, the internal combustion engine had been developed, first burning coal-gas (N. A. Otto, 1878), then oil (Priestman, 1886), and petrol (Daimler, 1885), with the carburetter (Daimler, 1885) and electric ignition (Karl Benz, 1885). The application of these devices to driving vehicles was almost immediate. Karl Benz built his first petrol-driven three-wheeler car in 1885 and his first four-wheeler in 1893. By 1900 Daimler cars were in full production in Germany (1894) and Britain (1896). Peugeot (1889), Panhard and Lavassor (1891) and Renault (1899) had built cars in France, Wolseley (1895), Lanchester (1895–96) and Austin were at work in Britain, and Henry Ford had built his first car (1896) in the United States. The first Model-T was to be produced eight years later, and the motor-car became the vehicle of the new middle class.

To mobility (and the car was to conquer deserts hitherto only accessible to the camel caravan), the west added ease in verbal communication. Submarine cables were laid in the 1850s after the invention of telegraphy and the morse code. The electric telephone followed in the 1870s (Bell, 1876), and in 1900 the world stood on the edge of long-distance wireless communication. Hertz had taken out his patents in 1887 and Lodge in 1897. The first successful trans-Atlantic transmission came in 1901 between St John's, Newfoundland, and Poldhu in Cornwall in the British Isles. The man responsible was the Italian Marconi, who, thereafter, settled in Britain.

Other major technological advances came in the widespread use of electricity for lighting purposes with the development of the electric dynamo in the 1880s, of street lighting, high-voltage transmission and the filament lamp. Other changes included the development of photography on celluloid film, the beginnings of the cinema in Britain and France, the invention of the rotary press and of rotogravure and the introduction of

31

steel and new types of cement and concrete for construction. The cities grew towards the sun as the Americans developed the skyscraper, and burrowed into the earth when the British pioneered the underground railway.

A significant development in this rapid advance of technology in all fields was the general shortening of time between the original innovation and its general application to the needs of society. In part this was due to the great effort put into research, in that the same innovation would emerge from widely separated laboratories and workshops more or less simultaneously. But it was much more the product of the industrial enterprise of the west, and the ease with which the device of the joint stock company made available the stored savings of the multitude rather than the inherited wealth of the individual few. Moreover the technological initiative had begun to pass from Britain to Germany in the last decades of the nineteenth century, the only major British inventions being Parson's steam turbine and Dunlop's pneumatic tyre to compare with the great German lead in electric engineering, in the motor-car and in dye stuffs and chemicals. Germany, however, was handicapped by Britain's and America's capture of the great new source of power, oil. Indeed, British capital was engaged in oil exploration throughout the world, including such diverse places as Rumania, Russia, Burma, the East Indies, Mexico and above all the Middle East.

Despite the fact that Germany led Britain in many industrial fields, and also in the race for technological innovation, Britain remained the paramount source of capital for a developing world industrialization. In the first decade of the twentieth century, Britain was investing 10% of her national income overseas (one-half of her current savings), as compared with a mere 2% for Germany, and her total overseas investments stood at £3,763 million sterling, one-quarter of her national wealth. The London market offered the largest range of investment agencies, from the great commercial banks, with their overseas branches, and the old-established merchant banking houses, to the small specialized investment agencies. The Stock Exchange was a self-governing institution with rigid rules for the enforcement of financial probity. The three hundred thousand odd substantial investors included many who were inclined to take serious risks and finance long-term private investment abroad, the largest share going to investments in the Empire, in the United States and in Latin America.

The Paris market stood in direct contrast to that of London, except that there were even fewer opportunities for profitable investment in France than in Britain. French investment first stemmed from the *rentier* tradition, which had bred a class of small investors looking for income investment rather than capital appreciation as did their opposite members in London. The ten million would-be *rentiers* placed their money first of all with a small group of banks, the *Banques des Depots* and the *Banques des Affaires*, and preferred above all to invest in the security of governmental loans, especially those made to foreign governments like that of Tsarist Russia, which accounted for one-quarter of all French investment abroad. The Paris market was above all the market for foreign governmental loans. Unlike Britain, France lacked an industrial organization able to carry out great industrial enterprise overseas, and the French investor had therefore an added inducement to entrust his money to those who would absolve him of all risks.

To these two international centres of overseas investment funds, Berlin stood a poor third, mainly because of the great demands on German capital made by the domestic economy. Germany lacked both the *rentier* class of France or the large investors of Britain, and control of her investment funds was much more institutionalized than among either of her two rivals. Capital funds were concentrated in the hands of the great banks who acted in combination to take up large demands for investment loans rather than in competition with one another. This concentration of power made German investment leadership overseas much more dominant than that of Britain or France, though lack of funds circumscribed Germany's freedom of action.

A characteristic feature of German overseas investment was the expansion of German banks especially in the Balkans and in South America, a form of financial imperialism much more resented by its recipients than either the political direction of French funds by the French government or the *de haut en bas* inquisitiveness of British investors. The bulk of German funds invested abroad went to South-Eastern Europe, the United States and Latin America.

## The Characteristic Phenomena of Imperialism

Behind this last great spasm of European expansion and the immense technological advances which gave the European powers their strength lay a deeper drive, the will to Empire. As a mass movement imperialism affected the major powers at different times, coming mainly in two great waves, in the late 1880s and again in the following decade. Contemporary writers such as J. A. Hobson in Britain and Charles Sumner in America were to find economic causes for its strength and persistence, failing to recognize it for what it was, a peculiar and viciously atavistic form of nationalism. It dominated British politics first in the mid-1880s, and swept back in the 1890s to rule unchallenged until 1903–4, when the Liberal party began to regain its balance. In France it held sway in the 1890s until the entire country became absorbed in the Dreyfus case. Imperialism maintained its grip over Germany for a longer period until checked in 1908–9. United States imperialism lasted from 1898 to 1912 when Wilson's victory in the Presidential election marked the end of 'dollar diplomacy'.

In all countries the main strength of imperialism lay among a determined, oligarchically-minded minority who formed a number of middle-class pressure groups. In Britain the Primrose League, the Imperial Federation League, in France the Committee for French Africa, in Germany the German Colonial League organized demonstrations, lobbied MPs, influenced or dominated the press and raged generally at the pusillanimity of their governments and the lack of interest in imperial matters of the average citizen. In such a mood, Rudyard Kipling wrote his famous *Recessional*. But the reluctance of the governments to act was often circumvented by the drive and opposition of the imperialists in the field. Frequently these were consuls, such as Nachtigall who secured the German Cameroons, Roustan who played a major part in the French annexation of Tunis, Kirk at Zanzibar, Willard Straight, the American vice-consul, who played so large a part in involving America in her first clash with Japan over Manchurian railroads. Often they were explorers like Karl Peters who secured Tanganyika for Germany, Marchand who led his men half-way across Africa to the head waters of the Nile at Fashoda to provoke an international crisis with Britain, or Stanley who marked out the Congo for Leopold. Sometimes they were visionaries like Cecil Rhodes, sometimes concession hunters. Often they formed chartered companies which operated ahead of their own governments. Typical examples were Rhodes' British South Africa Company, which settled the Rhodesias and attempted unsuccessfully to annex the Boer Republic in the Jameson Raid of 1897, Sir George Taubman Goldie's Royal Nigerian Company, and the Imperial British East Africa Company that deliberately intervened in East Africa to keep the Germans out. Most believed they were serving the national interest, even when their countries disowned them. For most of them nationalism was their religion.

It is this ideological element in imperialism which at bottom casts doubt on the economic theories of the origin of imperialism so popular around the turn of the century and taken over lock, stock and barrel by Lenin. These theories sought to explain imperialism in terms of the marginal return to capital invested. When this return became too small in relation to opportunities at home, so it was claimed, capital was exported, and where capital went the government which represented the interests of those capitalists had to follow. There were, of course, instances of such economic and financial imperialism. The French action against Tunis, the British occupation of Egypt, the Anglo-German action against Venezuela in 1903, the American actions in Central America are examples of this debt-collecting, financial imperialism. But there are so many cases of imperialism which fail to fit this thesis; including that of Germany, where there was an actual shortage of capital on the home market and the returns on capital invested abroad were less than the profits earned at home, or those of Italy and Japan which were net importers of capital during the whole of their most imperialist periods. Moreover there are even cases such as those of the American banks in China under President Taft, or the French financial interests in Morocco which behaved in an imperialist manner only after their governments forced them to do so to provide them with an excuse for an intervention on which they had already decided.

The truth is that imperialism was an emotion which often clothed itself in economic arguments, often in pseudo-Darwinian racialist arguments, often in a historicist appeal to the 'world-historical' process, whatever that might mean. It represented an exaggerated form of nationalism from which it developed with awful inevitability. Where this emotion did not classify itself as imperialism, it took other forms, of irredentist nationalism like pan-Germanism or pan-Slavism. Its explanation had to be sought in the processes which were at work in Europe. For it was a social not an economic phenomenon, a product of the strains and stresses of Europe itself.

## Chapter II
## EUROPE AT HOME

### The Newness of Europe

As a collection of political units defined by geography, Europe is old. But the precise collection of these units which made up Europe in 1900 were all newly created, or had at least passed in the nineteenth century through social and political upheavals on such a scale as to make them comparatively young in appearance. In general the socio-political set-up within the individual states and the international system which held them together were barely thirty years old.

In Britain the electoral reform of 1867, taken with the beginning of universal primary education in the 1870s, had completely transformed the nature of British politics, ushering in an era of mass political parties. Party organization and discipline became of the first importance, and control of the party organization at the grass-roots the key to political power. To lead these parties, at first the charisma of a great personality was necessary. Such a charisma was won at this date only by personal appearance over as wide an area as possible and by the oratorical powers displayed, for example, by the British statesman, William Ewart Gladstone, whose great Midlothian campaign of 1879 marked the first tentative essay of the mid-nineteenth century parliamentary leader in the techniques of mass persuasion to be so widely used in the twentieth century. Under the organizatory talents of Mr Joseph Chamberlain for the Liberals, and his opposite numbers on the Tory side, Lord Randolph Churchill and Sir John Gorst, the two loose coalitions of the mid-nineteenth century grew into disciplined and unified parties, though the strain of maintaining a doctrinal unity was to prove too much for the Liberals who suffered their first, though not their last, great schism with the resignation of Mr Chamberlain in 1886. The Tory party had already been organizing support among the new industrial working class and the divisions in the ranks of its rival did much to consolidate their influence among them.

In France, the Third Republic was founded in 1871 amidst the ruins of Louis Napoleon's popularly-based Second Empire. Its first act was to suppress with the utmost rigour the attempt of the Paris working class districts to set up a Commune. The effect was to turn the new industrial working class irrevocably against the new Republic. On the right, the Catholics and monarchists failed, despite their initial majority, to capture the state in 1877, and in 1891 the new Pope Leo XIII destroyed their mass basis of support in proclaiming the *Ralliément* of the faithful to the Republic. Under the impact of the scandals that bedevilled the Republic, and the attempt of Republicans to obtain redress for a Jewish staff officer named Dreyfus, wrongfully convicted of espionage by an Army court, the authoritarian element in French politics turned towards a new proto-Fascism of armed street-fighters, the *Camelots du Roi*, and a brilliant anti-Semitic press, the *Action Française* of Maurice Barrés and Drumont, author of *La France Juive*, but failed, through the fundamental individual-ism of French politics, to produce a leader capable of exploiting it.

Germany herself was no older than France. Proclaimed at Versailles in the aftermath of the Franco-Prussian war, the German Empire was the creation of Otto von Bismarck, the Prussian Chancellor, who had solved the long rivalry for the leadership of Germany of the houses of Habsburg and Hohenzollern, by excluding the Habsburg dominions after defeating them in war in 1866. His action left the Germans of Austria and Bohemia outside the new state which, despite its popularly elected *Reichstag* and its apparently federal structure, remained essentially Prussian in character. The Catholics of the South and West had been reconciled with the new state by the tariffs of the 1880s and the abandonment of the attempt to attack their separate educational systems, but the Prussian state machinery had made no attempt to reach greater agreement with the mass political parties produced by universal suffrage.

The new Italian state was a little older. It had been created with the aid of France in 1859–60 by Cavour, the minister of Piédmont, and Garibaldi, the reckless guerilla leader. But Rome itself had not been freed of alien troops until 1870 at the cost of a feud between the new monarchy and the Pope which was to last until 1929. More serious were the continuing divisions between north and south which the roles of the north in unifying Italy and of the Church in the south perpetuated. Italy remained a political oligarchy.

The state of Austria-Hungary had been remade in 1867 by the so-called 'Compromise' between the Habsburg dynasty and the ruling *élites* of Magyar Hungary. The two states enjoyed a common monarchy, army, financial system and foreign policy but had little else in common, having separate parliaments and separate administrations and having to re-negotiate their mutual trade relations every ten years. Farther east the states of Greece, Serbia and Montenegro dated back to the early part of the nineteenth century. But each was enlarging itself so much at the expense of the declining Ottoman Empire as to seem in a constant state of creation. The same could be said of the states of Rumania, which took its origin from the end of the Crimean war, and of Bulgaria, set up after the Russo-Turkish war of 1877, and still nominally under the suzerainty of the

Ottoman Empire. In the north, Sweden and Norway lived in an uneasy union which had been set up in 1815 and which was soon to be broken. In the east, Russia was ruled by a weak and impulsive Tsar, in a state of impending crisis. The great reforms of the 1860s had freed the serfs and opened the universities. But they had not solved the problem of peasant land-hunger, nor found a place in the Tsardom's structure of social power and status for the new classes produced by these reforms or by the concurrent industrialization which was proceeding so rapidly.

The system which held these states together was also of recent origin. Fundamentally it was the creation of Otto von Bismarck. It rested upon a structure of alliances and conventions. The four continental powers, France, Germany, Austria-Hungary and Russia, were grouped in two alliance systems each with its commercial and political satellites. The older of the two was that of the Central Powers, based on the Austro-German alliance of 1879, and transformed by the alliance with Italy of 1883 into the Triple Alliance. Bismarck had tied Rumania into this alliance in 1883, and had maintained a strong connection with Tsarist Russia through the so-called League of Three Emperors of 1882 and the Reinsurance Treaty of 1887. He had also maintained a rather weaker connection with Britain through the Mediterranean agreements between Britain and his ally, Italy, and by exploiting Britain's need for German diplomatic support in the Egyptian question.[1] His Austrian ally maintained her own control over Serbia through a secret agreement of 1878 by which the ruling family of Serbia, the Obrenovich's, received a secret Austrian subsidy.

After Bismarck's dismissal in 1890, his successors lost touch with Russia and Britain, and allowed Russia to conclude in 1891 a political and, in 1893, a military alliance with France, which Germany imagined to be directed against Britain but which was, in fact, directed against herself alone. Britain had stood off a challenge in the colonial field from France at the Fashoda crisis of 1898 when a French expedition attempted to lay claim to the headwaters of the Nile, had built up a fleet capable of taking on virtually anything Europe could muster against her, and had retreated into a policy of splendid isolation, unsatisfactory in the extreme to her European rivals, who could only wait for the misgivings felt by differing sections of British opinion to bring Britain back to the point where some bargain could be struck with her.

The essence of the Bismarckian system was agreement among the great powers to settle their differences peacefully, and not to allow one country to score gains without the others receiving compensation. This principle had been laid down at the two Berlin congresses of 1878 and 1885 with first Russia and then Britain called to book. These congresses were not repeated, but short conferences, and other devices of co-operation such as international consortia of banks, standing conferences of ambassadors and the like made it possible for the great powers to continue their co-operation and domination of the smaller powers of Europe. Bismarck's

[1] See Chapter V below.

dismissal had, however, removed from the scene the one statesman who really understood how the system worked.

## The 'Weakness' of Europe

The new Europe might seem to the outside world to be so strong that its dominance of the rest of the world was unlikely to be shaken for a century or more. But in fact it contained a number of fatal flaws, both in its individual states and in the system as a whole, which were to make its period of world supremacy of remarkably short duration. The most dangerous of these was the failure of the European system to accept completely the new principle of nationality. Even in western Europe such obviously 'national' states as Britain and Spain had their problems. The Irish problem bedevilled British politics from 1885 onwards and was in 1914 to bring Britain to the verge of civil war. The twin problems of Catalonia and the Basques introduced extra complications into the tangled web of politics in Spain. In France alone centralist nationalism maintained its sway, and the small revival of enthusiasm for Provençal never translated itself from the cultural to the political sphere. As one moved eastwards so the problems of nationalism became ever stronger and more threatening to the established order. The most dangerous areas lay in the three great multi-national empires of eastern Europe, those of Germany, Austria-Hungary, and Tsarist Russia, and in the marches which separated them.[1]

The two states most endangered were those of Austria-Hungary and Tsarist Russia. The compromise of 1867 had divided the Habsburg Empire along the river Leithen and the Carpathians. Its Hungarian part was the more unified of the two and formed a logical entity dominated by the Magyars of the Hungarian plain. To the north lay the largely suppressed Catholic minority of the Slovaks, to the south the ancient kingdom of Croatia with its own Diet under rigid Hungarian control. The institutions of state employment in Croatia, especially the railways, were potent instruments of Magyarization. To the east lay the province of Transylvania, with Rumanian and German minorities under equally strong pressures to assimilate themselves to the Magyar nation. The so-called 'Austrian' side of the monarchy was far less unified. Magyar Hungary contained only one dominant racial group; Habsburg Austria contained three, and several provinces where no single group enjoyed any domination. The core of the Empire was formed by the German provinces of Austria proper, the Tyrol, the Vorarlberg, Upper and Lower Austria, Salzburg, Carinthia and Styria, the last two provinces extending some way into what is today northern Yugoslavia, and having, as a result, sizeable Slovene minorities. In the north were the three provinces of Bohemia, Moravia and Silesia,

[1] See map, European Alliances and Alignments, following p. 160.

where Czechs and Germans were locked in bitter contest for dominance over such issues as the language of state and the control of the provincial Diets. Eastwards lay the province of Galicia where Polish landowners and aristocrats held down a townsfolk consisting of Poles and Jews and a peasantry mainly made up of Ukrainians, especially in the east. Beyond that lay the Bukovina with a mixed population of Jews, Germans and Rumanians. To the south lay the provinces of Istria and Dalmatia, where the dominant racial group was Italian and the bulk of the population Slovene or Serb; Slovenia where a Slav population managed its own affairs; and the Austrian colony of Bosnia-Herzegovina, placed under Austrian mandate by the Congress of Berlin.

The Habsburg monarchy faced two private nightmares: one was the pull of pan-Germanism exercised on the Germans of Bohemia and Austria by the propagandists of Bismarck's Germany, a pull which expressed itself in such movements as the *Deutsche Nationalverein*, the *Deutsche Schulverein*, and the nationalist anti-Catholicism of Ritter Georg von Schönerer; the other was the growth of a southern Slav or Yugoslav movement which would unite the southern Slav lands of the monarchy around Serbia, as the Habsburg lands of northern Italy, the Milanese and Venetia, had been lost to Piedmont in the 1860s. The Czech-German struggle in Bohemia and Moravia, which was by far the more immediate and virulent of the racial troubles in the empire, always seemed containable by contrast, since it lacked any real external focus. The continuance of Habsburg control of Serbia thus seemed essential to Vienna as was the avoidance of any serious trouble with Russia in the Balkans. The Austro-Russian agreement of 1897 to preserve the *status quo* in the Balkans was thus of the first importance.

The Tsarist empire was second only to the Habsburg empire in the number of its alien nationalities and greatly ahead of them in the degree to which it sought their assimilation. In the north the state of Finland annexed in 1805 remained almost totally indigestible, its Swedish aristocracy and its Finnish middle and peasant classes proving equally impossible to assimilate. Along the Baltic coast lay the ethnically mixed territories of the Estonians, akin to the Finns, the Latvians and the Lithuanians, areas dominated by dynasties of German-Balt nobility from whom in the past the Tsardom had drawn many of its ablest administrators. South of these lay Russian Poland, Byelo-Russia, the Ukraine and Bessarabia, each divided between a local peasantry and nobility, a largely Jewish urban middle-class, a mixed Jewish-native working class, and a Russian-dominated administration. In Poland the bulk of the Polish aristocracy had gone into exile after the failure of the 1863 risings, without in the least extinguishing the Polish nationalist movement, whose leadership was being taken up by a new university-educated class, a mixture of the rural gentry and the new professional classes. Such elements were hostile to the Tsardom in Russia itself; in Poland they were not only hostile to the Tsardom but to Russian rule as such. In Byelo-Russia there were only the beginnings of a local nationalism, of lower-class origins, which was still a little unclear as to whether it was Lithuanian rather than Byelo-Russian. In the Ukraine, local nationalism consisted of a combination of regionalist resentment of Tsarist centralism, local feudal antagonism to Russian modernization, cultural nationalism centering on the ancient cities of Kiev and Kharkhov, and general feelings of Cossack solidarity. In Bessarabia, a small element of Rumanian nationalism fed itself on support from Bucharest. All this western belt of the Tsarist empire was undergoing a high degree of industrialization, and showing the first signs of trade union and political labour organization. All these areas had a large Jewish population which the Tsardom was using as scapegoats for its own mismanagements, and repeated pogroms were driving many of the Jewish minority (of perhaps some 3 million) into emigration westwards.

In contrast with these two empires, Germany faced only one serious racial problem. Of course, there were a Danish minority in Schleswig-Holstein taken over in 1864 after the Prussian war with Denmark and a small Belgian minority in Eupen-Malmédy. There was a very serious problem in Alsace-Lorraine, taken into Germany from France in 1871 and still garrisoned like the conquered enemy territory it undoubtedly was. But the most urgent problem concerned the Poles in eastern Germany, too large and solid a mass to be either assimilated or long dominated, a link with Russia and Austria-Hungary so long as it was in their joint interests to keep the Poles in subjection but a very potent source of subversion if this common interest should cease. The Poles of Prussia lacked leadership outside their Church, being largely agricultural. The working-class politician of Polish origin tended to join the German left rather than to act on his own. The first Polish political representation in the Reichstag was rural in origin.

More serious than the nationalist strains in western Europe were those which came from the industrial revolution, and from the class of industrial workers which that revolution produced. By 1900 this class had passed from industrial organization through the creation of trade unions to direct political activity in most of the countries of western and central Europe. In France and Spain, and to a lesser extent in Italy, their organizations were at such odds with the state that their activity took the form of savage strike action with strong political overtones; in Germany, Belgium and Austria-Hungary they organized themselves into mass parties with a membership well into the millions. Everywhere this political ferment heralded the emergence into political consciousness of two new classes, the educated skilled worker of George Bernard Shaw's *Man and Superman* and the semi-educated industrial worker of large-scale industry. The first provided the leadership and the doctrine, and was joined by the *déclassé* intellectuals from every level of the social scale. The second provided the mass force, the unmoving threat behind the active militants. Neither of these groups had a recognized place in the social hierarchy of any European state, whatever its actual social composition, and their self-consciousness and organization seemed to threaten the fabric of the existing state, based as it still was on what frequently amounted to chattel labour.

An added strain was provided by the emergence of an educated female class which the universities so reluctantly began to admit around the 1890s. Women however remained deprived of the vote, treated by the law in the same manner as those men in imperfect command of their reason, and exploited by their employers in the new world of business organization which swallowed so many of them up as secretaries and typists. Feminism was born as a movement among the educated leisured women folk of the upper strata of the *bourgeoisie*, a movement so potentially disruptive of established social mores as to pass easily into the violence of the suffragettes within a decade of its being launched in Britain. To the strains brought by the rapid rate of economic growth through which most European countries were passing was added one which struck at the most basic social institution in European society, the family relationship between male and female.


## European Political Exemplars


To those critics who looked with extreme dissatisfaction at the current political systems in Europe, three distinctive forms presented themselves: constitutional parliamentary democracy of the monarchical or the republican kind; constitutional autocracy of the central European, Prussian, German or Habsburg variety; and Russian Tsardom. For examples of constitutional monarchical democracy, Europeans turned most naturally to Britain, then to Belgium, the Netherlands and the Scandinavian states. The basis of these systems was in each case a constitutional fiction by which a cabinet of ministers, representing whichever coalition of political forces could obtain a parliamentary majority in an election, ruled in the name of a monarch whose powers were confined, in Bagehot's classic formulation, to advice and warning. The electoral system in each case provided for universal male suffrage. Parliament was bicameral, the upper chamber normally being hereditary, though in the cases of Belgium and the Netherlands it was of a federal character. France provided the main republican variant, the Third Republic expressing itself through a bicameral legislature, and a cabinet appointed by a prime minister in order to command, as far as possible, a parliamentary majority. The prime minister himself was appointed by the president as the figure most likely at that moment to be able to form such a cabinet. France provided the one exception to the rule that political life in western Europe was dominated by the disciplined mass party. The French electoral system did its best to perpetuate the fractionalism and ever-shifting political alliances which had shown themselves in British politics in the period before the second Reform Bill.

But French individualism played an even larger part, and power rested more with the two chambers of the French parliament than with any cabinet or prime minister, however powerful his personality.

In central Europe, constitutional autocracy was the norm. In this system the monarch ruled through a chancellor and a cabinet whose job it was to control and manage a parliament, which, at least where its lower chamber was concerned, stood in somewhat the same relationship to the monarch as Congress does to an American president; that is to say, parliament's role was to approve his legislation and to limit the exercise of his autocracy. Ministers could be, but were not necessarily, chosen from parliament. The orders of the autocracy, to which considerable powers of emergency action were reserved, were executed by a powerful and all-pervasive bureaucracy. The autocrat, like the American president, was commander-in-chief of his armed forces. In turn the military authorities regarded themselves as at least the equals of his civilian cabinet and advisers. As a result conflicts between chiefs of staff and chancellors occurred with some frequency.

Only in Imperial Russia was unbridled autocracy still to be found. The position of the Tsar was strengthened by his quasi-religious role as head of the Russian Orthodox Church in a state whose masses were profoundly devout and acknowledged the authority of the priest almost before that of the policeman. The sole traditional check on the Tsar was his need for the support of the princely families and the aristocracy generally, which gave him his ministers, his senior bureaucrats and his generals and officers. In past history this class had not been above removing individual Tsars who had failed to rule strongly and successfully, so that the Tsarist system had come to be defined as 'autocracy tempered by assassination'. Future events proved that the Tsar still needed this support in times of great stress. But it was already becoming apparent that he needed the approval of a rather larger segment of the ruling classes than before, including the new industrial and commercial bourgeoisie whose power and stake in the state increased *pari passu* with Russia's industrialization.

### *The Bases of Social and Political Power, Traditional and Emergent*

The fact that even in Russia a public opinion existed, although the 'public' was much less numerous than in the autocracies of central or the democracies of western Europe shows that the bases and instruments of political power were the same throughout the continent. What differed was the degree to which each was present. One may perhaps distinguish seven different bases of power in the world of 1900. First came the traditional basis of power, the status, noble and aristocratic, conferred by the owner-

43

ship of land, which carried with it the triple role of providing advisers to autocrats, an officer class and leaders for agrarian-based political parties in autocracies and democracies alike. Second came the ever-growing power of the bureaucrat, as the states of the world, both autocrat and democrat, increased radically the scope of state action in industry, in commerce, and in the newly-developing spheres of social insurance. Third came the power conferred by wealth or the command of wealth, a power which lay with the large-scale investor, the banking house, the brokers and those who controlled the movement of funds and the placing of investments. In an era of such large-scale movements of private capital and government borrowing on the bourses of Paris, Vienna, Berlin and London, immense power lay in the hands of a Schroeder, a Baring, a J. Pierpont Morgan, a Rothschild. Fourth was the power of the large-scale industrialist and trader, a Krupps or a Carnegie in steel, a Ballin in shipping, a Mond in chemicals, a Rockefeller or a Deterding in oil, a Rhodes in gold and diamonds, a Nobel in explosives, a Harriman in railways. Fifth came the power of the democratic political leader in parliament and in the country, the power of a Lloyd George, a Joseph Chamberlain, a Theodore Roosevelt, a Clemenceau or a Poincaré. Sixth was the power of the new leaders of mass movements, a Jaurés or a Bebel for the social democrats of France and Germany, a Lueger for the Christian Social party in Austria-Hungary, a Kramař for the Czech nationalists of Bohemia. Seventh came a new group whose influence sprang from the growth of the mass press in Britain and the United States, the newspaper owners and editors, like Alfred Harmsworth in Britain and William Randolph Hearst in the United States. Beyond these, further sources of wealth were to develop, first with new technological advances such as in radio (Marconi) and second, with the development of new techniques in the distributive trades such as the chain store and the department store (Sir Thomas Lipton and Gordon Selfridge in Britain, and the Woolworth family in America).

With the increasing importance of the masses, as consumers, as tax-payers, and finally as conscripts, there developed out of the aristocratic traditions of Britain, Prussia and Austria, concerned with the link between crown, aristocracy and people, a new and positive conception of the role of the state as the purveyor of welfare especially to the urban working classes oppressed by the appalling conditions in the new towns which grew up during the industrial revolution. In the regulation of industry and in the provision of social insurance and medical services for the poor Bismarckian Germany led the way, to be followed by the Austrian empire and the monarchical democracies of Britain, the Low Countries and Scandinavia. Such reforms were anathema to the pure liberal *bourgeois* as interfering with the processes of the market, but aristocratic benevolence and the new radicalism were too much for them.

## Political Movements: Pro-System

The dominant systems in the states of Europe rested upon a combination of four main political movements. The first of these was aristocratic conservatism in all its forms, linked in most countries with the agrarian interests. In Britain the landed interest still accounted for much of the Tory party's strength in Parliament, parson and squire combining to turn rural constituencies into safe Tory seats. In Belgium, in Germany and Austria-Hungary where aristocracy was far more strongly entrenched, the parties of this persuasion, the Prussian conservatives and their opposite numbers in German Austria, in Austro-Polish Galicia, in Magyar Hungary, even in Bohemia, were the basis of the government's majority in the various parliaments. Sometimes allied to them, often in opposition, the national-imperialist wing of the various liberal parties provided an alternative party in general support of the system. In Britain the imperialist wing of the Liberal party, Asquith, Haldane and Sir Edward Grey, challenged the Liberal leadership while in opposition and threw their energies into the development of Britain's armed forces and international position once they came into office. In Germany and in Austria-Hungary the National-Liberals were in office for most of the 1870s and remained in general support of their respective autocracies thereafter, resenting only their refusal to move towards a more parliamentary system of government.

Aristocratic conservatism was informed by a kind of benevolent authoritarianism which looked back in many respects to the ideal of the eighteenth century, of an idealized non-political administrative state opposed to the divisions of mere party politics. Liberal imperialism by contrast looked outwards, reform at home being seen mainly as a means of increasing the efficiency of the state. Liberal nationalists also viewed the world in terms of a historical system in which struggles between states and between social classes were the only roads to progress. Many sought to identify in these conflicts an inevitable historical process, by which class succeeded class or racial group racial group by some 'scientific' law of universal historical applicability. Marx foresaw the rise of the proletariat and the inevitable conflict with the capitalist *bourgeois*. Danilevski, the Russian journalist, writing in 1871 saw the era of the Slav about to supersede that of the German 'cultural-historical type'. More popular than these among the bourgeois were the social Darwinian writers who saw the social process and the relations between states and nations as an extension into human society of Darwin's laws of natural selection, 'the survival of the fittest', 'the struggle for existence', a doctrine which both justified the social groups and nations currently at the top of the existing scale of power-relationships and enjoined upon them the need for continuous exertion to prove themselves worthy of that position. One possible development they foresaw was the merging of racial groups akin to one another into larger

45

political entities, Pan-Slavism among the Slavs of Eastern Europe, Pan-Germanism, Pan-Anglo-Saxonism uniting the British Empire and the United States.


## Political Movements: Anti-System

Opposition to the existing systems of government was of two types. In the first place, each system of government bred its own brand of opposition movement. In the second, the growth of imperialism and Social Darwinism was rivalled by the rise of the new universalist movements, socialism, social catholicism, agrarian radicalism and integral or totalitarian nationalism.

In the limited autocracies of central Europe the bourgeois and nationalist parliamentary parties always retained an element of hostility to the *régimes* which denied them real political power and responsibility. Indeed in all cases there were radical democratic groupings in fairly permanent opposition. Within the western democracies the main division came on the issues of imperialism and social reform, those who opposed the former and advocated the latter often taking their inspiration from a parochial if not isolationist nationalism inherited from the *laissez-faire* radicals of the mid-nineteenth century. The Little Englanders in Britain found parallels in France and in Belgium, in their opposition to overseas adventures as being actions inherently wasteful of the nation's resources and in their belief that the main motive force behind imperialism was corrupt financial adventurism. As such, however, this element only represented one strand in the movement for social reform, which was backed equally by those who felt that radical reforms were necessary to improve the efficiency of the nation-state to fit it for the struggle for international existence. Although divided on most issues, the imperialist and isolationist wings of the British Liberal Party could unite behind an important programme of social and political reform after its electoral victory in 1905. The American movement for social reform, which culminated in the reforms introduced in President Wilson's first two years of office, covered both Theodore Roosevelt and William Jennings Bryan, respectively Republican candidate for the vice-presidency and Democratic candidate for the presidency, in the elections of 1900. And the co-founders of the Fabian Society and the famous London School of Economics in Britain included both the ablest of the younger imperialist Tories, L. S. Amery, and the arch-intellectual reformist radicals, Sidney and Beatrice Webb.

An interesting element in these movements for social and political reform, progressivism in America, Liberal radicalism in Britain and their analogies in France and the other European democracies, was their use of the press to mobilize public opinion against the abuses they sought to reform. The journalism of 'exposure', 'muck-raking' as it was known in America, flourished most, and became for a time extremely profitable in the United States; but it was by no means unknown in Europe where, especially in France, the scent of a scandal was meat and drink to the journalists of the new popular press. Against the sensationalism of much of the popular side of the movement, must be placed the quiet dedication of those actually engaged in work among the poor, the destitute and the forgotten of the nineteenth century, working in the so-called settlements of which Britain's Toynbee Hall was the best known.

Reformist liberalism, however, was essentially a transitory phenomenon, except in the United States and Great Britain. Historically of much more significance at the turn of the century was the growth in strength of the older and the newer universals, Catholicism and Socialism, to which extreme nationalism and the elements which supported it were to prove themselves militantly hostile in the twentieth century. Both social Catholicism and Socialism were mass political movements and as such accommodated themselves a little too easily to the divisions between nations. Neither were to prove strong enough to withstand the outbreak of international war in Europe in 1914. But both were sufficiently moderate, even in a sense conservative in relation to the political institutions and systems of Europe, that they eventually became an anathema to the integral nationalists and proto-Fascists and the totalitarian socialists of the twentieth century.

Social Catholicism had been strong in the 1840s in Germany and France, under Lamennais and Bishop von Ketteler. At that date it had been well in advance of the central direction of the Catholic Church which, it was felt, had identified the Church too closely with those social classes and interests which were being threatened by the processes of social and economic change at work in the early part of the nineteenth century. The advent of Leo XIII and the issue of the Encyclical, *De Rerum Novarum*, in 1891 set the stamp of Papal approval on Social Catholicism. In Belgium, Germany, Austria, the Netherlands and Switzerland, Catholic parties sprang into existence, or took on a direction which had previously been denied them. In France the Papally-backed movement known as the *Ralliément* ended Vatican support for monarchism and diverted French authoritarianism into proto-Fascist channels. Catholicism entered the trades union and co-operative movements. It took very strong hold among the peasantry of Central Europe, now becoming increasingly politically conscious. The Social Catholic programme included legislation to bar the exploitation of labour, and to foster the growth of small-scale property-ownership both on the land and in industry. Coupled with this programme were attacks on economic and political nationalism, on the concentration of economic power in a few hands through cartels and trusts, and on class warfare. Its leaders were an odd mixture of the aristocrat and the new *petit bourgeois*. In Austria, for example, leadership passed from the aristocratic Baron von Vogelsang to the first of the great modern demagogues, Dr Karl Lueger, three times Mayor of Vienna after 1896, and a violent, if not totally indiscriminate, anti-Semite. In Britain and in America, where aristocratic Catholicism had for obvious reasons never existed as a political force, the movement was much more closely allied with the embryo Labour movement. Cardinal Manning played a major part in this movement in Britain (his intervention in the bitter London dock strike of 1889 is just one example). In America, Social Catholicism was strongly entrenched in the Irish and Central European elements in the trades union movement. As a political force, Social Catholicism was to suffer both from the essentially limited nature of its aims, which in many cases were confined to maintaining the parochial system in education, and from changes in the Papacy itself. Pius X, for example, felt it necessary to keep a tight rein on the movement his predecessor had initiated, and, as a result, the Social Catholic movement in Italy developed in opposition to the Papacy, even to the point, in 1909, when its leader, Dom Romalo Murri, was excommunicated. The conflict between local social idealism and the changes of policy in the Vatican kept it from developing any real international character or organization.

The Social Democratic movement was, in form at least, much more committed to opposing nationalism and developing on an international basis. The First International had been broken in the 1870s in the aftermath of the suppression of the Paris Commune, amidst the bitter quarrels between Marx and Bakunin, the Russian pan-Slav anarchist, who brought into the European socialist movement hostility to the organized state, and an idea of collective freedom of a totally Russian and non-European kind. The First International had acted as a means of inflating the importance of the various national groups, none of which, save perhaps those of France, Switzerland and Belgium, amounted to very much in their own countries. The Second International came only gradually into existence, and achieved formal status with a permanent office and executive in 1900, after its component national parties had become firmly established in their native political surroundings. The largest single socialist party was that of Germany, founded in the late 1860s, and converted, by its experience of Bismarckian persecution, very firmly to the idea of parliamentary action as a means to securing the revolution. By 1900 it was a mass party of considerable size with 56 seats in the Reichstag, two million or so voters, and three-quarters of a million trades unionists supporting it. Its programme centred on the conversion of Germany to a popular direct democracy, and contained no explicitly socialist measures such as nationalization for fear of strengthening the capitalist state. Its dominant theorist, Karl Kautsky, defended the party's policy with the argument that the achievement of an absolute majority for the party was historically inevitable. The revolution would come once such a majority had been secured. The important thing was to maintain party unity until that date.

Other important socialist parties were the Austrian socialists (re-founded in 1888–89) who were dedicated first of all to the achievement of universal male suffrage and from whose ranks came the only socialists to attempt to reconcile the growth of competing national groups with the rigid social categories of Marxism; the Belgian Labour Party (1885), with 27 seats in parliament, deadlocked over educational and franchise issues with Belgian political Catholicism; the Swedish (1889) equally absorbed in the fight for universal male suffrage; and the Italian socialists, who elected 33 deputies in the 1900 elections in a lower house of 500, despite government repressive measures against the party and its leadership the year before. The French socialist movement, characteristically, was divided into six main groups, not to be unified until 1905 under the leadership of Jaurés. The British Labour movement was divided between the Independent Labour Party (1893) with strong regional, Scots, Welsh and minority elements, the Labour elements in the Liberal party, the Fabian Society with its middle-class intellectuals and belief in 'permeation', and the Marxist Social Democratic Federation. But in 1900 most of these groups came together with leading trades unionists in the Labour Representation Committee, with a declared policy of creating a 'distinct Labour Group' in Parliament. However, only two of its candidates were successful in the 'Khaki election' of 1900 which was fought in the jingoistic atmosphere induced by the South African War.

In the Socialist International the socialist groups in the two great non-European extensions of Europe, Russia and the United States, played a remarkably limited part, the central role being taken by the German Social Democrats. The comparative impotence of the Russian and American parties stemmed from the very different conditions each faced when contrasted with the parliamentary role of the European Social Democratic movements. But it also underlined the point that in their own countries they only represented one wing of the native radical-revolutionary forces; and that in choosing to embrace the European pattern of social democracy they were in some sense breaking with their own tradition. Both parties, moreover, were very weak in numbers compared with the mass parties of Europe. Neither could accept a parliamentary approach to their problems. Both faced systems of government which seemed at first sight analogous to those of Europe proper but were in fact as profoundly different from those of the European powers as they were from each other.

In the United States the labour movement was divided between the American Socialist party (founded in 1901, its main strength lying among German immigrants) and the various branches of the American trades union movement. The latter was itself in turn divided between the craft unions led by Samuel Gompers, and united into the American Federation of Labour, which concentrated entirely on limiting entry to the labour force as an essential preliminary to the use of economic action to raise the conditions and terms of labour, and the more violent syndicalist advocates of 'one big union', from the Knights of Labour of the 1880s to the International Workers of the World, the 'Wobblies' of the 1905–20 period. The trades union movement, in either of its manifestations but especially in

49

the syndicalist form, was strongly American in ethos and organization, and regarded the intellectuals of the American Socialist party with a contempt tempered only by the personal admiration and adulation all felt for the perennial Socialist candidate for the presidency, the railroad unionist-syndicalist Eugene Debs (1855–1926).

The Russian Socialist movement, like that of America, regarded itself as being part of the European international socialist movement. In America, however, the diffuseness of the political system and the comparative infrequency with which the power of Federal or State governments was used against the interests of the American working classes, made for direct strife between labour and employers and made the capture of the state's machinery by parliamentary means seem impossible because of the other interests involved and irrelevant to the problems faced by the working classes. In Russia, by contrast, the lack of a parliament to conquer, and the omnipresence of the Tsarist system made revolutionary activity inevitable, and only preserved the illusion of unity with the Socialist international by imposing on the would-be leaders of the Russian socialist movement the necessity of living in exile in Europe. The party was officially created in 1898 and its first congress, held that year in Pskov, included delegates from the Polish Socialist party and the Russian Jewish Socialist party, the Bund. When its second party congress met in London in 1903, there occurred the great schism between Mensheviks and Bolsheviks which was to lead to the Bolshevik victory in the Russian revolution of 1917 and the subsequent division of European socialism between democrats and totalitarians from which it has yet to recover.

In Marxist terms, Tsarist Russia had not yet passed through its *bourgeois* revolution, and the time therefore for the replacement in the seats of power of the *bourgeoisie* by the working-class lay in the distant future. What then were those who looked for the socialist revolution to do? Co-operate with the *bourgeoisie* in the overthrow of Tsardom? Create a mass movement to preach and wait for the time when the socialist revolution could be won by parliamentary means? Or concentrate on creating a disciplined, single-minded revolutionary *élite*? Or should they concentrate on the economic struggle, on building up the trades union movement, on strikes to improve the conditions in the factories and legislation to improve the social conditions in which they lived? Plekhanov (1857–1918) and those who were to be called the Mensheviks wanted a mass movement which would embrace all who called themselves Socialists. Vladimir Ilyich Ulyanov, who took the name of Lenin (1870–1924), preferred discipline and unity, unity in leadership, unity in doctrine, unity in membership. In 1903 at the second party congress in London he split the party over his refusal to behave in a conciliatory manner towards his opponents at a moment when he had secured a majority (hence the title of his section, the Bolsheviks, from the Russian word *Bolshoi*=large i.e. the majority) on the control of the party newspaper, *Iskra*. His minority opponents, the Mensheviks, went ahead with their efforts to turn the party into a mass movement.

The Mensheviks regarded themselves still as part of the international socialist revolutionary movement. But this itself was to be stirred to its roots by the issue which separated both Mensheviks and Bolsheviks from the third group of Russian Marxists. This group argued that the main effort of the Socialist movement should go into the economic front. They were themselves divided into two groups, the Economists arguing for the use of the strike, the Legal Marxists for political pressure for remedial legislation. The issue was formulated most clearly in Germany in the controversy between Karl Kautsky (1864–1938), the party theorist, and Edouard Bernstein (1850–1932), the leading exponent of the theory known as Revisionism. Bernstein argued that socialism could be achieved by an accumulation of piecemeal changes to be brought about by participation in the process of legislation in co-operation with other parties. His view was akin to those held by the Fabian Society in Britain, with their doctrines of permeation, legislation and social reform from above and their belief in the 'inevitability of gradualism'. It was carried to its logical extreme by the independent French socialists, Alexander Millerand (1859–1943) and René Viviani (1863–1925), the first of whom brought on himself the condemnation of the 1900 Congress of the Socialist International for taking a portfolio in the Waldeck-Rousseau cabinet in France the previous year. Millerand and those who followed his example were to be formally expelled by the Socialist International under German insistence following Kautsky's victory over Bernstein. The Fabians, never being affiliated with the International, were able at an early date to convert the British labour movement to their point of view.

But concentration on economic action could lead those who advocated it to an entirely opposite course, that of the revolutionary general strike, of industrial action to secure revolution, the abolition of the wage system, the expropriation of the capitalists, worker ownership and control of industry, in sum unremitting class war. Those who advocated such doctrines were known generally as Syndicalists. Their main strength lay in France, Spain and Italy, and, by reason of the diffuseness of government mentioned above, in the United States with the formation of the International Workers of the World, the IWW or 'Wobblies' in 1905.

A strong element in syndicalism was its fascination with violence; from this element was to develop a small but influential school of writers such as Georges Sorel (1847–1922), Vilfredo Pareto (1848–1923), Robert Michels (1876–1936), whose deification of violence, irrationalism and leadership by *élites* was to make the movement from extreme syndicalism to Fascism an easy step for intellectuals to take. Early forms of Fascism were in fact developing especially in France and in Central Europe in this period, though it was a Fascism which depended on racialism, the deification of the nation and the organized use of force rather than the ending of social conflict. Its leaders were the brilliant school of French writers grouped around the newspaper *La Libre Parole*; Leon Daudet, Maurice Barrés, Edouard Drumont, Charles Maurras. It expressed itself through organizations such

51

as Deroulede's *Ligue des Patriots,* the young wealthy political hoodlums of the *Camelots du Roi,* the *Action Française* movement, and Drumont's *Socialistes Chrétiens.* In Germany proper it was much less strong. Anti-Semitism existed, as did the traditions of violence and militarism expressed in the student duelling associations and in the Army. But the various ingredients of Nazism had still to come together. In Italy, where the poet, Gabriele d'Annunzio, and the Futurist, Marinetti, were active, there were already groups known as *Fasces.* In Vienna both Czech and German nationalist deputies had discovered the use of violence and rowdyism as a means of political obstruction. Anti-semitism flourished. Extreme nationalist students organizations had begun to imitate the *Camelots du Roi.* And both in Vienna and in Munich a crop of little-known writers had begun to extol the virtues of Germanism, Aryanism, selective breeding and the extermination of the Jews. But political violence was still the prerogative of the Anarchists. President Carnot of France in 1895 and President McKinley of the United States in 1901, were only the most notable victims of anarchist assassins.

A third type of socialism, apart from that of the Second International and the followers of Lenin, was the peasant agrarian socialism of Russia and Eastern Europe. The most important manifestation of this agrarian socialism was the Russian Social Revolutionary party which held its first congress in 1898, as a revival of the Russian Populists of the 1870s, under Victor Chernov (1870–1952). A Croat peasant socialist party was founded in December 1904 by Stepan Radić (1878–1928). And ideals of peasant socialism were very strong in the second Zionist *aliyah* leading to the inspiration of the *Kibbutz* movement. A somewhat similar though much less doctrinaire manifestation was the agricultural co-operative movement in Germany and Eastern Europe associated with the name of F. W. Raffeisen (1818–88).

Most of these movements spread only through Europe and overseas on the wings of the great European emigration to the United States. But there were some interesting counter-currents. One, alluded to above, was the spread of Russian peasant socialism to Palestine through a wing of the Zionist movement. A second was the extension of early American syndicalism, embodied in the Knights of Labour, to Canada, Australia and Latin America, to be followed later by a similar extension of the IWW movement. A third was the counter spread of Ethiopianism and early Afro-American nationalism from the American Negro community to Africa. A fourth was the movement of Islamic and Arab nationalism stretching from India to Morocco. The future shape of the new universalist movements, both genuinely universalist and universalist nationalisms, could be vaguely seen.

In the 1900s, however, the main universalist nationalisms were Pan-Anglo-Saxonism, Pan-Teutonism, Pan-Germanism and Pan-Slavism. Of these, Pan-Teutonism, however, was little more than an emotion, 'a nebulous thing which lent itself admirably to after-dinner speeches'. It inspired the British statesman Joseph Chamberlain in his speech of 1899 in which he spoke of the 'natural alliance' between Germany, Britain and the United States. It led Cecil Rhodes, the British millionaire visionary, to include Germans and Americans among those eligible for the Oxford University scholarships set up by his will. It played its part in arousing German sentiment in favour of the Boers and against Britain during the South African War. But as a movement Pan-Teutonism never got off the ground. Pan-Anglo-Saxonism was stronger, inspiring neo-imperialists both in Britain and in the eastern United States. It was evident in the works of Captain Mahan, the writer on naval matters, whose books spread the gospel of sea power throughout the world. It inspired such organizations as the Pilgrims, the English-Speaking Union and the 'Round Table' school of neo-imperialists which developed in the British Conservative and Liberal parties after 1906. It is to be found in the thoughts of President Theodore Roosevelt of the United States and in the writings of Rudyard Kipling. Its real influence on the policy of either Britain or the United States is difficult to determine. It did not so much rule out the possibility of war between the two countries as give such a war the added terrors and resentments of a war between brothers, a civil war within the Anglo-American community.

Pan-Germanism was a far stronger movement expressing itself through various organizations in both Germany and Austria-Hungary, of which the German Pan-German League itself was only one among several. To some degree the movement was stronger in Austria-Hungary than in Germany, especially in the areas of Bohemia disputed by the Germans and Czechs. Georg von Schönerer, leader of the Austrian pan-German party, was elected to the Austrian *Reichsrath* in 1873. In 1882 he united with the future leaders of the Austrian Social Democratic party to advocate a central European customs union between Germany and an Austria divested of her Polish, Rumanian and South Slav provinces. The foundation of the German National Union, *Deutsche Nationalverein*, in 1882 was followed twelve years later by that of the German People's Party, *Deutsche Volkspartei*. That same year the Pan-German League was founded in Germany. It had been preceded by the formation of the German School League, *Deutsche Schulverein*, and the funnelling of German money through the Reich German School League into the maintenance of German schools in Bohemia. Schönerer's nationalism was anti-semitic, anti-Catholic and anti-Slav. With him and his rival in the German nationalist movement, Karl Wolf, who was elected to the *Reichsrath* in 1897 from the Bohemian constituency of the Egerland, Germanism was on the defensive against the growing strength of Slav nationalism in central and eastern Europe.

The Pan-German League in Germany was most important as an anti-democratic pressure group. With its mere 15,000–25,000 members drawn mainly from middle-class backgrounds, its strength lay in its links with other similar groups and its support in the German press and within the junior ranks of the army. Its main importance in German politics was to come after the outbreak of war in 1914.

Pan-Slavism existed both in Russia and among the Slavs of Austria. The first Pan-Slav organization, the Moscow Slavonic Benevolent Committee dated back to 1858, the first international congress to 1867. It was hostile to both Germany and Britain and deeply opposed to the nationalism of the minor Slav races. Poland was not a nation but a 'poisoned dagger which the west thrust into Slavdom's heart'. In 1876 the Ukrainian Uniate Church was suppressed in the name of Slav unity. In the 1890s Russification was extended to the Germans of the Baltic provinces, to Finland and to the Caucasus. In the 1880s the first great pogroms of modern times were launched against the Jews of Kiev and Odessa. The Czechs were exhorted to embrace the Cyrillic alphabet and the Orthodox Church. Like the Pan-German movement, Pan-Slavism was less an outgrowth of the aristocracy than a movement of the upper *bourgeoisie* and its loyalty was reserved for Russia rather than to the dynasty ruling her. Its strength grew as the dynasty weakened. Its enemies were Germanism, Catholicism, Socialism and Zionism—the other universals—and of course Britain.

## Movements Within the System

With the possible exception of the two major ideological movements of Socialism and Social Catholicism, all the political movements discussed in the two preceding sections were national before becoming international. There were other movements which were more genuinely international in character. One could perhaps even call them intranational in that they operated among and between the peoples of the individual nations rather than between their governments. One can distinguish four important movements which partook of this character: the movement towards intellectual co-operation, the humanitarian movement which expressed itself in the campaign against slavery and prostitution and in the growth of the Red Cross movement, the pacifist and disarmament movements and finally in a class of its own, Zionism.

In the first of these one can distinguish five different fields: the movement towards intellectual co-operation *per se* of which the most significant example was the foundation in 1895 of the *Société internationale d'études, de correspondance et d'échanges*, otherwise known as Concordia, with headquarters in Paris, whose declared aim was to promote good international relations by study of their intellectual, moral and economic 'manifestations'; the movement towards the development of an international language which had by 1900 fathered two main artificial languages, *Volapük* (which had largely run its course by 1900) and *Esperanto*, the creation of Louis Zamenhof (1859–1917), a Jew from Russian Poland; the movement towards the development of an agreed body of international law and a community of its practitioners, of which the major figures were Franz von Liszt (1851–1919), a German, and L. Oppenheim (1858–1919), a Briton; the major journals were Belgian, French and German, and the guiding institutes, the *Institut de Droit International* and the International Law Association, were both founded in 1873, on a genuinely international basis; the movement towards international scientific collaboration which resulted in 1899 in the formation of the International Association of Academics which linked together the principal learned societies of the civilized world; and lastly the organization of international co-operation in the control of epidemic diseases which had resulted by 1900 in the signature of three conventions designed to prevent the spread of cholera from the Asiatic world to Europe along the Arab and Ottoman shores of the Mediterranean.

The humanitarian movement had many aspects, of which perhaps the most important were the campaigns against the slave-trade, and the traffic in women. The first of these had largely been a British campaign until the abolition of slavery in the United States in 1864 and in Latin America in the 1880s and the opening of Africa in the 1880s which united the European powers against the Arab slavers of the Indian Ocean and the Red Sea. In 1890, at Brussels, seventeen powers including the United States, the Ottoman Empire, the Congo Free State and Persia jointly established a code of anti-slave trade regulations and formed international bureaus in Brussels and Zanzibar. The function of the latter was to provide up-to-date intelligence on the movements and activities of Arab slavers. The second took two forms, the setting up of international organizations to protect women against the lures of the pimp and the pander, and the conclusion of international agreements for the exchange of information on the traffic in women and action against those who undertook to conduct the caravans of unfortunate women across Europe's borders to the brothels of Asia and Latin America. (The internal European trade had been largely eliminated by 1899.) A rather different though equally important element was the growth of the International Red Cross after the international Geneva Convention of 1864 had established the principle of the neutralization of ambulances and health personnel. The International Committee of the Red Cross, itself post-dated the formation of more than 22 national Red Cross Societies, being set up in 1880 as the successor to the *Comité internationale et permanent de secours aux militaires blessés*, with an entirely Swiss membership. At the Hague conference of 1899 a second convention was adopted extending the provisions of the Geneva conference to war at sea.

The movement towards the 'humanization of war' ran in very close harness with that towards its abolition by the proclamation of pacifism, disarmament and the substitution of arbitration for force as the solution of international disputes. This movement had its religious and economic adherents, but much more important was the growth of such bodies as the

Interparliamentary Union (1859) and the Universal Peace Congress (1889)ʾ the establishment of the Nobel Peace Prize (first awarded in 1901), and the Hague conference of 1899 on disarmament, arbitration and the laws of war, which achieved certain very limited successes especially in the establishment of a Court of Arbitration. This movement was to become the forerunner of the far more powerful organizations of the inter-war years.

The last of these international movements was of quite a different kind, that of Zionism, the movement to create a nation for the Jews of the world. Zionism, like other European nationalist movements, began as a cultural and historical force, among philosophers, writers and historians. The factors which differentiated Zionism from the other submerged European national-isms of the nineteenth century were the religious system it built on, the long historical self-conscious continuity of the Jewish communities, their differentiation according to the different nations in which the various Diasporae had caused them to settle, the solidarity of the major Jewish communities of Tsarist Eastern Europe, the terrible persecution these com-munities suffered under Tsarist rule from the 1880s onwards, their great emigration into western Europe and the United States, and, finally, the fact that the geographical area around which they built their national myth had not seen a Jewish political organization for eighteen hundred years.

As a Jewish phenomenon, Zionism depended on the inter-action of three elements, the emancipation of the Jews of western and central Europe in the first part of the nineteenth century, the collective consciousness of the Jewish communities in western Russia and Poland, and the fact of Tsarist persecution. The bulk of established western Jewry, in Britain, France, Germany, Austria-Hungary, the Netherlands and Italy, had embraced emancipation as a step towards assimilation. The Jews of eastern Europe reacted in the opposite direction. The Tsarist massacres pushed them further. The first Zionist groups, the *Hoveve Zion*, began in western Russia in the early 1880s. Their first president, Leon Pinsker, from Odessa, published his *Auto-Emanzipation*, in 1882. That same year the First *Aliyah*, the first wave of Zionist-inspired immigrants, arrived in Palestine, then under Turkish rule. They were followed by the most idealistic of all Zionists, the Russian *Bilaim*, who were determined to found Israel's destiny on the land of Israel, as agricultural workers.

The scattered Jewish communities that resulted from this first wave of immigration into Palestine, were kept going mainly by the moneys of the French *Alliance Israelite Universelle*, and their principal banker, Baron Edward de Rothschild of the French branch of that great Jewish banking family. The impetus which built these first stirrings into a major intra-national movement and which turned a Messianic dream into an effective political force on the international stage came from Theodore Herzl, a western Jew from Vienna. Like the Rothschilds, Herzl had been reared in the tradition of the *Hof-Jude* (the Court Jew), who protected his interests by the maintenance of good relations and the offer of personal service to the autocratic courts of western and central Europe, rather than in the collective solidarity of the East European ghettoes. In 1896, Herzl, Paris correspondent of the leading Viennese daily, *Neue Freie Presse*, published his appeal for a Jewish state, *der Judenstaat*. In 1897 he summoned the first World Zionist Congress in Basel in Switzerland. In 1901 the Jewish Colonial Trust was established to buy land in Palestine. And from 1899 until his death in 1904, Herzl paid assiduous court to the rulers of Europe and Turkey. His only offer of aid from those he courted came in 1903 from Britain, when the British government offered him Uganda as a place of settlement. Herzl wished to accept this offer. But it was indignantly rejected by the Russian Jewish delegates to the Zionist Congress. In 1904, the Second *Aliyah*, some fifteen to twenty thousand settlers, nearly all of Russian Jewish origin, left Europe for Palestine. They came inspired by the agrarian socialism of the Russian Social Revolutionaries, and with the aid of the Jewish Colonial Trust, they began to found the socialist land settlements, the *Kibbutzim*, for which Israel was later to become so well known. In addition, they succeeded, over the opposition of French and German Jewry, in making Hebrew their national tongue. Among them was David Grun, the future Ben-Gurion.

## Internal Political and Social Crises

As the nineteenth century ended, each of the major European powers was racked by its own internal stresses and strains. In Britain the movement for Irish Home Rule was temporarily in eclipse. One generation of leaders had been defeated or disgraced by personal scandal. The Irish parliamentary party had settled down into a respectable parliamentarianism. But beneath the surface a new generation of leaders, poetic extremists, were about to emerge and usher in the bloody series of events by which Ireland was to bring Britain to the verge of civil war and eventually to win independence. In Britain itself, the Whig and radical elements in the Liberal party were beginning to separate, and one could see also beneath the surface a similar parting of the ways between the agrarian radicals of the western Celtic littoral and the new labour movement of the Scottish lowlands and the English and Welsh industrial areas. Enmity for the established church, the hereditary aristocracy, and the House of Lords acted as a unifying theme, as did the memory of Queen Victoria's Diamond Jubilee and, for all but a courageous few, the hurrah-patriotism of the war in South Africa.

Across the channel, France was bitterly divided by the question of the guilt of the Jewish staff officer, Captain Dreyfus, wrongly condemned for espionage in 1894. On the one side stood the radicals and anti-clericals, driven by their desire at all costs to see justice done, on the other, the traditional patriots, concerned above all to see the Army, in which they felt France's soul and hope of revenge on Germany for the loss of Alsace-

Lorraine to be incorporated, preserved free of criticism and denigration. Violence, anti-Semitism and proto-Fascism allied themselves with the anti-Dreyfusards, Freemasonry, anti-clericalism and ambition with their opponents. In the meantime, the French working class movement remembered the Paris Commune and listened to the syndicalists who preached direct action.

In Germany, the system erected by the great Chancellor, Bismarck, was in steady decline; in election after election the total votes gained by the Democrats, the Social Democrats and the other parties hostile to the system increased; the Army leadership turned more and more in an anti-political direction; and the power and prestige of the chancellorship and the Kaiser ebbed away. In Austria-Hungary, Chancellor Badeni's attempt to solve the language issue in bilingual Bohemia was defeated by the increasingly intransigent nationalism of both Germans and Czechs alike. The municipality of Vienna three times elected the Social Catholic demagogue, Karl Lueger, as its Mayor against the Emperor's veto. In Italy thwarted nationalism, radical anti-Catholicism and suppressed Socialism were building up slowly towards an explosion. In every country a superficial view showed a calm sunset closing the nineteenth century. More penetrating eyes, however, could see clearly the signs that portended storm.

Nowhere was this clearer than in the arts. To the contemporary eye much in the music, printing and literature of the *fin de siècle* seemed both ethically and aesthetically unsound. The British academic critic, Ruskin, who died in 1900, could describe the painter Whistler's work as 'a pot of paint flung in the face of the public'. But in retrospect his work and that of his associates in the British literary world seem as romantic as those of their continental colleagues. In 1898, for example, J. K. Huysmans, the French writer whose study of decadent aestheticism, *A Rebours* (1884), had had so deep an influence on Oscar Wilde and Aubrey Beardsley in Britain, was still writing. Wilde, disgraced for homosexuality, published *The Ballad of Reading Jail*. The Prince of Wales, visiting an exhibition of the French painter, Toulouse-Lautrec, in London, found the pathetic cripple asleep on a sofa and refused to disturb him. Ravel, the last of the French romantic composers, published his first work, and the great Italian composer, Giuseppe Verdi, had his last work performed in Turin with the young Toscanini as its conductor. The French Impressionists, Manet, Monet, Degas, Sisley, Pissarro, Renoir, were finally achieving the popularity that so long had eluded them.

However, the dominant school in *avant-garde* Paris was that of the post-impressionists, Cézanne, Seurat, van Gogh, the Douanier Rousseau. Gauguin was dying in the Marquesas islands of French Polynesia, Toulouse-Lautrec was to die the following year (1901). And already the younger painters who were to dominate Paris for the next forty years were gathering: Picasso, Fernand Léger, Matisse, Utrillo, Raoul Dufy. All were still painting in what was essentially a nineteenth-century Romantic representational style, concerned above all with colour and light, as the name, Fauvism, soon to be applied to their work, suggests. In sculpture Rodin's romanticized realism dominated Paris. The revolt of the twentieth century artists and musicians, their obsession with shape, form and architecture, their attempts to demolish existing aesthetics and remake everything from first principles lay some seventeen years in the future with Cubism, Surrealism and Dadaism in painting and Atonalism in music. It was significant, however, that intellectually the separation between them and the aesthetic accepted by the society in which they lived had already been effected. And in their midst lived the two men whose scientific theories were to dominate the first half of the twentieth century, the mathematician, Einstein, and the psychologist, Sigmund Freud, who destroyed traditional physics and psychology to replace them with their exploration of the incomprehensible theory of relativity and the irrational depths of the sub-conscious.

Beneath the surface, however, the new forces were also at work. The main developments took place in the field of physics and philosophy. As early as 1887 a series of experiments had revealed the inadequacy of the mechanistic view of the physical universe, governed by a consistent and universal body of discoverable principles, to explain the phenomena of light and radiation. In the last decade of the century, scientists investigating radio-activity and nuclear physics were accumulating data of increasing complexity and inexplicability in the terms of existing science. At the same time the dominant schools of philosophy were suffering a series of distinctive attacks from three different directions. In the understanding of the nature of scientific argument, Ernst Mach in Prague and Vienna, Henri Poincaré in Paris, and Hans Vaihinger in Berlin, developing from Kant and the British empiricists, were destroying the idea that the intellectual activity of science consisted in the elucidation of 'laws'. In the examination of the nature and history of society, the position of Spencer, Marx and the Social Darwinists had already come under the concerted attack of Emile Durckheim in France who was, with Max Weber, one of the two co-founders of the new sociology, as well as from Vilfredo Pareto, an Italian exile in Switzerland, and Benedetto Croce in Italy. And the whole structure of nineteenth-century thought, with its optimistic belief in moral progress had already been savaged beyond hope of recovery by the German prophet and critic, Friedrich Nietzsche, writing in the late 1880s. For these writers, the problems of consciousness, of the meaning of time and duration, of the nature of knowledge and reality were all important. Between new philosophers and the natural scientists the 'observed realities' of the common-sense view of the world were to disappear. At the same time Europe's leaders were pulling down the accepted structure of the political world around them. In such a relativist world, it was not to be long before those who despaired of achieving certainty themselves would fall victim to lesser men who had no doubts.

## Chapter III
# THE IMPACT OF EUROPE ON THE EXTERNAL WORLD: THE AREAS OF ACTIVITY AND PROGRESS

## Introduction

IN 1900, the societies of the non-European world already had four centuries of contact with and conquest by the states of Western Europe behind them. In the process the great native states of America and West Africa had largely disappeared. Settlers had herded the North American Indians into a scattered collection of reservations, occupied the temperate highlands of Central Africa and largely taken over the grazing grounds of the Bantu in South Africa. The Ottoman Empire had been defeated and driven out of Central Europe. The Indian states system had been in a state of decay even during the establishment of the first puny settlements of Portugal, France and the British East India Company. The same processes of disintegration had also been at work in South-East Asia and in the islands of the Indonesian archipelago, and the Moslem Khanates of Central Asia.

But the events of the last quarter of the nineteenth century, with its immense increase in European pressure, had made the divisions in the external world infinitely more apparent. Both among those states which were essentially extensions of the European system, and among those which remained recognizably alien to it, one can detect the existence of a broad gulf between those who were already in the strongest reaction against that pressure, developing their own indigenous nationalisms, seeking solutions to their problems which would be their own and not imposed on them, trying to develop their own strength so that they could stand up to and take their part among the great powers of the European appendix, and those which still lay stagnant and whose major awakening was to come in the future.

European pressures presented themselves in three different forms. First, there was the pressure of trade, money-lending and investment, an experience which led state after state into bankruptcy and subordination to, if not occupation by, its European creditors. Secondly, there were the

60

varying pressures of European power-politics which led in some cases to direct conquest, in others to situations where it seemed advisable to seek the protection of the strongest, and protectorates, with their apparatus of resident advisers, were established and accepted. Only a small handful of states managed to retain their independence as buffers between the powers, one or two, notably Abyssinia and Afghanistan, proving themselves capable of permanently defeating a would-be conqueror in conditions where his superior military technology could not be brought to bear. Third were the pressures of European population, expanding themselves in an immense wave of emigration, involving something of the order of $55\frac{1}{2}$ million Europeans in the period 1820–1924, the bulk of which emigration was concentrated into the period before 1914. Of the emigrants, nineteen million came from Great Britain, six million from Germany, about the same number of Italians, over a million each from Sweden, Portugal, Austria and Hungary; and about $4\frac{1}{2}$ million Jews came from Poland and Russia into Western Europe and the Americas in the same period. There was also a very considerable internal migration of Russians into Siberia, about $2\frac{1}{2}$ million peasants moving eastwards, between 1891 and 1910. The only comparable movements of non-Europeans were: the emigration of Indians, largely, in the form of contract labour, which led to there being a total overseas Indian population of more than two million by 1924, mainly in Ceylon, Malaya, the West Indies, Mauritius and Fiji; the exodus from China, which by 1924 resulted in an estimated eight million Chinese living overseas, the majority residing in Formosa, Indonesia and South-East Asia (there was also a considerable Chinese emigration into Manchuria); the movement from Japan, which by 1922 accounted for over half a million Japanese living overseas, mainly in China, the United States, Hawaii, Canada and Brazil; and an unknown volume of African slaves taken by the Arab slavers from East Africa to destinations in Arabia, Egypt and the Moslem Middle East.[1] Within Europe itself, about 600,000 immigrants entered France in the period 1860–1911.

## Extra-European Europe

At the beginning of the twentieth century, Russia and the United States, the two great super-powers of the mid-century, enjoyed a peculiar status, being both within and beyond the European states system, at once accepting and rejecting the values, ideas and traditions of European culture. Both had been subjected to the pressures of European ideas and culture for at least two centuries, and both had had time therefore to develop their own native reactions to those pressures, including a brand of radicalism which rejected Europe. The parallels which can be traced between the

[1] See map, p. 25.

two countries' reaction to and relations with Europe, however, illustrate rather the overwhelming strength of the European impact than any similarity in their historical development, except for the presence of a strong tradition of agrarian radicalism in both. But even there the parallel is in form and not content, save in a common hostility to and rejection of European capitalism in preference to a nativist romantic idealization of the simple virtues of the agricultural community.

Of the two, **Tsarist Russia** was the major survivor of that alternative form of Christianity which grew out of the schism between Rome and Constantinople. It was a state, by this very token, whose rulers had had to force its native nobility into western forms and moulds. In its political system it was a hierarchical and aristocratically-limited absolutism with a strong element of theocracy, in that the Tsar was also revered throughout Russia as the head of the State Orthodox Church, and the 'Father of all the Russias'. In the early nineteenth century, Russia had come to dominate the European scene after the defeat of Napoleon, and to millions of Europeans, Tsarist Russia represented the blackest form of reactionary aggressive authoritarianism. As a great power, however, Tsarist Russia had feet of clay and her major encounters with the western powers in the Crimean War and at the Congress of Berlin in 1878 revealed such internal weaknesses that in each case the Tsardom was driven to attempt to reform itself. By 1900, in consequence of the piecemeal and partial nature of these reforms and the inevitable reaction against them, Tsarist Russia was on the edge of revolution.

In all, eight broad groups can be distinguished as engaged in the internal struggle for power. At their head stood the aristocracy, educated, cultured, westernized, largely French-speaking, providing the Tsarist empire with the higher ranks of both its military and civil bureaucracies. Below them came the country gentry and the civilian bureaucracy itself. These three groups alone had some stake in the continuation of the existing system of authority in Russia. Of the remaining five groups the most powerful potentially were the capitalist class growing up in the big cities, in Moscow, Kiev, Odessa and the industrial centres of Southern Russia. Russian industry developed very rapidly and on a large scale with the aid of French capital, and the cottage and small-scale industry phases of industrial organization, found in Britain's more leisurely industrial development, were largely avoided or short-circuited. Inevitably, however, the members of this group tended to a strong identification with the state which was their major customer and which employed tariffs to protect them against more efficient foreign competition. It is a measure of the incompetence of the Tsarist system that this class was so strongly opposed to its continuance.

Below them came four groups with no stake whatever in the Russian state. First and most important were the peasants, emancipated from serfdom in the 1860s but still labouring under the burden of the redemption dues payable to their former owners, dominated by hunger for land and the pains and strains of adaptation to a money economy, without any capital to tide them over bad harvests or to improve their extremely primitive agricultural methods. Gradually, in the villages, the richer peasants were separating themselves from the general ruck at one end of the scale and an agricultural proletariat was also developing at the other, but it was to be some time before the resultant strains were to make themselves felt. In 1900 most Russian peasants were little removed from the kind of despair which can produce a *jacquerie*, and their dominant emotions were hatred of the landlords and hunger for land. Second were the industrial workers, separating themselves since the 1880s from their peasant forebears, especially in Western Russia, Russian Poland and the industrial areas of the Caucasus and South Russia. Third were the subject nationalities. For Tsarist Russia, as noted earlier, was a multi-racial state dominated by its Great Russian element. Finns, German Balts, Estonians, Latvians, Lithuanians, Byelo-Russians, Poles, Jews, Ukrainians, Georgians, Armenians, Azerbaijanis, Kirghiz, Uzbeks, Kalmucks, Tatars, all had come or were coming to hate the Tsarist state and to look on the first sign of its weakening for a chance to assert their independence. Of all these the most striking case was that of the German Balts, imported in the eighteenth century to strengthen the bureaucratic element in Russia, but now moving steadily away from their loyalty to the Tsar as the Tsardom began to take on a Great Russian aspect.

The last group consisted of the intelligentsia, the university-educated class for whom there was no real place in the Tsarist system. This system denied them status, paid them little, and stultified most of their efforts to apply their intelligence to finding new solutions to Russia's problems. Small wonder that their more radically minded elements turned inevitably to assassination and revolutionary activities. As a class their hallmark was that they possessed little apart from their intellectual capital, though their members came from every social level in Russia.

All these groups looked to and at Europe in different ways. The aristocracy embraced French culture but, except for its more idealistic members, shied away from any imitation of European constitutional models. The gentry and the *bourgeoisie* in large measure joined in admiration for such models. The more public-spirited among the gentry had been developing a good deal of ability in the practice of parliamentarianism in the local Councils, the *Zemstva*, set up by the reforms of the 1860s; the industrialist-capitalist class could not but admire a system which, as in France or Britain, would give them so large a share in the political leadership of the state. Within the bureaucracy their viewpoint was shared and protected by the Ministry of Finance.

And yet among the gentry there were many who were disturbed by that competitive commercialism which they believed to be the hallmark of Western Europe. Some no doubt believed their own position would be threatened if the hierarchical system which kept their peasantry subservient was upset. Others embraced a romantic paternalism for which parallels were not lacking in Europe but which they professed to believe to be specifically Russian. Many were suspicious of or hostile to the new industrialist families whose wealth and manner of living offended the more traditionally minded. All these embraced a romantic Pan-Slavism, expressed within the bureaucracy by the police and the Ministry of the Interior, and embodied in Pobedonostsev, tutor to the young Tsar before his accession.

The main division between Europophiles and -phobes, or Westerners and Slavophiles as they were classified at the time, was to be found among the intelligentsia with its revolutionary critique of Russian society. The main point at issue was whether it was inevitable or desirable that Russia's economic and social development should parallel that of the societies of Western and Central Europe. Given their general dislike of the selfishness and individualism of western capitalist society with its horrors in the exploitation of man by man, its lack either of social conscience or of social justice, its anti-aestheticism, its ugliness, its slums, was there not perhaps, the Russian Europophobes argued, an alternative set of developments, a Russian way to the social millenium. Some of the revolutionary intelligentsia believed in Russian solutions and as a result became preoccupied with the peasant problem, central to considerations of social justice in Russia. Thus, though the first Russian revolutionary outbreak, the Decembrist revolt of 1825, had been entirely western in impulse, the activist wing of the revolutionary movement in the mid-nineteenth century, the so-called *narodniks* who had gone out to live and spread their doctrines among the peasants, had found in the village co-operative, the *mir*, and the cottage industrial co-operative, the *artel*, primitive but purely Russian models for the social organizations they wished to see supersede Tsarist autocracy. Their eclipse, and the subsequent resort of the intellectual revolutionaries to terrorism was also a very Russian phenomenon. But by the late 1880s this in turn had been superseded by the growth of Marxist socialism which marked a return to the revolutionary models of Western Europe discussed in Chapter I. But from the late 1890s onwards the *narodnik* tradition was revived by the Social Revolutionary party, and the single characteristic institution which was to emerge from the revolution of 1905, the *Soviet*, owed nothing to Western revolutionary models.

The **United States** differed from Russia first of all in being an *emigré* state, a society consisting of those whose dissatisfaction with Europe had led them to leave it, where Russia had been forced to join Europe by the admiration and envy of its rulers. Founded in 1776 by the *élites* of the thirteen rebellious British colonies, it had survived the ordeals of the revolutionary wars by adopting a federal structure which prevented centripetal forces from rending it apart in its early days. Thereafter this new nation had embarked on a policy of expansion westwards across the American continent which, after wars with Britain in 1812 and Mexico in 1846, had carried the Stars and Stripes to the Pacific, the 49th Parallel and the Rio Grande. The Atlantic ocean and the British navy between them had insulated it against any necessity to cramp its society into a military frame-work as the price of political survival. Without British sea power, the United States' adoption of the policy of avoiding European entanglements and warning the European powers off the Americas, enjoined in its first President, Washington's, Farewell Address of 1796, and embodied in President Monroe's proclamation of 1823, would have been largely pointless. It was doubly fortunate in that for much of the nineteenth century, including the critical period of the 1860s, Europe was absorbed in its own internal conflicts. The only major European intervention, that of France in Mexico in the 1860s, ended in disaster for the French, and the only other European power to make its pressure felt in the Americas was the decaying empire of Spain. Russia abandoned her pretensions in the 1820s and her presence in 1867 when the United States bought Alaska for $7,200,000.

Europe's preoccupation with the problems of Italian and German unification enabled the United States to survive its own moment of crisis without European intervention. But the Civil War of 1861–65 destroyed the socio-economic system of the southern states, and ushered in a period of industrial feudalism both in the north and the west which was to last for more than half a century. The temporary emancipation of the Negroes in political, though not in economic terms, and the break-up of the large estates into sharecropping and crop-lien small-holdings made the south an agrarian peasant economy dependent on a single crop, cotton, a develop-ment which had strong parallels with the state of affairs in late nineteenth-century Russia. However, the creation in America of an agrarian peasant economy was greatly complicated by the Negro question and the absence of a hereditary land-owning class. At the same time, the development of large-scale mining in gold, silver and copper, and of cattle ranching and, following this, the increasing role of the transcontinental railways as intermediaries between the federal government and the settlers in the distribution of land, introduced the same element of capitalist feudalism into the west. Although the new settlers owned their own land they were still effectively in the power of the railroads, the warehouses and the banks which controlled the terms whereby the produce of their land could be marketed. The latter part of the nineteenth century saw the growth of the great American fortunes and families, the Rockefellers, the Harrimans, the Vanderbilts, the cattle barons, the 'robber barons'. But it also saw the growth of an agrarian radicalism as potent as, and stronger than, the agrarian radicalism of Europe, although it was to be sixty years before the political strength of industrial feudalism was to come under serious assault.

This agrarian radicalism expressed itself in three great waves, the Granger movement which reached its greatest strength in the period 1868–76, the Farmers Alliances of the 1880s, and Populism in the 1890s. Of the three the Granger movement with its strong co-operative aspect was the only one with any element of collectivism. American agrarian radicalism was essentially democratic and individualist. It was also opposed to large-scale capitalism and trades unionism and quite as racialist and nativist as were the radicals of Europe.

It's other major difference from the peasant radicalism of Europe was in its obsession with cheap money, above all with bimetallism. Bimetallism, the use of both gold and silver to back the currency at a rate of approximately sixteen ounces of silver to one of gold, was normal international practice until the beginning of the 1870s when most of Europe adopted a simple gold standard, and the immense silver deposits of the American mountain states discovered in the previous decade lost any chance of a government market. Silver ceased to be coined in the United States in 1873 and the general effect was to limit drastically the circulation of money, depress commodity prices and raise interest rates. The United States had experimented with a paper currency during the Civil War, the so-called 'green-backs', and the 'cheap money' policy they represented was remembered with gratitude by the farmers of the new west. But at that time, the United States had not been so much a part of the international financial community, and it had been easier to sell American agricultural goods. In the post-1870s the United States was again borrowing heavily from Europe and the tariffs were going up against her agricultural products. Bimetallism in the United States would have involved limiting or suspending the international convertibility of the US dollar since there was far more silver in the world than the United States Treasury could cope with at the set rate of sixteen ounces of silver to one of gold. National bimetallism meant economic isolationism.

This was in some sense the greatest strength of the Populist movement. In 1890 the Populist movement elected 4 Senators and 50 Congressmen, ran its own Presidential candidate in 1892 and captured the Democratic nomination in 1896 for William Jennings Bryan. For the Populists were nativist and anti-European. The two Satanic forces in their universe were the Jews and the English. They were aided by a bad financial panic and widespread unemployment in 1894, and the resultant election of 1896 was fought out on the issue of agrarian radicalism and bimetallism against the economic and financial forces of the east and the industrial mid-west. Populism was, in fact, one aspect of the growth of a native American culture which was not only non-European but opposed to those elements in America for whom European mores were all. Its representatives in American literature at this time were Mark Twain, Stephen Crane, Frank Norris, Willa Cather and Walt Whitman. Their opponents were the Easterners, William Dean Howells, Whistler, Owen Wister (target of one of Mark Twain's most savage essays in criticism), and the novelist, Henry James, who applied for British citizenship in 1914. The populists were defeated in 1896 and again in 1900, but American politics and American culture have continued to oscillate between their American nativism and East Coast Europeanism ever since.

The main element in their defeat was the growth of American nationalism and imperialism. Populism was indeed a part of American nationalism, and the same men whose Americanism impelled them to castigate the East for its links with and dependence on the outside world, were among the first to react to the cry of the 'nation in danger' or to the idea of an American mission abroad. Their consciousness of American differences from Europe was fed in part by glorification of the Anglo-Saxon element in America, thus echoing the racialist element in other nationalisms. But it found much stronger fuel in the belief that the experience of 150 years of pioneering and the democracy of the American frontier had given the American branch of the Anglo-Saxon race something lacking to their cis-Atlantic cousins. While politicians like Senator Henry Cabot Lodge from Massachusetts and writers like Captain Mahan, the naval theorist, lauded the Anglo-Saxon race, the historian, Frederick Jackson Turner, was finding a justification for American national self-consciousness in his famous essay *The Influence of the Frontier in American History*. Together their sentiments and theories voiced a mood which the mass American press orchestrated and amplified. From 1895 when President Cleveland's message to Congress proclaimed American intervention against Britain in a complicated dispute between Britain and Venezuela over the Venezuelan border with British Guiana; through the issue of orders to the American Pacific squadron to attack the Philippines six weeks before the American declaration of war on Spain in April 1898; to the instigation of a separatist revolution in the Colombian province of Panama in 1903 when Colombia was giving the appearance of dragging her heels over the Panama Canal question; American politics were as much dominated by the ideas and politics of imperialism as those of any European great power. But along with the appeals to national interest and manifest destiny, a different point of view emerged, eventually flowering during the presidency of Woodrow Wilson. For want of a better phrase, it could be called 'educative and liberating imperialism'. This point of view appeared in the American support for the Cuban revolutionaries out of which the Spanish-American war had grown, and in the reasoning behind the annexation of the Philippines. The claim was then made that the Filipinos were not ready for independence and therefore it was up to the United States to 'educate . . . uplift and Christianize them'.

From 1900 onwards two new elements were added to Populism in the American radical tradition. The first of these was the revulsion against economic and political feudalism on the part of the new professional classes and their followers in the big American cities of the East and the mid-West. The ideas of the Progressive movement, which came to dominate American politics from 1902–16, were a curious mixture of belief in direct democracy, which harked back to some Jeffersonian ideal of small-town politics in the Revolutionary era, and a determination to strengthen the powers of the Federal Government against the 'bosses' of the big cities with their armies of corrupt and ignorant voters and the business barons who financed them. The period of the Progressive attack on concentrations of economic power saw the first great development of the American press aimed at checking,

67

by investigation and revelation, the illegitimate exercise of power. The movement's strength lay in the sophisticated political expertise of the Progressives and the 'muckraking' of American journalism. From their work sprang a doctrine of liberal pluralist democracy through state action to control the abuse of and concentration of economic power which, with the decline of liberalism in Europe after 1900, was to become the main alternative stream to social democracy in the European democratic tradition.

These developments took place against the background of a staggeringly rapid rate of economic growth. The population of the United States rose from 50 million in 1880 to 97 million in 1913, and 35 million of that increase was added between 1900 and 1913. In the same period coal production rose from 64·8 million tons to 517 million tons per annum. (British coal production was surpassed in 1900, when the rate for England was 244·6 million tons.) Similar growth figures were to be recorded in every other industry. With this growth went an immense increase in immigration which ran from 1902 onwards at between 750,000 and one million-plus a year, the previous peak figure (1882) having been 780,000 and that for only one year in a decade in which the normal figure had ranged between 300,000 and 600,000 annually. With all this one must add a stupendous increase in the rate of investment of European capital in the United States and in American indebtedness to Europe, which stood in 1914 at the then astronomical figure of 7·2 billion dollars. The first decade of the twentieth century was to make the United States the major industrial power of the world. By the end of the second decade America would be transformed from the world's greatest debtor to the world's greatest creditor.

In the remainder of the world the only other states which can be discussed under the same heading as the United States and Russia, that is as extensions of the European system, are the **settler states of the British Empire**, the Boer republics of South Africa, and the states of Latin America. Of these the Boer republics came under the category of escapist states and with the Latin American states are discussed in the next chapter. British colonial rule outside the Dominions and India was devoted principally to the maintenance of order, the passage of British trade, and the establishment and encouragement of local economic activity as a means of raising the contributions of local revenues to the cost of administration. German colonial rule lasted for so short a time in Africa that it hardly got beyond the establishment of order and power. Italian colonial rule penetrated just a little more deeply. Only in France can one trace the beginnings of a colonial policy before 1900, and it was to develop as an unstable blending of three conflicting ideas, mercantilism to promote French economic interests, assimilation of the native *élites* through education, and investigation, admiration and preservation of existing cultural and political organizations for all but a handful of the native populations.

The white settler states of the British Empire, Canada, South Africa, Australia and New Zealand all show the development of the same sense of nationalism, of separate identity already traced in the United States. In Canada and South Africa this was complicated by the existence of a second nationalism, that of the French Canadians and the Boers. In both cases this second nationalism produced difficult obstacles to the achievement of self-government. This phenomenon of double emergence, an emergent nationalism bringing with it another directly opposed to it is to be seen also in the Ottoman Empire after the Young Turk revolution of 1908 and in India. But in neither of these two cases was it to be complicated by white racialism as in the settler states. In South Africa the whites became very conscious of their own small numbers in comparison with the overwhelming majority of the natives they were displacing. And the white settlers in Australia and New Zealand felt the massive pressure of the surrounding Asian populations seeking entry.

**Canada** was the first of the British settler states to achieve self-government and independence within the general framework of empire; and the present structure of the Commonwealth owes more to Canada than to any other state. Her nationalism developed, as did that of all the white British settler states, by a process of differentiation within a continuing attachment to Britain and things British. But in the Canadian case the differentiation was governed not only by the presence of an open frontier and a constant though never overwhelming flow of immigrants. These factors were present in the development of all the white settler states. Nor was the presence of a long-established European community of great cohesion, with an entirely different language, laws, religion, mores and culture the factor which made Canada the pacemaker in the Empire. A similar factor was also present in South Africa, although in South Africa the ratios between the races were reversed, Boers greatly outnumbering British and non-whites outnumbering both. The factor which made Canadian development unique was the presence and the pull exerted against the normal relationship with Britain by her great neighbour, the United States. Thus though a factor in Canada's history was rivalry between *Canadien* and Canadian with the revolts of 1856, 1870 and 1885 in the Red River area; equally if not more important was the three-way relationship between Britain, Canada and the United States, and Canadian experience, as in the Anglo-American settlement of 1903, that Canadian interests would always have to provide the sacrificial lamb on the altar of Anglo-American unity.

Canada's development in fact grew out of an inter-action between the relations between Canadians and *Canadiens* and relations between Canada as a whole and Britain's general external policy. It was British reaction to the rebellions of 1837 inspired by French Canadian radicalism that led to the evolution of the Durham Report: the doctrine of colonial advance towards economic self-sufficiency and political self-government which set in motion the development of the British Empire into the Commonwealth. It was British Free Trade which led to the establishment of the Dominion of Canada in 1867. But it was the Canadian discovery that union could only

69

be maintained if party allegiances ran across the communal boundaries instead of parallel with them which really established Canada; and the principle thus discovered necessitated continuous compromise on external policy between the different communities. Canada could not lean too close to the imperial connection. Nor could the ultramontane *Canadien* separatists with their *emigré* Royalist clergy altogether succeed in turning Quebec into an eighteenth century agricultural sanctuary separated from the industrialism and urbanism of the twentieth.

In 1900 it was the Liberals who were in power, led by the French Canadian, Sir Wilfred Laurier. For a time Laurier had ended the control of the separatist *Ligue Nationaliste* in Quebec. And it was Laurier who withstood imperialist pressure in Britain at the Colonial Conference of 1902 to set up a 'real council of the Empire'. But after 1904, when the creation of the new provinces of Saskatchewan and Alberta led to a revival of that perennially disruptive issue in all part-Catholic countries— parochial versus secular state education—Laurier steadily lost control of his ex-*Canadien* supporters. In 1907, Laurier was again successful in imposing on the Colonial Conference the idea of the Empire as a 'galaxy of nations under the British crown'. However, in the crisis year of 1909 in Anglo-German relations, his acknowledgement that 'when Britain is at war, Canada is at war; there is no distinction' was directly challenged by the *Canadiens* in Quebec. In 1910 his nominee was defeated for election in his home constituency by aroused *Canadiens*, though it was his negotiations of a treaty of commercial reciprocity with the United States in 1911 which led finally to his defeat in Canada as a whole. Nevertheless, the long Laurier period of rule had set the pattern for Canadian politics in the twentieth century.

The Conservatives who replaced him in 1911 had in the past found support in Quebec and the other French-speaking areas from the anti-clerical urban elements. It had been Laurier's success in largely reconciling these elements with the Liberal party that had made it possible for him to break the long period of Conservative rule in 1897. In 1911 the Conservatives, the party of the expansionist imperialist English-speakers, descendants of the American loyalists, had been chastened by the events of 1903 into viewing the imperial connection in very Liberal terms. It was therefore easier for them to ally themselves with Laurier's enemies in Quebec in a political *mariage de convenance*: the more so as Canada had generally been doing very well economically in its trans-oceanic trade with Britain ever since the beginnings of imperial preference enforcements in 1897.

The Conservative interpretation of Canadian nationalism was, however, to prove impossible to reconcile with French Canadian isolationism. In 1912 the Conservative leader Sir Robert Borden went to London and, in return for assurances of a Canadian voice in British policy, agreed to raise $35 million to add three Canadian-owned battleships to be part of an Imperial squadron in the British fleet. Although this move was defeated in the Canadian Senate, the onset of war in 1914 immensely strengthened the whole Conservative position in Canada, and at the same time greatly exacerbated English-French relations. Canada prospered economically, transformed by the needs of Britain to finance not only her war effort but those of her allies from a net borrower to a net lender of capital. By sending nearly half a million men overseas and by suffering 61,000 dead and 175,000 wounded, Canada won a place in the Imperial War Cabinet and separate representation on the British Empire delegation to Versailles. But the political leaders of French Canada largely spent the war years fighting a bitter battle over the use of the French language in the schools of Ontario, and the introduction of conscription in 1917 gave rise to strong separatist manifestations, considerable obstruction, three days of rioting in Quebec itself and wide-scale desertion. Its effects on the Liberal party were to last for another five years or so, and to set a precedent which was to contribute very largely to the *immobilisme* of Canadian foreign policy between the wars.

The early establishment of the Canadian state, and the relatively small number of French Canadians living outside Quebec did at least preserve Canada from the war and civil strife which was to mark the creation of South Africa. But the development of nationalism in South Africa was complicated in a way almost unknown in Canada by the whole question of the non-white majority and of cheap native and immigrant labour. In Canada the original Red Indian population had been largely ousted and confined to reservations by the middle of the nineteenth century. The importation of slave labour from Africa had never been on a very large scale (though it had created in Nova Scotia for a short time the world's oddest linguistic anomaly, a small group of Negro Gaelic speakers), and the largely short-term immigration of labour from the West Indies left a legacy of goodwill between the British Caribbean dependencies and Canada on which the West Indian members of the Commonwealth still attempt to build a policy. The main problem for Canada was that of cheap Oriental labour from China and Japan, one complicated after 1906 by an Anglo-Japanese commercial convention. But after riots in British Columbia and wild talk of secession to the United States the Canadian authorities, with American encouragement, were able to negotiate a direct agreement with Japan for the voluntary limitation of immigration into Canada by the Japanese authorities themselves, without leaving any legacy of ill-will to complicate later Canadian-Japanese relations. This first Canadian step into the field of external relations was followed in 1909 by the creation of a Canadian department of external relations, marking the first break in the principle of centralized control of foreign policy within the British Empire. The negotiations with Japan also marked the first example of the Canadian preference for quiet negotiations in external matters which was to become the distinguishing mark of Canadian activity on the international scene in the mid-twentieth century.

In **South Africa** the development of a common nationalism was impeded for most of the nineteenth century by the existence of a large non-

71

European population which greatly outnumbered both main groups of European settlers. An added hindrance was the determination of a section of the original Dutch settler community to maintain an eighteenth, if not a seventeenth-century separation from the external world, a determination only given temporary quietus by the victory of the British forces in the South African War of 1899–1902. Furthermore, the majority of European settlers were of Dutch not British origin. Schemes of large-scale British settlement never quite succeeded except in the province of Natal. All these factors plus the non-European problem caused the English-speaking settlers to lean more heavily on British colonial rule and to inhibit the growth of the conviction that London neither knew nor cared anything for colonial interests which was the main guiding spirit in the development of settler nationalism in the other parts of the Empire.

Those who administered British colonial rule did their best to apply the principles of the Durham Report to South Africa. But for most of the nineteenth century they had to cope with the problems of a continuous military frontier of a unique type. In the late eighteenth and throughout much of the nineteenth century the main threat was from the southwards-advancing Bantu tribes whose talent for military organization, developed in the long centuries of movement across Africa from their cradle in the Cameroons, made them formidable opponents. But British colonial rule imposed a theoretical quality before the law for all the Crown's subjects; and insistence on this principle drove a section of the Dutch colonists to trek northwards into Africa, where the Dutch founded Boer republics whose precise degree of independence was a matter of constant dispute with the British authorities. And these republics, with their breakaway Synods and extreme sects like the Doppers, fundamentalist and pro-slavery, developed a degree of military organization and a skill in open warfare which the British underestimated at their peril. In the meantime those who stayed behind during this period (sometimes called Afrikaners to distinguish them from the Boer trekkers) developed the habit of co-operation with the British colonials: and it was out of the alliance of the Afrikaner leader, Jan Hofmeyr, and the Englishman, Cecil Rhodes, that a Canadian-style compromise began to emerge. But the discovery of gold on the Rand in the heart of the Transvaal, the largest Boer republic, and the development in Britain of a new wave of imperialism in the 1890s made a conflict between Boer and Briton inevitable. And once such a conflict began, Afrikaner and Boer together viewed Britain as the enemy.

The discovery of gold on the Rand brought a flood of British immigration into the Transvaal, and gave British imperialists a lever to move the Boer republics back under imperial control. The Boers did their best to exclude the new immigrants from participation in their own rather simple democratic political system. But nothing could disguise the fact that the new immigrants were paying most of the costs of state while being denied the franchise. Rhodes' attempt to use their grievances to stage a *coup d'état* by his company police, the so-called Jameson Raid, was a miserable failure. Its consequences were to convince both Boers and Afrikaners that Britain was planning to dominate and destroy their nationality.

The Jameson Raid took place in 1896. Three years later the British were at war with the Boer states in an all-out effort to suppress them. The ostensible reason was the position of the British immigrants, the so-called Uitlanders, in the Transvaal, heavily taxed and denied the franchise. The reason widely accepted at the time by radical opinion generally was that the war was fomented by Rand mining interests who wanted to rid themselves of Boer rule. The real reason seems to have been a conviction in the minds of a handful of British imperialists in dominant positions that there was no room in the British Empire for the separatism which the Boers represented and the conflict of loyalties with which they must constantly confront the Afrikaners under British rule. Sir Alfred Milner, High Commissioner in South Africa in 1899, who did more than anyone else to provoke the Boer nationalism which began the South African War, was determined to smash the Boer states and resettle them with a British majority. His scheme was destroyed by the military weakness of the British troops and the incompetence of their leaders. The first few months of war saw nothing but a series of major military disasters for the British.

Thereafter the tide of war turned, and the main body of armed Boer resistance collapsed. Unfortunately for South Africa that was not the end. The hard core of Boer militants turned to guerilla warfare. And, in the effort to suppress them, the British army authorities used methods of collective punishment, burning farmsteads, and concentrating the families of guerillas and their supporters into hastily improvised camps so unsanitary and poorly supplied with food and shelter that the death rate in some camps rose to 40% or more. By such methods the British alienated not only the Boers of the republics but many of the Afrikaners of the colony; and only exhaustion, war weariness and the fear of a native rising finally brought the guerillas to negotiate with the British. Even then they only came to negotiate and not to surrender. And the negotiations and the subsequent Treaty of Vereeniging (May 1902) confirmed the authority of the cammando leaders, the 'bitter-enders', over the moderates, the Anglophiles, the loyalists and the collaborators among Boer and Afrikaner as leaders of the Boer people.

Such a capitulation, for in many respects it was the British not the Boers who capitulated at Vereeniging, made the work of reconstruction in South Africa extremely difficult. A proposal to bring in Chinese coolies to fill the gaps in the labour force in the mines of the Rand brought Britain and Boer South African together again. In December 1904 Louis Botha, one of the leading Boer ex-generals, founded *Het Volk*, a new all-Boer party. In 1905 it allied itself with British advocates of home rule for South Africa against the survivors of Rhodes' Progressive party. In 1907, after the Liberal victory in Britain, elections in South Africa gave *Het Volk* with its Liberal allies, and some from a new white supremacist labour movement on the Rand, an electoral victory, with General Botha heading a joint

73

British-*Het Volk* cabinet. The British Liberals saw that their only hope of coping with Boer numbers and reconciling the Boers with the British minority was to bring in the solidly British-settled Colony of Natal. In 1910 the Union of South Africa joined together Natal and the Cape Colony with the two former Boer republics and Botha took his variegated coalition into a new party, the South African National Party. In 1913 an extremist wing broke away to fight against reconciliation of Boer and Britain. And South Africa, like Canada, was thereafter to resist any attempt to bring her into an Imperial Federation. In 1914 extremists led a pro-German rebellion. But Botha put them down and South African forces played their part on Britain's side in the Great War. But there were still two nationalisms, not one, in South Africa, British and Boer; and their only point of union was their common fear of the African, Indian and coloured population in whose midst they lived and whose abandonment by Britain was the price of the Liberal settlement in South Africa.

The two remaining dominions of the British Empire, **Australia and New Zealand**, developed without the complications of double nationalism which so bedevilled developments in Canada and South Africa. At the same time racial issues did exist in each of the Dominions. Resistance to Oriental immigration played a considerable part in the drawing together of the separate Australian colonies. And politics in New Zealand had to take cognizance of the continuing existence of the Maori people and culture. From an early stage New Zealand's history displayed that conflict between the British Colonial Office's commitment to equality before the law for all citizens, whatever their colour, and local white exploitation of the advantage conferred upon them by the fact that the law before whom all were equal was alien to the non-whites, which led to the initial conflict between Boer and Briton in South Africa; only in New Zealand the conflict was on a much less bitter level, since Maori civilization and culture were much less warlike than those of the South African Bantu. In addition the early settlers did not depend on Maori labour in the same way that the South Africans did. Moreover the Maoris became a minority in New Zealand fairly early in its history so that there was never the sense of being outnumbered which nagged even in their early days at the nerves of Boer and Briton alike in South Africa.

Thus Australia and New Zealand had largely become mono-racial societies. Indeed the original inhabitants of Australia were so primitive in culture and organization and so few in numbers as to have no impact on developments there. Both Australia and New Zealand were settled almost entirely by emigrants from the British Isles, and their development both in internal and external matters was dominated by this fact. Domestic politics became a struggle between the older and the newer immigrants over land ownership long before the issue of labour was injected. Both developed state socialism of a welfare kind and state arbitration of labour disputes long before Europe did. In external matters both Australia and New Zealand were dominated by their political ties with the 'mother-country' and their economic dependence on the British market, especially after the development of refrigeration. Their economies were essentially pastoral. Both too were recognizably island states. Their defence rested on British sea-power and their trade reached its markets by sea. Both too were Pacific powers who in the 1880s and onwards came into contact with that other great Pacific power, the United States. Their great fear centred around the only Asiatic sea-power, Japan.

In **Australia**, the growth of national feeling was a slow one. There was no external threat of any consequence to bind together the six colonies which developed out of the original scattered settlements or to drive them closer to Britain than normal sentiment would hold them. Nor was there any real conflict with Britain. The process of conjoining the six colonies into the Commonwealth of Australia, which came finally into being in 1901, was a slow one, and a significant factor binding the pro-federal groups together was their common opposition to the emergent labour movement. Even then progress really depended on there being even fewer compelling interests opposed to the process of federation than there were in favour. The process developed therefore into one of bargaining between the colonies.

In foreign and imperial affairs, Australian sentiment was imperialist and racist. Chinese and Japanese labour at first accepted, from the 1890s onwards was rigidly excluded. Australia was 'a white man's country, to be kept that way'. On imperial matters, Australia preferred to control their own armed forces, but regarded Britain's wars as their wars. Towards Britain, Australia developed an uneasy relationship of love and contempt mingled together. Their own country they regarded as a more virile, libertarian and socially egalitarian extension of Britain overseas.

This attitude can be seen very clearly in the doctrines of the Australian labour movement, which after holding office twice on a minority basis after 1907 finally achieved an electoral majority in 1910. Its opposition to large-scale capitalism, its emphasis on redistributive taxation and collective ownership of monopolies were all taken directly from Britain. Its more radical wing was held in check, however, once the party had taken office, by the purely industrial interests of many of its members, by the development of a strong Catholic labour movement, and by its inability to secure the necessary majority for a revision of the federal constitution. Under the leadership of William Morris Hughes, the Australian Labour Party developed therefore into a thoroughly imperialist, not to say jingoist, movement. And in the debates within the Empire on its future constitutional development, which were to take place during and after World War I, Australian spokesmen were to press as strongly for the transformation of the Empire into an imperial federation, as the Canadians and South Africans were to oppose it.

The true nature of Australian nationalism was revealed during World War I. Australia contributed over 300,000 volunteers for overseas service and lost 60,000 dead on Near Eastern and French battlefields. But when

Hughes attempted to introduce conscription in 1916 he completely split the Labour Party, as MacDonald was to split the British Labour Party in 1931. Australian labour opinion was thoroughly anti-conscriptionist, and it was overwhelmingly supported by those who had volunteered for overseas service. The rights of labour included, in their view, the right to be free of compulsion. And although Hughes contrived to stay in power by allying himself with his Liberal opponents, who formed a new National party and thoroughly beat Labour in the 1917 elections, the conscription proposals were thrown out by popular referendum. The war was Britain's war and Australia was in it to the hilt. But conscription was accepted only to defend Australia herself, and not to win a war in Europe. Australia was a Pacific power, and her only potential enemy, Japan, was Britain's ally.

**New Zealand** differed from Australia in three respects. First, it was even more dependent economically on Britain than Australia, especially after the development of refrigeration had opened the British market to New Zealand meat and dairy products. Second, the land ownership issue dominated internal politics since control of land purchase from the original Maori inhabitants rested in the hands of the government. Third, New Zealanders were not possessed by the contempt towards Britain which proved so significant an element in Australian national feeling. Self-governing since 1852, New Zealanders even more than Australians thought of themselves as 'Britons overseas'. New Zealand differed in two other respects: in its pioneering in the field of social legislation and in the existence of the small farmer-labour coalition which made that social legislation possible.

Under this coalition, which was managed by Richard Seddon, one of the outstanding political 'bosses' of the twentieth century, New Zealand initiated a type of egalitarian lower-middle-class mixture of small-scale capitalism and municipal gas-and-water socialism which became the forerunner of much of mid-twentieth century reformist conservatism in Europe and radicalism in the United States. Its main distinguishing characteristics were land reform, state credit for smallholders, maternity hospitals, a state health service, old age pensions and arbitration with powers of compulsion by industrial courts in labour disputes. It was adopted during a huge agricultural boom which occurred when the introduction of refrigeration opened the British market. Yet even this prosperity was unable to prevent the gradual break-up of the farmer-labour coalition on which the Liberal party was based. Labour moved leftwards as the arbitration courts began to turn against further wage increases; and as labour moved left so the farmers moved to the new conservative Reform Party. For a time Labour itself was divided into two separate and rival trades union organizations—the small craft unions uniting against the large-scale unions of the mining, railway and service industries. This split between the craft and industrial unions was similar to the division between the AFL and the CIO in the United States. In 1916 the New Zealand Labour Socialist party was founded; its first MP was elected in 1918.

In international matters New Zealand outdid Australia in its policies of imperialism, racialism and jingoism. Though always inclined to make a sentimental exception in the case of its own Maori population, New Zealand was thoroughly racialist in external affairs, adamantly opposed to Oriental immigration and anxious about Japan. Indeed, as far as New Zealand was concerned, Britain was her protector in the Pacific. Unlike Australia, New Zealand saw nothing incongruous in contributing funds to the cost of the Royal Navy. By the end of World War I she had enlisted nearly 20% of her male population, 40% of all men between the ages of 20 to 45, to service overseas. Over 50% of these troops were killed, wounded or became prisoners. During most of the war, the country was governed by a national coalition which carried conscription with little or no difficulty. Labour opposition was simply treated as sedition—and such opposition was a factor in the growth of a Labour movement that was to prove much more radical than its counterpart in Australia.

## The Non-European World

The impact of Europe's power, of its military and industrial technology, of its money and its methods of administration, of its ideas and culture on the external non-European world was so overwhelming that none of the non-European empires, states or cultures were able to withstand it. Their reaction usually followed a fairly standard pattern. In the first place came armed resistance, which was overcome by the use of force. Then came adoption of the obvious outward institutions and techniques of western power, military, technical and educational. To pay for the development of these institutions there had to be trade, which usually meant that the non-Europeans had to borrow European money. For many states, especially those with autocratic rulers, the experience was disastrous. The weak or the over-optimistic rulers plunged into headlong borrowing, which quickly led to bankruptcy and the imposition by the European powers of control over their finances. The ambitious rulers used this access to western military technology to destroy whatever traditional or social restraints on the misuse of autocratic power were indigenous to their society, and, sooner or later, provoked civil or external conflict which led to further western intervention. At the same time, native forces of discontent would borrow ideas from the west, often through missionary channels, to use against their own native overlords.

The second stage of partial borrowing was often followed by an outbreak of atavism, or reversion to whatever was believed to be the innermost essence of the native culture. If the ruling class were alien then opinion would turn against them. In more magic-based societies the appeal to indigenous magic would be very strong. Dependent on the strength of the native culture and, more importantly, on the political and social strength of the native political unit, one of two reactions would follow the inevitable defeat of the atavist movement. In the weaker cases there might be total withdrawal into a kind of spirit-religion, as among the Amerinds of North America or, to a lesser extent, the Maoris of New Zealand. In the stronger ones the westernizing element would come to the fore. Again there might be one of two reactions. In one type political thinkers would attempt to marry western culture with their own and to find institutions or precepts in their past histories which could be refurbished to seem analogous to the institutions and ideas of the all-powerful west. In the other type of reaction, opinion would turn violently against the native culture and seek to jettison it entirely for a total imitation and adoption of western methods of government and political organization. Either way a process of social change was set in motion which led sooner or later to the rise of new social groups, challenging the authority of those already in power. And these new social groups paradoxically would preach or practise a nationalism which, because it inevitably sought to differentiate its nation from the west, would contain atavistic elements and lead to a fresh clash with the powers of Europe. In this process one can find the seeds of the decline of European influence in the later decades of the first half of the twentieth century.

By a curious paradox the first Asiatic state to react positively to the overwhelming impact of European power was the one which for three hundred years had most rigidly shut its doors to European contacts, the island empire of **Japan**. In 1851 Commodore Perry of the United States Navy, barely forestalling similar Russian action, used a naval demonstration to force the opening of Japanese ports to Western trade. Alarm at the ease with which British and French forces were breaking down their great neighbour, China, had already given rise to a native reform movement, and in the next forty years the reformers remade Japan entirely from a feudal state of the late middle ages into a power capable of challenging and defeating one of the great powers of Europe. The feudal rule of the Shogunate, Mayors of the Palace, who governed in the name of a puppet Emperor, was overthrown, the Emperor restored and his prestige captured by the reformers. The armies of feudal retainers were bought out, and inflation and economic pressure forced them into the armed forces and the kind of administration necessary to run a modern state. Japan embarked on a major programme of industrialization, and deliberately reshaped her government, laws and administration on the most successful models in Europe. By 1896 she had a Cabinet, an assembly, a first class army and navy. United under an unsteady autocracy based on the Prussian pattern, the armed services held an unusually strong position. In Japan the ministers of the army and navy had to be serving officers. This meant that the formation of a Cabinet had to be approved by the senior officers of the armed services.

This revolution had not been accomplished without very serious internal pressures and strains. The effect had been to exaggerate the peculiarly

Japano-centric nature of Japanese culture, and to turn its settled convictions of Japanese superiority into a dangerously expansionist ultra-nationalism, liable to burst out into aggression which was sudden and violent even by European standards. Japan's foreign anxieties stemmed from concern over the stategic position of Korea, 90% of whose trade was carried on with Japan. At the time Korea was undergoing its own internal upheaval as its rulers attempted to follow the examples of Japan and China, as Japan and China put increased pressure upon her, and as Tsarist Russian influence spread southwards from Vladivostok. In 1895, the Japanese picked a quarrel with China over Chinese intervention in Korea, and obliterated the Chinese army and navy in a lightning campaign. The peace terms exacted from the defeated empire demonstrated the inability of the Japanese diplomats to control their militarists. Despite repeated warnings of the danger of European intervention, China was forced to cede Formosa, the Pescadores and Port Arthur, to pay a vast indemnity, to recognize Korean independence and to give far-reaching commercial concessions to the Japanese. The Russians did in fact intervene to force the Japanese to abandon their claims to Port Arthur, and the stage was set for the inevitable clash between Russia and Japan.

The defeated empire of **China** was perhaps the oldest civilized state in the world. For three thousand years it had been the centre of civilization as far as its experience could reach. It had been repeatedly invaded by barbarians from the north (its ruling Manchu dynasty dated from the last of these invasions), and had always absorbed what it could not repel. Its ruling class was arrogantly and uniquely conscious of its superior virtues in comparison with the new barbarians of Europe who came to the Asian mainland as traders and concession hunters. It was ruled in the last part of the nineteenth century by a young and inexperienced Emperor very much dominated by his mother, the dowager Empress Tsu Hsi. Beneath them, their vast empire was divided into a large number of provincial administrations, each with its viceroy. The empire was held together by a bureaucracy, the mandarin class, entry, training and promotion to which was rigidly controlled from the centre. The mandarins governed China in accordance with a very full and rigid code of conduct, with a very considerable downward devolution of initiative and responsibility.

Imperial China in the nineteenth century was not, however, the stable society it was often represented to be. The dynasty was alien and its control of the loyalties of the Chinese peasantry was not locked in that consciousness of racial identity which enables dynasties to survive foreign defeat. Thus whereas the Japanese imperial system survived the impact of western civilization, the Manchu dynasty did not.

China had been forced to open its ports to European trade in the 1840s after the so-called opium wars, in which Britain and France forced China to allow the import of opium from their Asiatic colonies as the only means of offsetting a persistently unfavourable balance of trade with China. The price of China's defeat was the establishment of extra-territorial concessions and large-scale European settlements in the main ports and centres of the Chinese coast and rivers, Shanghai, Canton, Hangchow and Tientsin. At the same time European aid enabled the Manchu dynasty to survive its first reversals. Europeans reorganized the Maritime Customs and so gave China a steady and reliable source of income which made it possible for the Asiatic empire to buy loans on the European capital market. This aid, in turn, helped the Manchus to outlast and eventually defeat the first great anti-Manchu movement, the Taiping rebellions of 1850–64. Meanwhile, European missionaries gave China its first taste of western ideas and education; though the gift was not an unmixed blessing and the attempt to marry it with Chinese traditions and culture a long and weary one. The Taiping rebellion had a strong ideological basis in misinterpreted Protestant Christianity.

The first period of European influence, which followed the second opium war of 1857–60, saw the gradual recovery of control over China by the Manchu dynasty, and the adoption of a number of western techniques, especially in military and naval matters. Armed with moneys from the Maritime Customs, and isolated from further European pressure by Britain, and by the absorption of France and Russia in events in Europe, China began to flex her muscles, extending her control in Manchuria and into Korea. In 1893–94 Chinese forces intervened in Korea after anti-Chinese disturbances. The intervention provoked a rapid and humiliating defeat at Japan's hands, the loss of Formosa and the Pescadores, and the incurment, under the Treaty of Shimonoseki which ended the war, of an indemnity so heavy as to necessitate recourse to the European money market. It brought, too, Russian and German intervention to force Japan to disgorge part of her spoils and stake their own claim on what everyone now took to be the disintegrating corpse of China. In 1895 Russia founded the Russo-Chinese bank and advanced China a loan to pay off the indemnity to Japan. There followed the grant to Russia of railway concessions in Manchuria, obtained by a large personal bribe to the Chinese foreign minister, Li Hung Chang. Not to be outdone, Germany used the murder of two missionaries as an excuse to force China to lease her a base at Kiouchou on the Shantung peninsula. Russia followed with the occupation of Port Arthur, France with that of Kwang-Chou-Wan, Britain with that of Wei-Hei-Wei. The scramble for railway and other concessions in China had begun.

The effect on China was overwhelming. The defeats in the opium wars and the long civil war of the Taiping rebellion had merely resulted in a policy of borrowing some western techniques on a purely practical basis to make up, as it were, some technical deficiencies. The basic confidence of China in the correctness of its own political and philosophical system had hardly been touched. Yet now China had been overwhelmingly defeated by the Japanese barbarians, whom all Chinese affected to despise, as a result of the Japanese adoption of a really far-reaching programme of westernization.

Chinese reaction took two forms. The first was outright westernization by decree. In one hundred days in 1898 no fewer than seventy edicts designed to westernize China overnight streamed from the Imperial palace. They challenged the traditional provincialism of China, and offended everyone. They led the Dowager Empress, Tsu Hsi, to stage a palace revolution and to take the reins of government firmly into her own hands. In the provinces the stream of edicts had merely strengthened the xeno-phobic and traditionalist forces which wanted to turn back the clock. These forces expressed themselves through a secret society which the Europeans came to call the Boxers. They sprang from discontent, unemployment, two years of dought, famine and a disastrous flood of the Huang Ho river in 1898. The target of their activity were the overt manifestations of Europe in China, missionaries, railways, telegraphs and the like. In 1900 the western powers demanded Chinese action to suppress the Boxer movement. Instead, the Empress allied herself with the Boxer movement and unleashed her troops against the European legations in Peking and the con-cession in Tientsin. The European powers replied by organizing an inter-national force which occupied Tientsin, marched on Peking, sacked the Manchu palaces and imposed, by the Boxer protocol of 1910, a crippling indemnity on the Chinese state. Russia, acting on her own, occupied Manchuria. Tsu Hsi fled and the Emperor was restored to power. China settled down to a slower rate of westernization, while revolutionary forces continued to seethe below the surface. A new Chinese revolution was not far away.

Like China, the **Islamic world** produced both atavistic and modernistic movements in response to the impact of European power and culture. The eastern wing of the Islamic world, in India, Malaysia, Indonesia and the Philippines had passed under western rule or influence before the opening of the nineteenth century. But in these areas Islam was a religion more than a total culture, in that it lacked both the crusading tradition of Arab and Turkish Islam and its embodiment in one Islamic empire. The main strength of Islam lay in the two states of Iran and the Ottoman Empire, embodiments respectively of the Shia and Sunni branches of Islam.

The **Ottoman Empire** of the nineteenth century was only the shell of what it had been in the great days of the sixteenth century. But it was still basically a military-religious autocracy centred around a Sultan who, since the eighteenth century, had also begun to claim and obtain both the status of Caliph, inheritor both of the mystic aura conferred on his successors as heads of Islam to the prophet Mohammed by the prophet himself, and of the mantle of the mediaeval Arab empires of the Ummayids of Damascus, the Abbasids of Baghdad, the Fatimids of Egypt and North Africa, and the Ummayid survivors of Moslem Spain. As the Ottoman Empire was basically 'an army which had conquered an empire and embraced a faith', the Sultan exercised his power through military and religious organizations and a variety of civil administrations adapted to the peculiar needs of each locality.

By the end of the eighteenth century the military organizations, the Janissaries in the Empire proper and the Mamelukes in Egypt, had got very much out of hand. As a result the Sultan was forced to eliminate the former by massacre in 1826, and to suffer the suppression of the latter by his Albanian officer, Mohammed Ali, and the development of Egypt under Mohammed Ali and his children to the point where it could challenge the Sultan's own power and become virtually independent of him. The religious organization rested as a double structure of schools and courts, the intellectuals, the *ulema* in the schools, the *Qadis* in the courts, instructing in and interpreting the law of Islam, the *Sharia*. At its head was the *Sheikh-ul-Islam*, the Grand Mufti, who, with his supporting muftis and the two *kaziaskers* acted as a kind of Islamic Supreme Court. The muftis would check on whether the Sultan's actions were in accordance with the law of Islam. No legislation could be promulgated without their approval.

The people of the Ottoman Empire fell broadly into two ethnic groups, Turks and Arabs. The language of state was Turkish, that of religion Arabic; but a wide variety of other tongues were tolerated, and many minor linguistic groups were virtually autonomous under their hereditary chiefs. Similarly, the heterodox Islamic sects, such as the Druzes of Mount Lebanon and the Alawis in Syria, were autonomous where they had the strength to maintain themselves. Local chiefs or sheikhs were appointed *qaimaqams* (or governors), while the provinces were each headed by *walis* (viceroys), who acted as chief tax collectors and heads of the local garrisons, and exercised power outside the towns via the local notables and feudatories.

A feature peculiar to the Ottoman empire was the protection it gave to Jews and Christians, the *Umm' al-Kitab* (the Peoples of the Book). They were organized into autonomous communities known as *millets*, choosing their own head subject to Turkish approval. In all there were fifteen *millets*, fourteen Christian and one Jewish. Their leaders were functionaries of state, *ex-officio* members of provincial administrative courts, autonomous in matters of spiritual discipline, control of property, education, marriage, dowries, divorce and wills. The sentences of their courts in such matters were executed by the state. This system in fact enabled Christian and Jew to play a considerable role in commerce and finance, as well as enabling them to own land.

Under the impact of the French Revolution the Ottoman Sultanate at first attempted to modernize itself from above by the exercise of the Sultan's power on absolutist lines. The process was begun by Mahmud II (1784–1839) who acceded to the Sultanate in 1808. Beginning in 1826, after the elimination of the Janissaries, he raised a modern-style professional army, and set up schools and sent a series of students to Europe to provide himself with an educated officer corps and an efficient civil service. He centralized the administration, abolished the old military system of holding land in favour of leases to tax-farmers, brought the funds of the great religious land-owning trusts or *waqf* under his control and set up western-style ministries. His successor, Abdulmecid (1839–1861), continued his work with a series of great reforming edicts, known as the *Tanzimat*. Abdulmecid began by proclaiming the abolition of tax-farming and the equality of all before the law. He also promulgated a new penal code in 1840, re-organized provincial administrations along French departmental lines, introduced commercial codes and a new land law, introducing western-style land-ownership and landlordism, founded an Ottoman bank and experimented with an advisory council of notables.

The effect of these reforms, though they seemed to many western observers the merest window-dressing to give an Oriental despotism a liberal appearance, was to destroy most of the internal checks and balances of Islamic Ottoman society and to accelerate the process of disintegration. The land reforms destroyed the Islamic concept of joint rights in the land shared between tenant tribesmen and their feudal overlords or sheikhs in favour of the western concept of the landlord-tenant relationship. And this institution of European concepts occurred at a time when, in the west itself, it was rapidly becoming apparent that without legislation to protect the tenant, he was open to the grossest kind of exploitation. In the cities many of the rights and powers of the communities were transferred to the imperial bureaucracy in the name of efficiency. Most important, as the reign of Abdul Hamid II (1876–1908) showed, the conventional limitations on despotic rule itself had been largely weakened.

At the same time the reforms which were introduced, even if they were only the introduction of western military techniques, were exposing a small but significant element in Ottoman and Islamic society to the ideas of western liberalism—and imposing upon them the task of attempting to reconcile Islamic modes of thought and the traditions of their own proud society with the obviously more efficient and more powerful ideas of western Europe. Abdul Hamid II did his best to isolate the Empire from such ideas. As a result many of the most articulate of Ottoman liberals were driven into exile in Paris. Against them he did his best to encourage an atavistic reaction against the west and an upsurge of pan-Islamic sentiment which he hoped would consolidate the loyalties of his subjects to himself as Sultan and Caliph. But at the same time he multiplied military and technical schools throughout the Ottoman empire to provide it with an efficient military and bureaucratic *corps d'élite*. By so doing he increased in number the would-be critics of his own rule. Within the Ottoman ruling groups he managed largely to divide and break up the first wave of liberal critics of the Tanzimat, the so-called Young Ottomans. But he was unable to prevent the clandestine growth in later years of the Young Turk movement which was to overthrow him. Finally, by opening these schools in the provinces he was to raise up an Arab officer class which unlike the Young Turks in the Ottoman areas was not drawn from the traditional ruling groups of the Empire.

A good deal of the trouble lay in the fact that the Ottoman Empire was more than merely Ottoman and less than totally Islamic. Ottoman Turkish sentiment thus could always turn against the Sultanate, even against Islam. (After 1920 Turkey was in fact to abandon Islam officially and embrace even more extreme a form of imitation of the west than Japan had done.) In the non-Ottoman parts of the Empire, on the other hand, those who followed Islam were exposed to currents of thought which originated beyond the areas of Ottoman control; and the Christian and other minorities tended to develop a nationalism which was totally secular and western, either to enhance their own position within the Empire, or, as with the Greeks, the Kurds and the Armenians, to separate themselves completely from it.

The main centres of Islamic thought outside Ottoman control were in Egypt, Persia and North Africa. Generally speaking these had been exposed to mild western pressures for some period of time before the 1870s; their reactions tended to follow the path of attempted synthesis of Islam with the ideas of the west. It is only in the less exposed fringes of Islam, in the Sudan, in Somalia and within the Arabian peninsula that one finds examples of atavistic reactions to westernization. And it is significant that in most cases what was being reacted against was not western rule but Islamic rule with western accretions.

Of all these centres perhaps the most important was Cairo where Mohammed Ali had established the virtual independence of Egypt under the rule of his dynasty in the first decades of the nineteenth century. An Albanian by origin, Mohammed Ali had eagerly turned to Europe for modern military, managerial and educational techniques. His successors had followed him by borrowing money and seeing Egypt tied to Europe by the great growth in the cotton market during the Civil War in the United States. The construction of the Suez Canal and the modernization of Egypt under Ismail at a rate too great for its financial strength to bear led, in 1882, to the British occupation of Egypt following closely on an Egyptian nationalist uprising among the army officers, led by Major Arabi Pasha, against the remnants of Ottoman control. The combination of these influences had led to the growth of a school of writers and thinkers who sought in varying degrees to discover in Islam's past parallels for what they took to be the main motives of the west. Their aim was to defend Islam against those who might seek to abandon it entirely in favour of outright westernization. In the main these writers, such as Rifa Badawi al-Tahtawi (1801–73) and Mohammed Abdu (1849–1905), were Egyptian in origin and their writings tinged with something which was to develop into an Egyptian view of Arab nationalism if not an Egyptian nationalism in itself. A very considerable influence was played throughout the whole Islamic world by the writer Jemal al-Din al-Afghani (1839–97), who was probably born in Persia and who spent his years of greatest influence in Cairo. Al-Afghani worked for a time in India, organized a secret pan-Islamic society in Paris in 1884 and eventually died in Constantinople as a pensionary of Abdul Hamid, who had thought to enlist his pan-Islamist preaching in the service of his own political propaganda.

Al-Afghani's influence spread to North Africa and into Syria and Iraq. In Tunis a school of modernists had already grown up before the French occupation in 1881. Their influence spread westwards into the last unoccupied Islamic state in North Africa, Morocco, and eastwards into the only area under Istanbul's direct rule, the Beyship of Tripoli. Throughout North Africa, Islam had fossilized far more than in the Near East, and the mystical dervish orders, the *tariqas*, through which popular discontent expressed itself, had become much stronger and more numerous. The reformers therefore found themselves obliged, like Luther appealing to the Bible in 1520, to appeal to the *salafa*, the early written sources of Islam, and their movement became known as the *salaffiya*. From it was to spring the early Tunisian and Moroccan nationalist movements of the 1920s and the idea of regional rather than pan-Islamic nationalism which was to develop with the movement for a unified Maghreb (a unified North-West Africa) in the middle of the twentieth century.

In **Syria** and the **Lebanon** the ideas of Al-Afghani and Mohammed Abdu were to find both support and opposition from Christian Arabs for whom the erection of a pan-Islamic state would mean a continuation of their second-class status. The matter was complicated by the existence of a large number of heterodox Islamic sects, the Druzes of Mount Lebanon and the Alawis of upper Syria being the most numerous. The pan-Islamists tended to take refuge in Cairo from the excesses of Ottoman rule, when they did not join the growing number of Ottoman exiles in Paris. The Christian Arabs were equally *persona non grata* with the Ottomans; and the intellectuals among them tended to precede the pan-Islamists in taking refuge in Cairo where the Arabic press was for some time almost entirely under the control of Arab Christian *emigrés* from Syria and the Lebanon. Christian Arabs could support that side of pan-Islamic writing which emphasized the historical achievements of Islam as a society. But they used these achievements as the historical basis for a secular nationalism in which liberty and equality for all citizens were claimed to be the essential basis of Arab unity. In general these writers spoke of an Arab nationalism, but if they were allowed they would press, as did Khalal Ganem among the 'Young Turks', also for an Ottoman nationalism on a quasi-federal, or, as they put it, 'administratively decentralized', basis. And there were those who spoke of a Lebanese or a Syrian nation. There were even some who preached a Pan-Arab state based on Egypt under the restored rule of the Khedive.

All these were Arabs, drawn mainly from the Maronite or Orthodox communities of the Lebanon and Syria. Other Christian communities, like the Copts and Armenians in Egypt, turned either to cosmopolitanism or to a local nationalism serving whoever happened to be the ruling power in the state. Thus Egypt's Prime Ministers before and during the British occupation included Nubar Pasha, an Armenian, and Butrus Ghali, a Copt. In general the Christian communities found it easier to adopt western techniques and adapt themselves to western pressures than did the Moslems.

Outside the Ottoman Empire and those areas in direct contact with European influences, the impact of Europe presented itself less as something European than as something alien in the rule of the Islamic state. The reaction to it tended usually to be violently atavistic and puritanical, in the belief that Islam would prevail if it stripped itself of all alien influences. Perhaps the greatest of these movements was *Wahabism* which, under the leadership of the house of Saud, was to conquer all but the eastern and southern extremities of the Arabian peninsula arïd raid regularly into Egypt, Syria and Iraq until the reduction of the Saudi kingdom by Mohammed Ali's son, Ibrahim, in 1819 to its original small patrimony around the town of Riyadh. Another atavistic movement was that of the *Ansari* in the Sudan, the followers of Mohammed Ahmed, who proclaimed himself the Mahdi (the anointed of God) in 1881, in revolt against the Egyptian rule which had been extended over the Sudan in 1820. The Mahdi's followers controlled what is now the state of the Sudan between 1884 and the British reconquest of the Sudan in 1898. A third consisted of the *Senussi*, founded in Cyrenaica in 1843 by Mohammed Ali el Senussi as a mystical sect with the same mission to redeem and purify Islam from the accretions of Turkish and Tripolitanian rule. Less bellicose than either the *Wahabis* or the *Ansari*, the *Senussi* preferred to consolidate their hold on Cyrenaica by a network of lodges, fortress-monasteries of a non-celibate order, while the leaders of the movement moved their headquarters into the remoter oases of the Sahara desert.

One element which distinguished all these movements is that they occurred largely within that part of the Islamic world which followed the Sunni branch of Islam. The other main branch, the Shia, dominated **Persia** and provided the principal minority group in Mesopotamia; breakaway sects dominated the Yemen (Zaidism), Mount Lebanon (the Druzes), and the state of Muscat and Oman (the Ibadis, though these strictly are neither Sunnis nor Shias). Of these the only one of major political importance are the Imamis, the main branch of the Shia, who dominated Persia.

As a religion Imamism reacted far less obviously to contact with the West than did the Sunni branch of Islam. In part this was due to its strength as an entity separate from the Persian state. Imamism was thus saved from the comparative ossification that attacked Sunni Islam within the Ottoman Empire. A part was also possibly played by the changes in dynasty in the eighteenth century, three separate families occupying the throne between the fall of the Safavids during the Afghan revolt in the 1720s and the accession of the first of the Qajar dynasty in 1779. Whatever the cause, the Persians themselves had little time for the ideas of al-Afghani; and the reaction to western pressure on Persia was to be political rather than intellectual.

This pressure came principally from Russia and Britain, as each sought to extend its power into the lands that lay between the borders of India and Russian Central Asia. By the 1880s Russia had extended her borders up to the northern frontiers of Persia and Afghanistan with the occupation of the last of the Moslem Khanates of Central Asia. Britain in her turn had 'persuaded' Persia to recognize the independence of Afghanistan in the Anglo-Persian war of 1856–57. Both countries were engaged in spreading their activities into Persia itself. Russia acted officially by forming the Russian-officered Persian Cossack brigade as an aid to the Shah, and by founding the Russian-capitalized Discount Bank of Persia in 1891. Britain was represented by individual concession hunters such as Baron Reuter with his Imperial Bank of Persia in 1889 and the tobacco monopoly which was placed in British hands in 1890. It was in the outburst of discontent with this award of the tobacco monopoly to foreign investors and its defeat by a smoking strike, led by the Islamic intellectuals of the Shias, that the Persian nationalist movement was born.

The impact of Europe on **Egypt** came in two forms, the French cultural influence which originated during the brief period of Napoleonic conquest in 1798, and the political impact of Britain after the occupation in 1882. France had done her best to foster Egypt's development as a national state. She had backed Mohammed Ali in his bid to invade Turkey in 1839–40 and she had largely financed the construction of the Suez Canal opened in 1869. Indeed the bulk of the £90 million of Egyptian public debt in 1890 was owed to French bondholders. But in the actual moment of crisis France had held back and British troops had occupied Egypt. British capital had bought 40% of the Suez Canal Company shares in 1874. British ships were by far the most numerous in passage through the Suez Canal. In 1888 France and Russia had imposed upon Britain an international convention for the management of the Canal. But they had also left Britain with no option but to take over responsibility for Egypt's affairs. And under British direction Egypt's army and administration were reformed and modernized and Egypt's finances made secure and efficient. For the Egyptians the experience was both salutary and humuliating. Particularly resented was the sublime assumption of their British overlords that the various racial and religious groups in Egypt could not coalesce to make an Egyptian nation. Britain played therefore an important part in the creation of a nationalist movement in Egypt. In the meantime British engineers and capital presented Egypt with a modern irrigation system which with the aid of fertilizers was to make the Nile valley capable of yielding four crops annually.

The decaying remnants of the Turkish province of **Algeria** fell easily into French hands in 1830. But it was to take another 50 years of sporadic fighting before the French finally pacified the country. During this period the French were bringing in colonists and building up a European settler community, a process which would have been impossible without the removal from its original tribal ownership of millions of hectares of the best arable land. Algeria was administered as a French *département*; and a small educated minority of Arabs was encouraged to see themselves as equal members of the French community. They were not, however, encouraged to become too assimilated unless they were prepared to renounce their religion: they were ruled by a separate Code for the Natives, and they had no political rights as such. French Algeria like Ulster, which in other respects it resembled, became a nursery for generals.

Under Ottoman rule, **Tunisia** had counted officially as a 'regency' with its head carrying the title of Bey. Its ruling *élite* tended to be Turkish, though in fact the regency was virtually autonomous. For a time it was in the forefront of the Ottoman reform movement, following the Turkish reforms of 1856 (the Tanzimat), with the issue of a constitution (*Destour*) in 1860. The experiment failed largely owing to the personality of the Bey and his inability to resist foreign loans. In 1869 an International Commission was established to administer its finances and from 1875 onwards the main point at issue was only whether France or Italy would succeed in taking over Tunisia. As the stronger, and backed by Bismarck's Germany, France won, using the pretext of tribal raids into Algeria to occupy Tunisia in 1881. The changing pattern of European imperialism may be seen in the fact that France did not annex Tunisia, preferring to establish a protectorate. Thereafter French colonists poured into Tunisia. To satisfy their desire for self-government they were granted certain representative institutions. A joint Franco-Tunisian Grand Council voted on the budget. A Franco-Tunisian colonialism was being substituted for the nominal sovereignty of the Tunisian Bey. Tunisian resentment was to lead in 1907 to the foundation of a 'Young Tunisian' party to maintain Tunisia's right to manage her own affairs.

The **Moroccan Sultanate** was unique in North Africa in never having passed under Ottoman rule. It was also unique in that its rulers, like the Stuarts in Scotland, rarely succeeded in making their authority felt among the mountain tribes of the High Atlas. Indeed the area was known officially as the 'Region of Dissidence', the *Bled es-Siba*, the division roughly corresponding to that between the Arabic tribes who acknowledged the law of Islam and, in return for privileges, provided the Sultan with his army, and the Berber areas which, though nominally Islamic, had their own system of customary law and followed various *marabouts* or saints. Throughout most of the nineteenth century Morocco stood off French and Spanish pressure in part with British aid. Towards its end, the last great Sultan, Moulay al-Hasan, began the same process of modernization that Mohammed Ali in Egypt had tried before him. But he died in 1894 before the process could really begin. His successor was only fourteen years of age and Morocco was soon to fall into the hands of the French.

Up to the beginning of the nineteenth century the north-eastern shores of the **Arabian peninsula** had been the home of a variety of small Arab tribes who lived by trade, piracy and pearl-fishing. The only large states had been the Ibadi state of Muscat and Oman, at the southern end of the Gulf, and the port of Kuwait at the north. The Ottoman Empire claimed a rather vague sovereignty over the central province of Al Hasa which ran down to the edge of the Qatar peninsula. The Wahhabis invaded and occupied much of the province during the first decades of the nineteenth century. The British East India Company had also established trading stations at Bandar Abbas, and later at Bushire on the Persian coast of the Gulf in the middle of the eighteenth century. The threat to its trade from piracy led to the maintenance first of a Company, then of a Royal Naval squadron, to control piracy and to put down the slave trade. By the middle of the nineteenth century Britain had found it necessary to bind all the states of the middle Gulf from Bahrein to the Muscati borders into a network of treaties, to establish peace and to put down piracy; and with these treaties Britain assumed a position as guarantor of political stability in the Gulf which was to endure into the middle of the twentieth century, long outlasting the circumstances in which it had been created. In 1873 the Ottoman Empire reasserted its claims to the al-Hasa province, occupying Qatar too and appointing the head of the sheikhly family as the deputy-governor. The British maintained their protection of the off-shore island of Bahrein, making it by agreements of 1880 and 1892 into what amounted to a protectorate. A political agent was appointed there in 1900. Kuwait did not fall under British influence until the end of the century when, in order to forestall what they believed to be German and Russian attempts to set up a coaling station and a terminus for the Baghdad railroad project, the British extended their protection to the Sheikh of Kuwait. Since the 1780s, Britain had been on amicable terms with the rulers of Muscat; these relations continued after the division of the Omani territories of Muscat and Oman and Zanzibar into their two parts in the middle of the nineteenth century. The entire affair represented the ultimate example of British free trade imperialism. British power was supreme, being maintained against all comers by a naval squadron, and the whole burden of administration in the area, such as it was, was carried by the local rulers with whom Britain had treaty relations.

The British had succeeded to the control of all the **Indian sub-continent** at the end of the Napoleonic Wars. Their victory had been achieved over a collection of mutually warring militarist states and they had inherited a ravaged, exhausted and bandit-tormented countryside. In its pacification and settlement Britain developed doctrines of administration, reform through legislation and education. Administration was to be thorough and paternalistic, reforms were to create western-style institutions alongside those of India, so that the Indians could be taught to accept or reject them on their own. Education, in the words of Macaulay's famous Minute of 1833, was to produce a 'class of persons, Indian in blood and colour, but English in taste, in opinion, in morals and in intellect'. The first British evangelical drive along these lines produced what was to be the only major outburst of atavism in the history of Indian contacts with the west, the Indian Mutiny of 1857, a military explosion whose force grew out of the feeling of the traditional Indian military classes that British policy was directed towards destroying the moral, economic and religious basis of their social organization. As such it was essentially anarchic and the attempt of the heirs of the Maratha warrior states, on the one hand, and the last remnants of the Mogul dynasty to cash in on it, on the other, were easily suppressed.

The mutiny had the effect of taking the steam out of the first drive of the early Victorian reformers, and of investing all further reforms with an aura of doubt and uncertainty. The reform of India was still the aim of the British, but it was now seen as a very long term aim indeed; and the authoritarian ethos of the professional administrators of India became very much stronger, so that the emergence of classes and movements within India which were the direct product of these reforms for a long time went unrecognized. Administration gave India a programme of road, railway and canal building, of irrigation and public works which first set India's feet on the road of industrial development. More important than this the new communications bound India together and, in conjunction with the use of the English language, made possible the development of a single national movement which cut across the fourteen major language groups and the immense distances of the country itself. This movement developed out of the new class of educated Indians coming from what in old India had been the lower states of society, and largely employed in the lower reaches of the bureaucracy. They were joined by men of the new mercantile and industrial classes, the lawyers demanded by the reformers' introduction of British court procedures and justice, and the journalists and teachers. In 1885 members of these new groups founded the Indian National Congress. It was to act as the spearhead of Indian nationalism thereafter.

Unfortunately, in the foundations of the Congress movement can also be seen the division of India along communal lines. Orthodox Hinduism regarded India as the land of the Aryan Hindus, a definition which made Moslem and outcast into second class citizens. Moslems, centring around the University of Aligarh, watched the Congress movement with suspicion. Within Congress a major split developed between the moderate reformists led by Gopal Krishna Gokhale, who were themselves overwhelmed by the magnitude of the task of westernizing India and were prepared to work with Britain towards this goal, and the extremists led by Bal Gangadhar Tilak, who wanted independence at once and social reform afterwards. The British swung between a cautious policy of introducing consultative and representative councils with Indian participation and a return to the driving administrative paternalism which had produced the Mutiny. The viceroyalty of Lord Curzon (1898–1905) represented the paternalistic policy and led to a complete break between Congress and the British which was to foreshadow the violence and non-violence of the 1930s.

The resignation of Lord Curzon and the Liberal victory in Britain paved the way for the next two great advances towards Indian self-government. The first was the Morley-Minto reforms of 1909 which introduced Indian membership into the advisory councils at all levels and set up an Imperial Legislative Council of 60 members of which 27 were indirectly elected, six of whom had to be Moslem Indians. The second advance was the Montagu declaration of 1917. In this declaration, Britain announced a policy for India aimed at the 'gradual development of self-governing institutions, with a view to the progressive realization of responsible government in India as an integral part of the Empire'. Behind the Montagu declaration lay British recognition of the loyalty of India to Britain in 1914 and the major Indian military effort in the war. But the experience of war was to release Indians from the sense of permanent inferiority to the West that had been built up by one hundred years of subjection to Britain. The year 1919 saw the emergence into the Indian scene of Mahatma Gandhi, the greatest figure of recent Indian history.

## Chapter IV
## THE IMPACT OF EUROPE ON THE EXTERNAL WORLD: THE AREAS OF REACTION AND IN-ACTIVITY

### Introduction

THE previous chapter surveyed the areas of the world where European impact had already produced a significant reaction and rate of development by 1900. This chapter covers rather those areas where this was not yet the case. They fall essentially into four groupings. First there are the residual empires of the sixteenth and seventeenth centuries, of Spain, Portugal, the Netherlands and France, empires where economic and political stagnation was the rule, where the settlers were too much enervated or economically depressed to indulge in political activity and the natives too much repressed even to envisage such action. Second are the escapist societies of French Canada and Boer South Africa, societies in deliberate reaction from the pressures of the nineteenth century, seeking to wall off the relentless advance of European liberal urban and industrial society. One could perhaps also class under this grouping the utopian societies of the nineteenth-century United States of which the Mormon settlements at Utah were the most spectacular. By 1900, however, the two republics of the Orange Free State and the Transvaal were the only significant survivors in this category.

The states of Latin America came into a third category, politically independent, economically as much bound into the economy of Western Europe and as much open to its intervention as Egypt, Tunisia or Iran. The original achievement of independence in Latin America had produced a system of states isolated and insulated from European power politics, and thus free to indulge in the most violent internecine wars without fear of major intervention. But within the individual states the original *élites* had perpetuated the social system of colonial Spain, with its thin veneer of education and Europeanism. This system dominated and exploited a mass of poverty-stricken, illiterate and superstitious peasants who represented a mixture, here of half-castes, there of Indians, the basic patterns of whose lives, economic and social organization and beliefs had not changed since

92

the seventeenth century. Although the Latin American countries were exposed to great waves of European immigration and were a major target for European and American investment, they remained essentially in a quasi-colonial relationship with Europe that their development of sizeable armies and navies could do nothing to hide.

The fourth great division comprehends the non-European world, or rather those areas where traditional social and political organization had not yet begun to give way to the pressures of westernization. Few political units in these areas had escaped European rule by 1900; only Abyssinia and Liberia in Africa, Siam in South-East Asia, Afghanistan and Tibet in Central Asia eluded or defeated European efforts to conquer and absorb them. In the areas under European control and dominion one can detect two different situations. In some areas the local political organizations, tribes, statelets and principalities were so small as to succumb very easily to direct European rule. Perhaps prolonged war had reduced them to a state of virtual anarchy and weakness. But whatever the particular circumstances the effect of European rule was to obliterate existing political loyalties. And where nationalism was eventually to emerge, it had to create its own political organisms. In the second situation, the European colonial powers found effective large-scale political organizations. In some cases these proved militarily so recalcitrant that they had to be smashed and drained of life. But in many others it was easier, cheaper and administratively more convenient to take over the existing political organization as a protectorate or protected state.

Among the states that fell into this latter category, the greatest single divide lies between the Asian societies which were literate and the African which had no indigenous script. For a state to possess a written language meant that it had records of its history, chronicles, codes of law and works designed to instruct the rulers, and cadres, possibly *élites*, of literates, trained to speculate, philosophize, intellectualize as well as to administer. In non-literate societies the *élites* tended to be either warriors or magical-artistic in character, prophets, miracle workers or witch doctors. In the former the native religion was based on scriptures and the body of its faithful remained only marginally open to western missionary activity. In the latter, religion was animistic, tutelary and protective; and its inability to protect its devotees against European power left their culture the more shattered and less able to survive. In the former type of society the impact of westernizing impulses, as has already been argued in the case of Islam in the previous chapter, meant for the intellectual *élite* an effort to acclimatize and harmonize their own culture with that of the west. In the latter no such saving process was possible. Native culture was left with only two alternatives, total withdrawal of the type practised by the Amerinds or the Maoris, or disintegration and conversion to the religion of the Europeans.

Westernization came mainly, though not entirely, through missionary education. And the degree to which the process of westernization was slow or fast depended to a great extent on the schools system which existed before western contact. Thus, although there was a high male literacy rate in areas where Buddhism was the dominant religion, the elementary nature of the Buddhist educational system, which concentrated on village schooling, adapted itself only with difficulty to the introduction of western ideas and techniques. The Koranic schools in Moslem areas, on the other hand, and still more the Koranic universities allowed a much faster rate of absorption. In the magical-religious areas of the pre-literate societies of Africa and the Pacific there was virtually no educational system at all before the arrival of the West, and education was taken over entirely by western institutions. At first, almost without exception, these were missionary schools, though after 1903 state educational institutions competed with church schools in French Africa.

The content of this education was mainly modelled on that given in the schools of the colonial powers which, being European, meant that it was mainly designed to produce good servants of the state, lawyers, doctors and administrators. There was at first very little technical or vocational training. These schools tended to produce an educated intelligentsia which was separated from the mass of the native population and 'looked always, even when protesting, towards their rulers'. It was, however, among these *élites* that the new ideas of nationalism first took root.

## The Methods of European Colonial Rule

The motives which led to the organization of colonies were, as has been argued above, far from simply economic. But, with the exception in part of the settler states, colonies, once acquired, tended to see the development of their administration governed in the last resort by considerations of cost or economic advantage to the colonial power. The dominant economic philosophy was mercantilist. Whatever the pre-colonial pattern of trade the tendency was to tie the colonial economy into that of the colonial power. Where mercantilism gave way, as it did in Britain, to Manchester School liberalism, the overriding question was still that of economic cost. The colony was expected to be as self-supporting as possible. Although mercantilism persisted in the colonies of France, Spain, Portugal and the Netherlands, a colony which failed to produce sufficient raw materials or local revenue to defray the costs of its administration could expect little in the way of a subsidy.

The pressure on colonial governors to produce something that could be turned into profit was therefore very strong. Where there existed obviously exploitable resources like gold, diamonds, silver and other minerals then the biggest problem was labour. Where there only existed agricultural resources like rubber, corn, sugar, again the major problem was labour. In a primitive, non-money economy, the inducements to labour were few and the demands of the colonial power inevitably could only be satisfied by heavy taxation, backed by punitive measures to ensure payment, by forced or indentured labour, by slavery or peonage, or by the importation of Indian or Chinese coolies. What developed in many cases was a policy of economic plunder of the existing human and physical resources of the areas brought under colonial rule, a policy of which the most flagrant case was that of the *régime* of Leopold, King of the Belgians, in the Congo.

In the more humane colonies of Britain and France, where public opinion could be mobilized against the grosser forms of exploitation, the emphasis was rather on economy in administration and the encouragement of trade as a source of revenue. The ideal of economy in administration led to the policy of indirect rule through local political organizations, especially in West Africa and in Malaya. The encouragement of trade led to the development of monopolistic trading companies which in turn stimulated the growth of a class of native agriculturalists, again especially in West Africa, where comparative affluence heralded the growth of an indigenous, property-owning and conservative *bourgeoisie*. This group was complemented by the native professional classes which gradually emerged from the small western educational institutions.

Two factors, however, were always inherent in this system. The colonial governments and western economic *entrepreneurs* usually prevented the retention of much wealth in the colonial territories which produced it. As a result profits and capital appreciation accrued to the benefit of the metropolitan power or to those who originally furnished the capital. Second, the economies of the colonial territories tended to develop essentially on a one-crop basis. Consequently the economic well-being of such territories became highly vulnerable to fluctuations in word commodity prices, a factor which was to play a terrible role in the world economic crisis between the wars.

## Europe Abroad: The Colonial Empires

The main colonial empires remaining, apart from those of Britain and France, were the residues of the old Spanish and Portuguese empires, the Dutch colonies in the East and West Indies and the personal dominions of Leopold, King of the Belgians, in the Congo basin. All of these embodied the crudest kind of exploitation of their colonial territories and in few of them could there be said to be any real attempt at colonial development to compare with the colonies of Britain and France. The exception is provided by the colonial policy introduced by the Dutch in Indonesia after 1900, the so-called 'New Ethical Policy' (see below) with which the colonial power attempted to repair some of the damages done by the policy of the previous century.

95

As the new century opened the **Spanish Empire** had just lost the Philippines and Cuba to the United States. All that remained were a few small settlements in West Africa to mark the end of an Empire which had once embraced most of the Americas. The fault was very largely that of the Spaniards themselves who seemed to have learned nothing from the loss of their Latin American empire at the opening of the nineteenth century. For a fresh wave of emigration to Cuba and the Philippines in the 1840s had produced what the Spanish Empire had never known in its hey-day, racial tension between the newly arrived Spaniards and the native-born inhabitants of Cuba and the Philippines, and racial discrimination practised against them.

Spain too sought to recoup her revenues by high imposts on trade with other nations and by heavy taxation, all of which was a great spur to local nationalist movements. In the 1840s and 1850s Spain had also indulged in outbursts of neo-imperialism, especially in relation to Latin America. In 1829 she landed a force at Tampico in Mexico; in the 1850s she menaced Venezuela; in the 1860s her fleet bombarded Valparaiso and Callao, collaborated with France in an effort to coerce Mexico, and her army occupied the Dominican Republic for five years in 1861–65. Thereafter Spain attempted to rally Latin American opinion to her side by emphasizing their common Hispanic culture, devoting a special effort to the congress held in the 1890s to celebrate the fourth centenary of the discovery of America. An Ibero-American Union was founded and a great revival of interest in the early history and culture of Latin America took place in the Spanish universities. There was a strong element of hostility to the United States in this Hispano-American movement. Its influence in Latin America, however, was of little real importance. Its main role was to salve the wounded pride of Spaniards at the loss of their empire to the United States.

The **Portuguese Empire** was more fortunate. Its main possessions were the settlements in East and West Africa together with a scattering of relics of its former empire in the Indian Ocean, such as the Indian settlement of Goa and the Indonesian island of Timor. In the 1880s a revival of imperial activity in Portuguese East Africa led to conflict with British expansion in Nyasaland and in Mashonaland but in both cases the Portuguese were forced to back down. The Portuguese did, however, establish effective occupation inland from the coast around Mozambique and gradually extended their control over the Arab sheikhs on the coast up to the borders of German East Africa. Internally Portuguese rule was totally exploitatory. The African colonies had originally been founded to take advantage of the slave trade. Angola went on exporting slaves to Brazil until 1879, and the slave trade from Portuguese East Africa to the French planters on Réunion continued into the 1880s. Even with its nominal abolition the system of forced labour within the two colonies and on the cocoa plantations of the offshore islands of Sao Tomé was virtually the equivalent of slavery. On various occasions it seemed as if the Portuguese

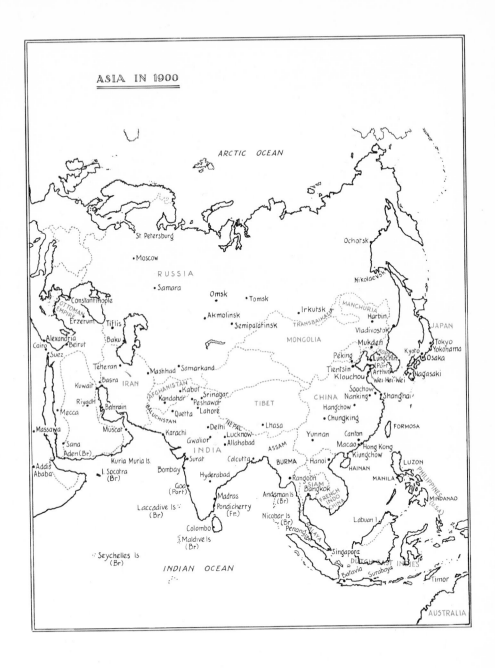

ASIA IN 1900

ARCTIC OCEAN

St Petersburg
Moscow
RUSSIA
Samara
Omsk
Tomsk
Akmolinsk
Semipalatinsk
Irkutsk
Ochorsk
Nikolaevsk
MANCHURIA
Harbin
TRANSBAIKALIA
MONGOLIA
Vladivostok
Mukden
JAPAN
Tokyo
Yokohama
Kyoto
Osaka
Nagasaki
Péking
Lungchin
Port
Arthur
Tientsin
Kiouchou
Wei Hei Wei
Constantinople
OTTOMAN EMPIRE
Erzerum
Tiflis
Alexandria
Cairo
Beirut
Baku
Suez
Teheran
Mashhad
Samarkand
Soochow
Nanking
Shanghai
CHINA
Basra
IRAN
Kabul
AFGHANISTAN
Srinagar
Hangchow
Kuwait
Kandahar
Peshawar
TIBET
Chungking
Riyadh
BALUCHISTAN
Lahore
Mecca
Bahrain
Quetta
Delhi
Lhasa
FORMOSA
Yunnan
Canton
Massawa
Muscat
Karachi
NEPAL
Lucknow
Macao
Hong Kong
Sana
Gwalior
Allahabad
Kiungchow
Aden (Br)
INDIA
Surat
Calcutta
ASSAM
BURMA
Hanoi
HAINAN
LUZON
Addis
Ababa
I. Socotra
(Br)
Kuria Muria Is.
Bombay
Hyderabad
MANILA
PHILIPPINES
Goa
(Port)
Madras
Pondicherry
(Fr.)
Andaman Is
(Br)
Rangoon
SIAM
Bangkok
FRENCH INDO CHINA
MINDANAO
(U.S.A.)
Laccadive Is
(Br)
Nicobar Is
(Br)
Labuan I.
Colombo
Penang
(Br)
MALAYA
Maldive Is
(Br)
Singapore
DUTCH EAST INDIES
Seychelles Is
(Br)
INDIAN OCEAN
Batavia
Surabaya
Timor
AUSTRALIA

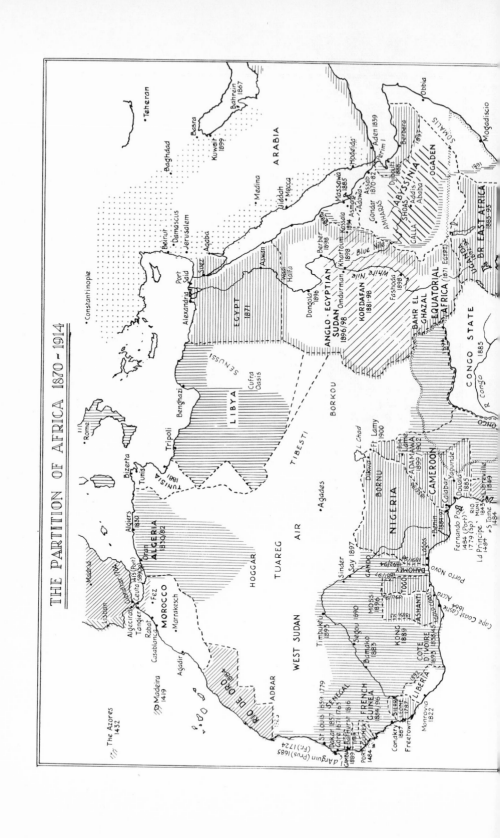

THE PARTITION OF AFRICA 1870 - 1914

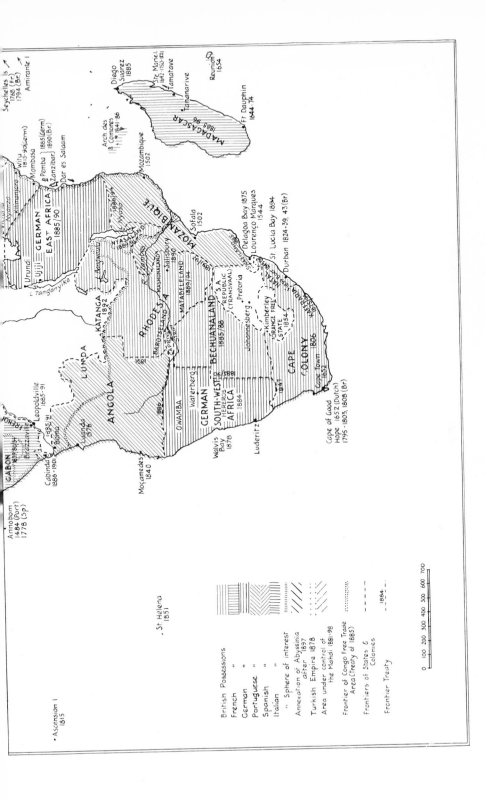

Ascension I
1815

Annobom
1484 (Port)
1778 (5p)

Seychelles Is
1768 (Fr.)
1794 (Br.)
Amirante I

Diego
Suarez
1885

Ste Marie.
1642 1750-82
Tamatrave

Reunion
1654

Arch des
Comores
1841-86

Tananarive

MADAGASCAR
1885-96

Ft Dauphin
1644-74

St Helena
1851

Nyanza

Urundi

Kilimanjaro

Witu
1815-90(Germ)

Ujiji

L Tanganyika

GERMAN
EAST AFRICA
1885/90

B Pemba) 1885(Germ)
Zanzibar) 1890(Br.)

Mombasa

Dar es Salaam

Mozambique
1502

Sofala
1502

NYASALAND

Nyasa

Bangweulu

Zambesi

Salisbury
1890

KATANGA
1892

RHODESIA

MASHONALAND

MOZAMBIQUE

LUNDA

BAROTSELAND

MATABELELAND
1889/94

1886/94

1886/94

Delagoa Bay 1875

Lourenço Marques
1544

ANGOLA

Luanda
1576

1886

OWAMBA

Waterberg

BECHUANALAND
1885/88

S A
REPUBLIC
(TRANSVAAL)

Pretoria

Johannesburg

Kimberley

ORANGE FREE
STATE
1854

St Lucia Bay 1894

Durban 1824-39, 43 (Br)

1681

Moçamedes
1840

Mocamedes

Walvis
Bay
1878

GERMAN
SOUTH-WEST
AFRICA
1884

HERERO'S

Luderitz

CAPE
COLONY

Cape Town
1652

1806

1847

Cape of Good
Hope 1652 (Dutch)
1795-1803, 1808 (Br)

Cabinda
1886-1901

Boma
1895/91

Leopoldville
1885-91

GABON

Brazzaville

British Possessions

French       "

German       "

Portuguese   "

Spanish      "

Italian      "

"   Sphere of interest

Annexation of Abyssinia
after 1897

Turkish Empire 1878

Area under control of
the Mahdi 1881-98

Frontier of Congo Free Trade
Area (Treaty of 1885)

Frontiers of States &
Colonies

Frontier Treaty          1884

0   100  200  300  400  500  600  700

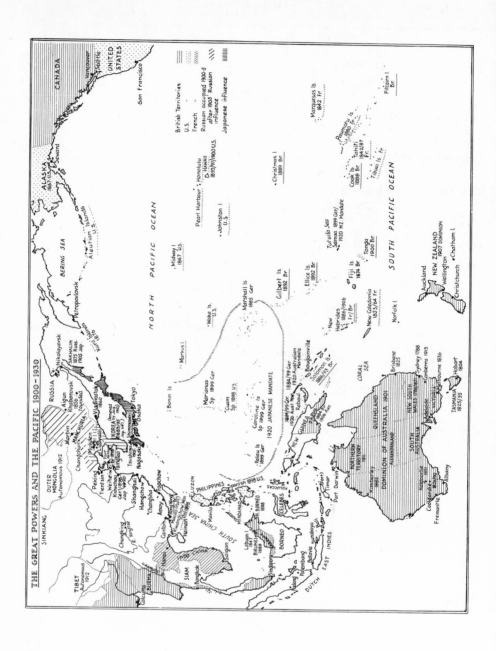

THE GREAT POWERS AND THE PACIFIC 1900-1930

Empire was about to break up. And on two occasions Britain and Germany signed or initialled treaties providing for its division between them in the event of such an occurrence.

**The Congo** provided the worst example of slavery and exploitation. In the early 1880s Leopold, King of the Belgians, had succeeded in setting up the so-called Congo Free State behind a smoke-screen of geographical and philanthropic sentiment and his dominion was recognized by the Berlin West Africa Conference of 1885. Its occupation, however, absorbed the bulk of his private fortune and to recoup his expenses he was forced to grant a series of railway and other concessions. To secure African labour, his hired mercenaries imposed heavy taxes on the African population which had to be paid in commodities like foodstuffs, ivory and raw rubber and in forced labour. The tribal chiefs were deposed in favour of *capitàs* (headmen) appointed by Leopold's administration, who inevitably used terrorist methods to maintain their power. Native uprisings were ruthlessly put down. The methods of Leopold's agents eventually attracted international notice, and the resultant storm of denunciation forced Leopold to allow the Belgian state to take over his private empire in 1908. By that date he had raised his original private fortune of $5 million to at least $80 million. Belgian rule abolished the worst of the cruelties and barbarities practised by Leopold's agents. But it cannot be said that Belgium made any effort to develop African social and economic advancement or encourage native participation in the colonial government. The large monopolies of Leopold's Congo were left untouched. And as a result of their efficiency, the general standard of living, including that of the African population, was higher than that of Africans in any other part of Africa. National feeling in the Congo turned to Messianic sects with Christian borrowings to express their own feelings of solidarity and hope.

## Europe Abroad: The Escapist Societies

Perhaps the oddest forms of European activity abroad were those communities that deliberately tried to remove and completely isolate themselves from nineteenth-century European civilization and advance beyond the frontier of that civilization to establish a state which could somehow be kept isolated from the contamination which they were trying to escape. In many cases such communities were purely religious like the Amish in Pennsylvania or the Mormons who trekked westwards out of the United States in 1846 to build an ideal state in Utah around Salt Lake City. It was anti-urban feelings of an analogous kind that drove many British to settle in Kenya and the Rhodesias and attempt to maintain there an agrarian, individualistic squirearchy of the kind which taxation and the advance of welfare politics were making increasingly impossible in

Britain. It is the tragedy of such states that they cannot hold the clock back; although they may advance for a time beyond the advancing frontier of western urban civilization, it is bound to catch up with them and engulf them. Only two escapist communities in this century have survived such engulfment to fight back against it, and to attempt to recover their earlier isolation, the *Canadiens* of Quebec in Canada and the Boers of South Africa.

The *Canadiens* differ from the Boers in never having had a state of their own, and in never having tried to trek beyond the European frontier. Rather as the nineteenth century advanced they became the more insistent on preserving the rural ultramontane Catholicism of their seventeenth and eighteenth century heritage. They represented France as it had been in the time of Louis XIV before the Enlightenment and before the French Revolution. They drew strength from the anti-liberal mood of the Papacy in the mid-nineteenth century and quietly ignored the modernism of Leo XIII. Their clergy were either native or *emigré* French royalists. And they grew gradually in strength in Quebec despite the success of the Liberals in maintaining themselves in power. They were, above all, protected from extinction by their extraordinary fecundity.

The Boers, by contrast, moved away from British rule in the 1850s in the Great Trek. Where the *Canadiens* were peasants, the Boers were pastoralists and their communities were partially nomadic. They represented an early rural form of Dutch protestantism that had been isolated from the main stream of European development even before emigration to South Africa, like the *Canadiens*, they missed both the Enlightenment and the French Revolution. They were reinforced by Huguenot *emigrés* from France and German protestants from the Rhineland long before English rule was established. And as they moved away from British South Africa so they broke with the synod of their own Church in Capetown which accepted and for a time was dominated by Scottish ministers with an awkward belief in racial equality before God. Eventually they developed break-away sects like the Nederlands Hervoormde Kirk and the even more extreme Doppers who preached a fundamentalist predestinarian Christianity, believing that the earth was flat and that the Bantu, having no souls, were destined for ever to be 'hewers of wood and drawers of water'. Their republics managed to maintain a semi-independent existence until the 1890s. It was their misfortune that the richest gold strike in a gold-hungry world was found in the centre of the Transvaal. The advancing frontiers of British rule had already bypassed them and engulfed them. The inrush of European speculators threatened now to outnumber them in their last reservations. And their attempt to maintain their own power by excluding the new immigrants from citizenship led directly to the war with Britain and their final defeat. (Their subsequent recovery is dealt with in Chapter III above and in Part II of this history.)

## Europe Abroad: Latin America

The third and greatest area of Europe abroad where little or no political or social progress was made in the nineteenth century existed in Central and Southern Latin America. The revolutions which established independence were essentially movements against what had become an alien bureaucratic tyranny. No more than the American revolution that formed the United States did the Latin American revolutions against Spanish rule produce any change in the social balance of power in Latin America itself. European Liberalism was imported. But in most cases it degenerated into a sterile and doctrinaire authoritarianism; and the history of the Latin American states in the nineteenth century is one of endless transition from one military dictatorship to another. In part this was simply a product of the immense distances, the poor communications and the thinness of the population in relation to the spaces of Latin America. But it had other causes too. The ruling groups in every state were bitterly divided by Liberal-Clerical conflicts. While they had adopted the trappings of Liberal republicanism from Spain and revolutionary France they only had the long absolutist traditions of Spanish rule to draw on. And when they were not racked by civil war and successive revolutions, they were involved in wars between themselves. Rule varied between authoritarianism with no real tradition of authority to call on and liberalism with no real popular support.

This internal instability prevented any major economic development except in the larger states such as Argentina, Brazil and Chile; and such economic development as occurred was financed almost entirely by foreign capital of which more than half was of British origin with French, German and United States capital following in that order. There was very considerable immigration from Europe with over 3 million foreign nationals living in Latin America by 1900. In economic and financial terms Latin America occupied virtually the same position as the European colonies themselves. The bulk of their financial resources and capital assets were in foreign hands and their economies in most cases depended on single commodity crops (as Brazil on coffee and rubber, the Argentine on beef exports, Chile on nitrates) in just the same way as did Britain's colonies in Africa. Latin American states were second only to Egypt and Tunisia in the recklessness of their borrowing, though they tended to default much more often than the Arab states were allowed to. Their defaults exposed them on a number of occasions to coercive action of the type we have come to term 'gunboat diplomacy' and even, on several occasions in the earlier part of the nineteenth century, to actual invasion by European forces. But the combination of European absorption in expansion elsewhere, a certain latent prejudice against imposing colonial rule on people of European descent, and the watchful power of Great Britain and the

United States preserved the Americas against any new European colonial ventures.

At the close of the century only three Latin American states, Argentina, Brazil and Chile, were beginning to emerge as powers in their own right. Of these Chile was racially the most homogeneous, Brazil the largest, and the Argentine possibly the most stable throughout the century. But all the Latin American states presented the same picture of violently divided congeries of oligarchic groups with regional political bosses and Army leaders prominently in the forefront. There was also emerging a small educated, Europeanized intellectual class among whom radical and Marxist ideas were beginning to catch hold. On the other side of an immense social abyss could be seen the labouring masses, illiterate, poverty-stricken and vulnerable to natural disasters. Their mortality rate was high and their expectation of life was brief. Only in the large cities, Buenos Aires, Montevideo, Rio de Janeiro, Valparaiso, did an urban middle class exist. The few signs of new forces coming to the surface were to be found in the growth of anarcho-syndicalism in Chile with the great strikes of 1905 and 1907 and the foundation of the Socialist Labour Party in 1912; in the socialism from above imposed in Uruguay after 1900; and in the growth of the Radical Civic Union, an American-style reform movement, in the Argentine. The reform movements of the mid-century in Mexico and Colombia seemed to have fizzled out. Everywhere else army rule, local bossism, civil war or demagogic government was the order of the day.

The exposure of the Latin American countries to European coercive measures had led early in the nineteenth century to a number of weak and tentative movements towards some kind of pan-American solidarity. Successive conferences, at Panama in 1826, at Lima in 1847–48, at Santiago in 1856, at Lima in 1864–65 and at Mexico City in 1896 had produced a number of collective agreements, but most of these pacts proved worthless almost at the moment they were signed. American influence led to the summoning of the first Pan-American Conference in Washington in 1889, but suspicion and fear of the United States made its deliberations fruitless. Moreover, Latin American opinion in general became profoundly alarmed over the course American policy took after 1898.

## Non-European States: Africa

In the mediaeval and early modern period in European history, Africa had witnessed a series of remarkable empires both in east and west Africa. In **East Africa** most remarkable was the Shona kingdom associated with the city of Zimbabwe, the remnants of which were destroyed in 1834 by breakaway Zulu rebels coming from southern Africa. At the time of the last great European scramble for Africa the main states were, firstly, the

100

Arab Sultanate of **Zanzibar,** relic of a wave of expansion in the 1830s from the Arab kingdom of Oman on the southern shores of the Persian Gulf; and, second, the inland states of Buganda, Ruanda and Urundi lying in a belt from the eastern shores of Lake Victoria Nyanza down to the shores of Lake Tanganyika.

**Buganda** was entirely a Bantu kingdom, which had succeeded early in the nineteenth century to the primacy of the region when the much larger kingdom of Bunyoro broke up. It was being challenged by a revival of political activity in Bunyoro when the Europeans first arrived. In 1875 the Kabaka Mutesa of Buganda invited Christian missionaries to counter the infiltration of Islam and Arab slave traders from Zanzibar and the Sudan. But his kingdom was speedily threatened anew as schism and civil war developed between the converts of Catholic and Protestant missionaries. Only British intervention and the establishment of a protectorate over all of present-day Uganda saved the Bugandan states from disintegration. Thereafter Britain's need to have some firm authority on which responsibility for minor matters could be devolved and with whom issues of land tenure and purchase could be negotiated preserved the kingdom of Buganda under British rule.

**Ruanda** and **Urundi** were multi-racial states where the more recently arrived Nilotic *emigrés* from the Ethiopian highlands, the Watutsi, ruled as an aristocracy over the earlier Bantu immigrants, the Bahutu and the aboriginal pygmies. They fell nominally into that part of East Africa which was awarded to Germany at the Berlin West African Congress of 1884–85. But in fact German influence had hardly made any contact with Ruanda and Urundi before the outbreak of war in 1914; in 1919 they passed under Belgian mandate since they adjoined the Belgian Congo.

In **Western Africa** the Negro empires of the early modern period had been larger and more powerful than the states of East Africa. In succession, Ghana, Mali, and the Songhai empires had ruled the savannah country south of the Sahara Desert. The Songhai were overthrown in the sixteenth century by invasion from Morocco and the *entrepôt* trade on which its wealth rested ended by the arrival of Europeans on the coast. The European arrival on the coast seems to have been preceded by a considerable movement of native tribes out of the reach of the savannah empires through the rain forests to the African coast, and a fresh growth of Negro states at Benin and in Dahomey and, inland along the Niger river, the formation of sizeable city states among the Hausa. In west Central Africa a large nation appears to have developed in the Congo basin around the Meni Congo tribe. But the advent of huge markets for slaves in the New World stimulated a state of continuous warfare and slave raiding among the African states themselves which over the three centuries it raged reduced all but a few states to disintegrated tribalism. Those which survived turned into militarist confederacies, such as that of Dahomey with its Amazon corps of virgin women.

When the last phase of European expansion in Africa opened, the main

African states consisted of military autocracies in the interior, the Tucolor in Senegal, the Mandingoes in the upper Gambia, the Ashanti Confederacy with its capital at Kumasi and the state of Dahomey, already mentioned, and a chain of Moslem emirates among the Fulani and Hausa on the savannahs, of whom the Sultan of Sokoto was the nominal overlord. The coastal tribes were subdivided into hundreds of petty chiefdoms. (There were something like eight hundred alone in the area lying to the east of the Niger delta.) The British penchant for indirect rule, using the local political structures to do most of the work of maintaining local law and order and collecting taxes, easily preserved the larger political units in the West African interior. But on the coast the political units were so small that detribalization began with the establishment of colonial rule. And the West African coast was to prove one of the earliest stamping grounds for pan-Africanism.

In **South Africa** the largest African political units at the time of the collision between the advancing Boers and the Bantu tribes were all more or less organized along military lines, since they had been the spearhead of the Bantu migrations and the instrument used to roll up the Hottentot aborigines before them. Of these militarist states by far the most remarkable was that of the Zulus in what is today Natal, built up out of a group of tribes by Chaka Zulu, who became great chief in 1818, into one of the most effective military machines in history. Some of his regiments broke away from his control and fled his wrath in two directions. One wing under Mzilikasi moved deep into the Transvaal before swinging northwards into what is today Rhodesia where they set up the Matabele State. Others moved directly northwards, destroying the last shadow of the Zimbabwe empire on the way, and ranged north as far as Lake Victoria before settling along Lake Nyasa. Their murders and raids laid waste much of Central Africa; and what destruction they had begun, the Arab slave raiders from Zanzibar completed. Apart from the Bechuana and the Basuto, whom Matabele pressure forced to band together for their own survival, the whole of southern and central Africa presented no political system capable of standing up to the advance of European influence and settlement apart from the Zulu whose military power was finally broken in 1879–80.

By 1900, there were only two independent African states south of the Sahara, Ethiopia and Liberia. **Liberia,** like its neighbour the British colony of **Sierra Leone,** was originally founded as a settlement for Negro slaves liberated by emancipationists in the New World and 'repatriated' to Africa. Of the two, Sierra Leone was the older, having been founded as a refuge for Negroes who remained loyal to the Crown during the American revolution and deportees from the great Negro rising of the 1790s in Jamaica. To these were added slaves seized by the British naval anti-slavery patrol. The first Sierra Leone settlements were made in 1787–91 and a distinctive Creole culture developed there.

Liberia was the product of American emancipation in the 1820s–30s and, unlike Sierra Leone, gained its independence (in 1841). Both faced the same problems, the impossibility of reuniting the Europeanized culture of the former slaves with the tribal structure among the natives. British rule in Sierra Leone preserved the two cultures side by side and developed a distinctive 'Creole' culture, as it was called, among the ex-slaves and their descendants, with Creoles associated with the executive and legislative councils of British rule and the first West African institution of higher education at Fourah Bay. In Liberia, an adroit policy of balancing between Britain and the United States preserved its independence. But the ex-slave element, modelling themselves on the ante-bellum South, created what was in fact a totally colonialist *régime*, and between 1914 and 1919 accepted American military aid as the only means of suppressing a succession of native uprisings.

**Ethiopia** was a very different matter. The Ethiopian Empire traced its independence and civilization back to pre-Christian times. It embraced Monophysite Christianity as the state religion in the fourth century AD. It had survived the onset of Islam, mainly because of its geographical isolation, though on one famous occasion only the providential arrival of a ship-load of Portuguese soldiers saved the day. In the late nineteenth century it was preserved mainly by the infusion of energy from the frontier kingdom of Shoa. The last emperors of the old Ethiopian empire, Theodore II and John IV, had in turn been killed, the one in conflict with Britain which led to a British expedition against his capital, Magdala, the other while fighting with the Mahdist forces in the Sudan. John's death made it possible for Menelik II of Shoa to claim the title of Emperor and to extend his rule outwards from Shoa's capital of Addis Ababa. Not only did Menelik II take over the traditional centres of the Ethiopian empire in Gondar and Tigré, but he also acquired the Moslem kingdom of Harrar to the south and a congerie of petty kingdoms to the west. He accepted some aid from France and Russia, and allowed his territory to be used by French expeditions against the headwaters of the Nile at the time of the Fashoda crisis. Even more significant was his crushing defeat of a major Italian invasion at Adowa in 1896, the first defeat inflicted by a non-European state on a European power since the days of the Ottoman invasions of Europe.

The state he attempted to rule was largely feudal. The barons of the north, especially the hereditary princes, the *Ras* of Tigré, were bitter enemies of the house of Menelik. The annexationist policy he pursued brought under Shoan rule not only members of the dominant Amharic race but also Galla and Danaquil tribesmen of Moslem and pagan faiths. The task of integrating the various aristocracies into the Ethiopian system was long and difficult and Menelik's need of western capital, if only to pay for the arms used to maintain his position, always left him vulnerable to a repetition of the British expedition which had overthrown Theodore II.

By 1906 the three powers which had established themselves around the Horn of Africa, Britain, France and Italy, signed a treaty agreeing to maintain the integrity of Ethiopia, but at the same time providing for its division among them in the event of its breakdown. The death of Menelik in 1913 and his succession by an unbalanced Emperor who shook Ethiopia to the core by embracing Islam, the faith of his mother, could very well have led to such a division. However, Ethiopia was saved by the fact that the European powers were absorbed in the Great War, and its survival owed more to the balance of interests between the European powers than to any inherent ability on Ethiopia's part to repeat the victory of Adowa. In 1900 Ethiopia, in comparative terms, was barely entering the sixteenth century.

## Revolts Against the West

The imposition of colonial rule over the better organized and more self-conscious African cultures and states was not an easy process. In some cases the impression of western power was so great that it was accepted passively as a kind of divine imposition. This was especially the case where European occupation had followed or taken advantage of a long period of chaos or civil war. In other situations wise and intelligent colonial administrators, particularly those who employed the methods of indirect rule first developed in Nigeria by the British, were able to obtain the active participation of the traditional leaders of the local African political units. In still others passive opposition was the initial reaction. But in a very large number of instances the imposition of colonial rule was followed within at most two decades by violent revolt led by the traditional political and religious African leaders.

The occasions for these revolts were numerous and varied. In a great many cases it was simply harsh and unimaginative colonial administration that was at fault. Brutality by native police and violence directed against native women figured high on the list of accepted explanations for these uprisings. In other instances there was a definite clash of interpretations of the existing *status quo*. In the hut tax war in Sierra Leone in 1898, for example, the chiefs of the inland protectorate regarded the imposition of a levy on them by the colonial government as derogatory to their sovereignty, which they did not feel they had surrendered simply by signing a treaty of protection with the colonial power. The Matabele and Mashona risings of 1896 in Rhodesia, like the Herero risings of 1904 in German South-West Africa, seem to have arisen from a conflict between European ideas of ownership as applied to their cattle herds, and the much more complex concepts of their own society. The Ashanti revolt of 1900 arose from a total misconception on the part of the British Governor of the nature of the Golden Stool, the mystical symbol of Ashanti unity, which led him in public council to offend grossly the deepest feelings of the Ashanti people. Other uprisings, as for example, the Maji-Maji rising in

German East Africa in 1905, the Zulu rebellion in Natal in 1906, and the Makombe rising of 1917–20 in Portuguese East Africa arose from protest against the draconian invasions of local tribal authority by the representatives of the local colonial power, invasions which included loss of lands, the imposition of heavy taxation and the introduction of severe labour laws, if not of forced labour as such.

The violence with which so many of these rebellions were conducted and the central role played in so many cases by witch-doctors, spirit-mediums, semi-mystical secret orders and charms supposed to protect the wearer against European bullets reveal the atavistic religious convictions of the rebels who believed they were fighting to preserve the very essence of their culture. And the violence and bloodshed with which they were so often put down reveal an equally strong, if more racialist, conviction on the part of the Europeans that it was the authority of their culture, their *mana* as the Maoris of New Zealand would say, which had been attacked. In South-West Africa over 90,000 natives, 80% of the Hereros and about half the other tribes drawn into the revolt, were killed. In German East Africa, an estimated 120,000 natives died from bullets or starvation. And the defeat and destruction of tribal authority in most cases only speeded up the process of pauperization and detribalization which the introduction of western rule, the western money economy and western systems of employment brought with them.

## The Beginnings of African Nationalism: Pan-Africanism and Ethiopianism

The atavistic revolts of the tribes represented only one form of African reaction to the European conquest, and one that was only possible in the rural areas where the traditional political structure was not immediately affected by western industrial civilization. But where that civilization struck roots in Africa, in the seaports, in the industrial towns and in the mining areas, there was an insatiable demand for labour. Africans were lured, bribed, shanghaied and conscripted to work in the new centres, and, once engaged as workers, came to stay and live where they worked. The experience was in most cases a traumatic one, since the labour forces were a mixture of many tribes and deprived of all traditional patterns of religious or political leadership and authority. The process of detribalization was a long and painful one. But generally among the detribalized, especially among those exposed to European education through mission schools and the like, there began to develop a new feeling, one of African nationalism, of a separate African identity.

As South Africa was the most advanced area in the continent in 1900, these new feelings showed themselves there first. But they were also to be

105

found in British West Africa, where Fourah Bay College in Sierra Leone had been producing a small number of university-educated Africans since the middle of the nineteenth century. The new feelings showed themselves first of all in two different forms, in the preaching of pan-African sentiments by a few intellectuals, with the development of an African press, and in the formation of break-away African churches. In the early stages those responsible were profoundly influenced by contact with Negroes from the more advanced cultures of the United States and the British West Indies. The American influence showed itself mainly in the religious field, the West Indian in the political. A major role in the political field was played in South Africa too by the half-caste Cape Coloureds and by the Indian community.

Ethiopianism, that is the foundation of African Negro churches, originally struck root among the freed slaves of the American South in the decades after the American Civil War. In the 1880s the first of a number of American Negro missionaries from these churches came to Africa to play their part in the great missionary effort all the Christian churches in Europe and America were devoting to the new-found continent. The first Ethiopian churches as such developed in Nigeria in 1891. But South Africa had already seen the break-away of individual African Negro priests from the Anglican communion, to be followed by a similar break-away from the Wesleyans in the Transvaal. In 1896 Bishop H. M. Turner of the African Methodist Episcopal Church in the United States sponsored the union of these groups into the African branch of his own church. But more Ethiopian churches continued to form and by 1918 there were more than 76 in South Africa alone. These Negro missionaries took a number of Africans back to the United States to be educated before returning to Africa to continue in the mission field. John Chilembwe, who led the Nyasa revolt of 1915, was one such.

Political pan-Africanism came first of all from the British West Indies. One of its earliest propagandists was E. W. Blyden, a West Indian who emigrated to Liberia in 1850, whose books asserting the existence of a unique African personality had a profound influence both in West Africa and among the educated Negroes of the United States. From Liberia, John Payne Jackson came to Lagos in 1891 to found the first pan-African newspaper, the *Lagos Weekly Record*, in 1891. The first Bantu language newspaper, *Llanga Lase Natal*, was founded in Durban in 1902. That same year a leading Moslem in Capetown, Abdullah Abdurahman, founded the African People's Organization to work for the extension of the rights enjoyed by the Cape Coloured community or coloureds in other parts of South Africa.

A second wave of pan-Africanism originated in the United States in 1905 with the rallying of the leaders of the American Negro community against the spread of 'Jim Crow' segrationist legislation in the American Southern states after 1900. In 1905 a number of prominent American Negro leaders, including the historian W. E. B. du Bois, set up the Niagara movement, which was to develop five years later into the National Association for the Advancement of the Coloured People.

In 1908 the two strands of West Indian pan-Africanism and American Ethiopianism came together with the organization of the first Pan-African Conference by a West Indian barrister, H. Sylvester Williams, who had developed a legal practice in London based in part on representing African chiefs negotiating with the Colonial Office and other organizations, and Bishop Walters of the African Methodist Episcopal Zionist Church in the United States. Du Bois produced a memorial of this conference. Later he became editor of the NAACP journal, *Crisis*, which was to develop a significant circulation in Africa. But the outbreak of war in Europe prevented the holding of any further conferences until 1919, though the Great War was largely responsible for developing African political consciousness and diminishing the European *mana* in Africa.

## Non-European States: Asia and the Pacific

The principal independent or semi independent states in Asia still surviving in 1900 were the Kingdom of Siam, the States of Malaya, and the theocracy of Tibet. **Indo-China** finally passed under French rule in the 1880s, although the French allowed a shadowy existence to continue for the Kingdom of Cambodia and Laos within the *Union Indochinoise* which they set up in 1887. **Siam** managed to avoid a similar fate despite a major crisis with France in 1895 which involved the loss of one-fifth of her territory, largely because Britain and France were agreed for most of the latter part of the nineteenth century on the desirability of maintaining Siam as a buffer state between their respective possessions in Burma and Indo-China. A very considerable role was played in maintaining Siamese independence by the long and liberal rule of King Chulalangkom (1868–1910), who used his semi-divine status and his traditional powers and prestige as the legal owner of all land to carry through a great many reforms. He bound the best of the military class to him by setting up Councils of State to advise him, made much use of foreign technicians and advisers and made considerable administrative reforms. He was aided by the opening of the Suez Canal in 1869 which linked the Siamese economy more closely to the European market. He avoided, however, a lavish commitment to public investment, and the tight money policy practised by his advisers, while preventing Siam from running up the kind of debts which would inevitably have brought European intervention, put a damper on economic expansion at a rate which would upset the normal tenor of Siamese life.

**Malaya** presented a rather different picture. In the south, Singapore had been entirely created by the British as the greatest commercial *entrepôt* for all South-East Asia, it population consisting largely of *emigré* Chinese

To Singapore were added in 1826 other British trading settlements at Penang and Malacca, the whole being known as the Straits Settlements. In up-country Malaya, the latter half of the nineteenth century saw an immense development of tin-mining by European and Chinese capital with the growth of a large and rowdy Chinese labour force. By 1900 Malaya was producing half the world's supply of tin and the various sultans of the Malay states were rich enough to be able to give a battleship, HMS *Malaya*, to the Royal Navy in 1911. To all this was added the cultivation of rubber which enjoyed a fantastic boom in 1910–12. By 1914 Malayan rubber had captured the world market from Brazil.

From the 1850s then developments had been casting an increased strain on the relations between the various Malay sultans; piracy, inter-state war, faction fights between Chinese secret societies, pressure from the Netherlands in the south and Siam in the north led to the gradual extension of the British residential system, first introduced into the state of Perak in 1874. Under the residential system each Sultan's position was guaranteed by the British, who undertook to help maintain order. In return the Sultan accepted a British resident, whose 'advice' had to be asked and acted on in all administrative matters, and who became responsible for overseeing the collection and control of all revenue. By 1895 British residents were installed in all the central and southern Malayan states except Johore. In 1895 four states in central Malaya were persuaded to come together into the Federated Malay States with a common administrative structure, and a capital at Kuala Lumpur and a resident-general. There followed an immense economic development, revenue tripling itself in ten years. In 1909 the Sultans formed a Federal Council to advise the resident-general. That same year the four northernmost Malay states were ceded to Britain by Siam in return for a £4 million loan and the abandonment of British extra-territorial rights. They preferred, as did Johore, to remain outside the Federation and to accept a British adviser rather than a resident. Johore did not even accept an adviser until 1914.

The advance of rubber cultivation brought a fresh wave of immigration from Southern India, and by 1911 Malays themselves constituted a bare 51% of the population. But whereas the opposition of capital to labour divided the Chinese and Indian communities, Malay society showed itself remarkably resistant in the face of this invasion. The sultans and the Malay peasantry remained dominant in the general fields of agriculture and fishing and proved able to expand the food supply in step with the increase in population. Islam gave them its remarkable powers of cohesion. But, above all, the main force in preserving the traditional structure of Malay society was the rule of Britain, whose overriding concern for the maintenance of law and order here as in India preserved the structures it found on conquest virtually unaltered, like flies in amber, until the moment of its withdrawal.

In **Burma,** British rule was not so beneficent in its effects. The three British wars in 1826, 1852 and 1855 were to destroy entirely the traditional system of divine royalty and the authority which went with it. The five years of anarchy, dacoity and piracy which followed necessitated military action and the introduction of direct British rule down to village level. The degeneration of Burmese society was accelerated with the introduction of large numbers of Indian coolies to aid in the commercial development of agriculture to serve the Indian market. The Burmese authorities gradually lost control of their land to Indian capital. There was a rapid rise in crimes of violence and xenophobia. Burmese opinion took added exception to being governed as a province of India, even though Burma benefited from the general advance of India towards self-government. An advisory Legislative Council was set up in 1897 and a Burmese civil service on Indian lines developed slowly thereafter. The ascent from the depths of 1900 was a very slow one, greatly retarded by the decline in native monastic culture and the absence of any significant European educational effort to replace it.

**Tibet** was the most remote of all Asian states, isolated both by geography and by an inward-looking religion whose principles left its devotees largely uninterested in the outside world. It was a theocratic state, governed for two hundred years by regents from the nobility chosen by the lamas (the monks of Tibet). A peculiar amalgam of Mahayana Buddhism with Tibet's own magical-mystical shamanism, Lama rule had been finally established in the seventeenth century AD by Mongol princes from Central Asia, under the head of one of the competing lama sects to whom a Mongol prince gave the title of Dalai Lama. Although the Chinese intervened to expel an invasion from Central Asia in 1720 and remained in active occupation of Tibet until the middle of the eighteenth century, their withdrawal left Tibet autonomous again under the religious hierarchy and until the advent of the thirteenth Dalai Lama in 1895, the Dalai Lamas were mere figureheads. The thirteenth Dalai Lama, however, was determined to make Tibet completely independent. But his attempt to achieve independence by playing off the British in India, the Russians and the Chinese against one another proved disastrous. His entertainment of a Russian agent in 1903 caused the Indian government to take up traders' complaints and launch an expedition which reached Lhasa in 1904, and led to his temporary deposition by the Chinese. Reinstalled, he appealed to Britain for aid against China in 1909, only bringing down on his head a Chinese expedition, from which he fled to exile in India in 1910. Tibet remained under direct Chinese occupation for two years until the Chinese Revolution of 1911 so weakened the Chinese authority as to enable the Tibetans to expel the Chinese garrison. The Dalai Lama returned to independent rule even though he received British aid in the reorganization of his armed forces.

## The Beginnings of Nationalism in South-East Asia

The **Philippines** were the scene of the only major nationalist movement in South-East Asia before 1900. Its causes can be traced to the wealth that flowed into the islands, after nearly three hundred years of stagnation under Spanish rule, with the opening of the Chinese ports to European trade in 1840. At the same time friction gradually developed between the native Filipino clergy and the large Spanish monastic orders which, having originally converted the Philippines to Catholicism in the sixteenth century, had come to own large quantities of land on the islands. There were clergy-led rebellions in 1843 and 1872 and a Messianic break-away movement, the Colorum movement, in the 1840s. By the 1890s a new movement had grown up which represented a coming together of three separate groupings, a gathering of native magical traditions in a secret society, the so-called *Katipuran,* led by one Emilio Aguinaldo, of a schismatic religious movement, such as the Independent Filipino Church, and of European liberal anti-clericalism represented by José Rizal who founded the *Liga Filipina* in 1892. In 1896 these various forces revolted against Spain. Rizal was executed and in 1897 the Spanish bought off the rebel leaders with 800,000 pesos. It was at that moment that the outbreak of the Spanish-American war led the Americans to enlist Aguinaldo's support against the Spanish garrison of the islands. When Spain withdrew, nationalist leaders raised the flag of independence. But neither their Catholicism nor their easy corruptibility convinced the Americans that they were 'fit for self-government'. Commercial, strategic and imperialist reasoning reinforced this basically Protestant Anglo-Saxon conviction of the backwardness of the Catholic Hispanicized Malay-Moro-Chinese population of the Philippines, and the islands were duly annexed to the United States in the sacred name of the American mission to 'uplift them and civilize them and Christianize them' (the words were those of President McKinley). There followed two years of bloody rebellion as violently put down. American opinion, however, took its mission seriously. In 1903 local elections were held and in 1907 the Philippines were given a general assembly on a restricted franchise. By 1918 the Philippines were well on their way again to self-government.

In **Indonesia,** the nationalist movement took much longer to develop than in the Philippines, and when it came it was Islamic rather than Catholic. In other respects, however, it represented a similar admixture of western and indigenous ideas. Dutch economic exploitation in the nineteenth century had created a large and restless labour force. Dutch control had also destroyed much of the authority of the traditional rulers, while at the same time producing a population increase in Java on such a scale as to outstrip the rate of expansion of agricultural production. The main resistance to Dutch rule in this period came from the *ulemas*, the intellectual leaders of Islam. In 1900 the Dutch reversed their stand to

110

introduce the so-called New Ethical Policy. Its aims were to expand and develop a new educated Islamic *élite* and to improve the social services and welfare of the islands. But the Dutch were unable to overcome the opposition of the resident European population who were unwilling to curtail their economic privileges. And administrative convenience dictated the continuation of direct rule through local sultans throughout all but the principal islands of the Indonesian archipelago. The effect of the New Ethical Policy was to create a semi-educated group not easily disposable into a system of administration dominated either by the Dutch or by local sultans. At the same time Chinese merchants were invading Java and establishing a stranglehold on the rural economy.

The combination of Islamic resistance to Dutch rule, European liberal ideas expressing themselves through the products of the New Ethical Policy and Javanese economic grievances led in 1906 to the establishment of the 'High Endeavour' Society, the aim of which was to establish schools and regenerate Javanese culture and in 1911 to the establishment of *Sarekat Islam* (the Islamic brotherhood), which at first was supported by Dutch officials. At its second conference, in 1916, the first to be held on a nation-wide basis, the leaders of *Sarekat Islam* passed a resolution demanding Indonesian self-government. At the same time Dutch socialists were beginning to proselytize in Indonesia, and after the Russian Revolution of 1917 Indonesian nationalism was to pass through a predominantly Marxist phase.

## *The Decline of Polynesian Society*

Worst hit by the arrival of western ideas and influences were the island cultures of Polynesia, the Maori states of New Zealand and the kingdom of Hawaii. At the time of the first contacts with European culture in the Pacific, Polynesian political organization was based on decentralized tribal kingdoms with a considerable record of internecine war. The introduction of European firearms only made these wars more bloody. At the same time the isolated Polynesian communities proved highly vulnerable to European diseases.

Thus in **New Zealand,** the first of the large Polynesian-inhabited areas to fall under European rule, eighteen years of tribal warfare and epidemics (1821–38) reduced the population of North Island from 200,000 to 100,000. At first European occupation did not bring a unified resistance until European encroachment on Maori-held lands had already become irreversible. Maori opposition ranged from a relatively benign attempt to achieve Maori unity in the 'King' movement to the racial-magical fanaticism of the *Hau-hau* movement with its attempts to appropriate the magical element in Christianity which the Maoris thought to be the secret of

European strength. Maori resistance, however, was easily defeated. Thereafter, despite the British policy of attempting to draw the Maoris into the economy by the construction of railways and the appointment of Maori members of the New Zealand parliament, the Maoris withdrew into isolation within their communities and by 1896 their numbers had dropped to a mere 42,000. At this point the white New Zealanders spoke of eventual disappearance of the Maori people.

After 1896, however, a new leadership, based on the Maori seats in the New Zealand parliament, stemming partly from half-caste Maoris like Sir James Carroll, partly from missionary-educated Maoris, began to bring about a revival. In 1897 the formation of the Young Maori party began to replace the declining traditional leadership. And its rediscovery of Maori language and culture through the methods of western ethnology led to a revival of pride in the Maori national heritage and the growth of a sense of Maori unity over and above tribal differences. The population trend was very slowly reversed. And Maoris began to work for a synthesis of European knowledge, ideas and practices which was made the more difficult for the lack of any but oral Maori traditions.

The state of **Hawaii**, by contrast, managed to maintain its independence until the end of the nineteenth century. In part this was due to the achievement of Kamehameka I who, by the close of the eighteenth century, had managed to unify most of the islands under his rule prior to all but the first European landfalls. Hawaii, however, remained open to trading and missionary contacts, and indeed by the 1860s had adopted Christianity on such a vast scale that it no longer constituted a field for missionary activity. The islands had also accepted American and British settlers and American, French and British consuls. And periodic descents on the islands by warships of these three powers in pursuit of national aims and a short period of British occupation led in the 1840s to a joint Anglo-French guarantee of Hawaiian independence. Thereafter British and French activities gradually declined and Hawaii became economically dependent on the United States, particularly after the Reciprocity Treaty of 1876. But with the increase in commercial wealth came an invasion of American, Chinese and Japanese settlers, smallpox and the decline of the native population from 200,000 in 1800 to barely 40,000 in 1890. In 1884 in order to secure extension of the Reciprocity Treaty a coaling station at Pearl Harbour on Oahu Island was ceded to America. In the effort to assert their sovereignty the monarchs of Hawaii inevitably came into conflict with the American settlers, and from 1887 to 1891 there were a series of political disturbances in the islands. In 1892 the white residents finally revolted against Polynesian rule, and set up a temporary government and applied for annexation by the United States, which followed, after an initial rebuff, in 1898 in the wave of imperialism fostered in America by the Spanish-American war.

*The West Indies*

Nowhere did the impact of European colonial rule and European mercantilist policies produce a political pattern more contrary to geography than in the islands of the Caribbean. Few areas showed less signs of economic, social or political progress at the opening of the twentieth century. The interaction of Spanish, French, Dutch, British and United States imperialism produced a chain of islands divided from one another by language, culture, political system, religion, trade and finance, and even by racial composition. Indeed, each was tied so firmly to its metropolitan economic system that neighbouring islands might well have been on separate continents for all the intercourse between them. The British-owned Bahamas lay next to Cuba, which was to win its independence from Spain in 1898, only to pass at once under the equally unwelcome protection of the United States. South of Cuba lay British Jamaica, east the independent Negro republics of Haïti and the Dominican Republic, the American colony of Puerto Rico, taken from Spain, and the American Virgin Islands. Next came the long chain of Leeward and Windward Islands with French, British and the occasional Dutch islands interspersed with one another, British-held Trinidad and Tobago, the Dutch Curaçao and the three Guianas, one British, one French and one Dutch (Surinam).

Throughout the area the largest population group was made up of descendants of the African slaves brought there in the sixteenth, seventeenth and eighteenth centuries. The next most numerous group was that composed of the products of union between slaves and European settlers. In the nineteenth century the British brought in Chinese coolies and Indian indentured labour to British Guiana and to Trinidad and Tobago, and the Dutch imported both Indians and Javanese to Surinam. Cuba and Puerto Rico contained large colonies of Europeans of Spanish origin, and there were British, French and Dutch planter minorities in the remaining islands. American rule brought in American businessmen, some planters and technicians for the American-owned and controlled fruit-producing plantations. The largest single crop was sugar, followed by coffee, cocoa and, in the south, oil and bauxite. The single most important reason for the stagnation of West Indian society for the first three decades of the twentieth century was the decline in the world price of sugar.

The **French West Indies** were largely governed in the nineteenth century according to the general pattern of French colonial practice. French slaves were emancipated in 1848 and in 1875 the islands were permanently incorporated as departments of Metropolitan France. The inhabitants were assimilated into France; adult male suffrage was introduced and the French educational system imposed as an inevitable accompaniment to the incorporation of the islands into the departmental organization of Metropolitan France. Yet sugar, the main product of

113

Martinique and Guadeloupe, competed on the French market with French-produced beet-sugar, the production and marketing of which was heavily subsidized in France by the French government. France's West Indian colonies became a permanent drain on the French economy and as a result economic and social development in the colonies stagnated for lack of funds.

The **Dutch West Indies** suffered equally from the slump in world demand for cane sugar, and the economies of Surinam and Curaçao were also run at a loss to the metropolitan exchequer. Dutch rule, however, was more paternalistic than that of France, though Surinam had a legislature of thirteen members, nine of whom were elected, left over from the days when it was run by a Dutch Chartered Company. An Assembly whose members were nominated rather than elected was set up to rule the Dutch island possessions in 1865. Such a system was not designed to stimulate political activity among the local inhabitants, and in 1900 the Dutch West Indies showed even less signs of any social or political ferment than the French colonies.

The **British West Indies** had enjoyed representative institutions at the beginning of the nineteenth century, though the only interests represented were those of the planter oligarchy. The Negro uprisings in Jamaica in 1865 led, however, to the abolition of the old assembly and the adoption of the standard British policy of Crown Colony rule. However, British opinion prevented an extension of the franchise to cover the illiterate and propertyless Negro masses. The Governor ruled through a legislative council, a number of whose members were, after 1884, elected on a property-owning basis which let in the small property owners of Negro or Creole blood. The effect was to destroy the political power of the small white oligarchy and to remove from the West Indies the prospect of racial strife. The Crown Colony system spread to the other British West Indies with the exception of Barbados and the Bahamas which preserved their eighteenth-century assemblies. But any chance of social or political progress was destroyed by the drastic slump in the world price of cane sugar with the invasion of the British market by European-produced and subsidized beet sugar. By 1900 only 2.5% of British sugar consumption came from the West Indies and the concurrent outbreaks of disease among Trinidad's cocoa and Jamaica's banana plantations left the islands virtually destitute.

West Indian labour emigrated to New York and the United States generally, and political consciousness tended to manifest itself among the *emigrés* in the form of Ethiopianism. Educated West Indians came to Britain and played their part in the early stages of the Pan-African movement. In their culture the masses of the people reverted to a more primitive form of Africanism, with *obeah*, spirit worship, the Shango cult, poco-mania and other degenerate forms of half-remembered, half-invented African-type superstitions taking hold. Destitution was their lot and a high birth rate produced a level of over-population which made the alleviation of poverty quite beyond the resources of the colonial power. Only among the small middle-class could the first stirrings of a distinctive West Indian political consciousness be found. Otherwise the West Indian remained proud to be British, and it is significant that only one out of four of West Indian immigrants to the United States chose to take out American citizenship, to the disgust of the American Negroes among whom they lived.

**Cuba** provided the real exception to this record of stagnation, though the revolutionary forces in the island were essentially those that had succeeded in casting off Spanish rule on the American mainland in the period after 1800. The revolutionaries were an admixture of Hispanic and Creole elements determined to free themselves and their island from a rule at once paternalistic, inefficient, corrupt and dictated by metropolitan considerations quite alien to Cuba. They resented the heavy Spanish taxation, the huge imposts on Cuban trade with the United States, the biggest market for Cuban sugar, and the discrimination practised against the Creoles by the new wave of Spanish immigrants in the 1850s. The conspiracies of 1848–51 were followed by the ten-year war of independence in 1868–78 in which over 200,000 lost their lives. It was a fresh Cuban rebellion in 1895 which did so much to turn American opinion against Spain in the period before the outbreak of the Spanish-American war in 1898. But when the war was over, Cuba had achieved nominal independence only to pass under the domination of the United States. The energies of the Cuban revolution seemed to have been dissipated, and Cuba, having fought for a century, only managed to achieve the status and ambitions of a Latin American *caudillo-* and army-ridden oligarchy.

# SECTION TWO    THE BREAKDOWN OF THE EUROPEAN SYSTEM

*Chapter V*
## THE NATURE OF THE EUROPEAN SYSTEM

*Centripetal Forces*

By 1900, the European great powers had managed to survive eighty-five years without a major war, though there had been numerous crises, minor wars, and war-scares; especially in the middle of the century after Louis Napoleon had succeeded in breaking the old ties between Austria and Russia, and initiated a succession of small but violent wars, which were to end with his own defeat at the hands of Bismarckian Germany in the Franco-Prussian war of 1870–71. Thereafter Bismarck had succeeded in re-establishing much of the old ethos of co-operation between the European powers established in 1815, the idea of the 'Concert of Europe' as it has been called, to deal with the strains consequent on the increasing disintegration of the Ottoman Empire, and with those arising from the scramble for territory in Africa.

The basic idea underlying the concept of the Concert of Europe was the principle of the balance of power and the maintenance of parity of force between the Great Powers. Its motive force was fear of a major disturbance of the *status quo* that would raise any one of the powers to a position of such quasi-Napoleonic supremacy over its rivals that only a costly and long-drawn-out major war could restore the balance. The Concert of Europe therefore called for co-operation to prevent disturbance of the *status quo* by the smaller powers. It also provided agreed compensation to the other great powers, in those instances when one great power enlarged its area of dominion to a degree which the others found excessive. Thus at the Berlin Congress of 1878 Tsarist Russia was forced to revise the peace terms it had imposed on Ottoman Turkey after the Russo-Turkish war of 1877. At the Berlin West Africa Congress of 1884–85, British claims to exercise a Monroe Doctrine over the African continent were set aside in favour of the doctrine of effective occupation. Another case in point was the joint intervention of Russia, France and Germany in Tokyo in April 1895 to secure modification of the Japanese peace terms at the end of the Sino-Japanese war. At the same time, in 1880, 1886 and again in 1897, international naval demonstrations and, in the last case, a blockade, were used to enforce the position of the great powers against Greece and Turkey.

An element in the Concert system was the negotiation of agreements to maintain the *status quo* or, failing that, to reach prior agreements to change it. The two agreements of February and December 1887 on the maintenance of the *status quo* in the Mediterranean and the Austro-Russian convention of April 30th, 1897, on the maintenance of the *status quo* in the Balkans are examples of this kind of co-operation. The instruments of the system included also Congresses and councils of ambassadors. Such councils were called into session repeatedly at Constantinople to control and intervene in the process of disintegration of the Ottoman Empire. They drew up or approved numerous schemes for the reform and modernization of the Ottoman administration, none of which, it is true, proved capable of covering the basic problem of reconciling that empire with the rise of Balkan nationalism, but which were continuously successful in restraining the rate of its disintegration and in preventing the outbreak of a major war.

A major factor in this process was the authority and control of foreign policy enjoyed by the various foreign ministries of the major powers and the secrecy in which the processes of their diplomacy were carried out. Bismarck affected to distrust the British government as a partner in negotiations because British governments insisted that treaties had to be disclosed to and ratified by Parliament. But British governments could play their cards in negotiations as close to their chests as any one else. It was only treaties they insisted on publishing. British foreign secretaries and British diplomats could and did hold their own with the diplomats of the Quai d'Orsay, the Wilhelmstrasse, the Ballhausplatz or the Tsarist Foreign Ministry. And the British cabinet system, so long as it was secure in its command of a majority in Parliament, proved no more (and no less) apt to dither when it was undecided than the chancelleries of any continental power. In France the impermanence of individual cabinets was compensated for by the continuity of ministers in the same office in one cabinet after another.

Elements in the maintenance of the balance of power were the armed forces of the great powers and the commanding position across the European exits to the oceans of the world exercised by British bases. British naval superiority was often threatened during the last decades of the nineteenth century, but never challenged. And it proved adequate in times of crisis, as for example, during the Boer War, to prevent any question of European intervention.

While the British fleets confined the major play of international power politics to Europe, the balance inside Europe was maintained by the institution of large conscript armies, with reserves rapidly mobilizable by means of the railway networks laid down in the 1860s–70s. The conscript armies gave the military leaders of the eastern autocracies equal say in the formulation of foreign policy with the foreign ministries, and their tendency to think at times in terms of a quick *coup d'armes*, especially in Tsarist Russia, added a note of peril to the formal manoeuvres of the diplomatists, though it was really only after 1900 that they began to play a major part in the formulation of foreign policy outside Tsarist Russia.

A second element of instability was provided by the growth of a nationalist public opinion in most of the great powers, and a press which could be muzzled and advised, 'inspired' even by government direction, but which could also sit in judgment on governments which it felt had betrayed the national interest. The press unfortunately fed on its fellows in other countries, and came to act as an echo chamber for rumours and an instrument for inflaming opinion against potential enemies. A 'press war' or a war of insults between the newspapers of two countries, each repeating accusations made by its opponents prior to returning them with interest, could, if left unchecked, bring public opinion to the verge of war. The continental autocracies tended to keep their press in line by censorship and subsidy. Much of the French and Italian press was open for sale to all comers. The British press fell into two parts, the quality press which was not unamenable to the quiet appeal to the national interest, and the more popular press which could in some instances be managed by the judicious distribution of honours. It was the heyday of the great editor and the great foreign correspondent. But it is difficult to argue that the role of the press was not that of a peril rather than a support to international peace; though public opinion, even in Tsarist Russia, acted as an effective brake against the more outrageous forms of horse-trading.

An essential element in the international scene too was the ubiquity of royalty and its tendency to be related to the English crown. In the autocracies the person of the Kaiser of Germany, the Austrian Kaiser Franz Josef, or the Tsar was of extreme importance in the dual role of head of state and commander in chief of the armed forces. Bismarck's strength lay in the unbroken faith placed in him by the Kaiser, William I. He did not long survive his master's death. Kaiser William II was a very different figure, irascible, impetuous, often silly, arrogant and hasty in his judgments and obsessed by power. His cousin, Tsar Nicholas II of Russia, was a weak and ambitious man, open to bad counsellors, fervently anti-British, determined to hang on to power, and a bad judge of men, preferring the second-rate and the sycophant to the few first-rate officials in his service. In Austria, the aged Kaiser acted always as a brake on adventurism, his main discoverable emotion being a conviction that he was himself the Austrian state. Even in Britain the personality of the Crown counted for a good deal, especially when the cabinet was hesitant or divided. Nor were any of the monarchs and emperors beyond personal diplomacy from time to time.

Great power co-operation in the political sphere was paralleled very often by similar co-operation in the financial sphere. This was especially the case when one of the smaller powers threatened to default on her debts, or, in the resultant action to prevent such default, one power seemed likely to obtain an advantage the others regarded as excessive or offensive.

Perhaps the first instance of the establishment of an international financial administration was the creation of the Chinese Maritime Customs after 1853. This was a Chinese institution with a British Inspector-General and a partly European staff which collected dues from all European merchants in the Chinese treaty ports and paid the revenues direct to designated Chinese banks. The British were able to gain international acceptance for the Inspector-General remaining a British subject so long as Britain retained the dominant position in European trade with China. A second instance was Anglo-French co-operation in the late 1870s to enforce on Egypt a government willing to give the first priority to the service of Egypt's debts to British and French creditors. And after the British occupation of Egypt in 1882, Germany joined France and Russia at London in August 1884 to insist on the principle of international agreement to any British proposals to re-organize Egypt's finances. Similar action was taken in 1880–81 with the establishment of an international Council of Administration of the Turkish debt with seven members named by foreign banks or groups of bondholders with the presidency of the Council alternating between the French and British representatives. And when in 1898 an international Financial Commission was appointed on German initiative to control the servicing of Greek foreign indebtedness, three governments, Russia, Austria and Italy, were invited to nominate representatives to the British, German and French organized council although little or no share of the indebtedness was held by their nationals. Banking syndicates and international consortia tended to be run on similar lines.

The most far-reaching, though not necessarily the most successful, of these joint international actions involved the Mürzteg programme for reform in Turkish Macedonia. This programme, begun in 1903, called for the division of Macedonia into five police districts, under Austrian, Russian, Italian, French and British command, with the *gendarmerie* directed by an Italian officer. Austrian and Russian civilian officers were also to be attached to the staff of the Turkish Inspector-General for Macedonia. In May 1905, the ambassadors of these powers were joined by the German ambassador in demanding that this *régime* should be tightened up by the appointment of four Financial Delegates to be attached to the Inspector-General, the Delegates to be appointed by France, Germany, Great Britain and Italy, and to co-operate with the Austrian and Russian Civil Agents. When the Turks refused, an international squadron under an Italian admiral occupied the Turkish customs house on the island of Mytilene, and the Turks accepted the new proposals.

## Centrifugal Forces

Beneath this surface appearance of co-operation lay those long-standing rivalries and enmities between the great powers which made its continuance so important. Some of these rivalries dated back to the three crucial events of the mid-century: the defeat of Russia in the Crimean war of 1854–56 by Britain and France; the Italian use of the Franco-Prussian war of 1870–71 to end the French occupation of Rome and to isolate the Pope in the Vatican City; and the German defeat of France in that same war and the annexation of Alsace and Lorraine. Between Austria and Russia there lay Austria's failure to support Russia in the Crimea and the question of who was to be dominant in the Balkans. Between France and Britain there lay since 1882 the British occupation of Egypt and the French determination to end it.

After 1871 Bismarck had used these enmities to keep Europe divided and peaceful. At first he had relied on the hostility to republican institutions common to the three eastern autocracies, united in the League of the Three Emperors, to keep France isolated. He engineered French expansion in Africa and pressure on Egypt as a means of embroiling France with Britain. After 1878 he built up a structure of alliances, first with Austria in 1879, then with Austria and Italy in 1882 (the Triple Alliance), then with Austria and Rumania in 1883. In 1884–85 he taught Britain the need for German support to counter-balance French pressure on the international control of Egypt's finances. The two Mediterranean agreements of 1887 between Britain, Austria and Italy, were made with his encouragement as the best way of tying Britain into his alliance system, which he crowned that same year with the negotiation of the Reinsurance Treaty with Russia. The Reinsurance Treaty, in turn, put him in the position of being able to maintain the balance between Austria and Russia, since in each case the question of whether his alliance with Austria or his guarantee to Russia became operative depended on him alone.

His successors in 1890, not perceiving the decisive position these treaties gave to Germany, allowed the Reinsurance Treaty to lapse. Bismarck had already allowed France and Russia to meet on the common ground of their enmity to Britain over Egypt and the British support for Ottoman Turkey. In 1891 and 1893 political and military conventions were signed between France and Russia (the Dual Alliance) which bound the two nations to support one another if either were involved in Europe. With this guarantee of their position against Germany in Europe, each felt free to pursue their respective colonial policies, France against Britain in Egypt, Russia against Britain in central Asia and in northern China. Bismarck's successors, misunderstanding the position, believed the Franco-Russian alliance to be directed against Britain. Indeed, they congratulated themselves that their central and neutral position would enable them to extract advantages from either side in return for diplomatic and military support in whatever crisis might ensue. But in truth their policy of the 'free hand' left them little chance of success, since they had little or nothing to offer either France or Britain, or Russia or Britain in the event of a conflict between them. In its search for links with France and Britain Germany accepted, in 1893 and 1894, frontier settlements in Africa which cut off the colonies of the Cameroons and German East Africa from further expansion into the African interior. And such concessions as could be wrung from Britain simply irritated successive British governments into thinking Germany to be an incompetent and annoying blackmailer.

The Franco-Russian alliance showed its strength in the Near Eastern crises of 1895, when for once the British did not feel free to send a fleet to the Dardanelles. But the upshot of the crisis was the abandonment by Britain of her own efforts to find an emenable way of withdrawing from Egypt. There followed the direct confrontation of French and British troops at Fashoda on the Upper Nile in 1898 from which France had to retire ignominiously. The crisis was provoked by the arrival of a French expedition, which had set out from West Africa the preceding year, at Fashoda, on the Upper Nile. Its dispatch was inspired by the idea of obtaining a pledge which might be used to secure a British evacuation of Egypt. But by the time it arrived at its destination, the international position had changed. A British army had invaded the Sudan and stood ready to arrest the French expedition. France herself was in the grip of the Dreyfus scandal. And France's Russian ally was unwilling to support her. In a conflict with Britain, France could do nothing without the support of another major naval power and in 1898 the German fleet was, in international terms, a negligible quantity. Nor could Germany offer Britain any real support against Russia in the Far East. There was no German interest there adequate to recompense Germany for the risk of a war on her eastern frontiers with Russia. Nor were Bismarck's successors the least sure of what they wanted out of the mediatory role they hoped to play.

Lacking any decisiveness in Berlin, the Bismarckian alliance system was perceptibly weakened. In the Near Eastern crises of 1895–97, Austria found herself without German diplomatic support and therefore virtually powerless. Thus, it is hardly surprising that in the latter stages of the crisis provoked by the revolt in Crete in 1896 the Concert of Europe functioned fairly well, or that in April 1897 Austria and Russia agreed to respect the *status quo* in the Balkans. And if Austria felt weakened Italy felt still more weakened. In the 1894–96 period Britain was grateful for her support against French pressure towards the upper reaches of the Nile. Britain encouraged Italian activity in Eritrea and in Somalia as a means of countering French attempts to find a route towards the headwaters of the Nile from Djibuti on the Red Sea coast. But in 1896 the Italians met disaster at the hands of an Abyssinian army at Adowa, and Britain's decision to bid for control of the whole Nile valley herself and the subsequent diplomatic defeat of France at Fashoda meant that Britain also no longer had any real need of Italian support. The Italians, isolated and weak, began to make their peace with France. In 1896 Italy recognized the French position in Tunis, and two years later a ten-year-old tariff war between the two countries was ended.

The outcome of the decade of diplomacy following Bismarck's dismissal had been to destroy the balance of power which he had given Europe, and to leave Europe divided into two alliance systems, the Triple Alliance of Germany, Austria and Italy with Rumania as an appendage, and the Dual Alliance of France and Russia. In Bismarck's system Britain was tied to Germany by her need for German support on the question of Egypt's finances, and through the joint interest she shared with Austria in resisting Russian expansion in the Balkans. After Bismarck's fall, both these ties disappeared. In 1895–96, she abandoned her old policy of opposing Russian expansion in the Balkans. And from this followed the decision to remain in Egypt, one which greatly diminished her need for German support in the administration of Egypt's finances. Britain had, in short, reverted to the isolated role which had so defeated Bismarck after 1870, before Disraeli's intervention in the Near Eastern crisis of 1877 and British involvement in Egypt had given him a means of pressuring her. As a result Austria had virtually retired from international politics, and Italy, Germany's other partner in the Triple Alliance, had felt obliged to edge towards France. The Triple Alliance was in disarray, and Germany's international position was isolated and without influence commensurate with her military and industrial strength and her central position in Europe.

## Chapter VI
## THE DIPLOMATIC REVOLUTION. STAGE I: THE ISOLATION OF GERMANY, 1899–1904

INTERNATIONAL politics in the last decade of the nineteenth century were dominated by the colonial rivalries of France and Russia with England, and governed by the Franco-Russian alliance. For its two signatories the Franco-Russian alliance had the effect of strengthening each of them and freeing them from any fear of a European attack. For France it was a protection against Germany and for Russia a shield against Austria. It enabled France gradually to wean Italy away from the Triple Alliance, since it made her almost strong enough to challenge Britain in the Mediterranean. And by freeing Russia of direct anxieties in the Balkans it converted the Tsar's advisers to the view that it would be better to attempt to keep the Ottoman Empire a going concern rather than allow the European complications which might follow its break-down to distract Russian energies from expansion in Korea, Manchuria and North China, and in Persia. The Tsar's advisers toyed with the idea of seizing the Dardanelles by force if the collapse of the Ottoman Empire seemed inevitable. But they preferred to co-operate with the other members of the Concert of Europe to prevent such an event from taking place. The Austro-Russian convention of 1897 led logically to the co-operation of the two powers in attempting to find a solution for the spread of nationalism to Turkish Macedonia, where widespread disturbances broke out in 1902.

As Russia turned to expansion in China and to pressure on Persia, and France to a decade of attempts to secure either an end to the British occupation of Egypt or compensation elsewhere for acquiescence in its continuation, both parties came inevitably into conflict with Britain, the one true imperial power. The British reaction first of all was to strengthen the fleet, which Gladstonian economizing and hostility to expenditure on armaments had gravely weakened. Then, once the naval programme initiated in 1895 had begun to remedy the deficiencies and restore the British navy to the two-power standard (by which Britain's naval strength was to be kept equal to the combined fleets of the next two largest sea-powers), the British government made strenuous efforts to find some kind of a *modus vivendi* with each of its two challengers. Of the two, France was the easier to stand off. And the French bid for the Nile headwaters was forestalled by the

124

occupation of the Sudan and the defeat of the Mahdi, and went off at half-cock in 1898 at Fashoda, when France herself was bitterly divided by the Dreyfus affair, and had made no diplomatic preparations whatever to face a crisis with Britain.

Russia was a more formidable proposition, since the Russian empire was by no means as defenceless in the face of British seapower as France seemed to be. It was true that until the Trans-Siberian railway was completed, Russia's military position in the Far East was at least in part dependent on the sea-route to China. But Britain was also vulnerable to Russian overland pressure in Persia and on the Indian-Afghan border. The Salisbury government attempted therefore to reach an understanding with Russia over the Far East. In 1897 a joint Anglo-Japanese naval demonstration prevented the Russians from occupying a port in Korea. But after the Russian occupation of Port Arthur in the same month, Salisbury proposed an agreement on spheres of preponderance in the Chinese and Ottoman Empires. In April 1899, agreement was in fact reached on railway concessions in China, using the Great Wall as the division between the areas within which each country would seek railway concessions. But the Boxer risings proved too great a temptation for the Russian administration, and the British government was forced to look elsewhere for an ally to restrain Russia.

Britain's need for an ally seemed the more necessary at the end of the nineteenth century in the light of the trouble Britain was facing in the South African war, the challenges issued to the British position in North and Central America, and the beginnings of German large-scale naval construction. British governmental opinion at the end of the century was an odd mixture of arrogant and self-confident isolationism and strained nerves. There can be no doubt that the ignominious military failures in South Africa which marked the second week of December 1899 shook British self-confidence badly. The steady development of American pressure in the Caribbean, when coupled with the major development of the American navy, combined sentimental and strategic reasons for reaching agreement with the United States. Involvement in South Africa meant that Britain could spare only a handful of troops to take part in the relief of the Peking legations during the Boxer risings. And, on June 12th, 1900, the German *Reichstag* voted the second navy law in three years, providing for the construction of a fleet of 38 battleships over the next two decades. The vote was taken amidst a storm of anti-British oratory and press comment following on British interception of the German mailship SS *Bundesrath* on suspicion of carrying contraband to the Boer republic in January 1900.

Since the early 1890s the Kaiser's advisers on foreign affairs had been conducting a foreign policy which, being embarrassed by the difficulty of choice between the various colonial contestants and restrained by the Franco-Russian alliance, had given Germany various small colonial prizes, but had gained her nothing of importance. But more significant was

125

the lack of any real thought among the Kaiser's advisers on what Germany's objectives should be. By 1895 Germany had sacrificed any chance of a large colonial empire in Africa by the agreements of 1890, 1893 and 1894 which delimited the frontiers of her African colonies so as to cut them off from the still-unclaimed interior of the continent. The agreement with Britain of August 30th, 1898, on the reversion of the Portuguese colonies in the event of a break-up of Portugal, briefly promised the chance of more colonial expansion. But the next year Britain concluded a direct agreement with Portugal which secured that small state from the dangers which had seemed to threaten it. Once again the Germans found themselves in the cold. The *condominium* with the United States in Samoa which Germany extracted from the agreement with Britain of November 1899 was hardly adequate compensation.

Germany's aims had to be European, since the balance of power was tilted against her by the Franco-Russian alliance. This implied one or two alternative courses, either the attraction of Britain to the side of the Triple Alliance, or the offer of a German alliance to France and Russia against Britain, in return for a formal French recognition of the loss of Alsace-Lorraine. But the unfortunate truth was that to attract Britain to the side of the Triple Alliance meant Germany had to be willing to fight Britain's battles against Tsarist Russia; while to join France and Russia against Britain was to offer France a strength she did not need, in return for Alsace-Lorraine which she could not abandon.

Thus when British statesmen approached Germany for an alliance as they did in 1897, in 1899 and again in 1901, the negotiations failed essentially for want of any real meeting of minds and interests. On the other hand when Germany made gestures designed to convince France and Russia of their mutual hostility to Britain, as for example in the dispatch of a congratulatory telegram to President Kruger, the Boer leader, after the collapse of the Jameson raid, the effect was to exacerbate British feelings without making any real impression on France or Russia. Nor were British statesmen thoroughly convinced Germany had anything to offer. As Lord Salisbury commented in 1901: 'It would be hardly wise to incur novel and onerous obligations to guard against a danger (that of isolation) in whose existence we have no historical basis for believing.' The point had already been made in 1897 when the British reply to the German telegram to Kruger had been to mobilize a 'flying squadron', a move which made any talk of German intervention in Africa seem stupid.

It was hardly surprising therefore that the Kaiser's advisers should have concluded that only a large fleet could improve the German position, one big enough to make it too risky for Britain to challenge Germany and at the same time make it worthwhile for France or Russia to offer concessions to secure either Germany's neutrality or its support in the event of their finding themselves at war with Britain. Thus successive German Navy Laws in 1897 and 1900 projected a force divided into three fleets, Home, Foreign and Reserve, comprising no fewer than 38 battleships, 14 large cruisers and 38 small cruisers to be built by 1920. Between 1900 and 1905, 12 battleships were laid down, and 14 launched.

The creation of a large German navy, when taken with the pre-eminence of the German army in Europe, could not but be taken in Britain as a direct threat to British security. And the British Admiralty, in fact, began quiet preparations to build up to a three-power standard, and to shift the principal home fleet bases from the English Channel to the North Sea coast where they could guard against Germany. The most dangerous situations, however, were in China and Persia where events were getting out of control. In Persia, the Russians secured in 1900 a virtual monopoly of all Persia's foreign loans for ten years. There was also talk of a Russian-Persian railroad with a terminal on the Gulf, and Russian ships actually appeared in the Persian Gulf itself. In China, the Russians used the excuse of the Boxer rising to send 100,000 troops into Manchuria and to use their position there to secure a monopolistic position in Manchuria, Mongolia and Central Asia, and railway concessions south of the Great Wall as a price for their withdrawal. Still worse by Japanese standards was the appearance of Russian ships at the South Korean port of Masampo, where they hoped again to set up a coaling station. The Tsar's entourage was coming to be increasingly dominated by a group of senior army commanders and concession-hunting adventurers, known as the 'Korean group'.

The British tried direct negotiations with the Russians and a new approach to the Germans, but both were in vain. They therefore took up the offer of an alliance made in the summer of 1901 by the Japanese. The signature of the Anglo-Japanese alliance on January 30th, 1902, struck the British as providing at last the diplomatic stop against Russia they had so long been seeking. Moreover, London felt it gave England control over Japanese policy, as it was believed to be impossible for Japan to defeat Russia in war, but not impossible that Japan's naval hotheads might involve Japan in a war in which Russia might well defeat her. The Germans took the signature of the alliance as indicating that Britain had broken from the policy of splendid isolation. In this they were mistaken. The signature of the Anglo-Japanese alliance marked not the ending of British isolation but its reinforcement; and a very welcome reinforcement it was to those whose nerves, unlike Salisbury's, were becoming a little strained. The British also gained confidence from the way in which Canadians and Australians had come to Britain's aid in South Africa and in the vision they derived of the new nations of the Empire reinvigorating Britain herself and lifting some of the burdens of imperialism from the shoulders of what Chamberlain in 1902 called 'the weary Titan'.

At the same time the British felt impelled to settle matters in the western hemisphere, especially in relation to the outstanding issues connected with the Canadian frontier with Alaska and the question of the concession to build a canal through the isthmus of Panama. In the British approach to the United States three elements were prominent. The first was a pan-

Anglo-Saxonism which persisted in thinking of the United States as still being part of the colonial domains of Britain, and in putting its inhabitants, especially its *élite*, in the same category as the *élites* of the emergent Dominions, Canada, Australia or New Zealand, rather than in the category of aliens and foreigners. This sentiment, imperialist, jingoist and essentially racialist, had been increased by a vicarious pride in America's display of strength and ruthlessness during the Spanish-American war. It made disputes with the United States of a different order entirely from those with European powers. Thus President Cleveland's message to Congress over Venezuela struck British opinion as surprising but not outrageous; whereas the Kaiser's telegram to President Kruger struck that same opinion as outrageous but hardly surprising.

A second element in the British decision to reach a *modus vivendi* with the United States was a cold military calculation of the same type which had impelled the British government to attempt to settle its differences with Russia in the Far East. The Admiralty's view was that Britain could probably defeat the United States in war, but that such a war would bring with it a dangerous weakening of Britain's position *vis-à-vis* Europe. In fact, the Admiralty, as part of its advance preparations against the development of German sea-power, was gradually weakening the West Indies squadrons. The Government's advisers had no desire to suffer from a revival of the Continental League of the War of the American Revolution. Third, the issues involved with the United States were comparatively unimportant for Britain (though not for Canada).

The United States was already flexing its own muscles. In the Presidential election of 1900 the Democratic-Populist candidate, William Jennings Bryan, was defeated by the incumbent, President McKinley, in a straight fight over imperialism. In March 1901, the United States Senate, under the Platt amendment, agreed to an American withdrawal from Cuba on terms which turned Cuba virtually into an American protectorate. In September 1901 President McKinley was assassinated by an anarchist and Theodore Roosevelt (for all his Americanism, the most European of American presidents save only John Kennedy) succeeded him. In December 1901 the Senate ratified a very much revised Hey-Pauncefote Treaty between Britain and the United States. The treaty called for American construction of a canal through the Isthmus of Panama, and at the same time abrogated an agreement of the 1850s which provided that any such canal should be run jointly, and be left unfortified. In November 1903, losing patience over Colombian delaying tactics, Roosevelt assisted a revolt of the isthmian part of Colombia, and set up the Republic of Panama, in what must have been one of the most flagrant examples of imperialist intervention in this century.

Roosevelt's leadership in foreign affairs was well established in what was to become a twentieth-century tradition of diplomacy by rhetoric and well-publicized gesture. But behind this rhetoric was a careful appreciation of the balance of strength and the need for quiet negotiation. And he was to display this combination of *fortiter in modo, suaviter in re* (of violence in rhetoric and caution in action) in his domestic policy, as he was also to demonstrate his dislike of being coerced. This aversion to being coerced was illustrated by his reaction to the miners' strikes of 1902, and in his revival of the anti-trust legislation of the 1890s in prosecuting the Harriman railway empire in the Northern Securities case of 1902. In his more general approach to the problems of the United States he was at this stage so cautious, that an American historian has written of him 'the straddle was built, like functional furniture, into his thinking'. But his indecisiveness reflected that of American opinion generally, unable to decide whether the massive concentration of economic power into trusts or controls was bad in itself, or merely abominable when misused.

Roosevelt was, however, an excellent associate for Britain, even if his behaviour in appointing politicians rather than legal assessors to the commission of arbitration set up in 1903 to settle the disputed Alaskan-Canadian border was regarded as rather sharp practice. Britain needed a strong friend. This need was the more apparent as the Conservative leadership in Britain, the senior military and naval advisers and the inner circle of informed lay opinion began to reflect on the appalling revelations of British military incompetence and of the politician's ignorance of military matters experienced during the South African war. The outcome of the Esher commission set up to investigate and report to the Cabinet on the lessons of the South African war was the foundation in 1904 of the Committee of Imperial Defence, in which civilian political and military personages were united with the responsibility of overseeing Britain's readiness to meet force with force and of maintaining a balance between Britain's foreign policy and her military strength. A parallel search for the improvement of the nation's efficiency underlay in part the great Education Act of December, 1902, which marked not only the nationalization of Britain's primary education system, but the invasion by the state of the field of secondary education.

The failure of the negotiations for an Anglo-German agreement, the Anglo-Japanese alliance and the limited Anglo-American *détente* all increased Britain's freedom of action and marked the defeat of the German hope that Britain would eventually come to Germany cap in hand. But their combined effect on the diplomatic balance was less than that of the virtual defection of Italy from the Triple Alliance, thus weakening the other two signatories, Germany and Austria. The causes of Italy's defection were part diplomatic, part internal, but there can be no doubt that, of the two, internal weakness was the more important. This weakness stemmed from the Italian failure to carry through an economic and social re-organization of Italy to correspond with the political re-organization involved in unification. Its effects were, on the one hand, to give politically conscious Italians an unrealistic conviction of the importance of Italy on the world scene, a conviction which rested essentially on a fiery national egotism that made no real calculation of strength. Its other effect was to

129

accentuate the poverty of the Italian south and Sicily. In the mid-1890s, the two strands came together. Strikes and minor agrarian risings in Sicily caused the dispatch of 50,000 troops, the proclamation of martial law and a state of siege. Crispi, premier and strong man, pushed the interpretation of a treaty with Abyssinia to claim an Italian protectorate and drove the Italian commander in Eritrea, under charges of lack of initiative, into a rash and ill-considered advance into Abyssinia, which ended in the disaster of Adowa. Eight thousand dead and five hundred million lire spent, and nothing to show for it, caused Crispi's downfall, but the social disorders in Italy increased and multiplied. By 1898 order was only being maintained in Italy's main cities by the use of the army and martial law. Eighty people were killed in Milan in May 1898, when the army turned cannon and grape-shot against the crowd. In 1900 the Left and the Left Centre in the Italian parliament walked out rather than vote the government quasi-despotic powers. The same year the King himself was assassinated by an Italian anarchist.

This internal weakness was complemented by a similar weakness in Italy's external position. The defeat of Adowa at the hands of the 'savages' meant that Britain no longer needed Italian support. Without Britain Italy was isolated and the Triple Alliance useless to her as a means of resisting French pressure. After 1894 the French position in the Mediterranean had been much strengthened by the alliance with Russia. And unable to stand off French pressure, Italy felt herself obliged, in 1896 and 1898, to recognize France's position in Tunis, and end the ten-year tariff war with France. In 1900 an agreement was reached on the French interest in Morocco, and Italy's ambitions in Tripoli. In 1902 the Triple Alliance was renewed, but five months later, on November 1st, 1903, a secret note to France reassured the French government that Italy would remain neutral in any war in which France was involved. The Triple Alliance was virtually at an end.

For France the Italian defection from the Triple Alliance represented the accidental achievement of something which ten years earlier would have represented a major gain. But at least since the death in 1894 of the Sultan, Mouley Hassan, who was the last strong ruler in Moroccan history, French eyes had been turned on the idea of rounding off their North and West African possessions by obtaining a protectorate over Morocco. After the humiliation of Fashoda, the acquisition of Morocco as compensation for the loss of Egypt became the main aim of French foreign policy. The experience of Fashoda made it seem essential to the new French foreign minister, Delcassé, to make the diplomatic preparation for a move against Morocco as thorough and meticulous as possible. Thus when the time came for French action, France would have the equivalent of a mandate from the majority of the interested European powers. These powers included Italy, Spain, Germany and Britain. Of the four, Britain was the most important, since the young Sultan leaned heavily on British advisers. There were also considerable British economic interests in Morocco, and local British influence was being placed behind the idea of reforms in Morocco on lines similar to those introduced into Egypt.

Delcassé's method was gradually to tackle the less important of the powers concerned and to reach an understanding with each of them until Britain could be dealt with in isolation. The agreement with Italy was achieved on December 14th, 1900. At the same time the French initiated approaches to Spain and began to encroach from the south-east into the tribal areas of Morocco which no Sultan had ever entirely succeeded in pacifying. In 1901 they secured an agreement with the Sultan on French control of the police on the frontier with Algeria. In 1902 the tribes, incensed by the Sultan's well-meaning attempts to introduce a European system of taxation, rose under a pretender. That November the French got as far as drawing up a draft agreement with Spain, but found themselves stymied by a Spanish refusal to sign unless their own international situation was improved either by their admission to the Franco-Russian alliance or by a British guarantee of Spain's Moroccan claims. So far as Germany was concerned, German spokesmen repeatedly declared that her interests in Morocco were trifling and insignificant. Germany seemed more interested in the Russian-English confrontation in the Far East, and at one time negotiating with Britain for an agreement on a projected railway to Baghdad from Constantinople, and at another approaching Russia with an offer of aid against Britain.

The approach of a seemingly inevitable clash between Britain and France's ally, Russia, in the Far East and in Persia added urgency to the French schemes. The outcome of the Boer war had done nothing to abate the hatred for Britain dominant among the Tsarist administration. Its members were still preoccupied with Manchuria and Korea, and with their desire for a warm-water port on the Persian Gulf. Within the Russian administration the conflict raged between Count Witte, the Minister of Finance, who favoured a policy of peaceful penetration of China by diplomatic and financial methods, and the Ministries of War and the Interior who thought in more militant terms. In 1902, a new element was added to their internal struggle. An aristocratic adventurer, an officer in the Tsarist guards, Bezobrazov by name, had captured the Tsar's mind in 1898 with a scheme for exploiting the timber resources of the Yalu river valley which divided Korea from Manchuria. A concession had been obtained from the Korean court in 1899. However, during that same year, Witte and Lobanov, acting for the Tsar's Foreign Ministry, had succeeded in burying Bezobrazov's Yalu scheme, while substituting a plan calling for the penetration of China proper by economic means.

Since 1900, however, Witte's own position with the Tsar had been growing steadily weaker. The Ministries of War and the Navy despised the commercial nature of his imperialism and hankered after more direct methods. They were able to argue, too, with some effect, that this was a game at which Russia was always grotesquely handicapped in contrast with Britain. The Boxer uprisings had enabled them to convert the Tsar to the more direct policy of force and the occupation of Manchuria. But again Witte and the Foreign Ministry were able to argue that to provoke a conflict with Britain and/or Japan would be unnecessary folly as long as the double-tracking of the Trans-Siberian railway was not completed. The Alexeiev-Tseng agreement of November 1900 on Manchuria, which restored its administration to China in return for extensive concessions to Russia in the matter of railways, represented a victory for their school. But Russia found herself under continuous diplomatic pressure from Japan and Britain to withdraw her troops from Manchuria.

Such pressure defeated its own purposes. The Alexeiev-Tseng treaty was followed by the negotiation of a draft Russo-Chinese agreement reflecting the demands of the Russian military, providing for the retention of the Russian forces in Manchuria indefinitely, and granting a monopoly of concessions in Manchuria to Russia in direct contravention of the doctrine of the 'Open Door' principle propounded in 1900 by the American government. At the same time came the Russian naval attempt to seize a base at Masampo on the tip of the Korean peninsula, a move which led to a direct Japanese naval demonstration and a Russian withdrawal. The European crushing of the Boxer rebellion, and the humiliating terms demanded by the European powers for the indemnity, had made the Chinese authorities anxious to do anything to evade too great a surrender to the 'barbarians'; they therefore took advantage of the Japanese intervention to publish the draft of their second agreement with Russia, and to plead Japanese pressure as a measure of avoiding the necessity of accepting it. There followed direct negotiation between Japan and Russia, in which the Japanese, conscious of their own weakness *vis-à-vis* Russia, proposed a division of Korea into spheres of influence and the application of the 'Open Door' principle to Manchuria, in effect its neutralization between Russia and Japan.

The Japanese intervention and the rejection of the draft Russo-Chinese agreement represented a defeat for Witte and his policy, and was followed by a marked revival of Bezobrazov's influence. A temporary coalition of the three Ministries of Finance, Foreign Affairs and War, of Witte, Lamsdorff and General Kuropatkin, held him in check long enough to secure the signature, in April 1902, of a second Russo-Chinese agreement which provided for the evacuation of Manchuria in three six-month stages. But the succession of shifts and compromises to which Japanese pressure was driving the Russian ministers was beginning to grate on the nerves of the Tsar and his military advisers. Bezobrazov succeeded in capturing the support of Admiral Alexeiev, the principal naval adviser, for a hare-brained scheme to use the existing forestry concessions on the Yalu river as a screen for a Russian military advance into Korea, the Russian troops being disguised as foresters. In November, 1902 Admiral Alexeiev was dispatched to the Far East to develop the scheme. In the meantime, although the first stage of the Russian evacuation of Manchuria was completed on schedule, no attempt was made to put the second into operation, and by April 1903 it was clear that the Russians were in breach of the 1902 Agreement.

The Russian government had not in fact abandoned their ultimate intention to evacuate Manchuria. They now advanced seven further conditions for the continuation of evacuation, conditions which would have established a Russian commercial primacy, if not a virtual commercial protectorate over Manchuria. Much to Russia's surprise, the Chinese rejected these conditions as the result of Japanese and American pressure. This rejection, when coupled with the increase in peasant disorders in Russia, the growing strength of the Russian liberal constitutional movement and the increasing activity of the Social Revolutionary terrorist wing, greatly weakened Witte's position. The Tsar felt increasingly oppressed by the various challenges to the absolute exercise of his powers. At the same time he was being seduced by the vision of a new Tsarist empire in the East, an Asian empire, which would emphasize Russia's rejection of Europe. In these views he was greatly encouraged by the Kaiser, and by those advisers who felt, like Count Plehve, the Minister of the Interior, that Russia needed a 'little victory now to stop the revolutionary tide'. A Japanese proposal in July for direct negotiations was therefore left unanswered for three months.

The turning point came in August 1903, when Admiral Alexeiev was appointed Viceroy in the Far East and Count Witte was dismissed and ordered to hand over control of the railways in the Far East including the Chinese Eastern Railway to Bezobrazov. In September a special committee for Far Eastern affairs was set up and General Kuropatkin joined the 'Koreans'. After all, they argued, the South African war had revealed the military weakness of Britain, and the Japanese were beneath contempt. A regiment of Tsarist cavalry could sweep the Japanese army aside. Even the belated collapse of Bezobrazov's financial schemes and his flight to Switzerland could not disturb their determination to descend upon Korea, consolidate the Russian position in northern China and put an end to Britain's humiliating obstruction of their plans.

The French, appreciating the urgency of the situation, did what they could. In July 1903, therefore, direct conversations were opened with Britain, after a much publicized and highly successful visit by King Edward VII to Paris. Pressure on Britain's exposed nerves in Egypt proved an infallible weapon in securing British concessions in Morocco, although final recognition of Britain's position in Egypt was a difficult pill for the French to swallow. The Anglo-French *Entente* was duly signed on April 8th, 1904.

It was in essence a settlement of differences between the two powers, of a sort Britain had often attempted to get but had hitherto failed to secure for want of an equal will on the side of the French. It was secured at a sacrifice of British interests in Morocco and a recognition of the impending Franco-Spanish agreement, actually concluded in October 1904, on the eventual partition of Morocco. In return Britain secured

French support for her position in Egypt and her schemes for a reform of Egyptian finance and administration. And a number of minor disputes on Madagascar, Siam and the New Hebrides were adjusted. It was the kind of settlement Britain had desired for years as a diplomatic way to end the pressure from both ends of the Franco-Russian alliance. It was Germany who turned the *Entente* into an alliance directed against herself.

By 1900 the Kaiser's advisers were beginning to be a little impatient with the failure of the policy of the free hand to show any results. The concessions wrung from Britain in the colonial sphere represented only a minor gain when compared with Britain's decreasing need of Germany and refusal to get involved in a continental alliance except on terms which would have benefited Britain but involved Germany directly with Russia. And every German attempt to secure a continental league with France against Britain broke down for lack of any real gain to France from such an alliance. The French defeat at Fashoda and the obvious approach of conflict in the Far East turned German attention to Russia, and between 1897 and 1903 there were a number of German attempts to get an agreement with Russia; but again the Germans wanted the one thing the Russians could not concede, either Russian abandonment of her alliance with France or pressure on France finally to abandon her claims on Alsace-Lorraine. In the meantime the Germans were careful not to alienate either of the two partners in the alliance. France was given a free hand in Morocco and Germany was careful not to become involved in the attempts and rivalries of Britain, Russia and Austria over the reform of the Turkish administration of Macedonia. Germany had an added inducement to keep out of the Macedonian problem in that, since 1897, she was beginning to win a favourable position within the Ottoman Empire itself. In October 1898 the Kaiser had toured the Empire from Constantinople to Jerusalem and had proclaimed his affinity for Islam. The following year German interests had secured the initial concessions on the Berlin to Baghdad railway, and German banks were moving into the Ottoman Empire.

The signature of the Anglo-Japanese alliance in 1902 was therefore welcomed in Berlin, as a sign that German policy was on the right track. There would soon be a direct conflict between Russia and Britain, both would turn to Germany for support and Germany would then be able to make her own terms.

## Chapter VII
## THE DIPLOMATIC REVOLUTION. STAGE II: THE WEAKENING OF THE FRANCO-RUSSIAN ALLIANCE, 1904–1906

THE signature of the Anglo-French *Entente* marked, though its signatories would have denied this, the first great step in the realignment of Europe. But in itself it was only a partial step, and by itself it contained a contradiction, since it left France united with two powers, Britain and Russia, who were virtually at war with one another, in Central Asia and the Far East. The victory of the Korean school in Russia made a clash between Japan and Russia seem virtually inevitable. The prospect of such a war was viewed with barely disguised alarm in Britain and the United States, who together shared the universal conviction of Japan's inability to stand up to Russian military force. But their efforts to restrain the Japanese and to secure the conclusion of some kind of agreement were frustrated by the arrogance of the Russians and the Japanese capacity for rapid decision once negotiations had proved fruitless. The Russo-Japanese negotiations collapsed on February 5th, 1904. Five days later the Japanese fleet staged a surprise attack on the Russian squadron at Port Arthur.

The military odds in the Far East were heavily weighted in Japan's favour, once the universal illusion of Japanese military backwardness had been exposed. The Japanese Navy, officered and trained on the British model, was more than a match, both in morale and in the modernity of its vessels, for the Russians. The geographical position of Japan enabled it to control the Russian access to the open seas both from Vladivostok and from Port Arthur. The Russian Far Eastern squadron was easily bottled up in Port Arthur, once its flagship and commander had been blown up by a mine on April 13th. On land the Japanese army disposed of some 270,000 men with the colours and some 200,000 more in reserve. The Russian forces in the Far East numbered a mere 80,000 men, and their reinforcements from European Russia were limited to 30,000 men a month by the carrying capacity of the Trans-Siberian railway, whose double tracking was not yet completed. The first engagement, at Kuraki on the Yalu river, in May 1904 resulted in a major victory for Japan, the Russian armies losing over one-third of their effective strength. A second

Japanese victory at Liaoyang in August isolated Port Arthur and drove the main Russian forces northwards in retreat to Mukden. In July 1904 Port Arthur was surrounded, and a grisly war of siege, bombardment, mine and counter-mine began to which there could only be one ending unless a Russian relief force could break through.

In October 1904 the Russians took the decisive step of dispatching their Baltic fleet on a long and, as it transpired, disastrous voyage to the Far East. Before the Baltic fleet could reach the scene of action, Port Arthur surrendered in January 1905. In February and March the long and desperately fought battle of Mukden, with over 300,000 men engaged on each side, resulted in a further Russian defeat and withdrawal. And on May 27th, 1905, the Russian Fleet, tired, disorganized and demoralized by its long voyage round the world, met the flower of the Japanese Navy under Admiral Togo in the Tsushima Straits, and was obliterated. For the first time since the sixteenth century a European power had been decisively defeated in war by an Asiatic. Not that the Russian commanders in the field accepted this. Russian reserves were still filtering along the Trans-Siberian railway, and Japan's resources both in manpower and money were being steadily exhausted. But at home, in European Russia, the steady succession of defeats had destroyed whatever credit the decaying Tsardom possessed, and revolution was in full swing. The Tsar was driven to accept an American offer of mediation made in June 1905, and Russian and Japanese emissaries met thereafter under American supervision in Portsmouth, New Hampshire.

The task of making the two combatants accept a reasonable settlement was not an easy one. The Japanese, flushed by victory, were inclined to push their claims beyond what Russian opinion could be brought to accept or Britain and America to condone. Neither of the two latter powers wished to exchange the threat of a Japanese hegemony in Asia for that of Russia. Britain's effectiveness was reduced by her anxiety that Russia, defeated in the Far East, would recoil on to India and Persia, where revolution was imminent. Britain's statesmen saw themselves impelled to re-negotiate the alliance with Japan, hitherto conceived of as being confined to the Far East; moreover, it only came into operation if a second non-signatory intervened in a war in which one of the signatories was engaged, so as to cover a Russian attack on India. The spectre of an Anglo-German war had begun to form on the horizon, and the British were concerned with the threat of a Russo-German alignment or of a Russian exploitation of Britain's increasing preoccupation with the balance of naval and military power in Europe. The growth of German naval power was beginning to necessitate a concentration of the Royal Navy in European waters. At the same time the Japanese victory had fired the Japanese with the idea of establishing direct control over Korea where the United States had certain entrenched rights and interests and raised the dangerous possibility of conflict between Japan and America.

The deadlock was broken by two moves. In July 1905, Roosevelt's

Secretary of War, William Howard Taft, visited Japan, which then agreed that its suzerainty over Korea would directly contribute to the maintenance of peace in the Far East. In return, the Japanese declared that they had no designs on the Philippines. The Japanese also gave Britain assurances that they had no plans which would bring them into conflict with the United States and that the Alliance would not operate in the event of a conflict with the United States, arising out of a violation of the latter's rights in Korea. On August 12th, 1905, the Anglo-Japanese Alliance was formally renewed, and Britain was free to turn her attention to Europe.

The task of getting the Japanese to see reason over the exaction of a large indemnity from Russia was more difficult. For a time Britain acted as a go-between, but President Roosevelt's personal impatience with the British ambassador in Washington led to a break between London and Washington. Instead Roosevelt exerted direct financial pressure on Tokyo by withholding action on Japanese requests for a loan, desperately needed to repair the country's financial exhaustion by the war. As a result of this pressure the Japanese demand for an indemnity was withdrawn, and on September 5th, 1905, the Treaty of Portsmouth was signed. Southern Sakhalin and the Liaotung peninsula were added to Japan. Korea was identified as being within the Japanese sphere of influence despite Korean protests. And the Russians undertook to evacuate Manchuria.

The Treaty represented a major success for President Roosevelt. At no real cost to America, and in a position where American opinion would certainly have made the use of American force virtually impossible, he had secured the establishment of a balance of force between Japan and Russia which thwarted the previous attempts of both powers to establish commercial monopoly and political domination in the Far East. What he had not guarded against and what the future was to hold was a combination of the two powers to exploit Manchuria and north eastern Asia, one in which Britain's increasing preoccupation with the balance of power between France and Germany in Europe would force her to acquiesce, and which diplomatic pressure from America alone would be inadequate to prevent.

The effects of the Japanese defeat of Russia were far-reaching throughout the Asiatic world. In China, the Japanese victory confirmed the reformers in their pressure to modernize the empire, and the revolutionaries in their determination to overthrow it and purge China of the alien, Manchu, dynasty. Steps were already under way to modernize the Chinese army, and two of China's future leaders, Yuan Shih-kai and Hsu Shih-ch'ang, were engaged in building up an *élite* force of six divisions called the Peiyang army. Major efforts were undertaken to modernize the Chinese educational system. The classical examination system was abolished in 1905, and command of the 'new learning' became the essential to advancement within the bureaucracy. Increasing numbers of Chinese students were going abroad to Japan, Europe and the United States to study. These students developed various movements aimed at transforming the empire into a constitutional monarchy, the erection of a republic and the destruction of the system of land-ownership from which Chinese conservatism drew so much of its strength. In 1905 Sun Yat-sen, a political *emigré*, organized the Alliance Society (T'ung Men Hui) among the Chinese community in Tokyo. Its fourfold aim was to overthrow the Manchu dynasty, restore a Chinese national state, establish a republic, and equalize the system of land ownership. But the effect of these developments was to lie in the future. Far more serious for the balance of power in Europe was the outcome of the internal revolution in Russia and the development of a direct Franco-German confrontation in the first Moroccan crisis of 1905–06.

One of the pressures under which the Tsardom had laboured before the outbreak of the Russo-Japanese war and which had contributed to its intransigence was a constant and continuous current of dissatisfaction with the Tsarist system as such. Tsardom was viewed as being incompetent, inefficient and above all unenlightened. The factors and events which had brought Russia to a situation where the least false step would entirely destroy the Tsardom's credit in the eyes of the Russian people included: its inability to deal with the causes of peasant unrest, or to suppress effectively the widespread peasant disturbances of 1902–03; the constant threat of Social Revolutionary terrorism culminating in the assassination of the repressive Minister of the Interior, Count Plehve, in July 1904; the overthrow of Count Witte, and the snub to the aspirations of the increasingly wealthy industrialist and commercial classes of St Petersburg, Moscow and South Russia; the senseless nationalist repression of the minority nationalities of Finland, Georgia and the German Baltic, and the fresh outbreaks of anti-Semitism embodied in the Kushynov and Crimea pogroms of 1903; some 45 Jews were killed, which was small-scale by Nazi standards, but frightening in 1900, when a state's total abandonment of a section of its citizenry to the baser passions and hatreds in man's breast was considered alien and revolting.

The assassination of Count Plehve had already led to a marked loss of Tsarist courage. Censorship was relaxed, state workmen's insurance on the German model was introduced and the Zemstvas' jurisdiction was enlarged. But all this was not sufficient. In November 1904, a great congress of Zemstva representatives in St Petersburg demanded the convocation of a representative assembly and the granting of civil liberties. Pressure was building up and with it the nerves of the police and repressive forces in the Tsardom were stretched taut. On January 22nd, 1905, the so-called 'police' trade unions got out of hand. These unions were founded with the secret acquiescence of the Ministry of the Interior as a means of limiting the threat from the trades union movement, and at the same time preventing their employers, the industrialist class, from turning against the state. In January, the St Petersburg union, led by Father Gapon, a priest in police pay, was permitted to demonstrate against the rising price of food brought about by the inflation caused by the war with Japan. Troops sent to keep order panicked and fired on the crowd, wounding or killing over three hundred people. Protest strikes spread in all the big cities. A month later the Tsar's uncle, the Grand Duke Sergei, was assassinated by a Socialist Revolutionary.

In March 1905, under the continuing stress of defeat in the Far East, the Tsar announced his intention of constituting a 'consultative' assembly. Various concessions were made to the minority nationalities, especially to the Jews and Poles. But the Tsar still dragged his feet on reforms and such concessions as he made could only be interpreted by Russian opinion as the occasion for more pressure. In May Prince Miliukov brought together all strands of liberal aristocratic and *bourgeois* opinion into the 'Union of Unions' with a programme calling for universal suffrage and a Russian parliament. In the meantime strikes and insurrections multiplied throughout Russia. In Finland a nation-wide general strike paralysed the Russian administration. A full-scale revolt broke out in Georgia. Peasant disturbances spread throughout the Ukraine, White Russia and the Baltic in a curiously similar pattern, which seemed to indicate Social Revolutionary influence. The crew of the battleship *Potemkin*, stationed at Odessa, mutinied. In August the Tsar recalled Count Witte to office and published a manifesto creating a national assembly with deliberative powers only and elected by a rigidly limited property franchise, but this move failed entirely to stem the upsurge of revolutionary activities. In October a nation-wide general strike and the setting up of the first Soviet, a council of workers which claimed sovereign powers, in St Petersburg paralysed the government and forced the Tsar to yield. The 'October Manifesto', issued over the Tsar's signature on October 30th, appointed Count Witte prime minister, and set up a Russian parliament, the Duma, to be elected on a wide franchise and with real if limited legislative power (very far-reaching powers, it developed, were to be reserved for the Tsar).

The effects of the October Manifesto when coupled with the breakdown in economic activity produced two conflicting groups. On one hand there were the liberals and on the other the more conservative elements drawn from the aristocracy, the gentry and the *bourgeoisie*. Two parties emerged from Miliukov's Union of Unions, the more conservative Octobrists and the Liberal Constitutional Democrats or Cadets who still pressed for a constituent assembly. The Social Democrats and the St Petersburg Soviet, led by Trotsky, rejected the October Manifesto as a whole and fought back with strikes and an insurrection in Moscow. On December 16th, the entire St Petersburg Soviet were arrested. In the meantime Witte floated a new foreign loan of about $400 millions, so that the government would not have to depend upon the Duma for funds. With this loan Count Witte had outlived his usefulness and the Tsar dismissed him in May 1906, shortly before the first meeting of the Duma.

Four days before the Duma met, Nicholas II promulgated the so-called Fundamental Laws, which proclaimed the Tsar to be the supreme autocrat and which permitted him to resume complete control over the armed forces, foreign affairs and the executive branches of the government. An upper house was created, half of whose members were to represent various

139

corporate bodies throughout the country, half to be appointed by the Tsar. The elections to the lower house of the Duma had made the Cadets the largest party, with 179 out of 497 seats, but their hopes that the setting up of the Duma would lead to the adoption by Russia of a genuine parliamentary system of government had been bitterly disappointed. They devoted most of their time to criticizing the government and on July 21st the new prime minister, Peter Stolypin, dissolved the Duma and arrested several of the Cadet leaders. The remainder adjourned to Viburg in Finland, which, though part of the Tsar's empire, was not strictly under Russian jurisdiction. There they issued a manifesto calling on the Russian people to refuse to pay taxes. But their appeal fell largely on deaf ears. The effects of the peasant and working-class risings of 1905–06 had only frightened the bulk of the *bourgeoisie* who again supported the Tsarist state. In the countryside, the more right wing among the gentry had organized their own strong-arm groups, the so-called Black Hundreds, against peasant disturbances. Stolypin was left to clean up the mess.

Meanwhile, the outbreak of the Russo-Japanese war roused the German government once more to hopes of an Anglo-Russian confrontation. It was not long in coming. In October 1904, the Russian Baltic fleet, while passing through the North Sea, mistook a group of English trawlers off the Dogger Bank for Japanese torpedo-boats and fired on them, sinking one of the trawlers. The Germans immediately offered the Russians a draft treaty of alliance against attack by a European power. The Russians accepted this alliance in principle but refused to sign before they had consulted with their French allies. The Germans refused this demand. They also turned down a Russian attempt to secure German aid against Japan which would have brought the Anglo-Japanese alliance into action. This attempt broke down on the German conviction that Britain was only waiting for an opportunity for a pre-emptive strike against the German fleet. Once again the Germans found themselves confronted with what was to be their dilemma until 1907; there was nothing they could secure from the colonial powers of Britain, France and Russia which would compensate them for the fact that in any colonial war Germany would have to fight on her land and maritime frontiers. The Germans returned to the charge in July 1905 when the Kaiser met the Tsar at Björkö in the northern Baltic. But the Tsar had second thoughts on his return to St Petersburg and repudiated the draft agreed on at Björkö, thus bringing to nothing yet another German scheme for a triple alliance against Britain (in which the Germans had even briefly hoped to enlist the United States).

The weakness of Russia revealed by the Russo-Japanese war and the 1905 revolution left France desperately exposed to German pressure. The Third Republic was still a long way from recovering from the strains of the Dreyfus affair. The Dreyfusards, Radical, Radical Socialists, Independent Socialists, supporters of the Republic, had been shaken by the strength of political Catholicism revealed in the French officer corps. But this had been nothing compared with the hostility aroused in republican circles by the activities of the religious orders which had sprung to the support of the Army in its battle with the Republic. The Waldeck-Rousseau government of 1900–02 had taken the initiative in legislation for the protection of the Republic against these religious orders. Waldeck-Rousseau himself had wanted all associations to be registered and supervised by the state. But he had been overruled by the radical anti-clericals and the law of July 1901 had required special legislation by the French parliament to authorize the formation of any religious order in France. And the attempt by the existing orders, the 'congregations' as they were called, to fight the 1902 elections on the basis of reversing this legislation resulted in a last resounding defeat for the French Catholic right. Waldeck-Rousseau resigned in June 1902 before the new Chamber met and was replaced by Emile Combes.

Combes applied the Law of Association against the congregations with extreme rigour. More than this, in 1904, the new Pope, Pius X, chose the occasion of an official visit by President Loubet to Rome to protest to the European powers that such a visit was an offence to Papal dignity. As a result the majority in parliament created by the 1902 elections turned even against the Catholic church as such, and a bill was introduced ending all connection between the French state and the church, including appointments and payments of salaries, and transferring control of all church property to special private corporations at the parish level. But before this law could be enacted, the parallel attempt to purge the Army backfired. General André, Republican Minister of War since 1900, had turned to the Masonic lodges for information on the political sympathies of the officer corps as a means of producing a General Staff loyal to the Republic. In the process he had built up a system of spying and witch-hunting which shocked France when it was exposed. The Combes government fell in January 1905, to be replaced by one under Rouvier, and a new bill of separation had to be steered through the Assembly by the former Socialist, Aristide Briand. The law separating church and state was finally promulgated in December 1905. These developments did nothing to sweeten French political life, and the years 1900–05 saw a great upsurge in the political strength and effectiveness of the extreme French right, the *Action Française* and the *Camelots du Roi*, forerunners of Fascism with their virulent anti-Semitism, their violence in the streets and in Parliament, and their denigration of everything connected with the Republic.

The increasing bitterness of French political life made it the more important for successive Republican governments to avoid charges of incompetence and neglect of the national interest in their conduct of foreign affairs. Delcassé, French Foreign Minister since 1897, thought he had avoided such charges. Although Delcassé himself could never be described as a friend of Germany, a considerable section of the French republican left were, by and large, well disposed towards Germany. Many of their more *bourgeois* elements came from the *milieu* of French commerce and finance (as did Rouvier himself), which infinitely preferred

141

combinations and consortia to conflict. Moreover, these same French financial groups were greatly interested in persuading Germany to let them take a share in financing the Baghdad railway. The French socialist left, united in one party in 1905 under the leadership of Jaurés, were equally anti-nationalist and inclined to trust the country which produced the largest Social Democrat party in the world. The general attitude of both groups to super-patriotism was reflected by the passage in 1904 of a bill reducing the period of service in the army to two years.

Ever since 1900, Delcassé had been preparing the ground for a French take-over in Morocco. After the conclusion of the Anglo-French *Entente* in April 1904, he had returned to his courtship of Spain, and in October of the same year had signed a secret convention which provided for the eventual partition of Morocco between the two countries, Spain taking part of the Mediterranean coast of the Sultanate. In January 1905, everything seemed ready. A French emissary was dispatched to Tangier to put before the Sultan a programme of reforms which would have given France a protectorate over Morocco.

It was at this stage that the German government chose to intervene. What seems to have irked the Kaiser's advisers was a feeling that here was yet another colonial division which would give them no profit. The Germans also were alarmed by the closeness of Franco-Italian relations displayed in President Loubet's visit to Rome and angered by the failure of their first attempt to secure an alliance with Russia during the Dogger Bank crisis of October 1904. On March 31st, 1905, the German Kaiser disembarked from his yacht at Tangier. There he publicly asserted German interest in Morocco, insisted on the full independence of the Sultan of Morocco and demanded an international conference. Rouvier and Delcassé, concerned and touched at their most vulnerable point, attempted to buy off the Germans with assurances of France's willingness 'to dissipate any misunderstandings', but in vain. Delcassé tried to interest the French Cabinet in an alliance with Britain, a possibility which he professed to discover in British proposals for 'full and confidential discussions'. Again he failed and his resignation followed. But Delcassé's fall had no effect on German pressure on France, which continued unabated. French opinion, aroused at last, began to harden. Rouvier was forced to accept the demand for a conference. But the conclusion of the German-Russian treaty at Björkö on July 24th, which the Germans hoped would lead to a continental alliance, and the consequent German *volte-face*, the relaxation of pressure on France, and recognition of French 'special interests in Morocco' came too late. France set herself steadily against the Björkö Treaty and the Tsar was forced to abandon it.

The Conference itself met at Algeciras in January 1906. But by the time it gathered, Europe as a whole had taken a look at the prospect of a European war for the first time since the 1880s and had not liked it. No one wanted war less than the high command of the German Army. The Franco-Russian alliance faced them, in military terms, with a war on two fronts against numerically far superior forces. The only solution they had found to this military problem was the use of Germany's interior lines of communication, the speed of her mobilization and her excellent railway system to concentrate the bulk of their armies against one of their two enemies so as to knock her speedily out of the war. This done, the German armies could be reconcentrated against the surviving enemy. The slowness of Russian mobilization and the sheer distances involved before any major Russian cities could be reached by a German offensive in the East made France the obvious first target. The knock-out blow would have to be delivered in the first six weeks of war; otherwise the Russian armies would be free to strike for East Prussia or Berlin. In the 1890s when this scheme was first elaborated, the German war plan called for a break-through at the southern end of the Franco-German frontier through the Belfort gap. But in 1905–06, in the aftermath of the Moroccan crisis, this plan was changed. The main weight of the German attack was now to be placed in the north and the southern flank would be deliberately weakened to draw the French armies away from the areas of German concentration. The French would be out-flanked and the road to Paris would be wide open. In military terms, the need to outflank the French required that the great fortresses of the north, such as Verdun, would have to be circumvented. Military logic led to the conclusion that to be really effective the German offensive would have to go through Belgium. And the final orders so provided, embodying the Schlieffen plan, named after General von Schlieffen who drafted it.

The other power to be shaken by the Moroccan crisis was Britain. The dismissal of Delcassé disgusted British opinion and alarmed it as to the state of French military strength and morale. The unprovoked nature and the intensity of the German pressure on France was added confirmation of Britain's own incipient anxieties over Germany. The growth of the German navy had continued unabated, and the Admiralty was steadily changing the world-wide dispositions of the British fleet to match this new threat. The design of the German battleships, with their heavy armour and short cruising range, struck naval observers in Britain as peculiarly suspicious. The naval display staged by the Germans in 1904 on Edward VII's state visit to Kiel caused an outbreak of anxious comment in the British press. In 1904 Admiral Fisher became First Sea Lord, and introduced sweeping reforms in naval organization. Even then Britain's military and naval authorities felt the balance of power all over the world swinging slowly against them.

The resignation of the Conservative government in Britain in December 1905 brought into office a Liberal cabinet, which represented an alliance between imperialism and social reform, with the latter element predominating. The general election of January 1906 which followed gave the Liberals a landslide majority and launched them on a programme of political and social reform which was to preoccupy the energies and interests of all but a few imperialists. The bulk of Liberal opinion was suspicious of France, violently hostile to Russia, once the wave of revolution had begun to subside, and friendly towards Germany. However, the handful of imperialists were able to use Britain's power to bolster the ailing position of France and to oppose the growing strength of Germany, without their cabinet colleagues really being aware of what was happening. The personality of the new Foreign Secretary, Sir Edward Grey, with his strong respect for international law and morality and his intense Francophile sentiments, was particularly important. His conservative predecessor, Lord Lansdowne, had been inclined to give the Germans the benefit of any doubt. Grey was not so inclined, and the first action he and his few imperialist colleagues undertook was to authorize the opening of military staff talks with France as a means of reassuring French morale against Germany. The Foreign Office were now preoccupied with the balance of power in western Europe in a way they had not been since the 1850s.

The steady withdrawal of British naval strength from the rest of the world was accompanied by a steady and on the whole welcome increase in American strength under Theodore Roosevelt and a willingness to use it on the world scene in a way utterly without precedent in American history. Roosevelt had begun by the consolidation of the American position in the Caribbean noted in an earlier chapter. Indeed, he became even more determined to resist further European encroachment in that area. The joint Anglo-German naval action in 1903 against Venezuela in the name of debt-collection proved particularly unwelcome. The threat of a similar situation in the Dominican Republic the following year led Roosevelt to formulate what came to be known as the 'Roosevelt corollary' to the Monroe Doctrine. Chronic violations of their international obligations by powers in the western hemisphere, he said, would compel the United States to intervene as the only alternative to a European intervention to enforce recognition of those obligations. Under this doctrine, US Marines were sent into the Dominican Republic in 1904, despite Congressional opposition, and the Customs administration of the Republic was taken over to service its international debts. Similar intervention was to follow in other countries in the Caribbean in the years to come.

On the domestic front, Theodore Roosevelt's strength was greatly enhanced by the 1904 Presidential elections which for the first time made him President in his own right with a majority of over two and a half million votes over his conservative Democratic rival, Judge Alton D. Parker. This victory gave him the confidence to move to embrace with greater enthusiasm the doctrines and policies of the Progressive movement. The anti-trust legislation was more strictly enforced, and the powers of government to regulate and inspect inter-state commerce were greatly increased, especially in the fields of railway rates, food and drugs. Also the first steps were taken to conserve American natural resources against the wasteful, inefficient rapacity of those who were exploiting them.

Roosevelt then was busy building an image of America which would be recognized by Europe as a strong and capable power. His rewards came in the manner in which European opinion accepted his intervention in the

Russo-Japanese war and in the Moroccan crisis of 1905–06. Germany particularly went out of its way to secure his participation in the critical Moroccan situation. And it was American assurances of support against unreasonable demands which played a crucial part in persuading the French government in July 1905 to accept the proposal for an international conference. But the strength of Roosevelt's position in these years lay in his intelligent use of what was still disinterested isolationism. He could intervene in European problems and causes because of the combination of strength and non-involvement in his position, secured by the exclusion of European influence from the New World, the 'Roosevelt Corollary', his own personality and reputation and the size of the American navy, which by 1906 was the second largest in the world. So soon as the United States became drawn into international politics by its own actions or interests, to that extent America became vulnerable and her strength the more easily discounted. And the years 1904–05 in fact mark the highest point American influence in Europe was to attain for a good ten years to come.

A noticeable feature of these years of Roosevelt's Presidency was the growth of the Progressive movement throughout the United States. Progressive machines were built up in state after state, paving the way for the great Progressive election of 1912. It seemed that America was following the example of Europe in building a Socialist party and a trades union movement which was made up of conservative craft unionists and a radical anarcho-syndicalist movement. As usual in American politics though, the similarities with European developments had significant differences. As noted in Chapter II above, the craft unions in the United States were conditioned by the flood of immigrants to restrict entry and unionize only those industries where casual labour was the exception rather than the rule. The masses in the large-scale industries, especially the miners, were left on their own. It is significant in this context that the one big union which represented the miners of the west, the Western Federation of Miners, formed in 1893, broke away from the American Federation of Labour in 1897 and changed its name in 1902 to the American Labour Union. In 1905 the American Labour Union formed the basis of the main American contribution to the anarcho-syndicalist movement, the International Workers of the World (the IWW), nicknamed the 'Wobblies'.

Despite its name, the only international element in the IWW was the ethnic origin of its members. Its only international action was to spread across the 49th Parallel into Canada. Besides the WFM, three other groups were represented in its formation; the American Socialist Labour party of Daniel de Leon (1852–1914), which from its formation in the 1890s opposed the AFL, with its unionist wing, the Trade and Labour Alliance; Anarcho-Syndicalists, mostly recent immigrants from Russia, followers of Bakunin and Peter Kropotkin, their aim the destruction of all government and its replacement by the communal organizations of workers which they expected to spring up spontaneously in its place; and, finally, emotional Socialists attracted by the personality of the main Socialist Presidential candidate, Eugene Debs. The main force in the IWW, however, was 'Big Bill' Haywood of the Western Federation of Miners. His version of syndicalism concentrated on industrial action as the most important, though not the only, weapon to achieve labour's aims and he preached the formation of 'one big union', centrally-directed and disciplined, to be the main planning agency for the new proletarian society. But the main characteristic which distinguished the IWW from the other branches of the labour movement (from which both the WFM and de Leon broke away in 1907–08) were its tactics which involved the mobilization and concentration of union members wherever there was trouble. Its main influence lay among its migrant miners, loggers and the seamen of the middle and far west. It was to reach its greatest strength in 1915.

The course of the diplomatic revolution of 1899–1906 had resulted in a complete change in the alignments of the Great Powers, an alignment which was rapidly approaching bi-polarity. The old division at the centre between the Austro-German alliance and France and Russia was confirmed by the course of the Moroccan crisis and the failure of the German attempts to seduce Russia and persuade France into a continental union. Instead Russia, defeated in the Far East, was on the road to settling the outstanding issues between herself and Britain and her Japanese ally. The three oceanic powers, Britain, Japan and the United States, had achieved a temporary understanding with one another. Britain had achieved a stronger understanding, one which continued to approach the reality, if it avoided the appearance, of an alliance with France. And France in her turn had succeeded virtually in detaching their ally, Italy, from the Central Powers and, by the making of the Mediterranean an Anglo-French lake, still further confined German ambitions to the European mainland. The German action at Tangier had in fact ended the period of European pressure on the external world and marked the first real shot in a European civil war which in its turn was to make inevitable the decline of European power and the revival of the rest of the world.

The division of Europe into two major power groupings was to be accompanied by a further division, the gradual separation of the Scandinavian powers into what was eventually to become a neutralist, social democratic, anti-colonialist bloc north of the Baltic. The process was to be a long and devious one, which, for most of the decade before 1914, was in fact to bring Denmark and Sweden closer to Germany than to neutralism. It was initiated, however, by Norway, with the break of the Norway-Sweden Union in 1905. The two countries had been united under one crown, that of Sweden, in 1815, Norway retaining its own Parliament, the Storting, and armed forces, but with control of foreign policy, as a monarchical prerogative, being exercised by the Swedish foreign office. During the mid-nineteenth century, successive Swedish monarchs had considered creating a Scandinavian League of Neutrals, even of a union of Denmark with Norway-Sweden. Sweden had intervened in the first Schleswig-Holstein crisis in 1848 and had in fact formed in 1853 a League of Neutrals with Denmark during the preliminaries to the Crimean War. By a treaty of November 1855 France and Britain had guaranteed Norway-Sweden against Russian attack, and for good measure had included in the treaty which ended the Crimean War a clause demilitarizing the Aaland Islands. Thereafter Sweden drifted away from this kind of pan-Scandinavianism, and indeed it was by repudiating rash promises made by Charles XV to Denmark in 1863 that the Swedish Council did away with direct monarchical rule and established itself as a proper Swedish cabinet. The unfortunate Danes were left alone to face Prussia and Austria in the war of 1864 over Schleswig-Holstein.

The essence of Scandinavianism was an attempt to take Scandinavia and the Baltic out of the clash of the Great Powers. Before German unification in 1871, the two Great Powers most concerned with the Baltic were Britain and Russia, and Scandinavianism represented a revulsion against Russian pressure. After the advent of Germany, the Swedish government began to move towards Germany and abandon the old connections with Britain. In part their actions reflected the internal struggle for power through which Norway and Sweden were now passing. In Norway this struggle lay essentially between the large land-owners and the peasants, fishermen and *petit-bourgeois* of the towns who were united in the Liberal party. It was complicated by the Swedish issue, with the land-owners leaning more and more towards Sweden, their opponents experiencing the revival of a specifically Norwegian nationalism, expressed in the growth of a major Norse school of literature. This revival of Norwegian cultural nationalism included the playwrights Ibsen and Björnson, and the composer Grieg, and expressed itself in the revival of the local dialect, the *landsmaal*, which in 1884 was made equal with the Swedish language in the schools and in official usage. In 1884 the Swedish king was forced to accept the Liberals as the dominant party in Norway and appoint a Liberal cabinet which would be responsible to the Norwegian *Storting*.

Sweden had had her constitutional revolution in the 1860s when the Council had taken over the management of foreign affairs from Charles XV, and the old *Riksdag*, divided into four Estates, had been replaced by a bicameral legislature. But it had been a conservative revolution, carried through under conservative auspices, and the electorate for the new lower house was severely limited by the imposition of a property qualification. The revolution had serious consequences for the union with Norway. While the conduct of foreign affairs was the prerogative of the Crown, foreign policy could be represented as the affair of both countries. But now the conduct of foreign affairs was clearly in the hands of a Swedish ministry and cabinet. Conflict between the two countries inevitably developed, with the Norwegians, convinced that their widespread maritime and commercial interests were being neglected by the aristocrats of the Swedish foreign service, pressing for the introduction of a separate Norwegian consular service. Matters came to a crisis in 1895, and only the setting up of a Union Committee could postpone the inevitable clash.

An element in Norway's withdrawal was fear of Swedish military force. Between 1896–1904, the Norwegian cabinet bought four new ironclads and modern artillery, strengthened the voluntary rifle clubs which had come to form a substantial 'Black' army, and built fortifications to defend Oslo from Swedish overland attack. In 1904, the negotiations on the Union Committee broke down. Norway announced the formation of its own consular service which was vetoed by the Swedish King. The Norwegian cabinet promptly resigned as a body, and the *Storting* passed two resolutions dissolving the union and declaring Norway to be an independent monarchy. The Swedish cabinet decided not to use force and approved Norwegian independence on September 23rd, 1905. The throne of Norway was offered to the Danish prince Charles, who accepted it, taking the title of Haakon VII after a plebiscite had confirmed his popular support.

The Norwegian action introduced a new element into an already complicated situation. The rise of German naval power had already upset the whole Anglo-Russian balance in the Baltic, and German policy joined that of Russia in wishing to exclude British influence permanently from the Baltic. As negotiations opened for a new international guarantee for Sweden and Norway, Sweden began to suspect that British influence had been behind Norway in the dissolution of the union. For a time it seemed that Swedish suspicions played into German and Russian hands. A guarantee treaty for Norway was in fact signed, but the Swedes refused to have anything to do with it, maintaining that it was directed against them. For a time, the Germans hoped for a Baltic *entente* with Russia and Sweden which would exclude Britain completely from the Baltic, but a Russian attempt to write into the draft treaty a clause allowing the remilitarization of the Aaland Isles belatedly awoke Swedish suspicion of Russia. The Germans proposed separate North Sea and Baltic conventions guaranteeing the *status quo*, which were eventually signed in April 1908. That same year the pressure of the Swedish radical forces finally broke through and universal suffrage was introduced in Sweden. Even then the conservatives scored a victory by writing into the new electoral laws a provision for proportional representation. On the outbreak of war in 1914, Sweden reverted to Scandinavianism, aided by a British failure to stage the naval break-in to the Baltic which their regular summer naval manoeuvres in the Baltic had previously foreshadowed, and a German decision that their purposes were best served by Danish neutrality and by using Denmark to bar the Baltic entrances. The Norwegian revolution thus foreshadowed a great decline in British influence in the Baltic, which was only to be restored after Germany's defeat.

## Chapter VIII
## EUROPE TURNS ON ITSELF: THE WEAKENING
## OF THE DUAL ALLIANCE, 1906–1909

THE beginning of 1906 ushered in a period of four years during which European affairs increasingly dominated world politics. Over these years the position of the Central Powers, Germany and Austria-Hungary, deteriorated markedly both in domestic and foreign affairs, and both absolutely and relatively in relation to their opponents, Britain, France and Tsarist Russia. No sooner had the Algeciras Conference on Morocco met on January 16th, 1906, when it quickly became evident that the German bid to turn the Moroccan issue to their favour had boomeranged. The German delegation found itself faced with a permanent line-up of Britain, France, Russia, Italy and the United States, and supported only by its Austrian ally. Some German leaders, notably Baron von Holstein of the foreign ministry, wanted to use force to obtain their ends; but the Kaiser and the Chancellor, Bülow, refused to countenance war, and von Holstein resigned in disgust. The final act of the Conference, signed on April 7th, 1906, gave France and Spain substantial control of Moroccan reforms, but still left intervention by the Great Powers a possibility.

The internal situation in Morocco deteriorated under the French pressure, and, after French occupation of the whole Atlantic coast in August 1907, civil war broke out between the Sultan and his brother Moulay Hafid which only ended in December 1908 when, on German initiative, Hafid was recognized as Sultan. This German intervention proved no real advantage. In 1909 Germany was forced to sign an agreement recognizing French primacy, and in 1910 Moulay Hafid was forced to ask for French assistance against another claimant to the throne.

The German position was further weakened by the progress of Anglo-French and Anglo-Belgian staff talks. Even though the British emphasized the absence of any treaty commitment, and the bulk of the British cabinet remained uninformed, the knowledge of British support made the government of Clemenceau in France, who succeeded Rouvier as premier in 1906, strong enough to ride out all the German pressure, despite the growth of extremism both on left and right after 1906. The unification of the various factions of the French socialist movement in 1905 under the leadership of Jaurés had been followed by a considerable increase in the parliamentary strength of the Socialists in the 1906 elections in France. This growth in socialist representation had aroused the advocates of direct action, who feared that socialism was about to become a parliamentary movement which would collaborate with those they should be preparing to overthrow. The inclusion of Briand and René Viviani, both former independent Socialists, in the Clemenceau cabinet added fuel to their fears. A wave of strikes led by the militants of the Trades Union movement, the *Confederation General du Travail*, followed through the years 1906–10, splitting the Socialist party again at the Limoges conference of 1906 on whether to attempt to reconcile the party with the CGT. Nevertheless Clemenceau was able to weather these strikes without difficulty.

France's ally Russia was similarly experiencing a revival of governmental strength and stability. Peter Stolypin, prime minister since June 1906, dealt easily with the first Duma in July. In August he instituted severe measures to suppress the continuing peasant disorders. The Tsarist Army commanders were virtually given a free hand in suppressing the nationalist risings in the Baltic, in the Caucasus and in Siberia, and new anti-Jewish pogroms were now instituted.

In October–November 1906 Stolypin promulgated a series of decrees designed to strengthen peasant ownership of land and weaken the old system of communal ownership. The pattern of consolidating individual land holdings in the villages was begun under the supervision of Land Commissions. In October 1906, Stolypin instituted conversations designed to form a new parliamentary ministry. But the second Duma elected in February 1907 was even more extreme than the first; the Social Democrats and Socialist Revolutionaries, having ended their boycott of the elections, won a total of 99 seats, the Octobrists and the extreme right 95 seats, and the Cadets 92 seats.

In June 1907 Stolypin demanded that the parliamentary immunity of the Social Democrats be cancelled on the grounds that they were implicated in a plot against the Tsar's life. He then dissolved the second Duma. Fresh elections were held on a much narrower electoral law which weighted the representation of the land-owners and wealthy industrialists much more heavily than anyone else. To elect a deputy it took only 230 landowners, compared to 1,000 wealthy business men, 15,000 *petit bourgeois* townsfolk, 60,000 peasants or 125,000 workers. The new Duma was heavily dominated by the right with 127 Rightists, 154 Octobrists and 54 Cadets. Only 33 deputies representing the left were elected. In foreign relations the new parliament was to prove violently anti-German and excessively, indeed embarrassingly, nationalistic.

Thus Germany found herself confronted with much stronger governments in both France and Russia. And this happened after it had already proved impossible for Germany to divide them even at the moment of Russia's greatest weakness.

Russia's position in the Far East was greatly strengthened by the Russo-

Japanese agreement of 1907, which marked out spheres of influence in Korea and Manchuria. More important, however, was the conclusion of the Russian *Entente* with Britain in August 1907. For the British government this was definitely an anti-German move. Stolypin's Russia, with the Dumas suppressed, had little popularity in Britain in contrast to Germany and Austria-Hungary, where parliamentary forces seemed to be in the ascendancy. But the increase in German armed strength, and, in the eyes of the British, the irresponsible manner in which the Germans were prepared to use it, made it desirable to end the obvious causes of friction between Russia and Britain. Actually the *Entente* itself was entirely concerned with Central Asia. Persia was divided into British, Russian and neutral zones of influence. Russia recognized Britain's primacy in the Gulf and in Afghanistan and Britain made encouraging noises about revising the Dardanelles agreements in Russia's favour.

For Russia, paradoxically, the main aim of the *Entente* was to regain a certain freedom of action in the Baltic and in the Balkans and Izvolski, Russian Foreign Minister since May 1906, went to considerable pains to reassure the Germans that it was not directed against them. Despite these reassurances the *Entente*, by ending British and Russian anxieties in Central Asia, could only strengthen their positions against Germany in any future crisis.

This was the more unfortunate in that, in Britain, opinion in the armed services was now thoroughly convinced of German enmity. In 1906, the British Admiralty initiated a fresh wave of naval competition with the launching of the Dreadnought, a new type of battleship which carried ten heavy guns in its main battery, in contrast to the four guns found on all previous battleships. At one stroke the value of all existing battle-fleets was reduced to nil, and a new and highly expensive form of competition, both in quality and in quantity, instituted. So rapid was the technological revolution in both the size of capital ships and in the calibre of the guns they carried, that by 1914, the Dreadnought itself was unable to take its place in the first line of Britain's battle fleet. The 1905–06 naval construction programme contained one Dreadnought and four battle-cruisers of an equally revolutionary type. Thereafter the official programme envisaged the construction of four of these capital ships annually.

The advent of the Liberal government brought into power a cabinet, part of which greatly objected to diverting monies from social reform to arms production. With the Admiralty's reluctant approval they dropped one ship from the 1906–07 programme and planned to drop two from the programme of 1907–08. This decrease in ship construction accompanied proposals that the Second Hague Peace Conference, due to meet in June 1907, should consider disarmament on land and at sea. The British gesture went unanswered in Germany. The German Chancellor denounced disarmament proposals as impractical in a speech in April 1907. The Conference itself proved largely abortive, save for reaching a number of minor agreements on the laws and conduct of war. None had been completely ratified by 1914 and most were ignored by the belligerents during the 1914–18 war.

In October 1907, therefore, the British restored one of the two Dreadnoughts dropped from the 1907 programme. In November, the Third German Navy Law was published. It provided for the construction of four capital ships annually in place of a previous rate of three and projected a fleet of 58 capital ships for 1917–18. There was considerable alarm in Britain. But the Admiralty kept its nerve. Indeed it only secured the cabinet's agreement to a programme of one Dreadnought and one battle-cruiser for 1908–09 after a major cabinet crisis.

None of these developments could be at all welcome to the German government, whose position in internal affairs was weakening steadily with the growth of the parliamentary forces in the *Reichstag*. In the 1898 elections the balance of forces in the *Reichstag* had been roughly equal, 138 Prussian Conservative and National Liberal deputies facing 102 in the Centre Party and 139 on the left, including 56 Social Democrats. But the 1903 elections had seen the forces of the left rise to 152 deputies, with 81 Social Democrats, while right and centre remained virtually static, save only that the balance within the Centre Party was slipping towards the left. This became evident in December 1906 when the Centre joined the left to defeat a government bill calling for the re-organization of the Colonial Office and the provision of funds to help the suppression of the Hereros rising in South-West Africa. It was true that the subsequent dissolution of the *Reichstag* produced, after fresh elections in 1907, a reversal of the 1903 results with 159 deputies on the right to 121 (with only 43 Social Democrats) on the left. But the victory was of little advantage to the *régime* when compared with the growth of parliamentary sentiments among the National Liberals.

The real state of affairs was revealed in 1908 when the Kaiser published an interview with the British newspaper, *The Daily Telegraph*, in which he boasted of the part he had played during the Boer War in preventing the formation of an anti-British coalition. The *Reichstag* exploded in a storm of criticism in which only the Prussian conservatives remained silent. The Kaiser was forced to issue what amounted to a public apology, in the form of an announcement that he would respect his constitutional obligations. Chancellor Bülow was able to govern for a time as the virtual parliamentary head of a democratic coalition, but the episode, while discrediting the Kaiser, did nothing really to strengthen the Chancellor's position or to introduce a genuine parliamentary coalition. Bülow fell over a minor defeat in the *Reichstag* in 1909, and his replacement, Bethmann-Hollweg, was, as usual, the Kaiser's nominee. In the long run the episode shook the credit of all three institutions, Kaiser, Chancellor and *Reichstag*, and only served to increase the tensions between German authoritarians and parliamentarians.

The steady deterioration in the position of the Austro-Hungarian government was more marked in foreign than in domestic affairs. The years 1903–07 were, it was true, years of considerable crisis in Austria-Hungary's internal politics, involving not only further strains in Czech-German relations in Bohemia, but also a major crisis in relations with Hungary, a crisis moreover which involved the resurrection of the South Slav movement.

In 1897, the Austrian Prime Minister, Count Casimir Badeni, had attempted to solve the Czech-German struggle in Bohemia and Moravia by making knowledge of both languages obligatory for all members of the government service. But the Germans throughout Austria had raised such disorder that the Emperor dismissed Badeni and rescinded the offending legislation. This action only embittered the Czechs and made a settlement of the language issue virtually impossible. Dr Koerber, appointed Premier in 1900, attempted to solve the nationalities problem by a progressive economic policy. But the elections to the *Reichsrath* in 1901 greatly strengthened the Pan-German and Young Czech parties, and national rivalries broke out equally strongly between Poles and Ruthenians in Galicia, and the Italians of the southern Tyrol and the German majority in the whole province. Riots in Innsbruck over the proposal to establish a separate Italian-speaking law faculty at the university caused Koerber to resign. His successor, Baron von Gautsch, was successful, however, in securing a compromise between Czechs and Germans in Moravia in 1905, which divided the province between the two nationalities. But an attempt to negotiate a similar compromise in Bohemia broke down again in riots and obstruction at the provincial Diet.

Austria's relations with Hungary were governed by the rise of separatist sentiment in the so-called Independence party led by the son of Kossuth, the rebel leader of 1848 who had died in 1894. The decennial negotiations of the quotas for common expenses, and of the customs and commercial treaties were already exacerbating relations between Vienna and Budapest, when, in 1902, the Kossuthists introduced a bill increasing the Hungarian contingent in the common army and chose at that time to stage demands for the total Magyarization of the language, officers and flag of the Hungarian regiments. They were backed by the strongly Catholic and aristocratic National Party. Their demands were flatly rejected by the Emperor himself, and in November 1903, Stephan Tisza, leader of the Liberal Party, was appointed by Franz Joseph to drive a compromise bill through the Hungarian parliament. In 1905 Tisza finally dissolved parliament and called for elections. Stimulated by the example of Norway's secession from the union with Sweden, Kossuth's party, linked with a large anti-Tisza coalition, swept to victory with 163 seats against 152 for Tisza's Liberals. On Tisza's resignation, the Emperor adjourned parliament and appointed his own premier. In addition he threatened the Kossuthist coalition with the introduction of universal suffrage, a device which would have destroyed the strength of the Kossuthites and greatly increased that of the non-Magyar minorities, Croats, Rumanians and Slovaks, whose combined strengths in the Chamber had already risen from 8 to 24 in the 1905

153

elections. The Slovak nationalists had already thrown up Dr Milan Hodza, a future premier of Czechoslovakia, and the extremist Catholic nationalist, dictator of the German puppet state of Slovakia from 1939–44, Father Hlinka. Six Slovak deputies and eight Rumanian nationalists, demanding autonomy for Transylvania, were among the twenty-four victors of 1905. In Croatia, in the meanwhile, the South Slav movement had been revived and strengthened by the formation of the Peasant's party of Stepan Radić. In 1903 peasant risings had expressed their discontent with their Magyar overlords, and in the following year deputations from Croatia joined deputies from the Austrian provinces of Istria and Dalmatia to complain to the Emperor, but were barred by the intervention of Budapest. In 1905, at the Congress of Fiume, the advocates of a union of Dalmatia and Istria with Croatia in a third, south Slav, member of the Dual Monarchy, on a level of equality with Austria and Hungary, offered their aid to the Kossuthite coalition, if the latter would accept the separation of Croatia from Hungary and its union with Dalmatia.

Nothing was less welcome in Kossuthite circles. In February 1906, the lesson was brought home when the reassembled parliament was closed with the aid of a battalion of Rumanian soldiers from the Bukovina. The coalition yielded at once. Internally the 1906 elections strengthened their position, giving Kossuth's Independence party alone an absolute majority, although the election of twenty-six minority deputies, sixteen from the Rumanian nationalist party, contained its own warning. The Hungarian quota of common expenses was raised by 4·9% to 36·4%, and the extremists' demands for the Magyarization of the Army were quietly buried. So too were the proposals for universal suffrage.

The mere discussion of universal suffrage in Hungary, however, left the way open for its introduction into the Austrian provinces of the Dual Monarchy. In court circles many saw in such revolutionary action a means of breaking the strength of the middle class nationalists and of advancing the Christian Socials and the Social Democrats, mass parties both committed in theory to a multi-national approach, and both devoted to the survival of the Habsburg State. The first elections to the *Reichsrath* on a basis of universal male suffrage came in May 1907, and resulted in the reduction of the middle-class nationalist parties to approximate parity with the Christian Socials and the Social Democrats.

The electoral reform of 1907 did not however produce the expected result in Bohemia. The cabinet of Baron von Beck, appointed by the Emperor to introduce universal suffrage in Austria, had a considerable success in other fields. It succeeded in carrying through new compromise negotiations with Budapest, in carrying the budget through the *Reichsrath*, in securing an increase in the Austrian armed forces and in legislating for the nationalization of the Austrian railways. But Beck himself was accused by the heir-apparent, the Archduke Franz Ferdinand, and his circle of having betrayed the interests of the monarchy in his negotiations with Budapest; and his attempt to negotiate a Moravian-style compromise in

Bohemia broke down entirely. In November 1908, Beck resigned. From 1908 the internal cohesion of the Empire entered a further stage of disintegration.

Beck's resignation, which came at the height of the Bosnian crisis of 1908–09, made apparent to all the deterioration in Austria's international position since 1900. This deterioration had begun with the military nationalist *coup d'état* of June 1903 in Serbia, in which King Alexander and his Queen had been brutally murdered by a group of young officers, and Peter, heir of the rival Karageorgovich dynasty, had been elected to the Serbian throne in his place. In December 1904, the extreme nationalist pan-Slav Radical party had won command of the Serbian Assembly and its leader, Nicholas Pasic, became Premier. Austro-Serb relations deteriorated. Serbia awarded a large arms contract to French rather than Austrian interests, and turned to preparing for a customs union with Bulgaria. Austria secured its abandonment; but her attempt to use a tariff boycott to re-establish her position of commercial and political dominance in Serbia—the so-called 'pig war' (Serbia's exports to Austria consisted largely of pig-bristles, leather and pork products)—proved a failure.

The issue of Serbian independence seemed particularly dangerous to Vienna because of the link between Belgrade and the Serbo-Croat elements in the southern Austrian provinces, in Croatia and in southern Hungary, and the 'South Slav' movement which sought to bring them together. Both the Habsburg Monarchy's anxiety over Serbia and the temptation to assert strong leadership in foreign policy combined to produce a course of action which was to end in disaster. The two main figures in this *débâcle* were Conrad von Hötzendorff, the Chief of the Austrian General Staff since 1906, a violent anti-Slav, and Baron Aehrenthal, the new Foreign Minister, who succeeded Count Goluchowski the same year. Aehrenthal began, it is true, by ending the 'pig war' with Serbia. Yet he was very soon driven to the conclusion that nothing could be done with Serbia, and he again tried to modify Serbian policy by diplomatic means. Although some anxiety had been caused in Vienna in 1902 by the conclusion of a secret Russo-Bulgarian military agreement, Austro-Russian co-operation in the Balkans, especially over the Macedonian issue, had gone very well. In the summer of 1907 therefore Aehrenthal played with the idea of reducing the six-power control of Macedonia virtually to a two-power Austro-Russian control by excluding Britain. In October 1907 Aehrenthal and Izvolski, the Russian Foreign Minister, discussed a Russian proposal to revise the Straits convention in Russia's favour and Aehrenthal obtained Izvolski's support for a projected railway through the Sanjak of Novibazar, which lay between Serbia and her fellow Slav monarchy, Montenegro, to Salonika. In February 1908 the two countries combined to block a British proposal for a six-power note to the Ottoman sultan demanding judicial reform in Macedonia. The Concert of Europe was for the moment at an end.

Aehrenthal unveiled his Novibazar railway project in January 1908. It was at once denounced by the Serbs as designed to split Serbia from its fellow Slavonic kingdom of Montenegro. Serbian protests were taken up in Russia, where the third Duma was strongly pan-Slav in sentiment and the Russian press even more so. Izvolski was forced to protest publicly, although he was at pains to control the protests of the Russian press as soon as he could. But the reception of the railway project in Europe was ominous for the future. In France and Britain it was seen, quite unjustly, as inspired by Berlin and even welcomed, as a revival of Austro-Russian rivalry in the Balkans. In Serbia it reinforced the enemies of the Dual Monarchy, already doing their utmost to spread subversion in the twin provinces of Bosnia-Herzegovina, Turkish in their nominal sovereignty but under Austrian rule since 1878. Together with the rejection of the British proposal in Macedonia it marked the end of European co-operation in the Balkans for the moment and cleared the way for the major crisis over Bosnia-Herzegovina which was to begin later in the year. It played a major part in the Russian move towards Britain after the Anglo-Russian *Entente* of the previous year, and the crucial meeting of King Edward VII and the Tsar at Reval in June 1908 at which Russia agreed to new British proposals for the extensive reform of the Macedonian administration and for the strengthening of their mutual position in Persia.

Russian pressure had already produced an explosion in Persia, as the news of the Reval meeting was to do in Ottoman Turkey. The Persian revolution, which broke out in 1906, was essentially Shi'ite in character, the Messianic nature of this branch of Islam making a direct assault in the name of the Sharia on the Shah's exercise of his despotism, the vehicle for expressing Persian dissatisfaction with a Shah whose insensate profligacy was misusing the national treasury and delivering Persia over to Russian control. The revolutionary movement organized itself in a number of semi-secret associations, the so-called *anjumen*, which united merchants and professional men, with ideals culled from the western liberal tradition, with the *ulemas*, religious intellectuals. In 1905–06 their agitation broke out into the open, and the attempt of the Shah's advisers to suppress them led many of their number to seek religious sanctuary in the shrines of Quum, and, more sensationally, in the British Embassy.

The Shah found himself forced to grant a constitution, and to summon a national assembly, the *Majlis*, in December 1906. Shortly thereafter he died, to be succeeded by his despotically inclined brother, Mohammed Ali Shah, and a long struggle ensued between the *anjumen*, which had now shed their secret character, and the new Shah, in which the latter twice, in December 1907 and again in June 1908, suspended the constitution. The subsequent disturbances revealed the *anjumen* to be well established in the country. The *anjumen* in Tabriz led a revolt against the Shah in July 1908, and were able to resist efforts to suppress it until Russian troops intervened in April 1909 to raise the siege. In the meantime the association in Isfahan, which had gone underground in 1908, had opened negotiations with the powerful Bakhtiari, the greatest of the Persian mountain nomad tribes. In January 1909, tribal forces drove the Shah's troops from Isfahan, and in

July entered Teheran, and the Shah took refuge in the Russian legation. The nationalists deposed him and set up a Regency for his twelve-year-old son.

The events of 1906–09 had shown the strength of the *anjumen* against the Shah. They had not unfortunately revealed any constructive ability on the part of their leaders, nor any agreement, or even any clear views as to the *régime* which they wished to see established, after the overthrow of the Shah's despotism. The result of their revolution, despite its origins in injured nationalism, was to weaken rather than strengthen Persia against foreign intervention. And the introduction of American financial advisers in 1910 was to prove an inadequate substitute for a properly worked out scheme of reform with public support behind it.

The weakness of the Persian revolution stands out the more strikingly when contrasted with the success of the Turkish revolution of 1908. The revolutionaries in Persia were an amalgam of the wealthy merchant classes with western contacts and Moslem intellectuals of the reformist variety. As such they had far more in common with the Arab nationalists of Syria and Egypt at this date, than with the revolutionaries of the Committee of Union and Progress. In part this was due to the fact that the ruling *élite* of the Ottoman Empire had kept the unique system of recruitment by talent which had been the secret of Ottoman success in the greatest days of the Empire. Abdul Hamid, normally represented as the most reactionary of Sultans, had in fact outdone his predecessors in opening schools throughout the Empire. The revolutionaries in Ottoman Turkey were drawn from the ruling *élite*, in revolt against a system of despotism which prevented them from ruling effectively. They were patriots for an Empire with a religious, not a racial basis, nationalists for the Ottoman state, and constitutionalists because the old controls on Ottoman despotism had broken, and constitutions seemed to work in the West. Their nearest parallel can be found among those groups who took Japan from isolation to world power in two generations. It was the Japanese defeat of Russia which fired their imaginations. And in the future they were to prove second only to the Japanese in their imitation and adaptation of European models.

Their greatest strength developed from 1908 onwards, not among the exiles in Paris but among the officer groups in Macedonia and Anatolia. For these the Anglo-Russian meeting at Reval in June 1908, which seemed to foreshadow a new *Entente* at the expense of Turkey, was the breaking point. Already a number of young officers, feeling the Sultan's police on their trail, had preferred to go into hiding in the hills of Macedonia. On July 4th, mutiny broke out among units of the Third Army Corps in Macedonia and spread rapidly to the Second Army Corps in what is still today European Turkey. On July 21st, 1908, under the threat of a march on Istanbul, the Sultan gave way and proclaimed the restoration of the constitution of 1876. The way now seemed open for the liberalization and democratization of the Ottoman Empire. The reason such reform failed to materialize was largely due to the European powers for whom the prospect of a revival of Ottoman strength was so unwelcome as to call for immediate action.

Five powers were involved, Russia, Austria, Serbia, Bulgaria and Greece. The main blow to Turkish democracy was struck by Austria in October 1908 with the annexation of Bosnia and Herzegovina. The decision had been taken as a result of a Russian initiative in July proposing discussion of the Novibazar issue, and Bosnia and the Straits. Aehrenthal felt this move would prove an essential counter to the growing pan-Serb propaganda organized in the two provinces by emissaries from Belgrade. It was discussed between him and Izvolski in September 1908 at Buchlau in Bohemia, at a meeting in which Izvolski failed to grasp the imminence of the Austrian action, believing he had been promised Austrian support for his ambitions for a revision of the Straits agreements. Neither man seemed to have realized that the action they were discussing was contrary to the spirit of the Concert of Europe in that it was not being done with the agreement of the other powers, and no question of corresponding compensation to them was suggested. Only Ferdinand of Bulgaria, as a result of a meeting later that month with Aehrenthal, grasped what was going on. Isvolski in the meantime continued his long planned visits to Rome and Paris, London and Berlin, to organize support for his claims.

Ferdinand's intuition (for he does not seem, as was believed at the time, to have been in collusion with Aehrenthal) enabled him to anticipate the Austrian action by one day and proclaim the independence of Bulgaria from the Ottoman Empire. Aehrenthal's action came on October 6th. The next day Crete proclaimed her union with Greece, thereby adding to the crisis.

Isvolski's reactions were governed by his belief that he had been deceived by Aehrenthal and by the intensity of pan-Slav reaction in Russia, an element he had misjudged, as before over Novibazar. The Austrian action included a declaration of withdrawal from Novibazar. But this was by no means adequate to appease Russian opinion, and his own schemes for the Straits were defeated by British insistence that Turkish agreement was essential. And Aehrenthal now refused Isvolski's call to attend a conference to discuss Bosnia, which he affected to believe to be a *chose jugée*. Isvolski had nothing therefore to defend himself with against charges that he had been out-manoeuvred by Austria, and had agreed to sell the interests of a fellow Slav state (Serbia) down the river. It seems doubtful whether he had obtained the prior backing of his cabinet and prime minister for his schemes. Aehrenthal, in his turn, had secured the assent, but by no means the support, of either his premier in Vienna or the cabinet in Budapest. The German Kaiser rejected his action as contrary to Germany's interests in Turkey, while Britain and France regarded the whole affair as a total departure from the rules of the game.

The strongest reactions came from Italy and Serbia. Italian opinion regarded the Austrian action as an unwarranted increase in Austrian power. The Serbs saw it as virtually an act of war. Guerilla bands were organized, Austrian goods boycotted. The Serbian government, backed by the assurances of the pan-Slav Russian press, demanded compensation in the strongest terms. Serbian military strength was built up until the Serbian army was virtually in total mobilization. These manifestations were viewed with growing rage in Vienna where pressure grew in turn for a preventive war against Serbia. In Germany these manifestations strengthened those who had welcomed the Austrian action against the Kaiser. Assurances were given to Aehrenthal, notably by Bülow, the German Chancellor, which amounted to an unconditional promise to restrain Russia in the event of an Austro-Serbian war.

On the other aspects of the crisis Germany did her utmost to be conciliatory, especially in relation to Turkey. By February 1909 Austria and Bulgaria had agreed to pay financial compensation to Turkey. But Russian support still enabled Serbia to threaten Austria and to run the danger of provoking an Austro-Serbian war. Germany therefore first assented to an Austrian proposal for military staff conversations and then in March forced the Russians to abandon support for Serbia and declare their formal acceptance of the annexation by threatening to let 'matters take their course', that is, to allow an Austrian invasion of Serbia which Russia was not prepared militarily to resist. Serbia, isolated, was forced to back down and promise to check anti-Austrian propaganda in a note of March 31st, 1909.

The effects of the Bosnian crisis were principally in the psychological field. It was easy to argue that Aehrenthal had no more acted against the spirit of European co-operation than German, French or Russian statesmen before him; that he could not have acted as he did without a concomitant eagerness on Isvolski's part for a major *coup* which would establish his own position, and that of his government, after the decline of Russia's position among the Great Powers. But the fact remains that Aehrenthal had acted without any consideration for the interests of the other European powers, and had subsequently managed to avoid paying any compensation other than to Serbia and Turkey. He had bitterly offended Russian, Italian and Serbian opinion, and left Britain convinced of his dependence on Germany. In fact, this was the exact opposite of the impression he had wished to convey. The German intervention in March 1909, designed as much as anything to demonstrate Germany's commanding position, offended everybody without any gain to herself.

The diplomatic consequences of the Bosnian crisis were therefore far-reaching. Italy and Russia drew together, and concluded at Racconigi in October 1909 a secret understanding designed to preserve the *status quo* in the Balkans, and, failing this, to favour the division of Ottoman Turkey on a basis of self-determination, with Italian support for Russian ambitions in the Straits and Russian support for Italian claims in Tripoli further began a long-term military build-up of her position on Austria's southern borders. In France, the first Briand cabinet, which succeeded Clemenceau in 1909, began long-term consideration of the improvement of France's military position, as did Russia. The Russian government in fact turned to diplomacy in the Balkans, to the encouragement of Balkan nationalism against Austria and the attempt to create a Balkan alliance which would bar Austria's way to the Balkans.

Perhaps the most serious consequences were to be felt in Austria and in Ottoman Turkey itself. The Bosnian action gravely exacerbated both German-Slav relations in Bohemia and Carniola, and Hungarian relations with the Croats. In 1909 the Hungarian Governor-General in Croatia placed more than fifty Croats and Serbs on trial in Agram on charges of treasonably plotting with Serbia, and condemned thirty of them to hard labour on evidence so patently inadequate that a higher court annulled the sentences. Still worse, in March 1909, at the height of the Bosnian crisis, the Austrian Foreign Minister allowed the publication of an article by the historian, Friedjung, which accused Croat and Serb leaders of trafficking with Belgrade. At the subsequent libel trial the documents he had used were shown to be blatant forgeries. In Hungary, the Independence party continued its pressure for still greater devolution of powers, and when Kossuth tried to be conciliatory, his radicals repudiated him. Fresh troubles broke out in Galicia in 1908 with the assassination of the Polish Governor-General by a Ruthenian nationalist. And at the height of the Bosnian crisis, the Prime Minister's disagreement with Aehrenthal's foreign policy brought down the last strong cabinet to hold office in Austria before 1914.

The strongest effects were felt in Ottoman Turkey. The immediate loss of territory and prestige to Austria underlined the position of the liberals and would-be parliamentarians in Istanbul, and, on the one hand, enhanced the position of the committee of Union and Progress which now emerged as the power behind the liberal statesman, and, on the other hand, caused a revival of extreme Moslem reaction. In April 1909 the First Army Corps mutinied under the influence of Moslem propaganda and marched on the Turkish Parliament, affording the Sultan the opportunity to rid himself of the Committee's nominee as Grand Vizier and replace him by a more pliable man. Modernism in the provinces was halted by a circular instructing provincial governments to safeguard the law of Islam, the *Sharia*, and outbursts of Moslem extremism culminated in large-scale massacres of Armenians in the province of Adana. The Committee's reaction was swift. From Salonica, troops loyal to the Committee of Union and Progress marched on Constantinople, deposed the Sultan, appointed his brother to replace him and in August reduced his constitutional powers to those of a French president, able to appoint the Grand Vizier but no more. The Vizier with his cabinet was supposed to be responsible to parliament, though the maintenance of military rule until 1911 made this position largely academic.

The manifestations of Serbian, Greek and Bulgarian nationalist aggressiveness from the time of the Russian crisis onwards convinced the extreme leaders of the Turkish revolution, especially the leaders of the Committee

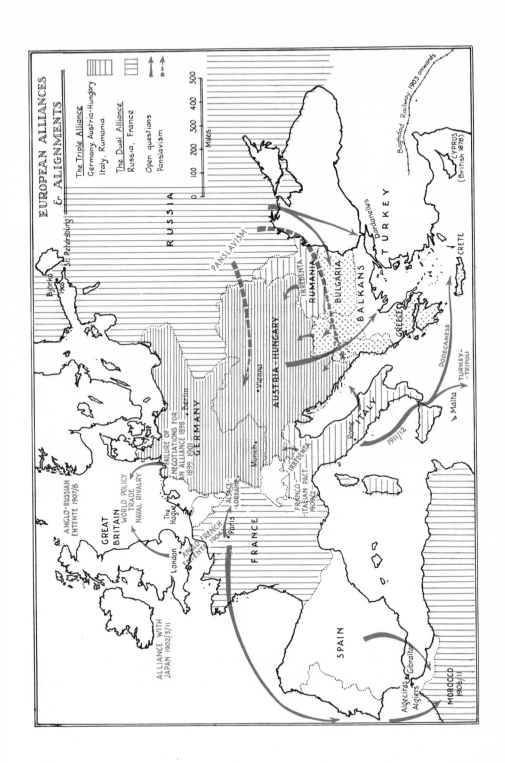

EUROPEAN ALLIANCES & ALIGNMENTS

The Triple Alliance
Germany, Austria-Hungary
Italy, Rumania

The Dual Alliance
Russia, France

Open questions
Panslavism

Miles
0  100  200  300  400  500

RUSSIA

St. Petersburg

Björkö 1905

PANSLAVISM

GREAT BRITAIN

ANGLO-RUSSIAN ENTENTE 1907/8

WORLD POLICY
TRADE
NAVAL RIVALRY

London

ALLIANCE WITH JAPAN 1902/5/11

The Hague

FAILURE OF NEGOTIATIONS FOR AN ALLIANCE 1898, 1899, 1901

GERMANY

Berlin

Munich

ANGLO-FRENCH ENTENTE 1904

ALSACE-LORRAINE

FRANCE

Paris

SPAIN

Algeciras  Gibraltar
Algiers

MOROCCO 1906/11

FRANCO-ITALIAN PACT 1900/2

IRREDENTA

Vienna

AUSTRIA-HUNGARY

ITALY

Rome

1911/12

Malta

TURKEY-TRIPOLI

IRREDENTA

RUMANIA

BULGARIA

BALKANS

GREECE

Dardanelles

TURKEY

Baghdad Railway 1903 onwards

CYPRUS (British 1878)

CRETE

DODECANESE

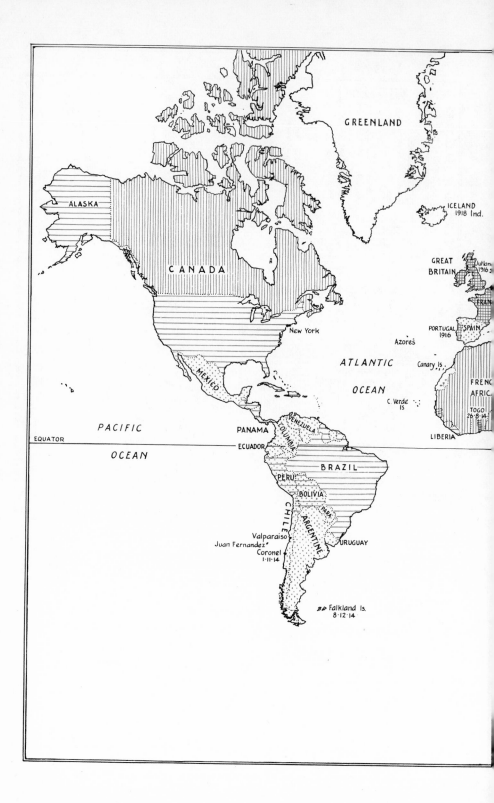

GREENLAND

ICELAND
1918 Ind.

ALASKA

CANADA

GREAT
BRITAIN

Jutland
1916 31

FRAN

New York

PORTUGAL
1916

SPAIN

Azores

ATLANTIC

Canary Is.

MEXICO

OCEAN

C. Verde
Is

FREN
AFRIC.

PACIFIC

PANAMA

COLUMBIA

VENEZUELA

TOGO
26·8·14

EQUATOR

ECUADOR

LIBERIA

OCEAN

BRAZIL

PERU

BOLIVIA

CHILE

PARA.

ARGENTINE

Valparaiso

Juan Fernandez

URUGUAY

Coronel
1·11·14

Falkland Is.
8·12·14

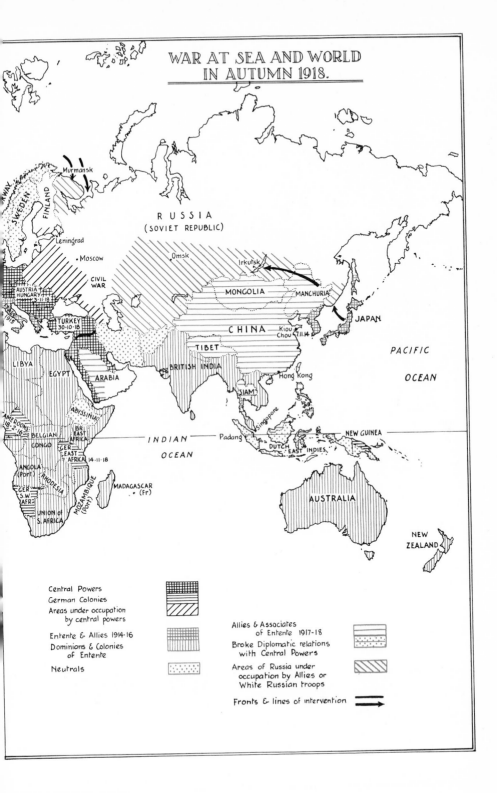

# WAR AT SEA AND WORLD
# IN AUTUMN 1918.

Murmansk

RUSSIA
(SOVIET REPUBLIC)

Leningrad
Moscow
Omsk
Irkutsk

NORWAY
SWEDEN
FINLAND

CIVIL
WAR

AUSTRIA
HUNGARY
3-11-18

MONGOLIA
MANCHURIA

TURKEY
30-10-18

CHINA
Kiou
Chou 7.11.14

JAPAN

TIBET

LIBYA
EGYPT
ARABIA

BRITISH INDIA
Hong Kong

PACIFIC

OCEAN

ABYSSINIA
CAMEROONS
18-2-16
BELGIAN
CONGO
BR.
EAST
AFRICA
GER.
EAST
AFRICA 14·11·18

SIAM

INDIAN

Padang

Singapore
NEW GUINEA

ANGOLA
(Port.)
RHODESIA
GER.
S.W.
AFR.

OCEAN

DUTCH
EAST INDIES.

MADAGASCAR
(Fr)

UNION of
S. AFRICA

MOZAMBIQUE
(Port.)

AUSTRALIA

NEW
ZEALAND

| Central Powers | | |
|---|---|---|
| German Colonies | | |
| Areas under occupation by central powers | | |
| Entente & Allies 1914-16 | | |
| Dominions & Colonies of Entente | | |
| Neutrals | | |

Allies & Associates
of Entente 1917-18
Broke Diplomatic relations
with Central Powers
Areas of Russia under
occupation by Allies or
White Russian troops

Fronts & lines of intervention

AUSTRIA ~ HUNGARY
POLITICAL & ETHNOGRAPHICAL

• Hamburg
LOW GERMANS
• Stettin
GERMANY   KASSUBS
• Hanover    • Berlin
MIDDLE GERMANS
• Wittenburg        • Posen
• Leipzig        POLES
THURINGIANS
SAXONY   • Dresden        • Breslau        • Lublin        RUSSIA
FRANKS   SAXONS • Carlsbad        • Prague        • Sadowa        PRUSSIA        • Kiev
BAVARIA   • Pilsen CZECHS        W. SILESIA        • Cracow        JEWS        EAST
• Stuttgart   • Ratisbon   BOHEMIA        • Iglau MORAVIA • Olmütz        RUTHENIANS        • Tarnow        • Przemysl POLES   • Lvov        SLAVS
HIGH GERMANS   • Budweis        • Brünn        SLOVAKS        GALICIA        • Tarnopol        RUTHENIANS
• Munich   • Passau        • Austerlitz        • Czernowitz
BAVARIANS        AUSTRIA        • Wagram        HUNGARY        RUMANIANS        BUKOWINA
VORARLBERG   • Innsbruck        • Salzburg   • Vienna   • Pressburg        • Jassy
TYROL        • Eisenerz        • Raab        • Budapest        • Debrecen        R. Pruth
• Meran   • Baren FRIULI        AUSTRIANS        Graz        (Györ)        • Szekesfehervar        • Bistritz        SAXONS   • Galatz
• Trent   VENETIA   CARINTHIA   • Klagenfurt   STYRIA        MAGYARS        • Kolozsvar        TRANSYLVANIA
• Verona   SLOVENIANS        • Arad        • Kronstadt        RUMANIANS
• Padua   • Trieste   • Zagreb        SOUTH        • Temesvar        BANAT        Vulkan        RUMANIA
R. Po        ISTRIA • Fiume   CROATIA        • Belgrade        Pass        WALLACHIANS        • Bucharest
• Bologna        CROATS        SLAVS        Iron        • Kraiova
ITALIANS        DALMATIA   BOSNIA        SLAVONIA        SERBIA        Gate        R. Danube
• Florence        • Zara        • Spoleto        • Sarajevo        • Nis
ITALY   Ancona        DALMATIA   • Novibazar        BULGARIANS        BLACK
ITALY        • Ragusa   HERZEGOVINA        MONTENEGRO        • Sofia   BULGARIA        SEA
• Rome        ADRIATIC        • Cetinje        • Philoppopolis
SEA        Scutari        • Adrianople
• Naples        Durazzo        TURKEY   Constantinople
• Brindisi   ALBANIA        ALBANIA        • Salonika        TURKS
TYRRHENIAN        GREEKS        TURKEY
SEA        GREECE        AEGEAN        TURKS
IONIAN        SEA
SEA        • Athens
SICILY        • Corinth

• Malta
MEDITERRANEAN   SEA

0        100        200        300
Miles

of Union and Progress, that the liberal Turks' hope of creating an Ottoman Empire on a basis of equality between Christian and Moslem, Turk and non-Turk was an illusion. A ruthless policy of centralization and Turkisation was the answer, one which, as events in the external relations of the Ottoman Empire sharpened the lesson, gradually alienated the new *élites* of the Arab and other non-Turkish communities in the Asiatic empire. From 1909 Arab nationalism in the *vilayets* (provinces) of what were to become Syria, the Lebanon, Palestine and Iraq, previously concealed between the twin currents of the Liberal Islamic movement and hostility to Hamidian despotism, begins to emerge in its true colours. On their side, the Turks began to exalt their Turkishness, expressed in organizations such as the Society 'Turkish Hearth', founded in 1912, and in the rise to prominence of the writer, Ziya Gökalp, with his gospel of pan-Turanianism, of Turkish kindom with the Turkic-speaking peoples of the Crimea, the Transcaspian emirates, Iran, Afghanistan and Chinese Central Asia.

The Turkish *élites* under the Young Turk movement were basically those of the old Ottoman Empire. But Hamid's educational reforms, especially his wide scattering of military schools, was producing by the turn of the century a new educated Arab group of young officers and intellectuals not necessarily drawn from the old land-owning families of the Arab provinces of the Empire. These young men eagerly greeted the 1908 revolution and embraced the Ottomanism of the Liberal Turks. But even in the first election to the Ottoman Chamber of deputies they found themselves prejudiced against. Between them the new intellectuals and the western educated Arabs of the Lebanon (see Chapter III) only secured 60 seats to 156 for the Turks in the Chamber of Deputies and a mere three seats out of 40 in the Senate. And after the 1909 *coup*, the Committee of Union and Progress banned all non-Turkish political organizations and began to tighten the powers of the central administration. Arab nationalism thereafter went underground or into exile. In Syria the only overt manifestation was the Arab Literary club which came to act as a kind of demi-official intermediary between the Committee of Union and Progress and Arab leaders. The most important of many secret societies was *Al Qahtani*, founded in 1909, with the declared aim of turning the Ottoman Empire into a dual Arab-Turkish monarchy, with an Arabic language state with its separate parliament and administration. Its strongest adherents were among the young Arab army officers. However, this secret society was soon penetrated by the Turkish police.

More important were the two organizations formed in exile. The first of these, *al Fatat*, or the Young Arab Society, was founded in 1909 by a group of Syrian Arab Moslems in Paris with aims roughly similar to that referred to above, of Arab independence within an Arab-Turkic monarchy. A more overt group, since, though it operated in exile, it cultivated contacts among the members of the Turkish governments of 1909–12, was that which came together in the so-called Ottoman Decentralization Party, founded in 1912 among Syrian *emigrés* in Cairo, in contact with the leaders of the Islamic Liberal movement among the Egyptians such as Mohammed Abdu. Prominent among these Syrians were Rashid Rida, who was to follow Abdu as the leading exponent of Islamic Liberalism, and the Emir Shekib Arslan, a Druze from the Lebanon, who, from his exile in Switzerland, was to become one of the most prominent figures in the pan-Arab movement, his influence spreading from Morocco to Palestine in the decade before World War II. Perhaps most significant were the conversations opened in 1911 between a group of thirty-five of the Arab deputies in Constantinople and the newly appointed Sharif of Mecca, Hussein ibn Ali, in which the Arab deputies promised Hussein their support if he rose against the Turks, and recognized him as 'Caliph of the prophet, the one man responsible for the interests of all the Arab countries'.

The Arab nationalist movement, as it was to manifest itself in the twentieth century, had at this time two other important elements, the Egyptian nationalist movement and the Arab sheikhs of the Arabian peninsula. It was in the years 1906–10 that the Egyptian nationalist movement began to separate itself out from the early development of Arab Liberal and nationalist thought, and to develop along purely Egyptian lines. In so doing it was following the logic of Egypt's separate position in the Arab and Ottoman world, a position which could be dated back to the middle ages, but which took its modern form from the work of Mohammed Ali. The separation of the Egyptian movement from the mainstream of Arab Liberalism is at first sight odd in view of the presence in Cairo of the main figures in the Arab Liberal movement at this time, the *Salafiya* leaders Mohammed Abdu, Rashid Rida, and the Syrian, al-Kawakibi, and the Christian nationalists Shummayil, Faris Antun and Negib Azoury. The difference sprang from the British presence in Egypt. Without that presence, Cairo could hardly have become the centre for Arab nationalist exiles from the Ottoman Empire. But to the Egyptian nationalists, Britain appeared as the mainstay of the rule of the Khedive, and the supporter of that oppressive oriental despotism against whom Arab liberal writers preached resistance.

Two events led to the estrangement of the young Egyptian national movement from British rule. The first was the British refusal to restore the Sudan to Egyptian control after the British reconquest in 1898. The unity of the Nile valley became an essential element in the nationalists' programme. The second was the Denshawi affair, in which the murder of a British officer after a shooting incident was made the occasion for a Draconian visitation on the inhabitants of the village in which the incident had occurred. In 1907 Lord Cromer retired, his policy of ruling Egypt on strict administratively imperialist lines in ruins. His successor, Sir Eldon Gorst, attempted to create a coalition of moderate opinion behind the Khedive, and did his best to divide the nationalist movement. In this he was greatly aided by the death in 1908 of Mustafa Kemal, the young nationalist leader (who should not be confused with the Turkish dictator of the same name). Those Egyptians who followed the *salafiya* for a time co-operated with the new Governor-General, and he was successful also in splitting away from the nationalist movement the leaders of the Coptic minority and the 'party of nobles', the mainly Turkish members of Cairo's ruling classes. Cromer had already shown the way by appointing Sa'd Zaghlul, one of Mohammed Abdu's pupils and friends, as Minister of Education in 1906.

In 1908 Sir Eldon Gorst appointed Butrus Ghali Pasha, the principal political figure among the Copts, as Prime Minister. There were then three main political parties in Egypt, all founded in 1907, the People's Party which followed Abdu, the Kemalist National Party, and the Khedive's party, which was the party of Constitutional Reform. Only the Nationalists remained anti-British. But Gorst, in turn, succeeded in alienating the moderates as well as the nationalists. The moderates hoped for a continuation of Liberal reform in alliance with the British. Instead they saw British support given to a Khedive who seemed to want to restore the absolutism they regarded as an alien accretion on Islam. And in 1909 the British ruined all chances of a successful outcome to their policy by forcing Butrus Ghali's government to propose a revision of the Suez Canal Company's concession, due to expire in 1968, to make it run a further forty years. There was an outburst of nationalist agitation, public order declined terribly and Butrus Ghali was murdered by a fanatic. His successor allowed the Assembly to throw the bill out. Sir Eldon Gorst died within the year from cancer, and Lord Kitchener came to replace him. After a period of repression he was able by 1913 to restore good relations with the moderate nationalists by introducing a revision of the constitution, giving the Legislative Council of the National Assembly the powers to suspend and initiate legislation. Sa'd Zaghlul resigned his ministry and was elected vice-president of the new Assembly.

In these years too the Arab monarchies of the twentieth century first began to take their shape. In 1908, under pressure from the Ottoman Liberal Turks of the revolution, the Sultan released from captivity in Constantinople Hussein ibn Ali, the head of one of the two branches of the house of Beni Hashem, the direct descendants of the Prophet Mohammed, from which families alone could be appointed the Grand Sharif of Mecca. At this date the position was largely titular, since Mecca, the holy city of Islam, was the capital of a Turkish province, with a Turkish Governor-General and garrison. Nevertheless the claims of the Grand Sharif to be head of Islam could technically be considered strong. And in securing his own appointment as Grand Sharif, Hussein was responding cannily to the pan-Islamic currents which were then sweeping the Middle East. On arrival in Mecca, he took steps to reassert the temporal position of the Grand Sharif as Amir of Mecca, soliciting the support of the *bedouin*, rebuffing a Young Turkish delegation, quarrelling with the Turkish governor of the Hejaz, and defeating a Turkish proposal to destroy the special status of the Hejaz as exempt from taxation and conscription. At the same time his youngest son, Abdullah, future King of Jordan, was elected deputy for

Mecca to the Turkish parliament, and made it his business to build up contacts with the Arab nationalist societies of Syria. It was probably Abdullah who secured the opening of contacts with the Arab deputies in Constantinople mentioned above. And it was in these years that Hussein and his family began nurturing plans for an Arab kingdom independent in all but name of the Ottoman Empire.

On the other side of the Arabian peninsula, in the country then called Nejd, another future Arab monarch, Abdul Aziz ibn Saud, had recaptured his ancestral capital, Riyadh, from the Rashidi of Hail in 1901, and beat them in battle in 1903. He was faced in 1904 with an attack by Turkish troops called in by the Rashidi to restore their position. After an initial defeat he succeeded in obliterating the Turkish army. But he nevertheless felt it safer to sue for formal submission to the Sultan. This submission did not prevent him catching and killing the Rashidi sheikh in April 1906; and thereafter the Turks withdrew their troops from the Nejd. From 1906–10, ibn Saud was gradually consolidating his desert realm, terrorizing the minor sheikhs into acknowledging his supremacy and putting down uprisings against him with a severity beyond the normal practice of *bedouin* politics. In 1913 he began to use the Wahhabi faith of his followers to settle them in religiously-governed settlements, gathering them together in a kind of religious brotherhood known as the *Ilkhwan*. In 1911 he contacted the British in Kuwait and proposed an alliance to expel the Turkish garrison from the Hasa, the coastal province south of Kuwait. His proposal was turned down. In May 1913 he undertook the conquest of Hasa himself. But after expelling the Turkish garrison, in May 1914, he again insured himself against the possibility of Turkish support for his tribal rivals by accepting the nominal appointment of a Turkish Governor-General of Nejd.

The third of the Arab rulers to assert himself in this period was less successful. This was the Imam Yahya of the Yemen, who, in 1911, with Italian encouragement, rose against the Turkish garrison on the coast. The rising provoked full-scale Turkish intervention and the capture of his capital, Sana. A treaty re-established his rule as a Turkish agent in the highlands, but left a Turkish army of some 14,000 men in the coastal strip. Further north, the Asiri tribes under that now-vanished dynasty, the Idrisi, also rose against the Turks and managed to establish some degree of independence, which they were to maintain until their absorption by ibn Saud in 1925.

## Chapter IX
## EUROPE TURNS ON ITSELF: THE ANGLO-GERMAN CRISIS, 1909–1912

BY 1909 the pattern of events which was to lead the European powers to mutual self-destruction was already beginning to be established. In the Bosnian crisis can be seen the first of the three elements in that pattern which played the largest part in the outbreak of the war in 1914, the attempt of the Habsburg monarchy to stifle Balkan nationalism, its inevitable enemy, before the monarchy itself began to fall apart; and a second element, the challenge of Imperial Germany to Russian pan-Slavism in the Balkans and at the Straits had also made an appearance. The third element, that of Germany's challenge to Britain, underlay and antedated both of these. With the intensification of Anglo-German naval rivalry and the second Moroccan crisis of 1911 it was now to emerge as the most significant element on the international scene. For the first time since the Kaiser's telegram was sent to President Kruger in 1897, British opinion beyond the closed circle of the Foreign Office, the Admiralty and the War Office, the Cabinet and the few journalists in the know began to echo the wondering words of the Liberal Premier, Asquith, who told his chief Conservative opponent Balfour in 1908: 'Incredible as it might seem, the Government could form no theory of the German policy which fitted the known facts, except that they wanted war.'

The main elements in this change of opinion were the growing realization of German naval strength coupled with the increasingly assertive role played by Germany in European politics. Of these by far the more important was the naval issue. Agitation began at the time of the publication of the British 1908–09 naval programme in February 1908, a programme which seemed absurdly small in relation to German construction. It was fanned by a highly imprudent personal letter addressed by the Kaiser to the First Lord of the Admiralty, Lord Tweedsmouth, attempting to reassure Lord Tweedsmouth that the German programme was not directed against the British. In April 1908 Tweedsmouth's successor as First Lord, Reginald McKenna, was persuaded by the Admiralty that the next annual programme should include no fewer than six Dreadnoughts, the Kaiser's letter having played its part in converting the Admiralty to the policy of laying down two keels for every one laid down by Germany. This proposal was fought bitterly by the advocates of economy in the Cabinet, of which the two strongest were Lloyd George, the Chancellor of the Exchequer, and Winston Churchill. In June 1908 Churchill was the Kaiser's guest at the German Army manoeuvres, and returned to Britain convinced of Germany's pacific intentions.

That was not the conviction which their meeting with the Kaiser at Kronberg in August 1908 left on King Edward VII and Lord Hardinge, the permanent head of the Foreign Office. The Kaiser refused point-blank to consider any reduction in the German naval programme, which was, he said, a point of honour with Germany. He would rather go to war than submit to British dictation. Thereafter navalist agitation increased in Britain. It fed on the Kaiser's *Daily Telegraph* interview, and the Anglo-phobe reaction in Germany that followed, and was compounded with rumours that the Germans were planning a secret acceleration of construction so as to give them in 1912 not the projected thirteen Dreadnoughts built and building, but on some estimates seventeen, on others twenty-one to the British figure of eighteen. The British Cabinet compromised on this news, by laying down four Dreadnoughts in the 1909–10 programme with four more to be laid down before April 1910 if the necessity was proven. In March 1909, the Cabinet revealed its estimate of German naval strength to a hushed and shocked House of Commons. There followed a major outburst of public opinion in support of an eight Dreadnought programme for 1909–10, an outburst compounded by the news which broke in April 1909 that Germany's two allies in the Triple Alliance, Austria and Italy, were each about to lay down four Dreadnoughts. In July 1909 the Cabinet decided to lay down all eight Dreadnoughts.

The British decision, in turn, resulted in a major Cabinet crisis in Germany between Chancellor Bülow and the Chief of the German naval staff, Admiral von Tirpitz. It was the latter who was the main driving force behind the German programme. A convinced navalist, he had evolved a variation of the Mahan thesis as to the connection between seapower and great power status. According to Tirpitz's theory all that was necessary was to build a fleet sufficiently large as to make it too dangerous for the larger naval powers to attack, since their resultant naval losses would leave them weaker than their more immediate rivals. This so-called 'risk theory' was conceivably valid in a polycentric, multi-polar, great power system. But such a system, even if it had existed in Bismarck's day, was beginning to disappear at least five years before Tirpitz began to formulate his theory, with the conclusion of the Franco-Russian alliance and the gradual bi-polarization of the great power system into two alliance systems. And nothing, so it turned out, was more calculated to accelerate this process of bi-polarization than German naval construction, since British opinion gradually took on the conviction that the German fleet was directed solely against Britain.

Bülow did his best therefore to persuade Tirpitz and the Kaiser of the need to reduce naval construction in the interests of an Anglo-German *rapprochement*. He failed completely and resigned in July 1909. His successor, Bethmann Hollweg, was if anything more anxious for agreement with Britain, but negotiations, which began in October 1909, were hampered by the German insistence that a naval agreement could only be accompanied by a political agreement which would bind each to benevolent neutrality, if the other were attacked by a third party. The aim was clear, to disrupt the Anglo-French *Entente*, which British official opinion was coming increasingly to see as essential to the balance of power in Europe. The British government could only counter this German thrust by postponing negotiations until after the 1910 General Election. The 1910–11 naval programme introduced into Parliament in May 1910 included five Dreadnoughts and provoked a fresh outburst of opposition from the radicals in the cabinet led by Churchill. Australia and New Zealand each volunteered to pay for an additional capital ship. A further five capital ships were to be included in the programme for 1911–12.

A second German overture to Britain had been made in June 1910, and a further eighteen months of negotiation followed. It broke down again because of the conflicting aims of the two sides. Britain wanted an *Entente* on the lines of those concluded with France and Russia which would put an end to the existing sources of tension between the two countries, of which the naval issue and the Baghdad railway line were the most important. The Germans wanted to detach Britain from the Franco-Russian alliance. Nothing less would compensate them for agreeing to modify their naval plans. The British entered the negotiations with little hope of their success and great suspicion of their opponents. The Germans entered with an entirely exaggerated idea of Britain's willingness to negotiate and of her vulnerability to economic considerations. Even then there was a chance that German pressure might have been partially successful but for Germany's own action in July 1911 in provoking the second Moroccan crisis.

The British Liberal government, on whom the German pressure was to be exerted, were, as had been earlier remarked, an odd mixture of conservatism in world affairs and social reformism at home. That minority element in the cabinets of Sir Henry Campbell-Bannerman, and his successor, Herbert Asquith, who were interested in foreign affairs, are normally described by historians as imperialists: but they had little of the aggressive drive for annexation which is regarded as essential in imperialism. Theirs was much more the imperialism of the satisfied, and their aim in international affairs was to preserve the *status quo*. What offended them most and also aroused their suspicions, in German and Austrian actions, was the lack of respect they felt was so often shown by those two powers for the interests of the other European powers and for the conventions of international intercourse. In the pattern of European politics, they were the conservative element, Aehrenthal, Bülow, Izvolski even, the radicals. They were, however, only one element in a party which included many much more genuine radicals than these foreign statesmen, men fairly and

167

squarely in the English radical tradition of resentment of externally-imposed limitations on national freedom of action in domestic affairs, simplists who saw the task of British foreign policy to be that not of maintaining the checks and balances of the international power system, but of finding some once-and-for-all solution to all international problems which would enable them to return to the serious business of pressing for internal reform and lambasting as reactionaries those who opposed them.

As a result the British government felt unable to play as determined a hand as they might otherwise have done. And a great many of the more vital issues and decisions were never thoroughly discussed by the Cabinet. Instead, the bulk of British energies were concentrated on those internal battles which by 1914 were to bring Britain to the verge of civil war. The roots of these lay in the determination of the Liberal movement in 1906 to secularize the education system, introduce a system of redistributive taxation, grant a degree of Home Rule to Ireland, reform the system of land revenue and taxation, reduce the political power of the brewery and drink interests and protect the position of the Trades Unions, a programme which involved tackling head-on the power of the main corporative organizations which had hitherto dominated those large areas of governmental activity in which previous governments had been content to devolve responsibility upon private persons and voluntary organizations. Many of these organizations were well represented in Conservative circles. The Liberals' reforms would have greatly reduced their power; indeed the main Liberal objection to most of them was that they represented undemocratic concentrations of power. And the permanent Conservative majority in the hereditary House of Lords remained determined to obstruct and thwart all the Liberal reforms which were intended to serve this Liberal purpose. Thus the 1906 Education Bill was reduced to such a travesty of itself in the House of Lords that the Commons refused to proceed with it. Only the Trades Disputes Bill and a Workmen's Compensation Act of the major programme of 1906 went through without emasculation. In 1907, the Irish Devolution Bill and two bills designed to deal with the land problem in Scotland were defeated. In 1908 the Budget and the Old Age Pensions Bill got through the Lords in deference to the constitutional convention in which in matters of finance the Commons were sovereign. But the principal bill of this session, one designed to reduce progressively the number of public houses and a new education bill were again thrown out by the Conservative majority in the Lords. Talks designed to reach a *modus vivendi* between the two Houses seemed to be getting nowhere. And greatly to the alarm of the Liberal Party, there seemed to be no very great public outcry among the electorate at this wanton thwarting of the democratic process.

It was in these circumstances that the new Chancellor of the Exchequer in 1909, the Welsh radical, the one-time small-town lawyer, David Lloyd George, came to draft the 1909 Budget. He needed to increase the Budget by £14 million, about 10% on its 1908 level, to cover the cost of the eight Dreadnoughts to meet the German challenge, and to build up the revenue to finance the schemes of social insurance on the German and Continental model under discussion in Liberal intellectual circles. His task was made to seem much more difficult by the fact that a trade recession had actually reduced the revenue from Customs and Excise by 15% of the total Budget. He chose to use his need to raise more revenue both for social and defence purposes to attack the main interests behind the Conservative opposition in their weakest position, their liability to taxation. Not only did he penalize the brewing interests for their opposition to temperance reform by a six-and-a-half million pound increase in duties; he also raised Income Tax progressively and introduced a supertax on incomes of £5,000 and over for that portion which exceeded £3,000 per annum. Most daringly, he introduced four taxes on increases in land values, and a capital gains tax confined to gains in the capital and rental value of land. Together these constituted a direct attack on the principle of property and the position of the hereditary land-owning peerage and gentry, on which so much Conservative support in the rural areas was based. In November 1909, after six months of heightened tension, the House of Lords broke the precedents of 250 years and rejected the Budget. The Liberal Government at once dissolved Parliament and were returned with a majority of 124 including 84 Irish Home Rulers.

The Budget was presented again to the new Parliament, and duly passed by the House of Lords. But the Liberals were now determined to democratize the House of Lords, and break the corporative powers which in their view stood behind it. Their ultimate weapon was to be the power of the Crown to create a sufficient number of Liberal peers to swamp the Conservative majority in the House of Lords; but they were bound by the King's belief that he would only be correct in doing so if a second General Election had given the Liberal Party a specific mandate for such a step. At this critical moment King Edward VII died and was succeeded by his son, the 46-year-old King George. For six months a last attempt was made to reach agreement between the two Houses, or to find a way out of the *impasse* by the creation of a new Centre Party; but these manoeuvres were in vain. In December 1910 a second General Election confirmed the Liberal majority, and left the way open for a new Parliament Bill linking the powers of the House of Lords to a suspensory vote which could only delay a Bill for three sessions before it should finally become law. When the House of Lords realized that the Liberals had secured the new King's consent to a mass creation of peers, the majority gave in, leaving a diehard minority of just under a hundred irreconcilables to record their votes against the government.

The Parliament Act of 1911 had broken the power of the House of Lords to obstruct the Liberals' reform programme. It had by no means crushed the resistance of the British right to what they regarded as subversive and socialist doctrines, inspired by the spirit of class warfare rather than of public service. The Liberal Party programme of 1911 included the major schemes of sickness and unemployment insurance foreshadowed by

Lloyd George in 1909. That of 1912 included a major measure of Home
Rule for Ireland and the disestablishment of the Anglican Church in Wales.
If the land taxes of 1909 were considered subversive, these were regarded
by the Conservatives as positively revolutionary. They had already turned
on their leader, Arthur Balfour, and forced him to resign, replacing him
with a Canadian Scottish business man, Bonar Law. Their decision ushered
in what was to be perhaps the greatest crisis in British politics since the
Jacobite Revolt of 1745, a crisis which began with the arming of Conservative Unionists in the six Protestant counties of Northern Ireland or
Ulster and the raising of a volunteer force of 100,000 men. This was
essentially a political move designed to force the Liberal Government to
think again—but it was accompanied by alarming and unscrupulous
invocations of physical force. What transformed their move from a reckless game of bluff to a preparation for civil war and insurrection was the
parallel growth of extremism in the South of Ireland, where volunteers
were also being raised and drilled, and arms collected. Most of the major
powers in Europe stood on the edge of civil strife in the decade before
1914. But not even Austria-Hungary, only Russia in fact had reached a
state of disorder and division similar to that of affairs in Britain.

Nor was this the only source of disorder in Britain. The Trades Union
movement, like its opposite numbers in France and elsewhere, had embarked on a programme of militant industrial action which threatened to
paralyse the country. The most discontented were the railwaymen and the
miners, followed by the dockers. Then there was the movement to secure
the suffrage for women, which in 1905 had abandoned ordinary methods of
propaganda for the use of publicity and violence, its supporters chaining
themselves to railings, invading Parliament, assaulting Ministers and even
breaking shop windows and burning down country houses. Nor were there
lacking charges of corruption, charges which publicly crystallized in
1912 around Ministers' dealings in the American Marconi Company's
shares, at the very moment its British parent company was concluding a
large and lucrative Government contract. The scandal was somehow
smoothed over by the Liberal Party leadership, but it shook the position of
the Liberal Government severely, and did much to exacerbate feelings on
both sides of the party division.

These internal developments greatly undermined Britain's international
position which was being weakened in other directions. The two most
serious developments were the breakdown of the Anglo-Russian understanding on Persia and the increasing threat of serious trouble between
Japan and the United States, trouble which could disrupt the settlement
in the Far East and face Britain with the impossible choice between her
Japanese ally and her 'cousins', the Americans, with whom it was axiomatic
now that war was unthinkable.

The breakdown in Anglo-Russian understanding in Persia was partially
connected with the Russian fear that the constitutional revolution of 1909,
which overthrew the Shah, was basically directed at them, and was favour-

able to Britain. In 1908 Russian troops had intervened in the disturbances and occupied Tabriz, one of the revolutionary centres. Although they evacuated Tabriz at the end of the year, the subsequent hostility of the population to the Russian colony in the city drove them to a second occupation in May 1909, and, in October, Russian troops invaded Persian Azerbaijan in force, making little effort in the field to hide their annexationist intentions. An element in the Russian action was anxiety over the growth of German influence in Persia, over the activities of the German bankers with whom the concession for a German bank in Persia was under discussion, over reports that Germany was about to ask for a railway concession in Persia, and over the increase of German arms trade with Persia. Britain reacted by pressing for closer co-operation with Russia in Persia, especially in a joint Anglo-Russian loan to the new Persian Government. In May 1910, the British and Russians together demanded that Persia submit any European requests for concessions in the English or Russian zones of influence in Persia to the power concerned for its advance approval.

This move provoked such strong German pressure on Russia (the Germans having again perceived a chance of using the Persian issue to pry open the Anglo-Russian *Entente*) as to bring the new Russian Foreign Minister, Sazonov, on a visit to Potsdam with the Tsar. During the visit, the inexperienced Sazonov, led by his desire to reduce German-Russian tension, verbally promised Germany that Russia would not support Britain in an anti-German policy, in return for similar German reassurances regarding Austrian policy towards Russia. The two countries further agreed to link the Berlin-Baghdad railway to a projected Russian railway system in Northern Persia, and Germany gave assurances that she would not intervene in the Russian Zone in Persia. Sazonov retreated very rapidly from the most far-reaching of these reassurances, which somewhat naturally caused considerable alarm in Britain and France when they became known. But the appointment of Shuster, an American financial expert, as adviser to the Persian Government in 1911, and his appointment in turn of a British officer to command the *Gendarmerie* in northern Persia caused a fresh crisis, which was not ended until the threat of a Russian invasion of Central Persia caused Shuster's dismissal, something in which Britain was forced to acquiesce, albeit with very bad grace. The conclusion in August 1911 of a German-Russian agreement on the railway issue in Persia, at a time when the Agadir crisis was at its height, did nothing to ease Anglo-Russian relations.

Britain's position in the Pacific was equally precarious owing to the development of major tension between Japan and the United States; tension in which the British Pacific Dominions were also closely involved. The conflict sprang in part from the growth of anti-Japanese feeling on the west coast of the United States and in Canada, which expressed itself both in opposition to fresh immigration from Japan and in measures designed to make the position of immigrants as difficult as possible. Japanese emigration to the United States and to Canada began in the late 1890s. In 1907 no fewer than 30,000 Japanese arrived in the United States from Japan, and in the period 1902–06, about the same number of immigrants, most of whom were Japanese, came from Hawaii to the United States. The number of Japanese residing in the US rose from 2,000 in 1890 to 24,000 in 1900, 72,000 in 1910, and 111,000 in 1920. The immigrants were mainly males and employed as labourers, but once established they sent back to Japan for brides. In October 1906, the school board in San Francisco acted to segregate the Japanese children in the city's schools. In effect, they were only transferring to the Japanese the anti-Oriental racialism from which the Chinese had suffered since the 1880s (see Chapter III above). The Japanese had not failed to observe the troubles of the Chinese in the United States, and had tried discreetly to discourage immigration from Japan to America by controlling the issue of passports. But they were unable to stop the migration of Japanese labour from Mexico, Canada and Hawaii to the United States, and there had already been vain attempts by Californian interests to influence Congress to restrict Japanese immigration. The action of the San Francisco school board followed the frustration of this pressure for action on a national scale by the Federal authorities.

The school board's action caused a considerable exacerbation of Japanese-American relations. President Roosevelt, however, realized the dangers in the situation and brought extreme pressure to bear on the San Francisco school board to rescind their order. While discreetly preparing the American fleet, he was able to negotiate an agreement with the Japanese, the so-called Gentleman's Agreement of February 24th, 1907, by which Japan bound herself not to issue passports to would-be immigrants to the United States. At the same time he acted on his executive authority to exclude from the United States all immigrants who held passports not valid for the US, thus shutting off immigration from Hawaii. On March 13th, 1907, the school order was rescinded. But before his retirement from the Presidency in March 1909, he was forced to intervene on several other occasions to scotch further Californian anti-Japanese legislation.

The crisis had however been an alarming one, and led Roosevelt to attempt to enlist the support of Canada (where anti-Japanese riots had broken out in Vancouver in September 1907) to bring pressure to bear on Britain, Japan's ally. His efforts were negated by the action of the Canadian Government in sending an unofficial emissary to Japan to negotiate an agreement by which the Japanese Government would restrict immigration to Canada on its own. For at least a year Roosevelt was partially convinced of the imminence of a Japanese-American war; and his convictions led him to order the US Fleet to the Pacific as the first stage in a world cruise which demonstrated to the world the position of strength the US Navy had come to occupy. In October 1908, at Japanese invitation, the fleet visited Tokyo; in November the Root-Takahira agreement pledged both powers to maintain the existing *status quo* in China and the Pacific. The conclusion of the Root-Takahira agreement greatly eased American-Japanese relations, and the US fleet was moved back to its Atlantic bases. But the agreement bound only the Roosevelt administration; and his successor, President Taft, was to institute a forward policy in China and Manchuria which was difficult to reconcile with the spirit of the Root-Takahira agreement.

The main element of this new policy was the active encouragement of American overseas investment, dollar diplomacy, as it has been called. In 1908 American investment in the Far East was generally made in Japan, and not in China. The appointment of the former American Consul in Manchuria, Willard Straight, as head of the American State Department's Far Eastern Division, began a deliberate attempt to reverse this trend. Straight was perhaps the first of the American ideological China lobbyists. His most important field at first was railways, where his ally was the American railway tycoon and millionaire, Harriman. In 1905 Harriman had attempted to buy the South Manchurian railway. In 1909 he joined with Kuhn, Loeb and Co., the American bankers, to persuade Straight to leave Government service and to act as their chief negotiator. Their aim was to force the Japanese to sell the South Manchurian railway, by purchasing from Russia the Chinese Eastern railway, and building on to it a line which would run parallel with the South Manchuria railway from Chinchow in the south to Aigun on the Siberian border. These were tactics of the sort which Harriman had used to create his American railroad empire. In this instance they received the full backing of the United States Government, which approached Britain in November 1909 with a proposal to effect the complete neutralization of the Manchurian railways, or failing that to support jointly the projected Chinchow–Aigun line, in other words to join in a dubious commercial manoeuvre, the aim of which was to injure the principal Manchurian interests of Britain's ally, Japan. This gratuitous attempt to drive a wedge between Britain, her Japanese ally and her Russian partner in the *Entente* was supported only by Germany, as another move in her constant struggle to break up the alliances and understandings which Germany believed kept her from playing her proper part in world affairs. A similar approach to Russia only provoked the Russian and Japanese Governments, with British and French acquiescence, to conclude in July 1910 an agreement which resulted in the practical closing of Manchuria and Mongolia to all but Japanese and Russian capital. Thus, Roosevelt's policy of maintaining a judicious balance between Japan and Russia, while never offending Japan, was in ruins. Inevitably the Americans heaped on Britain much of the blame for the failure of this ingenuous, unnecessary and ill-considered manoeuvre.

A similar effort was made by Straight to force American participation in the Anglo-French-German consortium engaged in 1909 in negotiating a loan for the projected Hukuang railways from Hangchow into the Kwangtung and Szechuan provinces of China. Failing to make any impression in London the American Government turned to direct pressure on Peking. By means of using this pressure to block a Chinese grant of the Hukuang concession, the American Government was able to force the three European

Governments to admit the American banks to the consortium. The main effect of the pressure was to contribute greatly to the sequence of events which led to the 1912 Revolution in China.

This course of events was the most embarrassing to the British Government in view of the need to renew the alliance with Japan which was due to expire in 1915. The renewal of the alliance in 1905 had enabled the British among other things to withdraw all their capital ships from the Far East to face the rising menace of Germany. By 1910 the Japanese Navy had become so powerful as to make Japan wholly unassailable. Whereas, in 1905, Japanese strength was a useful means of restraining Russia from any attack on Britain's Asiatic possessions, by 1910 Britain could not afford to risk a break with Japan unless she was quite free of any anxiety as to her naval position in Europe. The anxieties aroused by this growth of Japanese seapower among the British Dominions in the Pacific, whose policy of Oriental exclusion rendered them easy victims for Japan to pick a quarrel with, were she so inclined, reinforced this argument. The breakdown in Japanese relations with the United States caused by the racialism of the Californian state legislature and the dollar diplomacy of the Taft administration made it essential for Britain to renew the Anglo-Japanese alliance only on terms which would effectively prevent its ever becoming operative against the United States.

The British thought they had found a means of securing these safeguards when President Taft publicly proposed the negotiation of a universal arbitration treaty, or, failing that, a series of bilateral arbitration treaties. Negotiations were taken up simultaneously in Washington and Tokyo, and an Anglo-American arbitration treaty was signed in August 1911, less than a month after the conclusion of a revised version of the Anglo-Japanese alliance, which specifically excluded it from operating against any nation with whom Britain had an arbitration treaty. The American Senate's failure to ratify the arbitration treaty was dealt with by a British declaration that they would still continue to act as though it were in force. This face-saving device concealed but did not eliminate the fundamental dependence of the British position in the Pacific on Japan and the United States, neither of whom Britain could afford to offend. This was to be a major source of anxiety, weakness and distraction to Britain in the post-war years.

The dilemma faced by the British Government was underlined by the effects of Japan's growing power on the British Pacific Dominions, Australia, New Zealand and Canada. Since the Dominions' participation in the South African war, a strong current of opinion in Britain had pursued the idea of creating out of the Empire a kind of super-confederation, and of enlisting the aid of the Dominions to lighten Britain's increasing burden of defence. At the 1902 Colonial Conference, the then Colonial Secretary, Joseph Chamberlain, had appealed for aid to the Dominions, depicting Britain in harsh tones as a 'weary Titan', bowed down under the 'too vast orb of its fate'. His reward was a slight increase in the subsidies paid by

Australia and New Zealand for the auxiliary squadron maintained by Britain in their waters, and their reluctant agreement to British control of these forces. The growth of Japanese strength after 1905 was viewed in Australia and New Zealand with great alarm, amounting on at least one occasion to near panic, and the US fleet was given a tumultuous welcome on its visit to Sydney in 1908.

The increasing of the German threat to British security was marked principally by the removal of the British battle squadron from Chinese waters in 1905, and it was only in 1909 that the naval agitation in Britain made a real impact on the Dominions. The result was the undertaking by Australia, New Zealand and the Federated Malay States each to provide one Dreadnought or battle cruiser for the Navy. The Admiralty, then suffering from a double anxiety as to the forthcoming end of the Anglo-Japanese alliance, argued that each Dreadnought or battle cruiser should form the nucleus of a battle squadron, of which, in all, four were contemplated, respectively for the East Indian, Australian, Far Eastern and Canadian Pacific stations. The creation of separate Dominions fleets, however, only enhanced the need for Britain to secure agreement on a unified imperial foreign policy, and in May 1911 the British Foreign Minister, Grey, made a general *exposé* to Dominions delegates of British policy and the menace Germany was felt to constitute to the heart of the Empire; he obtained their wholehearted support for the renewal of the Anglo-Japanese alliance. This consultation marked a major stage in the evolution of the old relationship between Britain and her colonies towards the modern Commonwealth. There is no necessity to consult colonies.

The renewal of the Anglo-Japanese alliance and the signature of the Anglo-American arbitration treaty relieved Britain of a pressing extra-European anxiety at precisely the moment at which Germany chose to provoke a fresh crisis with France. The occasion for this crisis was the steady disintegration of the Sultan's *régime* in Morocco, where the increasing resentment of the inland tribes against the growth of French influence in the country had led them into revolt against the *régime*. In 1910 Sultan Moulay Hajid appealed to the French for military assistance. However, the organization of this assistance had not ended the revolt, and in the spring of 1911, Moulay Hajid found himself besieged by tribesmen in Fez. His appeals to the French resulted in the organization of a French relief column which raised the siege of Fez on May 21st, 1911. The French Government was aware that this action was difficult to reconcile with the terms of the Algeciras agreement of 1906 which had reaffirmed the independence and integrity of Morocco. The central figure in the current French Cabinet, the Finance Minister, Joseph Caillaux, was an advocate of economic co-operation between Germany and France; and the French Government, under his prompting, did its best to appease the Germans in advance of the relief of Fez. But their slowness in producing serious proposals, and the parallel action of Spain in occupying two towns in the zone secretly allocated to her in the Franco-Spanish agreement of 1904,

175

led the Germans to overplay their hand out of a mixture of suspicion, misunderstanding and over-confidence. On July 1st, the German gunboat, *Panther*, arrived in Agadir, a port on Morocco's Atlantic coast, with the declared aim of protecting German interests there. This somewhat forceful statement of German interests was followed on July 15th by a demand for compensation, in the shape of the cession to Germany of the whole of the French Congo, in return for the grant of a protectorate over Morocco to France; the pill was sweetened by the offer to throw in German Togoland with Morocco as France's share of the deal.

By contrast with the crisis of 1905 the Agadir crisis provoked by these demands caused little panic in France. The Caillaux government met them with a firm refusal to cede the whole Congo, but with an apparent willingness to haggle over a detailed agreement. But in London the sheer scale of the German claims raised fears not only that Germany would secure a naval base at Agadir, but, much more seriously, that this was yet another German attempt to humiliate France and destroy the *Entente*. These fears were instrumental in bringing over to the side of the Germanophobes in the Cabinet, David Lloyd George, the most powerful and controversial figure in British domestic politics. In a speech at the Mansion House on July 21st, 1911, he issued a warning that Britain would prefer war to a European pacification achieved at the cost of her national honour. The German-French crisis in fact passed off quite smoothly with a minor Franco-German exchange of territory, and German recognition of a French protectorate over Morocco in November 1911. But its effects in Europe were quite different. In France the French nationalist and colonialist right wing raised charges of timidity against Caillaux and secured his replacement in January 1912 by the right wing chauvinist anti-German Lorrainer, Poincaré, who was determined to strengthen France against Germany.

In Britain the crisis had revealed a lack of preparation for war and a total disagreement between the Admiralty and the Army authorities on the strategy to be followed should war occur. On October 1911, Winston Churchill was appointed to the Admiralty, and thus the other great opponent of an Anglo-German naval race was converted to the need to outbuild Germany. The moment was significant. The British intervention in the Agadir crisis had enabled the German navalists to argue that a larger German fleet would have restrained Britain; and in the autumn of 1911 discussions began on a new German navy law, the *Novelle*, designed to provide Germany with a fleet two-thirds the size of the Royal Navy. Advocates of economy in both countries were able to secure one last attempt at an Anglo-German agreement before the *Novelle* was submitted to the German *Reichstag*. But the conversations held during the visit of Lord Haldane, the German-educated, Scottish-born War Minister, to Berlin in February 1912 broke down again on Germany's refusal to modify her building programme except in exchange for a British guarantee of neutrality in any war in which Germany might be embroiled. Churchill, at his most bellicose, announced Britain's intentions of building Dreadnoughts so as to maintain a superiority of 60% over the German Navy, and laying down 'two keels for one', for every supplementary ship Germany might lay down.

At the same time measures were taken to counter the other alarming element in the *Novelle*, its intimation that the vast bulk of these ships would be immediately available for action throughout the year. When taken with new increases in Austrian and Italian Dreadnought construction, the new German naval construction faced Britain with the necessity of so concentrating her battle fleets against Germany as to leave an inadequate margin of strength against Germany's allies in the Mediterranean.

The British chose to deal with this new menace in four ways. First, they appealed to the Dominions, and succeeded in persuading the Canadian Government to offer the construction of three new battleships to play the main part in an Imperial squadron to be stationed at the western mouth of the Mediterranean at Gibraltar. Secondly, they increased construction with the aim eventually of providing a Mediterranean fleet capable of matching the Austrian and Italian fleets. Thirdly, they did their best to build up the Turkish fleet, for which they had already laid down two Dreadnoughts in 1911. And finally, and most significantly, as an interim measure, they concluded in November 1912 an agreement with the French, by which the French fleet would take over the defence of the Mediterranean. As a further element in strengthening the British position the Admiralty decided to increase substantially the speed of their latest battleships by converting them from coal to oil. To secure fuel supplies, the Admiralty in 1914 bought a controlling interest in the Anglo-Persian Oil Company, formed six years earlier after the discovery of oil in commercial quantities in South-West Persia, and forced a partial agreement between Anglo-Persian and its main competitor, Royal-Dutch Shell. Their action involved Britain much more seriously in Persian politics than before, and necessitated an agreement between Britain and the South Persian tribes over which the Persian Government's control was sketchy at best, which further weakened the Persian Government's position.

These years 1910–12 were marked also by the advance of liberalism in the Iberian Peninsula. In Portugal republicanism had fed on the contrast between her mighty imperial past and the pitiful showing made by Portugal during the last stages of the scramble for Africa. As a last resort to avoid the establishment of a republic, King Carlos, in 1906, had come to entrust Franco, the strong man of the Regenerationist Party, with quasi-dictatorial powers. His rule had been brought to an end in 1908 when it was beginning to show signs of success, by the assassination of the monarch. He was succeeded by his son Manuel, a weakling of nineteen. Two years later, in October 1910, the Republicans staged a *coup d'état*, and King Manuel took refuge in Britain. Royalist uprisings followed in 1911 and 1912; but the absence of any encouragement from the exiled King made it impossible for the rebels to win the necessary public support. The revolution was in fact the last result of a political struggle for power which

177

had by 1911 largely lost its *rationale*. The new Republican *régime* was challenged almost at once by the nascent Portuguese labour movement. The ensuing labour troubles revealed the lack of any popular basis for the rather Victorian parliamentary system the Republicans now introduced. Inevitably Portuguese republicanism degenerated towards a new dictatorship.

*Chapter X*
# THE BREAKDOWN OF THE SYSTEM, 1912–1914

FROM 1909–11, the Committee of Union and Progress had remained in virtual control of the Ottoman Empire. In 1911, however, the longing of the intellectuals and would-be parliamentarians in the movement for a more constitutional *régime* threw up an opposition group, the New Party, within the Young Turk Movement. A Party Congress failed to thrash out the differences within the movement and in November 1911 the malcontents linked with other Parliamentary figures to create a separate party, the Liberal Union. At the same time venerable survivors of the Parliament of 1878 raised their voices against the Committee. The Committee's action in virtually suppressing the parliamentary opposition by calling a General Election in January 1912 and so arranging the election so that all but six of their opponents lost their seats only threw opposition back into the complicated byways from which they had themselves emerged. Young officers in Rumelia took to the hills, and a secret committee, the 'Saviour Officers', was formed in Istanbul with the aim of overthrowing the CUP and calling new and free elections. In August 1912 they ousted the Committee from power and formed a new parliamentary *régime*. But by January 1913 the *régime* had slipped so badly in resisting European pressure that the officers of the Committee were able to stage a new *coup d'état*. From June 1913 until 1918 Turkey was governed by a military *junta* headed by three men, Enver Pasha, Talat Pasha and Cemal Pasha.

Despite these internal struggles for power, the Ottoman Empire had been showing considerable signs of life and reform in the years 1909–11; so much was this so, when taken with the progress of the French occupation of Morocco, that the Italian Government, which had long had designs on Tripolitania and Cyrenaica, was gravely alarmed. In September 1911, Italy picked a quarrel with Turkey over the treatment of Italian interests in Tripolitania and declared war on her. At the outbreak of the Italo-Turkish war, an Italian invasion force landed on the coasts of the two Ottoman provinces, and in November 1911 claimed Libya to be annexed to the Italian crown. However, Italy failed to beat the Ottoman forces in Libya, which were strongly supported by the local Arab population. The Italians chose, therefore, to widen the war. In April 1912 an Italian squadron bombarded the Dardanelles, and the following month, Italian troops occupied the Dodecanese islands off the Aegean coast of Turkey. The Ottoman position in Europe meanwhile was steadily deteriorating. Clandestine negotiations with Italy, opened in July, resulted on October 18th, 1912, in the signature of the Treaty of Lausanne, by which the Turks agreed to withdraw their forces from Libya and Cyrenaica on the understanding that, once the withdrawal was complete, the Italians would withdraw from the Dodecanese.

It was, however, already too late to save what remained of Turkey in Europe. Rebellion in Albania, the increasing activity of Serbian and Bulgarian *comitadjis* in Macedonia, the ambitions of Serbia, Bulgaria, Montenegro and Greece, all combined to make the end seem imminent. The only thing needed was agreement on action against Turkey between the would-be successor states. Occasion and encouragement for this was provided by Russia, intent on repaying Austria for the humiliation of the Bosnian crisis of 1908–09 by encouraging the formation of a Balkan alliance to bar further Austrian expansion into the Balkans. The Russian Foreign Minister, Sazonov, was apparently convinced that only in this way could stability be achieved in the Balkans and a further deterioration in Russia's position in Europe be avoided. In fact, his conviction that the disintegration of the Ottoman state was only a matter of time can be seen in his disavowal of a proposal made by the Russian ambassador in Constantinople in October 1911 to secure from the Ottoman state Russian control of the Dardanelles in return for a Russian guarantee against any attack on them or adjacent Turkish territories.

Thus when Serbia and Bulgaria concluded in March 1912 an alliance against any Great Power intending to invade or attack Ottoman territories in Europe, which included secret provisions for the partition of Macedonia between them and for mediation by the Tsar in the event of any dispute, Sazonov accepted this agreement in the belief that it would act as a stabilizing factor in the Balkans. In June, an alliance between Greece and Bulgaria followed, though without any secret clauses. In August 1912, Austria and, in September, Sazonov, who suddenly panicked, asked Constantinople to accept concessions in Macedonia in order to avoid a Balkan war, but the Turks refused to make the concessions. That same month Bulgaria and Serbia decided on war, in order not to miss the favourable advantage conferred by Turkey's preoccupation with Italy. On October 8th, in a last effort to avert war, a joint Austro-Russian note was presented to the Balkan governments promising Great Power intervention to secure reforms in Macedonia. But this proposal, the last thing the Balkan states desired, came too late. The same day Montenegro jumped the gun and declared war on Turkey. Bulgarian, Serbian and Greek declarations followed ten days later.

The armies of the new Balkan states proved infinitely more effective than either European or Turkish opinion had expected. A month after the outbreak of this first Balkan war, Serbian forces had reached the Adriatic, and the Bulgarian armies closely invested the Chatalja line, the last Turkish lines of defence before Constantinople. An Albanian assembly proclaimed Albania's independence at Valona on November 28th. On December 3rd, Turkey, Bulgaria and Serbia signed an armistice; the Greek and Montenegran forces continued hostilities however, the Montenegrans besieging Scutari, the Greeks Janina. The disappearance of all but the residual extremities of Turkey in Europe confronted the Great Powers with the most serious upset the Concert of Europe had yet experienced. Before it was clear that the Turkish lines of Chatalja would hold, Russia was constrained to warn the Bulgarians against any occupation of Constantinople on pain of being fired on by the Russian fleet. But pan-Slav sentiment in Russia was such that the Russian Government felt obliged to support the Serbian claim for an outlet to the Adriatic. To this the Austrians, with Italy's support, remained adamantly opposed. The Austrian Government began preparatory military moves, and the Russians retained certain troops due for demobilization.

Peace was maintained by the good sense of all the powers confronted with the possibility of war. At Russia's suggestion, Britain called a Peace Conference; and a conference of the ambassadors of the Great Powers in London met to discuss the territorial changes which the final defeat of Turkey in Europe would involve. Austria insisted on the rights of the newly-proclaimed Albanian state to full control of all the Adriatic coast between Montenegro and Greece. In the face of this insistence British, German and French advice was able to secure Russian abandonment of her support for the most far-reaching of Serbian claims. But the Peace Conference proved unable to reach agreement on a settlement agreeable to Turkey, for whom the mere discussion of surrender of Turkish claims on Adrianople sufficed to provoke the *coup d'état* of January 1913 by the leaders of the extreme nationalists, Enver Pasha, Cemal Pasha and Talat Pasha.

The *coup d'état* in Constantinople was followed by a renewal of the war. But the new Turkish rulers were no more successful than their predecessors, and a new armistice was concluded at the end of April 1913. The Peace Conference re-opened in London on May 20th, 1913. As before, the main difficulty proved to be restraining the victors. A naval demonstration was required to secure Serbian evacuation of Durazzo and Montenegran evacuation of Scutari, two cities which Austria regarded as essential to Albania's existence. On May 30th, 1913, the Treaty of London brought to an end the first Balkan war, Turkey ceding to the victors all her European territory except a strip of about thirty miles north of the Straits, and abandoning all claims to Crete.

The division of the spoils among the victors was to lead in less than a month to the second Balkan war. The central issue was the division of Macedonia. Baulked in the Adriatic, Serbia now demanded more compensation in Macedonia than Bulgaria, dominated and terrorized by the terrorist International Macedonian Revolutionary Organization, was in any mood to grant. At the same time Greece refused to evacuate Salonica,

181

which the Bulgarians also claimed. Rumania claimed Silistria, awarded to her by an ambassadors' conference in St Petersburg on May 9th. On June 2nd, Serbia and Greece concluded a new Treaty of Alliance against Bulgaria. Encouraged to excess by Austrian attempts to build up Bulgaria against Serbia, the King of Bulgaria ordered his troops to attack both Greece and Serbia on the night of June 29th, without the knowledge of his government. This foolhardy action exposed Bulgaria to the full onslaught of all her neighbours. Rumania occupied the Dobruja. Greek troops cleared most of the Aegean littoral. Serbian troops occupied all the territory Bulgaria had gained in Macedonia. And Turkey re-entered the lists to recover her former territory up to and including Adrianople. Defeated on all sides, Bulgaria was forced to sue for peace. The Treaty of Bucharest, signed on August 20th, 1913, deprived her of the major part of her gains in Macedonia and in Thrace as well as all the Dobruja. A separate Treaty of Constantinople, signed on September 29th, 1913, with Turkey, confirmed the Turkish re-occupation of Adrianople and set the frontier on the Maritza river.

There followed a similar period of megalomania on the part of Serbia and Greece in connection with their continuing occupation of Albanian territory. Serbian intransigence on the frontiers when set against the mildness of Serbian reassurances to Austria provoked the gravest of suspicions in Vienna, and led, in October 1913, to the dispatch of a direct Austrian ultimatum to Belgrade demanding the evacuation of Albania. Faced with this direct threat, Serbia withdrew her troops, but it was to take another six months to settle the Albanian frontier with Greece, and even then the dispute over the Aegean islands remained unsettled.

This series of defeats at the hands of their former subjects could only enhance the tendency of the new Turkish *régime* towards centralism and Turkism noted in Chapter VIII and increase the strain on relations between the dominant Turkish *élite* and the other races of the empire. The worst sufferers were to be the Armenians whose own reliance on terrorism was to make them only too vulnerable to similar methods. In brief, their presence in villages inextricably interwoven into the Anatolian heartland of Turkey made their nationalist claims, their Christian faith and their links with the west insupportable to the Young Turks. From 1912 onwards the Turks embarked on a policy of deliberate repression of the Armenians, which was to culminate, under the spur of war, in the terrible massacres of 1915–17 in which an estimated million and a half Armenians perished.

With the Arabs, the Young Turk leaders had to be more subtle. Various abortive military measures, as described in Chapter VIII, were undertaken to deal with the peripheral chiefs of the Yemen, Asir and the Nejd. Negotiations were opened through his son Abdullah, one of the surviving Arab delegates to the Turkish parliament, with Hussein, the Sharif of Mecca. In April 1914 Turkish pressure drove Abdullah to approach the British Governor-General of Egypt, Lord Kitchener, to ask, unsuccessfully, for arms for defence against the Turks. This pressure eased somewhat the same month when, in a scene reminiscent of Canossa, the Turkish governor of the Hejaz, being under instructions from the Turkish government who did not wish to alienate Hussein entirely, was forced to kiss the Sharif's robe. But the Turkish determination not to tolerate Arab pretensions was shown by their stiffening attitude to the Arab nationalists of Syria, the Lebanon and Palestine and of the Arab exile.

In January 1913, immediately before the Young Turks' *coup d'état*, a Committee of Reform was formed in Beirut to demand both the recognition of Arabic as a language of state for the province of the Lebanon and a high degree of decentralization to the provincial level. Similar demonstrations elsewhere in the Arab provinces led the new leaders of the Turkish government to announce various decentralizing measures in May. In June 1913, an Arab Congress met in Paris under the auspices of the Decentralization Party, and the secret society, *al Fatat*. The Turkish junta immediately entered into negotiations with the Arab Congress leaders, offering to include three Arab ministers in the Cabinet, to appoint five Arab governors of provinces and to concede the use of Arabic as a language of instruction in the elementary schools. Once the leadership had been won over, however, these concessions were withdrawn, and a decree of August 1913 scaled down or rescinded all the promised concessions.

In the international field, the new Turkish junta's resentment of their defeats turned them to further measures of modernization of their armed forces. In the naval sphere they turned to Britain, the leading naval power, who had in fact been maintaining a naval mission in Constantinople, at their request, since 1908. In 1911 two Dreadnoughts were to be built for Turkey in British yards, and in early 1913 a project of selling Turkey two pre-Dreadnoughts of the *Royal Sovereign* class was discussed between the two countries.

In the military field, the Turks naturally turned to the leading power on land, Germany. In June 1913, General Liman von Sanders was named head of a military mission of forty-two German officers to train the Turkish army. The Turkish government chose to appoint him a member of the Turkish War Council, to grant him the rank and powers of a general in the Turkish army and to give him command of the First Turkish Army Corps which was guarding Russia's Black Sea life-line to the outside world, the Black Sea Straits. In November, the news of his appointment became known to the Russians. Protests couched in the strongest language were made in Constantinople and Berlin. For a time military measures were apparently contemplated; but milder counsels prevailed, which was just as well for Russia as her army turned out to be unprepared for hostilities. In January 1914, Germany and Turkey agreed to promote Liman von Sanders to Field Marshal in the Turkish army and thus remove him from direct command over the Straits. This brought the crisis to an amicable end. The incident, however, left a lasting impression of German enmity on the mind of the Russian Foreign Minister, Sazonov, an impression which was to play its fateful part in the events of July 1914.

Nor was this the end of the deplorable consequences of the second Balkan war. Rumania had been bound to Germany and Austria-Hungary by a secret alliance since 1883, and the alliance was in fact renewed in February 1913. But the role of Germany and Austria in supporting Bulgaria during the second Balkan war had caused a great deal of annoyance and resentment in Bucharest. In the autumn of 1913, at the instance of the Austrian heir-apparent, Count Czernin was sent as ambassador to Rumania to attempt to win her support against Serbia. But Czernin found himself confronted with a series of complaints about the treatment of the Rumanian minority in Transylvania by the Magyars; the King of Rumania proved unwilling to acknowledge the secret alliance in public or to lend himself to Austrian schemes for a Rumano-Bulgar-Greek coalition against Serbia. Instead he laid himself open to encouragement from the French and Russian ministers, encouragement which culminated in a visit by the Tsar to Constanza in June 1914 and discussion of a possible marriage of one of the Tsar's daughters to the Rumanian Crown Prince, Carol. Rumania's adherence to the central powers was clearly one of form only. The unhappy Austrians also managed at this time to offend their Italian allies by announcing measures designed to strengthen their own position in the Mediterranean as well as that of their new creation, Albania. All in all the Balkan wars had been an unmitigated disaster for the Habsburg monarchy.

The events of 1912–13 had, on the whole, responded remarkably well to the procedures of the Concert of Europe. But 1914 was to prove that its fundaments had been shaken beyond hope of their functioning again. Austria-Hungary felt herself encircled by enemies intent on disrupting her internal order. Germany revealed a growing anti-Slav feeling and an increasing readiness to back Austria-Hungary against Russia without enquiring too closely into the merits of any particular issue. Britain still seemed capable of playing a mediator's role, but only when no direct quarrel between France and Germany was involved, and there had been no diminution in French suspicion of Germany, rather the reverse. Perhaps the worst feature of the Balkan crisis was the increasing difficulty the civilian elements in the three eastern empires were having in controlling their military commanders. They were to prove incapable of resisting the demands of the military for more armaments. In January 1913, a new arms race began on the European continent.

Once again the prime offender was Germany, or rather the German General Staff. In 1911 and again in 1912 they had insisted upon a larger German army. In January 1913 they demanded the formation of three new army corps. Although this demand was resisted on financial grounds, legislation passed in the *Reichstag* in July 1913 increased the peace-time army by 100,000 men at once, a figure which was to rise to 150,000, giving a total of 810,000 men by October 1914. The strain on Germany's financial resources was such that her naval construction programme had to be drastically cut, and Admiral Tirpitz attempted to make a virtue of necessity by offering to accept the ration of sixteen capital ships to every ten German ships proposed the previous year by Winston Churchill.

But Britain, now worried over Austrian and Italian construction, was in no mood to accept a proposal made *before* the passage of Germany's 1912 bill and based not on post-Dreadnought construction as Tirpitz made it, but on a figure which included Britain's overwhelming superiority in pre-Dreadnought ships. Britain's programme for 1913 added five new super-Dreadnoughts to the Fleet, the ill-fated *Royal Sovereign* Class. In addition, Churchill announced the formation of an Imperial squadron formed of the New Zealand, the Malayan and the three projected Canadian battleships. As an alternative, Churchill renewed his proposal for a 'building holiday' in capital ships, a sop to the radicals in his party. However, the proposal was indignantly rejected by Germany. The German rejection led Churchill to warn in October 1913 that the naval estimates for 1914 would have to be markedly increased (the Canadian Senate had meanwhile rejected the proposal to build three Canadian Dreadnoughts). And a bitter battle ensued both within and outside the Cabinet. As a result Churchill only succeeded in securing the four battleships of the 1914 programme by greatly cutting the light cruiser construction, creating a deficiency in this class which was to show itself markedly once war had begun.

More serious for the peace of Europe were the repercussions of the German army increases. In Russia, under the additional impact of the Liman von Sanders crisis, the Tsarist government adopted at the end of the year a vast new army programme, designed to make good the deficiencies revealed in munitions and artillery and to add half a million men to the one million three hundred thousand already under arms.

The reaction to the German army increases was faster in France than in Russia. In July 1913 the new French President, Poincaré, called for a credit of five hundred million francs and an increase in the length of army service from two to three years as a means of matching the lower French birthrate of the classes of 1895 onwards, now being called to the colours, with the intake of conscripts from the same classes in Germany. The increase gave France 790,000 men under arms on January 1st, 1914. It was bitterly fought in the French parliament and press and opened the way for a pronounced movement of French opinion towards the Radical and Socialist parties, united, as they were, on an anti-militarist platform. In December 1913 the patriotic Barthou ministry was overthrown and replaced by a middle of the road ministry including Caillaux, who had voted against the three year term of service.

Austria-Hungary followed the Russian increase in armaments in March 1914, raising her annual intake from 175,000 to 200,000 men. In 1912–13 staff talks also began between the High Commands of the Triple Alliance. A naval agreement was reached between Austria and Italy in June 1913 on operations against France. Italian anxieties in Libya delayed the conclusion of a military agreement, and one was still under consideration in June 1914. But in the course of the discussions the German and Austrian

Chiefs of Staff agreed in May 1914 that 'any procrastination' in the opening of a war against the Triple *Entente* 'led to a lessening of our chances'; they also expressed a good deal of scepticism of Italy's readiness to march, correctly as it happened, since the Italian Chief of Staff proved totally ignorant of the foreign policy position then being occupied by Italy's political chiefs. The increases in the effectiveness of the Russian army were agreed by the Italian Chief of Staff as well as his allied partners to increase the chances of defeat every year. And it was he, in fact, who in these conversations first voiced, in April 1914, the idea of a pre-emptive strike against the Triple *Entente*.

The increasing intransigence of the militarists in the Great Powers was in part a consequence of, in part given the lie by, the immense growth in strength of the radical, conciliationist, internationalist, often anti-militarist forces in each country. There is a good deal to be said for the view that the principal cause of the tragic European breakdown in July 1914 was the inability of the democratic forces in central and eastern Europe to establish control over the militarist elements in their society and the abdication of the autocrats not to their loyal democratic subjects but to their irresponsible military advisers. Under the French and British systems, the soldiers were at least formally under the control of the civilian cabinets and parliaments, though even here the events of 1914–18 were severely to try that control. The main danger came from an alliance of soldiers with the political nationalists of the right. In Italy, as we have seen, the Italian Chief of Staff was kept totally in ignorance of his government's foreign policy. In the eastern autocracies, the control of the armed forces was vested in the position of the autocrat alone, who could back Chancellor against Chief of Staff or *vice versa*, providing he had the personality to remain in control. In 1914, to Europe's eternal loss, neither the Kaiser nor the Tsar possessed that degree of personality, and the oldest of the three, Franz Josef, no longer cared.

This does not mean that the democratic anti-militarist reaction was without interest. It was certainly strong enough to preclude in every power save Austria-Hungary the idea of pre-emptive war. Its growth was in fact impressive. In France, the appointment of the Doumergue cabinet and Caillaux did not stem the flood. The general elections of April – May 1914 produced an increase in Socialist strength of 34 seats to 102 and a Radical party of over 160. President Poincaré's efforts to keep a ministry committed to the three year term of service were ignominiously defeated and on June 14th, the ex-socialist, Viviani, took office with a compromise cabinet. On June 28th, the murder of Franz Ferdinand was to render his efforts superfluous.

In Italy, events were following a parallel course, though with much more violent reactions than those in France, owing to the weaker state of Italy's liberal-radical constitutional parties of centre and left. In 1911, Giolitti, the veteran radical leader, had increased the electorate from three to eight million, by introducing what was virtually universal male suffrage for all above the age of thirty. As in France, the previous years had seen the growth of an extreme Right dedicated to the ideas of violence, authoritarianism and expansion abroad. And as in France, the years 1911–12 produced a great rise in jingoist nationalism throughout Italy. This expressed itself not simply in support for Italian participation in the arms race but also for the Libyan adventure, and this manifestation of imperialist nationalism on the right was to produce an equally violent reaction among its opponents. The Socialist party swung violently to the left, rejecting any collaboration with a parliamentary system that could so easily be won for *bourgeois* imperialism; so violently that the reformist wing was expelled, and the young revolutionary, Benito Mussolini, was pitchforked into the editorship of the party newspaper, *Avanti*.

In 1913, therefore, the elections in Italy were to produce a rise in the Socialist vote so as to give the party 78 seats and a full quarter of the total vote cast. The middle class radical vote rose proportionately, forcing the dominant liberal leadership under Giolitti into a coalition with the clericalists to maintain themselves in power. This coalition broke down in February 1914 with the withdrawal of radical support, and in June 1914 popular discontent broke out in a wave of violent strikes and peasant risings. Bologna, Ancona and other towns declared themselves independent communes and a republic was declared in the Romagna. Violence bred violence and the new cabinet of Salandra put down the risings with great severity. It was to prove even more nationalist than the coalition it had superseded.

In Germany, the introduction of the armaments programme of 1912 in the *Reichstag* had been accompanied by elections which made the Socialist party with 110 seats the single largest party, and in the subsequent election of a President and Vice-President for the new assembly, a Progressive was elected President, and for a brief period a Socialist was elected Vice-President with some National Liberal support. In November 1913 an incident between the military garrison of the Alsatian town of Zabern and the civilian population produced an outburst of indignation against the Army, the officer Junker class and the system they embodied, which showed how desperately devoid of support they were in Germany as a whole. By a majority of 293 to 54, the *Reichstag* censured the actions of the Government. Only the onset of war was to rally the nation to the support of Imperial Germany again.

Even in Russia a similar reaction against the system could be traced. By 1914 nearly one and a half million industrial workers were on strike. A growing Great Russianism in the Dumas and in the administration and a relentless rise in Russification led to an increase in anti-Russian sentiments among the subject nationalities. The election of the fourth Duma in 1912, despite gerrymandering and widespread corruption, saw a growth in the Cadets and the left from 87 seats to 123, and a corresponding growth in the nationalist Right from 127 to 145 seats. The victims of this squeeze were, as in Italy, the conservative centre, the Octobrists whose vote fell from 154 to 121 seats. The Social Democratic share dropped slightly from 17 to 13 seats.

The growth in the extreme right was due in part to heavy Tsarist subsidy. But the extremists were far from being creatures of the *régime*, being as or more radical in their nationalism as the Social Democrats were in their socialism. Loyalty as such figured far lower on the rightists' scale of virtues than among traditional conservatives, and failure or defeat remained as dangerous for the Tsar and the *régime* as ever. Among the aristocracy an additional factor augmented the opposition to the *régime*. This opposition stemmed from the increasing dominance exercised over Tsar and Tsarina by the drunken and lascivious peasant monk, Rasputin, through the effectiveness of his unusual hypnotic powers on the haemophilia of the Tsarevich, the heir to the throne.

In Austria-Hungary discontent with the system expressed itself as always in a sharpening of the demands of the various national groupings. In the 1911 elections the ministerial parties, especially the Christian Socialists and the Poles, sustained severe losses. The Social Democrats saw the virtually total secession of their Czech wing and showed themselves as violent as any once the new *Reichstag* met. The German *National Verband*, a coalition of nationalistically inclined parties, saw a considerable increase in their strength. Italians, Slovenes and Ruthenes displayed increasing resistance to the Habsburg *régime* and there was an ominous growth among the Ruthenes of secessions from the Uniate Church, which though orthodox in rite, acknowledged the supremacy of the Pope, and was therefore in some way identified with the Habsburg monarchy, to the Russian Orthodox Church. In late 1913 the police of Austria and Hungary arrested a considerable number of Ruthenes on charges of conspiring to unify the Ruthenian areas with Russia.

Among the Czechs there was a marked growth in neo-Slavism, a version of pan-Slavism which saw Austria's Slav population as the leaders of the Slavs against the German menace. Kramář was the uncrowned leader of Slav Bohemia. The realist, western-looking Masaryk was important only in the effectiveness of his own personal interventions into Hapsburg politics, his party being a comparatively minor splinter group. Yet apart from Masaryk no section of Czech opinion took seriously the idea of secession from the Habsburg state. Among the southern slavs, secessionism and union with Serbia were sentiments often encountered, but the dominant opinion sought a Trialist solution, a separate Slav kingdom within the Empire, which would transform the Dual into a Triple Monarchy.

In Hungary, the 1910 elections had brought to power a revived and reconstituted Liberal party under the title of the party of National Work. Its directing genius, Count Tisza, who became premier in June 1913, was determined to maintain the link with the Habsburg crown and restore the dominance of the Government over Parliament. The Magyar separatists were routed in debate, their filibustering tactics effectively ended. Though the franchise was extended, it was done so on a combination of educational, occupational and property qualifications which still disenfranchised the labouring and artisan classes, small farm-owners and traders and the lowest levels of the salaried class and this prevented the non-Magyars from effectively challenging Magyar supremacy. But despite Tisza's victory over the separatist elements in Parliament, separatism and Hungarian nationalism remained as sentiments so deeply rooted in the Hungarian people that Tisza could not afford to ignore or contravene them.

In Croatia, the era of the Balkan wars saw a new outbreak of separatist nationalism, after the passage of a bill widening the franchise slightly in 1910. In April 1912, the constitution of Croatia was suspended by the Magyar viceroy, in the face of a two-thirds majority in the Diet hostile to the administration. Extremists, one a Bosnian student, in contact with a Serbian secret society, the *Black Hand*, twice attempted to assassinate the Viceroy. But Tisza, replacing their target by a new Viceroy (who was himself gravely wounded by an extremist shortly after taking office), managed in the last months of 1913 to assuage Croatian feelings sufficiently to make it possible for the constitution to be restored and new elections for the Diet held. Despite a further attempt, again by a Bosnian student with connections in Belgrade, on the Viceroy's life, Croatian opinion was much quieter in the first months of 1914. Count Tisza did not, however, feel strong enough to make any real concessions to the Rumanian and Ruthenian minorities in eastern Hungary, and the state of agitation and suppression in the Rumanian inhabited areas of Transylvania did a good deal to influence the *rapprochement* between Rumania and Russia mentioned earlier in this chapter. Tisza's skill, ruthlessness and courage were capable of controlling the nationalist fervour of his own and the other national groups under Magyar rule, but not of reconciling them to it. There were those who believed that with time this could be achieved, but time was the one element Tisza could not dispose of.

The tides of liberal reformism and countervailing nationalism were at their strongest in Britain, where, by June 1914, the nation was on the edge of civil war and its army had been shaken by mutiny. The Liberal programme of 1912 had included a bill setting up a Parliament in Dublin to be entirely responsible for Irish domestic affairs, including those of the six largely Protestant counties of Ulster. The bill, vigorously fought by the Conservatives in the Commons amidst scenes of near-riotous disorder, was passed in January 1913 and was sent to the House of Lords where it was inevitably rejected. Under the new Parliament Act it needed therefore only to be passed again by the Commons in the sessions 1912–13 and 1913–14, that is, without any new General Election having to be called, to become law.

In July 1913, the new leader of the Conservative and Unionist party, a Scots Canadian, Bonar Law, who had succeeded Balfour in 1912, promised Conservative support to any measure of resistance Ulster might take. In September 1913 a mass meeting of Ulster supporters near Belfast signed a

'Covenant' pledging themselves to use 'all means which may be necessary to defeat the present conspiracy to set up a Home Rule Parliament in Ireland'. Steps were taken to raise, drill and arm the 'Ulster volunteers', a force of about 100,000 men. And the War Office and the officer corps of the Army generally, where Ulstermen had always played a disproportionately large role, saw themselves faced with a situation in which they might have either to enforce Home Rule and shoot down their fellow countrymen or refuse to obey orders and commit mutiny. In March 1914, as the Government felt it wise to take precautionary military dispositions against a possible rising in Ulster, the large majority of officers of the 3rd Cavalry brigade, already in Ireland at the Curragh, replied to questions put by the Army Commander in Ireland that they would sooner be dismissed from the Army than take part in operations against Ulster. The question was hypothetical, as no orders for operations against Ulster had been issued or drafted; but the subsequent parliamentary and cabinet crisis gravely shook the morale of both army and country alike.

The new King, George V, brought the political leaders of both parties together, but was unable to make any headway against those on the Conservative side who saw their task not so much as that of preventing Home Rule coming about as that of using the issue to overthrow the Liberal party and reverse the course of the parliamentary revolution the Liberals had set in motion. The counter-revolutionaries, led by two prominent lawyer-politicians, Sir Edward Carson and F. E. Smith, used conciliatory language in Parliament. But in April 1914 they ran into Ulster a large consignment of arms purchased from Germany, the country which they professed to believe the biggest threat of all to Britain's imperial position. Talks continued, on the basis of a temporary exclusion of Ulster from the terms of the Home Rule Bill (which was in the course of passage through the Commons for the crucial third time, after which it would become law despite the veto of the House of Lords), but the Conservative and Unionist leadership only supported such a solution in the expectation that it would be rejected by the Irish nationalists, and the bill therefore would become void. On the day the news of the Austrian ultimatum to Serbia was received, the Cabinet were still earnestly debating the Irish issue, and civil war in Ireland still seemed only a hairsbreadth away. Irish opinion was moving steadily away from the parliamentary nationalist party and towards those extremists who since the 1860s had been asserting that only violence and murder would rid Ireland of Anglo-Saxon rule.

The growth of the Home Rule crisis, with its increasing evidence of Army support for the Conservative-Unionist position, was accompanied by a parallel growth in strength of the radical, anti-militarist, anti-imperialist wing of the Liberal party. As noted above, the naval estimates of 1913 and 1914 ran into considerable opposition both inside the Cabinet and parliament, led by the radical Chancellor of the Exchequer, Lloyd George. There was a corresponding easing of Anglo-German tension as a result of the revived co-operation between Britain and Germany during the Balkan crisis of 1912–13. In this atmosphere, a new Anglo-German colonial agreement on the future of the Portuguese colonies in Africa was initialled in October 1913, in view of the expected break-up of Portugal's colonial empire as a consequence of the revolution in Portugal. Negotiations for a settlement of the long-standing dispute over the German-planned Baghdad railway took longer to conclude, but they too were brought into an agreement in June 1914. Most important for the European balance of power, however, was the thwarting by parliamentary opposition of a Russian move to conclude a naval staff convention with Britain similar to that concluded between France and Britain. In July 1914 the bulk of Liberal opinion in Britain was as pro-German as it was anti-Russian.

These movements of liberal-radical opinion against militarism and imperialism in Britain, France, Germany and Italy were paralleled by the growth in activity and concern with the avoidance of war on the part of the Socialist International. Since its foundation in 1900 the Socialist International had gone through two successive stages. In the first, from 1900–06, it had principally been concerned with the fight against party disunity, that is against revisionism and reformism in Germany and for a unification of the various socialist parties in France. With this achieved in 1906, and under the shock of the first Moroccan crisis of 1905–06 with its threat of war in Europe for the first time in thirty years, the Socialist International turned to discovering ways and means of preventing war. At the Stuttgart conference of 1907 and again at Copenhagen (1910), Basle (1912) and Berne (1913), there were repeated discussions of proposals for calling an international general strike, the moment any power began to mobilize its forces. The main resistance to such proposals came from the German leadership, who, while agreeing with their opposites in France, Britain and the western democracies that war in Europe could only be imperialist in origin, had distinct reservations on the subject of war with Tsarist Russia, the embodiment in their eyes of autocracy and barbarism. Such resistance delayed the passage by these conferences of resolutions which would unequivocally commit the constituent parties to industrial action to thwart war; but the Basle conference passed a manifesto of action against the Balkan wars, and at Berne the French and German delegates discussed a settlement of the Alsace-Lorraine question.

The years 1910–13 saw similar movements for progressive reform, if not revolution, in the United States, in Mexico and in the Chinese empire. In each case, however, their effect was, in international terms, to reinforce their differences, their separation from the main stream of European civilization. In America, the Progressive movement had been markedly growing in strength since the Presidency of Theodore Roosevelt. As noted in Chapter III, it combined in its beginning two potentially contradictory strands in American political thought, a belief in 'direct' democracy, which inevitably made its protagonists suspicious of too great a growth in the powers of the central government, and a conviction that in the strengthening of the powers of a democratically-elected government and the capture of the legislative power from the alliance of corrupt politicians and large-scale business interests lay the only hope of a preservation of American democracy against the growth of a capitalist oligarchy or plutarchy. The Progressive's belief in direct democracy was expressed in the evolution of various devices such as the referendum, the initiative, the recall, direct primaries to select political candidates and direct election of Senators, designed to bring back to politics the direct contact between political leaders and the citizen body of the town meetings of revolutionary America. By 1914 over twenty States had adopted the initiative and the referendum, and ten the recall. Two-thirds of all the States had adopted the direct primary in State elections, and in 1913 the Seventeenth Amendment made direct election of Senators part of the American Constitution. Increasing numbers of posts in the Civil Service were being put beyond the scope of political appointment; municipal home rule and commission government were placing city government beyond the reach of corruption.

In 1910, however, the conflict between this belief in direct democracy and the concomitant drive to strengthen the powers of the Federal Government as the only means of taking progressivism from the state to the national level, broke into the open. The leadership in provoking this conflict was taken by Theodore Roosevelt, who, in the two years since his resignation of the Presidency to Taft, had evolved a long way from his old hesitancy. He allied himself that year with the progressive wing of the Republican party in proclaiming what he called the 'New Nationalism', the essence of which was a whole-hearted use of central government powers to serve social justice and alter existing economic relationships. His intervention was never supported by the Republican rank-and-file and was bitterly opposed by the party bosses. And failing to capture the party's nomination for the Presidential election of 1912, he broke away and founded his own, the 'Bull Moose' party, taking with him most of the out-and-out Progressive wing of the party. The Democrats, themselves divided between a party machine candidate and the perennial candidate of the Populists, William Jennings Bryan, adopted as their compromise candidate, the democratic conservative, Woodrow Wilson, Governor since 1910 of New Jersey. An electoral minority (42%) gave him and his party all but eight States in the Electoral College, 290 to 145 seats in the House of Representatives, 51 to 49 seats in the Senate and 21 State Governorships; and once in power he initiated a campaign of major reforms comparable in American terms only to that of the British Liberal party between 1909 and 1912.

As a reformer, however, Wilson was hampered by his respect for the rights of the States and his belief in the essential rightness of the normal processes of American politics, providing they were used in a democratic way. He distrusted the new nationalism of Theodore Roosevelt as being essentially paternalistic; and his remedy for the concentrations of economic power against which Roosevelt had campaigned was not to develop the powers of government on a comparable scale but the more traditional

American approach which called for the dispersal of power and reduction in size through anti-trust legislation. He believed in the 'organization of the common interest', 'the people' against the 'special interests' who were corrupting American democracy; and the two themes of respect for States' rights, and belief in the unalterable virtue of the common people given strong executive leadership were central both to his domestic and his foreign policy.

His reform programme consisted essentially of four proposals, the reduction of tariffs, the reform of the banking system, the introduction of income tax and the regulation of business. The first he carried by a bold campaign of public oratory against the pressures of all those special interests which had grown up behind the tariff barrier. But to reform the banking system was much more difficult. The issues involved did not lend themselves easily to being dramatized in public, and his own dislike of centralization of economic power restrained him from the radical reforms really required to make the system effective and invulnerable to panic. A casualty in his banking legislation was the easing of farm credit, so much a part of the agrarian programme; he did not feel strong enough for the head-on collision with the banking interests necessary to force this through. In the regulation of business the main items on his programme were the establishment of the Federal Trade Commission in 1914 to prevent unfair methods of competition, the Clayton Anti-Trust Act, and the Rayburn Securities Act, defeated in the Senate and not reintroduced. To carry these proposals through he felt obliged to make his peace with the machine politicians. The principal figure in the Progressive wing of the Democratic party, Louis Brandeis, the natural candidate for the Secretaryship of Justice, was therefore excluded from office.

Comparison with both the reform programmes of European liberal and radical movements and with the platform on which Theodore Roosevelt had campaigned underlines the gap which divided Wilson's reforms from the mainstream of European radicalism at this period. Wilson used the language of radical anti-capitalism in Europe; but his programme displayed none of its concern for social justice, none of its determination to attack the economic foundations of capitalism, none of its identification with the organization of the working class. Government in Wilson's view should be concerned with regulation. Individuals rather than institutions were to be penalized for the infliction of social injustice. Liberty rather than equality was his concern. And his views on tariffs and trade struck European observers as being those of a mid-nineteenth century Liberal. In this Europeans were mistaking the basis on which his position had been attained. He shared with the Manchester school their belief in the essential pacifying nature of free trade. But his objections to tariffs and to trade subsidies were less economic than political, being directed against the distortions of power that were introduced when the Federal government became the tool of particular interests. His foreign policy like his trade policy stemmed essentially from his belief in the rightness of the common

193

people if given strong and disinterested leadership. It was in this field that he was to suffer his worst defeats and disappointments.

The greatest disasters of his career in foreign affairs were to be deferred until the year 1919 towards the end of his second term. But they were foreshadowed in his Mexican policy, where he came for the first time into conflict with radical nationalism. Revolution had in fact broken out in Mexico in May 1911, nearly two years before Wilson came to power. Its origins were complex, its occasion, a loss of nerve and judgment on the part of the dictator, Porfirio Diaz, too simple; the revolution swept away the dictatorship without offering anyone of real strength to put in his place. Those who made the revolution, and made the Liberal, Francisco Madero, President, came at first, almost without exception, from that small property-owning class which Diaz himself represented but barred from power. But the forces they used: the discontent of the copper mine and mill workers, whose strikes had been so bloodily repressed in 1906–07; the land-hunger of the peasants; the ambitions of the discontented and underpaid military; the resentment of the Mestizos and the Indians against the Church and the Creole aristocracy which oppressed and exploited them; these proved far more than Madero could control. What began virtually as a palace revolution among the dominant social *élite* swiftly developed into a prolonged civil war. This conflict was greatly complicated both by the interventionist anxieties of the major foreign investors, who wanted to find and back some strong man, capable of re-imposing order and national stability, and by the traditions of brigandage to which agrarian rebellion so often turned once its chances of success had disappeared. Almost immediately, agrarian risings broke out in the south, of which the most famous was led by Emiliano Zapata. Madero himself was compromised by the greed of his relations, who took the adage 'to the victors belong the spoils' only too seriously. And in February 1913, General Huerta, Madero's senior officer, seized power for himself and had Madero executed.

It was at this moment that Woodrow Wilson took office as President of the United States. The Huerta *régime* was immediately accorded recognition by Britain and most of the other military powers. But Wilson, revolted by the judicial murder of Madero, refused recognition to Huerta's *régime*, on the grounds that Huerta's claim to represent Mexico's legitimate government rested on force and not on the consent of the governed. Huerta, however, obstinately refused to fall, and in considerable exasperation, Wilson eventually, in April 1914, provoked an incident in the port of Vera Cruz and landed marines. From this *impasse*, he was rescued by the mediation of the three major South American powers, Argentina, Brazil and Chile. And a deal concluded with the British government the previous autumn secured the gradual withdrawal of British support from the Huerta *régime*. In August 1914, Huerta fled Mexico, and the vacant reins of power were seized by the American candidate, a landowner from the north, Venustiano Carranza. But this was far from the end of this troubled

194

chapter in American-Mexican relations. It is worth noting that Wilson's determination, in his own words, 'to teach the South American republics to elect good men', led him, despite his denunciation of dollar diplomacy, and his desire, proclaimed in March 1913, to 'cultivate the friendship and deserve the confidence of our sister republics of central and south America', to a much more far-reaching policy of intervention in the affairs of the Caribbean and Central American republics than that practised by his predecessor. The virtual protectorate over Nicaragua was continued. In the Dominican Republic American intervention to secure free and democratic elections led eventually, in 1916, to a military occupation of the island which was to last eight years. At the other end of the island, American warships and troops intervened to keep order in Haiti in January 1914, and, the following year intervened again to establish by treaty what was in all but name a protectorate over the island. Their intervention was to give the island fifteen years of comparatively efficient and orderly government.

But these blessings are more normally used to defend colonial rule of the kind the Wilson administration usually denounced as 'interested and self-seeking' when practised by the colonial powers of Europe. Wilsonian interventionism was more high-minded than that of his Republican predecessors—and in many ways was probably in the best interests of the populations of the weak, ill-governed and poverty-stricken states on whom it was practised. Only it was difficult to reconcile with Bryan's and Wilson's view of international justice and impossible to reconcile with the aspirations and anxieties of the Latin Americans. Nor was it in the long run effective in solving the internal political difficulties of the Caribbean and Central American states. As an instrument of progress colonialism has to be full-blooded, generously and forcefully applied over a prolonged period of time. Otherwise it is apt to secure order not by removing the internal causes of disorder but merely by putting them into suspended animation, to revive when the source of external control is removed.

Mexico was not the only state to slip at this time from the control of the Great Powers into a civil war which was to lead at length to its standing on its own feet. A similar case, that of China, proved to be far more decisive in its long-term implications for the world balance of power. By 1912, the effects of the reform programme undertaken by the Manchu emperor in 1905 had begun to make their mark. In 1908, one of the last acts of the emperor before his death had been to issue a decree outlining a proposed constitution including the introduction of parliamentary government in China by 1917. The emperor was succeeded by his three year old nephew, the Regency being exercised by the new emperor's father, Prince Ch'un. The next year, provincial assemblies were convened, and in 1910, the proposed National Assembly was called in its turn, with half its delegates elected, half appointed by the Prince Regent.

The new National Assembly's main role was to oppose further Chinese involvement with European finance and to urge the participation of Chinese finance in the development of the Chinese railway system. In 1911, the central government nationalized the main Chinese-owned railway running into Szechwan as a preliminary to its development with funds provided by the European Consortium. Risings followed in Szechwan, where local feeling was inflamed against further European investment, and on the middle Yangtse, and the Prince Regent in despair turned to the principal military reformer, Yuan Shih-kai, to re-establish order. Yuan, a man of devouring ambitions, used the invitation of the Manchu court to establish himself as Premier of the provincial Parliament, and to seize full powers from the dynasty, while at the same time opening negotiations with the rebels. In February 1912, he forced the abdication of the Manchu dynasty and his own appointment as President of the new Chinese republic; a representative of Sun Yat-sen's T'ung Meng Hui was appointed as Prime Minister.

At this stage, the control of China was divided between three main forces. In the south, especially in the maritime provinces, control was exercised by followers of Sun Yat-sen, or by military leaders sympathetic to him. In the north, Yuan Shih-kai's control was nearly absolute. In the western provinces, power lay in the hands of the provincial military governors who tended to exercise it as they saw fit. At this stage, the leaders of the T'ung Meng Hui, now transformed into the Kuomintang (Nationalist) party, came to regret their first backing of Yuan Shih-kai. After the elections of the winter of 1912–13 had made the Kuomintang the majority party in both Chambers of the main Chinese parliament, Yuan viewed the Nationalists as the strongest enemy to his own autocratic ambitions. However, Yuan was fortunate early in 1913 in negotiating from the European consortium a new loan of over $100 million. In March therefore he had the parliamentary leader of the Kuomintang assassinated. In mid-July the pro-Kuomintang generals in the south rose in revolt. They proved unable to stand up to Yuan's superior military and financial resources. In November 1913 Yuan outlawed the party, and in January 1914 dissolved parliament. In May 1914 he introduced a new constitution which, by purporting to model itself on that of the United States, established Yuan as virtual dictator in China. He had achieved the recognition of the Great Powers. But this was not to prove of much avail to him after August 1914 had concentrated their attention on Europe, and left him alone and weak to face the anxiety-prompted imperialism of Japan, for whom a strong and united China would mean an end to her hopes of pre-eminence in the Far East.

*Chapter XI*
THE ONSET OF WAR

*The Mood of Europe in 1914*

SINCE the early years of the new century, the intellectual and philosophical movements dominant in 1900 had been challenged by a whole cluster of new movements which stressed all that those they challenged had suppressed. As argued in Chapter II, those movements dominant in philosophy and intellectual life in 1900 had been rationalist and positivist, while those dominant in music, art, architecture and literature had been romantic and intuitive. There was now to be a curious reversal. Rationalism and positivism were to be challenged by pragmatism and intuitive philosophy, while in the arts the great romantic traditions were to be challenged by the restoration of an intellectual aesthetic interested first of all in form and formal relationships. These challenges were to lead, especially among the arts, to a half-century of internecine warfare, in the course of which the gap between the participants on both sides and their public was to widen to an almost impassable chasm.

The origins of these challenges lay in the decades before 1900. The critical developments in many fields seem to cluster around the years 1905 or later. It was in this year that Sigmund Freud published his *Three Essays on the Theory of Sexuality*, perhaps the most effective embodiment of his exploration of the unconscious, outlined in his earlier *Interpretation of Dreams*, and his consequent emphasis on the pre-eminence of pre-rational sexual drives in the explanation of human motives and behaviour. That same year the amateur German mathematician, Albert Einstein, by publishing his famous *Theory of Relativity*, pulled together all the various developments and discoveries of the previous two decades in physics and mathematics, and provided them with a new basic theoretical matrix to replace that which had been destroyed in 1887. The effect of his work was to re-establish the scientist's faith in the ability of man's mind to comprehend the nature of the physical world; though the physical world as hypothesized by Einstein bore little or no relation to that experienced by the senses of the ordinary man or to the matrices into which he fitted that experience. The divorce between intellect and science and the perception of the average man

197

widened rather than narrowed as a result of Einstein's work, and even sixty years later, very many educated men could not either comprehend or expound his theories so that others would comprehend them. There was more than a little justice in the doggerel rhyme,

> Nature and Nature's laws lay hid in night;
> God said, 'Let Newton be', And all was light.
> It did not last. The Devil, shouting 'Ho,
> Let Einstein be', restored the *status quo*.

But for the world of science, Einstein's work was to provide a basis for new progress, which has still not proven outmoded.

The revolt against positivism took place less from any appreciation of the physicists' earlier destruction of their own previously held view of the universe, than from a discontent with mechanistic theories of volition and the physicists' attack on religion, which had turned philosophers and psychologists to examining and considering the nature of the religious motive as such. It is curiously significant that of the two most dominant figures in the revolt against positivism, one, the American, William James, was a psychologist who had written on varieties of religious experience and the other, Henri Bergson, began by studying unconscious memory through speech defects, thus following the same route that Freud did. In philosophy the central years of the new challenge were thus 1906, the year in which William James published his *Pragmatism*, and the following year in which Bergson propounded his theory of the *élan vital, Creative Evolution*.

In the worlds of painting, architecture and music, the most critical period seems to have opened in 1906. In painting Europe was divided between the two great schools of Paris and Central Europe, schools with hardly a single point of intellectual or other contact with each other, yet moving from opposite ends to a similar meeting ground. In 1900 Germanic painting, divided as it was between Berlin, Munich and Vienna, was dominated by the first great revolt against the art of the academic, the *Sezession*, a Central European equivalent to *Art Nouveau*. In 1904 the group, *die Brücke*, in Dresden, launched itself into a decade of the most violent experimentation with the architectural balance of simplified forms and violent colours. Their nearest equivalent in Paris was the *Fauve* school, following the Post-Impressionists. For them the great year was 1907, the year of the Cézanne memorial exhibition. The introduction to the catalogue enunciated two great precepts, which had come to Cézanne only a year or two before his death: 'To paint is not solely to copy an object; it is to seize a harmony between the numerous relationships' and 'Everything in nature models itself upon the sphere, the cone and the cylinder.' The first of these led Henri Matisse to the exploration of rhythms in colour, and to the development of an architectural treatment of colour analogous to the work of Nolde, Kirchner, Schmidt-Rottluff and Mueller in Germany. (A minor member of *die Brucke*, Hans Purrmann, actually studied for some years in the school Matisse founded the previous year in Paris.) The second principle led Picasso and his friend, Braque, into Cubism and beyond. Both lines of development saw the painter progressively detached from the object painted. And in both the painter was becoming more and more interested in imposing a form, a structure on his work. The first line of development, that followed by Matisse, can perhaps best be distinguished as the exploration of decoration, of visual sensation, the second, followed by Picasso and the Cubists, that of design.

In architecture meanwhile the main departure from *Art Nouveau* (*Jugendstil* in Germany) was being taken by a German school of designers and architects, intent on returning to simple unornamented design which would be relevant to the purpose for which the artifact was designed (*Sachlichkeit* was the German catch-word), based on modern materials and techniques with its individual parts in harmony with one another. In 1907 they founded the *Deutsche Werkbund,* to promote *Sachlichkeit* and *Qualität* (quality). And the *Deutsche Werkbund* was followed by the foundation of similar *Werkbünde* in Austria in 1910 and Switzerland in 1913. The movement culminated in the Cologne exhibition of 1914 at which for the first time the full genius of Walter Gropius, founder of the principal seminal centre of modern architecture, the *Bauhaus* (1919), first attracted the public. In painting, however, the Central Europeans continued to reject the machine for an ever increasingly violent exploration of colour. In Munich in 1912 a group of painters founded the *Blaue Reiter* school which included Franz Marc, August Macke, the Russian Wassily Kandinsky. The Swiss surrealist, Paul Klee, was to exhibit in this school in the early 1920s.

The virtues which Gropius preached, simplicity, science and technique, hard struggles and no personal security, the architecture of the machine, carry a curiously positivist ring about them; although what the modern German architects were interested in was to come to grips with modern engineering techniques rather than with science itself. Among them the greatest controversies raged on the issue of standardization or individualization. In their interest in new and imaginative forms they were close to the intellectual approach of French Cubism, which following Cézanne's seminal aphorism broke the multifarious shapes and outlines of the observed world into the simple cones and cylinders of three-dimensional geometry. In their attempt to reconcile art with the machine they parallel the Italian Futurists, whose first manifesto was issued in 1909. But here again the Italians introduced a third approach to the intellectualism of Gropius and Picasso. The Futurist manifesto of 1909 deified the violence as well as the clean lines of the automobile: and geometry expressed itself in a temporary obsession with its instruments such as the set square and the T square in the so-called 'metaphysical' phase of Italian surrealism, of which di Chirico was perhaps the best known painter; this was, however, a war-time development.

In France, surrealism, that of Odilon Redon, the Russian painter

Chagall, James Ensor and others seemed to belong to the less intellectual-
ized line originated by Matisse. It was greatly enhanced by the terrific
impact of Russian ballet, which began with the first season of the Diaghilev
company in Paris in 1909, the decor of which by Benois and Bakst, highly
coloured, often semi-oriental fantasy, had an overwhelming impact on
popular taste. The extraordinary combination of violence and delicacy
which distinguished the choreography of the Diaghilev company and its
principal dancers were highly characteristic of the last years of European
culture before 1914. That same year, 1909, saw in Paris the first outbreaks
of *apachism*, an unbridled, underworld violence of a type new to Europe.

In social philosophy and in literature one can trace a new irrationalism
developing after 1905. Here the influence of Freud and Einstein is unimportant. Those involved were often followers of Bergson. But the crucial
event was the first Moroccan crisis, which for the first time since 1870 confronted the young with the possibility of war in Europe. In France this
expressed itself in a revival of intellectual Catholicism, of which the writers
Charles Péguy and Alain Fournier, prophets of a return to the mediaeval
order of the city or the idealized innocence of youth, are perhaps most
significant. In Italy it led to the violence of the Futurists, and the flam-
boyant heroism of the poet, Gabriele d'Annunzio. In Germany one can
trace a rather similar development which, however, began earlier and was
not so clearly a reaction to the events of 1905. This was the development of
the cult of youth by youth in the *Jugendbewegung*.

The central element in this movement was a reaction against the close
intellectual discipline of the German home and school, a reaction towards
an indefinable sense of freedom; but it was a freedom within a small group
of peers with a chosen or recognized leader. Its main manifestation was the
institution of the *Wandervögel*, hiking and rambling groups rediscovering
the beauties of the countryside and the simplicities of folk-song. But it was
also intensely nationalist in sentiment, and upper *bourgeois* in origin, and
the freedom it sought had no political or parliamentary content. Its intellectual mentors were a curious duo of political and cultural critics of
Bismarckian Germany, Paul de Lagarde and Julius Langbehn, its main
literary voice the poet of the aristocratic *élite*, Stefan George. War came to
it as to Péguy and Alain Fournier, and the young poets of Britain, Rupert
Brooke and Julian Grenfell, as the final, only too easily welcomed, challenge and release from their earlier hesitations.

These poets, indeed the whole youth itself, operated at a far shallower
level of literary consciousness than those two writers from Austria-Hungary,
offspring of the great and still not thoroughly understood centre of culture
which was Habsburg Austria, who explored most fully the new depths of the
unconscious to which Nietzsche and Freud had pointed. These were the
poet, Rainer Maria Rilke, and the writer, Franz Kafka. Not that either of
them was deliberately impelled to his choice of subject by his philosophical analogues. Far from it. Rather that their inspiration led them into
these realms of the unconscious. For Rilke, insulated by the aid of a circle

of well-to-do friends from the grosser necessities of economic man, the task he set himself was primarily one of reconciliation with and acceptance of the ancestral terrors of these new depths, a task brilliantly achieved in his ultimate work, the *Duineser Elegien* (1922). For Kafka the terrors themselves had to be charted. That itself was almost more than he could tolerate. And he left behind him two nightmare accounts of the terrors of a world in which all seemingly settled points of reference failed to provide the individual with anything to which he could relate, of which he could actually make sense. These two works, *The Castle* and *The Trial*, were written during the period after 1913, and only published after the author's death. They were to outdo even the horrors of the totalitarian states of the 1930s.

The achievement of these writers must not, however, be allowed to obscure the continuance of the older rationalist-humanist tradition of the late nineteenth century. A link is perhaps provided between them by the French novelist Proust, whose major investigation of the nature of time and continuity, *À la Recherche du Temps Perdu* (Remembrance of Things Past), was conceived and in part written before 1914 (the first of the ten volumes, *Du Côté de chez Swann* was published in 1913). They were concerned with the predicament in which Kafka found himself, with the problem of reorientation to a world where, as the physicists had discovered a generation earlier, nothing was as it seemed, and intellectual truth was difficult to recognize. And driven like the physicists to the recognition that relative truth is all that could be discovered, they found a certain security, as the physicists had done, in the process of intellectual activity itself, providing this activity was itself honestly practised. Perhaps the most significant examples of this approach, which was to produce some of the greatest figures of Europe in the 1920s, were the early work of André Gide, the French writer who founded the *Nouvelle Revue Française* in 1908 and the publishing house of Gallimard in 1911, which were to become the literary academy for modern writers in France, and, in Germany, of the novelist, Thomas Mann.

In the field of music, events and ideas were to turn away from the Romantics' preoccupation with the totality of experience. In Italy, the followers of '*verismo*' began, even before the turn of the century, to seek to relate their post-Verdian music dramas to the common and the contemporary. Mascagni and Leoncavallo turned to the life of the Italian village, Puccini, the last of the great Italian opera composers, to Paris (*La Bohème*), to Japan (*Madama Butterfly*), even to the American Wild West. Among the Germanic and French composers, romanticism was, however, still burning itself out in the work of the post-Wagnerians in Germany and France, with Richard Strauss and Hugo Wolff, in Gustav Mahler's immensely over-orchestrated all-embracing symphonies, and lastly, perhaps the final lunacy of the post-Wagnerian romantics, in Arnold Schönberg's *Gurrelieder* (completed in 1911 and orchestrated for ten different violin parts, eight different parts each for violas and 'cellos, three four-part male choirs, one eight-part choir, and, as well as immense wood and brass sections, a percussion section which employed 32 performers including six tympani and an iron chain!). A third school, in revulsion to this, grew up in France in the Impressionism of Débussy, Ravel and Fauré.

An interesting separate element is the development of various national schools of music, or rather of composers in individual national traditions other than those of France, Germany and Italy which make up the mainstream of European classical music. The most important single national tradition was that of Russia. Moussorgsky's songs played their part in the development of Débussy's impressionism. More important was the work of Rimsky-Korsakov and of the principal Russian recruit to the new music of twentieth century Europe, Stravinsky whose music for the ballets *Firebird* (1910), *Petrushka* (1911) and the *Rite of Spring* (1913) added immeasurably to the impact of the Diaghilev ballet. Bartok and Kodály in Hungary, Manuel de Falla in Spain, Sibelius in Finland, Janacek in Slovakia, Nielsen in Denmark, Vaughan Williams in Britain were all experimenting with a tonality which owed as much or more to the folk music of their own countries as to the main schools of European music.

These various strains were, however, all running out by 1914, as composers turned to the exploration of form, reverting, as Ravel did in 1911 with *Daphnis and Chloe*, to a new classicism, or moving on to atonalism, as Schönberg did with his *Erwartung* (1909), and *Pierrot Lunaire* (1912), and to the twelve-tone row of Josef Hauer, propounded in Vienna in 1914, and followed by Schönberg's two best known colleagues, Anton Webern and Alban Berg.

It is, perhaps, still too early to bring all these various intellectual movements under one theoretical roof. What is noticeable and significant at this time is the gulf which divided the culture based on Paris from that based on the cities of Central Europe, a gulf of considerable ignorance despite the opportunities for contact which were available. The culture of Paris remained virtually untouched by the movement in architectural design which was to eventuate in Gropius and the *Bauhaus* school. The painters of Central Europe visited Paris and saw the preliminary exhibitions of Impressionist and Post-Impressionist art which visited Munich, Stuttgart and Vienna—yet there seems to have been little or no contact between the giants of the Central European and Parisian schools of painting, and such contact as there was was all one way, towards Paris.

A second point to notice is the degree to which art and music, and, to a lesser extent, literature, from the peripheral states of Europe, came to play a fertilizing role in the two European cultures of Paris and Central Europe. The theorist and publicist of the *Blaue Reiter* group was the Russian painter, Kandinsky. Diaghilev and Stanislavsky came to dominate the stages of Europe in ballet and acting style. Chaliapin, the great Russian bass, bestrode the operatic stage, and a generation of dancers, Nijinsky, Pavlova, Karsavina, Lopokova, and their stage designers were to pass into legend. From Scandinavia, the dramas of Ibsen and the writings of Strindberg swept the theatres of Europe. In literature Dostoievsky and Tolstoi were the principal Russian influences. In philosophy, William James's pragmatism has already been mentioned. And in the realm of popular culture, shortly before the war, ragtime, the first great innovation in popular music and dancing since the waltz and the polka, invaded Europe from the United States, a forerunner of the true American jazz and folk music which was to make so profound an impact in the 1920s.

These influences were only a symptom of the growing eclecticism of much of European culture. More significant perhaps of the gradual damming up of some parts of the stream of European creativity, or perhaps, of the dissatisfaction of Europe's artists and musicians with inherited forms and ideas, was the eagerness with which they turned to the African and Oriental for models. Not that at first sight there was anything new in this. Eighty years earlier Ingres, Delacroix and the French romantic painters had turned to the scenes and colours of North Africa, to escape the *bourgeois* classicism of their predecessors. But the painters of the new century were finding more than models from the Japanese, Javanese, Negro and Polynesian art which influenced them so profoundly; they were borrowing ideas of form and balance from the Japanese, themes and motifs from the Negro art of West Africa. At a different level a dreadful mish-mash of misunderstood Buddhism and Yoga was invading the salons of London and Paris, fads and fashions to some, but to others signs of a lack of confidence and security in the continuity and fertility of European thought and philosophy, an ironic and revealing sidelight on the apparent serenity, security and unshakability of the European way of life in 1914.

These movements, outlined in the foregoing passages, with the single exception of the youth movement, took place and hold only among a series of intellectual and academic *élites* who were becoming progressively more and more isolated from the main body of educated opinion in Europe. At this latter level the main conflict was between the irrational nationalism and love of violence originally propagated by Nietzsche, and the continuing belief in scientific progress and social improvement of the positivists. Neither Freudianism nor the seething intellectual chaos out of which the theory of relativity was to emerge had begun to filter through to the great middlebrow mind, which can be seen perhaps at its clearest in Britain, convulsed between the pseudo-scientific optimism of H. G. Wells and G. B. Shaw, whose play *Man and Superman* was a kind of bowdlerized Nietzsche for the intellectual nursery, and the gentle romantic corporativism of G. K. Chesterton and Hilaire Belloc. The pernicious Oxford school of Platonic anti-democratic corporativism of Bosanquet and Jowett was translating itself into the neo-imperialist collectivism of the Round Table group. In France Bergson and Sorel were influencing the dominant school of military theorists into the belief that France's *élan vital* in attack would outweigh Germany's superiority in men and materials. In Germany, the popular philosophy was nationalist and patriotic, if not chauvinist, in its attitude to non-German ideas, peoples and culture. Nationalism, historicism, anti-modernism were everywhere strong. They were opposed by a growing consciousness of what was common in European culture, strongest among the university-educated of Europe, and an equal consciousness of the way in which economic forces were tying Europe so together so that war in Europe would come close to economic suicide. When, at the end of July 1914, the outbreak of war seemed inevitable, those nationalist patriots in every country who gave the war an enthusiastic welcome were opposed by those who thought war was stupid and suicidal. A group of British liberals protested to *The Times* that if Britain fought on Russia's side against Germany, she would be embracing the cause of barbarism against civilization. It was indeed the end of a Europe.

## The Immediate Causes of the Outbreak of War in 1914

In the controversies which have raged around the origins of the 1914–18 war and the responsibilities of the various belligerents for its outbreak, it has not often been recognized that there were not one but three wars which broke out in that year, and that each school of national historians has tended only to focus on that in which his own country was first involved. Of these three the first was that between Austria and Serbia, the second that between Germany and her Austrian ally on the one hand, and Russia and France on the other, and the third that between Britain and Germany. The first followed on the Serbian failure to accept the Austrian ultimatum provoked by the assassination of the heir to the Hapsburg throne, the Archduke Franz Ferdinand, by one of a group of terrorists trained in Serbia and armed and organized by a nationalist secret society run by the head of the Serbian Army intelligence service. The second followed on a German ultimatum to Russia demanding the cessation of Russian preparations for mobilization, begun as a means of diplomatic pressure on Austria to abandon her punitive war on Serbia. The third followed on the German violation of Belgian territory in the course of an offensive designed to knock Russia's ally, France, out of the war, before Russian military strength could be completely mobilized and hurled against Prussia's eastern heartlands. What needs to be explained are the links between these three wars.

These links were provided almost exclusively by military considerations. The Tsar and the Russian Foreign Ministry, concerned to save Serbia from the consequences of her folly, only intended to mobilize on their frontiers with the Austrian empire. Their military advisers said that to confine mobilization to the Austro-Russian frontier was impossible, and perilous if it were possible, in view of Germany's alliance with Austria. More disastrous for the peace of Europe, however, were the war plans of the German military. Obsessed since the conclusion of the Franco-Russian alliance with the peril of war on two fronts, they had concluded that

Germany's only hope of evading simultaneous invasion and defeat was to take advantage of Germany's internal lines of communication, her strategic railway system and her speed of mobilization. Germany could mobilize in 36 hours, France in 48. Russia needed nearly three weeks. In these three weeks the bulk of Germany's armed forces could be thrown against France, the French armies overwhelmed by superior numbers, France defeated and Russia confronted with a reconcentrated and victorious German army on the east. The time limits set by the plan were impossibly slender. Their effect was to make of Russian mobilization the signal for a German attack on France. Every hour wasted in diplomatic contacts thereafter brought the Russian armies an hour nearer to East Prussia and Berlin and gave the German armies in the west an hour less in which to achieve victory, the French an hour more in which to prepare their defences. The whole German war plan was based on the idea of a pre-emptive first strike against France.

But there was more to it than that. The French frontier with Germany was defended for much of its length by difficult hilly country, by the Rhine and by a series of fortresses. And classic German military doctrine called always for a victory through encirclement of the enemy. The original German plans of the 1890s envisaged a breakthrough in the south, through the so-called Belfort gap. But in the aftermath of the Moroccan crisis of 1905 the scheme was revised. France's great eastern chain of fortresses were to be circumvented by a drive through the plains of Belgium and Luxemburg, a drive which would give the Germans still more room in which to deploy their extra manpower and divisions. The consequent violation of Belgian neutrality of which Germany and Britain were guarantors by a treaty of 1839 was to the military not their affair. It was a political matter on which they did not feel competent to pronounce. The effect of this military decision was to confront Germany's political leadership in the hour of crisis with no choice but defeat or the acceptance of a plan for victory, called the Schlieffen Plan after its drafter, which would violate what they were pledged to honour.

The German violation of Belgium in its turn brought the possibility of war with Britain into account. The German military had largely discounted this possibility. The record of the British army in the Boer War was not such as to earn it the respect of the foremost military power in Europe. The reforms of the Haldane *régime* went unnoticed or were dismissed as not having been tested in battle. In any case the British army was a minute professional force compared with the great conscript armies of Central Europe. The six divisions of the British Expeditionary Force were a drop in the bucket by comparison with the eighty odd divisions which the Germans proposed to throw against France. In any case, there was a good deal of reason to doubt how seriously Britain would take a treaty that was seventy-five years old at the time of its violation. Moreover, all of Germany's plans were predicated on a victory so quick that British strength would simply come too late to be of any military use to France.

205

In this the Germans were making two serious mistakes. The first was to misunderstand the contingent nature of the British staff arrangements with France. They were, as has been seen, the product of divided counsels and interpretations as to the ends of German policy. One section of the Cabinet, a minority, but a consistent and well-organized one, believed that Germany was intent on the hegemony, not only of Europe, which she had when she chose to exert it, but also of the outside world. An equally small minority, as doctrinaire in its beliefs but less well organized, was composed of out-and-out pacifists and isolationists who saw no useful purpose to be served by intervention in Europe's quarrels. The floating middle was inclined by ideological conviction to the latter point of view, or could be expected to be so inclined, unless its members could be shown that international justice and Britain's vital interests were both involved. The German invasion of Belgium was admirably designed to combine both these issues; being unprovoked aggression at once against a small power of which Britain was a guarantor, and against a strategically important area which British policy for the last four hundred odd years had insisted should not fall under the dominance of a Great Power. The German invasion of Belgium was to destroy Germanophilia in Britain for three generations.

These military plans and attitudes were important, especially in the three autocracies of Germany, Austria-Hungary and Russia, because of the dual role of the sovereign as head both of the civilian and the military sides of the state, and the consequent unstable nature of civil-military relationships. In Germany and in Russia, the autocrats, Kaiser and Tsar, were adolescent, unstable personalities, and felt themselves as much soldiers as civilians. Their openness to military advice and the degree to which they shared their generals' dislike of their civilian ministers was greatly to weaken the effectiveness of the civilians' advice. In Austria the aged Franz Josef saw events not in nationalist but in dynastic terms—and he was therefore the more amenable to the arguments of the military. In both Germany and Austria the military classes were convinced of the inevitability of a war and the advantage of staging one before Russian strength was really built up. In Russia the military were convinced of the duplicity of Germany and deeply suspicious of German intentions. In every case there was an element of deceit in the arguments used to secure from the autocrat the orders to mobilize.

The immediate occasion for the Austrian attack on Serbia was provided by the Serbs. It is now established beyond a peradventure that the assassination on June 28th, 1914, of the Archduke Franz Ferdinand and his wife during an official visit to the provincial capital of Bosnia Herzegovina, was organized by a Serbian secret society, the Black Hand, whose effective head was Colonel Dragutin Dmitrievich, the head of Serbian military intelligence; and that the Serbian government, at least in the person of the Premier, N. Pasic, had foreknowledge of the plot. Indeed Pasic made an attempt, albeit a remarkably feeble one, to warn the Austrian authorities in

Vienna in advance. The assassins were all recruited from the disaffected student youth of Bosnia. The aim behind the assassination plot will probably always be unknown. This much is clear, that Franz Ferdinand was regarded in Belgrade as the most dangerous man on the Austrian side, since his dislike of the Hungarians had led him to support the idea of making the Habsburg dual monarchy into a triple monarchy by the erection of a third, Slav, state. But the possibility cannot be excluded that it was Colonel Dmitrievich's scheme to provoke a war between the Habsburg monarchy and Serbia in which Russia would be forced to come to Serbia's aid. He was in regular touch with the Russian military attaché in Belgrade from whom he had received explicit assurances of Russian support in such an event. Whatever the truth of this, 'the shots which echoed round the world' were fired by a tubercular student below the age of twenty-one, fired with the ideals of pan-Serb nationalism to whom the disruption of European peace was of little consequence compared with the advancement of his ideal. And he was incited by a man who was himself an assassin (he had taken part in the bloody murder of the Obrenovichs in 1903), a barbarian of intrigue, violence and terror himself, to whom peace was a meaningless and unwelcome abstraction, a man only one step removed from the professional bandits and brigands for which the Balkans were then infamous.

The murder caught the Austrian administration at its weakest point. Not that there was much love lost for Franz Ferdinand himself; indeed the comparative obscurity of the funeral arrangements scandalized all Vienna. It was immediately assumed that Serbia had a hand in the assassination and all Europe united to condemn Serbia for allowing its territory to be used by terrorists for attacks into Austrian territory. Under any circumstances a *prima facie* case existed for the Austrian state to take the severest police measures and demand far-reaching guarantees of Serbian good behaviour. Unfortunately for the peace of Europe, this was not enough for the Austrian government and military. Moreover the investigating judge was slow at getting the conspirators to confess, and the part played by Serbian officials did not emerge immediately or in such a way as to carry conviction and stifle opposition. The result was to delay Austrian action against Serbia, so that the first flush of anti-Serbian feeling in Europe was weakened, Russian pan-Slavism was aroused, and opinion in Europe saw instead of the chastisement of a nest of terrorists and brigands, an assault on Serbian national independence.

The root of the trouble lay in Vienna. The years of the Balkan wars, especially the months following the second Balkan war in which the Austrian authorities had striven to prevent the increase of Serbian territory at the expense of Albania, had convinced the Austrians of Serbia's fundamental hostility. An ultimatum had already been necessary in October 1913 to secure the withdrawal of Serbian troops from Albania's territory. The Austrian Chief of Staff saw the assassination as a declaration of war by Serbia. Count Berchtold, the Foreign Minister, was converted to the military view of the need for a preventive war against Serbia, and the

Emperor wrote to the Kaiser that 'the continuation of the situation is a chronic peril for my House and my territories'.

The first task was to secure German support lest Russia intervene to prevent the chastisement of Serbia. Assurances of German support were obtained from the Kaiser and the German Chancellor on July 5th–6th, and the terms in which these assurances were expressed suggest that the Kaiser and the Chancellor did not believe the danger of Russian intervention to be very serious. There followed a period of a week in which Berchtold had to meet and overcome the severe opposition of Count Tisza, the Hungarian premier, anxious not to add to the Empire's internal Slav problem. The visit of the French President to St Petersburg further delayed matters. The Austrian demands were not in fact presented in Belgrade until the evening of July 23rd. Their terms amounted to the establishment, at pistol point, of a police protectorate over Serbia. And they were to be accepted or rejected within forty-eight hours. Their tenor did more than anything else to win support for Serbia as the gallant little nation being bullied by her over-mighty neighbour, where she had previously been seen as a backward and near anarchic state whose territory was a nest of bandits, brigands, terrorists and would-be assassins.

The Austrian ultimatum caught the Serbian government in an unresolvable dilemma. To yield was impossible on a variety of counts. Serbian nationalist opinion very largely approved of the assassination. The *Black Hand* was well organized among the Serbian officer corps. The Serbian government moreover had very good reason not to wish to see the question of links between those who plotted the assassination and themselves subjected to any real investigation. On the other hand, they faced for the first time an obviously aroused and militant Austria. In their dilemma they had already appealed to Russia on July 22nd. On receipt of the ultimatum they directed a fresh appeal to the Russian government.

In St Petersburg, the reports of impending Austrian action against Serbia had already caused a good deal of alarm. The Serbian appeal of July 22nd caused Sazonov, the Foreign Minister, to wire a warning to Vienna not to address unacceptable demands to Serbia. The Austrian ultimatum itself was greeted with shocked horror. Russia immediately appealed to Britain and France. A Council of Ministers, convened in the afternoon of July 24th, decided on a partial mobilization of the Russian army and a full mobilization of the Black Sea and Baltic fleets. The Serbian government was advised to give a moderate answer; and every Russian diplomatic effort was bent to securing a withdrawal of the time limit in the Austrian demands; an especial appeal was directed to Britain to make her position plain.

On the evening of July 25th, the Serbian reply was handed to the Austrian Minister in Belgrade. With a great show of moderation it accepted all the Austrian demands save those involving Austrian participation in the investigation of the conspirators' connections in Serbia. The Austrians had not expected their demands to be accepted; and the Serbs did not expect their reply to satisfy them. The Serbian army was in fact given its orders to mobilize three hours before the delivery of the reply to the Austrians. The Austrian Minister broke off relations and asked for his passport. Three hours later the Austrian emperor ordered the mobilization of eight army corps against Serbia, to begin on July 28th.

The events of July 24th–25th in Vienna and St Petersburg mark the link between the Austro-Serbian war and the Russo-Franco-Germano-Austrian war. The actual linking event was the combination of miscalculations in the two capitals. In Vienna, Russia's reactions had been taken for granted. German was relied on to give Russia pause in 1914 as she had during the Bosnian crisis. In St Petersburg, Sazanov apparently hoped to produce a diplomatic line-up which would isolate Vienna. Germany's possible action in support of her ally does not seem to have been given much thought at this stage. Sazanov's hopes were pinned on a hostile demonstration by Britain, perhaps another Mansion House speech. This he soon found was unattainable. The main idea in the British mind was mediation. Britain and France would restrain Russia and Germany would restrain Austria. With this aim, on July 26th the British proposed a four power conference, Italy, Germany, France and Britain to meet in London immediately.

This proposal was the product of the British Foreign Secretary's knowledge of the divisions in his own Cabinet, where an influential section were for neutrality on all issues. With it, the scene of miscalculation shifted to London. The British plan depended on the ability of Germany to hold Austria, and Britain and France to restrain Russia. In fact neither Austria nor Russia could be restrained. Although Germany, in the person of her Chancellor, backed the British plan for a conference, the Chancellor's hand was weakened by the military anxieties of the German General Staff lest the European war they dreaded should open before Germany could strike the pre-emptive blow on which German strategy rested. And the Austrian authorities proved unwilling to pay any attention to representations. On July 27th they declared the Serbian note totally unsatisfactory. Russia in her turn accepted the British idea of a conference. But this acceptance was vitiated by the Tsar's telegram to the King of Serbia promising support. The only method of restraint which would now have worked would have been a declaration from one or more of Austria or Russia's allies that they would *not* support them in the event of war. No such statements were forthcoming. On July 28th, the Austrians declared war on Serbia, the Emperor being induced to sign the declaration by a false report of Serbian firing on Austrian troops.

The next two days were crucial, and provide a clear demonstration of the strength of the two forces which brought Europe to ruin, the Russian drive into the Balkans and Austria's reaction to it, and the failure of the civilians to control the military in Berlin. The news of the Austrian declaration of war on Serbia, and still more of the bombardment of Belgrade the following day (July 29th), provoked a crisis in St Petersburg. The

Foreign Minister, Sazonov, decided that partial mobilization was what was called for, but the War Minister and the General Staff were so convinced that war with Germany was inevitable that they persuaded the Tsar to order general mobilization. A warning from the German ambassador that mobilization would mean a general European war only confirmed them in their views; but at the last moment an appeal from the Kaiser induced the Tsar to recall the order for general mobilization and substitute only partial mobilization against Austria.

During this breathing space, the German and British governments each did their best to work out a compromise. On the evening of July 28th, the German Chancellor had done his unavailing best to restrain the Austrians, but without success, the German *démarche* not taking place in Vienna until after the Austrian declaration of war. The German proposals envisaged the Austrian troops halting in Belgrade, and made their occupation of the Serbian capital the guage for Serbian good behaviour. On the 29th, the Germans were impelled to repeat their proposals by a series of events which greatly weakened their own position. During the course of the day it became obvious that neither of their two remaining allies, Italy or Rumania, would support them, and for the first time it became clear that Britain would in all probability back France and Russia. The probability of British action in this sense was made clear to the German ambassador in London in the afternoon of July 29th, as an accompaniment to the proposal that Germany should mediate with Vienna perhaps on the basis of an Austrian occupation of Belgrade. The German Chancellor reacted during the night of July 29th–30th by bombarding Vienna with telegrams threatening German inaction if Austria refused to enter into conversations with the Russians.

The German Chancellor seems, however, to have been already convinced of the inevitability of war. On July 29th, the draft of the ultimatum to Belgium demanding the passage of German troops through Belgium was sent to the German embassy in Brussels. And that evening the Chancellor made a first bid for British neutrality, saying that in the event of a victorious war Germany did not aim at any territorial acquisitions from France. He was unable to give similar assurances about the French colonies and he prevaricated over Belgium. And his control over his military was slipping, as Moltke, the German Chief of Staff, took the opportunity on July 29th of hinting strongly to the Austrians that they should answer the Russian partial mobilization by a general mobilization.

On July 30th, in fact, independently of each other, Germany and Russia both decided on general mobilization. The Russian decision was an agonizing one for the Tsar to take, and he was only induced to take it by allegations, quite untrue, that the German measures of preparation for mobilization were already secretly in a very advanced position and that Russia was in serious jeopardy of surprise attack. The Russian Army and Foreign Ministry were of one mind on the desirability of and the inevitability of war with Germany. The German decision was not so immediate, in that the Crown Council of July 30th after lengthy argument decided to issue the preliminary order for mobilization, the notification of a so-called 'threatening danger of war', by noon on July 31st. The Chancellor fought a losing battle against the Kaiser and his military advisers, who were convinced that mediation was pointless, and themselves alarmed at the evidence of French and Belgian preparations for war, preparations which could well put the whole German war plan in danger. That same evening the Austrian government also decided on general mobilization. Their decision was greatly influenced by two telegrams from the Chief of the German General Staff urging them to mobilize against Russia and advising that such action would bring the German alliance into operation. 'Every hour of delay makes the situation worse. . . . A European war offers the last chance of preserving Austria-Hungary. Unconditional support by Germany.' The Austrian government had already rejected the proposals for a halt in Belgrade, as had the Russians. War was now inevitable.

News of the Russian mobilization reached Berlin on July 31st. It made any further resistance by the German Chancellor to the military impossible. That afternoon the Germans addressed an ultimatum to Russia demanding the suspension of all military activity on pain of German mobilization and war. At the same time the order 'threatening danger of war' was issued. Almost simultaneously the French were given a time limit to say whether they would stay neutral in a Russo-German war. If they were to declare themselves neutral then they were to be requested to surrender to German occupation the fortresses of Verdun and Toul as guarantees of their neutrality. The Schlieffen Plan would only work if France entered the war at once and the Germans, by advancing these totally unacceptable terms, made sure of her entry. Belgium issued the order for general mobilization that evening, and a French decision to mobilize was also taken at that time, though the order was not issued until the afternoon of August 1st. With this, war became for all the powers a matter of waiting for the ultimata to expire.

For all the powers, that is, except Britain. Since July 27th, it had become apparent that the Liberal Cabinet and the country were deeply divided. Over half the Cabinet were against British involvement and most of the rest undecided. Only a handful favoured British intervention on the side of France, though these few included Grey, the Foreign Secretary, Churchill, the First Lord of the Admiralty, and Haldane. The Liberal press and all the radical side of the parliamentary party were neutralists and the City and the Bank of England were appalled at the prospect of war. As the ultimata expired and the declarations of war followed, Germany on Russia (August 1st), and on France (August 3rd), the debate continued. It was aggravated by the agonized representations of the French who had left their northern sea coasts to be defended by the Royal Navy under the Staff Agreements of 1912. A vain attempt was made to secure German agreement to French neutrality but the German general staff proved unable to alter its plans despite the Kaiser's intervention. On August 2nd, the British officially promised the French that their northern sea coasts would be protected against German attack, and the Royal Navy was officially mobilized.

The position was changed by the German ultimatum to Belgium which was officially presented on the afternoon of August 2nd. The Belgian rejection was followed by a German refusal to accept it, and at 7 a.m. on August 4th, German troops crossed the Belgian frontier *en masse*. The news of the German ultimatum to Belgium was crucial. On August 4th, the British ultimatum was despatched to Berlin. No answer being received, Britain entered the war at midnight. The Army was mobilized at 4 p.m. that afternoon. Only two members of the Cabinet resigned. Britain's ally, Japan, followed with a declaration of war on Germany at the end of August.

There remained the strange anomaly of Austria-Hungary. The German intervention against Russia had in fact prevented any use by Russia of her mobilization against Austria-Hungary. And for five days after the German declaration of war on Russia, both the original protagonists, Austria and Russia, remained strangely reluctant to go to war with one another. This did not suit Germany's strategic plans at all. If the main weight of the German army was to be brought against France, Austria's role was to help the weak German forces opposing Russia to ward off the expected Russian offensive. The Austrians, however, had been looking to Germany to protect them against Russian diplomatic pressure. And as the bulk of their armed forces were to be deployed against Serbia they expected Germany to continue to protect them against Russia militarily. It took the Germans until August 6th to overcome the resistance of the Austrian general staff and secure a declaration of war against Russia from Vienna. The Russians on their side were so little concerned with the Austro-Serb dispute which had provoked their original intervention that they were content to wait. As for France and Britain, it was August 12th before either brought themselves to declare war on the Austrian empire, and then it was false information of Austrian troop movements towards the Franco-German frontier which turned the trick.

This delay in 'regularizing the situation', more than anything else, underlines the hiatus between the Austro-Serbian war and those between Germany, France, Russia and Great Britain. The foregoing account shows that there were three main factors in bringing about the German declarations of war on France and Russia. First was the Russian conviction that she could not afford an Austrian take-over in Serbia, and that not only Austria but Germany was determined on securing this, whether this involved war with Russia or not being a matter of indifference to them. Russian moves to head off Austrian pressure on Serbia were first made before the Austrian ultimatum. Though they can be explained in part by the rumours which began around July 14th or so of impending Austrian action against Serbia, there was never any disposition in Russia to share in the almost universal European condemnation of Serbian support for the assassination. With this attitude Russia demonstrated her detachment at all but the *élite* level from the main currents and values of European civilization. Once the Austrian ultimatum to Serbia was delivered the Russians reached the substantially correct conclusion that this had been concerted with Berlin. Thereafter the Tsar's advisers were unanimous in seeing Germany as the enemy, and rejecting any mediation except on terms which preserved Serbia's freedom to continue to threaten the cohesion and interests of the Austrian state.

The second factor was Germany's inability to exercise any restraining influence in Vienna. This inability was the result of the previous assurances given to Vienna, the conviction of the German military that war with Russia was inevitable, and their consequent contradiction of the diplomatic pressure brought to bear on Vienna by the Chancellor, and the determination of the Austrian Cabinet not to allow anything to prevent their planned chastisement of Serbia. In giving their original assurances to Vienna, the German Kaiser and Chancellor misjudged both the degree to which Vienna would take advantage of them and the strength of the subsequent Russian reaction.

The third factor was simply the failure of the German Kaiser and of his Chancellor properly to control their military, and their willingness to countenance military planning which left Germany no alternative but pre-emptive war not only against Russia, not only against France, but also involving an invasion of Belgian neutrality and a breach of Germany's own guarantee to Belgium. This was the more disastrous in that, while in Russia and Austria the only obstacles to war were the reluctance of Tsar and Emperor to send their peoples to destruction, in Germany the Kaiser and his Chancellor belatedly realized where their ally was leading them and did their best to find a way out.

On this showing the main responsibility for the outbreak of war between Germany, France and Russia must lie between the Tsar's advisers in Russia, who never hesitated in their drive for war, and the German military's fears, in that they could consider no alternative but a pre-emptive strike against France through Belgium. The main responsibility for war between Britain and Germany must lie squarely with the same military men, and with the Kaiser and Chancellor who failed to restrain them. A dominant school of historians have long argued that had Britain made it clear that she would enter the war on the side of France, Berlin would have been given pause; but these arguments run counter to the evidence. The German authorities did what they could to secure British neutrality, but they had already accepted the possibility of British entry on the side of their enemies and discounted it. British hesitations did the British very little credit, but their main effect should have been felt in Paris and St Petersburg. There is no evidence that this was the case.

There remains the responsibility for the original outbreak. And here we return to the actions of the Serbian extremists, whether in the *Black Hand* or the Serbian government. They planned the assassination. They willed the destruction of Austria. They were prepared to hazard a European war and the destruction of Europe to secure a union with the South Slav peoples under the Habsburg crown, who, it is fair to say, were a long way from sharing their desires. They relied on Russian backing which was freely given them. Never can the essentially destructive anarchic element in nationalism have been so well demonstrated as in the barbarian determination of this handful of ambitious politicians, unscrupulous military and sick-minded and -bodied adolescents to pull down a civilization which seemed to overshadow them.

Second only to them in the responsibility for the outbreak of war is the despair of the advisers, civilian and military, to the Austrian Emperor. Their inability to control Serbia or to resolve the internal conflict between Slav and German had driven them to a state bordering on paranoia. The two Balkan wars had seen a considerable deterioration in Austria's position in the Balkans; but this deterioration was not so serious that a determined diplomatic offensive based on Serbia's enemies might not have countered it. The assassination of Franz Ferdinand, unpopular as he was with them all, struck them with a shock that is rarely given its proper weight in a world where nationalism has always been taken to be in the right. It led them to an unshakable determination to excise the Serbian cancer. They knew the operation would be perilous to the patient. But their main efforts were directed to thwarting those who might stop them, efforts which involved misleading not only their German ally but their Emperor. If they had been content to secure guarantees of good behaviour, more effective in prosecuting their examination of the assassins, and swifter to act they might well have succeeded in neutralizing Serbia for a decade. But their over-estimation of their freedom of action was only matched by their incompetence in playing their hand; and they were to prove almost as criminally indifferent to the continuance of that European civilization of which Vienna was one of the principal props as the barbarians outside.

Studying the decade before 1914 in Europe, one is struck by the growth of violence, of anarchism that demanded victory-or-death, of recklessness and dissatisfaction with the existing atmosphere of civilization and society not merely among those who had little or no place in it, but among those who ruled or dominated it. These phenomena were essentially nationalistic and have to be set against a corresponding growth in internationalism, in Europeanism, in the centripetal forces of European civilization. The tragedy was that for a crucial month these destructive centrifugal forces gained control, aided by the pressures and challenges of that great power which had only in part been absorbed into Europe, Tsarist Russia. The autocrats played an equivocal part in this disaster, it is true, all three contributing in some degree to the sense of urgency which accompanied the weeks immediately after the assassination of Franz Ferdinand and then attempting to rein back when they realized how near to the abyss they had come. All three then had to be cajoled or cheated by their advisers into signing the fatal mobilization orders.

A major part in the initial processes which led to the unleashing of the armed forces was played by a kind of desperate and irrational conservatism seizing what it felt to be its only chance of avoiding social or political revolution. This anarcho-conservatism, for that was what in essence it was, was to continue into the war years, to render any chance of a compromise peace impossible, to ensure that revolution, when it came, would be violent, bloody and republican. When peace came it was not to be a peace of the dynasties. The age of the emperors, kaisers and tsars, of imperial courts and chancellors, of aristocratic advisers and noble generals, was over.

*Chapter XII*

# THE GREAT WAR: THE DISAPPEARANCE OF VICTORY, 1914–1916

THE outbreak of the war was greeted with wild scenes of popular enthusiasm throughout Europe. In Vienna, Berlin, Paris, St Petersburg and London the scenes were the same: with the sides of their railway carriages plastered with slogans, trainloads of garlanded reservists left to join their units amidst hysterically cheering crowds drunk with hurrah-patriotism. Volunteers swarmed to the colours both in Germany and in Britain, from those who had escaped conscription in the one country, and those to whom Continental ideas of universal military service had always seemed mere militarism, in the other. Young women made drunk with patriotic fervour paraded the streets of London, handing out white feathers, the badge of cowardice, to all young men not in uniform. 'Now God be thanked, who has matched us with this hour', wrote the English poet, Rupert Brooke; he voiced the sentiments of his generation.

In this welter of patriotic emotion, the old sentiments of class solidarity and loyalty disappeared overnight. Of the member parties of the Second International, those of Italy, the Netherlands and Scandinavia remained neutral. The French party, deprived of leadership by the assassination of Jean Jaurès in the week before war broke out, did nothing collectively. The German party, for years the largest and most dominant socialist party in Europe, voted to a man for the credits necessary to finance Germany's war effort. All the long denunciations of war as a capitalist-imperialist plot, which the workers of the world could defeat in its opening stages by a concerted General Strike, were forgotten. Individual pacifists disappeared behind bars or were metamorphosed into ultra-patriots of the most violent kind. Socialist international solidarity gave way to what the Russian revolutionary, Lenin, watching sourly from his exile in Switzerland, dubbed 'social patriotism'.

In those heady days the idea that party strife was unpatriotic dominated the political leadership of the belligerents. In Germany the Kaiser proclaimed a 'court peace' (*Burgfrieden*). In France the parties joined together in the *Union Sacrée*. In Britain the parties declared a truce. The civil war which threatened over Ulster was suspended as the Liberals agreed not to implement the Home Rule Bill until the war was over. In Austria the

216

pressure on the Czechs was relaxed a little. Even in Russia the parties of the Duma rallied behind the Tsar.

This voluntary cessation of activity on the part of the political parties in Central and Western Europe foreshadowed the primacy of the military which was to hamstring the political direction of the war in Britain, lead to violent political strife in France, and produce a virtual military dictatorship in Germany. With the concentration of public attention on the battlefields the leading military men, particularly those whose names were associated with military success, were to come to enjoy a degree of popular support that in many cases amounted to idolization, making it virtually impossible for the civilian governments to remove them from office. Their power was increased in France and among the Central Powers by legal precedents of some antiquity which placed part or all of the country under military juris-diction in time of war. In France, one third of the Chamber of Deputies were of military age and in fact rejoined their regiments on the outbreak of war. From August to December 1914 the French parliament did not meet. Patriotism was leading to the abdication of civilian rule. All of this was based on the hypothesis that the war would be a short one, and that there would be 'victory by Christmas'. Only the British, advised by Field Marshal Lord Kitchener, the victor of the Boer War, whom the Cabinet made Minister for War, began to prepare for a long conflict. Yet final victory eluded the Generals in 1914. Not a single one of the prewar military plans succeeded.

The opening months of the war were dominated by four great battles of collision between the opposing forces. The army staffs of Europe had spent the years before the war elaborating and perfecting plans for victory through attack. Germany pinned her hopes to the modified Schlieffen Plan of 1912 which swung the main weight of the German armies in a great turning movement through neutral Belgium and western France with the aim of encircling and driving the bulk of the French armies against their own frontier. The French, imbued with an irrationalist belief in the primacy of morale above material things, prepared to fling themselves into the offensive to regain the lost provinces of Alsace and Lorraine. In the East, the Russian armies planned to drive into East Prussia and into Austrian Galicia, to break out of the great Polish salient and to prepare for an invasion of Silesia. The Austrians planned two offensives, one, on their northern front into the centre of the Polish salient, aimed at Brest-Litovsk, and another on the southern front, to pinch off the northern end of Serbia. The Germans preferred to stay on the defensive in the East, stationing the bulk of their forces in East Prussia on the northern flank of the great Polish salient. Of the four armies the French were really the only equals to Germany in military science. But they lost any chance of making this equality tell by their senseless devotion to the offensive à l'outrance.

The western front, accordingly, was dominated by the great German offensive movement. The German armies swept through Belgium, using enormously heavy artillery to demolish the great Belgian fortresses of Liege and Namur. The Belgian army withdrew to the flanking position of Antwerp, and the French Fifth Army and the small British Expeditionary Force moving into Belgium to their aid were forced back deep into France. The French frontier offensives into Alsace-Lorraine and in the Ardennes were repulsed with enormous losses (over 300,000 killed and wounded), and the whole French line pushed back on a great arc between Verdun and Paris. The French Supreme Commander, General Joffre, however, kept his nerve, and purging the less successful army commanders, waited for the right moment to go over to the attack.

In their pursuit of the retreating French armies, the individual German armies over-reached themselves, not only exposing their flank to the forti-fied camp that was Paris, from which the French government had prudently removed itself to the safety of Bordeaux, but allowing a gap to open between the two armies in their centre. Into this gap, in the engagement known as the Battle of the Marne, moved the revivified British Expeditionary Force and part of the French Fifth Army. At this moment the nerve of General von Moltke, the German Supreme Commander, proved less strong than that of General Joffre, and he ordered a general retreat to the line Noyon–Verdun along the river Aisne, which he ordered to be entrenched and fortified. Thereafter each of the two opposing armies tried desperately to envelop the other's western flank, in what has come to be known as the 'race to the sea'. The fighting was bitter, bloody and inconclusive. Both sides dug themselves in, and by the end of November 1914 an unbroken line of trenches, dugouts and barbed wire stretched between the two sides from the Swiss frontier to the North Sea. In these battles, the French lost 380,000 killed and 600,000 wounded, including 80% of their infantry officers. The German casualties were a little less, but on much the same scale.

On the eastern front, the Russians did not wait for their full mobiliza-tion to become effective. After initial successes on the borders of East Prussia, their armies were lured into a rash attempt to break through to the sea and isolate the Germans into a pocket around Königsberg. But by brilliant manoeuvres the Germans evaded the trap, turning the tables on the Russians. In the successive battles of Tannenberg and the Masurian Lakes one Russian army was destroyed and a second badly mauled. The remnants of the Russian forces then withdrew from East Prussia. Russian casualties in dead and wounded were enormous and the Germans took over 150,000 prisoners.

On the Galician front, the Austrian and Russian offensives met head on. There followed nearly a month of confused fighting, in the course of which the Austrians' deficiency in leadership was demonstrated. At its end the Austrians retreated precipitately over more than 200 miles to the river Dunajec in front of Cracow. In the south the Austrians fared even worse. Their invasion of Serbia was rolled back by the Serbian Army. By December 15th, 1914, their forces had been completely expelled from Serbian territory. The Austrian collapse forced the Germans to form two new armies to attack towards Warsaw in the hope of relieving Galicia of some of the Russian pressure. But a new Russian offensive caused their withdrawal; and only Russia's extraordinary weakness in arms, munitions and means of transport saved the German and Austrian armies from disaster. At the end of 1914 Russian troops had regained all but the most westerly section of Russian Poland, and lay along the foothills of the Carpathians. And a joint offensive in the snow in January 1915 by German and Austrian troops failed to dislodge them.

The end of 1914 then saw virtual stalemate on both the major fronts. In the west all chance of a war of movement had ended, and for three years siege conditions existed all along the line. The ability to overcome fortifications requires a heavy weight of artillery, trained assault troops capable of taking heavy casualties, meticulous planning and long preparation before an assault is made. But the generals were for long deceived by the absence of recognizable fortresses. And it was only gradually that they learned that siege warfare on a front stretching several hundred miles against trenches, barbed wire and machine guns required a weight of war material in shells, artillery, bombs and motor transport which only a major industrial mobilization of a nation's entire economic resources could provide.

Throughout 1915 the British armies, which were prepared only for field warfare, unlike their German and French counterparts, were desperately short of these essentials. Manpower was the one thing as yet they had in abundance, owing to the enthusiasm with which the pick of the nation's youth responded to the call for recruits launched by Lord Kitchener, whose photographed figure, grimly moustached, finger pointing at his audience with the slogan 'Your Country Needs You', adorned every public wall. But manpower meant human lives, which were spent in the years 1915–17 with a prodigality whose cost to Europe can never be properly calculated.

Every Allied offensive in the west took the same form. First came a bombardment which, it was hoped, would silence the enemy's artillery and machine guns, cut a way through his barbed wire defences and take a heavy toll of the garrisons of his trench systems. Then the guns moved on to bombard the rear positions while the infantry attacked through the barbed wire, and the enemy's machine guns. Ideally the infantry should first break in to the enemy's trench-line and then break through. But they never did. And the cavalry, which had been brought up in anticipation of a break-through and a pursuit, would retire disconsolate but comparatively undamaged to their camps, while the infantry counted their losses. The Germans tried poison gas to secure an easy break-through in April 1915, and the British employed tanks for the same purpose in 1916. But in each case the new weapon was used in penny packets and on an inadequate scale. And the generals on all sides remained obstinately devoted to the frontal assault. And in every case where initial successes were scored the defenders' reserves arrived more quickly to plug the line than the attackers could regroup to break through.

This stalemate in the west was used by both sides during 1915 to divert forces to other fronts. The Germans decided to turn their main efforts against Russia in the hope of saving the disintegrating Hapsburg Empire. At the end of April 1915 a joint German-Austrian offensive broke through the Russian lines near Gorlice in Galicia. There followed a steady German advance and an equally steady Russian withdrawal. By December 1915 the Central Powers had advanced nearly to Riga in the north and their front ran due southwards from the River Dvina through the Pripet Marshes in Central Poland to the eastern Galician frontier. The Russian armies managed to evade the successive German attempts to envelop them, but all the same they lost an unknown number of dead and wounded and over three hundred thousand Russian prisoners were taken.

The disappointment of the hopes placed by each of the belligerents in an early victory and the stalemate which was established in the west after November 1914, with the Germany army so firmly entrenched in Northern France that only a long and protracted war seemed likely to expel them, naturally led the *Entente* Powers to search for allies, especially from those powers which could most effectively bring pressure to bear on the Central Powers. Such allies, it was very quickly realized, could be found not only among the nations already in being but also among the suppressed nationalities of the German, Austrian and Turkish Empires. The Central Powers on their side tried naturally to thwart the approaches of the *Entente* Powers to the neutrals. But they also realized the extreme vulnerability of the Tsarist Empire to encouragement of the subject nationalities; and they toyed too with the support of the Irish, and attempted to enlist the support of Islam, to subvert Persia, Afghanistan and India, and to raise Abyssinia against the rear of the British position in Egypt.

The first of the neutrals to enter was the Turkish Empire. The 'Young Turks', the military junta which had full command of Turkish affairs in August 1914, were already thoroughly committed to Germany, with the Liman von Sanders mission re-organizing their army, German capital heavily engaged in developing the Turkish railway system and Krupps acting as their main supply of armaments. But they had little to lose and much to gain from staying neutral. They were tipped towards war partly by their hatred of Russia and partly by their confidence in a German victory. But the action of the British Navy in commandeering two modern battleships they had under construction in British shipyards, and the successful evasion of the British Mediterranean squadron by the German battle cruiser *Goeben* with its attendant cruiser the *Breslau*, which sought refuge in the Sea of Marmora and were promptly transferred by Germany, together with their crews, into Turkish service, finally decided them to declare war on Russia in November 1914.

By this time Japan and Portugal, as Britain's allies, had formally entered the war on the side of the *Entente* Powers and interest shifted to Italy.

Nominally a member of the Triple Alliance with Germany and Austria-Hungary, Italy had in fact virtually abandoned the Alliance around the turn of the century; and at the outbreak of war Italy proclaimed her neutrality. Italian entry into the war was determined by a kind of auction of Austrian territories in upper Italy in which inevitably the Germans, inhibited by the fact that they were dealing with the territory of their allies, came off second best. In April 1915, by the Treaty of London, Britain and France promised the Italians the Trentino, the South Tyrol, Trieste, Gorizia, Istria and Dalmatia and the Turkish province of Adalia if Italy would enter the war on the Allied side. Italy declared war on Austria on May 23rd, 1915.

The Italian entry into the war was preceded in Italy by a debate between the advocates of the doctrine of *sacro egoismo* (holy egotism) and those of *parecchio* (much) who argued that Italy could obtain most by staying neutral. This spirit of unashamed and admitted desire for national aggrandizement was not rewarded by any immediate gain. The Austrian position was very strong naturally and had been systematically prepared. By the end of 1915 the Italians had lost over 250,000 men in successive battles on the river Isonzo and had advanced only as far as the Austrian main defences.

More success attended the next entrant into the war, Bulgaria. The *Entente* Powers made desperate attempts to keep her neutral. But Bulgaria's ambitions lay all in the territories Serbia and Greece had taken from her in 1913 in the second Balkan war. Under German pressure Turkey ceded her land west of the Maritsa river. On September 6th, a secret German-Austrian-Bulgarian treaty committed Bulgaria to join in operations against Serbia. On October 14th, Bulgaria entered the war. The German and Austrian offensive against Serbia had already begun, and the Bulgarian forces succeeded in cutting off the Serbian escape route to Salonika in Greece, where two *Entente* divisions had landed. The Serb army was driven into a desperate retreat across the mountains to Durazzo on the Adriatic where the survivors were evacuated to the Greek island of Corfu. A quarter of a million Serbian casualties, killed, wounded and prisoners, were lost in this campaign.

The course of events in Greece was less smooth, the country being deeply divided between the pro-German King Constantine and his followers, whose main strength lay in those sections of Greece which had gained their independence in the early part of the nineteenth century, and the Liberal leader, M. Venizelos, whose main support came from the Greek islands. In January 1915 the *Entente* Powers offered Greece the Turkish city of Smyrna and its hinterland in return for Greek concessions to Bulgaria and Greek support of Serbia. Venizelos wished to accept but the King would not agree and dismissed him. Elections in June 1915 returned Venizelos to power again but the Allied failure to carry Gallipoli made him less enthusiastic to intervene in the war unless the presence of a large *Entente* force at Salonika could be guaranteed. The obvious move of Bulgaria towards the Central Powers also made him more cautious. Greece refused to come to Serbia's aid against Bulgaria but connived at the landing of two Allied divisions at Salonika. The *Entente* troops in fact came too late to save Serbia; and uncertainty as to the intentions of the Greek armed forces made them abandon their first offensive. They did, however, stay in Salonika. Venizelos resigned yet again and the Greeks moved back towards an occupied neutrality.

The Turkish armies meantime were engaged on their only front with Russia in the Caucasus. Here megalomania on the part of Enver Pasha drove the Turks into a winter offensive towards Kars in which the Turks lost 77,000 men out of an army of 95,000. The Turkish defeat was quickly repaired by German direction and the Russians, in their turn, were caught early in 1915 and only brilliant Russian generalship defeated the subsequent Turkish offensive.

In the meantime the Turks and Germans between them had been attempting to preach a *Jehad*, a holy war of Islam, against the British and French. The position of the Ottoman Sultan as Caliph gave them a springboard and his proclamation of a *Jehad* was duly endorsed by the *Ulemas* of Istanbul. But the *Jehad* floundered without the support of Hussein, the Sharif of Mecca. And Hussein saw in British support the chance of forming an Arab kingdom which would comprehend the whole of the Arab east. In October 1914 the British, desperately anxious for the security of the Islamic population of their empire, and remembering Abdullah's approach to Kitchener in February 1914, opened contact with Hussein and promised him aid and support in the event of an Arab rising against the Turks. The Indian government at the same time began similar approaches to ibn Saud. As the Turkish forces in the Yemen were preparing an offensive against Aden which was to take them as far as Lahej before it petered out, the matter was urgent.

There followed, however, a year or more of negotiations in which the British authorities in Egypt offered Hussein an outright alliance and the recognition of a single Arab state in the Arabian peninsula. But Hussein's ambitions stretched to Damascus and Baghdad; in return for British support of these ambitions, he offered the British a defensive alliance and economic hegemony within the new Arab state. The British, however, were in no position to accept such proposals, in view of the interests and ambitions of their French ally in the Lebanon and Syria. And the final British note sent to Hussein in October 1915 reserved the Syrian areas west of Damascus, Homs, Hama and Aleppo, and provided for a 'special form of administration' with British participation in the provinces of Basra and Baghdad. Even that did not settle matters and the negotiations dragged on into 1916. In the meantime the only Arab forces to take the *Jehad* seriously were the Senussi of Cyrenaica, especially after their self-styled overlords, the Italians, joined the *Entente* Powers. A joint Turkish-Senussi force caused considerable trouble with its irruptions into Egypt, until the capture of its able Turkish commander in February 1916 brought its effective activities to an end.

In the war at sea, the balance of power lay overwhelmingly in favour of the *Entente* Powers. The British battle fleet, the Grand Fleet as it was called, consisted of 35 Dreadnoughts, 27 pre-Dreadnoughts and 10 battle cruisers, 72 ships in all, which from their bases at Rosyth and Scapa Flow effectively bottled the German fleet into the North Sea. The German fleet with its 22 Dreadnoughts, 16 pre-Dreadnoughts and 8 battle cruisers was thus completely unable to exert any strength against Britain's supply lines, all of which terminated in ports on Britain's south and west coasts. And the naval folly of Admiral Tirpitz's construction policy, with its concentration on gun-power and heavy armour at the sacrifice of range of operation, was revealed. For so long as the Grand Fleet survived, Britain's commerce was largely invulnerable to attack by surface warships, once the few German warships outside the North Sea in August 1914 had been hunted down. It was for the German battle fleet, numerically the weaker of the two, to lure the Grand Fleet into action, in the knowledge that unless it was exceptionally well-handled and fortunate in the lottery of war, it faced inevitable defeat by superior numbers. Not surprisingly, sorties by the German battle fleet tended to be few and far between.

The hunting down of the German warships outside the North Sea was only a matter of time. The German Mediterranean squadron, as related above, evaded British capture and took refuge in the Sea of Marmora. The German Pacific squadron under Admiral Graf von Spee caught its weaker British equivalent at Coronel off the coast of Chile in November 1914 and destroyed it. But thereafter, except for the cruiser *Emden*, which managed for a time to terrorize British and Allied shipping in the Pacific, Graf von Spee's squadron was lured by faked German signals sent out by British Intelligence to the Falkland Islands, to be destroyed in December 1914 by a superior British force. The *Emden* was caught and sunk by an Australian cruiser, the *Sydney*, in the Indian Ocean in November 1914, and the *Dresden*, sole survivor of Graf von Spee's squadron, was sunk in March 1915 in the Pacific. The last German cruiser, the *Königsberg*, was caught in African waters in July 1915. Thereafter only German U-boats and the occasional German merchant cruiser appeared outside the North Sea to harass British commerce.

The German battle fleet was handled with extreme caution in these first two years of war; though isolated German cruiser and battle cruiser raids were made into the North Sea, their fate precluded more large-scale operations. In August 1914 and again in January 1915 at the battle of the Dogger Bank, British battle cruisers caught German cruiser squadrons engaged on such raids and damaged them severely. A German battle cruiser attack on the British coast in December 1914 managed to evade interception; but their fate in general convinced the German Naval High Command that the only hope of victory at sea lay in U-boat raids on all shipping engaged in supplying Britain. In February 1915 therefore the German Naval High Command issued a formal warning that all shipping found in the waters around the British Isles would be liable to be sunk

223

without warning, neutral shipping included. But the Germans lacked the numbers of U-boats as yet to make their threat real, and its only effect was greatly to exacerbate German relations with the United States, especially after the sinking of the passenger liners *Lusitania* and *Arabic* in May and August 1915 with considerable loss of life to the passengers, who included American citizens. American protests were so strong that in September 1915 the German government greatly modified its orders to U-boat crews and U-boat attacks in the waters around Britain notably diminished.

This was the first sign of the issue which was eventually to bring the United States into the war. On its outbreak in August 1914 the United States had proclaimed its formal neutrality. In practice, most American opinion, save among the members of the German, Irish and Jewish minorities, were either indifferent or profoundly pro-Ally. And their pro-Allied sentiments were reinforced once Britain began placing large orders with arms and steel manufacturers, raising loans on the New York money market to finance these orders and making pre-emptive bids for the whole American cotton crop in order to prevent it from falling into German hands. The combined effect of all the Allied orders for war material and supplies in America was to introduce a general upswing in the American economy which up to the summer of 1914 had been in the throes of a depression. British and Allied orders which were largely financed by the mobilization of Britain's immense overseas investments were to keep American industry operating at full capacity for the next three years.

The British blockade of Germany, however, also had its repercussions on Anglo-American relations. As Britain had failed to ratify the pre-war conventions on contraband, the British Navy was free to issue its own lists of goods whose export to Germany was forbidden, and, as always, it arrogated to itself the right to stop and search any neutral ship suspected of carrying contraband to its enemies, the Central Powers. This right was extended to include shipment to the ports of neutrals such as the Netherlands or Scandinavia, where trans-shipment to Germany, because of the territorial contiguity of the neutral to Germany, could not be checked. Shippers found it safer to clear their cargoes with British blockade authorities in advance and arm themselves with certificates, 'navicerts' they were called, against boarding and search by British warships. And such boarding and searching with its constant reminder that the seas could only be used with British permission grated deeply on the nerves of the one world power that was not yet involved in the war.

In addition to making possible the blockade of Germany, Britain's dominance of the sea made the conquest of the German colonies merely a matter of time. Those in the Pacific fell to Australian and New Zealand action. The naval station at Kiou Chou on the Shantung peninsula of North China was reduced by Britain's Japanese ally. German South-West Africa fell easily to South African forces once a rebellion by Boer extremists in South Africa itself had been put down. Togoland was caught between British forces moving from the Gold Coast and the French

THE BALKAN WARS 1912~1913.

Albania independent 1912/13
          Princedom 1914
Macedonia  Serbian
          Greek   } 1914
          Bulgarian
Bulgarian acquisitions
          between 1886 & 1913
Greece
   Greek acquisitions  1913
Gains to Serbia in 1913
      Montenegro in 1913

RUMANIA

• Kronstadt

• Ploësti

Belgrade
• Bucharest

Silistra

R. Danube
Ruschuk

BOSNIA
Annexed 1908

• Kragujevac

• Sarajevo

HERZEGOVINIA
Annexed 1908

SERBIA

• Nis

BULGARIA
1908 Ind. Kingdom

Varna

BLACK
SEA

• Novibazar

• Sofia

Burgas

MONTENEGRO
Ragusa
Cattaro
• Cetinje

• Kumanova
• Skopje

• Philippopolis

Kirk Kilisse

Adrianople

Constantinople
Chataldja

ADRIATIC
SEA

Durazzo  • Tirana

• Strumnitsa

Dedeagatch

MACEDONIA

Salonika

GALLIPOLI

ALBANIA

IMBROS

TURKEY

Valona

LEMNOS

ITALY

CORFU

Larissa

LESBOS

AEGEAN
SEA

CHIOS

GREECE

SAMOS

• Athens

Corinth

0          100
Miles

DODECANESE
1912 Italian
RHODES

CARPATHOS

MEDITERRANEAN SEA

Greek 1908/12

CRETE

ENGLAND

London

Doggerbank
✕ 24.1.1915

SKAGERRAK

Jutland ✕
31.5 – 1.6.1916

Stockholm

DENMARK

Göteborg

Malmö

Heligoland ✕

Kiel

Hamburg

Bremen

Danzig

Stettin

Thorn

Berlin

Wloclawek
Poznan

English Blockade 4.8.1914 – 12.7.1919

NETHERLANDS

Ostend
BELGIUM
Ypres
28.9.18
Antwerp
Brussels
Arras
St Quentin
Soissons
Compiègne
Reims
Verdun
Le Havre

Versailles

Orléans

Cologne

Coblenz

GERMANY

Leipzig
Lützen

Dresden

Glogow

Prague
28.10.18

Cracow

FRANCE

Le Creusot
3.8.1914

Épinal
Belfort

Strasbourg

Altenburg

Munich

Wagram
Vienna

AUSTRIA-

SWITZERLAND

Innsbruck

Graz

Budapest

Trente

Milan

Venice

Trieste

Zagreb

Fiume

Genoa

Spezia

Marseille

Toulon

ITALY

BOSNIA

Belgrade

Sarajevo

SERBIA

Novi Bazar

MONTENEGRO

Cetinje

Scutari

Durazzo

ALBANIA

0    50   100        200        300
Miles

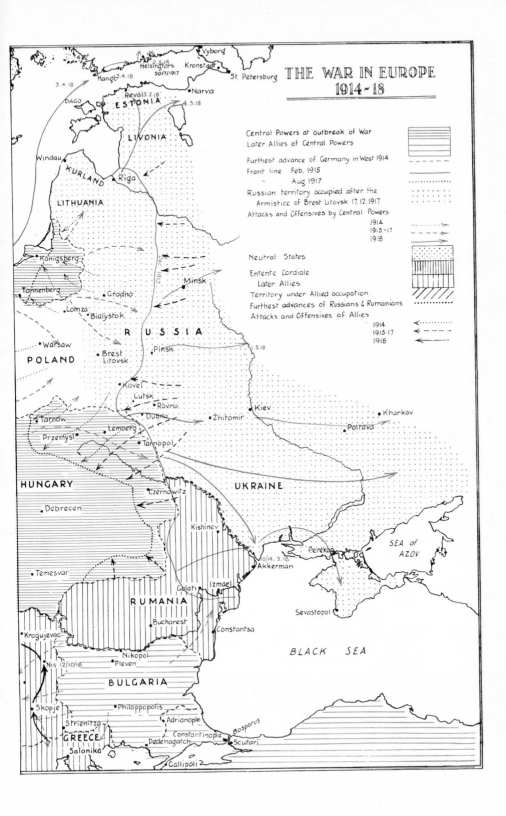

THE WAR IN EUROPE
1914~18

Central Powers at outbreak of War
Later Allies of Central Powers

Furthest advance of Germany in West 1914
Front line   Feb. 1915
    "        Aug 1917
Russian territory occupied after the
    Armistice of Brest Litovsk 17.12.1917
Attacks and Offensives by Central Powers
                                    1914
                                    1915~17
                                    1918

Neutral States

Entente Cordiale
    Later Allies
Territory under Allied occupation
Furthest advances of Russians & Rumanians
Attacks and Offensives of Allies
                                    1914
                                    1915-17
                                    1918

Vyborg
Helsingfors 9.4.18   Kronstadt
Hangö 7.4.18   20/7/1917   St. Petersburg
3.4.18   Narva
DAGO   Reval 25.2.18   4.3.18
ESTONIA
LIVONIA
Windau
KURLAND   Riga
LITHUANIA
Königsberg
Tannenberg   Grodno   Minsk
Lomza   Bialystok
Warsaw   R U S S I A   Pinsk
POLAND   Brest   Pinsk   1.3.18
    Litovsk
Kovel
Lutsk
Rovno   Kiev   Kharkov
Tarnow   Dubno   Zhitomir   Poltava
Przemysl   Lemberg
    Tarnopol
HUNGARY   Czernowitz   UKRAINE
Debrecen
Kishinev
Perekop   SEA of
                    AZOV
Temesvar   10/14.3.18
    Akkerman
Galati   Izmael
RUMANIA   Sevastopol
Bucharest
Kragujevac   Constantsa   BLACK   SEA
Nikopol
Nis 12/10/18   Pleven
B U L G A R I A
Skopje
Philippopolis
Strienitza   Adrianople
GREECE   Constantinople   Bosporus
Dedeagatch   Scutari
Salonika
Gallipoli

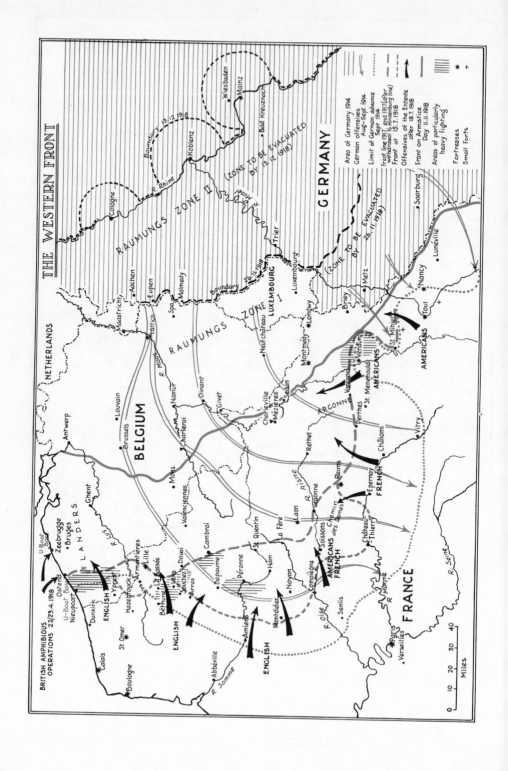

# THE WESTERN FRONT

**GERMANY**

RAUMUNGS ZONE II
(ZONE TO BE EVACUATED BY 13.12.1918)

Boundary 13.12.1918

Cologne

R. Rhine

Wiesbaden

Mainz

Bad Kreuznach

Koblenz

Trier

RAUMUNGS ZONE I

LUXEMBOURG

(ZONE TO BE EVACUATED BY 26.11.1918)

Boundary 26.11.1918

Luxembourg

Longwy

Briey

Metz

Saarburg

Montmedy

Neufchâteau

Verdun

St. Mihiel

Toul

Nancy

Lunéville

**AMERICANS**

ARGONNE

Varennes

St. Menehould

Perthes

AMERICANS

Vitry

Sedan

Charleville

Mézières

Rethel

R. Aisne

Reims

Épernay

Châlons

**FRENCH**

Givet

Dinant

Namur

Charleroi

Mons

Valenciennes

Laon

La Fère

Soissons

Chemin des Dames

Château-Thierry

AMERICANS

FRENCH

Senlis

Compiègne

Noyon

Ham

St Quentin

Péronne

Montdidier

Bapaume

Cambrai

R. Oise

R. Marne

Versailles

Paris

R. Seine

**FRANCE**

NETHERLANDS

Antwerp

Louvain

Brussels

Ghent

**BELGIUM**

Maastricht

Aachen

Spa

Eupen

Malmedy

Lüttich

R. Meuse

**FLANDERS**

Zeebrugge

Bruges

Ostend

Nieuport

U-Boat Base

U-Boat Base

Ypres

Armentières

Lille

Douai

Lens

La Bassée

Souchez

Béthune

Arras

Abbéville

Amiens

Albert

**ENGLISH**

Hazebrouck

R. Lys

Calais

Boulogne

St. Omer

Dunkirk

R. Somme

R. Scarpe

**ENGLISH**

**ENGLISH**

BRITISH AMPHIBIOUS
OPERATIONS 22/23.4.1918

Front at 15.7.1918

### Legend

Area of Germany 1914

German offensives Aug–Sept 1914

Limit of German advance Sept 1914

Front line 1917 and 1917 (after withdrawal to Hindenburg line), Front at 15.7.1918

Offensives of the Entente after 18.7.1918

Front on Armistice Day 11.11.1918

Areas of particularly heavy fighting

Fortresses

Small Forts

### Scale

0   10   20   30   40
Miles

advancing from Dahomey. The Cameroons fell after eighteen months fighting to British, French and Belgian forces moving in from three sides. Only in German East Africa, where disease took a frightful toll of the Allied troops, did the German garrison, led by a genius, General von Lettow-Vorbeck, succeed in holding out until the end of the war. The very considerable body of African troops, twenty-two battalions in all, raised by the British to conduct this campaign, had a considerable impact on the development of African nationalism in East Africa in later years.

In the war at sea, British naval supremacy, as was pointed out in an earlier chapter, rested not only on her superiority in the actual strength of her fleet but also in her control of most of the major 'narrows', outlets for European seapower to the open oceans, bottle-necks through which maritime commerce virtually had to pass. Of all these narrows, only one, and that perhaps the most vital to Britain, the Suez Canal, was really vulnerable to attack by land. Once the Turks had entered into the war, Suez was an obvious target for the Ottoman forces in Palestine. Expecting such an attack the British authorities moved two Indian divisions to Egypt in November 1914 and used Egypt as the assembly point for the first two divisions from Australia and New Zealand. They were thus easily able to repel a Turkish attack across the waterless Sinai desert in February 1915.

Before the Turkish entry into the war the British government moved troops to the frontiers of Mesopotamia at the head of the Persian Gulf to protect the oil installations at Abadan, which was commanded by a Turkish fortress on the island of Fao on the opposite side of the Shatt-al-Arab. On the Turkish entry into the war, the Turkish fortress was captured. From this there developed a full-scale advance up the Euphrates river towards Baghdad. But at the end of 1915 the British forces, rebuffed before Ctesiphon some twenty-five miles south of Baghdad retired on the town of Kut-al-Amara where they rashly allowed themselves to be besieged by the Turkish forces and were eventually, in April 1916, forced to capitulate.

The main use made of Britain's command of the sea in 1915, however, was in the amphibious assault on the Dardanelles which became the Gallipoli campaign. The scheme represented a deliberate attempt to get away from the 'continental' strategy to which Britain had committed herself before 1914 in order to return to the traditional 'maritime' strategy of the past; in this traditional strategy British seapower was used to land British armies wherever on an enemy-dominated European coastline they would create the maximum disruptive effect and could secure the most important immediate success. It had as its immediate aim the opening of a direct supply route to Russian warm-water ports so that the manifold and paralysing deficiences of the Russian war industry could be made up from the Allies. The British Admiralty before the war had wanted to launch the Army in an amphibious assault on the German North Sea coast. In late 1914 it toyed briefly with the idea of using Britain's great store of pre-Dreadnoughts to force a way into the Baltic. But in January 1915 the decision was taken to attempt to force the Dardanelles. A purely naval attempt in February 1915 failed with the loss of three British and French capital ships; its only success was to draw Turkish divisions away from the Caucasus front, and to give warning of Allied interest in the Dardanelles area.

Thus when in April 1915 amphibious landings were made on the Gallipoli peninsula at the mouth of the Dardanelles they ran into heavy Turkish resistance organized by the future president of the Turkish Republic, Kemal Ataturk. And a second landing in August came to grief when the British troops failed to exploit the initial surprise achieved by the landing. In December 1915 the Allied forces were secretly and safely evacuated. British losses totalled 213,980 killed, wounded, hospitalized and missing, of which two out of three were casualties from disease rather then enemy action. As an exercise in 'maritime strategy' the Dardanelles campaign was a costly failure.

The effects of the first days of war in enhancing all the nationalist centrifugal forces in European society and opening fissures between nation and nation were greatly intensified by the hardships, privations and strains of war, above all by the impact of the ever-lengthening casualty lists upon the morale of the middle-classes from whom the bulk of the volunteer and reservist officer corps of the new mass armies in Europe were recruited. These feelings of internecine hatred of English and French for German and *vice versa* were only exacerbated by the growth of considerable propaganda machines on either side designed to convince both domestic and neutral opinion of the justice of the nation's cause and the barbarism of the enemy. To this effort all but a very few of Europe's intellectuals lent their aid; and their efforts aborted for most of the following generations the development of any common European intellectual culture except among a small and *avant-garde* minority. The British were particularly effective, so all agreed, at this novel form of European intellectual *hari-kari*; so much so that, from a country where German intellectual influences had once been overwhelming, knowledge of contemporary German intellectual developments became almost as esoteric an accomplishment as expertise in Indian ceramics or the writings of Lao-Tse.

This was, however, only of significance in that it accentuated the long-term development of fissiparous as against unifying forces in Western and Central Europe. Of more immediate importance was the accentuation of internal divisions, the revival of party strife in Britain, France and Germany under the increasing strains of 1915's succession of sanguinary and unsuc-cessful attempts to break the strategic deadlock.

In Britain the main lines of the struggle became clear from January 1915 onwards. On the one hand was a small group in the Liberal party, led by David Lloyd George, which was becoming appalled by the rate at which Britain was dissipating her financial resources and the calm with which the military commanders, backed by Lord Kitchener, the Field Marshal whom Asquith had made War Minister, were prepared to take extremely severe casualties and yet have nothing to show for it. For this group the main urgency was to re-establish civilian control of the military. The Conservatives were increasingly dissatisfied with their exclusion from power, and had lost confidence in the abilities of all but a handful of Liberal ministers. Both groups were highly critical of Asquith's powers of leadership. In May 1915 the Conservatives forced a coalition on the Liberals. The casualties, however, continued and by the end of 1915 it was clear that Britain would have to introduce conscription.

In France, Parliament did not meet at all during the months of crisis in the autumn of 1914, and the French High Command flourished without criticism. When Parliament did re-convene it was obvious that General Joffre, with the help of the Minister of War, Millerand, was determined to tolerate no parliamentary interference with the conduct of the war. In June 1915, General Joffre precipitated a crisis in internal politics by summarily dismissing the commander of the Third Army, General Sarrail, who had a strong parliamentary following that wished to see him Commander-in-Chief. The failure to restrain Bulgaria and the need to make some gesture towards Serbia led to Sarrail's appointment as commander of an Allied expedition to Salonika. In the resultant crisis, Briand replaced Viviani as Premier, and General Gallièni became War Minister. The *Union Sacré* between left and right had been disturbed: but the real crisis was to follow in 1916–17.

In Germany, it was the unequal social effects of the British blockade that were mainly to blame for the gradual ebbing away of the feeling of social unity which sprang up so spontaneously in August 1914. Although there was an official rationing scheme for food, it was easily circumvented, and rationing tended to operate according to the size of one's purse rather than on the basis of one's need. The Chancellor, Bethman-Hollweg, did his best to satisfy the Social Democrats, who were, after all, the largest party in the *Reichstag*. But his only reward was to induce in the conservative right the conviction that victory was essential as a means of restraining the further advance of parliamentarianism, so that social discontent could be sublimated in the exultation of an annexationist peace. The revival in social tension within Germany was not reflected in the *Reichstag*, however, until December 1915, when the left wing of the Social Democrats began to break away and opposed the vote for war credits.

In the Far East, the absorption of the Great Powers in the war in Europe left Japanese expansionists virtually a free hand. Japanese troops expelled the Germans from Kiou Chou and Japan fell heir to the German sphere of influence in the Shantung peninsula. In January 1915 Japan secretly presented to China a list of 'Twenty-one Demands' in five groups, Chinese agreement to the last of which would have given Japan an economic protectorate over Northern China and effective control of the Chinese armed forces. China managed to mobilize a certain amount of diplomatic support, which enabled her to evade discussion of the last group of demands, but she was forced to make very considerable concessions in the economic sphere.

The effect was to exacerbate internal tensions in China. Yuan Shih-kai was encouraged by the overwhelming support he received from all branches of Chinese opinion to proceed with his ambitions to found a new dynasty in China, despite international opposition from the *Entente* Powers. With Japanese support, however, the republicans rallied and anti-Yuan forces raised revolt throughout the south of China. The controversy ended in part at least with Yuan's death in June 1916.

At the end of 1915 the war was beginning to move into a new and more extreme phase. Up to that date a negotiated peace might have been possible, and the losses which Europe had so far suffered in men and material, though extremely serious, could possibly have been overcome. But in each of the major countries the tides of parliamentarianism and anti-militarism which had flowed so strongly in the years immediately before the war were in retreat, and the military leaders, with their instinctive preference for social conservatism and political authoritarianism and their almost universal contempt for civilian parliamentarianism enjoyed the strongest popular support. For their part they had reached in all countries virtually the identical conclusion, that victory could only come when the forces of their enemies had been numerically worn down and their morale broken in the process, in short, a strategy of attrition. For Europe as a whole, however, attrition meant self-attrition; and as the process continued the world balance shifted inevitably, irretrievably, away from Europe.

*Chapter XIII*
# TOTAL WAR AND THE SELF-MUTILATION OF EUROPE, 1916–1917

## *1916, The Year of Attrition*

As 1915 ended the supreme commanders in France and Germany were both convinced that ultimate victory could only be reached on the Western Front. Joffre planned a great Anglo-French offensive in the summer to be supported by simultaneous attacks on the Russian and Italian fronts. He secured the reluctant agreement of the British commander in France, General Haig, to that offensive taking place along the river Somme, an area selected not for any strategic importance but because, being in the area in which the French and British forces touched one another, it would make the problems of command easier. The aim of the offensive was principally that of attrition. The German commander, von Falkenhayn, who had replaced von Moltke after his failure at the Marne, had a similar aim, to bleed the French army white in the hope of knocking France out of the war. With this aim he proposed to concentrate his attacks on the fortress of Verdun, which lay in a salient with poor communications easily commanded by the German artillery, and which, he correctly estimated, French sentiment would make it impossible to abandon. He was unable to carry his Austro-Hungarian allies with him; they preferred to concentrate on knocking Italy out of the war by an Alpine offensive.

The German attack on Verdun began on February 21st. Its strategic aim succeeded magnificently. French troops were poured into the defence of the great fortress system which General Joffre had previously dismissed as outmoded, and many of the reserves he had earmarked for the great summer offensive were killed or wounded. The Germans, however, became equally committed to Verdun, as the final casualty total, 362,000 for France and 336, 831 for Germany, reveals. Neither side made any significant gains in territory.

As a result the planned Anglo-French offensive on the Somme became virtually an all-British affair. Launched with insufficient artillery preparation, the Somme offensive was based on a system of attack better fitted to the battlefield of Waterloo than to one dominated by the machine-gun.

The first day's casualties amounted to nearly 60,000 British killed and wounded. But the battle continued until mid-November when the advance of winter made further fighting impossible, with heavy reserves being committed on both sides, the Germans using 161 divisions to 20 for the French and 55 for the British. The German casualties outnumbered those suffered by Britain and France, and the German professional army was said by historians on both sides to have been virtually destroyed in the battle.

The failure by either the French or Germans to achieve victory led to the dismissal of Joffre and his deputy, General Foch, and Germany's General von Falkenhayn. Nivelle, the hero of Verdun, succeeded Foch, and Hindenburg, the victor of Tannenberg, succeeded von Falkenhayn. The British commander, General Haig, was promoted to the rank of Field Marshal. All three promotions reflected more on the effectiveness with which their beneficiaries had built up their military reputations at home than their actual military capabilities, and Nivelle's ill-judged optimism was soon to lead France to the edge of collapse.

If the British forces had secured a partial victory in France, the rest of the Allied fronts in 1916 showed nothing but disaster. On the Italian front, it is true, the Austrian offensive in the Trentino was repelled with heavy losses on both sides. But four further Italian offensives on the Isonzo advanced the Italian lines only a few miles around Gorizia at the cost of very heavy casualties.

On the Russian front, the great offensive planned to coincide with Joffre's originally planned assault in the Somme was advanced in date to ease Austrian pressure on Italy in the Trentino. Under General Brusilov's leadership, it was at first amazingly successful and over 400,000 Austrians were taken prisoner. But the Russian casualties were extremely severe and they lacked the reserves of men, material and mobility to exploit the victory. Germany's command of the interior lines enabled her to move troops from the Western front; although the German counter-offensive was unsuccessful, these fresh German troops were able to control the new Russian offensives launched in July, August and October 1916. Ultimate victory continued to elude the Russian armies; and in the meantime the Russian will to victory was being steadily eroded by the lack of materials, Tsarist bureaucratic mismanagement and the appalling casualties. About one million men were killed, wounded and missing on the Russian side in 1916.

The worst *Entente* disasters occurred in Rumania and Iraq. In Iraq the British forces at Kut were forced to surrender to their Turkish besiegers. In Rumania the apparent success of the Russian summer offensive brought the Rumanian government to a hasty abandonment of their neutrality in return for promises of post-war gains at Austria-Hungary's expense in Transylvania and the Bukovina. But by the time Rumania's claims had been finally conceded by the *Entente* Powers, by the Treaty of Bucharest of August 27th, 1916, the Russian offensives had lost their momentum and a force of German, Austrian, Bulgarian and Turkish forces was being rapidly assembled to deal with her. The Rumanians chose to ignore *Entente* pleas for a southern offensive to link up with the *Entente* forces at Salonika so as to cut the Central Powers' link with Turkey. Instead they concentrated their forces against Transylvania. Here they caught the Austrians off balance and advanced in some places over forty miles; but the effect was only to exhaust and scatter their forces and leave them less able to stand up to the German counter-offensive when it came. The German attack duly began in October 1916. By December the Rumanians had been pinned into the north-eastern corner of their own country at a cost of over 300,000 casualties. And Rumania's oilfields, granaries and her great wealth of wheat-lands fell into German hands.

In the meantime the Greek government continued to give trouble to the Allied forces in Salonika. In June 1916, Anglo-French forces blockaded Athens and demanded and secured the demobilization of the Greek army and the dismissal of the pro-German government. In August, reinforced by the survivors of the Serbian army from Corfu, the *Entente* forces launched an offensive against the Bulgarians. But it was repelled and the British flank was weakened when a German-Bulgarian counter-offensive was accompanied by the voluntary surrender of a Greek army corps to the Germans on the Graeco-Bulgarian border.

With *Entente* encouragement, Venizelos, the Greek Liberal leader, then raised a revolt in Salonika and the islands, established a provisional government and declared war on the Central Powers. The *Entente* Powers sent an ultimatum demanding the dismissal of the representatives of the Central Powers and landed troops near Athens in support. They withdrew only after the Greeks had agreed to withdraw all Greek forces from Thessaly. In December the British decided to recognize the Venizelos government, and a second offensive re-established Serb forces on Serbian territory in the town of Monastir. Troubles with the Greek Royalist government in Athens continued until, in June 1917, after fresh French landings on the isthmus of Corinth, King Constantine abdicated in favour of his second son, Alexander, and a Venizelist government was established. In July 1917 the new *régime* declared war on the Central Powers and the Greek army joined the *Entente* forces on the Salonika front.

The Caucasus saw major Russian victories in 1916. Under the Grand Duke Nicholas, transferred to this theatre in disgrace after the Russian defeats in Poland in 1915, the Russian winter offensive caught the Turks completely off balance. By mid-July the Turkish fortresses of Erzerum, Trebizond and Eringhian had fallen and the Russian armies had advanced into the heart of Anatolia. But the primitiveness of the communications and the general weakness of the Russian supply system brought them to a halt. The Turkish forces in the Caucasus were in a complete state of demoralization and a new army was sent to replace them.

The Suez and Palestine fronts saw a further Turkish defeat in August 1916 when a Turkish offensive against Suez was stopped by superior

British forces on the Mediterranean coast of the Sinai peninsula. The British forces were in the meantime engaged in solving the engineering problems of launching a campaign through the Sinai desert. In December 1916 they advanced up to the borders of Palestine. And the same month a new British offensive was launched in Mesopotamia and by February 1917 Kut had been recaptured.

At sea, the year 1916 began with a new man in command of the German High Seas fleet, Admiral Scheer. He began by intensifying cruiser and submarine warfare against British shipping. But the sinking of the Folke-stone–Dieppe packet, the *Sussex*, in March 1916 with the loss of several American lives led the Kaiser to one of his rare, and as it proved his last, interventions in the conduct of the war and the temporary rescinding of the order for unrestricted submarine warfare under the threat of an American break in diplomatic relations.

Scheer then attempted to lure the British Grand Fleet into battle. There followed two German sorties in March and April 1916 with the bombardment of seaports on the British North Sea coast. A third sortie at the end of May, made with the deliberate intention of luring the Grand Fleet into action off the coast of Norway, resulted in collision between British and German battle cruisers. A rather confused engagement between the main battle fleets, known to British historians as the Battle of Jutland, to Germans as the battle of the Skaggerak, followed, from which the Germans managed to escape under cover of night. Both sides claimed a victory. Tactically, perhaps, the Germans had the edge, having sunk three British battle cruisers for the loss of one battleship and one battle cruiser, and three cruisers for the loss of four light cruisers. One further German sortie in July passed without an engagement between the two fleets. But the strategic success scored by the British at Jutland was underlined by the fact that this was the last move by the German High Seas fleet for the rest of the war. Its existence continued to dominate the Baltic entrances and to tie up a large mass of British light craft in the North Sea. But effectively, Jutland marked the end of the German High Seas fleet as an offensive weapon of war. Its crews were to become the main objects of the decline in morale and the growth of revolutionary feelings in Germany. For Britain Jutland was hailed as a success by her propagandists; but it was difficult for public opinion to accept it as something to place alongside the classic naval victories of British tradition.

The impact of the campaigns of 1916 and the progressive destruction by death, disease, capture or nervous breakdown ('shell-shock' in contemporary parlance) of the whole eighteen to thirty-five year old age group in the principal belligerent countries resulted in a marked intensification of the strains that had already begun to show themselves. As previously noted, the war losses were particularly felt among the educated middle and professional classes from whom the junior officers in the new mass armies were largely drawn, an infantry lieutenant's expectation of life on arrival at the front being reckoned at about a month. In Germany the effect was mainly to drive these classes towards the right, war-service giving their members admission to the class and status of a member of the pre-war Prussian ruling class, and to accentuate the divisions between these classes and the German industrial and agricultural workers.

In Britain the main effect was to drive enmity for Germany deep into the national sub-conscious. On the conscious level, the main strains worked themselves out in the battle for the unorthodox but inspired leadership of Lloyd George as against the uninspired committee chairmanship provided by the Liberal leader, Herbert Asquith. The Conservatives found them-selves increasingly dissatisfied with his personality; pressure built up within political circles for the creation of a small streamlined War Cabinet, without the large and lengthy debates of which no real record was kept, which were the main feature of Asquith's cabinets. Asquith himself proved unable to understand the real nature of the criticism directed against him; and when in December 1916 a gathering together of the most dynamic members of his own and the Conservative party broke up the coalition, he virtually defied his opponents to form an alternative government. David Lloyd George, his War Minister, succeeded in bringing together the Conservatives, Labour and a large section of the Liberals under his leader-ship. The split in the Liberal party was never quite healed again, and Lloyd George, losing control of the party political machinery, lacked the organiz-ing genius to create his own. For the moment, however, he was supreme, except in his relations with his generals.

In Italy, similar discontents were beginning to break out. Salandra, the Italian premier, had by no means had a majority of the Italian people behind him when he took Italy into the war. The hope of immediate victory had, however, silenced opposition and as late as February 1916 he had secured an overwhelming vote of confidence from the Italian parlia-ment. The Austrian offensive in the Trentino in May 1916 was, however, too much for Italian opinion, and the King turned to a seventy-eight year old nonentity, Signor Boselli, in the hope that he would prove a successful leader of a national coalition which embraced all but the consistently pacifist Italian Socialist party.

In Japan a similar crisis broke out in May 1916. Count Okuma's cabinet had failed to push through the most far-reaching of the Twenty-One Demands, while at the same time its increased reliance on parliamentary support rather than that of the elder statesmen of the court deprived it of the patronage necessary to enable it to withstand the nationalist extremists in the armed services. Okuma was replaced by a non-party government under Count Terauchi which, despite its use of official influence, was unable to secure a general majority in the parliamentary elections which followed.

Japan, however, remained free to pursue a more active policy in the Far East by securing the political support of its allies for its continental ambi-tions. The accession to power of the Terauchi government was followed by a prolonged press campaign against the Anglo-Japanese alliance which included a discussion of an alternative German connection. At the same time Russo-Japanese negotiations led in the summer of 1916 to a secret agreement by which Russia recognized Japan's gains in China. A similar agreement was reached in February 1917 with the British government recognizing Japan's general rights to the succession of the German position not only in the Shantung peninsula but also in the Central Pacific.

These internecine strains in the domestic politics of the *Entente* Powers were accompanied by far greater activity on each side in subverting the minority national groups within the rival political groupings. The Easter 1916 rising in Ireland provided the most effective example, though the arms sent by Germany were captured together with the renegade Anglo-Irish diplomatist, Sir Roger Casement, as he attempted a clandestine landing in Southern Ireland. The would-be revolutionaries in Ireland represented a much younger generation than the Irish leaders in England's parliament, a generation which had lost all confidence in the chance of obtaining anything for Ireland by parliamentary methods; nor would they have been satisfied by Home Rule alone had they got it, being out-and-out advocates of Irish independence. The Easter rising was put down with that peculiarly drastic brutality which was so often the hallmark of British policy in Ireland; but its occurrence made it impossible for post-war Ireland to be content with Home Rule.

The Arab revolt broke out formally two months later, in June 1916. In all but form it was a revolt of the Arabs of the Hedjaz alone. The Sharif of Mecca, Hussein, and his three sons, Feisal, Abdullah and Zaid, had been in contact with the Arab nationalist secret societies in Syria, where the Turks had been exercising their own peculiarly drastic methods of dealing with local discontent. The need not to be challenged by these, much less Anglophil, Syrians, played its part in making Hussein both all-embracing and unwilling to compromise in the territorial side of his negotiations with the British. But the revolt itself provoked little response in Syria and the only Arab officers to join Hussein were volunteers from those captured by the British in Mesopotamia. They included the future Nuri es-Said, for twenty years the dominant figure in Iraqi politics.

The revolt came in time to thwart a new Turco-German military mission aimed at the capture of Aden, the subversion of Ethiopia and the setting-up of a tenuous link with German East Africa. But after the initial capture of Mecca and Jeddah the revolt came to a dead halt and for a year or so was only kept going by frequent injections of British money and advisers, and the constitutional inability of the Turks to fight desert campaigns.

The divided country of Poland saw an equally dramatic change of fortune. At the beginning of the war the Polish nationalist movement was divided into three main strands, the Russian Polish, the Austrian Polish and the German Polish parties. The first was the most revolutionary, the second the most sophisticated and the last was the weakest. Of the four Polish leaders who set up the Polish state in 1918, Joszef Pilsudski, who had led the Polish socialists in the 1905 rising, and Roman Dmowski, leader of the Polish National Democrat party in the Russian Duma, came from Russian Poland; Professor Jaworski, the leader of the Polish Conservatives and Ignacy Daszyński, the veteran Socialist, came from Austrian Poland.

The main motive forces in the Polish movement in the first years of the war were first Pilsudski's National Socialists, and the Polish legions he raised to fight at first on the side of the Central Powers, and, second, the Polish *emigré* movement in London, Paris and, ultimately, in the United States. The main division of opinion in the movement was whether to back Russia or Austria-Hungary. Pilsudski's supporters were thoroughly anti-Russian; Dmowski and the majority of Russian Poles saw Germany as their worst enemy. Polish military units fought on both sides at different times.

The Polish movement offered obvious chances of exploitation to all three of the Eastern autocracies, though none of the three wished to see a situation in which Polish aspirations could get out of hand. And with their decisions to exploit the Polish question against their opponents, there was raised at once the question of frontiers. A Russian-backed Poland could advance its frontiers deep into Germany and Austria-Hungary. But it would have to abandon all its claims in Lithuania, White Russia, the Ukraine or Austrian Ruthenia (Eastern Galicia). A German-backed Poland could push its frontiers deep into the Ukraine and Byelo-Russia: but only at the price of abandoning its claims on Prussian Poland, on Danzig and on Lithuania.

The Russians were, in fact, first in the field with their proclamation made by the Grand Duke Nicholas, commander-in-chief in the west, on August 16th, 1914, promising religious, linguistic and administrative autonomy to the Poles, within the general framework of the Tsarist empire. But the great Russian retreat from Poland in 1915 made those promises seem remarkably unconvincing. The Germans on their side began by inclining to an 'Austro-Polish' solution, one which envisaged the inclusion of most of Russian Poland into a Polish state within the Hapsburg empire. The Convention of Teschen of September 15th, 1915, which established boundaries between the German and Austrian zones of occupation in Russian Poland, represented a part of this policy. But the Austrian military, who were progressively increasing their power *vis-à-vis* the civilians in Vienna, disliked even the dualism of the *Ausgleich* with Hungary and thus were unlikely to look with favour on the addition of a third Polish element to make the dual monarchy into a trinity. The Austrians preferred outright annexation.

The Germans, therefore, turned increasingly towards the idea of a satellite Polish kingdom under German protection, an idea they were encouraged in by those who hoped to recruit Polish manpower to swell German armies. The Polish legionaries fought excellently against the Brusilov offensive in July 1916, and converted to their support the increasingly powerful and otherwise very pan-German and annexationist High Command in the East, Hindenburg and Ludendorff. The main obstacles the Germans had to face were the continuing anxieties of their Austrian allies and the resistance of those who still hoped for a compromise peace with Tsarist Russia. The collapse of secret negotiations with Tsarist representatives in the autumn of 1916 removed the objections of this latter group. Austrian resistance, however, restricted German action essentially to their zone of occupation. The German proclamation of November 5th, 1916, promising the erection of an independent Polish kingdom with its own constitution and army was thus effectively confined to the provinces of Warsaw and Lublin. This was followed on January 14th, 1917, by the setting-up of a Polish Council of State in Warsaw. But the German hopes of a large Polish army were disappointed. And soon the revolution in Russia made it seem less urgent to them than it had appeared in 1916.

Inter-allied relations also underwent severe strains in this period, particularly in the near East. The pre-eminence of British forces in military matters in this theatre, in the Gallipoli campaign, in Sinai, the Arabian peninsula, Persia and Mesopotamia was far from universally welcomed in St Petersburg or Paris; especially as the Turkish choice of the Central Powers as her allies seemed to have removed all reason for any British or Russian acquiescence in the perpetuation of the Turkish Empire. As early as January 1915 when the Dardanelles operation was still under consideration the Russians had asked their allies to agree in principle to the post-war Russian control of the Turkish Straits. The British and French concurred by secret agreements, signed on March 12th and April 12th, 1915, subject to the satisfaction of their own aspirations in the region. And the Treaty of London with Italy promised her the province of Adalia, if the Ottoman Empire were to be partitioned.

Egypt had already been formally proclaimed a protectorate in December 1914, and Britain concluded agreements in 1915 not only with the Sharif of Mecca, but also on December 15th, 1915, with ibn Saud, recognizing him as ruler of Nejd with a British subsidy. By all the accepted laws governing Great Power relations, these advances of British interest demanded the granting of compensation to France. On May 16th, 1916, the so-called Sykes-Picot agreement recognized Russian claims to Turkish Armenia and Northern Kurdistan, and French claims to Turkish Cilicia. French pre-eminence in Western Syria and the Lebanon was recognised up to the Damascus, Homs, Hama and Aleppo line. Britain in return was to be granted primacy on the Palestininan coast, and the provinces of Basra and Baghdad. The area between was to be divided into a French zone covering northern Syria and Mesopotamia and a British zone covering the rest of Arabia and what is now Jordan. These terms were difficult if not impossible to reconcile with the promises made to the Sharif of Mecca—and the British negotiations in Cairo, seeking a new British empire over the whole Arab world, may well have been deliberately out of step with the Foreign Office in London. Nor could the assurances given to ibn Saud by negotiators responsible to the government of India be altogether reconciled with those promises made to the Sharif.

The Sykes-Picot agreement contained one very odd provision, that Palestine, or rather the old Turkish province of Jerusalem, should be under an international administration. This clause represented a combination of three rather different lines of thought in London. The first was the theory that it would be desirable to have a buffer between the French zone of influence in Syria and the Suez canal. The second was a genuine wish to internationalize this land which was holy to every brand of Christianity as well as to Islam and Judaism. The third was the influence of British sympathies with Zionism.

The international Zionist movement had been split by the outbreak of war into separate German and western sections, supposedly co-ordinated by a bureau in neutral Copenhagen. The German wing had devoted itself systematically to pressure on the German government to secure concessions from its Turkish ally; but its efforts had been largely in vain. More successful was the British wing, led by a brilliant industrial chemist, Chaim Weizmann, whose war work brought him into contact with Lloyd George during his days as Minister of Munitions. Playing on the sympathies of those British leaders whose Anglican or non-conformist religion had made them familiar with the Old Testament, and arguing for the for something to combat the hostility aroused among the large Jewish minority in the United States by the anti-Semitic measures of England's ally, Tsarist Russia, Weizmann gradually converted one member after another of the British government to the Zionist cause.

In October 1916, Weizmann opened formal negotiations with the British Foreign Office, while a colleague, Nahum Sokolow, won the support of France and Italy. In March 1917 matters had gone far enough for Weizmann to speak openly of British support for the establishment of a 'Jewish Commonwealth'. His announcement, however, stirred up the opposition of all those Jewish citizens of Britain who had been working so long for equal rights in Britain, who felt that the creation of a Jewish state with a 'secular Jewish nationality' would again make them aliens within a strange country. For them their Judaism was a messianic religion, and their Jewishness of the same significance within Britain as if they were Scots, Welsh or Cornish. Much of their support lay, it should be added, among the older Sephardic Jewish communities of Britain; while Zionism was much more the creed of the refugees from Russian Poland. With the support of Edwin Montagu, the Jewish Secretary of State for War, they succeeded in modifying the text of the British declaration designed to satisfy Zionist aspirations so that instead of a reference to Palestine 'as the National Home of the Jewish People', the British government pledged itself to 'the establishment *in* Palestine of a national home for the Jewish people'. Palestine's Arab inhabitants appeared only in the text among the 'existing non-Jewish communities in Palestine', whose 'civil and religious rights'

237

were reserved. This pledge was duly issued on November 2nd, 1917, in the form of a letter from Arthur Balfour, the British Foreign Secretary, to the Jewish financier, Lord Rothschild, and is known as the Balfour Declaration.

Neither side had much doubt at this time that what was foreshadowed was a Jewish state. The British either dismissed the Arabs as natives on a par with the Bantu of Africa or expected that the Jews, themselves Semites, would lead to a regeneration of the Arab world in a Judean-Arab union. Weizmann himself believed that agreement could be reached with the Arabs. And he was able to present the Zionist movement, despite the strong radical populist anti-imperialist sentiments of both its Russo-Polish and American wings, as a possible vehicle for British liberal imperialist policy. It was to be twenty years before the vision of Israel as a self-governing dominion within the British Empire was finally to expire, ten before Weizmann's hopes of Arab-Jewish co-operation were revealed to be hopeless. Zionism was not strong enough as a movement, and the Arabs were far more advanced in their disunity, for the ideals behind the Balfour Declaration to be realized. And the state of Israel had to be established against the opposition of Britain and the Arabs alike.

Prospects of a successful mediation by the United States were greatly reduced during 1915–16. Outraged by the contempt with which both the German and British Admiralties treated American neutral rights at sea, President Wilson had called in November 1915 for a great rearmament effort by the United States under the slogan 'preparedness'. The National Defence Act of June 1916 enlarged the American regular army; the Naval Appropriation Act of August 29th satisfied the long-term aspirations of American navalists in setting out a major battleship construction programme designed to secure 'a Navy Second to None' (i.e. equal in strength to that of Britain) by the year 1925; the US Shipping Board Act of September 7th satisfied the aspiration of those navalists who maintained that greatness at sea could only rest on a large nationally-owned merchant marine.

The approach of the Presidential elections on the other hand demanded a rather different kind of policy. In February 1916 Wilson dispatched his intimate adviser, Colonel House, on a tour of exploration of the prospects of a mediated peace in Europe. House visited Britain; but his main efforts were devoted to obtaining a statement of Allied peace aims sufficiently moderate for Wilson to be able to use them to bring the Central Powers to negotiation. The British agreed, in the hope of securing American entry into the war on their side after the refusal, which they took for granted, of the Central Powers to accept such terms as a basis for peace talks. But their hopes were disappointed. Lacking a slogan of mediation to campaign on, Wilson chose to campaign in October 1916 on the slogan 'He kept us out of war', a slogan which he used narrowly to upset what promised to be an inevitable Republican victory.

Wilson's re-election encouraged the German Chancellor, who was under very strong pressure from the General Staff to reverse the Kaiser's decision of May 1916 and authorize the renewal on a far larger scale of unrestricted submarine warfare, to appeal to Wilson on December 12th, 1916, to mediate between the Central Powers and those of the *Entente*. Wilson, the balance of whose suspicions of the belligerents were still weighted against Germany, chose to appeal to both sides to state their terms for peace.

In their reply of December 26th the Central Powers chose to ignore this request to define their war aims in detail. The *Entente* Powers replied on January 10th, 1917, in terms which made it clear that they had irrevocably chosen to destroy the structure of pre-war Europe. Belgium, Serbia and Montenegro were to be evacuated as was the German-occupied territory of France, Rumania and Russia. Alsace-Lorraine was to be returned to France: and, more significantly for Europe's future, they demanded that Europe be re-organized 'on the basis of nationalities'. Italians, Slavs, Rumanians and Czechoslovaks were to be freed from foreign (Habsburg) rule. All the subject nationalities of the Turkish Empire were to be liberated, and Turkey was to be expelled from Europe. The terms did more credit to the *Entente* Powers' ideals than to their military realism, considering the strategic circumstances of January 1917. They must be seen, therefore, as making explicit a definite ideological choice, already largely made in domestic discussions of war aims, against any continuation of the system of balance between the Great Powers in Europe such as had made the limited stability of the Concert of Europe possible in the previous century. They made the war in Europe essentially a revolutionary struggle; and, as such, they also represented a renewed bid for the ideological sympathy of the United States.

In this they went a good deal further than Wilson, who was essentially a realist save where he was himself making ideology his own weapon. His preference was still for 'peace without victory'. The German terms given to him confidentially on January 29th, 1917, were much more his idea of reality save in their colonial chapters where Germany demanded the granting of colonial territories to accord with her population and needs. The territorial clauses on eastern Europe, which envisaged the creation of a large Polish satellite for Germany, represented no more than Germany controlled politically already. But the whole discussion was made almost academic by the German decision taken on January 8th, 1917, three weeks earlier, to risk everything, including American entry into the war, on six months unrestricted submarine warfare against Britain, and to attempt to distract the United States by fomenting Mexico against her.

In Mexico, the Germans had discovered an easy target. By the end of August 1914, the Huerta *régime* had collapsed and General Huerta himself abdicated. Carranza, Huerta's successor, was, if anything, even less amenable to American views than Huerta had been. The American government began therefore to support his general and would-be rival, Pancho Villa. But Carranza was more than a match for Villa and drove his forces steadily into the wild country of Northern Mexico, and the United States found herself forced, on October 19th, 1915, to recognize the Carranza *régime*. Villa thereafter turned violently anti-American and began to kill all the American citizens who fell into his hands. Still worse he raided American territory in March 1916.

Public opinion in the United States was now violently anti-Mexican. President Wilson, under strong pressure to intervene in force, pursued Villa by sending a large-scale punitive expedition into Mexico under General Pershing. Alarmed by its size, Carranza called in April and May 1916 for its withdrawal. A second raid into New Mexico on Villa's part made this impossible and there followed in June 1916 the inevitable incident between a unit of Pershing's so-called 'Punitive Expedition' and Carranza's forces. Wilson managed, however, to restrain his hotheads, and new negotiations with Carranza opened. In October 1916 a general election gave Carranza a Constitutional Assembly, and in March 1917 Carranza was elected President of Mexico. The Punitive Expedition was finally withdrawn at the end of January 1917 and Carranza's government recognized *de jure*. But the whole incident had placed Mexican relations with the United States under a strain from which they were only to begin to recover in the late 1920s, and in January 1917 the Germans might be forgiven for feeling that Mexico could be incited against the United States.

Their feelings were, however, mistaken; disastrously so. The instructions to the German Minister in Mexico City, known to history as the Zimmermann Telegram, fell into the hands of British Intelligence. The announcement of the German decision to wage unrestricted submarine warfare had already led President Wilson to break off relations with Germany and propose the arming of American merchantmen. The publication of the Zimmermann Telegram and the sinking of American ships led inevitably to the declaration of war by the United States on April 6th, 1917. It was, however, to be more than a year before the real weight of American power was to be felt by Germany.

In the meantime the German submarine blockade of Britain raged at full force. British losses rose monthly, until in April 1917 over 169 British merchant ships totalling 849,000 tons, one out of every four ships that left the British Isles, were sunk by German submarine attack. The tide turned slowly with the introduction of the system of convoying merchant ships with escorts of warships in May. But at first this system was only confined to ships coming into British waters and was not extended to outward-bound vessels until August 1917. The losses of ships by torpedo fell slowly to a mere 90 a month in December 1917; and the coupling of the convoy system with the introduction of a really effective control of shipping, and the concentration of British and American naval resources on anti-submarine warfare gradually gave the naval powers the upper hand. But it proved a necessary part of the battle that those senior naval officers in the British Navy to whom traditional objectives and conventional methods were all-important should be removed from office. And for most of 1917 the battle was touch-and-go.

## 1917, The Year of Disaster

In 1917 the process of European self-immolation continued and intensified. America entered the war, dragged in by German miscalculations. In Russia, the Tsarist *régime* dissolved into revolution, and the parliamentary *régime* that followed disintegrated, falling into the hands of the Bolsheviks. American influence was asserted in the Pacific. China entered the war. The French armies mutinied and the British took a mauling in Flanders that added the word 'Passchendaele' to the English language. German submarine warfare brought Britain to the edge of defeat. Yet the advocates of a war to the bitter end were strengthened in France and Germany. The Pope's attempt to mediate was much less successful than even Wilson's effort had been.

On the Western front, General Nivelle had succeeded Joffre with a great fanfare of optimism as to the chances of a major break-through in France. Tactically he pinned his faith as a gunner to a colossal bombardment preceding the attack. But when the plans for the attack had all been settled the Germans destroyed their main base by executing a strategic withdrawal to a carefully prepared system of fortifications known as the Hindenburg Line. The line was much shorter and enabled the Germans to release many divisions to the reserves. Nivelle insisted, however, on continuing his offensive, which took place in April. The French losses were high and the territorial gains negligible. German losses were even higher. But the defeat of the hopes pinned on Nivelle and the apparent failure of the French command to evolve any variation in their offensive tactics led to a total breakdown of French army morale and widespread mutinies in no less than fifty-four of the French divisions. The secret of the mutinies was well kept, not even a whisper of them reaching the Germans.

Their effect, however, was to throw the main burden of fighting on the Western front on to the British. In April British forces had attacked near Arras in an offensive intended to act as a diversion for that of General Nivelle, and had scored some success at the cost of 160,000 casualties. But the French mutinies called for a much greater effort. The British admiralty, unable to cope with the great German submarine offensive, urged that the coast of Flanders be cleared of the German submarine bases. On June 7th the Messines ridge, the principal geographical obstacle to an offensive into the plain of Flanders, was successfully captured. But the main British offensive, six weeks later, ran into heavy rain; and the prolonged bombardment which generals now thought essential to any offensive merely resulted in the complete destruction of the natural drainage system of the Flanders plain, not to mention all sign of metalled roads. The offensives now known as the battle of Passchendaele made some significant advances around the town of Ypres. But the cost to each side was approximately one quarter of a million casualties. In November, the British launched a frontal offensive at Cambrai with no preliminary barrage and behind massed tanks, the first heavy use of the new British arm. The initial success was overwhelming but Passchendaele had denuded the British army of adequate reserves and the Germans were able to recover most of the ground the tanks had taken.

In Italy even greater disaster was to strike the *Entente* Powers. Two further offensives on the Isonzo had secured little or no gain when on October 24th a joint German-Austrian force attacked in heavy fog. They scored an immediate break-through, in what became known as the Battle of Caporetto, and the Italian army collapsed. A new front line was not established until the Italian forces had withdrawn to the river Piave, over one hundred miles to the rear. The Italians lost over 300,000 casualties, and eleven British and French divisions had to be rushed from France to Italy to stiffen the new Italian line. The Italians were, however, able to hold the line of the Piave and the crucial pivot of Monte Grappa against very heavy Austrian and German attack. As a result, Italian morale recovered as quickly as it had broken.

In Rumania, greater disaster struck in August 1917 when German and Austrian troops began to clear the remainder of the country. In December 1917 a truce was signed to be followed in May 1918 by a definite treaty of peace between Rumania and the Central Powers. The Treaty of Bucharest of May 7th, 1918, ceded Dobruja to Bulgaria and the Carpathian passes to Austria-Hungary. Germany took a ninety year lease on the Rumanian oilfields. Rumania was allowed, however, to annex Bessarabia which had broken away from Russia in the Russian revolution.

Iraq and Palestine saw the only real victories on the *Entente* side. In October 1917 General Allenby, appointed to Palestine after the part he had played in the Arras battles in April 1917, finally pierced the Turkish positions at Gaza. The break-through was well-exploited and on December 11th the British forces entered Jerusalem and held it easily against Turkish counter-attack. Earlier in 1917, British troops had cleared Lower Mesopotamia and on March 11th, 1917, entered Baghdad. New advances began in December 1917. At the same time, Colonel T. E. Lawrence succeeded in revitalizing the Arab revolt and in raising its guerilla activities to the dignity of minor military operations.

The increased strains of war, which had already shown themselves in the overthrow of the Asquith government in Britain in December 1916, expressed themselves among the other belligerents in 1917. In France, the end of 1916 had seen the removal from office of the French commander-in-chief, General Joffre. In March 1917 the cabinet of Briand was overturned by a parliament suspicious of its subordination to the French military. Its successor, headed by Alexandre Ribot, an aged nobody, Finance Minister in the outgoing government, was dominated by the Minister of War, Paul Painlevé. Painlevé had the gravest doubts as to the success of the Nivelle offensive. With its failure he replaced Nivelle with

Pétain and Foch, under whom French strategy turned into a waiting game predicated on the arrival of American troops in force on the battle-field, an event which was not expected to occur until the summer of 1918. The Ribot cabinet proved vulnerable, however, in its failure to act decisively against defeatism and German fifth column activity. Painlevé succeeded Ribot as Premier in September 1917. But the scandals continued and the gradual uncovering of the full truth of the Nivelle failure and the subsequent mutinies led to Painlevé's succession in November 1917 by Georges Clemenceau, the ruthless, patriotic, embodiment of victory, whose one policy was, 'I wage war'.

In Germany, the decision to wage unrestricted submarine warfare was made despite the opposition of the Imperial Chancellor, Bethman-Hollweg, and marked the victory of the military. Germany became virtually a military dictatorship. Field Marshal von Hindenburg had succeeded to the supreme command in August 1916. His deputy, the Chief Quartermaster-General, General Ludendorff, was able to use Hindenburg's prestige thereafter as an infallible weapon of political power. Those whom he distrusted or disliked, those who opposed Army policy as he formulated it, those who advocated a policy with which he disagreed, were denounced to the Kaiser as persons for whom, or for whose policy, Ludendorff 'could not assume the responsibility'. And the implied threat of resignation left the Kaiser no option but to get rid of the offenders. It was with this weapon that he secured the resignation of the German Chancellor, Bethman-Hollweg, in the summer of 1917 and his replacement by an obscure Prussian bureaucrat, Dr Michaelis.

In the German parliament and country, the continuance of the war was now linked to the increasing social dissatisfaction with the existing system of power. The parliamentarians of the *Reichstag*, National Liberals, Centre Party and majority Social Democrats, began to agitate for the establishment of parliamentary control over the government and army. On the left revolutionary factions broke away from the Social Democrats, first the extremists who were to organize themselves into the *Spartacus League*, and then the so-called Independent Social Democrats, the USPD. The parliamentarians succeeded in obtaining in April 1917 an undertaking that the Prussian electoral system, on which the power of the German right was based, would be reformed after the war. Their attempt to establish civilian control, even in principle, over the Army was ignominiously rebuffed. In July 1917 therefore, the Centre's leader, Matthias Erzberger, chose to challenge the Army head on, with the introduction into the *Reichstag* of a motion demanding a compromise peace without annexations or indemnities. It passed the *Reichstag* on July 19th, 1917, by 212 votes to 196.

The resolution was rendered pointless by the new Chancellor's acceptance of it with the rider, 'as I understand it'. The *Reichstag* thus remained powerless even when, in October 1917, the new German Chancellor, Michaelis, over-reached himself in attempting to secure its approval for the suppression of the USPD. Michaelis' defeat led to his replacement by what appeared to be a parliamentary *régime* under Count Hertling, a member of the Centre Party, and von Payer, of the Progressives. But as real power remained with Ludendorff the significance of 1917's events lay in the creation of a united middle-class and Social Democrat opposition to his military dictatorship, which would be able to take over power when the defeat of Germany broke the power of the military.

That year saw two other significant events in German politics. With Ludendorff's encouragement the right wing Conservatives and National Liberals began to gather together in a new party, the Fatherland party, determined to prevent a compromise peace. Only a peace with major annexations could, in their view, save Germany from a social and political revolution. On the left the USPD came into contact with discontent in the German navy. There were disturbances and political demonstrations in which the sailors' suspicion that their officers did not share their own poor food rations played a part. They signified the growing social discontent in Germany, discontent which went so deep as to give revolutionary Communism deep and almost permanent roots in Germany between the wars.

In Austria-Hungary, the war had aggravated the bad relations between Hungary and the non-Magyar parts of the Empire. It had also driven the Czechs into passive resistance to the central government, elevated the military authorities, dominated by pan-German sentiments, and had brought upon the Empire a series of defeats which discredited the monarchy both in the eyes of its German allies and of the peoples of the Empire. At the opening of the war the military authorities took over, the *Reichsrath* was prorogued, and there began a long struggle for political power between the military and the civil powers in the Czech, Ruthene and Slovene provinces of the Monarchy. The military, however, were unable to impose their will in Hungary, and the Hungarian government, in control of the major part of the Empire's food supplies, gave so little food to Austria that privation was already raging in Vienna by the middle of 1916.

In October 1916 the Austrian premier was assassinated. A month later the aged emperor, Franz Josef, died of pneumonia. The Archduke Charles, who succeeded him, did not feel strong enough to challenge the Hungarians head on. Moreover, he felt bound by his coronation oath as King of Hungary. On the non-Magyar side, however, he took severe steps to reduce the power of the military. General Conrad von Hötzendorff was dismissed and Charles set himself the task of winning back the loyalty of the non-German nationalities. An essential part of this plan was the convocation of the *Reichsrath*, which met in May 1917. Its meeting showed that the military authorities had already succeeded in completely alienating the main Slav groups. The Czech spokesman demanded that the Empire be changed into a federation of free and equal states. The Yugoslavs demanded the union of Serbs, Croats and Slovenes into an autonomous democratic state under the Habsburg crown. The Emperor did his best to conciliate them. And it is just possible that he might have succeeded had it been possible for Austria to make peace at that time, though he would have faced stiff resistance from the German population of Austria proper.

It was the desperate condition of the Monarchy in fact which drove the Emperor to open secret peace negotiations with France through his brother-in-law, Prince Sixte of Bourbon. France and Britain were very interested. But their promises to Italy stood in the way; and it proved difficult to persuade Charles to make sufficiently far-reaching concessions to satisfy the Italians. Individual negotiations continued through the summer, culminating in a meeting in Switzerland in December 1917 between Count Mensdorff, the former Austrian ambassador in London, and General Smuts, the South African premier and member of the British War Cabinet. But an actual Austrian break with Germany would have been impossible at this time unless Austria was prepared to fight Germany. The *Entente* Powers on their side were unable to win over Italy. The main effect of the secret negotiations was to postpone for nearly a year effective British, French and American support for the Czech and Yugoslav *emigrés*.

On their side the *emigré* leaders of the Czechs and Yugoslavs had an uphill task trying to win support for their aims. The vast mass of the Czechs were passive rather than active. They resented having to fight against the Russians and deserted or surrendered to them in large numbers. But their principal leaders preferred to persist with their policy of inactivity in the hope of a Russian victory rather than to take an active part in winning support for their cause in the West. It was left to the leader of the small Czech Realist party, Professor Thomas Masaryk, to go into exile to win support for Czech independence in France and Britain.

The southern Slavs in the Empire were in greater difficulty, since the principal enemy in the south was Italy, whose far-reaching claims on the Dalmatian Coast involved Slav territory. Moreover, they were still very much divided between advocates of a Greater Serbia and Croat advocates of a Federal Yugoslav state. Not until Italy's great defeat at Caporetto did the future begin to appear more cheerful. The year 1917 was a grim period for every section of opinion in Austria-Hungary.

However, these signs of strain and incipient revolution in France, Germany and Austria-Hungary were very minor incidents compated with the events of 1917 in Russia. During 1916, dissatisfaction with the Tsar and his entourage had been rising in all sections of Russian society, even among the aristocracy who had been disgusted with the Tsar's reliance on the drunken and lecherous self-styled holy man, Rasputin. The capitalists, merchants and industrialists of Moscow had been outraged by the total breakdown of the Tsarist bureaucracy under the demands of total war. The old Tsarist army, officers and men alike, had been virtually destroyed by the casualties of three years of war. And in March 1917 strikes and bread riots in St Petersburg led to a complete collapse of the dynasty and a take-over of power by the politicians of the Duma.

The new Provisional Government consisted of a coalition of the Constitutional Democrats, the Cadets, and the Social Democrats. But its claim to power was disputed throughout Russia by the spontaneous formation of councils, *Soviets* in their Russian name, dominated by left wing Socialists, Social Revolutionaries and Bolsheviks. And the Social Democrats felt obliged to express the mood of the soldiers, workers and peasants who had elected them to the Soviets. For these the revolution involved much more than the mere transfer of power from the Tsar to the Duma. It involved the destruction of the whole police apparatus of the Tsarist state, from the oppressive military discipline of the army to the land ownership and taxation system in the villages. And under their demands Russia slid steadily downhill into chaos, disturbance and civil war.

The effect of this steady disintegration was to drive the middle class parties and the Social Democrats steadily apart from one another, and to alienate them from that section of the army that wished to continue the war and maintain order at home as an essential part of this. The Provisional Government might have been able to save itself if it had immediately concluded peace with the Germans, no matter what sacrifice was demanded. But the Provisional Government were both patriots and realists. To modernize and rebuild Russia after three years of war would necessitate large amounts of foreign capital, and Russia was already heavily in debt to the *Entente* Powers. Moreover both Miliukov, the leading spirit in the first Provisional Cabinet, and Kerensky, who became premier in July 1917, hoped that a victorious offensive might recreate the sense of national unity which the revolution seemed to have destroyed. The Russian offensive of July 1st, 1917, was at first successful. But German counterattacks soon reduced it to the status of a major disaster; and the Germans followed their victory by a major offensive into the Baltic coastlands which took Riga in September and overran most of Latvia.

In March 1917 the Bolshevik party had very little influence in Russia, and all its leading figures were in exile in Siberia or Switzerland. In April 1917 the German authorities, hoping deliberately to accelerate the breakdown of order in Russia, offered Lenin and the other Russian revolutionaries in Switzerland passage through Germany to Russia. On Lenin's arrival at St Petersburg, he immediately took control of the Bolshevik party, and began building up Bolshevik military units, or Red Guards, in the factories. In June and July his supporters got out of hand, and Lenin was forced to seek refuge in Finland for safety. Allegations that Lenin was largely financed by German money and the revelation of the Bolshevists' desire to seize power temporarily discredited him.

But peasant disturbances and desertions from the army continued to spread, and the collapse and defeat of the July offensive only accelerated the process. In September 1917, alarmed at the deterioration on the home front, General Kornilov, commanding the remaining Russian armies in the west, attempted to seize power. To resist him, Kerensky was forced to turn to the Red Guards and release those Bolshevik leaders he had arrested. The way was now clear for the Bolsheviks to take over control of the congress of Soviets in St Petersburg, to arrest the members of the Provisional Government, and to establish a nominal coalition government dominated by the Bolshevik leadership. With this Russia passed under the control of a *régime* that thought of itself as the spearhead of revolution in Europe, but was in fact to isolate itself from, and be isolated by Europe, so as to become something quite different and apart from the main stream of European culture and civilization.

In the Far East, the Chinese government was lured into abandoning its neutrality and declaring war on Germany in the hope of extracting a diminution of foreign influence in her territories. Chinese labourers were in fact widely used behind the front in France. But the main effect of China's entry into the war was to increase Japanese domination, since only Japan was prepared to supply China with loans to cover her additional financial expenses. Only the United States remained as a check on Japanese ambitions in China. By an exchange of notes in November 1917 between Lansing, the US Secretary of State, and M. Ishii, Japan's Special Ambassador to the United States, America recognized Japan's special interests in China in return for Japanese assurances that the Open Door policy and China's integrity would be maintained. The Lansing-Ishii agreements were to prove a very inadequate check, however, on Japan's ambitions in the Far East.

The Russian revolution gave new impetus to a series of movements which had been stimulated by the earlier strains of war: the casualty lists, the constant flood of abusive propaganda, the reckless dissipation of Europe's reserves of manpower, money, materials and morale, and the destruction of her cities and countryside in the war zones. These movements represented a new series of efforts on the part of the three most important supranational movements of the pre-war era, firstly, that which had produced the Hague conferences and the World Court, secondly, the second, socialist, international, and thirdly, the Papacy, to re-establish themselves against the forces of nationalism and to secure a negotiated peace.

The first movement was the strongest in the English-speaking countries and in France where it was infused with utopian aspirations. It centred on the settlement to be obtained when peace negotiations should eventually be entered upon; and it looked to a world so re-organized as to make it impossible for any war, on the scale of the one on which they were engaged, ever to break out again. The desire most favoured in discussions in the Anglo-Saxon countries was a 'League of Nations', as it was called in Britain, a 'League to enforce peace', as it was called in the United States. The sponsors of the movement in these two countries came from two rather different and previously opposed groups. One group represented a continuation of the radicalism which had begun to express itself prior to 1914 in international organizations and in a persistent critique of conventional diplomacy and power politics. The second embodied an aroused conservatism, particularly strong among international lawyers, but well represented elsewhere, which had come to regard modern war as essentially subversive of the established order. Lord Robert Cecil, who was to make himself the driving force behind the idea in the British government, typified this approach. In 1917 the Lloyd George government was induced to set up a committee under Lord Phillimore to consider and report on a possible draft constitution for a League of Nations. And the theme of such a league was to play a large part in Allied propaganda thereafter.

The movement was to see its agitation crowned by success; although it had little support among the Central Powers. Here the moderates chose to press for a compromise peace, without annexations or indemnities, as in the *Reichstag* Peace Resolution of July 1917. Their slogan was originally taken from the Bolsheviks. But the movement for a compromise peace enjoyed only limited support in Britain. The most spectacular support came from the former Conservative Foreign Secretary, the aged Lord Lansdowne, who appealed, in a letter published by *The Daily Telegraph* on November 29th, 1917, for a negotiated peace as the only alternative to a war of attrition which was eliminating an entire generation in Britain and Europe and preparing the way for chaos and revolution. The letter caused no little stir in Britain. But its main effect again was to play a part in forcing the British Government once more to define its peace aims. The terms, as defined, could only have been acceptable to Germany as an alternative to outright defeat; and few in Germany outside the innermost circles of government contemplated this possibility.

The only support any movement for a compromise peace secured in Britain was that sponsored by the Social Democrat parties of the Netherlands and Scandinavia, which reached its culmination in the so-called Stockholm peace conference in September 1917. This conference was the last of a series at which the remnants of the old Second International had sought to restore their movement's shattered internationalism. Earlier conferences had met in Switzerland, at Zimmerwald in September 1915 and at Kienthal in 1916, where Lenin's influence had secured the publication of a *communiqué* saying that there could be no real solution of the conflict without the conquest of political power and the ownership of capital by the peoples of Europe themselves. Such a resolution, even if valid, was unlikely to lead to a negotiated peace, and in July 1916, at a second conference confined to delegates from the European neutrals (thus excluding Lenin and the Russian Social Democrats) the Dutch Socialists attempted to persuade their colleagues in the belligerent powers to agree to attend a conference to discuss the terms of a possible peace.

In this effort the Dutch were abandoning their own earlier inclination, in which the influence of the Belgian Socialist, Vandervelde, the chairman of the Second International, can be seen, to feel that there could be no peace without a total German withdrawal from Belgium. The influence of the belief that the German invasion of Belgium made the war a just war and not an imperialist manifestation could be seen still at work in the preference, expressed by the Labour movement in Britain and the

Socialists of France, for working for an agreed statement of Allied war aims.

The Russian revolution of March 1917 provided a new spur to the Dutch efforts, more effective in that, since January 1917, there had been a Labour member of the British War Cabinet, Arthur Henderson. But divisions within the British Labour party, which refused to have anything to do with the breakaway Independent Labour Party, prevented the assembly of a British delegation, and the whole project was most bitterly opposed by Lloyd George and the Tories in the War Cabinet. Henderson resigned from the War Cabinet in August 1917 as a result, to be replaced by another Labour leader, George Barnes. But no British delegation, and no French delegation, came to Stockholm; and the conference as such never met. Instead the Dutch-Scandinavian committee held a series of discussions with delegations from the German, Austrian and Russian parties, and a good many individuals. But these meetings had little or no effect.

A rather similar fate befell the Papal Peace Message of August 1st, 1917. The Pope had been waiting for some time for the right moment to intervene, and the stalemate of the summer seemed to offer the best opportunity. But the moment was in fact ill chosen. The *Reichstag* peace resolution, as has been seen, was virtually ignored by the German Government, and the conjunction of the Papal intervention with it merely laid the Pope open to accusations of allowing himself to be used as a German catspaw. The real stumbling block at this stage was the determination of the Lloyd George government and the Americans to overthrow the German Empire and secure Alsace-Lorraine for France, and the equal determination on the German side not to abandon their gains on the Belgian coast and frontier, let alone give up Alsace-Lorraine.

The fact of the matter was that in Britain, France and Germany, the governments were now dominated by those who were determined to fight *à l'outrance*. Alone among the leaders of these three countries, Lloyd George was capable of thinking internationally. But being the nominee of a coalition of Conservatives and Liberals determined on victory he could only express his international leanings in terms of redevelopment of the world after victory. In the United States, President Wilson was grimly determined now on the punishment of aggression and the overthrow of autocracy and militarism as necessary pre-conditions to a just peace. American opinion was indulging in an orgy of nationalism and chauvinism to which, among others, the IWW, pacifists to a man, were to fall victim. Their leaders disappeared behind bars, all save one, who was lynched. Everything was set for the collapse of Europe.

## Chapter XIV
## 1918—VICTORY AND THE COLLAPSE OF EUROPE

THE winter of 1917–18 was a long and hard one in Central Europe; and its privations made themselves felt in a wave of strikes of a semi-political nature in Austria-Hungary and in Germany. By January 1918 the flour ration in Vienna was reduced to 165 grams a day. The spontaneous demonstrations that followed developed into a major strike movement which spread into Lower Austria and to Budapest. The strikers usually combined political demands with their demands for more food. Echoes of the November revolution in Russia could be heard in Austria where extreme criticism met the severe peace terms being demanded of Russia by the Austrian and German governments. In February sailors of the Austrian fleet mutinied, demanding peace. In March Austrian ex-prisoners of war began returning from Russia bringing with them a ferment of ideas and stories of the Russian revolution. From May onwards there was a succession of mutinies among Austrian army units especially among the Czechs and Slovenes.

The strike movement in Germany broke out almost at the same time as the demonstrations in Vienna, though the fact that these events occurred almost simultaneously seems to have been a coincidence. As in Austria the strikes were on a very large scale and dominated the large cities such as Berlin, Hamburg, Essen and Leipzig. The strikers, as in Austria, published a series of protests against the unfairness of the food rationing and the excesses of military government which were combined with demands for the reform of the Prussian electoral system and the conclusion of an immediate peace 'with no annexations and no indemnities'. The strikes were more easily suppressed in Germany than in Austria-Hungary. But in both countries they revealed that the determination of the autocracies to secure an annexationist peace as the only alternative to social revolution had become self-defeating; it had created instead a large group of citizens for whom nationalism and loyalty to their rulers were no longer relevant. The German ruling *élite* in the military and ultra-patriotic circles had produced what was to be a permanently revolutionary element in their country; they had alienated a section of the working class tradition permanently from its national roots.

At the time the military authorities in both of the Central Powers were inclined to see behind this wave of strikes the influence of the 'new diplomacy' introduced into European affairs by the two non-European powers represented in the Bolshevik leadership in Russia and the Democratic President of the United States. On November 8th, 1917, the new *régime* in Russia had adopted a 'Decree on Peace' proposing the immediate opening of negotiations for a 'just and democratic peace without annexations and without indemnities'. On November 21st they had called for an armistice on the Eastern front, and on December 15th an armistice was signed. On December 22nd, peace negotiations were opened at Brest-Litovsk. The Bolshevik negotiators chose deliberately to conduct the negotiations in open session and to accompany them with a barrage of appeals to the peoples of Europe and the colonial territories under European rule. In their view revolution was imminent in Europe; and they did their best to subvert the German units with which they came into contact. They found themselves confronted instead with demands for the attachment to Germany of Poland, Lithuania, Kurland (Latvia) and the Ukraine. There followed a prolonged and agonizing debate within the Soviet government. On February 18th the Germans denounced the armistice and resumed their advance towards St Petersburg. On March 3rd, 1918, the Bolshevik government gave way and signed the peace of Brest-Litovsk.

The treaty of Brest-Litovsk accelerated the process, which had already begun, of the separation from Russia of the subject nationalities. In March 1917 the Provisional Government had abolished the restrictive legislation passed by the old Tsarist *régime* against the so-called national minorities, and had announced the beginning of national self-rule. The administration of the border-lands had been placed in the hands of prominent local figures. But the same factors which in Russia proper were to make the triumph of Lenin possible, popular restlessness, the demand for land and peace, the inability of the Provisional Government to provide firm authority, led to an immense growth in separatist national movements in the non-Russian areas. In the Baltic, White Russia and the Ukraine the landlords were Russian. In the eastern border-lands beyond the Caspian Sea, nationalist feeling expressed itself against the Russian colonists brought in by the Tsars. Under such circumstances the Bolshevik party inevitably became the party of the Russian colonists and the arm of Russian colonialism. The collapse of the Tsarist empire and the failure of the Provisional Government left pockets of Russian troops, sailors and settlers scattered throughout the non-Russian territories. Civil war between them and the nationalities was virtually inevitable. Until the fall of the Provisional Government, Lenin's followers collaborated with the 'nationalities'. Thereafter they were to become their bitterest enemies. The fate of the nationalist movements thereafter depended on the degree to which they could call on German and then Allied support against first the Bolshevik Red Army and then the White counter-revolutionaries. Finland and the Baltic states, Lithuania, Latvia and Estonia were to establish and maintain their independence. The Ukraine, Byelo-Russia, the Crimea, Transcaspia, Turkestan, cis-Caucasian Daghestan and the three Transcaspian states of Georgia, Armenia and Azerbaijan at various times proclaimed their independence, but none proved able to maintain it; though isolated resistance to Soviet rule was to continue in the Turkic areas of Transcaspia until the middle of the 1920s.

Among the non-Russian members of the Tsarist empire, Finland was the most successful in winning independence. The Finnish achievement of independence began after a vicious civil war which lasted from January to May 1918, in which the anti-Communist forces, the Whites, were greatly aided by the German Baltic division under General von der Goltz. Thereafter, the Finnish 'Whites' became involved with the Allied intervention in Northern Russia, and suffered a serious defeat in the course of an attempt to annex East Karelia from Russia. On the German signature of an armistice with the *Entente* Powers in November 1918 they found themselves abandoned by Germany; but they managed to re-establish friendly relations with the *Entente* Powers by intervening to help the Estonians beat back a Soviet invasion while wisely refusing to intervene in the Civil War in Russia. Estonia, Latvia and Lithuania, being much weaker than Finland, survived through 1918 only under the occupation of German forces intent on annexing the whole area to the German crown. The German collapse in November 1918 left them still under German occupation, which the *Entente* Powers tolerated as a means of protecting them against the Red Army. A British naval squadron was eventually to play a large part in aiding native forces to beat off the combined attacks of German, Soviet and 'White' Russian counter-revolutionary armies. Polish troops also participated in the last stages of the fight with the Soviet Red Army.

The Ukraine and Byelo-Russia were not so fortunate. Both operated in areas claimed by other minorities, the Lithuanians and Poles having designs on Byelo-Russia, the Cossacks of the Don and the Poles operating at various times across the territory of the Ukraine. Both had large Russian elements hostile to native nationalism. Both built up national councils, *Radas*, in 1917, both claimed their independence after the November Revolution, both found themselves under attack from Bolshevik forces, and both turned to the Germans who forced the Soviets to recognize their independence at Brest-Litovsk. However, after Brest-Litovsk, the Ukraine and Byelo-Russia found themselves forced to accept German-sponsored puppet governments and to be exploited for German supply purposes. German withdrawal in November 1918 left the Ukraine the main theatre of civil war between the White Russian armies of General Denikin, native Ukrainian forces, Poles and the Soviet Red Army. Byelo-Russia's fate was similar, save only that the very weak nationalist movement collapsed completely during the German occupation. In both territories the sole lasting monument to local nationalism was their establishment as separate Soviet republics in a Soviet Federation with nominally separate Communist parties under central Russian control.

The Moslem element in the Tsarist empire was divided between those liberal reformists who hoped to unite the sixteen million Moslems of the Tsarist empire either on a basis of national cultural autonomy or within a federal state, and the advocates of independent nationhood for the separate parts on a more orthodox Moslem basis. By December 1917 the pan-Moslem element had succeeded in setting up an Executive Council, the *Shura*, in St Petersburg, and an Assembly, the *Medzhilis*, at Kazan on the Volga. The seizure of power by the Bolsheviks in November 1917 was followed by the capture of this machinery by Moslem Communists, who, against the wishes of the Bolshevik leaders, evolved a grandiose plan for an autonomous Moslem republic to cover all Russian Central Asia. The Moslem Communist movement collapsed, however, in June 1918 when the Czech legionaries originally recruited by the Provisional Government to fight on the Eastern front, clashed with the Bolsheviks in the course of their immense withdrawal across Russia and Siberia to Vladivostok. The Kazan *Medzhilis* collapsed and the Moslem Communist movement with it. The survivors were ruthlessly absorbed into the Russian Communist party in November 1918.

Only the Turkic separatists, the Crimean Tatars, the Kazakh and Kirghiz who, in 1916, had staged a major rebellion against the loss of their lands to Russian colonists, the Turkestanis, the Circassians, Chechens and Ingush of the Caucasian mountains were left to fight the battle for independence on their own. Some fell victim, especially in Turkestan, to the panic-stricken violence of the Russian soldier and settler population. Some fought for a time for the White Russian armies of General Kolchak. However, they were eventually driven to the Bolshevik side by the ultra-nationalism of the White Russian officers. Some rallied, especially in Turkestan, into the *Basmachi* movement of mounted partisans, defying Soviet forces until well into the 1920s. In the Kazakh-Kirghiz areas famine was to kill over a million natives in 1921–22. The Crimean Tatars, occupied first by Germans, then by Soviet forces, then by the White armies of General Denikin, suffered a fate similar to that of the nationalists of the Ukraine. Throughout these areas Soviet victory meant a resumption in a new and more oppressive form of the colonization of the Tsarist days; and the network of Autonomous Regions, Autonomous Soviet Socialist Republics and People's Soviet Republics, set up by the victorious Bolsheviks, were to be autonomous in name only.

The Transcaucasian states of Georgia, Armenia and Azerbaijan were divided from one another by language, race and religion, and caught between the Russians and the Turks. The Armenians were virulently anti-Turk, the more so as in 1915 the Ottoman government had set itself deliberately to exterminate the Armenian minority in Eastern Turkey, over one million Armenians perishing between 1915–17. Georgia with its own language and alphabet was thoroughly Social Democrat. Azerbaijan was Moslem. All three were in the front line of the war with Turkey; and the Russian armies on the Caucasus front did not begin to disintegrate until after the Bolshevik revolution in November 1917. By the Treaty of

Brest-Litovsk the territories of the Transcaucasus found themselves handed over to the rule of the Ottoman Empire. To proclaim their independence was the only alternative.

To maintain their independence proved more difficult. For a time the Azerbaijanis looked to their Turkish co-religionists and the Georgians to the Germans. The armistice of November 1918 brought British and White Russian forces in their stead. British withdrawal in the autumn of 1919 left them open to division between the Red Armies from the north and the revived military power of the new Turkish republic. Here again separate Federal Socialist Soviet Republics were continued after the Russian reconquest. But the return of Bolshevik rule meant the return of the old centralism practised by Tsarist Russian nationalists. Nationalism now only expressed itself within the Communist movement.

The Russian revolution had thus run full circle from the enlightenment towards the subject nationalities shown in the early days of March 1917 to the repression of their independence from 1919 onwards. The Bolshevik party similarly had begun as the extreme Russian wing of the European socialist movement. In capturing Russia it became more and more separated from that movement and less and less European in its socialism. Soviet Russia was to retire into and be isolated in the non-European traditions of Russia.

Before this process of withdrawal was well under way, the Soviet leadership was to bequeath to Europe a new style in diplomacy, one concerned not with relations between governments nor with influencing governments, but with influencing peoples behind and against their governments. The 'new diplomacy' was essentially subversive, not to say revolutionary; and it was to play a very considerable part in the destruction of pre-war Europe brought about in the year 1918, in ensuring that defeat brought not reform but revolution. This 'new diplomacy' was not, however, directly the creation of the Soviet leadership. Rather it was adapted by them from the European radical left, especially from the intellectual radicals of Great Britain, particularly from that group which had drawn away from the Liberal party and had not yet joined Labour, the radicals of the Union of Democratic Control.

In the circumstances of 1917 the 'new diplomacy' was essentially concerned with peace. For the Soviet leadership it took two forms, publication of the secret treaties concluded by the western *Entente* Powers with the Tsarist Empire during the war, and the public demand for a peace 'without annexations or indemnities'. The Soviet leadership also announced its intention of abolishing secret diplomacy and conducting all negotiations 'absolutely openly before the entire people'. The peace decree was directed not to governments but to their peoples. It was to be coupled with a series of appeals to the peoples of Europe's colonial empires in the sacred name of 'self-determination'.

These Soviet moves found an immediate reaction in Britain and the United States. In Britain the impact of the Soviet peace decree was observable well beyond the radical and Labour circles to whom it might be expected to appeal. It certainly influenced Lord Lansdowne to publish his peace letter which was to find a considerable echo in other conservative circles. Further it drove the British premier and those who felt that war *à l'outrance* was essential to define British war aims in such a way as both to make them accord with the radical-populist ideals of the British Labour movement and to make it inconceivable that there could be any peace with Imperial Germany without there first being a major revolution. In a speech of January 5th, 1918, made significantly not to Parliament but to the British Trades Union Congress, Lloyd George called for a territorial settlement based on 'government with the consent of the governed', 'national self-determination', and the creation of an international organization 'to limit the burden of armaments and diminish the probability of war'.

Lloyd George's appeal was almost immediately taken up by President Wilson for the United States. In the election campaign of 1916 Wilson had moved much closer to the American progressives; he had indeed only defeated his Republican opponent with the support they gave him in 1916 and refused him in 1912. Once engulfed in war his aim, like those of the Union of Democratic Control (UDC) in Britain, was to use the war to bring about reform in the international system. Wilson himself drew a great many of his ideas and much of his programme from the UDC either directly through emissaries in Britain or indirectly through UDC influence on his Progressive supporters. He was determined to use the position of military and financial pre-eminence in which he knew the United States would end the war to secure acceptance of his ideas. Ironically however he did not represent more than a minority of the American electorate in this plan. Majority opinion in America at this time was thoroughly martial and chauvinist, dominated by the kind of war psychosis which had swept Europe in August 1914. Like his Soviet opposites, Wilson was acting as an immense amplifier for the ideas and notions of Europe's progressives.

Wilson's vehicle was the famous 'Fourteen Points', set out in an address to the American Congress on January 8th, 1918. These were to be followed by the 'Four Principles' of February 11th, the 'Four Aims' of July 4th, 1918, and the 'Five Particulars' of September 27th, 1918. They represented much the same ideas of national self-determination, justice and open diplomacy through a League of Nations as Lloyd George had voiced; though Wilson was precise where Lloyd George preferred to be vague. Wilson added two favourite ideas of American progressivism, the Freedom of the Seas, so that maritime traffic might pass in peace and in war without interference by belligerents, and the removal of all economic barriers to trade. But the first was defeated by British obstructionism (to British opinion it could only seem an attempt to deprive them of the blockade weapon, the major weapon in their armoury as a Great Power). For the second it was impossible to obtain public acceptance in the United States itself.

The British and American replies to the Soviet appeal to open diplomacy both represented an implicit determination, whatever the qualifications introduced into the speeches, to destroy the German, Austro-Hungarian and Ottoman Empires; though so long as there still seemed a chance of a separate peace with the Habsburgs, reference to Czech and Yugoslav nationalist aspirations was muted. It was apparently assumed that these could still be accommodated within the framework of a Hapsburg state reconstituted on federal lines. Only the Poles, wǒrking through representatives in London and America, had secured Allied support for the creation of a Polish state, and such support figured prominently in both Lloyd George's and President Wilson's pronouncements. Hopes of detaching Austria-Hungary from Germany were, however, revealed as baseless on April 2nd, 1918, when Count Czernin, the Austrian Foreign Minister, in an unhappy attempt to turn the techniques of the new diplomacy against the Western powers, revealed the peace talks with them, and sought to ascribe their failure to France's insistence on the recovery of Alsace-Lorraine. He also denounced the Czech political leaders within the Monarchy as no better or, by implication, no less treasonable than the exiles in France, Britain and Russia.

The Czech answer came very quickly. On April 9th, Czech, Croat, Serb, Rumanian and Polish exile leaders met in Rome. Italian ambitions in Dalmatia and along the coast of the Adriatic, as expressed in the Treaty of London in 1915, had long stood as a barrier to Allied recognition of Serb and Croat national aspirations. But the defeat of Caporetto in 1917 had caused the Italian government to change its attitude, and had ended the Serbs' attempt to put Serbian aggrandizement before union with their Croat and Slovene brethren. The Pact of Corfu in July 1917 had already bound its signatories to form an independent 'Yugoslav' national state. Now the Italians were prepared to back this movement for its disruptive effect on the Hapsburg empire. In February 1918, a meeting of Allied experts on propaganda in London decided deliberately to encourage all the anti-German minorities in Austria-Hungary as a means of breaking her power as the weakest link in the German alliances. The meeting at Rome now styled itself the 'Congress of Oppressed Nationalities' and demanded the abolition of Austria. On April 13th, the Czech leaders within the Empire convened a meeting of Czech and Slovene notables in Prague and adopted a National Oath, and on May 16th a second meeting in Prague brought together representatives of the Czechs, Poles, Yugoslavs, Slovaks, Italian and Rumanian minorities in a pledge to work together for independence and democratic government. At the same time Czech and Polish national units were forming with Allied encouragement in France and Italy. In addition the terms of the Treaty of Brest-Litovsk had alienated the Polish units that had hitherto been fighting on the German side. In February 1918 the Polish Council in Warsaw broke off relations with Austria-Hungary and a brigade of the Polish legion deserted to the Russians. Almost simultaneously the Czech legion in Russia obtained

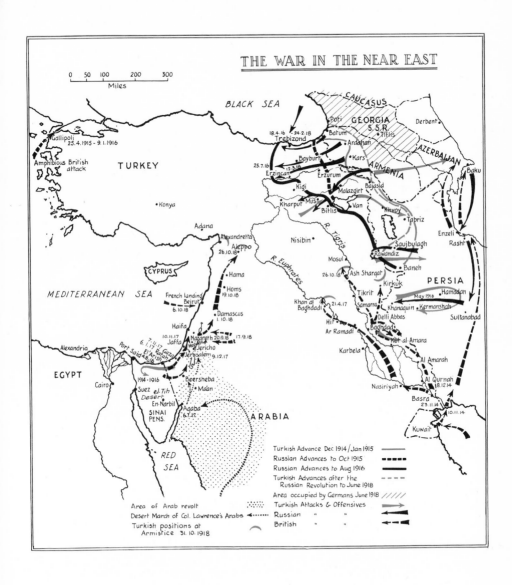

# THE WAR IN THE NEAR EAST

0  50  100      200      300
Miles

BLACK SEA

CAUCASUS

GEORGIA S.S.R.

Poti · Derbent
Batum
18.4.16   24.2.18   Tiflis
Trebizond   Ardahan   AZERBAIJAN

Gallipoli
25.4.1915 - 9.1.1916
Amphibious British
attack

TURKEY

Bayburt · Kars   ARMENIA   Baku
25.7.16   12.3.18   Bajasid
Erzincan   Erzurum
Kiği   Makzgirt   Khvoy
Kharput · Muş   Van   Tabriz   Enzeli
Bitlis   Saujbulagh   Rasht

Konya

Adana

Nisibin ·   Rawandiz
Mosul   Ash Sharqat   Baneh   PERSIA
26.10.18   Kirkuk

Alexandretta
26.10.18
Aleppo

CYPRUS

· Hama

MEDITERRANEAN SEA   French landing
Beirut
6.10.18

Homs
19.10.18

Damascus
1.10.18

Haifa
10.11.17   Nazareth 20.9.18   17.9.18
6.1.17 Jaffa   Jericho
El Arish   Jerusalem 9.12.17

Alexandria   Port Said   Rafah

EGYPT

Cairo   Suez el Tih   Beersheba
Desert   · Ma'an
En Narbil
SINAI   Aqaba
PENS.   6.7.17

ARABIA

RED SEA

Tikrit
May 1916   Hamadan
Khan al   21.4.17   Samarra
Baghdadi   Khanaquin · Kermanshah
Hit   Delli Abbas   Sultanabad
Ar Ramadi   Baghdad
Kut al Amara
Karbela

Al Amarah
Nasiriyah   Al Qurnah
18.12.14
Basra
23.11.14
10.11.14
Kuwait

Turkish Advance Dec 1914 / Jan 1915
Russian Advances to Oct 1915
Russian Advances to Aug 1916
Turkish Advances after the
   Russian Revolution to June 1918
Area occupied by Germans June 1918
Turkish Attacks & Offensives
Russian    "    "
British    "    "

Area of Arab revolt
Desert March of Col. Lawrence's Arabs
Turkish positions at
   Armistice 31. 10. 1918

EUROPE, NORTH AFRICA, THE
NEAR AND MIDDLE EAST circa 1923.

0   100  200  300  400  500
                              Miles

SWEDEN

NORWAY

Oslo

Stockholm

DENMARK

BALTIC SEA

Memel

DANZIG

E. PRUSSIA

NORTH
SEA

Edinburgh

ULSTER
Belfast

IRISH
FREE
STATE

Dublin

London

The
Hague

Brussels

R. Elbe

Berlin

R. Oder

Warsaw

GERMANY

RUHR
Cologne

SILESIA

UPPER

ATLANTIC

OCEAN

Paris

Metz

SAAR

Strasbourg

Prague

CZECHOSLOVAKIA

Teschen

Munich

Vienna

Geneva

SWITZERLAND

AUSTRIA

Budapest

HUNGARY

Locarno

TYROL

Trieste

Marseille

Venice

Rome

ITALY

ADRIATIC SEA

YUGOSLAVIA

Belgrade

Lisbon

PORTUGAL

Madrid

SPAIN

CORSICA

Rome

ALBANIA

GREECE

Gibraltar

BALEARIC IS

Naples

Tangier

SARDINIA

FRENCH
MOROCCO

Algiers

Tunis

SICILY

Malta

ALGERIA

MEDITERRANEAN

Tripoli

LIBYA

Territory lost by Russia
    "     "   Germany
    "     "   Austria-Hungary
    "     "   Bulgaria
Neutral Zones

Murmansk

Archangel

R. Dvina

FINLAND

Sverdlovsk

Helsinki
(Helsingfors)

L. Ladoga

Leningrad

•Vologda

Tallinn
ESTONIA

Riga
LATVIA

R. Volga

LITHUANIA
Kaunas
Vilna

•Moscow

Samara

Orenburg

R. Dvina

•Minsk

•Smolensk

U S S R

Saratov•

KIRGHIZ

POLAND

•Orel

R. Ural

•Kiev

R. Don

•Kharkov

Tsaritsin
(Stalingrad)

ARAL
SEA

GALICIA

BUKOVINA

R. Dnieper

•Rostov

Astrakhan

TRANSYLVANIA

R. Dniester

BESSARABIA

Odessa

RUMANIA

•Bucharest

Sevastopol

CAUCASIA

CASPIAN SEA

R. Danube

BLACK SEA

Batum

GEORGIAN
S.S.R. Tiflis

Baku

AZERBAIJAN
S.S.R.

•Sofia

BULGARIA

Istanbul
(Constantinople)

Erivan

ARMENIAN
S.S.R.

•Tabriz

Athens

•Ankara

•Teheran

Smyrna

TURKEY

I R A N

SYRIA

CYPRUS

R. Tigris

Baghdad

SEA

CRETE

Haifa

LEBANON

•Damascus

IRAQ

R. Euphrates

Basra

PERSIAN

Alexandria

PALESTINE

JORDAN

TRANS

Jerusalem

GULF

Cairo

Suez Canal

SAUDI ARABIA

E G Y P T

RED SEA

TREATY OF
BREST~LITOVSK

Russian Frontier 1914 – – –
Central Powers &
  their Allies
Allies of the
  Entente
Neutrals
Areas occupied
by Central Powers
Armistice Line
15·12·1917
Areas in nationlist
revolt against
Russia.
Security Zone occupied
by Central
Powers in 1918
Soviet Republic
of Russia

NORWAY
SWEDEN
DENMARK
Neutral
FINLAND
(Ind. 28.7.1917)
Romanovsk
(Murmansk)

St Petersburg (to 1914)
Petrograd (1914 – 1924)

RUSSIA
Feb.1917 Parliamentary Republic
16.9.1917 Republic.    24/25 Oct Russian Calender
                       Bolshevik Revolution
· Moscow
(Capital since
1918 )

ESTONIA
LATVIA
LITHUANIA

GERMANY
WHITE
RUSSIA
POLAND
· Brest Litovsk

AUSTRIA
HUNGARY

Kiev
INDEPENDENT
UKRAINE
22.1.1918 Ind.
2.1918 Peace with
Germany

· Kharkov

· Rostov

RUMANIA

SERBIA
ALBANIA
GREECE
BULGARIA

BLACK  SEA

CAUCASUS

TURKEY

Soviet agreement for its withdrawal from Russia via Vladivostok. In June 1918 the French recognized the Czech exile National Council as 'the basis for a future Czechoslovak government'. And in America, Masaryk concluded at Pittsburgh an agreement with representatives of the Slovak *emigrés*, looking to the establishment of a Czechoslovak state. Recognition by Britain and the United States followed soon thereafter.

These developments took place against the background of the German spring offensives on the Western front. It was on these attacks that the German military leadership pinned their final hopes of victory. The aim was to force the British to sue for peace. New infantry tactics had been developed, involving infiltration by independent battle groups, using smoke to hide their movements. Known strongpoints were to be encircled rather than assaulted from the front. Thirty-five divisions from the Eastern front were to be committed to the first offensive. The initial assault fell on the British Third and Fifth Armies in the Somme area. It did not succeed in separating the British and French forces but scored an advance of forty miles and inflicted a quarter of a million casualties on the Allies. A second offensive in Flanders in April scored a complete breakthrough and the Germans were only contained by the greatest effort, and a further three hundred thousand casualties. In May a third German offensive struck the French on the Aisne river, broke through and advanced to within thirty-seven miles of Paris before being halted. Two more major attacks in June and early July scored minor successes but were soon contained. The German army had shot its bolt at a cost of eight hundred thousand casualties to itself. However, Germany had inflicted over one million casualties on the Allies, captured great quantities of guns and war material and carved three immense salients in the Allied line. But Allied morale had held, the armies though badly mauled had not collapsed, and American divisions, fresh, strong and vigorous, were now pouring into France. Two such American divisions had in fact held the third German offensive in front of Paris. The initiative now passed inexorably to the Allies.

This was the more welcome in that the German offensives had at last forced the Allied generals to agree to a system of unified command. The Caporetto disaster in October 1917 had led to the formation of a Supreme War Council the following month. But the British and French generals had refused to give it powers of command over themselves or to furnish it with a central strategic reserve, and the British and French prime ministers had felt themselves unable to override their refusal. The British defeat in March 1918 was compounded by Pétain's refusal to send more than a few divisions to the aid of the British, and an announcement that French troops in the event of a retreat would withdraw to the south-west to cover Paris. Such an action would have given the German general staff the separation of British and French armies for which they were working. It led the Supreme War Council to give General Foch supreme command over all Allied forces in France.

Under Foch's direction the Allies now prepared for the counter-offensive. In the second half of July, four French armies, into which considerable American and British contingents were incorporated, drove the Germans back from their great salient pointing towards Paris. On August 8th, the 'black day' of the German army in the view of General Ludendorff, the British Fourth Army, with large Canadian and Australian contingents, over 600 tanks and very heavy air support, broke clean through the German front at Amiens and drove the Germans back to the starting line of their first spring offensive. For the first time the morale of the German army was seen to crack. And on September 12th, the first all-American offensive (though it had heavy air and artillery support from the Allies) obliterated a salient at St Mihiel which had persisted since the fighting in 1914.

The turn of the tide on the Western front came, however, too late to forestall the opening of Allied intervention in Russia. Small elements of British and Allied troops had been landed in Murmansk as early as March 1918 at the appeal of the local revolutionary forces, to protect the large quantity of Allied stores landed there against possible German attack through Finland. They received military reinforcements in May 1918. And the Japanese military authorities had long been nursing plans to intervene in Siberia and take over the Russian Maritime Provinces, with the aim of making the whole North China Sea into an 'inland sea' surrounded by Japanese controlled territories. There were half a million tons of Allied war stores in Vladivostok too. Since November 1917 there had been discussions in Allied circles centred on the idea of using Japanese troops to recreate the Eastern front which Russia's collapse had destroyed. But the Japanese refused to move without American agreement, although naval units were sent by Britain and Japan to Vladivostok in January 1918.

The desperate state of the Western front under the impact of the German spring offensives stirred the British and French authorities into renewed pressure for Japanese intervention in Siberia. Their proposals which envisaged a mass movement of Japanese troops along five thousand miles of Trans-Siberian railway to the Urals and beyond were so unreal as to indicate more the depths of despair to which Britain's military planners had been brought in the early summer of 1918. In April, small Japanese and British units were landed at Vladivostok to prevent local Bolshevik forces from shipping the war stores in the city out of Allied reach. And in May the Czech Legion, retreating across Russia under an agreement made by the Czech exile leadership with the Bolsheviks, clashed with Red Army units, and seized control of the whole Central Russian railway network from the Volga to Irkutsk. A section of the Legion had already reached Vladivostok. The rest determined to fight their way across Siberia to join them. At the end of June 1918 the Czechs already in Vladivostok seized the city.

The need to come to the aid of the Czechs overruled American objections to intervention in Siberia. Japanese troops began landing at Vladivostok at the beginning of August 1918 and within three months there were over 70,000 Japanese troops in Siberia. They were to be joined by much smaller contingents of American, British and Canadian troops. By this date the Czechs had established complete control from the Pacific to the Urals. The Japanese, however, made no move to come to their aid but simply entrenched themselves in Manchuria and the Siberian Maritime Provinces. West of them were the Czechs now gradually retreating in the face of Bolshevik attack; authority was exercised by various anti-Bolshevik governments. In November 1918 these were to be united under the leadership of Admiral Kolchak. The stage was set for civil war in Russia.

The intervention in Siberia was important principally because of its scale. There had been other British landings in Northern Russia, where at the beginning of July 1918 the Murmansk Soviet had broken with the Bolshevik leaders in Moscow, and a Social Revolutionary government had been set up in Archangel. American troops were added to those of Britain in August 1918, and the combined forces advanced deep into North Russia. Their original aim had been simply to protect Northern Russia against German and Finnish invasion; and they had been dispatched *before* the break between Murmansk and Moscow. Thereafter they were, willynilly, embroiled in the civil war. Other small British forces were sent into the Caucasus and into Transcaspia to aid in the protection of the oilfields against Turkey and to forestall a possible German-Turkish drive into Persia and Afghanistan. Their presence did not outlast the year 1918. It was to be more difficult to extricate the British troops in Northern Russia.

The Allied interventions in Russia were conceived in panic and borne of too much study of small-scale maps. Their effect was to embroil the West with the new Soviet government and to accentuate the division between Russia's new rulers and Europe; to plant the Japanese military firmly in Eastern Asia and to exacerbate relations between Britain and America; and all to no avail. As has been shown previously, by the time the Japanese troops had begun to invade Siberia, the German forces were already in retreat on the Western front. In September 1918 three great offensives, in Palestine, on the Salonika front and on the Western front were to bring total defeat to Germany and her Eastern allies, and dissolution to the Habsburg monarchy.

In Palestine, the British forces had been considerably weakened during the spring of 1918 by the withdrawal of British troops to bolster the armies in France and repair the losses they suffered during the German spring offensives. They were replaced by Indian troops, who needed a good deal of training before Allenby felt it safe to go over to the offensive again. The British offensive opened on the plains of Megiddo (the biblical Armageddon) on September 19th. A complete breakthrough was scored and Allenby unleashed his three cavalry divisions and the Hejazi Bedouin forces in a pursuit which was only to end with the conclusion of an armistice by Turkey on October 30th. Damascus was 'liberated' by Arab forces on October 1st, a day after Australian cavalry had passed through in pursuit of the fleeing Turks. The Turkish Cabinet then resigned, Enver Pasha retiring in favour of a non-partisan Cabinet appointed by the Sultan. By the terms of the armistice, for which the Turks sued on October 14th, and which was signed on October 30th on the isle of Lemnos, the Turkish authorities agreed to open the Dardanelles, surrender all garrisons in Cyrenaica, Tripolitania, Arabia, Syria and Mesopotamia, and withdraw all forces from Northern Persia and Transcaucasia. The bulk of the Turkish army was to be demobilized and the Turkish fleet surrendered. British troops entered Mosul in late November, and British forces moved through to the Caspian Sea, reoccupying Baku. The Ottoman Empire was destroyed.

The Arab nationalists believed themselves now to have British support for setting up an Arab government in Damascus. Among the secret treaties published by the Bolsheviks in November 1917 was the Sykes-Picot agreement of 1916 providing for the division of the Arab provinces of the Ottoman world into spheres of influence between Britain and France. The Ottoman Governor of Syria lost no time in turning this disclosure to the propaganda advantage of the Turks and against the forces of the Arab revolt and their supporters in Syria. The pro-Arabs in the British administration in Cairo and Palestine and in the Arab Bureau responsible for relations with the Arab forces were encouraged by the effect of these revelations to resume their campaign for a unified Arab monarchy under British protection. Various statements were made by these pro-Arab elements (most notably the so-called 'Declaration to the Seven' of July 1918 made to the leaders of the Party of Syrian Unity formed among the Syrian exiles in Cairo), promising that the government of the territories liberated from the Turks would be based on the principle of the consent of the governed. Where the Arab forces had themselves (i.e. without British military participation) 'emancipated' former Ottoman territories the Declaration promised that their 'complete and sovereign independence' would be recognized. It was presumably to fit in with this provision that Arab forces were allowed to 'liberate' Damascus, British troops being deliberately held back to make this possible. This chicanery, for there is no other word for it, encouraged the Arabs to believe that Britain would protect them against French claims. They were to be rudely disillusioned the following year.

The offensive on the Salonika front began on September 14th, 1918. The front was defended primarily by Bulgarian troops, the German and Austro-Hungarian contingents having been withdrawn to bolster the French and Italian fronts. By September 17th the Allied forces had advanced over twenty miles; by September 26th the Bulgarian army was in a state of total collapse and the road to Sofia, the Bulgarian capital, lay open. That day the Bulgarian government requested an armistice, which was signed on September 29th. The Bulgarian army was to be demobilized and all Allied territory evacuated. Free passage through Bulgarian territory and the control of Bulgaria's transport facilities were surrendered to the

Allies. The way was open to attack Germany and Austria-Hungary from the rear.

On the Italian front, the armies of Austria-Hungary had staged their last offensive across the river Piave in June 1918. The offensive involved crossing the river on pontoons within range of the Italian artillery; and although the Austrians fought with vigour and determination their margin of strength was too small to bring victory. The Italian counter-offensive was not launched until October 24th, twenty days after the Austrian government had enquired of the American government about an armistice. The Austrian forces bravely held out for five days, inflicting heavy losses on the attacking forces. But on October 30th they began to crumble, and the Italian cavalry started a pursuit which carried them right up to and across the old Italo-Austrian frontier and which ended on November 4th, the day the Austrian armistice was finally signed. On November 3rd Italian sea-borne forces occupied Trieste. Half a million Austrian prisoners were taken on this final offensive, known to historians as the Battle of Vittorio Veneto.

The collapse and disintegration of the Habsburg Empire was already in full progress. On September 14th, the Emperor had published a last appeal for peace which had simply been ignored. On October 1st the *Reichsrath* convened for the last time, all the national delegations taking advantage of the occasion to issue declarations in favour of independence. On October 4th, the Austrian government dispatched a note to the United States requesting an armistice and offering to make peace on the basis of the Fourteen Points. On October 16th, in a last attempt to save the Habsburg state, the Emperor issued an Imperial Manifesto proclaiming the re-organization of the non-Magyar part of the monarchy as a federal state with complete self-government for the subject nationalities. Even at this late date the government in Budapest was able to prevent its application to the territories under Hungarian rule.

But the move came much too late. On October 14th Beneš had already announced the formation of a provisional Czech government in Paris. On October 21st, in America, Masaryk proclaimed Czech independence and on October 28th in Prague the local Czech leaders had no difficulty in formally taking over the administration of Bohemia with tacit Austrian acquiescence. The following day Serb and Croat leaders meeting in Zagreb proclaimed the establishment of a Yugoslav state. On October 30th a German National Council was set up for the German provinces of Austria. The next day, after the assassination of Count Tisza, strong man of the old *régime*, a Radical-Social Democratic government under Count Karolyi proclaimed Hungary's independence. Polish independence had been proclaimed in Warsaw on October 7th; and the administration of Polish Galicia was taken over from the Austrians together with that of eastern Silesia and the Austro-Hungarian zone of occupation in eastern Poland by the end of October. It was to be some time, however, before the Polish exiles and the Warsaw Poles were to be reconciled and a single

Polish government recognized by the Allies. On November 12th the last of the Habsburg emperors abdicated his throne. Balkanization, the division of Eastern and Central Europe into a congerie of small, weak, mutually suspicious and inimical states, a natural prey to Great Power pressures and ambitions, was completed.

Of all the belligerents there remained only Germany. During the spring and summer of 1918 the hold of the military over German affairs had become virtually absolute. In June 1918, at the height of Germany's victories in the West, Ludendorff had forced the Kaiser to dismiss the State Secretary in the Foreign Ministry, von Kuhlmann, for daring to suggest that the Supreme Command should conduct peace negotiations. He followed this *coup* by forcing the Kaiser to dismiss the head of his own Civil Secretariat. The Kaiser was reduced to bitter complaints, scribbled on the margin of Foreign Ministry dispatches, that he could not obtain a hearing for his views from the Chief of the General Staff. But the events of August 1918 shook Ludendorff's nerve badly; and his encouragement of the Prussian conservatives and German nationalists through the Fatherland party and the whole movement for an annexationist peace meant that any resignation of power on his part would mean at least a parliamentary, if not a socialist revolution in Germany.

The final Allied offensives in the West opened on September 26th with a massive attack by the new American armies on the Argonne forest area. On September 27th–28th a British offensive on the Cambrai sector broke into the Hindenburg Line, and on October 5th they had forced a total German withdrawal to new positions along the Selle river. In Flanders Anglo-Belgian forces were on the advance from Ypres. Throughout October successive offensives threw the German forces back along the line. Ostend, Zeebrugge, Roubaix, Lille, Valenciennes, all fell before the advancing armies. By the end of October, Allied troops were approaching Sedan. The events of September 27th–28th, when taken with the collapse of Bulgaria, were enough for Germany.

On September 29th, Hindenburg and Ludendorff informed the Emperor and the Chancellor that the military situation demanded the immediate institution of negotiations for an armistice. It was decided to address an appeal to President Wilson to bring about an armistice on the basis of the Fourteen Points. The generals believed that if the Allied terms should prove too onerous then Germany would fight on. At the same time they realized that there would have to be a change of government in order to provide one that would be both acceptable to the Allies and able to maintain order in Germany. Since the only alternative source of authority was the *Reichstag*, a German staff officer was sent to tell the party leaders that the army had lost the war and that the *Reichstag* would have to make the peace. A new Chancellor was found in Prince Max of Baden, the one German state where the ruling house had established a compromise with the middle classes. This action by General Ludendorff, for he was the prime mover, represented the complete abdication of power by the army leadership. When Ludendorff came thereafter into conflict with the new Chancellor he was easily forced to resign. The real German revolution occurred between September 29th and October 3rd, 1918.

On October 4th the new Chancellor sent a note through neutral channels to President Wilson asking for an armistice to be concluded on the basis of the Fourteen Points. The German government was to find President Wilson a stern and unbending task-master, insistent on proof that the new government was speaking not merely for the old imperial authorities but for the German people. There followed further exchanges of notes, Wilson demanding that submarine operations cease immediately and that the armistice should confirm the 'present military supremacy' of the Allied armies. He remained so obstinately unconvinced that any real transfer in power had been effected in Germany that pressure began to build up in favour of the Kaiser's abdication. On October 26th the *Reichstag* adopted a series of resolutions which made the Chancellor and his Cabinet responsible to the *Reichstag*, established civilian authority over the armed forces and swept away the three-class system of voting in Prussia.

In the meantime, the plans made by the German naval command for a large-scale raid on the British coast led on November 3rd to mutiny in the German fleet and the setting up of workers and sailors councils on the Russian model. Mutiny spread to the army and on November 7th in Munich the Independent Socialist leader, Kurt Eisner, proclaimed a Bavarian republic and the overthrow of the ruling house of Wittelsbach. On November 9th, the revolution spread to Berlin and the Kaiser abdicated. The Social Democrats overthrew Prince Max of Baden's Cabinet and a new Cabinet under a Social Democrat Chancellor, Friedrich Ebert, took office. On November 10th the Republic was proclaimed in Berlin. The Kaiser took refuge in Holland. The Supreme Command of the Army pledged its support to the new *régime*. The German revolution was over; though attempts both from left and right to overthrow it were to be a constant feature of its first five years of life.

Throughout this period the Allied Supreme War Council was in session at Versailles, debating the terms of the Armistice. None of the Allies had ever formally accepted the Fourteen Points; and President Wilson's assumption of the leadership in negotiating unilaterally with the Germans was much resented. The British and French leaders turned therefore to writing armistice terms which would make it impossible for Germany to resume the fight again. All but a handful of Germany's modern warships and all her submarines were to be surrendered. Allied armies were to occupy all the land between the existing front and the river Rhine, including Belgium, Alsace-Lorraine, Northern France and Luxemburg; they were in addition to occupy the bridgeheads over the Rhine. Germany was to disgorge her gains in Eastern Europe. The blockade would continue in force. The American authorities made no complaint over the terms and the German delegation accepted them over army protest. On November

11th the armistice was signed in a railway carriage at Compiégne. At 11 a.m. that day the Great War was at an end.

The war losses were immense. In all sixty million men were mobilized by the belligerents excluding the United States and Japan. Of these 57·6% became casualties, with over eight million killed, twenty-one million wounded, and seven and three-quarter million taken prisoner and incarcerated behind walls and barbed wire fences until the armistices released them. The highest casualty rates were suffered by Austria-Hungary (7 million casualties, 1·2 million dead, 3·6 million wounded, 2·2 million prisoners, 90% of all mobilized), Russia (9 million casualties, 1·7 million dead, 4·9 million wounded, 25 million prisoners, 76·3% of all men mobilized), France (6 million casualties, 1·3 million dead, 4·3 million wounded, 0·5 million prisoners, 73·3% of all mobilized), Rumania (535 thousand casualties, 335 thousand killed, 120 thousand wounded, 80 thousand killed, 71·4% of all mobilized), Germany (7 million casualties, 1·8 million dead, 4·2 million wounded, 1·2 million prisoners, 64·9% of all mobilized), Serbia (45 thousand killed, 133 thousand wounded, 152 thousand prisoners, 46% of all mobilized), Italy (650 thousand killed, 947 thousand wounded, 600 thousand prisoners, 39·1% of all mobilized), the British Empire (908 thousand killed, 2 million wounded, 191 thousand prisoners, 35·8% of all mobilized), Belgium (13 thousand killed, 44 thousand wounded, 34 thousand prisoners, 34·9% of all mobilized) and Turkey (325 thousand killed, 400 thousand wounded, 250 thousand prisoners, 34·2% of all mobilized). The direct costs of the war have been estimated at over one hundred and eighty billion dollars, or forty-five thousand million pounds sterling, the indirect costs at one hundred and fifty-one billion dollars, or just under thirty-eight thousand million pounds sterling. But these figures are purely notional. The casualties, to be put in their clearest light, must be seen as falling entirely on the age groups entering into the eighteen to thirty-five years range between the years 1914–18, in terms of an average expectancy of life in the front line of one month for an infantry officer, six to eight weeks for an ordinary soldier. A significant proportion of a whole generation in Europe, especially of those with courage, dedication, and initiative was killed or scarred physically and mentally. And attempts made today to belittle these figures go contrary to all the contemporary evidence.

The war produced many new means of battle. It was, in fact, the first industrialized war in history. Poison-gas, the tank, the submarine have all been mentioned. Another major development was that of war in the air. In 1914 aircraft were primitive, unarmed, slow and used merely to extend the scouting range of the armies' cavalry. In 1918 the Allies were preparing for a major bombing assault on Germany's cities; ground attack techniques had been developed and proved especially effective in France and Palestine. The Allies had some eight thousand aircraft to the Central Powers three and a half thousand. Aerial combat techniques had become advanced, air aces with tens of 'kills' to their credit were national heroes. German dirigible lighter-than-air balloons, the *Zeppelins*, and German aircraft had bombed London, causing a certain amount of panic among its citizens. The more imaginative had already leaped forward to visualizing the scenes that were to mark World War II, Warsaw, Rotterdam, Coventry, London, Belgrade, Lübeck, Hamburg, Berlin, Cologne, Dresden—even to Hiroshima.

In the world of art and literature, the war accentuated that division of the creative and artistic intellectual groupings from the remainder of society referred to in Chapter XI above. For many artists, of course, the war period was too short to introduce any really startling changes in doctrine or technique. But the development of 'metaphysical painting' (*pittura metafisica*) in Italy, a curious combination of cubist method and surrealist themes, pointed forward to the developments of the next decade. Marc Chagall continued his surrealist exploration of dream-life fantasy in Russia to which he returned on the outbreak of war. In Britain Italian Futurism had a brief influence in 1914–15 on the so-called Vorticist school, one which united painters and sculptors such as Wyndham Lewis, Jacob Epstein, Henry Gaudier-Brzeska, and E. Wadsworth, with Anglo-American writers such as Ezra Pound, Ford Madox Hueffer, Rebecca West and Osbert and Edith Sitwell, a school which if it can be said to have had any theme, preached a revolutionary *élitist* assault on the received values of their own society.

The most significant development, however, began in neutral Switzerland in 1916. This was the so-called 'Dadaist' movement, an anarchist and nihilist assault on any notion of order, restraint or aesthetic in art and culture. For a time 'Dada', which spread rapidly to Berlin, Paris, Barcelona, New York and Cologne, embraced artists and writers as variegated as Picasso, the Italian Futurist, Marinetti, the Russian philosopher of the Central European *Blaue Reiter* group, Kandinsky, Paul Klee, Max Ernst, André Breton and Louis Aragon. It cleared the way for the post-war development of the extreme forms of cubism and surrealism, especially the work of Paul Klee, the Swiss surrealist. For others, especially in Germany and France, it opened the way to a personal re-involvement in political activity on the side of the extreme revolutionaries, an involvement itself so anti-political as to hinder rather than help the re-integration of the artist with society. In general it marked the revulsion and disgust of the artists and writers in Europe with the society in which they lived but with which they felt little or no identification, a society which seemed to have decided to immolate itself in an orgy of hatred and self-destruction.

The war of 1914–18 marked for Europe the end of an era of peace, stability and co-operation between the established ruling social groups of the continent's leading powers. The forces which expressed themselves in these years were divisive and destructive, both between the powers and within them, and in each case they reflected the discontent of the social groupings which, under the existing systems of socio-political power, were denied any participation in, or identification with, the processes which governed their destinies. For those social groups which thought along individualist rather than collectivist lines, peasants, professional men, small traders and business men, white collar workers, the main enemy seemed to be the forces of cosmopolitan Europe and the foreign powers whose activity, they thought, hampered and stunted their own national development. For those who thought on collectivist lines, the alienated intelligentsias and the organized industrial workers, the main enemies became, under the privations of war, the ruling groups who seemed to want to prolong the war to satisfy their own annexationist demands. Between these two forces, political Europe as it was organized in 1914 fell to pieces to be replaced by the spurious internationalism of the League of Nations, all things to all men, in theory world-wide, in fact European in composition, which sought to outlaw war by the threat of making it universal, and ensured only that any future employment of force for national ends would be deliberate, conspiratorial, and less hindered by the checks and balances of the Concert of Europe system which had broken down in 1914. The League was to last only twenty years, until a second world war destroyed what the first had left undamaged of Europe's supremacy and introduced a new balance of terror, rather than power, between the super-powers on Europe's periphery, the Soviet Union and the United States, with Europe divided between them.

# SELECT BIBLIOGRAPHY

Albertini, Luigi, *The Origins of the War of 1914*, 3 vols., translated and edited by Isabella M. Massey, Oxford University Press, London, 1952–57.

Anderson, M. S., *The Eastern Question, 1774–1923*, Longmans, Green and Co., Ltd., London, 1966.

Avery, Peter, *Modern Iran*, Frederick Praeger, New York, 1965.

Ayearst, Morley, *The British West Indies*, New York University Press, New York, 1960.

Barbour, Neville, *A Survey of North West Africa (the Maghreb)*, Oxford University Press, New York, 1962.

Barraclough, Geoffrey, *Introduction To Contemporary History*, Basic Books, Inc., New York, 1965.

Black, C. E., and Helmreich, E. C., *Twentieth Century Europe: A History* (2nd ed.), Alfred A. Knopf, Inc., New York, 1963.

Brogan, D. W., *The Development of Modern France*, Hamish Hamilton, Ltd., London, 1959.

Bullard, Sir Reader, *The Middle East: A Political and Economic Survey* (3rd ed.), Oxford University Press, London, 1958.

Cady, John F., *South-East Asia: Its Historical Development*, McGraw-Hill Book Co., New York, 1964.

Cargill, Oscar, *Intellectual America: Ideas on the March*, Macmillan and Co., Ltd., London, 1941.

Carr, Raymond, *Spain 1808–1939*, Oxford University Press, London, 1965.

Chambers, Frank P., *The War Behind the War*, Faber and Faber, Ltd., London, 1939.

Clubb, Oliver E., *Twentieth Century China*, Columbia University Press, New York, 1964.

Cole, G. D. H., *A History of Socialist Thought*, Vol. III, *The Second International, 1889–1914*, St. Martins Press, New York, 1956.

# SELECT BIBLIOGRAPHY

Craig, Gordon A., *The Politics of the Prussian Army, 1640–1945* (rev. ed.), Oxford University Press, New York, 1964.

Dozer, D. M., *Latin America, An Interpretative History*, McGraw-Hill Book Co., New York, 1962.

Edmonds, Sir James E., *A Short History of World War I*, Oxford University Press, London, 1951.

Edwardes, Michael, *Asia in the European Age, 1498–1955*, ill., Frederick A. Praeger, Inc., New York, 1962.

Esposito, Brigadier-General Vincent J. (ed.), *A Concise History of World War I*, Frederick A. Praeger, Inc., New York, 1964.

Feis, H., *Europe, The World's Banker*, 1870–1914, Kelley, New York, 1961.

Gooch, G. P., *Before the War: Studies in Diplomacy*, 2 vols., Longmans, Green and Co., Ltd., London, 1936–38.

Gratten, C. H., *The South West Pacific Since 1900: A Modern History*, University of Michigan Press, Ann Arbor, Mich., 1963.

Griswold, A. W., *The Far Eastern Policy of the United States*, Yale University Press, New Haven, Conn., 1962.

Hodgkin, Thomas, *Nationalism in Colonial Africa*, New York University Press, New York, 1957.

Hofstaedter, R., *The Age of Reform, From Bryan to F.D.R.*, Alfred A. Knopf, Inc., New York, 1955.

Hourani, Albert, *Arabic Thought in the Liberal Age, 1798–1939*, Oxford University Press, London, 1962.

Hughes, H. Stuart, *Consciousness and Society*, Alfred A. Knopf, Inc., New York, 1958.

Hurewitz, J. C., *Diplomacy in the Near and Middle East, A Documentary Record*, Van Nostrand Company, Inc., Princeton, N. J., 1956.

Jones, A. H. M., and Monroe, E., *A History of Ethiopia*, Oxford University Press, London, 1955.

Kann, R. A., *The Multinational Empire: Nationalism and National Reform in the Hapsburg Monarchy, 1848–1918*, Columbia University Press, New York, 1950.

Kedourie, Eli, *England and the Middle East: The Destruction of the Ottoman Empire, 1914–1921*, Bowes and Bowes Publishers, Ltd., London, 1956.

Kelly, John B., *Eastern Arabian Frontiers*, ill., Frederick A. Praeger, Inc., New York, 1964.

King, J. Clemens, *Generals and Politicians*, University of California Press, Berkeley, Calif., 1951.

Komarnicki, Tytus, *Rebirth of the Polish Republic: A Study in the Diplomatic History of Europe, 1914–1920*, William Heinemann, Ltd., London, 1957.

Langer, W. L., *The Diplomacy of Imperialism, 1890–1902* (2nd ed.), Alfred A. Knopf., Inc., New York, 1956.

Lewis, Bernard, *The Emergence of Modern Turkey*, Oxford University Press, London, 1961.

Lewis, Cleona, and Schottebeck, Karl T., *America's Stake in International Investments*, The Brookings Institution, Washington, D.C., 1938.

Lindberg, Folke, *Scandinavia in Great Power Politics, 1905–1908*, Almkvist och Wiskell, Stockholm, 1958.

Link, Arthur S., *Woodrow Wilson and the Progressive Era, 1910–1917*, Harper and Row, Evanston, Ill., 1954.

Little, Tom, *Egypt*, Ernest Benn, Ltd., London, 1958.

Mack Smith, Denis, *Italy: A Modern History*, University of Michigan Press, Ann Arbor, Mich., 1959.

Marder, Arthur J., *The Anatomy of British Sea Power*, Shoe String Press, Hamden, Conn., 1940.

Marlowe, John, *The Persian Gulf in the Twentieth Century*, Frederick A. Praeger, New York, 1962.

May, Arthur J., *The Habsburg Monarchy, 1867–1914*, Harvard University Press, Cambridge, Mass., 1961.

Mayer, Arno J., *The Political Origins of the New Diplomacy*, Yale University Press, New Haven, Conn., 1959.

Mazour, Anatole G., *Finland Between East and West*, ill., Van Nostrand Co., Inc., Princeton, N. J., 1956.

Morison, S. E., and Commager, H. S., *The Growth of the American Republic* (5th ed.), Oxford University Press, New York, 1962.

Morton, William L., *The Kingdom of Canada*, Bobbs-Merrill Co., Indianapolis, Ind., 1958.

Mowat, R. B., *The Concert of Europe*, Macmillan and Co., Ltd., London, 1930.

Mowry, George E., *The Era of Theodore Roosevelt, 1900–1912*, Harper and Row, Evanston, Ill., 1958.

Mumford, Lewis, *Technics and Civilization*, ill., Harcourt, Brace and World, New York, 1963.

National Bureau of Economic Research, *International Migration*, The Bureau, New York, 1931.

Nelson, Harold, *Land and Power: British and Allied Policy on Germany's Frontiers, 1916–1919*, University of Toronto, Toronto, 1963.

Nowell, C. E., *A History of Portugal*, Van Nostrand Co., Inc., Princeton, N. J., 1962.

Page, Stanley W., *The Formation of the Baltic States*, Harvard University Press, Cambridge, Mass., 1959.

Pevsner, Nicolaus, *Pioneers of Modern Design, From William Morris to Walter Gropius* (2nd ed.), Simon and Schuster Inc., New York, 1949.

Pipes, Richard, *The Formation of the Soviet Union: Communism and Nationalism 1917–1923*, Harvard University Press, Cambridge, Mass., 1964.

Reshetar, John S., *The Ukrainian Revolution, 1917–1920*, Princeton University Press, Princeton, N. J., 1952.

Rippy, J. Fred, *Latin America: A Modern History*, University of Michigan Press, Ann Arbor, Mich., 1958.

# SELECT BIBLIOGRAPHY

Rosenberg, Arthur, *The Birth of the German Republic, 1871–1918*, Russell and Russell, New York, 1962.

Sachar, Howard M., *The Course of Modern Jewish History*, World Publishing Co., Cleveland, 1958.

Schapiro, Leonard, *The Origin of the Communist Autocracy*, Frederick A. Praeger, Inc., New York, 1952.

Schmitt, Bernadotte E., *The Coming of the War, 1914*, Charles Scribner's Sons, New York, 1930.

Seton-Watson, Hugh, *The Decline of Imperial Russia*, Frederick A. Praeger, New York, 1952.

Seton-Watson, R. W., *A History of the Czechs and Slovacks*, Hutchinson and Co., London, 1943.

Shwadran, Benjamin, *The Middle East, Oil and the Great Powers* (2nd ed.), Council for Middle Eastern Affairs Press, New York, 1959.

Singer, Charles, Holmyard, E. T., Hall, A. R., and Williams, Trevor I., *A History of Technology*, Vol. IV, Oxford University Press, London, 1955.

Smith, C. Jay, Jr., *Finland and the Russian Revolution 1917–1922*, University of Georgia Press, Athens, Ga., 1958.

Spear, J. G. P., *India: A Modern History*, University of Michigan Press, Ann Arbor, Mich., 1961.

Spender, J. A., *Great Britain, Empire and Commonwealth, 1866–1935*, Allen and Unwin, Ltd., London, 1936.

Taylor, A. J. P., *The Habsburg Monarchy, 1809–1918*, Humanities Press, New York, 1964.

——, *English History, 1914–1945*, Oxford University Press, London, 1965.

Ullman, Richard H., *Anglo-Soviet Relations 1917–1921*, Vol. I: *Intervention and the War*, Princeton University Press, Princeton, N. J., 1961.

Vinacke, Harold, *A History of the Far East in Modern Times* (6th ed.), Appleton-Century-Crofts, New York, 1961.

Walker, Eric A., *A History of Southern Africa* (3rd ed.), Longmans, Green and Co., Ltd., London, 1957.

Wiedner, Donald L., *A History of Africa South of the Sahara*, Random House, New York, 1962.

Wilenski, R. S., *Modern French Painters*, Harcourt, Brace and World, New York, 1963.

Winkler, Henry R., *The League of Nations Movement in Great Britain, 1914–1919*, Rutgers University Press, New Brunswick, N. J., 1952.

Wolfe, Bertram, *Three Who Made a Revolution*, The Dial Press, Inc., New York, 1948.

Yanaga, C., *Japan Since Perry*, McGraw-Hill Book Co., New York, 1949.

Zeine, Zeine M., *Arab-Turkish Relations and the Emergence of Arab Nationalism*, Khayat, Beirut, 1958.

Zeman, Z. A. B., *The Break-Up of the Habsburg Empire, 1914–1918*, Oxford University Press, London, 1961.

# PART TWO
## 1918-1945
# FRANK SPENCER

*Chapter I*
# INTRODUCTORY

## (i) *Europe and the World between the Wars*

THE collapse of the eastern European and Turkish empires in World War I left the map of Europe east of the Rhine to be entirely redrawn and the Middle East to be reshaped, while the disposal of Germany's Far Eastern interests also posed major problems. New forms of government for the successor and defeated states had to be found. The economies of the combatants had to be restored to a peace-time footing in the aftermath of a war which had made heavy demands on their human and material resources, and in a world subject to radical economic and political changes throughout the postwar years. In the cases of Soviet Russia, Greece, Turkey and to a lesser extent Poland, economic reconstruction had to be deferred for some years after the November 1918 armistices, thereby retarding not only their own economic recovery but that of Europe generally. Even the non-European powers, Japan and America, suffered considerable economic dislocation in the early postwar period, though during the war they had undergone few difficulties and had gained great economic advantages. Germany was subjected to especially heavy strains both because of defeat and the penalties which defeat brought, and because her war effort had been far greater than those made by her allies and enemies. But extensive economic dislocation also followed the political disintegration of the Austro-Hungarian and Tsarist Russian Empires, and all the European manufacturing countries had to re-equip and modernize their existing major industries in order to replace damaged or obsolescent plant, and build up new industries. And all this occurred while these countries encountered revolutionary political changes in Europe and radically altered patterns of European and world trade.

The shifts in political and economic strength between the leading European powers, and between those countries and their non-European competitors, whether initiated or accelerated by World War I, were still largely unaccommodated when its successor broke out. In 1939 the most destructive war in history followed upon the heaviest mass unemployment, the worst economic depression and the most brutal political tyrannies which the world had known. However, the inter-war years also saw great economic progress, though not at the rate achieved in the world economy in the generation before 1914. In all the advanced countries of the world standards of living rose with the advent of full mechanization, rapidly developing technology and improved educational, medical and other social services. Increases in agricultural and manufacturing productivity, and with them higher standards of living, have taken place in proportion to the amount of mechanical energy available. By the middle of the twentieth century this was estimated as corresponding to the work done in a forty-hour working week by about fifty billion adult male workers, a figure about twenty times greater than that of the total world population. In the United States, the richest and technologically most advanced country, mechanization had been widely used after World War I for economic production and for domestic purposes and pleasure on scales not approached in the most advanced European countries. By 1950 half the mechanical energy used in the United States was used for domestic heating, lighting, appliances, and private transport, while more than half the world still lived in the pre-industrial age.

In addition technology, accompanied by the medical sciences and services, saved since 1900 more lives than the destructive wars of the twentieth century have taken. In most under-developed countries, however, the expectation of life at birth in 1950 was still under half that enjoyed in advanced countries, while the advances which the latter made in technology and in industrial and agricultural production during the inter-war years continually increased the gulf between themselves and the under-developed regions. Even the European continent, economically stagnant in the inter-war period, saw general improvements in the standard of living despite the effects of World War I and the great depression. Before the Nazi dictatorship in Germany began to slow down the pace of Europe's economic recovery and her advances in education, social services and medical and physical science, Europe was reducing the gap between her own and American economic power, and thereby inevitably widening the gulf between European living standards and those of the backward countries of Asia and Africa.

Europe's partial economic recovery in the inter-war years could not, however, check the shift in the balance of economic power from Europe to America and to a lesser extent to Soviet Russia, which accompanied a corresponding shift in the balance of political power. The outcome of World War II ensured that the trend would be irreversible, though as partial compensation for the crippling of European power in the world and the destruction of the balance of power within Europe by World War I, the last war brought in its closing stages the resumption of the American-Soviet global rivalry initiated by Lenin and Wilson in 1917. In their competition to secure the allegiance of mankind for their respective ideologies, Wilson tried to create a world of sovereign democratic nations collaborating to secure peace and progress within the framework of the

League of Nations, the first attempt at an international organization, while Lenin envisaged world proletarian revolution as the means of bringing about classless societies in a world which by abolishing capitalism would also have ended imperialism and war. In fact both visions were utopian. Though the struggle was rapidly abandoned after 1918, and was not resumed until after 1945, and then under greatly altered circumstances, it nevertheless introduced global revolutionary and ideological factors which had major consequences for the post-1918 generations. Soviet Russia in practice abandoned attempts to bring about world revolution almost as quickly as America after the Paris peace conference of 1919 repudiated the peace settlement and the League of Nations. While America disclaimed obligations to support the forces of democracy in Europe, and to oppose the Japanese expansion in the Far East which Wilson had been preparing to meet even before the end of the war, Soviet Russia showed not only a parallel preference for isolationism, but an increasing suspicion of all forms of Socialism which she did not herself control. Foreshadowed long before the outbreak of the war, the Bolshevik breach with democratic Socialism was marked in March 1919 by Lenin's establishment of the Third International, or Comintern. This was designed partly to replace the Marxist Second International, which had been disrupted when the war had shown that the primary allegiance of most Marxists was to their respective national states, and not to the cause of mythical proletarian solidarity. Comintern's chief objective from the beginning was to ensure that the foreign Communist Parties which were affiliated to the Comintern followed lines of policy which conformed to the Soviet government's strategic directives. By formalizing Lenin's breach with Social Democracy, the Comintern divided the Socialist movement into Communists and crypto-Communists who placed Soviet Russian national interests before all others, and Social Democrats who preferred evolutionary and constitutional methods of bringing about Socialism within their own countries.

## (ii) *The Challenge to European Imperialism: Communist Utopian Theory and Bourgeois Nationalist Practice*

The foreign Communist Parties established after World War I gained a significant following in only three of the advanced countries (Germany, Italy and France), and by 1923 the Bolsheviks had practically given up hope of being able to promote the proletarian revolutions in the west which they had originally thought necessary for the success of their own revolution. The under-developed countries seemed to offer better prospects, This also had been foreshadowed before the Russian Revolution by Lenin.

who, while in exile, had groped towards a theory of imperialism which he set out in a study entitled *Backward Europe and Progressive Asia*. In the Leninist theory 'backward countries' are not insulated primitive societies, but societies made revolutionary by foreign capitalist exploitation. By 1921 Soviet policy included among revolutionary societies 'the whole colonial world, the world of the oppressed peoples of Asia, Africa and South America, that is of that sector of the world by the exploitation of which the capitalist society of Europe and the United States maintains its power'. Soviet policy had few practical proposals for taking advantage of this situation, however. On the contrary, until the potentialities of the Chinese Revolution became apparent to them in 1922, Japan had been regarded as affording the best prospects for promoting Soviet action and revolutionary activities in Asia, and the Bolsheviks had practically no concrete objectives in China except regaining and extending old Tsarist interests. Yet whereas China and the western colonial territories in Asia fitted the Leninist stereotype of backward countries, Japan did not. Japan indeed strove to harness Asiatic anti-western imperial movements to further her own imperial ambitions.

The Leninist theory of the revolutionary potentiality of backward nations argued that their domination by western capitalism, either by direct rule or by economic exploitation, provided an opportunity to copy capitalist technological and economic development without adopting the capitalist organization of society, proceeding instead directly to Socialism —whose political aspects might indeed be easier to establish. In contrast to classical Marxism, Leninism argued that backward countries are more revolutionary than advanced ones, though it saw the revolutionary temper of the 'exploited' classes from a Marxist standpoint, and also in a sense equated backward societies with the 'exploited' proletariats of advanced countries. Hence after November 1917 Lenin regarded himself as a Russian national liberator and the Bolshevik victory as marking a Russian national awakening. He saw the emerging nationalism of the colonial peoples and their struggle against 'world imperialism' as part of the international proletarian revolution which it was the Marxist aim to promote. However, Lenin's views had gone far beyond those of Marx and Engels even before the war, and at the Comintern's second congress in 1920 Lenin argued that as the class struggle regarded by them as the dominant factor in history had merged with the struggle between nations, the 1848 *Communist Manifesto*'s famous slogan had become obsolete. He therefore extended it to read: 'Proletarians of all countries, and oppressed nations, unite!' The revolution of the colonial peoples envisaged by Lenin would combine national liberation with social and economic progress through programmes of industrialization, which would extend the process already begun by foreign capitalist exploiters, though the aims were totally different aims. The new Leninist theory was elaborated slowly from 1911, when Lenin had recognized Asia's importance for his evolving ideas, and it was still further elaborated after his death. Lenin, however, was loath to transfer priority for Soviet revolutionary activities from Europe to Asia, and in March 1923 coupled Germany with the East as the great areas of revolutionary activity even while noting that 'Russia, India, China, etc. constitute a gigantic majority of the population of the world'. In April 1923 Stalin more boldly argued that only by revolutionizing the 'eastern colonial and semi-colonial countries' could Soviet Russia 'hasten the downfall of imperialism'; otherwise 'we shall fail, and thus strengthen imperialism and weaken the force of our own movement'. The defeat of the 1923 German Left Wing risings and the continued momentum of the Chinese Revolution, appeared to confirm Stalin's view of the immediate possibilities. From 1924 the East played a major part in Soviet calculations. But the activities of both the Comintern and official Soviet foreign policy continued to concentrate on the western capitalist world, and especially on Europe. The Bolshevik leaders' belief that the 'fundamental contradictions' of the capitalist world would inevitably drive it to war remained unaffected, though they were uncertain whether it would take the form of war within the capitalist world, or of attack on the Socialist citadel of the Soviet Union prompted by capitalism's allegedly irreconcilable hostility. In any case, Soviet policy aimed at weakening the capitalist world by the activities of Comintern through foreign Communist Parties (activities which could be, and were, officially disavowed when necessary), by Soviet diplomacy within the capitalist countries themselves, and by striking at them through their colonial Achilles heel.

In the Near and Middle East, Africa and Latin America these anti-capitalistic activities had little success in the post-World War I years, though conditions in those regions would have offered golden opportunities if the Leninist analysis of the potentialities of backward countries had proved correct. Lenin believed that the exposure of such countries to capitalist pressures, as Russia had been exposed before the Bolshevik seizure of power in 1917, and as backward countries were still exposed, produced revolutionary situations of great intensity by telescoping into one epoch developments which western societies had taken centuries to complete. The simultaneous existence in backward countries of what Marxists called 'non-contemporaneous' indigenous 'feudalism' and foreign capitalism would create two separate class struggles: proletariat against *bourgeoisie*, *bourgeoisie* against feudalism (or other pre-capitalist elements). Hence there existed two 'non-contemporaneous' revolutions directed against western capitalism, and *'bourgeois* national' revolutionaries should be encouraged together with proletarian revolutionaries, in order to speed up capitalism's defeat. However, the supreme aim was to utilize these conditions to drive forward to a Soviet form of political organization, by-passing the *'bourgeois* democratic' stage now rendered superfluous despite the existing low stage of development of the backward countries. As these 'non-contemporaneous' forms of development reflected the situation obtaining in the world as a whole, one practical deduction was that the success of the Bolsheviks in 1917 in establishing a Soviet form of society uniquely fitted them to lead the world revolutionary movement. In addition to ruling the world's only Socialist country (Socialist, that is, by their standards and by those of their admirers) they had the only practical experience in successfully promoting revolution in backward countries. Moreover, their propaganda in the early 1920s deliberately included Soviet Russia's Asiatic lands among these backward countries. There they were forcing through programmes of rapid industrialization, educating the illiterate masses (naturally simultaneously indoctrinating them in Marxism-Leninism, but this was no more than they were doing in western Russia) and in general pointing the contrast, which became sharper as Soviet reforms increasingly took effect, between their treatment of backward Asiatic nations and that of western imperialism. They also claimed the right to direct the vanguard of the proletariat (their obedient tools of the foreign Communist Parties and foreign sympathizers) in the advanced western capitalist countries. These countries, with the help of Soviet Russia and the successful revolutions in the backward countries, would now undergo the proletarian revolutions which classical Marxism had been predicting for over half a century as the inevitable and imminent result of capitalist contradictions. Prevented because the political structures of the capitalist states had (allegedly) become too rigid, these revolutions could now be achieved. Finally, and most important of all from the standpoint of Soviet Russia's interests and of her security, such revolutionary victories would strengthen her against the capitalist world.

The pronouncements of Lenin, his colleagues and their successors were made less often in general terms than in response to specific problems, and Soviet external policies lacked an intelligible blueprint for engineering a world revolutionary movement, to which indeed no more than lip service was paid after Stalin's rise to power. Even in Lenin's time those policies had revealed the Bolshevik leaders' overriding concern with Soviet Russian national interests, especially Soviet Russian security, and above all with maintaining their dictatorship. This produced rapid and bewildering shifts in official foreign and Comintern policy, though the frequent discrepancies were the product of decisions by the Politburo which controlled both. Though Soviet official and Comintern methods varied, no valid distinctions can be drawn between their objectives. Foreign Communists and the cause of world revolution were sacrificed by the Comintern and the Soviet foreign ministry to the internal necessities of Soviet leadership. Yet if the foreign Communist Parties were deceived, they deceived themselves even more. The conditions of admission to the Comintern drafted in 1920 prescribed 'unconditional support of every Soviet republic in its struggle against counter-revolutionary forces', which in the circumstances could, and did, only mean unconditional support for the policies and interests of Soviet Russia as the only Soviet republic. Further, an immediate practical demonstration of the fact was provided. In 1920 Soviet foreign and Comintern policy laid great stress on fostering revolutionary movements in the Near and Middle East, with the particular aim of weakening British imperialist power, but after the conclusion of the Anglo-Soviet agreement of March 1921 Moscow showed markedly less zeal for the revolutionary cause in those regions. On the other hand, the Bolshevik's predilection for viewing the outside world in the light of what their dogmas insisted was taking place there, instead of in the light of actual circumstances, was apparent from the beginning. Yet few foreign Communists were prepared to take issue with them, even before the ghastly purges decreed by Stalin in the 1930s rigidly subordinated all parties to the Moscow line of the moment. The Indian Communist, M. N. Roy, who had indeed first suggested that Asian revolutions could promote European social changes, failed to convince Lenin and the Comintern that the Indian *bourgeoisie* was not, as the new Leninist line taught, the ally of Communism against British imperialism, but that it had vested interests in maintaining a capitalist form of society. The Bolsheviks, however, insisted on pinning their hopes on Congress (and indeed Indian Communism was very weak) just as later they backed the Chinese '*bourgeois* nationalist' Kuomintang.

Many gross miscalculations made by Soviet Russian eastern experts were the result of sheer ignorance of actual conditions. Further, reluctance to abandon preconceived positions was strongly reinforced by conservative dogmatism. Hence Lenin throughout the early years of the Bolshevik *régime* regarded India under Congress's leadership as a great hope of the masses of Asia in their progress towards the confidently predicted proletarian revolutions. In 1922 the theses of the Comintern's fourth congress, bearing the stamp of Lenin's ideas, listed in order of importance in the Asian revolution India, Mesopotamia (Iraq), Egypt, Morocco, China and Korea. However, the Bolsheviks rightly attributed the strong postwar Asian revolutionary tide not merely to the war's disruptions, but also to the promotion of national reactions by nineteenth century imperialist aggression, and to the fostering by western capitalism of the growth of business and proletarian classes hostile to it through the capitalists' policies of industrialization and urbanization.

The Bolsheviks successfully camouflaged their own imperialism, which succeeded in maintaining practically undiminished the Tsarist imperial heritage (apart from unequal treaties with China, largely worthless, which they voluntarily renounced) and were soon successfully manoeuvring to extend it. More obvious blind spots in the Leninist view of postwar imperialism were Japan's imperialist aggressions. Moreover, though Soviet Russia and America already looked forward, though for very different reasons, to the destruction of European imperialism in Asia, their tacit and hesitant collaboration for that purpose during World War II was not yet foreshadowed. However, America in the early inter-war years had overcome her opposition to Bolshevism sufficiently to recognize a certain community of interests with Soviet Russia in checking Japanese expansion in the Pacific and on the Chinese mainland. America's dominance of the Pacific after 1918 and Soviet Russia's position as the strongest land power in Asia presaged the further decline of European influence while simultaneously involving Asia more closely than ever in world affairs.

Even though European political influence in Asia was declining, America showed surprising reluctance to exploit her strength there. Soviet Russia's attacks on western capitalism and the success of her Five-Year Plans in the 1930s in forcing through rapid industrialization greatly appealed to many colonial leaders, but most Asian countries had ties with the West which were not easily broken. This was true of 'backward countries' in general, in China, and even in Latin America, though it was most obvious in India and Ceylon, where revolutionary movements not only ante-dated the Bolshevik seizure of power, but had been permeated by British democratic ideas. Moreover, Britain during the war had promised India eventual independence, and had long been training Indians and Ceylonese in government and administration. Hence while Britain herself created a westernized *élite* capable of using her own liberal democratic values against her, she also went a long way towards denying Marxism-Leninism the advantages of a clear ideological field which it found in Indonesia, in most of South-East Asia, and among some Arab national movements.

However, Britain's generosity in these respects was extended to few of her other colonial territories, and it found no parallels in the policies adopted by the other European imperialist powers during this period. Yet effective anti-imperialist activities were limited to the more important Asian countries, and to the Arab lands of North Africa and the Middle East, where war-time Allied propaganda in favour of democratic ideas had sapped old imperial positions and endangered those gained after 1918, and where Pan-Arabism and Islam constituted potent anti-western rallying points. Italy did not finally suppress the resistance of the Senussi sect until 1930. The growing strength of Egyptian nationalism further contributed to the decline of British imperial self-confidence visible during the war. The significance of Abdel Krim's Riff rising, first in Spanish and then in French Morocco, was exaggerated by the Soviet government, which at first thought it offered to the revolutionary movement in 'the east' greater potentialities than did the simultaneous intensification of unrest in China. The Riff rising, however, certainly required a considerable French military effort before it was crushed in 1926. By the late 1920s the Tunisian national movement had become actively revolutionary in its quest for independence. The Algerian national movement sought the integration of Algeria into France until the closing stages of World War II, and it required the weakening of European power by that war before the Arab nationalist movements could exploit the mass social discontent and anti-western sentiments of the Arab world with sufficient force to end European imperialist domination.

In the Negro lands of Africa, European political and economic control were opposed by few viable nationalist and social revolutionary movements until World War II. In the British West African territories, where such movements first appeared in strength, their original aim was to achieve self-government within the British Empire. Before the 1930s, moreover, their leaders, like the Negro intellectuals who founded the weaker movements in French West Africa, appealed as much to public opinion in the imperialist countries as to fellow Africans, to most of whom their nationalist and socialist arguments were unintelligible. There were, in any case, no African nations with educated and nationally conscious *élites* comparable to the Chinese, Indians, Burmans, the Indo-Chinese or the Ceylonese. Therefore the slow African struggle against white domination could not be accelerated by consciousness of a national existence in pre-imperial times. On the contrary, Negro 'national consciousness' had to be artificially propagated and carefully nursed before it could transcend old tribal divisions. Moreover, as indigenous Negro civilizations comparable to those of China, India and the Arab world had never existed, there was no resentment against the claims to superiority of European culture which might reinforce this tenuous nationalism. Though Pan-Africanism had held its first formal congress in 1919 in an attempt to press on the Paris Peace Conference the demand that Africans should share in their own government, it had no organization campaigning in the inter-war years for independent Negro states. Only in 1945 did Pan-Africanism begin to appear as an effective political organization, when the future chiefs of state Kwame Nkrumah and Jomo Kenyatta began to play leading roles in the movement.

Even in the Union of South Africa, where in the inter-war years a large Negro proletariat developed, no mass Bantu national movement appeared, though here the 'contradictions' of capitalist rule were more evident than anywhere else in Africa. Afrikaner nationalism was intent on destroying the British imperial connection. Not only Bantu, but Coloureds and Indians were repressed by the dominant white settlers, of both Afrikaner and British stock. The predominantly rural economy of the pre-war years, when the only heavily populated areas had been found in the mining regions and the ports, rapidly gave way to an urbanized society after 1914. In addition, the growth in urban white population was far exceeded by that of Negro labour, a fact which had important racial, political, social and economic consequences. Negro labour swept in great waves into the old and new urban centres, and in 1919 founded its own trade union, the ICU or Industrial and Commercial Workers' Union of Africa.

As the Communist Parties in the imperialist countries themselves originally showed little sympathy for their oppressed colonial brethren (a phenomenon as marked in Great Russian attitudes to backward Soviet Asian peoples, as in western European Communists' disinterest in Asian and African subject peoples), so the white South African Communists at first resented the rising Bantu claims. In the 1922 Rand Revolution, white miners resorted to strikes and violence after the Rand Chamber of Mines, because of rising costs, had cut their wages and begun to replace them with grossly underpaid Negroes in certain skilled and semi-skilled operations. The Communists were among the strikers who came out for a 'White

South Africa', and in 1923 there was widespread white trade union opposition to the employment of skilled Negro labour, which was so cheap that its extension would inevitably have dragged down white working-class living standards. Most white South Africans endorsed the white trade unionists' line, although the Union government was entirely confident of its capacity to keep all the non-whites in their place and many leading industrialists and commercial magnates shared its contempt for the ICU. The ICU's early successes in improving Negro conditions of employment were in fact relatively small, and made no impact on the crucial racial problem. Furthermore, it soon became apparent that the organizers of Negro labour faced insuperable difficulties. To the pass laws and the existing restrictions was added in 1926 the Mines and Works (Amendment) Act, popularly and correctly known as the Colour Bar Act. This excluded Negroes and Asians from many skilled and semi-skilled trades, and it was clear that eventually Coloureds must also be discriminated against. Settlers of British stock, and the Afrikaner supporters of the British connection who also shared Smuts' outlook, disapproved of the Act and the trend which it exemplified, but they did not accept Indians, Coloureds or Bantu as political, social and economic equals. Trade unionists of British origin, however, joined with Afrikaner workers and farmers in supporting the Colour Bar Act, and this meant a considerable advance towards Premier J. B. Hertzog's ideal of the fusion of English and Dutch-speaking South Africans as Afrikaners forming a consolidated nation independent of Britain.

Indeed, the anti-imperialism of South Africa took the form of repudiating the British connection which offered the only real guarantee of protection for the non-whites. Moreover, as the Afrikaners moved in the twentieth century towards ending the political and economic hegemony of the British element, they were supported by British South African trade unionists who were equally hostile to the predominantly British mine-owners, industrialists and commercial leaders. Hence while urbanization was transferring most Afrikaners from farming to mining, manufacturing or commercial operations, it pursued a parallel course of integrating Briton and Boer. Here, however, its inevitable tendency towards integration ended: non-whites were not to be integrated, but separated and subjected. *Apartheid* was the corollary of industrialization as well as of the old Boer ideology. However, it could be applied only in an independent Afrikaner South Africa, for the British 'white settler' colonies to the north were too firmly controlled by the imperial government in London to be able to prevent power from passing after World War II to the African Negro.

The complexities of the situation in South Africa and in the rest of the colonial and 'semi-colonial' world did not prevent Stalin, whose confidence only matched his ignorance, from proclaiming in 1925 a formula whereby the future development of all backward countries would be determined. The first essential step towards the international victory of the proletariat over capitalist imperialism was, of course, the founding of a Communist

Party to lead the proletarian national struggle and to establish a bloc of workers, peasants and 'revolutionary intellectuals' under its leadership. This bloc would utilize the 'national *bourgeoisie*' for its own purposes, but would wage war on two fronts: against the 'national *bourgeoisie*' and against capitalist imperialism. Finally, the imperialists would be overthrown by a violent proletarian revolution, and a Soviet form of workers' and peasants' government would be established. In fact, when the great process of decolonization began after World War II, this formula worked only in the case of North Vietnam. In 'semi-colonial' Latin America Marxism-Leninism was overshadowed by the rival authoritarian Fascist dogma, which made great progress after the world depression of 1929, and by western democratic ideas. It was also physically opposed by United States military, economic and political power. Developments in the Asian and African national movements further falsified Stalin's predictions. Communist Parties in Asia played important roles in the World War II resistance movements against Japanese occupation, though they had strictly subordinate parts in the Indian and Ceylonese national movements. Certainly, Japan's sweeping victories in the early stages of World War II did incomparably more to shatter European imperialist power than Marxism-Leninism and its Asian practitioners, including the Chinese Communists. Moreover, Soviet Russia's physical and ideological interventions in the Chinese revolution did more to retard than to promote Mao's eventual triumph. In South-West Asia Marxism-Leninism could never appeal to the Arab masses as Pan-Arabism, Islam and in some cases even Fascism could, and among Palestinian Jews it could never compete on equal terms with its old enemy Zionism.

After Ireland and the successor states of central and eastern Europe, India was the first victim of European imperialism to secure freedom in the generation after World War I. The Indian nationalist movement's resort to violence certainly speeded up the collapse of British rule, but there was no proletarian revolution, and Mohandas K. Gandhi, the architect of Indian independence, was a living reproach less to the British imperial rule which he defeated, than to Soviet Russia's Bolshevik dictatorship and her materialism. While Gandhi repudiated the technology, industrialization and commerce together with the imperialist rule brought by the British, he respected their achievements in India, and wanted to maintain after independence the political unity which they had imposed. He admired the British constitution, and thought its values compatible with those of Hindu civilization though he hoped to base the new central government firmly on the support of the masses by establishing the Indian villages as the basis of popular sovereignty in an independent India. It was an aspect of his libertarian and individualistic spirit that he should turn his back on the mass age, and seek to restore India to the idyllic pre-industrial past of his dreams. Yet it was Gandhi who brought the Indian masses for the first time into the political reckoning, and he allowed Jawaharlal Nehru to ensure that India should move towards industrialization as the only possible basis in the long run for social equality, and towards a parliamentary system of government, which could not be based on the village, as the only way of combining political freedom with national independence. Gandhi also admired the British habit of compromise, and indeed regarded readiness to compromise as an essential part of his principle of *satyagraha*, or passive resistance, which became India's principal weapon in the struggle against British rule.

In sharp contrast to the Marxist-Leninist bigots, Gandhi believed that 'we win justice quickest by rendering justice to the other party'. Even as leader of a revolutionary national movement he could distinguish between the underlying principles of British justice, which he admired, and its perversions in practice. His readiness to recognize the strengths of his opponents' case was shown at the height of anti-British demonstrations in 1930, when the British Viceroy, on grounds of public security, rejected Gandhi's demands that police activities should be restricted. Gandhi replied: 'You do not deny that I have an equitable claim, but you adduce unanswerable reasons from the point of view of Government why you cannot meet it. I drop the demand.' During World War II he was to push his opposition to British imperial rule and adherence to the *satyagraha* principle to the absurd but logical conclusion of deciding that if the Japanese attacked India they must not be resisted by the national movement. However, he usually eschewed such pedantry and short-sighted obstruction, and his political legacy of an India adhering to the basic tenets of western parliamentary democracy was to prove crucially important for the future of Asia, and of major significance for the rest of the world.

Most of the Asian countries after World War II falsified the Marxist-Leninist prediction of the trend to proletarian revolution. Indeed, the absurdities and contradictions of the Marxist-Leninist analysis had been increasingly apparent since the early 1920s, when Kemal Ataturk, who made a new national Turkish state from the remnants of the old Ottoman Empire, and the Egyptian Wafdist national leader Zaghlul, had been praised by the Bolsheviks as 'progressive' anti-imperialist nationalist leaders, though they were avowed enemies of Communism. Similarly, the Soviet leaders found it necessary to condone the course taken by the majority of national movements a generation later, when the new independent Afro-Asian nations chose non-alignment between Soviet Russia and the capitalist west, instead of unconditional support of the Soviet line.

However it was Soviet policy in China, after it had come under Stalin's direction, which provided the most striking instances of the inadequacy of analysis, the wishful thinking and the rigidity which underlay Soviet views on the backward countries, and provided the supreme example of the bungling which afflicted Soviet diplomacy before Stalin almost fatally mishandled relations with Nazi Germany. In 1927 Stalin unwittingly promoted the massacre of large numbers of Chinese Communists by the Kuomintang leader Chiang Kai-shek, a humiliating defeat for Soviet policy, and a fair comment on its claims to be able unerringly to analyse present and predict future events. For the Chinese Communists the disaster would have been even greater had not Mao Tse-tung gradually reshaped their political and military strategy by basing the Communist revolution on the Chinese peasant. That Mao himself was often hesitant, opportunist and contradictory was not a sign, however, of uncertainty about his final goal: an independent, strong and prosperous Chinese Soviet Republic. The Long March of the mid-1930s took the Red Army deep into the interior and out of the Kuomintang's reach, while its small remnant of 40,000 gathered its strength for the counter-attack. This was the turning point of the Chinese Communist Revolution, and one of the decisive events of world history. Yet Stalin was not alone in failing to understand how, by adopting the traditional Chinese methods of peasant insurgence and indoctrinating the peasants with his own modified brand of Marxism-Leninism, Mao was shaping a force of great potential power. Not that the policies of America and of the European democracies towards Mao's movement, or towards China in general were any more acute and far-sighted than Stalin's. But then, oddly enough, the imperialist countries had less to lose than Soviet Russia from an unsuccessful policy towards China. Perhaps, also, the Chinese question really was insoluble for the outside world, capitalist or Soviet. The refusal of all Chinese *régimes*, Imperial, Republican, Kuomintang and Communist, to surrender old Chinese imperial territorial claims to reconstitute the former Middle Kingdom, and to renounce pretensions to cultural, and more than cultural, superiority, presented problems which might be contained, but never resolved.

In addition, the Europe of the inter-war years was equally remote from the stereotypes manufactured by the Bolshevik leaders. World War I delivered blows to the fabric of pre-1914 society from which it never recovered. It introduced degrees of state intervention into the economies of the belligerents which had enduring consequences. It brought political, economic and social chaos to eastern and central Europe on a scale which appeared to enemies as well as followers of Bolshevism to create the necessary preconditions for its triumph there. Even the victorious western Allies faced onerous tasks of economic and political reconstruction which produced serious discontent, and in Italy the propertied and conservative classes were sufficiently frightened by the red spectre of Communism to support the Fascist dictatorship of Mussolini in 1922. The poor 'peasant' countries of eastern and south-eastern Europe, closer in political and social structures to Tsarist Russia than to western Europe though western in their general culture, were also to embrace Fascism in the inter-war years instead of Communism. Only Hungary, the core of the eastern half of the former Habsburg Empire, actually had a Communist *régime* before the westward advance of the Soviet Russian armies in the closing stages of World War II. There, only a brief and extraordinary conjunction of circumstances permitted the rise in 1919 of Bela Kun's transient Bolshevik dictatorship, which was easily crushed by the old ruling class once it had outlived its usefulness by helping to destroy the incipient Social Democracy of Michael Karolyi.

## (iii) *The European Civil War: Political and Ideological Conflicts*

Germany, which had developed a form of state Socialism to meet the economic demands of World War I, underwent a revolution in October–November 1918 which aroused great hopes among the Bolsheviks. Lenin, in particular, predicted that the combination of the economically advanced Germany and Bolshevik Russia, which he regarded as having instituted a politically Socialist *régime*, would lead the rest of Europe towards proletarian revolution. But though the German, like the previous Russian Revolution, had been born of defeat in war, it produced not a Soviet-type *régime* but the *bourgeois* Weimar Republic. Weimar Germany was indeed to find a community of interests with Soviet Russia against the western European democracies in the early inter-war period, but on the basis of power politics and of their depressed status as the pariahs of Europe.

After 1918, as before, the central political issue in Europe was the German question, and the failure to solve it by peaceful methods was the major disaster of the inter-war years for Europe, and so for the whole world. Yet a more lenient treatment of Germany by the Paris Peace Conference would not have reconciled Germany to the military defeat of 1918. This would have required in the first place a total recasting of the balances of political and economic forces within European analogous to those effected after Napoleon's defeat a century earlier, which had prevented further French attempts to seize the hegemony of Europe by military power. It would also have required a change of heart by the Germans themselves, of all colours of the political spectrum from extreme Left to Right Wing Nationalists, before the verdict of the Paris Peace Conference could have been accepted.

Though the post-World War I arrangements were the fairest which Europe had ever known, they still left burning resentment in Soviet Russia, Hungary, and even in victorious Italy as well as in Germany. Italy soon adopted a revisionist policy which tended to place her on the side first of Hungary, and then of Germany against her former allies. Poland, receiving on the whole less than her due from Germany, and far more than her due from Soviet Russia, was also dissatisfied when most of the former duchy of Teschen was allocated to the neighbouring successor state of Czechoslovakia. She finally connived at Czechoslovakia's partition in 1938, as did Yugoslavia and Rumania, the other beneficiaries in eastern

Europe from the Paris settlements, thereby establishing the pattern which was to see each of Germany's World War II victims abandoned by neighbours with vital interests in their survival. That Germany would seek to regain the mastery of eastern and central Europe which she had enjoyed before her defeat was a foregone conclusion, though whether it meant renewed conflict with Britain and France depended on the methods employed to achieve it. It certainly meant in the long run resuming the struggle with Russia, though a preliminary period of co-operation with Russia was not thereby precluded, especially as Russia in the inter-war period was placed on the defensive by pressing internal political and economic problems, as well as by military weakness.

France, deeply conscious of her permanent military inferiority to Germany, was refused the punitive settlement against Germany which she demanded from America and Britain in 1919. This would in any case have been beyond French power to maintain for any length of time, a fact which, however, redounds all the more to the discredit of the Americans and British, who subsequently abandoned their offers of an alliance with France in return for which France had already modified her demands against Germany. With these offers were repudiated first American and then by degrees British obligations for maintaining the Versailles settlement itself. Most Americans approved of America's return to isolation by disavowing the Versailles Treaty, and its corollary the League of Nations, Wilson's instrument for preventing further war and estabilshing an international organization. While Britain guaranteed France's retention of the restored provinces of Alsace-Lorraine, and recognized that France's continued existence as a Great Power was a vital British interest, Britain maintained serious reservations about the settlements in central, and, more particularly, in eastern Europe.

Though World War I had not reduced Britain's physical and economic power as severely as it had France's, the assistance of the British Dominions had been necessary during both the war and the Peace Conference to maintain Britain's role as a world power. The Dominions were even less concerned than Britain in maintaining the eastern and central European territorial settlements in their entirety. Furthermore, the Dominions reinforced British arguments that France was taking dangerous risks in promoting the allocation of former enemy territories on so large a scale to the successor states. Traditional British policy towards disputes in these areas was one of non-involvement, and Britain moreover wanted a rapid revival of German economic power to recreate the pre-war international economy on which British prosperity depended. Since Germany lost her navy and overseas colonies as the result of the war, Britain seemed to be able to afford a more generous attitude towards German interests east of the new Franco-Belgian-German frontiers. As Anglo-French differences widened in the 1920s, the French were forced to rely increasingly on their system of alliances with the successor states, thereby increasing the resentment already felt by the British at what appeared an unnecessarily vengeful and a short-sighted attitude towards Germany. This British attitude was found quite as much among the Left as the Right, and the pattern of Neville Chamberlain's later appeasement of Nazi Germany was established in these years by Labour, Liberal and Conservative politicians alike. The same Conservatives who in the closing stages of the war had preferred German interests to those of Poles, Czechoslovaks, Yugoslavs and other 'successor' peoples, took the ominous line that once Germany was beaten in the west and was no danger to the British Empire, she could be allowed to dominate eastern and central Europe. They added to these arguments the consideration that Germany might also be allowed to dominate Russia, for their greatest anxiety towards the end of World War I revolved around Bolshevism, which they feared might sweep across Europe and affect the British working classes.

However, the prospects of the 'Bolshevization' of the whole of Europe were possibly as much exaggerated by the Bolsheviks themselves as by their enemies. The new Polish Republic was violently anti-Russian in general and anti-Bolshevik in particular, as were the new Baltic states, Hungary and Rumania, while Bulgaria and Yugoslavia had *régimes* implacably hostile to the Bolsheviks. Czechoslovakia, who saw her own future security against Germany, as well as European peace, best upheld by a *rapprochement* between Soviet Russia and the western European democracies, looked essentially to the West and to free parliamentary institutions when forming her own political system.

France sufficiently shared the anti-Bolshevik views of the British Right to make her system of postwar alliances with the eastern successor states into a *cordon sanitaire* against 'Bolshevik infection', as well as a barrier against further German aggression. But the Bolsheviks, afflicted to the point of obsession with the traditional Russian governmental sense of inferiority and insecurity in dealing with the western world, were far more afraid of the West than the West was of Soviet Russia. Soviet Russian hostility to the West also far exceeded Western hostility to the Bolsheviks, as was shown by the Comintern's attempts to promote revolutionary movements in western countries which constituted no physical danger to Soviet Russia. Bolshevik policy gratuitously made enemies of the Social Democratic parties which still adhered to the ineffective Second International, and made the western trade unions, organized into the International Labour Organization, a major target for the vituperation and splitting tactics of its Communist counterpart Profintern.

The basic Leninist thesis of the impossibility in the long run of peaceful co-existence between Soviet Russia and the capitalist world, including the United States, did not, however, preclude Soviet attempts to establish useful relations with capitalist states even in the early and most dogmatic Bolshevik period. Therefore, while Fascism was branded as the final *bourgeois* reaction, as an attempt by the *bourgeoisie* to win over some of the masses and prevent the collapse of the *bourgeois* state (incidentally, the same definition was applied on occasions to Social Democracy), the interests of the Italian Communists were always liable to be sacrificed by the Comintern on the altar of Italo-Russian official relations. The Italian Fascists' murder of the Socialist leader Matteotti in 1924 strengthened Italian Socialist and *bourgeois*, but not Italian Communist opposition to Mussolini, partly because Italian Communists were gravely embarrassed by the callous and self-regarding treachery of Soviet policy when only a few weeks later the Soviet Ambassador gave a banquet for Mussolini.

However, the blackest betrayal of all the foreign comrades was reserved for the German Communist party. Stalin first facilitated Hitler's rise to power in 1933 by ordering the German Communists to treat as their main enemy the Social Democrats, then being abused as 'Social Fascists', instead of Hitler's Nazis. Six years later he handed over to Nazi vengeance German Communist refugees to signify his good faith in the Nazi-Soviet pact which signalled the outbreak of World War II. During the inter-war years, the Soviet leadership wooed and abused the Social Democrats for its own purposes and not in the cause of proletarian revolution, in which it had for all practical purposes ceased to believe after Lenin's death. The 'united front' with German Social Democracy was pursued from December 1921 to suit the exigencies of Bolshevik domestic and foreign policies. In 1924, with the Labour Party in office in Britain and the 'Left bloc' in France, the 'united front' was vigorously followed in those countries, but the line was entirely abandoned to suit Stalin's purposes as he began to consolidate his power in 1926. In the middle 1930s, when Soviet miscalculations that Hitler's *régime* would speedily collapse became apparent, similar use was made of the 'popular front', which included 'anti-Fascist' *bourgeois* as well as Socialist elements, both hitherto branded as inveterate enemies of the masses in general and of Soviet Russia in particular. The outbreak of the Spanish Civil War in 1936 caused the great crisis of conscience for the non-Communist European Left in the inter-war years, and it ceased to be predominantly pacifist in face of German and Italian Fascist intervention in the war. However the resulting impetus to the popular front movement was soon ended by Soviet brutalities and perfidies in Spain, which disgusted many of the Bolsheviks' leading sympathizers among the non-Communist groups.

An equally fertile source of Soviet miscalculations in policies towards the European states and America was the Leninist dogma that unless the capitalist world's 'contradictions' impelled it to attack Soviet Russia, it would be driven to war within its own ranks; war between the major imperialist powers, Britain and the United States, was often favoured as a possibility in these predictions. Certainly World War I had increased the tensions within the capitalist states of Europe, though none of them, including Nazi Germany until World War II was well under way, thought of attacking America, and she did not think of attacking them. It was partly from rigid adherence to this dogma, though partly also from knowledge of Soviet military weakness, that Stalin in August 1939 preferred to come to terms with Hitler, whom he distrusted even more than he suspected the motives of Britain and France in seeking Soviet aid against Nazi Germany. Though he did not doubt the seriousness of Hitler's proclaimed objective of basing a Greater Germany on control of eastern Europe and western Russia, Stalin went on to handle relations with Nazi Germany in a manner which might have proved fatal to Soviet Russia. So unrealistic had Stalinist policy become because of its own dogmas, and the lack of objective information about the outside world, that in June 1941 Stalin was preparing a diplomatic campaign to appease Hitler, while Hitler was launching the military campaign of 'Operation Barbarossa' to conquer the whole of western Russia from Archangel to the Volga.

The western capitalist powers, allegedly irreconcilable enemies of the Soviet *régime*, now saved it from extinction at the hands of Nazi Germany —a genuine capitalist 'contradiction'! Stalin's war-time pronouncements of community of aims with his Anglo-American allies in building a peaceful and democratic world were not apologies for past misrepresentations and actual or attempted injuries, still less recognition of the obvious international realities. Yet his views had a certain underlying theoretical consistency as did their application, though against his will and predictions, in his supreme follies on crucial points from August 1939 to June 1941. Only, however, if Nazi Germany, Imperial Japan, and, less important, Fascist Italy are regarded as capitalist states, can the Nazi-Soviet pact of August 1939 be regarded as having fulfilled the primary Marxist-Leninist objective of increasing the contradictions within the capitalist world by opening the door to World War II. And since the war substituted for Japan, as the strongest Asian power, a Communist China whose independent line in the nuclear age was to bring forth a kind of Soviet Russian *cordon sanitaire* in Asia as well as a dangerous split in the emerging Communist world, Soviet Russia faced graver problems in Asia than ever before. Again, Soviet aggressive policy in eastern Europe in the closing stages of the war, by ensuring that American forces remained there in strength after it had ended, more than offset the territorial and immediate political gains which it brought. Above all, by conferring on America overwhelming political, economic and military power, and by preparing the way for large-scale social reforms in the countries of western Europe, World War II went far towards realizing the aims of Wilson and the European idealists which had been disappointed after 1918.

Apart from the all-important German question, the most pressing problems of the early post-World War I years in Europe were those of social and economic reconstruction—a pattern which was repeated after the great depression of 1929, until the beginning of Nazi Germany's aggressions overshadowed all other issues. Though the work of the Paris Peace Conference was concerned largely with the territorial settlements, economic problems occupied much of its time, and they were the primary concern of the European masses. It was social and economic issues, far more than political problems as such, which from 1919 brought Communism to the rank of a major political movement, and produced the

Fascism which was itself largely a reaction against Communism. The disappointment of the wartime hopes of the European peoples for wider measures of political democracy also contributed to the rise of Communism and Fascism. But the major factors were the disintegrating effects of the war on the European states' social and economic structures. A considerable measure of disappointment was inevitable even among the victorious western nations whose leaders had encouraged exaggerated hopes of a 'brave new world' dedicated to peace, prosperity and democratic freedom.

However, it must also be said that the postwar betrayals were greater than postwar difficulties justified. The western countries did not experience the mass poverty and social and political upheavals caused by the war in the defeated countries of central and eastern Europe, and to a lesser degree in the successor states also. At the same time, they shared the prevailing feelings of disillusionment and betrayal, and even Italy shared the wounded national pride felt by the defeated peoples. Above all it was the mass unemployment, the social and economic dislocation which war brought in its train, which provided the fertile breeding grounds for Communist and Fascist advocates of revolutionary, or counter-revolutionary violence in both victorious and defeated states. Therefore, although the new states adopted the parliamentary institutions, whose superiority over the authoritarian systems of the defeated empires was generally deduced from the outcome of the war, only Czechoslovakia and Finland established viable democratic governments, and the inadequacy of parliamentary government in solving the socio-economic problems of the west raised doubts about the future of democracy itself.

Communism did not gain control of any country, inside or outside Europe, in the generation between the Bolshevik coup and the closing stages of World War II. Even then its successes were limited to the economically, socially and politically retarded eastern European countries; and among these, revolution was secured by Soviet Russian military occupation in every instance except those of Yugoslavia and Albania. Violently though they campaigned against the ineffectiveness of the Social Democrats, the European Communists achieved far less. Experience of the inter-war years reinforced the lesson of 1917–18 that Communism was only for backward societies, composed in the mass of ignorant and poor peasants, with a proletariat large enough to provide revolutionary groups to overthrow the central government and seize control of the urban centres, and with a revolutionary leadership formed from a discontented intelligentsia persecuted by a reactionary and unintelligent despotism. Yet though Communism achieved no practical political triumphs in Europe, it was an important factor in all the leading states except Britain, and in Italy and Germany before they succumbed to Fascist dictatorships. It made a strong appeal to intellectuals rebelling against the failure of other ideologies to explain the contemporary world's chaos and poverty, and to those sections of the middle and working classes which rejected the social values, economic structures and political institutions which surrounded them. It offered certainties to those seeking ideological security and reassurance in a world whose stability had ended in 1914. It attracted an active and devoted leadership in all countries, including those which officially proscribed it, and its carefully chosen rank and file exerted an influence in politics and in trade union movements out of all proportion to their numbers, though Communists' obedience to directives from Soviet Russia exposed them to embarrassment and charges of inconsistency when the Bolshevik *régime* made its rapid changes in line. A notable illustration of Soviet inconsistency was the Stalin-Hitler pact made in August 1939. Overnight the Fascist aggressor became a peace-loving power for all Communists, and Britain and France imperialist warmongers. Communists were also forced to use conspiratorial methods even in democracies which allowed normal political freedoms, because the Bolshevik leadership could never throw off its former habits even after it had seized power: having begun as a conspiracy against Tsarism, it became a conspiracy against the Russian people. When Stalin imposed unquestioning obedience on the European parties after the purges, they rapidly lost much of the respect which they had hitherto commanded from the non-Communist Left.

Fascism was a much more potent, though a short-lived, rival to liberal democracy. Apart from gaining adherents from the same socio-economic disturbances as did Communism, it also derived strength from inflamed national susceptibilities—hence its victories in defeated Germany and Italy, whose chauvinism was aroused by Allied lack of warmth towards her wartime achievements and excessive territorial demands. Paradoxically, whereas Communism was avowedly an international movement, yet achieved practically nothing outside Russia, Fascism stridently insisted on its national origins and nationalist exclusiveness, yet became a factor of the greatest importance in international relations. In part this was due to the hatred of Communism by the ruling classes of the countries in which Fascism flourished (for example in Spain, Portugal and the 'royal dictatorships' of eastern Europe), and in part because of the support furnished first by Mussolini and then by Hitler to the native Fascist movements of other European countries. Nevertheless Fascism made its greatest gains, as it had done since its early beginnings in the French Second Republic, in conditions of economic crisis: in Italy in the postwar years, in Germany in 1923, and in Germany again, this time in combination with advances in most eastern European states, after the great depression of 1929. So rapid was Fascism's advance, despite its intellectual shabbiness and its failure to achieve the ideological solidity of Communism and political potency of the Russian Communist Party, that Fascism was regarded in the 1920s and 1930s as 'the wave of the future'. These years were, indeed, in a very real sense the age of Fascism, and not only in Europe. Instead of the age of democracy predicted by American and European idealists as the inevitable outcome of World War I, the age of the political mass ruler supervened, and the war's most striking political result was the proliferation of dictatorships. Indoctrinated at school in the prevailing ideology of the dictatorships (Marxism-Leninism in Soviet Russia, Fascism elsewhere) the masses were thereafter ceaselessly manipulated through the media of modern mass propaganda. Even where it had not captured state power, which was an essential ingredient in its political triumph, Fascism had advantages over both Communism and democracy in appealing to the masses, except in politically mature countries, where democracy outshone both its rivals. Like Bolshevism, once Fascism achieved power it began to suppress all opposition, though the degree of repression varied considerably from country to country. Even in Nazi Germany, however, where Fascism was most bestial in its treatment of political opponents, it never achieved the full flower of totalitarianism proper. That was, indeed, found only in Soviet Russia, and only after Stalin consolidated his dictatorship.

Europe, the home of all three ideologies, and finally the scene of their triangular conflict, exported her ideological tensions with her capital, manufactures and technology to the backward countries. There the struggle was made cruder, though not more violent, by social and economic retardation. In the end, Fascism was eliminated from the extension of the struggle overseas, except in Latin America where it continued to be a formidable force from 1930. However Fascism's defeat overseas only intensified, as in Europe, the struggle between liberal democracy and Communism.

The defeat of Fascism was by no means inevitable. As Fascism spread into European countries which had been economically dislocated and psychologically disorientated, even if they had not also been militarily defeated in World War I, Europe gave good grounds for Mussolini's predicting Fascism's eventful victory there. The adoption of many Fascist characteristics by some Middle Eastern nationalist movements and Latin American states, by Afrikaner Nationalism and by Japanese militarism, indicated further that Fascism was no longer purely a European phenomenon, though it won its greatest victories in its European home. Here, within a bare two years after the outbreak of World War II, only the citadels of the rival ideologies, Britain and Soviet Russia, and the permanently neutral states of Sweden and Switzerland, were not under Facist rule.

## (iv) *Scientific, Technological and Economic Change*

Although European ideologies dominated the world political scene more than ever after World War I, the world was no longer dominated by European technology and economic power. European science remained supreme, notably in physics, and it was during the inter-war years in Weimar Germany and in Britain that scientists developed the essential theoretical basis for the application of nuclear energy later employed in atomic bombs by the United States. Again in the inter-war years, when science was still international, the flow of ideas and experiments between Britain, Germany, Denmark, France, Italy and the United States helped to revolutionize physics. The invention in 1919 of the mass spectroscope, which made possible the identification of over two hundred isotopes (variant forms of the basic atoms), and Lord Rutherford's vindication in Cambridge of the alchemists by his transmutation of matter, ushered in a period of great advances. These led through the discovery of the neutron, key to atomic fission, to the unsuspected splitting of the atom and the equally unsuspected discovery of chain reaction by the Italian scientist Enrico Fermi in Rome, who first split the uranium atom in 1934. Then came the definite discovery of uranium fission in December 1938. It was, however, only because of the impact of World War II, and President Roosevelt's decision to accept scientific advice that at all costs Nazi Germany (which did not realize the potentialities of nuclear energy for war) must not be the first to make the atomic bomb, that America did so.

In the 1920s other European scientific discoveries in biophysics and biochemistry inaugurated a generation of great progress in medical science (the most notable being Fleming's discovery of penicillin in 1928) which eclipsed all earlier advances. In the technology of death also Europe remained supreme in the inter-war years. Aviation, which because of World War I grew from a sport for enthusiasts to a concern of state, was developed for both military and civil purposes in Europe. America lagged far behind until the eve of World War II. In 1919 the German firm of Junkers built the first all-metal cabin airplane. The potentialities of flying, which became so important during the second war, were only slowly realized. In June 1919 two RAF men, Alcock and Brown, made the first non-stop flight across the Atlantic, but in 1939 ships still carried practically all Atlantic traffic. The first round-the-world flight was made in 1924. In 1927 the heroic age of flying ended when Charles Lindbergh flew on a non-stop solo flight from New York to Paris in under thirty-four hours. However, commercial flying, requiring heavy state subsidies, developed slowly, and airships continued to operate until the mid-1930s.

The greatest technological advances in aviation were made for military purposes, or with military potentials very much in mind. This partly explains why the American aircraft industry did not achieve predominance until after American involvement in World War II, and why it was the German Messerschmitt aircraft which produced a world speed record of 450 m.p.h. for Nazi Germany in 1939. (The record for 1919 was 196 miles an hour.) Interestingly, the Messerschmitt speed record was not broken until the development of jet aircraft after World War II. Air power, as an independent arm and as an instrument of land and sea warfare, was to revolutionize war after 1939, first and most notably by its combination with the rapid onslaughts of heavily-armed, fast moving tanks and mechanized divisions in the German *Blitzkrieg*. However, the death-dealing power of bombing aircraft was grossly exaggerated before World War II. At the same time, the bombers' capacity for material destruction was under-rated before the war, though also greatly exaggerated during it by Germany, and by the Allies once their strategic bombing attacks had got under way. British expert advice in the autumn of 1938 that German bombers could drop 100,000 tons of bombs on London in fourteen days (more than they dropped on London throughout World War II), thereby causing 5,000,000 casualties and 500,000 deaths, doubtless reinforced, though it did not determine, the British government's decision to make the Munich agreement.

Nevertheless the employment of air power added a new dimension to war, as an independent arm and as reinforcement of traditional forces. It enforced on armies, navies and civil populations alike the necessity of adopting effective anti-aircraft measures, among them radar, fighter aircraft and artillery defences. Radar was first developed in Britain in barely sufficient time to make a major contribution to the defeat of Nazi Germany in the Battle of Britain, which ensured that Hitler could not win World War II, though not that he would lose it. The dropping of poison gas on the civilian population, which had been feared, fortunately did not materialize, but by bringing civilians, ports, industrial centres, the whole war industry, lines of communication, and great centres of population of the enemy into the direct line of fire, air power imposed a form of total warfare far exceeding in intensity that of 1914–18. It might have gone even farther, and produced the collapse of civilization which the experiences of 1914–18 had suggested that the next great war would do. The appearance of the German long-range rockets launched against Britain in 1944, and of the atom bombs dropped on Japan a year later, feeble though those were in comparison with the later hydrogen bombs, showed the shape of things to come—or which might come.

In the peaceful uses of technology the United States had a clear lead in the inter-war years with further refinement of the conveyor belt system and other methods of mass production; the development of radio for serious and leisure purposes (in the decade following the opening of the first American broadcasting station at Pittsburgh in 1920 over 13,000,000 radio sets were built); the development of television in the next decade, slower because of its greater cost (it was the British engineer Logie Baird who in 1928 first transmitted television pictures across the Atlantic but in this field also America gained a commanding position); the development of heavy engineering methods and of electrical appliances for the home; and the extraordinary growth of the automobile industry, possibly the most important of all for its economic impact and its social consequences in promoting the urbanization of America. This made the car so essential a part of American life that between the end of World War I and the onset of the great depression the number of motor vehicles increased from 9,000,000 to 26,000,000, a figure which was to continue to grow, though naturally more slowly, during the depressed thirties.

America possessed an unparalleled domestic market, as well as great resources in manpower, raw materials and finance. These advantages combined with the severe shocks administered to European former economic predominance by World War I to emphasize Europe's economic decline after 1918. Although America was already the greatest single industrial power in 1914, Europe remained the industrial, financial and commercial centre. As this predominance depended on the economic strength of Germany, Britain and France, all of whom were debilitated by the war, Europe's later position was seriously impaired. If Soviet Russia is excluded from consideration, it appears that if pre-1914 economic trends had not been interrupted or checked by hostilities, Europe would have reached in 1921 the level of manufacturing output attained in 1929. On this calculation, admittedly unreal since factors other than those directly attributable to war operated, Europe lost eight years of industrial development. On any likely hypothesis, therefore, if the war had not intervened, there would not have been so great a disparity between Europe's and America's levels of production on the eve of the great depression, when America's manufacturing output was 81% and Europe's only 28% above their respective 1913 levels. The war also severely affected Europe's export trade, though again its consequences cannot be accurately determined. British, French and German exports all declined considerably, notably the exports of British textiles. As British industrial, commercial and financial strength were major constituents of European economic power, their decline was a general European misfortune, for Britain's heavy net imports from Europe had to be reduced. Their decline was a misfortune also for world trade, for British prosperity had promoted the stability and flow of international trade before 1914 to a degree achieved by no other country after 1918; indeed, once the debilitating effects of the depression had been added to those of World War I, Britain's once world-wide role as a banker and main pillar of international exchange was restricted after 1931 to acting as the leader of the sterling bloc, containing nearly the whole Commonwealth and a few outside countries, and two years later co-operating with France and America to maintain until 1939 a minor kind of gold standard.

The fact that the great depression which began in 1929 originated in a financial crash on Wall Street, and by involving the whole world proved to be the single most important international event of the inter-war years, demonstrates the changes in the balances of economic power which had taken place since 1914. The violent fluctuations in capital investment made by the European states at home and abroad, and the increased vulnerability of their foreign trade to the competition of hitherto negligible rivals in the inter-war years, further contributed to Europe's decline. Moreover, apart from the direct effects of the war on Europe's manufacturing production, the European states found insuperable difficulties in attempting to match American war-time advances in products and manufacturing techniques—for they had been obliged to concentrate on military production while the United States developed such industries as those of automobiles, rubber and electrical engineering more suitable to the years of peace. The sheer cost of financing the war, though in the end largely borne by Britain, who could not afford it, and by America who could, was another major disadvantage for the Continental states, including Germany, who transferred her burdens to other shoulders by obtaining foreign loans which more than covered the reparations which she paid. However, Germany suffered more economic dislocation than any other European country in the early inter-war years, and again between 1929 and 1932; and because of her commanding economic position in central and east-central Europe, this had wide repercussions.

While the political consequences of World War I are clear in regard to Europe, its economic consequences are still a matter for dispute, even in respect to the apparently identifiable factors introduced by the rise of the successor states, consisting of six new republics and one enlarged kingdom. Before 1914 the five leading European powers (excluding Tsarist Russia) each had populations of between thirty and fifty millions, or three-quarters of the total European population. Tsarist Russia's total population was about 170,000,000—a figure not reached again until 1939, and then within smaller western territories. With the disintegration of Austria-Hungary, in the inter-war period there were four major powers (excluding Soviet Russia) with populations of between forty and seventy millions, or just over half the total European population (about 401,000,000 in 1920 and about 543,000,000 in 1940). Moreover, their share in the growth of population between 1920 and 1940 was only about 40%, despite the fact that the great decline in European emigration after 1918, as compared with the pre-war movements, affected the eastern and south-eastern countries more than any major power except Italy. One clear-cut economic consequence of World War I was the decrease in the number of small states and the increase in the number of medium-sized countries. Before 1914 Europe had twelve states with populations of under six million, as against five after 1918. However postwar Europe had thirteen states with populations ranging from six to thirty-five millions, and this group accounted before 1939 for 44% of Europe's total population. These medium-sized states were vulnerable because of their size and political difficulties to the economic fluctuations of the inter-war period. The addition to their number by the peace settlements, marking the breakdown of the great economic units formed by the old eastern empires, was the most unfortunate economic consequence of the 'Balkanization' of eastern and central Europe by the war. The new states would in any event have faced formidable economic as well as taxing political problems, as they were situated in the poorest and most backward areas of Europe along the eastern Mediterranean and the German-Russian borderlands. Of the new states only Czechoslovakia inherited an adequate industrial, financial and commercial base, and her foreign trade was seriously handicapped by her smaller neighbours' poverty, Germany's rivalry and the virulent economic nationalism which complemented the strong political nationalism of the inter-war years. Among the pre-World War II states of medium size—Greece, Bulgaria and Rumania—which were situated in these zones, only Rumania had natural resources capable of sustaining a reasonable standard of living, and these resources first required considerable capital investment and development. The neutral Scandinavian countries, like Spain and the nominally belligerent Portugal, had profited from the war, as had Switzerland, but their contribution to inter-European and overseas trade had been small, and was to remain so after 1918.

Europe's economic convalescence depended in the first instance on the revival of the economic strength of her three leading industrial powers, for Italy, though comparable in population, was of second-rate economic importance. Yet, despite their economic stagnation, the European countries on the eve of the depression enjoyed appreciably higher standards of living than in 1913. That Soviet Russia did not was the result of government policy. The Five-Year Plans started in 1928 began to transform the Soviet economy, but at such high human and economic cost as to make them a model of dubious validity for the backward countries, though long-term economic planning began to be more widely accepted as being desirable and feasible, except in the conservative capitalist countries. Even the backward peasant countries of eastern Europe improved their standards of living, though mass poverty remained. Except in Hungary and Poland, extensive land redistribution was carried out, and those two countries already possessed industrial bases which were extended, though at an inadequate rate, during the inter-war years. However restrictions on emigration, lack of western capital, low standards of education and of technological development, made eastern Europe perennially backward, and an easy prey for Fascist propaganda directed at racial antagonisms (notably anti-Semitism) and social tensions. And as the setbacks caused by World War I to the European economy were possibly more serious in agriculture even than in industry, the peasant nations suffered in proportion.

Before the slump, and especially from 1925, Europe was slowly recovering from the problems posed by war dislocation, changing patterns of foreign trade and the obsolescence of many of her industries—especially the British coal and cotton industries, which remained depressed practically throughout the inter-war years. British exports of coal, chiefly to Europe, faced severe competition from oil and European coalfields, and a declining market after 1918. The greatest competition to her cotton exports came from within her own Empire and Commonwealth and above all from Japan, which by the mid-1930s was the world's biggest exporter of cotton goods. British exports fell from 576,000 tons in 1913 to 377,000 in 1925, and slumped to 135,000 by 1938; Japan's rose in the same period from 3,000 to 234,000 tons. Admittedly cotton's decline exceeded that of other European export trades, but nevertheless it was the classic illustration of that decline and the symbol of Europe's and especially Britain's rapidly ebbing economic power in the backward areas in general and in Asia in particular, for China and even India were gradually lost as British cotton markets in the 1930s. Similarly Germany, though she recovered her position as the leading chemical technologist, never regained her former dominance in the chemical industry, which was taken over by America during the war, thanks in part to German preoccupation with more pressing problems. The chemical industry, however, was not an important factor in international trade after 1918, its strategic importance in war economies ensuring that the major countries remained self-sufficient in that field. And further evidence of Europe's decline in the world economy was provided by her continuing inferiority in automobile production, despite large-scale adoption of Henry Ford's conveyor belt and methods of rationalizing manufacture. Here the gap between the three major European industrial powers and America was certainly narrowed, and moreover Europe depended far more on railways and coastal shipping than did America, where road transport rapidly achieved predominance. In America the 1920s were pre-eminently the age of the mass automobile. But whereas in 1923 America's production of private cars (about 3,625,000) was over thirty times greater than Europe's, and of commercial vehicles (409,000) about ten times greater, by 1929 the ratios had dropped to about 9 to 1 and 5 to 1 respectively (about 4,590,000 cars and 771,000 vehicles). By 1938, the depression had further reduced the disparity, so that America was then producing 2,001,000 cars and 488,000 vehicles against Europe's approximate total production of a million cars and a quarter of a million vehicles.

In the production of electricity Europe also made great progress, though here, as in the case of her expanding automobile industries, disappointing use was made of the opportunities provided for extending trade and industry. Nevertheless the use of hydro-electric power on an increasing scale as technical difficulties were surmounted compensated such countries as Italy, France, Switzerland, Sweden and Norway for their dearth of coal resources and the high cost of oil imports. Together with the increased use of electricity from power stations, it revolutionized European agriculture and industry, and helped to lay the basis for western Europe's great economic advance after 1950. In 1920 the total European production of electricity had been 52·8 billion kWh as against America's 56·6 billion, but by 1925 the figures were 79·9 against 84·7, and in 1929 114·0 against 116·7. Henceforth American production was overtaken, so that in 1939 it was only 161·3 billion kWh against Europe's 199·0 billion kWh, and America exceeded Europe's production subsequently only as the result of World War II.

As the corollary of her industrial, financial and commercial decline in the face of American and other overseas competition, Europe's share of world trade declined in both value and volume. Admittedly world trade was stagnant in the inter-war years, and its rate of increase between 1880 and 1913 (when in every decade it had increased by about a third) could not have been approached unless America, Europe's heiress, had set out to stimulate it as a matter of policy. This America did not do until after World War II, though before the onset of the great depression her great investments in Europe had been largely responsible for the economic revival which took place from 1925. Repudiation of the peace settlement and of the League of Nations did not connote in the 1920s economic isolationism, nor even total abandonment of political responsibilities by America in Europe, though in her own interests America could, and should, have shouldered far more responsibilities in both respects.

Nevertheless, the major responsibilities for Europe's political and economic decline lay with the European states themselves. Europe's share of world trade dropped from its figure of over 50% in 1913 to about 45% as the average of the inter-war years, and the world trade in which she had no share increased more quickly than that in which she participated. The growth of American protectionism had much to do with this decline, but far more important were the protectionist measures of the European powers themselves. More important still were the conservative and rigid adherence to outmoded economic patterns by Britain and France, and widespread reluctance to adopt necessary measures of state intervention— except in Soviet Russia, Germany and Italy, where it took place in politically and socially undesirable ways. Indeed, the manner in which German political objectives distorted the economy of the greatest European industrial power, and hence the European economy also, was the most important drawback of all. Moreover American productivity, massive though it was, must not be over-estimated, for although American *per capita* production was over twice the European average by 1937, that of Britain and Sweden was not much inferior. Had it not been for Germany's return to the path of aggression under Hitler, Europe's great powers of economic recuperation could have halted the trend towards American (and in the distant future, perhaps Soviet) economic predominance. Instead, Europe set the seal on her economic, and next her political decline.

# SECTION ONE  THE POSTWAR ERA

*Chapter II*
## THE MAKING OF VERSAILLES EUROPE

(i) *The Peace Treaties*

THE major business of the peace conference which opened in Paris on January 18th, 1919, was to make the peace treaty with the major enemy, Germany. To Wilson's mind, however, the most essential matter was the establishment of the League of Nations. On January 25th the conference unanimously resolved to create the League and appointed a committee to draft its constitution; other committees were assigned to the various territorial questions and to work out reparations from Germany. The Covenant of the League of Nations was based on a British draft. It was presented by the constitutional committee's spokesmen, led by Wilson, on April 28th. All signatory states were members. New members who wished to be admitted must obtain two-thirds of the votes cast by existing members. Each member was to have one seat in a General Assembly. An executive Council was to contain delegates from the five Great Powers (America, Britain, France, Italy and Japan) and from four states chosen by the Assembly (Belgium, Brazil, Greece and Spain were the first choices). This number was raised to eleven by 1933. To assist the League a permanent secretariat was established in Geneva. The Covenant provided that members should give mutual protection against aggression according to means decided upon by the Council, submit to arbitration, judicial settlement or Council enquiry into any disputes likely to lead to a rupture, and abstain from war until three months after an award. All treaties between members which conflicted with these obligations were invalid, but not 'treaties of arbitration or regional understanding like the Monroe doctrine, for securing the maintenance of peace'. The League was to seek solutions to problems of disarmament, run the new Permanent Court for International Justice, to which it was hoped all nations would submit disputes, create the International Labour Organization, which non-members might also join, and direct health, educational and administrative commissions.

The non-political aspects of the League's activities did much to improve social conditions and to promote enlightened public opinion on such issues as slavery, vice, health and educational needs in backward societies, as well as giving financial and economic advice and assistance to poorer countries, including some in eastern Europe. Its accepted political activities, such as its Minorities and Mandates Commissions, also performed valuable services. The Minorities Commission supervised plebiscites in disputed territories during the early inter-war years and this Commission was also entrusted with overseeing the treatment of minorities, except in Germany. The Mandates Commission was composed of entirely independent members nominated by the Council to advise on conditions in the mandated territories so far as they related to the terms of the mandates. This Commission did much to arouse national consciousness and support claims for greater political freedom among the people under the mandates.

The Covenant of the League was an integral part of the European settlements, and it provided for their revision by suggesting that 'treaties which have become inapplicable' and 'international conditions whose continuance might endanger the peace of the world' might be reconsidered. Wilson, who rightly thought Versailles a good treaty, expected thereby to provide for any necessary revisions, and indeed hoped that the European states which had grievances against any parts of the peace treaties would be more disposed to accept them temporarily because the League machinery existed.

But America's refusal to ratify the Versailles Treaty, and thereby join the League, crippled it from the beginning. As both Germany and Soviet Russia were members for only seven years, Japan only until 1933 and Italy's membership practically ended in 1936, the League was never a truly international organization. Most Latin American states were members, though not throughout its effective existence from 1920 to 1940, but it was largely a European concern, and above all an Anglo-French one. But whereas France tried to use it as an instrument for maintaining the peace settlement against the revisionist powers, Britain saw it mainly as an instrument for conciliation. In fact it was essentially a talking shop, for none of its members would sacrifice any of their sovereignty, and no major power allowed the League to shape its policy, though British governments sometimes talked as though they did. The League had no military or even police forces, and had to rely on individual members' loyalty in carrying out economic or military sanctions against aggressor states. The League achieved some successes in settling minor disputes between small powers (for instance, that between Greece and Bulgaria in 1925) or in clothing a great power's brutality against a smaller one with fine words (as when Italy attacked Greece in 1923). But when faced with real test cases, as in 1931, when Japan seized Manchuria, and in 1935 when Italy attacked Ethiopia, the League failed, as it had always been bound to do. Its supporters argued that it was not the League but its members who had failed the test, a casuistry which deceived only themselves. Great Powers could use League formulae of collective security and other phrases to impose their will on small countries, or to rally support against bigger transgressors or would-be transgressors. They would not entrust their security or major interests to the safe-keeping of Geneva, nor allow votes of small powers to launch them into actions which they opposed.

The Treaty of Versailles, which was rightly regarded as the sanction of the League and the basis of the postwar settlement, was negotiated solely by the victors. According to the pre-armistice terms of November 5th, 1918, agreed upon by Wilson with Allied approval, and by the Germans, the peace was to be based on Wilson's Fourteen Points and his subsequent enunciations of principle. These amounted to 'no annexations, no contributions, no punitive damages' and no undemocratic *régimes*. Germany was to restore the invaded territories, and to pay compensation for all damage inflicted by her aggression on land, sea and in the air on Allied civilians and property—not the entire direct cost of the war to the Allies, as some vindictive politicians demanded. Germany was not allowed to negotiate terms and the Allies interpreted the agreement unilaterally, though generally fairly. By the armistice terms Germany surrendered immediately her submarines and most of her battleships, her guns and railway stock, evacuated the territories annexed at Brest-Litovsk, and evacuated the left bank of the Rhine and bridgeheads opposite its large cities. None of these terms could be disputed, though when the Germans later learned the terms of the peace treaty they scuttled their battleships, interned by the British at Scapa Flow. Allied occupation was not unduly onerous, and the mass starvation suffered during the winter of 1918–19 was not caused, as German propaganda claimed, by the Allied blockade but by the refusal of German shipowners to offer their vessels for bringing in food, which therefore had to await Allied shipping in April 1919.

Wilson had arrived in Europe determined to bend what he conceived to be undemocratic associated governments to his will, and to make a genuinely democratic and just peace settlement, as a reward for the wartime sacrifices of the peoples and as an assurance that there would be no more war. Except for the insistence on freedom of the sea—formally the cause of American belligerency—Lloyd George warmly endorsed the Fourteen Points, and Wilson agreed not to press this one point of disagreement. Effectively Versailles was based on the principle of self-determination, so far as that could be reconciled with economic, strategic, geographical and political considerations. Essentially Wilson got his way, though his idealism became badly tarnished during the negotiations and Lloyd George produced most of the results. The treaty was a moderate one except for the insistence on Germany's and her allies' unique war guilt (the famous Article 231), introduced as a compromise between American insistence to honour the pre-armistice agreement by excluding war costs, and the Anglo-French necessity to satisfy public opinion by at least some theoretical declaration of German liability for complete reparation. Indeed it was generous in comparison with Brest-Litovsk, and the treatment planned for the west had Germany been victorious. However, the Germans convinced themselves that to 'dictate' and not negotiate peace was immoral (it was certainly not customary), that Article 231 was false instead of being largely

303

true, that the reparations were intended to destroy Germany and that her territorial losses to Poland were intolerable.

The Versailles Treaty was essentially the work of President Wilson, the British Prime Minister, Lloyd George, and the French Premier, Georges Clemenceau, who acted as president of the conference. Negotiations began in the Council of Ten which consisted of the heads of state and their foreign ministers: Wilson and his Secretary of State Robert Lansing, Lloyd George and Arthur Balfour, Clemenceau and Stephen Pichon, Vittorio Emanuele Orlando and Sidney Sonnino (who eclipsed his Premier), and Kimmochi Saionji and Shinken Makino, Japanese Premier and Foreign Secretary. The Council proved too unwieldy for the purpose and, as Japan was interested chiefly in acquiring former German assets in the Far East and Italy sulked because her claims were scaled down, the Big Three made the decisions on the basis of expert reports from their various advisers and committees. They also had to take note of previous agreements, to Wilson's chagrin. Though this affected the Versailles Treaty less than the settlements with Austria and Turkey, it provoked a major issue, since in 1917 Britain, Italy and France (and Tsarist Russia) had agreed that Japan should take over Germany's Shantung concession. Wilson yielded reluctantly, for this flagrantly contradicted his stand on self-determination and national rights. The Chinese delegation denounced Wilson's surrender, and refused to sign the treaty. Though a minor issue at Versailles, the problem had important consequences. In America it was seized upon by Wilson's opponents, who denounced the commitments of the Versailles Treaty, including the League of Nations. It was in this way that the 'China Question' entered American politics.

Wilson, in fact, suffered successive defeats over the question of Germany's colonies. He agreed that she should not retain them as she was 'unfit' to rule them, but successfully insisted that they should not be annexed in the old imperialist fashion. They were to become League mandates, held in trust by Britain, the Dominions, Belgium, France and Japan. Britain thereby took over Tanganyika and shared the Cameroons and Togoland with France, Belgium took Ruanda-Urundi, South Africa held South-West Africa, Australia took New Ireland, north-eastern New Guinea, New Britain, the Solomon Isles and Nauru (on behalf of the British Empire), New Zealand took Western Samoa, and Japan was given the mandates for the Marianas, Caroline and Marshall Islands. Wilson was well aware of the danger to America from Japanese control of these islands. But he could not deny British and Dominion demands that if outright annexation were refused they should enjoy mandates (in any case the practical differences were small). He liked even less his naval officers' contention that America should take the islands, and Japan have as compensation a free hand on the continent of Asia.

On reparations Wilson also made concessions. Belgian and French demands for reparations were justified, for the western war had been fought in Belgium and France, and the Germans in retreating had wantonly added to the damage, whereas Germany had built up and modernized her industrial plant. Britain also had justifiable claims in view of her shipping and general economic losses. No allowance, however, was made for German property (including colonies) seized after the war, and Britain's demand that war pensions should be treated as civilian damage was unparalleled. Lloyd George succeeded in having the decision on the amount of reparations deferred, expecting that later it could be examined more dispassionately. John Maynard Keynes, the economist, who resigned from the British delegation over reparations, attacked them in a brilliant book, *The Economic Consequences of the Peace*, which attracted great attention, especially in Germany. Keynes proposed that because of Germany's commanding economic position, reparations totalling £2,000,000,000 would prove feasible and would not ruin either Germany's or Europe's economy. The Reparation Commission fixed total liability at £6,600,000,000 in April 1921, by which time Germany had defaulted by about £600,000,000 on the first instalment of £1,000,000,000 due by May 1st. Because Germany had failed to co-operate over reparations in kind, the Allies had extended their occupation in March to Düsseldorf, Ruhrort and Duisburg. They now threatened to occupy the whole Ruhr unless the rest of the instalment was paid. It was paid in August, but the incident caused a breach between France and Britain. Britain thought French insistence on reparations both vindictive and short-sighted, since it held back general European recovery. Britain also wanted to combine reparations and war debts in one settlement. She had made heavy loans to her Allies before America entered the war, and had then assumed responsibility for loans made to them by America. Hence when Congress in February 1922 appointed a commission to collect war debts by 1947, Britain offered to forego her share of reparations and the war debts due to her if all war debts were cancelled. Wilson had always refused to consider cancelling war debts, and his successors (except briefly Hoover ten years later) endorsed his view. France also rejected the proposal. She was denied priority in the payment of reparations, though the reconstruction of her northern provinces swallowed up half her government expenditure.

When in 1922 Germany obtained a partial financial moratorium and also defaulted slightly on payments in kind, France and Belgium determined to exact reparations themselves. In January 1923 they occupied the Ruhr, in the face of violent British protests and German passive resistance. The German government now increased inflation, in order to avoid reparations, to such an extent that in November the dollar was worth 4,200,000,000 marks. Raymond Poincaré's object, however, was not to exact the missing reparations but to gain control of the Ruhr, which contained 80% of Germany's coal production, 80% of her steel capacity, and 10% of her population. This would have made France the greatest industrial power in Europe, destroyed Germany as a power, and rendered British influence in Europe insignificant. The French policy was defeated, though considerable reparations were exacted, and Germany at the end of September gave up the policy of passive resistance. Before inflation was checked in November it had wiped out the savings of the middle classes, who rightly ascribed their ruin to the politicians, and had set off a social revolution which led to Communist and nationalist rebellions. Of these the chief was in Munich where Hitler, hitherto the unknown leader of a minor nationalist party, launched an abortive *putsch* against the Bavarian state government.

A rapid German economic recovery then ensued, and an international enquiry presided over by an American, General Charles Dawes, produced a plan for the payment of reparations. The Dawes Plan of April 1924 arranged for a gold loan by American bankers to Germany, whose aim was to balance the budget and to stabilize German currency by placing it on a gold standard. Germany in return was to pay reparations up to the 1921 total in instalments rising in five years from £50,000,000 to the standard rate of £125,000,000. Foreign, especially American, loans made repayment possible, and also revived the German economy, but on highly unstable bases. In 1929 another committee, headed by another American, Owen D. Young, reduced total payments to just over $28,800,000,000 or about £6,000,000,000, exclusive of interest, to be paid by 1988, with provision for varying annual instalments. It was also agreed that if America reduced claims on her debtors, two-thirds of the benefit would be passed on to Germany in the first thirty-seven years, and all benefits in the next twenty-two. In fact before reparations ended in 1932 Germany had paid perhaps $6,200,000,000, but this was a paper transaction. Her actual payments were only those in kind, for America and other creditors lent her far more than she paid. Nevertheless reparations remained a burning grievance, even when she had stopped paying and had a comfortable profit.

The territorial settlement and its implications created greater grievances. Clemenceau, though more moderate than Poincaré and many other French leaders, was intent on guaranteeing French security by weakening Germany permanently, for he foresaw that however leniently Germany was treated she would not forgive her defeat. He demanded that France should annex the Saar, as well as regain Alsace-Lorraine (to which the Allies agreed), and that the left bank of the Rhine should be separated from Germany to form a buffer state—obviously under French control. Wilson and Lloyd George argued that this would create a more dangerous problem than Alsace-Lorraine had done after 1871, and it was finally agreed that Alsace–Lorraine should return to France; that Belgium should annex Moresnet, Eupen and Malmédy (with provision for a plebiscite in Malmédy); that the Allies should occupy the left bank of the Rhine and the major bridgeheads for fifteen years; that a League of Nations commissioner should administer the Saar, allowing France to exploit its coalfields, for fifteen years, when a plebiscite would be held; and that a thirty-mile belt on the right bank of the Rhine should be demilitarized. The German army was reduced to 100,000 men and was forbidden artillery and military aircraft; the navy was limited to six obsolete capital ships and some small craft. To compensate France for the rejection of her claims, America and Britain offered treaties of mutual aid pledging them to help her in case of a German attack, but this promise also was dishonoured as America refused to ratify Versailles and Britain therefore repudiated her commitment. Demands for the trial of war criminals, including Wilhelm II, were conceded by Germany, but Wilhelm remained in Holland and the trials, as conducted by the Germans, were a farce. They also claimed that the Allies had pledged themselves to disarm. There was indeed a moral obligation, but this was cancelled by Germany's shiftiness over reparations and her illegal rearmament.

In the west Germany surrendered part of Schleswig to the Danes, who themselves carried out a plebiscite. Outwardly the Germans accepted their losses in the west, though with what sincerity cannot be determined. They freely re-affirmed the territorial clauses and disarmament obligations of the Versailles *Diktat* after the British Labour government, in order to satisfy French demands for security which it privately thought nervously exaggerated, had drafted an abortive general agreement known as the Geneva Protocol. This would have pledged all League members to disarm by mutual agreement, to support each other against unprovoked attacks and to accept compulsory arbitration in international disputes. As this bound Britain to guarantee every frontier in Europe and a great many outside it, and the Americans expressed fears that Britain might be obliged to transgress the Monroe Doctrine by observing the Protocol, the Conservatives immediately dropped it on taking office in November 1924. However, Austen Chamberlain, their Foreign Secretary, unlike his half-brother Neville and most British politicians, was better disposed towards France than towards Germany. His German opposite number Gustav Stresemann, saw that Chamberlain would seek to honour the British promise of 1919, and that 'a security agreement without Germany would have been a security agreement against Germany'. He therefore proposed an Anglo-French-German-Italian pact pledging the signatories not to attack each other. This developed into the Locarno Treaty of December 1925, whereby France, Belgium and Germany confirmed the Versailles settlement in the west (except Schleswig), and Britain and Italy stood guarantors.

The treaty prevented staff talks (if they had been desired) between Britain, France and Belgium on the pre-1914 pattern. It further thwarted the enforcement of the Treaty of Versailles, as Stresemann intended, by limiting it to the west. Britain refused to underwrite France's eastern alliances, though Locarno laid down that action against Germany under the alliances would not constitute aggression. Nevertheless Locarno was regarded as a sign of growing confidence and better relations in the west. Eastern Europe disliked the treaty, especially when Austen Chamberlain asserted that the Polish Corridor was something for which no British government could risk 'the bones of a British grenadier'. It was, however, the prelude to Germany's entry into the League of Nations on September 10th, 1926, and Stresemann's proposal to Aristide Briand a week later for the closest possible Franco-German economic collaboration. Stresemann hinted at more relaxations of Versailles in return for German economic support for France, and Briand, who first gave currency to 'appeasement' by his efforts to establish Franco-German friendship, was willing to pursue the matter as an important step towards his great goal of a United States of Europe. However, neither his nor Stresemann's colleagues favoured the idea. Neither did public opinion in their countries, nor American economic interests.

Stresemann's aim as foreign minister until his death in 1929 was to 'drive France back from trench to trench as no general attack is feasible'. Stresemann was just as much a nationalist after 1918 as he had been during the war, when he had been a leading annexationist. Only in the self-deluded twenties could he have been thought of as a 'European', and then only in the west. He never dropped his derisive gibes at Poland and Czechoslovakia, whose existence as independent states barred the way to old German ambitions. Immediately after Locarno he publicly asserted that Germany had not agreed to refrain from attack in the east. 'Membership of the League does not exclude the possibility of war,' he declared. Germany had ceded little territory to Czechoslovakia, and the Germans in Czechoslovakia were unpopular in Germany, but Stresemann made his hostility unmistakable.

However, it was Poland who constituted an unforgivable reminder of defeat, and Polish greed and obduracy during the peace negotiations had alienated every power except France, who encouraged Poland in order to weaken Germany. The Poles had promised to put themselves in Allied hands but refused the terms offered to them at the conference. Their reasoning was frequently specious, even dishonest and sometimes contradictory: their arguments supporting their claim to Upper Silesia destroyed their claim to East Galicia, but they intended to have both. Nevertheless the Polish-German frontiers made ethnic and economic sense, and certainly did Germany no injustice. Poland was given Posen and West Prussia, with the 'corridor' to the Baltic providing access to the sea, as promised by the Fourteen Points. The Germans made this a major grievance since it 'cut off' East Prussia, but East Prussia was perfectly accessible from west of the corridor by sea. Danzig, a wholly German city, was first assigned to Poland but on the protests of Lloyd George was made a Free City under the League, while economically united to Poland. The Danzigers remained obstinately German and Poland built up Gdynia as her major port so that, if Danzig were eventually lost to Germany, Polish trade would not be disrupted. Yet in Polish eyes Danzig remained until World War II the touchstone of relations with Germany. Again on British insistence plebiscites were held in Upper Silesia, Allenstein and Marienwerder to discover the wishes of the inhabitants. Marienwerder and Allenstein voted to remain with Germany and Upper Silesia was partitioned despite a Polish uprising against the League's decision. By the final settlement of October 1921 Germany got more of the territory, but the richer industrial zone went to Poland. Germany also ceded a small part of Silesia to Czechoslovakia, and Memel to the new Lithuanian Republic.

Germany lost altogether about $13\frac{1}{2}\%$ of her prewar territory, including Alsace-Lorraine. Her loss of economic productivity was of the same order, and she gave up about 7,000,000 subjects, the vast majority of whom were Slavs only too pleased to leave. When the terms were given to Germany there was a nation-wide outburst. Right Wing Nationalists and Social Democrats alike denounced them. A spokesman for the latter asserted that they would never abandon their compatriots: 'Unbreakable is the bond which ties us to the Germans in Bohemia, Moravia and Silesia, in Tyrol, Carinthia and Styria.' Germany was to claim first under the new Republic, later under Hitler, and then after World War II in the form of the Federal Republic, the right to speak for all Germans living beyond the frontiers, but for the moment she had to accept the terms. Wilson insisted that the 'real case was that justice had shown itself overwhelmingly against Germany', but there was a government crisis in Germany before her delegates signed the treaty on June 28th, 1919. Thereupon Wilson, Lloyd George and Orlando returned home, and left the completion of the peace-making to their foreign ministers. But Wilson's vanity, obstinacy and tactlessness allowed his domestic enemies to defeat his attempts to obtain Congress's ratification of the treaty, which meant also that America did not participate fully in what Balfour called 'the immense operation of liquidating the Austrian Empire', and in making peace with Bulgaria and Turkey. America's abdication of responsibility was still more marked when the ambassadors took over near the end of the year and America had only an observer present.

It was in the settlement of the old Habsburg lands that the principle of self-determination was first seriously violated, and particularly in drawing the frontiers of the new Austrian Republic. The 1915 Treaty of London had promised Italy South Tyrol (to give her the strategic Brenner frontier), Istria (including Trieste) and northern Dalmatia. But the northern part of South Tyrol was solidly German-Austrian, and its cession to Italy was a grave injustice. The principle of self-determination was also denied when the Austrian Republic at its inception on November 12th, 1918, demanded union (*Anschluss*) with Germany and was refused. Austria also lost her Czech and Slovene lands, both Galicias, which went to the new Poland, and Sopron which went to Hungary, though she kept the Burgenland. These losses, however, were inevitable, and the great problem after the signature of the Austrian treaty (St Germain-en-Laye) on September 10th, 1919, was how to make the rump state politically and economically viable.

The Treaty of Neuilly with Bulgaria was settled on November 27th without much difficulty, for she had no friends and several enemies at the conference. Rumania coveted southern Dobrudja which was largely Bulgarian; the Macedonian annexations by Yugoslavia (at this time called the Kingdom of the Serbs, Croats and Slovenes) in 1913 were confirmed and slightly increased, but the worst blow was the loss of Western Thrace to Greece. This was predominantly Turkish, but it contained many Bulgars and it gave Bulgaria access to the Aegean. She was promised 'economic access' but never received it, and the real purpose of the move was to satisfy the imperialist ambitions of Lloyd George's Greek *protégé*, Eleutherios Venizelos.

The settlement with Hungary was made next. By the Treaty of Trianon (June 4th, 1920) Rumania annexed Transylvania, part of the Hungarian plain and part of the Banat of Temesvar (the other part went to Yugoslavia). Ruthenia, Slovakia and some territory where there was a considerable Hungarian minority went to Czechoslovakia. Hungary violently disputed all these decisions. However, the greatest disputes over the division of her territories were caused by Italian claims. Wilson rejected Italy's claim to northern Dalmatia and the former Hungarian port of Fiume, which had not been promised in 1915, but accepted the claim to Istria. Orlando angrily withdrew from the conference, though later an Italian delegate returned. Yugoslavia put in a counter-claim to Istria and, while they were disputing, the Italian poet d'Annunzio launched a comic-opera (or proto-Italian-Fascist) attack on Fiume in September 1919. In November 1920 a compromise was reached in the Treaty of Rapallo whereby Fiume became a Free City and Italy renounced Dalmatia except for Zara and four islands, but received Istria. This did not satisfy her. Fiume was ethnically Italian and strategically important, and in September 1923 she annexed it. Yugoslavia acquiesced in 1924, but more bad blood was caused by continuing disputes over Albania. Albania had been occupied by Austria during the war, but in 1920, despite Italian, Yugoslav and Greek encroachments, the Albanians had vindicated their claim to independence and had been admitted to the League. An open struggle for influence followed in which Yugoslavia had the upper hand until 1925, when economic penetration by Italy won for her considerable political influence, and in November 1927 she made Albania virtually a protectorate. Even then Albania refused entirely to submit, and only as a result of Italy's attack on April 7th, 1939, did her independence disappear.

The negotiations for the Turkish peace treaty were complicated, more than the others, by the problems of dealing with Bolshevik Russia. The Allied fleet (America did not declare war on Turkey) had arrived in Constantinople on November 13th, 1918, and the Sultan's government had begun to co-operate with the victors. But then in April 1919 the Italians landed at Adalia to claim the Anatolian booty granted by the London Treaty. There followed the landing of the hereditary enemy, the Greeks, at Smyrna on May 14th, 1919. This brought numerous recruits to the nationalist leader Mustafa Kemal, when on May 19th he organized resistance to Turkey's further dismemberment. Despite being outlawed by the Sultan in July, Kemal went on to fight the Allies, establish his Nationalist Congress at Erzerum, and assert first Turkish territorial integrity, and then, on September 13th, the principles of the National Pact: the right to self-determination, the security of Constantinople (coveted by Greece), the opening of the Straits, preservation of minority rights and the annulling of the capitulations.

The Allies were embarrassed both by Kemal's military and political successes and by the Russian attitude. The Bolsheviks had published the Tsarist secret treaties with their plan for partitioning the Turkish Empire. America disliked the plan, and refused suggestions that she should take charge of either the Straits or Armenia. Lloyd George, too deeply committed to withdraw, continued to spur on the Greeks. In March 1920 Constantinople was occupied in order to put pressure on Kemal, keep open the Straits and protect the Armenians against the Nationalists. In June peace terms were finally given to the Sultan's government by the Treaty of Sèvres. This ratified Arab 'freedom' from Turkey, common ground among the Turks, and demanded the partition of Asia Minor, which the Sultan also accepted. He agreed to the treaty on August 10th, but Kemal, with overwhelming national approval, rejected it and fought on. In March 1921 the Italians sensibly decided to cut their losses, a few days before Kemal agreed that Batum should go to Soviet Russia. Russia in turn accepted Turkish possession of Kars and Ardahan, already formalized in the Turco-Armenian treaty of December 3rd, 1920, by which Armenia's and Turkey's frontier disputes had been settled, the day after the Bolsheviks had set up their Armenian Republic. In October France followed Italy's example, but Lloyd George held fast to his Greek friends despite mounting protest in Britain. In the Chanak crisis of September 1922 he appealed to the Allies and Dominions to help to defend the Straits against Kemal, but got frosty replies from all except New Zealand and Newfoundland. Soon afterwards he was defeated and a Conservative government took office. Kemal had merely to hang on to obtain his terms, which were entirely reasonable.

By the Treaty of Lausanne (July 24th, 1923) the Turks confirmed their cession of the Arab lands, but regained Eastern Thrace from Greece; there was also separate provision for Greek-Turkish population exchanges. They accepted Italian retention of the Dodecanese islands, British retention of Cyprus, and Greek retention of all but two of the Aegean islands. They also agreed to demilitarize the Straits, which were to be open to all nations in peacetime, and in war as well, if Turkey was neutral; if she was at war she had to keep them open to neutral ships.

The Turkish *imbroglio* was the great blot on Lloyd George's moderating and statesmanlike role at the conference. Over the Polish question especially he sought a reasonable compromise, though his later readiness to intervene against Soviet Russia when she temporarily turned the tables on Polish imperialism caused a storm of protest in Britain. But, unlike the French, he clearly saw the dangers which threatened when the Poles refused the Allied suggestion that the Polish-Russian frontier should run along the so-called 'Curzon line'. This followed the rivers Niemen and Bug towards the Carpathians, and was as ethnically and geographically valid as any frontier could be in the mixed populations of the eastern border-lands. The Russians did not attend the Paris conference, and the Curzon line was drawn without reference to them. Hence neither they nor the Poles had accepted it, when the Poles in May 1920 exploited Russian preoccupation with the Civil War by invading the Ukraine. The Russians had been reluctantly obliged in February to renounce imperialist claims to Estonia, but despite the Polish invasion they hung on to the other Baltic states as long as possible, releasing Lithuania in July, Latvia in August and finally Finland in October 1920.

Lord Curzon, British Foreign Secretary since October 1919, confirmed a common suspicion when he told the Lettish foreign minister in January 1921 that, while Britain hoped the Baltic states would remain independent, she could never forget that they were small in power and population; that the Soviet *régime*, as it shed its Communist principles and increasingly developed imperialist leanings, was determined to regain them; and that the powers might find themselves, as in Poland, involved in obligations to fight for them in 'impossible circumstances'. The powers had not in fact fought for Poland when Russia first held the Polish advance, and then in August 1920 advanced to Warsaw. France theatrically rushed out supplies and General Weygand's military mission, but the Poles did the work of defeating Russia. France, however, busily helped them to spread the myth that a great battle of world history had been fought before the gates of Warsaw, which had saved the freedom and civilization of the world from Bolshevik hordes. Within six weeks the Poles had pursued the Russian army back into Russia, and the Bolsheviks offered to make peace. By the terms finally agreed at the Treaty of Riga on March 18th, 1921, the Poles retained the territory which they held. They regarded this as merely a compromise solution, for it did not restore the 1772 frontier held before the first partition of Poland, though it was half-way between that and the Curzon line. The Riga line doubled the area of territory allotted by the Allies to Poland, which also had not included Vilna, seized by Poland from Lithuania in flagrant breach of faith and in defiance of the Allies in October 1920. The preposterous Polish chauvinism did not displease France, but it greatly diminished British friendship for Poland.

The Poles also refused to give up East Galicia, which unlike West Galicia was almost entirely non-Polish in character, and rejected the offer of a League mandate. But although Poland had waged a vicious civil war before suppressing the Russians in East Galicia, the Allies in 1923 recognized that *fait accompli*, together with Poland's other frontiers, in return for a promise to set up an autonomous *régime* in East Galicia. This promise Poland never intended to honour, and her refusal to disgorge ill-gotten gains did her no good when Germany later attacked legitimate Polish interests. The Poles hoped to safeguard their booty by playing off Germany and Russia against each other. Germany would never be reconciled to territorial losses which, except for Danzig (indispensable to Poland in the early inter-war years only), were justifiably enforced. Russia would never be reconciled to the loss of about 7,000,000 White Russians, Ukrainians and Ruthenes. Her greed condemned Poland to a non-stop balancing act between her powerful neighbours which ended in August 1939 with a fatal fall when they came to terms. Moreover, one reason for the rapid collapse of Poland thereafter was that in nearly half the country the Poles were in a minority, and more than a third of the population was non-Polish. Even these gains left extreme Polish nationalists unsatisfied. They continued to dream of a revived Polish empire which would include Lithuania and stretch from the Baltic to the Black Sea.

## (ii) *Political, Social and Economic Problems*

The complex of peace treaties was generally known as the Versailles settlement, though it was not Versailles to which serious objection could be made. Apart from Riga, the greatest injustices were done by Trianon, which repaid Hungary, unwisely if not in full, for her ill-treatment of the subject races before 1918. On strictly ethnic grounds the 1919–23 settlement was the best ever made in Europe. The 'Balkanization' of central Europe was the work not of the peace conference but of the collapse of the Austro-Hungarian empire. Even if the delegates had wished to reverse that process they could not have done so. The violent reversal of centuries of German and Hungarian aggrandizement within the space of a few years inevitably left deep scars, but Czechoslovak and Yugoslav claims to independence were irresistible. A few prescient British politicians argued that independence might not in fact give more liberty to the 'successor states' than would autonomy in a federation, and feared that Russia would in time take over the smaller Slav nations if they broke away. Some French generals, though not Foch, whose views counted for most, also doubted whether the new small states could long resist Germany's pressure. Yet 'home rule' was no more practicable as the solution to Austro-Hungarian problems than it was in Ireland, which was used by British critics of the treaties to bolster up the shaky argument. It was rightly said that a young state wanted more than frontiers—'It wanted internal harmony, external peace and some outlet for its trade'—but these could not be found in association with the Habsburgs. If the Allies were to stand by the 'democratic' aims which they had professed, their only course was to accept the situation. They did not attach undue importance to self-determination as against economic and geographical factors, though they certainly rejected it in two cases where it worked in favour of Germany. They would not allow Austro-German union for political and strategic reasons. They also refused to allow the Sudeten Germans, who for geographical reasons could not be included in the rump Austria, a plebiscite on the issue of incorporation into Germany. The Sudetenland was economically,

313

strategically and geographically an essential part of the Bohemian lands and therefore had to go into the new Czechoslovakia.

The peace conference certainly did not overlook economic problems, and its Supreme Economic Council was anxious to establish organizations to ensure international economic co-operation. However little could be done against flat American opposition to attempts to establish a common European policy towards America in such matters as currency, or against the insistence of new and old European states alike on coupling political with economic nationalism. The 1921 Portorose conference attempted to replace the old Austro-Hungarian economic union with a Danubian tariff union, but succeeded, despite American, British, French and Italian blessing, in solving only minor problems. In any case Europe's great economic problems were not capable of being handled by a peace conference, nor were they even mainly the results of the war. The effect of the war was not to introduce new trends, nor to reverse established trends, but to accelerate processes already apparent before 1914—which is not to say that the war had no important direct and indirect consequences. The mere fact of territorial changes carried significant connotations. The distribution among countries of natural resources such as coal, iron, oil and hydro-electric power was altered; their complementary industries, which had been developed as integral parts of large economies, had to be adapted to narrower national frameworks; and agricultural production and marketing patterns had changed. The Austrian Republic, cut off from the old manufacturing centres in Bohemia and from Hungarian agricultural products, was an extreme example of these consequences. At the other extreme was Poland, whose industrial central region had been tied to the great Russian market, and whose eastern lands were relatively poor. Poland's western and southern neighbours could not and would not replace that market; hence Polish industry had only just struggled to its 1913 level of productivity when World War II broke out.

There was little justification for reproaching the peace conference for failing to establish democratic *régimes*, though it was unduly tender to Magyar reactionaries through fear of the spread of Bolshevism into eastern central Europe, where Lenin was competing with Wilson to become the prophet of the new age. Few of the 'new' peoples had had any experience of parliamentary institutions or of self-government, and none had combined the two before 1918. There was no reason to suppose that western parliamentary democracy was exportable to these areas when it had never consolidated its position even in Italy, while Germany failed after 1918 to build democracy on the basis of existing parliamentary institutions and a new constitution which was theoretically the most perfect ever devised.

The Poles, like the new nations, adopted a parliamentary system, which was popularly supposed to have proved its superiority over the pre-1914 autocracies (even in Japan this idea took political form). But Polish parliamentary traditions were anarchic, and adoption of the French model, unstable in its own country, was a further handicap. Poland's provisional

Premier, Ignace Paderewski, the great pianist, failed to reconcile the anti-Russian Josef Pilsudski and the anti-German Roman Dmowski factions, and the Socialist, peasant and *bourgeois* groups. On Paderewski's resignation in December 1918, Pilsudski as chief of state had matters very much his own way for a time, especially in foreign policy. On this he imprinted the stamp of the military adventurer, setting a precedent which Poland later had cause to regret. Even over Vilna, where Poland had a good ethnic case, Pilsudski's treachery spoiled it. Moreover he stimulated Lithuania to emulate him by seizing Memel, a solidly German city, from East Prussia.

The Bolshevik invasion of Latvia in January 1919 was repulsed by Latvian and German forces, the latter under General Gotmar von der Goltz, whom the Allies recalled when Germany revealed ambitions to control Latvia. By January 1920 all Germans and Bolsheviks had been expelled from the country and by the Treaty of Riga of August 1920 Russia recognized Latvian independence, which was also accepted by the Allies in January 1921. The Latvian constitution of May 1922 established a parliamentary democracy which endured until May 1934.

Estonia took a similar course, except that she did not have to contend with German freebooters. She achieved a democratic constitution and independence more rapidly, but had to contend with more Communist activity. Even after a Communist rebellion was suppressed in December 1924 Communism remained a major issue, provoking the rise of a reactionary coalition which included Fascists. In the mid-1930s there was a dictatorship, but parliamentary democracy was finally being consolidated when Russia re-annexed Estonia in 1940.

Lithuania's attempts at parliamentary government ended in November 1923 with a Right Wing military coup, and successive governments veered towards Fascism. In March 1923, Memel was constituted an autonomous region at the League's demand. In December 1938 the local Nazis gained 90% of the vote, but Nazism made little headway in Lithuania herself. Germany's seizure of Memel in March 1939 frightened the government of General Jonas Cernius, which took office immediately afterwards, into accepting as partners the previously prohibited opposition parties. But this *régime* also was given no time in which to establish itself before Stalinist imperialism recouped another Russian loss.

Finland's territorial settlement was not completed until 1921. The attempt of Bolsheviks and Finnish Communists to seize power in January 1918 led to civil war against the White Finnish forces led by Baron Karl Gustav Mannerheim and aided by von der Goltz. Germany gained considerable influence over the Finns, who in October 1918 elected a Hessian prince as King, but Germany's defeat led to Mannerheim's becoming head of State in December and launching a brutal 'White terror'. Russia's renewal of the fighting in June 1919, when the Finns would not surrender Karelia, led to another Russian defeat, but she was in no position to resume the struggle until November 1939. In the meantime the Finns consolidated their parliamentary democracy, received the Aaland Islands from the

315

League in June 1921 (one of the League's few successes) and established a stable and prosperous society. They resumed as rapidly as possible their old Scandinavian orientation and regarded themselves, and were soon regarded by all except Russia, as a member of the Scandinavian neutral bloc.

That the failure of democracy was not due to adverse economic or territorial provisions is shown by the way in which the free institutions of others—Greece, Rumania and Yugoslavia as well as Austria, Hungary and Bulgaria—alike succumbed. Greece, of course, was victor in one war and vanquished in another. Alexander, made king by Venizelos in 1917, was bitten by a pet monkey and died in October 1920, a bizarre fatality with a farcical *dénouement*. Opposition to Venizelos's Anatolian adventure led to his defeat in the elections held in November, and a plebiscite on December 5th voted overwhelmingly for the return of his enemy, King Constantine. The Allies immediately withdrew aid from Greece, but Constantine continued the war against Turkey. Turkey's offensive against Smyrna in August 1922 was followed by a Venizelist offensive against Salonika and demand for Constantine's abdication in September. Constantine returned to exile again, to die the following January, and his successor George II was merely an instrument of the successful generals, who also disliked Venizelos' pretensions. In December 1923 the generals virtually expelled George II, and when Venizelos attempted to save the monarchy, they forced him out also. A plebiscite in April 1924 favoured a republic as overwhelmingly as the December 1920 result had favoured Constantine. Anarchy and military dictatorships followed until Venizelos returned in May 1928 to establish in July a stable government which lasted for four years. But Greek political fickleness remained a major factor in the 1930s.

In Bulgaria defeat brought the abdication of King Ferdinand in favour of his adroit son Boris III, but it also brought thousands of refugees from Thrace and Macedonia. Both influxes proved dangerous to the government, but more particularly the Macedonians, with their terrorist IMRO organization. The ruthless repression of Macedonian nationalism by Greece and Yugoslavia in their Macedonian territories stimulated IMRO to continual outrages against the government of the Peasant Party leader Alexander Stamboliski. The Bulgarian peasants, constituting 80% of the nation, demanded a political and social revolution, and Stamboliski tried to meet their wishes by breaking up crown lands and large estates. Thus Bulgaria rapidly acquired a stable agricultural society. His relations with the middle class parties and the Communists were difficult because of his insistence on peasant predominance, but Communists enjoyed more political freedom than in any other eastern European country except Czechoslovakia. Stamboliski tried to heal the breach with Yugoslavia and unite the two countries in a South Slav Union, but this was rejected by both Serb and Bulgarian nationalists. His arrogance also made him enemies, and he was overthrown and murdered in June 1923, certainly with Boris's complicity, after he had talked of establishing a republic. Stamboliski's reforms were soon largely undone, and with them ended what small hope there was of democracy in Bulgaria. By degrees a police state was established, though IMRO continued its terrorism even when it split into two major factions, with a third small one encouraged by Russia. A bomb outrage in the cathedral of Sofia in April 1925 provoked rigorous suppression of Communists, two of whom were responsible, though without Party knowledge, and the murder of Communists and Peasant politicians. IMRO terrorized Bulgaria for over ten years, and in July 1926 launched a mass raid into Yugoslavia. The authorities could check neither this adventure, nor daily gun battles between the terrorist factions, the chief of which was protected by the war minister and possibly by Boris, because of its opposition to the Moscow-directed faction which sought an independent Macedonia. Italy subsidized both the Bulgarian government and its favoured IMRO faction in order to make trouble with Bulgaria's neighbours, and in October 1930 the Italo-Bulgarian connection was strengthened when Boris married Princess Giovanna, daughter of Victor Emmanuel III.

Even in western Europe democratic standards often lapsed. Belgium survived the strains of war, but demands that the Flemish language should be put on a par with French impaired national unity. In July 1926 a financial crisis brought temporary suspension of parliamentary government in favour of a six-month royal dictatorship, but Belgium rapidly recovered. The Socialists, rising in importance under Paul-Henri Spaak, who in 1938 became Belgium's first Socialist Premier, gave staunch support to parliamentary democracy in coalitions with the Catholics. King Albert himself was both immensely popular and strictly constitutional, and, except for Flemish separatists and insignificant Right Wing groups, opposition to Belgian democracy hardly existed until the 1930s when Fascist groups arose.

Holland, like the other maritime neutrals, suffered heavy shipping losses during the war but these were soon made good, and only the great depression and occasional colonial disturbances such as the East Indian rebellion of 1926–27 affected Dutch phlegm, until the rise of Nazi Germany stimulated measures against Dutch Nazis and revolutionary Left Wing groups.

Portugal, though she had fought with the Allies and was nominally a democracy after December 1918, was ripe for military or Fascist coups because of her economic backwardness, staggering illiteracy and governmental corruption and inefficiency. One military coup in April 1925 failed only because of inadequate leaders, for the government was hopelessly discredited. A second, in May 1926, succeeded and dissolved parliament and the political parties, but proved itself equally inept and was overthrown in July by a rival junta under General Antonio Carmona. He appointed an extremely able finance minister, the former economics professor Antonio de Oliveira Salazar, who by 1929 was to establish a clerical dictatorship of remarkable longevity and efficiency.

Spain, neutral in the war, also underwent a period of military dictatorship. After 1917 the army played a prominent political role, and indeed made and overthrew governments. The failure of the politicians to solve the thorny problems posed first by Catalan demands for home rule, and then by the Moroccan Riff rebellion against France and Spain, weakened their already precarious position. In July 1921 the Riff leader Abdel Krim humiliatingly defeated the Spanish army at Anual. A political crisis followed immediately and an enquiry was held. The army and the king, Alfonso XIII, were the chief culprits, but the parliamentary system was virtually moribund. Hence the Captain-General and virtual dictator in Catalonia, Primo de Rivera, suppressed the enquiry's report, and with Alfonso's blessing and considerable popular support established a military dictatorship. Though he admired Mussolini, he hoped to restore the parliamentary *régime* which he had destroyed. In December 1925 he stepped down as dictator to become Premier in a largely military cabinet, but he could not win over the old politicians. In 1926 therefore he began to build a new party, for he disliked the army's assumption of its divine right to supply the backbone for what the Spanish philosopher Ortega y Gasset called an 'invertebrate' country, but Primo's 'Patriotic Union' could not supply the deficiency. Influenced by his Italian model (though in fact Primo resembled Pilsudski, not Mussolini) he established a corporative assembly in 1927, to prepare the way for a new constitutional *régime* which he hoped would be endorsed by plebiscite in 1931. But in 1930, discouraged at his lack of popular support, he resigned and his defeat meant the end of the quasi-constitutional monarchy.

Although few solid democratic political structures were created in Europe as the result of a war officially fought after America's entry to secure democracy, at least until the 1930s there was a greater measure of freedom and of social justice than there had been in 1914. Moreover, conditions seemed worse than in fact they were, because of the unduly high hopes entertained after the defeat of the authoritarian empires, and because of the golden promises of peace and prosperity made by the democratic leaders, including Wilson. Wilson had been the hope of European liberals and democrats when he had crusaded for settlements based on 'clearly recognizable lines of nationality', 'impartial adjustment of colonial claims', diplomacy conducted 'always frankly and in the public view', and even 'removal, so far as possible of all economic barriers'. No doubt he attempted too much, and he showed peevish ingratitude when the slippery but realistic Lloyd George saved him from many of the consequences of his ill-considered promises. His goal of establishing a democratic Europe, well-intentioned though it was, was not without an element of Messianic megalomania. However he left Europe much better than he found her, a success achieved by few statesmen. Neither was he responsible for the bitter disillusionment which characterized the inter-war years.

The social and economic devastation wrought by the war necessitated large-scale relief for Belgium and the countries of central and eastern Europe. Only the non-European states, especially America, could provide

318

this. In the four and a half years after the armistice America supplied a total of $1,415,000,000 in relief, approximately 86% of this sum before the Versailles treaty. Only America could have intervened to such effect to give Europe time to recuperate. The economic dislocation was far more serious in eastern than in western Europe, and most serious of all in Russia, which underwent virtual economic collapse. Little could be done to relieve Russia for physical and political reasons, but central and eastern Europe would have revived more quickly had raw materials been provided as well as food and medical aid. Repayment of relief aid was not in fact a burden, for, though only 8% of it was given free, only 29% was actually repaid; repayment of the remaining 63% was practically unenforceable. Cessation of Russian foreign trade cut off the central and eastern countries from one major supply of the raw materials needed to restart their industries, and overseas supplies were largely monopolized by America and western European countries who had the money to pay for them. Only Czechoslovakia, which had a well-balanced economy, a prosperous middle class, and considerable financial strength (the banking system had largely emancipated itself from Vienna before 1918) enjoyed anything like the western boom of 1919–20.

Central and eastern Europe was also handicapped by the economic disturbances caused by her social revolutions, and by the great population migrations. The greatest of these was the flood of refugees from Soviet Russia, which numbered over a million and a half by the end of 1920. When America restricted emigration through the 1921 and 1924 quota laws she blocked a great outlet for these people (and for Italians and others who had gone in large numbers to America before the war). Germany absorbed refugees from both east and west, but these were mainly Germans. France, with a pressing demographic problem caused by a population which was declining before 1914, welcomed foreign workers, but among these immigrants, Italians, Swiss and Belgians far outnumbered Poles and other eastern Europeans. Latin America took eastern Europeans among her approximately 3,000,000 immigrants before 1929, of whom about half remained permanently, but the British Dominions followed the American example of restricting immigration to northern Europeans. This had the effect of increasing the already wide gap in living standards and general economic development between the prosperous and advanced countries of north-western Europe and the poor, retarded southern and eastern European countries.

On the other hand the war opened up possibilities of improving the national economies, though these were often neglected. War-time exigencies had forced widespread government intervention in social and economic life, and, though pressure from business and industrial interests brought rapid dismantling of the apparatus of state economic regulation after the war, the older system of *laissez-faire* could not be entirely restored. Rationing, price-fixing and subsidy machinery were largely abandoned, but regulations for wages and working conditions remained, and the position of governments in the economic life of the nation had been permanently altered. After mobilization for total war the national economies could never be the same again. Walter Rathenau, who had directed Germany's war economy, had insisted that the economic task was a national, not an individual concern, and that collectivization of the 'commanding heights' of the national economy must endure after the war. In 1917 Rathenau had foreseen the economic chaos that would result from the war and had realized that only state control could enable Germany—and other countries —to make the efforts required to check inflation, solve balance of payments problems, make good the great capital losses, and establish an international machinery of economic co-operation, without which the international economy would founder. But he rejected socialism, insisting that state direction of industry would produce better results. Indeed the continuing chaos of Soviet Russia discouraged the adoption of socialism.

During the war Germany had reached a stage in controlling the economy not approached elsewhere. Britain and France followed her example at a more leisurely pace. America, who had least need to plan her resources, hardly followed it at all, and remained the bulwark of economic individualism. Inevitably, therefore, after World War I America led the return to what President Harding in his 1920 election campaign called 'normalcy', 'the good days of prosperity and peace'. This was economic lunacy in the closely integrated national economies and straitened circumstances of Europe after November 1918, as it was in America after 1929. Britain attempted to return to pre-war patterns, jettisoning most of her war-time controls and maintaining a largely free-trade system in a world of high tariffs and quotas. She hoped to restore thereby the flow of international trade which had been so marked a feature of the pre-war international economy, but in the prevailing atmosphere of economic chauvinism she won little support.

France retained some measure of government control over the economy as the best method of ensuring the economic revival of her devastated northern provinces and the economic integration of the regained provinces of Alsace-Lorraine. Pre-occupation with maintaining the value of the franc, for purposes of general international prestige as well as of economic recovery, also entailed considerable governmental intervention. Even so, French public finance remained one of the worst among the major economic powers, with its deficits, bad budgetary system, and anti-social taxation structure, which was due to its refusal to enforce a socially fair level of income tax. However, government-controlled finance did help to save France from the mass unemployment which afflicted Britain in the inter-war years. The large-scale wartime destruction enforced a heavy level of investment (necessitating some measure of government supervision) and considerable modernization in the important steel industry. The vigorous French economic expansion until 1929 was largely due to increased coal mining and steel production and expansion in the related railway and canal systems.

Germany's course was different, partly because of reparations. These were actually paid by creditors and by America as creditor of Germany's creditors, but they distorted German economic development as well as increasing the instability of the international economy. Germany, like the other powers, rejected Keynes's argument that governments should shoulder responsibility for full employment and economic growth, but gave legal recognition to the increased power of the trade unions. They had legal rights to share in drawing up conditions of labour and to negotiate collective wage contracts. The constitution guaranteed the eight-hour day, and the state remained arbiter between highly organized labour and industrial organizations. Although the state fostered investment, it left industrial organization to the huge cartels, notably the steel trust and the chemical IG Farben trust. These were formally constituted in the second half of the decade, though their origins went back to imperial Germany, and the trend to cartelization was unmistakable in the early twenties. The limits of governmental power were shown very clearly when the great German industrial magnates refused to tolerate the amount of direct taxation necessary to meet the heavy costs of keeping the Ruhr workers on unemployment pay when France and Belgium invaded the Ruhr in 1923, though the object was to deny these countries as far as possible any economic advantages.

Italy also gave free rein to private capitalism, even after the inflation had destroyed what little sense of national unity existed immediately after the war. Bread subsidies and inordinate expenditure on the army and government services threatened the country with bankruptcy. Italy was ripe for social revolution, but the Socialists lost their opportunity by waiting for the *bourgeois* state to dissolve. Their former leader Mussolini, whom they had expelled, rightly saw that of the three major forces strengthened in Europe by the war—democracy, nationalism and socialism—nationalism was by far the most potent as it thrived on hatreds. Accordingly, after briefly proclaiming socialist objectives in the early days of Fascism, he abandoned them in order to gain the support of capitalists, industrialists and big landowners whose interests were involved in maintaining the *status quo* against revolutionary peasants and urban workers.

Although World War I accelerated processes of decline, it also increased the rate of technological and economic advance in certain sectors. Even the static trench warfare had not prevented the increasing motorization of the armies, except for the Russian army, which lagged behind in that respect just as Russia lagged behind in the automobile industry during the inter-war years with disastrous consequences during World War II. This stimulus to the automobile industry had major social and economic effects after 1919, as did military development of the airplane, which in Europe became an economic source of transport earlier than in America. Thanks to the revolution in transport brought about by the automobile, and to new developments in the use of electricity, Europe after 1918 had the opportunity to exploit immensely increased potential productive capacities. Admittedly the essential technological bases for both automobile and electrical industries had been laid before 1914, but the inter-war period saw such extensive developments that transport, agriculture and industry were revolutionized. The transformation was at least equivalent to that produced by the earlier development of steam power.

Moreover, progress in electrification is one of the great exceptions to the picture of inter-war stagnation, for in this field Europe certainly kept pace with America, and the relatively backward European countries advanced more quickly than the others. Between 1910 and 1920 technological difficulties in exploiting hydro-electric sources, using coal more economically and increasing voltage were largely overcome, as were problems of distributing electric power considerable distances from the generating stations. This exploitation of electric power improved agricultural productivity and made it possible to locate industries close to large areas of urban consumption. Increased electrification facilitated new methods of mass production in industries, specialization of manufacturing and assembly plant within industries, production of greater ranges of both capital and consumer goods, and in consequence the growth of new mass markets for cheap, standardized products. Aided by war-time (notably German) developments in all kinds of synthetics, above all in chemical synthetics, the great new industries of plastics, rubber, electro-chemical processes and rayon (barely coming into production in 1914) expanded rapidly. Electrical welding introduced to speed wartime shipbuilding, employment of diesel engines in ships and the development of the aircraft and radio industries were also major inter-war advances. So were the use of continuous steel rolling mills and introduction of electricity as the normal method of public and domestic lighting. The social consequences of decentralization in urban housing, of radio and the cinema as the first genuinely mass media of entertainment, and, in a more restricted field of pleasure, of motoring, were also of the first importance.

Most of these developments would have taken place in any case, though not so quickly or extensively without the war, which stimulated demands for social reform, and gave a considerable impetus to rationalization and mass production to meet the unprecedented demand for munitions. Nevertheless, in politically and economically conservative Britain the older industries put up strong resistance to changes in manufacturing methods and the use of new materials, while in the leading European countries taken together the rate of progress was far too slow, though it would have been slower still without the impact of the war.

Problems of postwar reconstruction and re-integration of the European states into the world economic community overshadowed all other problems in the 1920s. For America these years were the 'New Era', for Europe years of economic insecurity even in the boom of 1919–20 and the longer and more solid boom which came after 1924. Much of the insecurity of the new gold standard was due to British losses of overseas investment and markets in the war, and it never worked as smoothly after 1925 as it had done before 1914. Even more troubles stemmed from the foolish hopes, admittedly not shared by Britain, first that German reparations would solve western Europe's financial difficulties, and then that inflation would. Hence Europe, and especially her masses, paid for the war twice over: in blood from 1914 to 1918, and in economic privation thereafter.

## Chapter III
# THE EUROPEAN STATES AFTER 1918

## (i) *The Victorious Western Allies*

BRITAIN emerged from the war with her major objectives secured. Germany's navy had been destroyed, her overseas empire dissolved, and her Napoleonic ambitions in Europe checked. But Britain had had to pay a heavy price on the battlefield, and in her losses of overseas trade and imperial power. The war in fact made the Commonwealth a reality. The 1917 Imperial Conference had asserted the Dominions' and India's right to an adequate voice in foreign policy, and the Commonwealth's constitution existed before its members signed the treaties and joined the League of Nations. When Balfour in 1926 defined Britain and the Dominions as 'autonomous communities within the British Empire, equal in status, in no way subordinate one to another in any aspect of their domestic or internal affairs, though united by a common allegiance to the Crown, and freely associated as members of the British Commonwealth of Nations', he described a situation already firmly established in 1919. The Dominions merely insisted more than they had in the past on an independent voice in matters of foreign policy affecting them, without being more willing to admit that the right to share in determining foreign policy entailed the obligation to share its burdens. When Lloyd George attempted to involve the Dominions in war with Turkey by the Chanak incident of 1922 the assertion of Commonwealth independence was unmistakable, and again in the same year Canada demonstrated the supreme importance to her of good relations with America by independently negotiating a treaty with Washington. Similarly in 1925 the Dominions and India excluded themselves from British obligations under Locarno. Equality, however, was a pretence. Britain could not treat the Dominions as equals because of her greater population, resources, geographical position and rank as a Great Power, with its concomitant defence, foreign policy and economic burdens.

Lloyd George's immediate task after the armistice was to win the peace as, he flattered himself (with some justice), he had won the war, and to make good his wartime promises to the British people. A general election was long overdue. The electorate had been greatly increased by enfranchising all adult males and many women, and obviously the government had to obtain a mandate before negotiating peace. Lloyd George wanted the coalition to continue into peacetime, but he made no discreditable bargain by agreeing to the 'coupon' election. Agreed candidates, Liberals, Conservatives and a Labour sprinkling, were officially endorsed, and their candidatures unopposed by loyalists. But for this device the Lloyd George Liberals would have been wiped out earlier than they actually were, although it saddened many radicals who had hitherto supported them. Lloyd George's demands for 'hanging the Kaiser' and recovering full costs of the war from Germany coincided with popular sentiment. He did not exploit it; he merely voiced it. Doubtless he was equally sincere in promising a country fit for heroes to live in. He certainly wished to conciliate Ireland and carry out sweeping social reforms, but he was the prisoner of the Conservative Party, the majority party in British politics until 1945. The election of 1918 returned 339 Conservatives (Coalition Unionists), only 136 Coalition Liberals, 26 Asquithites, and 59 Labour members, most of these trade unionists. Labour's anti-war leaders, MacDonald, Henderson and Snowden, had been defeated in the jingoistic election atmosphere, and returned to Parliament through by-elections.

Lloyd George found it hard to relinquish dictatorial habits assumed during the war, and was soon at loggerheads with the Conservative ministers, but he was indispensable for the moment. His return after concluding the Versailles Treaty was a triumph, soon to be tarnished when he tried to moderate its application. However, most Labour men and many Liberals deplored Versailles' treatment of Germany and tenderness to the agents of French 'imperialism' in Europe—with some justice in Poland's case but not in Czechoslovakia's. In 1919 the domestic economy experienced an unexpected boom instead of the expected depression and 'social revolution'. Intervention on the White side in the Russian Civil War raised angry protests from radicals as well as Socialists, for there was then considerable popular sympathy for the Bolsheviks. Proposals in 1920, after intervention was practically over, to fight on Poland's side were hurriedly dropped in face of the threat of a general strike. Yet though the Russian example stimulated the extreme Left, the foundation of the Communist Party in July 1920 had little effect on the solid mass of Labour supporters, and the Labour Party refused to allow Lenin's Trojan horse to enter its ranks through affiliation, a refusal which was to be maintained in the future. Nevertheless, Communism gained ground among the Durham and South Wales miners when Lloyd George refused to nationalize the coal mines, as the miners demanded. Government control over the mines was retained until March 1921, when they were in serious difficulties because of reduced overseas markets. The problem of the mines remained serious until it exploded into the 1926 general strike. The miners had wanted a general strike in 1919, but their railwaymen allies under J. H. Thomas and the dockers under Ernest Bevin, soon to be the great figure in British trade unionism, had preferred collective bargaining. A miners' strike in

October 1920 brought them concessions, but the industry was obviously running down. In 1921 the boom ended when the artificially high demand caused by wartime restrictions on consumer goods had been satisfied. Loss of overseas coal, textile and engineering markets then took a heavy toll and in June 1921 unemployment exceeded 2,000,000 and never again between the wars fell below 1,000,000. To alleviate distress high rates of unemployment benefit were paid, and Lloyd George pursued conciliation abroad more strongly than ever in order to restore the international economy on which British prosperity depended.

Though he never achieved that objective, Lloyd George finally made a settlement with Ireland. In December 1918 73 Sinn Feiners were elected. Instead of coming to Westminster they established an Irish parliament, the Dail, in Dublin. Ireland's cause was not heard in Paris, though it was put to Wilson, and his different sets of values for Irish and Continental national claims alienated Irish-Americans in the 1920 Presidential election. Admittedly only 47% of the Irish electorate had voted for Sinn Fein in December 1918, but the Dail acted as if it had the overwhelming support of the southern Irish and the right to speak for Ulster also. It made De Valera its president and formed a republican government which exercised real control. It hoped to win independence peacefully, but the Irish Republican Army under Michael Collins began 'the troubles' by launching a small-scale war against the British. The British government replied to IRA terror by bringing in the notorious Black and Tans to reinforce the police, and then the Auxiliary Division ('Auxis'), who together rivalled the excesses of the German freebooters on the new Polish-German frontier.

Civil war began at Easter 1920, and continued to ravage Southern Ireland after Lloyd George in December partitioned the country into the South, which continued the rebellion, and the six counties of Northern Ireland, which henceforth were comparatively peaceful. He offered home rule to both, and Ulster accepted this, but not the suggested Council of Ireland, composed of members from Ulster and the south. The south refused outright and civil war intensified. On Smuts's advice and with Lloyd George's approval, King George V, when opening the Northern Ireland parliament in June 1921, appealed for an end to war. De Valera responded, and, though the IRA continued to fight, agreement was reached in December that Ireland should become the Irish Free State, with Dominion status as Smuts had suggested. Ulster had the right to withdraw and did so. De Valera refused to accept the treaty, and civil war continued in 1922 between his new Republican Party, supported by IRA irreconcilables, and Collins' more moderate faction.

After Collins' murder in August 1922 the government was run by W. T. Cosgrave, on behalf of the now dominant Catholic *bourgeoisie*. In December 1922 the formal decease of the Union was ratified, giving the Free State Dominion status on Canada's model, which meant in time power to end all connection with Britain. Britain held only three 'treaty ports' (Lough

Swilly, Queenstown and Berehaven) but Ulster retained her connection and her Protestant ascendancy. In the Free State the system of proportional representation was instituted at the demand of the British Parliament, but not in Northern Ireland, which adopted the electoral system common throughout the United Kingdom. Partition remained to disrupt harmony between Dublin and Belfast, and between Dublin and London. Though IRA atrocities matched British brutalities they had more justification, for they had aimed at ending foreign domination, and the Conservative-dominated British Parliament would never have conceded independence without Ireland's resort to force. The worst atrocities, however, were those inflicted by Cosgrave and De Valera supporters on each other. Before the civil war ended in the spring of 1923 Cosgrave's government executed far more nationalists than the British had done between 1919 and 1921. It was not until 1927 that De Valera returned to political life, but then he rapidly dominated it. In 1932 he became Premier and at once began to work towards taking the Free State out of the Commonwealth.

The Irish question, together with failures to revive the British economy and Lloyd George's unpopular foreign policy, discredited the Coalition government, and many radical Liberals went over to Labour. Moreover by 1922 the Conservative rank-and-file in Parliament and some of its leaders wanted a wholly Conservative government. The Chanak incident provided the opportunity. Bonar Law became Prime Minister in October 1922, with Stanley Baldwin as Chancellor of the Exchequer. Neither Austen Chamberlain nor Winston Churchill was in the cabinet, Churchill still being a Liberal as well as a Coalitionist. In March 1923 Neville Chamberlain became Minister of Health, a very minor post, but his energy and ability were at once apparent. On Law's death Baldwin became Prime Minister, retaining the Chancellorship until he turned it over to Neville Chamberlain in August 1923. Though both Austen Chamberlain and Churchill returned to the Conservative fold, their belief that there were more important things in politics than Conservative retention of office meant that they never won the loyalty shown to Neville Chamberlain and Baldwin, who between them dominated British politics from the mid-1920s until 1940.

The general election of November 1922 gave the Conservatives a strong majority, and marked the continued decline of the Lloyd George and Asquith Liberal factions. The Conservatives could have served their full five-year term had not Baldwin rashly abandoned his usual safety-first policy. Convinced that Britain would never restore her economic strength unless she entirely abandoned free trade, he held a general election in December 1923 on protection. The Conservatives suffered widespread losses but retained 258 seats against Labour's 191 and the Liberals' 159. The Free Trade issue temporarily reunited the Liberals, and they held the balance of power. As they could not accept protection, especially when the electorate had rejected Baldwin's specious argument that it was the only remedy for unemployment, Labour under Ramsay MacDonald was given its first opportunity to govern.

Against all expectations MacDonald's government pursued solidly Liberal policies instead of indulging in an orgy of nationalization and planning. It was essentially a trade union and proletarian government, and as such reformist, not Socialist. It carried out a successful housing programme, laid the basis for a good system of secondary education, adopted a strictly orthodox financial policy with Philip Snowden as Chancellor of the Exchequer, and tried to follow a foreign policy which offered genuine support for the League instead of the lip service paid by the Conservatives. MacDonald, who was not prone to undervalue himself, was Foreign Secretary as well as Premier.

A coherent domestic policy might have overcome some of the handicaps imposed by the ministers' inexperience in government, but a Socialist policy would have repelled more voters than it attracted, and without a parliamentary majority was out of the question. MacDonald publicly proclaimed that profiteering was as rampant among trade unionists as among capitalists, declaring that strikes for increased wages and limitation of output were contrary to the Socialist movement's spirit. His capacity for meaningless but noble generalities was seen to perfection at Geneva. Practical mastery of foreign affairs eluded him. He recognized Russia without improving relations with her, and conciliated Germany at French expense without improving relations with Germany either. He was brought down because he mishandled a minor matter involving a Communist editor who had published seditious articles.

The general election of October 1924 was notable for the first use of radio broadcasting in a campaign, and for the 'Red Scare'. Grigori Zinoviev, head of the Comintern, was alleged to have ordered the British Communist Party to start seditious activities. The 'Zinoviev letter' was probably forged; it violently attacked Labour; but the Conservatives seized on it as evidence that Labour was in league with Communism. The Conservative technique was worthy of the post-World War II witch-hunt of Communists and Socialists in America, but it had no effect on the election's outcome beyond inducing some Liberal or uncommitted electors to vote Conservative. MacDonald was rattled and ineffective, yet Labour made a net gain of a million votes from Liberals, who lost even more to the Conservatives. Baldwin's blatant pursuit of electoral advantage by dropping protection within a year paid handsome dividends. Conservatives now numbered 419, among them Churchill, who was made Chancellor of the Exchequer. Neville Chamberlain, Baldwin's only serious rival, was ruthlessly relegated again to the Ministry of Health, while Austen Chamberlain became Foreign Secretary. The Liberals, united under Lloyd George again as Asquith lost his seat in the Commons and went to the House of Lords, had only 40 seats, a further stage in their decline. Labour blamed its defeat on the Red Scare instead of on its own incompetence. James Maxton, leader of the Independent Labour Party faction, attributed defeat to the abandonment of Socialism, and took his group out of the main Party. However the Conservative victory was decisive, and marked the end of the postwar period.

France in 1919 elected an even more conservative lower house than Britain had done, in fact more conservative than any other in this century. This reversal nevertheless marked no genuine change in electoral allegiance. Left Wing parties polled a higher popular vote than in 1914, and until World War II won every election except that of 1928. But the Left-Centre dominated these groups as the Right-Centre dominated the Right. The French Socialists never obtained more than a quarter of the votes in the inter-war years, and were no more a working class party than they had been before 1914. The establishment of the French Communist Party made moderate Socialists more respectable in Radical eyes, but destroyed the Left's electoral prospects in November 1919 by hopelessly dividing it. Although France remained solidly conservative throughout the 1920s, the 'Horizon Blue' Chamber, with its ex-servicemen predominating, was an electoral fluke, and the victorious Right-Centre and Right Bloc National rapidly disintegrated. On the other hand the Communists, now the only genuinely revolutionary party, divided the Left still further and simultaneously strengthened the extreme Right. A great Socialist and Communist demonstration in November 1924, when Jaurès's ashes were transferred to the Pantheon, led to a crop of Right Wing leagues with Fascist orientations, supported by many former Socialists. As they were not then necessary to the enemies of the Left they died down, to be revived again in the 1930s.

The republican system remained unaltered until the grant of quasi-dictatorial powers on the eve of World War II, and it operated much as it had done before 1914. Clemenceau was overthrown in January 1920 largely because of dissatisfaction at the comparative lenience of Versailles towards Germany, and the Presidential election went not to him but to the nonentity Paul Deschanel. Alexandre Millerand succeeded first Clemenceau as Premier and then Deschanel as President on Deschanel's death. Two short ministries intervened, one headed by Briand, before Poincaré formed his second and third ministries (January 1922–June 1924). He was mainly concerned with obtaining maximum reparations from Germany, stabilizing the franc and ensuring French hegemony in Europe. In February 1921 Briand made a defensive treaty with Poland on both anti-Soviet and anti-German bases, but Poland was no substitute for Tsarist Russia. Far from redressing French numerical inferiority towards Germany, the Franco-Polish treaty underlined it by giving Germany better opportunities for good relations with Russia, and the 'haggard France which faced the dawn' of victory in 1918 enjoyed less security than she had before 1914. Poincaré attempted to reinforce the alliance by underwriting the Little *Entente* coalition of Yugoslavia, Czechoslovakia and Rumania, formed on an anti-Hungarian basis, and then by a separate treaty with Czechoslovakia in January 1924. But the two mainstays of France's system of eastern alliances, Poland and Czechoslovakia, were not on good terms because of Poland's claims to Teschen and generally anti-Czech line. The abortive Franco-Belgian invasion of the Ruhr in 1923 in any event demonstrated the failure of the intransigent line towards Germany. Moreover, by raising the spectre of war, Poincaré played into the hands of the Left, which capitalized on the nation's anxieties to win the May 1924 election.

As in Britain, little was done to reduce the backlog of social reforms. The General Confederation of Labour, the CGT, was temporarily dissolved by court order in January 1921 because of its domination by syndicalists, though it constituted no real danger to the state. National morale had survived the shocks of war, and syndicalists and Socialists alike were improbable imitators of Bolshevism. Indeed postwar politics were too much like the prewar variety for France's well-being.

Industrial and agricultural production had declined during the war, exports had slumped by 75%, and France had suffered relatively more during the war than any other European power except Russia. However, of the major causes of weakness in her economy after 1918, only losses in manpower and her declining birth-rate were ineradicable. The devastated areas were soon re-equipped, and the recovery of Alsace-Lorraine enabled France to enlarge and strengthen her industrial base. The war did not make France a poor country despite the loss of investments in Turkey and Russia. But this, with government failure to repay war loans, severely hit the *rentiers*, and was one of the major causes of inter-war political instability.

France did not seize her opportunities to reshape her economy, though the way had been prepared. German occupation of the north-eastern industrial zone had forced France to build up new industrial regions in central and southern France, and especially around Paris itself. Again, though the war had stimulated heavy industry and steel production increased rapidly after 1918, economic transformation did not go far enough. However, the economic changes had considerable political consequences. They swelled the ranks of the proletariat, again especially around Paris, whose 'red belt' formed the most radical section of the inter-war labour and trade union movement, and gave Left Wing Socialists and Communists a solid measure of support.

Nevertheless Paris continued to be the chief stronghold of the *petit bourgeoisie*, and revealed the stresses and strains of economic and political structures which were really designed to suit the small man. The high-tariff system both allowed many more peasant proprietors to survive in France than in any other western European country, and favoured the small industrialist. By 1931 only half the industrial proletariat worked for firms employing over 100 men, only a quarter for those employing over 500; nearly two-thirds of French firms had no paid employees, and most of the remainder were small family businesses. As France remained essentially a *petit bourgeois* country both politically and exonomically, she continued on the whole to be ruled by centre coalitions which disliked Right, but more particularly Left, extremists. These coalitions pursued the common objectives of defending the Republic against its enemies, defending the franc, and preserving French security. Until the great depression and the rise of Nazi Germany this was done successfully, if sometimes precariously.

But in one respect, that of overseas empire, France reached her zenith in the inter-war years. Accessions from Germany's African and Turkey's Middle Eastern empires increased French overseas territory to about 4,500,000 square miles, and overseas population to practically double that of France herself. However, the French empire had no territories comparable to the British Dominions, and its civil service had no concepts of trusteeship. Some members of the native *élites* were given high posts in the colonial service, but only in Martinique, Guadeloupe and Réunion were serious attempts made to integrate the native societies into French political life, although the conciliatory Lyautey strove hard to create a common Franco-Moroccan culture. The closed imperial economic system worked almost entirely to France's benefit; even colonial public works were financed for the benefit of French capital.

The system of colonial administration was rigidly bureaucratic, and the kind of effective criticism of imperial policies voiced in Britain was seldom heard in France, for the Communist, Socialist and Radical Socialist critics were practically powerless to alter the system. Their protests in support of the Indo-Chinese peasantry, struggling under an intolerable burden of debt, carried no more weight than those of the Indo-Chinese themselves, who had been urged by French officials after 1914 to enlist in the struggle for freedom; German militarism was then the enemy; now it was French imperialism. The future Chinese Communist Premier, Chou En-lai, was among those who came to France in this way, and there absorbed Marxist and anti-imperialist doctrines. In 1919 the Tunisian Destour nationalist party was formed clandestinely; it emerged openly as a political party in 1920. In 1922 France was obliged to give some economic power to mixed Franco-Tunisian councils in an attempt to satisfy the growing demand for self-government. In Algeria the *Etoile Norde Africaine* followed a similar line. In Morocco, however, an attempt by Spain and France in 1925 to subdue the Riff country provoked Abdel Krim to attack the French. The Riff campaign ended in May 1926 only after a major Franco-Spanish onslaught under Pétain; even so French control of Morocco was not completed until 1934.

Another area of serious disturbance was Indo-China. The Vietnamese reacted vigorously to principles of national self-determination preached during the war, and the Kuomintang had contacts among the Annamese. In 1930 there were widespread outbreaks of violence, and a mutiny in Yenbay. The French put down the disturbances with great severity, and took the opportunity of dissolving the Annamese nationalist party and driving the Communists underground. By 1925 French indifference to the interests and national susceptibilities of subject peoples also brought the leading families of Syria to the point of rebellion, though at first they had been ready to accept French rule. The insurrection by Sultan Pasha's

Druzes which began in July 1925 lasted for almost two years. In the meantime France proclaimed the Great Lebanon a republic, but a Syrian settlement was made only in 1932 with the election of an assembly and a president approved by France. However, in the Middle East the French were no more maladroit than the British, only weaker, and the nationalist movements in the Mediterranean region made little headway except in the North African territories before the outbreak of World War II.

Italy's political and economic structures had been unstable before her entry into the war, which probably cost Italy 148,000,000,000 lire, equivalent to double the total of her 1861–1913 government expenditure, while war-time needs also caused considerable exhaustion of the soil. Conversion from war-time to peace-time economy was mismanaged, so that 1919 saw more hardship than had any of the war years. With living standards depressed by shortages and inflation, civil servants and urban workers resorted to strikes. Anarchists, Bolshevik sympathizers and other extremists advocated the seizure of factories and land, sabotage and a concerted effort to paralyse the economy in order to prepare for social revolution. Had the Socialists been revolutionaries they might easily have made 1919 the Italian '1917', but the economic breakdown which constantly threatened never took place. On the contrary, there was a slow but general growth of economic activity from 1918 to 1922. In 1920, though strikes were endemic, there was virtually no unemployment. 1922 was the worst year, with bad crops and industrial failures, but before Mussolini made his 'march on Rome' the crisis had been overcome. The governmental debts piled up during the war had been wiped out by the mercilessly heavy taxes imposed since 1918, a policy which no French government dared to adopt. The heavy budget deficits of 1918–22 resulted from paying off war debts, as even the Fascists originally acknowledged. This, not Mussolini's advent, explains why the 1922–23 deficit was only 3,620,000,000 lire as against the average for the previous four years of 18,250,000,000 lire, figures later used to explain how Mussolini had miraculously saved Italy from bankruptcy after October 1922. In 1921 the Italian government for the first time since 1915 did not need foreign loans.

In 1922, though Italy was not a Great Power (and could never become one because of her shortage of natural resources), she was economically stronger and richer than in 1915, and territorially was grossly over-rewarded for her relatively small war effort. The war, while dislocating her economy, had stimulated industrial re-equipment, and had encouraged the building of new power stations; on balance it was a good business deal. Nevertheless extensive economic and social reforms remained to be carried through, especially in the depressed agricultural south, before the country could realize her potentialities. The parliamentary *régime* made a beginning, but it was only a beginning, and it fell to Mussolini to continue the work. In fact he merely made a show of reshaping the economy, though for a long time he deceived many people, Italians and foreigners alike. His Fascist *régime* had many foreign well-wishers, including both Chamberlains,

Churchill, and—for he appealed to the Left also—Ramsay MacDonald.

It was not economic crisis but political collapse which brought Mussolini to power. Parliamentary government was discredited first by its failure in foreign policy. Orlando's government foolishly encouraged its excitable and chauvinistic supporters by making excessive claims. These claims lost it the favour of the Allied leaders, and in particular of Wilson, who in exasperation unwisely appealed to the Italians over the head of their own government; he was savagely derided by the Italians for his pains. Italy also sacrificed a great opportunity to make a friend of her new Yugoslav neighbour. She demanded complete control of the Adriatic, partly from territorial greed, but also because she felt insecure while the eastern Adriatic was controlled by a Great Power, as Austria-Hungary had been in relation to Italy, or by a state supported by a Great Power, as Yugoslavia was by France. Some of the wiser Italian generals doubted Italy's capacity to control the eastern Adriatic coastline, but insatiable territorial appetite and old dreams of a new Roman Empire carried the day. The issue of the Yugoslav frontier brought down Orlando's government in June 1919 and formed the bitterest political problem until 1920. The Italo-Yugoslav Treaty of Rapallo marked the effective end of parliamentary government as well as the end of claims on the Allies, except for minor colonial adjustments. However, parliamentary government would probably not have survived, even had there been no crises over foreign policy.

General postwar distress was a natural breeding ground for Fascist as well as Communist movements, but Italy was particularly vulnerable to adventurers prepared to take risks and exploit the revolutionary situation. The ruling classes had lost their power and the middle classes feared for their property and security in the face of anarchy and inflation. Demobilized soldiers provided recruits for the Fascist strong-arm squads which Mussolini and his lieutenants formed when his movement had been established in Milan in March 1919. His *Fascio di Combattimento* had no real political programme beyond its appeal to nationalism, for Fascism, unlike Socialism, was never an international movement, though it made headway in many countries after Mussolini had given the example. Italian Fascism, moreover, did not become a mass movement until after it had taken power. In the 1919 elections the major parties were the Socialists, and the Christian Democrats or *Popolari*, a Catholic party with a strongly Socialist platform demanding land redistribution and better conditions for the urban working class. The Church preferred Mussolini's black-shirted *squadristi* as allies against Socialism, though Right Wing elements controlled the Christian Democrats. Opposition to the anti-clericalism of Giovanni Giolitti's Liberals prevented clericals from allying with *Popolari* and as they could not work with the Socialists either, parliamentary anarchy eventually permitted Mussolini to take over the government. Also Giolitti preferred Mussolini to *Popolari* or Socialists, who in 1919 were the biggest party. Socialists, in their turn, not only would not collaborate with Liberals or *Popolari*, preferring to voice revolutionary slogans which they had no intention of implementing, but also were deeply divided among themselves. They could not force themselves into office, but could prevent others from governing while they waited for the 'inevitable' proletarian revolution to establish a Socialist republic. The radical Francesco Nitti, who succeeded Orlando as Premier, did not understand the changes made in the political system by the development of mass Catholic, Socialist and nationalist parties instead of the old, small groups with which it had been possible to strike realistic political bargains. He also failed to foresee the consequences of his introduction of proportional representation for the elections of November 1919, the freest and fairest which Italy was to have until after World War II.

*Popolari* then secured 100 seats, the Socialists 156, Giolitti's Centrists 91, the Radical Liberals 67, Right Liberals 23, Ivanoe Bonomi's Independent Socialists (moderates who accepted the parliamentary framework) 21 as before, and the Republicans only 9. The Fascists were humiliatingly defeated, with only 4,000 votes, and Mussolini appeared to have no political future. He revived by rapidly abandoning his remaining Socialist ideas, and taking up nationalism in the highly dramatic form just exhibited by Gabriele D'Annunzio in seizing Fiume. D'Annunzio's legionaries, with their daggers, death skulls on their insignia and massed bellowings before their leader, strutting and declaiming from a balcony, provided the pattern for Mussolini's Blackshirts, and many of their recruits. D'Annunzio also provided Mussolini with a model in the technique of 'balcony choreography'. Hence while the Socialists refused to collaborate with the democratic parties, thereby ensuring that universal suffrage would lead to dictatorship, Mussolini abandoned his anarchist postures, and sent his strong-arm squads into operation against Socialists and the new Communist Party formed out of their extreme Left elements in January 1921. However, the majority of the Socialists still refused to support the government, which Giolitti had again taken over in June 1920, and with justice, for Giolitti had decided to destroy them.

Giolitti's proposals in September 1920 for tax reforms threatened the rich and the Church and led *Popolari* to withdraw their support. Doubtful of his power to retain office without them, Giolitti held another election in May 1921. His electoral coalition included nationalists and Fascists, and used the Fascist symbol. Fascist attacks on Communists, Socialists and even *Popolari* in the elections were made with police connivance, and with official backing Fascists won 35 seats. Though the Socialists had alarmed many people by greeting the king's speech in the last parliament with shouts for a republic, and had sung the *Red Flag*, they retained about 123 seats, with another 24 moderate reformists. *Popolari* had 107, Radicals 64, and Giolitti's 'National bloc' just over 100. To secure this Giolitti had made Fascism politically respectable, and brought Mussolini himself into parliament. (Hitler, in contrast, led the German Nazis without ever being a *Reichstag* deputy.)

Mussolini was still a republican, though many of his Fascists were monarchists, but otherwise he had made his peace with conservatives. In 1921 he concluded his open alliance with landowners and industrialists, who supplied the money he needed to pay his gangsters and run his propaganda machine. He was also becoming popular with army officers and Right Wing politicians. These elements were the counterparts of the groups in Germany which were to support Hitler later, and, like them, they expected to control the noisy demagogue whom they had subsidized. They had become seriously alarmed in 1920 when proletarian 'soviets' were being set up in factories, ironically often with Fascist approval. Privately Mussolini remained hostile to capitalism, but he knew how to present himself publicly as capitalism's only safe defence against Bolshevism. He proclaimed his Blackshirts the mainstay of law and order, though in fact they alone threatened it by beating up Socialists and Communists, wrecking their opponents' meetings and headquarters, and using less public methods of intimidation such as the refined torture of forcing victims to swallow large doses of castor oil. Though the May 1921 election, the first conducted under universal suffrage, showed the limits at this time of Fascism's popular appeal, by 1922 Mussolini's squads dominated northern Italy. Exaggerated fears of Bolshevism, and even of Socialism, neither of them real threats after 1920, led the old ruling classes to connive even when Fascists attacked Giolitti's government. The Liberals, including the politician and philosopher Benedetto Croce, completely misunderstood one of Fascism's major strengths, by declaring that it could not succeed because it had no programme.

In June 1921 Giolitti resigned after parliament refused him full powers to carry out budget reforms. Bonomi, who took over until February 1922, was even weaker in parliament, but it was under the Liberal Luigi Facta that all pretence of parliamentary government collapsed. In May 1922 the Fascists seized control of Bologna, and in August of Milan. However, Mussolini's nerve failed him, as it had done in December 1920 when Giolitti had been forced by Allied pressure to call D'Annunzio's empty bluff and drive Mussolini's ally from Fiume. Mussolini would have reneged on the 'March on Rome' agreed with his lieutenants, because of his ineradicable physical cowardice. He took no part in the march, arriving in comfortable safety by train after it was all over. The cabinet asked King Victor Emmanuel to declare martial law and put down the Fascists. Constitutionally he was bound to concur, and militarily it would have been a simple matter. However, the army, preferring the Fascists to their enemies, advised against martial law, and he concurred. Thereupon the parliamentary leaders advised him to invite Mussolini to form a new government, expecting that the experience would either tame or break Mussolini. Hence, despite the 'March on Rome', there was nothing unconstitutional about Mussolini's advent to power, and many parliamentarians wanted to give the Fascist experiment a chance, particularly as nobody, including Mussolini himself, yet knew what it would amount to, and there was a surprisingly widespread belief that Fascism was the essence of law and order. At this time Mussolini was intent on making an impression as a man of moderation and reason, and moreover did not fully control the Fascists. Local bosses like Dino Grandi, Italo Balbo, General Emilio De Bono and Michele Bianchi were largely independent—as they showed in 1921 by preventing Mussolini's alliance with Bonomi. Very respectable men of property as well as demobilized unemployables, landowners as well as land-hungry farmers and farm labourers, thought that Mussolini, with his remarkable political talent for being all things to all men, ought to have his opportunity. Catholics thought him their sure shield against atheistic Bolshevism, though Mussolini was an unbeliever. Above all, the lower middle classes and those proletarians who were ashamed of their origins, the predestined supporters of Fascism in all countries, gave him their support when they saw that his time had come.

His first cabinet was a coalition of Nationalists and Fascists, with the latter greatly outnumbered. On November 25th he was given dictatorial powers until December 31st, 1923, to restore the law and order which his thugs had overthrown. He did so by appointing Fascists or Fascist sympathizers as prefects. In May 1923 *Popolari* gave him their support. His followers showed their gratitude by continuing to attack the Church. In July he made his first great appeal to Italian chauvinism by instituting a vicious de-Germanization of South Tyrol. Hitler, then coming into prominence in Germany, endorsed this brutality out of deference to his admiration for Mussolini and belief in an Italo-German alliance. The South Tyrolean Germans were the worst-treated minority in Europe, but Hitler never objected even after he himself came to power. In August 1923 Mussolini chose another small victim by occupying Corfu in retaliation for the murder, allegedly by Greeks, of some Italian officials on the Albanian border. However, when Britain and France pressed for Corfu's evacuation he complied, despite his contempt for the League. He encouraged Hungarian revisionism out of hostility to France and Yugoslavia, and championed Austria and Bulgaria as well, but he mingled bellicose utterances on the themes of the military virtues and Italian claims, with assurances of friendship for the democracies whose political and cultural values he publicly derided. In November, still too weak to enforce the Fascist monopoly of power, he carried an electoral law giving the party which secured the largest number of votes two-thirds of the seats, provided that it had received 25% of the total votes; the remaining seats were to be distributed proportionately. This law, combined with Fascist electioneering techniques, would obviously produce a permanent Fascist majority.

But the 'capture' of Mussolini by Fascism, which was created much more by his ruthless lieutenants than by himself, was still far from complete. Until the spring of 1924, despite the verbiage and bluster, much of his domestic policy could be accepted by Liberals as well as Conservatives, and he had even made what could be presented as a reasonable compromise with Yugoslavia. Hence the shock was all the greater when Fascism revealed its true face in June 1924 with the murder of the moderate Socialist deputy, Giacomo Matteotti, who had published details of Fascist atrocities. Mussolini, who had thought of reverting gradually to coalition with some of the opposition elements—admittedly not in order to have a parliamentary system—was stunned. In the 'Aventine Secession' most non-Fascist deputies vowed not to return to the Chamber until the affair had been cleared up and the government's innocence proved. He implored them to return, and even considered resigning, according to some reports. Probably he never intended to do so. Certainly king, Pope, Senate and big business were confident that he would not yield the field to their Left Wing enemies.

Once the Matteotti crisis had been surmounted Mussolini advanced steadily towards dictatorship. On January 3rd, 1925, Mussolini surrendered to the Fascist extremists who demanded 'totalitarian' rule. In fact totalitarianism was never achieved in Fascist Italy, or even in Nazi Germany. Fascist ruling parties never assumed all state functions, as the Bolsheviks did under Lenin. Mussolini's dictatorship began with a cabinet reorganization, which made the ministry his personal instrument. He now even claimed responsibility for Matteotti's murder. He outlawed all other parties, repressed opposition, controlled the press, and, when the Aventine seceders returned, refused them admission. The full power of the state supported the Fascist squads' atrocities, the Fascist militia duplicated the army, Fascist tribunals were superior to the law courts, and the Fascist party with its innumerable racketeers became a burden on the tax-payer, while its functionaries became local tyrants. Open political opposition met with imprisonment, sometimes murder, and underground opposition did not effectively exist until the later 1930s. But until World War II the *régime* was not unpopular. The monarchy was retained and the law of December 1925 made the Premier responsible to it, though he had a new function as head of state. In January 1926 Mussolini took powers to rule by decree. A new electoral law of May 1928 simplified matters by abolishing universal suffrage in favour of qualifications based on tax payments, and by restricting candidates to the choices of the party's leading organism, the Fascist Grand Council, in turn nominated by Mussolini. In November the Council was made an official state body, and in December the king lost his formal right to select the Premier, the Council being empowered to choose Mussolini's successor. In practice it failed to act as his mouthpiece on only one occasion: in July 1943, when under Grandi's leadership it removed him.

While the system of Fascist government was clear enough, Fascist ideology remained an incoherent jumble. Some of its ideas were borrowed from the Marxism which it execrated. Others were blurred echoes of Nietzsche and Sorel in Mussolini's early days, though he repudiated anarchism's abstention from parliamentary activities and its obsession with general strikes. Fascism's love of violence derived from the bloodthirsty traditions of the class war of the Italian countryside. Mussolini's attempt to harness it first in the squads and then by military discipline fitted in with his rejection of anarchy in favour of unquestioning obedience to the strong military state embodied in himself as *Duce*. Marxism, though Fascism's ideological origin, was its first enemy; next came 'internationalism', because it conflicted with the state's claims to unquestioning obedience, then liberalism and pacifism. Fascism's continual emphasis on the military virtues so obviously lacked by the Italian people was Mussolini's own contribution, possibly because he also conspicuously lacked them. His mania for reviewing troops from horseback or from a tank turret revealed at least unconscious doubts. War and heroism were recurrent propaganda themes, but he waited thirteen years before attacking an enemy who was hopelessly inferior, and entered World War II only when he thought its issue had been decided.

Mussolini's major contribution to politics was the 'corporative' state. The Italian parliament retained a nominal existence until 1939, but Mussolini retained some elements of popular consent for his 'Caesarian democracy', and was *Duce* to most Italians until he involved them in World War II. He had some qualities of popular appeal and, until bombast and megalomania led him to destruction, he had qualities of wit, of objective observation, and even of deep political insight, as when he observed of the Germans that they were a dangerous people because they dreamed collectively. His 'corporative' device, whereby private enterprise was permitted, but regulated in the interests of the state through 'corporations', was proclaimed by him to be 'destined to become the civilization of the twentieth century'. In fact it was never more than a façade, though had it been operated through independent trade union representatives in collaboration with management and state representatives, it might have contributed considerably to economic development. Such, at least, was the view of other Fascist states which adopted the device to suit their own conditions. In Italy, however, its effects were negligible when they were not frankly injurious. Its further objectives of preparing the economy for aggression and territorial expansion were equally unrealized.

## (ii) *The Defeated Central Powers*

On November 11th, 1918, the Emperor Charles renounced his rights in the government of 'German Austria', though he did not renounce his crown. On November 13th, under pressure from a group of Hungarian nobles anxious to salvage what they could from the wreckage of the Dual Monarchy, he repeated the procedure in respect to Hungary. On November 12th the Provisional German-Austrian Government proclaimed the German-Austrian Republic as 'a component part of the German Republic'. On November 16th the winding up of the broken Habsburg empire was completed when the Hungarian parliament dissolved itself and transferred its powers and duties to the National Council. This immediately proclaimed the Hungarian Republic with Count Michael Karolyi as provisional president. But the disappearance of the Habsburg Monarchy replaced an insoluble set of problems with an intractable one. The nationalities problem which had devoured the old empire remained to destroy the independence of the new national states, truncated Austria and Hungary, and successor states alike. The new states did indeed govern themselves, with varying degrees of success and internal harmony, but they were incapable of safeguarding their independence when this was threatened first by Nazi Germany and then by Soviet Russia. They were also to show a remarkably consistent callousness in pursuing their own imperialist ambitions, standing aside when one after another was destroyed.

Austria was reduced to the purely German lands—and not all of those. Her population was only 6,455,000, of whom nearly a third lived in Vienna. Austria attempted to evade reparations by arguing that she also was a successor state, and not responsible for the war. The war guilt clause was nevertheless written into the St Germain treaty but without practical effect, for the Allies were obliged to keep Austria in being by extensive relief and economic aid, to avoid her incorporation into Germany. There was no distinct 'Austrian' national consciousness until the Austrian renegade Hitler created one after 1938, by subjecting Austria to his German Nazis. Loyalty was to the province, or to pan-Germanism, not to federal government in Vienna. The psychological trend to separatism was strengthened by economic circumstances. Vienna and industrial Lower Austria had hitherto been fed from all parts of the empire. Now they depended on the other provinces for food. There was not enough and this was resented. Moreover Vienna, which was a province as well as the capital, was Social Democrat, and the other provinces were predominantly Christian Social, that is Catholic Agrarian. Until the Civil War smashed the Socialists in the 1930s, they and the Christian Socials were the only mass parties. The Socialists talked of proletarian dictatorship and invincible hostility to the *bourgeoisie*, but in practice were reformists. The Christian Socials were the pillars of the *bourgeois* first Austrian Republic as they were of the second after 1945, but in the first they moved steadily towards a brand of clerical Fascism in hostility to the Socialists. Though a great deal was made of the 'Communist danger' in the early days of the Republic, this was a myth. Nonetheless it was alarming in view of Soviet-type *régimes* in Bavaria and Hungary and some unrepresentative and ineffectual but vocal 'Red Guards' and Soviet 'Councils' in Vienna.

The first Austrian government contained the Socialist Karl Renner as Chancellor, five other Socialists, five Christian Socials and four non-party men. On March 12th the assembly voted Austria an integral part of Germany, but St Germain expressly forbade *Anschluss*, as Versailles had done. The relief and financial aid without which Austria would have starved was granted only on condition that she remained independent.

The assumption of the name of Republic of Austria instead of German Austria by St Germain underlined the bargain. In June 1920 the Renner cabinet was replaced by an all-party government until the constitution was completed. From the first election held under it in October 1920 the Christian Socials dominated all coalitions, and their leader Mgr Seipel was the ablest politician of the first Republic. In October 1922 Seipel made the Geneva Protocols with Britain, France, Czechoslovakia and Italy which guaranteed loans and territorial integrity for Austria as well as her independence, while she agreed to reform her finances and balance her budget. The Socialists unsuccessfully opposed this as a betrayal of the national cause. Drastic reforms and economies were introduced, but they failed to improve production for some time. Only after 1927 did matters improve, and then chiefly because of tourism.

Seipel managed to exclude the Socialists from office, his main political ambition, but they controlled Vienna, and they had the strongest and best party organization in Austria. They used their control of Vienna to exact heavy taxes to pay for an expensive but highly popular health, education and housing programme; in fact Vienna's working class flats became a red Mecca for foreign Socialists and a red rag to the Austrian Christian Social and pan-German bulls. The enmity became irreconcilable after 1927, when the courts acquitted members of the Fascist para-military *Heimwehr*, who had shot some Socialists. This gave rise to the belief that Socialists would never get justice, and caused riots. The authorities handled them badly, and henceforth Austria moved steadily towards authoritarianism. The *Heimwehr*, hitherto insignificant, began to play a major role in politics, fostered by Seipel, other clerical reactionaries, and big business. It armed its members on a large scale, especially when Mussolini subsidized it, but never gained mass support. The Austrian peasants generally disliked it, but they equally detested its Socialist rival, the *Schutzbund*, formed in retaliation. Other Christian Socials, among them the future Chancellor Schuschnigg, distrusted the *Heimwehr*, and set up their own movements. The Socialists adopted obstructive parliamentary tactics after 1929, and in 1930 the *Heimwehr* pledged itself to destroy parliament and set up a Fascist dictatorship. 1931 was a comparatively quiet year, apart from the *contretemps* over the projected Austro-German customs union, but in 1932 the storm broke. The Austrian Nazis emerged for the first time as a strong political force. The pan-Germans welcomed them and the *Heimwehr* split, its larger faction openly or covertly favouring the Nazis. Austria's democratic western friends therefore came to rely on Italy to maintain Austrian independence for them, believing that Italy would always be anti-German.

Count Michael Karolyi hoped to establish in Hungary a genuinely democratic *régime*. Although he denounced the territorial settlement, he hoped that Hungary would accept it to atone for greater past injustices perpetrated by her. Internally Hungary emerged from the war comparatively unscathed, but her peasants had had a low standard of living before 1914, and now were poorer still. The upper classes came out of it very well, with some of their members far richer than before. By ordering the soldiers to lay down their arms Karolyi had increased the poverty and confusion which followed defeat, and had set loose a dangerous and undisciplined element. Hungary's obvious weakness encouraged the Rumanians to advance their frontiers, further increasing discontent with Karolyi.

Anxious to settle the land problem, the great issue in all the 'peasant nations' of eastern Europe, he handed over his own estates for redistribution in March 1919. He began to draft a land law to break up all the big estates, but without Allied backing he was helpless against his conservative and reactionary enemies. When prisoners of war returned from Russia describing the Revolution's achievements in glowing terms, the situation became dangerously revolutionary. He was too humane and sensitive to use force to crush his oppponents. In their struggle to defeat Karolyi's democratic programme, and more particularly to retain their estates, the old ruling classes provoked nationalist agitation over the territorial question —on which, indeed, they and nearly all Hungarians felt strongly. The Allies' ultimatum of March 20th, 1919, demanding Hungarian withdrawal to the frontier with Rumania fixed by them, immediately produced an explosion. Right Wing nationalist and Left Wing revolutionary tendencies came together under the bizarre leadership of Bela Kun, a Hungarian Jew who had participated in the Russian Revolution. His aims were simple: to retain Hungary's existing frontiers, and make Hungary a Soviet republic. Karolyi's moderate 'Third Force' was crushed between Bela Kun's Bolshevik adherents and the extreme Right. As the Communists were gaining control of the trade unions, Karolyi's moderate Socialist allies deserted him to avoid being outbid for working class support. Whether or not the Allies' ultimatum 'stabbed Hungarian democracy in the back', as Karolyi claimed, it certainly destroyed his government. A Communist-Socialist coalition was formed in which Bela Kun wielded dictatorial powers.

He immediately proceeded to inaugurate a Soviet state and combined this hopeless task with waging war first on Rumania and next on Czechoslovakia. Some conservatives and reactionaries established a provisional government of their own under Michael Karolyi's reactionary brother Julius, Count Stephen Bethlen, Admiral Nicholas Horthy and the Habsburg Archduke Joseph at Szeged, then occupied by France. On June 24th Bela Kun proclaimed his Soviet republic, but his readiness now to accept Allied terms over the frontiers would in any event have ranged his Right Wing associates against him. The army officers who had supported him against Rumania went over to the rival White government. He lost control of the unions, the peasants revolted, and in a desperate effort to save himself he launched a Red Terror. On August 1st he fled to Vienna and the Soviet republic collapsed with him, but a White Terror ensued which far surpassed Kun's campaign of violence. The Whites crushed an attempt at a Social Democratic government, and then held elections early in 1920

341

under open terror. Their predictable victory gave them some basis for making Admiral Horthy on March 1st commander-in-chief of the armed forces, and head of state. It was impossible to restore the Habsburgs because of Allied hostility, so it was decided that, though there could as yet be no king, Hungary should remain a kingdom with Horthy as Regent. Charles in fact twice failed ignominiously in 1921 to regain the Hungarian throne. Legitimist support in Hungary, as in Austria, practically collapsed before World War II, though the restoration spectre could always alarm their neighbours, including Nazi Germany until 1938.

With Horthy as Regent, and Bethlen as Premier until 1931, Hungary settled down more rapidly than Austria or Germany. There was a measure of freedom of speech and of the press, though no attacks were allowed on the foundation of the *régime*. Right Wing nationalist groups formed so strong a bloc with the so-called Small Landowners Party (the party of the 'gentry'), that they could tolerate with equanimity the various opposition groups of the radical Independent Small Landowners Party (representing the 'yeoman' class), Liberals and even Social Democrats. The Social Democrats were permitted to control the trade unions at first, though after 1921, when a law was passed dethroning the dynasty, and the Legitimists could be disregarded, there was no need to concede anything to the Left. As voting was open everywhere outside the municipalities, the government coalition won every election. Land reform was minimal and benefited chiefly the landlords. Urban and rural workers were rigidly controlled.

The major preoccupation of the ruling classes in the inter-war years was to revise the Treaty of Trianon, though the early years saw great distress because of the disturbances caused by the war, and general economic backwardness. The Hungarians in 1924 swallowed their pride by accepting foreign financial help. Britain, Italy, France and the Little Entente guaranteed Hungarian territorial integrity and political independence, while Hungary promised to fulfil Trianon and pay moderate reparations, with the help of a substantial loan. Immediately Bethlen was able to stabilize the currency and stimulate industry and agriculture, especially the latter. Hungary shared, though unevenly, in the general prosperity of the late 1920s. She never degenerated into the kind of police state which flourished in Rumania and Yugoslavia, though she was never reconciled to Trianon, and her treaty of friendship with Italy in April 1927 and continual revisionist agitation foreshadowed the final disaster.

Germany also underwent political disintegration as the result of the war. Led by Independent Socialists and the extreme Left Spartacists, but with strong Majority Socialist support, workers', soldiers' and sailors' councils appeared on the model of the Russian soviets before the Bolshevik dictatorship. Bavaria and Saxony were declared Socialist Republics by the Independent Socialists, with Majority support. However, the Majority Socialists, who controlled the central government in Berlin under the Chancellor, Friedrich Ebert, soon broke with Independents and Spartacists. Ebert honoured his pre-armistice agreement with Ludendorff's successor,

General Wilhelm von Gröner, to support the officer corps' efforts to maintain army discipline in the field, and fight 'Bolshevism'. Even the Independent Socialists reluctantly agreed to prevent the army's disintegration, since an undisciplined rabble would have been incapable of retreating in good order, and would accordingly have been taken prisoner by the Allies. A crucial problem was posed in the early postwar period by the ambiguity in Ebert's position as both head of a revolutionary government and legal Chancellor recognized by the army and conservatives. Ebert could attract full loyalty from neither Left nor Right, and the Republic depended for its existence on the support of an army whose leaders were reactionaries. But the army leadership retained its control because most of the German people between 1918 and 1920, Majority Socialists included, feared Communism far more than the reactionary militarists, and Gröner immediately seized the opportunity. Within two years the army had recovered its prestige. Majority Socialists like Ebert vied with Right Wingers in fulsome praise of its 'victorious' defence of the homeland.

Ebert's immediate tasks were to establish a democratic political system and to socialize the economy, but the latter objective could have been achieved only by setting up a revolutionary dictatorship. For this neither the Majority Socialists nor Right Independent Socialists were prepared. Moreover they approved the popular demand to call a constituent assembly, though Right Independents wished to retain the councils for the time being as the instrument of socialization. They accepted the decision by the national congress of councils which met in Berlin in mid-December to hold elections for an assembly in January 1919, whereas Left Independents correctly predicted that the assembly would end the revolution. In fact most Socialists feared that the Allies would immediately take any socialized property for reparations, that refusal by the industrialists to work a socialized economy would bring chaos and mass unemployment, and that land redistribution would endanger the 1919 harvest. Yet the decision of the national congress was clearly in favour of moderate socialism carried through under a parliamentary system 'forthwith'. This was impossible under existing political conditions, and the Majority Socialists rejected the idea. They also rejected the congress's demand for the democratization of the army, which Ebert's military allies would never accept. In fact Ebert had difficulty in convincing his supporters that the government could not rely on the disorganized and weak republican forces which had come into existence.

On December 23rd, 1918, the revolutionary sailors, believing that Ebert intended to disband them, captured the members of the government. The army forced the sailors to surrender, but the Independent Socialists resigned from the government in protest against Ebert's handling of the affair and his neglect to consult them before calling on the army. However, the army itself, from Gröner's viewpoint, was no longer reliable, for the troops who repressed the sailors had shown some sympathy for them. As the Spartacists openly demanded revolutionary seizure of power and denounced the assembly even before it met as counter-revolutionary, civil war became inevitable. Under Karl Liebknecht and the Polish-born Jewess Rosa Luxemburg they formed at the end of 1918 the German Communist Party (KPD), in combination with some small extreme Left Wing groups. Ebert did not engineer the departure of the Independents but they attempted to bring him down and prevent the Spartacists from dominating the extreme Left. This strengthened Ebert when Berlin on January 6th, 1919, began to undergo the 'Battle of the Marne' of the German revolution. The Spartacists then proclaimed the overthrow of Ebert's government, and called a general strike. Mass demonstrations by Spartacists and Majority Socialists led to clashes and Spartacist occupation of important buildings. On refusing to evacuate the buildings, the Spartacists were attacked by government forces on the order of the new *Reichswehr* Minister, Gustav Noske, brought in after the Independents had resigned. Noske relied on the notorious Free Corps, groups of ex-servicemen, chiefly unemployed officers, whom Gröner had begun officially to favour after the December 23rd rising. These troops showed as little mercy to Spartacists as they did to the Poles on the eastern borders where they were often employed. They murdered Liebknecht and Rosa Luxemburg in cold blood. Their methods were later copied by the Nazis and many of them indeed became Nazis.

During the insurrection preparations for the election went ahead, and it was held on January 19th, 1919, shortly after the Spartacist defeat, on the basis of universal suffrage with a qualifying age of twenty. The Communists boycotted the election. The former Conservatives and Free Conservatives combined in the German National People's Party, and showed the general tendency by declaring themselves 'a new party' which rejected 'all responsibility for the past'. They polled 3,121,500 votes and returned 44 deputies, promising to support socialization of the big industries if production would not suffer, denouncing the revolution as a crime, and hoping for the monarchy's restoration. The former National Liberals did not promise loyalty to the republic, and remained capitalist and nationalist when they formed the German People's Party (1,345,600 votes and 19 deputies). The old Progressives united with some Left Wing National Liberals and independent intellectuals to form the republican and nationalist Democratic Party (5,641,800 votes, 75 deputies). The biggest *bourgeois* party was the old Centre, which now and for a short period called itself the Christian People's Party (5,980,200 votes, 91 deputies). It altered neither its policies nor its methods, attacking principally the Socialists as a class party and a danger to Catholic educational and social interests. It accepted the democratic republic with rather less enthusiasm than it had accepted Bismarck's Germany, as a disagreeable reality. Majority Socialists formed the largest party with 11,509,000 votes and 165 deputies, and remained the largest Socialist party in Europe despite the breach with the Independents (2,317,300 votes and 22 deputies). But Ebert's continued reliance on the army, which remained bitterly opposed to a democratic republic, weakened the democratic forces. Yet the alliance did not doom the republic, which lasted until January 1933 and there was plenty of time in which to consolidate democratic institutions. Moreover, the alliance was forced on Ebert by the extreme Left's resort to revolutionary methods. Ebert and Noske's methods merely completed the breach between Independent and Majority Socialists, just as the result of the election dictated a coalition between Majority Socialists and Centre.

The republic was nevertheless severely handicapped from the beginning. Like the German revolution, it was the product of defeat, and its supporters could be plausibly branded as traitors by the Right. A second Spartacist rising in Bremen was defeated by Noske and the Free Corps. There were further disturbances in Berlin and the Rhineland in 1919 by industrial workers who felt that Ebert and the Majority Socialists had cheated them out of Socialism, while the Majority Socialists gained the undying enmity of the Right by signing the Treaty of Versailles. The Communist Party increased in strength and the Independents repudiated parliamentary government, most of them joining the Communists. The republic accordingly occupied the dangerous position of having not the normal opposition with which to contend under parliamentary rules, but irreconcilable enemies of both Left and Right extremists pledged to its destruction. Hence the Majority Socialist chancellor, Philip Scheidemann, graphically described it as a candle burning at both ends.

In addition it had to suppress separatist tendencies from states which had never fully accepted being ruled from Prussian Berlin. After its defeat in Berlin, the extreme Left pinned its hopes on Bavaria. Here the Socialists remained united longer, and moreover had peasant support. Kurt Eisner's Independent-Majority Socialist coalition called for a federal Germany based on Socialist principles. Eisner was no 'Red dictator', as enemies alleged. He intended to accept the decision of the Bavarian electors, who returned a *bourgeois* majority to the Bavarian Diet, while retaining the Soviets to exert pressure for Socialist measures. But on February 21st, when the Diet was due to open, he was murdered by Bavarian Monarchists.

There were soon three governments claiming authority: the legal coalition under the Majority Socialist Johannes Hoffmann, Eisner's Independent heirs who proclaimed a Bavarian Soviet in emulation of Bela Kun, and a Spartacist Soviet. Hoffmann used Right Wing officers, the Free Corps under Ritter von Epp, and forces of the new Provisional *Reichswehr*, created by the assembly's decree of March 6th, to defeat the Independents and Spartacists. After brutal fighting and atrocities on both sides the revolution ended in May, but its results were far-reaching. The defeat of the radical elements turned the youth of Bavaria towards Right Wing nationalists who here, as elsewhere in Germany, dreamed of overthrowing the republic, tearing up the Treaty of Versailles, avenging the defeat of 1918, and restoring Germany to her rightful place in Europe.

The Bavarian revolution paved the way for the final success of the

345

Right Wing nationalists. Munich became the centre for Bavarian nationalistic and militarist adventurers, who saw in the Independents and Spartacists of the 'republics', many of them Jews as well as Marxists, their own
and Germany's enemies. From these beginnings came the National
Socialist (Nazi) movement, developed in Munich by Hitler, at first a
political agitator in army pay. Hitler, sent by his army superiors after the
revolution to investigate the German Workers' Party, a small working class
nationalist organization, joined it and took it over. In February 1920 he
renamed it the National Socialist German Workers Party and gave it the
ideology which, as an Austrian subject, he had acquired in Vienna before
the war among the pan-German nationalists and anti-semites. Among
Hitler's *Reichswehr* masters was Captain Ernst Röhm, who had joined
the German Workers' Party before Hitler, and was soon to be one of his
lieutenants. Röhm enrolled into the party ex-servicemen and Free Corps,
the beginnings of the Nazi Brownshirted SA (storm-troopers) which he
later led. Hitler's contribution was a phenomenal mastery of the art of
demagogy and propaganda techniques. He had no original political ideas,
and never needed them. The Right continually denounced the 'November
criminals' who had overthrown an Imperial Germany with victory in its
grasp, by 'stabbing in the back' the soldier at the front and launching a
Jewish-Marxist revolution, but nobody was so effective in this kind of
demagogy as Hitler, with mass-oratorical and mass-hypnotic powers that
have never been equalled, before or since. But his rise to power was slow,
and when the *Reichswehr* officers in Bavaria decided to overthrow Hoffmann
in March 1920 and appoint an illegal Right Wing coalition under Gustav
von Kahr, they did not need Hitler. However he and his friends flourished
under the benevolent eye of a Bavarian government which approved their
treason against the central government in Berlin.

The first assembly of the German republic proclaimed its faith by
meeting not in Berlin but in Weimar, an old citadel of German liberalism
and the home of Goethe. It also proclaimed its continuity with Imperial
Germany by retaining the designation *Reich* for Germany, instead of
adopting the official title of *Republik*. It faced a heavy task. A new constitution and system of government had to be framed; the aftermath of the
world war and of civil war had to be cleared away; Germany's internal
economy and her position in Europe had to be restored; and peace had to
be made with the Allies. The sense of shock at the suddenness of defeat still
remained. This encouraged a revulsion against militarism, but the stronger
reaction was to hold fast to the militarist traditions of Imperial Germany
and to nurse feelings of resentment. This sense of grievance was fully
shared by the Weimar politicians, and intensified with the rootlessness
and the sense of insecurity prevalent now that the old order was destroyed.
These factors combined to produce the infirmity of purpose which paved
the way for the Weimar Republic's overthrow.

The Versailles terms were not punitive, but Germany had devoted so
much more of her national power and resources to the war than any other

country had done, that economic and political recovery after defeat was all the more difficult. Hence the war's social, economic, political and psychological legacies dominated German history for the next twenty years. Though Majority Socialists, the Centre and the Democrats had all sponsored the 1917 Peace Resolution and combined to form the first coalition under the Majority Socialist Scheidemann, they accepted neither military defeat nor Versailles as Germany's just deserts. Scheidemann resigned rather than sign the treaty, but the *Reichswehr* leaders insisted that there was no choice. Indeed there was no alternative, as Germany could not regain her territories, did not intend to pay reparations, could only secretly evade the disarmament clauses, and could not eject the Allied occupation forces. A Socialist-Centre coalition under Gustav Bauer submitted and the Democrats returned to the fold in October.

At this time the *Reichswehr* was still chastened, though it was essentially the old army in miniature. It was officially limited to 100,000 men but actually it was much larger, and already had the nucleus for an even bigger army, as it consisted of picked commissioned and non-commissioned officers, and clandestinely retained its forbidden General Staff. All ranks were obliged to take an oath of allegiance to the republic, but did so while feeling no loyalty to it. The *Reichswehr* was 'above politics', which meant that it retained in its own eyes the right to redress them if necessary. The President, Ebert, controlled the army and could use it in crises to maintain order. He could even suspend civil rights for that purpose, though only with the *Reichstag*'s permission. Officially the *Reichstag* had some control over the *Reichswehr*, as all Presidential decrees had to be counter-signed by the Chancellor or the responsible minister—in this case the *Reichswehr* minister. The *Reichswehr* minister now organized the whole *Reichswehr* since the old Saxon, Bavarian, Württemberg and Prussian war ministries had disappeared. The civilian government also was more centralized than it had been before 1918, for the Berlin government controlled central finance and the means of communication as well as the *Reichswehr*, and the federal council representing the constituent states had little power. In fact Berlin interfered with state governments mainly when they showed Left Wing tendencies. Hence no opposition came from Berlin when Hoffmann was overthrown, though dissident officers, backed by part of the *Reichswehr* under the Northern commander General Walther von Lüttwitz, tried in the simultaneous Kapp *putsch* to overthrow the central government. This attempt by the army and big business leaders to recover the power lost in 1918 failed ignominiously. The High Command's disloyalty was patent, but the traitors were leniently treated, the government failed to press its advantage, and the *Reichswehr* emerged as the real victor.

For the German masses the great problems were economic, and the greatest was inflation. A few days after the Kapp *putsch* there were disturbances in the Ruhr, which the *Reichswehr* blamed on the Communists. They were principally due to working class distrust of the *Reichswehr*'s obvious reactionary intentions, and the justification for this distrust

347

became increasingly apparent in the next few years. The Bavarian government sheltered the notorious Free Corps Ehrhardt Brigade when it hurriedly left Berlin after the Kapp *putsch*. The Free Corps made arrangements in Bavaria for the murder of Matthias Erzberger, who had signed the armistice, and of the Foreign Minister Rathenau, considered doubly obnoxious for being a Jew and for attempting to fulfil the Versailles Treaty. The Free Corps led the way in subjecting Germany to the political murders and terror which became endemic between 1920 and 1924, and again after 1929 when the Nazis became prominent.

Pressure was finally applied on the Bavarians to abandon their barbarous habits after Erzberger's murder in August 1920. A new Bavarian government made Hitler serve a term of imprisonment for acts of violence, but the inflation accelerated out of control after reparations were fixed—not that many efforts were made to control it. By the time of Rathenau's murder in June 1922 the mark had dropped from its December 1918 rate of four to the dollar to 400. Outcries against the central government's attempts to suppress terrorism brought down the Bavarian government and led to an extreme Right Wing Bavarian government in November. Ludendorff, now living in Bavaria, linked northern Nationalist elements with the Bavarian chauvinists, but the Bavarian Right Wing, in which Hitler had now achieved some prominence, hesitated about its strategy for a year. Meanwhile the nationalist tide swept on, strengthened by the Franco-Belgian invasion of the Ruhr in January 1923. The non-party government of Chancellor Wilhelm Cuno from November 1922 to August 1923 fell, however, because of a general strike, organized by the workers in reply to its policy of deliberate inflation.

Gustav Stresemann of the German People's Party, Cuno's successor, had to contend with several nationalist risings, including Hitler's famous Munich beer-hall *putsch* in November. By this time Hitler had practically completed the oratorical repertoire which was to make him a serious contender for power after 1929. Following his admired model Mussolini, he put increasing emphasis on the leadership principle, and on the supreme importance of the leader's will in overcoming obstacles before which democratic politicians trembled. He had not yet fully elaborated the old racial myth whereby only 'pure' Aryans could be members of the state. But he was groping his way to the concept of the great German people, the *Volk* in its atavistic sense of the tribal community of blood and soil. His basic concept of *Volk* as the source of authority expressed through his Nazi Party and finding its supreme embodiment in himself as *Führer* (Leader) was being insistently propounded. He had also gathered around himself most of the lieutenants who were to come into power with him: Hermann Göring and Rudolf Hess, the ex-officers, Joseph Goebbels and Alfred Rosenberg, the former intellectuals, and the Jew-baiter and pornographer Julius Streicher. Heinrich Himmler, his chief instrument of mass murder in World War II, did not come on the scene until 1929. With Himmler's advent the monolithic development of the Party which Hitler sought was brought within reach, though he had known for some time what he wanted.

However, when Hitler, Ludendorff and their allies launched the Munich *putsch*, Stresemann was in firm control of the situation. Moreover General Hans von Seeckt, as head of the *Reichswehr*, would have nothing to do with Bavarian separatists who wanted to destroy the *Reich*'s unity, and thereby the prospects of restoring its, and the *Reichswehr*'s, former glory. Hjalmer Schacht, who as President of the *Reichsbank* largely controlled finance, also came out firmly against Hitler and other rebels. Hitler's *putsch* collapsed ignominiously, a clear sign of what modern state power meant. Imprisoned for his revolt, Hitler followed up the magnificent propaganda platform given by his trial for attacking the 'November criminals' by composing his political testament, *Mein Kampf*. This revealed not only his pan-German and anti-semitic ideas, but also his proposals for a great new Germany which, in alliance with Italy and Britain, would first destroy Versailles. Next he would conquer eastern Europe to subjugate the sub-human Slavs, and incorporate in the Third *Reich* all Germans, beginning with those in Austria. But the great objective was to seize from Russia's western lands a living-space (*Lebensraum*) which would both form the essential basis for the Continental empire which he envisaged, and mark the beginning of the destruction of Russia. Intensely Austrian in his outlook, Hitler had hated the Russians before they became Bolsheviks, but now as the arch-apostle of nationalism and anti-Bolshevism in Germany he could work these strands of emotional hysteria into a compelling political pattern.

Hitler's eclipse, however, appeared conclusive, and he did not become a national figure again for almost seven years, Stresemann's (second) cabinet, and with it his 'hundred days', ended on November 28th, 1923, and two cabinets followed under the Centre politician Wilhelm Marx. Von Seeckt, suspected of harbouring dictatorial ambitions, readily surrendered his emergency powers when the crisis was over and went back to building up the *Reichswehr*, in collaboration with Soviet Russia. Stresemann, who became foreign minister on resigning as Chancellor, disapproved of what he considered von Seeckt's excessive readiness to commit Germany to Russia, for Stresemann liked at least two strings to his bow. As the German economy recovered under the Dawes Plan, and unrest died down, an era of political stability was established. Stresemann succeeded in restoring Germany's position as a power accepted on equal terms in Europe, and convinced many western Europeans of his good faith. He could present Locarno as a triumph, which from his standpoint it was, and himself as a friend of the west, though he took care not to cut the wire to Moscow.

In the stable, peaceful years from 1924 to 1929 Germany spent more on armaments than Britain did; the Nazis in May 1924 polled nearly 2,000,000 votes; and when Ebert died in February 1925, the Germans elected as President the unregenerate Junker Field Marshal Paul von-Hindenburg, nominee of the republic's Right Wing enemies. Actually Hindenburg owed his victory to its Communist foes, who nominated their leader Ernst Thälmann, who had no chance, in order to keep out Marx, and weaken the republic, by endangering its democratic system of government.


## (iii) *The Successor States*


Germany's neighbours, the successor states, were bound to France. However, at the heart of the French system of alliances there lay a dangerous ambiguity, symbolized by the construction from the later 1920s of the great defensive system known as the Maginot Line against attack from Germany. Like the system of alliances, it was designed to prevent any recurrence of the 1914 onslaught which had carried the Germans almost to Paris, but the unspoken premise was that the eastern allies existed to draw off German troops from France, not to involve France in an attack on Germany on their behalf. Yet it was obvious from the beginning that no German government would freely accept the consequences of Versailles, and that Russia, no longer even a potential French ally in the 1920s, was as hostile as Germany to Versailles. Britain, the only other European Great Power, had made it abundantly clear by 1923 that she would not condone French attempts to enforce Versailles, and implicit in British policy was the belief that in course of time Germany would dominate eastern Europe by sheer economic and political weight, and that nothing either should or could be done to prevent this, provided that this domination was achieved peacefully. In this way appeasement was being foreshadowed within at least two years of Germany's defeat, though it became reality only twenty years after the armistice. Hence France, unless she was to acquiesce in the prospect of German hegemony in Europe, was bound to try to increase her security by increasing her commitments.

Poland never achieved the economic strength or financial and political stability which were necessary to make her a real military factor. Much of her land was poor, yet nearly three-quarters of her gainfully employed population worked in agriculture. Her small and inadequate industry could not equip a modern army. Her middle class was not sufficiently strong to give competent economic or political leadership. Dangerous political and social tensions found their roots in the violence of political life, the depressed situation of the predominantly Russian peasantry of the eastern lands, and poor economic and social conditions among the urban workers, notably in Warsaw itself. Socialism was strong among the working classes, though Communism was not. The Socialists had recognized in 1918 that Socialism must be postponed if independence and territorial unity were to be achieved. The Polish Communist Party, founded in December 1918, was active in Warsaw and in the Dombrowa coal-mining area but could never compete with the Socialists, especially when the nature of the Soviet Russian *régime* became clear. Pilsudski therefore had little opposition from the Left, when as provisional president in 1919 he consolidated a *bourgeois* democratic *régime* and formed a Polish national army.

Pilsudski, like most western and eastern European leaders in the turbulent postwar years, feared the spread of Communism—not unnaturally, as conditions of distress and upheaval favoured it, and as the Soviet government's avowed aim was to promote Communist revolution in Europe. Though the failure of the Hungarian and German, but especially the German, revolution temporarily blighted Soviet hopes, they were not renounced even during the Russian Civil War. Pilsudski's decision to invade the Ukraine, however, was not precautionary, but chauvinistic. In April 1920 he agreed to help the Ukrainian nationalist leader Semyon Petlyura to reconquer the Ukraine from the Bolsheviks, in return for Petlyura's renunciation of East Galicia. The subsequent Russian advance into Poland encouraged Trotsky's hope of setting up a Bolshevik *régime* there, though Lenin doubted the feasibility of establishing Communism 'with bayonets'. However, a committee of Polish Communists was set up in Bialystok under the Polish Communist Feliks Kon, and, more important, under Feliks Dzierzhinski, the Polish-born chief of *Cheka*, the Russian secret police. The Russian government began to hope that a Soviet Poland could be used to link Russia with the Communists in Germany, and so establish a solid base from which to launch proletarian revolution into western Europe. With the Russian retreat later in 1920 these hopes collapsed. The Poles rallied round Pilsudski in a great burst of national enthusiasm and Russophobia, and for nearly twenty years barred Bolshevism's advance to the west.

In March 1921 Poland received a formal constitution. It rapidly proved impossible to conduct parliamentary government under it because of the weakness of the executive, the violence of party warfare, and the proliferation of the parties themselves—fifteen were represented in the *Sejm* after the elections of November 1922. Pilsudski denounced the constitution, and retired to his country home, where he plotted its destruction. After 1921 there was a gradual increase of prosperity with good harvests and better exploitation of Upper Silesian resources, but political harmony remained unattainable. In November 1925 an economic crisis brought rising prices and unemployment, caused numerous bankruptcies, and almost destroyed the *zloty*, the new currency unit introduced in 1924.

A kaleidoscopic coalition government partially restored the economy, and in December 1925 enacted legislation providing for the annual redistribution of 500,000 acres during the next ten years, with full compensation for landowners. A severe deflationary policy, however, aroused massive discontent, and the Socialists deserted. Wincenty Witos, leader of the great Peasant Party, formed a Centre and Right coalition on May 10th, 1926, but was deposed within a few days by Pilsudski, with the aid of the army, old 'legionaries', Socialists who remembered his former Socialist tendencies, and even Communists. But finding that opposition increased as *bourgeois* democrats, Socialists and Communists rejected his authoritarianism, he soon started to persecute his opponents. He bullied the *Sejm* into passing the laws he wanted, and relied until his death in 1935 on the 'colonels', a group of reactionary militarists and landowners. Though Pilsudski's powers were never unlimited, his dictatorship encouraged quasi-Fascist tendencies.

Poland benefited from the general prosperity of the later 1920s, and even enjoyed an industrial boom between 1925 and 1929, but the great depression brought widespread distress. Pilsudski's rule was too strong to permit any recurrence of the postwar disturbances, but it had no solution to the problems posed by under-development and a phenomenal rise in population, which both nullified the advantages gained by land redistribution and exacerbated the urban unemployment problem. The colonels were intellectually and temperamentally unsuited to grapple with such issues, and prevented economic, social and political progress.

In foreign policy Poland acquired a measure of success and stability through alliances with France and Rumania. The latter alliance was purely anti-Soviet, for the Poles were well-disposed to Hungary and detested Czechoslovakia, while Rumania had no quarrel with Germany. On the contrary, it was through German good offices that she had regained Bessarabia from Russia in May 1918, an acquisition which the Allies confirmed in 1920. After Rumania had made a separate peace with the Central Powers in March 1918, she had declared war on them again barely in time to appear as an Allied state in Paris. Had it not been for Allied—or rather French—fear of the Bolshevik bogey, Rumania would have done much less well at the expense of Hungary, Bulgaria and Russia. Her gains, however, were almost as dangerously excessive as Poland's. Apart from her unassimilated Jewish minority (only about half a million but they largely ran Rumanian finance and commerce, so helping to produce an anti-semitism just as violent as Poland's) she had strong Hungarian, Bulgarian and Ukrainian minorities. She had more than doubled her prewar territory and population, which had been ethnically Rumanian. The Dobrudja contained no Rumanians. The province of Transylvania had a small, though absolute Rumanian majority over Hungarians, Germans and some other minor nationalities. The province of Bukovina also had an absolute majority, though northern Bukovina was entirely Ukrainian. Rumanians constituted under half Bessarabia's population, though they outnumbered the Ukrainians there. Probably 4,500,000 out of a total Rumanian population of about 16,000,000 were dangerously disgruntled minorities.

After the territorial problems were settled, the main task of Marshal Alexandre Averescu's People's Party government of Right Wing nationalists was to suppress 'Bolshevism'. Averescu, with the Liberals' support, initiated land reforms, chiefly in order to prevent Communism from gaining ground in the countryside, though the urban, *bourgeois* Liberals also wanted to destroy the land-owning Conservatives. There was widespread discontent in the towns, but whereas the peasants, constituting 75% of the population, were bought off, the urban workers were merely repressed. Averescu resigned in 1922 to make way for his Liberal allies. They ran Rumania until 1928, apart from a brief Averescu interlude of 1926–27. Their aim was to industrialize the country by heavy taxation and export duties, at the expense of the large class of peasant proprietors, and by depressing working class wages. They did not intend to make any contribution themselves, and would not even admit foreign capital. Moreover, to ensure their political and economic control they imposed a strongly centralist and nationalist constitution in March 1923 which made the minorities second-class citizens, and clipped the wings of the Nationalist Party coalition led by Iuliu Maniu. Henceforth the *régime* and its bureaucracy aroused such bitter opposition that the old days of Austrian rule in Bukovina and Hungarian in Transylvania were recalled with affection. The Liberal policy overreached itself, however, by forcing the opposition to unite. First small groups of Conservatives, then the Peasant Party of the Regat (the old Rumanian kingdom) under Ion Mihalache combined with the Nationalists. In October 1926, therefore, the National Peasant Party was formed under Maniu's leadership. Fusion was all the more necessary because in March the Liberals had passed a new electoral law which gave half the seats to the party with 40% of the votes.

The year 1927 saw political and economic crises. Agrarian depression had already produced rural tensions, and after the death of King Ferdinand peasant pressure on the government intensified. Prince Nicholas, the Regent, did not share his father's irreconcilable hostility to the National Peasant Party, and after a great peasant 'march on Bucharest', made Maniu Premier in November 1928. In the December general election, the freest during the inter-war years, Maniu's supporters got a majority of over 75%. He made minor agrarian reforms, but, instead of improving peasant conditions, the free sale of land which he encouraged produced a rural proletariat with uneconomically small farms. These labourers, who numbered about 75% of the peasantry by 1930, were practically ignored by Maniu's and later governments. Maniu's government, however, greatly improved industry by admitting foreign capital. It was generally more successful than its predecessors, and not notably more corrupt.

The Czechs set up partnership with the Slovaks in a unitary state—a partnership dominated by the Czechs, who numbered in 1921 roughly 6,800,000. With the Slovaks, who numbered about 2,000,000, they formed about 65·5% of the population. However, the former Austrian Germans living in Bohemia, Moravia and Silesia numbered about $24\frac{1}{2}$% of the population, or about 3,275,000 (the official Czechoslovak census credited them with 3,123,624). Hungarians numbered over 745,000, Ruthenes under 462,000, Jews about 181,000, Poles 76,000 and Rumanians 14,000. The Slovaks, poor, backward and agrarian, grudgingly accepted Czech hegemony for the material advantages it brought, but developed no 'Czechoslovak' consciousness. Whether Germans, Hungarians and Poles could in time have been brought to accept minority status remains uncertain. They would certainly have used any autonomy granted under a federal system to make it plain that Czechoslovakia was not a unitary, and therefore unhyphenated state, but hyphenated Czecho-Slovakia, as it formally became when Nazi Germany partitioned it in October 1938. That these minorities were the best-treated in Europe made no difference. Their conviction of innate superiority to the Czechs was ineradicable. The Germans had immediately demanded self-determination, attempting to establish a 'Government of German Bohemia', and similar *régimes* in Southern Moravia and old Austrian Silesia. The last pretender claimed jurisdiction also over Northern Moravian and Eastern Bohemian Germans, and invented the name of Sudetenland for the whole area which it claimed. (Sudeten Germans, strictly speaking, lived in the Sudeten Mountains, but the name was used indiscriminately in the 1930s for all Germans in Czechoslovakia.) Germans and Hungarians, pinning their hopes on national re-unification, had in any case not been invited to the National Assembly which met in Prague on November 14th, 1918. Consequently the Assembly proceeded without hindrance first to confirm the Czechoslovak Republic under Thomas Masaryk's Presidency, next to redistribute large landed estates, with fair compensation, and then to draft the parliamentary constitution of February 1920. This guaranteed freedom of the press, of political organization and assembly, but only Czechs, Slovaks and Ruthenes were 'peoples of state', and the country was formally declared the 'Czechoslovak national state' and home of the 'Czechoslovak nation'. Despite these shortcomings, Czechoslovakia was the only state east of the Rhine capable of realizing even in part the hopes of the wartime democratic idealists.

Once the great estates had been redistributed, breaking the power of the old land-owning class, the finances reformed, and a capital levy enforced to redistribute more equitably the burdens imposed by deflation, Czechoslovakia made steady economic progress. She possessed 70% of the total manufacturing production of the old Dual Monarchy, with only 26·4% of its population. The Czech lands developed powerful heavy and machine industries, and prosperous engineering, automobile and electrical industries, though the German lands remained unduly dependent on the glass, china and textile industries which became increasingly vulnerable to foreign competition. Agriculture flourished, though its prosperity was less solidly based.

Politically Czechoslovakia was stable. The early inter-war period saw the predominance of Left Wing parties, but the Social Democrats under Vlastimir Tusar split in 1920, the extreme Left majority forming the Communist Party. Karel Kramář, whom Masaryk had made provisional premier in 1918, led the National Democrat Party, which represented the wealthy *bourgeoisie* and was bitterly hostile to the minorities, but this continually declined in importance. Eduard Beneš's National Socialists were radical—not Nazi. They appealed chiefly to the middle classes, but always had extensive lower class support. The largest party was the

(Czechoslovak) Agrarian Party, officially called the Czechoslovak Republican Party. Based on the Czech peasantry and *bourgeoisie*, it also had Slovak support. Except for the Communists, who rejected national divisions, all other parties were, at least originally, strongly influenced by nationalism. The Social Democratic parties, however, began to drop national animosities some time before the 1925 elections, when the Communists won so large a vote as to leave them little choice. Certainly the solid and broad bases of the Agrarians were partly due to overcoming the national barrier. The Slovak National Party under Milan Hodza, who was to be premier during the crisis of 1938, accepted union with the Czechs, but wanted more self-government than the Czechs were at first willing to concede. Fusion with the Agrarians brought it most of its desires, whereas Father Hlinka's Slovak People's Party was anti-Czech as well as anti-semitic (though also anti-Hungarian), and developed an eastern brand of clerical Fascism. Hlinka never carried even half the Slovak votes, but secession was never actually an issue during the elections.

Coalitions were unavoidable because of the proliferation of parties under proportional representation. This explains why Beneš was permanently foreign minister until he succeeded Masaryk in 1935, though he was also exceptionally well qualified for the post. Beneš was a staunch supporter of the League and genuinely internationalist in outlook, though force of circumstances would in any case have led him to make Czechoslovakia the cornerstone of the Versailles settlement in central Europe. Beneš believed also that only friendship between Soviet Russia and the western democracies could maintain the peace of Europe, and strove continually to bring them together. But he regarded Czechoslovakia as sharing in the cultural heritage of the west, and his orientation was always to the western democracies, particularly to France. When in August 1920 he inaugurated the Little Entente with Yugoslavia to oppose a Habsburg restoration and Hungarian revisionism, this accorded entirely with French policy. If restored, the Habsburgs were bound to revive old claims and bring chaos again to central and east-central Europe—as would Hungarian revisionism, whether it involved the Habsburgs or not. In April 1921 the Little Entente was completed by bringing in Rumania. Beneš would have liked to extend his alliance with France by one with Britain. However, the British politicians (Labour, Liberals and Conservatives alike) were cool to Czechoslovakia, and were determined to refuse commitments east of the Rhine. Hence the Czechs were forced to rely on the Franco-Czech treaty of 1924 too much for their own interests.

Czechoslovakia had seven nationalities. Yugoslavia had nine. Its original name of Kingdom of the Serbs, Croats and Slovenes concealed the existence of Bosnian Muslims, Albanians, Germans, Hungarians, Rumanians and Macedonians. The Macedonians were denied official nationality because most of them demanded autonomy and hated the Serbs. The Serbs had the physical power to dominate the whole kingdom and they used it ruthlessly. Out of a total population of about 11,895,000 they numbered 5,953,000, the Croats 3,221,000 and the Slovenes 1,134,000. Of the other nationalities the Germans numbered 505,790, the Hungarians 467,652, Albanians 439,657, Rumanians 231,068 and Italians 12,533. There were other small groups and Croatia provided a further division by using both Latin and Cyrillic scripts. Religion was another divisive factor. Serbs and Macedonians were mainly Greek Orthodox, Croats and Slovenes Roman Catholic, but there were Serb and Croat Muslims. The Yugoslav peoples had also widely different historical, political and social traditions, and both Croats and Slovenes thought the Serbs barbarians. Only when an exclusive loyalty was imposed by the Communist Tito after 1945 was there any hope of uniting so diverse and complex a mass.

The new Kingdom was formally proclaimed on December 4th, 1918, eight days after the Montenegro national assembly had deposed its own king Nicholas, who had opposed the union. A centralist constitution was drafted which was officially designed to create Yugoslav political unity, but actually became the political instrument of Great Serb chauvinism. Presented by the Serb leader Nicholas Pašić, it was accepted (January 1st, 1921) mainly because 161 delegates, including the Croat leader Stepan Radić, walked out of the constituent assembly without even voting. Had they stayed they might well have defeated the constitution, and almost certainly could have modified it in the direction of federalism. Pašić, who might have been forced to compromise, no longer saw any necessity to do so. Henceforth national problems, particularly the Serb-Croat conflict, dominated Yugoslav politics. Pašić, as Serb Radical leader, and Radić, as Croat Peasant Party leader, both concerned themselves chiefly with it. Alexander I, who succeeded in 1924 though he had ruled from 1918 as Regent, tried, as his predecessor Peter had done, to end the racial antagonisms, but the Croats were soon justifiably complaining that they had been better off under the Habsburgs. Yugoslavia's external problems made the nationalities question particularly dangerous. Italy, Hungary and Bulgaria were openly hostile and involved in Macedonian and other dissident movements. Albania was an uncertain quantity, though not dangerous unless backed by Italy.

A 'strong' régime was essential from the moment of Yugoslavia's foundation because of the backwardness of her peoples and the nationalities problem—which is not to say that a Great Serb dictatorship was the only solution. However, it was in fact the violence and unreasonableness of the party politicians, culminating in the murder of the stiff-necked Radić in June 1928 and the Croats' attempt in consequence to set up their own diet, which impelled Alexander in January 1929 to establish his dictatorship. Even without the nationalities problem, however, it would have been difficult to establish parliamentary government. The poverty, backwardness and illiteracy of most of the people put them at the mercy of politicians who were exceptionally bloody and corrupt even by the standards of their time and place. The freedom for which the South Slavs had fought turned out to be freedom for reactionary Great Serb politicians to impose a police state on the other nationalities, and on their own democrats, radicals, peasants and Communists.

Yugoslavia had virtually no industry except that which sufficed for meeting rudimentary demands for processed food and clothing, and in consequence practically no urban proletariat, or middle class. Nearly 80% of the total population was agricultural, mostly smallholders, for there were few large estates or even prosperous yeoman farms. On the other hand there was little social tension. In the 1920 elections the new Communist Party gained 58 seats, against the Croat Peasant Party's 50, the Serbian Radicals' 98 and the Democrats' 94. The Communists at this time had considerable strength in Belgrade and Zagreb, so Radicals and Democrats (themselves dissident Radicals) united to repress them. In 1921 the assassination of the Minister of the Interior by a Communist provided a pretext for dissolving the Communist Party, which rapidly diminished in size. However, Serbs, because of old ties with Russia, felt some sympathy for Communism, while Croats and Macedonians in particular, as well as other nationalities, sympathized with it because of its opposition to the *régime*. Hence as time passed Serb intellectuals and proletarians who had adopted Communism found themselves in alliance with *bourgeois* and upper class anti-Serb nationalists. Police repression accordingly came to be directed impartially against Communism and subversive nationalism.

But while Communism appealed in the towns to the socially and spiritually uprooted, rather than to intellectuals and proletarians as such, it eventually acquired considerable peasant support. As the peasant masses alone were numerous enough to be a genuinely revolutionary force in Yugoslavia, this was one of the principal reasons why the Communists were so cruelly repressed and hunted out. Another reason was the strength of the ties of respect and gratitude which still bound many Serbs to their old protector Russia.

## Chapter IV
# THE EXTERNAL WORLD

## (i) *Russia under Lenin*

THE Bolsheviks' success in holding together an empire embracing far more numerous and diverse nationalities than the Habsburg and Turkish empires, bears witness to their political skill and ruthlessness, as well as to Trotsky's organizing genius in building up the Red Army when Soviet Russia's political, social and economic structures were disintegrating. However, had the Central Powers not collapsed in November 1918, thereby reducing the value for the Allies of the Whites as well as removing German and Austrian troops from Russia, the Bolsheviks might not have been able to hold out much longer. It remained uncertain for some time whether they or the Whites would move into the vacuum left by the Germans, and whether the Allies would extend the scope of their intervention.

At the end of November 1918 the British landed at Baku, on December 18th the French occupied Odessa, and at the end of December the British took Batum. The British agreed to supply General A. I. Denikin, and supported the White Generals N. N. Yudenich in Estonia and E. K. Miller in Archangel, as well as Admiral A. V. Kolchak, who had assumed supreme power on November 18th at Omsk. The Whites expected the British and French to launch full-scale offensives; the Allies proposed merely to send supplies and hold the ground until the Whites attacked in force. In any event, the Allies could not commit large forces to the Ukraine or to southern Russia, and Japanese intervention was strictly limited.

In January 1919 the Bolsheviks treacherously attacked the Ukrainian Directory which they had agreed to support, but which was working for an independent Ukraine on the basis of the right of self-determination proclaimed by them. On January 3rd the Red Army occupied Kharkov, and it also began to make progress in regaining the Baltic states, though this was soon checked. Byelorussia, which the Red Army had entered when the Germans left, was combined with Lithuania in February into the Litbel or Lithuanian-Byelo-Russian Soviet Republic. In April, however, the Poles captured most of Litbel, and the Bolsheviks soon infuriated the Ukrainians because of the ruthless enforcement of collectivization and War Communism, which they combined together with their hostility to Ukrainian nationalism. The Ukrainians, however, were divided among themselves. The followers of the Socialist Petlyura distrusted the peasant leader N. I. Makhno as much as they hated the Bolsheviks and the Whites. Ukrainian history between the opening of the Revolution and the ending of the Civil War saw an unparalleled diversity of *régimes* established, and eventually the complete disintegration of the region. In 1919 it existed merely as a number of separate communities. The Makhnovites after October 1919 temporarily succeeded in attracting mass support, after the Whites under Denikin, who had taken supreme command in south-eastern Russia on February 15th, 1919, had made themselves even more hated than the Bolsheviks. But the Makhnovites controlled only the disorganized and unreliable countryside with its anarchist peasants. The towns, where the issue was decided, were Russian and despised Ukrainian nationalism, and here the Bolsheviks developed a strong party apparatus.

French evacuation of Odessa on April 8th, 1919, following British withdrawal from Transcaspia three days earlier, in no way eased the difficulties of the Bolsheviks, which in January had induced them to accept an offer by the peace conference, made on Lloyd George's initiative and transmitted by Wilson, who still saw democratic potentialities in Lenin. This proposed a meeting of Bolsheviks, Whites and western delegates on the island of Prinkipo to end the Civil War. Though the Bolsheviks' reply was insulting and evasive, and their ultimate aim was to annihilate the Whites, they needed a truce so that they could establish control of western Russia. The Whites, confident of success, and privately assured by France that they could count on Allied support if they refused the offer, unhesitatingly rejected it. Kolchak's spring offensive in March 1919 was their reaction to the holding of Comintern's First Congress in Moscow on March 2nd–7th. The European extreme Left Wing groups failed, however, to exploit the postwar conditions in Europe, and the Comintern itself was never much more than a means of manipulating foreign Marxists to suit the needs of Bolshevik internal and external policies, and a bugbear to the western democracies whose governments it tried to subvert. However, the myths of the 'world Communist conspiracy', and of 'Moscow's bid for world domination' became securely established.

In mid-March the Bolsheviks again showed their readiness to compromise temporarily with the Whites. They promised an amnesty for Allied supporters and an end to hostilities, if the Allies ended their intervention and blockade of Russia. The Allies would have been well-advised to accept. Intervention was achieving no military success, while it gave excellent material for Bolshevik propaganda against the Whites as the agents of foreign interests, and for Bolshevik appeals to the minority nationalities. Basing their policies on information supplied by the Whites, the Allies thought that Kolchak's offensive was still proceeding when it was actually being repulsed by Frunze's counter-offensive of April 26th.

Denikin did open another offensive on May 19th, while the Hungarian and Bavarian attempts at Soviet republics had already alarmed the west. On May 27th, therefore, the Allies offered recognition to Kolchak as ruler of all Russia if he would recall the Constituent Assembly, recognize Polish and Finnish independence and the autonomy of the minorities, and promise not to restore Tsardom. Kolchak agreed to everything except Finnish independence, which the Assembly must decide, but his military power was already largely destroyed, and he could not link up with Denikin in the south. The Social Revolutionaries, with their slogan 'Neither Kolchak nor Lenin', crippled Kolchak's authority in Siberia, and so opened the way for Lenin. On June 9th Kolchak's power on his central and southern fronts was shattered, his northern units were contained and his major forces driven eastwards into Siberia. At the end of June Denikin, in a great offensive, captured Kharkov, Ekaterinoslav and Tsaritsyn, but instead of turning to help Kolchak, decided to take Moscow. He moved steadily forward, and by mid-October had taken Orel and his vanguard was approaching Tula. Simultaneously Yudenich moved against Petrograd, where Trotsky organized the defence. Probably it was beyond Yudenich's strength to take Petrograd; Denikin certainly had over-extended his lines. The Whites had now been brought to defeat by their failures to concert their strategy, to win over the peasantry in the face of their identification by the Bolsheviks with dispossessed landowners seeking revenge and the return of their lands, and to obtain effective Allied help. The decisive counter-blows against Denikin's offensive, and with it against the White cause, came in the second half of October, though more than a year passed before the Civil War ended.

Most of the British troops had already been withdrawn. The Allies left Archangel on September 30th and Murmansk on October 12th, 1919. Lloyd George was quick to recognize that the mid-October victories meant that the Civil War, after bringing the Bolsheviks to the brink of destruction, had finally consolidated their power, and that it was now impossible to defeat them by force. On November 14th the Red Army scored further triumphs in the east by capturing Omsk and pursuing the Whites towards Irkutsk. In January 1920 the Allies completed the evacuation of all but a few troops and ended the blockade. Kolchak gave place to Gregory Semenov, and was executed next month by the Bolsheviks. The Red Army tried to exploit its advantage by seizing Vladivostok, but the Japanese were there in strength, and were not inclined to abandon their Siberian ambitions merely because the western powers had been forced to withdraw and the Americans had voluntarily left Siberia. The Whites had no prospects there now. Most of them went to Manchuria or China, though Semenov set up a puppet *régime* for the Japanese in Chita, east of Lake Baikal, until October 1920. Western Siberia, the area between Lake Baikal and the Urals, declared for incorporation into Soviet Russia. Eastern Siberia was gradually taken over by pro-Bolshevik partisans, and in April 1920 Lenin found an ingenious expedient by promoting its establishment as the

'Far Eastern Republic', ostensibly independent of Moscow. It sent delegates to the Washington naval conference. American and British delegates readily accepted their argument that the Japanese had no right on the northern mainland. Under American pressure the Japanese finally evacuated Vladivostok in October 1922. The Bolsheviks immediately entered it and the Whites fled. Thereupon the coastal region joined the Far Eastern Republic, which in turn on November 10th proclaimed its dissolution and incorporation into the Russian Soviet Republic.

This completed the territorial reconstitution of the Tsarist Empire until 1939. The Ukraine and Byelorussia were partitioned with Poland by the Treaty of Riga. In the south Denikin's last stronghold fell in March 1920, but Denikin was succeeded by General P. N. Wrangel, one of the few great generals on either side, and the only White comparable to the former Tsarist officer M. N. Tukhachevsky, whom Trotsky had made a general despite protests from Bolshevik purists who could not understand Tukhachevsky's patriotism. Wrangel in a brilliant offensive overran large southern areas before the ending of the Polish war in October freed overwhelming Red Army forces, who drove him first back to the Crimea, and then out of it to Constantinople in November 1920. The Allies had granted *de facto* recognition to the Caucasian republics of Armenia, Georgia and Azerbaijan in January 1920. But they had no intention of helping the republics, though a small British garrison held the Black Sea port of Batum until July 1920, and the Bolsheviks cut off all chance of effective help by making a military agreement with Kemal. In April 1920 Azerbaijan capitulated. In December, after Armenia had been involved in war with Turkey, an Armenian Bolshevik *régime* was installed. Georgia was subdued in March 1921, but considerable Menshevik opposition to the Bolsheviks remained. Stalin, himself a Georgian, suppressed this in what was soon to be recognized as a characteristic manner. The south-eastern Muslim countries, never integrated into Tsarist Russia, were integrated into the Soviet Union by a combination of promises of self-determination, persuasion of intellectuals, and bloody repression of recalcitrants. Fighting continued against the Turkestan partisans, the Basmachi, until 1926, but Turkestan was largely in Bolshevik hands by the autumn of 1922, and control of Central Asia was assured.

The misery of the workers and peasants during the Civil War was intensified by War Communism and its accompanying apparatus of terror and dictatorship. Lenin would not in any event have tolerated opposition to the *régime*, but the Civil War in his view necessitated the destruction of its enemies. Hence, while he envisaged the eventual establishment of a Utopian socialist *régime* which could dispense with coercion and rely on voluntary acceptance, Leninist society provided the base on which Stalinism was built. This was true also of Lenin's nationalities policy, which worked for the establishment of a centralized despotism, though it was to produce great material benefits for the backward nations of eastern, central and southern Russia by giving them industries and educational opportunities which never existed before. The principle of equality and non-discrimination on national grounds was never fully enforced, nor were the Jews the only race to be discriminated against, but national differences became less important. Bolshevik centralization entailed enforcement of accepted standards which in the nature of things had to be Great Russian standards. Of course 'Russianization' facilitated the tightening of Moscow's control over the constituent republics, but centralization was at the heart of Marxism, and without it the tremendous achievement of re-uniting all but a few of the peoples formerly subject to the Tsar would have been impossible. There were also good practical as well as good Marxist reasons for the extension of Great Russian predominance. The proletariat, the official leaders of the revolution, was largely Great Russian, and so were the directors of the Red Army and trade unions.

The new constitution of July 1923 which formally constituted the USSR gave to the All-Union Soviet Congress complete control over foreign policy, foreign trade, defence, industry, agriculture, education, justice and public health. In effect these powers were given to the Central Committee of the Party, acting through the Praesidium and the Council of People's Commissars; which meant that they were given, as in 1918, to the Politburo. A significant gloss on the right to secession under the constitution was made when it was demonstrated that demands for secession could arise only from class feelings on the part of those who were hostile to the proletariat. An even more brutal gloss appeared five years later, when Stalin inaugurated the first of his Five-Year Plans, calling for collectivization of agriculture and massive industrialization. This could only be achieved over the dead bodies of many of the nationalist leaders who had survived Civil War and Bolshevization.

Lenin was forced to relax the political and economic terror in 1921. The urban proletariat had grown too restive to submit to enrolment in labour battalions so that it could more easily be disciplined as conscripted labour. The peasants defied the requisitioning of crops and cattle, and as there were no manufactured products to buy in the collapsed economy which seven years of war and revolution had brought, they farmed only at subsistence level. Apart from physical devastation which had left large areas of towns gutted and pillaged, factories destroyed, communications practically at a standstill and the countryside prostrate, the towns were being depopulated by starving people leaving to scavenge the rural areas for food. Bands of demobilized soldiers spread further ruin and rapine. There were great peasant outbreaks in southern and eastern Russia. Tsarism at its worst had never been so execrated as Bolshevism was in early 1921, but unco-ordinated dissatisfaction of urban and peasant masses had no influence on the Bolshevik dictatorship. A mutiny in March 1921 by the staunchly revolutionary sailors in Kronstadt, however, showed that the Bolsheviks must immediately make concessions.

Famine in 1920 had caused the death of about 3,000,000 people. By

January 1921 industrial production was only just over one-eighth of 1913's total and, like trade, was coming to a halt. The government had no plans for reviving the economy, though a planned economy had naturally been an original Bolshevik objective. Trotsky had been working for one throughout 1920, but he also wanted to combine it with what came to be called the New Economic Policy (NEP). Lenin had bombastically declared in 1920 that 'Communism is Soviet power plus electrification of the whole country', but in 1921 he adopted Trotsky's New Economic Policy in modified form, though not Trotsky's idea of planning, insisting: 'We are paupers. Starving, destitute paupers. A comprehensive plan for us = "bureaucratic Utopia".' NEP as introduced in March 1921 set out first to encourage food production, which was possible only if the peasants were given inducements to produce for the market. This could only be done if there were a free market in food, and if the peasant were paid in something more substantial than inflated paper currency. Or, as the official jargon put it: 'Exchange of goods is recognized as the basic lever of the new economic policy', 'starting from the existence of the market and accepting its laws', and 'alleviating and expanding the exchange between towns and villages'. The re-introduction of small-scale peasant farming was formalized in the 'fundamental law' of May 1922 legalizing private property in land. The collective farms introduced by War Communism were officially favoured, but peasants were not compelled to join them, and by 1927 less than 1% of peasant households was collectivized. Peasants could sell or lease their land and hire labour, and whereas hitherto the Party had insisted on the primacy of industry, now it had to admit the predominance of agriculture. By 1927 gross agricultural and industrial outputs slightly exceeded the 1913 levels, though agricultural *per capita* production was slightly smaller. But the situation was unhealthy. The peasant economy was still largely self-sufficient, and production would not continue to rise when prices discriminated against agricultural products and taxation against the more prosperous peasants. Also, the pre-war level was likely to mark a plateau in agricultural production as the artificially high demand for manufactured goods decreased during the years of recovery.

'Capitalist', or rather free-market agriculture, was not to be accompanied by capitalist heavy industry or wholesale trade. Inauguration of a state planning commission, Gosplan, in April 1921 indicated this, though it was some time before Gosplan actually produced a plan. Large-scale industry remained almost wholly socialized (about 97% in 1923) as did wholesale trade (about 93%). Heavy industry, transport, foreign trade and banking were all in the socialized sector. Foreign capitalists were encouraged to invest not only in small-scale industry where private enterprise now flourished (owning about 82% in 1927) but also in large-scale. The intention was to permit peaceful competition between public and private sectors of the economy. At first the government favoured the latter, but from 1927 discriminated severely against it. Both sectors, particularly the private, operated at high costs, but the socialized was notably inefficient—and would have operated at relatively higher costs if the private sector had not suffered from high taxation and scarcity of raw materials. One reason for higher costs was the ideological conviction, abandoned only with the Five-Year Plans, that manual workers in nationalized heavy industries, as the cream of the proletariat, should have high wages. The growth of productivity did not justify them; admittedly it increased considerably, but it started from a very low level, and little attention was paid to costs or quality as the market was assured. In addition, the disparity between the prices of industrial and agricultural products created a crisis (the 'scissors' crisis, Trotsky called it after the shape formed by intersecting curves of rising industrial and falling agricultural prices). Towards the end of 1923, therefore, the government finally forced down industrial prices, and a degree of economic stability was attained, though at a very low level.

In January 1923 Lenin argued that NEP's compromise with the peasants was essential to the revolution's success, and that they could gradually be converted to socialism. It was demonstrably true that the economy depended upon the small-holder, and Lenin believed until his death on January 21st, 1924, that NEP must be retained for a long time to ease the transition first to state capitalism and next to socialism. NEP and planning were generally regarded as incompatible, but Trotsky, as usual far ahead of his colleagues, insisted that the introduction of price fixing necessitated planning. But Lenin, his only powerful ally among the leaders, was dying, and the economic dispute became entangled with the struggle for the succession. During the Civil War Russia had been ruled by the Politburo of Lenin, Trotsky, Kamenev, Bukharin and Stalin, but Stalin was largely ruling Russia before Lenin's death by virtue of his posts as commissar for nationalities, commissar for the workers and peasants inspectorate, which gave him immense patronage, his membership of the Organization Bureau (Orgburo) which carried out the Politburo's decisions, and his post as secretary-general to the Party's Central Committee, which was to form the stepping-stone to his dictatorship later.

Even before Stalin became secretary general there had been growing criticism of the 'bureaucratic malformation' of the Party organization and demands for a return to 'democratic centralism'. Both Lenin and Trotsky had some sympathy for these views, and Trotsky illogically proposed to reduce the bureaucrats' powers by enforcing more rigid control on the trade unions through selected personnel. The most vocal union leaders, constituting the 'Workers' Opposition', argued more sensibly that as the workers under Marxism should dominate the state, their unions ought to control it. Lenin maintained that the unions had a right to independence as Russia was not yet socialist, and the workers therefore needed defence. However, as NEP permitted capitalism, and the Bolsheviks were the only party, it was feared that capitalism might seek within the Communist Party the channels of political expression which it could not find outside, so letting in the counter-revolution. Lenin would allow no reduction of the

Party's power, but the Kronstadt rising and NEP indicated the need for greater Party unity. At the 10th Party Congress in March 1921 Lenin denounced both Workers' Opposition and 'Democratic Centralists', and imposed a ban on 'fractionalism', that is, organized opposition to Party decisions. The Central Committee was empowered to expel leaders elected by Congress. Lenin did not intend to stifle free discussion; neither did Trotsky, who voted for the ban unaware of how it would be used against him. Under these circumstances, Stalin's particular gifts had full scope, and he rapidly became in the Party caucus, though not in the public eye, the second man to Lenin. In the Civil War he had been eclipsed by Trotsky, and had already learned to hate him. Political differences, however, now became more important. Moreover, in the Party caucus Trotsky was largely isolated, when Lenin suffered his first stroke in May 1922. Trotsky had never been an 'Old Bolshevik', and had quarrelled violently with Lenin. Lenin was prepared nevertheless to work with him for the revolution, whereas Lenin's *epigoni* were not. The Bolsheviks also feared that their revolution, like the French, would throw up a military dictator, and Trotsky as the creator of the Red Army was the only likely Bonaparte. Finally, Stalin knew how to keep in the background when necessary, and give the appearance of a loyal, safe and unambitious servant while he gained control of the Party machine. Lenin had been head of both Party and state; Stalin's control of the Party after a few years also gave him control of the state.

After Lenin's second stroke in March 1923 incapacitated him, bitter quarrels broke out in the Politburo—chiefly, though not openly, over the succession. Stalin joined with G. E. Zinoviev and L. B. Kamenev to set up the 'triumvirate'. Zinoviev and Kamenev feared Trotsky with his ideological and intellectual brilliance, but they despised Stalin who had neither. In his last year Lenin came to suspect Stalin's dictatorial tendencies, particularly when Stalin suppressed the Georgian national movement with unnecessary ferocity. He prepared to 'break' Stalin, and wrote a political testament which proposed to give the post of general secretary to a man 'more patient, more loyal, more polite and more attentive to comrades'. The testament, however, also criticized Zinoviev and Kamenev, and praised Trotsky as the ablest man in the Party. As Trotsky had been vigorously denouncing the triumvirs for their economic failures and 'secretarial bureaucratism' yet refused to organize an opposition which would cheerfully have followed him, the triumvirs successfully held together. On December 15th, 1923, Stalin in *Pravda* denounced Trotsky for being 'in a bloc with Democratic Centralists and a part of the Left Communists'. At a meeting that evening Zinoviev coined the word 'Trotskyism', and though he added that Trotsky was indispensable to the leadership, 'Trotskyism' had begun to be presented as the treacherous enemy of 'Leninism', of which the triumvirs were the defenders and exponents.

In January 1924 the triumvirs pilloried the opposition as a 'petty bourgeois deviation' and Trotsky as its leader. Lenin died a few days later.

His widow, an enemy of Stalin, wanted the testament brought before the 13th Party Congress of May 1924. It is uncertain whether the leadership's decision, foolishly endorsed by Trotsky, to suppress the testament prevented Stalin's ruin. Certainly Stalin would not have gained the power which he did had it been published. Lenin well knew Trotsky's political incapacity, and clearly wished a form of collective leadership to follow his own. So did Zinoviev, Kamenev, Bukharin, Trotsky, and possibly even Stalin at first, though it was not long before the temptation to assume supreme power proved irresistible.

## (ii) *Africa and the New Middle East*

The European colonial powers could not foresee in 1918 that Africans would within fifty years be able to establish independent states over large areas of the continent. Lord Lugard, the leading expert on Britain's African colonies, and the French colonial minister Albert Sarraut succeeded in introducing into the League Mandates the principle that the colonial peoples must be advanced by their rulers both politically and economically to justify colonial rule. But they thought that it would be a very long process before the primitive, superstitious African Negro would be capable of running his own affairs. Attempts were made to direct economic development on lines suitable to the African peoples in the tropics, while social services like education and medicine, as well as the propagation of improved agricultural methods, were introduced more widely by colonial officials, but chiefly to promote the economic interests of the colonial powers. Some progress was made in the British colonies and Mandates towards instituting representative government, but indigenous Africans were in a small minority on the councils, and little was done elsewhere, least of all in the Belgian and Portuguese colonies and Mandates. The colonial services were in any case undermanned and underequipped to deal with the older problems of suppressing slavery, establishing courts of justice and maintaining law and order. They had neither the knowledge nor the financial resources to carry out large-scale developments, and such finances as were available came from taxation of European-owned enterprises and trade. These were centred mainly in the mineral-bearing lands of South Africa and Northern Rhodesia, where the value of the 'copper belt' was realized in the mid-1920s, though railway systems were extended in the inter-war years to open up most of the colonies which had not had them before 1914. Indeed most of the European capital invested in African railways, which were essential for administrative purposes, was put up by governments. Private investors were dubious of getting any returns.

Investments went mainly to South Africa and the British territories (especially Northern Rhodesia), which altogether accounted for about 80%

of the total before 1936 of approximately £1,222,000,000 or about $6,100,000,000; Belgian Congo took about 12% and the rest went to French territories. If this invested capital chiefly benefited the industrialists, planters and white settlers, particularly those in the Rhodesias and Kenya, it also brought advantages to the Africans, though not nearly enough. Northern Rhodesia remained a Crown Colony, but Southern Rhodesia in 1923 was given self-government, though not Dominion status. Henceforth white Northern Rhodesia wanted union with the south in order to evade the restrictions imposed by Britain. In the same year the important decision was made that it was no longer automatic British policy to give self-government to whites, British or not, merely because they appeared to be capable of maintaining a government. Over Kenya, where Indians outnumbered British, it was declared that, while minorities must have safeguards, the major consideration was the welfare of the African majority, and Britain must assume responsibility for discharging this trust.

In British West Africa Lugard's programme of dual rule prevailed. British ideas and influence were promoted by introducing British law and customs, while British officials tried to preserve the old tribal systems. But in southern and British eastern Africa (Kenya, Uganda, Tanganyika and Nyasaland) the prevailing idea was to 'keep the kaffir in his place', and the British official attitude accordingly aroused great resentment. This was also true of South Africa, where Afrikaner ambitions for ending the British connection added complications. General J. B. M. Hertzog had led a delegation of Nationalists to demand independence at the peace conference, but this was then obviously a minority view, and the chief South African concern had been to have South-West Africa ceded outright instead of mandated. On the central issue, that of race, there was a difference only about the tactics to be used in dealing with the Bantu; the British and General Jan Christian Smuts preferred more humane and discreet methods of repressing black nationalism. Though the Germans had been deprived of their colonies on the grounds of 'unfitness', Smuts disregarded the mandatory provisions and introduced into South-West Africa racial policies differing little from the German. He could do nothing else, unless he denounced the system which he operated in the Union; indeed the Africans in the colony were worse off economically than they had been under German rule. He set out to incorporate the German settlers into the Union's system, explaining to a German government representative that he admired the work of the German settlers, which would materially promote the building of 'an enduring European civilization on the African continent, which is the main task of the Union'.

Tripolitania and Cyrenaica (formerly Libya), were economically poor, and they were always liabilities, like the eastern colonies of Eritrea and Somaliland. At the peace treaty Britain ceded Jarabub to Italy and promised Jubaland, which was handed over later, in 1924, and France handed over a small area to Eritrea from French Somaliland ten years afterwards.

But though Italy's sole contribution to colonial enterprises during the war had been a hurried retreat from Libya, she burned with indignation at Allied ingratitude. However, since quarrels with the neighbouring European colonies were then unthinkable, she encroached on the backward independent African state of Ethiopia (Abyssinia). She offered to do so in concert with Britain, but Britain had enough difficulties across the Red Sea in Aden and southern Arabia and disliked the Ethiopian proclivity for slave-trading. Britain opposed the Franco-Italian sponsorship of Ethiopia for admission to the League in 1923, but Ethiopia promised to stop slavery, and Ras Tafari, Regent for the Empress Zauditu, was attempting to modernize the country. In December 1925 Britain agreed to assist Italy's development of her sphere of influence in Ethiopia, but when the Ethiopians protested at this manifestation of old-fashioned imperialism both Britain and Italy reassured them, and in August 1928 Mussolini signed a treaty of friendship with Ethiopia, also promising co-operation in building a road from Assab to Dessié. Two months before Ras Tafari had made himself king over the protests of several important chiefs, and extended his programme of modernization, notably of the army. After the old empress's death in April 1930 he declared himself Emperor Haile Selassie, and next year attempted to transform Ethiopia into a rudimentary constitutional state. As it transpired, it was not Ethiopia's barbarism to which Mussolini objected, but the Emperor's attempts to modernize and strengthen her.

On the conclusion of the war a delegation of Egyptian nationalists proposed to go to Paris to demand independence, but they were arrested by the British. To meet the ends of British politicians and their service advisers, Egypt could serve her essential purpose of providing bases for defending the Canal and the route to India, only if controlled by British forces. Only during World War II were British interests in India threatened by external forces, but India with her British and Indian troops served as the major source of British military power in the inter-war years. Hence it was vital to ensure communications between Britain and India. Egypt, and to a lesser extent Iraq, though not parts of the British Empire, were strategically essential for this purpose. This was why Britain, though for centuries a Mediterranean power of sorts, after 1914 dominated the Mediterranean for nearly forty years. Oil, to which so much significance was later attached, was a factor of only limited importance in the inter-war years. The whole of the Middle East oil supply amounted to under 5% of the world production in 1938; 57% of British oil imports came from the western hemisphere and only 22% from the Middle East. The British government certainly drew considerable advantages from its oil interests in the Middle East, especially in Iran, but these also carried disadvantages, as any British move in the area tended to be seen in terms of concern for oil shares. Britain's record of promises broken and friends betrayed in the Middle East did nothing to weaken this view.

The Egyptian nationalist (Wafd) party was not concerned with oil, nor were the British much concerned about it in their Egyptian policy.

However, Egypt constituted a pressing problem from March 1919, when the deportation of the Wafd leader Saad Zaghlul Pasha provoked rebellion. General Sir Edmund Allenby suppressed it fairly quickly, but the Egyptians recognized only military defeat. In 1922 Britain was obliged, in unique circumstances, to declare the independence of a country with which she could not come to terms, reserving for herself rights for the 'defence of Egypt and the Canal and continuation of her administration of the Sudan'. A parliamentary system was installed in April 1923 by Ahmed Fuad, the former Sultan, who had assumed royal status in March. The Egyptian parliament was dominated by the Wafd when elections were held in September. Popular support for Zaghlul and his anti-British line was unmistakable, and this blocked Fuad's attempts to reach a compromise with the British. The Wafd would not yield on the reserved points, and some of its leaders were involved in a murder campaign against the British and in engineering mutiny among the Sudanese troops. The Wafd thought control of the Sudan essential to ensure Egypt's Nile water supply, and British threats in 1924 to divert Nile waters after the Egyptian nationalists' murder of the Sudan Governor-General Sir Lee Stack merely strengthened Zaghlul's determination. However Fuad, a Europeanized Turk who despised the *bourgeois* Egyptian politicians as demagogues, dissolved parliament and tried to rule through his friends. It proved impossible to rule except through the Wafd or with its acquiescence, and when Zaghlul died in August 1927 the new leader Nahas Pasha was as intractable to Fuad as to the British. That a party so corrupt, essentially anti-democratic, and reactionary in social questions as the Wafd had become, could nevertheless win sweeping victories in any free election, was an indication of nationalism's supreme importance in Egyptian politics. In 1933 Fuad set up a virtual dictatorship as the only way out of the *impasse* —for him. The young Farouk, who succeeded him in 1936, came to terms with the Wafd, and British readiness to compromise on something less than 100% military security brought an agreement with Egypt in August. Thereupon the Wafd, deprived of its *raison d'etre*, began to disintegrate rapidly.

Iraq (formerly Mesopotamia) and Iran (formerly Persia) were also British concerns. British policy in Iran was designed to produce a stable *régime* in place of its warring factions, to ensure that Iran could not be used to threaten either Iraq or India, to maintain the oil supply, and to prevent the spread of Bolshevik ideology among the poverty-stricken masses. Curzon, to forestall Lenin, induced Iran in August 1919 to sign a treaty which served as model for those later made in the Middle East, providing for British financial and military supervision. But Bolshevik victories in 1920 in the Civil War induced the Iranians to have second thoughts. Moreover they hoped that their rising military leader, Reza Khan, would turn out a second Kemal. In the event they handled the matter extremely skilfully. They substituted American for British advisers since the State Department, while resisting Wilsonian commitments in

369

the Middle East, had no objections to supporting domestic oil interests. The Iranians could hardly reject Soviet offers of a treaty in 1921, even though it involved entry of Red Army units. They solved this problem by appointing a pro-Russian as governor of the northern provinces, and replacing him when the Red Army left.

Iraq was a bone of contention between the British and Indian governments; the British ministers were tired and over-burdened with work; there was for a long time uncertainty about American intentions in the Middle East, so that it took a year before British and Arabs alike realized that Wilsonian self-determination was not going to be a factor there; and of course there were the problems posed by Turkey even after she had renounced the Arab lands. Britain obtained the mandate in May 1920, but in July the Iraqis, encouraged by Syrian nationalist and Islamic agitation, struck out for independence—and for smaller taxes, which afflicted fellahin, landlords and tribes as well as dignitaries. It had been known for some time that trouble was coming, but no precautions had been taken. The British in Iraq, also, did not want to assume mandatory responsibilities, and found a temporary way out of their difficulties by attempting to make reparation to the Emir Feisal. Feisal had been promised rule over a self-governing Syria, but the nationalists distrusted him for conceding too much to France. In September 1919 Britain agreed to French control of coastal Syria, on condition that Feisal had the four inland towns, with the desert beyond them. However the French broke their promise, and the British gave Feisal no support. In July he was deposed by the French and fled, whereupon France in September re-organized Syria, giving separate status to Great Lebanon, and recognizing Jebel Druze as autonomous in March 1921. Britain and France delimited the Syrian-Palestine-Iraq frontiers in December 1920, and in August 1921 Britain managed a plebiscite in Iraq which accepted Feisal as king.

An Anglo-Iraqi treaty of March 1922 gave Britain financial and military control, but Iraq remained politically unstable and the northern Kurds never accepted Iraqi rule. In October Britain ostensibly exchanged mandatory responsibilities for senior partnership in an alliance, which was finally ratified in March 1924. The Turks, however, had claims on Mosul, which the British wanted Iraq to have for strategic reasons, before it was certain that it contained oil, though not before this had been suspected. The League eventually awarded Mosul to Iraq in 1926, but French and American oil interests were appeased in 1929 when they joined in a consortium to form the Iraq Petroleum Company. Similarly Aden colony, Aden protectorate, Muscat and the Trucial states, later discovered to be rich in oil, were retained for strategic reasons. Bahrein, Kuwait and Qatar had come under British protection long ago, and the last two looked to Britain to maintain them against the encroachments of the great Arab imperialist, ibn Saud of the Nejd. Ibn Saud in the inter-war years conquered most of the Arabian peninsula not already seized by him. His great rival Hussein of the Hejaz, Feisal's father, was forced to abdicate by his subjects because of incompetence in 1924, but his son Ali was equally incapable of resisting ibn Saud. By 1926 ibn Saud had completed the conquest of the Hejaz. Next year the British, who had shown their friendship continually to the Hejaz, recognized ibn Saud's independence. Only the old kingdom of the Yemen, the coastal areas, Palestine and Transjordan held out.

Palestine and Transjordan became British mandates, with provision for a Jewish national home in Palestine. The terms of these mandates, as of the other Middle Eastern mandates, prescribed that the mandatory powers should render administrative advice and assistance until the states could stand alone. This special 'A' type mandate was established only in the Middle East. The 'B' types established in Africa (except for South-West Africa, which was a 'C' type like those in the Pacific) did not specifically prescribe autonomy, but on the other hand the decisions of the Allied Conference at San Remo in 1920 which awarded the Middle Eastern mandates disregarded both the promises of freedom of choice and the desire of the Arabs for independence. Over Iraq the British had a bad conscience, and the British general election of 1922 had revealed considerable opposition to keeping the mandate. Therefore it was slowly whittled away until it ended in 1932, with Britain however still in a strong treaty position. The British could rely on Feisal's brother Abdullah, first emir and then king in Transjordan. They recognized his independence in 1928 while retaining financial and military control. This new kind of imperialism 'by treaty', reasonably successful though it was in Transjordan and Iraq, could not be employed in Palestine, where irreconcilable Arab–Jewish antagonism and conflicting British promises to both sides produced a witch's brew which had led even Wilson to agree that for 'the time being' Palestine must be excluded from the area destined for provisional independence. But though conditions were from the start disturbed, and the problem insoluble on terms acceptable to both sides, nobody could foresee the Nazi persecution of the 1930s and the anti-semitism in other countries which would send Jews in large numbers to Palestine. Finally in May 1939 the British proposed to end Jewish immigration after another 75,000 had been admitted, for Arabs outnumbered Jews, and Arab resort to violence frightened the British government into making concessions which it would otherwise not have considered.

In Afghanistan the national forces won resounding victories, and also sought, unlike Iran, which remained theocratic and backward, to reform the state on modern and western lines. The Afghans won their freedom from the British as early as 1919. The British were tired of war and its expense, and against Curzon's protests withdrew voluntarily, whereas American and French pressure was required to force them out of Iran. The Afghan ruler, Emir Amanullah, attempted to raise the Indian Muslims against the British, but his invasion was defeated and the British were not prepared for a long and difficult occupation of Afghanistan. From 1921 Amanullah looked to Russia for support against Britain—unnecessarily, and from the domestic viewpoint also foolishly. Emulating Kemal, in April 1923 he promulgated a new constitution as preliminary to western-type economic and administrative reforms, but the religious leaders and tribal chiefs disliked this even more than his friendship for the Bolsheviks. They rebelled against him in 1928, and he abdicated in January 1929. The ensuing civil war, however, was ended in October 1929 by a western-ized general, who carried out under the title of Mohammed Nadir Shah a more thorough-going programme than Amanullah's, but with tact and caution. Afghanistan remained, however, a strongly Muslim country, and was not westernized even in the sense in which Kemal succeeded in westernizing Turkey.

Kemal's achievement in Turkey was to make a compact national state out of the remnants of a multinational empire in such a way as to restore Turkish self-respect after the humiliating disaster of 1918, while leaving no foundation on which a revengeful chauvinism might arise. In the old empire the Turks had been a minority. In the secular Turkish Republic which he established, less than 2% of the population, if the Kurds are excluded, was non-Turkish. His ambition to transform Turkey into a western parliamentary democracy was not realized, but he made her into a secular state recognizing the rule of law and the equality of women, and participating in the civilization of the west, which alone could give the material and social basis which Turkey needed.

British policy towards Turkey, mistaken from the start, was doomed when America's resort to isolationism defeated Lloyd George's plans for her assumption of mandates over Armenia and the Straits region, and then of Anatolia also. The worst that can be said about American policy is that it should have been as sparing in giving advice as in assuming commitments, when it was pressed by the Allies for both. After the American Senate refused in May 1920, very properly, to accept Lloyd George's recom-mendation that America should accept the Armenian mandate, he could do no more than accept the Allies' offer to arbitrate the Turkish-Armenian border. Immediately afterwards Kemal's forces overran Armenia, but the revival of Soviet power prevented the perpetration of a great national injustice by Turkey—who could less afford it than Russia. After driving the Greeks from Anatolia in September 1922 and regaining Smyrna in a bloody massacre which was the last manifestation of Turkish military barbarism, Kemal advanced to surround the small British garrison in Chanak on the Straits. Aware that a peace conference would certainly restore Chanak, Kemal did not attack, but waited for the British with-drawal. The armistice of Mundania in October gave Kemal what he wanted, and next month he proclaimed the abolition of the Sultanate, whereupon Mohammed VI left Constantinople (soon renamed Istanbul) on a British warship. In October 1923 Kemal was proclaimed President of the Turkish Republic, with his lieutenant Ismet Inönü as Premier. In March 1924 the caliphate was abolished, though Islam remained the state religion until April 1928. After abolishing the caliphate Kemal secularized education and destroyed the power of the ulema, the Muslim priesthood who were the bitterest enemies of reform. A rebellion in February 1925 by the Kurds, who were urged on by the dervishes to overthrow the godless republic and restore the caliphate, was quickly suppressed. He exploited the situation to make his first great symbolic revolution, the abolition of the fez, which was still worn as a proclamation of their faith by Muslims who had otherwise adopted western dress. Kemal regarded it as an 'emblem of ignorance, negligence, fanaticism and hatred of progress and civilization'. He made it an offence to wear it, using the emergency powers voted against the Kurds to enforce the ban. It was not a trivial matter to either Kemal or his opponents, but symbolized repudiation of the theocratic past. The veil took longer to displace, and this was not done forcibly. In 1926 he introduced a new code of civil law based on the Swiss civil code. Polygamy and repudiation of wives were forbidden and civil marriage, divorce and equality between the sexes enforced. The changes took years to enforce, especially in villages and smaller towns. But the forces of reaction, though not destroyed, could put up no active resistance after their last attempt in 1926 to displace him.

Kemal's was a unique dictatorship, constantly sustained by his conviction that it embodied the sovereignty of the people, which, in view of his immense authority, it did. Though it originated in war and rebellion it was not a military dictatorship. He permitted only his own People's Party, and banned political opposition, but tolerated some degree of freedom of speech and of the press, and respected personal liberty. As soon as possible he abandoned the ruthless and autocratic methods used to defeat his enemies—who were more ruthless than he.

But he transformed only the state and its economy, not the Turkish people, though he laid the basis for their transformation by his educational reforms and programme of industrialization. Turkey's industrial development was founded on her mineral resources which were to be state-controlled, though private enterprise was fostered in consumer goods. Foreign businesses were nationalized, and the state itself, with great difficulty, financed Turkish industry. Lack of technicians, management and skilled labour also retarded industrial production. Agriculture, which should have had greater attention as 78% of the population still worked on the land in 1930, was largely ignored, and the peasants remained depressed. The peasants were Turkey; and they were not westernized. When, twelve years after Kemal's death, Ismet held free elections, they voted into power the enemies of democracy, reform and secular forms of society. The Turkish intellectuals and the middle classes in general—businessmen, managers, bureaucrats and professional people—had become westernized. So, though to a smaller extent, had the urban workers. The peasant masses, for whom the *régime* had done little, preferred Islamic theocracy.

## (iii) *Asia and Australasia*

From the viewpoint of most Asiatics the war of 1914–18 was a European civil war. Certainly its first result was to show that there was no solidarity among the European powers in Asia, and that they willingly collaborated with Asiatic powers to destroy each other. The operation of the Anglo-Japanese alliance before 1914 had not been comparable with war-time collaboration, and Sir Edward Grey's initial reluctance as Foreign Secretary to bring Japan into the war against Germany showed that he had some suspicion of what the consequences might be. Japan, indeed, declared war on her own account and for her own purposes: the destruction of German power in the Far East and the acquisition of German interests. Germany's defeat there was largely due to Japanese intervention, and though Far Eastern fighting was relatively insignificant, it was of the first importance for Asia's future relations with the west. The Japanese also drew the inevitable lesson from the revelation of the limits of British naval strength. Even before 1914 Britain had practically abandoned control of Far Eastern waters to Japan, as she had abandoned the Caribbean to America, but her Far Eastern possessions had not been at Japan's mercy, as they were after 1918. The Allies even found it necessary to enlist the aid of China, inducing the Chinese—who originally were unwilling to be involved—to close German industrial, banking and commercial interests, end German extraterritorial rights and recover the concessions. This was a procedure which the Japanese were to exploit during the war and the Chinese to extend after it to Allied disadvantage.

America pressed Japan to withdraw from Siberia, and maintained that during the war she had recognized only such Japanese interests in China as would not conflict with Chinese territorial sovereignty and the principle of the open door. The Allies were ready to honour their wartime bargains, but Britain was in a particularly ambiguous position. Her Far Eastern interests exceeded France's, but America's repudiation of Wilson's offer of an alliance largely freed France from the need to follow America's lead outside Europe, whereas World War I had focused British interests on non-European fields more than before. Therefore the major concern of British foreign policy was to maintain good relations with America, a tendency reinforced by pressure from the Dominions, which relied to a great extent on America for their security. When forced in effect to choose between the alliance with Japan and the uncertain support of an America opposed to all forms of territorial imperialism which hampered her own economic variety, Britain abandoned the alliance. America's tremendous industrial expansion and growing naval power after 1918 made this inevitable, but British freedom of movement was restricted in other areas besides the Pacific. There was a difference of opinion between the Dominions, however, over the Anglo-Japanese treaty. Canada supported

America in opposing its renewal. New Zealand and Australia supported Britain in wanting to retain it. They were more vulnerable than Canada, and less certain of American aid.

Moreover, at the peace conference, there had been considerable disagreement between Wilson and Australian and New Zealand delegations over the mandates question and the Japanese proposal to introduce clauses on racial equality in the League Covenant. Canada wanted to make no annexations, and refused Lloyd George's suggestion that she should take over the West Indies. On the issue of racial equality, Sir Robert Borden, Canada's Premier, was prepared to compromise, on condition that Canada could impose such restrictions on Oriental immigration as she thought fit— which Japan did not dispute—whereas New Zealand and Australia remained intransigent. In the end Lloyd George and Wilson had to yield the point, as Wilson had to concede their colonial demands under the guise of the 'C' class mandate conferring powers to administer mandated regions as part of their own territories. This gave them effectively what they wanted. The Japanese forgave neither the Australian Premier W. H. Hughes' intransigence nor Wilson's treachery, but they were able to extract some advantage for their defeat over racial equality by making effective use in Asia of the propaganda points thus presented, and by making good claims to former German islands. Their acquisition placed Japan astride America's strategic communications with the western Pacific.

Except for subsequent pressure on Britain to reject American demands over the Japanese treaty, the Pacific Dominions concentrated almost entirely on domestic problems in the 1920s. Australia had a stable, essentially two-party system, for though the Country Party was founded in 1919 in protest against the growing political power of the cities (Australian wealth has always been based on the countryside), in practice it sided with the Nationalist Party (Liberals) against Labour. The Communists on the extreme Left were ineffectual, and no rival to Labour. Labour was trade-unionist, not Socialist, and least of all internationalist. Its high-tariff policy in 1921 had general support, as did the establishment of a rudimentary planned economy to protect primary producers against fluctuations of demands in the world markets for their products. In 1922 the Country Party, which held the balance of power, forced out Hughes, whose New Guinea mandate had made him unpopular. His wartime policy of expanding and diversifying industry was continued, though unfortunately care was not taken to maintain a sound balance, and Australia therefore became more vulnerable to outside pressures. Heavy foreign borrowing and continued dependence on wool, wheat and metals made Australia one of the first countries to succumb to the depression, though the 1920s were on the whole prosperous, as was shown by the development of the new federal capital at Canberra in 1927.

New Zealand was less prosperous and less stable. Her party system was based essentially on sectional alliances and regional hostilities, though there was also strong conservative resistance towards further welfare state developments, led by the Reform Party under W. F. Massey until his death in May 1925, and then by the extremely able J. G. Coates. Liberals in the United Party competed with Labour for the votes of urban middle and working classes, as well as for the farmers who normally supported Reform. There were good reasons for Reform and Liberals to coalesce, especially when Labour dropped its demand for extensive nationalization, including land, among its objectives, and demanded higher credits for farmers. Reform, however, also represented business interests, which thought government economic intervention during the war had gone too far. The exceptionally high 1919 prices which farmers hoped to have guaranteed never returned, but farmers benefited from increased markets provided by encouragement of British immigrants and the development of secondary industries. Moreover though the Reform Party ranked as conservative, and certainly wanted to go no further than necessary with economic planning, it was more radical than Lloyd George's Liberals or American Progressives. It did not neglect welfare services, and even to some extent increased them, especially in education and public health. It diffused the benefits of the welfare services more widely among the Maoris. The Maoris did not become integrated, but they were accorded full equality of rights.

For India the Montagu-Chelmsford reforms were worked out to implement the 1917 promise of eventual self-government. They proposed a system of dyarchy, establishing central and provincial governments which would include both British and Indian ministers. The central government, headed by the viceroy, would contain a council of state with 60 members, of whom 26 would be officials, and an assembly of 140 members, 100 of them elected. In the provincial governments major matters were reserved for the governors and executive councils. Minor matters were to be dealt with by Indian ministers responsible to elected councils (70% of their members were elected on restricted franchise), and these responsibilities included public health, agriculture, local self-government and education. At first the proposals were well received by Congress leaders, including Gandhi.

Gandhi had just returned from South Africa, where he had campaigned against racial discrimination and developed the technique of *satyagraha* (passive resistance). On returning he had carried out an enquiry into peasant conditions in Bihar, during which he had developed another technique of using the moral values of western civilization to secure psychological ascendancy over British officials who knew they were transgressing their own code by relying on methods of brute force to suppress resistance. However, post-war distress, including the effects of the influenza epidemic, created general unrest, and at Amritsar in April 1919 British troops were ordered to fire on a crowd, killing 379 Indians. British rule in India never recovered its prestige after this tragedy. However, Congress continued to co-operate until the publication of the Treaty of Sèvres produced a pan-Islamic reaction among Indian Muslims which Gandhi, declaring himself openly against the British Raj, immediately exploited to increase Hindu-Muslim solidarity.

Gandhi transformed the Indian Congress movement, using it to give a sense of national solidarity which the Ceylonese Congress movement, founded in 1919, never acquired. Ceylon's peaceful and constitutional progress towards independence reached a decisive stage as early as 1924, when the elected members in the Council had a majority, though officials still controlled the executive. India might have moved in the same way but for Gandhi. As it was, a large section of Congress retained its faith in constitutional, gradualist methods, and broke away as Liberals to contest elections for the new provincial governments. Gandhi established a mass following by force of character and propaganda. He insisted that independence must also mean self-sufficiency, which, he bizarrely argued, entailed a return to the old Indian outlook and ways of life, and hence restoration of the old handicrafts. At the opposite pole in nearly every respect to Kemal, he abandoned western dress and technology. However, Gandhi found that his civil disobedience movement was getting out of hand—as it would have done even if he had not deliberately linked it with the violent Muslim Khilafat (caliphate) movement. The Khilafat campaign collapsed in 1924 when Kemal abolished the caliphate, though not before the south Indian Moplah tribe had launched a rebellion in which hundreds of Hindus were murdered.

Hindu Congress mobs showed that they also did not understand how to conduct civil disobedience. The Moplah incident caused a breach between the Muslim League of the Ali brothers and the Hindu Nationalists, which later had major consequences. After the cold-blooded murder by Hindus in February 1922 of twenty-two policemen Gandhi called off his campaign. His sentence in March to six years' imprisonment ended resistance, and in 1923 the moderate Congress group under C. R. Das formed the Swaraj (home rule) Party and contested elections so that its representatives could obstruct the legislatures. However, once elected, many of their members forgot their purpose was to force the grant of home rule and began to co-operate. In addition rivals to Congress appeared, among them the Madras Justice Party for non-Brahmins, as Brahmins dominated Congress. Most opposition groups made little headway, though the Punjabi Unionist Party including Hindus, Muslims and Sikhs controlled Punjabi politics.

Gandhi was released in February 1924 because of ill-health. He continued to urge boycotting dyarchy, while Das's friend Motilal Nehru campaigned for Dominion status instead of independence, but came over to Gandhi's side after the British in 1926 set up the all-party Simon Commission. The Indians decided to boycott the Commission, which made no provision for enrolling Indian members, and the ensuing tension erupted into industrial as well as nationalist disturbances.

In transforming Congress into a mass movement, Gandhi hoped also to give it a social conscience, and to shatter the callous indifference of the Indian middle classes and Brahmins to the plight of the untouchables.

There were also political reasons for Gandhi's attitude. Untouchables as well as Muslims might be organized against the Brahmin-dominated Congress. (In the 1930s they were.) Another important point was that during the war the growth of Indian industry had greatly increased the numbers of the urban working class. The All-India Trade Union Congress had been founded in 1920. It had originally been closely tied to Congress, but it came under the influence of Marxist groups. In 1924 the Communist Party of India was founded, and in 1926 Indian Communists also established the Workers' and Peasants' Party to promote their aims. However, it was not until after they had gained control of the Trades Union Congress in 1927, and played a leading role in the widespread strikes of 1928, which showed that the Indian proletariat was at last being organized, that the British authorities took them seriously. A Trade Disputes Act and the Public Safety Act of 1929 provided legal grounds for the arrest of many of their leaders, among them some Britons, who were tried at Meerut for conspiracy. With Congress resolved on another *satyagraha* campaign under Gandhi's leadership unless India were granted independence by the end of 1929, the country was already moving towards economic and political upheaval before the depression made itself felt in late autumn.

China had attended the Paris conference relying on Wilson's promise of a just settlement, a promise which in Chinese eyes was immediately violated by the decision that Japan should keep Shantung. This aroused storms of protest among youthful Chinese nationalists which provoked the mass Peking demonstration known as the May Fourth Movement. This in turn produced a nation-wide movement of protest—hence the later Communist *régime*'s well-founded belief that the demonstration marked the beginning of China's anti-imperialism. Japan's legal case was strong, and China's argument, that her concessions under the 1915 treaties were invalid because made under threat of force, should logically have applied to all the 'unequal treaties'. The Peking government, however, had equally grave difficulties to overcome in dealing with the Canton government and the Manchurian ruler Chang Tso-lin. The Paris delegation had spoken officially for both Peking and Canton, but there was no unity between them. Moreover, the Peking warlord *régime* did not control all north China and was displaced in July 1920. The Canton warlords collapsed immediately afterwards when attacked by Sun Yat-sen's forces. In November 1920 he took possession of Canton, declaring himself Provisional President of China on May 5th, 1921, with the approval of a rump of the old parliament. He promulgated a programme of peaceful national unification, local autonomy, the open door and industrial development. However he had no power in the north, where Chang Tso-lin was disputing with other generals, and he could not trust his own generals. His *régime* crumbled in October 1922, by which time new Peking rulers had a puppet President of their own, and had reconvened the 1913 parliament there. Sun had no prospects of success unless he adopted fresh methods.

In July 1919 Sun, disappointed in the western powers, had turned his back on western democracy, declaring in a manifesto that if the Chinese people 'wished to be free, like the Russian people ... its only allies and brothers in the struggle for national freedom are the Russian workers and peasants of the Red Army'. The Chinese Communist Party had been founded by two intellectuals and a Comintern agent in Shanghai (in July 1921) before Sun's defeat. Its Chinese founders had a low opinion of Sun, but another Comintern agent had reported to Moscow in the spring of 1921 that Sun was leading the most important trend of Chinese nationalism, and in 1922 again reported favourably on his relations with the trade unions. In July 1922 the Chinese Communist Party was affiliated to Comintern, and in August its members were instructed to join the Kuomintang, as they did next year. Russia's recovery of her Far Eastern territories in 1922 facilitated intervention in Chinese politics, and in January 1923 the Russian diplomat Adolph Joffe met Sun in Shanghai and they issued a joint manifesto to mark Soviet-Kuomintang collaboration. By the terms which Sun worked out with his Soviet political 'adviser', Michael Borodin, the Communists entered the Kuomintang as individuals and retained their own party organization. They at once infiltrated the Kuomintang and its administrative organs, while they also held high posts in the trade unions and at the Whampoa military academy established by Sun's military 'adviser', the Red Army General, Vassili Blücher (Galen). Borodin taught the Kuomintang rather too well, for it learned how to counter Bolshevik techniques of infiltration when these came to be used by the Chinese Communists against the Kuomintang. However, the prospects of the Kuomintang, still less the Communists, subduing the anarchy which ravaged nearly all China in 1923 were remote.

At the Paris peace conference Japan ranked after the Big Three, and was well on the way to becoming the predominant Far Eastern power. But in many respects she was treated at Paris as an upstart, and her defeat over racial equality left resentment against America which a permanent seat on the League Council did not diminish. Moreover, while she got the substance of her claim in Shantung, she was embittered by the American attitude on this question also. This hostility was strengthened when she was obliged to evacuate Siberia, for which the retention of North Sakhalin (until 1925) was small compensation. Yet Japan's contribution to the defeat of Germany was amply rewarded, and she derived great economic advantages from the war. Apart from her penetration of some markets hitherto controlled by European powers, the stimulus of war had made her a fully industrial state, though at the price of increasing the political, psychological and economic tensions in Japanese society. Industrialization had increased her urban proletariat, which was growing more restive, though it was still heavily outnumbered by agricultural and forestry workers (5,300,000 in manufacturing in 1920, against 14,128,000 out of a total working population of 27,261,000). Moreover Japan's unbalanced wartime development created serious problems of readjustment, and these were intensified by the rapid growth of population (from 51,000,000 in

1914 to 56,000,000 in 1920, and 64,500,000 in 1930). National income probably quadrupled between 1914 and 1930, and real incomes increased for peasants and proletariat alike until 1927, when a slump in the price of rice hit the peasants. Between 1914 and 1929, however, the trebling of raw silk production, Japan's next important agricultural product, created a more solid and extensive prosperity.

Allied wartime contracts for Japanese shipping and manufactures produced prosperity and a first-class industrial base, but they brought serious problems. In 1914 Japanese shipbuilding yards had launched 85,000 tons; in 1919 they launched 650,000. Her merchant fleet rose in the same period from just over a million and a half tons to just under three million; her net shipping receipts from just over four million yen to just over 380 million yen. However Japanese shipbuilding costs were high, and the return of foreign competition led to a long decline, so that in the fairly good year of 1929 she launched only 165,000 merchant tons. Naval building was reduced after 1922 by the Washington naval treaty, but war contracts had helped to turn her from a debtor into a creditor country, and stimulated her heavy, engineering and chemical industries, as well as equipping her textile industry to compete with Britain's. The crucial heavy industry, however, still lagged behind that of her major competitors, and her iron and steel failed to achieve the relative importance among Japan's industries that they enjoyed among her rivals'. In addition Japan throughout the inter-war years had to import a great deal of foreign machinery, though in proportion to home-produced machinery these imports did decrease.

Banking and financial facilities lagged behind industrial developments, constituted major weaknesses in the economy, and were inadequate for Japan's enhanced international position. The 'rice riots' of 1919 were due to falling urban standards of living caused by inflationary policies which had raised prices. Weaknesses in the financial structure increased the dislocation caused by the collapse of the post-war boom in March 1920, which brought the wholesale price index down from 322 to 190 by April 1921. Japan possessed neither the financial skill nor means to carry out the deflationary policy needed to remove the distortions in her economy, nor would the *zaibatsu* have tolerated it. However the nation on the whole benefited considerably, and the *zaibatsu* could hardly have been expected to foresee that so many of the developments which they fostered in overseas trade (e.g. in textiles) would prove ruinous after 1929. Japan's foreign trade trebled in value and more than doubled in volume between 1913 and 1929, and when trade with her colonies is considered, the increases are even greater, and it becomes even more apparent that foreign trade chiefly reflected the interests of Japan's manufacturers. Coupled with the growth in production was an increase in the size of *zaibatsu* undertakings, though small-scale shops in 1930 still employed about 2,500,000 workers and produced about 30% of Japan's manufactures. However the great iron and steel plants, and the cement, chemical and heavy engineering firms were all growing.

Agriculture remained the preserve of the small man, or rather of small family holdings. In 1920 about half the farmers held under one and a quarter acres, and two-thirds of them were wholly or partly tenants. This made radical changes in technique difficult, though as cultivation was already so intensive, probably productivity could not have been further raised. The increased population, therefore, when the outlet of emigration was closed, had to find employment in the towns, and Japan followed the general twentieth century pattern of urbanization. Towns of under 10,000 contained 72% of the population in 1913 and only 59% in 1930; those of 50,000 contained about 14% in 1913 and 25% in 1930. Agriculture could provide neither more employment nor more food by 1930, and this was partly responsibile for Japan's expansionist tendencies.

Urbanization increased social tensions among the proletariat, though the early trade unions were remarkably moderate. Faithful to the traditions of Japanese hierarchical society, they sought to co-operate with employers instead of striking, a matter of great concern to the Marxists who began to exert considerable influence on trade unionism after the war. After the Communist Party's foundation in July 1922, however, the increasing number of strikes received close attention from the police. The limits of toleration of the liberal *régime* during the 1920s then rapidly became clear. There was a highly successful police drive against the Communists in June 1923, and most of their leaders were arrested. The police followed this anti-Communist campaign with another drive against trade unionists and suspected Left Wing sympathizers, and were so confident that subversion was suppressed that later they released the Communists. This was premature, for though the Communists made little impression on the peasants, their various front organizations managed to poll almost half a million votes in 1928. Thereupon the police redoubled their activities, but the depression and resentment of the wars in Manchuria and China produced conditions which favoured the Communists until the late autumn of 1932. Then the police again carried off most of the Communist leaders, and the intensifying repression of the dark years before 1945 reduced the party to insignificance.

Until the depression Japan seemed to be gradually moving towards parliamentary democracy. The victory of the democratic powers over the authoritarian states during the war, and the Japanese militarists' unpopularity after the failure of their Siberian intervention, made it difficult for the latter for some time to pursue their old pretensions. In 1918 Japan had for the first time a commoner, that is non-*samurai*, as Premier in the person of Takashi Hara. Hara regarded himself as a party politician of a quasi-western type by virtue of his leadership of the conservative *Seiyukai*, or Constitutional party. Hence he had an exclusively *Seiyukai* cabinet, except for the service ministers and a career diplomat as foreign minister. Until his assassination in November 1921 he managed to hold his party together, but he could not impose the concept of strong party government when the party structure was itself so precarious. Moreover his government

381

was essentially undemocratic. He opposed constitutional reforms, and made no attempts to root out the corruption rife in the political system—he could not have held his party together without it. He was too conservative to seek support from the more radical elements, and too committed to *zaibatsu* groups. To the spread of Left Wing thoughts encouraged by the Russian Revolution and events in central Europe, his only answer was repression. Industrial unrest with its propagation of 'dangerous thoughts' presented problems which he could not solve. Nevertheless he had made a breach in the old system, but had no able successors to widen it.

The new system attracted little support beyond the circles of interested politicians and *zaibatsu*. Strong, though at first covert, contempt and hatred developed for big business and its instruments in the Diet, which was increasingly identified with it. The beginnings of Japanese military Fascism of the 1930s were already apparent. However traditionalism was also rooted deeply, and opposed changes of any sort. Traditionalists deplored western industrialization and urbanization because these destroyed the disciplined older form of society and weakened the peasant whom they regarded as embodying the old Japanese virtues of frugality and modesty. They denounced foreigners with their 'dangerous thoughts' (pacifism and liberalism as well as Marxism). These elements regarded as symbols of decay big business and trade unions alike, the spread of western innovations like dance-halls and imported luxuries, and the 'new standards' of all kinds. A Radicalism of the Right developed, fostered by the secret societies, some elements of which favoured state ownership to destroy the *zaibatsu*, others a revolution based on agrarian idealism. Other secret societies existed to protect Japan from Marxism, such as the Japan National Essence Society, founded in 1919 by Hara's minister of the interior, and the National Foundation Society of 1924 which included three future premiers, several leading generals, politicians and *zaibatsu*. This society had diverse and sometimes conflicting aims, but its central purpose was to champion the 'national' cause. Other societies were essentially criminal strong-arm squads levying political blackmail. Others wanted a military dictatorship, of either conservative or revolutionary character. Chief of these was Kita Ikki's 1921 Society for Preservation of the National Essence. Kita wanted Japan to nationalize her industries, redistribute surplus private estates, and lead the revolution in Asia, which he thought was inevitable, as a proletarian nation dispossessing the rich. But whether 'collectivist-industrialist', agrarian-centred or merely anti-western, anti-capitalist and anti-parliamentarian, all these societies wanted an expansionist policy on the mainland both for Japan's own needs and for her future status as the leader of Asia.

More conventional politicians shared this aim. It might be achieved by finding Chinese who, by the use of bribery and intimidation (including the use of Japanese troops when other persuasions failed), could be induced to do Japan's work in China, and co-operate in setting up an Asian league to expel western influences from the Far East. Others, service chiefs particularly, thought Japan could not rely on co-operation and must create a mainland empire containing Korea, Manchuria and possibly Mongolia, from which she could draw the necessary resources—the policy which led to the industrialization of North Korea and Manchuria. Others favoured the 'peaceful' economic exploitation of China, and some of these saw no reason why China should not provide what they thought India had provided for Britain, apparently unaware that after World War I India was not an asset to Britain but a liability and an irritating trade competitor. Yet even this policy would need force, and thereby raise the possibility of disturbances in China which would involve America and Britain. Finally the 'southern school' thought Japan's prospects lay not in north China and Manchuria, where Russian hostility was sure to be considerable, but in a great drive to the south and the East Indies. However all were expansionist, believing that pressure of population and economic needs made imperialist adventures of some sort essential.

## (iv) *The Western Hemisphere*

The United States, like Canada and Latin America, experienced after November 1918 not the aftermath of Armageddon but the sweeping away of wartime restrictions. Unfortunately, while America had matured economically she had not matured politically. She could not understand, still less accept the burdens which her gain and Britain's loss of world pre-eminence had thrust upon her. As far as possible she repudiated them, for isolationism was the normal American outlook. Americans wanted to trade with the rest of the world, and otherwise to be left alone by it.

This was not entirely their fault. The conduct of the Allies during the peacemaking had not been irreproachable, though sometimes they had been justifiably irritated by American hypocrisy. Yet Wilsonian idealism, for all its woolliness, ignorance of practical realities and occasional treacheries, had offered prospects to Europe and the Middle East, if not to Africa and Asia, which could have been realized in part. American 'internationalists' who had seen the reception given by European and Middle Eastern peoples to the original Wilsonian message, were disillusioned, and if they did not become isolationists themselves, at any rate no longer opposed isolationism. Moreover much so-called isolationism concealed old anti-British or pro-German sentiments on the part of hyphenated Americans, while the struggle against Wilson's attempts to commit America to the Versailles Treaty and the League of Nations was also an aspect of the struggle against his 'new freedom' and general Progressive domestic policies. It was no coincidence that it was in the Republican, big business era of Harding and Coolidge that hysterical American nationalism became reactionary as well as anti-foreign, and that the slogan of '100% Americanism' meant repudiation of liberal standards as well as opposition to Socialism. The average annual total of European immigrants between 1907 and 1914 of about 862,000 was reduced first by the 1921 Quota Act to about 356,000, and then by the 1924 Act to about 163,000. In addition, it was believed (by social workers and others who thought themselves humane) that Oriental and southern European immigrants created grave social problems which could best be dealt with by stopping the evil at source. The National Origins Act of 1921 therefore not only prohibited Oriental immigration, which had alarmed the south-western states before the end of the war, but restricted European immigrants to 2% of the foreign-born population according to the 1890 census. This would keep out eastern Europeans, whose dangerous mixture of supposed Jewish and Marxist characteristics alarmed the Ku Klux Klan and other '100% Americans', and southern European Catholics whose presence was unwelcome to Anglo-Saxon and other Protestant groups. Yet though the Act discriminated in favour of British and German immigrants, it also favoured the Southern Irish Catholics, because of the great Irish influx into America during the nineteenth century.

Despite wartime hysteria and intolerance which continued into the early post-war period, more tactful handling of his opponents and dubious supporters by Wilson might have saved the internationalist cause. However Wilson had grown more autocratic and suspicious of opposition (as Lloyd George remarked, he believed in mankind but distrusted all men). Moreover, he had driven himself to the brink of nervous collapse. He failed to see the opportunity which was his even after the isolationists had won mass, but not overwhelming, support by a propaganda compounded of straight misrepresentations of fact and deliberate scares. The Republicans regained control of Congress in 1918, and the isolationists among them dominated the foreign relations committee. Its chairman, Senator Henry Cabot Lodge, may have been concerned less to defeat the Treaty than to see that Wilson got no credit for it, but certainly acted as if both Wilson and the Democratic Party were enemies of the state. American opinion in July 1919 favoured accepting the Treaty and thereby League membership. Accordingly Lodge held up ratification while the irreconcilable isolationists flooded the country with propaganda, and Wilson in reply embarked on the speaking campaign which finally incapacitated him.

However, well into 1920 it would have been possible to carry ratification with reservations on American sovereignty which, while important, would have been worth tolerating to ensure entry into the League. Wilson refused to compromise, though most Democratic senators were only too anxious to do so. Ratification was defeated on March 19th, 1920, by 49 votes to 35—that is, if seven Democratic Senators had not deserted him, America would have joined the League, and the 'great crusade' would have ended in victory. Wilson proclaimed that the Presidential election would be a 'great and solemn referendum' on the issue.

The election was not what Wilson promised, though it emphatically endorsed the Senate's decision. The Democratic candidate, the former

Governor of Ohio James M. Cox, was a nonentity, and his vice-Presidential candidate Franklin Delano Roosevelt, Secretary of the Navy, as yet carried only small guns. But their opponents, Warren G. Harding and Calvin C. Coolidge, were little better as electoral prospects. The economic recession of 1920 militated against the Democrats, but Republican propaganda against foreign entanglements and traditional dislike of government interference were equally important, and Harding's call for a return to normalcy was irresistible. Possibly the complete enfranchisement of women by the nineteenth amendment, approved in June 1919 and effective in August 1920, had some effect, but higher tariffs and lower taxes, fewer immigrants and more aid to farmers counted for more. Certainly the quality of the successful candidates could not account for the landslide in November 1920 which gave Harding 16,152,000 popular votes and 404 electoral votes against Cox's 9,147,000 and 127. This landslide gave the Republican candidate every state outside the south, and Tennessee.

The old Progressive alliance which Wilson had built up over the years had clearly disintegrated, and indeed there was little room for Progressive ideas in the 'roaring twenties' of Harding and his successor Coolidge. The scandals of gangsterism and corruption fostered by the eighteenth amendment of 1919 prohibiting the sale, manufacture or transportation of intoxicating liquor could not be fairly blamed on the Republicans. Profits from 'bootlegging' and vice brought the Chicago gangster boss Al Capone a gross annual income of $60,000,000, and 'speakeasies' flourished—but so did private and respectable cocktail parties. Moreover, though Democrats carried repeal of prohibition in 1933, most of them approved of it in the 1920s, among them William Jennings Bryan, who also endorsed attempts to prohibit the teaching in schools of Darwinian 'atheist' evolutionary theories. Neither could the Republicans fairly be blamed for the recrudescence of the Ku Klux Klan, which flourished in the Democratic South; for the Red Scare, strongly in evidence before Wilson returned from Europe; or for the judicial murder in 1927 of two avowed anarchists, Sacco and Vanzetti, after they had been awaiting execution since 1921 on a murder charge of which, to say the least, their guilt had not been proved beyond doubt.

The 'gilded' years from 1922 to 1929, however, were fairly characterized by their association with Republican defence of big business and neglect of the small man and the national interest. The Republican attitude to Progressive attempts to regulate the growing use of hydro-electric power in the national interest was summed up in its attitude towards Henry Ford's bid to lease the facilities undertaken by the War Department at Muscle Shoals on the Tennessee River. Both Harding and Coolidge supported the bid. Hoover after them vetoed an attempt to preserve the Valley's water resources for the nation.

Nevertheless the Republican era was one of unprecedented prosperity, even though it was unevenly distributed. It was also, for all its brashness (in which it differed from the twenties in Europe only because its wealth made its vulgarity more ostentatious), an age of considerable intellectual and cultural achievement. The development of the American cinema in the days of silent films (that is, effectively before 1929) though not comparable with the great period of the thirties, introduced to the world in Charlie Chaplin a comedian and social critic of genius, and came nearer, despite national idiom, to providing an international form of entertainment than had been achieved before. This turbulent decade saw also a considerable native literature and architecture develop. It was not only in material and technological development that America became a leading power after 1918. Sinclair Lewis's novel *Babbitt* (1922) was a universal protest against the *bourgeois* nihilism of the first truly mass age. Ezra Pound and T. S. Eliot, Europeanized though they became, were the greatest poets of the inter-war years and great poets by any standards, and Eugene O'Neill a superlative dramatist.

Despite their lack of social conscience, the twenties made possible higher living standards for the masses than had ever been achieved before. The expansion of the automobile industry made a major contribution to the transformation of both social and economic scenes. From just over a million and a half in 1921, automobile production increased to over five and a third million in 1929, and the use of the private automobile was both absolutely and relatively far greater in America than in any European country. Its development not only stimulated steel, rubber, electrical and other ancillary industries, but also opened up new areas and promoted further economic developments. Electric power became in this period America's second industry, with consequent expansion of all other major industries, especially radio and electrical appliances. This expansion, like all the industrial developments of the twenties, was financed largely by small savings; hence the widespread disasters when the slump came.

Agriculture and coal mining did not share in the prosperity caused by the increase of 70% in iron and steel, 94% in chemical products and 86% in rubber products. Moreover it was estimated that out of a total of about 27,500,000 American families in 1929, about 71% had incomes below the $2,500 thought necessary for a decent living standard—though over large areas of the world this would have seemed luxurious. This inequality was largely due to vicious repression of labour unions by violence and intimidation, enforcement of 'company unions', declaration of the illegality of strikes, and use of strikebreakers. However, despite the phenomenal rate of urbanization after 1920 (temporarily reversed in the early thirties because of the depression), with an urban increase of 14,600,000, chiefly in or around the largest existing cities, there was little mass dissatisfaction, and no danger of disturbances even in the early postwar period. The tensions which arose came less from the activities of the insignificant Communist Party, founded in September 1919, than from the difficulties of assimilating immigrants and the migration of Negroes from the South. Even in 1920 the percentage of Negroes living outside the South was 15%; this compares with under 24% in 1940.

Isolationism implied neither refusal to play a considerable share in the re-establishment of the economies of the European states after 1918, nor reluctance to pursue American power interests elsewhere. American-Japanese relations became so strained over the Siberian incident and immigration that a naval arms race developed which highly embarrassed Britain. Some governments became so alarmed as to believe that there was a danger of war between America and Japan. Lloyd George actually considered retaining British naval supremacy after the war even at the cost of a naval race with America, and he certainly preferred Japan to America as a partner in the Far East. However, the removal of German and the weakening of Russian power, meant that the Anglo-Japanese alliance lost much of its value for Britain. Both British and American moderates, especially their diplomats, deplored their respective naval experts' demands for bigger navies, and there was a general desire in both countries for disarmament.

Certain that the British would accept the offer, Secretary of State Charles Evans Hughes invited the British to a naval conference at Washington, which was attended also by Japan, France, Italy, Holland, Belgium, Portugal and China, while the Dominions sent representatives as part of the British delegation. Holland, Belgium, Portugal and China attended only the Pacific and Far Eastern section of the conference, not the important naval limitation section, which established the 5:5:3 ratio in capital ship tonnage between America, Britain and Japan, with absolute limitation of French and Italian tonnages to 175,000. The same proportions were retained for aircraft carriers and no limitation was imposed on other classes. As Britain was obliged to drop her Japanese alliance in favour of a useless Anglo-Japanese-American-French Four Power Treaty imposing merely the obligation to consult and not to act, America had strengthened her Far Eastern position at British and Japanese expense. The British suffered most. The whole of their empire east of Suez was at the mercy of a power which was potentially at least as hostile to them as to the Americans. Over China the other eight powers promised respect for integrity, independence and sovereignty, but undertook no commitments, though they agreed to enquire into ways of ending extra-territorial rights. Japan refused to have Shantung discussed at the conference, though privately she agreed to restore Chinese sovereignty in return for economic concessions. The Chinese were still dissatisfied, for their goal was complete sovereignty over China and Manchuria, and the end of all foreign imperialism in their country. All except China, however, regarded the conference as a great success; Hughes was particularly pleased and justifiably so.

His victory over the Anglo-Japanese alliance, however, was largely due to the help of Canada, whom he repaid by denying, with the other Dominions, separate representation on the mistaken grounds that the Dominions took orders from Britain. Canada was in fact of all the Dominions the least dependent on Britain and the most reliant on America. She took the lead among the Dominions in the movement towards partnership enunciated in the 1926 Balfour definition of Dominion status, and this was supported by a great increase in her economic power. Canadian agriculture and industry had both profited from the stimulus of war, though agricultural expansion could not proceed much farther. Canadian industry on the other hand continued to develop and diversify rapidly. In 1911 capital invested in Canadian industry had amounted to 127,000,000 Canadian dollars but by 1921 it exceeded 3,000,000,000. Mineral mining offered great opportunities which were widely exploited, and war-time trends were continued by extending textile, chemical and secondary iron and steel industries. Ontario and Quebec became urbanized, with important social and political consequences. By 1921, indeed, the federal structure seemed likely to disintegrate because of the intensified quarrels between French and British Canadians, urban and rural districts, and eastern and western provinces.

The wartime coalition broke up and Conservatives dominated the Union government under Sir Robert Borden until 1920, when illness forced him to give way to Arthur Meighen, one of the prime movers in ending the Anglo-Japanese alliance. Meighen was unpopular because undeservedly he was considered responsible for the wartime restrictions, and then for the effects of the 1920–21 world-wide industrial and agricultural depressions on Canada. To avoid defeat in the 1921 elections the Conservatives called themselves National Liberals and Conservatives. The Liberals nevertheless defeated them, though not with an overall majority, and Mackenzie King's 1921–30 cabinets had to rely on splinter parties. King had earlier campaigned for a large measure of state intervention in the economy, but beyond encouraging state development of hydro-electric power and wheat co-operatives, he left the development of the economy to private enterprise. Until the depression this sufficed. Foreign trade, of which about 60% was with America in the 1920s, was 149·3% of the 1913 level by 1929. American investment exceeded British, though it never controlled Canada's economy as it did that of many Latin American countries, where wartime exigencies also reduced British investment.

In the early postwar years America abandoned many of the more disagreeable aspects of economic imperialism in the Caribbean, though not her protectorate over Panama. The marines were withdrawn from Cuba in 1922, the Dominican Republic in 1924, and Nicaragua in 1925. The war had brought the republics into much closer participation in international affairs, and many joined the League. Several remained loyal members; others wanted merely a platform from which to air grievances against their neighbours and America. The common hope that the League would interpret the Monroe Doctrine to exclude American interference in Latin American affairs was quickly dispelled: in 1927 the marines were back in Nicaragua. However, the general stimulus given to nationalism by the war made the republics less disposed to accept political subordination to Washington and economic dependence on American or European capital. The war had stimulated the ABC states into manufacturing their own textiles and establishing canning industries, but until the depression forced most republics to seek economic self-sufficiency, the impetus was lost.

The major consequence of the war for Latin America was to strengthen America's economic influence at Britain's expense, though both countries increased their Latin American investments between 1913 and 1929 (from $1,242,000,000 to $5,587,000,000, and from $4,983,000,000 to $5,889,000,000 respectively). Britain's South American investments were much larger than America's, but America had bigger holdings in Mexico and Central America. In Brazil, the largest and potentially strongest republic, American capital now predominated, as American manufactures had done before 1914. Brazil profited considerably from the war, and largely because of her comparative prosperity remained politically apathetic until army officers tried unsuccessfully to establish a military dictatorship in 1922. The abortive revolt formed the prelude to endemic disturbances, some of them led by the army officer Luiz Carlos Prestes who later turned to Communism. However, conditions improved after 1926 under the presidency of Washington Luiz Pereira de Souza: coffee and cotton production prospered and American investment increased. Argentina's varied resources enabled her quickly to rectify the economic dislocation caused by the smaller postwar demand for her beef and the effects of wartime breeding of inferior cattle. Fluctuating demands for Chile's copper inflicted great hardship on the miners, but demands for her other great product, nitrates, which had been heavy in the war, slumped as other states for strategic reasons followed Germany in developing synthetic nitrates. Argentina and Chile were ruled by dictators in the *caudillo* tradition. Hipólito Irigoyen made way in Argentina for his own nominee Marcelo T. de Alvear in 1922, but resumed office in 1928. Arturo Alessandri could not solve the problems posed by the poverty and backwardness of Chile's lower classes and her lack of resources, nor end her political instability. His new constitution strengthening presidential powers merely produced military coups until his follower Carlos Ibáñez in 1927 formed a modified military dictatorship. This improved working conditions, prevented a civil war between landowners and working class, and promoted education and foreign investment.

Mexico resumed her revolutionary course under Alvaro Obregón in 1920, though he was no longer a revolutionary at heart. He distributed about 3,000,000 acres of land and made extensive educational reforms, but the trade unions remained government instruments in the Latin American tradition, and the peasants remained too poor and badly equipped to cultivate their land. His nominated successor Plutarco Elias Calles continued his policy, except that Calles' land redistribution was more extensive (though not more effective in improving peasant conditions), his repression of the Church more violent, his manipulation of the trade

389

unions more blatant, and his defiance of American oil interests more profitable and more skilful (in 1923 America recognized his government). Under Calles the revolution became institutionalized. In 1929 he formed the Partido Nacional Revolucionario (PNR) to unite the local organizations and party bosses—and to complete the transformation of the *régime* into a racket.

*Chapter V*
# YEARS OF HOPE

## (i) *The Internationalist Illusion and the Europe of Locarno*

FROM the mid-1920s there was widespread and growing prosperity in the western world. There was more international co-operation in economic and political affairs among its peoples. They even nourished comforting expectations of disarmament. Except among the realists there was a belief that collective security would soon become a reality, and that something resembling pre-war stability would be achieved.

By 1929 hopes of economic co-operation were dashed; by 1931 the international political structure had sustained its first shock. Yet the manner in which the zenith of the twenties' illusions was reached ironically fore-shadowed their collapse. Aristide Briand, foreign minister in Poincaré's fifth cabinet, and Coolidge's Secretary of State, Frank B. Kellogg, signed their celebrated Pact of Paris on August 27th, 1928, which all other countries except Argentina, Bolivia, Brazil, Saudi Arabia and the Yemen rushed to join (even anti-*bourgeois* Soviet Russia ratified it).

Briand had wanted to draw France and America together in a bilateral treaty assuring France of American neutrality in all circumstances. Kellogg was not prepared for that—not that he intended America to aid Germany in the unlikely event of a French attack. His idea was to conclude a series of bilateral agreements proposing arbitration between the signatories except over conflicts involving their internal affairs, conflicts with third parties, conflicts involving the Monroe Doctrine, and conflicts which would produce action in the League of Nations. This was a formidable list of exceptions. However, Briand and Kellogg were forced to yield to American public opinion after certain American pacifists and 'outlawers of war' extensively publicized Briand's message of April 6th, 1927, to the American people, in which he proposed that France and America should commemorate America's entry into the World War by forever renouncing war to settle differences.

Briand had wanted to increase French security, not to make a pious gesture. Kellogg hated the pacifists and 'outlawers of war' who forced his hand, and whose delusions he thought dangerous to American security, but for reasons of domestic politics he had to do something, and he accepted Senator Borah's suggestion that war should be outlawed not merely for America and France but for all nations. Briand would have contented France with a bilateral treaty just because it was a treaty, but he could not refuse Kellogg's suggestion, especially when Stresemann adroitly stepped in, applauded it and declared Germany's eagerness to adhere. In February 1928 Kellogg's arbitration treaty was signed. In March Briand agreed to Kellogg's suggestions for the Pact of Paris: America and France 'solemnly declare ... that they condemn the resort to war for the settlement of international disputes and that they renounce the resort to war as an instrument of national policy in their mutual relations' and promise to settle all disputes between them by peaceful means. Stresemann thought the occasion of the pact's signature an excellent moment for raising the question of termination of the Rhineland occupation, but Poincaré insisted that reparations must first be settled. Hence the moves were made which produced the Young Plan next year.

An interesting anticipatory comment was made on the Kellogg-Briand Pact in the Pan-American Conference held at Havana in January 1928. The Latin American countries overwhelmingly supported a demand that Hughes, brought from retirement to head the American delegation, should unequivocally promise that America would renounce rights of intervention. This Hughes refused, for international law recognizes that there are cases where intervention is legitimate, but he agreed that intervention should be limited. Coolidge and Kellogg went farther, and in December 1928 adopted the view that the Monroe Doctrine did not justify the Roosevelt Corollary, though this fact was not published until June 1930. Nevertheless, by early 1928 America had set out on what was to become the good neighbour policy.

But the Pact of Paris was worthless, and indeed deleterious, for it raised popular hopes which could not be realized. Indeed Kellogg and Briand, for all their early scepticism, came under the influence of the propaganda which surrounded it, and made it the symbol of the illusions of a war-weary age. On its signature Briand said that it was 'a beginning, not an end', but in fact it was merely a bromide. In 1931 Kellogg, recognizing its worthlessness, said that he felt that he was living in another epoch.

Even the international economy's recovery from the mid-1920s was insecure, for it depended on an unstable American prosperity. American industrial expansion was symbolized by a great building boom (in 1927, its peak year, 12% of the gross national income went on building construction); rapid expansion of automobile, electrical and other major industries; unprecedentedly high levels of investment (21% of gross national income as early as 1923 and rising until 1929); and greatly increased productivity per man hour in industry through rationalization and greater and more efficient industrial plant. Even agricultural productivity increased by 15% between 1923 and 1929, though here the first signs of the coming depression were apparent by the mid-twenties.

Britain attempted, despite her reduced financial and economic power and the burden of debt repayments to America, to encourage the flow of international trade by making considerable concessions to her own debtors. In the financial year 1927–28 Britain paid £33,000,000 to America while receiving only £25,000,000 in war debts and reparations. Though the settlements were burdensome all round, they ended previous uncertainty about liability and contributed to the growing confidence which by 1929 brought Europe's share of world production to its 1913 percentage. However, the financial system on which the revival depended was only superficially comparable to the pre-war structure. The 'new' gold standard established from 1924 was incomplete, insecure and clumsy in operation, and largely nominal when it came to the internal convertibility of paper money into gold. Above all, the new American foreign investment and lending, on which the economic advance depended, was chiefly short-term. British pre-war lending, which had formed the cement of the old international financial system, had been mainly long-term and therefore more reliable. Thus, although between 1925 and 1929 the post-war difficulties seemed to have been finally surmounted, the new system was precarious. Productivity increases were remarkable: world production of food and raw materials increased by 11% and manufactures by 26%, while the flow of world trade rose by 19%. But the economic well-being of the world could be, and was, destroyed for years by a speculative mania on the part of American investors.

The prosperity chiefly affected the western world, but it was unevenly shared even in that restricted area. Germany profited from the American boom in the form of loans, especially after her currency had been stabilized in the middle of 1926, but calling in of American loans began to affect her at the end of 1928 and reduced her economic well-being. Nevertheless before the depression it remained considerable, even though her manufacturing index was then only 117, while the world average was 153. The manufacturing index of Britain however was only 100, a sad commentary on the Conservatives, the party of businessmen which had held power since November 1924, and which yielded office to the second Labour government in June 1929 barely four months before the collapse of the international economic structure. Italy under Mussolini was discovering more new difficulties than solutions to old problems. In western Europe only France, building up heavy gold reserves under Poincaré's frugal stewardship and improving her industrial output, really consolidated economic power. If the special case of Soviet Russia is ignored, as she pursued autarchy and rapid industrialization regardless of economic cost, only Japan of the major countries produced an economic spurt comparable to America's; and with the death of Kato in 1926, such prospects as still existed of Japan's evolution into a peaceful parliamentary *régime* suffered an irreparable blow.

Politics in Britain were dominated between 1924 and 1929 by economic problems, which reached the height of their intensity in the general strike of 1926, yet Parliament devoted more time and oratory to the archaic issue of the revision of the Anglican Prayer Book than to the plight of the unemployed and the depressed areas or to industrial disputes. During the two years (1927–28) of this storm in a teacup, industrial disputes still numbered 610, and real wages were not rising. At the end of 1928 they stood at the same level as at the end of 1924, which was only about 9% above that of 1913. Only Neville Chamberlain in Baldwin's ministry could claim solid achievements. His reforms of local government services, connected with improvements in poor law, health insurance and pensions schemes for orphans, widows and the aged, transformed local government from an incoherent jumble into a logical pattern. The reputation for clarity of mind and efficiency thereby earned (he carried twenty-one bills in the 1924–29 parliament) in turn brought him the premiership in 1937. The only other major political reform was the establishment of universal adult suffrage in 1928 when the vote was extended to women over the age of twenty-one—the 'flappers' vote.

Mass unemployment proved an intractable problem and Keynesian methods of solving it were unacceptable to the Conservative government and its financial advisers. The solution in fact depended on a greater degree of government economic control than any government but a Socialist one could then have countenanced. Unemployment derived from the continued decline of the coal industry with the loss of overseas markets after 1914, from foreign competition to textiles and steel, and from government failure to promote changes in the economic structure to suit Britain's altered position in the pattern of world trade. However the general strike resulting from the coalminers' dispute with the mineowners was touched off also by the political tensions and social stresses of a country which had not yet surmounted the dislocation of the war. The industry had an unenviable strike record, and in 1925 a royal commission was appointed to report on the miners' grievances. Its report dissatisfied both miners and owners, particularly the latter, and when the miners rejected cuts in wages they were locked out by the owners on May 1st, 1926. The cabinet was divided in its views; Baldwin was anxious to compromise, but Churchill was eager for strong measures. The central organization of the British trade unions, the TUC, was as anxious as Baldwin to avoid a general strike. It might have been avoided had not Baldwin decided that he needed to go to bed when one of the cabinet's major demands was being conceded by the Trade Union Congress's general council. He awoke next morning to find the general strike in progress.

In fact there was no 'general strike', for though all forms of transport were involved, as were the gas, electricity, building, printing and heavy industries, only about 2,500,000 workers walked off their jobs, and a million of those were miners. Road transport, manned by volunteers, could now in emergency supply essential services, and only the large cities were much affected. One beneficial result of the strike was that radio, in the form of the British Broadcasting Company, or Corporation, as it became after 1926 (in Europe the radio services were from the beginning public services), established itself as a largely impartial source of news to a population deprived of its press. The BBC thereby began to build up the reputation for probity which was to be of major political importance during World War II, when it constituted for a Europe under German occupation a source of hope as well as of information. Otherwise the strike had surprisingly little effect. Miners, owners and government all adopted exaggerated postures. The government claimed that the strike was a threat to the constitution and to legally constituted authority. The unions showed a remarkable degree of solidarity, but had no intention of challenging the government's authority. The general strike ended on May 12th, though the miners continued with their own strike for another six months before they admitted total defeat. Britain was not close to revolution; the essential democracy of the British working class ensured that. In the end the miners lost about £60,000,000 in wages, and had to work longer hours for lower wages. In 1927 the government meanly underscored its victory by passing a Trade Disputes and Trade Union Act making sympathetic strikes illegal, and placing on unionists the onus of ensuring that they contributed to political funds, that is, to the Labour Party, of which the unions were the paymasters.

However, there was no more talk of a general strike; even the customary individual industrial strikes became rarer with the depletion of union funds and the drop in union membership, and other employers did not repeat the errors of the coal-owners. The economy recovered rapidly before 1929, once union leaders such as Bevin adopted the arguments of the more progressive employers that only higher productivity could pay for higher wages. The strike's political consequences were far-reaching, and on the whole beneficial. The Labour Party and trade unions were irrevocably committed to democratic parliamentary Socialism and its political processes. That the British people had cooler heads and greater political maturity than some of their rulers was shown in June 1929 when they rejected Baldwin's 'honest Stanley' image and demand for 'safety first', in the sure conviction that MacDonald and his followers were no revolutionaries. The result on the whole reflected national opinion as well as the vagaries of the electoral system: Labour 288, Conservative 260, Liberal 59. The defeat was a blessing for the Conservatives. Their enemies had to face the depression.

Under Poincaré's National Union ministries of July 1926–July 1929 France achieved a measure of political stability. Having abandoned his punitive policy towards Germany, Poincaré concentrated on restoring financial stability. Under Briand's three ministries (November 1925 to July 15th, 1926) the franc had declined until it was worth only two American cents. Apart from Briand, to whom Poincaré entrusted foreign affairs, there were five other former Premiers in the cabinet—though this was not necessarily a strengthening factor, as their pretensions exceeded their capacities. The Radicals had to accept his strong personality, and, even more difficult, heavy taxation of the kind that they should have imposed years before, but they preferred this to letting in the Socialists. The ease and speed with which Poincaré ended the financial crisis demonstrated all too clearly where the blame for it lay, and the emptiness of Radical political rhetoric.

Effectively what Poincaré surmounted in the summer of 1926 was a crisis of confidence. He made few reforms, but sharply cut government expenditure, and increased taxation—as usual, chiefly at the expense of the poor, but if the fetish of balancing the budget was to be observed and confidence restored, this was the only way which the iniquitous taxation system allowed. However, the shibboleth of restoring the franc to pre-war parity, as the British pound had absurdly been restored, was abandoned. In the end the franc was fixed at about a fifth of its pre-war value, that is, at four American cents. In fact so much money had been brought back from abroad by the patriots who had sent it there during the inflation that it could have been re-established at a higher rate, had not the government stepped in. Henceforth the franc was stable, albeit at the expense, among others, of those who had invested in war bonds and lost accordingly 80% of their investment. Though the franc was stable it was not regarded as secure, and the inflationary experiences before Poincarist orthodoxy saved the day had unfortunate repercussions. Devaluation and abandonment of the gold standard were regarded with such horror that it was difficult for governments to take the necessary steps during the depression.

Poincaré, however, at last completed the work of economic reconstruction, aided by the payment of reparations from Germany. Though the nagging and justified fear of eventual German ambitions still remained, the building of the Maginot Line gave a sense of greater security, however illusory. The French at last also experienced a measure of economic prosperity and security, though on a tenuous basis. The effort to maintain the franc's stability in perpetuity was doomed to failure from the start in the international financial quicksands of the inter-war years. Establishment of real military security would have meant heavy outlays which Poincaré could never have accepted. Balancing the budget meant restriction of already inadequate social services, refusal to introduce necessary new ones, and continued refusal to inject enough public money into the economy to end the stagnation. However, the French people had suffered much since 1914. They were only too willing to be deluded, and even to delude themselves into half-believing that they had found salvation in Poincaré's unimaginative financial orthodoxy, in the eastern frontier fortifications begun by the former sergeant of World War I, André Maginot and in Briand's comforting and magnificent rhetoric.

Far from being Socialist, as its Right Wing extremist elements alleged, Weimar Germany was not even liberal in its political temper. Though in terms of its political leadership it did not deserve the gibe that it was 'a republic without republicans', this came dangerously near the truth in respect of the masses. Paul von Hindenburg's election as President in early 1925, however, reduced until 1930 the dangers to the Weimar Republic from all sections except the extremes of Left and Right. Hindenburg's reputation as monarchist, nationalist, conservative and anti-democrat was unimpeachable—better than Ludendorff's, whom Hitler had backed in the first ballot, but abandoned when Ludendorff polled under 1% of the votes, thereby producing an irreparable breach between them. Hindenburg naturally did not give an example of allegiance to the Republic, but until the Republican politicians showed their inability after Stresemann's death to operate the constitution, Hindenburg respected it.

Stresemann, the former adherent of constitutional monarchy and bitter enemy of the October-November revolution which had destroyed its prospects of success, had favoured the Kapp *putsch* of 1920, but he had rapidly altered his view that overthrowing the Weimar Republic was the quickest way to restore Germany's former greatness. His vigorous stand in 1923, when extreme Left and extreme Right both conspired—though hating each other as much as the Weimar *régime*—to overthrow the *bourgeois* Republic, showed his political temper. A dictatorship of either Left or Right would destroy the conservative forces of which he was the leading spokesman. Just as Thiers, in the analogous position of leader of a France defeated by Germany in 1870, had established a Republic in the ashes of defeat, he recognized that a Republic would divide his countrymen least, while insisting that it must be conservative to survive. His aim was to make himself the bridge between Imperial and Weimar Germany, and unite all moderates in support of his policy of fulfilment of those parts of the Treaty of Versailles which could not be ended or evaded for the present. The clandestine German rearmament which was conducted with the aid of Soviet Russia he fully approved, as did the great majority of Germans. He merely disliked the readiness of the *Reichswehr* chief, von Seeckt, to reject the possibility of securing concessions from the west, and the noisiness of the extreme Right. His aim was to create a great new centre party which would not be exclusively Catholic, but would rally moderate conservatives to the Republic. He died before he could begin the task, but in any case his neglect of responsibilities as leader of the German People's Party meant that he failed to make his own party unquestioningly loyal to the Republic. After his death in October 1929 it was taken over by its rightist elements, who exemplified the general trend of Germans in their political outlook, by gravitating first to the Nationalists, whom Stresemann had tried for his own purposes to manipulate. Finally, after the elections of March 1933 brought the party only 432,300 votes and two deputies, it endorsed Hitler's dictatorship in July 1933 and then dissolved.

However, after 1923, and especially after concluding Locarno (denounced by the Nazis as another 'Versailles'), Stresemann was chiefly instrumental in holding together the German political system, as the one permanent member of rapidly changing coalitions. Germany's entry into the League of Nations in 1926 was postponed from March to September because of Polish fears and Spanish and Brazilian jealousy over her having a permanent seat on the Council, but Stresemann's appearance in Geneva as an equal of the British and French leaders was a personal as well as a national triumph. Oddly enough, his completion in April 1926 of negotiations with Soviet Russia for a new agreement reaffirming Rapallo and pledging both parties to neutrality in the event of a third party's attack on the other, was unhesitatingly accepted by all parties in the *Reichstag* in June. Evacuation of the first zone of the Rhineland by the Allies and departure of their Military Control Commission in January 1927 were further triumphs, though the Control Commission had long given up the attempt to prevent rearmament. His confidence that German economic expansion would prove irresistible in central and eastern Europe was being vindicated by the rapid development achieved under the Dawes Plan, which reduced difficulties over reparations and provided investment and loans. Stresemann privately rejoiced that Germany would probably never meet her obligations, yet simultaneously would ensure continued foreign interest in her economic well-being because she had such heavy foreign debts. Nevertheless both the political and financial stability of Stresemann's *régime* were precarious, and for the former at least Stresemann's Right Wing sympathies were largely responsible. Von Seeckt, dismissed from the *Reichswehr* in 1926 because of his indiscretion in permitting the eldest son of the former crown prince to attend army manoeuvres, found his political home in the People's Party after the death of his enemy Stresemann. The rightest elements in it formed, with the German Nationalist Party, the political expression within the *Reichstag* of respectable opposition to the Republic itself, though Stresemann often tried to make the Nationalist Party an integral part of the Weimar system. Stresemann always felt more sympathy for the Nationalists than he did for the Socialists, though the latter were as nationalist as he was, and far more reliable allies for his major purposes.

Germany's economic stability was dependent on foreign loans and on the development of heavy industry, whose chief function was to produce arms. In May 1925 it was public knowledge that the *Reichswehr* planned an army of 35 divisions, which was in fact its size when Hitler in March 1935 repudiated the disarmament clauses of Versailles and brought into the open the largely Weimar-built army for which he claimed the credit. The Nationalists were above all the party of big business, and especially of heavy industry. They were connected with the first paramilitary organization officially blessed by the Right, the Stahlhelm. Alfred Hugenberg, who took over the Nationalist Party's leadership in 1928, was unbalanced and drove away many of its more moderate members, but his connections with Krupps, ownership of a press empire, and ties with the steel cartel were characteristic of its affiliations. By 1928 the official budget of the *Reichswehr* was 726,000,000 marks, which meant that, allowing for the increased cost of living, the cost per man was almost double that of 1914. Of course the official budget did not tell half the story. The *Reichswehr* was conducting big business on its own account inside Germany. German armaments plants were operating in Sweden, Denmark, Holland, Spain, Switzerland, and, above all, in Russia. Though the Russians failed in their attempts to control Germany, they obtained important short term benefits from military collaboration as well as German industry's assistance when it was badly needed by them. Indeed, of all foreigners the Russians made the greatest contribution to building up the Weimar armed forces, as they did later to the building up of those of the Nazis.

Russian interventions in German politics also tended to foster German nationalism. The failure of the Cuno government in 1923 to maintain decent living standards for the German people had led the Comintern's German expert, Karl Radek, and the German Communist Party to make overtures to certain Fascist groups and ex-officers, and adopt what came to be called National Bolshevism, by appealing to the most violent nationalist resentments of the Germans. However, in the early 1920s Moscow fomented uprisings in the Rhineland and elsewhere only when the German workers, from misery and despair, were likely to revolt in any case, and when Stresemann sought a *rapprochement* with the west. Although these insurrections represented the Comintern's last attempt to promote a German revolution, the German Communists continued their attempts to outbid even the Nazis by denouncing the Treaty of Versailles, promising to free Germany from its chains, and resortir g to anti-Semitism. From February 1925, if not earlier, they set out to destroy the Socialists, as the first and indispensable prerequisite for the establishment of the dictatorship of the proletariat. For this purpose they collaborated on several occasions with the Nazis, sharing the belief of other politicians, at the opposite end of the political spectrum, that the Nazis could be discarded when they were no longer useful.

Hitler allowed Goebbels and other radicals such as Röhm and Gregor Strasser to take seriously the Left Wing elements of the original Nazi programme with its defiance of capitalism and 'state socialism', but his aim was to produce a mass party of the Right. Partly for that reason, and partly because he did not want the Party to own allegiance to anybody else, he allowed the dispute between Nazism's Left and Right to continue unchecked while he was in prison between November 1923 and December 1924. In February 1925 he could therefore begin to rebuild the Party on his own lines, and with the clear goal of achieving power by peaceful methods (that is, merely, non-revolutionary) and what he called legal means. Dubious even before the Munich *putsch* took place of the rising's chances of success, he was now resolved to gain power constitutionally, and also as leader of a national party, not of southern separatists. The prosperity which came to Germany under Stresemann, however, made it difficult to get mass support. In the 1928 elections the Nazis secured only 810,000 out of 41,224,700 votes, and 12 seats out of 491 in the *Reichstag*.

Though Hitler was only a minor political figure after ten years in politics, he was still convinced of his eventual victory. He scented the insecurity of German prosperity, though he predicted another annihilating

399

inflation, not the slump induced by the great depression. His chief asset, however, was his political flexibility. He had nothing in common with either Left or Right. He allowed Goebbels' posters to depict Brownshirted proletarians marching to revolution under the 'red storm banner' when he was on the eve of taking power as the defender of German capitalism. He seized every useful opportunity of coming to terms with the capitalists, and the first opportunity established him as a national figure. In 1929 the Nationalists, who were still the party of big business, came out against the Young Plan, because it derived from Versailles, and in effect re-asserted German war guilt by providing a means of paying reparations. Because the Nationalists lacked mass support, they decided to enlist the aid of the Nazis. Hitler still had to contend with Gregor Strasser and a strong prejudice in the Party against Hugenberg and other reactionaries, but he got his way. Between July 1929 and Hindenburg's approval in March 1930 of the acts embodying the Young Plan, Hitler had at his disposal the resources of Hugenberg's propaganda machine, and used them to make himself known to the German people. He was now in a position also to outbid and divide the Nationalists. The glories in his campaign against the Plan were not tarnished by its failure, for he blamed that on Hugenberg— who had indeed committed some wretched blunders. He now attacked the Nationalists as bitterly as he had 'fulfilment' politicians like Walter Rathenau, though he took good care not to antagonize big business. This bore fruit as the depression deepened and the banker Hjalmer Schacht and Hugenberg's old friend Albert Vögler, chairman of the steel cartel, gradually became convinced that Hitler was their man.

## (ii) *The Rise of Stalin*

Soviet Russia's Stalin understood his peasant nation's need for a substitute to replace the ritual of the Orthodox Church. As a former acolyte, Stalin also knew how to provide it. The ceremony of Lenin's funeral and the subsequent worshipping of his embalmed body in the shrine of the great tomb in Red Square were foretastes of the cult of Leninism which Lenin himself had tried to forestall, and which Stalin was supremely fitted to institute as a matter of policy, and to exploit as a means of strengthening his dictatorship when he saw its potentialities.

However, the process was slow and Stalin was hesitant over its completion. Moreover, he could not possibly have appreciated what a precedent was being set when he and his two allies reacted in 1924 to Trotsky's criticisms not only by denouncing Trotsky's heresies, but by beginning to write Lenin's indispensable lieutenant out of the Bolshevik Revolution. There thus began the distortion of the history of the Revolution in order to magnify Stalin's minor role into one of crucial importance, second only to

Lenin's. It should, however, be added that Stalin did not exempt even his own earlier works from revision where they conflicted with his later policies. This was the case with his *Foundations of Leninism,* which he published in April 1924 to establish his absurd claim to have been Lenin's closest disciple, and therefore to be the man best fitted to expound Leninism.

The Bolshevik leaders had expected when they seized power that their revolution would be the spark to set ablaze proletarian revolutions in western Europe. However, they had had no coherent policy for governing Russia herself. While striving for the goal of a socialist Soviet Russia, they had doubted whether it could in fact be achieved without the help of successful foreign revolutions. Lenin, in particular, had feared before 1917 that the Russian revolution would get off course and lead Russia into an Oriental despotism more backward than Tsarism unless great care was taken to prevent this. However, first the Civil War, next the failures of the European revolutionary Left, and then sheer exigencies of government, had converted the Bolshevik leaders into the heirs of the Tsars instead of the directors of a great international revolution. Nevertheless, until 1924 no Bolshevik leader had doubted that outside help was necessary to establish a socialist society in Russia, and the first version of *Foundations of Leninism* said exactly that.

But even the most dedicated of revolutionaries—and Stalin must certainly be numbered among them—like to taste the fruits of their labours for themselves. Moreover, with the failure of the German Left Wing uprisings in 1923 there was little prospect of successful—or indeed, of any—western proletarian revolutions. Therefore, as Lenin and other Russian Marxists, including Trotsky, had adapted Marxism before 1917 to provide the ideological justification which they needed before they seized power on behalf of a practically non-existent Russian proletariat, so Stalin now groped his way to a new formulation of the revolution's character. That this new theory provided ideological weapons against Trotsky, who adhered to the older viewpoint, was only one of its advantages, and not the most important. Stalin could not know that Trotsky, hitherto so flexible in changing his viewpoint, would adhere with rigid conservatism to an exploded dogma. He himself was never averse to taking over Trotsky's ideas, after first deriding their author, once he had become convinced of their utility.

In the autumn of 1923 Gosplan had prepared a five-year plan for the metal industry, and in December it was studying the operation of the NEP market. The attempts after the scissors crisis to establish better balance between town and country by controlling the prices of certain goods led gradually to the extension of controls to other sections of the economy, and finally after 1928 to the successive five-year plans. In 1924 many of the planning measures which Trotsky had advocated were slowly put into practice, though the triumvirs gave him no credit for that. His argument that the government must begin to accumulate the capital necessary for further expansion by imposing heavy sacrifices on the Russian people was not taken up till later, for the Bolshevik leadership was not yet prepared for it. Stalin's ideas in 1923–24 still reflected the confusion within the Party over whether it ought to combine central planning with the continuation of NEP. NEP, as a retreat from socialism, had always been unpopular within the Party. However, Trotsky was regarded by most Bolsheviks as demanding the end of NEP while it was still, on Lenin's own authority, thought indispensable, and as advocating a return to the even more unpopular War Communism. This interpretation was crude but it contained more than a measure of justice. In addition, whereas Trotsky was known to have been a leading architect of War Communism, in order to create the Red Army and win the Civil War, his contribution to the adoption of NEP had been obscured by his opposition to certain of its features as Lenin had finally presented them. In addition, the improvement in conditions from the end of 1923 produced general agreement that the triumvirate was pursuing the right policy.

In fact, when Zinoviev told the 13th Party Congress in May 1924 that expansion of heavy industry was a principal objective and must be carried through at full speed, Russia was committed to establishing a planned economy at the expense of her workers and peasants. The full consequences of the decision were not seen for at least five years, and it was also a laborious process to translate plans into action. But planning was well under way when in January 1925 the triumvirate secured Trotsky's resignation from the post of Commissar of War. Trotsky was too loyal to consider using the Red Army against his opponents, and made no resistance. One of the greatest dangers to Stalin was thereby ended, and so was his dependence on Kamenev and Zinoviev, who discovered too late their error in taking the lead in disposing of Trotsky.

In April 1925 Stalin took a decisive step towards consolidating his position by putting before the 14th Party Conference his theory of socialism in one country. Its thesis was that under Bolshevik leadership and with its rich resources in raw materials and manpower, Russia could build a socialist society, unless the capitalist powers again intervened. The appeal to Russian pride in the achievements of the revolution and faith in its future successes were backed by quotations from suitably modified texts of the Leninist scriptures. In fact there were no practical reasons for supposing that the course of events inside Russia need be affected in any respect by the failure of foreign proletarians to overturn capitalism. Lenin himself might well have drawn that conclusion, as he had jettisoned Marxist shibboleths in 1917, though without abandoning the Bolshevik internationalist outlook or subscribing to the crudities of Stalin's formula and the brutalities of its execution. However, it was time to reshape the Bolshevik sense of purpose, as the 14th Party Conference showed by its endorsement of the new line. Zinoviev, though head of the Comintern, and Kamenev at first largely ignored it, but in the summer Stalin's theory was endorsed by three Old Bolsheviks: N. I. Bukharin, an eminently respected theoretician, A. I. Rykov, successor to Lenin himself as Chairman of the Council of Commissars, and M. P. Tomsky the trade union boss.

These allies constituted the Right Wing leadership, which argued that NEP need be abandoned only by degrees, as socialism's success was assured. In fact the April Conference had marked the high point of NEP, but in the autumn, when Zinoviev came out publicly against it, NEP still had considerable support. Zinoviev's and Kamenev's manoeuvres that year, when they belatedly realized what Trotsky's removal meant, brought them round to the Left Wing view of NEP propounded by Trotsky, and they began to furnish quotations from Lenin designed to prove that capitalism, not socialism, formed its basis. Zinoviev especially attacked official tenderness to the 'rich' peasants, the *kulaks*, and demanded a return to the rigorous methods of 1918 in dealing with them. However their attack on Stalin at the 14th Congress in December 1925 miscarried, for the Right supported him strongly. Kamenev was reduced from full to candidate member of the Politburo (even Trotsky remained a full member for a time), and when Zinoviev tried to organize the Leningrad machine, which he headed, against Stalin, Stalin put it under the control of Kirov, then his henchman.

At the Congress Stalin proclaimed the government's intention to make the Soviet Union economically self-sufficient by making the countryside 'march behind the town, behind heavy industry'. This was the decision on which the five-year plans were based, but Stalin had been reluctant to reach it almost to the end. Moreover, he could not foresee how far events and his mastery of them would take him, though he certainly solved problems as they arose in ways which increased his own power. By 1926 Trotsky understood that 'socialism in one country' presupposed a closed economy and therefore economic isolation from the west, and Stalin may also have done so. Everybody understood that 'planning' meant the subordination of agriculture to heavy industry, but this did not yet entail illtreatment of the peasants. On the contrary, the period between 1925 and 1927 saw them very favourably treated. The 'pro-peasant' policy of these years, however, was popularly associated with Bukharin, who actually exhorted the peasants to make themselves rich. The battle for planning was finally won in April 1926 when it was decided that planning should be undertaken by all state economic organs. In 1927 a start was made in clearing the way for the inauguration of the first five-year plan. The 15th Party Congress of December 1927, later known as the Industrialization Congress, called for higher rates of industrialization and collectivization. This virtually ended NEP, though in July 1928 the Party's Central Committee denied that NEP was to be scrapped, rejecting as 'counter-revolutionary blabber' stories to that effect.

Trotsky had held aloof from the 14th Congress controversies. He despised Zinoviev and Kamenev, while recognizing the sincerity of their internationalist outlook. But because Stalin's combination of isolationism and

403

neo-Populism had a formidable appeal, he joined them in leading the 'united opposition' of 1926–27. In 1925 their coalition might have succeeded; now Stalin's grip on government and Party was too strong. In July 1926 he had Zinoviev expelled from the Politburo. In October he forced all the opposition leaders to promise to honour the 1921 ban on opposition. When they broke their promise he forced Trotsky and Kamenev out of the Politburo and Zinoviev out of the Comintern, replacing Zinoviev with Bukharin. The opposition was still not silenced.* It denounced Stalin for betraying the proletarian to the *kulak* and the NEP profiteer, abandoning the Chinese Communists to the Kuomintang, and deserting the cause of international revolution.

Then in the autumn of 1927 Trotsky demanded the removal of the government if its foreign policy led to war, as was thought likely. Stalin had Trotsky and Zinoviev expelled from the Central Committee, and after they had organized street demonstrations against the government to celebrate the tenth anniversary of the Bolshevik Revolution, he had them expelled from the Party also. In January 1928 the opposition leaders were exiled from Moscow, Trotsky to Alma Ata in Central Asia, whence he continued the attack. In January 1928 signs of serious trouble over the collection of grain from the peasants were apparent. Stalin, however, was determined to push through his policy of rapid industrialization and collectivization, and the discontent increased in the countryside. In June Zinoviev and Kamenev again recanted, and were re-admitted to the Party. In the first half of July, however, the dispute between the Right and Stalin over the reversal of the pro-peasant policy came to a head, and Bukharin and Kamenev got secretly in touch. Stalin, though hard-pressed because of the strength of support for the Right, managed between July and October to outmanoeuvre it. In November he got the Central Committee to condemn it, and next month defeated the Right Wing trade union leadership. He pursued his advantage, securing Bukharin's, Rykov's and Tomsky's condemnation by the Politburo on February 9th–10th, 1929.

Then, flushed with success, he committed a grave error. On February 11th he had Trotsky exiled from the Soviet Union, instead of waiting a little longer and 'liquidating' him. Trotsky was thus able to build up his 'Fourth International' and denounce Stalin's betrayals of the Russian revolution and of international Communism. However he remained convinced both that the Russian revolution had been proletarian, and that the Bolsheviks had been justified in suppressing all political opposition, Socialist and 'counter-revolutionary' alike—if indeed there was 'objectively' any distinction. He had approved the operation of the terror, first under the Cheka, and then under its successor the OGPU, long after even the specious justification of Civil War conditions had disappeared. He and Lenin had created the monstrous apparatus of tyranny which Stalin inherited, and his only defence was that they had chastised with whips where Stalin chastised with scorpions. He had ordered requisitions under War Communism in the knowledge that it would mean mass starvation.

and had thereby caused the death of hundreds of thousands. The bloody tyranny of Stalin against which he protested was worse than his own only in scale, and because it was exercised over Bolsheviks in the political sphere, and not over Liberals, Social Revolutionaries, Mensheviks and Whites.

Trotsky's criticisms of Stalinist foreign policy were more to the point, though his own role in encouraging the German revolutions in 1923, when Stalin had been doubtful of their success, suggests no sureness of touch on Trotsky's part. Moreover Stalin was following, if ineptly, the basic line agreed on before Lenin's death. The constitution drawn up in 1923, and adopted practically simultaneously with Lenin's death, had recognized that relations with foreign powers posed special problems. Stalin followed pretty faithfully its dogma that with the establishment of the Bolshevik *régime* the world had been divided into two camps: capitalist and socialist. The belief was that while the capitalist camp remained implacably hostile the socialist camp should not use force in order to spread revolution—which was in fact no more than a recognition that it could not. The ultimate objective of promoting socialist revolutions was not formally abandoned by Stalin: he merely recognized that it was not immediately practicable, and concentrated on a policy of defence of the Soviet Union which had never been ruled out in theory, still less in practice. His policy after 1923 of penetrating and exploiting the '*bourgeois*-democratic' states' mass workers' organizations was also a return to tactics adopted, though admittedly unsuccessfully, by Lenin himself in 1921. The change from NEP to the planned economy in the end made no difference, so far as foreign policy was concerned. Whether the *régime* accepted the predominance of the peasantry as under NEP, or adopted large-scale industrialization, the first objective was to concentrate both on the internal interests of Soviet Russia and on her external 'national' interests, to the exclusion of the international revolution; the next was to advance Stalin's own interests.

The first objective could be best achieved by regularizing relations with foreign powers, impossible if Soviet Russia allowed her foreign policy to remain dominated by Lenin's assertion under the quite different circumstances of 1919: 'We are surrounded by people, classes, governments, which openly express their hatred for us. We must remember that we are always within a hairsbreadth of invasion.' By 1924 Comintern leaders had accepted the view that 'world capitalism', far from being threatened with imminent collapse, had entered a new phase of stabilization. They had accordingly deduced that there were no immediate prospects of revolutionary situations arising in Europe or elsewhere. This did not, however, entail abandoning the view that Russia's greatest security lay in the contradictions within the capitalist world, nor hopes that these might lead to wars between her enemies. In 1925 the Soviet view was that the world had entered on a 'long period of so-called peaceful co-existence between the USSR and the capitalist countries'. Dubious of Germany under Stresemann's direction, the Russians in 1924 had pinned their hopes on MacDonald's Labour government, and then when that proved a broken reed, actually made overtures for the renewal of Tsarist Russia's alliance with the arch-imperialist France. This reversion to normal methods of diplomatic intercourse did not in Russian eyes preclude instructing foreign Communist parties to do everything in their power to provoke unrest and disaffection. On the contrary, in their view the first duty of all foreign Communists was to demonstrate their immunity to '*bourgeois* nationalism' by putting the interests of the socialist fatherland above everything else. Though the 'Zinoviev letter' used in the British general election of 1924 was a forgery, substantially it said what Zinoviev had been saying in the Comintern for some time. The readiness of the various Communist parties to accept Bolshevization did not surprise the rival Social Democrats and Labour parties in Europe, though the Russians were surprised at the unpopularity of their policies, and put the blame on incompetence in Berlin, Paris, Rome or London instead of in Moscow. An offer of financial aid to assist the British general strike was only one of the most blatant Soviet miscalculations, and aroused hostility equally among the British trade union leadership, which the Russians wished to supplant, and among non-trade unionists.

In 1927, after the Russians had openly admitted their intention of using China as a means of weakening Britain, and were conducting blatantly subversive activities inside Britain and her imperial territories, the premises of the Soviet trade delegation in London (Arcos) were raided, evidence of subversive activities was allegedly found, and diplomatic relations broken off. The French, who had similar grievances, also broke off relations, and in Warsaw the Russian envoy was assassinated while engaged in negotiations for a non-aggression pact. There was no danger of war with Britain, but Stalin and his opponents in Russia appear to have believed there was. One consequence of the 'crisis' was to bring Russia into the disarmament negotiations of the next few years. Russia proposed 'universal disarmament' partly because she herself was militarily so weak, and also for propaganda purposes, to expose the insincerity of the leading League powers which were taking it up.

By 1928, however, the Comintern was almost moribund. Always used as a battlefield on which to fight out Russian domestic quarrels, it now had to abandon the 'Right Wing' policy of 'alliance' with non-Communist parties abroad which it had followed for the last few years. Trotsky's attacks on its ineffectiveness in Britain and China had proved only too well-founded. Moreover, Stalin was now engaging in a struggle with new opponents: the Comintern leader Bukharin, the Russian Right, and the elements in foreign parties espousing moderation whose support had been necessary in the struggle with Trotsky. The Comintern therefore decided that a new revolutionary upsurge was on the way, and hence that it must pursue abroad a revolutionary class policy. It was decreed that Right 'reformists' inside the foreign parties were the main enemies of the loyal Communists, and that Social Democrats, especially 'Left' ones preaching unity with the Communists, were 'the most dangerous enemies of Communism and of the dictatorship of the proletariat'. The Comintern came out against these elements, as likely to support Bukharin's views, and Bukharin was replaced as Comintern chairman by Stalin's faithful Molotov.

## (iii) *The Victory of Kuomintang*

Stalin's gravest miscalculation in the field of foreign policy was his handling of relations with China, which brought near-disaster to the Chinese Communists in 1927. Lenin had talked for years of the importance of Asia as a revolutionary factor, but no policy towards the Chinese revolution had been worked out. Certainly in the early 1920s there were no plans for using China against the western powers, beyond utilizing the Kuomintang as a means of weakening foreign imperialism, and before Borodin came as adviser to Sun Yat-sen in October 1923, Soviet envoys had been sent to the Peking warlords. In May 1924 Soviet Russia made a treaty with the Peking *régime* establishing diplomatic relations with it as 'the government of the Chinese Republic'. It was not realized for some time that relations with the Kuomintang were to be the decisive factor for some years. Neither did Stalin suspect the wiliness of Chiang Kai-shek, who exploited the military support given by Soviet Russia to extort concessions from Britain while he used Soviet military equipment to attempt to destroy the Chinese Communists. And had it not been for the independent-minded rising Chinese Communist leader Mao Tse-tung, Chiang might well have succeeded.

In January 1923 one of the kaleidoscopic changes then typical of China's political scene had seen Sun Yat-sen's usurpers themselves evicted from Canton. By early March Sun had re-established Kuomintang headquarters there, with himself as generalissimo. After that he appealed unsuccessfully to America to persuade the other interested foreign powers to join in a military occupation of China for five years, so as to permit an overhaul of central and local government and preparations for democratic elections. Though disappointed at America's rejection of the proposal, he saw new prospects opening up in the summer from the outbreak of another war between the Peking warlords, and a favourable Soviet attitude to the Kuomintang. Committing himself finally to Russia, in August 1923 he sent Chiang to lead a political and military mission to Moscow, which contained prominent Chinese Communists, but Russia continued to deal also with Peking.

The treaty which Russia signed with the Peking warlords in May 1924, however, was more than an insurance against Sun's and the Kuomintang's suffering another, possibly fatal relapse. In addition to abrogating Russia's special rights and privileges in China under the 'unequal treaties', it recognized Chinese sovereignty over Outer Mongolia, which Russia had long coveted. This did not prevent Russia from turning Outer Mongolia into the puppet Mongolian People's Republic, though in deference to Chinese susceptibilities it was not annexed outright. Rights in the Chinese Eastern Railway were also reserved for a future settlement and the railway was administered jointly in the meantime. Chang Tso-lin, the Manchurian warlord, was infuriated by the agreement over the railway, which ran through Manchuria, and he refused to subscribe to it until the Russians threatened dire consequences if he tried to prevent the working of the pact. He submitted in September 1924, but rapidly regained prestige by securing Peking's recognition of his predominance in Manchuria. At the end of 1924 Sun arrived in Peking to wind up negotiations which he had been conducting for some time with Chang and the Peking warlords, to restore the unity of China. However, of Chang's two Peking warlord allies, Tuan Ch'i-jui did not intend to share power with Sun, and Feng Yü-hsiang had quarrelled with his partners. Sun therefore had little prospect of 'saving the country' in collaboration with the northerners, and his death in Peking in March 1925 probably preserved his reputation as a national hero.

It also opened up a struggle for the succession in the Kuomintang, and civil war might have developed in the south but for the 'May Thirtieth incident' in Shanghai, when police at the orders of a British officer fired on a demonstration, killing twelve students. This provoked a boycott of British goods, and both Kuomintang and Communists used the incident to obtain support, the Communists very skilfully, and they gained many adherents in the towns. In July 1925 the Canton *régime* transformed itself from a Military Government into the Nationalist Government of China, and called its army the National Revolutionary Army. The rapid growth of Communist and Left Wing influence, however, alarmed the Kuomintang's Right Wing. Of the triumvirate which took power in August 1925 Chiang Kai-shek occupied a centre position, seeking first the unity of the Kuomintang, as he had shown in October 1924 when his Whampoa cadets and the Communist-led Workers' Militia had defeated a Right Wing revolution against the Sun *régime*. Another triumvir was of the Right, but the chairman Wang Ching-wei was a Left Winger and highly sympathetic, as were most Left Wingers, to the Communists. Chiang knew that the Communist aim was to dominate the nationalist revolutionary coalition, and he decided to strike first. His rapid rise had been due both to his close relationship with his brother-in-law Sun, and to Borodin's belief that Chiang was less likely to be dangerous to Soviet interests than the other leading Kuomintang officers. Borodin was surprised when in March 1926 Chiang declared martial law, dismissed Communist political commissars from the army and arrested Communist trade union leaders. Wang resigned and went into exile, and Borodin threatened to stop Soviet aid. However Chiang secured a compromise which gave him much the better of the bargain: he would check the Right Wing extremists, but the Communists must reduce their agitation among the peasants, replace their class-war slogan with 'social peace', and, instead of demanding rent reduction, agitate for land redistribution. Borodin agreed also to reduce the number of Communists at Whampoa and in the higher bureaucracy. Finally the Russians, anxious not to alienate Chiang, agreed to allow him to conduct the expedition to the north which he had demanded before the coup. In June 1926 he further consolidated his power by becoming commander-in-chief.

Even now Stalin adhered to the policy of insisting that the Chinese Communists must learn to work within the Kuomintang as the best means of progressing towards the Chinese Socialist revolution, and the Communists co-operated in the northern expedition on which Chiang set out in July 1926. This, as Chiang had predicted, was a Kuomintang triumph. His forces were well received because the northern warlords' tyranny and exactions had done as much as the Communist propaganda among the peasants to prepare the way for them. Not only the peasants but the dis-integrating armies opposing the Kuomintang came over. The Peasants' Associations, which the young Communist Mao Tse-tung had helped to organize, claimed almost 10,000,000 members by early 1927 in four central provinces. However they came over largely because of promises of land made to them by the Communists, and as the Kuomintang increasingly became the *régime* of the landlords and business interests and shed its revolutionary radicalism, the peasants went over to the Communists. In Hunan, where Mao had been active, peasants began to redistribute land in December 1926, but it was a long time before the Chinese Communist Party took its strategy from him.

In November heavy fighting in Kiangsi province ended in Chiang's victory over the local warlords after a struggle which had lasted over two months, and Chiang established his headquarters in Nanchang, its capital. The Kuomintang political leadership, still predominantly Left Wing, left Canton for Wuhan in December, and on January 1st, 1927, operated from the central Wuhan city of Hankow. Here, as in the other great central cities and in the countryside, there were the beginnings of a social revolu-tion. There were strikes for higher wages in Hankow, and Left Wing trade union and political leaders organized great demonstrations, culminat-ing in the allegedly spontaneous demands by the working class for the seizure of the British concessions in Hankow and Kiukiang, and in anti-foreign riots in Foochow. Chiang Kai-shek, now firmly on the Right, disapproved of these radical trends. He was closely connected with moneyed interests in Shanghai, which was his next objective. In February 1927 the Shanghai Communist trade union leadership defeated the local warlord, establishing what was effectively a municipal revolutionary government. Instead of aiding it, Chiang halted his troops near Shanghai, while the warlord regrouped his forces and counter-attacked. The Comintern nevertheless ordered the Shanghai Communists to trust him, as to their cost they did. When Chiang finally entered Shanghai at the end of March he received financial loans which made him independent of the Russians.

He was not only independent of the Kuomintang government in Hankow but at loggerheads with it. After April 1st it was joined by the Left Wing Wang Ching-wei, whom the Communists had pressed to return. The Hankow government, as Wang himself admitted, was dominated by the Communists. Only in the army were they weak—and this was true in Hankow as well as in Nanking, which Chiang made his 'capital' on April 18th. Stalin's orders to the Chinese Communists to collaborate with the Left Wing were meaningless: except for its leaders, their friends and relatives, the Left Wing was already Communist, and Communists controlled the mass organizations of peasants and workers. Trotsky demanded that the Communists should strike against the Kuomintang and establish Soviets in the towns and countryside, but he based his opinion on misleading reports. There was no great surge of town and countryside towards the Communists, and when Chiang's forces appeared after his breach with the Hankow Kuomintang, the 'solid masses' of the workers' and peasants' associations disintegrated. In Peking, which Chang Tso-lin controlled as well as Manchuria in early 1927, the Soviet Embassy was searched on April 6th, Chinese Communists found there were executed, and papers were seized which made clear Russian policy in China. As Chang had already halted Russian activities in Manchuria (including legal economic undertakings), when control of Peking increased his self-confidence, Russia had suffered a humiliating defeat in the north.

To complete Stalin's mortification, on April 12th Chiang Kai-shek's troops put down a Communist rising which had been provoked by his arrest of some leading Communists. The trade unions were destroyed together with the Communist Party organization in Shanghai, and the only Communist-led urban insurrection ended in disaster. On April 5th Stalin had asserted that Chiang was submitting to Kuomintang discipline and had no choice except to lead his forces against the foreign imperialists. Chiang, Stalin had added, must be used as long as possible by the Communists, and then 'squeezed like a lemon and thrown away'. Chiang in fact followed his Shanghai massacre of the Comintern's innocents by opening the first of his 'annihilation campaigns' against the Communists. The Communists, attacked also by the Wuhan military leaders, withdrew from the Wuhan government but tried to follow Stalin's incoherent line by remaining in the Kuomintang. On July 13th the Kuomintang, under pressure from its military chiefs, outlawed the Communist Party, and the first 'United Front' collapsed. Thereupon Chou En-lai was sent to organize an insurrection in Nanchang, but this proved a fiasco. So did Mao's raising of the Kiangsi and Hunan peasants in the 'autumn harvest' insurrection.

Mao then retreated with the remnants of his forces deep into the interior, proscribed by the Kuomintang and dismissed from the Chinese Politburo. There he began to elaborate his strategy of basing the revolution on the peasantry. Since its goodwill was essential, he incurred the hostility of urban Marxist zealots by not 'burning and killing' with sufficient vigour in the countryside. As the Chinese proletariat was small and largely anti-Communist, while the Kuomintang controlled the towns, Mao's was the obvious strategy. It was also based on the classic Chinese pattern of the peasant war, adapted for Marxist purposes. It was not his intention, as his Communist opponents feared, to allow the peasants' *petit bourgeois* characteristics to distort the revolution. Moreover, the Chinese Communist movement which he created in the countryside in the next few years was not a peasant movement, any more than Lenin's Bolsheviks had headed a proletarian movement, but harnessed peasant discontents for Marxist purposes as the Bolsheviks had harnessed proletarian discontent.

The difficulties of securing the new strategy's acceptance lay in the hidebound ideology of the Chinese Communists, and above all in Moscow. Stalin needed a victory in China to flourish before the 15th Congress in December 1927, so, even though the revolutionary tide had ebbed, the Chinese Communists were ordered to take Canton. They did, but the proletariat which they claimed to represent ignored them. In three days Kuomintang troops smashed the uprising and murdered thousands of Cantonese. Nevertheless this coup was represented in Moscow as evidence that 'the movement is growing', and that the '*bourgeois* counter-revolutionaries will be defeated'. The Chinese Communist movement was indeed growing, though not in a manner which Moscow was ever to find acceptable. Early in 1928 Communist contingents began to make their way towards Mao's growing nucleus for a Red Army in Chingkangshan, lying between Kiangsi and Hunan. Chu Te, Mao's future leading general, arrived there in April 1928, and in May they routed the Kuomintang troops sent in pursuit. The first 'annihilation campaign' had set the pattern for its successors. In these years Mao achieved the only Communist successes of importance, though other leaders also built up bases in the interior. His rivals' insistence that the urban proletariat must play the leading role became more absurd as time passed and Mao's strength grew in the rudimentary rural soviets which he was establishing. Crude though Communist 'education' of the peasantry was, the rapid improvement of peasant conditions produced by a fairly moderate measure of land redistribution and by the ending of landlord rapacity and warlord exactions, soon won popularity and brought Mao hundreds of thousands of recruits. He employed them not as wandering insurgents, but as both concentrated forces holding revolutionary bases against their enemies and as emissaries dispersed among the peasantry to win it over. Mao's guerrilla strategy was to

'Disperse the forces among the masses to arouse them, and concentrate the forces to deal with the enemy.

The enemy advances, we retreat; the enemy halts, we harass; the enemy tires, we attack; the enemy retreats, we pursue.'

Against Mao's wishes Communist forces were sent in July 1930 into the great Hunan city of Changsha, and as he had predicted the larger and better equipped Kuomintang forces overwhelmed them. Even when the

411

Provisional Government of the Chinese Soviet Republic was established with Mao as chairman in Juichen in November 1931, the Central Committee's main aim was to gain control over the soviets. By then the Party was practically defunct in the cities, and in 1932 the Central Committee had to leave Shanghai for Juichen, but the issue remained undecided. The decision came as the result of the Kuomintang victories of the next two years, which by forcing the Red Army out of Juichen even farther into the interior, left the Communists with no feasible alternative policy to Mao's.

Chiang, however, was contending with difficulties nearly as great as Mao's. In December 1926 the British had shown themselves ready to revise the 'unequal treaties' even before a strong central government was established to guarantee foreign lives and protect foreign rights, and next to transfer recognition from Chang in Peking to Chiang in Nanking. Chiang, after establishing his own government in Nanking in rivalry to the Hankow Kuomintang, had sought to improve relations with the western powers. These had lately been strained by his troops' excesses in Nanking (conveniently blamed on the Communists). Nevertheless, both America and Britain accepted his good faith. Indeed, American tenderness towards him, and refusal to join in the defence of the international settlements against Kuomintang attack, had exposed these settlements to serious danger. Refusal of American support drove Britain reluctantly between 1927 and 1929 to look for Japanese assistance, and caused a temporary coolness in Anglo-American relations. The chief consequence of the Kuomintang encroachments, however, was to increase Kuomintang hostility to the Japanese. The British military concentration could be overlooked, but not Japan's intervention in Shantung in May 1928 against the Kuomintang, and continued reluctance to surrender her privileges in China.

However, by the late summer of 1927 it seemed as if the whole Nationalist camp would collapse. Both the Wuhan and the Nanking governments appeared to be disintegrating. In August Chiang went to Japan, ostensibly to remove one cause of dissension within the Nationalist ranks by absenting himself, but in November yet another splinter government appeared in Canton. Paradoxically, however, the growing disunity on the Nationalist side opened the way for a strong leader, and in December 1927 Chiang decided that the time had arrived for his return. The Stalinist Canton *putsch* of that month conveniently weakened Wang Ching-wei and the Left. In January 1928 Chiang regained the posts of commander-in-chief and of chairman of the Kuomintang Central Executive forfeited because of his Shanghai activities in 1927. In June 1928 he set the seal on his political triumph by capturing Peking despite the Japanese intervention.

Before Chiang's troops entered Peking, Marshal Chang decided to return to Manchuria before that also was lost. The Japanese in Manchuria, however, who had made him warlord there, had no further use for him, and they blew up the railway coach in which he was returning. His son and successor, the 'Young Marshal' Chang Hsüeh-liang, was willing to work with Chiang, and to recognize the Kuomintang as the Chinese central government. Yet Sinkiang, Outer Mongolia and Tibet as well as Manchuria were outside its jurisdiction. In addition large regions were preyed on by bandits. Others were controlled by Communists or warlords, whose membership of the Kuomintang did not guarantee subordination to Nanking. Nevertheless, though Chiang's rule extended only to five lower Yangtse provinces, his achievement was considerable. By 1928 most western powers had recognized his government, and he had scored diplomatic and financial victories by regaining control of China's tariffs. In 1929 Chiang was negotiating to end extra-territorial rights when the 'Young Marshal's' resentment of Soviet economic imperialism in Manchuria led Chang unwisely to seize the Chinese Eastern Railway and arrest Russian citizens. There were good reasons why such actions were entirely different from ending western imperialist concessions in Hankow and elsewhere. These arguments were massed in Red Army uniforms on the Soviet border under the command of Chiang's old teacher, Blücher.

By then the character of the Kuomintang *régime* was clear, even though it had not had time to consolidate. Of Sun Yat-sen's revolutionary Three People's Principles, the only one which it really represented was the nationalist, now interpreted as meaning anti-foreign imperialism of all kinds, Japanese and Soviet as well as western. Its Right Wingers were as hostile as Chinese Communists to western and Japanese encroachments on Chinese territorial and political sovereignty, though Communists as yet did not resent Soviet exploitation. Chiang's hope that the democratic principle might be realized in time was probably sincere at first. After two decades of anarchy and civil war, the basis of the government could be widened only when order and stability had been restored. But in practice the Kuomintang's Organic Law of October 4th, 1928, established a system of 'tutelage', nominally exercised on behalf of the people, which entailed Kuomintang dictatorship in a one-party *régime*, operated by Chiang with the support of his military chiefs, reactionary politicians and leading financiers and businessmen. The National Government of China established in Nanking on October 10th represented no return to its predecessor's spirit under Sun by reverting to its name. It was a monolithic dictatorship, as Borodin had wanted it to be, though under different management. It was not, however, an unregulated dictatorship, and originally the Kuomintang had wide popular support from intellectuals who shared its nationalist outlook and hoped that it would carry through the kind of social reforms envisaged in Sun's Principle of the People's Livelihood. It also won a considerable following among the urban proletariat, and it could certainly have challenged the Communists for the allegiance of the peasants by carrying out land reforms. Wang, and other Left Wingers continued to demand such measures. Other Kuomintang leaders who shared the outlook of Chiang's business and great landowning supporters disliked the pampering of the army, and especially his partiality for old Whampoa friends. Others of both the Left and Right factions disliked the manner in which the Kuomintang came to provide patronage in the bureaucracy.

413

The Kuomintang's breach with the Chinese Communists had not meant abandonment of the Russian Bolshevik's view that the Party was the highest embodiment of the state, and should therefore control all aspects of government. However, the identification of Party and bureaucracy could not proceed so far as it did in Russia; the Kuomintang was neither as powerful nor as pervasive as its Russian model. Moreover, it degenerated rapidly as the profiteers and racketeers gained more influence in its upper and lower echelons. Its leadership in fact constituted the greatest obstacle to the reforms in the land system and agricultural credits which became essential if the *régime* was to survive, though they were bound to transform it beyond recognition if carried out. In the end its corruption as much as its tyranny prevented the efficient operation of its military and civil forces.

Economic reform would have been immensely difficult even without these handicaps, because of the insoluble population problem (probably about the 400,000,000 mark in 1929 and not much affected by mass emigration to South-East Asia) which meant heavy pressure on land, a permanently depressed peasant population, and chronic under-consumption. Hence China's internal market, potentially the biggest in the world, was actually one of the smallest. Chiang's brother-in-law T. V. Soong was an able finance minister, but his attempts to stabilize the currency were handicapped by America before 1934, and then destroyed by Japanese aggression in 1937. The League's advice was asked for in connection with problems involving national reconstruction, public health, control of the opium trade and educational reforms, in which a small beginning was made along western lines. In 1933 the National Economic Council was established to create a viable 'mixed' economy, but these developments were only in the exploratory stage by 1937, and subsequently never got beyond it. Attempts to emulate western methods of industrialization were partly successful in textile and other consumer industries, despite unscrupulous Japanese competition. However, Manchuria contained most of the Chinese heavy industry, and after 1931 Manchuria was lost, and with it the best hope of achieving a more balanced economy. In 1931 China was economically almost as self-contained as she had been before the opium wars. Indeed the great inland agricultural provinces had not much altered in the last century, apart from improved rail and road communications designed to further military and political rather then economic progress. The eastern coastal regions had a hectic brief period of comparative prosperity, but were the obvious prey of Japanese expansionists.

## (iv) *The Parliamentary Experiment in Japan*

By the end of 1931 Japan had outstripped her western competitors in China proper, in addition to monopolizing Manchuria. British exports to

China had been overtaken also by those of America, and British economic influence further declined because the Chinese were now increasingly handling their own commerce and finance, so that Hong Kong's share of China's trade dropped appreciably. In investment Britain was still ahead of America, with $1,045,000,000 against $340,000,000, but Britain's investment was nearly stationary while America's was rising, and Japan's at $2,096,000,000 was increasing at an even faster rate. In addition nearly all China's iron mines were in Japanese hands, and Japan had a large share of her coal output, of which over half was foreign-owned. Hence the external difficulties in the way of making China economically independent were considerable. Even an efficient and enlightened *régime* would have found them almost intractable. For the Kuomintang they were insuperable.

Japan's concessions to China and America at the Washington Conference in 1922 were regarded as signs that a period of peace and stability could be expected in the Far East. Her agreement to withdraw from Siberia reinforced those impressions, though evacuation of north Sakhalin and restoration of diplomatic relations with Russia had to wait until January 1925. However, British refusal to renew the alliance humiliated Japan, forced her into isolation and damaged the standing of western political institutions in Japanese eyes. The resentment was not assuaged by the extensive American and European aid furnished after the catastrophic earthquake of September 1st, 1923, which killed about 100,000 people, destroyed over half of Tokyo, most of Yokohama, and devastated neighbouring towns and villages. America's breach in 1924 of the 'gentleman's agreement' over immigration by discriminating against Orientals, further hurt national pride.

This American act did not, however, greatly increase Japan's problem of over-population, as large-scale Japanese emigration was to Asia. The population pressure alone was a powerful reason for ending the interlude in Japanese overseas expansion which had lasted since the war. Manchuria and China were old objects of nationalist ambitions, and also areas where Japanese commercial, industrial, government and military organizations had built up extensive interests. The army, and its Kwantung forces especially, was the dominant force behind the renewed overseas expansion. Moreover a mere two decades of parliamentary government and *laisser faire* economic policy could not reverse the trends established by centuries of authoritarian government and state regulation of the economy, unless reinforced by overwhelming external pressures, as occurred after 1945. The Nine-Power Treaty guaranteeing the Open Door and Chinese integrity was an affront, and if it were implemented, would increase the damage done to Japanese interests by the surrender of Shantung. Conditions in China were also likely to provoke Japanese intervention, either by continued anarchy which jeopardized Japanese trade, or by the possibility that the Kuomintang would succeed in its efforts to unite China and end her exploitation by foreigners. It was mainly the army which resented the policy of conciliation towards China propounded by Kijuro Shidehara, who served as foreign minister from June 1924 to April 1927, and again from July 1929 to December 1931. The army thought this conciliation was 'damaging to its prestige', a phrase which gained ominous significance after the 'Manchurian incident' was exploded in 1931, in order to gain complete control of Manchuria, but the state of mind giving rise to it had been clearly shown during the period of the Washington Conference.

The more important *zaibatsu*, however, favoured peaceful expansion. They had not even approved the disgust at the Washington naval limitations expressed by the navy, which was invariably less expansionist than the army. In contrast, less well established capitalists, and even some members of the Mitsui, the greatest capitalist combine, wanted opportunities which could be secured only by expansionist policies. They found allies among nationalist politicians and some army factions. Other army factions, while equally expansionist, were connected with politicians of the radical anti-capitalist Right. Both these elements despised capitalism and its profit motive, which they condoned only with reluctance, to forward their policy of building a great Japan. Even Communism they opposed for its attack on the Imperial system, the basis of Japanese society, and because it was the ideology of Japan's great enemy in the north; hence they regarded its adoption by Japanese as treasonable. They did not oppose Communism because of its antipathy to capitalism, which they largely shared, nor dislike its emphasis on a planned economy, and indeed many officers were attracted by state socialism. However as they needed wealthy allies, they swallowed their distaste for the *nouveaux riches*.

There was general approval of the view that, because of the isolation into which America had forced her, Japan's only possible policy was to build up her strength and await opportunities to improve her position— by peaceful or warlike means, according to taste, though the industrialization which was essential for Great Power status brought grave dangers to peace. Industrialization made Japan more dependent than ever on imported raw materials. Indeed, the most dangerous feature of her industrialization drive was that Japan imported 85% of her iron and steel, 79% of her oil, 74% of tin, and all her rubber; all these materials were vitally important strategic commodities. Further, by fostering production of raw silk when her population was rapidly increasing, Japan also increased her dependence on imported foods. This situation increased the temptation to expand further into Manchuria and also into China. It also helped to justify in Japanese eyes the argument that Japan had a right to a greater share of the world's resources.

Despite these growing expansionist tendencies, Japan seemed to be moving into an era of liberal parliamentary government. The result of the general election in May 1924 made it inevitable that Kato Takaaki should be made premier as head of the now dominant Kenseikai party. Kato realized an old ambition in May 1925 by extending the franchise to all adult males. This increased the electorate from 3,000,000 to 13,000,000, and thereby allowed the growth of lower-middle and working class parties.

However, these parties were too small to rival the *bourgeois* liberal Kenseikai and the conservative major rival party, the Seiyukai. Radical non-Communist parties were able to develop little strength before reaction set in again from 1932. Moreover, only political institutions, not the political climate, became more liberal after May 1924. Kato had to take members of other parties into his cabinet, and its composition was in fact mainly Seiyukai. It was one of its reactionary Seiyukai members who introduced the Peace Preservation Law of April 1925, whereby 'dangerous thoughts' could now be held to include even academic discussions of political and constitutional problems. The law's major target was the growing Left Wing movement, for it prescribed imprisonment for anybody forming or joining organizations which sought to change the Japanese form of government or way of life, or which advocated abolition of private property. Kato's well-intentioned efforts to reform the bureaucracy, end the spoils system and root out political corruption, remained ineffective after a promising beginning. Kato's war minister, General Ugaki, was exceptionally liberal for an army officer with Ugaki's background, and he even reduced the military budget. Ugaki also reduced the army by four divisions, but as the displaced officers were employed as instructors at higher and middle schools in a bigger system of compulsory military training, the army was actually strengthened, and its political power remained formidable.

Kato's domestic and foreign policies continually antagonized the Seiyukai and its Mitsui *zaibatsu* connections. Kato's and Shidehara's own *zaibatsu* connections were with the rival Mitsubishi combine, which strongly favoured their conciliatory policy towards China. General Tanaka Giichi, the Seiyukai leader, attempted to bring down Kato, but Kato held another election, which enabled him to form a more loyal and liberal cabinet in August 1925, and then to embark on a programme of radical social, economic and political reform. Kato aimed at eventual labour and major land reforms, and a more efficient working of the parliamentary system. His death in January 1926 brought in Reijiro Wakatsuki, the second non-*samurai* premier, and an admirer of Kato's policies. Shidehara remained as foreign minister to continue the established policy towards China despite the Kuomintang's anti-foreign line, but Wakatsuki's position in both party and cabinet was weaker than Kato's, who had met Privy Councillors, nobles, great bureaucrats and oligarchs on equal terms. He was less able than Kato to counter army opposition to the Chinese policy, but his fall in 1927 was caused by a great financial crisis. This ruined many small firms, which were swallowed up by the Mitsui and Mitsubishi, further enraging a section of the nation which had never favoured the Diet politicians and their *zaibatsu* friends. When the Privy Council refused the emergency powers which Wakatsuki requested, he resigned on April 17th, 1927.

The Kenseikai were joined in opposition by Seiyukai dissidents to form a new party, the Minseito, still connected with the Mitsubishi, while Tanaka formed a Seiyukai cabinet. Tanaka decided to attempt to improve

417

his position by holding a general election in 1928, which he won only by resorting to the use of police intervention and strong-arm squads against his opponents. Nevertheless, the parliamentary precedents were being established whereby the resignation of one party's cabinet would put its rival in office, and it was also being recognized that the government must have a majority in the Diet.

The old emperor had died on December 25th, 1926. His successor Hirohito adopted the regnal title *Showa* ('enlightened peace') with what seemed to be fair prospects of justifying it. Japan refused to participate in such international sanctions against Chinese attacks on foreign concessions as the Anglo-American bombardment of Nanking on March 24th, 1927. However, the advent of Tanaka meant that Japanese pursuit of hegemony in China would take the form of a 'positive' policy, as advocated by Tanaka's military, nationalist and Mitsui associates. The so-called 'Tanaka memorial', which allegedly called in the summer of 1927 for completion of the conquest of all Asia as a preliminary to the conquest of the whole world, was not his work, if indeed it ever existed. Tanaka was concerned not only with the threats to Japanese interests posed by the Kuomintang advance, but also with Russian Communism. In the 'Shantung crisis' Tanaka temporarily blocked the Kuomintang's progress by halting Chiang's advance on Peking. In 1928 Tanaka advised Chang Tso-lin to withdraw to Manchuria, where Japan could protect Chang's forces while they regrouped. The Kwantung forces, however, had become dissatisfied with Chang, and with Tanaka's policy of extending Japanese rights by collaborating with him. They decided to seize Manchuria by force, and to prepare the way they engineered Chang's murder, planning to replace him with his son, the 'Young Marshal' Chang Hsüeh-liang, and then force the Tokyo government to accept the *fait accompli*. They murdered Chang Tso-lin, and their plan brought about Tanaka's resignation in July 1929, but otherwise their scheme miscarried. Nevertheless it marked the first instance of the army's attempting to force on the Japanese government a major change in national policy, though in this case it was the Kwantung army, and it had to convince the Tokyo General Staff as well as the government. It convinced neither, but the precedent was set for 1931. More important still, the overthrow of Tanaka's cabinet marked a decisive stage in the destruction of the feeble system of constitutional government which was slowly taking shape.

## (v) *The 'Roaring Twenties' in America*

In the America of the 'roaring twenties' also, the moral fabric of society was attacked together with its political institutions, though the novelist Scott Fitzgerald thought that the age of jazz and of big money had no interest in politics, and that all that America knew was that she was going on 'the greatest, gaudiest spree in history'. That it was perfectly possible to combine the two, however, was shown by sensational scandals implicating members of Harding's cabinet. If Harding, incapable but far from unpopular, had not died in August 1923, the scandals would almost certainly have ruined Republican chances in the 1924 election, as well as his reputation. There were gross irregularities concerning the provision made for ex-servicemen by the Veterans Association. The Attorney-General was involved with bootleggers and other undesirables. The Secretary of the Interior was exploiting the federal oil reserves at Teapot Dome and Elk Hill for private interests. However there was no evidence that Harding was involved, and the administration hoped to bury the scandals with him. His Vice-President, Calvin Coolidge, who succeeded him and went on to win the 1924 election, handled the crisis expertly. Though it was clear that the public had been defrauded on a scale not seen since Grant, the conservative press played down the scandals, and branded as 'character-assassins' those who had exposed them. As the administration contained figures who were above all suspicion, Teapot Dome and the rest were gradually forgotten.

It was with Coolidge that the great and frenzied era of American prosperity began, with production reaching such heights that high-pressure advertising had to be invented to cope with it. Coolidge's victory in 1924 would have been a foregone conclusion even if the Democrats had not been hopelessly split over the nomination. Their most obvious choice, the popular Governor Alfred E. (Al) Smith of New York, was of Catholic Irish extraction, and passed over for the colourless lawyer John W. Davis, who decided to campaign on the issue of corruption. Senator Robert M. La Follette diminished Davis's already slim chances by standing as a Progressive, and Coolidge won by the margin of 382 electoral votes against Davis's 136 and La Follette's 13. But though there was no prospect of success for a Progressive platform in Coolidge's America, it was not for want of issues. Coolidge and big business would do nothing for the farmers, who remained the semi-depressed half of the economy, dismissed by Coolidge with the reflection that they had never made much money and nothing much could be done about it. Urban wages were too low because of the restrictions on trade union activities, so that productivity per man-hour rose four times faster than hourly wages under Coolidge.

At least in its official philosophy the New Era of the 1920s was not selfish, and Henry Ford, who came closest to epitomizing it, proclaimed that its purpose was to serve the community both by providing an abundance of products and by increasing purchasing power to extend the flow of trade. His concept of what would later be extended to become the affluent society was based on a dynamic and self-charging economy of private enterprise. In Ford's world there was no place for intervention by the government nor for organized labour; they did not understand what was involved, and would stop the flow of demand on which the economics of mass production depended. The new America which he had done more than any other man to create was symbolized by his scrapping in 1927 of the phenomenally successful Model T. As the first cheap, mass-produced automobile the Model T had transformed the world's transport system. Now his plant was temporarily closed down to prepare for the new Model A. This manifestation of buoyant optimism and prosperity had also an ominous significance, for it brought down the Federal Reserve index of industrial production. The tension and insecurity never absent even at the height of the boom, found a general if brief expression in fears that depression was on the way. So indeed it was, though there was nothing wrong with the capacity of American industry and agriculture to deliver the goods.

The danger lay in the investment mania now gripping America and in the exchange crises set off by Winston Churchill's decision in May 1925, as Chancellor of the Exchequer, to restore the pound sterling to the gold standard at the prewar rate of $4·86. Keynes thought this over-valued sterling by 10%, which was clearly an exaggeration. Even before the return to parity, Britain's ability to sell abroad had declined. Now it slumped more than ever, and gold from Britain came in increasing quantities to America. The British, French and Germans alike successfully urged America in 1925, and again in 1927, to adopt an easy money policy to discourage this trend, and the Federal Reserve Bank of New York in 1927 vigorously cut its rediscount rate from 4% to 3·5%. Subsequent heavy selling of government securities freed large sums of money for speculative purposes. The mania could have been checked but only Hoover and a few other men of prominence thought that it should be.

The Coolidge administration's readiness to leave big business and high finance alone was popular at the time. Indeed, in 1918 Wilson himself had resolved to remove government economic controls and revert to a *laisser faire* economy as soon as possible. The consequent postwar rise in prices and unemployment, leading to violent fluctuations in the economy and industrial unrest, had provided lessons which were forgotten in the easy boom after 1922, except when the wrong deductions were drawn from them, and it was decided to give big business its head while organized labour was repressed. But this was not an issue between Democrats and Republicans. In fact there were hardly any issues between them in the 1928 election, though it was not therefore any less significant.

Coolidge's intimation that he would not run for re-election was ambiguously phrased, but he was given no chance to clarify it. The Republicans nominated Herbert Hoover with alacrity, and with justice. More than anybody else the trained engineer and apostle of 'rugged individualism' represented New Era America in her strengths and weaknesses. In the campaign he took it as self-evident that more of the same policies would produce bigger and better results, though Coolidge had realized at the end of his term that 'From this time on, there must be something constructive applied to the affairs of government, and it will not be enough to say, "Let business take care of itself".' However, Coolidge took care not to say so publicly and Hoover campaigned on the 'fundamental rightness' of America's economic system, and predicted the certain abolition of poverty if the Republicans were 'given a chance to go forward with the policies of the last eight years'. Protectionism was endorsed for industry, but Congress's proposals for agricultural relief were not. Hoover paraded the small successes of the new good neighbour policy towards Latin America, but paid more attention to vigorously enforcing prohibition, 'a great social and economic experiment, noble in motive and far-reaching in purpose'. His Democratic opponent, Al Smith, by attacking prohibition lost more votes in the South and Middle West than he gained in the more liberal East. But it was Smith's attacks on religious bigotry which more than anything else lost him the solid South. There the nomination of a Catholic brought about an ugly recrudescence of the Ku Klux Klan. Smith's forces had introduced a resolution condemning the Klan as un-American during the 1924 convention. It had been defeated then by only 543 votes to 542. Now the Klan had its revenge.

However the essential reason for Smith's defeat in the 1928 election was that prosperity had defeated the Progressives. He recognized this fact by adopting an essentially conservative approach, and in effect asking, as did Hoover, for a mandate to carry on business as usual. In such circumstances Hoover was the obvious choice and he won by 21,392,190 popular votes against Smith's 15,016,443. Yet, though Smith was resented as a Tammany Hall machine politician as well as a Catholic, he polled more votes than any previous Democrat, and carried the twelve largest cities. He also did far better in the Middle West, and especially in the corn belt, than Cox and Davis, and he carried Massachusetts and Rhode Island. The loss of the solid South could be, and was, made good by another candidate next time, and there were even signs in the Republican Middle West of dissatisfaction with the Republican leadership's conservative outlook. Equally there could be no doubt that 'Republican prosperity' had won the election, and therefore that continued prosperity was a necessary ingredient in Republican success. The margin of Hoover's success, on the other hand, appeared to indicate that there was little future in America for Progressivism, liberalism and radicalism and that big business had triumphed in politics as it had in industry and commerce. There was little opposition when the Federal Trade Commission, organized to prevent unfair business practices and inform Congress and the nation about them, ranged itself on the side of the enemy, as it had done under Coolidge. The Department of Justice was equally tender to trusts, and the Supreme Court no less diligent in tempering the wind of the law to them. Franklin D. Roosevelt, as Governor of New York, thought even when the depression's malignancy was unmistakable, of making new anti-trust legislation one of his major election planks for the 1932 Presidential contest. For him, as for Hoover, recognition that the economy was not fundamentally sound, and needed something more than palliatives to restore it, was gradual and belated. But he had learned, as the architect of prosperity had not, the supreme importance of high-pressure salesmanship, and the onset of the depression gave him his opportunity.

# Chapter VI
## YEARS OF DEPRESSION

### (i) *The Crisis in the International Economy*

THE great depression was a unique event, arising from a combination of economic and political complexes which it modified beyond recognition and in some cases destroyed. It began quite unremarkably, with a rapid acceleration of the fall in American and Canadian agricultural prices which had been causing alarm for some time. However, agriculture throughout the world had been in a semi-depressed state for a decade; the general American economic recession which had manifested itself in 1927 was brief; Canadian difficulties were not a matter of global consequence. The American boom was on again in 1928 and continued into 1929. An American slump had been prophesied, but of only normal proportions, and chiefly because business cycles were supposed to make one inevitable after the long boom of the 1920s. Little notice was taken when the most reliable measures of economic trends, the monthly Federal Reserve indices of industrial activity and factory production, began a continued decline in July 1929. Only in October did the general downward trend become noteworthy, and it was still not alarming. America possessed gigantic agricultural resources, the greatest skilled labour force and the most advanced industrial plant in the world, and unrivalled financial strength. Until the crash came in October it seemed that only recession was involved.

Depression was signalled by the collapse of the American speculative mania in the middle of October. If the American economy had been fundamentally sound it could have withstood the Wall Street panic which led to the shattering of the self-confidence of the whole American nation. Hoover's belief that the American economy was fundamentally sound and would therefore recover if left to its own devices, was modified far too slowly by the pressure of events. His failure to react quickly and vigorously enough was largely responsible for the depression's length and intensity in America. When it did end it left permanent psychological scars. Moreover, so commanding had America's position in the world economy become by 1929 that it was bound to have far-reaching consequences.

American industrial production accounted for 46% of the total production of the twenty-four biggest producers in 1929; American consumption in 1928 of nine principal primary products represented 39% of the total of the fifteen leading countries; America's foreign investments were essential to the world economy. In 1929, even though foreign lending had contracted because speculation in domestic stocks had led to withdrawals of money placed abroad, the United States still provided for the rest of the world the staggering sum in imports and investments of $7,400,000,000, just over one-fifth of the value of world imports. In 1929 America's favourable balance of trade, despite the depression, was still $842,000,000 (in 1928 it had been $1,037,000,000) and war debt repayments brought in $800,000,000. Without American foreign investments many countries, and especially Germany, could not remain solvent. Admittedly in global terms the proportion of foreign investment to trade was only about 6%, and in 1928 Britain had lent $569,000,000 and France $237,000,000 to America's $1,099,000,000. However the loans were major factors in the economies of the debtor countries—again especially Germany, who had debts of $1,007,000,000, Australia of $193,000,000, Argentina of $181,000,000, Canada of $164,000,000 and Poland of $124,000,000. As most of this lending was short-term, it was called in with catastrophic suddenness when the crash came. American withdrawals totally eclipsed the comparatively small foreign withdrawals from America.

Despite this tremendous predominance over the world economy, international trade formed a very small part of American economic activity. In 1929 American imports were only 5% and exports only 6% of the national income; hence, as far as America was concerned, the crisis had to be solved in domestic terms. Yet America continued until Hoover's June 1931 moratorium to exact payment of war debts (though when Roosevelt tried to resume the exactions in 1933 the stream had dried up except for a trickle from Finland). Debtors could achieve solvency only through trade, but in June 1930 America imposed the Hawley-Smoot tariff which increased the average agricultural import duties from 20% to 34% and the general average of duties from $33\frac{1}{3}$% to 40%. In 1933 when gold was flowing into America and she still had a large favourable balance of trade, Roosevelt increased international difficulties by devaluing the dollar. America, however, suffered longer and more severely from the depression than other countries.

In its progress through the world the depression brought down governments—even in stable Britain—altered the bases of many national economies, and permanently affected international trade. Though the rest of the world was affected less severely than America, most countries, and especially the primary producers, suffered large rises in unemployment and sharp falls in prices. Hence between 1929 and the third quarter of 1932, when recovery was slowly starting, the international trade of the non-European countries fell by over 70%. However, large parts of the world were not greatly affected by the depression. Soviet Russia's catastrophic slump from 1929 was mainly due to her government's policies, for her economy largely shut her off from the outside world. In addition many peoples lived largely or entirely as agrarian producers, subsisting on their own produce, and so were not affected by the great falls in agricultural prices which were so marked a feature of the slump. These were, however, largely the backward nations of the world which already had very low standards of living—and even some of those suffered severely.

The only countries to emerge comparatively unshaken were the Scandinavian countries and Japan. Japan introduced inflationary measures which included not only heavy armament expenditure but war itself— indeed it was partly from economic motives that zealous junior army officers precipitated the Manchurian incident in 1931 and thereby ended the postwar era. Scandinavian countries fared reasonably well on the whole because of relatively stable agriculture and fishing resources, fairly constant foreign demands for their raw materials, and intelligent government policies. Though their multi-party systems tended to produce political instability, their Socialist parties, which frequently held office either singly or in coalitions before the depression, had produced balanced mixed economies which reconciled private enterprise and state planning with conspicuous success. When the depression struck they extended government intervention where necessary, but left the private sectors largely independent while their activities did not conflict with national objectives. Sweden adopted the Keynesian principle of increasing purchasing power with marked success, but all Scandinavian countries extended their social security services. When in 1930 and 1932 it seemed that Finland, the poorest country, might resort to the Fascism stimulated by the depression elsewhere in Europe and the world, the Finnish *Lapua* Fascist revolts were suppressed.

One of the regions most affected by the depression was Latin America. In Latin American history the year 1930, when the depression bit severely, marks both a political and an economic divide. Chronic political instability, lack of productive capital and excessive reliance on a few primary products made her particularly vulnerable. It was under the depression's impact that Latin Americans as a whole awoke to their countries' underdevelopment and sought to remedy it. Argentina had made some progress towards industrialization before and after World War I, and other republics after 1918 had done so on a small scale, but only in 1930 did the move towards industrialization become widespread and determined. In addition the depression convinced most Latin American governments of the need for a planned economy. Only Uruguay in the early 1900s and Mexico after 1910 hitherto had accepted the necessity of government economic planning. Now the depression enforced its adoption, if the republics were to escape from the dependence on overseas markets which had put them at the mercy of recent violent fluctuations. This entailed the reconstruction and diversification of economies, and most republics began this process in the 1930s. The constriction of foreign markets and capital (especially American) by the depression had exposed the inadequacy of existing *laisser faire*

425

economies. Hence they reverted to older patterns of paternalistic government intervention, though adding Socialist, or more often Fascist, variations derived from European models.

These developments were remarkably rapid, but they were not unexpected, for World War I had clearly shown the benefits of industrialization even with the limited expansion then achieved. However, few republics possessed the resources for large-scale industrialization, while this alone could not refloat their shipwrecked economies. Land, agrarian, commercial and fiscal reforms were also needed. These were introduced in various ways in the different republics, though there was an unmistakable general pattern, which derived from the common objective of restoring their economies from within.

In some republics foreign interests, especially American, also played their part as manipulators, accomplices or victims of the 'economic policy revolution'. Anti-American sentiments increased, often with official encouragement. America was justifiably regarded as chief practitioner of the international capitalism which had brought unemployment to Latin America and exacerbated the problems of her largely mono-cultural economies. American companies were expropriated or limited, as were British, wherever their own vulnerability or the republics' interests invited it.

The device of building up state-controlled trade unions as instruments of the *régimes* was often greatly facilitated by using them as spearheads in an anti-foreign campaign. This was a useful stratagem also in those states where it was possible to limit the excessive power of the landowning class, which was justified neither in economic nor in political terms now that agriculture's contribution to the economy had decreased. Therefore land-hungry peasants, as well as urban workers and *bourgeoisie*, were mobilized in some countries against the big landowners, and the depression introduced shifts in economic and political power to the benefit of *bourgeoisie*, bureaucracy and even proletariat. The major result of these upheavals, however, was to increase the power of the military. Many military dictatorships became adept at providing the masses with bread and circuses, often with considerably increased security and improved living standards. Some learned the techniques involved in nationalizing banks, public utilities and major industries, in establishing controlling state interests in big corporations, in marketing agricultural products and controlling their levels of production, and in fostering agriculture and industry by subsidies, tariffs and currency manipulation.

The British Dominions as primary producers also suffered in the world-wide collapse set off when American faltered. Canada took the lead in pressing for the policy of imperial preference, to restore her shattered agriculture and acutely distressed industries. Henceforth this was to regulate the international trade of the Empire and Commonwealth countries. Her solvency depended on reasonable price levels and stable demands for her staple exports, especially wheat, whose price fell from

$1·60 Canadian a bushel in 1929 to $0·38 at the end of 1932. Mining remained comparatively prosperous by depression standards as silver and nickel were in good demand, though at greatly reduced prices, but demand for her other main exports of fish, lumber and newsprint dropped sharply. Canadian industry slumped less because of foreign tariffs, though these rose to unprecedented heights after 1929, than from the declining purchasing power of the predominant agrarian community, which brought heavy unemployment in the train of the rural disaster.

The 1930 general election was fought chiefly on the Liberal government's failure to arrest the slump. The Conservatives promised effective counters to the American Hawley-Smoot tariff, which had hit Canada particularly hard. They also insisted that Britain would receive preferential tariffs only in return for concessions. The election gave the Conservatives a clear majority, and their leader, Richard B. Bennett, fulfilled his protectionist promises, and also carried emergency legislation to provide a public works programme and relief for unemployed (by 1935 10% of the total population was receiving relief). At the 1930 Imperial Conference Bennett proposed imperial preference on terms protecting Canada against British and Dominion as well as outside competition. After the crisis had brought down Britain's free trade Labour Government in August 1931, Conservative protectionists dominated the sham National Government which succeeded under the largely nominal Premiership of MacDonald.

The British National Government agreed to the holding of an economic conference in Ottawa in July–August 1932 when imperial preference was finally accepted. Britain had wanted this to introduce mutual tariff concessions, but its chief result was discrimination against extra-imperial goods. It produced not imperial consolidation but increased economic nationalism, chiefly to Canada's benefit. Her protected agriculture and industry benefited at Britain's expense, and Britain gained no advantage from the agreement. The other Dominions did, but world trade in general suffered and the solid recovery even of the Dominions came with general world recovery.

Australia was already severely depressed when the October 1929 general election put the Labour Party under J. H. Scullin back in office after twelve years in opposition. Labour had made promises of prosperity during its period of opposition which it could not have fulfilled in normal times. Now it had to deflate, reduce wages and the standard of living, and cut government expenditure. Australian food production increased during the slump as did its volume of exports, but prices fell. The currency was devalued at the end of 1931; higher tariffs and flat prohibitions cut imports, but nevertheless unemployment mounted. In mid-1930 J. T. Lang, the Labour leader in New South Wales, opposed the federal Labour Party's retrenchment programme. This and other dissensions hopelessly split Labour in 1931. Joseph A. Lyons, leader of another small splinter group, united with former Nationalists to form the United Australia Party. In the December 1931 general elections Labour was heavily defeated

427

and Lyons took office with the support also of the Country Party. The Centre and Right then controlled Australia until after World War II had broken out. Lyons' measures did little to promote recovery, which came first from rising gold prices, next from rising wool prices and finally from general world trends.

In New Zealand, the United (Liberal) Party had won the November 1928 general election by promising a period of great prosperity, and until October 1929 optimism had been widespread despite growing unemployment and erratic agricultural prices. The awakening was particularly shattering as New Zealand's national debt was already high (by 1933 interest charges amounted to 40% of total government expenditure). Moreover she depended entirely on agricultural exports, which declined by two-fifths in two years.

The government adopted the normal and ineffective remedies of the period: cuts in government spending (except for agricultural subsidies), reduction of wages, reduction of public works, restriction of imports, crippling of the social security services, and lower interest rates. From 1929 to the end of 1932 national income fell from about £150,000,000 to about £90,000,000. In September 1931 the United and Reform (Conservative) Parties coalesced and easily won the December elections, but they were helpless in the face of the calamity. In 1932 the situation was desperate: approximately 15% of a total population of 1,500,000 unemployed; dangerous rioting in some cities; personal rights circumscribed by a frightened government; and a witch-hunt against even moderate Left-Centre critics. However in January 1933 Joseph G. Coates, as finance minister, further devalued the pound and made effective efforts at last to curb the depression. These foreshadowed much of the activity of the successful Labour government elected in 1935, but did not forestall the electorate's justifiable repudiation of the coalition.

South Africa's major problems in these years were not economic but racial. The wool and diamond industries slumped, and a costly but essential campaign was launched to keep the farmers on their holdings. The gold mines cushioned the depression's worst effects, and South Africa's distress would have been much less if she had gone off the gold standard with Britain in September 1931. General J. B. Hertzog, the Premier, thought that abandoning gold was equivalent to breaking trust, but despite almost dictatorial currency and exchange rate powers South Africa also abandoned gold in December 1932 to prevent further loss of capital. When in mid-1933 America, though herself off gold, continued to buy it at inflated prices, a gold boom began which largely financed a minor industrial revolution.

Relations between whites and Bantu on the other hand constantly deteriorated. Hertzog's Afrikaner Nationalist Party had won a clear majority in the June 1929 'Black Peril' election on the issue of 'White South Africa'. White mobs demonstrated what this entailed by attacking Bantu and Coloured meetings. The government underlined the lesson in 1930 by taking statutory power to deport or expel from any given area, persons born outside the Union who incited trouble between Europeans and non-Europeans. This was used to destroy the Bantu political and union organization, the Industrial and Commercial Union (ICU), of which only small scattered trade unions survived. Oswald Pirow, the German-born Minister of Justice, was notably zealous in this work, as he was in harassing white Left Wing trade unionists and later in promoting Nazi ideology. Hertzog rejected extremist Nationalist demands to disfranchise the Bantu, but enfranchisement of white women in 1930 and extension in 1931 of the racial franchise to the Cape, hitherto liberal in its attitude to non-Europeans, were steps towards the racialist solution. The 1931 Natives' Urban Areas Amendment Act further limited Bantu rights to live and move freely in towns. In December 1931 the Statute of Westminster formally embodied the 1926 Imperial Conference's provisions, thus ending the British parliament's technical sovereignty and making the Crown Britain's sole link with the Dominions. As a result the Bantu's future in South Africa looked even bleaker, though the Bantu of Basutoland, Swaziland and Bechuanaland Protectorate gained because the British High Commissioner shielded them from the Nationalists. By this time the Nationalists were in serious difficulties with Smuts, and with Labour which had left the coalition in August 1931. They were clearly failing to curb the depression, and in 1932 an explosion seemed likely. Many Bantu were becoming even poorer and some faced actual mass starvation, while nearly 20% of the white population lived in extreme poverty. Hence in 1933 Smuts called for a coalition, nominally to settle imperial problems, and Hertzog agreed. In March Smuts duly became Hertzog's deputy, before recovery had started.

In the world economy the collapse of primary product prices caused the heavy industrial slump, and checked the incipient revival of early 1930. There had been over-investment in most primary products, and over-production in many. Hence the 1929 financial crash brought smaller orders and lower prices, which caused further bank failures. These discouraged investment in both agriculture and industry when it was needed. Production of foodstuffs did not contract between 1929 and 1933, though world trade of agricultural products dropped by 11%. Production of raw materials, on the other hand, slumped by 26% and world trade in them by 19·5% as industry reduced orders. One general result of the depression was the increase in trade barriers, and primary producers reacted to their diminishing markets by reducing industrial imports. By the end of 1932 world industrial production had fallen by 30% and world trade in manufactured goods by 41·5%.

## (ii) *The Crisis in Europe*

These factors, however, only partially explain the depression's effects in Europe. Most of the debtor countries of 1929 were primary producers, and were therefore heavily hit by withdrawals or reductions of foreign investments, but Germany, whose collapse was second in importance only to America's, was heavily in debt as a result of reparations, or rather of her method of dealing with them and with her industrial investment. While modernizing her industry with American and other foreign loans, she had also borrowed American managerial methods. Chief among these methods was 'rationalization', to standardize production and cut labour costs by extensive use of machinery. This had increased production and wages (in 1929 wages in real terms were 6% higher than in 1913) but technological changes had caused widespread unemployment. With the 1929 crash import controls were inevitable, but Germany made them by resorting to an unnecessary degree of deflation. Memories of the inflation of the early 1920s suggested this device, instead of direct restriction of imports to levels which Germany could afford, and of replacement of foreign by domestic credit at levels possible for German investors. These methods were finally adopted in 1932, after unnecessary political and economic damage had been done.

The depression made a major political party out of the Nazis, and their 107 seats in the September 1930 elections frightened foreign investors and brought another run of withdrawals from Germany, which however lasted only until March 1931. Then international economic and political factors combined to start a new, and for Europe greater, crisis. This grew out of German-Austrian attempts to exploit the situation by rushing through an already prepared scheme for a customs union. France, Italy, the Little *Entente* and other countries would have opposed the suggestion however discreetly they had been approached, but its bald announcement by Austria and Germany on March 21st provoked an uproar. Because of the international crisis the drain of credit from Germany re-started. France also withdrew money from the Austrian Kreditanstalt Bank, starting a run which made it insolvent by May. Thereby France forced Austria to drop the union, but started a financial crisis which brought in its train agricultural and industrial slumps in central and eastern Europe. Austria's financial collapse caused further pressure on Germany, which intensified when a German official financial memorandum of June 5th gave a pessimistic view of German finances and suggested that it might be impossible to continue reparations payments. This produced another panic. Within the next ten days £50,000,000 of gold and foreign exchange were withdrawn from Germany, and another £17,000,000 in the next week despite a rise in the discount rate. As Germany's first reparations instalment under the Young Plan was due on July 1st, Hoover tried to limit the disaster by proposing a year's moratorium on reparations and war debts. With loans from Britain, France and the Bank of International Settlements as well as from America, Germany was saved from financial collapse. Provision for further credit was made by the western governments and, together with German exchange and currency restrictions, this allowed her to resume restricted financial activities. However her foreign trade was still further crippled, and unemployment rose even higher (1,368,000 in 1929; 3,144,000 in 1930—source of many Nazi votes; 5,668,000 in 1931; 6,014,000 in 1932).

Britain had given extensive credit to Austria and Germany, though confidence in sterling's strength had diminished. In August there was heavy pressure on sterling. British bankers confessed to owing foreign creditors £250,000,000 but they probably owed twice that amount. The government split over the handling of the crisis and on August 23rd resigned, to make way for the National Government. This secured American and French credit, but in September there were such heavy gold withdrawals that Britain was forced off the gold standard and sterling was allowed to depreciate. Sterling's collapse ended all hope of recovery from the slump in 1931 and destroyed the international financial system built in the 1920s. Canada, India, Iceland, Denmark, Egypt, Norway and Sweden immediately followed Britain off the gold standard. America, Germany, France, Italy, Poland and some other countries retained it but, except for America and France which had large gold reserves, only by most stringent restrictions on currency and trade. Some countries tied their currencies to sterling, while others allowed theirs to depreciate freely. Hence at the end of 1931 there were three groups of countries: gold standard adherents, sterling's followers, and countries with freely depreciating currencies. This made concerted efforts to restore financial stability an urgent necessity. A beginning was made with a projected war debts settlement at the Lausanne Conference in June 1932. The European nations agreed to waive most of Germany's reparations and war debts owed to them if America would waive her claims. America refused, but her debtors soon ceased paying after Germany's reparations ended. International attempts to reduce tariff barriers had been made since February 1930 without success, and further attempts also failed.

The eastern European agrarian states had been so badly hit by low prices for their products even before the financial crisis, that proposals had been made under League of Nations auspices for treating their cereals preferentially. These proposals were vetoed, notably by America and Britain, for infringing most-favoured-nation treatment, whereby countries bound by commercial treaties with each other had to pass on to all their partners any advantages granted to one. However, this principle did not worry Britain when it came to formulating imperial preference. America checked the 1931 run on Austrian, German and Hungarian reserves with six-months' moratoria, which were renewed early in 1932, but this did not solve their difficulties or the basic eastern European problems. The depression ruined the international trade of the Eastern European primary producers, and crippled their internal economies. Even if the wheat-producing countries managed to sell abroad, prices were so low as to yield virtually no profit, and internal price levels slumped. Seasonal labourers on the big Polish and Hungarian estates who were paid in fixed proportions of crop yields did not suffer unduly, however, neither did remote Balkan, Carpathian or eastern Polish villagers who had always lived by subsistence production and barter. As the slump progressed more Eastern European areas adopted this pre-monetary economy, while farming communities ceased to buy manufactured goods or utilize the services of professional classes. Between 60% and 80% of the population effectively ceased to be consumers, and the middle classes were as much affected as farmers, peasants and urban workers. In this way the depression provided both rank and file and leadership for the Fascist movements which grew apace in eastern Europe after the slump. Urban discontent, however, was less proletarian than middle class. Rural discontent came less from labourers than from big landowners and small and medium farmers. These were to be the supporters of Fascism, and were impelled towards it all the more easily by its anti-semitism—which was indeed never far below the surface. Farmers who mortgaged their land to 'finance capital' in practice dealt almost entirely with Jewish bankers. In addition, in many Eastern European countries large-scale trade and industry were largely in Jewish hands because these were only the fields open to them. Generally they were not allowed to become civil servants or army officers, positions which were originally preferred by non-Jews of the middle classes. Furthermore, when the Poles, Rumanians and Hungarians lost their civil service jobs, they discovered that desirable positions in trade and industry were no longer available since these posts had already been filled by Jews. Hence the depression made anti-semitism a force again in eastern Europe, with fearsome consequences in the later 1930s and in World War II. On the other hand it brought some progress by forcing Hungary, Poland and Rumania to expand their industries (admittedly in order to replace previously imported manufactures), and Austria and Czechoslovakia to extend their agriculture. However, Austria and Czechoslovakia were outside the general European pattern. Neither suffered from anti-semitism until overrun by Nazi Germany. Austria remained economically unviable, and the depression had dangerous political repercussions for Czechoslovakia of another sort. Sudeten German areas suffered particular badly from her industrial and foreign trade losses, and this brought recruits to Konrad Henlein's Nazi movement.

Greece was hit as hard as any other Eastern European country. Though she was not predominantly agrarian (about 46% of her population depended on agriculture) she did depend heavily on agricultural exports. However she too had heavy war debts, and her finances were insecure before 1929. Premier Venizelos's failure to deal adequately with the depression led to mass discontent and his defeat in the 1932 elections. His defeat was the prelude to the restoration of the monarchy and the advent of General Metaxas's military dictatorship.

Metaxas' *régime* was a different proposition from the royal dictatorships of Rumania and Bulgaria, and above all different from King Alexander's *régime* in Yugoslavia. In Yugoslavia the already distressed condition of the peasants (75% of the population) deteriorated further under the depression's impact. An Agrarian Bank was founded to provide credit, and a Privileged Export Institute to protect cereal export prices, but these were of little help to the smallholders. The police ruthlessly repressed all forms of discontent, agrarian, urban and national—especially Croat nationalism. Though the government proclaimed the existence of a Bolshevik conspiracy, Communism represented no threat for another decade. Moreover, it was Croat demands for federalization which led Alexander on January 6th, 1929, to establish his royal dictatorship and to take complete responsibility for the country. Its change of name from 'Kingdom of Serbs, Croats and Slovenes' to Yugoslavia meant no concessions to nationalist aspirations. On the contrary, the country was divided into nine new provinces drawn according to geographical features and bureaucratic convenience.

Spain, permanently semi-depressed, was the only south European country to achieve freer political institutions during the depression, but this was purely coincidental. The dictator Primo de Rivera fell in 1930 not because of failures to curb the depression, but because the pampered Spanish army withdrew its support. In the April 1931 municipal elections the monarchists carried the countryside (admittedly with the aid of fraud and violence) but republicans carried the cities. Without awaiting the rural results Alfonso XIII precipitately abdicated, declaring that he would not set Spaniard against Spaniard in fratricidal civil war. Civil war over the monarchy was improbable, but the situation was revolutionary, and the new Spanish Republic never controlled either the depression or internal anarchy. It imposed strict exchange controls, but could not stabilize the country until 1934. It never got the agrarian crisis under control. Falling prices, rising unemployment and land hunger could not be overcome by the small-scale land redistribution effected. In the towns the slump intensified already explosive discontent, and violent strikes became endemic. The Republican Action (Liberal) coalition government under Manuel Azaña responded with mild reforms. Even its Socialist supporters until 1933 were reformists, not revolutionaries. The Left-Centre Radical Socialists were *bourgeois*, and Alejandro Lerroux's Right-Centre Radicals were uncertain Republicans. Nevertheless Azaña's moderate reforms won undying hostility. Admittedly his anti-clericalism alienated many moderate supporters, but the Church was from the beginning hostile to the Republic and to social reform, and would not have tolerated the infringement of its rights by secular education, let alone some unnecessarily provocative measures. Reduction of the army's privileges, and the granting of autonomy to Catalonia aroused the fury of the army which had always been strongly centralist. Then in 1933 the moderate Socialists under Prieto Indalecio and extremists under Largo Caballero left the coalition, seriously weakening Azaña. Anti-clericalism had united the Right against him, while granting female suffrage gave it further adherents for the November elections. The Right, in which the Catholic CEDA Party played a prominent part, thereupon started the clerical reaction, the *Bienio Negro*. Azaña's reforms, including the Catalan Statute giving autonomy, were undone. No serious programme for solving Spain's over-riding economic problems could be devised under these conditions. The Civil War in 1936 struck a country still in the grip of depression.

Before the world depression began Italy was experiencing a slump, thanks to Mussolini's disastrous financial policy and his efforts to make her self-supporting. His answer was still more autocracy. However, he scored a great success in February 1929 by settling the relationship between the Papacy and the Italian State for a time. Despite future discord, both sides on the whole benefited, Mussolini first. He regarded the elections due in March as a plebiscite, and though the government would naturally win, he wanted an overwhelming victory to show the world that 'Italy is Fascist and Fascism is Italy'. Fascism did in fact receive 8,517,838 votes against only 135,773.

The period between this triumph and the Ethiopian adventure in 1935 marked the period of his greatest popularity, despite his economic failures. He retorted to the great crash by launching the 'Battle of the Lira' to defend the currency, and he managed to keep Italy on the gold standard. In 1930 he established the National Council of Corporations, thereby eliminating remaining elements of economic liberalism. The trade unions, as well as employers and the state, sent representatives, but the trade unionists were Party nominees instructed to call for sacrifices from labour. Wages were reduced and hours increased; otherwise the corporations' major achievement was to regiment the labour force. As it was necessary to reduce imports, and especially wheat imports, a highly publicized 'Battle of the Grain' was also launched, and also officially won. In fact the drift from the land to the cities was as bad as ever, despite the settling of hundreds of peasant families in the land reclamation scheme which was a genuine (though not novel) Mussolinian contribution. The 1936 census showed that the trend to urbanization had brought an increase of two million town-dwellers since 1921. The drift might have been partially checked if Fascism had broken up the great estates, but Mussolini had too many obligations to their owners.

In 1933 the 'Battle of the Grain' ended with the declaration that in that year only 1,798,050 kilograms had been imported as against 10,918,660 in 1932. Actually Italy was still heavily dependent on imported grain, and her own increased production was achieved only by cultivating uneconomic marginal land previously used for cattle, fruit and olives, thereby disturbing the economy still further. Another much publicized activity was the

434

rebuilding of much of Rome, which he undertook to provide public works and to glorify his *régime*. He also built major arterial highways (*autostrade*) between the main towns. Nevertheless his great aim of making Italy a self-sufficient industrial and military power was as far from achievement as ever in 1933. Italian manufacturing production then had improved by only 8% on the 1923 figures.

Much of the improvement was due to general world trends. Early in 1931 international trade was worth only about 60% of its value in early 1929, but by the end of 1932 recovery was unmistakable. Even the primary producers felt the pressure relax, as did America, Germany and those countries, including Italy, which had been particularly badly affected because they were Germany's neighbours. Even so, Italy's record was under average, as the figures for industrial production show. Based on 1929 as 100, the 1932 figures were: Japan 98, Norway 93, Sweden 89, Britain and Holland 84, Hungary and Rumania 82, France 72, Belgium 69, Italy 67, Czechoslovakia 64, Poland 63, Canada 58, Germany 53 and America 53. Less successful still was Mussolini's 'Demographic Battle', intended to produce a population of 60,000,000 by mid-century. Despite prizes for babies and taxes for bachelors the birth-rate fell from 27·5 in 1927 to 23·4 in 1934; and 1932 was the only year since 1876 when live births numbered less than a million. Had it not been for restrictions on Italian immigrants imposed by America and other countries the increase of 6,000,000 between 1922 and 1939 would not have been achieved, and would almost certainly have been turned into a net loss even without counting the emigrants who returned in old age.

In political as well as economic international co-operation the depression years marked a turn for the worse. This was made increasingly clear after 1930. In the London Naval Conference of April 1930 the British had yielded to America's demand that they should have only 50 instead of 70 cruisers, as the Americans wanted to achieve parity cheaply, by reducing British, not increasing American cruiser strength. It was then agreed fairly easily to allot the British, American and Japanese navies tonnage roughly in the ratio of 5:5:3 for cruisers, destroyers and submarines, to have a five year interlude in battleship construction, and to scrap some battleships in the near future. However it was impossible to get agreement between France and Italy. France would not concede Italy's demand for parity unless French Mediterranean security were guaranteed by a naval version of Locarno. Britain, despite her views on eastern European guarantees, would not guarantee the western Mediterranean only, as her major interests were then in the Levant, not a major French concern. Moreover both powers wished to involve America in the guarantee, which was out of the question. Britain's chief concern was to regain economic and financial strength, which she thought would best be achieved by promoting international economic and political conciliation. France's insistence on security, which had prevented a comprehensive naval agreement, was further manifested to British annoyance by her diplomacy in

435

eastern Europe. Hence while France sought security, Britain pursued financial solvency and disarmament, despite Japan's attack on Manchuria and blatant German evasions of disarmament provisions.

However, it was not economic weakness alone which induced MacDonald's Labour government to make naval concessions which encouraged Japanese encroachments in the Pacific and Italian in the Mediterranean, and which left Britain with inadequate escorts for her vital shipping convoys in World War II. MacDonald continued to press for the holding of the Disarmament Conference first proposed in 1924 for 1925, but postponed ever since. Both Labour and Conservative politicians believed German demands for equality justified, and MacDonald's National Government pressed as firmly as its Labour predecessor. The April 1932 budget, presented by the Conservative Chancellor of the Exchequer, Neville Chamberlain, introduced the lowest arms estimate of the inter-war years to encourage other countries to reduce arms expenditure. Despite protracted sessions in London between February 1932 and its dissolution in June 1934, the Conference failed because of the impossibility of reconciling German demands for equality with French demands for security, when Britain would not underwrite the latter. In March 1933, after Hitler's accession to power had made the German problem infinitely more dangerous, the British Foreign Secretary Simon dropped some ominous hints to Beneš, his Czechoslovak counterpart. After declaring that if Germany were denied equality in armaments she might take the law into her own hands, Simon added that if she were denied the Sudetenland, Germany might try to take it by force. Few British politicians would have dissented from Simon's assessment, nor his implicit readiness to allow German use of force. However, if the British were already on the road to Munich, the French were not.

The first political result of the depression was to strengthen French power in eastern and central Europe, though in the long run it enabled Germany and Italy to destroy the peace settlement. France's temporary financial supremacy over Britain, and Germany's political, economic and military weakness were fully exploited, and it was not until 1935 that Germany's position began to assume real strength. Until 1933 the only effective resistance to France was supplied by Italy, for Soviet Russia was first preoccupied with pressing internal problems, then with the Far East, and finally with Germany herself. Russo-German relations were uncertain after 1928, and especially after France had evacuated the Rhineland in June 1930, five years ahead of time, providing Stresemann's last (posthumous) triumph. Just before the completion of the evacuation, Stalin had called France 'the most aggressive and militarist country of all aggressive and militarist countries of the world'. However Soviet foreign policy remained faithful to the principle of opposing the strongest European power within comfortable safety margins, and always leaving open the door for an understanding. When in July Litvinov became Foreign Minister his suppleness gave Russia further room for manoeuvre, especially as he had always been cool to the Rapallo policy of friendship with Germany. Stalin nevertheless made the major decisions, and Soviet policy was essentially his.

Germany had reacted to the Rhineland evacuation with increased demands for revision of the eastern frontiers and ending of reparations. The Austro-German customs scheme of March 1931 alarmed the French sufficiently for them to suggest a Franco-Soviet non-aggression pact—a proposal unsuccessfully made several times before by Russia, and even now France demanded that Russia must also conclude non-aggression pacts with Poland and Rumania. The Poles had in fact been discussing such a pact for some time, and the September 1930 Nazi election successes had spurred them on. Above all, for both France and Poland the negotiations with Russia marked reduced reliance on the Franco-Polish treaty. On Poland's insistence, the Baltic states too were brought in, though at first Russia adhered to her old policy of not negotiating with blocs. Eventually the long complex of Soviet non-aggression pacts materialized in 1932: with Finland in January, Latvia in February, Estonia in May, Poland and Rumania in July, and France in November. Thereby Russia hoped to prevent use of neighbouring territories for intervention by the capitalist west, and also to split the capitalist camp, for Britain's resumption of relations with Russia in October 1929 and the ensuing commercial negotiations had not improved their relationship. It was essential for Russia to gain security in Europe, for while Japan could inflict heavy damage on the Soviet Far Eastern position, only an attack launched from Europe could be fatal to the survival of the *régime*. Therefore Stalin sought reinsurance immediately after the Franco-Soviet pact was concluded. Germany was publicly assured that the Franco-Soviet and Polish-Soviet pacts meant no alteration in Soviet foreign policy. In fact none of the new treaties provided for co-operation 'in all political and economic questions jointly affecting' the signatories, as the 1926 Soviet-German agreement had done. They were also purely defensive, though this was a blow to Germany, for it ended, at least temporarily, prospects of Soviet-German partition of Poland which had helped to sustain the Rapallo policy. In addition, the Soviet-Polish pact pledged that Russia would not aid the aggressor if Poland were attacked. This strengthened Poland against Germany, but Russia also benefited by limiting her reliance on Germany. She could now seek to restore her former extensive influence in eastern Europe with two strings to her bow, the French and the German. She did not, however, intend to quarrel with Germany. On January 23rd, 1933, a week before Hitler became Chancellor, the Soviet Premier Molotov emphasized Russia's special relationship with Germany. Hitler's advent naturally increased the value of the pacts for Russia, especially when he liquidated the German Communists. Hitler pursued an ambiguous policy because his position was weak and uncertain in his first months of power, but he was not alarmed when the Russians made the breach with Rapallo in the summer because of exaggerated fears of Germany. Now, however, that Russia could not count on Germany, she sought to promote better relations with France, while for France the November 1932 pact with Russia was useful chiefly as a means of keeping Germany and Russia apart. The Franco-Soviet pact certainly did not lessen the reciprocal antipathy of the two signatories for some time. Even then it was Nazi anti-Bolshevik fanaticism, and other manifestations of aggression which turned the fragile *rapprochement* of 1932 into the Franco-Soviet alliance of 1935.

Moreover, the French would not have made the alliance if they had not expected to be able to achieve also an understanding with Italy, though Mussolini throughout the inter-war period displayed the traditional Italian hostility to France's North African and Balkan interests, despite occasional friendly gestures. Only over Austria was there real identity of French and Italian interests in their common opposition to Germany, and even here conflicts were also apparent. Italy sought to replace France as Austria's guarantor in order to set Austria against France's Little *Entente* allies, Czechoslovakia, Rumania and Yugoslavia, as well as to protect Austria against Germany. Mussolini was actually attempting in 1929 and 1930 to disrupt Yugoslavia by fostering Croat separatism, and was deeply involved in Alexander's murder in 1934. Italian and Hungarian intrigues strengthened the ties binding the Little *Entente* countries to each other, and France under the 'Plan' of Premier André Tardieu in March 1932 proposed to utilize Austria's precarious economic situation by uniting Austria, Hungary, Czechoslovakia, Rumania and Yugoslavia economically through internal free trade and perhaps a common currency. The Little *Entente* countries would inevitably have dominated the union, to France's economic and political advantage as well as their own, for all members were to renounce revisionism. Germany and Italy, with British approval, vetoed the proposed union. France in turn rejected Germany's proposal, which offered preferential tariffs to Austria and the other eastern states. The German scheme was carried through by the Nazis from early 1934 as part of their policy of controlling central and eastern European economic life, but the sole immediate result of the negotiations was the Lausanne Agreement of July 1932. By this agreement the League of Nations agreed to an international loan to Austria, in return for Austria's accepting League financial supervision, and for agreeing not to promote any form of union with Germany for twenty years. However, this set off an anti-French reaction which brought to office as Chancellor the clerical-Fascist Engelbert Dollfuss. When the Social Democrats and pan-Germans refused to join him, he brought in the para-military *Heimwehr* whose chief, Prince Ernst Starhemberg, was a close friend of Mussolini, and it could be only a matter of time before Austria looked to Italy. Almost simultaneously, Hungarian reactions against similarly French-directed League intervention in return for financial aid brought to the premiership Julius Gömbös. Gömbös' first aim was to promote Hungarian revisionism; his next goal was to bring together Hitler's Germany, Mussolini's Italy, and his own Hungary.

This proved impossible, but he firmly committed Hungary to supporting Mussolini.

After Poincaré's resignation because of ill health in July 1929, France was subjected to thirteen government changes and eight different premiers before Hitler's rise to power. This was due only in part to the depression, which did not begin seriously to affect France before the consequences of sterling's depreciation made themselves felt after September 1931. Under the depression's impact France's exports had fallen and her imports had risen, like those of the other industrialized countries, but her level of industrial production remained high for two years. Instead of devaluing the franc (already devalued with harsh consequences for the *rentier* class in June 1928) France increased tariffs and extended import quotas. France did not suffer heavy 'official' unemployment as foreign workers were first dismissed, and they returned home, while many French urban workers returned to their previous rural homes to work on family farms. France was also financially strong, as the franc was not subjected to the same strains as the dollar and pound: moreover French investors had chosen their foreign investments more discreetly, and France had built up strong gold reserves. She was thereby able to remain on the gold standard long after America abandoned it, though with increasing difficulty. France also suffered less than Britain because she was not economically so advanced. Her numerous small independent farmers could sustain themselves and their unemployed relatives, and her numerous small businesses could survive without radical reorganization if they were protected by tariffs. In addition, the franc had been stabilized in 1928 below its real value, thereby bringing in foreign orders which enabled France to maintain high productivity into 1931. Yet again 1930's harvest was poor; this was fortunate because it deferred for another year the burning problem of agricultural surpluses caused by overproduction, which afflicted other countries. However, when the crisis came it stayed longer than in any other major industrial country except America, and in 1935 industrial production was 27% below 1929's figure. Exports stood at $2,042,000,000 in 1928, and in 1938 had slumped to $882,000,000.

The franc's artificially high price before its eventual devaluation in September 1936 severely curtailed exports, and brought a heavily adverse balance of payments as well as continuing deflation in an attempt to balance the budget. Much of the political instability of the 1920s was caused by inflationary efforts to balance the budget. Deflation now had much the same results, except that more people suffered. As France could either export or 'rusticate' some of her unemployed, unemployment never exceeded the 500,000 mark. Nevertheless unemployment posed serious social and political problems, and contributed to the growing popularity of the Left Wing parties which promised to end it. Farmers were also discontented with falling prices, as were the landowners. *Rentiers*, financiers, industrialists, small businessmen and shopkeepers nursed grievances, as did civil servants whose salaries had been cut. Enemies of the Republic grew more numerous on both Left and Right. The Socialists remained loyal to the Republic, but the Communists, pledged to its destruction before Russia launched the Popular Front movement in 1935, increased their support among intellectuals, *bourgeoisie*, working class and even peasantry.

On the Right the Action Française, though no longer a dominant force, was still important, as its contribution to the 1934 anti-Republican riots showed. The Croix de Feu, founded in 1928, was comparatively moderate, even in its anti-Communism. It numbered several hundred thousand by 1936, when it was suppressed with other, more Fascist-oriented organizations, but reappeared as the Parti Social Français. Of the new Fascist Leagues which appeared only the Parti Populaire Français, founded in 1934 by Jacques Doriot after his expulsion from the Communist Party, had a mass following (possibly half a million). From 1936 Mussolini subsidized Doriot, but the other Leagues were noisy rather than dangerous, except for the Cagoulards (hooded men) of the later 1930s. The essential mass *bourgeois* and working class basis for a successful Fascist movement never appeared in France, though the danger was far greater than in Britain. Even under the strains of the thirties French society never disintegrated, and most Frenchmen retained their acute sense of the ridiculous. A French Mussolini would have been an absurdity; a French Hitler an obscenity.

Even without the perennial economic crisis after 1931, the Centre coalitions which did the positive work of sustaining the Republic would have been too narrowly based for stability. Though the Socialists were the major Communist target ('Social Fascists' in Communist jargon here as elsewhere) until mid-1934, Léon Blum continued to refuse support to the Radical and Radical Socialist coalitions, and waited until he was in a position to control the cabinet himself before he would take office. Additional weakness stemmed from the fact that with Poincaré's departure in 1928 and Briand's death in March 1932, there were no political leaders of real stature. André Tardieu, Pierre Laval and Pierre Étienne Flandin, all later to be involved in Fascist intrigues, competed for the premiership with Edouard Herriot and Blum, Laval most successfully because of his greater pliability and unscrupulousness. Tardieu was Premier three times between 1929 and 1932, and dominated the political scene before January 1933. His proposals for reforming French political institutions, on either British or American lines, in order to produce the strong executive needed to solve the economic problems and ensure political stability, were rejected by the anarchic deputies. Laval, who like many French politicians had gravitated from Left to Right, owing to ambition and growing wealth, typified the prevailing temper.

Elections in May 1932 put Herriot and the Radicals in power, though the Socialists had a larger popular vote. Herriot fell in December after demanding that France should pay her war debt instalment to America. There ensued a period of political instability rivalling that between 1924 and 1926. Five cabinets were destroyed before the February 1934 riots temporarily frightened the deputies into some sense of responsibility. Among these cabinets were two led by Edouard Daladier, who had replaced Herriot as the Radical leader. Daladier was readier than Herriot to work with the Socialists, but Blum's attitude towards the Radicals did not change. The Left-Centre cabinets could not control the Chamber, which was too far to the Left for them. They dissipated most of their strength, moreover, in hopeless struggles to maintain the franc and balance the budget, as Right Wing coalitions like Laval's did later. Yet the violence and oscillations in the Chamber and in Paris did not reflect French realities accurately. Despite economic stagnation, financial crisis and political turmoil, provincial France remained surprisingly stable.

Nevertheless the collapse of capitalism and the Republic was constantly predicted, and social discontent ran dangerously high thanks to the endemic class warfare preached by the Left and practised by the Right. The refusal of all French governments before the Popular Front to carry out social reforms even of the New Deal type left labour hopelessly embittered, and the selfish greed of industrialists and financiers made reconciliation of the two sides impossible. The depression years provided France with an opportunity to reshape her economy by fostering new industries, to replace the luxury industries which inevitably suffered badly in times of depression, and which could not create the mass domestic market necessary for a healthy economy. Lack of social cohesion and persistent political immobility precluded radical reform, which was unacceptable to the upper classes. Working class hostility to capital remained ineradicable. Peasants and small businessmen were inimical to change. When reform was finally attempted by Blum's Popular Front government it neither satisfied the working class nor was tolerated by the reactionary upper class. However the 'two hundred families' who were alleged to hold such wealth and power that they could dictate to governments were as much a myth as their nicely-rounded number would suggest, and Blum's reforms failed for a formidable number of domestic political reasons: irresponsible or treacherous trade union leadership, lack of bureaucracy capable of accepting and implementing new ideas, and incapacity on the politicians' part, as well as refusal by the propertied classes to accept infringements of their power and prerogatives.

They also failed because of France's international position, which had become increasingly vulnerable. Obviously nothing could have averted the collapse of French hegemony in Europe with the rise of Nazi Germany, the growth of Soviet strength, Mussolini's ambiguous policy, and British coolness to French views on security. The collapse first of Poincaré's independent policy and then of Briand's 'Europeanism' limited France's freedom of manoeuvre, though it did not dictate the paralysis which overtook French policy. The loss of French nerve which led to the collapse of the system of alliances after 1933 long preceded depression, and was not much increased by it. Hitler was wrong, though not very far wrong, when

441

he predicted civil war in France as one of the factors which would enable him to begin his programme of expansion. The defeatism of 1940 was not yet apparent, but after the losses of World War I France had adopted a thoroughly 'defensive' outlook. In 1934 an army officer, Charles de Gaulle, would argue against derision, that if France were to remain a truly Great Power she must build up an offensive tank force—not only because of military, but political necessities. But his argument that a country permanently on the defensive had neither the military nor the political force required to confront potential enemies was not then acceptable to France. The Socialists denounced such pernicious doctrines as much as did the future collaborationist elements of the Right, who gravitated to Vichy after France's defeat in 1940. The attempt of Jean Louis Barthou, foreign minister in Gaston Doumergue's cabinet, to revive France's system of eastern alliances in 1934 was probably doomed before he was assassinated with Alexander of Yugoslavia in October of that year. Pilsudski, for one, perceived the trends which underlay the surface toughness of Barthou's policy when he told him that the French would yield to Germany: 'You would not be what you are if you did not.'

Britain faced the depression's onset with a Labour minority government which depended on Liberal goodwill. Failure to adjust her economy to changing patterns of world trade and production had been largely concealed before 1929, because her overseas income had covered her imports and allowed a considerable, though reduced export of capital. From 1929 income from such invisible exports as payment for shipping and other services generally declined. In 1933 income from foreign investments was about £150,000,000, though by 1938 it had risen to about £185,000,000—roughly the 1913 figure, though not its equivalent in purchasing power. Shipping tonnage by 1925 had exceeded the pre-war level of 19,145,000; it reached 20,332,000 in 1930, then declined by 1935 to 17,298,000, and rose again to 18,046,000 in 1939. The British share of the world total, however, and of the carrying trade fell throughout the inter-war period. In the 1920s this was offset by higher prices so that income exceeded the prewar level, which was about £100,000,000, but then it fell to £65,000,000 by 1933 and only recovered in 1938 to the prewar level. Other invisible earnings from insurance, banking and trading services averaged annually roughly £77,000,000 for 1924–28, £54,000,000 for 1929–33, and £42,000,000 for 1934–38. This decline would not have caused much distress if it had not been accompanied by a slump in manufactured exports, due in part to world stagnation but above all to the predominance in Britain of declining industries, notably textiles and coal. Before 1914 British exports had accounted for 13·1% of the world total, but only 11·1% in 1927, 9·92% in 1932 and 9·87% in 1937. Before the war over three-quarters of European coal exports had been British, shipped chiefly to Europe. The long-term decline in textiles was even more apparent. In 1938 coal exports were under half those of 1913, whereas cotton exports dropped from 576,000 tons to 135,000. Yet in 1938 cotton still accounted for about a quarter and coal for about a tenth of total exports. Europe as a whole also reacted slowly to changes in world demand, but Britain lagged very far behind, and would have been worse off but for largely captive markets in Australasia, which took about a tenth of British exports in the later 1930s, and in Africa and Asia, which each took about a sixth.

The slump's chief effect in Britain was to increase unemployment in the export trades, which nevertheless left the majority of workers, and even whole areas, such as the south-east, largely untouched; next it reduced Britain's active balance of payments from a surplus of £103,000,000 in 1929 to a debit of £104,000,000 in 1931 (by 1937 only £56,000,000); and then it set off the financial crisis in the summer of 1931. Sir Oswald Mosley, a junior minister, drafted a scheme for a planned economy, to give the government control of credit and foreign trade, and direction of industry. This proved too radical for his colleagues, especially as he wanted to abandon free trade, and in 1931 he left the Labour Party. In 1932, despairing of parliamentary government, he founded his Fascist Blackshirt organization. This immediately resorted to brawling and violent anti-semitism on the Continental pattern, and seriously menaced public order for four years. Yet Britain's economic situation was not nearly so bad as orthodox financiers, economists and politicians believed. In 1930 unemployment rose from 1,500,000 to 2,000,000, but real wages also rose. Despite the declining exports, reduced import costs meant a net balance of payments liability of only £25,000,000.

The damage came in 1931 with loss of political and financial self-confidence caused by American and Central European crises, nervousness about sterling and pedantic demands for a balanced budget. Fears reached feverish intensity in late summer. Unemployment of over 2,750,000 in July seriously strained a budget already weakened by falling tax receipts. Orthodox financiers demanded reductions in unemployment relief and other government economies. British bankers' misguided foreign credit policy had made the problem insoluble by orthodox measures, but those were to be applied. MacDonald favoured cutting the 'dole' (unemployment relief) and government expenditure. He called for his ministers' resignations when a cabinet split had produced deadlock on these issues on August 23rd. Instead of yielding to a Liberal-Conservative coalition, as he was expected to do, he formed a National Government with Baldwin as his deputy. The Liberals, whose temporary leader Sir Herbert Samuel had suggested the idea of a National Government to George V, also gave support. Had Lloyd George not then been ill, the National Government would not have been formed, but the Labour Party would have been irremediably split.

After an emergency economizing budget the National Government held a general election on October 27th which produced an enormous majority. MacDonald had only twelve National Labour supporters, but the Labour Party lost about 2,750,000 voters as well as its incurably vain leader. MacDonald and his adherents were expelled from the party, which now

443

numbered only forty-six in the House of Commons, and had lost most of its chiefs in the electoral slaughter. However it had kept its separate identity, and was still a mass party. The Liberals had expected to share power, but they were as much prisoners of the Conservative majority as was National Labour.

Probably the National Government's abandonment of the gold standard on September 21st was inevitable because of the shortage of liquid reserves. The consequent depreciation of sterling temporarily aided exports, but other currencies also depreciated, and dollar devaluation in 1933–34 offset any sterling advantages. The pound's decline from $4·86 to $3·40 on abandoning gold was preceded by a 10% cut in unemployment benefits, and greater reductions in salaries of teachers and government employees. However the whole crisis was over before the general election gave the Conservatives a virtual blank cheque. They used it to introduce protection, as they had promised. This split the Liberal Party into thirty-five Simonite Liberals accepting protection (Sir John Simon was rewarded with the Foreign Secretaryship) and thirty-three free-traders. The Liberal decline continued when Labour began to recover. After October 1931 Lloyd George was supported by only three members, all relatives. The Conservatives' 472 seats represented about 11,800,000 votes against Labour's 52 seats and 6,600,000 votes.

The National Government's first major act was the uncontroversial passing in December 1931 of the Statute of Westminster, giving formal independence to the Dominions. It also continued its predecessors' conciliatory policy towards India, despite Gandhi's second civil disobedience campaign of March 1930, which had led to violent riots, and his arrest with other leaders. In June 1930 the all-party Simon Commission's report had recommended administrative changes, but not responsible government, thereby arousing violent condemnation in India. The Labour Government had called the first round-table conference (November 1930–January 1931) which had proposed federation with some measure of responsible government. In January 1931 Gandhi had been released and negotiated with the British, calling off civil disobedience in return for release of political prisoners. He attended the second round-table conference of September–December, held by the National Government against Churchill's protests. This however also failed to meet Congress's demands, and in January 1932 Gandhi was again arrested, and Congress declared illegal. The National Government nevertheless was anxious to grant self-government, as soon as this could be done with safety to minorities. Churchill's opposition to the Conservative party line over India led to his exclusion from the National Government. Neville Chamberlain was consequently next in the Conservative hierarchy to Baldwin, and therefore also effectively second man in the government after Baldwin—for MacDonald was a straw Prime Minister. As neither Baldwin nor MacDonald, still less Chamberlain after them, was capable of providing the leadership in foreign affairs which Britain was still strong enough to give, the 1930s became the 'locust years' when Britain's morale was continually, though gradually sapped by her political leaders. The government's domestic policy was equally unenlightened. Neville Chamberlain introduced protection in March 1932 against all but Empire goods but this aroused little public interest. Its development in his subsequent budgets did nothing to improve exports, while little was done to reorganize and stimulate industry.

Though foreign investments had made Germany highly susceptible to the depression, these investments had been largely used to modernize and extend her industrial plant. Hence in 1929 her exports stood at 95% of the 1913 total, whereas Britain's were only 87%. In 1913 terms Germany's manufacturing index was 117 and Britain's only 103. Although unemployment mounted rapidly after October 1929, German recovery was also rapid. By slightly increasing exports and sharply reducing imports Germany built up a substantial balance of payments credit before the financial crisis in the autumn of 1931. Even before the end of 1929 the balance of payments was going into credit, and at the end of 1930 it was 1,644,000,000 reichmarks to the good. However, sterling devaluation in September 1931, coming on top of the Austrian and German financial crisis, produced stringent credit restrictions within Germany. Instead of devaluation the government resorted in December to deflation. The foreign exchange controls established in July on a temporary, and then in November on a permanent basis, did nothing to check the decline of exports evident since the summer. However, the system of 'special' bilateral arrangements with south-eastern European and Latin American countries, later extended by the Nazis, improved German exports, by allowing Germany's partners to increase exports to her in return for taking more German manufactures. This system benefited both sides, though Germany more than her weaker partners. Restriction of imports by licensing and attempts to increase agricultural production and establish industries to replace raw materials with synthetic substitutes achieved little success. Whereas Britain's exports were recovering by the end of 1932 Germany's continued to decline until 1934, after which the discrepancy rapidly disappeared, so that in 1938 her recovery had exceeded Britain's. Germany's other major success was in dealing with unemployment. In mid-1932 she abandoned deflation in favour of resuming on a larger scale the public works programme initiated in 1925. This policy was further extended by Hitler after 1933. He accompanied it with an armaments programme which also contributed largely to recovery, though Germany would in any event have recovered without adopting a war economy.

Certainly it was not the depression which destroyed the Weimar Republic. That was the work of its friends; and it was accomplished in March 1930 by Social Democrats, not in January 1933 by Hitler. Just as in 1931 in Britain the watershed of the inter-war years was marked by the advent of the National Government, so the refusal of some German Social Democrats in March 1930 to accept decisions to reduce social

445

benefits brought down Chancellor Hermann Müller's Social Democratic coalition, the Weimar Republic's last parliamentary government. Müller was succeeded by the army's nominee, the Centre leader Heinrich Brüning, no friend of democracy, though less of the Nazis. As Brüning had no parliamentary majority, he resorted to extensive emergency powers, relying on Presidential and army backing. The Social Democrats tried to repair their error of March by offering to negotiate but he refused, even after the September elections returned 107 Nazis in place of the previous 12. The Socialists were still the largest party with 143 seats; the Communists had 77, the Centre 68, Nationalists 41, and there were numerous splinter parties. Brüning's parliamentary position was therefore impossible without Socialist support, which was forthcoming on a 'passive' basis— that is, refusal to vote against him. For this the Communists vigorously denounced the Socialists.

The Nazi success was partly due to the unpopularity of Brüning's deflationary policy, but chiefly to Hitler's breaking with the Nazi socialist wing. This enabled him to bid more strongly for middle class votes, and also to get the support of great industrialists like the steel magnate Fritz Thyssen and bankers like Kurt von Schröder, who later helped him into office. They hoped to use him against the radical and socialist forces in Germany—which he intended to destroy, but for his own purposes. They thought he was on their side, a patriot and conservative who would reassert the authority of army officer, businessman and bureaucrat. They did not consider his violence excessive, for Hitler's defeat in 1923 had shown him that to make his 'revolution' he needed the power of the state, and that he must get that power by constitutional means. These included beating and terrorizing opponents so long as the army and police would tolerate it, for one of the essential ingredients for Fascism's success is the complicity of the state authorities. His progress to power was eased by Stalin's dogma that the Socialists, not the Nazis, were German Communism's main enemies, but the major factor was the army's readiness to tolerate and use the Nazis (under safeguards which soon proved illusory).

Nevertheless Hitler was also a popular figure and had mass support from urban and rural lower middle classes. It was small businessmen and peasants who provided this support, together with some unemployed white-collar workers and struggling professional men—in other words those elements who were unfavourably treated under capitalism but felt no bonds of sympathy with the proletarians. These last remained largely loyal to their former Socialist, Communist or Centre Party allegiances, and indeed the bulk of Nazi support came from the countryside. The Nazis also gained at the expense of small splinter parties, and from middle class parties in eastern areas where originally conservative support had had a strongly nationalist basis. Perhaps the most striking features of the Nazi success were that many Nazi votes came from people who had not voted before, though again in rural areas, and that their urban gains came chiefly from the ranks of the unemployed.

In 1931 Hitler became an even more formidable figure when the Nazis made further advances in state elections. His extraordinary powers as a speaker, the effectiveness of Nazi propaganda aimed at mass emotion and prejudice, his insistence that a man of iron will alone could save Germany, and his effective reiteration of a few points—mostly lies, but he proved his point that people were more willing to accept great lies than small ones—led Brüning in the autumn to offer a deal. Brüning's aim was to restore Germany's economy and end reparations; then he would retire in favour of somebody more acceptable to the Right Wing parties. Hitler refused, whereupon Brüning reconstituted his cabinet, making his Defence Minister Wilhelm Gröner also Minister of the Interior, at the suggestion of Gröner's *protégé* General Kurt von Schleicher. Schleicher was in effect under-secretary in the defence ministry, and on intimate terms with Paul von Hindenburg. He had indeed been largely responsible for Brüning's own appointment.

The winter was a grim one; unemployment exceeded 5,000,000 and Nazi Party membership rose to over 800,000. Schleicher wanted to have Hitler in the government, but when Brüning repeated his offers in January 1932 Hitler again rejected them. Moreover, Hitler offered Nazi and Nationalist support to Hindenburg for the March 13th Presidential election, if Hindenburg would dismiss Brüning in favour of a Right Wing National government. When Hindenburg refused Hitler challenged him for the Presidency. As the election did not give any candidate a majority a second ballot was held on April 10th. Hitler then polled 11,339,285 votes against Hindenburg's 18,650,730 and the Communist Thälmann's 3,706,655. Hindenburg would have been defeated had not Brüning campaigned vigorously on his behalf, and had not the Socialists supported him. This need for Socialist support was a humiliation for which Hindenburg blamed Brüning, who had insisted that he should stand again.

On April 10th Gröner, against Brüning's wishes, ordered the dissolution of the SA and SS bands, though the Nazi Party remained legal. Despite this check, in state elections on April 24th the Nazis became the strongest party in Bavaria, Hamburg, Württemberg, and above all in Prussia, though the Socialist-Centre coalition there retained office. There were, however, signs that though the Nazis were still gaining strength, their rate of progress was declining. There was no political crisis, for Gröner loyally supported Brüning, and the Socialists could be relied upon against Hitler. However Schleicher hoped to gain control of the SA for the army— either through Röhm, or by dealing with Hitler. As Gröner remained loyal to Brüning, Schleicher engineered Gröner's fall on May 13th and then induced the senile and treacherous Hindenburg to withdraw his support also from Brüning. The industrialists had already been protesting to Hindenburg about Brüning's economic policy, which they thought conceded too much to labour. When Brüning proposed to redistribute insolvent East Prussian estates for colonization, Hindenburg gave a ready hearing to the Junkers who denounced Brüning as an 'agrarian Bolshevik'. Brüning refused to fight to retain office, and Schleicher suggested Franz von Papen as Brüning's successor. He assured Hindenburg that Papen had the army's confidence, and that the Nazis would support him—hence Papen could work through the *Reichstag*. In fact Papen never attempted that, relying on Hindenburg and the army as Brüning had done, but without the support of the Centre, which resented Bruning's shabby dismissal. Schleicher expected to dominate Papen, an amateur jockey with excellent Nationalist Party social and business connections, but Papen revealed capacities for intrigue which exceeded even Schleicher's.

Papen intended to rule for himself, even though he could form his 'non-party' cabinet—the 'cabinet of barons'—only with Hindenburg's help. It was the most unpopular and inefficient government since November 1918. Its two triumphs of negotiating the formal end of reparations and the Disarmament Conference's recognition of Germany's claim to equality were the fruits of Brüning's diplomacy. The Nazis suffered it temporarily while they manoeuvred to destroy it. Papen dissolved the *Reichstag* and raised the ban on the Nazi paramilitary forces in June, thereby, as Thälmann predicted, issuing an open provocation to murder. Seizing the pretext of electoral disturbances, Papen dissolved the anti-Nazi Prussian state government in July. In the election campaign of the same month the Nazis succeeded as never before in satisfying the emotional needs of the German people, gaining 37·3% of the total votes, with 13,745,000 against the Socialists' 7,959,700, the Communists' 5,282,600, the Centre's 4,589,300 and the Nationalists' 2,177,400 (a drop of a million and a half). This was not the outright victory for which Hitler had hoped, and he had still not captured the greatest state of Prussia. Henceforth Nazi mass support declined, but Hitler's political position was still strong. The Nationalists were too weak to sustain Papen, who moreover had rejected the claims to office of their leader Hugenburg. Papen's government could not rule through the *Reichstag* without Nazi support, and Hitler would accept nothing less than the Chancellorship—on the grounds that his was the strongest party, for he could talk parliamentary language when he liked. Papen and Schleicher rejected the demand, though Hitler had offered to form a coalition. Schleicher nevertheless still bargained with the Nazis, hoping to get their support after he had disposed of Papen, whose position in the *Reichstag* and the country was impossible. Papen also kept in touch with the Nazis, hoping to reduce their price.

By the autumn the Nazis' unbridled violence lost them much popular support. More important, big business interests were wondering whether the Nazi leadership took its radical and socialist propaganda seriously, as speeches by Gregor Strasser, the Party organizer, and other radical Nazis suggested. Hitler faced dangerous discontent in his party. If he did not give his thugs the kind of employment they wanted they might leave him in disgust; if he did, he might frighten off the 'respectable' people whose money and support were essential. Papen's belief that the Nazis had shot their bolt appeared to be confirmed when he dissolved the new *Reichstag* (which had sat for only one day) in September, and the general election of November 6th saw Nazi votes drop to 11,737,000 (33·1%). Furious with Papen though he was, Hitler still manoeuvred skilfully. He rejected Papen's renewal of the offer made in August to appoint Hitler Vice-Chancellor. He also refused Schleicher's overtures through Gregor Strasser for Nazi entry into a Schleicher cabinet—though Göring and Goebbels were chiefly responsible for this refusal. Papen's only resort was to ask Hindenburg for extensive emergency powers to frame a new constitution, rule by decree, and forcibly repress opposition. Schleicher advised Hindenburg that this would produce civil war, for the nation's opposition to Papen was unmistakable. Schleicher offered to form a government with Nazi support—if not from Hitler, then from Strasser—and also win over the small *bourgeois* parties, Centre Party and trade unions. This last proposal antagonized Hindenburg, but when Schleicher convinced him that the army would not tolerate Papen's proposals, Hindenburg appointed Schleicher Chancellor on December 2nd. However Schleicher's personal hold over Hindenburg was gone, and he failed to get Nazi or any other support. Hitler thwarted his offer to make Strasser Vice-Chancellor with responsibility for handling the trade unions. Thereupon Strasser resigned control of the Party's organization, which Hitler immediately entrusted to the faithful Hess. Radical elements under Strasser and Röhm nevertheless remained formidable.

Denied Nazi support, Schleicher made a public bid for popular and trade-union backing over the radio on December 15th. This destroyed his chances of support from large sections of the army leadership and the industrialists. Schleicher's enquiries into the Junker landowners' racket in agrarian relief infuriated them, and threatened to implicate the Junker Hindenburg and his son Oskar. The Nazi danger declined further as economic conditions improved and Nazi funds dried up, but Papen had won Hindenburg's senile affections, while the army repudiated Schleicher in favour of giving Hitler the power refused in November. Finally big business stepped in. At a meeting in the banker Schröder's house on January 4th, 1933, Hitler and Papen agreed to combine to overthrow Schleicher. Hitler was promised extensive funds in return for promising to respect German industry's interests. Papen was still reluctant to concede power to Hitler, but the Nationalists were too weak for the industrialists' purposes, as defined by Schröder: 'The feeling common to the whole of industry was the fear of Bolshevism and the hope that, once National Socialism was in power, it would provide Germany with solid political and economic foundations. There was another point in common: the desire for realizing Germany's industrial programme. This programme (i.e. heavy rearmament) was known to industrial circles and was well received.'

Hard bargaining and intrigue still lay ahead before Papen consented to act as Vice-Chancellor and renounced his scheme of making himself 'Presidential Chancellor' with the help of Hugenburg, who also resented Hitler's pretensions. There was also danger of Schleicher's seizing power by a military coup, after Hitler had rejected on January 29th Schleicher's last-minute suggestion that they should combine against Papen. However, Papen's influence over Hindenburg finally induced him to agree to make Hitler Chancellor, if General Werner von Blomberg would act as Defence Minister. Blomberg had long been assiduously wooed by the Nazis, and he agreed, bringing Hitler the indispensable support of the army. On January 30th, 1933, Hitler was made Chancellor, with Papen and Hugenburg under him. These two, with their industrialist friends and the generals, thought that they had bought Hitler and could control him—and that if he refused to be managed they could get rid of him by methods similar to those employed to bring him in. They had no conception of the evil depths of the paranoiac Hitler. They thought that the physically nondescript Führer, with his hysterical outbursts, would be a mere instrument in their hands. However Hitler represented German dreams and ambitions as no other ruler had ever done. He found a disjointed, incoherent nation awaiting the leader who could give it shape and purpose, and he provided both.

### (iii) *The Crisis in Soviet Russia: Collectivization and the First Five-Year Plan*

After the Soviet Party Congress of December 1927 preliminary moves were made for the all-out drive of the autumn of 1929 to increase industrialization and the collectivization of agriculture. Instead of the advances called for by the first Five-Year Plan, this drive brought the disaster which culminated in the terrible winter of 1932–33. At least 5,000,000 people died as a result of collectivization, and even the greatly increased industrial investment could not halt the slump in industrial output. Nevertheless Soviet Russia proclaimed that she had suffered no such depression as had afflicted the capitalist world since 1929 (which was true in one sense) and that she had solved the problem of unemployment (also true in a sense).

The first Five-Year Plan began on November 7th, 1929, with Stalin's call for mass murder under the cry 'Annihilation of the kulaks as a class'. This inaugurated the Second Bolshevik Revolution. Stalin's purpose was not liquidation of kulaks, who were numerically insignificant, but destruction of the independent peasantry. The rate of industrialization envisaged could not be achieved without destroying the existing village system, and the working definition of kulaks during collectivization was peasants who opposed it. Those who resisted, however, could not all be deported to Siberian concentration camps, or liquidated more directly by murdering individuals and launching military operations against whole villages. Official statistics listed over four million peasant families collectivized by January 20th, 1930, and another ten million by March 1st, in all about 55% of the total. As the brutality was excessive Stalin on March 2nd blamed his executioners for 'dizziness from successes', but it was his own policy which was chiefly responsible for Russia's change after 1928 from a country with a population growth of nearly 3,000,000 a year into one with only about 100,000 growth in 1933. The peasants burned crops and killed livestock to prevent their seizure, and gross farm output declined between 1928 and 1932 by about 15%. In 1932 Soviet agriculture probably achieved only half of the first Five-Year Plan's target for that year. However collectivization achieved its political objective by enforcing Stalinist totalitarianism on the peasants, about 60% of whom had been collectivized by December 1932. Most of these peasants, however, were on the 'artel' collectives and not on the officially favoured 'state farms', which made the peasants landless labourers. The 'artel', the commonest form of collective (about 96%), permitted peasants their own livestock and smallholdings, which they might cultivate for either subsistence farming or for sale on the market. This 'private' sector of the agrarian economy was by far the most productive.

Collectivization nevertheless achieved important economic objectives. It provided much of the heavy investment in agriculture, and especially in the Machine-Tractor Stations (MTS's). Above all it was the essential precursor of Stalin's industrialization programme, which he defined as intended 'to create such an industry in our country as to be able to re-arm and re-organize not only industry as a whole, but also transport and agriculture—on the basis of socialism'. Stalin achieved not socialism but a more ruthlessly exploiting system of state capitalism than Lenin, by greater concentration on heavy industry, and especially steel production. Much of the labour for the industrial surge and some of the investment capital came from collectivization, but the virtual strangulation of consumer goods production also made a major contribution. This was partly the result of the genuine conviction that the 'imperialist interventionists' were bound to attack the only 'socialist' state. (Japan's attack on Manchuria produced a great increase of expenditure on Soviet armaments.) However it also derived from the belief that only a tremendous industrialization policy could make Russia a great power. This could not be achieved while independent peasants formed the mass of her population. Bukharin was expelled from the Politburo in November 1929 for advocating what were strictly Leninist views on the need for their cautious handling.

The first Five-Year Plan's objectives were unreal. It proposed to increase industrial production between late autumn 1930 and late autumn 1933 by 90%, and to exceed 100% in the next quarter. Even when it should have been clear that a very bad start had been made, the 16th Party Congress of June–July 1930 announced that the Five-Year Plan would be achieved in four years. When it became clear that something had gone seriously wrong (factories had been erected for which there was no machinery, and machinery was spoiled by unskilled workers or inadequate

451

housing), blame was laid on foreign 'spies' and saboteurs, or disgruntled intelligentsia. Steel production, which the plan particularly favoured, actually stagnated. From late autumn 1930 to late autumn 1932 a 2% increase in steel output was achieved, and the planned increase in the output of steel for 1932 of 3,900,000 tons became an actual increase of 300,000 tons. At the end of 1932, when Stalin's Second Bolshevik Revolution had led to his Second Civil War against the peasantry, and the *régime*'s crisis reached its height, he claimed that the plan had been fulfilled. There certainly was an increase in industrial production, but this must be set off against the catastrophic decline in consumer goods, and the tremendous losses in the private agricultural sector. Much of the excessively heavy investment in industry was wasted by inefficient direction, the incapacity of transport to meet the demands made on it, and the shortage of skilled labour. Moreover, had it not been for the repressive nature of the *régime*, which could enforce a sharp decline in real wages by allowing heavy inflation in the private consumer goods market, production costs would have increased rapidly from mid-1930, when price statistics ceased to be published. The prices of rationed food doubled between 1928 and 1932, and it has been estimated that bread prices in the free (i.e. private food) market increased to about fifty times those of 1928. For the ordinary citizen, these aspects of the plan's operation counted for far more than deflationary policies intended to halve industrial construction costs by 1933 and cut wholesale prices of producers' goods by nearly a third. In fact neither these aims, nor the promised reductions of retail prices were achieved.

Indeed, none of the plan's major aims was achieved by 1933. Crop production declined markedly between 1930 and 1932—and in 1930, a good year for grain, Russia dumped grain abroad, undercutting already severely reduced world prices. Total industrial production increased by about 40% instead of the planned target of over 100%—though this was certainly a considerable achievement, and the basis had been laid for the second Five-Year Plan which was to make Russia a great industrial power. To facilitate the task the unions were brought to heel. They had enjoyed the legal right to strike against Nepmen 'exploiters', and had been allowed to protect their members in the socialized sector, but NEP's abolition and Stalin's totalitarianism doomed this independence. Tomsky, the trade union chief, joined Bukharin and the 'Right Opposition' in protesting against the anti-union policy. Stalin accordingly removed Tomsky from his post in 1929. Union functions now were to increase productivity. Though the profit motive was still frowned on, in production the economic motive was quickly restored by re-introducing differences of income. From 1931 piece rates replaced time rates wherever possible, while differentials between skilled and unskilled workers soon exceeded those found in the west. In accordance with the totalitarian trend the powers of management were greatly extended, a process to be carried even further when the great purges began during the second Five-Year Plan. Nevertheless official dissatisfaction with the achievements of the first Plan, despite public boasting, was shown when the targets for major commodities were fixed for 1937, though even the more moderate demands were not achieved in the overwhelming majority of cases until the 1950s.

| Product | 1932 targets | 1932 pro- duction | 1934 targets | 1937 pro- duction | Years when 1932 targets were reached |
|---|---|---|---|---|---|
| Electric power (billion kw-h) at least | 100 | 13·5 | 38·0 | 36·2 | 1951 |
| Coal (mil. tons) | 250·0 | 64·4 | 152·5 | 128·0 | 1950 |
| Pig iron (ditto) | 22·0 | 6·2 | 16·0 | 14·5 | 1952 |
| Crude petroleum (ditto) | 80–90 | 22·3 | 46·8 | 30·5 | 1955 |
| Grain (ditto) | 130·0 | 66·4 | 105·0 | 96·0 | 1956 |
| Sugar beet (ditto) | 19·8 | 6·6 | 27·6 | 21·9 | 1937 |
| Seed cotton (thousand tons) | 2,542 | 1,271 | 2,125 | 2,582 | 1937 |

Though the economic revolution eventually established Stalin's dictator-ship, this outcome was uncertain for some time. The Rightist opposition was defeated in 1929 and forced to recant on several occasions later, but its complaints against the harshness of the Five-Year Plan were real and commanded wide sympathy. Stalin pursued it as vigorously as he dared. After Tomsky's removal from the Politburo in the summer of 1930, A. I. Rykov was displaced in December, and the trusted Molotov succeeded him as Premier. In March 1931 Stalin carried out a 'show trial' of alleged Menshevik 'wreckers', to discredit former Mensheviks employed in economic planning, who had criticized Stalinist cruelties and crudities, and exiled Mensheviks who had exposed collectivization, as well as to intimi-date other potential opposition elements within Russia. After this dis-ciplining, criticism of Stalin died down until late autumn 1932. Then the great famine and increasing industrial difficulties provoked further Right Wing criticisms and demands were secretly voiced for his removal. Large-scale 'wrecking' activities were immediately discovered. The Left Wing leaders Kamenev and Zinoviev were alleged (probably correctly) to sympathize with Right Wing demands for an end to collectivization and for Stalin's removal. Stalin wished to launch the kind of terror which came later in the purges, but a majority on the Politburo opposed this. Kamenev and Zinoviev were again expelled from the Party, and forced like the Rightists publicly to recant, while Stalin seized the opportunity to enforce his own ideological line more strictly. Yet before the crisis ended, Stalin was sufficiently shaken to offer in November his resignation to the Polit-buro, thus forcing it to declare its confidence in him. Further to strengthen himself he instituted in January 1933 a bloodless purge which lasted for three years, and reduced Party membership by half. N. I. Yezhov, another Stalin henchman who achieved notoriety as head of the secret police in the blood-letting which came afterwards, took a leading part in this purge. In March 1933 Stalin put on another trial of 'wreckers', this time of British engineers, to cover up his failures. However he had to make concessions to both peasantry and proletariat. The second Five-Year Plan was less brutal and more realistic than its predecessor.

The first Five-Year Plan dominated Soviet foreign as well as domestic policy, and not only because economic problems generally dominated international relations in the early thirties. Soviet Russia needed peace no less desperately after 1929 to allow her to implement the plan than she had done when recovering from the First Bolshevik Revolution and Civil War. Comintern continued to preach subversion abroad, and from 1928 there could be no doubt that it was the instrument of Moscow and not of foreign Communist Parties. But though Stalin continued to denounce capitalist imperialists and sought to prevent what turned out to be their imaginary attempts to establish a bloc against Russia, he proclaimed his desire for friendship with all countries which would assist in strengthening Russia's economy. On July 5th, 1930, Stalin declared, as he was to do consistently for years, that 'Our policy is a policy of peace and strengthening of trading relations with all countries'.

The plans certainly implied good relations with the capitalist world and necessitated Russia's reappearance on the world market, though they also sought to make her an autarchic as well as a great military power. The slump hampered the improvement of economic relations, and great efforts were required to raise her percentage of world trade from 1·36% in 1928 to 1·95% in 1931, after which it dropped back to 1·44% in 1932 (in 1913 it had been 3·8%). After the resumption of Anglo-Russian diplomatic relations in 1929 trade with Britain increased until late 1931, when the British exchange controls reduced it, and in 1933 British resentment at the engineers' victimization led to the suspension of trade for a time. With France little could be done at first because of the slump and resentment at Lenin's repudiation of Tsarist debts, but Russia's bargaining position was strong because of her oil exports to France, French anxieties about Germany, and French hopes that Russia might form some sort of counterpoise to Germany in eastern Europe. Hence a combination of economic and strategic factors led France in 1931 to consider *rapprochement* with Russia.

However it was above all with Germany that the first plan necessitated good relations, for Germany supplied much of the equipment for it as well as purchasing raw materials and giving military advice and aid. Despite her own difficulties as the depression deepened, and despite the reduction of Soviet export trade in face of the slump, Germany retained a dominating position in Russian foreign trade. This had important political consequences when relations between the two countries became difficult after 1932.

America, best placed of all for trade with Russia, did not take advantage of the opportunity, though some large industrial firms gave credit before and even during the depression. In 1930 America was responsible for 25% of Russia's import trade, against Germany's 24%, but in 1932 the figures were 5% and 46% respectively. It was only when Roosevelt became President that America granted recognition to the Soviet government. Even after that there was no improvement in economic relations, though the fault for that lay mainly with Russia. Russia's anxiety about her Far Eastern and European positions was clearly manifested in the early thirties with the establishment of her Far Eastern base against Japan, the drive to improve communications throughout the Soviet Union for strategic as well as economic reasons, and the building up of new industrial complexes in the Urals, away from the exposed western frontier. America was suspect in Soviet eyes as the citadel of capitalism but she was not considered an opponent in either theatre. America was indeed wooed by Russia after Japan had attacked Manchuria, but even in dealing with an unmistakably isolationist America, the Russians could not bring themselves to drop the crudities of their ideological and cultural outlook on the outside, capitalist world. Especially during the early years of the second Five-Year Plan, when the Ural-Siberian region was being transformed by the development of such industrial centres as Stalingrad and the opening up of remote areas, American economic and technological aid would have been invaluable. Russian xenophobia and ideological antipathy to America prevented this aid from being given.

## (iv) *The Crisis in Manchuria: The End of the Postwar Years*

Russia dealt one of the earliest blows at world peace in November 1929 with her punitive expedition into Manchuria, after attempts by Chang Tso-lin to end Soviet 'special interests' there, and after Kuomintang attacks on her interests in China. General Blücher, formerly Chiang Kai-shek's military adviser, needed only one division and sixty planes to rout Chinese forces in Manchuria within ten days. Russia did not seek to press her advantage, demanding only that China should respect treaty obligations. Russia indeed vigorously denounced 'probable' capitalist instigation of the Chinese, and got her own way in Manchuria, though not in China proper. When the Japanese, intensely interested observers of Russia's reaction to Chinese encroachments, launched their Manchurian incident, Russia began to react only after they occupied Changchung, junction of the Japanese-owned South Manchurian Railway and the Soviet-controlled Chinese Eastern Railway. As Japanese ambitions became more obvious Russia became more alarmed, but accompanied threats with offers of a non-aggression pact, both of which Japan ignored. Even Japan's military occupation of Manchuria and establishment of a puppet *régime* provoked only Soviet assertions that a new capitalist war of intervention was being planned, but that capitalist forces were divided, since behind the American-Japanese imperialist conflict loomed the greater imperialist clash between Britain and America. How much of this the Russians believed is uncertain, but they were serious when they warned Japan on March 1932 against encroaching on Soviet territory—which was admittedly unlikely in view of Japan's other commitments. From May 1932 Russo-Japanese tension began to diminish as a Japanese attack could obviously be no longer considered likely. Russia remained eager to restore the diplomatic relations with China which had been broken in 1929 (they were in fact restored in December 1932), and to establish good political relations with America. Radek in July 1932 asserted in an American learned journal that Japanese aggression would be resumed with British blessing as anti-Chinese and anti-American, and that Russia would collaborate with any power desiring the peaceful development of the Far East. There was no response. America would not resist aggression even in Britain's company, and certainly not in Russia's, whose motives she then suspected far more.

Japan had not differed greatly before September 1931 from other countries with interests in China, in her reactions to Chinese attempts to destroy her rights and privileges in Manchuria, Shantung and the Yangtse. She had, however, realized that Chinese nationalism, if victorious, would first expel foreigners from China, and then try to reassert old imperialist claims to neighbouring territories—hence to Manchuria and Korea. She was also concerned at the growth of Chinese Communism and at Soviet expansion in Outer Mongolia.

When the depression began, the *zaibatsu* had reached the height of their power in Japan. They were intimately connected with the political parties and the government. They had extensive interests in every important branch of industry as well as dominating finance and commerce, and the party governments had to give considerable attention to their demands. The finance minister of the Minseito cabinet which took office in July 1929 had married into the leading Mitsubishi family, and Shidehara was also related to it. The onset of the depression, however, destroyed the cabinet, and the alliance of politicians and *zaibatsu*.

Japan's chief economic difficulty was the fall in raw silk prices. Raw silk formed two-fifths of Japan's exports, most of it to America, so the American collapse had catastrophic effects. In 1930 raw silk exports declined in volume by 18% and in value by 47%. Japan further depended heavily on cotton and silk manufactures, which represented 28% of the 1929 total, and also went mainly to America. To increase Japan's difficulties, her orthodox financiers restored her to the gold standard at par in 1930 when her prices were far too high to justify it and the world depression was gathering speed. The fall in prices ruined silk farmers, the decline in cotton manufacture meant unemployment for their daughters, and low rice prices further depressed the peasantry.

Peasants formed the rank and file of the army, and Northern Japan, which was hardest hit, supplied many recruits. The middle and small landowners also provided many officers, so that the army felt immediate and deep concern. To reduce the budget deficit, the government proposed in the summer of 1931 to decrease military and naval expenditure—this after having already infuriated the Naval General Staff by accepting at the London Naval Conference of 1930 a smaller ratio of ships than the navy wanted, though it sufficed for Pacific naval supremacy. Japan did not have the resources to maintain both a large army and a large navy without seriously straining her economy, but acceptance of the terms provoked an outcry in which many politicians joined. The premier, Hamaguchi Yuko, however, insisted on maintaining the cabinet's supremacy in matters of high policy even when they affected the navy—and so by implication the army also. Army officers stirred up opposition to the cabinet not only on this account, but for its policy in Manchuria. A nationalist fanatic shot Hamaguchi in November 1930. He attempted for a time to retain office, but made way in April 1931 for the much weaker Wakatsuki, and died that year from the effects of his wounds.

In 1931 the army's protests came to a head with parliamentary government weak and discredited. The Kwantung Army launched the Manchurian Incident on September 18th, three days before Britain's abandonment of the gold standard, and the two actions combined to depreciate the Japanese *yen* so severely that the government fell in December. With its fall ended attempts to pursue orthodox financial and economic policies. The depression also stimulated the young officers in Manchuria to try to redress Japan's economic balance by increasing the exploitation of Manchuria and thereby helping their own and their men's families, but the triangular conflict between Japan, China and Russia for control of Manchuria had long threatened an explosion. Defeat at Russian hands in 1929 had merely stimulated the new Manchurian ruler, the Young Marshal Chang Hsüeh-liang, to act more vigorously against Japanese interests. Moreover, the Kwantung Army could not tolerate his readiness to co-operate with the Kuomintang. Junior officers in Manchuria, not the Army General Staff in Tokyo or the government, ordered the blowing up of a section of the South Manchurian Railway as the pretext for taking Mukden on September 18th. The next step was intended to be the taking over of all Manchuria.

This attack forced Chiang Kai-shek to drop his anti-imperialist drive against the west and appeal to it for help against Japan. His idea was simple. He instructed Chang not to resist the Japanese, on the grounds that resistance would enlarge the incident, while Chiang himself appealed to the League to end the incident. The League twice demanded Japanese withdrawal, but the Kwantung Army was not susceptible to moral pressure from Geneva, and the Japanese government could not control it. Hence the incident led Japan into what her people called the 'dark valley', the period of ten years between the Manchurian Incident and Pearl Harbor. If the emperor had ordered the Kwantung Army to withdraw it would probably, though not certainly, have done so. Doubtless army extremists would have resisted, and this led senior officers and even cabinet ministers to shrink from decisive action of the sort that Hamaguchi could have enforced. The militarists immediately saw how to exploit their advantage both against their own moderate superior officers and civilian politicians. Henceforth they could force on the cabinet the line of policy which led to the attack on China in 1937, and later to entry into World War II.

The Manchurian crisis seriously damaged the League's prestige and marked the first major breach in the international structure established after 1918. However, its effects on collective security were exaggerated at the time, and even more so after World War II had begun. Collective security had had only a limited existence in Europe, and none elsewhere. Britain deplored Japan's forcible methods but recognized that Japanese complaints had considerable justification. Britain would do nothing without American support, and America even originally opposed the sending out of the Lytton Commission by the League to investigate the situation in Manchuria. Britain, the only League power with extensive interests involved, was preoccupied with the financial crisis and thought the League's function was to conciliate. Indeed, China herself did not break off relations with Japan, though she enforced an economic boycott. The major League powers never considered economic, still less military sanctions. Apart from splutters by Secretary Stimson, which President Hoover suppressed, America's voice was firmly against interference with American-Japanese trade, which provided most of Japan's strategic imports and even in 1936 took 22% of her exports (as against 43% in 1929). As no outside opposition developed, the Kwantung Army rapidly occupied all southern Manchuria, ignoring its own government. Wakatsuki's promises to the League and to America that Japanese troops would return to their former bases once order had been restored were sincere, but in December his government fell. The new cabinet of Inukai Tsuyoshi was dominated by the army and Japan moved rapidly towards a police-state *régime*. Most politicians and members of the old *zaibatsu* were terrorized into acquiescence, as the militarists proclaimed themselves guardians of the nation's 'essence' against foreign capitalism and democracy. New *zaibatsu* arose who collaborated wholeheartedly with them, especially in Manchuria.

All Japanese, liberals or militarists, regarded Manchuria as essential for Japan's economy and for defence of her strategic interests against Russia, and it was only a matter of time before it was completely absorbed. It was not the policy of even the militarists to attempt to conquer the whole of China, still less to attack western powers. However, once embarked on the Manchurian adventure, the militarists found that they could neither abandon it on 'honourable' terms nor end it by defeating Chinese resistance. By January 1932 the Kwantung army controlled all China north of the Great Wall except for Jehol province. To give some legalist substance to Manchuria's annexation they called on February 29th an all-Manchurian convention in Mukden, as a preliminary to establishing the former Emperor Pu-yi on March 9th as ruler of their puppet state, which they named Manchukuo. By then fighting had spread to Shanghai and affected its international settlements. By the time British forces reached Shanghai the fighting there had died down, and Japan gave satisfactory assurances to Britain about the settlements. The proclamation of the Manchukuoan *régime*, however, which had the full backing of the Japanese government, was a different matter. In February Stimson had revived Bryan's 1915 doctrine of non-recognition of territorial and political changes made by force, and invited other powers to support his stand. Hoover, who had suggested the move, refused to go further. Britain proposed the League's acceptance of the doctrine and this was duly carried in March, but nobody dreamed of forcibly preventing the Japanese from tightening their hold on Manchukuo. In September 1932 agreements between Japan and her puppet formalized the exploitation. Effective control, however, stayed with the Kwantung army.

Exploitation of Manchukuo's resources and the building up of an extensive industrial base there were important elements in Japan's new economic policy starting in 1932. This policy introduced a virtual war economy, and reshaped her foreign trade. Inukai's murder on May 15th by naval officers and army cadets ended party cabinets, for henceforth the army refused to provide war ministers to cabinets headed by party leaders, and promoted the militarization of the nation as well as of its economic life. The new policy nevertheless brought considerable gains to the industrial and commercial classes in general, as well as to the new *zaibatsu*. By 1933 the depression had been mastered. The economy would probably have recovered if governments had spent money on public works instead of on armaments, but it was in fact based on an armament boom. The volume of exports in 1936 exceeded 1929's by about 60% when world trade was still stagnating, and much of the increase was at the expense of western competitors in the Asian markets, especially of British textile manufacturers. Losses in the United States market were more than replaced by gains in Latin America, Africa, Europe, Australasia, India, the Dutch colonies, and above all in North China and Manchukuo. This showed remarkable flexibility in face of a world catastrophe. It also demonstrated increasing dependence on imports from America of strategic materials, as war needs swallowed up more of the economy after 1932, thereby eventually putting before the militarists irresistible temptation to gamble for higher stakes. If it was not too late in 1931 for Japan to retrace her steps, it was after the Manchurian crisis.

## (v) *The Crisis in American Capitalism: the End of Laisser Faire*

Even during the height of the prosperity of the later twenties there had been signs of weakness in America's economy. Large areas of the South remained depressed, and others semi-depressed. Nothing was done to stop the slump in agriculture that set in during 1920, and by 1929 gripped large areas of the mid-west. The decline of certain old industries such as textiles had caused unemployment in the north-east, and in the pre-depression months of 1929 unemployment had been about two million. Also, prosperity had been unevenly shared. Manufacturing productivity had increased by approximately 43% per worker between 1919 and 1929, but wages had remained comparatively stable. Costs and prices fell, while profits rose. Much of the profits was invested in industry, though not enough, especially when the mania for speculation mopped up nearly all the available money. But there was under-consumption of consumer goods. The 5% of the population with the highest incomes in 1929 took about a fifth of the available income, so the middle and lower classes, buying in the mass markets for food and other essential or non-luxury goods, had too little purchasing power. Moreover, in the general prosperity lax banking practices had become widespread, and the Federal Reserve Board's easy money policy had encouraged them as well as the speculation itself. Though Hoover had foreseen since 1925 that a speculative mania would develop, he had not foreseen its extent or the consequences of its collapse. Neither as Secretary nor as President had he taken restraining action.

The government's financial policy was largely responsible for fundamental weaknesses in the economy. Rigid adherence to the gold standard made it difficult to control the supply of money; no supervision was maintained over the Federal Reserve Board's policy; and the idea of establishing in the national interest a balance between public and private financial sectors was inconceivable to orthodox financiers, Democratic and Republican. More important still was the Republican administration's refusal, following Wilson's unfortunate precedent, to admit responsibilities in international finance. Instead it left to private banks the responsibility of establishing the credit system for European recovery. The official contribution was to keep high tariff barriers, to make it as difficult as possible for foreign debtors to sell in the American market in order to make repayments of war and postwar debts more tolerable. In 1929 these repayments still depended in the main on fresh credit supplies to Europe, so the ending of these credits would inevitably bring international disaster. The 1929 figures of American foreign trade and credits made that clear. America had for 1929 a favourable trading balance and war debt repayment totalling $1,642,000,000, but to maintain the system she had to invest abroad $1,037,000,000, since European earnings from American sources were comparatively insignificant.

Europe was not the only great field of American investment, nor the most dangerous. Extensive credit was given to Latin American governments of dubious financial and political stability, and many of these loans could not be recovered even in part. At the end of 1930 investments in Latin America totalled $5,243,986,000 as against $4,929,277,000 in Europe, $3,941,693,000 to Canada and Newfoundland, and $1,560,072,000 to Africa, Asia and Oceania. The overwhelming majority of investments were made in speculative deals on the New York Stock Exchange. In 1925 the market value of stocks listed there had been $27,000,000,000 but by October 1st, 1929, this had risen to $87,000,000,000. In September some anxiety had been shown about the stability of the market but it had steadied. Then from October 15th considerable withdrawals were made, though discreetly, until prices began to fall quickly on October 21st. After a brief rally, panic selling on October 24th ('Black Thursday') of nearly 13,000,000 shares knocked the bottom out of the market, and ruined many brokers and hundreds of thousands of small investors who had hoped for quick profits. So ludicrously inflated had stock prices become that immense losses were certain when the bubble inevitably burst, but a sound economy and financial leadership could have averted the national disaster which now ensued. After another rally due to intervention by some leading banks, the greatest upheaval came on October 29th. Nearly 16,500,000 shares were involved and the bottom was again knocked out of the market. Matters then got progressively worse, for future rallies were more than cancelled out by relapses. By the end of October the average stock loss was 40%, or the paper equivalent of $15,000,000,000. From September to the end of 1929 the loss had reached about $40,000,000,000. The loss to the American people was incalculable, for the financial collapse turned the recession into depression, by exposing the fragile structure of the credit system.

Hoover and other orthodox financiers continued to assert that the economy would right itself. Hoover had created in June 1929 a non-partisan Federal Farm Board by his Agricultural Marketing Act to lend money to agricultural co-operatives, so that they could market products efficiently and hold them if prices declined. Under Senate pressure Hoover agreed that the Board could intervene to stabilize prices. It might have been able to underwrite efficient and economical farming in normal conditions, and it succeeded in keeping domestic prices slightly above world prices until mid-1931. Then the European crisis and wheat dumping by Russia, Argentina and Australia brought wheat prices down still further, from $1.04 a bushel in 1929 to $0.67 in 1930 to $0.39 in 1931. The Hawley-Smoot Tariff of 1930 was equally ineffective except for supporting meat and dairy prices, but this slight advantage to agriculture was far outweighed by the reactions towards higher tariffs which it stimulated abroad, and industry gained nothing from it. In mid-1932 the Board openly admitted failure, and in December asked Congress to restrict acreage and production to prevent further disaster. By that time gross farm income had dropped from its 1929 level of $11,941,000,000 to $5,331,000,000.

In 1929 there were 659 bank failures involving nearly $250,000,000 deposits, rising in 1930 to 1,352 banks with $853,000,000 deposits and in 1931 to 2,294 banks with $1,700,000,000 deposits. This forced Hoover to act before the financial system completely disintegrated. Against opposition from politicians even more conservative and *laisser faire* in their views, he established in January 1932 the Reconstruction Finance Corporation with $500,000,000 capital and power to borrow another $1,500,000,000 to underpin banks, financial houses, railways and building and loan associations. This stemmed the collapse so that in 1932 only 1,456 banks with $750,000,000 deposits failed, and in February the Federal Reserve Banks were allowed to expand the currency, and release $1,000,000,000 for foreign withdrawals of gold, to help to restore the international economy. In addition the Federal Home Loan Bank Act in July provided $125,000,000 to permit savings banks, insurance companies, and building and loan associations to obtain cash without foreclosing on homes. All these moves, like the agricultural regulation powers demanded by the Board, foreshadowed the New Deal, but they were too little and too late. Hoover's tardy niggardliness was partly due, however, to the general belief in the summer of 1931 that the recession was ending. His appeals to employers to maintain wage rates had been observed until then so far as possible, though in the summer of 1930 production had been cut. Hoover still strove to balance the budget, but this was an article of faith for Democrats also, and they demanded in the 1932 Presidential campaign an 'immediate and drastic reduction of government expenditure' to cut the cost of government by at least 25%. Added to the difficulties imposed by this shibboleth was an irrational fear of inflation which kept interest rates high and credit tight. In March 1930 Roosevelt, as Governor of New York, had worked to stabilize unemployment, relieve distress and expand public works, measures which bore fruit in considerably alleviating the state's economic problems and giving him a great majority when he stood for a second term in November. This put Roosevelt in the running for the Presidential nomination, though in the end it was attained with great difficulty. As Governor of the greatest state he challenged Hoover while agreeing with him on fundamentals like objecting to federal relief expenditure, because it assumed tasks that properly fell to state and private agencies, and demanding balanced budgets and reduced government expenditure. First for the gubernatorial and then for the Presidential election, however, he attacked Hoover's immobility and strengthened his own reputation as a man of action. After Presidential nomination in July 1932, won with the aid of some dubious allies (including Huey Long, who supported him 'only because he had seen the other contenders'), Roosevelt pledged his party and himself to 'a new deal for the American people' and promised work, security and fairer distribution of incomes. His electoral campaign did indeed vaguely foreshadow the future New Deals, but it was his self-confidence and belief in American powers of recovery which carried him to victory.

After the victory matters were nearly as bad as ever, but he refused

Hoover's invitation to approve the Republican policies—any credit they incurred would revert to Hoover, whereas Roosevelt would share Hoover's unpopularity while reducing his own freedom of manoeuvre. Moreover he had decided on inflation to meet the deepening crisis, and could not make this known yet. In October 1932 another financial crisis began to loom. By January 1933 there was panic again. In February nearly all states closed their banks or restricted banking operations. When Roosevelt took office in March national income and industrial productivity were half those of 1929; manufacturing wages were 60% lower; salaries were 40% lower and dividends nearly 57% lower; foreign trade had slumped by about two-thirds; unemployment was again about 12,000,000. Although Hoover had, as he pathetically claimed in the election campaign, weathered the worst of the storm, there was a continuation of mass evictions of farmers and houseowners who had mortgaged their properties, and of tenants who could not pay rents. Hospitals, schools, public services of all kinds and the railways were still being inadequately maintained. The bread lines and vagrancy of the destitute, the shanty slums of the poverty-stricken whites which had been called Hoovervilles in derision of the President who had promised prosperity, were as much in evidence as before.

There were, however, signs of recovery. Otherwise Roosevelt's rapid moves towards balancing the budget by heavy cuts in federal expenditure (in strict Hooverite fashion) and measures to control banking would not have had such immediate effect in restoring confidence, and inspiring the trust which was soon to make him the hope not only of his own people but of most of the democratic nations who faced the prospect of either Fascism or Bolshevism if democracy failed.

*Chapter VII*
THE NEW DEAL AND THE AMERICAS

(i) *Roosevelt's 'Conservative Revolution'*

BY MARCH 1933 America's economic machinery had broken down, her system of government had proved inadequate, and even the fabric of American society was threatened. There were an estimated 12,000,000 unemployed, and possibly twice as many relying on public relief or private charity. Mid-Western farmers were forcibly resisting foreclosure on their farms. The notorious Senator Huey Long demonstrated for two years before his assassination in September 1935 that a Fascist dictatorship could gain control of Louisiana, and therefore possibly of other states. Strong action was needed to avert economic, political and social catastrophe, and Roosevelt promised to provide it. His inaugural address of March 4th, 1933, proclaimed that Americans had not failed, that 'the only thing we have to fear is fear itself', that 'direct vigorous action' would bring recovery, and that America's essential democracy would survive.

The unprecedented burst of legislation of Roosevelt's First New Deal of 1933–34 gave the leadership which his people craved, and made him the most dominating and dynamic president in American history. Yet much of its programme was long overdue, most was conservative rather than radical, and none was really revolutionary. It altered neither the basis of the economy nor that of the system of government, but strengthened and improved both by bringing finance, agriculture and industry under firmer federal control, exercised by more effective executive and presidential leadership. Its insistence on protecting the employment, general welfare and security of Americans had been foreshadowed under Theodore Roosevelt and Wilson, and it was the depression which finally convinced most Americans that state power must be invoked to safeguard the nation's economy and the citizen's livelihood.

The banking system was not overhauled, though the Banking Act of June 1933 extended the Federal Banks' operations in the open markets, and began on a small scale the practice of insuring deposits on federal guarantee to prevent recurrence of the 1929–33 panics. Currency manipulations and abandonment of the gold standard (until January 1934) were equally unorthodox measures but were widely approved. So was Roosevelt's decision to drop his attempt to balance the budget and reduce federal expenditure, in favour of deficit budgeting which increased the federal debt from its 1932 figure of about $20,000,000,000 to nearly $50,000,000,000 by 1940. Less popular, except with farmers, were attempts to plan agricultural production at the taxpayer's expense by the Agricultural Adjustment Act of May 1933, which the Supreme Court in January 1936 ruled unconstitutional. It was certainly, like the Tennessee Valley Authority Act (also of May 1933), a clear breach with traditional American insistence on a 'weak state' and *laisser faire* government as bulwarks of individual liberty. TVA was designed not merely to develop the region's water power but to promote its inhabitants' general welfare. Government operation through TVA of power-plant, industrial and agricultural undertakings further implied that American, like European, capitalism must accept some degree of Socialism in public utilities. Even though a running fight developed between 1935 and 1937 over the Supreme Court's nullification of some New Deal progressive legislation, the Court upheld TVA's use of the nation's resources for the people's own benefit over protests from vested interests and old-fashioned individualists.

Roosevelt did not seek dictatorship, as many reactionary or ultra-conservative Democrats and Republicans alleged. The eventual failure of the attempt by the Supreme Court's die-hard members to defeat the New Deal was rightly and generally regarded as a vindication of what he called 'new applications of old democratic processes'. He saved American political democracy from the gravest dangers facing it since the Civil War and strengthened American capitalism when its future was highly uncertain. His most controversial (and least effective) measure, the National Recovery Administration (NRA) of June 1935, aimed at promoting active industrial self-government while safeguarding general interests. It protected honest manufacturers against cut-throat competition by framing 'codes of fair competition' which even big business originally favoured, despite its distrust of the New Deal. NRA's first task was greatly to extend Hoover's grudging federal expenditure on public works in order to 'pump prime' the stalled economy and reduce unemployment. It further assisted labour through presidential fixing of minimum wages, maximum hours and conditions of employment, by guaranteeing freedom of trade union organization and collective bargaining, and by protecting consumer interests in general. However NRA's popularity and effectiveness rapidly waned, for it created more problems than it solved. The Supreme Court's 1935 ruling that the National Industrial Recovery Act which had established NRA was unconstitutional was widely approved, and probably relieved the administration of an embarrassment, though it denounced the ruling. NIRA's main impact, like that of most New Deal legislation, had been psychological and propagandist, though it conclusively demonstrated the lesson of preceding emergency legislation: that future American governments would not supinely tolerate the advent of another collapse like the one which had started in 1929. NIRA's labour provisions were eventually re-enacted in better and more acceptable forms, though no comprehensive government economic policy was formulated. Roosevelt was too staunch a supporter of free enterprise to attempt a fully planned economy. The reforms of the First, and more especially of the Second New Deal of 1935–38, were designed to make American capitalism more profitable and stable, not te replace it with Socialism or with the kind of 'mixed', Socialist-capitalist compromise economies generally established by western European countries after 1945.

The repeated contemporary charges that New Deal 'creeping Socialism' was destroying free enterprise had no solid basis; there was less Socialism in Roosevelt's America than in Bismarck's Germany. His attack on unemployment through the May 1935 WPA (Works Progress Administration) upheld the right to work, and together with the great Social Security Act of August inaugurated the Second New Deal. Few Americans regarded the demand for the right to work as specifically Socialist, or felt that in recognizing obligations to provide security for less fortunate citizens (the aged and children, disabled and temporarily unemployed workers) the moral fibre of a capitalist nation was being destroyed.

The nation's confidence in the New Deal was unmistakably demonstrated in the 1936 Presidential election when Roosevelt polled 27,751,597 popular and 523 electoral votes against the Republican Landon's 16,679,583 popular and only eight electoral votes. Yet in 1937 there were still over 7,000,000 unemployed, production and private investment remained low (partly from big business's distrust of Roosevelt, but mainly because the depression had been so long and severe) and another collapse began. Despite this, the Second New Deal cut the ground from under the feet of Long's heirs and other Fascists trying to organize lower middle and working class onslaughts on wealth and property. Roosevelt's defence of liberal democracy against these enemies (many of them Roosevelt's supporters in 1932 when they had mistaken his essentially democratic temper) and against the less numerous and dangerous Communists, was virtually complete before foreign affairs became his major preoccupation.

The New Deals also disappointed Roosevelt's more idealistic adherents by not creating a new form of American society. Nevertheless, their progressive trends proved irreversible: no Republican *laisser faire* reaction of the 1920s' type was henceforth possible. Their long-term effects were to give greater central control over the social and economic structures while avoiding a planned economy and an unacceptable degree of government regimentation, to redistribute national income more equitably through a more democratic system of federal taxation, and to give greater security to both capital and labour. Above all they equipped the United States to meet in time the challenges of World War II.

Neither Roosevelt nor his supporters foresaw this vindication of the New Deals, though in January 1939 he avowedly turned from New Deal internal reform to meet the dangers to American security from abroad.

467

Measures originally framed to counter the continuing depression were converted by pressure of events into the great industrial, agricultural and armament programmes which from the summer of 1940 formed the basis for the greater expansion developed explicitly to defend the western hemisphere. This in turn made possible America's decisive role in World War II and in the ensuing nuclear age, and was also popularly approved when Roosevelt stood for an unprecedented third term in the autumn of 1940.

The foreign policy thus endorsed had altered radically from its beginnings in 1933 when it had been avowedly isolationist. To gain the newspaper tycoon Hearst's support for the Presidential nomination, Roosevelt in February 1932 had disowned his Wilsonian internationalist past, and repudiated the League of Nations and all ideas of involving America in 'foreign difficulties'. Indeed, during his first four years as President he had too many internal problems to have much time to spare for foreign difficulties, as well as a strongly isolationist nation to govern. His first major step in foreign affairs, refusal to co-operate in international monetary regulations in case this hampered American economic recovery, destroyed the London Economic Conference. Next he reversed Hoover's attempts to bring about the cancellation of war debts. His *de jure* recognition in November 1933 of Soviet Russia implied no internationalist reorientation of American foreign policy, though in retrospect the renewal of American-Russian relations proved to be a major factor in bringing these two powers first to resume the interest shown by them in European affairs before isolationist trends had dominated their policies, and then to dominate European politics. Despite the tension created by Soviet economic and ideological obstructive tendencies, Roosevelt developed the illusion that he had a special understanding of Stalin. He did not share Wilson's genuine concern for Europe, and his readiness after both America and Russia were involved in World War II to believe in an enduring American-Russian partnership was no new miscalculation. Roosevelt's Far Eastern policy was at first no more than waiting on events. Japan's conquest of Manchukuo remained unrecognized, but no positive measures were taken against Japanese aggression, and as far as possible he ignored it.

Only towards Latin America was an active policy followed. Pursuing the 'good neighbour' ideas announced in his inaugural address, Roosevelt ended intervention in Latin American internal affairs, and at the December 1933 Seventh Pan-American Conference at Montevideo, Secretary of State Cordell Hull accepted the principle of non-intervention, now approved by all member countries, thereby greatly easing United States relations with her neighbours during the next critical years. The May 1934 Cuban treaty abrogated the objectionable Platt amendment; the worst manifestations of dollar diplomacy in the Caribbean in particular and Latin America in general came to an end; and the 1936 Buenos Aires Pan-American Conference, which Roosevelt himself addressed, agreed to consultation if the continent's peace was endangered, and to neutrality in any inter-American conflict.

Otherwise Roosevelt followed the trend of public opinion. He accepted the Neutrality Acts of 1935, 1936 and 1937 which actually abandoned neutral rights of trading with belligerents in order to ensure that America was not 'drawn into' foreign wars as in 1917, and which legally obliged him to follow this interpretation of neutrality when war came in 1939. By October 1937 Roosevelt was sufficiently impressed by the growing danger of unchecked aggression to American security to make his 'quarantine speech' calling for 'concerted action' against aggressors. This aroused such hostility from isolationists and others (including Hull) whose internationalism stopped short of risking trouble with aggressors, that Roosevelt hurriedly drew back. The renewed Japanese aggression against China in July 1937 which provoked the speech produced no more concrete American reaction than sending a little aid to China, which was legal as Japan insisted that there was no war, and the May 1937 Neutrality Act empowered the President to decide when a state of war existed. In November Roosevelt rejected Britain's offer of naval support provided that America, Japan's greatest source of essential strategic materials, would take the lead in imposing sanctions.

In January 1938 Roosevelt proposed an international conference to promote disarmament, revise treaties peacefully, uphold international law, and give all countries equal access to raw materials. However, Neville Chamberlain, now British Prime Minister, thought peace would be best preserved by his own recipe for appeasing aggressors. Roosevelt disliked this policy but could hardly oppose it when he could take no positive action against aggressors, although in January 1938, and again in May 1939, Anglo-American staff talks were held which laid the basis for the increasingly close collaboration which took place after the outbreak of World War II. Probably nothing would have been achieved by the projected conference, and Roosevelt went as far as his own political prudence and United States public opinion permitted in 1938 by verbally opposing aggression in Europe and, at the December Pan-American Conference, prodding the reluctant Latin Americans into making the Lima Declaration. This stated that the countries of the Americas would defend themselves against foreign (i.e. European Fascist) intervention or activities threatening them.

In 1939 Roosevelt abandoned his futile attempts at disarmament, improved America's own defences and vigorously sought to educate his people out of their isolationism. Although their sympathies, like his, were openly with European democracy against Fascist dictatorship, there was no question of even diplomatic commitment against Fascist aggression before war came in September. Roosevelt could do no more to aid the democracies than to revise the Neutrality Act in November to enable them by 'cash and carry' provisions to buy and transport American munitions in their own ships. He might not have been able to do more even if he, and most Americans, had not mistakenly expected an early victory for the democracies. It took the shock of France's defeat and Britain's knife-edge

469

survival in the summer and autumn of 1940 to teach America that isolation-ism would not be feasible if Europe fell under the power of countries hostile to America's democratic ideology.

## (ii) *Latin America's 'Economic Policy Revolution'*

The Latin American states were more affected by the depression than by the greater catastrophe of 1914–18. It underlined even more emphatically their dangerous dependence on foreign capital and markets, and the precariousness of their economies. Their natural resources sufficed, if properly developed, to give most of them reasonable living standards, but this development presupposed greater political stability, unprecedented readiness to co-operate among themselves and with an outside world pre-occupied with other problems, and the evolution of policies aimed at ending the mass poverty and social injustice traditional in Latin America. The depression's first effect on the policies of the Latin American states was to intensify their economic nationalism, but in most of them efforts were also made to improve living standards. These generally involved large measures of government economic control under authoritarian *régimes*—ranging from the quasi-Fascist 'disciplined democracy' of Vargas's Brazil to Cárdenas's semi-Socialist Mexico, and from the Dominican Republic's 'Trujillo era' to Justo's Argentinian version of the New Deal.

The depression added large-scale unemployment to Latin America's problems, and still further lowered working class living standards by reducing the prices of the primary products which dominated her economy (especially coffee, her 'black blood'). It intensified her economic anarchy, and helped to precipitate revolutionary disturbances of varying intensity in eleven states. However, Central America, though suffering severely, continued to attract notice mainly because of the strategic significance of the Panama Canal to the United States. The depression exacerbated Panama's perennial anti-American popular sentiments, but rivalry for the presidency between Panama's leading political families was chiefly responsible for her political turmoil. In 1933 the United States promised full commercial rights in the Canal Zone, and in March 1936 formally ended the protectorate, thereby creating embarrassment when in 1941 the pro-Nazi President Arnulfo Arias had to be deposed for rejecting pressing American demands for bases as well as because of numerous sins against his own people.

Nicaragua was for Latin Americans an even sterner test of the 'good neighbour' policy introduced by Hoover and proclaimed by Roosevelt. Coolidge's costly and largely unsuccessful 1926–27 interventions in Nicaragua had forced the Republican administrations to grope their way towards the non-intervention policy, but effective and generally acceptable

470

methods of protecting United States interests in Latin America had still to be found. Territorial conquest remained unthinkable even when in the 1930s the growth of Japanese and of European Fascist aggression gave a substance, hitherto lacking, to United States arguments that it was essential to prevent non-American powers from threatening her vital interests there. The Nicaraguan administrations of José Maria Moncada (1929–33), whom Washington supported, and of Juan Sacasa (1933–36), whom it disliked, failed to establish a free and democratic system of government. In June 1936 Anastasio Somoza seized power by a military coup, and retained it until his assassination in 1956. His police state combined brutality and corruption with some modernization of agriculture and improved living standards.

Roosevelt's administration did nothing to assist the coup, having withdrawn American forces from Nicaragua in January 1933, but his benevolent attitude to Somoza's bloody *régime* horrified Latin American democrats and many United States citizens. It also cruelly exemplified the central dilemma of United States' relations with Latin America, and especially with Central America. From Wilson's time all American administrations wanted Latin America to be free and democratic, and their Latin American policies had not been nearly so oppressive as they might have been in view of the overwhelming military and economic superiority of the United States. Nevertheless the United States had a far worse reputation south of the Rio Grande than her citizens, and even many of her politicians suspected. Yet Latin American states either could not, or would not achieve democracy; and freedom for their peoples would certainly have meant, among other things, freedom to express violent hatred of 'Yankee imperialism' from Mexico to Argentina. Hence during World War II the crucial United States contribution to defeating Fascist aggression outside the western hemisphere depended in part on friendship towards Latin American dictatorships which showed little respect for human rights and liberties, when they were not actually Fascist, but which satisfied the overriding American demand that they should co-operate with Washington.

Between the depression's onset and the outbreak of war only Costa Rica, among the Central American states, enjoyed settled and orderly democratic government (apart from minor disturbances in 1932). El Salvador's economy, though highly industrialized by Latin American standards, depended largely on coffee, and the slump helped to bring about the ruthless and openly Fascist dictatorship of Maximiliano Hernández Martínez (1931–44). Honduras, the 'banana republic' *par excellence*, was also badly hit by the price collapse, but remained firmly controlled by the military dictatorship of Tiburcio Carías (1924–48), who in 1933 formally assumed the presidency. With the United Fruit Company's financial and political backing Carías defeated his democratic and Communist opponents, the latter category being interpreted, as in El Salvador and Guatemala, to include most enemies of the *régime*. The depression also facilitated the

471

establishment of the Guatemalan military dictatorship of Jorge Ubico (1931–44). He collaborated closely with Martínez and Carías to repress all opposition, and he followed domestic policies similar to theirs, though his concern for the poor was more genuine. Communism, however, was not a major Latin American problem in the 1930s, despite the professional anti-Communism of this unholy trinity and of other dictators, though in Leninist terms Latin America was ripe for social revolution with her mass poverty, discontented intelligentsias, ready-made bogey in the form of 'capitalist imperialist exploitation', falling prices of primary products, and rising populations.

The Caribbean island republics had similarly suffered from America's propensity for 'sending in the marines' when disturbed conditions threatened her interests, and it was in Haiti that Hoover had first made practical reparation. After virtually initiating the tolerably constitutional *régime* of Stenio Vincent in 1930, Hoover had prepared to end the bitterly resented occupation (finally terminated in 1934), and inaugurated considerable economic, social and administrative reforms. Because of American aid in the 1930s, and above all in World War II, Haiti's poverty was partly relieved, and she remained comparatively peaceful, but this aid could make no real impression on her economic and political backwardness.

American occupation of the Dominican Republic had ended in 1924, though it remained a financial protectorate until 1941 and its government depended on the support of the American-trained army, whose leader Rafael Leonidas Trujillo seized power in 1930. A comparatively enlightened dictator of the Latin American Caudillo variety in his early period, Trujillo improved health and education services, fostered industry, diversified agriculture to strengthen the economy, and balanced the budget while allowing relations and hangers-on to assist his pillaging of the public revenues. In 1937 he ordered Haitian Negro immigrants and casual labourers to be liquidated or expelled (perhaps 20,000 were involved), thereby shocking the Roosevelt administration into forcing him to make financial reparation for the butchery; however, in accordance with the accepted American interpretation of non-intervention, the administration did not withdraw its favour.

In Cuba, which by ending Negro immigration had also increased Haitian over-population, Gerardo Machado's dictatorship was precarious before the depression added economic disaster to political upheaval. Disregarding non-intervention obligations, America promoted his downfall, and sent warships to Cuba during the disorders which followed his deposition by the army in August 1933. However they were soon recalled, and Roosevelt refused to intervene again when in September ex-sergeant Fulgencio Batista made himself first chief of the army and then real ruler of Cuba. Batista was, in fact, soon acceptable in both North and Latin America. Though he made and unmade presidents virtually at will, his Fascist corporative *régime* adopted a radical and popular programme of social reform and state control of the sugar and mining industries. He did not outlaw opposition, and in 1937 actually set out to democratize Cuba. Trade unions received favoured treatment and the Communist Party was legalized. In 1939 reasonably free elections were held, and Communists supported the coalition which secured Batista's election as president in 1940. In 1944 he surprisingly did not seek to perpetuate his own presidency and went into temporary exile voluntarily on his nominee's defeat.

Under the dictatorship of Plutarco Elías Calles, Mexico reacted to the effects of the depression and of foreign economic domination by adopting a system of governmental paternalism which greatly resembled Mexico's pre-*laissez faire* system, except for its admixture of economic planning. Calles' six-year plan of 1933 proclaimed the need for state regulation of the economy. His favoured model was Hitler, but his successor Lázaro Cárdenas (1934–40), though Calles' own choice, was a moderate Marxist. Their developing personal and political antagonism forced Calles into exile, while the Mexican revolution reached its economic climax. Calles had done little for the individual peasants or the collective farms, the *ejidos*, but Cárdenas distributed about 45,000,000 acres between them (compared with 18,000,000 acres distributed between 1917 and 1932), and increased the number of *ejidos* from 4,000 to 20,000. Though agricultural productivity did not greatly increase, his revolutionary policy began Mexico's real economic progress. He nationalized the railways, backed labour in the government-dominated trade unions against employers (especially foreign capitalists) and completed in 1938 the expropriation of the oil companies. The British government denounced expropriation so violently that Mexico broke off diplomatic relations, but Roosevelt refused to jeopardize the achievements of the good neighbour policy for the sake of American oil interests. The compensation given them in 1942 was in fact fair, and Roosevelt's reaffirmation of the non-intervention principle, whatever the political complexion of the governments involved, had beneficial effects on United States relations with Latin America as a whole. Cárdenas maintained good relations with Roosevelt, whose New Deal considerably influenced Cárdenas's economic policies. Avila Camacho (1940–46) strengthened American–Mexican understanding even further. Though nominated by Cardenas, Avila Camacho pursued a moderate conservative policy, ending the dispute with the Church, and taking his support from the urban middle class, whereas Cardenas had relied on peasants, proletarians and a purged army. Avila Camacho encouraged private enterprise within the generally Socialist economy and fostered industrialization, which was further stimulated by American contracts during World War II amd by the war's impact. Although the economic boom set off by the war greatly increased the national income, it did little to improve the condition of the lower classes, who were as badly off in 1945 as in 1934.

The ABC states, Argentina, Brazil and Chile, underwent both political and economic transformation with the depression's onset. Hipólito Irigoyen's *régime* aroused mass discontent by its brutal repression of strikes in 1930, and was overturned by an Argentinian army coup led by General José F. Uriburu. Uriburu favoured a Mussolini-type corporative system, but though democratic institutions were rapidly eroded after 1930, Fascism did not come to power until Perón's election in 1946. In November 1931 Uriburu's Conservative-dominated coalition fraudulently secured the election of his presidential nominee, General Agustín P. Justo. Justo and his successors, Roberto M. Ortiz (1938–40) and Ramón S. Castillo (1940–43), reverted to a nineteenth century type of reactionary conservatism, dependent on army support and hostile to lower middle and working class interests. Justo brought economic recovery, though before World War II the 'Fifth Dominion', as Argentina was sometimes called, failed to reduce its dependence on the British market. An Anglo-Argentinian barter agreement, made in 1933 and renewed in 1936 until 1939, saved Argentina's agriculture and foreign trade at heavy cost. She had to treat British investors preferentially, reduce tariffs on British goods to 1930 levels which were intolerable under the prevailing conditions, and use sterling payments for her meat and grain to discharge debts to Britain, who undertook only to import at least as much Argentinian beef as in 1932. The treaty was severely criticized in Argentina for perpetuating her economic bondage, but United States complaints of discrimination against American trade received short shrift—partly from traditional anti-Americanism, partly from a resolve not to exchange vassalage to sterling for subjection to the dollar.

Otherwise Justo's recovery policy was popular as well as successful. It established a controlled economy through a new central bank affording stronger government control over banking, and through price control and regulation of crops and foreign exchange. Industry was encouraged, so that by 1939 its output was worth a fifth of Argentina's agricultural production, a considerable achievement by Latin American standards. The major beneficiaries of the recovery policy were not the urban middle and working classes, despite concessions to trade unions and the belated introduction of an income tax, but the landowning oligarchy, which increased its economic preponderance and united with the army and the rising Fascist groups to repress Liberal, Radical and Socialist opposition. The trend to Fascism was briefly interrupted between 1938 and 1940 when Ortiz, the coalition-nominated president, unexpectedly attempted to restore democratic institutions and favoured the Allied cause. Ill-health forced his resignation and the pro-Nazi Castillo reverted to naked fraud and violence. Castillo, however, aroused such hostility that the army, fearing the election of a second pro-Allied president, deposed him in June 1943 in order to forestall it. However the Conservatives repudiated the ensuing military dictatorship, and in the absence of support from the urban *bourgeoisie* and industrialists, the army under its rising star Perón at last turned to the lower middle and working classes.

Brazil also resorted to Fascism, greater industrialization and a controlled economy. The practically bloodless 'gay revolution' which inaugurated

Getulio Vargas's 'authoritarian democracy' derived from the state of São Paulo's attempt to retain the presidency, breaking the tradition whereby it alternated with Minas Gerais. Vargas, nominee of Minas Gerais, his own state of Rio Grande and the army, thereupon overthrew the republic, and ended its loose federalism together with its democratic institutions. A strongly centralized government was probably necessary to revive the collapsed economy and industrialize his 'New State'. Agricultural production was stabilized and rationalized, albeit by such irrational measures as burning or dumping into the sea unsaleable coffee, as well as by forbidding excessive coffee production and diversifying agriculture. Brazil had largely overcome the depression before Vargas's 1934 constitution gave a legal and genuinely popular basis to his *régime*, which had shown its strength in 1932 by easily defeating São Paulo's rebellious attempt to dictate to the rest of Brazil. It also inaugurated a coherent and planned economy. Subsoil resources were vested in the nation; banks and large sectors of industry (especially mining) were nationalized and government corporations directed industry, agriculture and foreign trade. The policy was effective and popular, though its extensive housing programme, increased wages and insurance benefits, and reduced working hours did not prevent considerable political opposition. Communists, however, were no longer a threat after Vargas crushed their attempted coup of 1935, while Radical and Socialist groups were irritations rather than dangers. On the other hand the pro-Hitler and pro-Mussolini para-military *Integralistas* gained such strength through Vargas's own early sympathy and Brazil's permeation by German economic and political interests, that their candidate for the presidential election due in January 1938 seemed certain of success. Vargas forestalled this in November 1937 by promulgating a new constitution, conferring absolute power on himself as head of the 'New State's' corporative political structure—which he, however, argued was not Fascist. His resentment of the German embassy's complicity in the *Integralista* putsch of May 1938 strained relations with Nazi Germany, but did not induce him to make his government more democratic or to feel any genuine warmth towards the democracies. It was growing suspicion of Hitlerian ambitions in Latin America, with Brazilian dependence on United States markets and finance, which aligned Vargas with the Allies in 1942, and his ideological commitment remained ambiguous.

However, American aid was essential for Brazil's economy, despite its considerable recovery since 1930. Brazil's *per capita* income of $50 in 1939 was barely over half the Latin American average. American aid in establishing the great Volta Redonda steel works in 1941 and subsequent aid and contracts began Brazil's most rapid period of industrialization. Vargas's genuine concern for the Brazilian masses ensured that some of the profits went to public works and social security. Even before 1941 he had made public health and educational reforms of a scope exceptional in Latin America, and in 1943 he enforced labour regulations which gave Brazil's industrial workers their first effective protection against exploitation. Finally, the enlightenment of his despotism fostered Brazil's architectural renaissance of the mid-1930s, which, under the Swiss Le Corbusier's influence, for a time in the 1950s led the architecture of the world.

Chile felt the depression's effects comparatively slowly, but her excessive dependence on the declining nitrate industry and on copper mining left her particularly vulnerable. As her political stability, like that of the other Latin American states, was largely based on government customs receipts, her exceptionally heavy loss of foreign trade caused comparable political upheaval. President Carlos Ibáñez's 'corporatization' of the nitrate industry in 1930 set an example widely followed in Latin America but failed to restore its prosperity. After rising economic and political discontent forced Ibáñez to resign in July 1930, violent anarchy ensued until in December 1932 Arturo Alessandri Palma was again elected president. His government retained the 1925 constitution, restored by judicial decree before his election, but moved from rigid conservatism to reaction. He gagged the opposition press, and exiled political opponents who criticized his ruthless suppression of a railway strike and dissolution of congress in 1936. By an austere economic policy Alessandri and Gustavo Ross, his finance minister, balanced the budget in 1937 and greatly strengthened and expanded Chilean industry before the 1938 elections. However, this was done at the expense of social services and the economy remained depressed.

The combination of political and social discontent produced in 1938 the phenomenon of a Popular Front of Radicals, Socialists and Communists which was supported by the Chilean Nazis after Alessandri's brutal defeat of a Nazi putsch in September 1938. Despite official intimidation and electoral corruption in favour of Ross, the Popular Front candidate Pedro Aguirre Cerda was elected president. A moderate radical, Aguirre Cerda was soon attacked by his allies—the Nazis because of his essentially democratic outlook and support for the Allies; the Socialists because some of them favoured Communism while others feared its growing influence in the government and trade unions; and the Communists because their slavish adherence to the Moscow line made them patently disloyal, until Hitler's invasion of Russia in June 1941 compelled them to attempt to rebuild the Popular Front which they had helped to end in January. Even the Radicals distrusted Aguirre Cerda, and on his death in November 1941, their right wing allied with the conservative groups to replace him with Juan Antonio Ríos. Aguirre Cerda's only success was the establishment in 1939 of the Chilean 'WPA', the *Corporación de Fomento*. However, Aguirre Cerda's CORFO, with United States financial backing and World War II contracts, put Chile firmly on the road to self-sufficiency after Chilean public opinion forced Ríos to break diplomatic relations with the Axis Powers in 1943.

The 'Indian' countries of the Andes reacted characteristically to the strains of the depression decade. Colombia's Conservative government's failure to solve the economic crisis was due to the slump in coffee prices, not to incompetence, but it was already divided and discredited after its long period of office. For most Latin American countries 1930 marked the beginning of a revolutionary era, but the moderate Colombian Conservatives broadly agreed with the aims of the new Liberal president, Olaya Herrera: social security, economic recovery, education reforms and establishment of minimum wages and maximum hours for labour. His firm but conciliatory stand against Peru's renewed attempt in 1932 to seize the remote jungle outpost of Leticia in the Amazon region was justified when Peru withdrew in 1934, though Leticia was important only for reasons of prestige. This success, and recovery from the worst effects of the slump thanks to her oil resources and advantages derived from the Panama Canal, produced a Liberal congressional electoral victory in 1934, and under Alfonso López Colombia adopted a New Deal policy which by 1938 made her politically the most progressive, stable and respected Latin American state. Moreover, her strong line against Nazi infiltration and firm friendship with the United States during World War II paid handsome dividends.

Ecuador, on the other hand, endured thirteen presidential upheavals from 1931 to 1940, mostly instigated by the army. However its toleration of Nazi infiltration, refusal to sanction sufficient social reform to satisfy the poverty-stricken masses, and confusing alternations of crudely repressive and comparatively liberal presidents produced in 1940 Arroyo del Río's election and the army's own eclipse. Arroyo's constitutional government looked to Washington for political and economic aid. It achieved steady though unspectacular progress, but fell in 1944 through having accepted, under pressure from Washington and Latin American capitals, a frontier settlement which grossly favoured Peru's territorial ambitions.

In Peru the depression emphasized the financial and economic incompetence of Augusto B. Leguía's dictatorship, and facilitated Leguía's overthrow by the army in August 1930. Nevertheless its nominee, Luis M. Sanchez Cerro, restored Leguia's brand of *caudillismo* in December 1931, after an interlude which saw Sánchez Cerro succeeded by three more presidents, and Haya de la Torre's return from exile to propound his mystical APRA (*Alianza Popular Revolucionaria Americana*) programme. This envisaged a united Indo- (geographically Latin) America which by embracing egalitarianism would enfranchize its Indian majority and all its women, nationalize land, industry, and the Panama Canal, and defy foreign capital. Sánchez Cerro defeated APRA by electoral fraud and repression, by imprisoning Haya and other leaders, by launching minimum social reforms, and by appealing to Peruvian chauvinism against APRA's internationalism. After Sánchez Cerro's assassination (possibly by an APRA supporter) in 1933, Oscar Benavides continued his policy until 1939, though more adroitly. As free elections would have given APRA power, he and Manuel Prado (1939–45) rigged them, and imprisoned or exiled its leaders. By 1945 Prado's moderately enlightened dictatorship, with wartime American aid (not least against Ecuador's territorial claims) had brought stability to the government and prosperity to Peru, while

APRA had been transformed into the essentially *bourgeois* People's Party. A free election in 1945 was won by the opposition coalition, dominated by Haya and the People's Party. By 1947 Haya and his party had achieved most of their realizable aims through their popularization of democratic ideals and weakening of Peruvian 'feudalism'.

Bolivia's chief concern in the 1930s was not with its economic plight, though United States loans had ended in 1929, and by 1933 Bolivia exported only 21,000 tons of tin at $33 a ton, as against 47,000 tons at $96 in 1927. Bolivian energies from 1932 to 1935 were concentrated on wresting from Paraguay the Gran Chaco territory, partly from desire to gain access to the Atlantic, partly from hope of Chaco oil deposits, and partly from frustrated chauvinism. Despite her larger and better equipped army, Bolivia was humiliatingly defeated, suffering in the process heavier economic losses than the depression itself inflicted, for the sake of a useless river port. Moreover, the war produced a revolutionary crisis, inflaming peasants, urban workers, intellectuals, and even army officers against landowners and industrialists. In 1936 a 'Socialist Republic' was proclaimed by junior officers whose model was Hitler rather than Lenin, though Standard Oil was expropriated and social welfare promised. By 1940, however, the military had sided with Conservatism, the mine-owners and finally the United States, despite popular hatred for America as the alleged author of the Chaco *débacle*. During World War II violence was endemic, for the immense demand for tin brought no advantage to the tin-miners or the Bolivian masses. The 1942 'Catavi massacre' of striking miners, supported by the rising *Movimiento Nacional Revolucionario*, which incongruously combined radicals, Perónista-type Fascists and Trotskyites, cleared the way for MNR's seizure of power.

Paraguay's attention had already been concentrated in 1928 on securing the Gran Chaco, where she was technically the aggressor though Bolivia was equally ready for war. Paraguay was too backward to be seriously affected by the depression, apart from some urban unemployment. Discontent over the Liberal President Eusebio Ayala's readiness to concede some of the area to Bolivia, under League of Nations and strong Latin American pressure, in February 1936 brought Ayala's overthrow by Rafael Franco's neo-Fascist *Febrerista*, or New Paraguay movement. Franco offered land redistribution, social benefits for urban workers, and respect for traditional conservative interests. This programme was largely adopted by the Liberals, restored by anti-Franco officers in August 1937, and by the military dictatorship of Higinio Morínigo (1940–48), which considerably increased Paraguay's rate of economic progress.

Uruguay, politically and economically the most progressive republic before the slump, saw her exports drop after 1929 by over four-fifths, as against the Latin American average of two-thirds. Mounting unemployment and bankruptcies threatened to undermine her democracy. Gabriel Terra, a president in the Liberal tradition from 1931 to 1933, gradually adopted repressive measures against the rising political and economic discontent. In 1933 he forcibly dissolved the legislature and cabinet for opposing his plans to deal with Socialist and Communist opposition, and with army backing issued a new constitution in 1934 establishing a moderate dictatorship. However, he continued the economic and social policies of his democratic predecessors, and had brought recovery when his term ended in 1938. His successors restored the old constitution, and favoured democracy in the international field during World War II, in defiance of blustering Argentinian threats.

Venezuela, more typically Latin American, was nevertheless hardly affected by the slump, thanks to the profitable oil industry. By 1929 this produced over 10% of the world's output, and receipts from it had paid off Venezuela's public debt. The great event of the depression decade in Venezuela was the death in 1935 of her hated dictator, Juan Vicente Gómez, but this effected only a change of racketeers and not of *régime*, and British and American concessionaires still profited more than the Venezuelans from the oil industry. Gómez' minister of war, Eleázar López Contreras, ruled until 1941. He established the eight-hour day, tolerated trade unions and even a congress by his new constitution of 1936 so long as its political composition was not too radical, and in 1941 rigged the election of another Gómez general, Isaías Medina. Medina also ruled on behalf of the great landowners and business interests, which logically entailed co-operation with the United States. He went some way towards setting Venezuela on the road to democracy by permitting the organization of the non-Communist, but Left Wing *Acción Democrática*, which broadly sympathized with the aims of the British Labour Party. Supported by dissident army officers, *Acción Democrática* in October 1945 overthrew Medina and set out under Ròmulo Betancourt to convert Venezuela into a social democracy. Instead the traditional Latin American cycle of *coup d'état* and dictatorship was again quickly in evidence.

## (iii) *The Other Americas*

British Honduras and British Guiana, like Dutch and French Guiana, for all their poverty and backwardness, did not want incorporation into the neighbouring Latin American republics. Mainland and island Central American colonies alike suffered heavily from the slump as primary producers, while their connection with the collaborationist Vichy *régime* for some time after France's defeat in 1940 precluded her colonies from sharing in the considerable profits which the war boom brought to the British and Dutch colonies.

The depression, however, accelerated the British colonies' economic and political advance. The disasters suffered by their sugar, banana, cotton, rice and other staple industries added extensive rural underemployment to urban labour problems, but thereby stimulated a trade union movement which rapidly dominated West Indian politics. Middle class politicians like the Jamaicans N. W. Manley and W. A. Bustamante, and Grantley Adams in Barbados, used the developing trade unionism to voice demands for responsible instead of Crown Colony government. However none of the British colonies had sufficient economic resources to sustain alone the burdens of independence. Federation, favoured by Britain and the larger islands, was opposed by the smaller islands, and by Guiana and Honduras whose large tracts of uninhabited land were coveted by the over-populated islands. Nevertheless the British government from 1940 began to make considerable political concessions. Colonial Development and Welfare Acts of 1940, 1945 and 1948 laid the necessary economic basis for the future independence of the colonies as a whole, and the West Indies in particular.

The collapse of Newfoundland's credit through governmental incompetence and the slump, combined with the decline of her fishing and mining industries to force in 1934 what was intended to be a temporary relinquishment of dominion status, while a commission of official receivers reformed her finances and administration. After World War II, instead of regaining dominion status she became a province of Canada, where, however, the high tariffs of Richard B. Bennett's Conservative ministry (1930–35) had brought little improvement. But with an election imminent in 1935 Bennett prepared to appease America's vociferous protests against them in return for reduction of the even higher Hawley-Smoot tariff. The government handled wheat marketing, increased relief expenditure, passed minimum wage and social security acts, and instituted an industrial forty-eight hour week. This legislation, however, infringed provincial rights; its regulation of trusts and business standards alienated big business and unemployment remained high.

The Liberals promised greater social security while attacking Bennett for infringing the constitution (Canada's Supreme Court nullified most of Bennett's New Deal in 1936) and in 1935 they won the landslide victory which inaugurated William Lyon Mackenzie King's 'reign' of twenty-three years. He adopted Bennett's policy towards America by making the reciprocal trade agreement of November 1935, which gave concessions, including reduced tariffs, on two-thirds of Canada's exports by volume, in return for concessions on three-quarters of American dutiable exports. He even adopted part of Bennett's New Deal, though without advertising the fact, and with due regard for provincial rights. The slow improvement in world trade in the mid-1930s combined with imperial preference, the greater American market and American investment to increase Canada's wholesale price index by nearly a third before the 1937 recession began.

The 1938 American-British-Canadian commercial agreement further fostered Canadian trade, though it increased economic dependence on America. American proximity and economic strength were in any event certain to bring domination of the Canadian market. By 1939 Canada's trade with America eclipsed Canadian-British trade; Britain's exports to Canada were worth only a third of her imports from Canada, and approximately 40% of America's foreign investments of over $10,000,000,000 was in Canada. This investment contributed substantially to the rapid industrialization which made Canada a major industrial power by 1939, and lessened the impact of the agricultural distress on her economy. By 1939 industry employed over half Canada's population. Her iron, coal, oil and hydro-electric resources could be exploited, given sufficient increase in population, to form the industrial basis of a great power.

Yet Canada's defence still depended unduly on the imperial connection, before World War II showed Britain's declining military strength. Thereafter it depended more on America. Roosevelt had proclaimed on August 18th, 1938, the United States' determination to prevent any threat to Canadian soil, while King was attempting unostentatiously to reconcile Canada's American nationhood and determination not to be automatically involved in European quarrels, with the unalterable fact that British participation in them must involve Canada. In September 1939 isolationism remained strong in French-speaking Quebec, where a subversive Fascist minority was vocal, but most Canadians approved the declaration of war on September 10th. Canada contributed to the war effort over a million servicemen, extensive financial assistance to Britain and other allies, and armaments and merchant shipping on a scale exceeded only by America and Britain.

## Chapter VIII
## THE EXTENSION OF JAPANESE AGGRESSION

JAPAN replied to the Lytton Report on the Manchurian Incident and to continued Chinese resistance by occupying the rich northern province of Jehol between January and March 1933. League approval of the Report and adoption of Stimson's non-recognition formula on February 24th merely brought further Japanese defiance in the form of notification on March 27th of intended withdrawal from the League. The Tangku Truce of May 31st, whereby Chinese troops evacuated the Tientsin region, temporarily suspended hostilities, but gave openings into Hopeh and Chahar which Japan immediately exploited. Relations with America, Britain and Russia were further strained by Japan's 'Amau Declaration' of April 18th, 1934, proclaiming Japan's virtual protectorate over China and exclusive right to maintain 'peace and order in eastern Asia'. Installation on March 1st of her puppet P'u Yi as emperor of Manchukuo indicated the manner in which Japan would interpret these claims. Denunciation in December 1934 of the 1922 and 1930 naval treaties limiting Japan's forces emphasized the warning to the west. In March 1935 Russia, after two years' bargaining, appeased Japan by selling Soviet interests in the Chinese Eastern Railway to Manchukuo. Nevertheless, Manchukuo imposed heavy military and economic burdens on Japan, and further advances in North China became imperative. Japan failed to establish a puppet *régime* for North China, however, and had to content herself with the 'East Hopeh Autonomous Council' set up in November 1935 to rule from Peking to the coast.

Japan's growing economic problems, army political ambitions, the European crises and the prospect that Chiang might learn to co-operate with Mao, led to the decision to widen the conflict if necessary. A minor incident, staged at the Marco Polo Bridge, near Peking on July 7th, 1937 by local Japanese commanders, exploded into the full-scale, but undeclared war of the China Incident. By August fighting involved much of North China and foreign concessions in Shanghai. In November Chiang officially designated Chungking as his new capital. The Japanese, after ferocious fighting and atrocious bombing of civilians, captured Nanking on December 13th. But to the amazement of Japan and outside observers, continued advances in the north and towards south China in 1938 merely stimulated Chinese

482

resistance. Installation in March 1938 of the puppet Reformed Republican Government at Nanking made no difference, neither did growing Japanese control of the coast and large cities. Britain and America offered merely protests, despite attacks on their interests and shipping which included the sinking of the American gunboat *Panay* in December 1937, but Japanese encroachments from Manchukuo and Korea into Siberia were heavily repulsed in July-August 1938.

The southern advance, however, made good progress. In October, with European problems preoccupying the western powers, Japan captured first Canton and then Hankow as obvious preliminaries to moves against western interests. Hankow's fall forced Chiang's administration and army westwards along the Yangtse to Chungking. On November 3rd Japan proclaimed her 'New Order in East Asia', whereby she was to control China politically and economically and leave no room for European interests there. In addition Japan proposed to drive Russia from her trans-Baikal territories and rid Asia of Communism. Chiang replied by refusing Japanese peace terms, but other Kuomintang leaders, including Wang Ching-wei, saw no prospect of defeating Japan and in 1939 Wang headed her Nanking puppet *régime*. China would probably have been doomed without large-scale outside aid, but neither America, Britain nor Russia was prepared to give this for some time. In the summer of 1939 Soviet-Japanese hostilities were resumed, this time in Outer Mongolia. Japan was even more heavily defeated but this involvement did not prevent her from blockading Britain's Tientsin concession on June 14th, and declaring that Britain must denounce Chiang and help to establish the New Order. However, the conclusion of the Nazi-Soviet pact in August and the outbreak of World War II produced such uncertainty in Japan about her future course that she pursued an unusually cautious policy for almost a year.

This extension of aggressive militarism abroad was logically accompanied by growing militarism within Japan, which produced military dictatorship during World War II. It would have been established earlier, if the army had not been torn by its rival *Kodo-ha* (Imperial Way) and *Tosei-ha* (Control) factions. *Kodo-ha* wanted a form of national socialism and appealed mainly to the more radical younger officers, who were eager to destroy the political parties. *Kodo-ha* men in February 1936 murdered the former premier Admiral Saito Makoto, but the *Tosei-ha* crushed their attempt at a military dictatorship in favour of its own policy of subordinating the politicians by subtler means, and employing present economic and political structures as bases upon which to build the new Japan. *Tosei-ha* dominated the cabinet of Hirota Koki of March 1936, forcing on it heavy expenditure on the army and armaments in preparation for war, and secured Japan's adhesion in November to the anti-Comintern Pact with Nazi Germany, though unlike *Kodo-ha* it did not want early war with Russia. In January 1937 *Tosei-ha* destroyed Hirota's government, but public opinion was not yet sufficiently chauvinistic nor the politicians sufficiently cowed to tolerate Hirota's successor, General Hayashi Senjuro. The general election in April saw Hayashi's followers defeated, and the army made a tactical withdrawal by replacing him with Prince Konoye Fumimaro. It expected to control Konoye, while he hoped to restore constitutional government. In June the army forged ahead with war-economy measures and destruction of political and educational obstacles to militarism. Konoye's failure to end the China Incident made disaster inevitable. In October and November 1937 economic and military planning were practically freed from civilian interference, and the National Mobilization Bill of March 1938 gave almost dictatorial powers to the cabinet. In 1938 Konoye attempted unsuccessfully to check the army's power by reviving *Kodo-ha*, but in January 1939 he resigned, recognizing his hopeless situation. The army, nevertheless, could not force through the military alliance with Germany which it favoured. Civilian and navy members of the cabinet were still strong enough to veto a policy which certainly meant war with Britain, and possibly with America.

Despite Japan's failure to administer the *coup de grace*, China's chances of even bare survival deteriorated throughout the 1930s. Japan had recovered remarkably quickly from the slump, so that by 1936 her imports and exports were worth 25% more than in 1929, her iron, coal, shipbuilding and textile industries were booming, and she accounted for about a third of Asia's total production. In contrast, China was ravaged by civil war as well as by Japanese aggression. By 1940 Japan's Manchukuo and North China empires were providing coal, pig-iron, machinery, chemicals and cement in abundance, while Kuomintang, or 'free China' had to rely on the undeveloped resources of the south-west, and the Communist-held areas were small and economically insignificant. Chiang, convinced that eventually Japanese aggression would bring its nemesis by involving the western powers, refused until his kidnapping in December 1936 by the Young Marshal Chang to declare war on Japan and work with Mao against her. Instead he concentrated his attacks on the Communists. In August 1933 a massive Kuomintang attack was launched which brought the Red Army to the verge of annihilation before its 100,000 survivors in October 1934 began the famous Long March of 6,000 miles from their Fukien-Kiangsi bases to Shensi in the north-west. The march not only saved the Red Army. It forced the Chinese Communists to accept, in defiance of Moscow, Mao's strategy of basing their revolution on the peasants. In the year which was spent on the way to Shensi organizers were allocated the task of establishing Communist (in Kuomintang parlance, 'bandit') *régimes* which allocated land to the peasants, while simultaneously demanding a national war against Japan. Communist propaganda made great headway among both peasants and Kuomintang forces before Chiang's kidnapping produced the anti-Japanese coalition of January 1937, with Chiang as the admittedly indispensable leader. Civil war, however, ended only ostensibly with the agreement, for each side sought to manoeuvre its suspicious ally into taking the brunt of the hostilities which began in July. By 1941 the Sino-Japanese conflict had reached stalemate, but Kuomintang and Communists were preparing openly to resume their own struggle as soon as a favourable opportunity arose. In fact, though Japan controlled most of the coast, the great eastern cities and the lines of communication, she could overthrow neither Chiang nor Mao, while they lacked the military power and modern weapons essential for expelling Japan. On the whole the Communists were more loyal than the Kuomintang to the anti-Japanese line, from conviction as much as from the necessity imposed by their numerical and military inferiority to the Kuomintang. Moreover, despite the misgivings aroused among the middle classes and richer peasants by their domestic programme, the Communists' essentially nationalist line evoked widespread support.

## Chapter IX
# SOUTH-EAST ASIA, INDIA, CEYLON AND AUSTRALASIA

JAPAN had also long coveted south-east Asia's rich supplies of rubber, tin, oil and other strategic supplies. Japan sedulously increased her economic influence and stimulated the rising anti-colonial and anti-western movements there in the 1930s. Siam, the only independent state, exhibited chauvinistic hatred for French Indo-China which Japan used to bring Siam (or Thailand as she called herself from 1939) to her side in 1940. The Siamese were the most prosperous people of the region. Siam's industry and commerce were largely foreign-owned and her commercial class was Chinese, but her resources could not be so selfishly exploited as those of Burma, Malaya, Indo-China and the Netherlands East Indies, which helped to reduce their metropolitan countries' unfavourable balances of trade with America. America also invested in the area (though in 1939 only $330,000,000 as against Europe's $1,943,000,000, Britain's $860,000,000, China's $640,000,000 and Japan's $60,000,000).

America, however, sought to renounce her protectorate over the Philippines as soon as possible, and was preparing them for the self-government promised by Congress in 1934, subject to her control of foreign policy and defence. The other colonial powers were in no such hurry to transfer power.

Burma had a bi-cameral legislature after being separated from India in 1935, but was restive despite increasing grants of autonomy before World War II as Britons still held the senior administrative posts. Malaya comprised the Straits Settlements around Singapore, which were governed as a Crown Colony, the four semi-autonomous Federated Malay States, the five Unfederated Malay States, and some island territories. Malaya was economically important for its tin and rubber (it shared with Hong Kong the distinction of not being a charge on the British exchequer), and commercially and strategically important because of Singapore. However, too little money was spent on Singapore's defences and, as it was a naval base, the danger of attack from the landward side, from which Japan actually attacked in 1941, was regarded as negligible. Its British Governor co-ordinated the administration of all the Malay territories, and also of the British East Indian territories.

In the Netherlands East Indies Dutch officials adopted a paternalist attitude towards Indonesians which was made more intolerable by their perpetuation of privileges accorded to Chinese businessmen and European industrialists and planters. However, the establishment in 1918 of the *Volksraad* (or advisory people's council) led, though far too slowly, to greater Indonesian legislative participation. From 1927, with the foundation by D. P. Kusumu and Ahmed Sukarno of the National Indonesian Party, the Indonesian nationalist movement rapidly gathered strength. In 1937 the *Volksraad* demanded dominion status within ten years. Indonesia's nationalist movement was mainly non-Communist, though it had strong Communist support, but never possessed the mass following of the Indian Congress Party or the Kuomintang.

The Indo-Chinese movement looked for its model to either Congress or Chinese Communism, after it became clear that French talk of 'cultural association' and of the great revolutionary ideas of 1789 did not mean concession of even moderate liberal demands of self-government in the 1920s. Stern repression of nationalist groups, and especially of Communists, did not prevent serious disturbances in 1930 and 1931 in Tonkin, where the depression's economic effects were capitalized upon. Though it failed to secure anything like mass support in the 1930s, Ho Chi-minh's Indo-Chinese variety of Communism, the Viet-minh, led Indo-Chinese nationalism in World War II—and did so for some of the time with the approval of the Kuomintang and America. Both these wished to seee French power in Indo-China ended, though for different reasons: the Kuomintang in pursuit of old Chinese imperialist claims, America from dislike of European imperialism.

By 1933 most British people were prepared to see independence granted to India, for though other groups besides Churchill's Tory die-hards doubted Congress' right to speak for all India as well as its fitness to rule, the example of Ireland had suggested what might result from the denial of freedom. As most civil servants were Indians, the major problems were the reconciliation of Hindu and Moslem claims and the form of India's association with Britain, not the question of capacity for self-government. Despite Gandhi's resort to civil disobedience in August 1933, the 1935 Government of India Act provided for a federal all-India government, which, however, was never actually established; autonomy for the provincial governments; reserve powers for the governors, under which India was brought into World War II without her consent; and for the British Parliament's right to legislate for India. Congress, and especially its rising young leader Jawaharlal Nehru, denounced the new constitution's concessions to the princes of representation in the proposed central legislature, and its concessions to the racial and religious communities. As the princes refused to join the new federation, the intended dyarchy within it never took effect, and the federal provisions were stillborn.

Congress decided to contest the first provincial elections of 1937 on the platform of non-participation in the provincial governments, but absolute

Congress majorities in five provinces, and pluralities in three others out of the total of eleven, suggested second thoughts. Nehru continued to urge non-participation, but in July 1937 the eight Congress ministries took office. M. A. Jinnah's Moslem League won no election, and in the United Provinces Congress reneged on its pre-election promise to share power, as it gained a majority without League support. Nevertheless the League, to Hindu surprise, now became an effective political movement as Jinnah set out to appeal to the Moslem masses, while Congress purists under Gandhi's leadership replied to India's involvement in the war by instructing the eight provincial ministries to resign.

This brief tenure of power sufficed to ensure that Congress would follow the parliamentary road when independence finally came, and Congress resignations gave the League an opportunity to regain lost ground, so that within a year two ministries were League cabinets and three others were pro-League. World War II, in turn, both strengthened Congress's resolve to wrest complete independence, and established the League's programme of a separate independent existence for the Moslem, or predominantly Moslem areas which later formed Pakistan.

Ceylon achieved independence by constitutional and peaceful means. Richer, more stable and more manageable than the Indian mainland, with its huge and amorphous mass of races and religions, Ceylon had only three important peoples, Sinhalese, Tamils and immigrant Indians, and only Hindu and Buddhist religions. Its caste problems, though not negligible, were not socially disastrous like India's. The British remained Ceylon's economic leaders even after independence was granted, but the Sinhalese and Tamil political *élites* ran the bureaucracy as well as the independence movement in the 1930s. Despite racial antagonism towards each other, they shared a common 'western' outlook which made it easy for them to use British liberal political ideas against the foreigners who had trained and educated them. In the process, however, they became divorced from their own masses, who often saw little to choose between British and Ceylonese plantation owners.

The 1931 constitution gave adult suffrage for the first time to an Asian people, though it added safeguards for minorities. The Ceylon National Congress, distrusting the masses as the Indian Congress had done before Gandhi, had opposed full suffrage, but Labour, Ceylon's first real political party, had campaigned for it vigorously. The 1931 constitution was difficult to work as it gave the assembly both legislative and executive powers, but it stimulated the development of political parties, and provided the training in self-government which produced politicians such as W. R. Bandaranaike, D. S. Senanayake, N. M. Perera and Philip Gunawardene, whose acumen and power far exceeded those of older-style nationalists and trade union leaders. Ceylon's Conservative, Liberal and moderate Socialist leaders kept her stable during the depression, when some bitter plantation strikes caused serious alarm. The Left Wing Lanka Sama Samaja Party, founded in 1935, won many urban workers away from the Labour Party but was

Trotskyist, and in 1944 Stalinists formed the Communist Party of Ceylon. During World War II the Ceylonese democratic politicians showed themselves both capable and loyal to the British connection. The British promised to grant independence after the war, except for defence and foreign policy.

One of the first countries to succumb to the slump, Australia was also one of the first to recover. Indeed Australian and New Zealand *per capita* incomes were the highest in the world in 1939. Australian recovery was due to rising world prices, imperial preference, stimulation of agriculture and industry by flexible taxation measures, the natural resilience and capacity of the people for hard work, and by the end of the 1930s, the opening of the interior by developments in air transport, which by 1936 had also linked Australia with the rest of the world as a normal means of communication. Though Australia was chiefly concerned in the inter-war period, and especially from 1929 to 1933, with domestic problems, the rising danger from Japan led Joseph A. Lyons' United Australia Party government in July 1934 to institute a three-year defence programme to strengthen and modernize her armed forces. When in November Earle C. G. Page's Country Party joined Lyons' essentially Liberal government, defence policies remained unchanged. The coalition followed the tradition of relying on the British Navy as the first arm of Australia's defence. Most Australians realized as World War II approached that they would automatically be involved if Britain were at war, and in the October 1937 general election the coalition defeated Labour on the defence issue.

In foreign affairs the government supported Britain's appeasement policy. The Ministry of External Affairs (established in 1935) had no independent policy, though in 1937 it pointed out to Britain the probable future trend: war with Germany in Europe and with Japan in the Pacific, with Italy possibly threatening the Anglo-Australian lines of communication. The isolationist Labour Party sought to reduce dependence on Britain, whose power to give effective aid in the Pacific it justifiably questioned, but the Lyons government's only independent suggestion was that Australia should seek to appease Japan by making a treaty with her. The country went to war automatically in September 1939 under the leadership of Robert G. Menzies' minority United Australia Party government, and the war itself was widely supported. Even the Labour Party thought better of its demand in May 1939 for Australian neutrality if Britain were involved in European war.

Largely because of the New Zealand Conservative government's failure to solve the problems of the depression, the Labour Party won a sweeping victory in the 1935 elections, and formed the first New Zealand Labour government, under Michael Joseph Savage. Its aim was not Socialism, for it was essentially a trade union movement, but social security, and it carried out a minimum of nationalization. Railways and the Bank of New Zealand were taken over, and the government controlled mortgages and financing of overseas trade, but most of its measures were New Deal in character: an agricultural products marketing board, public works, regulations on minimum wages and maximum working hours. With the help of rising prices fostered by the world recovery, rapid progress was made before the 1938 election returned the government, and its heavily increased spending on social security combined with a fostering of secondary industries further to stimulate the economy. This made the economy less vulnerable to outside influences than before, but it remained dependent on imported manufactures, especially British. Her greater economic dependence made New Zealand even more reliant than Australia on the imperial connection for defence. Hence, though New Zealand was more conscious than Australia of her exposed position, she gave equally unhesitating support when Britain declared war on Germany.

# Chapter X
# AFRICA AND THE MIDDLE EAST

In 1933 the only independent African Negro countries were Liberia and Ethiopia. Neither of these offered leadership, or even political models, to the stagnant black African national movements of the inter-war years, and Italy's subjection of Ethiopia in 1936, though really marking the victory of a modern over a mediaeval police state, appeared to confirm general impressions that at least in Africa colonial rule was at its zenith. Moreover, before the revolutionary impact of World War II on Africa, none of her native leaders achieved the prominence of the Asian nationalists. Belgium's Congo territory had no parallel anywhere in the colonial world for paternalism, since neither its Africans nor its whites had the vote. Forced labour, heavy terms of imprisonment, and sometimes death for political agitators were imposed, but considerable economic progress was achieved. Primary and vocational education comparable to that of the British territories was provided, and after 1933 a modified version of British indirect rule employed native authorities in local administration, but no steps were taken to promote self-government. Official Portuguese policy by the 1933 Colonial Act aimed at economic and political integration of the mother country and her East Indian, Indian and extensive African territories, but under strictly centralized rule from Lisbon. This meant in practice selfish exploitation of colonial resources and repression of African national consciousness, under the pretext of fostering common Portuguese identity among all Portuguese citizens at home and overseas.

French policy, similarly, was to make Frenchmen out of *élite* Africans — before 1914 by 'assimilation', in the inter-war years by 'association'. Allegedly designed to promote African welfare by respecting African traditions while extending economic and political intercourse between metropolitan and colonial territories, this meant in practice denial, so far as possible, of any distinctively African identity. In French West and Equatorial Africa this was largely achieved by the colonial bureaucracy, which had to make only minor concessions in purely local matters. Except in Senegal, only an insignificant minority in the Negro colonies held French citizenship, and therefore could enter colonial administration. The position in Arab French Africa was different. Algeria's white population was so large that Algeria ranked as three French departments. The most prominent

Algerian Arab leader, Ferhat Abbas, denied in 1936 the existence of an Algerian 'homeland' and nationalism, and demanded that Algerians should seek their future in emancipated 'French Algeria'. Simultaneously, however, Tunisia's nationalist movement under Habib Bourguiba was repudiating both French sovereignty and the Bey's conservatism. In 1938 it was proscribed and Bourguiba jailed. French Morocco was not completely 'pacified' until 1934, but its nationalist movement was insignificant until after World War II. No active independence party was formed until the Istiqlal was established in 1944.

Britain's view that colonial rule could only safely be ended after a very long period of African evolution towards political maturity explains, though it does not excuse, the small number of her African subjects in responsible posts even in 1939. On the other hand, British emphasis on education, narrowly based though it was, made possible the founding in London in 1925 of the West African Students Union which bred a whole generation of political leaders, from the Nigerians in the mid-1920s to Kwame Nkrumah, who became Ghana's Vice-President at the end of World War II. The inter-war nationalist movements were led by African intellectuals, professional and literary men such as the Nigerian Benjamin N. Azikiwe, already a notable figure in 1933, and the Kenyan Jomo Kenyatta, with active encouragement from British politicians and certain colonial officials.

In South Africa Smuts demanded in January 1933 that Hertzog's Nationalist government should yield to a national coalition formed to carry out policies of imperial co-operation and internal harmony between whites. In the National Government formed accordingly in March, Smuts became Hertzog's deputy, and in June 1934 Smuts' South African and Hertzog's Nationalist parties combined to form the United Party. Henceforth economic progress was rapid, but the breach between Afrikaners and British was not healed, and it was Smuts who in 1936 moved towards *apartheid* by further restricting native land rights by the Native Trust and Land Act and enforcing segregation by the Representation of Natives Act. Even this did not satisfy extremist elements of the former Nationalists, who had annexed in June 1934 the Nationalist Party title. These extremists campaigned under Daniel François Malan for stronger measures against natives and establishment of an independent republic outside the Commonwealth. Many of the Malanites were receptive to Nazi ideas, which also gained ground among Hertzog's supporters. Though a German *Bund* was proscribed in 1934, Afrikaner extremists did not abate their sympathy for Nazi ideology. Continuing separatist tendencies made loyalty to Britain even more dubious, though Neville Chamberlain had been sympathetic to Hertzog's demand in 1935 to take over Basutoland, Bechuanaland and Swaziland. In September 1939 Smuts defeated by only 80 votes to 67 a proposal for neutrality supported by Hertzog and Malan, but subsequent events, including the 1943 election, showed that the overwhelming majority of South Africans were either pro-British or fearful of Nazi

Germany, and South Africa's contribution to victory in World War II was strategically, militarily and economically substantial.

In 1936 Egypt achieved a substantial measure of independence, though defence and foreign policy remained under British control. As Italy by then had added Ethiopia to Libya and her East African territories, and the peril from Nazi Germany was unmistakable, Britain made substantial concessions, notably in the Sudan. Egyptians were now eligible for its administration, they were to share in its defence, and their emigration into the Sudan was unrestricted. Farouk began rapidly to strengthen Egyptian relations with the Arab countries of the Middle East, which were anxious to end British and French control, and were moreover violently antagonized by Britain's plan to partition Palestine between Jews and Arabs, first proposed in 1937 and effected just after World War II.

The British and French positions in the Middle East were dangerously exposed when war came, and not only because of military weakness in the region. France's 1936 treaties with Syria and the Lebanon were uneasy compromises. British military power was strong in the minor Arab states along the Persian Gulf and the Arabian Sea, but Iran, with its important oil supplies and strategic position for India's defence, was restive, while American oil interests were offering not always scrupulous opposition to the British there and elsewhere in the Middle East. Transjordan was a reliable friend to Britain, but too weak to give effective assistance, while the ending of the British mandate over Iraq in 1932 facilitated the Nazi intrigues which assumed formidable proportions there by 1940. Indeed, on the eve of World War II the Arab world, although nervous of Italian ambitions, was already poised to throw off the Anglo-French imperial yoke. When the war ended, western political and military control of the region had become so corroded that within little more than a decade Egyptians and Arabs could secure full independence, even though they remained incapable of preventing the establishment of the small state of Israel in their midst.

# Chapter XI
## THE DEATH OF VERSAILLES EUROPE

HITLER'S dictatorship first transmogrified the political scene in the most important state in Europe; next it reshaped European and a good part of extra-European international relations; and finally it ended not only Versailles Europe, but also most of Europe's remaining power in the outside world.

The 'two fat men going down a dark valley', as a British diplomat described Britain and France in the years between 1933 and 1939, bear the heaviest responsibility for allowing the Nazi danger to reach such proportions. However, they acted from good as well as from discreditable motives. Their governments were preoccupied with unemployment and other pressing social and economic problems, and wished to spend money on something more socially useful than armaments, while their peoples were war-weary. Political quarrels were bitterly conducted, Fascist and Communist riots were frequent before 1936, and in France in 1934 actually menaced the government. In both countries large and influential sections of opinion either saw no essential difference between Soviet and Nazi barbarisms, or considered Nazi tyranny the less dangerous in the long run to western interests. Moreover, as general British and French opinion in 1933 was that Germany needed at least a decade to become a great military power again, there was marked lack of urgency in facing the Nazi portent.

In Britain the leading political figure was Neville Chamberlain, first as Chancellor of the Exchequer and then as Premier. His chief concerns in January 1933 were that unemployment was at nearly 3,000,000 and that general economic recovery was lagging. At Chamberlain's prompting, the government embarked on a programme of extended state intervention in the economy. Agriculture was subsidized as well as protected, overseas trade fostered by imperial preference and trade agreements (seventeen between 1932 and 1935) insisting on concessions to British exports. Light industry was encouraged, and Special Areas Acts were passed in 1934 and 1937 to relieve the derelict areas of the north and of Wales, ruined by their heavy dependence on the declining coal, steel and shipbuilding industries. However recovery was effected mainly by normal economic processes, and by a building boom for which the government deserved little credit, but which was the biggest factor in reducing unemployment to just over a million and a half in 1936. Large-scale unemployment still continued, alleviated by niggardly relief and unemployment pay. Yet the thirties were not so 'hungry' as the twenties, still less the pre-1914 years, but social conscience was more tender and the 'dole' was denounced as an affront to human dignity.

In June 1935 MacDonald resigned his purely nominal tenure of the Premiership to Baldwin, though the fiction of the 'National Government' was maintained in the general election of November 1935 (the last until July 1945). The government had 420 seats, plus eight National Labour supporters, while Labour had 154 and Liberals seventeen members. However Conservatives and their allies polled only about 11,500,000 votes aganst the opposition's total of 9,930,000; and Labour defeated Communist and Left Wing attempts to set up a Popular Front of anti-Fascist parties which would have impaired its mass following.

Baldwin won the election by exaggerating the government's economic successes (even in 1937 production was only about 20% over 1929's low level), by promising to support the League and collective security, and by playing down the need for re-armament—possibly from under-estimating the Nazi danger, not from electoral considerations of the continuing British dislike of heavy armament expenditure. However, the government blatantly dishonoured its League platform in December by agreeing with the French Premier Laval to give Mussolini two-thirds of Ethiopia. Leakage of the plan in Paris caused such storms that Hoare was replaced as Foreign Secretary by the undoubted League supporter, Anthony Eden. Baldwin weathered the storm, and even regained his popularity by his handling of the 1936 crisis caused by the desire of Edward VIII, who had just succeeded his father George V, to marry an American divorcee. On Edward's abdication his younger brother succeeded as George VI.

By then the British people were divided, as never before in the interwar years, by the issues posed by the Spanish Civil War. All Left Wing and most popular opinion favoured the Spanish Republic, while government sympathies were with Franco's rebel and Fascist side. It was not, however, Baldwin's weak foreign policy but his general indolence that made Conservatives welcome his replacement by Chamberlain in May 1937. Certainly his neglect of foreign affairs proved less damaging to them and Britain than Chamberlain's misguided activity and autocratic treatment of his critics. In happier times Chamberlain's earlier reforms and his government's industrial and housing legislation would have stamped him as a respectable early contributor to the framework of the welfare state. His Anglo-Irish treaty of April 1938 was a thoroughly enlightened measure. Churchill's die-hard opposition to its surrender of the treaty ports to Eire (as the Free State called itself by its new and independent constitution of 1937) for a time lessened the impact of Churchill's consistent and well-founded criticisms of Chamberlain's foreign policy. Churchill's criticisms won little support until after the Munich surrender to Nazi Germany for which Chamberlain will always be remembered.

The general election of May 1932 in France gave a majority to the Left. Herriot's Radical cabinet had Socialist support, but fell in December, when the Chamber defeated his proposal to pay the war debt instalment due to America. During the next fourteen months there were five cabinets including two led by the Radical Daladier. All five sought to retain the gold standard and avoid inflation. None of them could have succeeded even had they not faced growing threats from the Fascist Leagues. These Leagues combined with Right Wing organizations to exploit the political scandal of December 1933 connected with Alexandre Sacha Stavisky, who had been involved in a fraudulent bond issue by the municipality of Bayonne. Probably few of the leading politicians allegedly involved in the financial corruption exposed after Stavisky's death (officially suicide) were guilty, but the case struck blows at French democracy from which it had not fully recovered by World War II.

Daladier's second government defeated the riots of February 6th, 1934, which attempted to overthrow it and the Republic and which brought France to the brink of civil war, but Daladier was forced to yield to the conservative coalition of the veteran Gaston Doumergue. Rising dissatisfaction with the Radicals induced growing disrespect among moderate middle class and working class sections for democratic institutions themselves, while extreme Left and extreme Right sought to destroy them. To instil some sense of responsibility into the anarchic parliamentarians, in November 1934 Doumergue proposed constitutional reforms whereby governments' overthrows would result in general elections. This proposal immediately brought about Doumergue's defeat, and produced another conservative coalition under Pierre Étienne Flandin. In May 1935 Flandin fell after demanding almost dictatorial powers to save the franc, and was succeeded in June by Pierre Laval's ignominious ministry. Laval's adherence to economic orthodoxy—gold standard, drastic economies in public expenditure, salary cuts—deepened the depression. Worse still was his failure to suppress the Fascist Leagues and his initiation of the policy of appeasement towards Mussolini and Hitler. These policies stimulated the move towards a coalition of the Left and Centre, begun by the merging in November of socialist groups into the Socialist and Republican Union. The Communists, instructed by Moscow to combine with all anti-Fascist groups, then coalesced with the Socialists and Radicals in the Popular Front. However, it was not the Front's rising influence, but the obloquy incurred by his pact with Hoare which brought Laval down in January 1936. When Albert Sarraut, Laval's successor, failed to react to Hitler's violation of Versailles and Locarno in re-occupying the Rhineland on March 7th, general indignation was so aroused by the Front that the May 3rd elections gave it a handsome majority. Nevertheless, there was virtually no desire by the French people to expel the Germans forcibly, and the army thought itself too weak to do so.

The Popular Front government under Léon Blum was supported, but not joined by the Communists. It was no more willing than its predecessors to risk war against Germany and Italy, and indeed initiated the policy of non-intervention towards the Spanish Civil War which facilitated Franco's victory. Blum feared that if his government openly supported the Republic there might be civil war in France. In any case Blum infuriated the upper classes by his nationalizing of the Bank of France, railways and munitions industry, establishing of the forty-hour week, and enforcing of paid holidays and compulsory arbitration in labour disputes. These measures made no impact on France's economic difficulties. Production dropped while prices rose, and Blum's demand for emergency financial powers caused his overthrow in June 1937. By then the ugly cry, 'rather Hitler than Blum', was often heard from even the non-Fascist Right, which combined informally with the Republic's foes to bring France to the verge of social and political disintegration. A united France would have found it difficult to maintain her international position in these years. The Popular Front's reforms increased her divisions. The reforms left labour disgruntled and open to Communist propaganda because the strikes in which labour rashly indulged failed ignominiously. The discovery in November of an armed conspiracy by the royalist *Cagoulards* ('hooded men'), who had Fascist links, did nothing to make the democrats close their ranks. In January 1938 the Socialists defected from the cabinet of Camille Chautemps, in which Blum had been made vice-Premier as an empty gesture to anti-Fascist solidarity. The ensuing crises left France actually without a government when Hitler annexed Austria in March. Blum's attempt at forming a government of national unity in turn collapsed, and on April 10th the fake strong man Daladier formed another of the discredited, old-style coalitions which had neither unity, authority in foreign affairs nor even a foreign policy. Daladier followed Chamberlain's lead in the European crises which culminated in World War II, surrendering to him as well as to Hitler at Munich. France's future leader de Gaulle was to resolve that this spectacle of vacillation and abdication of national independence should not be repeated.

In Portugal Antonio de Oliveira Salazar consolidated the dictatorship which he had established with army support after 1929. In February 1933 he established a corporative *régime* which easily crushed the January 1934 revolt of Communist and trade-union opponents. He managed, unlike his predecessors, to keep firm control over the military elements which had put him in power. His Fascist one-party dictatorship aroused little popular enthusiasm, but it ensured that the anarchy instigated by the army's political ambitions in the 1920s should not recur. It was too efficient to be unseated by popular discontent and it offered a security which the Portuguese masses had rarely known. In foreign affairs Salazar steered an ambiguous course, sympathizing ideologically with Hitler, Mussolini and Franco—whom he helped to power. At the same time he suspected their ambitions, not least Franco's traditional Spanish yearning for control over Portugal, and maintained good relations with Britain. However, in his undying hostility to Soviet Russia Salazar has been entirely consistent throughout his political career.

When Spain plunged from endemic anarchy into Civil War in July 1936 the European triangular ideological conflict between Fascism, Communism and liberal democracy took physical form, and the full-dress rehearsal for World War II in Europe began. However internal Spanish conditions warranted neither the Civil War's international importance nor the War's becoming the bitterest crisis of political conscience of the 1930s in Europe, with repercussions even in America, where Catholic and Rightist groups favoured Franco, and Liberals and Left Wingers the Republic. But for German, Italian and Soviet intervention in the war, the Spanish people might have ended it quickly, if only from exhaustion, and struggled slowly towards some form of liberal democracy. The rebellion could not have got properly under way without Italian and German help. The Loyalists would have defeated Franco if Britain and France had not adopted 'non-intervention'.

The 1931 constitution had decreed universal suffrage, ministerial responsibility to a unicameral legislature, religious freedom, nationalization of Church property (which, contrary to common belief, was not extensive), State education and separation of Church and State. The Liberal Manuel Azaña's moderate coalition attempted to implement the radical social, economic and political changes entailed in constitutional advance along these lines. A long overdue reduction of the army's power and proposals for Catalan autonomy produced in August 1932 a military revolt which was easily suppressed, but the government did not pursue its advantage, with unfortunate consequences in 1936. Redistribution of the large southern and south-western landed estates went far enough to make active enemies of the land-owning classes without strengthening the peasantry.

Growing impatience from below at the slow pace of reform exploded in January 1933 into the Barcelona Anarcho-Syndicalist uprising. This revolt frightened not only Right Wing but also Centre opinion, and many moderates withdrew their allegiance from the Republic. Aided by the female vote—of the greatest importance now that anti-clericalism was an election issue—the Right Wing parties in the November 1933 election took 44% of the seats in the Cortes against the Left's 21%. In such conditions only unstable coalitions could result. In the anti-Republican coalition of the *Bienio Negro*, Alejandro Lerroux of the Radicals, and Gil Robles with the CEDA Catholic Party, emerged as the leading figures, Robles propagating a brand of clerical-Fascism similar to Salazar's. In protest against this trend towards Fascism Socialists (especially the Trotskyite POUM organization) and Anarchists resorted to strikes and violence. These disturbances were repressed by the government with unnecessary brutality, as was a working class rising in the Asturias which the Communists attempted to control. Finally the Left Centre and Left groups, ranging from Liberals, moderate and extreme Socialists and Communists to Anarchists, combined in a Popular Front in the February 1936 election to win a small popular majority over the anti-Republican National Front. However, not all adherents of the Popular Front were genuine Republicans, while Lerroux still regarded himself as a Republican, and some CEDA supporters were ready to accept the Republic if it would come to terms with the Church. This, however, was impossible—not least because the Spanish Church would never accept the Republic.

The Popular Front won 4,700,000 votes against its opponent's 3,997,000, but the peculiarities of the electoral system gave it 267 against the National Front's 132 Cortes deputies. The Basques supported Azaña's new coalition, hoping for home rule, but Largo Caballero and the Communists favoured rigid centralization as strongly as the army. Meanwhile the army prepared its rebellion and disgruntled Radical, CEDA, Monarchist and Fascist (Falange) Party adherents joined the plot. In May 1936 Azaña became President, to prevent the Socialists from forming a government on their own. But they were taking no active measures to promote revolution; instead the Right was. By July 17th, when the Moroccan garrisons raised the standard of rebellion under General Francisco Franco, anarchy prevailed in most of Spain, and the army expected an easy victory. Yet, though it soon controlled the south, the west, and the northern region around Burgos where its headquarters were established, it made little progress elsewhere.

The Civil War's outbreak changed the pattern on the government side, and with Largo Caballero's accession to the Premiership in September, revolutionary forces controlled it. These were too disparate to be held together. Separatism was rampant, especially on the part of the Catalan Anarchists. The Anarchists were the strongest group numerically, and their Barcelona stronghold (taken by the rebels only in January 1939, and then with Italian aid) was the real focus of Republican loyalty. Madrid was held, with the aid of foreign volunteers in the International Brigade, until the end of the war in March 1939, but it had ceased to be the Republic's capital by the autumn of 1936. The other major elements, besides the Anarchists, were the Socialists, Communists and POUM—whose members together with Anarchists were the major victims of Communist purges. Largo Caballero thought himself the Spanish Lenin, a delusion fostered by the Communists, who had cast him as Kerensky. As he failed to hold together the Loyalist forces, some of his *bourgeois* ministers, notably the finance minister Juan Negrin, and even the moderate Socialist Prieto Indalecio, supported the Communists against him. The crisis came in May 1937 when the Communists annihilated the Anarchist and POUM forces, and Negrin replaced Largo Caballero. But for the Communists' intervention, the Republican side would have disintegrated even earlier than it did, because of its own dissensions and Italo-German intervention. They checked not only Anarchist and POUM military disruption, but the social revolution, in order not to alarm the *bourgeois* democracies which Soviet Russia was still wooing.

Both sides conducted the war with appalling brutality as well as with such great feats of heroism as the Loyalist defence of Madrid, the rout of the Italians at Guadalajara in March 1937, from which the rise of an effective Italian resistance to Mussolini has been dated, and the rebel defence of the Alcazar fortress against overwhelming odds. The war totally devastated Spain, ruined her economy, and left her people hopelessly divided and dispirited for years. At least 700,000 lives were lost, the great majority Spanish, though there were heavy casualties among the 100,000 Italian Blackshirt 'volunteers', and among the genuine volunteers of the International Brigade on the Republican side. Particularly as the war developed the Loyalists came to be called Reds and Franco's supporters Fascists, but this grossly oversimplified the picture. Comintern agents came to play leading roles in Madrid, especially when Russia in the war's closing stages carefully regulated her aid to promote their activities, but Communists were always in a minority. In the spring of 1938 they became strong enough to establish in Madrid what has been termed 'the first of the Popular Democracies', but only with Soviet support. When this was withdrawn because of the exigencies of Russian foreign policy, which had always been Stalin's main concern, an internal civil war followed within the Popular Front, which ended in February 1939 with the Communist defeat. Similarly the Spanish Fascists had little influence over Franco, though they approved his appointment by the army as Chief of State in October 1936.

Though Franco would have lost the war without massive Italian support and high-level German technical and military assistance, he remained independent, and undisputed master of the insurgents. At the end Franco had achieved most of his objectives by destroying the secular and anarchic Republic, but his Fascist and monarchist allies were disappointed. Franco's government was at most semi-Fascist. The problem of the monarchy's restoration was adroitly shelved.

The war's major consequences were in the international field. Hitler succeeded, at very little cost, in strategically weakening Britain and France, diverting their attention from his Central European ambitions, increasing western suspicions of Russia, and above all preventing restoration of an Anglo-French-Italian front against Germany. The first fruits of joint German-Italian support of Franco came with the forging of the Rome-Berlin Axis in October 1936, a rude commentary on the Anglo-French sponsored Non-Intervention Committee of the previous month which failed entirely to prevent Axis aid to Franco. The second came with the growing dependence of Italy on Germany occasioned by Italian sacrifices on behalf of Franco. Stalin intervened in October, after the failure of non-intervention was apparent; first to save the still *bourgeois* Republic, next to perpetuate the war and German-Italian involvement in it. This, however, was the fault of the western powers, who had much greater interests in keeping Spain out of the Axis camp. It was no triumph of British forethought and statesmanship that kept Franco from joining Hitler for the kill in 1940 when Britain alone fought Nazi Germany, but Spain's weakness, Franco's doubts of Nazi victory, and his dependence on American aid to feed his people.

In November 1934 completion of the corporate state was decreed in Italy by establishing twenty-two corporations, drawn from employers, employees and the Fascist Party, to direct the economy. The system failed to make Italy self-supporting, but it had considerable success in further speeding up grain production, though at distinctly uneconomic prices. Fascism's hydro-electric and land-reclamation schemes were of permanent benefit, but Italian recovery from the depression was slow, apart from distorted developments in certain industries and agriculture due to the fact that the basic and avowed trend of the *régime* was towards war. Certainly it was not economic difficulties which, beginning in 1935, impelled Mussolini towards war. On the contrary, he deliberately ignored the economic realities of Italy's position, which would have dictated peace in any rational *régime*.

While Mussolini was flattered by Hitler's open admiration, his first reaction to Hitler's accession was distrust of the Nazi phenomenon, which he described in 1934 as 'Against everything and everyone: yesterday against Christian civilization, today against Latin civilization, tomorrow, who knows, against the civilization of the whole world'. There were obvious bonds of sympathy in ideological matters, and both countries wished to revise the peace settlements, but their territorial ambitions conflicted in South-East Europe. Moreover, Mussolini agreed with Britain's and France's desire to maintain the independence of Austria which Hitler planned to destroy. Mussolini even hoped to realize his dreams of conquering Ethiopia with Anglo-French consent. At the same time, he also hoped to exploit Hitler's accession to power for Italy's advantage. When France proposed a four-power agreement in which she would be joined by Britain, America and Italy to end German revisionism and rearmament, Mussolini countered by substituting Germany for America in a four-power pact which would bring Europe under the control of the four states. However when the pact was concluded in July it had been so emasculated by the other powers as to be effective only in scaring Soviet Russia into believing that the dreaded bogey of 'capitalist encirclement' was imminent. Mussolini's practical measures were first to make with Austria and Hungary the Rome Protocols of March 1934 for closer trade relations and a Fascist-led bloc to counter the influence of France and the Little *Entente* along the Danube. Next he reacted to the Austrian Nazis' murder of Dollfuss by moving troops to the Brenner and standing forth as protector of Dollfuss's successor Kurt Schuschnigg.

While Italy was hurling abuse at Germany, she seized the pretext of a clash on the undemarcated Ethiopian-Somaliland border at Wal-Wal in December to prepare to attack Ethiopia. Mussolini expected no opposition from Britain and France. He believed that he had secured French acquiescence in his ambitions from Laval in January 1935. Both Laval and MacDonald at the Stresa meeting of April 11th–14th raised no objections

501

to his obvious intentions. The meeting's purpose, in any case, was to proclaim support of Austrian independence and horror at Hitler's repudiation in March of disarmament—but not to act against it, though France and Italy agreed to joint defence of Alsace and South Tyrol. In June Britain prudently prevented some further Nazi breaches of disarmament by signing with Joachim von Ribbentrop, Hitler's rising diplomat, a naval agreement limiting Germany's surface ships to 35% and submarines to 45% of Britain's tonnage (parity, however, in submarines was granted in the event of danger from Russia). Though this diplomatic manoeuvre was accomplished without consulting Laval and Mussolini, this did not breach the Stresa front, nor was it treachery to France, for Britain recognized that French security was the prerequisite of her own. Immediately afterwards Eden journeyed to Rome and offered territorial and economic concessions at British expense if Mussolini would not attack Ethiopia. However Mussolini refused the offer, contemptuously rejected League attempts to provide a settlement, and on October 3rd formally invaded Ethiopia. Inevitably Italy was declared the aggressor and sanctions called for, to the embarrassment of the British and French governments. Economic sanctions were imposed, though they did not include oil, which Britain felt might have aroused Mussolini to the point of attacking her Mediterranean fleet. The British also refused to close Suez against the aggressor, a step which would certainly have ended the adventure, but Mussolini was justifiably outraged by British and French hypocrisy, not least over the Hoare-Laval plan to partition Ethiopia. In May 1936 Ethiopian resistance virtually ended, and the League completed its own humiliation on July 4th by voting the end of sanctions. Disgust with Britain and France threw Mussolini into Hitler's arms, but he himself restricted his freedom of manoeuvre even further by involving Italy in the Spanish Civil War, and thus making himself more dependent on German support.

However, the decisive event in Mussolini's loss of independence to Hitler was his visit to Germany in September 1937, when he was overwhelmed by the display of German military power. On November 6th the Duce joined the German-Japanese anti-Comintern pact, which had been made by Germany and Japan against Russia in November 1936. Though Hitler did not realize it, Mussolini's consent to Germany's annexation of Austria was now virtually a foregone conclusion. Mussolini's acceptance of the *Anschluss* of March 1938, which put Germany on the Brenner Pass, failed to serve as a warning to Chamberlain of what was in store. In pursuit of his aim of winning over Mussolini, Chamberlain had forced Eden out of office in February, because of Eden's insistence on the withdrawal of Italian troops from Spain and further proofs of good faith before Anglo-Italian relations could be improved.

Chamberlain's faith in Mussolini's desire for peace was sustained when at the height of the Czechoslovak crisis in September 1938 Mussolini backed Chamberlain's proposal for a conference. Mussolini played a leading role at the Munich conference, albeit by putting forward Hitler's demands. However in November, on the heels of British and French recognition of the conquest of Ethiopia and other concessions, the Italian chamber and people demanded cession of Corsica, Tunis and Savoy, though no formal demands were made. Nevertheless when Chamberlain and his Foreign Secretary Halifax visited Rome in January 1939 Mussolini expected that possible French concessions would be discussed. When these failed to materialize, he decided to accept the offer of a military alliance which Ribbentrop had been urging between Italy, Japan and Germany. No progress was made, however, before Hitler on March 15th annexed the remaining Czech lands, established a protectorate over Slovakia and allowed Hungary to seize Ruthenia. To assert his own status Mussolini annexed Albania on April 7th. On May 22nd the military alliance was signed with Germany despite obvious signs that Hitler was preparing to attack Poland next and that Poland would resist. When the Polish crisis reached the point of explosion in August, however, Mussolini still had sufficient prudence not to honour the May 'Pact of Steel', and to declare that he must maintain neutrality as Italy was unprepared for war. When he did join Hitler in June 1940, after nearly twenty years of glorification of war, Italy was militarily less prepared than she had been in 1915.

Except for Turkey, the small states of central and eastern Europe were all to be victims of Nazi Germany, if not as conquests then as satellites. Turkey escaped by a combination of geographical advantages and Nazi strategic decisions in World War II, for the Anglo-French guarantees given to her in 1939 would have been as valueless as those given to Greece and Poland had they ever been put to the test. Turkey was also exceptional in that while she was a one-party state, she was neither Fascist nor Communist, but was ruled according to Kemal's six principles of April 1931, which proclaimed that his Republican People's Party was 'republican, nationalist, populist, statist' (which meant that while private enterprise would be fostered, the state would take control wherever the national economic interest required it), 'secularist and revolutionary'. The first five-year plan of 1933, completed in 1939, was Soviet in inspiration, though it showed no Stalinist ruthlessness while establishing a largely state economy. Turkey made considerable economic progress under the plan, which assisted Kemal's westernizing policy. In 1934 Kemal engineered the Balkan Pact with Greece, Rumania and Yugoslavia to check German and Italian ambitions, and in 1936 secured a major diplomatic success with a new settlement of the Straits question by the Montreux convention, which allowed Turkey to re-fortify the Straits (at this time Germany and Italy, not Russia, were viewed by the western powers and Turkey as the threats to her security). On Kemal's death in 1938 Turkey was a stable and secure state, undemocratic but essentially aligned with the western democracies.

Bulgaria did not enter the Balkan Pact, for though she effected a reconciliation with her traditional enemy in Belgrade, she would not even implicitly renounce irredentist claims, especially those on Rumania and

Greece. When the army seized power in May 1934 and dissolved the political parties, it also took action against the Macedonian terrorists. The military dictatorship was moderate in its policies, and took the popular steps of continuing the *rapprochement* with Yugoslavia (which in 1937 produced a friendship pact), and resuming relations with Russia. However, King Boris managed to divide the military chiefs and replace them by civilians in April 1935, after which by skilful manoeuvres he rapidly broke the army's power, establishing his own dictatorship in March 1936. He promised to restore constitutional rule, and he managed to keep Nazi sympathizers powerless. As general elections in March 1938 brought in many of his opponents, the parliament which met in May was allowed only a consultative capacity. Boris strove for neutrality in the growing international tension, and maintained it for some time after the outbreak of war.

By January 1933 the Populists (i.e. monarchists) in Greece were at last getting the better of the Venizelist Liberals. The Populists won the March election convincingly, but their leader Panagiotis Tsaldaris rejected demands from Generals Joannes Metaxas and George Kondylis to restore the monarchy. In March 1935 the Venizelists rose in revolt, but were easily defeated by Kondylis. He proceeded to oust Tsaldaris, and held an obviously rigged plebiscite in November which voted for a restoration by a 97% majority. George II attempted at first to rule constitutionally, but as the balance between Populists and Venizelists was too narrow for comfort, he was persuaded by Metaxas in August 1936 to grant Metaxas dictatorial powers. Thereupon Metaxas began to institute a Fascist dictatorship, but though well-disposed towards Germany, he was concerned about Italian hostility and, after Mussolini's seizure of Albania, accepted an Anglo-French guarantee of Greece.

Rumania's Fascists, the Iron Guard, were of no significance until King Carol arrived in 1930, recalled by the premier, Iuliu Maniu, to claim the crown which he had renounced as Crown Prince in 1925. Until 1938 Carol tolerated parliament and even permitted elections, though naturally they were rigged. His *régime* took on an increasingly Fascist flavour, and deliberately adopted some Nazi economic policies, including the policy of creating an agrarian lower middle class by redistributing the holdings of peasants forced into industry, but Carol strove to remain independent of Germany. His non-aggression pact of July 1933 with Russia virtually secured her renunciation of Bessarabia, and this was clinched when in June 1934 the two countries and Poland guaranteed each other's frontiers. In 1935 and again in 1936 Carol agreed to allow Soviet troops through northern Rumania to aid the Czechs in the event of German attack, and he was surprisingly, though not foolishly, loyal to Czechoslovakia in 1938.

However Rumania's position was impossible. She kept friendly relations with France, even after the Rhineland coup made French help to eastern European victims of German aggression even more problematical. Yet Rumanian suspicions of Russia were ineradicable; Britain wrote off eastern

Europe to Hitler until it was too late to check his ambitions except by war; and Poland preferred revisionist Hungary to Rumania. On the other hand Hitler was well-disposed towards Rumania. He was her only effective support against Hungarian and Italian intrigues, and he was so interested in her economic resources that he took special pains to ensure that Rumania should not be harmed. The murder in 1938 of the Iron Guard's leader and its suppression after Guardist pretensions had become intolerable, aroused Germany's anger but did not seriously affect German-Rumanian relations. Britain and France, in fact, became alarmed at Hitler's increasing economic stranglehold on Rumania, as did the Rumanians themselves after he completed Czech annihilation on March 15th, 1939, and allowed Hungary to swallow Ruthenia.

On March 17th, alleging German troops might attack Rumania at any moment, the Rumanian envoy in London suggested forming a 'solid block of Poland, Rumania, Greece, Turkey and Yugoslavia' with Anglo-French support. This set off the most bizarre diplomatic negotiations of the interwar years. Rumania disowned her envoy's request next day, but Britain nevertheless approached the states mentioned, eliciting extremely cautious replies, and also approached France and Russia. France reluctantly followed Britain's lead, but Russia suggested a six-power conference in Bucharest, which Britain rejected as too slow, and also too dangerous if it did not reach agreement. Britain therefore proposed an Anglo-French-Polish-Russian declaration against further aggressions. France agreed, and Russia agreed if France and Poland accepted, possibly anticipating Poland's refusal. Poland did refuse. She would not commit herself publicly against Germany in company with Russia. She scented Rumanian ruses to get a guarantee against Poland's friend, Hungary. Poland also hoped to settle her own difficulties with Hitler peacefully. Having killed the declaration, Poland turned the talks into negotiations for the Anglo-Polish bilateral agreement which brought Britain into World War II. Hence Poland received as preliminary insurance an Anglo-French guarantee announced by Chamberlain on March 31st, while Rumania and Greece received their guarantees only on April 13th after Italy's seizure of Albania.

Hungary maintained her sham-parliamentary system despite the depression, the Premiership of the would-be Führer, Julius Gömbös, from October 1932 to October 1936, and the rapid growth of Nazism after 1935. Gömbös conferred some solid benefits, however, for his agricultural subsidies and stimulation of industry promoted considerable economic recovery, and in 1939 Hungary, Poland and Czechoslovakia were the only significantly industrialized eastern European states. However, his 1934 economic treaty with Germany distorted Hungary's economy by retarding her industry, since Germany wanted agricultural products, not industrial competition, and it also swept Hungary into Germany's economic net. Neither did Gömbös receive in return the German backing for Hungarian revisionist claims. On the contrary Hitler encouraged Mussolini to come to terms with Yugoslavia at Hungary's expense, and favoured Rumania over Hungary. When in 1937 Hungary retorted to German coldness by drawing closer to Austria and the Little *Entente*, Hungarian Nazis plotted to overthrow the government. The conspiracy was suppressed, but the Nazi agitators continued to alarm the government, especially when they called for redistribution of the big landed estates. In March 1938 the *Anschluss* forced Hungary to drop her anti-German tendencies, and efforts were made to appease the Hungarian Nazis with the institution of anti-semitic measures and land redistribution, both on a minor scale. The Hungarian demands on Czechoslovakia brought Hungary closer to Germany, though Hungary was too weak and too cautious to risk involvement in hostilities. Her claims would have gone by default but for Mussolini's continuing support, which secured parts of Slovakia for her in November 1938 after the Munich agreement. In February 1939 the Hungarian government finally plucked up the courage to suppress the Nazi Arrow-Cross Party, but it joined the anti-Comintern pact as a way of signifying Hungarian-German solidarity. Henceforward Hungary was a German satellite, though she did not join in the attack against Poland in September, nor drop her territorial claims on Rumania.

Yugoslavia's royal dictatorship officially ended in September 1931 with a constitution establishing a bicameral parliament, but the November elections saw the government nominating most of the candidates, and thereafter it carried on much as before by imprisoning its opponents, especially Croats, Slovenes and Communists. On October 9th, 1934, a Macedonian terrorist assassinated Alexander and the French Foreign Minister Barthou. The assassin was aided by the Croat Fascist Pavelić and Italian and Hungarian authorities. As a result of the outrage radical changes were made in foreign and domestic policies. Alexander had staunchly supported France and the Little *Entente*, but France's prestige in Yugoslavia was shattered when she hushed up Italian and Hungarian complicity for the sake of Franco-Italian relations. Yugoslavia gradually dropped her opposition to Italy and Germany, and became in effect an Axis economic satellite. By 1939 Germany supplied 54% of her imports and took 53% of her exports. The Regency of Alexander's brother Paul was less brutally repressive than the previous *régime*, and the relaxation allowed the Croats gradually to push their claims. In October 1937 Croat and Serb democrats formed the Agrarian-Democratic Party which called for democratic government. In the election of December 1938 the government won its usual majority, but Vladko Maček's Croat Peasant Party made such gains that Paul decided to try to solve the Croat problem by making Yugoslavia into a federal democratic state. In August 1939 a constitution was promulgated along those lines, with voting by secret ballot. The outbreak of war, however, meant that liberal democracy had no opportunity to establish itself in Yugoslavia.

The Austrian Nazis expected to take over Austria almost immediately after Hitler's victory in Germany, but instead Dollfuss established his own dictatorship, though his position within the Christian Social Party was at first insecure. He imposed strict press censorship, forbade political meetings and parades and combined the Christian Socials and Italian-subsidized *Heimwehr* into the Fatherland Front. Hitler and the Austrian Nazis demanded a general election, rightly confident that the Nazis would increase their parliamentary strength considerably. Hitler's purpose was to force the Austrian Nazis' entry into the government so that they could take it over and effect the *Anschluss*. However Dollfuss continued to repress them, and when Hitler ended German tourism in an effort to ruin Austria's economy, Dollfuss publicly humiliated Hitler's Nazi 'inspector for Austria', and replied to Nazi riots by dissolving the Austrian Nazi Party on June 19th. Dollfuss was equally hostile to the Socialists, and in February 1934 bloodily smashed their organization when they resisted his decree dissolving all parties except his Fatherland Front. This ensured that the Viennese working classes would not support the Front against the Nazis.

Dollfuss' new constitution of April 30th which established an authoritarian corporative state, and his cabinet changes on July 10th, emphasized the Fascist and pro-Italian nature of his government. When the Nazis finally attempted their coup on July 25th they were easily defeated, though Dollfuss lost his life. His lieutenant Kurt Schuschnigg rapidly restored order, and continued Dollfuss' policy, but Hitler's growing power made the dictatorship more dependent than ever on Mussolini's protection, and made Mussolini less willing to give it. In July 1936 Germany promised to respect Austrian independence while Austria agreed to follow a 'German' policy. The real situation became clear with the establishment of the Rome-Berlin Axis in October, and Mussolini's notice to Schuschnigg in April 1937 not to rely on Italian military help against Germany. Nevertheless, Mussolini did not formally abandon Austria to Germany even when on February 12th, 1938, Hitler bullied Schuschnigg into taking the Nazi Artur Seyss-Inquart into the government and ending repression of the Nazis. When Schuschnigg in March decided to explode Hitler's claim to speak for Austria, by holding a plebiscite on the independence issue, Mussolini was merely sceptical. Hitler could not tolerate the plebiscite challenge, and was reasonably sure that Britain and France would not intervene. However, only when assured of Mussolini's consent did he dare to order German troops into Austria on the invitation of the new Chancellor, Seyss-Inquart, who on March 11th replaced Schuschnigg at Hitler's behest. On March 12th Hitler crossed the frontier a few hours after his troops, to be tumultuously received. On March 13th Seyss-Inquart proclaimed the *Anschluss*. All the European powers except Italy protested formally, but their protests were disregarded, and on March 18th Hitler clearly indicated in a *Reichstag* speech his intention to 'redeem' the Sudetens next.

Control of Vienna opened the strategic and political gates to all South-East Europe, and the probability was that Hitler had already determined to complete Czechoslovakia's destruction after taking the Sudetenland.

As an Austrian Pan-German, Hitler had a settled hatred for the Czechs. Moreover, he could move neither east nor west until he had eliminated Czechoslovakia as a factor, and in 1937, when still uncertain about his method of taking Austria, he had considered taking Austria *en passant* in the event of war with Czechoslovakia. An additional reason for Hitler's hostility was that Czechoslovakia under first Masaryk and then Beneš was a focal point of the Versailles settlement and also served as a staunch ally of France. Before the Sudeten German Nazi Party under Konrad Henlein, formed in 1933, began its work of subverting Czechoslovakia from within, Beneš agreed to supplement the Franco-Soviet treaty of May 1935 with a Czech-Soviet treaty pledging Russian assistance in the event of German attack, though Soviet aid was made conditional on the prior assistance of Czechoslovakia's major and more congenial ally. In November and December 1936 Beneš rejected Hitler's offers to guarantee Czechoslovakia's frontiers in return for a promise not to carry out Czechoslovakia's Russian and French treaties if Germany were involved in war. The Czech fortifications were still formidable even after Germany's move into Austria had turned some of them. Since Czechoslovakia maintained a highly mechanized and well-armoured army of thirty-five divisions, she was not to be taken lightly, and Hitler proceeded cautiously.

Konrad Henlein, on Hitler's orders, won great sympathy in British Conservative circles by insisting at first that the Sudeten Germans wanted only self-government, not independence. However, after the *Anschluss*, under Hitler's direction Henlein's Nazis staged incident after incident to give the impression of Czech brutality, though the Sudetens were the best-treated minority in Europe. Until May 1938 Hitler's plan was to break Czech resistance as he had broken Austria's, and he decided that he would not act unless he was convinced that Britain and France would stand aside as they had over Germany's annexation of Austria. Britain had no obligations to Czechoslovakia (except under the now practically-defunct League Convention); traditional British policy was to avoid obligations in eastern Europe; and most members of parliament and of the public shared Chamberlain's view that war to keep the Sudetens in Czechoslovakia was unthinkable. Nevertheless, if France were drawn in as Czechoslovakia's ally, this would inevitably involve Britain.

As Daladier's government officially stood by its commitments but wanted to evade honouring them, the gist of Anglo-French discussions was that Czechoslovakia should be told to make concessions and Germany not to use force. In mid-May German troop movements in the border region suggested to the Czechs that they were about to be attacked, and they began to mobilize. The Germans protested their innocence, though it looked as if their moves were synchronized with Sudeten disturbances which died down on Czech mobilization. Certainly German moves did not amount to full mobilization, and the British and French governments soon concluded that Beneš had attempted to turn them against Germany. However, it was popularly believed in the west that when the Czechs had called Hitler's bluff he had retreated. Stung by this, he amended on May 30th the first sentence of a draft military directive dated May 20th, which renounced the use of force, to read: 'It is my unalterable intention to smash Czechoslovakia by military action in the near future.' Preparations were to be complete by October 1st. Sudeten incidents multiplied. Violent German press and radio campaigns against Czechoslovakia made Chamberlain even more certain that she must be made to yield the Sudetenland, and that he must ensure this happened. The French would not apply the necessary pressure, and Chamberlain saw that, if Hitler attacked, general war would ensue. Chamberlain therefore sent out as 'mediator' Lord Runciman, President of the Board of Trade, who had supported the establishment of Czechoslovakia in World War I, but was now a convinced appeaser. Runciman's reports at first demonstrated that the Sudetens, not Beneš, were to blame for the tensions, and that Beneš would make reasonable concessions. These concessions, however, would not satisfy Hitler, which was Chamberlain's object. While Runciman was still in Prague, Chamberlain decided, with French approval, to fly to see Hitler. At their first meeting in Berchtesgaden on September 15th Hitler demanded self-determination for the Sudetens, and Chamberlain promised to inform his colleagues, the French, and the Czechs of the demand. The British and French governments advised Czechoslovakia that if she refused, she could not count on aid in the event of a German attack. Russia, deliberately ignored by Britain and France, promised to honour her obligations—to fight if France did—but Beneš would not fight on such conditions, and therefore accepted the terms on September 21st. Hitler wanted not a peaceful settlement of the dispute but Czechoslovakia's destruction. At the next meeting, held on September 22nd–23rd at Godesberg, he made further demands: immediate occupation of the areas already agreed upon, plebiscites in others, and settlement of Polish and Hungarian claims on Czechoslovakia.

Faced with stiff opposition from his own cabinet and France, Chamberlain finally agreed to reject Hitler's crude blackmail. For a few days war seemed inevitable. France partially mobilized her army, Britain mobilized her fleet, and Russia denounced at the request of Czechoslovakia her non-aggression pact with Poland. Russia also moved troops towards the Polish frontier—whether to assist Czechoslovakia if war came, or to regain her lost lands from Poland remains uncertain.

Chamberlain, however, refused to give up appeasement. He refused to believe assurances that the German generals were ready to remove Hitler before Hitler could involve Germany in a war for which she was unprepared. Moreover, Chamberlain did not believe that Hitler was bluffing. Above all he did not believe, as he broadcast to the British nation, that war should come 'because of a quarrel in a far-away country between people of whom we know nothing'. Hence he appealed for Mussolini's intervention with Hitler, and Mussolini's approval of a four-power meeting led to the Munich settlement on September 29th. Hitler would not

509

allow the Czechs to participate, only to send envoys who would be told of the decisions. Nobody wanted the Russians present.

The British and French peoples, like most others—including the Americans—approved the Munich agreement. There was little support for Churchill's trenchant judgment: 'total and unmitigated defeat ... And do not suppose that this is the end. This is only the beginning of the reckoning.' Daladier expected on returning from Munich to be lynched, but was accorded a hero's welcome. Like Roosevelt, Daladier remained dubious about the implications of the Munich surrender. French and British prestige suffered disastrously in eastern Europe. Hitler achieved everything which he had demanded at Godesberg, since he was allowed to invade the Sudetenland on October 1st and demonstrate that German power had won the day, though he was cheated of a triumphal military entry into Prague. However, as the German military members of the international commission appointed to draw the new frontiers behaved with a brutality not seen since their predecessors at Brest-Litovsk, finally Munich gave him more than his Godesberg territorial claims.

The Czechs hesitated a few hours before accepting the terms. Beneš for a few hours thought of rejecting them and enquired if Russia would help if France dishonoured her obligations when Czechoslovakia resisted. There was in fact no chance that he would fight on such terms and Beneš changed his mind before his question reached the Kremlin, which had conveniently not been informed by its envoy of the request until after Beneš withdrew it. Thereupon communications between the Kremlin and its Prague Legation were coincidentally restored. Hence Russia emerged from the crisis unscathed by the obloquy which soon became attached to Munich as the symbol of craven treachery, and Beneš went into exile. Poland earned general contempt by demanding Teschen with its Polish minority while Czechoslovakia was still prostrate and could not resist, but the rump state rejected Hungarian claims to Slovak lands, until forced by Germany and Italy in November to concede the major Hungarian demands. The crisis, however, had already ended the unitary Czechoslovak state, by forcing recognition in October of Slovak autonomy.

Chamberlain secured from Munich essentially what he wanted. Peace was maintained, though not the 'peace with honour' which he proclaimed to rapturous crowds on his return, and he brought from Munich Hitler's written promise to work with him in strengthening Anglo-German relations by the methods of consultation as exemplified in the 1935 naval treaty and the Munich agreement. He was, nevertheless, keenly conscious of British unpreparedness for war, for which indeed as a leading minister since 1931 he bore major responsibility. He began a rearmament programme which had proceeded far enough by the time of the new crop of crises next spring to meet his service advisers' conditions of minimum preparedness for facing the Nazi tiger. It was not, however, until after the shock of Hitler's completion of Czechoslovakia's destruction and the growing Polish crisis that he accepted the domestic political risks involved in introducing conscription. Though both France and Britain had leading experts in the use of armoured divisions in Charles de Gaulle and Basil Liddell Hart, neither country sought with sufficient urgency to offset Germany's great gains in armoured and mechanized strength after Munich. Fortunately for the future Allied cause Hitler's penchant for quick and spectacular gains in re-armament as well as in foreign policy meant that he had not prepared for a long war. At the end of 1938 Germany produced about 25% more steel than Britain and France combined, but her armaments industry was geared for a brief *Blitzkrieg* war even when the likelihood of British intervention, and therefore of a long war, could not safely be discounted.

The destruction of Czechoslovakia was an integral part of German war-oriented economic and political strategies. Bohemia and Moravia were essential industrial bases. Even when the Czechs' fortifications were taken over in October, Germany could not run the risk of leaving them any opportunity of attacking when Germany was involved in war. Beneš' successor, Emil Hacha, was a straw president, and his government strove desperately to win Hitler's favour. But the whole former Bohemian-Moravian lands were indeed a physical and economic unit, as Masaryk and Beneš had argued, while complete German control was essential for further expansion. By mid-December Hitler had decided to annex Bohemia-Moravia. To expedite matters, and reduce still further the chances of Czech resistance, the Germans incited the Slovaks to demand secession, under threat of being abandoned to Hungary if they refused. When Slovakia's Fascist President Mgr Joseph Tiso was deposed by Prague for his secessionist moves on March 9th, he was summoned to Berlin and given until early afternoon on March 14th to proclaim independence—of course as preliminary to being taken under German 'protection'. On March 13th Hitler gave Hungary a free hand in Ruthenia. On March 14th Slovakia proclaimed her independence, and that evening Hacha was summoned to Berlin to accept Germany's 'protectorate' over Bohemia and Moravia. This was yielded early next morning, and German troops occupied the provinces. Slovakia came formally under German protection on March 16th.

Hitler rightly expected no active opposition. The four-power guarantee of Czechoslovak integrity promised to the rump state at Munich had never been given, and Chamberlain's first reaction was to argue that Czechoslovakia had disintegrated from within. Only growing internal opposition to Chamberlain and possibility of further German moves against Rumania and Poland convinced him that he should be horrified by Hitler's betrayal of the Munich promises, and reiterated assurances that Hitler wanted only to regain for the Third *Reich* the Germans living in Czechoslovakia. Nevertheless, the damage to Hitler's policy had been done. The 'rape of Prague' on March 15th was an error from which he never recovered.

It was generally recognized that Poland would be required to render tribute to Hitler after Czechoslovakia. However, there was justice in

Hitler's claim that so great was German national resentment against Versailles Poland, that only he could have signed with her the non-aggression pact of January 1934. Geographical, strategic and nationalist factors alike demanded settlement of the Danzig and Corridor problems. But the precariousness of Hitler's *régime* in its first year ruled out any risks. He had not consolidated his dictatorship, he was seeking to ward off foreign interventions—he could not be sure that they would not materialize—and Germany was not capable then of dealing even with Poland.

Indeed Hitler's greatest fear was Pilsudski, the only genuinely strong dictator in Europe apart from Stalin, Ataturk and later Hitler himself. Pilsudski suggested to France that they should prevent Germany from becoming too strong by occupying certain territories, notably East Prussia, and in March 1933 staged an incident in Danzig to provide the pretext. Hitler, however, would not be provoked, and France not only deplored the action but participated in negotiations for the four-power pact with Germany, Italy and Britain which was anathema to Pilsudski as well as to Stalin. Pilsudski proceeded to make preliminary soundings of Hitler's readiness to offer a bargain, and eventually, after Germany withdrew from the League, himself suggested a bilateral agreement in November, which produced the Polish-German non-aggression pact. In December 1933 the Russians, alarmed by Hitler's anti-Soviet line, suggested to Pilsudski a joint guarantee of the Baltic states in terms which would justify intervention in case they were envisaging any changes in their political, military or economic structures. The Poles put this proposal to the Baltic states, who naturally rejected it. Thereupon it was dropped until March 1934, when Russia made the offer to Germany, against whom it had been originally directed. It was pointedly refused.

Under the 1934 Polish-German pact, which was to last ten years both sides agreed not to use force to solve their grievances. Pilsudski and his Foreign Minister, Józef Beck, attached great value to it, believing that Hitler had realized the need for Polish friendship and would honour the agreement. Hitler had severely damaged France's eastern system of alliances and simultaneously gained great credit in Britain for his apparent renunciation of Danzig, the Corridor and Polish Silesia. France thought Poland treacherous, but French attempts to come to terms with Soviet Russia entailed the subordination of the Franco-Polish alliance.

The Poles made clear their intention to continue to balance between Germany and Russia by immediately re-affirming friendship for Russia, but answered France's sponsorship of Russian membership of the League of Nations with a denunciation of League supervision of Poland's minorities, and the torpedoing of France's projected Eastern Pact between Russia, Germany, Poland, Czechoslovakia and the Baltic States. The proposed pact was intended to maintain the eastern European *status quo* (with British approval but not participation). On Germany's expected refusal, Poland also declined, as she would have done in any event. The Franco-Soviet and Czech-Soviet pacts signed next year were detested as much by

Poland as by Germany, against whom they were directed. Yet Poland was well aware of their justification. In January 1935 Göring had proposed to Poland, on Hitler's orders, joint conquest of Russia, in which Germany would take North-East Russia and Poland the Russian Ukraine. Pilsudski stiffly ignored the preposterous suggestion.

After Pilsudski's death on May 12th, 1935, Beck and Pilsudski's other heirs, President Ignace Moscicki and the commander-in-chief, Marshal E. Rydz-Smigly, pursued Pilsudski's foreign and domestic policies, Beck almost completely running the former. France, on poor terms with Poland and reluctant to make the Soviet alliance viable, continued to work with the unreliable Mussolini to check Germany in eastern Europe until the winter. Beck meanwhile improved relations with both Italy and Germany. In March 1936 when Hitler fortified the Rhineland, Beck promised nevertheless to aid France if war broke out 'under conditions conformable to the spirit of the alliance', recognizing how seriously this affected eastern Europe. The Germans learned of the offer, and aware of Polish anxiety about the growth of Nazi power in Danzig, re-affirmed in August their respect for Polish rights there. In January 1937 Hitler publicly linked in friendship Poland, Germany and Italy, and sent Göring in February with assurances that Germany did not want the Corridor and would not attack Poland. On November 5th, when signing a minorities treaty with Poland, Hitler twice said: 'Danzig is bound up with Poland.'

The Poles needed the reassurances of German friendship. Their Ukrainian subjects were restive, and in December demanded autonomy. Glad to see Nazi interests diverted from the east, Beck approved Hitler's Austrian ambitions. Beck despised Czechoslovakia as 'a caricature of Habsburg Austria', and he knew that Britain and France would not fight for her—which did not excuse the manner in which he pressed the demand for Teschen. Yet Germany's tremendous accession of power in 1938 alarmed him, and he sought to check it in company with Mussolini and the Hungarians, but they were too wary. In pursuit of this aim, and of realizing his old dream of a common frontier with Hungary along the Carpathian crest, he supported Hungary's demand for Ruthenia. However when his Berlin ambassador, Józef Lipski, came to discuss the matter with Ribbentrop on October 24th, the Nazi Foreign Minister demanded Danzig, extra-territorial rail and road communications across the Corridor (Poland could have similar facilities to Danzig and a free zone there), and Polish adhesion to the anti-Comintern pact. To Poland he offered at first a territorial guarantee and then concession of her Ruthenian demands. These Lipski designated as intended to ensure repression of an allegedly strong Communist movement in Ruthenia, whereas the agitation which Poland wished Hungary to crush there was Ukrainian nationalism, which Germany was then encouraging. Beck rejected the demands in November 1938, but indicated that he could discuss everything but Danzig's cession.

The Germans expected to win Beck over by degrees. Early in January 1939 they repeated their offers and demands, virtually promising Russian

Ukraine to Poland. Beck refused to join the anti-Comintern pact, but gave the impression that he might bargain over Danzig for adequate compensation. If Hitler had continued to press his demands on Poland the course of history would have been very different, but he shelved them while he concentrated on the more immediate problem of finally 'solving' the Czechoslovak question. The Czechs submitted to his threats of force, as the Poles would never do. For the Czechs the Poles would do nothing, but the Poles' resistance on their own account would have forced the vengeful Hitler to turn his attention to them. In the circumstances of early 1939 he could not have run the risks involved in simultaneously 'solving' the Czech and Polish crises, for he knew only one solution when opposed: the use of force.

Though Czechoslovakia's obliteration satisfied the Polish desire that Ruthenia should go to Hungary, the common Polish-Hungarian frontier thereby achieved was valueless, since Slovakia simultaneously came under German control. German control of Slovakia completely exposed Poland's southern flank. Germany's seizure of Memel from Lithuania on March 23rd was not intended as an indirect threat to Poland over Danzig, but it was so regarded by Poland. Yet Hitler and Ribbentrop still hoped to make a deal with Poland, and Hitler was ready to bargain, with Slovakia as a counter for Danzig and his demands in the Corridor. On March 25th Hitler still hoped to get his way with Poland without war, but he seriously considered smashing Poland if she did not concede his demands. However on March 28th, in response to Ribbentrop's bluster, Beck told the Germans that if they touched Danzig it meant war, and on March 31st the Anglo-French guarantee of Poland was announced. Hitler now certainly could not withdraw his demands.

Like Chamberlain, Beck believed that the Anglo-French guarantee would deter Hitler from attacking Poland. Yet it was of questionable value without Soviet military aid to Poland, as the Germans fully realized. Chamberlain, however, both doubted Soviet willingness and capacity to help Poland, except by sending supplies, and sympathized with Polish reluctance to admit the Red Army into eastern Polish territories which Russia had ruled before 1918. At the same time it is unlikely that Stalin would have taken up arms against Germany on any issue short of a German attack on Russia. Moreover, Stalin believed that Poland would eventually be abandoned by the west as Czechoslovakia had been, a view shared by Ribbentrop and Hitler among others. Beck's adamant refusal to admit Soviet forces into Poland would in any case have prevented the western powers from coming to terms with Russia, and their attempts to make an alliance with Russia formally broke down on this point on August 18th. Their failure left Beck unconcerned.

Doubtless Beck was right to believe that cession of Danzig and of Hitler's demands in the Corridor would have made Poland Germany's satellite, for Hitler himself told his generals that the territorial demands were not the real issues. Certainly neither Beck nor Hitler had expected that World

514

War II would break out in the manner in which it did. Beck considered that Hitler could not possibly come to terms with Stalin, as Hitler actually did on August 23rd, by agreeing to partition Poland. Hitler expected Poland, in view of her hopeless position after that agreement, either to capitulate, or to be abandoned by the west.

## Chapter XII
## THE SOVIET AND NAZI TERRORS

WITH the second Five-Year Plan which was approved on January 10th, 1933, Stalin's dictatorship retreated from the worst brutalities which had characterized the economy of Soviet Russia since 1928. By the end of the famine winter of 1932–33—which was not admitted officially for thirty years—and the forced collectivization which had caused the famine, at least 5,000,000 peasants had died in the Second Russian Civil War. Between 1928 and 1934 the livestock population also dropped, in millions of heads: from 32·1 to 15·4 in horses; from 60·1 to 33·5 in cattle; from 22·0 to 11·5 in pigs; and from 97·3 to 32·9 in sheep. The much-vaunted tractor programme of the 1930s offset the loss in horses, but served principally to strengthen the dictatorship. Private livestock was allowed in 1934 and by 1938 accounted for three-quarters of Soviet cattle, over two-thirds of pigs and nearly two-thirds of sheep, but motive power could come only from the state-provided tractors, not from horses.

The *régime's* victory was not entirely complete. Stalin himself admitted in 1935 the need to formalize the private sectors on the collectives. Taxation and victimization forced into the collectives the few peasants who had withstood the 1928–32 holocaust, but each collectivized household was still permitted smallholdings with unlimited poultry and a small number of sheep and cattle, and also retained the right to market its produce in the free market. The 1936 constitution guaranteed these rights. The fully socialized state farms in 1937 occupied just over 12,000,000 hectares while the collectives had nearly 116,000,000, but the former contributed less than their proportionate share of production despite official favour. Moreover, within the collectives the private plots and private animal holdings were more productive than the communal sections. Between 1933 and 1937 the low level of 1928 agricultural production was at last exceeded. Then with the advent of Stalin's megalomaniac 'purge period' in the autumn of 1936 production again slumped, so that while the 1937 harvest was good and the total agricultural production exceeded 1928's, these gains were not maintained. The good 1937 figures probably permitted the intensification of the purge, as the good figures of 1935 facilitated its inception, and from 1938 attacks were made on both the livestock and land holdings of the collective peasants (*Kolkhozniki*). These attacks, and the *régime's* general brutality, ensured that when the Germans invaded western Russia in 1941 there was at first little disposition on the part of the peasants to die for Stalin's Russia.

Agriculture's unhappy state was due partly to inefficient direction and misconceived aims, but chiefly to the continued priority afforded to industrialization. Industrial planning remained unrealistic though the planned annual rate of growth was cut from 36% in 1932 to 16·5% in 1933. This was impossible to achieve, but industry expanded rapidly during the 'good years' of 1933–36. Steel production, stagnant under the first Five-Year Plan, at last forged ahead and all the major industries advanced even during the purge era.

The great industrial advances of the second Five-Year Plan (1933–38) did not achieve Stalin's major object of making Soviet Russia a great military power. This was secured only just before Hitler's attack in 1941, which naturally transformed the situation, but the economic basis was laid after 1928. In 1928 Russia was largely on the economic level of 1913, which put her among the under-developed countries, but by 1939 her total industrial production was exceeded only by America's and Germany's. Thus Soviet Russia was no longer backward, despite lagging consumer industries, and a grossly inadequate transport system, which was hampered by inefficient direction and Russia's vast size and physical features. The engineering triumph of the great Dniepropetrovsk hydro-electric dam testified to Soviet advances, and Russia could have competed for the lead in scientific research and technology, but for the activities of Stalin's secret police and the terror organized by the dictatorship, which deliberately cut off knowledge of the outside world to prevent independent thought and its corollary, disaffection. Foreign specialists who were imported to assist in carrying out the plans were made scapegoats for their failures, and sometimes accused of sabotage and spying. Soviet manpower experienced even worse abuses. In no other country were workers and peasants so viciously exploited as in the workers' and peasants' Socialist Republic, nor were wage differentials between unskilled and skilled workers higher (admittedly they had always been high in Russia). In 1935 the Stakhanovite system (named after a miner alleged to have cut single-handed a hundred tons of coal in a day) was introduced to give great rewards to workers exceeding official production quotas. Still greater privileges were offered to the successful managerial class. However defiance of the Stakhanovite movement and resentment caused by exploitation led in 1937 to a protracted purge of trade union central committees. In 1938 the carrying of labour books giving details of all employments was enforced. In 1940 labour was directed to specific jobs—this was also practised in Britain under war conditions, but in an entirely different spirit by the trade union leader Ernest Bevin as Minister of Labour. The last vestiges of trade union independence were abolished; unions became mere tools of exploitation, and workers could be sentenced to long terms of imprisonment for negligently handling or for sabotaging machinery. Nevertheless the Stalinist economic revolution

517

brought after 1933 a distinct improvement of living standards, though workers' housing remained squalid and consumer goods exorbitant in price, poor in quality and in short supply. Moreover, the brutal driving away from the land of excessive rural population eventually made possible better standards of living for both town and country.

There is no excuse, however, for the terror which gripped the whole country under Stalin's dictatorship, except his paranoid delusions. The first signs of the purges had been seen during collectivization. This had horrified some leading party figures, and their demands for moderation had been partly responsible for the less brutal second Five-Year Plan. Among these critics was, in all probability, the genuinely popular S. M. Kirov, head of the Leningrad party apparatus, and widely regarded as Stalin's heir. On December 1st, 1934, Kirov was murdered. Responsibility was officially attributed to Zinoviev, whose opposition had allegedly stimulated criminal and counter-revolutionary tendencies. He and Kamenev were arrested, and thousands of their real or alleged supporters liquidated or deported to Siberian concentration camps in the nightmare terror of the purges which Stalin ordered. Real or alleged Trotskyites shared the same fate. In 1956 Khrushchev blamed Stalin, probably correctly, for instigating Kirov's murder. From the summer of 1935 to the summer of 1936 the terror died down, and a constitution was promised.

Promulgated in November 1936, it was welcomed in the hope that it would end the lawlessness of the secret police and of other agents of the purge, but it merely enshrined Stalinist totalitarianism in constitutional trappings. In form it guaranteed individual rights. It enfranchized everybody over eighteen—to vote for Party lists. Constitutionally, power was vested in the bicameral Supreme Soviet, one chamber representing the whole Soviet Union, the other the republics and autonomous nationalities. The Supreme Soviet elected the Praesidium, whose chairman appointed the Council of Commissars or ministers. Simple majority sufficed to pass laws, but happily in the state of completed Socialism proclaimed by the constitution all important questions are settled unanimously. The subjection of judges to the law meant their subjection to the Party which, as before, was the state. Only Party members could be politically active and its Secretariat under Stalin's domination remained the real government. The freedoms guaranteed—religion and anti-religious propaganda, equality of sexes and races and so on—were explicitly granted to strengthen the system and not to allow opposition to it. There was no redress when letters and telephone messages were intercepted and arbitrary arrests carried out in private homes—for maximum effect in the small hours.

The 'Stalin constitution' was calculated both for its internal effect in Russia and to convince the outside world that the stories of tyranny were untrue, and that Soviet Russia was thoroughly democratic. However in 1937 the purge was more savage than ever under the direction of N. I. Yezhov, who succeeded G. G. Yagoda as head of the secret police after the 'show trial' in August 1936 of sixteen old Bolsheviks of the 'Left Opposition', accused of conspiring to remove Stalin and other members of the government. A. Y. Vyshinski as chief prosecutor demanded that 'all these mad dogs be shot', as they were. Zinoviev implicated only himself, Kamenev named others. Other people still became understandably nervous when the secret police 'uncovered' a new 'Anti-Soviet Trotskyite Centre' whose members included Lenin's old friend K. B. Radek. There was even then open opposition to Stalin's terror, but he removed his critics after the spring of 1937 by extending the purges in the ghastly *Yezhovschchina*, as they were called from their director. In June 1937 the purge spread from politicians and innocent citizens to the army. Marshal M. N. Tukhachevsky, chief of the general staff and architect of the new armoured and mechanized Red Army, was shot after being accused with other generals of conspiring with Nazi Germany against the Soviet Union. Numerous other high-ranking officers were executed. The Red Army had not recovered from the loss in leadership and morale when war came. The last great political show trials came in March 1938, at the time of the *Anschluss*. Now it was the turn of the 'Right Opposition' to have conspired with 'Trotskyites' also on trial (or absent) to open Russia to German attacks and overthrow the government. The chief victims now were N. I. Bukharin and the former Premier, A. I. Rykov. Yagoda was also liquidated, as was Yezhov a few months later when the blood-bath was practically over. With this onslaught Stalin completed the murder of all members of Lenin's Politburo except himself and Trotsky, who was murdered by Stalin's agent in Mexico in 1940. So monstrous were the charges against the victims, and so incredible the confessions of nearly all of them, that their capitulation was assumed abroad to have been secured by threats against their families, and physical and mental torture of the variety known as 'brain-washing' after the war. The final tally included not merely those who had at one time or another opposed the dictator, but loyal Stalinists. The purge was also extended to foreign Communists living in Russia, including Hungary's Bela Kun and practically the whole Polish Central Committee.

Whether Stalin believed all the charges is uncertain, especially in the case of the army officers, but the 'evil dwarf's' invincible suspicions of all potential opponents and the possibility that the army leaders might exploit the crisis to seize power were enough to determine their fate. However, it is also possible that the Nazis planted on Beneš the 'evidence' of army complicity with Hitler which Beneš turned over to Stalin, and which Churchill for one accepted. Be that as it may, not only could there be no opposition henceforth, but a climate of slavish adulation of Stalin had to develop. Stalin was portrayed as rather more than a demigod, infallible in ideology and political divination, the unchallenged arbiter of literary and artistic taste and the object of worship for all Soviet citizens. In the stifling atmosphere of 'Byzantine' adulation combining the worst features of the old Tsardom with Greek Orthodox religious ritual, a generation of Soviet citizens grew up which was taught to view its country as the standard-bearer of social, economic and political progress, and the stale, flat, essentially Victorian culture of Stalin's reign as the flowering of the arts and sciences. So tremendous were the Soviet technological and industrial developments and so wide the opportunities offered to the rising managerial, professional, scientific and intellectual *élites* that few were disposed to challenge these absurd artistic and scientific pretensions. Yet, as the ordeals of World War II were to prove, there was more behind the cohesion of Soviet society than mere repression. Loyalty to the Soviet form of society depended less on terror and rigorous indoctrination and more on patriotism and respect for the *régime*'s achievements than either its leaders or its enemies believed.

The effects of the purges on Soviet foreign relations before the outbreak of World War II cannot be accurately measured, but they must have been considerable. In purely physical terms they made a staggering impression. What was the real position and strength of a country which removed, by murder or concentration camps, 70% of the members and candidates of the Russian Communist Party's 1934 Central Committee, 75% of its Supreme War Council, nearly two-thirds of its senior officers, numberless party officials, and a total of ordinary and innocent people conservatively estimated at 7,000,000 ? If the charges brought against them were true, the *régime* was precarious; if they were false, its barbarism far eclipsed Hitler's. In either event, it was no bastion of democracy.

Soviet foreign policy seemed equally enigmatic, for it was capable of bewildering shifts, though its major objectives were remarkably coherent: defence of dangerously exposed territories in Europe and the Far East, regaining of territories lost because of World War I, the fulfilment of old Russian territorial desires, and sowing dissension in the 'capitalist camp' —whether democratic or Fascist did not matter in this respect. Hitler's professed anti-Bolshevik and annexationist policies were certainly the gravest danger which Russia faced after 1933, but they could be met either by reaching some form of temporary settlement or by joining a coalition against him. The chief point was to ensure that he did not attack Russia, with or without western approval or backing. Stalin's first move was to seek to strengthen relations with Germany, which had become less cordial in the last years of the Weimar Republic, and to threaten to come to terms with France if Germany did not respond. She did not, though Red Army-*Reichswehr* collaboration and mutual economic assistance continued for a time. In December 1933 the Soviet Foreign Minister, Maxim Litvinov, publicly expressed Soviet fears about German aims. He distinguished, as Soviet pronouncements were to do until the eve of World War II, between the varieties of *bourgeois* powers as seen from Moscow: 'actively aggressive', 'passively indifferent' and 'actively co-operative'. Common fear of Germany induced Litvinov to talk the language of collective security and French statesmen to overcome their repugnance towards Russia. Litvinov spoke the Geneva language to perfection—too well to have been wholly sincere if Soviet ideology meant anything—while continually dropping hints that

Russia too could make deals with aggressors, as indeed she demonstrated over the Chinese Far Eastern Railway. He also continually affirmed Soviet readiness to live in peace and to do business with any country, whatever its ideology, which would maintain peaceful relations with Russia.

Russia's entry into the League in September 1934 was designed to increase her security, not her commitments. In 1935 Stalin was again sounding out the Germans despite his pacts with France and Czechoslovakia. It would indeed have been extremely imprudent not to do so, especially as France intended to subordinate the Franco-Soviet treaty to a hoped-for agreement with Mussolini about eastern Europe, which, as it turned out, failed to materialize. In any event, from 1935 onwards France rebuffed every Soviet proposal for a military convention. During the Ethiopian crisis the Soviet attitude was that of a good League member, which did not preclude increasing oil sales to the aggressor. Whatever his motives, Stalin certainly in the early days of the Spanish Civil War wanted a victory for the Republican government which would have proved most damaging to Hitler and Mussolini and equally advantageous to the western powers. The end of 1936 and early 1937, however, saw him again making overtures to Hitler, this time through the devious machinery of commercial negotiations, but Hitler remained contemptuously hostile. On the *Anschluss*, Russia proposed a conference which would include America and which would decide what steps should be taken to prevent further aggression, a proposal which was either insincere or naïve. Then while Litvinov indicated that Russia would assist Czechoslovakia if France would, he privately told the American ambassador that Czechoslovakia might yield because she had no confidence that France would aid her and because Czechoslovakia was completely surrounded; that France had no confidence in Russia and Russia no confidence in France; and that only a change of British government or British policy could prevent Germany's victory in Europe. Russia, however, would be safe because Germany would 'have her hands full' on her long border with Russia. When the predicted Czechoslovak crisis arose, the western powers deliberately shut out Russia; in Britain's case less from distrust than from belief in Russia's complete military ineffectiveness, in France's case from both in equal measure. Stalin could not forget such an affront. Moreover he deduced from the incident, as did many westerners, that Anglo-French policy was to direct German aggression against Russia.

Chamberlain was equally convinced that Russia was trying to embroil the west with Germany, but his main objective was, as always, to maintain peace. He certainly did not desire Germany to gain control of western Russia's huge resources. He wished after mid-March 1939 to associate Russia with the guarantees to Poland and Rumania, not realizing how absurd and treacherous his proposals might sound, because he regarded Russia as no more than a useful economic reservoir for Poland and Rumania. Yet in the end Hitler made terms with Stalin not because of western maladroitness and arrogance, but because he was always able to outbid the west. He could offer peace instead of war, at least in the short run. After Munich, Britain and France were in a poor bargaining position with Russia. Britain's and France's bargaining position was even further weakened as a result of their Polish and Rumanian guarantees, which automatically obliged them to defend Russia's western frontiers. Anglo-French reluctance to turn the Baltic states over to Russia, which was clearly the implication of Soviet demands for joint 'guarantees' of those states, aroused Soviet distrust and animosity. In effect, Stalin was demanding the primacy in eastern Europe which was eventually conceded by America and Britain towards the end of World War II, but which Britain and France would never have yielded in 1939. (They would not resist Nazi aggression to promote Soviet imperialism; it needed Hitler's war to prepare the way for Stalin's peace.) Finally, Russia's alliance with the west would mean further difficulties for her in the Far East with Hitler's Japanese friends. On the other hand, an understanding with Germany could be expected to lessen the tensions in the Far East.

When on May 3rd, 1939, Litvinov, the Jewish advocate of collective security, was replaced by Stalin's *alter ego* Molotov, Stalin proclaimed Soviet readiness to bargain with both sides. Obviously Litvinov could not bargain with the anti-semites in Berlin, but Stalin had not yet decided to go in with Germany. However, once Hitler demonstrated readiness for serious bargaining, as he did in July, there could be little doubt of Stalin's reaction. Stalin's main concern henceforth was that Hitler might conclude another Munich agreement over Poland, which would allow Poland to be used as a springboard for an attack in due course on Russia. Thus his plan was to continue to negotiate with both sides to prevent their striking a bargain, and to defer his own agreement with Germany until there would be no time left for Hitler to come to terms with the west over Poland. Hitler, for his part, did not finally regard the Nazi-Soviet pact as unavoidable until mid-August, and he had to attack Poland no later than the beginning of September to avoid fighting in the mud of the late autumn. He sent Ribbentrop flying to Moscow on August 23rd, the earliest possible date after Stalin had signified willingness to make the pact.

By then the essential terms of the bargain had been agreed. In return for her neutrality Russia would obtain eastern Poland, Bessarabia and the Baltic states. In return for Russia's promise not to support the west against Germany, Germany would not aid Japan against Russia. Stalin had as much reason to believe that Hitler would honour the bargain as that Chamberlain would honour the guarantee to Poland, and no reason to believe that France, with her Maginot mentality, and Britain, promising 'two divisions now and two later', would wage effective war against Germany. Even if Russia had been ready for a major war (and her feeble showing against the already shattered Polish army in September and her humiliation by Finland in the later 'winter war' of 1939–40 suggest otherwise) she could not risk engaging from unprepared positions in Poland the bulk of the advancing German army. The fate of '*bourgeois-*

Fascist' Polish, Rumanian and Baltic *régimes* did not trouble Stalin. The west promised neither effective aid nor territorial gains in return for war. Germany offered peace and passionately desired, traditional territorial objectives. When Stalin concluded the Nazi-Soviet pact in Moscow on August 23rd he told Ribbentrop that he had 'long been in favour of a Soviet-German *rapprochement*'. Though he was speaking the truth, it was not the whole truth.

On March 4th, 1933, the day of Roosevelt's inauguration, Hitler wound up Nazi Germany's first and last contested election campaign with strident appeals to German nationalism. Nevertheless, and despite a month of intimidating opponents, torchlight processions and tremendous press and radio propaganda, Hitler next day got only 17,277,200 votes (43·9%), and had barely a majority with the Nationalists (3,136,800 and 8%) against the Centre Party (4,424,900), Social Democrats (7,181,600) and Communists, who even in that desperate hour still mustered 4,848,100 votes and 81 deputies out of 647. On March 21st Hitler pledged Nazi loyalty to Hindenburg and therefore to the army. On March 23rd the Reichstag passed the Enabling Act which established the legal basis for his dictatorship by giving him power to rule by decree. It was carried with the help of the Nationalist and Centre Parties, which misunderstood Hitler's purposes, and thought that it would be only a temporary measure, like its Weimar predecessors. Hitler used it to destroy the independence of the German states not already brought under his control after January 30th, by rigidly subordinating them to Berlin. Full rein was given to the SA and Himmler's *élite* blackshirt SS to destroy all opposition. Then Hitler dissolved first the Communist, next the Social Democrat and finally even the Nationalist Parties. The Centre Party dissolved itself. In October Hitler took his first steps in foreign policy by withdrawing from the League of Nations and the Disarmament Conference, on the pretext that Germany had not been treated as an equal in the matter of armaments. However he insisted that he hated war and would not wage it, that the Versailles 'injustices' should be ended peacefully, and that all powers should disarm. This line had some success with the British, despite their suspicions of him, and they felt that France ought to concede equality in armaments to Germany.

Hitler proceeded to pass on December 1st the law to safeguard the 'unity of Party and State', whereby unrestricted political power was legally secured, though it could not be fully exploited until the problems of the SA's political ambitions and the army's dislike of its unruly radicalism were solved. The SA greatly outnumbered the army. Worse still, many of its leaders and rank-and-file felt that Hitler had betrayed them, as he had, by allying himself with the conservative elements instead of carrying out the radical revolution which he had promised. The SA also enjoyed a great deal of independence from the Nazi Party, and its leader, Röhm, wished to make it both a political power and the basis of a new German mass army, by replacing reactionary army officers with radical Brownshirts who would lead the new united forces. Hitler knew the SA's ambitions and the discontent among radical Party groups over his broken promises. He saw the danger of a Brownshirt *putsch* heading a radical revolution. On June 30th, 1934, Hitler, loyally supported by Röhm's enemies, Göring and Himmler, purged suspect SA and Party members in what became known as the 'night of the long knives'. The former Chancellor, General Schleicher, was also murdered, but apologies were made to the army for this disrespect. Indeed, next to giving Hitler unchallenged authority over the party, the most important result of the murders was the army's conviction that Hitler was resolved and obliged to defend its interests and privileges. Hence on August 2nd, when Hindenburg died, it gave full support to Hitler's merging of the Presidency into the Chancellorship, and his assumption as new head of state of the office of commander-in-chief of the armed forces—never dreaming that he would turn the last post into a reality. It readily swore allegiance to Hitler personally, and though it had not respected its oath to the Weimar constitution, it found this new oath difficult to renounce when Hitler was leading it to destruction in World War II. Hitler did not, however, try for some time to exploit his new advantages. He did not seriously encroach on the army's power until the winter of 1937–38. Only after its conservative elements' opposition to his methods of solving the Czechoslovak problem did he show real hostility, and by then most younger officers were either Nazis or strongly inclined to Nazism.

The single-mindedness with which Hitler sought power and totalitarian fulfilment dominated all aspects of the political scene after March 23rd, 1933. The trade unions, and their assets, were taken over by the Party, but at the same time big business was reassured. By the end of 1933 the Nazi policy of *Gleichschaltung*, that is, of co-ordinating the whole national life under Party direction, had been largely achieved.

Yet there was more to Nazism than tyranny and destruction, as its economic reconstruction showed, and it could appeal to genuine idealism and readiness for self-sacrifice as well as to arrogance, self-pity and brutality—hence the considerable sympathy with which many foreign democrats received it before its inherent bestiality became apparent. Moreover Hitler's victory in 1933 was the victory of only half the German people. Germany had some traditions of political liberty and respect for individual freedom, whereas Russia had never seen the triumph of either. A resistance of sorts remained—not so much that of generals and conservatives which became active only after Hitler had failed, but of Communists, Social Democrats and moderates, so that Nazi indoctrination of youth failed to refashion the nation as Hitler desired. Nazism also lacked the coherence and solidarity of Marxism even in its debased Stalinist form, and the quality of its leadership was inferior. Hitler's genius was intuitive to the point of irrationality. He depended as much on the masses over whom he achieved unrivalled mastery as they did on him for inspiration, and as time passed fell victim to his own megalomania. Apart from his elaboration of the leadership principle, the *Führerprinzip*, whereby the German found his sublimest expression in total submission to the state in the person of the

*Führer*, Hitler's political gifts were exemplified by an unerring instinct for exploiting the weaknesses and resentments of others.

Hitler's technique for gaining and extending power was devastatingly effective, partly because of his own essential affinity with the hysteria and resentments of his audiences, above all because of his hammering home of a few propaganda points, best exemplified by the anti-Semitism which became central to the Nazi ideology and *régime* for both its propagandist and its practical advantages. Jews were officially persecuted from the beginning to the end of the *régime*. They were designated 'sub-human', stripped as quickly as was expedient of their property, deprived of citizen status and professional and business occupation and driven into exile if they were fortunate—to the advantage of America and other western states which received them—or else into concentration camps. Their posts and property went to Nazis and they were denounced as the guiltiest 'November criminals' and, in patent contradiction, as both Marxists and international capitalists. They were also alleged to threaten with defilement the purity of the non-existent Nordic race, 'the founder of culture' according to Hitler, whose superiority was maintained by the murder, sterilization and imprisonment of hundreds of thousands of German Jews before the war, and afterwards of millions of foreign Jews. Yet this bestial rubbish was one of the most effective pieces of Nazi mass propaganda, and extremely useful abroad, especially in eastern Europe. Fewer Germans and fewer foreign governments were appalled by anti-Jewish excesses than approved them.

Nazism could allow no other focus of loyalty, so the Christian Churches also were persecuted—and Nazism was in any event essentially pagan. At first the Catholic Church and its political instrument, the Centre Party, attempted to come to terms with Nazism, but the Nazis broke the 1933 Concordat promising freedom of worship and organization to the Catholic Church. Neither the Papacy nor the German Church as a whole came out against Nazi bestiality and murders before or even during World War II, though individual German Catholics showed great heroism, until it was too late for their opposition to achieve anything but martyrdom. A few great Churchmen were too important to be subjected to torture, concentration camps or liquidation, but they were very few. Some Protestants actually adhered to the new Nazi organization set up under the *Reichsbischof* (*Reich* bishop) Ludwig Müller to preach Nazified religion. A larger number gave allegiance to the 'Confessional' Church which denounced Nazism. Most retained their faith and Lutheran organizations as unostentatiously as possible.

Indeed the lesson of the Nazi terror was that with the growth in power of the modern state, tyrannies cannot be effectively resisted after they have consolidated their power. In the early Nazi period many Germans believed that the excesses would soon end and that Nazism would become respectable, but Hitler had an undying hatred of *bourgeois* decency and respectability. Nazi barbarism had achieved unique proportions by the time that the Nüremberg racial laws were passed in September 1935 depriving German Jews of citizenship and prohibiting marriage or sexual intercourse between Nordic 'Aryans' and Jews, defined as persons with even one Jewish grandparent.

The Nazis abolished personal freedom and allowed no legal redress against their tyranny. They inhibited opposition with the SS, their dreaded secret police, the Gestapo, and the concentration camps to which Jews, Communists, Socialists, democrats and other enemies of the *régime* were sent. But Hitler's Third *Reich*, as it was called (the First *Reich* was the mediaeval German Empire, the Second was the Empire of 1871–1918), was not unpopular with the German people until the last dark days of World War II. Hitler boasted that his Third *Reich* would endure for a thousand years, but it lasted for only twelve. Nevertheless it at once made Germany a power to be reckoned with again, and before it began to meet defeats in Russia and North Africa in 1942, it had created a military machine such as the world had never seen before.

Hitler's industrialist backers rapidly found after his assumption of dictatorial powers that they could not control him, but there were compensations. The Nazi Labour Front kept the German working class in line. Tremendous profits came from re-armament and from public works programmes (including the new roads, the *Autobahnen*). Industry and commerce were stimulated by the Nazis' great extension of the policy of trade agreements in eastern Europe which Weimar Germany had introduced. However, Goebbels' incessant propaganda service exaggerated both the degree of German prosperity under the Nazis and the extent to which it was due to their policy. Though agricultural production increased, purely economic considerations were subordinated to the policy of increasing the number of peasant smallholders. This policy provided both grateful adherents to the *régime* and useful propaganda, but it retarded agrarian progress. Unemployment almost disappeared, but this success was due to much concealed unemployment (Party officials and other economic parasites), to re-armament, and to conscription.

There was no nationalization of industry, but state control was exerted by controlling raw materials and investment, as well as by regulating the labour supply. The state also became a great (if inefficient) industrialist through the Hermann Göring Works set up in 1937 by Göring for his own aggrandisement and for the advancement of re-armament, with which he was entrusted. The economy was subjected to severe strains by the policy of attempting to make Germany self-sufficient for war purposes, but this also led to major advances in the creation of synthetic substitutes for textiles, rubber and oil. It had been predicted that financial disaster would inevitably result from the re-armament policy. However, the ability with which the Reichsbank under its expert, Schacht, financed it (until his conservatism and Nazi jealousy caused his dismissal in 1937) and the skilful direction of expert economists and industrialists, brought rapid results in re-armament. They would have been even better but for the rivalry between Göring's Four-Year Plan Office set up in 1936 to direct re-armament, and the Ministry of Economics, which opposed Göring's amateurish meddling. However despite the concentration on war production, German steel output in 1939 exceeded that of 1929 only because of additional plants acquired in Austria and Czechoslovakia. The scope and extent of German re-armament were grossly exaggerated in order to alarm potential opponents, though in terms of gross national product and proportion of total expenditure the armament increases were certainly staggering: 3·2% of the gross national product and 8·7% of the total expenditure in 1933, rising to 18·1% and 42·7% respectively in 1939. Yet Germany was still unprepared for a major war in September 1939, and though German armaments were extremely formidable in both quality and quantity, British war production was by then rapidly catching up with the German.

That Germany was unprepared for war in 1939 does not, however, mean that Hitler was forced into war then against his will, as he maintained—except in so far as he would have preferred to blackmail Poland into submission. His aims made war with at least Soviet Russia inevitable, though he expected to go a long way towards achieving them by the superior strength of his will, to which he attached great importance. The 'will to power' manifested in his triumph within Germany would be equally successful, he thought, in dealing with his foreign opponents. Moreover for some time he expected to have British and Polish, as well as Italian support for his European objectives. His early plans for winning in Russia the resources and *Lebensraum* which he needed depended above all on Polish and British support. Göring in 1935 offered the Ukraine to Poland, and the Germans had schemes for building up a great anti-Russian coalition, which would include England as well as Poland. This coalition, however, would open up for purely Nazi conquest and colonization the richest areas of southern Russia, including the Ukraine and the Caucasian oil fields. Hitler would not be satisfied merely with the restoration of pre-1914 German frontiers in Europe, nor was he greatly concerned, until the war opened up fresh perspectives, with regaining her colonies, which until 1939 interested him chiefly as a means of putting pressure on Britain. Even the Greater Germany secured by the *Anschluss*, Munich, Prague and the attack on Poland did not suffice. His eyes remained fixed on the greater gains to be made in the east, nearly secured in World War I.

It was chiefly with these greater gains in mind that Hitler strove to ensure that Soviet Russia and the western powers did not come to terms. As time passed he came to doubt the feasibility of the British alliance, for Britain would never commit herself to resigning eastern Europe to him in return for recognition of her overseas interests. For France he had a settled contempt. Italian friendship was consolidated after the Ethiopian crisis, but never yielded the results which he had expected from it. With Russia, of course, there could be only one settlement in the end, and not merely because of his anti-Marxist fanaticism, for even his most violent diatribes

527

against her were calculated from motives of power-politics. He would, of course, in any event have sought as one of his earliest aims to remilitarize the Rhineland, because of the vulnerability of Germany's greatest industrial regions of the west while the Rhineland was demilitarized. But he displayed his political genius in seizing on the ratification of the Franco-Soviet pact as the pretext for sending his troops into the Rhineland on March 7th, 1936. Contrary to rumours current at the time, and even to Hitler's and his generals' later assertions, the troops had orders to fight, not to retreat if the French opposed them. But there was little prospect of French opposition. Laval's friendly attitude over the plebiscite which restored the Saar to Germany in 1935 had shown the way the wind was blowing, and Hitler knew how strong were anti-Soviet and pacifist views in France. There was no chance that the British government would move. By this blow Hitler demonstrated the paralysis of French policy, even if he did not greatly affect the immediate relationship of France with her eastern allies.

The move also led to Belgium's prompt reconsideration of her strategic position and her consequent return to neutrality. The growth of Fascist groups like Léon Degrelle's Rexists, which were already allied with Flemish national extremists in order to destroy parliamentary government, did not affect the Belgian government's decision, though these dissidents brought Belgium to the brink of civil war before she was invaded by Germany in 1940. Then their 'fifth column' of collaborators (so-called, in Belgium and elsewhere, because when Franco's four armies were converging on Madrid in the Spanish Civil War, it was claimed that there was a 'fifth column' inside the capital) greatly facilitated the Nazi advance. When Belgium decided to disavow the Locarno obligations from considerations of military expediency after the Rhineland reoccupation, her political sympathies remained with Britain and France, but she was no longer an ally against Germany. The French, however, built no major defences to continue the Maginot Line from where it ended near Sedan, down to the Channel coast. The Maginot Line extension, as it was called, was virtually non-existent when war came in 1939. Such effective defences as were then thrown up along the Belgian frontier were built by the British Expeditionary Force. Germany constructed her own defences, the West Wall (or Siegfried Line), to face the French frontier only before the winter of 1939–40.

In 1936 the inauguration of the Four-Year Plan gave practical shape to the programme which Hitler then confided to his key government leaders: the army and the economy must be ready for war by 1940. As events favoured his ambitions, he became more impatient. He hoped that the Spanish Civil War would embroil the western powers with Italy; in any case he had realized the danger that Russia would grow too strong, and therefore she must be destroyed 'in 1943 at latest'. This entailed prior settlement with the west, either by diplomacy or force. By 1937 he was sufficiently satisfied with Germany's progress to consider that a war next year against the western powers might be feasible. On November 5th, 1937, he took the service leaders into his confidence. Explaining that the essential problem was Germany's lack of living space, he declared that this must be obtained between 1943 and 1945 at the latest. His immediate objectives were Austria and Czechoslovakia, but he still hoped to gain Austria by 'evolutionary methods', that is, by internal subversion, and he believed that Britain and France might stand aside while he destroyed Czechoslovakia. He could not then foresee that Schuschnigg's defiance would force the *Anschluss* crisis, nor that Britain and France would do so much of his work for him by forcing Czechoslovakia to yield. However, the programme required that Baron Constantin von Neurath, the Weimar politician whom he had allowed to be Foreign Minister for five years, should be replaced by a Nazi—Ribbentrop. It also necessitated greater control over the army, which was also secured in February 1938, when Hitler took over the Supreme Command and got rid of, or hobbled, independent-minded generals. With Göring in charge of the Luftwaffe, and Raeder controlling the navy, there were no difficulties.

In November 1937 Hitler had described Britain and France to his henchmen as Germany's hate-inspired antagonists, and he rather played down Russia. Next January, at Ribbentrop's prompting, he changed Nazi foreign policy from a predominantly anti-Soviet to a predominantly anti-western line, and this became only too clear in the negotiations of 1938 and 1939 for a tripartite alliance with Japan and Italy. This did not mean that he was committed even in his own mind to war against the west in the near future. His stand in the September Czechoslovak crisis was bluff, as was shown by his agreement to the Munich conference when Britain at last made unmistakable her determination to fight if France supported Czechoslovakia against German attack. Even then he had not definitely decided to attack the west, for he still did not consider this unavoidable, though it was now very likely. Certainly of all the demands which he made, those put to Poland in October 1938 were the most justified and the least designed to provoke a crisis, while his contempt for British and French leaders, the 'little worms' as he called them in August 1939, led him to believe that they would not react to the Prague crisis or to his subsequent threats to Poland after she had refused his terms. Then, however, following his hitherto successful methods, he tried to beat down Poland by a war of nerves and to frighten off the west. He rightly discounted prospects of a western alliance with Russia, though he sought to intimidate the partners of this unlikely coalition with the projected tripartite alliance. It was Japan's refusal of the proposals, not the arrival in Moscow in August 1939 of an Anglo-French military mission hoping for an impossible military alliance, which induced him to resort to what he had called in early 1934 the costliest solution of a pact with Stalin, though he had no idea even then how costly it would be.

However both Chamberlain and Mussolini surprised him: Chamberlain by reaffirming on August 25th British determination to stand by Poland,

Mussolini by refusing to join in the war. Astounded that the Nazi-Soviet pact should have no effect on Britain, Hitler called off the attack on Poland ordered for the next day while he again attempted to bludgeon Poland into submissiveness and the west into treachery. Poland, despite Anglo-French pressure, would not yield to his ultimatum, and the appeasers in the British cabinet dare not go too far, for opposition to another Munich was mounting inside and outside the British parliament. Hitler could not defer his attack too long, and it began at dawn on September 1st. This made impossible the second Munich which Hitler had always regarded as one possible solution of the crisis, and for which Mussolini worked until September 2nd, when British demands for Germany's withdrawal from Poland ended the attempt. Hence on September 3rd, Britain declared war on Germany, followed by a reluctant France. Although Hitler stumbled into a general war over the Polish issue, this was not an accidental development but the result of a deeper logic. It was the consequence not of external objective factors, but of the necessities of his own nature. On November 23rd, when urging his reluctant generals to attack in the west, he asserted: 'I did not organize the armed forces in order not to strike. The decision to strike was always in me.'

# SECTION THREE     THE SECOND WORLD WAR

*Chapter XIII*
## THE WAR BEGINS IN EUROPE

WHEN Germany attacked Poland at dawn on September 1st, 1939, she was inferior to her combined enemies in military, naval and economic strength. However, the divisions which defeated Poland within three weeks were better trained and better equipped than those of the enemy. Germany had decisive superiority in the air, and above all in political and military leadership. Against Poland she had forty-four front-line divisions, including six motorized and six armoured divisions, together with 1,500 combat aircraft. In reserve she held or was forming sixteen second-line divisions which saw no fighting, and about 500 aircraft. Poland had only thirty front-line infantry divisions, one poorly equipped cavalry division which boasted some obsolete tanks, a handful of brigades mounted on horseback, and ten reserve divisions. Of her 935 aircraft only 400 were modern enough to face the *Luftwaffe*, and as no steps had been taken to disperse and camouflage them, most were destroyed on the ground before the end of the day. Polish mobilization was still incomplete when the Germans attacked, but as the Polish army was dispersed along the whole length of the frontier, the delay was immaterial. Only well-prepared defences in depth could have held back the Germans on terrain so ideally suited to their new *Blitzkrieg* tactics. Except for the rivers there was virtually no natural obstacle in the vast Polish plains which stretched from the German frontier to the forests and marshes of the eastern borderlands. There was virtually no defence against the air attacks on cities, airfields, supply and communications centres, and terrible losses were sustained by civilians and troops alike.

Instead of the frontal assaults developed in World War I, the Germans concentrated their forces for rapid and deep penetrations of Polish territory. Motorized and light tank units exploited at high speed the devastation and confusion caused by massed air raids, followed by heavy tanks to obliterate any serious remaining pockets of resistance and the regular infantry to mop up and consolidate. These tactics were employed in two great pincer movements. General Fedor von Bock's northern army group seized the Polish Corridor, detaching enough forces to take Gdynia while the main body thrust to the south and east of Warsaw. The southern army group under General Gerd von Rundstedt attacked from Pomerania,

531

Silesia, Moravia and Slovakia to destroy the Polish southern forces, drive east of Cracow to Lvov, and push north to meet von Bock. Within this great encirclement further movements were developed to seal off Warsaw. On September 5th the German High Command decided that Poland was 'practically beaten'. Next day Cracow fell and the Polish government moved from Warsaw to Lublin. On September 8th the Germans were on the outskirts of Warsaw, and though Warsaw withstood a siege until September 27th, there was only isolated resistance after September 17th, when the Red Army also moved into Poland. The remnants of the Polish forces either followed their government into exile in Rumania, and eventually into France and Britain, or surrendered to the Red Army under the delusion that it was coming as a friend. However, President Ignacy Moscicki nominated from Rumania Władysław Raczkiewicz, who was in Paris, as his successor. Hence the legal continuity of the Polish Republic was preserved despite the Nazi-Soviet partition of Poland on September 28th.

The essential political and military prerequisite for the success of the Polish campaign, as both Hitler and his generals knew, was that Poland's western allies did not aid her by attacking the Rhineland. In the west Germany had only eleven first-line divisions, one division of fortress troops, thirty-five second-line divisions and no armoured or motorized units. The French had fifty-seven front-line divisions, forty-five reserve divisions, two mechanized divisions, one very heavily armoured and powerful tank division, and four British front-line divisions were also soon under the French commander-in-chief, General Maurice Gustav Gamelin. This immense Allied superiority on the ground was enhanced by the fact that the German troops were mostly either elderly reservists or raw recruits. Germany was inferior in the air both in bombers and fighters (except for dive-bombers, in which case French artillery superiority more than redressed the balance). With this tremendous superiority the French could have breached the Siegfried Line, as Gamelin himself later admitted, but they were haunted by memories of the bloody offensives of 1914–18, and remained on the defensive. Gamelin had promised the Poles a full-scale attack on the Siegfried Line by the sixteenth day after a German attack on Poland, but clearly the promise was never meant to be honoured. Had it been, the Rhine could have been reached within a fortnight, with incalculable consequences for the morale and military prospects of Germany and the Allies.

A western offensive would have impressed the Russians also. They had doubted, with good reason, until the British and French declarations of war had been made, whether the western powers would declare war, but they were equally uncertain of Nazi fidelity to bargains. They were anxious to seize their share of Poland ('this ugly offspring of the Versailles Treaty', as Molotov brutally called Poland on October 31st) but they were not ready for war even with Poland, still less with the west. Though Britain and France had guaranteed Poland only against Germany, not against

Russia, this was not officially announced until after Poland had fallen. The Russians resisted heavy Nazi pressure to move into the territory allocated by the Nazi-Soviet pact, until they suspected that unless they moved quickly a German-Polish armistice acceptable to the west might be made (a totally unfounded fear), and until they could be more certain of the truce which they actually signed with Japan on September 16th. On September 17th they felt safe enough to move into Poland, but did not neglect to inform foreign envoys (including the Polish) that the Soviet Union would remain neutral in the German-Polish war. They justified the attack on the grounds that as the Polish state had collapsed, they must defend White Russian and Ukrainian minorities—by implication against Germany. Indeed there was good reason for suspicion of Germany, for though Hitler was resolved not to quarrel with Stalin yet, German troops began on September 17th to occupy the extremely important oil-fields of the Borislaw-Drohobycz area near Lwow which the German generals coveted. Hitler immediately met Soviet protests by re-affirming the terms of the Nazi-Soviet pact of August 23rd, but this no longer satisfied Stalin. He decided that it would be too dangerous for Russia to tolerate the existence of the rump Polish state then envisaged, since the Nazis might in future use it against him. He therefore proposed that Poland should be completely partitioned along the lines made by the Rivers Pissa, Narev, Vistula and San. In return for this extension of the Nazi share of Poland, he demanded that Lithuania, allocated in August to Hitler's sphere of influence, should now fall to Russia's. Hitler, who had recently had his own doubts about leaving a rump Poland, made no difficulties. It was also agreed that Lithuania should recover Vilna, provided Lithuania ceded to Germany the Suwałki triangle on the frontier of East Prussia. The new Nazi-Soviet treaty of September 28th embodying these decisions was accompanied by important Soviet economic concessions to Germany, and a joint public demand that the western powers should make peace with Germany. However the mutual Nazi-Soviet distrust could not be overcome. When the marking out of the new frontiers began on October 4th each party at once began to fortify its side.

The economic negotiations which began in October were of great importance to both sides, and especially to Germany. Soviet assistance in providing Germany with food and strategic materials was invaluable. The grant of transit rights across Siberia enabled Germany to import from the Far East supplies of strategic materials, especially rubber. On September 1st she had only two months' supply of natural and artificial rubber, and the former was essential both for manufacturing the latter and for reclaiming rubber. Without the supplies of natural rubber transported to Germany across the Soviet Union the western campaigns of 1940 could not have been fought, nor could the later campaigns in Russia. German stocks of copper and other strategic materials were similarly built up with Soviet help. Before June 1941 immense quantities of grain, timber, oil and other essential commodities were exchanged by Russia, in some

533

cases in return for manufactured goods and munitions, including the uncompleted heavy cruiser *Luetzow*, in others for little return. Hitler's belief that his understanding with Stalin would enable him to circumvent the Allied blockade proved well founded.

But the territorial gains which Stalin began to make on September 28th, 1939, were of more lasting significance. Though Hitler annexed outright the areas of Poland held by imperial Germany, and placed the rest of his share under Seyss-Inquart in the 'Government-General' of Poland, Stalin's annexations went beyond the Curzon Line in the north and south, and cut Germany off from direct contact with Rumania. Moreover, even before the treaty was signed, Stalin announced to Germany his intention of 'solving the problem of the Baltic countries'—that is, of working for the annexation of Latvia, Estonia and Lithuania. At the end of September and the beginning of October they were accordingly forced, with reluctant German connivance, to grant military and naval bases to Russia, thus placing them under Soviet control. Immediately afterwards, German nationals living in the Baltic states were expatriated. However, Soviet demands on Turkey for territorial concessions and control of the Straits, and on Finland for naval bases and Finnish territory were rejected. Instead on October 19th Turkey signed a treaty with Britain and France, pledging support to them if they assisted Greece and Rumania against aggression, though the treaty was not effective against Soviet Russia. The treaty was, therefore, in the end a blow to Germany's prestige, though it had little practical importance for the west.

Indeed, there was by now little that the west could do except continue with its blockade and await the Nazi onslaught, which Hitler had fixed on September 27th to take place on November 12th. The speech in which he offered peace to the west on October 6th was patently insincere, but his generals dissuaded him from launching the attack, prescribed by him on October 9th in his directive for 'Case Yellow', on grounds of insufficient strength. This directive ordered an offensive through the neutral countries of Belgium, Holland and Luxembourg as soon as possible, seizing large areas of the Channel coast and northern France which were essential for air and naval operations against Britain. Next day he explained to them that his aim was 'the final military dispatch of the west', and he clearly believed that this would be achieved by a *Blitzkrieg* in France. The rapidity of his victory over Poland, and the west's supineness, had convinced him that he must exploit the unique opportunity to defeat Britain and France while he could still be sure of Soviet neutrality, but his final aim remained the destruction of Soviet Russia and the winning of *Lebensraum* in the east, to which attack in the west was the essential prelude.

Meanwhile even the French had tired of inactivity, though they did not intend to attack the Siegfried Line and end the *Sitzkrieg*, or 'phoney war', as the posturing on the western front had come to be known. Britain and France had eschewed air attacks on Germany from fear of retaliation, and only at sea was there any action. Even there the Allies confined their activities to enforcing the blockade, while Germany resorted to commerce raiding and sowing her new magnetic mines by submarines and aircraft, in an attempt to set up a kind of counter-blockade. At sea Germany was hopelessly outclassed. Even in ocean-going submarines, essential for the major German effort at sea, the Allies had a five to one superiority. In capital ships the ratio was three to one, though the German ships were faster and better armed. In cruisers it was ten to one, and very nearly the same in destroyers, while Britain had seven aircraft carriers, France one, and Germany none. Nevertheless, on October 14th the Germans scored the first naval success of the war with the sinking of the British battleship *Royal Oak* by a submarine which had penetrated into Scapa Flow—a humiliation not avenged until three British cruisers caught the German pocket battleship *Graf Spee* commerce raiding in the South Atlantic in December, and drove it into Montevideo harbour. There, on December 17th, it was scuttled by its captain's orders.

The only military action of the winter months took place in Finland. On October 31st Molotov publicly threatened the Finns with dire consequences if they did not submit to Soviet demands. They did not, and on November 30th the Russians attacked Finland, expecting easy victory. Germany maintained strict neutrality, but both the western powers and Italy sympathized with Finland, and the League of Nations expelled Soviet Russia. When Marshal Mannerheim's Finnish army inflicted humiliating defeats on the more numerous, but poorly led and equipped Soviet forces, the British and French governments gravely under-estimated Soviet military power. The French were especially anxious to help Finland, but chiefly from dislike of Russia, whom they would now much rather fight than Germany. The British wanted merely to use the pretext of an expeditionary force to aid Finland, with the League's blessing, to get troops across Norway and Sweden in order to cut off supplies of iron ore from Sweden to Germany. However, the British approved lunatic schemes by the French to synchronize this proposed expedition with air bombing of the Soviet Caucasian oil fields. Fortunately for the Allies they could carry out neither of these schemes. Norway and Sweden, despite sympathy for Finland, judged Allied military competence too accurately to offend Germany and Russia simultaneously, and they refused to allow western troops into their territories. Nevertheless in February 1940 the Allies assembled naval and military forces for Finland. The British intended them to seize *en route* the Norwegian port of Narvik, whence iron ore was shipped to Germany, and also destroy Sweden's iron mines. Invasion of Norway would be justified on the grounds that German naval forces were violating Norwegian territorial waters to avoid the Allied blockade along the Norwegian coast. By this time, however, the Russians had begun to rectify their military shortcomings, a factor which proved of great importance when they had to face the Nazi onslaught in 1941. The major offensive which the Russians launched on February 1st, 1940, defeated the Finns within a month. Finland concluded peace with Russia on March

12th at the cost of ceding Vyborg, some territory in the north and the naval base at Hangö.

This peace was a relief not only to Stalin but to Hitler. Sweden supplied nearly three-quarters of the iron ore used by Germany. In December 1939 Hitler had favourably considered his naval advisers' plans to seize Norway to protect the iron ore supply and to provide naval bases against the Allies. He had then been introduced to the Norwegian Nazi leader Vidkun Quisling, who had devised a scheme for seizing power in Norway with the aid of German forces. However, Hitler, still intent on 'Case Yellow', had continued to give that plan priority. On January 10th, 1940, he had ordered the attack on the west to begin on January 17th. On January 10th, however, a German officer carrying the operational plans had been captured when his plane, flying off course, had crashed in Belgium. He had not destroyed all his papers before his arrest, and these had confirmed the warning which Hitler's jealous friend Mussolini had leaked to Belgium and Holland in December 1939 of Germany's intentions to attack them. Belgium had sought, and obtained, Allied promises of help if Germany attacked, but Holland's dependence on neutrality was even more abject to the end. Hitler had naturally cancelled the orders on hearing of the crash —unfortunately for the Allies, as neither those instructions nor the state of the weather would have permitted the devastating *Blitzkrieg* launched later. Chamberlain had rightly predicted that Belgium would not allow access to Allied troops until Germany actually attacked, and Belgium refused to co-ordinate her defence with the Allies until Hitler's onslaught of May 10th. Then, vainly attempting to prevent Germany's turning of the Maginot Line by invading through Holland and Belgium, Allied troops went headlong into Belgium and disaster.

Postponement of 'Case Yellow' allowed Hitler on January 27th to order preparations for invading Norway and Denmark, but no urgency was shown until on February 16th the British seized in Norwegian territorial waters the *Graf Spee*'s supply ship, the *Altmark*. The *Altmark* carried captured Allied seamen, though the Norwegians denied this breach of neutrality. Churchill, who had taken over the British Admiralty on September 3rd, 1939, denounced Norway for allowing this and the other Nazi abuses of Norwegian territorial waters through the iron-ore traffic. The Allies had always ruled out moving into Norway against the Norwegians' wishes, but Churchill's denunciations strengthened Hitler's suspicions that if he did not occupy Norway quickly, Churchill might forestall him. On February 21st Hitler personally ordered General Nikolaus von Falkenhorst to complete the planning, and to lead the invasion if it took place. Falkenhorst was a mere corps commander, and knew nothing of Norway, though he had fought in the Baltic states twenty years earlier. According to his own later account, immediately after being appointed he bought a Baedeker (certainly the General Staff, never having studied Scandinavia, had no maps of Norway) and set to work with this. In fact considerable preliminary planning had already been done, and by March

1st the directive for 'Exercise Weser', the invasions of Norway and Denmark, was ready for Hitler's signature.

As Germany did not have command of the sea, it was essential that the invasion of Norway should be a surprise. Surprise was achieved although Britain and Norway had ample warning of German preparations, and the Allies expected a vigorous Nazi reaction to their decision to mine Norwegian waters and force the iron-ore ships outside them. Hitler, who genuinely regarded the invasion as a defensive move against Britain, on April 2nd fixed 'Weser' for April 9th. On April 4th Chamberlain confidently asserted that by not attacking while the west was unprepared, Hitler had 'missed the bus', a gaffe which helped to bring Chamberlain's fall from power the next month. On April 8th Britain announced that she was mining Norwegian waters, and British naval units skirmished with some of the Nazi warships escorting the invasion fleet. They sank a cruiser and a transport, but did not realize what was afoot, and next day, Denmark, Norway and Britain were all taken by surprise. Denmark did not oppose occupation. Norway's 'Quislings', as her and similar traitors in other countries were henceforth contemptuously called, assisted the Germans to seize ports, airfields and other strategic points. Molotov, told by the German ambassador of the invasions soon after they had occurred, wished Germany complete success in her defence of the 'rights of neutral nations' against British aggression. In previous months Soviet uncertainty about the course of future events had produced Russian assurances to Britain and France that Nazi-Soviet friendship was not eternal. It had also caused suspension of economic aid to Germany, and in early April restrictions on the use by Germany of the naval base which she had built near Murmansk. Now, however, Molotov promised that the deliveries of grain which had been held up would be made, and cordiality was restored.

The Germans on April 9th occupied the ports of Narvik, Trondheim, Bergen, Stavanger, Kristiansand, Egersund and Arendal against little or no opposition, but Oslo resisted long enough for the government to escape. As Allied troops were rushed out in response to Norway's appeal for help, the invasion turned into a bitterly fought campaign instead of the hoped-for walkover. Hitler indeed became so nervous that by the end of the first week's fighting he considered evacuating Narvik, the key to the whole campaign. However the Germans, brilliantly pioneering the new technique of combined air, naval and ground operations, established the air superiority which proved decisive. The Allies and Norwegians besieged Narvik from April 14th, but captured it only on May 28th. The Allies also inflicted very heavy losses on the German navy, though no more than the Germans had expected, and the British navy also suffered badly. Moreover, Germany had dealt a shattering blow at the prestige of the Allies and of the British navy. She had assured her vital iron ore supplies, gained absolute mastery of the Baltic, and had obtained excellent Atlantic air and naval bases. And although the campaign did not end until June 8th, by early May the Allies had been forced to evacuate their troops from

537

central Norway, and the Norwegian campaign did not interfere with Germany's major enterprise in the west.

For this thrust the portents were not ignored, though the direction of the blow was misjudged. In one respect France was better able to meet attack than she had been in January. On March 20th the feeble Daladier had been overthrown—not because he had failed to attack Germany, but because he had not ordered an attack on Russia through Finland. His successor, Paul Reynaud, proved no more competent, and he also had to include defeatists in his cabinet. However, in Britain a change of vital importance was made. The Norwegian fiasco, and the anxiety aroused by Chamberlain's obvious incapacity to meet the great danger now imminent, forced his resignation. A coalition government was a clear necessity in face of the Nazi peril, and as the Labour Party would not serve under Chamberlain, but would under Churchill, Chamberlain resigned on May 10th. Churchill assumed the responsibility for which he was supremely fitted, making the Labour leader, Clement R. Attlee, his deputy, and the trade union leader, Ernest Bevin, Minister of Labour, but retaining Chamberlain and most of the former appeasers, since sacking them would have split the Conservative Party, which had accepted Churchill with reservations because of his prewar record. These cabinet changes could not affect the outcome of the western campaign, but a competent Allied command might conceivably have done so, and could certainly have delayed it.

In May 1940 the Germans were not numerically superior in land forces or fighter planes. The 136 Nazi divisions, numbering about 2,000,000 men, had superiority only in morale and leadership. They faced ninety-four French divisions (another nine guarded the Franco-Italian frontier), ten British divisions, twenty-two Belgian, nine Dutch and one Polish division, totalling about 4,000,000 men. In armour the forces were equal, with about 2,400 tanks each. German armour, though faster, was lighter, but it was its disposition and employment, together with a superiority in bombers to exploit this, which gave German armour the decisive advantage. Despite Colonel Charles de Gaulle's appeals to group the French tanks into a single mechanized corps, more than half of them were dispersed along the 400-mile front as support for infantry. Hence France had only three armoured divisions against Germany's ten. Seven of Germany's tank divisions, with massed bomber support, decided the issue of the Battle of France within four days. Yet the Allied command had excellent defensive positions at its disposal, and an ample ratio of troops to space had it not allowed the Germans to throw it off balance.

Gamelin had expected the major attack to come through Belgium, as it had in 1914. This was indeed the strategy first adopted for 'Case Yellow', but the young General Fritz von Manstein produced a scheme for a main attack driving through the Ardennes to the mouth of the Somme, thereby splitting the Allied force and making possible its rapid defeat. Hitler, to whom the idea of an Ardennes offensive had already occurred, endorsed the plan. The German General Staff elaborated it, and it was employed in

May with devastating effect, though at considerable risk. Gamelin, as the Germans had predicted, reacted to their invasion of neutral Holland, Belgium and Luxembourg on May 10th by ordering the British Expeditionary Force under Lord Gort, and some of the north-eastern French forces, to advance from prepared defensive positions behind the Belgian frontier into Belgium. Luxembourg was taken within hours. Holland held out for only five days against German armour, parachutists and glider troops, and against her own numerous 'fifth column' of traitors, though her resistance would certainly have been more protracted but for the frankly terrorist bombing of Rotterdam on May 14th; Queen Wilhelmina and her government escaped to Britain to continue the war. The forces in Belgium managed to hold the German advance there at first. But by May 11th, a German tank division was across the lower Meuse, the great fort of Eben Emael which commanded the junction of the lower Meuse and the Albert Canal had been captured, and the Belgians' control of their major defensive barriers had been lost. Even more important, the Allied advance into Belgium had left a fatally weak force of only twelve divisions to hold the hundred miles of the Ardennes front, the oldest and shortest German route into France. Here von Rundstedt attacked with forty-four divisions, seven of them armoured. Gamelin had not considered the Ardennes impassable for armour, but he had not expected an attack there unless the Germans had first been held elsewhere, and expected none on the Meuse before the ninth or tenth day, thereby giving him enough prior warning. By May 15th Sedan was in German hands and the Maginot Line had been turned (it was not, in fact, breached, so that in this respect at least it justified itself) and German armour had crossed the Meuse and broken out into open country towards the Channel coast. This precipitated first the retreat and then the rout of Allied forces in Belgium and North-East France, for despite their numerical superiority, the Allies had no strategic reserve. In its dash for the coast, reached at Abbeville on May 20th, the German armour was often cut off from the infantry following up and both were open to counter-attacks. These were attempted by de Gaulle's patched-up armoured division on May 17th and 19th, but de Gaulle, now a Brigadier-General ('temporary'), had only a hundred and fifty tanks to pit against the now monstrous superiority of the German armour, as most of the French tanks had been lost by inefficient handling.

On May 19th Gamelin was succeeded by General Maxime Weygand as commander-in-chief. With the forces in Belgium almost cut off from the major forces in France, it was already too late to save France. Weygand made the only decision possible under the circumstances, by ordering the troops in Belgium to break south through the German line while he himself directed an attack to the north, but his forces were too weak for the manoeuvre. By the morning of May 25th the Germans had moved so far to the north-east through the Belgian front that they threatened to cut off the British not only from the Belgians but from the coast. Gort's immediate superior, the French General Georges M. J. Blanchard, immediately ordered his own troops, the Belgians and the British to make for Dunkirk. German tanks would have been there before them, had not Hitler, with von Rundstedt's approval, ordered them to halt just south of Dunkirk on May 24th. Hitler did not want to risk armour which he hoped to throw into the battle for France ('Case Red'), as soon as it had been refitted and regrouped. Göring, also, assured him that the *Luftwaffe* would prevent the evacuation of the British and French troops from Dunkirk.

The British and French were thereby enabled both to strengthen Dunkirk's defences, and to begin on May 26th the evacuation which by June 4th brought to Britain 225,000 British and 112,000 French troops, together with a few thousand Belgians who dissociated themselves from the surrender ordered by their king Leopold III on May 28th. They supported the Belgian ministers who fled first to France and then to Britain. Most of the heavy equipment taken into Dunkirk, however, could not be taken off, and Hitler had good reason for believing that British troops would see no more action against Germany in this war.

After Dunkirk the major preoccupation of the British government, apart from re-equipping and strengthening its army and air force and preparing to repel a Nazi invasion, was to persuade the French not to surrender but to continue the war from their colonies. Reynaud wanted to fight on but had little authority over his government. Weygand, as early as May 25th, had indirectly but clearly argued for an armistice, to preserve the French army as the only means of maintaining public order in the country. Pétain, whom Reynaud had made Vice-Premier on May 18th in a vain attempt to restore the morale of the army and nation, was the most powerful defeatist of all in the cabinet. Nevertheless, he certainly spoke for the majority of the shattered and demoralized French when he supported Weygand's demand that the government must make an armistice with Germany and remain in France, and not abandon the country to chaos, Communism and possible civil war. On June 9th the government left Paris, which it declared an open town, and went to Tours. Next day Mussolini, convinced that the war was won and that Britain must soon follow France into defeat, declared war so that he could share the booty. On June 14th the Germans entered Paris, and the French government moved to Bordeaux. The British reluctantly agreed on June 16th that France could negotiate an armistice, provided that during the negotiations her fleet sailed for British harbours. With the approval of de Gaulle, appointed Under-Secretary of Defence on June 5th, they offered to make a complete union of the French and British empires to keep the French colonies in the war. The French cabinet rejected the offer practically out of hand, although the originators of the proposal had been the French politicians Guy Mollet and René Pleven. Reynaud resigned, to be succeeded, in strictly constitutional fashion, by Pétain. Next day Pétain appealed for peace, de Gaulle flew to London, soon to make himself the leader of 'Free France', despite his low rank, and Hitler arranged a meeting for June 18th with Mussolini to agree on the armistice terms. Mussolini had neither won even a token victory over the shattered French army, nor fully considered what demands he should make on France. In any case the victory was Hitler's, and Germany would have the decisive voice. The French armistice delegation was summoned by the Germans on June 21st to the railway coach in the forest of Compiègne where the 1918 armistice had been signed, and on June 22nd they had their revenge. The French army was reduced to the 'Versailles' figure of 100,000 men. Alsace-Lorraine was annexed and the northern part of France with the whole Atlantic seaboard was occupied by German troops. Pétain's government controlled the Mediterranean coast and the rest of France, together with the colonies and the fleet, which was to remain in French ports and be disarmed. Harsher terms were not imposed in case the fleet and colonies went over to de Gaulle and the British. A separate armistice with Italy on June 24th gave Italy control of a strip of demilitarized territory along the Franco-Italian border. Of course these were only armistice terms. Moreover, Hitler wanted to make peace with Britain.

The non-combatant states had been as surprised as the Allies at the unprecedented speed and magnitude of Hitler's victory. The Russians were particularly taken aback, and as in September 1939 they had to move with unwelcome hurriedness to claim the reward of their bargain with Germany. On June 4th they cautiously sounded out the Germans about 'solving' the Balkan problems in conjunction with Germany and Italy, but though Hitler was willing to divide control of the Balkans with Mussolini he rejected Stalin as a partner there.

No objection could be made, however, to Soviet occupation of the Baltic states between June 14th and 17th, though as a precaution the Russians moved troops up to the German frontier. Encouraged by this success, and anxious to get what they could before the armistice was made with France and German troops could be brought back to the east, the Russians told Germany they intended to demand Bessarabia and northern Bukovina from Rumania. Hitler advised Rumania to yield to the Soviet ultimatum of June 26th, though only the cession of Bessarabia had been agreed upon by the August 1939 pact with Stalin. Hitler dared not quarrel yet with Stalin, nor risk the outbreak of hostilities in the Balkans. Despite the essential German economic interests in Rumania, especially in grain and oil, he had to yield, but he rightly regarded the move as a sign of Soviet hostility, though he did not recognize the nervousness which lay behind it. The breach in the Nazi-Soviet partnership had begun, though Hitler had, indeed, confided to von Rundstedt and others even before the French armistice that he intended to attack Russia. First, however, he had to settle with Britain, to whom he had made overtures for peace by devious methods even after Churchill's resounding speech of June 18th, affirming that the rights of Czechs, Poles, Norwegians, Dutch and Belgians would all be restored, and that if France left the British to fight alone they would so bear themselves 'that, if the British Empire and its Commonwealth last

for a thousand years, men will still say: "This was their finest hour." '
Hitler, and many others, thought these empty words.

Franco, like Stalin, wished to exploit the Nazi victory at no cost to
himself. He had given useful diplomatic support in countering Allied and
United States propaganda in Latin America, and more practical help by
allowing Germany surreptitious use of Spanish air and naval bases. On
June 19th he demanded from Hitler large areas of French African territory;
and if Britain did not make peace, German artillery and aircraft, under
strict Spanish control, were to attack Gibraltar. The demands were quite
explicit, but the offers to enter the war which he made before and after
June 19th were always predicated on conditions which could never be met.
Spain, of course, was too weak and impoverished after the Civil War to
fight. Moreover, America in close consultation with Britain doled out the
aid to Spain without which her economy would have been in even direr
straits. As the fortunes of war deserted the Axis Franco moved discreetly
over to the other side, though he continued to maintain his independence.
The British, who could easily have been shut out of the Mediterranean
had he allowed the Nazis to take Gibraltar, were well content.

Pétain's government, which Laval joined on June 23rd, was an equally
uncertain, and at first even more dangerous quantity from Britain's standpoint. It was determined not to surrender its fleet to Hitler, but the
characters and political views of its members were such that Britain
refused to run the risk of allowing Hitler to use the French fleet to invade
her. To forestall the danger, French ships in British home and overseas
ports were seized or immobilized on July 3rd, and strong British naval
units offered the French warships in Oran and Mers-el-Kebir the choice
of joining the Free French, internment in neutral ports, or sailing to the
French West Indies. On refusal of these terms the British opened fire.
Three battleships, an aircraft carrier and two destroyers were sunk. One
battleship and seven cruisers, which had been stationed in Algiers,
escaped to France. On July 8th a surprise attack disabled another battleship at Dakar.

On July 1st the French government had moved to Vichy. There Laval,
as premier, on July 10th got the National Assembly to pass a bill giving
Pétain's government dictatorial powers pending creation of a new constitution—which was never created, so the dictatorial powers were retained
until de Gaulle came back to rule France in 1944. Laval's methods were
unscrupulous and illegal, though not more so than those then used in
London for the nobler cause of establishing the Free French movement.
The Assembly had no legal power to destroy the Third Republic in favour
of the feeble imitation of the Italian corporate state which was set up with
Pétain as Chief of State, but the vote of 569 for the bill, against a mere
eighty convinced democrats, was both decisive and representative of the
wishes of the demoralized nation. However, the generals, royalists, near-
Fascists and reactionary civil servants who formed Pétain's court certainly
were not representative, though for a time some better men served him in

the hope that better days would come. At Vichy they never did. There was neither consistency nor resolution in Pétain's attempt to carry through a 'National Revolution' which would restore France's soul by recalling her to older, spartan and non-democratic ways of life. Nevertheless, the vain and senile Chief of State convinced himself that France could be 're-generated' by purges of Jews and Freemasons, and by the destruction of the trade unions and all other organs of political and social democracy. When he met Hitler at Montoire on October 24th he avoided giving any specific concessions, but he promised that France would 'collaborate' with Germany in setting up the Nazi New Order in Europe. He clearly believed that the ambiguities of his 'double game' were honourably preserving French independence. Laval, however, whom in July he had nominated as *Dauphin* and successor, drew the logical conclusions from the fact that the Vichy *régime*'s existence depended on Germany's victory. He became so friendly with the Germans that Pétain's courtiers suspected that he was working for an alliance against Britain in return for the release of French prisoners of war and the reduction of German occupation costs. They therefore secured his dismissal in December, but the Anglophobe naval chief who succeeded as *Dauphin* in February 1941 followed a more blatantly collaborationist policy. Admiral Jean François Darlan put French industry and manpower at Germany's disposal, and in May 1941 ordered Vichy's High Commissioner in Syria, General Henri Dentz, to give military facilities to the Germans when they were poised to destroy the British position in the Middle East. Only a speedy and risky Anglo-Free French reaction, and Hitler's refusal to spare more men from 'Barbarossa' (the plan to invade Russia) averted catastrophe for the Allies and put Syria and Lebanon under their control in July. Yet Vichy was a collaborationist, not a puppet government. The French Quislings—notably renegade Socialists and Communists, and their Fascist former enemies—were in Paris, urging the Germans to establish a thorough-going dictatorship over the whole country.

On purely military considerations Roosevelt was almost as justified in handling Vichy circumspectly as in following the more congenial policy of upholding Britain as the western hemisphere's strategic line of defence, and moving away from the policy of neutrality followed since the outbreak of war. Under United States leadership, the American republics had issued in October 1939 the Panama Declaration fixing a zone 300 miles into the Atlantic, except from Canada and the European Caribbean colonies, within which zone no belligerent acts must occur. They further agreed to consult each other if the security of any American republic was threatened by transfer of territories in the hemisphere from one European country to another. This had been mere verbiage. The republics would not enforce the zone's neutrality against German commerce raiders—nor against the conquerors of the *Graf Spee*. The amendment of the United States Neutrality Act in November had repealed the embargo on selling arms to belligerents only to the extent of imposing 'cash and carry terms' and this favoured the Allies. But it also signified United States resolution to keep out of war by minimizing the dangers of submarine sinkings of American ships, and indeed represented an isolationist rather than a neutral stand-point. The Allies, however, had money and ships, and both Roosevelt and his advisers had no doubts then of Allied victory. His declaration of April 18th, 1940, after Hitler occupied Denmark, that the Monroe Doctrine covered Greenland, was a necessary and obvious measure of precaution. His approval of Britain's occupation of Iceland on May 10th was qualified by a clear resolve that Iceland, like Greenland, must revert to Denmark after the war, and not fall under the control of either Britain or Canada.

By the middle of May, however, when France's fall was imminent and his service advisers doubted whether Britain alone could survive the Nazi onslaught, Roosevelt had to re-appraise American policy. He decided to run for an unprecedented third term as president, though he did not announce this until July. On his service chiefs' advice, and with popular approval, he stepped up armament production. Indeed he followed rather than led public opinion, for despite the vigour of isolationist propaganda two-thirds of Americans believed that Hitler's victory would menace their security. However he vigorously seized on Mussolini's cowardly attack on France on June 10th to exchange neutrality for non-belligerence by giving the Allies all aid possible short of war. On June 14th he signed a bill that had been under discussion for months for a 'two-ocean navy'. Next week he appointed the Republicans Frank Knox and Henry Stimson as Secretaries of Navy and War respectively to signify that a national emergency had arisen and national unity was essential. Obviously he exaggerated the Axis danger for, although some Latin American republics were receptive to Axis propaganda, while Hitler could not invade Britain, the western hemisphere was safe. On July 27th the Havana Conference of Pan-American Foreign Ministers issued a declaration that an attack on any American republic was an attack on all. (This measure proved to be of importance, however, despite the reservations of some signatories, when Japan and her European friends made war on the United States eighteen months later.) In August 1940 the Canadian-American Permanent Joint Board on Defence was established.

Tremendous and rapid strides were made in American war production, but they could not show results for many months after June 1940, and Britain's danger was immediate. Hitler was disappointed that she had not made peace. He was still well-disposed towards the British Empire so long as it did not block his schemes in Europe and would accept a German Empire overseas. On July 2nd Hitler ordered planning to begin for the invasion of Britain, and on July 16th he decided that operation 'Sea-Lion' (its code name) should take place in August. Hitler, like his army and navy chiefs, doubted its feasibility, but Göring insisted that the *Luftwaffe* could destroy the Royal Air Force and make invasion possible. The German navy had been so weakened by recent actions that it could not gain even temporary control of the Channel unless Göring could neutralize both the Royal Navy and the Royal Air Force. The British knew that the two keys to survival were national morale, which was upheld by native obstinacy and Churchill's resounding speeches, and a tremendous increase in the production of the Hurricane and Spitfire fighter planes. Despite the peril at home the British managed to send out men and tanks to General Archibald Wavell, commander in the Middle East, to meet the threats posed by Italy's belligerence. And after all, if the Nazis had got across the Channel in force, they could not have been thrown back.

The aerial Battle of Britain began on August 13th, after a month's inconclusive aerial dog-fighting over the Channel and German attacks on ports and shipping, and after Hitler had postponed (on July 31st) the invasion to mid-September. The primary Nazi objectives were to destroy airfields and aircraft factories, and force the British fighters into a battle of annihilation. Göring at first had about 1,000 bombers and 700 fighters available on any day. The British fighters were of superior quality, and were also directed on their targets by radar, without which the battle would probably have gone the other way. Hence Göring needed in the early stages two fighters to escort each bomber, and before mass raiding on London began, he rarely attacked with more than about 350 bombers and 700 fighters. The British began with about 950 Hurricanes and Spitfires (and some inferior planes). Despite damage to airfields and losses in the air they kept about 700 fighters operational even in the darkest days. British success in destroying bombers imposed heavy escort duties on the German fighters, and so thwarted Göring's attempt to force the British fighters into a battle of annihilation. Hence in the first eleven days the Germans lost 290 aircraft against 114 British planes, and no airfield was knocked out, while British aircraft production and training of pilots more than replaced losses.

Then on the night of August 23rd London was attacked by bombers, and the British retaliated by bombing Berlin for a week. At that time the Germans were heavily damaging airfields, and wearing down the British fighters by better concentration on targets. Göring, however, in the belief that mass bombing attacks would end British resistance, and also humiliated by the raids on Berlin, ordered on September 7th the commencement of mass raids on London. In the decisive stage of the Battle of Britain which now ensued, the Nazis lost 195 aircraft and the British 120 fighters, as against 380 and 286 respectively between August 24th and September 6th. As German invasion barges and transports had already been assembled and were being heavily attacked by British bombers, the British authorities at first thought that the massed bombers approaching London on the afternoon of September 7th, escorted by all available fighters, heralded the invasion. Other massed raids followed on September 9th, 11th and 14th. Because of weather conditions in the Channel, Göring had to win air superiority by September 17th if the Germans were to invade that year. On September 15th he sent over 200 bombers against London (over 300 had been sent on September 7th), but by changing his tactics he had lost the ascendancy which was being gained over the British fighters before September 7th. The British, sensing the crisis, made their supreme effort. Sixty planes (not 185 as claimed at the time) were shot down, mostly by fighters, of whom twenty-six were lost. Many more Nazi planes were damaged, and the *Luftwaffe* never recovered from this shattering defeat. On September 17th Hitler put off the invasion indefinitely. However, the terror which was to have accompanied it fell upon Russia in the following year on a much larger scale.

Hitler had been much preoccupied with Russia even during the Battle of Britain, partly from his vague and mistaken belief that Stalin was holding out to the British hopes of support. Hitler could not believe that Britain would otherwise have continued to resist. He had nevertheless good reason to be annoyed with Russia. Stalin's territorial demands on Rumania had provoked Hungary and Bulgaria to follow suit and regain the areas lost after World War I. Hitler exaggerated the dangers posed by this development, but Soviet incitement of Bulgaria against the country whose economic resources were needed for Germany's war machine was disquieting. Hitler also knew that Churchill shared his own belief in the strategic importance of the Balkans, and he feared possible Anglo-Russian collaboration there. On July 31st he declared that a *Blitzkrieg* would be launched against Russia (Operation 'Barbarossa') in May 1941, which must smash her within five months, as a standstill during the winter would be 'hazardous'. The reasons given to his service chiefs were that this would extinguish Britain's last hopes and make Germany the master of Europe, the Balkans and the Baltic. If 'Sea-Lion' did not succeed, Britain could be defeated by submarine and aircraft, though it might take two years.

Thereby Hitler had unconsciously committed himself to the war on two fronts which he had always said he would avoid, but he did not regard Britain as his chief enemy now. His real reason for attacking Russia was that this had always been his great objective in Europe, but his anger was further aroused early in August when Russia formally annexed the Baltic states, and almost at once proceeded to clear out the German Legations there. Hitler instructed Rumania to cede northern Transylvania to Hungary and southern Dobrudja to Bulgaria, but on August 30th he replied to Russia's southern advance by guaranteeing Rumania in concert with Italy. Russia was excluded, though the Nazi-Soviet pact entitled her to be consulted, and Molotov on September 10th complained of bad faith. There was, indeed, a kind of diplomatic Nazi-Soviet cold war already in progress in the Balkans, though Stalin continued with appeasement to the end. He not only rejected British proposals to co-operate in building up a Balkan front against Germany, but informed the Germans—thereby merely increasing their suspicions.

Hitler, however, was ready to overlook the real and important United States assistance to Britain, since he believed that the isolationists would keep America out of the war and that Britain must soon be defeated, though at the end of August Germany had only twenty-six submarines operational, and a heavy toll was being taken of the *Luftwaffe*. Yet Hitler's view of America was not entirely based on wishful thinking, for on July 10th Roosevelt had told Congress: 'We will not send our men to take part in European wars.' American aid did not affect the outcome of the Battle of Britain. No American-built fighter flew in it. There was no immediate importance in the celebrated deal of September 3rd whereby Roosevelt turned over fifty obsolete destroyers in return for long leases of air and naval bases in Newfoundland, the West Indies and Bermuda, and he rightly calculated that Hitler would not go to war over it. Nor were the old American rifles and light artillery pieces now sent needed to defend Britain. But Roosevelt was able to spike the guns of his isolationist opponents by pointing to the good bargain made for the destroyers, and when diminishing British assets in America were jeopardizing purchases of food and munitions in the hard winter of 1940–41, he was able to prepare the ground for the great Lend Lease Act of March 11th, 1941, which made America not only the 'arsenal of democracy' but its indispensable larder.

Hitler knew the extent of Roosevelt's aid to Britain, but dared not try to stop it directly. Germany therefore tried by indirect means to stop American aid by exploiting the close interconnection of European and Far Eastern events. Germany's victories had left the Dutch and French colonies in South-East Asia without any defence against Japanese pressure, and the British position was not much better. The Vichy authorities in Indo-China had been forced to allow Japanese military observers into the country to ensure that no supplies sent through Indo-China reached Chiang Kai-shek; heavy pressure on Batavia had given Japan a large measure of control over the products and commerce of the Dutch East Indies; and war had been threatened against Britain, unless she cut off supplies to Chiang through Hong Kong and the long and difficult Burma Road from Mandalay to Kunming. Until mid-June the Japanese had used the opportunities given to them in Asia by the European war with great caution, but the defeat of France and Holland, and the likelihood that Britain's demise would soon follow, presented irresistible temptations. At first the Germans had not given much encouragement to Japan, for she had infringed German as well as other foreign rights in China. At the same time, America had refused to promise Britain help against Japanese encroachments while withholding American approval of British surrender to them. However, Roosevelt and Churchill agreed to try to keep Japan quiet as long as possible, while America built up her military power and Britain recuperated from the recent German blows. In July Roosevelt had finally terminated the Japanese-American commercial treaty of 1911. He had also put under licence, but not under embargo, exports of some scrap metals, plus aircraft fuel and oil which Japan had been stockpiling. Roosevelt's two-ocean navy bill underlined these warnings against further Japanese advances.

These were entirely defensive measures and Japanese protests were disingenuous. Japan had determined to move to the south as soon as possible, and in September sent troops and aircraft into North Indo-China, somewhat embarrassing Germany. Germany wished neither to lose Japanese friendship nor to offend Vichy, whose fleet and North African colonies would be useful against Britain. Early in September, therefore, Ribbentrop was simultaneously refusing to put pressure on Vichy, as the Japanese wanted, while pressing Japan to make the alliance with Germany and Italy which he had urged for two years. On September 11th the Japanese Foreign Minister, Yosuke Matsuoka, who was eager to make the alliance, told the Germans that in addition to China and Manchukuo, Japan claimed as falling within the limits of what she (euphemistically) called the Greater East Asia Co-prosperity Sphere, French Indo-China, Thailand, Burma, Malaya, British Borneo, the Dutch East Indies and New Caledonia 'at present'. He added that Australia and New Zealand would be taken later. He did not reveal that Japan intended to retain the German former Pacific possessions taken after World War I, and to conquer India also.

By the terms of the Tripartite Pact signed by Germany, Italy and Japan on September 27th, Japan recognized the New Order in Europe, her partners reciprocally recognizing her New Order in Asia. They agreed to assist by all means within their power any of their number who was attacked by the United States. America was not named explicitly but it was well understood in the west who the potential enemy was. Neither Japan nor Italy, however, knew Hitler's plans against Russia, and before agreeing to the pact the Japanese government had decided to follow it with a non-aggression pact with Russia, for it would not be possible to move south unless Russian neutrality was assured. All three signatories agreed that the pact would check America in the Pacific and frighten her into ending aid to Britain. The pact was based on the hypothesis of a Nazi victory in Europe, but it was phrased in such a way that Matsuoka could rightly boast that Japan could remain outside the European conflict as long as she chose, and could decide for herself when the pact became operative. The events of 1941 vindicated Matsuoka's interpretation, though the pact's immediate effects were not encouraging for Japan. Roosevelt was aware before its signature that it would be anti-American. On September 25th America announced a new loan to China and the next day put under licence the export of all scrap iron and steel to Japan. Britain, who had closed only the Burma Road, and then only during the monsoons when it was impassable, reopened it on October 8th. Japanese reactions were restrained. While Russia was still so uncertain a quantity they had to be.

Meanwhile the territorial losses inflicted on Rumania had caused Carol's abdication on September 3rd, in favour of his son Michael, and the establishment of a Fascist government under General Ion Antonescu which sought German protection. In mid-September it asked Hitler to send in troops to defend Rumania against Soviet or Hungarian attacks, and to make a fighting force of the weak Rumanian army. Hitler agreed immediately, giving secret orders, however, that neither the Rumanians nor the German occupying troops were to learn that one major purpose of their activities was to prepare for an attack on Russia from Rumania. He also decided to occupy the Rumanian oil fields. These were clear breaches of his pact with Russia, and Molotov rejected the excuses that Germany sought only to secure essential supplies from Rumania and prevent Britain from stirring up conflicts in the Balkans. The moves were anti-Russian more than anti-British. Russia had accepted the argument that the Tripartite Pact was directed purely against the Americans, but the adhesion to it of Russia's hostile neighbours, Hungary, Rumania, Slovakia and Bulgaria, between November 1940 and March 1941 could have only one common purpose.

Even with his ally Mussolini, Hitler no longer bothered to maintain appearances. Mussolini had guaranteed Rumania with him, but had been ignored when Nazi troops had been sent in, even though he had vigorously seconded Ribbentrop's negotiations for the Tripartite Pact and German attempts to bring Franco into the war. It had even seemed that Italy was proving an active, though not very effective military ally. Wavell had not awaited Italy's attack on Egypt after Mussolini had entered the war on June 10th, but had launched harassing moves against Mussolini's Libyan forces. However this had only delayed the assault on Egypt, and the Italians had advanced rapidly in East Africa. On July 4th they took the Sudan frontier towns of Kassala and Gallabat, and on July 15th they occupied Moyale in Kenya. Exploiting their overwhelming numerical superiority, by mid-August the Italians had captured British and French Somaliland. British control of Suez, however, cut off Italian troops in East Africa, British agents were organizing Ethiopian tribesmen against the Italians, and Mussolini had not seized the key to the Eastern Mediterranean, Malta, when it was practically defenceless. On September 14th Marshal Rodolfo Graziani's 250,000 strong army drove from Cyrenaica into Egypt, and was soon at Sidi Barrani, sixty miles beyond the frontier. Instead of sweeping on, however, it halted there to dig in and regroup. Thereby it lost a great opportunity of destroying Wavell's Western Desert forces, which it outnumbered by about nine to one. Reinforcements of tanks and Commonwealth troops, British, South African, Indian, Australian and New Zealand reached the Western Desert and East Africa during the late fall and the winter, though the Commonwealth troops remained hopelessly outnumbered.

Because Hitler had ignored Mussolini when ordering the German occupation of Rumania, the Duce in a display of pique decided to assert his independence by attacking Greece and facing Hitler in turn with a *fait accompli*. Preparations were being completed while Hitler's demand to Franco that Spain should enter the war was being adroitly but humiliatingly rejected at their Hendaye meeting on October 23rd, and Hitler's conversation next day with Pétain was proving equally fruitless. When Hitler saw Mussolini on October 28th he was told that Greece had just been attacked. The news renewed Hitler's exaggerated fears of a British entry into the Balkans and of air raids on Rumanian oil fields. Moreover Mussolini's invasion of Greece was so bungled, and Greek resistance so heroically spectacular, that Axis prestige suffered heavily. Hitler, also, had to defer until next spring the help he had intended to give in North Africa, and had to prepare to rescue Mussolini from the Greek disaster. Yet despite Italian mismanagement of the North African and Greek campaigns, they provided excellent openings for driving the British out of the Mediterranean and Middle East by the spring of 1941. Moreover, the temporary disruption of Hitler's plans to invade Russia because of the Greek campaign was his own fault, for he had not told Mussolini about them.

The Axis sustained another reverse with Roosevelt's election for a third term on November 5th, 1940. Roosevelt's Republican opponent, Wendell Willkie, was no isolationist, though to counter Roosevelt's popularity Willkie depicted him as a warmonger. Roosevelt reaffirmed his determination to keep America out of the war. He insisted that the great measures taken in July to step up arms production and the decision in September to introduce limited conscription by the Selective Service Act (the 'draft') were purely defensive. However, he also insisted that aid to Britain was essential for America's defence. Roosevelt was re-elected with 27,243,000 popular votes against 22,304,400, and 449 electoral votes against 82. This was a much smaller majority than in 1936, but a clear vote of confidence nevertheless.

Hitler was not disturbed. He still believed that Britain's position was hopeless, and that Russia was so weak militarily and politically that she would disintegrate in a few months after his attack. He neither feared Russia nor, as he later alleged, offered her a fair bargain before he attacked her. He allowed Ribbentrop to propose that Russia should join in partitioning the British Empire, but Hitler did not believe that Russia would in fact abandon her schemes to control the Balkans, the Straits and Iran in favour of the move towards India which Ribbentrop projected. Ribbentrop took seriously the talks which he and Hitler had with Molotov in Berlin on November 12th and 13th, whereas Hitler on November 12th signed orders for operations against Britain and Greece next spring, and for continuing with preparations to invade Russia whatever the outcome of the talks.

Molotov also took the talks seriously, but could not commit Russia on the spot to adhesion to the Tripartite Pact and to carving up Asia and Africa in concert with its signatories. He also rightly doubted German good faith about the Straits. Yet Stalin was ready to negotiate. His counter-proposals of November 25th were stiff, and designed to ensure that Hitler kept on fighting for Russia's benefit, but they did not signify aggressive intentions towards Germany. He even agreed to sign the Tripartite Pact, apparently unaware how Germany was then using it in her dealings with Hungary and the Balkan countries. In addition, however, Stalin demanded Germany's recognition that Iran fell within his sphere of interest. He also demanded Japan's concessions in North Sakhalin as promised by Ribbentrop. Stalin further required the withdrawal of German troops from Finland (where the build-up for 'Barbarossa' had been going on since late September). Finally, he insisted on German acceptance of Soviet treatment of Bulgaria following the pattern established in the Baltic states, and Soviet control of the Straits. Hitler not only ignored the demands. In December he virtually ordered Italy not to negotiate with Russia about the Straits.

Hitler could not be diverted from 'Barbarossa' despite growing preoccupations in the Mediterranean. Britain had honoured her obligations to Greece by sending forces into Crete on November 1st and sending some aircraft to the mainland. On November 11th she had crippled an Italian naval squadron at Taranto, thereby entirely changing the Mediterranean naval balance. On December 6th Wavell opened a great offensive which drove the Italians out of Egypt by December 15th. Franco was becoming even more dubious about an Axis victory, and on December 7th made impossible conditions for entering the war. Hitler feared that Weygand might take French North Africa back to Britain's side. On December 10th Hitler signed operation 'Attila' for occupying Vichy France and seizing her fleet, but soon postponed this venture because of more pressing business in the eastern Mediterranean, as on December 11th, he had postponed operation 'Felix' for seizing Gibraltar because of Spanish obstinacy. Nevertheless, by December British financial reserves were running out and German aircraft and submarines were taking a heavy toll of shipping in the Battle of the Atlantic. On December 8th Churchill appealed to Roosevelt to use American merchant ships and warships to ensure supplies got through to Britain. He also asked the President to send to Britain heavy bombers for strategic bombing of Germany, and to devise some other means besides monetary remuneration for the payment for American supplies. Fully recognizing the danger Roosevelt, on January 6th, 1941, asked Congress for power to make and hand over munitions and supplies to countries resisting aggression, with payment to be made in goods and services after the war.

At this time Hitler was endeavouring to bring Bulgaria and Yugoslavia into line, by supporting Bulgaria's rejection of Soviet demands for a non-aggression pact of the type found so effective in the Baltic, and by offering Yugoslavia the Greek port of Salonika and a favoured position in the Balkans if she would join the Tripartite Pact. Then on December 18th, 1940, he signed a directive for 'Barbarossa' which formed the basis for the operations launched next June. Turkey resisted German blandishments, but her fear of both Germany and Russia (of whose claims she was well aware) ensured her neutrality. She also rejected British suggestions that she should aid Greece, and join with Greece and Yugoslavia to defend the Balkans against Hitler. British and Soviet pressure on Yugoslavia not to yield to Hitler could not be co-ordinated, because Stalin still sought to appease Hitler and did not trust the 'imperialist' British, even after German troops were preparing to move into Bulgaria in mid-January 1941. Their first objective was, of course, Greece, but Russia was next. On January 18th Greece agreed to accept British air and military forces in strength on the mainland if German troops crossed the Danube or entered Bulgaria. Turkey still refused aid to Greece, unless Germany attacked Greece and Russia would help Turkey. On February 4th the Soviet *Tass* agency showed there was no hope of such aid by denying that there was any Soviet undertaking to help Turkey against the Germans.

Yugoslavia courageously resisted Nazi pressure for some time after German troops entered Bulgaria at the beginning of March, but Churchill was distinctly dubious about the wisdom of going into Greece. So was Wavell, but obligations of honour and Eden's insistence as Foreign Secretary carried the day. For a brief period the enterprise did not seem entirely hopeless. Stalin even overcame his fear of Germany to the point where he negotiated a pact with Yugoslavia, after a revolution there on March 26th had deposed the government which had succumbed to German pressure and joined the Tripartite Pact on March 25th. King Peter took over from his uncle, the Regent Prince Paul, but the aim was to maintain Yugoslav neutrality, not to fight Germany. Nevertheless Hitler regarded the incident as defiance, and ordered that both Yugoslavia and Greece should be attacked on April 6th. This, by coincidence, was the day on which the Soviet-Yugoslav agreement was signed, but Hitler ignored it and Stalin virtually disowned it. Stalin would not have signed it had Hitler attacked a few hours earlier.

Britain could give no help to Yugoslavia and very little to Greece when the Balkan *Blitzkrieg* got under way. Obviously Hitler could not allow Greek resistance to Italy to continue. Whether it would have been safe to rely on Yugoslav neutrality while he attacked Russia is uncertain. He would not risk it, and postponed 'Barbarossa' from mid-May for a period of four weeks. In a brilliantly executed but bloody and vicious campaign he broke Yugoslav resistance in eleven days. King Peter with his government joined Free French, Polish, Belgian, Dutch, Norwegian, Czech and other exiles in London. Greek resistance on the mainland lasted another week. Then only Crete, where King George had gone for refuge, and some smaller islands held out. Crete seemed impregnable, but German air power first neutralized the British navy, and then an airborne attack captured the island between May 20th and 27th. Crete's capture was Germany's best feat of arms in World War II, despite its small scale, but because it was so costly Hitler forbade further airborne operations of this kind. However, Germany's possession of Crete was a thorn in the British flesh in the eastern Mediterranean, and Hitler now completely controlled the Balkans. He rewarded Italy, Hungary and Bulgaria by partitioning Yugoslavia and Greece, but left large areas of both victims under German military rule, and set up a puppet *régime* under Ante Pavelić in Croatia.

The British Commonwealth forces in the Mediterranean and Middle East were at Hitler's mercy immediately after conducting the first victorious

Allied campaign of World War II in East Africa. From February to May 1941 they had brilliantly overrun Italy's East African colonies, regained Britain's, and restored Haile Selassie to his capital of Addis Ababa on May 9th, though some Italians held out until November in the mountains and south of Ethiopia. From June 1940 to May 1941 they sustained only 1,154 battle casualties against 74,500 from accident, climate and disease (744 malaria fatalities), while enemy losses, Italian, and native, totalled about 289,000. Further west the Desert army on February 7th rounded up the remnants of Graziani's shattered forces and grouped to invade Tripolitania, while on March 27th a naval victory was won over the Italians off Cape Matapan in southern Greece. But the Commonwealth forces had gravely over-extended their North African lines of communication, they had seriously weakened themselves by aiding Greece, and the Germans were a different problem from the Italians.

On February 12th Hitler sent over to North Africa the crack troops of the *Afrika Korps* under General Erwin Rommel, a brilliant and hard-hitting tank commander in the Battle of France. Rommel brushed aside his timid Italian colleagues' objections to a speedy counter-offensive. Within five weeks the *Afrika Korps* was advancing on El Agheila, about 150 miles south-west of Benghazi. By early April Wavell's weakened forces were being pressed back to Benghazi. Within a fortnight Rommel had driven the Commonwealth forces back into Egypt, except for Australian forces which against heavy odds and constant attacks held the port of Tobruk for eight months until relieved. However, Rommel was refused the reinforcements which would have taken him to Cairo, for Hitler was obsessed with 'Barbarossa' and with his fears that if Germany became too heavily involved in the eastern Mediterranean Stalin would strike at her. Hitler even neglected the opportunity given by the pro-Nazi Rashid Ali's seizure of power in Iraq to throw the British out of Iraq and seize her oil. After two critical months the British crushed the Iraqi revolt on June 1st. A week later they and Free French forces entered Syria, whose Vichy authorities had been intriguing with the Nazis, and rapidly gained control of both Syria and the Lebanon.

By this time only the Soviet government doubted what was in store for Russia. It had had ample warnings from its own intelligence, from the British and from the Americans that Nazi invasion was imminent. The British Ambassador in Moscow was openly saying that the invasion date was June 22nd. This was merely guesswork, for he said so before Hitler had fixed it on April 30th—but June 22nd was the anniversary of Napoleon's attack on Russia in 1812, and of Hitler's triumph over France at Compiègne in 1940. However, Stalin was sufficiently worried to sign with Japan on April 13th a neutrality treaty, something he had hitherto refused to do. He also asked not only America but hard-pressed Britain for supplies, while he simultaneously poured food and raw materials into Germany, and shortsightedly gave Nazi intrigues in Iraq his blessing. When on June 13th Britain offered Russia a military alliance,

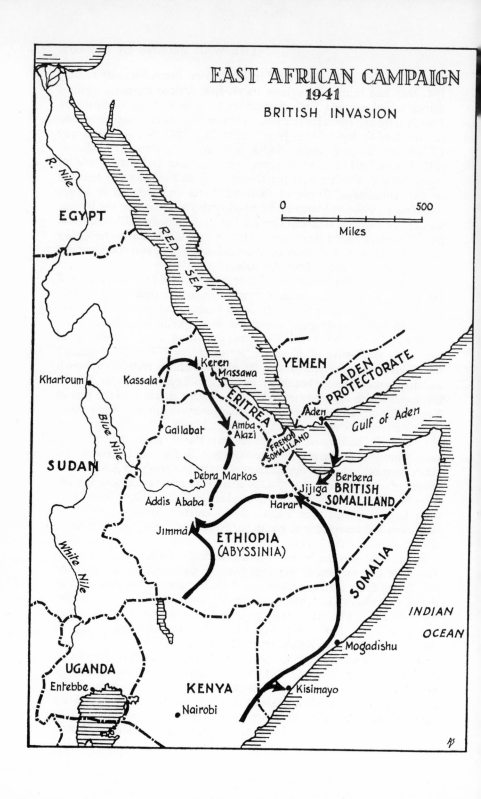

EAST AFRICAN CAMPAIGN
1941
BRITISH INVASION

0                    500
Miles

EGYPT

R. Nile

RED SEA

Khartoum

Kassala

Keren
Massawa

YEMEN

ADEN PROTECTORATE

ERITREA

Aden

Gulf of Aden

Gallabat

Amba
Alazi

Blue Nile

FRENCH
SOMALILAND

SUDAN

Debra Markos

Berbera

Jijiga

BRITISH
SOMALILAND

Addis Ababa

Harar

Jimma

ETHIOPIA
(ABYSSINIA)

White Nile

SOMALIA

INDIAN
OCEAN

Mogadishu

UGANDA

Entebbe

KENYA

Kisimayo

Nairobi

the Russians not only rejected it at once, but published the news the same day, and denounced British attempts to incite Soviet Russia against her trusted German friend. Hitler ignored this attempt to curry favour. On June 14th he settled the final details of 'Barbarossa'.

*Chapter XIV*

# THE WIDENING OF THE CONFLICT: THE ROADS TO MOSCOW AND PEARL HARBOR

HITLER'S defeat in the Battle of Britain and the postponement of 'Sea-Lion' meant that he could not win the war; they did not mean that he had lost it. But by strengthening his determination to destroy Russia and thereby free himself for the final struggle with Britain, they helped to drive him into launching 'Barbarossa' in circumstances in which it could not succeed. Nevertheless before Hitler attacked Soviet Russia his position in Europe was impregnable. He controlled the whole Atlantic coast from the tip of Norway to Franco Spain. In conjunction with Mussolini he dominated the Mediterranean. British bombers and the resistance forces within the occupied countries posed negligible military threats. German bombings of British cities (the 'blitz' in British parlance) were admittedly militarily no more significant, but German aircraft, surface raiders and submarines (heavily reinforced in 1941 and hunting in 'wolf packs') sank nearly 4,000,000 tons of shipping, mostly British, in the Battle of the Atlantic in 1941. By June ships were being sunk twice as quickly as they could be replaced, though one great menace had been dramatically overcome. The 45,000 ton *Bismarck*, the most powerful battleship on either side, had left Norway to wreak havoc on the convoys from America, but had been caught off Greenland on May 24th. She sank the World War I veteran battle-cruiser *Hood* and damaged the powerful new battleship *Prince of Wales*. The Royal Navy could not afford to allow this challenge to succeed, and the Home Fleet set out to hunt the *Bismarck*. She would, however, probably have got safely to a French port if aircraft from the carrier *Ark Royal* had not caught her and slowed her down with torpedoes for the British warships to close in for the kill. This lesson that the traditional role of battleships was over, was reinforced when the *Prince of Wales* was sunk by Japanese bombers off Malaya later that year; and again when *Bismarck*'s sister ship, the *Tirpitz*, was sunk by British bombers in a Norwegian fjord in November 1944 after attacking convoys to Russia, without being damaged, but after being torpedoed by British midget submarines in another fjord.

The increasing German havoc with the supplies sent to Britain under

556

the Lend Lease Act of March 1941, however, had forced Roosevelt in April to extend the operations of the Neutrality Patrol to longitude 25° west, a line running from west of Iceland to east of the Azores. In July American marines occupied Iceland with Icelandic and British approval. America now provided naval escorts for American and Icelandic ships sailing between America and Iceland. America also relayed submarine sightings to British ships, thereby beginning her 'undeclared war' with Germany in the Atlantic. But despite this vigorous prosecution of 'all measures short of war' in aiding Britain, Roosevelt remained determined to keep America out of war if he could—in the Pacific as well as in Europe. The Anglo-American staff agreement of March 27th indicated both countries' resolve to avoid war with Japan. This American-British Commonwealth agreement (called ABC-1) also stated that if America were involved in war with both Japan and the Axis she would concentrate on Europe. Though this decision largely determined the course of the war after America's involvement in it, she made no military and political commitments at the ABC-1 conference, nor at the ABCD conference in April where the Dutch also took part.

Stalin offered no such provocation to Hitler. Stalin even failed to order the measures needed to equip and deploy the Red Army to meet an attack. Steps taken to rebuild the Red Army after the Finnish fiasco were grossly inadequate. Soviet forces had been neither properly trained nor properly disposed to meet the kind of war which the Nazis had fought in Poland and France—and which, ironically, Soviet forces had pioneered in a small way in the Spanish Civil War, though it was the Germans who had drawn the right conclusion from that experiment. In numbers of men and mass of metal the Red Army exceeded the *Reichswehr*, as the French Army had done. Moreover the Soviet High Command, like the French, had expected to be able to halt the Nazi onslaught at the frontier and then hurl it back, though the offensively-minded Russians had made no defence plans. The Russians had no intention, however, of attacking Germany, as Hitler alleged to excuse his own aggression. Indeed the Red Army was caught at a grave disadvantage, because while many obsolete weapons had been withdrawn, not enough new weapons had been issued. Soviet military torpor was such that the January 1941 defence manual for Red Army training had not even mentioned the possibility of war that year. German planes reconnoitring Soviet western territory—with great advantage for planning 'Barbarossa'—were not fired on even as late as June 21st, when ample evidence of Hitler's intentions was available.

Hitler's invasion of Russia ranks as the greatest campaign in history in respect of the extent of the forces employed and the territorial area in which they fought. For 'Barbarossa' Hitler had withdrawn from the west nearly all his front-line ground and air forces. Stalin also suspected that Hitler had prepared for it by sending his deputy Hess to Scotland in May. In fact it was Hess's own idea to persuade the British to make peace at the price of dismissing Churchill and giving Hitler a free hand against Russia.

557

The visit puzzled the British, and Hitler repudiated and deposed Hess, but as the last bombing raid on London coincided with Hess's flight, the Russians retained their suspicions even though Churchill on hearing of the invasion had again offered a military alliance to them. Whether there would even be time to negotiate it, however, seemed highly uncertain. The general belief in London was that Russia might hold off the Nazis for two months, but even that assessment began to seem optimistic. Germany's early successes in Russia were so staggering that it was not apparent that the Nazis had failed to evolve a comprehensive strategic plan.

Nevertheless the Germans achieved complete strategic surprise along a front of over 1,200 miles, though they did not envelop the Red Army by their three major thrusts against Leningrad, Moscow and Kiev. Finns, Rumanians, Hungarians, Slovaks, Balts, Italians, and Spanish and French volunteers joined in the battle, which for a time constituted a genuine crusade against Bolshevism and seemed about to destroy the whole fabric of the Soviet state, as Hitler had predicted that it would. His generals, however, soon had their doubts. They had not opposed 'Barbarossa', as they had previously opposed 'Case Yellow'. Their subsequent complaint was not that 'Barbarossa' had been launched, but that Hitler had not followed their strategic advice. They certainly had not opposed the monstrous orders for the treatment of occupied Soviet territory which had been embodied in the 'Commissar Order' in March for a war of extermination. They were not directly responsible for the bestialities which dwarfed even those in Poland. However, without army connivance the mass murders by the SS would have been impossible. German civilian authorities were morally as culpable; they knew of the plans to starve millions of Russians to supply the *Wehrmacht* and meet the needs of the New Order. This ghastly plan failed in all its purposes. Russian resort to the 'scorched earth' policy caused inhuman reprisals, but shattered Hitler's scheme of basing his empire on Soviet resources. He gained incomparably more from his economic agreements with Stalin before June 1941 than he did from plunder afterwards. At first his troops had even been well received in western Russia as well as in the Baltic states, but there was a violent reaction as soon as the SS and the new civilian bosses arrived, and began the kind of treatment reserved for Slavs by the master race.

Yet it is doubtful whether Hitler could have succeeded in Russia in the circumstances of 1941, that is, with Britain still undefeated, America hostile and Japan neutral. He had realized earlier than many of his generals the importance of armour and of air power, and of striking with overwhelming speed and strength at the decisive point, but Russia had no decisive point, and was too big to be conquered even with the resources he commanded: 118 infantry, fifteen motorized and nineteen armoured divisions, comprising just over 3,000,000 men, and 3,580 tanks and 2,000 aircraft, together with about sixteen inferior satellite divisions (Rumanians and a few Slovaks). Against these Russia deployed nearly 4,750,000 men and well over 10,000 tanks (mostly obsolete but some heavier than the German tanks, and a powerful force if properly used, as by late autumn it was). Of the 6,000 Russian planes only about 1,100 could match Germany's, and nearly 2,000 were destroyed on the ground or in the air on June 22nd–23rd. Russia's size, however, and the lack of airfields prevented the German fighters from giving adequate support to the armoured thrusts after the first onslaught. Moreover, even if Hitler had kept his forces together, he could not have delivered the immediately decisive blow which he himself had said was necessary to settle the issue. The 'extra month' which he later said was lost in Greece and Yugoslavia would not have altered the outcome.

By the end of 1941 the Red Army had learned how to counter the German armoured thrusts; and after they had checked the initial renewed advances in 1942 the Russians' tremendous resources in reserves enabled them to counter-attack with devastating effect. Though the great industrial regions of western Russia were overrun in the first twelve months of the campaign, the industries of Siberia and the Urals combined with western supplies and Russian powers of recuperation to offset the damage. No help for Germany could be expected from Japan, who intended to strike for her own advantage, in her own time, and in the direction which she alone chose. From March 1941 until the attack on Russia the Germans had urged Japan to seize Singapore and break British power in the Far East. Japan had refused. After June 22nd they asked Japan to attack Russia. This was the second time within two years that Hitler had tried to treat Japan as a pawn and had deceived her. He had not consulted her before signing the Nazi-Soviet pact or before launching 'Barbarossa'. Japan honoured her neutrality pact with Russia until the end of the war. By so doing she made a crucial contribution to Stalin's eventual defeat of Hitler.

As Hitler had predicted, the world did 'hold its breath' at his early victories, but his essential amateurishness was at once apparent. Intoxicated by the speed of the advance, he was preparing on July 14th to reduce the Army's strength in the near future and concentrate on building up air and naval power against Britain. On July 19th he committed his first military blunder. Guderian's tank force was then poised at Smolensk to take von Bock's central offensive the remaining 200 miles to Moscow, and destroy the Russian forces massing before the capital. Hitler ordered Guderian south to help von Rundstedt's drive on Kiev, and sent a further tank force from the central sector to help von Leeb to take Leningrad. Hitler did not command the strength to crush the major part of the Red Army in the central sector, as his generals urged, and simultaneously to launch great offensive against Leningrad and Kiev. Leningrad was reached in mid-September with Finnish help, but despite great hardship held out until the investing armies retreated in spring 1943.

In a great tank battle for Kiev on September 14th, 1941, Guderian surrounded and captured 600,000 men to add to the 400,000 already taken on the central front. Von Rundstedt then moved on to Kharkov and

Taganrog in order to continue the capture of the Ukraine, and prepare to seize the other great prize of the Caucasus with its oil and agricultural resources. Guderian meanwhile rejoined von Bock, in accordance with Hitler's plan of keeping the three army groups moving forward more or less in line. Early in October von Bock resumed his advance. Another brilliant operation encircled 600,000 men near Viazma, and by mid-October Guderian was at Mozhaisk. After this great thrust, however, German progress was slow, and soon ceased.

With the unexpectedly early onset of winter the German position became untenable. The whole Ukraine and most of the Crimea were in German hands, but the Germans before Moscow were trapped, and the southern forces which had taken Rostov were retreating. The Russians had far more reserves than Hitler believed possible, despite accurate estimates by his intelligence service. With these Zhukov counter-attacked. He drove back the German vanguard which had reached the Moscow suburbs early in December. On December 8th German operations were officially suspended because of winter. Hitler had in fact no plans for a winter campaign; his soldiers were being frozen from lack of protective clothing; and his vehicles could not move in such low temperatures. His generals wanted to retreat, but he rightly refused. Retreat would have meant disaster now that the Red Army, so often declared 'annihilated' by Nazi propaganda, was attacking all along the front. His three commanders in the field were replaced. Hitler himself took over from Brauchitsch as Army commander-in-chief, asserting: 'This little matter of operational command is something anyone can do.'

When Roosevelt and Churchill had their first war-time meeting in August 1941 aboard the American cruiser *Augusta* off Argentia, New-foundland, it seemed unlikely that Russia could hold the German offensive. The British were giving what help they could by bombing Europe and by sending to Russia supplies which they themselves needed. Before the middle of 1942 they were to send over 2,400 tanks and over 1,800 planes, and America over 2,000 medium and light tanks and 1,300 planes, all of great value in holding Hitler's 1942 offensive. However the major decision at Argentia did not give much comfort to Stalin, for it was a manifesto of Anglo-Saxon idealism. The British had hitherto refrained from committing themselves to any war aims except the destruction of 'Hitlerism', repudia-tion of the Munich agreement on its second anniversary and a few hours after Chamberlain's retirement from the cabinet (September 30th, 1940) and promises to restore the freedom of Allied countries. In the case of Poland the promises were vague both before and after June 22nd, 1941, and no binding territorial commitments had been made. Nor were they now. The Atlantic Charter signed by Roosevelt and Churchill on August 12th declared that there should be no territorial aggrandisement during the war, and no territorial changes without the full consent of the peoples involved; that all peoples must be able freely to choose their own forms of government and to live in peace and free from fear, want and aggression;

that there should be economic co-operation between nations after the war; and that aggressor states were to be disarmed pending the establishment of a permanent system of general security. Though the Charter was mainly Roosevelt's concept, it ignored the freedom of worship and speech listed in his 'four freedoms' speech to Congress in January. Nevertheless it was an improvement on Wilson's Fourteen Points as well as a necessary reply to Hitler's New Order propaganda.

The Charter did not bring America's entry into the war any nearer, but Roosevelt's next actions did. After a German submarine on September 4th attacked the American destroyer *Greer* for assisting a British aircraft to locate the U-boat, Roosevelt declared that American ships and aircraft would 'shoot on sight' German and Italian submarines within the patrol area, which was now extended up to Iceland. In November he officially extended Lend Lease to Russia, and induced Congress to permit American merchantmen to be armed and sent through the war zone to Britain. Despite these open provocations Hitler still insisted that Nazi submarines could take action against American forces only if the submarines themselves had first been attacked. Doubtless this situation would have produced in time an incident which would have provoked war between America and the Axis, but a short cut was provided by the Japanese attack on Pearl Harbor.

Since March 1941 the Japanese had conducted curious and ambiguous negotiations with the United States. America refused to drop her demands for the restoration of the 'open door' in China, for a return to the position before the Manchurian incident of September 1931, and for an end to Japanese aggressions. In March Roosevelt had told the new Japanese ambassador, Admiral Kichisaburo Nomura, sent by Premier Konoye to try to reach an understanding, that another act of aggression might mean war with America. Japan's Navy chiefs, civilian ministers and even the more moderate Army leaders would have been glad to end the China Incident without loss of face. But as they meant to keep Manchukuo, and as America's demand for the 'open door' was unacceptable, deadlock was inevitable.

On July 2nd the Japanese government, now certain there was no danger from Russia, decided that in addition to trying to end the China Incident —that is, to defeat Chiang Kai-shek, and gain full acceptance of the puppet ruler Wang Ching-wei whom it had set up as Chiang's rival—it would advance south even at the risk of war with America and Britain. Accordingly, on July 21st, the Vichy authorities were forced to allow the Japanese to occupy the remaining, southern half of Indo-China. Japan thereby directly menaced Malaya, the Dutch East Indies and the Philippines. On July 26th America, Britain and the Dutch retaliated by 'freezing' Japanese assets; the Panama Canal was closed to Japanese ships; and in August the three governments combined to place embargoes on oil, rubber, tin and other strategic raw materials. The Japanese had built up considerable stocks of strategic materials over the last few years, but these would be exhausted after two years of fighting. The issue was therefore clear: unless she capitulated to American terms she would have to go to war, and seize the areas which would supply her needs. To avoid this outcome Konoye suggested that he should meet Roosevelt. America replied that she would agree to the meeting, providing a real basis of agreement had first been made. This meant Japanese withdrawal from China, among other things. When America gave this reply on September 3rd, Roosevelt still believed that firmness would peacefully end Japanese aggression, and that Japan was too well aware of her military and economic inferiority to risk war with America. At a meeting on September 6th where Emperor Hirohito himself presided, Konoye and the Navy chiefs wanted to continue negotiations with America. However, General Hideki Tojo, the War Minister, who carried most weight, insisted that Japan must fight Britain and America unless Japanese terms had been met by mid-October. As Konoye still insisted in October that the talks in Washington must continue, the Army forced his resignation. On October 17th Tojo became Premier. Obviously Tojo had come to power to make war, but in deference to the Emperor's wishes it was agreed to negotiate until the end of November. By then the decision for war or peace had to be made, for Japan could not risk being forced to fight after her strategic stock-piles had run down. The American government knew of these decisions even before the Japanese envoys in Washington, by intercepting and more speedily decoding their radioed instructions from Tokyo. What Germany's Washington *chargé d'affaires*, Hans Thomsen, called 'an absolutely reliable source', had told him in April that America had broken Japan's diplomatic coding system. But though Thomsen warned Berlin, Tokyo's wireless codes continued to be broken.

In early December the British informed the Americans that Japan had secured pledges of German and Italian support against the Anglo-Saxon powers. On December 6th the Americans knew war was imminent. They did not know when and where the attacks would come. They thought the great Pearl Harbour naval base was not a likely target because of its remoteness from Japanese bases, and because they considered carrier attacks inconsistent with likely Japanese tactics in a war against the United States. They expected attacks on the Philippines, Dutch and British East Indies, Burma, Malaya, Hong Kong and Thailand, but like the British and the Dutch they did not believe that Japan had the strength to attack these widely separated points almost simultaneously.

Japan achieved complete surprise on December 7th. The attack on Pearl Harbor was the heaviest blow physically and psychologically. Within an hour nearly half the American fleet was crippled, and more American naval losses were sustained than during 1917–18. Carrier air-craft sank or disabled seven battleships and sank three destroyers. It could have been worse, for the American carrier and cruiser forces were elsewhere, and naval installations and fuel tanks were not seriously damaged, so that the base was soon operational again. However, when two

British battleships were sunk by aircraft off Malaya on December 10th, Japan achieved immediate naval supremacy in the areas which she had destined for conquest. As Thailand did not resist, but made an alliance on December 21st, Japan had established a formidable position within a month.

However the Allied failure to appreciate Japan's military strength was far less important than Japan's own miscalculations. Chief of these was the belief that Roosevelt would automatically secure a declaration of war on Japan if she seized the raw resources for war by attacking British and Dutch colonies. Roosevelt and his advisers thought America should resist such attacks, but they might well have failed to convince Congress. The American people had genuinely sympathized for years with China's struggle against Japan, but had shown no desire to become involved in it. Moreover the blow at Pearl Harbor not only brought America into the war, but the treachery was so glaring that it gave a resolution and unity of purpose to the American people such as its own leaders could never have created.

## Chapter XV
# THE GLOBAL WAR BEGINS

WITHIN hours of launching their attacks the Japanese declared war on America and Britain, though not on the Dutch, with whom they were still hoping to come to terms. Britain and the Dutch declared war on Japan on December 7th. America did so the next day. Hitler could have decided that Japan's refusal to attack Russia absolved him from declaring war on America, but he welcomed the Japanese attack on America. He under-estimated the quality of the war effort which America could make. He believed that Japan could defeat her and that he could crush Russia before the United States could make any effective military contribution. Also, his failure to take Moscow needed some resounding stroke to offset it. Exploitation of Japan's victories would supply this. Hitler even feared that Roosevelt might steal a march on him and declare war on Germany before he could declare war on America. However, most important was his resentment of American actions in the Atlantic. The declaration of war made by Germany and her European allies on December 11th was preceded by orders to his forces in the Atlantic to attack American ships. It was, therefore, Hitler and not Roosevelt who ensured that the struggle would be a world war, instead of two separate though interconnected conflicts in Europe and the Far East.

Declarations of war on Japan by the exiled governments in London, and on Germany by China were merely affirmations of solidarity. So was the breaking off of relations, or declarations of war on the aggressors, by nearly all Latin American republics during the next few months. This was agreed upon by the Rio de Janeiro Conference of January 1942, but the total continental breach with the Tripartite Pact powers desired by the United States was not achieved. Chile, and more particularly Argentina, remained centres for Axis sabotage and espionage activities until Chile fell into line in January 1943 and Argentina a year later. Brazil gave some active aid by first moving against submarines in the Atlantic and later sending a division to fight in Italy. Her sister republics did little more than arrest Axis agents, furnish raw materials, and provide bases to assist in the protection of the hemisphere. Nevertheless, out of approximately $50,940,000,000 in all, the Latin American republics received Lend Lease aid before the end of July 1946 to the value of roughly $460,000,000, as against roughly $148,000,000 for the Belgians, $230,000,000 for the Dutch, $1,549,000,000 for Chiang Kai-shek, $3,208,000,000 for the French, $11,260,340,000 for Soviet Russia, and $31,270,000,000 for the British Empire and Commonwealth (the biggest single beneficiary and also the one which gave the biggest material return). There were also (comparatively) small amounts to other countries.

It was in Washington that the twenty-six founding nations on January 1st, 1942, signed the Declaration of United Nations formally constituting the Allied coalition. It was in Washington that most of the money and supplies to maintain it were obtained. It was also chiefly with American resources in mind that Churchill decided, on hearing about Pearl Harbor, that the Allied problem was henceforth 'merely the proper application of overwhelming force'. However, neither Churchill nor Roosevelt yet understood how far the aims of the Allies diverged, especially Soviet aims from those of the west. America's Far Eastern aims were indeed incapable of realization except in their negative aspects: defeating the Japanese, ejecting them from Chinese and other territories which they had overrun, and ensuring that they committed no further aggression. All this was achieved by America with very little support from her allies, except from Britain and the Commonwealth, but America did not secure her major purpose of promoting in China a stable, democratic and open form of society. Chiang was almost useless as a military ally and barely more eligible as a democratic partner, even by World War II standards. The opening of the Pacific war actually worsened the Kuomintang's position because Japan soon dominated the whole Chinese coastline and few supplies could get through. Chiang had not done much against Japan before Pearl Harbor. Now he concentrated almost entirely on defeating Mao. The American government paid little heed to the warnings from its agents in China of what was in store as the result of Kuomintang corruption and inefficiency. There was, in any case, not much that it could have done to alter the outcome of China's civil war. Mao's *régime* ruled less than 2,000,000 Chinese in 1937; in 1945 nearly 100,000,000. Roosevelt, however, did not lose faith in Chiang, though Chiang's *régime* failed the acid test, and Mao's dictatorship did not: Mao was not afraid to arm the Chinese peasant.

In Europe also the west's political prospects were clouded. After June 22nd Stalin had recognized the exiled governments in London which until then Russia had denounced as agents of the British warmongers, and had begun to negotiate treaties with them. Most of them had no political or territorial disputes with Russia, but the Polish question raised difficult issues. General Sikorski, the Polish Premier, was a politically moderate man. He was prepared to forget Soviet atrocities in Poland after September 17th, 1939, and the Soviet partnership with Hitler, but he demanded that the prewar Polish-Russian frontier must be restored. The British would not support that claim. They had welcomed the Soviet advance into Poland of September 1939 as a means of checking Hitler's further progress, yet had accepted neither the Nazi-Soviet partition line nor Soviet annexation of the Baltic states. However, they encouraged Sikorski to negotiate with the Russians. The Russians allowed the exiled government to recruit Polish prisoners of war in Russia for its own army, and promised to equip them, but would not yet renounce the gains made in 1939. When Foreign Secretary Eden went to Moscow in December 1941 to settle these and other problems, and to negotiate for a full-scale Anglo-Russian treaty, Stalin asserted that to demand surrender of eastern Poland and the Baltic states was equivalent to attempting to begin the partition of Russia.

Nevertheless Stalin was prepared to bargain. He offered to accept the Curzon Line (privately regarded by the British as the best solution), so retaining very large areas of prewar Poland, but not all his September 1939 gains. He insisted, however, on keeping the gains made from Finland and Rumania in 1940 but lost after June 22nd, and Molotov tentatively suggested Soviet annexations of some East Prussian territory. In return Russia offered to support demands for any bases which the British wanted their western European allies to surrender. There was, of course, little new in the Soviet proposals except for the last two, and nothing new about Soviet methods of negotiation. Stalin had paid lip-service to the ideals of the Atlantic Charter and subscribed to their re-affirmation in the United Nations Declaration. He would not allow this to interfere with Soviet territorial ambitions. Application of the right to self-determination would bring few volunteers for incorporation into Stalin's Russia. Stalin therefore was obliged to interpret Anglo-American reluctance to discuss post-war frontiers as a sign that while the western Allies would use Soviet human and material resources to defeat Germany, they wanted the exclusive right to draw the map of postwar Europe. His order of the day of February 23rd, 1942, to the Red Army rudely ignored Anglo-American aid to Russia, and clearly implied that his major aim was to clear the Nazis out of Russia, not to overthrow Nazi Germany. Roosevelt correctly rejected British fears that this portended a separate Nazi-Soviet peace once the June 1941 frontiers were regained. He wrongly believed that Stalin would respond if trust were placed in him, and would defer territorial claims in return for assurances that Russian security would be guaranteed. The British, with memories of the 1939 negotiations, knew better. At the end of March 1942 the British agreed to recognize in effect all Russia's June 1941 frontiers, except the Russo-German one through Poland.

Allied military prospects were equally uninviting until the autumn of 1942. The Battle of the Atlantic cost nearly 6,000,000 tons of Allied shipping in 1942, due to strong reinforcements of the 'wolf-packs' which gave Germany nearly 400 submarines in operation at the end of the year. Further losses were caused by the lifting of restrictions on operations against United States ships, and American inability at first to realize the seriousness of the problem, and to take such security measures as blacking-out eastern ports and coastal towns now that submarines were operating in the western hemisphere. The British, who suffered the heaviest losses in the Atlantic, also bore the brunt of Axis depredations in the Mediterranean, and on the Arctic route to carry supplies to Soviet Russia. (The alternative Lend Lease route from America round the Cape to the Persian Gulf was much safer, for Britain controlled East Africa and the Middle East.) Of a total 7,795,097 Allied and neutral shipping tonnage lost in all theatres in 1942, Britain lost 3,506,979 tons.

Japan's South-East Asian campaign, considering the size of her own and enemy forces and the physical problems posed, was the most brilliantly conceived and executed feat of the war. Her sensational early victories were achieved by fewer than 200,000 men and less than 1,700 planes. Only her naval forces were superior in strength. On December 8th (December 7th in Washington and London) Malaya was invaded. The sinking by aircraft on December 10th of the British battleships *Prince of Wales* and *Repulse* virtually sealed Malaya's fate. Japanese air superiority and skilful tenacity in jungle fighting, together with the failure in previous years to defend the great fortress and naval base of Singapore from attack by land as well as by sea, led to Malaya's capitulation on February 15th, 1942. Singapore's surrender then, with the loss of 73,000 prisoners, was a far bigger blow than Hong Kong's surrender on December 25th, 1941, to Britain's military power, prestige, and, above all, to her imperial future in the Far East. British North Borneo, attacked on December 24th, 1941, submitted early in January 1942, while Thailand on January 25th declared war on Britain and America. On January 11th–12th Japanese attacks began on the Dutch East Indies. A combined American-British-Dutch fleet under a Dutch admiral attempted to relieve Java, the richest economic prize of all, but was crushed in the Battle of the Java Sea of February 27th–March 2nd. Resistance on Sumatra was quickly wiped out after Singapore's surrender, and the entire Dutch East Indies surrendered at Batavia on March 9th. By then Burma, where the attack had begun on December 8th, was largely in Japanese hands. By mid-April British, Indian and Burmese forces under British command were retreating to the Indian border. India was not invaded, but the Burma Road was cut. To prevent that, the Allies after Pearl Harbour had made Chiang commander-in-chief of the China-Burma-India triangle, with the American General Joseph W. Stilwell commanding in the field. 'Vinegar Joe's' Burma campaign met disaster and, rejecting his American Air Force colleagues' offers of transport, he led some tattered remnants of his American, British, Chinese and Burmese troops on foot into Assam at the end of May, while others escaped into China. Within five months, therefore, Japan had secured the oil, tin, rubber and other strategic materials which she had sought in the south.

Both India and Australia seemed open to attack next, for the Japanese had occupied the Andaman Islands in the Bay of Bengal, and had secured footholds in New Guinea and at Rabaul in New Britain. The British government insisted on controlling India's defence during the war, but in March 1942 offered self-government and the right to leave the Common-wealth after the war. Congress had repudiated Britain's declaration of war on India's behalf without its approval, and Gandhi now demanded com-plete independence. He called for non-co-operation with the British and non-resistance to the Japanese if they invaded India; fortunately they did not. Some Indians set up a National Army to fight the British for inde-pendence, and Congress carried on a 'Quit India' campaign despite its leaders' imprisonment.

The Indian nationalists did not realize the nature of Japan's ambitions. The Australians did. Moreover, now that the Japanese peril was almost at their door, they became convinced of what they had hitherto only suspected: that the defence of Australia could no longer rest with Britain and the Commonwealth, but must rely on American strength. This, with the destruction of western imperial power in South-East Asia, was a direct result of the Japanese victories, but especially of the fall of Singapore, which the British had alleged to be Australia's shield, but had surrendered because of military incompetence bordering on levity.

Yet the American disaster was equally striking. Wake and Guam (the latter unfortified to spare Japanese susceptibilities) were conquered before Christmas 1941, leaving Midway the sole western Pacific base, and cutting communications between Honolulu and Manila, the capital of the Philip-pines and the headquarters of General Douglas MacArthur. The Philip-pines were bombed a few hours after Pearl Harbour. The first Japanese beachhead was established on Luzon on December 10th, and four others later that month. Manila, militarily indefensible, was repeatedly bombed, even after MacArthur had declared it an open city on December 26th. The Americans moved to prepared defences at Bataan and Corregidor, which were surrendered on April 9th and May 6th, 1942, respectively. MacArthur wanted to stay with his decimated troops but was evacuated, and in due course set up headquarters in Australia to organize a counter-offensive.

Japanese strategy was at first carefully adjusted to Japanese strength. Its original goal was to seize the areas needed for Japan's New Order, which it achieved by May 1942, and to establish a defensive perimeter. This would run from northern Manchuria through the Kuriles, then south through the Marshalls and Gilberts, west through the Bismark Archi-pelago and New Guinea, past Timor and west of Sumatra, turning north and finally halting on the Indian-Burmese border. These acquisitions would be exploited economically, while the perimeter would be made so strong that the Americans would refuse to pay the price to pierce it. The United States would therefore be forced to recognize the New Order and abandon Chiang. This strategy would have succeeded against any power but America, which alone commanded resources vast enough to overcome even the Pacific's immensity (San Francisco to Honolulu 2,400 miles; Honolulu to Manila 5,600). The Allied task was fortunately lightened by Japan's decision to exchange this cautious strategy for one of further

568

advances to capture Midway and the Western Aleutians (Attu and Kiska were occupied, pointlessly, on June 7th). Japan hoped thereby to complete the work begun at Pearl Harbour and destroy the remaining American Pacific fleet; next, to prepare Australia's invasion by seizing Tulagi in the Solomons and Port Moresby in New Guinea.

Tulagi was captured, but on May 8th the Port Moresby task force was sighted, and a totally new form of sea battle was fought by carrier planes in the Coral Sea. Despite heavy losses, the Americans threw back the invaders. Moreover, the American fleet's losses since Pearl Harbour were being replaced so quickly that the Japanese decided that by 1943 it would be too late to challenge it, though until the autumn of 1942 America was still too weak in the Pacific to undertake anything more offensive than the carrier bombing raid over Tokyo in April 1942. Then on June 4th the great carrier naval battle at Midway inflicted a defeat on Japan which restored the Pacific balance of naval power and prevented continuation of the campaign to move further south and cut communications between America and Australasia. To prepare for MacArthur's counter-offensive, the Americans launched a drive to clear the Solomons. On August 7th they established a beachhead on Guadalcanal, and Tulagi was also attacked. On August 9th the Japanese inflicted heavy damage on the Guadalcanal invasion fleet, and the struggle for the island lasted six months. But the Americans had recovered sufficiently to combine defence with the beginnings of their own offensive phase. The Japanese had dangerously over-extended their strength and lines of communication, and in October–November 1942 they suffered another great naval defeat in engagements off the Solomons.

The Japanese offensive which was halted at Midway had been launched partly because of Japan's belief that Germany would win the European war. In November 1941 the British had counter-attacked Rommel's army and by the end of 1941 had driven it back to Agheila. Churchill had expected Rommel's speedy destruction, but the pendulum of the desert fighting had again swung the other way. Rommel's skilful counter-thrust drove back the British, who evacuated Benghazi and regrouped around Gazala and Tobruk. From Gazala in May Rommel launched his last desert offensive, which took him again almost to Cairo. By capturing Tobruk, a week before he reached El Alamein in June, he had secured his rear. His position could not be outflanked, but his lines of communication were too long. The issue would be decided by numbers of men and tanks, and by supplies. These came in a flood from Alexandria, only sixty miles away, to General Bernard L. Montgomery, now commanding the cosmopolitan Eighth Army. In August at Alam Halfa Montgomery repulsed German forces of equal strength. Air and naval superiority in the south-eastern Mediterranean, largely due to British retention of Malta, now enabled Montgomery to achieve overwhelming power. On October 23rd, 1942, he attacked at El Alamein with superiority of 6 to 1 in tanks and 8 to 1 in men over the Germans (3 to 1 over Germans and Italians combined) and won the first decisive British military victory against the Germans in World War II. On November 4th Rommel began to retreat.

It was, however, the Russian campaign which attracted most Japanese interest. Despite Soviet recapture of Mozhaisk on January 19th, 1942, the February White Russian counter-offensive, and smaller Soviet advances in March in the north and centre, Hitler told the German people in March that the Red Army would be annihilated that summer. The Japanese thought this event entirely possible, though the Germans could now launch only one full-scale offensive at a time. It was decided to attack in the south. After containing a Soviet thrust around Kharkov in mid-May, the Germans straightened their front in a battle lasting from June 10th to 25th. On June 28th they launched from Kursk an offensive which by August drove into the Maikop Caucasus oil-fields, one of Hitler's major objectives. On July 27th Rostov was captured and the Germans advanced into Kuban territory, but the drive to the middle Volga was held at Voronezh.

Hitler's decision not to pursue the Voronezh thrust, but to strike at the northern Caucasus and 'Stalin's city', meant leaving intact the road, river and rail communications without which Stalingrad must have fallen from lack of reinforcements. The major oilfield at Grozny escaped capture, while Maikop's was destroyed. But though the economic resources of the Northern Caucasus could not be exploited, the superstitious Hitler determined that Stalingrad must be taken. Stalingrad was the third of the Soviet 'holy cities' after Leningrad and Moscow, and the symbol of Stalin's power. By mid-September the Germans had penetrated to the outskirts of Stalingrad, and the greatest single trial of strength of World War II began—and one which was recognized as such not only by Germany and Russia but by the rest of the world. Stalingrad was a great military as well as a great psychological prize. If the Germans took it they could turn back to take Moscow from the south-east; they would cut off the oil essential for the Red Army and for agriculture; and their southern armies would even be poised to sweep south and join Rommel in Cairo—if he got there.

Stalin, however, was as determined as Hitler to win the Battle of Stalingrad, and the tremendous Russian reserves of man-power—reserves in which Hitler still refused to believe despite the evidence of the battle—carried the day. On November 24th a huge Soviet encirclement cut off the German forces, though they might still have fought their way out. Hitler, whose lunatic rages were increasing with Nazi reverses, forbade retreat. After a battle which lasted five months and reduced Stalingrad to rubble, the German commander Friedrich Paulus was captured on January 31st, 1943. On February 2nd the 91,000 Axis survivors surrendered. The Germans and their allies lost in this battle over 300,000 men. Stalingrad has been compared with the even longer and bloodier struggle at Verdun in World War I, but its strategic importance was actually greater. Hitler lost the initiative there, and could never regain it.

Yet when the Germans had resumed the offensive in the spring of

1942 their defeat had seemed a very remote possibility. General George Marshall, Roosevelt's most trusted service adviser and chairman of the American Joint Chiefs of Staff, thought that before the tide turned later that year Germany and Japan were very close to securing domination of the world. As the German offensive gained momentum Stalin demanded with increasing bitterness that a Second Front should be opened in western Europe to relieve the strain on Russia. Roosevelt was anxious to comply, and ignorant of the difficulties involved in the operation, when he met Molotov in May rashly promised to invade Europe. The American Chiefs of Staff believed it possible to seize a bridgehead in northern France (Operation 'Sledgehammer') in 1942, and to build up forces from it to launch a full-scale offensive against Germany ('Roundup') in 1943. After first accepting this view, the British decided that Allied strength was unequal to the task of meeting the Germans in a frontal assault before they had been further weakened. In July they proposed instead to invade French North Africa (Operation 'Torch') and Roosevelt concurred. Churchill had to go to Moscow next month to inform Stalin of the decision. Stalin was unconvinced by Churchill's arguments, and it was not the time to recall how Russia had behaved when Britain alone was defying Germany.

The bloody repulse of the Canadian probe into the strength of German defences at Dieppe in August gave no conclusive evidence either way, for it was only a probe, not an assault in strength. From the western standpoint it would have been wiser to devote more attention to the Pacific theatre, instead of launching 'Torch', though 'Torch' did distract some German attention from Russia. MacArthur and the American Navy chief, Admiral King, argued for sending forces to the Pacific instead. MacArthur did not agree that Germany should be beaten first. King did, but also argued that the Japanese should be allowed as little time as possible to consolidate their gains. He also supported Marshall's contention that 'Torch' would consume so many Allied resources that it would prevent the invasion of France in 1943. This proved true, though Churchill and Roosevelt denied that 'Torch' would have that effect. Certainly an invasion of France launched in 1943 would have entailed far heavier casualties than were sustained in 1944. The building up of the invasion force would have had to contend with heavier submarine attacks than were met in the Atlantic in 1944, and it is even doubtful whether enough specialized amphibious craft could have been built before 1944 to give reasonable prospects of a successful landing in France.

In any case Russia's 1942 counter-offensive proved that a Second Front was not essential either for Russia's survival or for keeping Stalin from making a separate peace with Germany. Allied contributions in Europe in 1942 therefore were limited to sending supplies to Russia, continuing the blockade of Axis countries, and strategic bombing of Hitler's 'Fortress Europe'. American Air Force officers, who shared their British counterparts' exaggerated assessment of the role of strategic bombing in defeating Germany, began to take an important share in it after mid-1942.

571

On the night of November 7th, 1942, the Anglo-American forces of 'Torch' landed at Safi and Casablanca on Morocco's Atlantic coast, and at Oran and Algiers in Algeria. They could have landed even farther east at Bizerte, as the British and American navy commanders proposed, but General Dwight D. Eisenhower, who commanded the operation, erred on the side of caution. Bizerte's seizure would have prevented Rommel's reinforcements from reaching him through Tunisia, thereby shortening North African operations by some months, but Eisenhower could not predict that Vichy's resistance in North Africa would end so quickly, for this was due to the accident that Darlan, Pétain's *Dauphin*, was in Algiers when the landings took place. Roosevelt and Churchill both resented de Gaulle's methods of insisting on his status as leader of what he alone regarded as a major Allied power. De Gaulle was excluded from the 'Torch' operations by the Americans, who intended to win over Vichy's North African forces by using General Henri Giraud, whom they had smuggled out of France. Giraud was completely disregarded by the North African forces, and the Americans therefore persuaded Darlan to end resistance and bring Morocco and Algiers over to the Allied side. Churchill, despite his dislike of Darlan, admitted the importance and necessity of the deal. Darlan was made political chief in North Africa, with Giraud as military deputy, but Darlan was assassinated by a young anti-Nazi French Royalist on December 24th, and was at once succeeded by Giraud. In the course of 1943, however, de Gaulle became co-president with Giraud of the French Committee of National Liberation set up in Algiers, and was recognized by Churchill and Roosevelt at their 'Quadrant' meeting at Quebec in August as rightfully speaking for France.

Hitler reacted to 'Torch' by sending into Tunisia more men than had been needed six months earlier to enable Rommel to capture Cairo, and by ordering on November 11th the occupation of Vichy France, with the full approval of Laval whom the Germans had restored as premier in April. Mussolini scored his last feeble triumph by taking Nice and Corsica. On November 27th the Germans treacherously attacked Toulon, which Hitler had promised not to occupy, but the fleet there was scuttled to keep it out of his hands. Hence the Western Allies could exploit their growing strength in the Mediterranean without any naval opposition, as Mussolini's fleet dared not face battle. Western strategy in the Mediterranean and elsewhere was reviewed by Roosevelt and Churchill when they met in Casablanca in January 1943. Churchill wanted to follow up the North African campaign by invading Italy, Axis Europe's 'soft underbelly', but the American Joint Chiefs pressed for an invasion of northern France instead. It was finally agreed to compromise by invading Sicily in order to extend Allied control of the Mediterranean, and to gain further air bases for fighters and for the strategic bombing of Axis Europe, which was to be stepped up in 1943. The Italian mainland was not to be invaded, as that would defer once again preparations for invading France; and America was not to build up a Pacific offensive at the expense of the European theatre.

The only notable new feature at Casablanca was Roosevelt's public demand for 'unconditional surrender' by the enemy. He had previously discussed the formula with his advisers and Churchill, who were in general agreement with it though they were surprised at the haste with which Roosevelt announced it. The formula brought no advantages to the Western Allies. It certainly did not convince Stalin of their good faith, as Roosevelt hoped that it would, but it stiffened Germany's determination to fight on for nearly a year after the war had obviously been lost. Yet as the ineffectiveness of the German 'opposition' to Hitler was demonstrated conclusively by the failure of the July 1944 bomb plot, the formula was far less important than German and other critics of the policy alleged after the war. Hitler was immovably in command until Germany collapsed in the spring of 1945, and he would not have surrendered on any terms. It is equally unlikely that the moderate elements in Japan would have been in a position to negotiate for her surrender until she had been nearly destroyed as a military power, even if the demand had not been made. Moreover, unconditional surrender might never have been promulgated as a war aim but for the zeal with which the Germans after 1918 promoted the legend of the 'stab in the back', and Japanese treachery in December 1941, which Roosevelt thought merited condign punishment to deter similar future aggression. Anglo-American moral indignation and affronted national prides contributed more than military and political calculations to the making of the formula.

## Chapter XVI
## FROM STALINGRAD TO THE SECOND FRONT

### (i) The Resistance Movements

IN 1943 the Allies inexorably drove back their enemies in every theatre of war except the China-Burma-India command. The Nazi and Japanese New Orders, nevertheless, continued to exploit the European and Asiatic subjugated nations virtually unchecked, except for the Resistance Movements. Stilwell and MacArthur pressed for a great Far Eastern offensive at least partly from the desire to liberate China, the Philippines and other occupied territories. Not only the Russians and their sympathizers demanded a Second Front in Europe, but also anti-Soviet circles which saw no essential difference between Hitler and Stalin, yet saw in the New Order the most bestial tyranny in history. This last attitude was paradoxically reinforced even among the Right Wing London Poles when the Nazis announced in April 1943 their discovery of mass graves in the Katyń forest near Smolensk. The Nazis asserted that about 10,000 Polish officers murdered by the Russians in 1939 or 1940 were buried there. The Russians insisted that the Nazis were responsible for the massacre, and that Poles or others who asserted the contrary were Nazi collaborators. The London Poles, while aware that the Nazis were constantly committing worse atrocities in Poland, demanded an independent enquiry, and Stalin thereupon broke off relations with Sikorski's government. The Nazi disclosures were clearly designed to drive a wedge between Russia and the west, but Churchill and Roosevelt refused to let them affect their attitude to the Soviet war effort. This dispute had nothing to do with their decision at the Washington conference of May 12th–18th to postpone the invasion of France until May 1944.

Poland was the European country which suffered most severely from the war. About 1,500,000 Poles were deported from the Soviet zone before June 1941, chiefly to Siberian labour camps. In the areas annexed to Hitler's Greater German *Reich* about the same number went as slave labour to Germany or central Poland; the remaining 7,500,000 were treated avowedly as 'sub-humans'. The Poles in the 'Government-General' were also treated as slaves, but were less rigorously suppressed—they were, for example, allowed to use Polish in their schools. Property of Poles and Jews alike was everywhere liable to confiscation. Over 3,500,000 people, mostly Jews, were murdered in concentration camps or in such 'extermination' camps as the notorious Auschwitz, where mass executions by gassing were carried out daily. About another 1,250,000 died from starvation and brutality. During the war about 20% of the population, or about 6,500,000 people, were murdered. Yet the Poles maintained an extraordinary Resistance organization, taking orders from Sikorski's government, which kept in being an entire underground 'state' to resume control under Sikorski's direction when the Germans were at last expelled. The Polish Communists were generally hated for their conduct before June 1941 had made Russia an ally of the London Poles, but in the spring of 1942 they began to fight the Germans, and in November 1943 Władysław Gomułka became their leader. However, the Polish Resistance was essentially conservative and anti-Communist—though Gomułka was from the beginning no 'Muscovite' Communist, but an independent-minded patriot.

The Czechs, enslaved before the Poles had been, did not put up the same kind of Resistance to the Germans, though they too were plundered, seized as slave labour and subjected to mass murder, especially after May 1942, when the paranoiac Nazi Protector Reinhard Heydrich was assassinated. In retaliation the SS wiped out the innocent villagers of Lidice—not the first or the worst of such atrocities, but the name of Lidice came to symbolize the Nazi New Order. Slovakia was given favoured treatment, for she was an ally of sorts and too poor to attract much attention from pillaging Nazis.

Yugoslavia, the other Slav state which had opposed Germany, was a very special case. Croatia was given satellite status under Ante Pavelić. Pavelić's SS, the Ustaśe, carried out atrocities against Serbs and Jews exceeded only in number, certainly not in severity, by SS operations in Poland and Russia. The German puppet *régime* in Serbia was a parody of Vichy, and totally unrespected. The supporters of Peter's exiled government rallied round a former army officer, the Serb chauvinist Draža Mihailović, whom Peter made War Minister in January 1942, after his 'Ćetnik' resistance forces had already adopted an equivocal attitude to the Italians and Germans. The Yugoslav Communists had adopted an even more equivocal attitude until the Nazi attack on Russia converted them into Resisters. They then rapidly became the driving force. In November 1941 their leader Josip Tito, a prominent Comintern figure in the Spanish Civil War, adhered to Russia's orders by forming a united front with the other Resistance groups. For a time his Partisans and the Ćetniks collaborated uneasily, but they soon fought each other—in Mihailović's case in preference to fighting the Germans. Mihailović was never much concerned with the Italians, who, for their part, disliked the Germans' Ustaśe friends, while the Croats resented Italy's annexation of Dalmatia. Some Serbs were armed by the Italians against the Croats, and acted as liaison between Italians and Ćetniks. The Western Allies, ignorant of these

575

intricate manoeuvres, sent supplies to Mihailović even after January 1943, when his Četniks with Italian backing fought their only major operation of the war—against the Partisans, among whom there were few Serbs.

Apart from the peculiar circumstances created by Yugoslav national problems, the Partisan-Četnik struggle represented a continuation of the wider conflict between the Communist and anti-Communist elements in the European states which had enabled the Fascist *régimes* to bring about the war, and now helped them to continue it. The Četniks were neither pro-German nor pro-Italian, but first and foremost anti-Communist Serbs, and they subordinated their patriotism to their ideology. The Communists would normally work with any force which the Russians prescribed—whether Germans before June 22nd, 1941, or Resistance elements afterwards, unless either made co-operation impossible. Patriotism was adopted as a rallying cry only when it served other than purely national purposes, though Tito was one of the few politicians in Yugoslavia who thought in Yugoslav terms. But after all, Stalin himself now publicly beat the nationalist drum as a more effective means of rallying the Russian masses than Socialist exhortations. In May 1943 he even dissolved the Comintern to appease western *bourgeois* democrats—but also to enable the European Communist parties to operate more effectively within the Resistance movements, while still retaining their separate identities. Essentially this marked a return to the prewar Popular Front tactics.

The tactics were most clearly recognizable in France. The French were better treated by the Germans than were the conquered Slavs. Nazi racial theories credited them with some admixture of Nordic blood, and Laval persuaded the Germans to keep their looting of French industry and agriculture within just tolerable limits. Even so French 'occupation costs', as distinct from losses through plunder, amounted to more than half of those imposed on all Europe, which have been roughly estimated as reaching before the end of the war the total of $15,000,000,000. Laval also managed to reduce German demands for conscript labour, the most important requirement of all after June 1941, when the drain on the German army became so great that most able-bodied German men had to be sent to the front, and the gaps in Germany's labour force had to be filled by enslaving foreigners. Many men who joined the French (and other) Resistance forces did so to escape this fate.

After June 1941 the French Communists, with their excellent underground organization and their influence over the French workers, were able to exploit this situation in their bid to control the Resistance, which hitherto they had previously opposed as agents of Free French 'imperialist lackeys'. The Communists set up the *Front National*, which included groups from all areas, and men of all shades of political opinion from extreme Right to extreme Left, but de Gaulle defeated their attempt to control the Resistance, and therefore possibly postwar France. His prestige within France enabled his agents to weld by May 1943 the scattered and heterogenous resistance groups into the French Forces of

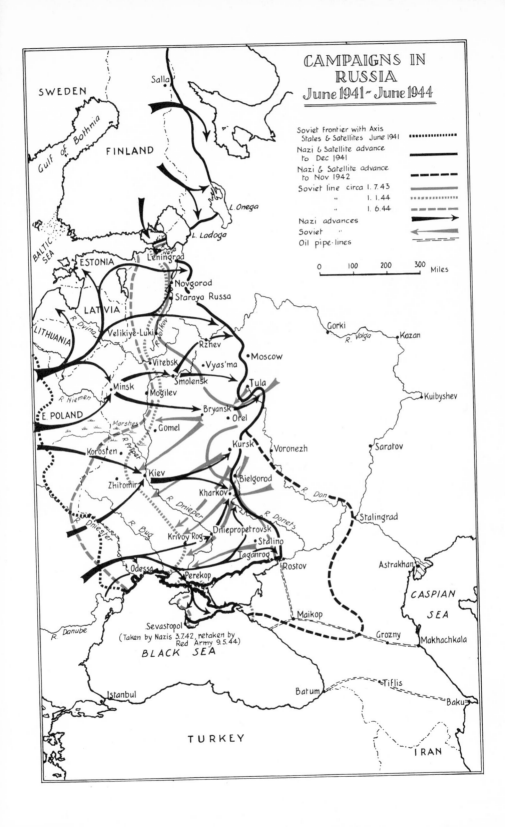

CAMPAIGNS IN
RUSSIA
June 1941 - June 1944

Soviet frontier with Axis
States & Satellites June 1941 ·············
Nazi & Satellite advance
to Dec 1941 ——————
Nazi & Satellite advance
to Nov 1942 — — — —
Soviet line circa 1. 7. 43 ············
   "      "   1. 1. 44 ············
   "      "   1. 6. 44 — — —
Nazi advances ——————▶
Soviet   "    ——————▶
Oil pipe·lines

0    100   200   300  Miles

SWEDEN

Gulf of Bothnia

FINLAND

Salla

L. Onega

L. Ladoga

BALTIC SEA

ESTONIA

Leningrad
Neva
Novgorod
Staraya Russa

LATVIA

R. Dvina

LITHUANIA

Velikiye-Luki

Rzhev

Moscow

Gorki

R. Volga

Kazan

Vitebsk

Vyas'ma

Smolensk

Tula

Kuibyshev

Minsk
Mogilev

R. Niemen

E. POLAND

Bryansk

Orel

Gomel

Korosten

Marshes

R. Pripet

Kiev

Zhitomir

Kursk

Voronezh

Saratov

Bielgorod

R. Don

Kharkov

R. Dnieper

R. Donets

Stalingrad

Krivoy Rog

Dniepropetrovsk

Stalino

R. Bug

R. Dniester

Taganrog

Astrakhan

Odessa

Perekop

Rostov

CASPIAN
SEA

R. Danube

Sevastopol
(Taken by Nazis 3.7.42, retaken by
Red Army 9.5.44)

Maikop

Grozny

Makhachkala

BLACK SEA

Istanbul

Batum

Tiflis

Baku

TURKEY

IRAN

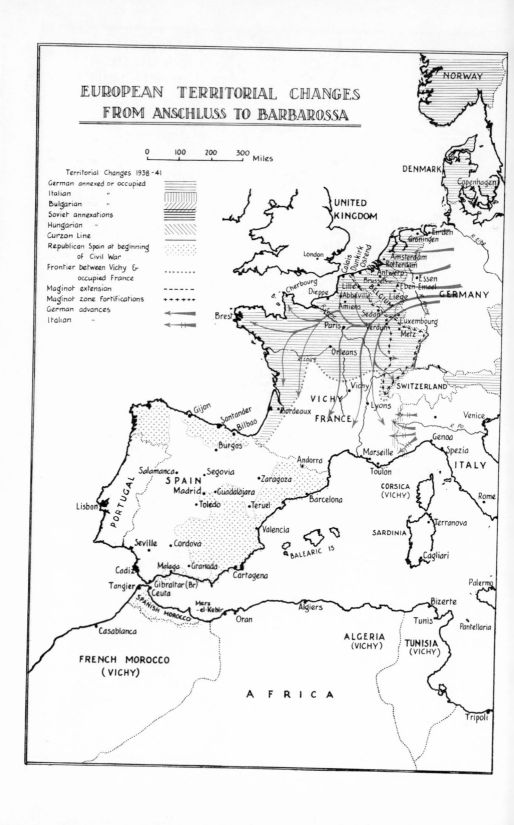

# EUROPEAN TERRITORIAL CHANGES
## FROM ANSCHLUSS TO BARBAROSSA

0    100    200    300    Miles

Territorial Changes 1938-41
German annexed or occupied
Italian          "
Bulgarian        "
Soviet annexations
Hungarian        "
Curzon Line
Republican Spain at beginning
    of Civil War
Frontier between Vichy &
    occupied France
Maginot extension
Maginot zone fortifications
German advances
Italian      "

NORWAY

DENMARK
Copenhagen

UNITED
KINGDOM

London

Emden
Groningen
Amsterdam
Rotterdam
Antwerp
Essen
Brussels
Lille Eben-Emael
Liège
GERMANY

R. RHINE

Calais
Dunkirk
Ostend
BELGIUM

Cherbourg
Dieppe
Abbeville
Amiens
Sedan
Luxembourg
Metz

Brest
Paris
Verdun

R. LOIRE
Orleans
Vichy
SWITZERLAND

VICHY
FRANCE
Lyons
Venice

Gijon
Santander
Bilbao
Bordeaux

Marseille
Toulon
Genoa
Spezia
R. PO

Burgos
Andorra

Salamanca
SPAIN
Madrid
Segovia
Zaragoza
Guadalajara
Toledo
Teruel
Barcelona

CORSICA
(VICHY)
ITALY
Rome

PORTUGAL

Lisbon

Valencia
Seville
Cordova
BALEARIC IS
SARDINIA
Terranova

Malaga
Granada
Cadiz
Cartagena
Cagliari
Palermo

Tangier
Gibraltar (Br)
Ceuta
Mers-el-Kebir
Oran
Algiers
Bizerte
Tunis
Pantellaria

SPANISH MOROCCO

Casablanca
ALGERIA
(VICHY)
TUNISIA
(VICHY)

FRENCH MOROCCO
(VICHY)

A F R I C A

Tripoli

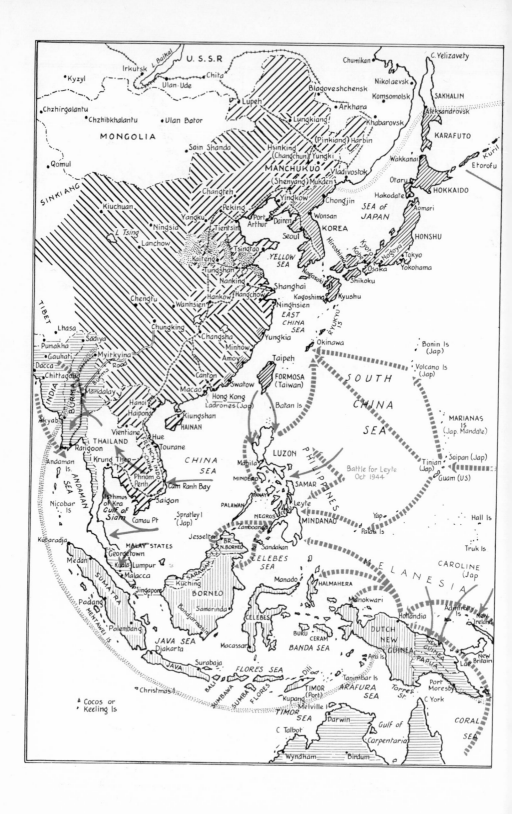

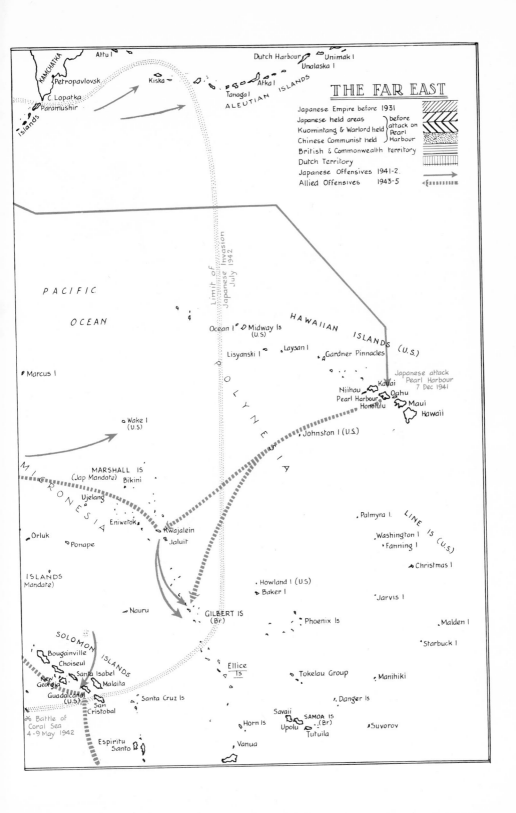

# THE FAR EAST

Japanese Empire before 1931
Japanese held areas      } before
Kuomintang & Warlord held { attack on Pearl
Chinese Communist held    } Harbour
British & Commonwealth territory
Dutch Territory
Japanese Offensives 1941-2.
Allied Offensives    1943-5

KAMCHATKA

Attu I
Petropavlovsk
C. Lopatka
Paramushir
Islands

Kiska
Tanaga I
Afka I
ALEUTIAN ISLANDS

Dutch Harbour   Unimak I
Unalaska I

PACIFIC

OCEAN

Limit of Japanese Invasion July 1942

Ocean I  Midway Is (U.S)

Lisyanski I   Laysan I   Gardner Pinnacles

Marcus I

HAWAIIAN ISLANDS (U.S.)

Japanese attack
Pearl Harbour
7 Dec 1941

Kauai
Niihau        Oahu
Pearl Harbour   Maui
Honolulu    Hawaii

Wake I
(U.S)

Johnston I (U.S)

MARSHALL IS
(Jap Mandate)   Bikini

Ujelang
Eniwetok

Orluk   Ponape

Kwajalein
Jaluit

ISLANDS
Mandate)

MICRONESIA

Palmyra I.    LINE IS (U.S.)

Washington I
Fanning I

Christmas I

Howland I (U.S)
Baker I

Jarvis I

Nauru

GILBERT IS
(Br)

Phoenix Is

Malden I

Starbuck I

SOLOMON ISLANDS

Bougainville
Choiseul
New Georgia   Santa Isabel
Guadalcanal   Malaita
(U.S)     San
Cristobal

Santa Cruz Is

Battle of
Coral Sea
4-9 May 1942

Espiritu
Santo

Ellice
IS

Tokelau Group

Manihiki

Danger Is

Horn Is   Savaii   SAMOA IS
Upolu   (Br)
Tutuila   Suvorov

Vanua
POLYNESIA

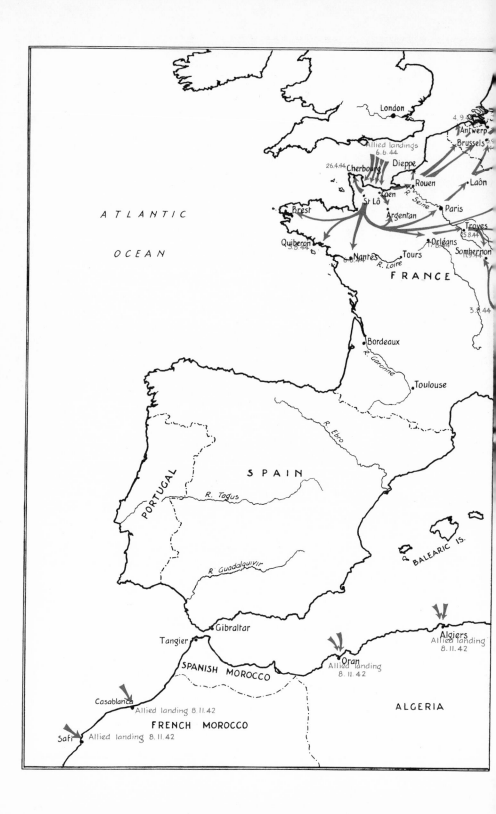

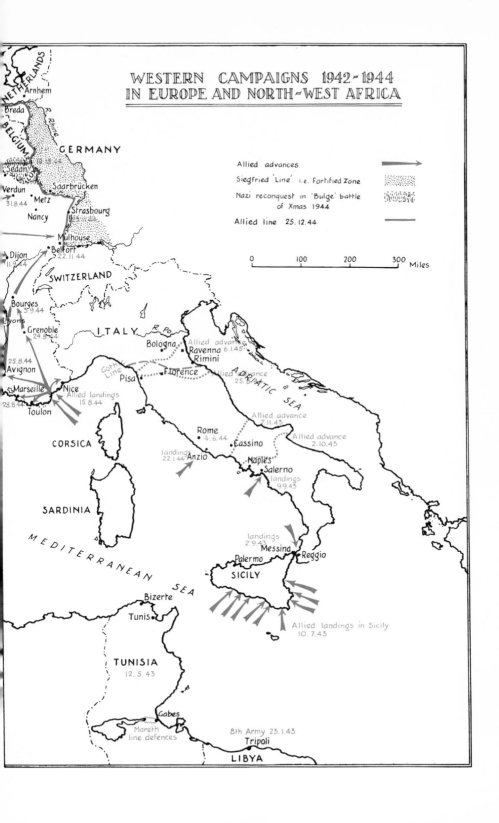

# WESTERN CAMPAIGNS 1942~1944
# IN EUROPE AND NORTH~WEST AFRICA

Allied advances

Siegfried 'Line' i.e. Fortified Zone

Nazi reconquest in 'Bulge' battle
of Xmas 1944

Allied line 25.12.44

0        100        200        300  Miles

NETHERLANDS
Arnhem
Breda
R. Rhine
BELGIUM
GERMANY
Sedan
Saarbrücken
Verdun
31.8.44
Metz
Nancy
Strasbourg
Mulhouse
Belfort
22.11.44
Dijon
11.9.44
SWITZERLAND
Bourges
3.9.44
Lyons
Grenoble
24.8.44
ITALY
R. Po.
25.8.44
Avignon
Gothic Line
Pisa
Florence
Marseille
Nice
28.8.44
Allied landings
15.8.44
Toulon
CORSICA
Bologna
Ravenna 6.1.45
Rimini
Allied advance
Allied advance
25.8.44
ADRIATIC SEA
Allied advance
2.11.43
Rome
4.6.44
Cassino
Allied advance
2.10.43
landings
22.1.44
Anzio
Naples
Salerno
landings
9.9.43
SARDINIA
landings
2.9.43
Messina
Reggio
Palermo
MEDITERRANEAN SEA
SICILY
Bizerte
Tunis
Allied landings in Sicily
10.7.43
TUNISIA
12.5.43
Gabes
Mareth
line defences
8th Army 23.1.43
Tripoli
LIBYA

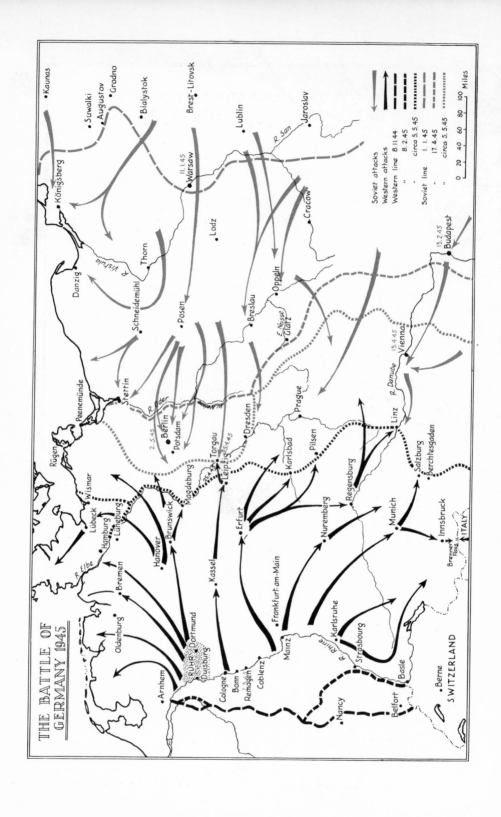

THE BATTLE OF GERMANY 1945

Soviet attacks
Western attacks
Western line 8.11.44
" " 8.2.45
Soviet line circa 5.5.45
" " 1.1.45
" " 17.4.45
" " circa 5.5.45

0   20   40   60   80   100 Miles

the Interior, taking orders from the Gaullist-dominated National Resistance Council. After Corsica was freed by Free French from North Africa in September 1943, the name 'maquis' (from the Corsican scrub) was given to the Resistance bands which, operating from the wild interior regions of France, launched their attacks on the Germans and the brutal Vichy Militia. The Militia, however, was controlled by Paris Quislings. Laval and Pétain had virtually no power by 1943, and in January 1944 the Germans forced them to take some Quislings into the government. By that time Giraud's political *naiveté* had allowed de Gaulle to take virtually complete control of the Committee of National Liberation in Algiers, and in March he was its official chief. He spoke for all Frenchmen inside and outside France who rejected Vichy, except for Right Wing and Left Wing diehards, and collaborators.

The most effective Resistance appeared in Russia, though many of the Partisans, particularly in the Ukraine, were less pro-Soviet than anti-German. Increased Partisan activity was noted whenever the Germans made fresh attempts to collect slave labour, and Partisans were not much in evidence until early 1942. Stalin's appeal for guerrilla warfare aroused little response from Russian civilians until there seemed reasonable prospects that the Red Army would return and eject the Germans. By the autumn of 1941 Red Army prisoners escaping from almost certain death at their captors' hands, were forming Partisan bands and maintaining liaison with their High Command. Large-scale guerrilla warfare developed in 1942, most effectively behind the central front and in northern Ukraine. In 1943 it was tying up about a tenth of the German field divisions, and may possibly have prevented a general German offensive that year.

On the other hand, nearly a million soldiers deserted to Germany from hatred of Stalin's *régime*, which indeed nearly collapsed in 1941. A more humane German policy would have made possible the establishment of an independent Ukraine—though whether it could have lasted is another matter. In 1944, when it was too late, the Germans saw their opportunity and sponsored an anti-Stalin movement, the Committee for the Liberation of the Peoples of Russia. Perhaps fear of another deadly Stalinist terror helped to preserve the loyalty of Nazi-occupied areas when it became likely that, as Stalin had promised, the Red Army would return. Certainly the practical demonstration of what the New Order entailed for Russian 'sub-humans' was effective in reinforcing patriotism. Nearly 4,000,000 Red Army prisoners died in German hands. At least 750,000 Russian Jews were 'exterminated'. Between 3,000,000 and 5,000,000 other Soviet citizens died in one way or another because of the occupation—so monstrous was the slaughter that estimates have to be made in millions. The Germans systematically devastated the Ukraine and the Donetz basin, Russia's greatest industrial and agricultural region. They inflicted wanton and incalculable damage on the other occupied areas. Yet so inefficient was their economic exploitation, as distinct from their cruelty, that in 1943 they estimated their exactions as worth only $1,000,000,000—less than one-seventh of the annual French 'occupation costs'. Never was so brief a victory paid for so dearly, or the final reckoning so well deserved.

By the winter of 1941–42 the Nazis' rounding up of slave labour, and their seizure of industrial plant, manufactures, food and assets of all kinds, had exploded the pretence that Hitler's New Order would create a genuine partnership of the European nations (Slavs of course excepted). Japan's New Order of the Greater East Asia Co-Prosperity Sphere also dissipated the stock of goodwill at first accorded by the gullible. Japanese propaganda of 'Asia for the Asians' and demands for assistance in overthrowing western imperialism were originally well received. Except for the Communists, the political intelligentsia in South-East Asia was pro-Japanese, until it realized that the region's function under the New Order was to furnish supplies for Japan's war economy on the model of Manchukuo. Some Japanese politicians sincerely believed that the New Order would in fact free the colonial peoples of South-East Asia from imperialist exploitation, just as they had convinced themselves of the justice of Japan's actions in China. However, the military elements which actually wielded power and made the decisions were men of the type who had fabricated the Mukden incident and been responsible for the rape of Nanking. The ferocity with which their subordinates now committed atrocities against European prisoners of war and Asians profoundly affected Allied attitudes towards Japan for the rest of the war.

Within a year Japan was provoking Resistance movements of a size and character unknown under western imperialism in South-East Asia. Japan thereby helped to establish the political pattern of Communism and nationalism, operating through guerrilla warfare, which later became so prominent a feature of the region. Asian Communists, unlike their European comrades, had been early in the forefront of the Resistance movements. They had been anti-Japanese before their own countries were invaded, for Britain and the Dutch were Soviet allies before Pearl Harbour. Japanese brutality was largely responsible for the growth of Communism in this region. In Indo-China the former Comintern agent, Ho Chi-minh, founded the Vietminh Resistance Movement to fight the Japanese and their Vichy puppets. The Malayan Resistance Movement was led by Communists, most of them Chinese residents. Filipino Communists took the lead in organizing another local variety of the anti-Japanese coalitions, the Anti-Japanese People's Army. In Burma, where the movement for national independence had been strong before the invasion, Resistance developed much more slowly, and most Burmese politicians collaborated. Only at the end of 1943 did a small Burmese Resistance Movement, also under Communist leadership, come into being. The Thai Resistance looked exclusively to the Free Thai movement in Britain and America, and was even less effective. In Indonesia only Communists and extreme Socialists went into Resistance. The leading Indonesian nationalists, notably Ahmed Sukarno, collaborated with the Japanese to the end.

The popular support secured by Resistance leaders was, nevertheless, due not so much to emergent nationalism or Communism as to the privations inflicted by the Japanese. Under their exploitation the economy of the region was seriously dislocated. They could not maintain the level of production reached before the invasion. They commandeered the tin, oil, rubber and other materials which they needed, but could not replace the imports formerly supplied by Europe and America. As American air and submarine attacks on Japanese shipping increased, South-East Asia became a liability, in the same way as Russia by late 1942 took far more out of Germany's war machine than Russia put into it. It was not the failure to make an economic reality of the Co-Prosperity Sphere, nor fear of Communism, but the advance of the Western Allies in 1943 which forced the Japanese to adopt a less brutal policy.

## (ii) *The Allied Offensives*

In the winter of 1942–43 in North-West Burma the British offensive in Arakan was repulsed with heavy losses, but Stilwell's persistence secured in December 1942 the beginning of the construction of the Ledo Road from India to north Burma to join eventually the old Burma Road to Kunming. Progress was slow, but the building up of Allied forces in India showed what was intended. Supplies were flown to Chungking over the Himalayan 'hump' to sustain Chiang's forces. Chiang, however, made no move to attack the Japanese, who in May drove his forces on the south coast into the interior, thereby ending Allied hopes of landing an army in South China. It was also impossible to launch an offensive from Burma, as Stilwell desired. He had to content himself with using his Chinese troops to neutralize Japanese forces around Myitkyina, on the River Irrawaddy and 150 miles south-east of Ledo. In March British guerrillas ('Chindits') under Orde C. Wingate penetrated far behind the Japanese lines and kept the enemy off balance, and Americans under Frank D. Merrill later adopted similar tactics. These measures sufficed to prevent an invasion of India, as Japan no longer had the seapower necessary to launch an amphibious operation of the size required. Since India did not rise in rebellion against the British, and China had allied herself with the west, Japan could not present herself as the leader of a united Asian movement against western imperialism.

Until July 1945 it was expected that only an invasion of the Japanese islands could conclude the Far Eastern war. A strategy to secure this victory was elaborated by Churchill and Roosevelt with their advisers' assistance in May 1943, but it had to be modified almost immediately. The Japanese May offensive precluded a landing in South China. The British disliked the idea of the offensive from Burma to which they had agreed. Even though Lord Mountbatten was given the new South-East Asia

579

Command in August, with Stilwell as his deputy, Churchill weakened its forces to provide reinforcements for the Mediterranean operations which he favoured. These setbacks, however, proved immaterial, for the offensives mounted by the Americans in the South-West and Central Pacific proved brilliant successes. The first major objective was Rabaul, the great air and naval base which was the key to Japanese control of the strategic Bismarck Archipelago, and therefore of the South-West Pacific. The American strategy was not to launch frontal assaults on every Japanese stronghold, but to neutralize the major bases by 'leap-frogging' operations which by-passed them wherever possible. Only unavoidable frontal assaults were undertaken. In this way Japan's error in over-extending her strength was most economically exploited, and thousands of Japanese troops were left to 'wither on the vine' as the American offensive swept past their positions. This strategy would have been impossible without naval and air supremacy, and without the tremendous supply resources which enabled new airfields to be built wherever they were needed.

The offensive began in June 1943. Under MacArthur's command American and Australian troops, supported by the American Seventh Fleet and Fifth Air Force, advanced in New Guinea. Progress there was slow because of the difficulties of the terrain and Japanese tenacity, but Lae was captured in mid-September, and by the end of February 1944 the eastern part of the island was in Allied hands. In the Central Pacific Admiral William F. Halsey's amphibious forces gained control of the Solomons in heavy fighting which ended with the capture of the Green Islands in February 1944; another major blow was struck in November 1943 by capturing bases on Bougainville from which to bomb Rabaul— the only kind of operation now needed to keep Rabaul innocuous. When MacArthur's forces completed the occupation of the Admiralty Islands (February 29th–April 3rd, 1944) Rabaul was encircled. Nearly 100,000 well-armed Japanese were left to 'wither on the vine' there until the end of the war.

Meanwhile a strong Central Pacific force drove simultaneously to the north-west. Makin and Tarawa in the Gilberts were taken in November 1943, and in February 1944 Kwajalein, Eniwetok and other bases in the Marshalls. Heavy blows were struck deep into Japanese defences by bombing attacks on February 16th on Truk (another formidable base which was by-passed), and on February 21st on Saipan in the Marianas, from which long-range bombers attacked Japan itself after July. Even on the mainland Japanese power was being blunted. In March 1944 a major Japanese assault was directed against British and Indian forces in North Burma to seize Imphal in Assam, strike from there into Bengal, and cut off Stilwell, now ready to move against Myitkyina. Stilwell's capture of Myitkyina's airfield in mid-May, and the Chindits' capture of his other main objective Mogaung, west of Myitkyina, at the end of May, made a Japanese repulse certain. The long drawn-out Imphal-Kohima battle in Assam ended next month with decisive Japanese defeat, and Myitkyina itself fell in August. The former Indian Congress leader Subhas Chandra Bose, who had gone over to the Japanese, assured them that there would be great disturbances in Bengal, and that victory in North Burma would mean the rallying of India to gain freedom. The actual result was that the Japanese collapse in northern Burma, which was accompanied by the loss of Saipan after desperate resistance, meant the resignation of Tojo's cabinet on July 18th. The Americans rightly believed that Tojo's disappearance would not make much difference to the war.

In the European theatre the Western Allies scored some resounding successes early in 1943. In what Churchill regarded as the decisive struggle, the Battle of the Atlantic, the end of March saw the crisis surmounted, with 693,389 tons of Allied shipping sunk in that month; 344,680 in April; and 299,428 in May. Except during July there was a practically constant decline in the amount of tonnage sunk while German submarine losses increased. In North Africa Montgomery's Eighth Army drove through Rommel's Tunisian defences of the Mareth Line at the end of March. Instead of ordering the evacuation of the Italo-German forces, which were also menaced by Anglo-American troops coming from the north-west, Hitler insisted on having another Stalingrad, though Rommel was recalled before his army of about 250,000 men surrendered on May 12th. This was the first great victory of the Anglo-American alliance which was to prove the most successful military and political alliance of the war—perhaps in history. But the planning which at once began to exploit the victory immediately revealed major strategical differences. Churchill wanted to follow the invasion of Sicily, to which Roosevelt agreed, with advances into Italy and into the Balkans. Instead, the Americans wanted to prepare for the greater task of a cross-Channel invasion as soon as Sicily had been captured.

The Sicilian invasion (Operation 'Husky') began on July 10th, 1943. Its execution went well after some early uncertainties, and it had major political repercussions almost immediately. Both Mussolini and the Fascist *régime* were now detested in Italy as the result of reverses at Allied hands, virtual occupation by the hated Germans, and privations on the home front caused by the war. Strikes and disaffection were rife. To forestall a revolution which might sweep away the monarchy as well as Fascism, the king, supported by the army and dissident Fascists, dismissed Mussolini on July 25th. The new *régime* of Marshal Pietro Badoglio wished to take Italy out of the war, but was hampered by the formula of unconditional surrender and fear of savage German reaction. Before Sicily's conquest was completed on August 16th, Churchill convinced the Americans that Italy should be invaded to take advantage of the political opportunity. Eisenhower was accordingly instructed on August 18th to carry out this decision, and the first landings were made in Calabria, opposite Sicily, on September 3rd. Badoglio's government, which had been secretly negotiating with the Allies, concluded an armistice as a 'co-belligerent'. Italy then pledged that she would surrender the remnants of her fleet,

581

turn over the country's administration temporarily to the Allies, and help them occupy strategic points. On the same day an all-party National Liberation Committee was established in Rome because of the widespread distrust of Badoglio. On September 8th the news of the armistice was published, but Hitler had used the lull in the fighting after September 3rd to prepare for undisguised military occupation. On September 10th the Germans took Rome (which the Allies should have taken first, instead of landing in Calabria), disarmed Italian forces which they encountered and occupied strategic points north of the Allied lines. The Allies were to push laboriously over one mountain range after another to advance a bare seventy miles before the end of 1943. Mussolini by a skilful airborne operation was rescued by German troops on September 12th and set up the Republic of Salò, a new *régime* under German protection in the north. Here he reverted to some of the Socialist ideas of his youth, but he had no power, for the Germans were the masters. To make the point abundantly clear they put the frontier provinces of South Tyrol and Venezia Giulia under two Nazi Gauleiters, and the SS guarded Mussolini's villa at Ciangano on Lake Garda. A very effective Resistance developed in the German occupied areas, in which the Communist Partisans played a notable part. Indeed, though Italians had not shown much heroism in fighting for Mussolini, they displayed great courage and tenacity now in fighting against him.

Despite its slowness, the advance to the north forced Germany to commit twenty-five divisions which could not really be spared from the Russian front. Heavy Allied losses, however, were sustained because of the terrain and the great skill of the Germans in exploiting it, notably exemplified by their defence of Monte Cassino, which was first attacked in January 1944 to mask Allied landings at Anzio whose purpose was to get behind the German lines. The superior mobility of the Germans meant that heavy losses and four months were required to break out from the Anzio beachhead. German positions on Monte Cassino and inside its monastery were attacked from the air and by ground forces until the end of May, though in mid-May the Allies outflanked it, and advanced to enter Rome on June 4th—the first European capital to be freed from Hitler. Victor Emmanuel at once handed over his powers to his son Umberto, hoping to save the dynasty, as he himself was discredited by long collaboration with Fascism. Badoglio's suspect *régime* also was replaced. Ivanoe Bonomi, chairman of the National Liberation Committee, headed an anti-Fascist coalition. The struggle for Italian democracy now began. Its progress owed little to the Allies, who had more pressing problems in Italy and elsewhere.

## (iii) *Allied Political Problems*

During Eden's visit to Washington from March 12th to 20th, 1943, the British and American governments had started seriously to discuss the problem of European resettlement after Germany's defeat. The Soviet offensive which had regained Kursk on February 7th, Rostov on February 14th and Kharkov on February 16th had then been checked, and Kharkov was again in German hands on March 15th. This did not affect the western attitude towards Russia, except in so far as it strengthened British suspicions that the Russians might consider a separate peace with Germany. Even so Eden re-affirmed strongly held British views, which called for the partition of Germany. The details, Eden said, could be settled later, but East Prussia should be promised to Poland. This would force the London Poles, whose obduracy over the frontier with Russia was causing great annoyance to Britain and America, to accept a frontier somewhere along the Curzon Line. On this Roosevelt reserved judgment, though he declared that the Polish question would be settled by the Great Powers.

Roosevelt fully endorsed the proposal to partition Germany, and was prepared to accept British views that the Baltic states, Bessarabia and the territories taken from Finland in 1940 should be guaranteed to Russia. The crisis over Katyń, and Soviet annoyance when in May the west postponed the Second Front again, led to Stalin's rejection of Roosevelt's invitation to a meeting. Stalin's suspicions were further increased by Churchill's obvious preference for Mediterranean or Balkan offensives, over the broad frontal assault on northern France desired by both Russia and America. Repulse of a strong German attack against Kursk on July 5th and Russia's resumption of the offensive on July 12th made the matter less urgent on both political and military grounds for the west, but Stalin continued to press for the Second Front to be promised without reservation for 1944. As the Allied offensive moved into Italy he also demanded that Russia should share in the administration there.

From October 19th to 30th, 1943, the three Foreign Ministers, Hull, Eden and Molotov, held a series of meetings in Moscow, at which the Western Allies promised to invade France the next spring. It was also agreed to establish a European Advisory Council in London to settle the surrender terms for Germany and her allies, and a separate Advisory Council for Italy meeting in Naples. This would include a Free French, Greek and Yugoslav representative in addition to those nominated by the three major powers represented on the European Advisory Council. The Commander-in-Chief in Italy, however, kept ultimate authority under the general supervision of the Anglo-American Combined Chiefs of Staff—a device which rebounded against the Western Allies when the Red Army occupied eastern Europe. It was decided without difficulty that Austrian independence would be restored. Poland was not discussed specifically, though Molotov made it clear that Russia would insist on having the kind of eastern European settlement which she wanted, and Hull and Eden did not react unfavourably. Relations between them and Molotov were in fact cordial. Molotov even promised that Russia would join in the war against Japan after Germany's defeat, though Russia had not been asked to do so.

The chief purpose of these meetings was to prepare for the first, 'summit' meeting of Roosevelt, Churchill and Stalin, which took place at Teheran between November 28th and December 2nd. By that time the Red Army was capable of making major advances during the winter. The Germans were fighting very skilfully, but faced odds of more than five to one and could no longer replace losses from reserves. On the central front, by the end of October, Smolensk and Gomel were firmly held by the Red Army, as were Kiev and Dniepropetrovsk, though the Germans still occupied most of the Ukraine. Stalin's self-confidence, badly shaken in 1941, was growing with his army's advances, and was further strengthened at Teheran by the attitude of Roosevelt and his advisers. They came convinced it was essential to have the friendliest possible relations with Russia, since she was the decisive factor in the European theatre, and she would certainly dominate eastern Europe after the war. Roosevelt himself had decided that by showing trust for Stalin, and giving every concession needed to ensure Russia's security, Stalin might be induced to make no annexations but to 'work for a world of democracy and peace'. On the crucial Polish question Roosevelt took no stand, but as he did not oppose the Russian interpretation of the Curzon Line, which was much more favourable to Russia than the line shown on British maps, the Russians logically assumed that he had accepted their view. He definitely supported compensation for Poland's losses in the east by moving her western frontier to the Oder. Stalin promised Churchill minor concessions to Poland in the north, but insisted on keeping Lwów in south Poland, and claimed Königsberg and northern East Prussia from Germany. The London Poles and their Resistance forces in Poland rejected these terms. Stalin thereupon took the opportunity in January 1944 to form a 'Polish National Council' made up of Polish Communists inside Russia. The Council immediately accepted Stalin's terms, which were in fact reasonable. However, Stalin went on to use these 'Muscovite' Poles against the London Poles to gain Soviet control of Poland—the first open step towards the 'sovietization' of eastern Europe.

The major business of the conference was to settle future strategy against Germany. The promise of a cross-Channel invasion in May 1944 was reaffirmed, and Stalin definitely promised to join the Far Eastern war after Germany's defeat—but not as a means of obtaining the Second Front, and he fixed no date. Churchill wanted to accompany the cross-Channel operation ('Overlord') with a drive through Trieste into Yugoslavia and Austria, instead of into southern France ('Anvil') in support. Roosevelt's insistence on 'Anvil' instead of a Balkan campaign was sound militarily and politically. It would have been a long and costly matter, as the Italian campaign was proving, to push through the Balkans, and the major western thrust must go through France.

Moreover, at this time British suspicions of Soviet designs on the Balkans were exaggerated. The western victories in the summer of 1943 prompted Greek Communists to save their ELAS private army for use against the nationalist (and largely Republican) elements in the Greek Resistance, instead of fighting the Germans. However, this was the Greek Communists' decision, not Stalin's. The British government refused to abandon King George II of Greece, but knew that general Greek opinion, not only Communist, was opposed to his return. Italy's surrender gave ELAS enough arms for them to have obliterated their rivals, had not Britain sent arms to the Nationalists after the Communists launched a civil war in October. In February 1944 the British negotiated an armistice between the two sides in Greece, but the Communists proclaimed a provisional government there, and in March the king was forced to leave Cairo, to put his case for returning to Greece before the British government in London. This provided the signal for the mutiny next month of his troops in Egypt. When the political crisis was surmounted by a compromise agreement in September, it was partly through Soviet good offices.

In a similar fashion Stalin had prior notice that Tito's Anti-Fascist Council of National Liberation (set up in November 1942) intended to declare itself a provisional government on November 29th, 1943. Nevertheless, the Soviet line for Yugoslavia was still that there should be a united front between Peter's adherents and Partisans. When Tito's Council followed the Greek Communists' example, and forbade Peter in December to return to Yugoslavia until 'the people' had made their wishes known, Stalin resented this sign of independence.

Stalin's reversal at Teheran of his previous view that Turkey ought to be brought into the war was prompted by military considerations. It was also for military reasons that the British tried, though in vain, to bring Turkey into the war at the meeting which they and the Americans held at Cairo with the Turkish president from December 4th to 6th, 1943. Until 1945 there were no significant differences between British and Americans as to where their forces should meet the Red Army in eastern Europe. Stalin's promise at Teheran to greet 'Overlord' with a Soviet offensive meant the saving of heavy western casualties while the main body of western troops consolidated the Normandy beachhead. It was not until the autumn of 1944 that the timing and direction of Soviet thrusts justified western concern.

Before that time Russian moves were dictated by military considerations. The February 1944 thrusts which preceded the offensive into Poland had no political undertones. In March Zhukov began the major offensive which virtually liberated the Ukraine; and northern Bessarabia, which also fell, had been accepted as a legitimate Soviet territorial aspiration. In May the liberation of the Crimea was complete. On the eve of

'Overlord' the Red Army was poised to strike into the Baltic states, East Prussia, central Poland and the Danube valley. By then Poland was certain to be sovietized, but Stalin made doubly sure by allowing the Germans to crush the Warsaw rising in August unhindered, and so directed his strategy henceforward as to ensure maximum political gains in eastern Europe. The Western Allies could not have landed in Trieste, for logistic reasons, much before Rumania's surrender to Russia on August 30th opened the Red Army's way into Bulgaria and Hungary. Hence only Prague and Berlin of the eastern capitals might have fared differently from a different western strategy. A race between the Red Army and the Western Allies for Vienna would have had no lasting political and military consequences.

A major reason why Roosevelt made his concessions to Stalin was his conviction of the overriding importance of Allied co-operation first to win the war, and then to secure a lasting peace. Conscious of Wilson's errors in preparing neither the American people nor Congress for participation in the League of Nations, Roosevelt had worked with Hull ever since Pearl Harbour to replace it with a vigorous international organization in which America would play a leading role. These ideas harmonized with those of the British government, which readily agreed to make the embryonic United Nations organization serve the aims of peace as well as of war. However, the British doubted whether China should be regarded as one of the Big Four in the new organization, as Roosevelt insisted, since her contribution to the war fell far short of the American, Soviet and British efforts. The British yielded that point reluctantly, but readily agreed to concluding a treaty with China on January 11th, 1943, ending the 'unequal treaties', and America signed a similar pact with China on the same day. At the Foreign Ministers' Moscow meeting in October 1943 a Four-Nation Declaration was adopted, which embodied Anglo-American views and which was accepted by Molotov and the Chinese envoy. This declaration provided first for common action in matters concerning the enemy's surrender and disarmament, and the occupation of his territory. It also called for the establishment 'at the earliest practicable date' of 'a general international organization, based on the principle of the sovereign equality of all nations, and open to membership by all nations, large and small, for the maintenance of international peace and security'. This marked the real beginning of the United Nations Charter.

Before the Teheran conference, a meeting was held at Roosevelt's initiative in Cairo from November 22nd to 26th to discuss Far Eastern problems. Chiang Kai-shek appeared as the Far Eastern equivalent of Stalin in Europe, to determine the postwar settlement. Roosevelt's attitude to territorial changes in the Far East differed radically from his reluctance to endorse new frontiers in Europe. The Cairo Declaration issued on December 1st by the three Allies was drafted by the Americans with British and Chinese approval. It insisted on Japan's unconditional surrender and her return of all conquests made after 1894: Formosa, Manchuria and the

Pescadores. Japan must surrender Pacific islands taken since August 1914 (Roosevelt wanted some of these, but under United Nations trusteeship) and withdraw from all territories 'taken by violence and greed', while Korea would in due course become 'free and independent'. Stalin approved the declaration, though not publicly, as Japan was not yet Russia's enemy. It could be interpreted as giving Russia the Kuriles and south Sakhalin, but not Manchuria, which she also coveted.

Chiang had further claims. He had asserted in his book *China's Destiny* (March 1943) that China needed Tibet and Mongolia for defence purposes, and that no area could 'of its own accord assume the form of independence'. His demand for 'self-determination in Asia' was subject to China's over-riding interests, but was certainly not comparable to Japan's interpreta-tion of 'independence' as manifested by Japan's puppet *régimes* in Man-chukuo and China. The governments which Japan set up in Burma (August 1943) and the Philippines (September 1943) were mere agencies, and the Indonesian Central Advisory Council of Sukarno and the Malayan Consultative Council of September 1943 were only mouthpieces for Japanese propaganda. In South-East Asia only the Filipinos had been promised independence by the former ruling power. The Cairo declara-tion held out no hopes to these peoples. Japan's promises of equality and freedom were not meant to be honoured, but she made it more difficult for the European nations to continue to deny real independence after the war, by setting up even these façades of self-government.

## (iv) *Allied War Production*

The strategy which defeated Japan, like that which defeated Germany, depended as much on war production as on the forces in the field, and particularly on American war production. Despite the delay in putting America on a war footing (and even then not on a total war footing), her war production in 1942 at $30,200,000,000 equalled the whole of the enemies'. By 1944 it was double theirs, and was more than equal to the demands made on it by the offensives in Europe and in the Pacific. In the crucial field of merchant shipping American construction by the late autumn of 1942 had outpaced losses in the Atlantic. So quickly did American shipbuilding increase that the 1943 maximum of over 19,000,000 tons did not need to be maintained, and fell next year to 16,500,000 tons— though this reduction was partly due to success in sinking German submarines.

The Pacific war was mainly a naval one, and was won essentially by aircraft carriers and submarines. The major reason for deferring the offensive of 1943 until June was the dearth of aircraft carriers, which neutralized the Japanese island bases and escorted convoys from the air, as well as winning the decisive battles of Midway and the Philippine Sea. American submarines sank nearly a third of the Japanese warships lost in the Pacific, among them a battleship, four aircraft carriers, four smaller escort carriers, and three heavy cruisers. They sank 60% of the Japanese merchant ships lost, against 30% sunk by aircraft, and 10% by mines and surface craft. The Japanese merchant fleet of nearly 6,000,000 tons in December 1941 was reduced to 1,800,000 by August 1945, despite 3,300,000 tons built and 800,000 captured by Japan during the war. By August 1945 it was practically restricted to the Inland Sea, and the home islands' communications with each other were nearly ruptured. By then submarines and land and carrier based aircraft had blockaded Japan so effectively that her stocks of fuel and food were on the point of exhaustion. From November 1944 until her surrender nearly 160,000 tons of bombs were dropped on Japan. Air raids destroyed two-thirds of her war economy and two-fifths of the densely-occupied zones of her major cities; the March 1945 fire-raid on Tokyo destroyed its entire centre, leaving 185,000 casualties.

Airpower in World War II was not a mere adjunct to military and naval strength but a major arm of attack, defence and supply in its own right, and a substantial factor in increasing the effectiveness of the armies and warships. The vulnerability of armies and navies to an enemy possessing superior airpower was shown in Norway, France and the Pacific war by the aggressor powers, but the Allies quickly learned the lesson. Between September 1939 and September 1945 the American aircraft industry built some 296,000 service aircraft of all kinds. Britain from January 1939 to the end of March 1945 built about 115,000. German figures are highly uncertain because of the confusion caused by the western strategic bombing offensive when it reached its climax between October 1944 and May 1945, but from January 1939 to the end of March 1945 at least 120,000 planes were built.

The crucial significance attached to airpower is shown especially by the strategic bombing offensive, which from July 1943 to May 1945 dropped 2,700,000 tons of bombs, mostly on Germany, but also on enemy and enemy-occupied Europe. Allied air forces exaggerated the damage which it caused—German aircraft and tank production were higher in 1944 than in 1943. Nevertheless the German armaments chief, Albert Speer, stated after the war that American precision daylight attacks on industrial targets caused the breakdown of the German armaments industry. In the late autumn and winter of 1944 Allied bombers won what was in effect the third battle of the Ruhr. German war production would certainly have been much higher than it was, but for the offensive. In addition to disrupting communications in Germany, thereby hampering production, it facilitated the Russian advance in the east before and after the Normandy landings. The bombing of German production of synthetic oil and petrol made a major contribution to the success of the landings of June 6th and the subsequent break-out into France, for the *Luftwaffe* was even shorter of fuel than of planes and pilots. The pre-'Overlord' bombings in France both helped to deceive the Germans about the point of invasion and prevented them from moving up the forces needed to meet the invaders. Without overwhelming air superiority 'Overlord' could not have been launched.

The basis of Allied material superiority, apart from American technological feats in applying mass production methods to armament production and shipbuilding, lay in greater economic and industrial resources. The Allied powers possessed 86% of the world's oil, a crucial advantage in a war fought so largely with machines, 64% of its iron deposits, 67% of its coal, and had a 3 to 1 advantage in manpower. The early Axis victories reduced these margins, for in January 1943, when Britain and America were nearing peak production, Germany held nearly all Europe and territories containing a third of the Soviet population, and the shattered remnants of what had been half of Russia's heavy industry and coal production. However, these capital resources could not be exploited to the extent to which the Allies could harness their human and industrial strengths. In late 1944 Germany suffered a major crisis of production because of the bombings and the inadequate basis of her economy for a long war. Hitler had known before attacking Poland that Germany could not face a long war. He failed to deliver against Britain and Russia the knock-out blows on which he had counted. Japan, with one-tenth of American industrial power, could not conceivably win the Pacific war if America refused to make a compromise peace. The early German and Japanese triumphs had encouraged the delusions of grandeur already prevalent in Berlin and Tokyo, but the reckoning was inevitable.

The Western Allies added greater scientific skill to physical and material superiority. The British invention of radar, essential for winning the Battle of Britain, was developed by British and American scientists to provide bomb-sights for day and night bombers, to vector fighters on enemy aircraft, to direct artillery fire and to detect submarines—or their periscopes. The British also invented asdic for detecting submarines under the water, but Vichy betrayed this to the Germans. The German invention of the magnetic mines, which exploded when a ship's hull completed an electric circuit inside their fuses, was countered within a day of recovering unexploded samples, by running electric cables around ships to 'degauss' them. British scientists also won the 'battle of the beams' by 'bending' the radio beams along which the German night bombers flew to attack British cities, to send the bombers off course. The British began to develop the 'proximity fuse' for shells which the greater resources of America enabled her to perfect and bring into production for the Pacific war, and to use against the German flying bombs (V-1s) sent against Britain in 1944. American development of rockets for air, ground and naval purposes greatly increased the fire power of the Allied forces. However, in rocket missiles Germany established a monopoly, in the shape of the V-2s launched against London and southern England after the Normandy landings. Fortunately for the Allies, strategic bombing reduced the production of this weapon, which carried a warhead of a ton at a speed

589

of 3,400 m.p.h. and was then impossible to intercept. Had the Germans put it into production sooner they could have inflicted devastating damage not only on Britain but on the Anglo-American invasion fleet. As it turned out, the western armies overran the launching sites before the weapon's real potentiality could be shown. Fear that Germany was capable of producing in time an even more deadly weapon, the atom bomb, led Einstein and other scientists to urge Roosevelt to order the research necessary for building it. They assumed that Germany (who was not in fact capable of making the bomb and had not tried to do so) would use it if she made it. There can be no doubt that she would have done so if she could, nor that it would have been used against her if that had been necessary to bring her to surrender.

Only America could have allocated during a world war the financial, technological and industrial resources necessary for producing the atom bomb, or have gathered together the scientists (refugee European, American and British) of the numbers and quality required to provide the theoretical bases for the 'Manhattan project'. The British government first began to develop the bomb, but lacked the resources, and after sharing its information with the Americans in 1940 agreed to make it a joint Anglo-American project in 1942. On December 2nd, 1942, the controlled chain reaction was discovered at Chicago University by the nuclear fission of plutonium, the new element derived from uranium 238. As a result in March 1943 an international team of scientists could begin to work on the bomb itself at Los Alamos, New Mexico. At a cost of nearly $2,000,000,000 the bomb was completed and ready for its successful test on July 16th, 1945. Roosevelt's first appropriation in 1942 had been for $6,000.

*Chapter XVII*

# FROM THE SECOND FRONT TO JAPAN'S SURRENDER

THE speed and ferocity of the Nazi offensives in 1939–42 occasioned the belief that the new weapons of war gave attack a clear superiority over defence, in contrast to the experience of World War I, when defence had triumphed. The true lesson of World War II was that despite the increased mobility and fire power given by armoured and motorized divisions, and by aircraft used both for direct attack and for landing troops at strategic points in the enemy's rear, determined and skilful defence in depth could be overcome only by so wearing down his economy and by employing so overwhelming superior a strength that a successful counter-attack was impossible. This was demonstrated when the British learned the new technique in North Africa, when the Russians learned how to meet the German thrusts, and when the Americans in the Pacific deployed massive air, naval and ground power in their amphibious operations. Above all, the Germans demonstrated it after June 6th, 1944, when they faced superior forces in both east and west, and the Japanese at much the same time showed such determined will to resist that the American government decided to drop atomic bombs on Japan, rather than incur the casualties thought inevitable if Japan had to be subdued by invasion.

General Eisenhower, designated commander of 'Overlord' in December 1943 at Cairo, deferred the invasion of France from the beginning of May to the beginning of June 1944 because of the shortage of landing craft— the only shortage from which the Allies then suffered. Despite loss of a good campaigning month this proved an advantage. It allowed the invasion force to be better trained and greatly increased, and Eisenhower to obtain more heavy warships to batter the strong concreted coastal defences. Most of these could not be knocked out by air bombardment, and in fact only about a seventh of the gun positions in the landing zones were destroyed on D-Day. However, the air bombardment and the more terrifying naval fire very effectively pinned down the German defences on D-Day and then hampered German reinforcements.

The invasion force included seven battleships, two monitors each carrying two 15-inch guns, twenty-seven cruisers, 164 destroyers, over 500 light warships (frigates, gunboats, torpedo boats and other small craft), about 350 minesweepers, and some 4,300 landing ships and craft. German naval forces ready for action on D-Day were thirty-five submarines, three destroyers, six torpedo boats and thirty-four fast motor-torpedo ('E') boats, but on D-day there were only a few torpedo boat attacks. Allied control of the air was also absolute with 3,500 heavy bombers, 2,300 medium and light bombers, and 5,000 fighters. On D-Day the Germans flew only 319 sorties, and by June 10th mustered only about 750 operational planes.

Since March Allied bombers had been disrupting German road and rail communications with Normandy, but these attacks were so skilfully directed that they concealed the fact that the landings would be made there. However, the Germans had in the west fifty-eight divisions, ten of them armoured. This force was strong enough to throw the Allies back into the sea if the point of invasion had been known, or if the Germans could have massed quickly enough to counter-attack the assault troops. Before midnight on D-Day about 75,000 troops had landed in the British sector, and about 57,000 in the American, but the build up of armour, transport and supplies was slow. Fortunately for the Allies, though Hitler had suspected the invasion might come in Normandy, the German command had greatly over-estimated the size of the invading force, and elaborate Allied strategems misled Rundstedt, the commander in the west, into believing the Allies would take the shortest sea crossing and also invade the Pas de Calais. The Germans had thought this the likeliest invasion area, and dummy installations were built in England opposite to it and feints made in Dover Straits to strengthen that impression. Rommel, Rundstedt's deputy, also expected the main landing there, though Rommel thought there might be a diversion farther west. As air reconnaissance had been impossible, against all reasonable expectation the largest fleet ever assembled met only a few torpedo boats and scattered fire from coastal batteries before the first assault troops landed at 6.30 a.m. on June 6th.

The coastal defences were alerted by airborne landings in the early hours of June 6th, and by the air bombardment which had continued throughout the previous night. The bombings were aided, and often directed to their targets, by French Resistance forces. These forces had been previously briefed by secret agents of the Gaullist movement and of the British Special Operations Executive—the 'SOE' which had helped train and equip European Resistance movements since June 1940. Two American parachute divisions had landed in the eastern Cotentin peninsula in the early hours to cut it off from the south. They failed in this objective, but protected the American assault troops' flanks and seized some strategic points, though they did not link up with the assault troops for two days. A British division dropped east of the lower Orne seized its objectives: the bridges over that river and over the Caen canal.

German intelligence had given earlier warning still by recognizing the significance of coded BBC messages calling out the French Resistance, but because of the bad weather in the Channel the German command had not expected an invasion then, and Rommel and some other generals were actually absent from their posts when it began. Moreover, the Germans were slow to realize that the main invasion had come; there were no reserves behind the beach defences; and the order to attack was not given to the key armoured divisions until late afternoon. The best opportunity to repel the invasion, by immediately counter-attacking it on the beaches, was therefore lost. Rommel had urged this strategy in vain, and the beach defences had not been made as strong as he wished. As he had predicted, Allied air supremacy prevented quick and adequate reinforcement of the coastal defences. By late afternoon of D-Day only one armoured division had engaged the Allies. Allied air superiority, naval gunfire, armour and artillery, and French Resistance forces held up further armoured and infantry reinforcements. So did the lack of fuel, whereas the Allies obtained their vital fuel supplies from underwater pipelines. Moreover the Germans expected further landings in force in the Pas de Calais in the third week in July, thanks to Allied bluff, and held large forces in reserve while the Allied troops built up overwhelming superiority. By the end of July the Allies had landed thirty-six divisions (about 1,600,000 men), but the eight German divisions originally facing the invasion had increased to only twenty-eight divisions (about 400,000 men, for the German divisions were under strength).

However, it was not until July 25th that the Allies firmly established the initiative, because of the slowness of building up on the British sector of the bridgehead, and the heavy losses inflicted on the Americans. The Allied delay in advancing enabled the Germans to throw up defences around Caen, the road centre through which their armour must advance. The Allies had intended to take Caen on D-Day, but the Germans held Caen for six weeks. However, Montgomery's assault on Caen by drawing heavy German counter-attacks enabled the Americans to strengthen their bridgehead and capture the port of Cherbourg on June 27th. Cherbourg was urgently needed, for storms frequently threatened to prevent unloading of supplies on the beaches. Indeed, storms destroyed one of the two artificial harbours ('Mulberries'), built to offset the lack of ports in the landing area, within two days of their coming into operation on June 18th. It was not until July 16th that even small supplies could come into Cherbourg, so badly had its installations been damaged by the retreating Germans, with some help from the Allied bombardment. However, on July 18th Montgomery captured Caen after three heavy assaults against the German armour concentrations. On July 25th General Bradley's American First Army launched an attack which captured St Lô after even heavier fighting and broke into open country next day. Bradley then sent Patton's Third Army driving west into Brittany, which was reached on July 31st.

Normandy and western France were obviously lost, but Hitler forbade retreat, still hoping to throw the Allies back into the sea by counter-attacks. These German thrusts were no more effective in stopping the Allies than the flying-bomb offensive which Hitler had begun against

London on June 13th, in the hope that Eisenhower would attack the strong German forces still holding the Pas de Calais, where the bomb launching sites were located. The bombs (called 'V-1s'—V for *Vergeltung*, 'vengeance') were left to fighter and anti-aircraft defence to destroy. Out of about 9,000 launched before early September nearly 3,500 were destroyed, many went off course or exploded prematurely, and less than 3,300 caused material damage. Hitler's generals in the west urged surrender, and for this advice von Rundstedt was replaced on July 5th by Field-Marshal Hans Gunther von Kluge. (Rundstedt, Kluge and ten other generals had been promoted to field-marshal rank after the June 1940 victories, and Rommel during his North African campaign.)

Other leading officers, including Rommel, went farther than merely advising surrender, and plotted to depose or assassinate Hitler and end the war. The attempt was made on July 20th by Colonel Claus Schenk von Stauffenberg, a staff officer of Hitler's headquarters at Rastenburg in East Prussia. However, because Stauffenberg's bomb was not placed close enough to Hitler, Hitler suffered only shock and minor burns, and was more convinced than ever of his divine mission. Stauffenberg and the other conspirators failed to seize power, and were executed as the penalty for their failure—except for Rommel, whose popularity with the army and people was so great that he was allowed to commit suicide. This abortive plot made Hitler stronger than ever in Germany, and left no hope to the opposition, which could not even decide whether to work for a separate peace with the west or with Russia. In fact this dilemma was hypothetical. The west maintained its demand for unconditional surrender to all the Allies. Stalin's ambitions could be achieved only by Germany's destruction as a power in eastern Europe, and Soviet occupation of the whole region.

This was clearly realized by the London Poles and their supporters in Poland. The Polish Premier, Stanislaw Mikolajczyk, who had succeeded Sikorski (killed in an air crash in July 1943), had been told by Roosevelt in June 1944 that Poland might have all Silesia, the Pomeranian coast up to Stettin, and perhaps all East Prussia, but Roosevelt had been very evasive about the Polish-Russian frontier. It seemed that the Russians would overrun the whole of Poland within a short time. The Russian offensive launched in White Russia on June 23rd took Vitebsk in two days and Mogilev in four. Minsk fell on July 3rd, Kovel on July 6th and Vilna on July 13th; a Galician offensive began on July 16th. With Soviet armies pushing forward, the Polish Resistance (the Home Army owing allegiance to the London Poles) decided to act before Russia's military advance settled the political issues also. Stalin rejected the London Poles' claim that their representatives should administer Polish territory as it was 'liberated' by the Red Army, and set up a satellite *régime* of Muscovite Polish Communists at Lublin on July 25th, to rule under Red Army direction. The Home Army leaders who, on orders from their London chiefs, presented themselves to the Red Army, were arrested, and some of them were executed.

The Home Army leaders in Warsaw, despite the hesitations of Mikolaj-czyk's government, decided to free Warsaw themselves and hold it for the London government. On August 1st the Warsaw uprising began. The Germans were determined to hold Warsaw, and launched counter-attacks against the advancing Red Army. Stalin would not have his hand forced by avowedly anti-Soviet Poles, and though the Praga suburb of Warsaw on the eastern side of the Vistula was occupied by the Russians on August 15th, they remained there while the Germans systematically wiped out the Home Army, and thousands of civilians also. There were good reasons for the Red Army's pausing to consolidate before storming so formidable an obstacle as the Vistula, but Stalin's refusals of facilities to western aircraft to drop supplies into Warsaw and of Soviet tactical support to the Poles there indicate that political motives were predominant.

On the other hand easier openings for further Soviet advances were being made to both north and south. On August 25th Finland requested an armistice. Its conclusion on September 19th led to Soviet-Finnish co-operation in expelling the Germans from Finland by December. The Baltic offensive then being waged led to Russian control of Estonia by the end of September and Latvia in October.

Stalin's chief concern, however, was to exploit the opportunities created by the offensive of August 20th against Rumania, which led to Michael's dismissal of Antonescu's pro-German government on August 23rd. The new government was a broadly-based coalition acceptable to America and Britain but not to Russia. Stalin proceeded to treat his allies in Rumania as they had treated him in Italy, but Roosevelt was preoccupied with his campaign for a fourth term. In any case the Red Army was the decisive factor in Rumania and Stalin's promise not to alter her 'social structure' was dishonest, but Churchill could not insist that it be kept. Before the formal armistice was signed on September 12th with Rumania, Russia declared war on Bulgaria (September 5th), though Bulgaria had not joined Hitler against Russia, whereas she had declared war on Britain and America. Rumania's defection exposed both Bulgaria and Hungary to the Red Army. Before Bulgaria could conclude negotiations with the British authorities in Cairo for an armistice—the delay was due to Bulgarian as much as to Anglo-American obduracy—the Russians overran the country, and the Bulgarian armistice concluded at the end of October installed the Russians in power. Hungary tried to escape paying the penalty for assisting Hitler by throwing out the Germans on October 15th and seeking peace, but the Germans imprisoned the Regent Horthy and set up a puppet *régime* in Budapest. The Russians replied by setting up a rival puppet *régime* at Debreczen under General Béla Miklos, and launching an offensive against Budapest.

The only western success in this region was won despite Roosevelt's disapproval. The British, after moving into Greece in early October, pro-posed a deal in power politics to Stalin. He accepted it, and subsequently honoured it. By the so-called 'percentages agreement', he and Churchill on

October 9th arranged in Moscow their spheres of influence in the Balkans: Rumania 90% to Russia, 10% to the others; Greece 90% to Britain in accord with America (an option refused by Roosevelt, who disapproved of spheres of influence except in the Far East), and 10% to Russia; Yugoslavia and Hungary each 50% to Russia and 50% to the others; and Bulgaria 75% to Russia and 25% to the others. These bizarre percentages were unenforceable, but for some time Stalin did not make difficulties for the British in Greece, Rumania and Bulgaria logically fell into his sphere of influence, the percentages for Yugoslavia really did come to represent the independent position of that country in time, and Hungary was bound to fall under Soviet control by force of geography. Churchill recognized that he could do nothing for Poland. On returning to London he told Mikolajczyk that the Curzon Line had been conceded at Teheran to Russia, which was essentially true.

For the next two months the Russian advance made little progress except in Yugoslavia and Hungary; consequently there were military and political standstills for a time in the east. The Red Army's progress had indeed already become so slow that at the Moscow meeting Stalin had encouraged the British to drive through Istria towards Vienna, and meet the Red Army there. British commitments in Italy and France precluded this, but in any case Tito would have objected, perhaps forcibly. The Russians, however, openly looked down on him, and Molotov on October 10th told Eden that Tito (whom Molotov, with curious Marxist overtones, called 'a peasant') should make terms with Peter's supporters. Tito's Partisans captured Belgrade with Soviet assistance on October 21st, but they did not need the Red Army after that. It soon moved into Hungary, where it met stiff resistance from the Germans.

In any event the political outcome in eastern Europe would not have been much different even if the western campaigns in France had produced a German collapse in 1944, as seemed possible at one time. By mid-August the main body of German troops in northern France had been trapped in a narrow pocket around Falaise by an Allied pincers movement. Kluge was dismissed by Hitler, for failing to do the impossible and on suspicion of treason, but his successor, Field-Marshal Walter Model, could do no more than extricate the survivors and retreat east. Patton's armour meanwhile swung off towards Paris. Here the Resistance rose on August 19th–20th against the Germans, whose commander disobeyed Hitler's savage orders to destroy the city, and surrendered it to the Resistance. Allied troops entered Paris on August 24th, and next day de Gaulle led the formal entry. The Americans had hoped to the end to be able to deal with Vichy, because of de Gaulle's touchiness and delusions of French grandeur. However it was apparent after D-Day that de Gaulle had the overwhelming support of the French people. It was impossible and unnecessary to set up an Allied administration, for Gaullist authorities took over as soon as areas were liberated from the Germans, except in the south-west where the Communists seized power before the new central authority took over. On

August 26th de Gaulle's Committee of National Liberation was accepted by Britain and America as *de facto* authority, though not as provisional government until late in October. Many of de Gaulle's later actions should be seen in the light of his shabby treatment by Roosevelt and Churchill's acquiescence in it.

After several postponements the forces of operation 'Anvil', renamed 'Dragoon', landed between Toulon and Cannes on August 15th, 1944. Toulon, Nice and Marseilles were captured within a fortnight, and the Franco-American forces then moved rapidly north against comparatively weak resistance to join the northern armies around Dijon on September 12th. A continuous front was now established from Belfort to Antwerp, the Anglo-Canadian forces having driven into the Netherlands. They captured Brussels on September 3rd and the town of Antwerp the next day (the port was not taken until late in October).

Montgomery had argued since August 23rd that instead of attacking on a broad front, which would be difficult to supply, the armour should be concentrated for a 'big thrust' either under himself in the north or under the American General Bradley in the centre. Eisenhower agreed that the major advance should go through Belgium, but adhered to the broad-front strategy laid down before D-Day. On September 4th, however, the British Second Army had covered two hundred and fifty miles within a week, and was only ninety miles from the Ruhr, a great strategic and supreme industrial prize. A massed drive by the British Second Army and General Hodge's First American Army had excellent prospects of enveloping the Ruhr and opening the road to Berlin before the Germans could recover. But Eisenhower insisted on maintaining a broad front, and consequently an alternative operation ('Market Garden') was launched on September 17th to outflank the Siegfried Line defences to the north and cross the Rhine near Arnhem, though by then the Germans had regrouped and reinforced their front. Supporting American airborne landings at Eindhoven and Nijmegen were successful, but the crucial British airborne landing at Arnhem failed, and on September 26th only 10% of the paratroopers could be brought out.

Meanwhile American armour had crossed into Germany near Eupen on September 12th, but was held up by unexpectedly strong resistance. The Americans captured Aachen on October 21st, but German defence was becoming increasingly effective, and Allied resources of fuel and ammunition were inadequate for so long a front. Already it was impossible to break into the Ruhr that year, and American attacks towards the River Roer in November and December were repulsed. Antwerp, however, was opened to shipping in late November, and could be used to build up further offensives. This was one reason why Hitler launched a counter-offensive on December 16th into the Ardennes against the Americans. The Americans had under-estimated German strength and were taken by surprise. Moreover they were holding part of their Luxembourg line with inadequate forces, and were thrown off balance by the Germans. Hitler

597

proposed not only to take Antwerp but thrust into Alsace, though his generals thought they would do well to reach the Meuse.

To give coherence to the Allied defence, Eisenhower entrusted to Montgomery its co-ordination in the north, while Patton in turn surprised the Germans with the speed and power of his armoured thrust from the south against the German salient. On Christmas Day von Rundstedt, who had by then been re-instated as commander-in-chief, saw that the 'Battle of the Bulge' had failed, but Hitler continued to throw in reserves until mid-January 1945, by which time the Russians were attacking in the east. He thereupon moved all divisions that could be spared to meet the Russians. The failure of the counter-offensive meant that for the sake of retarding the western advance for a month, Hitler had facilitated his enemies' advance on both eastern and western fronts, and had virtually no reserves left.

In order to make good the losses in the eastern and western campaigns of the summer, Hitler had ordered Goebbels to mobilize all available men. Goebbels, given far-reaching power as 'Plenipotentiary-General for Total War' after the July bomb plot, did so only at the cost of weakening Germany's war production, already seriously dislocated by shortages and bombing. The mobilization of 200,000 men ordered in July was followed by that of another 100,000 in September, for Hitler decided that priority must go to putting men into uniform. The proclamation of October 18th calling up all able-bodied males between the ages of sixteen and sixty for the *Volkssturm* (or Nazi Home Guard) also had shattering economic consequences.

Goebbels' propaganda machine worked feverishly to maintain morale, and with considerable success as its effectiveness was increased by an official terror against defeatists, and by a leakage of the American 'Morgenthau plan'. Morgenthau, Secretary of the Treasury, proposed that in addition to partitioning Germany after her defeat the Allies should destroy the Ruhr's heavy industry, thereby 'pastoralizing' Germany and preventing her from becoming a military power again. Roosevelt and Churchill endorsed this plan at their second Quebec conference of September 11th–17th, 1944. Churchill did so reluctantly, and Roosevelt immediately had second thoughts, but news of the plan strengthened Goebbels' arguments that Germany must not surrender, as neither east nor west would show any mercy.

In any case, Hitler believed almost to the end that if he held out long enough his enemies' coalition would disintegrate, and he could defeat them. He also hoped for victory from the V-2 rocket campaign launched after September 8th against Britain (a few were dropped on Antwerp), and from 'secret weapons', many of which were imaginary. However faster and heavier types of submarines were developed, and these were fitted with the 'snorkel' breathing tubes which were also put into the older types, to enable submarines to complete their operations without surfacing. These developments might have inflicted shipping losses in the range of those suffered in 1942 had Germany not been defeated in time. It was also fortunate for Allied air forces that the inflexibility and deterioration of German aircraft production prevented large-scale construction of the jet fighters developed in 1944. This could not have altered the final outcome, but it would have made Germany's defences even more formidable. As it was, in early September the German army numbered over 7,500,000 men, and it was as well for the Allies that the needs of Germany's war economy, Hitler's refusal to abandon conquests, and expectations from the new submarines, led Hitler to keep strong forces in Denmark, Norway, Hungary and Yugoslavia which could have strengthened Germany's own defence. Surrender was, or course, impossible for Hitler personally, and he would not sacrifice himself for Germany and let others make peace. After Russia opened her greatest offensive across the Vistula on January 12th, 1945, he left the western front for the *Reich* Chancellery in Berlin. There he rapidly degenerated into the shambling lunatic who in April was ordering non-existent armies into battle, yet still controlled absolutely those around him.

The Russians captured Warsaw on January 17th, and two days later Stalin's Lublin puppets moved there. They had already declared themselves the Polish Provisional Government on December 31st, 1944, and Stalin had recognized them as such on January 5th, 1945. Britain and America continued to recognize the London Poles, even though Mikolajczyk had resigned on November 24th, because his colleagues had insisted on retaining the prewar frontiers. The new offensive sealed Poland's fate. By mid-February Zhukov's forces had driven from Warsaw to the River Oder near Frankfurt, only forty-five miles from Berlin. By the end of January the offensive in southern Poland had penetrated to the old Czechoslovak border east of Cracow, and the Russians had captured the Silesian industrial belt on which war production depended after the bombing of the Ruhr.

Resistance in East Prussia was stronger: Danzig was captured only on March 30th and Königsberg on April 9th, while in Hungary on March 3rd Hitler ordered a counter-offensive which nearly reached the Danube. Its failure, like that of the Ardennes offensive, did not affect Hitler's determination to fight on, though the Polish front had been gravely weakened to produce reinforcements for Hungary. Budapest, finally captured by the Russians on February 13th, was not retaken. By mid-March the Russians were advancing again; on March 29th they entered Austria, and on April 13th they captured Vienna.

Prague they took symbolically, though their occupation was real enough. A rising against the German troops in Prague on May 5th coincided with the crossing into Czechoslovakia of Patton's armour. As Stalin insisted that the Red Army, though meeting heavy resistance seventy miles from Prague, must 'liberate' the capital, the Americans halted at Pilsen, some fifty-five miles distant. Fortunately for the Czech insurgents, there happened to be in Prague surviving units of the renegade Red Army soldiers recruited by the Germans to fight the Stalinist *régime*. They had gained an unenviable reputation for excesses, but by attacking the Germans on May 7th they saved the local population. The Red Army arrived when the fighting was over, and with Partisan help rounded up some of the renegades. Others who fell into western hands were later handed over to the Soviet authorities, together with Russian deserters and prisoners of war.

In Italy the Western Allies in September 1944 had at heavy cost broken through the Gothic Line defences which ran from Pisa to Ancona, but the Germans held them off with great skill and determination until the early spring of 1945. Militarily the advance to the north was wasteful from the western viewpoint, but it hastened the collapse of Mussolini's *régime*. While trying to escape to Switzerland in company with some Germans Mussolini was captured by Partisans, and summarily shot on April 28th at Dongo, near Lake Como. On May 2nd the German commander in Italy capitulated, and the Allies swept north through the Brenner Pass into Austria, and east to meet the Yugoslav Partisans.

In the Rhineland the Americans met strong resistance until they finally regained in early February 1945 the line held before the Ardennes counter-offensive. Until February the Western Allies had not improved on the positions held in September 1944, for Hitler still wanted to hold both fronts, whereas the German people and most of his generals wished to see the western powers advance more quickly than the Russians, in order to save as much of Germany as possible from the 'Red hordes'. His reinforcement of the eastern front after mid-January did, however, facilitate the success of the western offensive which Montgomery opened on February 8th to clear the lower Rhineland. On February 23rd, after hard fighting, the American Ninth Army began to break through the Siegfried Line, and on March 2nd reached the Rhine near Düsseldorf.

On March 8th German carelessness in leaving a Rhine bridge intact at Remagen, and immediate exploitation of the opportunity, let the Americans cross the Rhine and at once they consolidated their advantage. On March 24th, Montgomery's divisions forced their way across the lower Rhine in strength and drove towards Bremen and Hamburg. On March 28th Patton's and Hodge's forces drove towards Kassel, east of the Ruhr, while a second American enveloping movement to the north completed on April 1st the encirclement of the Ruhr. After the defending forces had been split into two to facilitate their annihilation in twin operations, the centre of the western front, and with it the Ruhr's industry, lay completely shattered on April 18th. Montgomery's armies meanwhile drove on to cross the Elbe at Lüneberg on April 29th and reach Wismar on May 2nd. American and French forces in the south launched thrusts which captured Nuremberg on April 20th, Stuttgart next day, Munich on April 30th, and took the French into Austria on April 30th. The major American forces under Bradley drove through Kassel and Hanover to cross the Elbe on April 12th at Magdeburg, only fifty-three miles from Berlin.

Churchill had urged since March that Berlin, 'the most decisive point in Germany', should not be left to Russia to capture because of the political implications involved. Stalin's breaches of agreements made in February at Yalta with Roosevelt and Churchill had revealed Soviet ambitions in eastern Europe, but Berlin was within the zone of Germany allocated then for Soviet occupation. Roosevelt had become worried about Soviet activities before he died on April 12th, 1945, but still accepted Marshall's views that Eisenhower's decision to move against Leipzig instead of Berlin was sound. The new president, Truman, concurred and therefore the Americans awaited the arrival of Russian vanguards at Torgau on April 25th. As Zhukov could not attack Berlin until April 20th, the Americans could clearly have forestalled him. Eisenhower disregarded political considerations, and he attached no military significance to Berlin, but a great deal to an imaginary stronghold in the south, the 'National Redoubt', which Goebbels' propaganda was manning with last-ditch Nazi resisters. If Eisenhower was at fault in altering the direction of his main attack, the real responsibility for failing to derive political advantages from the western offensive rests with the Roosevelt and Truman administrations in the first place, and secondly with the British for having accepted the Yalta agreement. But what really mattered was that the American-Soviet meeting at Torgau symbolized the end of Germany's bid to be the greatest power in the world, and the end of Europe's greatness.

On April 25th the Russians completed the encirclement of Berlin. Hitler could still have escaped to the south by air, but even on April 28th he was expecting relieving armies to break through to Berlin. News that night of Himmler's treachery in trying to negotiate peace with the west made it obvious even to Hitler that the end had come. After making Admiral Dönitz his successor he committed suicide on April 30th. Goebbels and Martin Bormann (Hess's successor) tried on their own account to negotiate with the Russians, but were repulsed. On May 1st Goebbels himself committed suicide, while Bormann was either killed in the fighting or escaped. Dönitz in turn attempted to divide the Allies by offering to surrender to the west. His transparent manoeuvres failed, and on May 7th the Germans surrendered unconditionally at Eisenhower's headquarters in Rheims to American, British, French and Soviet representatives. At Russian insistence the proceedings were repeated next day—in Berlin, under Russian auspices.

There was no novelty in this demonstration of Soviet views on the political implications of military power. Stalin had not protested when British troops in December 1944 and January 1945 had prevented the Greek Communists from seizing power, and had safeguarded the Varkiza agreement of February 12th establishing political liberties for all Greek political parties. For their part the Russians interpreted democracy according to their lights. They used the inter-Allied armistice commissions, despite the protests of the western representatives, to lay the basis of the future Communist *régimes* in the Balkan countries occupied by the Red

Army. In January 1945 Soviet occupation authorities and local Communists in Bulgaria began to destroy the independence of the main non-Communist parties, the peasant Agrarian Union and the Social Democrats.

Nevertheless both Roosevelt and Churchill believed that their Yalta meeting of February 4th–11th with Stalin had paved the way for a lasting understanding with Soviet Russia. The meeting did in fact mark the period of greatest goodwill between Russia and the west. Stalin disposed of the major difficulties raised by the Soviet delegation at the Anglo-American-Russian Dumbarton Oaks Conference (August–September 1944) which was held to draft the constitution for the United Nations, actually based on the general structure of the League of Nations. He dropped the demand that all sixteen constituent republics of the Soviet Union should have seats in the General Assembly, and instead accepted just two additional seats (for the Ukraine and White Russia). He also agreed that the permanent members of the Security Council (France, China and the Big Three) could not veto discussion of any matter affecting themselves. (That they could veto action affecting themselves was as indisputable to Roosevelt and Churchill as to Stalin, and Churchill had been equally reluctant at first to allow Britain to be put in the dock to justify her actions before the United Nations.)

Stalin also accepted Roosevelt's suggestions for opening membership of the United Nations to all states at war with Germany on March 1st, so that they could attend the full meeting (held at San Francisco, April–June 1945) to draft the charter. This brought in Turkey and some other small states as nominal belligerents, but did not affect the course of the European war. On the treatment of Germany Stalin also made some concessions, chiefly to Churchill. He agreed to French participation in controlling Germany, though America and Britain were to yield parts of their zones to give France a zone of her own. He did not press at this stage his demands for reparations and participation in control of the Ruhr. It was decided unanimously to break up Germany into separate states, though to Churchill's relief this idea was soon dropped.

Stalin essentially got his way on the Polish question, the major European issue at Yalta. Roosevelt now formally accepted the Curzon Line as the Polish-Soviet frontier. A vague phrase in the agreement effectively fixed the western frontier at the Oder-Western Neisse Line. In fact the Polish Provisional Government was already operating up to that line. Stalin agreed to re-organize this government to include some non-Communist Poles from London and from inside Poland, and promised 'free elections' in Poland as soon as possible. He agreed to a similar enlargement of Tito's government to include Peter's nominees. By the 'Declaration on Liberated Europe' the Big Three promised to co-operate in assisting the liberated and former satellite peoples to create democratic institutions through representatives chosen in free elections. The actual significance of these pledges was soon shown. On February 27th Vyshinski, Stalin's deputy Foreign Minister, ordered Michael of Rumania to dismiss his Right Wing Premier,

General Nicolae Radescu. Radescu and his colleagues were suspect because of their prewar and wartime activities, but his successor, Petru Groza, was an equally odious example of the new type of eastern European Muscovite Communist, despised by his masters as much as by his own people.

Clearly the Communists and their sympathizers would reign supreme in eastern Europe unless Soviet influence there could be countered. Hence Churchill suggested from March that the western forces should drive as far to the east as possible, and hold their positions until Stalin agreed to recognize Western interests in eastern Europe. Roosevelt still took the view that eastern Europe was bound to fall under Russian control. He was moved to protest only when Stalin accused the Western Allies in March and April of attempting to use their negotiations for an armistice in Italy as a means of obtaining a separate peace with Germany.

Later the Yalta agreement was to be compared with the Munich surrender, and it is true that Roosevelt deliberately conceded domination of eastern and central Europe to Stalin, as Chamberlain had conceded it to Hitler. It is also true that the West had only Stalin's word, as it had once had Hitler's, that the agreement would be honoured, and that it had had six years' prior warnings of Stalin's aims and methods. On the other hand, by February 1945 only Czechoslovakia could conceivably have been prevented from falling under Soviet control by methods short of war against Russia, and such a war, after the long common struggle against Hitler, was out of the question.

In Russia's darkest days after June 1941, Stalin had played for western benefit the role of the Russian nationalist leader, renouncing 'world revolutionary' objectives. This was not wholly deceitful. Even his present activities promoted old Russian national aims. His view of the political consequences of World War II was that 'Whoever occupies a territory also imposes his own political system.' Though he was too discreet to put this in so many words to the west, he expected the principle to operate in Greece, Italy and Belgium just as much as in Eastern Europe. Of course this did not alter the fact that with Germany's defeat certain, he had reverted to the struggle against the capitalist enemy only temporarily suspended since June 1941. Churchill soon realized this. Roosevelt never realized it, though not because of secret pro-Soviet sympathies. His belief that Churchill, not Stalin, was the dangerous imperialist was shared by the unwaveringly anti-Communist military advisers in the Pentagon. On their advice, at the Anglo-American meeting at Malta which preceded the Yalta summit conference, he rejected Churchill's pleas for a joint approach to Stalin. This advice reinforced Roosevelt's preference for Stalin over Churchill as a partner in establishing a democratic postwar Europe, and for Chiang as America's most promising ally in giving liberty to the peoples of the Far East. Moreover, these opinions had some support from sections of opinion, in both America and Britain, which had never entirely overcome distrust of the 'Old Tory', Churchill.

Roosevelt at least secured his two major objectives at Yalta: to bring

Soviet Russia into the United Nations and into the war against Japan. On the other hand, he could have left it to Stalin to take both steps. Geneva had afforded a very useful platform for Soviet propaganda if for nothing else. Stalin would in any case have soon settled accounts with Japan, and avenged the humiliating Russian defeats by Japan in 1904–05. Stalin was still a reliable, if critical ally of Chiang, and though Russia had not been able to spare much help for China since 1941, between 1937 and 1941 she had supplied five times as much material as America had done to help the Kuomintang against the Japanese. Since 1941 no Russian aid had gone to Mao, whom Stalin regarded much as Molotov viewed Tito—except that Stalin did not conceive Mao's triumph as being remotely possible. Chiang was relieved that at Yalta no stipulations had been made about the Chinese Communists, and that Stalin had re-affirmed support for the Kuomintang. Stalin offered to declare war against Japan within three months of Germany's defeat, for what both Roosevelt and Chiang regarded as a fair price: the return of Russian rights 'violated by the treacherous attack of Japan in 1904'. Roosevelt agreed, subject to Chiang's own approval, though Roosevelt promised to get Chiang's agreement. In fact the 'rights' demanded were Tsarist imperialist extortions from China repudiated in the 1924 Sino-Soviet treaty, and the return of the Kuriles, which Russia had ceded to Japan in 1875 in return for recognition of Russia's control of southern Sakhalin. Stalin now demanded both the Kuriles and southern Sakhalin. From Chiang he wanted, and on August 14th obtained, the lease of Dairen and Port Arthur, control of the Man-churian railways (though recognizing formal Chinese sovereignty over Manchuria) and control over Outer Mongolia.

Mao's military chief, Marshal Chu Teh, had declared in October 1944 that he could see no way of expelling the Japanese, and that the Chinese Communists could 'carry on a war of attrition only'. Mao himself did not dispute as yet the Kuomintang's legal sovereignty, though the Japanese 'Trans-Continental Drive', launched in June 1944, had seemed by the end of 1944 likely to eliminate the Kuomintang completely. It captured eight Kuomintang provinces, secured control of the coast, made most of the American airfields useless, and very nearly established land communications between Manchukuo and Indo-China to offset American command of the sea. In October Stilwell had been recalled at Chiang's insistence, after reporting home that, since the Kuomintang was hopelessly corrupt and incompetent, Kuomintang, Communist and possibly bandit forces also must be combined under the command of an American general. The Japanese could not, however, sustain the offensive now that so many other demands were being made on their resources. It was apparent early in 1945 that they would fail to capture Chungking and their two other major objectives, Sian and Kunming with its great American airfield. On January 26th, 1945, Kuomintang troops from Yunnan met Chinese divisions which had driven into North Burma with Indian and British troops, and the land route into South China was reopened.

Even before the Japanese drive petered out its purpose had been defeated by the American advances into the Philippines and Central Pacific. Between mid-June and mid-August, 1944, Operation 'Forager' secured American control of the Marianas, with their air and naval bases for attacks on Japanese towns and shipping. On June 19th a Japanese fleet attempting to defend Saipan was attacked. Its carrier planes, together with aircraft from Guam, were shot down in the 'Marianas Turkey Shoot', and though most of the ships escaped to the west, aircraft and submarines severely mauled them next day in the Battle of the Philippines.

In September carrier raids on the Philippines showed the weakness of the Japanese air defences there. After taking the Caroline islands of Angaur and Pelelieu and neutralizing Yap in September, the Americans invaded the Philippines at Leyte on October 20th. The greatest naval battle of the two world wars ensued (October 23rd–25th) and destroyed most of the remaining Japanese warships. Before MacArthur redeemed his promise of 1942 to the Filipinos to free their islands from the Japanese, Japan had lost over 400,000 men and about 9,000 aircraft, in a series of battles lasting until July 5th, 1945. Japanese resistance at Leyte gave a foretaste of future Japanese tactics, for it was here that aircraft piloted by suicide pilots (*Kamikazes*) were first used against American ships. The Philippine invasion, however, cut Japanese communications with South-East Asia, while from November long-range bombers from Guam, Saipan, Tinian and bases in China could bomb Japan on round-trip missions. Nevertheless the Japanese were determined to resist to the end. The island of Iwo Jima, needed as a staging post for bombers attacking Japan from the Marianas, was defended desperately from February 19th to March 16th, 1945. Okinawa, required as a base from which to invade Japan, was invaded on April 1st with covering fire from British as well as American warships. The battle here lasted until June 21st, costing Japan about 120,000 casualties (nearly 110,000 of them fatal) and about 4,000 aircraft, including 3,500 flown by *Kamikaze* pilots.

Japan was already on the verge of collapse. In February the emperor had supported the peace party in Japan, which had recognized as early as the autumn of 1943 that she could no longer win the war. On April 8th he appointed Suzuki Kontaro premier with orders to end it. This was impossible, however, for another four months. The demand for unconditional surrender was difficult even for the peace party to accept, while the army insisted on fighting to the end. In May the government asked Russia to renew the neutrality pact, due to expire in April 1946, but unlikely even to be honoured until then. It was hoped, however, to use the negotiations to induce Russia to mediate, and in both June and July the emperor requested Russia to arrange peace talks between Japan and America. To this even the War Minister and Chief of the Army General Staff agreed. The Russians delayed their reply to the Japanese while informing the Americans of the request. The Japanese were finally told that the answer must await Stalin's return from the Potsdam conference. There Stalin told Truman and Churchill of the overtures. Truman already knew of them from intercepted Japanese radio messages, but he distrusted Japanese good faith. He was unaware that the refusal to surrender unconditionally was prompted mainly by desire to save the imperial throne, which the Japanese regarded as the indispensable basis of their whole society.

News of the successful testing of the atom bomb on July 16th merely strengthened American insistence on unconditional surrender. Truman accepted the advice of his military specialists that Japan would surrender only after invasion, unless the bomb could induce capitulation, and thereby save a long struggle and perhaps a million American casualties. Some military and civilian advisers urged that its use might make it unnecessary to pay Stalin's price for attacking Japan, and might even force him to behave fairly in Eastern Europe. Nevertheless, it was the rigidity of American policy towards Japan which made the biggest contribution towards the Potsdam Declaration on Japan of July 26th. In this declaration Truman, with Churchill's and Chiang's support, demanded Japan's unconditional surrender under threat of 'prompt and utter destruction'— but the means remained unspecified. On July 28th the Japanese government announced that it would ignore the message, though its civilian members wished to surrender, and did not expect that Truman would take their reply literally. Their desire to save the throne, and to save face also, gave the impression that they could never admit defeat—which was indeed true of some army elements.

It had been decided on July 22nd by Truman and his military advisers, with Churchill's approval, to use the bomb if Japan did not surrender. The opinions of the 'Manhattan' scientists on the matter were conflicting, but the consensus of scientific opinion favoured it, though an important minority both opposed its use and advocated that so dangerous a weapon should be under international control. Truman told Stalin with studied casualness on July 24th that America had 'a new weapon of unusual destructive force', to which Stalin replied with equal lack of emphasis that he hoped she would make 'good use of it against the Japanese'. The Russians were in fact well informed from agents in America of the bomb's existence, and they had themselves been working since 1943 to make atomic weapons. Truman regarded the atom bomb as only a new weapon, not one whose use posed moral questions of an unprecedented kind. He did not explore the possibilities of bringing Japan's surrender by diplomatic means, nor give Japan any indication of what was in store, before authorizing the use of the bomb. On August 6th a bomber from Tinian dropped the first atom bomb on Hiroshima, killing over 78,000 people and destroying three-fifths of the city. Even then the Japanese would not surrender.

On August 8th Russia declared war on Japan and invaded Manchuria. Admittedly the Russians had warned Japan in April that the Neutrality Pact would not be renewed, but this action was unprovoked aggression. In its bearing on Japan's decision to surrender it may have been as important as the atom bombs and the destruction of her economy. On August

9th, while the inner directing group of the Japanese government, the Supreme Council for the Direction of the War, discussed on what terms to seek peace, news came that a second atomic bomb had been dropped on Nagasaki. Next day Hirohito and the full cabinet agreed to make peace, providing only that the monarchy was retained. On August 11th the Allies replied that the authority of the emperor and his government would be subordinated to the Allied Supreme Commander, and it was not until August 14th that this vague and pedantic formula was accepted. A small group of military fanatics tried to prevent the surrender, but on August 15th it was broadcast as an imperial message to the nation. By the end of August the Japanese forces in Manchuria had surrendered to the Russians, those in China to the Kuomintang or Communists, and the South-East Asia forces to Britain's Mountbatten. On September 2nd the ceremonial surrender was made to MacArthur, as Supreme Commander, on board USS *Missouri* in Tokyo Bay.

Undoubtedly the Americans' independent decision to drop the atomic bombs was the most momentous reached at Potsdam, but the main problems of this lengthy conference (July 17th–August 2nd) concerned Europe and relations between the Big Three. Disputes over Poland had nearly prevented the San Francisco conference from meeting, and there had been long wrangles before Russia had conceded the major American demands embodied in the United Nations Charter signed on June 26th. However, in June the western troops had occupied their zones in Berlin, and a Four-Power Kommandatura had been set up to rule the city. Despite the unrepresentative character of the Polish Provisional Government established on June 28th (sixteen Muscovite or fellow-travelling Poles and only five non-Communists), the Western Allies recognized it on July 6th, for they had reluctantly helped to create it. At Potsdam they drew the logical conclusions from their previous concessions to Stalin over Poland. They agreed that the Oder-Neisse Line should be Poland's western frontier, that northern East Prussia should be annexed by Russia, and the rest of the province by Poland. These were only interim agreements, like all those made at Potsdam and the other Big Three conferences, and were subject to confirmation by the general peace conference when it should be held. In fact they proved to be binding. The uprooting of populations started by the Germans now recoiled on their own heads when both Czechs and Poles expelled Germans whom they did not wish to allow to remain inside the new (or restored) frontiers.

No change in British policy resulted from the general election in July, which returned a Labour majority and replaced Churchill as Premier by Clement Attlee midway through the conference. Truman similarly followed Roosevelt's general line. It was agreed at Potsdam that Germany should be ruled as an economic unit by the Four-Power Allied Control Council in Berlin, though each occupying power would administer its own zone. It was also agreed that German war industries should be dismantled, war criminals be brought to trial, and denazification measures be vigorously pressed. Reparations were not fixed, but each power could take them from within its own zone as delimited on July 26th. Russia in addition could receive 10% of industrial equipment from the western zones which was not needed for Germany's 'peace economy', and another 15% in exchange for food, coal and other agreed commodities from her zone. Russia's demand for a share in controlling the Ruhr was again rejected, more from political than from economic considerations. The eastern zone was already being sovietized, and neither Britain (whose zone contained the Ruhr) nor America would allow that process to extend into western Germany. They had, however, also rejected in May France's demands for her strategic control of the Rhineland, or alternatively for the internationalization of the Ruhr.

Truman, as much as Churchill, welcomed Stalin's statement of May 9th, 1945, that Russia did not intend to dismember Germany, and the assumption at Potsdam was that Germany would one day again be ruled by a central German government. It was only after Potsdam that the developing conflict between Russian and western interests prevented Germany's reunification on mutually acceptable terms. It became obvious only gradually to the British and Americans that the Russians would not deny their revolutionary heritage, nor abandon the possibility of using eastern Germany as a base from which to sovietize western Germany, and then to use the whole of Germany as a base for communizing western Europe. In turn, the Russians would not allow Germany to be reunited on *bourgeois* democratic lines, for this would imperil the advantages gained by denying eastern Europe to both a resurgent Germany and the western powers.

Western obstinacy in trying to achieve an impossible total victory by demanding unconditional surrender admittedly favoured the establishment of Russian control of eastern Europe, and the rise of a Communist *régime* in China also invincibly hostile to western interests. However, the major responsibilities for those developments lay on the one hand with Germany and the undemocratic prewar *régimes* in eastern Europe, and on the other with Japan and Chiang. The destruction of Nazi tyranny in Europe and of the Japanese menace in the Far East were inescapable necessities for the western powers. It was equally beyond their power to remove, or even to ameliorate the implacable hostility of Soviet Russia. The limited hostilities of the cold war, stripped of their ideological overtones, were more the expression of Russia's rivalry with the United States, the greater world power, than a consequence of World War II. World War II did, however, mark the beginning of the most critical stage ever reached in international relations by restricting great power status to nations so ideologically motivated as Russia and America, and simultaneously extending their areas of conflict almost literally throughout the world.

This bipolarization of the world had indeed been foreshadowed in 1917, when America and Russia had begun to compete for the ideological leadership of the world under the rival banners of liberal democracy and Marxism. Nevertheless, the decisive contribution to the overthrow of Europe's political and economic primacy was made by the defeat of Germany's two bids to become the dominant world power. A German victory in World War I would have meant the creation of a European imperialist domination invulnerable to American or any other pressure, and would have prevented the rise of any government capable of transforming Russia into a great military power. Nazi Germany's defeat of Soviet Russia, which was entirely within the realms of possibility if Britain had followed France into submission in World War II, would have meant the creation of a German-dominated European military colossus invulnerable to anything but a nuclear holocaust—to which even the bestialities of Hitler's New Order would have been preferable. As it was, in the dawn of the nuclear age which was World War II's most terrifying legacy, the future of mankind depended on the frail hope that the American-Soviet global balance would be more effective in maintaining the peace of the world than the European primacy which it had replaced.

# SELECT BIBLIOGRAPHY

Allen, G. C., *A Short Economic History of Modern Japan, 1867–1937*, Frederick A. Praeger, Inc., New York, 1963.

Aron, R., *The Century of Total War*, Beacon Press, Boston, Mass., 1955.

Ashworth, W., *A Short History of the International Economy, 1850–1950*, Methuen and Co., Ltd., London, 1952.

Brenan, G., *The Spanish Labyrinth* (2nd ed.), Cambridge University Press, Cambridge, England, 1950.

Bullock, Alan, *Hitler, A Study in Tyranny*, Harper and Row, Evanston, Ill., 1964.

Burns, James McGregor, *Roosevelt, The Lion and the Fox*, Harcourt, Brace and World, New York, 1956.

Butow, R. J. C., *Tojo and the Coming of the War*, Princeton University Press, Princeton, N. J., 1961.

Carr, E. H., *A History of Soviet Russia*, Macmillan Co., New York, 1951.

Churchill, Winston S., *The Second World War*, 6 vols., Bantam Books, New York, 1962.

Cole, G. D. H., *A History of Socialist Thought*, Vol. V, *Socialism and Fascism 1931–1939*, St. Martins Press, New York, 1960.

Cole, J. P., *Geography of World Affairs*, Penguin Books, Baltimore, Md., 1963.

Dallin, A., *German Rule in Russia, 1941–1945*, St. Martins Press, New York, 1957.

DeGaulle, Charles, *War Memoirs*, 3 vols., Viking Press, New York, 1955–60.

Deutscher, Isaac, *Stalin, A Political Biography*, Oxford University Press, New York, 1949.

————, *The Prophet Armed, Trotsky, 1879–1921*; *The Prophet Unarmed, Trotsky, 1921–1929*, Oxford University Press, New York, 1954 and 1959.

Duroselle, Jean-Baptiste, *From Wilson to Roosevelt, Foreign Policy of the United States, 1913–1945*, trans. by Nancy Roelker, Harvard University Press, Cambridge, Mass., 1963.

Earle, E. M. (ed.), *Modern France*, Princeton University Press, Princeton, N. J., 1951.

Eyck, E., *A History of the Weimar Republic*, 2 vols., Harvard University Press, Cambridge, Mass., 1963.

Feis, H., *Churchill, Roosevelt, Stalin, the War They Fought and the Peace They Sought*, Princeton University Press, Princeton, N. J., 1957.

————, *Japan Subdued*, Princeton University Press, Princeton, N. J., 1961.

Galbraith, J. K., *The Great Crash, 1929*, Houghton-Mifflin Co., Boston, Mass., 1955.

610

Greenwood, G. (ed.), *Australia*, ill., Tri-Ocean Books, San Francisco, Calif., 1964.

Hailey, Lord William, *African Survey*, Oxford University Press, New York, 1957.

Hancock, K., *A Survey of British Commonwealth Affairs, 1918–1939*, 2 vols., Oxford University Press, New York, 1940.

Hart, B. H. Liddell, *Memoirs*, 2 vols., Cassell and Company, Ltd., London, 1965.

Hoover, Herbert, *The Ordeal of Woodrow Wilson*, McGraw-Hill Book Co., New York, 1958.

Hughes, H. Stuart, *Contemporary Europe, A History*, Prentice-Hall, Englewood Cliffs, N. J., 1961.

Jacobsen, H. A., and Rohwer, J. (ed.), *Decisive Battles of World War II*, G. P. Putnam and Sons, New York, 1965.

Jasny, N., *Soviet Industrialization, 1928–1953*, University of Chicago Press, Chicago, 1960.

Joll, J., *Intellectuals in Politics*, Pantheon Books, Inc., New York, 1961.

Kinross, Lord, *Ataturk*, William Morrow and Co., New York, 1964.

Kirkpatrick, Sir Ivone, *Mussolini: Study of a Demagogue*, Odhams Press, Ltd., London, 1964.

Langer, W. L., and Gleason, S. E., *The Challenge to Isolation, 1937–1940*; *The Undeclared War, September 1940–December 1941*, Harper and Row, New York, 1952–53.

Link, A. S., *American Epoch* (2nd ed.), Alfred A. Knopf, New York, 1963.

Ludowyk, E. F. C., *A Modern History of Ceylon*, ill., Frederick A. Praeger, Inc., New York, 1966.

Macartney, C. A., and Palmer, A. W., *Independent Eastern Europe*, Macmillan and Co., Ltd., London, 1962.

Masani, R. P., *Britain in India*, Oxford University Press, New York, 1961.

Miller, Harold, *New Zealand*, Hillary House Publishers, New York, 1950.

Milward, Alan S., *The German Economy at War*, Oxford University Press, New York, 1964.

Myere, A. G., *Leninism*, Harvard University Press, Cambridge, Mass., 1957.

Nolte, Ernst, *Three Faces of Fascism*, trans. by L. Vennewitz, Holt, Rinehart and Winston, Inc., New York, 1966.

Panikkar, K. M., *Asia and Western Dominance* (rev. ed.), ill., Hillary House Publishers, New York, 1959.

Pipes, R., *The Formation of the Soviet Union* (rev. ed.), Harvard University Press, Cambridge, Mass., 1964.

Reynaud, P., *In the Thick of the Fight*, Simon and Schuster, New York, 1955.

Rogger, H., and Weber, E., *The European Right: A Historical Profile*, University of California Press, Berkeley, Calif., 1965.

Schwartz, B. I., *Chinese Communism and the Rise of Mao*, Harvard University Press, Cambridge, Mass., 1951.

611

# SELECT BIBLIOGRAPHY

Seton-Watson, Hugh, *Eastern Europe Between the Wars, 1918–1931* (3rd. ed.), Shoe String Press, Hamden, Conn., 1963.

Sherwood, R. E., *Roosevelt and Hopkins: An Intimate History*, Harper and Row, New York, 1948.

Snyder, L. L., *The War: A Concise History, 1935–1945*, Messner, Inc., New York, 1960.

Storry, R., *A History of Modern Japan*, Barnes and Noble, New York, 1962.

Taylor, A. J. P., *English History, 1914–1945*, Oxford University Press, New York, 1965.

Teichert, Pedro, *Economic Policy Revolution and Industrialization in Latin America*, University of Missouri Press, Columbia, Mo., 1959.

Thomas, Hugh, *The Spanish Civil War*, ill., Harper and Row, New York, 1961.

Treadgold, D., *Twentieth Century Russia*, Rand McNally and Co., Chicago, Ill., 1964.

Ulam, Adam B., *Lenin and the Bolsheviks*, Secher and Warburg, Ltd., London, 1966.

Vatcher, W. H., Jr., *White Laager: The Rise of Afrikaner Nationalism*, ill., Frederick A. Praeger, Inc., New York, 1965.

Walters, F. P., *A History of the League of Nations*, 1 vol. ed., Oxford University Press, New York, 1952.

Wilmot, Chester, *The Struggle for Europe: World War II in Western Europe*, Harper and Row, New York, 1952.

# PART THREE
## 1945-1963
# NEVILLE BROWN

*Chapter I*
# THE MARCH OF SCIENCE

## (i) *Space Research*

Too much account should not be taken of the interplay between science and politics. Science is a minority quest for neat explanations that will stand the test of time; politics is concerned with resolving, postponing, or moderating the transitory conflicts of interest and attitude that arise between large human groups. What a scientist does today may well influence the military and economic competitiveness of his country five years hence. It may, alternatively, help shape the material and mental horizons of future generations. Either way his work will have real political effects but these effects will be indirect, somewhat intangible, and comparatively long-term.

To these generalizations space programmes are a partial exception. They can be so melodramatic and can make such high demands on quality resources that they tend to appear as indices of overall national prowess. Propaganda strongly promotes this tendency. The Russians, in particular, have heavily emphasized their space achievements. This is because they can thereby suggest that the West's technological advantage has been eliminated, and perhaps also because they may thus persuade themselves and others that Scientific Materialists can, in some sense, reach out to heaven. They certainly succeeded in the first objective in the months after the launchings of *Sputniks I* and *II*, the first artificial earth satellites. Many people thought at the time that these triumphs automatically implied Soviet military supremacy. Many people think even today that they ushered in an era of strategic stalemate. The myth about the significance of *Sputnik* has been so widely believed that it has acquired a certain validity.

Soviet rocket crews placed the first two *Sputniks* in orbit in the autumn of 1957, soon after the start of the International Geophysical Year.[1] The *Sputniks* preceded by several months their American equivalent, a much lighter vehicle called *Explorer I*. Two years after their release one Russian space vehicle hit the moon and immediately afterwards another one took

[1] See Section ii of this chapter.

close range photographs of its reverse side. No American probe hit the moon until 1962. The Russians placed a man in earth orbit in April 1961 and the Americans in February 1962.

The United States later recovered much of the national confidence and international prestige which it lost at the beginning of the space age. She increased her space budget from $500,000,000 in 1956 to $4,000,000,000 in 1963, and used this expansion of resources to promote a variegated programme that exploited fully her supremacy in electronics and other relevant technologies. Meteorological observation began with the launching of *Tiros I* in April 1960. 1962 witnessed the arrival of booster-relay communications and the close observation of Venus by means of the *Mariner* space probe; these observations, it may be noted, strongly suggested that Venus could not support life. By July 1963 the Americans had launched 119 satellites, including two with British equipment, and the Russians 20.

The phrase the 'conquest of space' has been bandied around far too freely in connection with this rocket exploration of a small fraction of our tiny solar system. If any such conquest is being achieved it is by the radio astronomers rather than by the rocket engineers. Their science has made fantastic advances in the last fifteen years and its progress is accelerating the whole time. Already they handle information collected from thousands of billions[1] of billions of miles away.

## (ii) *Science in General*

The fifties was a decade in which all aspects of science gathered momentum ever more rapidly. Perhaps, through the exacting demands they made on many skills, the space and military programmes helped force the pace. Perhaps it would have been yet faster in their absence; in Britain in 1956, for example, nearly half of all those engaged in research and development were concerned with defence.

Central to the whole movement were the advances made in electronics, and in particular the evolution, early in the 1950s, of the transistor—a source of free electrons that was smaller, tougher, and cheaper to run than the valve. And the symbol of man's new electronic prowess was the computer. Fifteen of these machines were operating in the United States at the close of the Korean War; five years later the figure was well over 1,000. Even little Switzerland employed about 200 early in 1964; the American total was then 17,000. Radio astronomy depended upon computers to pick out incoming signals—sometimes of the order of a billionth of a watt—from a background of ambient noise. Meteorology was improved by them, the processing of clerical data made easier, and

[1] One billion = 1,000,000,000 throughout.

the automatic control of heavy industrial processes made increasingly feasible. But there were many other devices, ranging from diagnostic pills to radar sets, that were either made possible or rendered more manageable by the advent of the transistor. Indeed the word 'transistor' came popularly to be used as the name for the most highly portable types of radio sets and so to characterize an impending age of affluence and leisure or, to take a different tack, of aimless noise and cultural monotony.

Electron microscopes had been constructed by 1956 that could magnify almost three million times. With machines such as these it was possible to carry out detailed examination of molecules that might, in the most complex cases, be composed of thousands of atoms arranged in the most intricate patterns. And by 1963 molecular biology was approaching a threshold that promised to open up very exciting, if somewhat disconcerting, prospects for understanding the exact mechanics of memory and heredity and to suggest ways in which congenital and virus disease might be controlled. Typical of the progress being widely made was the artificial synthesis of molecules of chlorophyll, which each contain 140 atoms, in 1960. This was effected almost simultaneously, but quite independently, at Munich and Harvard.

Applied medicine forged ahead meanwhile. Several approaches were tried in the quest to eliminate cancer and along some of them significant progress was made. Between 1947 and 1957 the tuberculosis death rate among young adults in Britain, for example, dropped by 95%, thanks largely to improved diagnosis and to the use of efficient drugs. Vaccination helped to bring poliomyelitis under control. In many areas malaria was curbed by the use of new drugs and by systematic campaigns against the mosquito larvae. But the progress was not unqualified. Lung cancer, which by 1957 had been shown to be closely linked to heavy cigarette consumption, and coronary thrombosis were among the diseases whose incidence rose as that of certain traditional major killers declined. And medical science was more directly responsible for some misfortunes. Both lay and professional opinion was shocked by the discovery of a German doctor in 1961 that a strong correlation existed between the administering of thalidomide to expectant mothers and the birth of deformed children. Soon other tranquillizers and certain antibiotics were made the subject of warnings and investigations.

This kind of soul-searching in medicine can be related to the growth of a strong, though often ill defined and ill informed, unease about what a Director of the World Health Organization called the 'unprecedented interference with the balance of nature'. Heavy use of pesticides, intensive rearing of farm animals, and, of course, the incessant growth of motor transport were among many trends that attracted unfavourable notice as being perhaps incompatible with an environment being morally, physically or aesthetically sound.

Quite the most dramatic manifestation of world-wide co-operation in science was the International Geophysical Year staged, in order to coincide with exceptionally intense sunspot activity, between the middle of 1957 and the end of 1958. The decision to launch the IGY, which involved the manning of over 3,500 observation posts and the release of hundreds of research rockets, had been taken by the International Council of Scientific Unions as early as 1950. Among its more outstanding accomplishments were the crossing of the Antarctic via the South Pole by a Commonwealth expedition and the discovery, as the result of a co-ordinated effort by survey ships from various nations, of several deep, broad and powerful submarine currents, the existence of which had not previously been suspected.

## (iii) *Weapons of War*

Russia exploded her first fission bomb in 1949—four years after America but several years earlier than most Western experts anticipated. She was followed by Britain in 1952 and France in 1960. By 1963 all these nations except France had attained thermonuclear status as well—that is to say they had exploded hydrogen bombs. These are the weapons that derive their energy principally from the fusion of hydrogen nuclei; their special characteristic is that they can be made up to any required size. The first American hydrogen device was exploded in November 1952, and some nine months later a rather more developed Soviet one was released. Britain achieved thermonuclear status in 1957.

The USA had accumulated thousands of nuclear warheads by the end of 1963 and their combined explosive yield amounted to many billions of tons of TNT equivalent. Britain had c. 1,000 warheads equal to one to three billion tons. Estimates of the Soviet stockpile are less easy to make but its explosive yield was of a similar order. It has been said that the total high explosive released by all combatants in World War II was seven million tons.

The nuclear nations can now obtain increments in firepower comparatively cheaply; the United States, for example, can manufacture a megaton bomb (i.e. one of a million tons of TNT equivalent) for about $1,000,000. But, in general, defence has become progressively more expensive. It is research and development costs that have risen the furthest and this, indeed, largely explains why the smaller nations have found it ever more difficult to meet their weapons requirements without large overseas purchases. Even at the stage of mass production, however, there has often been an accelerating cost inflation. In 1945 each *Mustang* fighter plane cost the United States Air Force $21,000. By 1957 it was paying $1,000,000 for F–100 *Super Sabres* and by 1963 over twice that for F–110 *Phantom II*s. The next generation aircraft—the F–111—will be purchased for something in excess of $4,000,000. Warplanes have been, of course, an especially bad example because they have incorporated so many of the electronic advances, but other weapons systems have also made heavy demands. During the Kennedy era the United States alone spent over fifteen billion dollars on military research and development.

Some of the American development programmes, such as the billion dollar nuclear-powered aircraft one, have been total and obvious failures. Others have been controversial, and of these perhaps the best example is the anti-missile missile. Since about 1957 both America and Russia have been developing anti-missile missiles which neither of them is likely ever to deploy on more than a token scale. The American effort has come under domestic criticism both from those who believe that early deployment could be the only logical outcome of the research effort and from those who think that the whole quest for missile defence is mistaken. Arguments can be advanced, however, for retaining anti-missile deployment as an option to be taken up under certain circumstances. They might be of value, for example, against the small and unsophisticated long-range rocket force that China might acquire in the late 1970s.

Certain trends can be detected in the evolving pattern of military technology. One is that it is getting progressively more difficult to conceal objects. Darkness and shade can be penetrated increasingly by radar and by infra-red. Salt water remains relatively opaque but submarine detection ranges have multiplied several times since 1945. Between 1956 and 1960 Lockheed U–2 aircraft reconnoitred the USSR in great detail. Late in 1961 surveillance was resumed with orbiting satellites. Their work has been of lower quality but it showed, for example, that the USSR had only 75 intercontinental rockets in mid-1962 as compared with the 2,500 or more predicted for that year by American intelligence in 1959.

A trend that some influential Western military commentators have discerned is one towards a supremacy of the defence in 'conventional' (non-nuclear) war. They argue, in particular, that the advent of guided missiles has enhanced the vulnerability of the two main offensive weapons, the aircraft and the tank. This thesis can be objected to on technical grounds but there is, on the other hand, no doubt that the inherent threat of nuclear action now works to the psychological advantage of the defence because a dramatic advance may lead not to final victory but simply to nuclear reprisal.

America's nuclear capability has remained generally superior to Russia's throughout the Cold War. The USSR has made the largest hydrogen bombs—perhaps her largest have been unduly large—but she has not been able to rival the USA in respect of warhead compactness; this has meant that the USA has been able to produce tactical nuclear systems of better quality and variety. Also, although the USSR led the USA by about two years in the acquisition of liquid-fuelled intercontinental rockets, she was outclassed in respect of the solid-fuelled versions which are much easier to mass produce, to install in concrete emplacements, and to fire at short notice. Thus while the American *Minuteman* entered service in 1962, its Soviet counterpart had not appeared by early 1964.

The strategic relationship between the two super-powers may be fundamental to the origin and outcome of the Cuban missile crisis. By late in
1962 several factors had combined to render the Soviet Intercontinental
Ballistic Missile force rather vulnerable to destruction on its launching
pads. The USA already had 200 ICBMs and was rapidly acquiring more;
the USSR had far fewer, their positions were accurately known, and they
were of a type that would have been relatively easy to destroy on the
ground. It is likely that a Soviet anxiety to correct this strategic imbalance was among the factors that precipitated the crisis.[1] It is certain
that it helped the USA to control it.

[1] See p. 706.

*Chapter II*
# ECONOMIC CHANGE

THE most important economic fact about the 'post-war'world is that its population grew at an accelerating rate. Expectation of life at birth rose to seventy years or more in parts of the Atlantic area and the average size of families ceased to fall. In some cases indeed—notably the USA, Canada, France, and Britain—it started to rise. Parallel trends were evident in the underdeveloped regions. Several countries that had life expectations of forty or fifty years in the 1940s had raised them by about a third by 1960. During the fifties the annual percentage growth of population was 1·9 in Asia and 2·4 in Latin America. For Europe, exclusive of the USSR, and for North America the respective figures were 0·8 and 1·8. The world total seemed likely to double during the rest of the century.

Another trend was an increase in the proportion of town dwellers with all that this implied in terms of physical congestion, social instability, and demands on public investment. Places with over 20,000 inhabitants apiece increased their share in the total population from 10 to 13% in Africa and from 25 to 32% in Latin America during the 1950s. The corresponding shift in North America was from 43 to 46%.

Food production per head may have risen 12% between, say, 1936 and 1960 but this increase was concentrated almost exclusively within the temperate zones. Whether any overall per capita increase at all occurred after 1958 is doubtful; it is certain that the vast mass of humanity remained very hungry in 1963. British experience has suggested that 2,800 calories a day is a threshold of average national consumption below which general health and efficiency are impaired. Variations in climate and stature affect the threshold, of course, but it is, nevertheless, most significant that only 20% of mankind lived in territories above the 2,800 level and as many as 45% in ones below the 2,000 line. Tables of protein consumption suggested an even greater mean deficiency and a graver geographical imbalance.

Mining and manufacturing output rose faster than that of basic food-stuffs—30% being the approximate global increase between 1958 and 1962. For non-Communist Europe the figure was 25% and for the USA 20%. Russia and Japan registered 45% and 120% respectively. The growth in overall energy consumption is linked closely with this forward move-ment. Estimates of energy rise are of their nature somewhat arbitrary, but the best available suggest strongly that the volume grew by well over one half in the decade after the Korean War. It was, in addition, employed more efficiently. The amount of coal typically needed to generate one kilowatt hour of electricity fell by almost one quarter in, for example, the United States after 1950. Yet oil was often replacing coal as a prime source of electric power as well as in spheres such as transport and domestic heating. Oil's contribution to the recorded energy consumption of Western Europe rose in the course of the fifties from 13 to 30%. In Latin America the proportion provided by oil and natural gas came to exceed 90%. Proven world reserves of oil had multiplied tenfold since 1938 but were still, when consumption trends were considered, equivalent to less than twenty-five years supply.

Britain, who lacked adequate indigenous reserves of cheap fuel, brought the world's first large breeder-cum-power nuclear reactor—Calder Hall—into full commission in 1958, but it was not until 1962 that technicians were able to say with any assurance that the break-even point between nuclear and conventional power was within a few years of realization. Reports occasionally appeared from the three thermonuclear states which seemed to suggest that controlled fusion—which would, of course, solve the energy problem forever—was becoming a real prospect. Such reports proved to be much too sanguine.

The rise in the output of those industrial nations that still operated, albeit in modified forms, free market economies was, by past standards, remarkably smooth. Historical precedent could have led one to expect a slump to develop soon after the war but this did not happen. Western Europe experienced only two general recessions—1951–2 and 1957–8; neither was severe. The average rate of unemployment in the USA was 4·8% after 1945—as compared with 18·3% in the 1930s—and all but two of the years in question—1958 and 1961—had yearly averages below 6%. 1949 and 1954 also contained low turning points in output but the cycles that produced them were of but moderate amplitude. Annual unemployment percentages in Britain were almost entirely confined to the 1·2 to 2·6 range. The exception was 1947 when the figure kicked up to 3·1 largely as a result of the severest winter for a century.

Some of the explanation lies in the fact that managerial psychology, particularly outside the United States, was becoming less morbid. This in its turn can be partly explained in terms of shifts in the balance of industry. Big businessmen evaluating capital projects that might take years to complete, and that are likely to be financed out of ploughed back profits or from fixed interest loans, tend to be comparatively insensitive to the vagaries of a stock market. They often also have a strong sense of public responsibility as well as of marginal profit.

Yet more decisive, however, was the acceptance by governments and legislatures of the proposition that it was their duty to ensure the maintenance of full employment, even when this appeared to be a threat to stable prices. Thus Congress passed an Employment Act in 1946 designed to 'promote maximum employment, production and purchasing power'. This established a Council of Economic Advisers responsible to the American President and also a Joint Congressional Committee to study the Presidential Economic Reports. Swift action to smooth out trade cycles has thereby been made easier.

As high employment came to be taken for granted, interest began to focus more on improvements in productivity. France was a pioneer in this respect with her close central co-ordination of all investment, a policy facilitated by the existence of a large nationalized sector and by a free use of public capital within the private one. The Monnet Plan of the 1940s emphasized basic industry. A second one, which operated from 1952 to 1957, concentrated more on manufactures, housing, and agriculture. These two programmes ensured that France had one of the fastest rates of expansion in the Atlantic area during the middle fifties. This, one may note, was despite the extremely heavy burdens imposed by the Indo-Chinese and Algerian Wars.

Full employment was not, of course, the only aim that governments sought to fulfil in the sphere of economic activity. More importance was attached than previously to the progressive redistribution of income and capital and to the maintenance of basic standards of welfare and security; and, of course, defence expenditure soon became an important factor again in many cases. Thus the proportion of the American gross national product spent by the federal government became 15% in 1960 as against 11·5% in 1940. Central government taxation absorbed 16% of the Spanish national product in 1960, 29% of the British and 34% of the Federal German.

Trade between nations outside the Communist camp was encouraged by an early and general reversion to something of a free trade philosophy. Twenty-three countries signed a General Agreement on Tariffs and Trade in 1947 and approximately as many again have acceded to it since. Various kinds of obstacles have been removed through the operation of GATT but its main achievement has been the lowering, as a result of a succession of tariff conferences, of the duties on about half of the world's imports. The average tariff on goods entering the United States was 18% in 1934; in 1959 it was 7%.

Reserves of those forms of currency that were normally used to finance international trade—i.e. gold, dollars and sterling—tended to expand more slowly than did the value of that trade. This, plus the internal inflationary pressure that full employment seemed often to generate, meant that many trading nations frequently ran into balance of payments difficulties which could usually only be resolved by restricting imports either by physical controls or by internal deflation. But this did not prevent a vigorous expansion in the volume of international trade, an expansion that was, indeed, larger proportionately than that of production or of population. Trade increases were greatest in the field of manufactured goods, however, and greatest between the manufacturing countries themselves. The way in which intracontinental commerce grew more quickly than intercontinental reflected these trends. Falls in the relative prices of many primary products characterized the middle years of the period in question.

So the primary producers remained highly vulnerable to fluctuations in world price levels and, because of the inelastic nature of the supply patterns, the downward fluctuations could be severe even when import demand slackened only a little. The profoundly hostile reception Richard Nixon encountered in Latin America in May 1958 was largely due to the marked effect a comparatively mild American recession was having on Latin American export prospects. International commodity agreements were drawn up at various times to cover coffee, sugar, tea, tin and wheat. Their value was limited.

The weak trading position of the primary producers of Afro-Asia and Latin America made the governments of the 'metropolitan' countries more aware of an obligation to help finance their development plans by means either of grants or of loans made, as a rule, on easy terms. This meant for them higher taxation, perhaps the export of skilled manpower, and perhaps also foreign currency losses. Another inhibiting factor was the limited ability of many recipients to absorb aid effectively. Nevertheless the monetary value of official aid to the developing countries[1] doubled in the five years after 1956. The total for 1962 is estimated to have been $6,500,000,000[2] and this was then being supplemented by a private capital inflow of $2,500,000,000. Just over one half of the former figure, which includes funds channelled through international institutions, came from the United States; France contributed 15% and Britain and Germany some 6% each. About 5% came from the Communist states. If the gift of surplus food and the provision of military assistance is included in the scale, the American programme appears to increase by about a half.

Twenty per cent of the foreign exchange received by the developing countries in 1962 took the form of aid or private investment. Ghana and Senegal were implementing five-year plans that were drawing about a quarter of their capital from these sources; Tanganyika was implementing a three-year one that was 80% dependent upon them for its capital supply. How important all such plans were may be gauged from the fact that, in 1960, the less developed parts of the world contained 71% of its population but consumed a mere 21% of its income. And this was an imbalance that appeared to be getting worse.

---

[1] Using the OECD definition which excludes North Korea, Mongolia, China and North Vietnam.

[2] $1·0 US = seven shillings and twopence (£0·36) in British currency after 1949 and four and elevenpence (£0·24) until then.

# SECTION ONE    FROM HIROSHIMA TO PANMUNJOM

*Chapter III*
# RUSSIA UNDER STALIN

STALIN was possessed of a jealousy that may ultimately have reached the pitch of clinical madness. He resented independent and original minds. He even resented—suggests Milovan Djilas—any subordinate who was taller than his diminutive self. Envy isolated him from his more able colleagues and this isolation encouraged, in its turn, a withdrawal from the world at large. He rarely appeared in public and when he did so he was always surrounded by a heavy bodyguard. Absence of the flesh aided the cultivation of the myth of an ever-youthful shepherd, benignly guiding a willing flock.

Could the Soviet regime have survived the war and its aftermath without the cult of personality or without, at any rate, some legends to rally the loyalists and confuse the dissenters? Subsequent Soviet statistics have implied that twenty million people died of injury or privation during, or immediately after, the Great Patriotic War. In the summer of 1945 one person in every eight was homeless. Stalin's policies were the product not only of his own idiosyncrasies but also of an exceptionally brutal and chaotic national environment.

Some months after the fourth Five-Year Plan was launched in the spring of 1946, Zhdanov emerged from a spell of comparative obscurity[1] to lead a great drive for ideological purity and revolutionary enthusiasm. With his return to prominence seems to have gone a waning of the influence of Malenkov[2]—a man to whom ideological discussion meant almost nothing. To talk of two competing factions within the Communist Party of the Soviet Union would be unreal. The policy differences between Zhdanov and Malenkov did not lend themselves to clear definition, and, besides, both men depended too heavily on Stalin's approval to act the part of a group leader. It is noticeable, however, that Kaganovich[3] and the economist Voznesensky rose and fell with Zhdanov and that Kruschev[4] seemed then to be hitched to the Malenkov star. Thus, Voznesensky was brought into the Politburo Commission for Foreign Affairs in October 1946, the time when Stalin, seeking to reduce the authority of the full

[1] e.g. work on the Allied Control Commission in Finland.
[2] Then a Deputy Chairman of the Council of Ministers.
[3] Then a Deputy Chairman of the Council of Ministers.
[4] See p. 627.

Politburo, extended that Commission's responsibilities to the domestic sphere. The other members of the Septet, as the Commission then came to be known, probably included Molotov, Zhdanov, Beria, Bulganin and Mikoyan.

Zhdanov began his new work with a demand for greater orthodoxy from the intellectuals of Leningrad, where he had served as Communist First Secretary until 1944. Soon he spread his net wider. Alexandrov's *History of Western Philosophy* was condemned for its objectivity. The Society for the Dissemination of Political and Scientific Knowledge was persuaded to adopt a charter that committed it 'to inculcate national pride, to combat obsequiousness to foreign culture . . . and to unmask warmongers, imperialists, and the falsity of bourgeois democracy'. After Eugene Varga had asserted that economic advances were possible under capitalism the institute that he had directed was placed under Voznesensky's State Planning Commission.

The most famous beneficiary from the Zhdanov decrees was, of course, the biologist Lysenko. He propounded a view of evolution that, if correct, would have meant that it was faster and more controllable than had generally been assumed. Classic doctrine said that there will always be random variations in inherited characteristics between the individual members of any one species found in any given environment, and that, as generation succeeds generation, those characteristics that best match the environment will come to predominate. No, said Lysenko, an environment can induce within any one individual during its lifetime conspicuous changes that can be transmitted to that individual's descendants. Since Western scientists have never observed the pattern of inheritance that Lysenko described and since the reports on his case studies suggested that he has confused environmental change with grafting, the great majority of Western scientists have dismissed him as a charlatan.

Why was he backed by Stalin and Zhdanov? To advertise the solid achievements of the Tsarist scientist Michurin, improperly claimed by Lysenko as his John the Baptist? To humiliate Soviet intellectuals? To discredit the Nazi distortion of classical genetics in the interest of racialism? Whatever the mix of reasons, the Lysenko controversy that had begun in 1939 was revived with a vengeance in 1947. In the August of the following year Lysenko, with the overt support of the Communist Central Committee, hectored the Academy of Agricultural Sciences. Soon afterwards many Soviet biologists lost important posts, among them A. A. Zhebrak. Four years earlier Zhebrak had written a mild article in an American journal in which, like Kruschev later on, he had given Lysenko the practical agriculturist the benefit of the doubt, but had drawn attention to the naïvety of Lysenko the theorist. Other Central Committee initiatives around this time included the condemnation of Shostakovich and Prokofiev for the 'formalism' of their music. Meanwhile, physicists were told to study Einstein's concrete results but to ignore the bourgeois idealist philosophy that was said to permeate their presentation.

Estimated industrial production overtook the pre-war level during 1948 but agriculture fared less well. 1946 witnessed a terrible drought and also the illicit seizure for private exploitation of millions of acres of collective farmland, not merely in the 'liberated areas' but in districts like the Lower Volga as well. Guerrilla activity persisted in the new provinces of the Western Ukraine for some years after the war. Bitter armed clashes were precipitated by the Lithuanian collectivization law of 1948. Moscow launched a sustained ideological offensive against Catholicism among the Balts and the nationalism of the Ukraine, which it rightly regarded as contributing to Communist unpopularity. One or two million Balts and Ukrainians were deported to join the several million Soviet citizens and prisoners of war already in labour camps. Kruschev was temporarily displaced as First Secretary of the Ukrainian Communist Party in March 1947.

This phase of the Stalin era was not one of great innovation in civilian technology but on the military side things were different. Official figures state that, between 1944 and 1948, the armed forces were slashed from 11,000,000 men to fewer than 3,000,000, but, in the meanwhile, vast sums of money and much talent was ploughed into weapons research and development. Over 80% of the Nazi aircraft factories had fallen into Russian hands in 1945 and so had 200 Peenemunde rocket specialists. The MIG–15 jet fighter that first flew in 1947 was in most aerodynamic respects superior to its American contemporary, the F–86. The first Soviet atomic explosion came in 1949; and much of the credit for it must go to Communist spies. Agents are known to have gleaned important nuclear information from both the United States and Britain. In Canada, also, a big spy ring had been uncovered.

To what extent was Soviet foreign policy conditioned by the temporary Western atomic monopoly? Stalin's indifference at Potsdam to the news of the Los Alamos test proves nothing, for his agents had forewarned him. In 1946 he said that the atomic bomb was only a terror weapon and Mao said that it was but a paper tiger. But in that same year Molotov cautioned the Yugoslavs after they had intercepted and shot down two planes belonging to the sole nuclear nation. Eighteen months later Stalin discussed the atom bomb with Yugoslav leaders in highly enthusiastic terms. Did the Russians seek to dominate Eastern Europe principally in order to place Western Europe at their strategic mercy so as to ensure themselves against nuclear blackmail? Were they deeply interested in the exploitation of the uranium deposits of Saxony, Bohemia, and Rumania, deposits perhaps more workable than those of the Soviet interior? Perhaps, but it should be remembered that Stalin himself was something of a military traditionalist. He solemnly justified lavish investment in the Volga-Don canal on the grounds that it would enable the Black Sea Fleet to fall back to cover Stalingrad in the event of renewed hostilities.

Zhdanov is often regarded as the architect of a forward foreign policy, but this may well be erroneous. As he acquired more power, Russia discontinued her rather cavalier expansionist activities in the Middle East. She had already pulled her army out of Manchuria, having left Chiang Kai-shek's armies enough time to replace it and herself enough unilaterally to collect, according to the United States Economic Commission, some $850,000,000 worth of reparations. Soviet troops closed the frontier between Bulgaria and Greece in July 1946, apparently as a gesture of support for the Greek Communist rebels. At the same time, however, Stalin was letting the rebels know that he regarded their recourse to violence as premature. The Berlin election results of that autumn seem to have led to a basic reconsideration of the whole forward policy in Germany. Earlier that year both Stalin and the Socialist Unity Party had been optimistic about the prospects of taking over the whole of Germany, which they apparently regarded as a classic case of monopoly capitalism in decay, but thenceforward this optimism visibly waned. Molotov was still pressing for a strong all-German central government at the Foreign Ministers conferences of 1947, but his demands were imprecise, and were mainly directed, one suspects, against Western plans for the reform of their zones. Early in 1948 Stalin observed in private that a Sovietized East Germany and a Westernized West Germany would inevitably come about. All that remained in some dispute was West Berlin.

What then of the Communist Information Bureau? This idea was discussed with certain East Europeans early in 1946, that is before Zhdanov's days of power. However, Zhdanov was easily the most active Soviet participant in its inaugural meeting of September 1947. The Cominform was intended to facilitate a full exchange of facts and opinions between the parties of the USSR, Eastern Europe, France and Italy, and for their concerted action as required. At the first meeting in Warsaw a fiery declaration was approved that spoke of the division of the world into two camps. But perhaps this should be regarded as reflecting a combination of a tactical offensive and a strategic consolidation. Perhaps it should be related to the Communist withdrawal from coalition governments in Belgium, France and Italy in the course of that year and to the July crisis over the Marshall Plan conference. On July 9th, after some days of silence, Poland declined an invitation to attend; this decision had been predicted by Moscow Radio the previous day. Peaceful penetration of Western Europe through nominal co-operation was discarded. A new emphasis on Eastern Europe was soon reflected in numerous bilateral pacts, between the countries concerned, stronger economic ties with the USSR, and moves to resolve the Czech-Hungarian minorities dispute. The option of mass industrial action in Western Europe was retained, but this was now seen as an instrument of obstruction rather than conquest.

Just after Christmas 1947 Kruschev regained his party post in the Ukraine and a month later *Pravda* did a conspicuous *volte-face* over the Tito-Dimitrov proposals for a South Slav federation. These events are linked, for the deepening Moscow-Belgrade split led to, or was caused by, Stalin's rejection of Zhdanov. He was given a leading part in the Cominform meeting of June 1948, but this was probably in order that he would be obliged to denounce the Yugoslavs, lately his warm friends. He died, perhaps as a result of his heart disease, in August. His memory was thenceforward revered but, once the Lysenko affair was concluded, his cultural policies were applied with less vigour. Voznesensky was dismissed in March 1949, and killed soon afterwards; he had added the sin of implicit criticism of the national allocation of resources to that of identification with Zhdanov. Hundreds of people were dismissed from official and party positions in Zhdanov's old base of Leningrad in the course of 1949. Some were killed.

By 1953 overall Soviet industrial production was, according to the official records, two and a half times the pre-war level whilst electricity generation, for example, had quadrupled. But agriculture was said to have only just exceeded its 1940 output and even this claim, Kruschev later admitted, was excessive. One interesting fact is that by 1953 both Stalin and Kruschev had become identified with solutions to the agrarian question that strongly reflected a simple Marxist-Leninist faith in the economies of clean sweeps and large scales. Stalin's name was closely linked with the planting, from 1948, of belts of trees hundreds of miles long in order to speed up the water cycle and check soil erosion—objectives which they could not have realized to any but the smallest degree. Kruschev, who in 1950 seems to have assumed certain All Union agricultural responsibilities, advocated the grouping of the peasantry into large and well appointed new villages—'agro-towns', as some called them. His scheme experienced a cool official reception, however, and was condemned by Malenkov at the 19th Party Congress. But piecemeal amalgamation of the smaller collective farms continued to be encouraged.

The armed forces began to expand in 1950 and by the peak year of 1955 numbered over 5,000,000 men. Meanwhile, extensive modernization was carried out; in 1950 about half the army was horse drawn, in 1955 none of it was. Perhaps 5,000 Soviet military advisers and technicians served in rear areas during the Korean War.

One of the last traces of a forward policy in Europe can be seen in the 1948 attempt to subvert Finland by diplomatic pressure and by the illicit shipment of small arms to the local Communist Party, one of whose members was the Minister in charge of the secret police. Severe Communist setbacks in the General Election of July 1948 demonstrated, and the subsequent disbandment of the secret police confirmed, the failure of this attempt.

But from 1948 the effort to shatter West European morale, in order to impede the development of the Marshall Plan and the arrangements for collective defence, was stepped up. The instructions to intensify the class and anti-colonial struggles that were given to the Communist Party of France in the spring of 1952 were an example of it. So, in part, was the Peace Offensive. A conference of intellectuals from forty-six countries was held in Wroclaw (formerly Breslau) in Poland in August 1948. One

Frenchman noted that some delegates 'tried to divert the Congress along channels of colourless cosmopolitanism, with the aid of which certain groups servilely camouflaged American imperialism's fantastic plans for world domination'. But all such attempts failed and the conference resolved to fight the 'fascist revival' and to establish in Paris an International Liaison Committee of Intellectuals for Peace. By 1950 this had become known as the World Peace Council. In that year it launched the Stockholm Appeal against all use of atomic weapons in war, and the following one it heavily supported the Soviet call for a Five Power Peace Pact—a pact, that is to say, that would have Communist China as a participant. Both proposals were endorsed, it was said, by over 500,000,000 petitioners, mostly from within the Communist bloc.

No direct connection has yet been established between the Calcutta Youth Conference of early 1948 and the spate of revolutions that hit Asia later that year. But the Sino-Soviet interest in promoting unrest within that region was made clearly manifest during the Peking congress of the World Federation of Trade Unions held late in 1949. Among the committee activities of that congress were studies of guerrilla war, arms smuggling and the dislocation of shipping in the Pacific. Resentment at the way in which the WFTU, which had been formed in 1945, had become involved in Cold War polemics led to the establishment of the International Confederation of Free Trade Unions. The British Trade Union Congress was among the many labour movements that transferred to it.

The figure who became most closely identified, in Russia and elsewhere, with Stalin's internal policies was Laurentia Beria. He had been appointed a Deputy Prime Minister with special responsibility for internal security in 1941 and he remained in that post until after Stalin's death. From this it does not follow that he enjoyed Stalin's perpetual and unqualified confidence. He seems to have been in disfavour in 1946 and 1947 and there is little doubt that it was his supporters in his native Georgia who were the intended targets of the purge that began in that Soviet republic in November 1951. This was the month of the arrest of Slansky, his chief colleague in Czechoslovakia.

1952 saw the long awaited 19th Congress of the Soviet Communist Party. Though the guiding text was Stalin's 'Economic Problems of Socialism' which predicted, among other things, that wars would occur between the capitalist states, rather than between them and the Soviet bloc, most of the official *rapporteurs* laid stress on the menace of capitalist encirclement. This was linked with the threat of subversion and this in its turn was linked, both at the Congress and in a vast press and radio campaign, with embezzlement by 'Jews' and others. On January 13th, 1953, *Tass* announced the arrest of several medical practitioners on charges of working as assassins for an American-Jewish intelligence net or for British espionage. They were blamed for the death of Zhdanov and accused of the attempted murder of several senior and well trusted army officers. Their arrest may have heralded a purge of Stalin's immediate political subordinates.

Stalin died quite suddenly on March 5th. Like Zhdanov and Dimitrov, he did so soon after he had alienated some prominent personalities.

# Chapter IV
# EASTERN EUROPE

## (i) *Russia Makes New Allies*

By January 1946 the Polish provisional government was bitterly and openly split. The dominant faction was composed chiefly of the Communist Party, which described itself as the Polish Workers' Party or the PPR and the Polish Socialist Party (the PPS). Against it stood the liberal radical Polish People's Party (the PSL), led by Mikolajczyk. Already the campaign of terror against the PSL had begun. Two of its leaders had been assassinated—one of them by uniformed members of the Communist controlled security police. The party as a whole was continually represented as being just a front for the guerrilla resistance, which, on the admission of the authorities themselves, was to claim the lives of over 1,000 members of the security forces in the course of that year. Terrorism by thugs and police officers effectively disrupted a farm co-operative movement with which the PSL was associated. The PSL was, in fact, alternatively known as the Peasant Party.

The general election of the following winter was, in many respects, a flagrant violation of the Yalta agreements; Mikolajczyk demanded the right to appoint 5,000 Peasant Party scrutineers—in fact, he was allowed 300. Many of his candidates were disqualified and well over 100 were imprisoned. PSL spokesmen said that a total of 10,000 of their members had been arrested; the government conceded that this was so. Open collective ballots were held in many places. The National Front, which included the PPR and the PPS, won almost 90% of the seats on a 90% poll.

After these results were announced the Peasant Party went into official opposition. Cyrankiewicz, the very Left-Wing General Secretary of the PPS, became Prime Minister whilst the Communist Gomulka became a Vice-Premier in place of Mikolajczyk. May Day was made the occasion to issue a joint Socialist-Communist Manifesto. That autumn Mikolajczyk fled to the West and so was branded a traitor by the new parliamentary majority. At the end of 1948, after over 50,000 Socialists and some 25,000 Communists had been expelled in a series of preparatory party purges, a new Polish United Workers' Party was formed by the fusion of the PPR and the PPS. Several months earlier the demoralized rump of the Peasant Party had joined the National Front. All the party candidates in the 1952 elections were Front representatives; 99·8% of the recorded vote was in their favour.

Loyalty to the Soviet Union rapidly became the simple unifying theme behind Polish foreign policy. Gomulka resigned from the government in 1948 and was made to confess that he had not taken a strong enough line towards Tito. Three years later he was arrested for alleged association with foreign agents. In 1949 Marshal Rokossowski was made Minister of Defence. He was the Red Army commander of Polish birth who had failed to aid materially the Warsaw Rising of 1944.

Major domestic changes were also effected. All the voluntary youth organizations were brought under official control and at the beginning of 1948 a new compulsory State youth corps was formed. Later that year collective farming was introduced and an offensive against rich peasants begun. This took the form of overt discrimination in respect of taxation and credit allowances.

But peasant hostility made the government take collectivization very slowly. Only 1% of the 1949 harvest came from collectives, and three years later the proportion was only about 10%. Part of this hostility arose out of dislike of the official attitude towards Roman Catholicism. The authorities sought to remedy this by depicting the Pope as a Germanophil. They did this by placing a tendentious interpretation on his refusal to establish bishoprics in the new Western Territories until the Oder-Neisse line had been internationally recognized. In 1951 the government abolished the papal administration in the Western Territories and in February 1953 it announced that all clerical appointments throughout Poland were to be subject to its approval.

These revolutionary initiatives were facilitated by sustained police terror. Trials were staged at Cracow in January 1953 in the hope of implicating the Catholic hierarchy in espionage. Guerrilla activity had faded out but sundry 'enemies of the people' were still being hunted down. A professor, who defected from the United Nations delegation that autumn, put the number of forced labour camp inmates at 300,000.

The once powerful Agrarian Party of Czechoslovakia had been banned because of its collaborationist record. Otherwise the elections that were held there in May 1946 appear to have been both free and secret. Over a third of the seats were won by the Communists and about a fifth by their chief opponents, the Social Nationalists; the remainder split almost equally between the Czech Social Democrats, the Slovak Democrats, and the Czech People's (Catholic) Party. A Communist, Klement Gottwald, became Prime Minister; the Ministries of Information and of the Interior were retained by Communists.

Communist support in Slovakia was comparatively weak and equivocal, presumably because Slovak society was relatively Catholic and agrarian.

Soon after the elections were over the Communists began to accuse the Slovak Democrats of harbouring Fascists. It was not, however, until 1947 that the Communist political offensive really got under way in Slovakia and elsewhere. In April of that year Josef Tiso, the ex-quisling President of Slovakia, was executed despite Democrat and People's Party appeals for clemency. Early in July the Czech government reversed a decision to attend the first Marshall Plan conference immediately after Stalin had told a strong official delegation that he would regard participation as severing the Soviet-Czech pact of friendship and mutual aid. That autumn the Minister of Information said that the anti-Communism within the universities was tantamount to treason and that dissident undergraduates should be excluded. Meanwhile, large scale round-ups of 'subversives' began in Czechoslovakia.

On February 17th, 1948—a date very close to the centenary of the *Communist Manifesto*—the Communists called for political change through extra-parliamentary mass action. Three days later the Social Nationalist, Democrat and People's Ministers resigned in protest against the inaction of the Communist-packed police in regard to the dispatch of parcels containing bombs to three ministers, including the distinguished Foreign Secretary, Jan Masaryk. Their hope was that Eduard Beneš, the gallant and distinguished President, would not permit the Communist caucus to reform the government without fresh elections.[1] But sickness had rendered Beneš acutely apprehensive of national disunity and of the absence of Soviet military support in the event of a German military revival. On February 25th he agreed to the immediate formation of a new Communist controlled administration. On the 29th, Mr Zorin, a Soviet Deputy Commissar for Foreign Affairs, ended a ten-day visit to Prague.

The death in March, apparently by suicide, of Jan Masaryk symbolized the Communist triumph. Single list elections in May confirmed it. Industrial nationalization was then greatly extended; during the next four years a third of the arable land was brought within the 'socialist sector'. Successive purges were conducted within the youth organizations, the universities, the army, the administration and even the Communist Party. They culminated in 1952 in the trials of thirteen former leading officials of the government and the Communist Party. Among them were Rudolf Slansky, who had been Secretary-General of the Party, and the former Foreign Minister Vladimir Clementis. All but three of the accused were executed. All but two of them were Jews.

Negotiations between the Roman Catholic Church and the State about matters such as land confiscation and the financial support of church schools broke down in 1949. Thereupon, the government formed its own Catholic Action Committee in an attempt to by-pass the bishops. After Archbishop Beran had forbidden priests to do business with it on pain of excommunication he was placed under house arrest. In 1951 he was deported.

[1] Beneš had been an active member of the Social Nationalist party before the war.

Much the same plot unfolded in Hungary. If there was any important respect in which the experience of this Magyar nation differed from that of its Slav neighbours, it was that it was subject to more blatant Red Army intervention on behalf of the Moscow-trained Communist clique. Their victory was facilitated here, as elsewhere, by the appointment of one of their number to be Minister of the Interior. It was assured when the Small Farmers' Party was subverted in 1947. In February of that year a leading anti-Communist Small Farmer politician named Béla Kovács was arrested by the Red Army on an espionage charge. He was never seen again but soon the authorities had claimed that he had implicated the Small Farmer Premier Ferenc Nagy. When his 'revelations' were published Nagy was on holiday in Switzerland. He resigned and went into exile in the United States.

Confirmation of the Muscovite triumph came with the single list elections of 1949 and with the two major trials of that year. The first was that of Cardinal Mindszenty, a deeply conservative prelate who had been arrested after refusing to allow priests to continue work in the newly nationalized church schools. Mindszenty confessed to plots against the state after the prosecution had presented a case that consisted of little more than trivial gossip; his sentence was life imprisonment. Next Rajk, a Communist and former Minister, was charged with such crimes as plotting with Marshal Tito and working for the American Secret Service. He duly confessed and was executed. Rajk's real mistake had been to spend the war in the Hungarian anti-Fascist resistance and not in the seminaries of Moscow.

1946 seemed to start well as far as Rumanian democracy was concerned. After representations had been made by the Potsdam powers, the ruling National Democratic Front was broadened by the inclusion of one Independent Liberal and one National Peasant representative. Britain and the United States decided to recognize the reconstructed provisional government on receipt of assurances that free and secret elections would be held not later than May.

But all the illusions of the moderates in Rumania and their well-wishers abroad were soon to be shattered. The two new ministers were without portfolios and had no influence. Their respective parties became subject to systematic hooliganism which, aided by extensive ballot rigging, made a mockery of the elections eventually held in November. All that the 90% poll and the 85% pro-Government vote showed was the effectiveness of intimidation. Encouraged by this display of its own strength the government bloc began to crush all opposition. The highlight of its effort in this direction was the trial of Maniu, the National Peasant leader, which began in October 1947. He was arbitrarily adjudged responsible for some contacts which some of his followers had apparently had with American agents and so was sentenced to solitary confinement for life. In fresh elections held the following March such remnants of parliamentary opposition as still survived were almost entirely obliterated. Shortly afterwards a Soviet-pattern constitution was introduced and most industrial concerns were nationalized. Agricultural collectivization began in 1949.

In Rumania, as elsewhere, the early years of Communist rule were ones of considerable terror. The death penalty was imposed for quite minor economic misdemeanours. The Communist Party itself was heavily purged, about a fifth of its million members being expelled before the middle of 1950. Here, as elsewhere, Stalin's anti-Semitic sentiments were pandered to. A ban on emigration to Israel in 1949 marked the beginning of a campaign against 'Zionism'. The arrest in 1952 of Mrs Ana Pauker, the Moscow-trained Communist who was then a Vice-Premier, can be regarded as part of this persecution.

Members of the Communist-dominated Fatherland Front secured nearly 80% of the votes and seats in the Bulgarian elections of October 1946. These elections had been timed to follow a September plebiscite on the monarchy in which the republican policies of the Fatherland Front were endorsed by 95% of the voters in a 91% turn-out. Both polls had, of course, been conducted in an atmosphere of high tension. Thus, by the autumn the Communist Minister of the Interior had arrested nearly half of the members of the Supreme Council of the Agrarian Union, a party that commanded considerable support in rural areas.

Resolutions passed by the Fatherland Front in January 1947 opposed the continuation of independent political parties. Accordingly, Nikola Petkov, leader of the anti-Communist majority group within the Agrarian Union, was arrested on a flimsy treason charge. A bench of Communist judges condemned him to death in August and ten days later the Agrarian Union formally dissolved itself. Vigorous Anglo-American protests against 'judicial murder' did not prevent Petkov being executed in September, after another bench of Communist judges had rejected his appeal. Early in 1948 a Social Democrat rump elected to fuse with the Communist Party. Their decision followed hard upon a public warning from Georgi Dimitrov the Communist Premier, that dissident Socialists might experience the same fate as Petkov.

In Bulgaria, as in Rumania, the Orthodox Church fell quickly into line with the new political establishment. So once parliamentary opposition had gone the only serious obstacle to Muscovite supremacy came from within the Communist movement itself. But, as in Rumania, over a fifth of the party members had been expelled by July 1950. Among them was Traicho Kostov who had, in fact, been executed for 'Titoism'—i.e. for some display of independent-mindedness. Meanwhile, Dimitrov fell from Stalin's favour because of his love of country. Back in 1946 he had openly evinced his annoyance at Stalin's refusal to support formally Bulgaria's territorial claims on Greece. Then early in 1948 he made a speech that looked towards an East European federation as a long term objective. For this he was berated by *Pravda*. Next came a brutal dressing down by Stalin in the Kremlin for his encouragement of further Communist resistance in

Greece and for his attempted promotion of a bilateral customs union with Bucharest. On the matter of the customs union his luck was badly out; he had submitted his draft proposals to Moscow but Molotov had omitted to refer them to Stalin. Dimitrov went on sick leave to Moscow in April 1949 and died there in July. His embalmed body was accorded a ritualistic funeral.

Through its wartime resistance campaign Enver Hoxha's Democratic Front had secured an unshakable grip on Albania. The elections of December 1945 served to demonstrate this. No opposition candidates were allowed and almost 90% of all the electors voted for the Front. Albania soon became one of the most militantly anti-Western of the East European states.

## (ii) *Russia Loses a Friend*

Marshal Tito once said that all the new Communist countries except Yugoslavia and Albania had been liberated by party cliques who flew in after the fighting was over, smoking their pipes. In this remark he gave the explanation for the great inner strength of his Communist Party. National enthusiasm had been fired by the epic wartime resistance, and during that resistance a remarkable network of spies and informers had been established which could now be used to ensure that the enthusiasm did not falter. A savage official terror was not needed to obtain the overwhelming vote in favour of the People's Front registered at the general election of November 1945.

One can assume much genuine popular approval for the execution for treason in 1946 of Mihailović, wartime head of the Right Wing Četnik forces. Likewise for the harsh prison sentence passed on the Roman Catholic Archbishop of Zagreb, Aloysius Stepniac; he had had his wartime contacts with the Fascist authorities officially represented as active collaboration after he had opposed Front decisions to confiscate large Church land plots and to end religious education. Any such assumption may, however, be invalid in respect of the heavy prison sentences meted out to various radical but non-Communist peasant leaders in 1957.

From its popular roots the Yugoslav Communist Party drew a purity of thought and militancy of spirit unique in the Communist world. In 1947 a Five-Year Plan was launched that was even more ambitious than the first Soviet one had been. Tito hoped, among other things, that it would provide the economic foundation for the formation of a Balkan federation under his leadership. One step towards this federation, as it was envisaged by Tito and his friend Dimitrov, was the carving of a united Macedonia out of Yugoslavia, Bulgaria and Greece; it seems that the quarrel that Markos Vafiades, the leader of the Communist rebellion in Greece, had with Tito in 1949[1] arose in part out of a Yugoslav tendency to favour the Macedonian element among the Greek rebels.

The basic hostility of the Yugoslavs towards the West was well revealed in the constituent meeting of the Cominform when they sharply criticized their French and Italian colleagues for their lack of ruthlessness. This hostility had been considerably strengthened by the Trieste dispute. The Partisans had laid claim to the whole Istrian peninsula in 1943, contending that it could serve as a reparation, was a necessary commercial outlet, and was, in any case, largely Slav. But the Soviet Union agreed to a Western proposal that, under the Italian peace treaty, part of this area should be temporarily designated a free territory under the Security Council. Zone A of this territory, which included Trieste itself, would continue to be garrisoned by Anglo-American troops and Zone B by Yugoslav. On March 20th, 1948, a few weeks before a critical Italian election, the Western powers submitted that the Free Territory should go entirely to Italy. No surprise was occasioned by the united Soviet and Yugoslav opposition to this suggestion. What would have surprised the outside world would have been the degree of disunity that had recently developed on more general questions between Moscow and Belgrade.

Two days previously all Soviet experts had been withdrawn from Yugoslavia on receipt of a Belgrade demand that they conform to local pay scales. This demand had been made as an act of defiance following Russian prevarication over the signature of the next annual trade pact. Moscow had hoped by such economic pressure to induce the Yugoslavs to stop their aid to Greece and to federate with, and only with, their poverty-stricken neighbours, Bulgaria and Albania. After the withdrawal of the experts, a series of letters were exchanged between Moscow and Belgrade but their style and substance were such that they served only to broaden and deepen the disagreement. In May Tito arrested two Ministers whose criticism of his ambitious economic schemes had previously met with Soviet approval. In June Yugoslavia was expelled from the Cominform. By December even Dimitrov had branded Tito a traitor.

As though in order to demonstrate that he sought to bully rather than reason, Stalin levelled utterly contradictory criticisms at Yugoslavia. He accused her of Trotskyite militarism and of appeasement to the West; he said she collectivized her farms over hastily and pandered to the rich peasants. Yugoslav remonstrances against Russia, on the other hand, were factual and concise. A major one was that Soviet secret police were recruiting agents inside their country. Another was that the Red Army had failed to supply a balanced quota of good quality military equipment at reasonable prices and that its military mission had waxed too large. Yet another was that the USSR had not supplied her due share of capital to some bi-national industrial concerns that had been established in Yugoslavia and that she had manipulated their freight charges in favour of herself.

[1] See page 640.

By 1949 trade between Yugoslavia and the rest of the Communist world had fallen to a mere fraction of the previous yearly totals. Commercial contacts with the West were rapidly strengthened and half a billion dollars of Western aid was accepted in the course of the next several years, but the dislocation produced still caused inflation and balance of payments crises and forced the abandonment of the first Five-Year Plan. Diplomatic reorientation was similarly a painful process. Western votes enabled Yugoslavia to beat Czechoslovakia for a place on the Security Council in 1949, but in 1950 she opposed the sending of military assistance to South Korea. Later in that year, however, she denounced as aggressive the Chinese march across the 38th Parallel.

Meanwhile, Tito initiated a major departure from the Soviet model in the internal organization of society. A new fundamental law provided that the Managing Committee of each industrial enterprise should be drawn from a Works Council elected by the whole staff. This committee was to run the enterprise competitively with, in principle, no government control other than some over general investment plans. This innovation was considered by Belgrade closer to Marxist-Leninism than the 'state capitalism' of Russia.

## (iii) *Greece*

British support enabled Themistocles Sophoulis, a spry octogenarian with radical and republican sympathies, to become head of the Greek provisional government in November, 1945. His immediate task, the preparation for a general election, was complicated by the fact that in the course of the civil warfare of the previous winter the Gendarmerie, the Police and the Civil Service had been largely taken over by a zealous and unscrupulous Right Wing. Sophoulis hoped to offset this by the systematic appointment of liberals to key bureaucratic positions but he was dissuaded from doing so by traditionalist British advisers. The latter probably made another mistake when they insisted on elections being held as early as March 1946. Legalized bullying had become rampant in the rural districts and so had manipulation of the electoral roll. The Communist Party boycotted the elections on the grounds that the right environment had not been created.

Be all this as it may, 60% of those registered voted in a poll which, in the opinion of an Anglo-French-American observation team, was fairly conducted. The outcome was a convincing victory for the Right Wing Populist Party led by Tsaldaris and this was capped in September by a large plebiscite majority in favour of the return of King George. Faced with a slump in their popular support and with increasing political surveillance and constraint, the Communist Party repaired to the Northern Mountains and the Second Civil War began.

639

For some months 10,000 British troops and a good deal of sterling currency served to stiffen the Government effort, but, after Britain announced, late in February 1947, that she could little longer bear the economic strain involved, the United States assumed the chief burden of support. By 1949 she had 400 commissioned officers in Greece and her post-war aid bill, including contributions through the United Nations Relief and Rehabilitation Administration, had topped $800,000,000. The influence that this aid conferred on its donor was used without inhibition. Stern counsel was given on such matters as budget details and army Staff appointments. Above all, in August 1947 the recall of Sophoulis was arranged. All this meant, among other things, that civil liberties were not entirely eroded by the exigencies of war. Though the leading Communist newspapers were ordered to close in October 1947, both the government and its official advisers were still subject to much open press criticism.

Despite the deep American involvement, a near stalemate persisted for some time. Operating from sanctuaries in Albania, Yugoslavia and Bulgaria, 20,000 rebels kept at bay government forces ten times their number. But then, in 1949, disaster overtook them. Their leader Markos Vafiades was removed in February because of deteriorating health and, apparently, the discord over the Macedonia question. In July Tito forbade the rebels to operate from Yugoslav territory. Soon afterwards the rebel leaders announced the cessation of hostilities and Albania and Bulgaria 'interned' all insurgents on their territories.

*Chapter V*
# THE CREATION OF TWO GERMANIES

THE Potsdam Declaration of August 1945 seemed to lay adequate found-ations for the co-ordinated reconstruction of the four occupation zones into which Germany had been partitioned. All agreed that Stalin's advance of the Polish frontier to the Oder-Neisse Line was to be regarded as provisional. Reparation levels became a matter of individual zonal policy but a quarter of the capital assets dismantled in the West were to go to the USSR in exchange for certain bulk deliveries. No national political institu-tions were envisaged for the time being but there were to be central authori-ties to supervise such activities as finance and transport. They were each to be directly responsible to the Allied Control Council, which was composed of the four national army commanders. A common currency was established.

But behind this general statement lay big differences of attitude and of interest. Reparations policy was left flexible simply because the Russians had already taken extensive unilateral action in this regard. The French, resentful of their absence from Potsdam and keen to detach the Saar and perhaps the Ruhr from the rest of Germany, used the unanimity rule under which the Control Council operated to inhibit the creation of any central authorities except one for transport. No blueprints were ever prepared for the routine enforcement of Control Council authority. In its early days it played an important part in the return from Germany of over five million displaced persons and in the resettlement of the ten million Germans expelled from Eastern Europe. But soon it became little more than a forum of gamesmanship and dispute. When, in March 1946, it ruled that German industry should be kept permanently at half its pre-war level it merely illustrated how little it had remained a centre of effective power.

Zonal commanders were left free, under the Potsdam Declaration, to recreate local democracy as and how they saw fit. By Christmas 1945 some private newspapers were operating in the Western zones, many local councils had been elected and the Americans had appointed a German federal cabinet in Bavaria. During 1946 elections were held in the American zone at *Länder* (i.e. provincial) level. The Christian Social Union (CSU) was triumphant in Bavaria, the Christian Democrats (CDU) in Wurtem-berg-Baden, and the Social Democrats (SPD) in Greater Hesse. Com-munal elections in the relatively urbanized British zone gave roughly equal honours to the CDU and SPD. Meanwhile, the authorities pushed ahead with the purging of ex-Nazis from business, government, and education. Their achievement in this regard was substantial, although they succumbed to the natural temptation to treat with comparative leniency those with scarce and useful talents.

Because of their preoccupation with the Saar, the French revived democracy more slowly. For the same reason they did not participate in the economic fusion of zones conducted by Britain and America late in 1946. Instead they placed a customs barrier between the Saar and the rest of Germany.

Mr Byrnes—then US Secretary of State—announced the impending zonal fusion in his Stuttgart speech of September 6th, 1946. This reflects the fact that 'Bizonia' was partly intended to serve as an instrument of the Cold War that was developing in Central Europe. One of the mainsprings of this Cold War was Western unease about Soviet policy in the Eastern Zone and Berlin. Tens of thousands of German labourers, many of them highly skilled, were deported to the USSR. By 1948 the Russians had taken as reparations capital assets and produce worth, according to one informed Western source, some ten billion 1936 Reichsmarks.[1] Rather over half this wealth was retained within the country, in contravention of the Potsdam agreement, by the Soviet-owned enterprises called SAG. By 1947 these represented about a fifth of East Germany's industrial potential. In May 1946, in protest against these and other policies, the Americans halted the Eastward movement of reparations from their zone.

The SAG helped tie East Germany to the USSR. So did its economic and political reconstruction along lines that were essentially, though not avowedly, Marxist. By 1948 all the mines and over a third of the factories had been nationalized through the seizure of 'Fascist' assets. Confiscation of all landholdings in excess of 250 acres began in the autumn of 1945; within three years seven million acres had been redistributed to half a million people. Soon after land reform began the Socialist and Communist parties in the Soviet Zone were welded together to form a new Socialist Unity Party (the SED). From it came four of the Premiers of the five coalition governments formed after the *Länder* elections of 1946. A feature of these elections was that the SED fared best not in the traditionally radical industrial towns but in the remote rural areas where official interference was easier to contrive. In Saxony they got only 48% of the votes as against 69% in Mecklenburg.

In Berlin, as in the Eastern Zone, German Communist leaders back from Russian exile turned denazification to their own advantage. Anti-Fascist committees were formed to distribute food and to act as auxiliary police and within those committees Communist representation was strong. By the time the four power Kommandatura was established in Berlin the Soviet authorities had appointed a Magistrat—i.e. a city assembly—and had formed the auxiliaries into a People's Police. After its establishment they continued to try to treat Berlin as an integral part of the Soviet zone. Both

[1] Approximately four Reichsmarks could be exchanged for one US dollar in 1936.

GERMANY AND AUSTRIA IN 1945

0 20 40 60 80 100
MILES

NORTH SEA

BALTIC SEA

AMERICAN ZONE

NETHERLANDS

Hamburg

Bremen

BRITISH

ZONE

Hanover

G E R M A N Y

SOVIET

ZONE

Berlin

U.S.S.R.

BELGIUM

Cologne

Bonn

Dresden

LUX.

FRENCH

ZONE

AMERICAN

ZONE

Nuremberg

CZECHOSLOVAKIA

Prague

Pilsen

FRANCE

Strasbourg

FRENCH

ZONE

Stuttgart

Munich

AMERICAN

ZONE

SOVIET

ZONE

Vienna

Berne

SWITZERLAND

FRENCH ZONE  A U S T R I A

BRITISH ZONE

ITALY

YUGOSLAVIA

ADRIATIC

SEA

the SAGs and the land reform scheme were extended to it and the University of Berlin was required to accept students from all over East Germany.

This usurpation was gradually checked. Precise agreement was obtained early in 1946 on what access routes the West were to have to Berlin, and, at about the same time, the Red Army's right of entry into the Western sectors was sharply curtailed. The French publicly declared in March that their sector was quite separate from East Germany. But one check that was not effective was that introduced in October 1946 of having a four-power inspectorate to curtail intimidation by the People's Police. The police headquarters were in the Soviet sector which meant, under a pre-existing arrangement, that only the Red Army could dismiss any key police officials. The Western authorities extended more and more direct protection to non-Communist politicians but by March 1948 the number of people who had been kidnapped by the police had risen to 1,600.

A referendum held among SPD cardholders in West Berlin and West Germany in March 1946 decisively rejected the idea of fusion with the Communists. But despite this Marshal Zhukov, the Soviet member of the Control Council, vetoed the attempt of his colleagues in the Kommandatura to defer indefinitely the proposed autumn elections to the Magistrat.[1] The elections were, in the event, a disaster for the Russians—on a 92% poll half the votes went to the SPD and only a fifth to the SED.

1947 was very much a year of decision. On the world plane it was marked by the failure of two Foreign Ministers' Conferences and the Soviet rejection of the Marshall Plan; within Germany it was marked by a growing determination on the part of the non-Communist parties to resist Soviet encroachment even if it meant the division of the country. Foremost in this resistance movement was the eloquent idealist-cum-political crafts-man, Ernst Reuter—a Socialist whose election as Mayor of West Berlin was vetoed by the USSR in the Kommandatura in August. But the anxiety many Germans felt about the prospect of schism was clearly reflected in several of the resolutions passed by the conference of Länder Premiers held in Munich in June—a conference that was boycotted by those from the Eastern Zone because they felt unable to discuss exactly how to create a unified and sovereign German state. A few months later the SED sponsored a National Congress to which all the political parties and organs of 'direct democracy' were invited. The Christian Democrats declined politely; the Social Democrats refused bluntly. The Eastern wing of the Liberal Demo-crats attended. So did many trade unions from all over the country. The Congress, which opened on December 7th, called for the signature of a peace treaty by an elected central government.

Economic recovery began slowly. Thus as late as October 1947 the official ration scale of 1,550 calories per day was not being reached in certain parts of Bizonia. Each zone had been left free to regulate its own note issue and from 1946 the East indulged in heavy printing in order to

[1] Marshal Zhukov returned to the USSR in the autumn of 1946 and went into oblivion until just after Stalin's death.

finance reparations deliveries. This, plus the persistence of a vigorous black market throughout the country, impeded export recovery and so produced a Bizonia balance of payments deficit in 1947 of $400,000,000. Half this deficit was financed by Britain and half by the United States.

February 1948 was a month of tension in Berlin. Ernst Reuter used the 1848 centenary celebrations to predict to a vast crowd that the Communist flood would break on the 'iron will of Finland and Berlin'. Marshal Sokolovsky advised his fellows on the Control Council that Berlin belonged to the Soviet zone and that they might not be permitted to stay if they abused their position. Sporadic Soviet interference with road and rail access routes began in March. But after that tension subsided for a while.

Early in June representatives of the Western Occupation Powers and of the 'Benelux'[1] countries met in London and declared themselves in favour of the internationalization of the Ruhr under the Western powers, and of a Federal Government for West Germany. They also—and this was the really explosive issue—came out in support of currency reform. On the 18th of the month, three days after the Russians had closed for 'repairs' the Helmstedt–Berlin access road, a new currency was introduced into West Germany. However, the Western powers, who remained too aware of Berlin's military vulnerability to take undue political risks, were still prepared to regard the old Reichsmark as the sole legal tender for West Berlin, provided it was brought under strict quadripartite control. But on June 22nd the Russians announced a reform of the East zone currency and so the following day the West declared itself willing only that both currencies should circulate in West Berlin. Both sides knew, of course, that this would result in the Eastern Deutsche Mark falling to but a minor fraction of its official exchange value. That night the Russians, for 'technical' reasons, stopped all electricity supplies to West Berlin and closed every access route. The Western response was to develop an airlift of supplies.

By September less than 2% of the West Berliners had taken advantage of an opportunity to register for food in the Eastern sector. By then the airlift had grown beyond almost everybody's expectations and the Russians, as well as the West, began to accept the prospect of two Berlins and two Germanies. On September 6th the bulk of the Magistrat, after repeated exposure to organized mob violence in East Berlin, transferred to the British sector, leaving an SED rump behind. Within a few months all city government under inter-allied control was little more than a legal fiction. Early in 1949 the Russians, now much embarrassed by increasing Western restrictions on exports to their zone, sought negotiations. These led in May to the lifting of the blockade and to the acceptance of the Western currency as the sole legal tender in West Berlin. The conclusion of the Nuremberg War Crimes Trials in April symbolized the end of the attempt by the victors of 1945 to work together to remould their major foe.

The East German political scene altered considerably in the course of 1948. The SED was extensively purged. Jacob Kaiser—a prominent

[1] 'Benelux' = Belgium, Luxembourg and the Netherlands.

national figure on the Christian Democrat Left—was ejected from the leadership of the East German branch of the CDU. The Liberal Democrats were cowed into submission. Two new parties—the National Democrats, which openly enlisted the support of ex-minor Nazis, and the Peasant Party—were formed under pro-Soviet leaders. The ground was thus laid for the elections that the People's Congress arranged for the spring of 1949. The voters were presented with only one list of candidates for a new Congress and were obliged to vote either for the list, and so for unity and peace, or against it and against those obviously laudable objectives. One third of the ballots were, none the less, cast in opposition. Despite, or perhaps because of, this disquieting result, the new Congress hastened to found the German Democratic Republic.

In 1947 the Frankfurt Economic Council was created in Bizonia. This Council, whose policies remained subject to Anglo-American approval, consisted, by the spring of 1948, of 104 members, all elected by the *Länder* legislatures. These legislatures also provided the members of a Parliamentary Council that met in September, under the presidency of the CDU leader Konrad Adenauer, to prepare a draft federal constitution. Almost complete three-power approval of this draft (the only important exception being the proposed inclusion of West Berlin in the Federal Republic), together with the integration of the French zone with the other two, paved the way for a general election in the late summer of 1949. The CDU/CSU axis—compaigning on Ludwig Erhard's *laisser faire* economic philosophy of *Soziale Marktwirtschaft*—won only eight more seats (139 *v.* 131) than the Social Democrats. They owed their ability to form and maintain a government to the general support of the 52 Free Democrats, a group that on domestic issues stood rather to their Right. Extreme nationalists won 17 seats and the Communists 15. Economic recovery had clearly begun in time to weaken the appeal of the moderate Left and of extremists of either shade. Since the currency reform industrial production had risen from 45% of the 1936 level to nearly 90%.

Under the revised Occupation Statute of April 1949, tripartite control was retained over the industrial Ruhr, overseas trade, and foreign affairs. The Allies were also able to continue to pursue, by means of a Military Security Board, the policy of German demilitarization. But in almost all its aspects supervision rapidly became less stringent. Because of the flow of refugees from the East, unemployment remained quite high, and this, in its turn, fanned resentment against Allied dismantlings sufficiently to precipitate sporadic physical resistance in the course of 1949. Faced with this discontent, and increasingly alive to the value to the West of German industrial strength, the Western Allies slowed dismantling down. Meanwhile, by the Petersberg Agreement of November 1949, they approved the Federal Republic's becoming a full member of the International Ruhr Authority and seeking to join the Council of Europe. Konrad Adenauer said in December that Germany had no desire for a national army. His assurances were welcomed by the leading Western governments.

## Chapter VI
## WESTERN EUROPE REVIVES

In October 1945 an assembly was elected in France with the mandate that, within seven months, it was to draw up a constitution and have it judged by a national referendum. And within a month this assembly had unanimously elected Charles de Gaulle head of the provisional government—a government which included representatives of all the major parties. Its Foreign Minister was Georges Bidault of the *Mouvement Républican Populaire*—a new liberal Catholic party that had been formed in 1944 by a section of the resistance movement.

But de Gaulle soon proved too inflexible, and too easily bored, to adjust himself to multi-party politics. On January 20th, 1946, shortly after he had been forced to water down his plans for army reconstruction, he retired and a new government was formed by a Socialist, Felix Gouin. Maurice Thorez, the Communist leader, remained a Minister of State and other members of his party retained control of the Ministries of Armaments, Industrial Production and Labour. Most of the other ministries stayed in the same hands.

In the referendum in May and the election in June the MRP secured the defeat of a draft constitution, sponsored by the Socialists and Communists, that provided for no second chamber. Bidault then formed a new government with stronger MRP representation and this prepared a new draft that did incorporate a second chamber—to be known as the Council of the Republic—which was to be chosen by a most elaborate electoral procedure and which was to be able to delay ordinary legislation and resist constitutional changes. This draft was accorded a modest majority on a low poll in the referendum of October 13th, but, in the meantime, Gaullist protests that the President should have been given important reserve powers had helped to weaken the general MRP standing in the country. It was the Communists who came best out of the Assembly elections of November 1946. They won 163 of the 574 seats, as against the MRP's 160 and the Socialists' 93. But it was a Socialist, Paul Ramadier, that led the government which took office in January 1947. The Communists would not have served under anybody from the political Right; few other elements in the coalition, on the other hand, would have served under a Communist.

In France, as in so many lands, 1947 was a year of bitterness. The heavy investment in basic industry that was the key feature of the recovery plan Jean Monnet had launched in 1945 had yet to yield much fruit. Inflation and tax evasion were rife; up to 75% of the average urban wage was being spent on food. In May the Communists left the government after disputes over almost every aspect of policy; they thereby lost all ability to influence from the inside French governmental attitudes towards such matters as the 'Cold War' that was now obviously in progress between Russia and the West. They became free, on the other hand, to use their grip on the *Confédération Générale du Travail* to promote industrial action for political ends. Ramadier was driven from office in November in a series of strikes and riots that involved two million workers. But the feeling that the CGT was now being used mainly for political ends led to the breakaway *Force ouvrière* being formed in December. This split weakened the trade union movement as a whole. Six million workers were affiliated to the CGT in 1946; by 1955 the combined total for it and the *Force ouvrière* was below two million. The Catholic movement, the *Confédération Française de Travailleurs Chrétiens*, also slumped below its post-war peak of one million members.

Another dramatic expression of the tension prevailing in 1947 was the formation, under the auspices of de Gaulle, of the *Rassemblement du Peuple Français*. Speaking in Strasbourg in April de Gaulle depicted the RPF as a national movement 'above party differences and within the framework of the law'. That autumn it swept the board in the municipal elections and, despite the implacable hostility of the Socialist and MRP leaders, secured the nominal allegiance of 80 deputies. But after this it started to lose its momentum.

The next administration, which was led by Robert Schuman of the MRP, was also based on the Socialist–MRP–Radical axis, or the 'Third Force' as it now styled itself. But this government disintegrated over the questions of economic policy and aid to Catholic schools. After a long political crisis in the summer of 1948 another Third Force *régime* was formed which was led by the Radical veteran Henri Queuille and so inclined more to the Right. Schuman had now displaced Bidault as Foreign Minister and he was to hold that post until Bidault recaptured it at the end of 1952. There was, one may note, a tendency for all ministries to change hands less frequently than did the leadership of the government itself.

Frequent violent clashes between Communists and Gaullists, coupled with industrial unrest, made Queuille's first weeks of office parlous. However he survived to lead the country for over twelve months. This success was made possible by a happy combination of rising production and mild deflation and, in particular, by the humiliating collapse of the too overt attempt the Communists made to generate a strike wave as a protest against the plan that General George Marshall had launched to aid European recovery. Bidault formed the next ministry. He lost his

Socialist ministers in February 1950 but was able to stay in office until the eve of the Korean War.

The elections held for the Italian constituent assembly on June 2nd, 1946, confirmed the supremacy of Alcide de Gasperi, the moderately conservative leader of the Christian Democrats. And that same day, in a national referendum, Italy decided to abolish her monarchy. As a private poll taken on April 25th had shown, there was, even among Christian Democrat members, a republican majority.

1947 witnessed the signature of a peace treaty that, among other things, deprived Italy of her colonies. It witnessed, also, the emergence of a sharp dichotomy between Right and Left. De Gasperi finally dropped both the Communists and the orthodox Socialists from his administration some months after 50 Socialist deputies broke away from their party in protest against the strongly pro-Communist policy of its leader, Pietro Nenni.

The Popular Front of Communists and Nenni Socialists had to fight the April 1948 election against the background of the Socialist split, the Czechoslovak coup, the promise of Marshall Aid and the Western commitment to Trieste. So it only secured a third of the seats in each House, whereas in the lower one the Christian Democrats secured a comfortable overall majority. That summer it resorted to strikes for political purposes but these simply led to a splitting of the trade union movement. This did not mean, however, that the militant Left could be discounted. Unemployment hovered obstinately around the two million mark.

But the pressure of immediate events in Western Europe was not such as to crush all faith and aspirations; the concept of European unity, for example, was one that flourished as it had not done for generations past. In his Zurich speech of September 1946 Winston Churchill called for a United Europe based on Franco-German partnership. Late in 1947 an International Committee of the Movements for European Unity was formed and the following May it convened a Congress of Europe at the Hague. A year later the Council of Europe was set up under a statute signed by ten governments. Its main deliberative body was a Consultative Assembly composed of representatives from national parliaments who, through a Committee of Ministers sent recommendations back to the respective national governments. Leon Blum, Alcide de Gasperi, Paul Reynaud and Paul-Henri Spaak were among those active in the European Movement by this time.

The most important step towards European integration taken before 1950 was the establishment of the Organization for European Economic Co-operation. This was, of course, a by-product of the Marshall Plan. General Marshall's proposal, made in the summer of 1947, had been that all those European states who shared a genuine interest in mutual recovery should receive, over a period of three or four years, large scale assistance from North America. His initiative led to the Paris conference of that July and so to the creation, in April 1948, of OEEC and of the Economic Co-operation Administration—the agency through which American funds were channelled. The OEEC founder members were Austria, Belgium, Denmark, France, Greece, Iceland, Ireland, Italy, Luxembourg, the Netherlands, Norway, Portugal, Sweden, Switzerland, Turkey and Britain. West Germany became a full member in 1949. These nations received a total of twelve billion dollars in Marshall Aid and this assistance played a key part in the expansion of just over 50% that took place in their industrial production between 1948 and 1953. With this expansion came a much greater ability to meet both the internal and external Communist challenges.

During 1948 and 1949 ECA tried to use its influence to promote European economic integration. But, thanks, in part, to British refusal to impair her Commonwealth trading pattern, it made little headway. However, the quantitative restrictions on mutual trade were reduced and, in September 1950, the European Payments Union was created to facilitate the redevelopment of a full multilateral trading pattern among OEEC members.

All the OEEC signatories bar Austria, Greece, Ireland, Sweden, Switzerland and Turkey were founder members of the North Atlantic Treaty Organization, which was created in April 1949. NATO was the logical extension of the Brussels Treaty signed by Britain, France, Belgium, the Netherlands and Luxembourg in 1948. But it was more formalized than the Brussels Treaty as well as more comprehensive. Ultimate alliance authority was vested in a Council that was composed of representatives of all member governments. In 1951 General Eisenhower was appointed as the first Supreme Allied Commander, Europe.

Western anxiety to create a viable ground defence in Europe was much increased by the outbreak of the war in Korea in June 1950. European economic recovery had been the chief priority before then; from then on the main emphasis was on military deterrence. In 1951 the American army in Bavaria began a build up from two to six divisions, and Marshall Aid was superseded by a global programme of military and economic aid run by a new Mutual Security Agency. Of the $7,500,000,000 of aid authorized for the world as a whole in the first fiscal year only a fifth was economic. Between 1949 and 1955 the USA gave $17,500,000,000 in military aid to NATO Europe, and Canada gave well over a billion. Defence expenditure by the recipients themselves during this time was around seventy billion dollars.

Two months before the Korean invasion the American Joint Chiefs of Staff recommended that West Germany be rearmed. That August the Council of Europe called for an international European army. NATO Council decided in September to urge West Germany to rearm and, in order to persuade her to do so, committed itself ultimately to adopt a Forward Strategy, i.e. to prepare to fight the main battles near the Iron Curtain and not on the Rhine. Within a few weeks France produced the Pleven Plan; this provided for a European army in which the largest national unit was to be a battalion. The French government had wanted integration to be that thorough because it had felt that it would make a

German military contribution more acceptable to the French public. But German and American opposition killed all hope of international military integration below divisional level.

Nevertheless on May 27th, 1952, the day after the signing of new conventions which made West Germany virtually an independent sovereign state, the European Defence Community Treaty was signed in Paris by France, Germany, Italy, the Low Countries and Luxembourg. However, by the end of 1953 neither the Italian nor the French parliaments had ratified it.

But the six nations reacted more swiftly to the suggestion, made by Robert Schuman in May 1950, that they establish a European Coal and Steel Community. By the treaty that came into force in July 1952 a free trade area was to be established in these products and a High Authority and a Council of Ministers set up to curb monopoly abuse and co-ordinate development. Each year an assembly, the members of which were to be elected by national votes or delegated by parliaments, was to meet to assess the High Authority's work. Jean Monnet became the Authority's first President. He had done more than anybody else to prepare the original Schuman Plan.

NATO's decision to seek German rearmament came after years in which sports like gliding and fencing had been banned in the Occupation Zones because they were considered conducive to militarism. It was not, therefore, an easy one for Chancellor Adenauer to adapt himself to. He had himself pressed for the creation of the 30,000 militarized border police that was authorized in September 1950, but his initial preference had been to leave matters there. He came soon to realize, however, that the EDC might become a useful device for building up his country's world position. But this it would only be if the Federal Republic could successfully play the role of a tough bargainer. Early in 1950 relations with France became delicate over the establishment of a semi-autonomous Saar republic under French suzerainty. So Adenauer had to resist, for example, the original French suggestion that the formation of the EDC should be contingent upon the ratification of the Schuman Plan. Such bargaining power as Adenauer possessed in this and other matters derived from the acute feeling of military peril that beset the Allies. At its meeting in Lisbon in 1952, NATO Council called for the early assembly of 96 active and cadre divisions in, or available for, NATO Europe. Sixty of these were to stand West of the Stettin–Trieste line in the event of war. In 1950 about twelve ill-accoutred divisions held that central sector.

It was two or three years before a solid majority of Germans was prepared to accept the need for rearmament. Kurt Schumacher, a man whose intellectual and moral fibre was steeled by terrible physical disabilities, initiated SPD opposition to such a move. He also persuaded many of the SPD deputies to oppose the Schuman Plan. Doubts about whether integration with the West was compatible with reunification with the Eastern Zone were not, of course, confined to the SPD. The Soviet proposal, made in March 1952, that there should be a united and neutral Germany with its own national army was presumably intended to encourage such doubts. So, perhaps, was the marked strengthening of East German border security that took place two months later. But the East German refusal to admit the United Nations Neutral Nations Supervisory Committee that had been set up in 1951 to establish the conditions for all German elections weakened the strength of the Soviet appeal.

France was finding the quest for stable government as difficult as ever. The coalition of the centre that René Pleven had formed in July 1950 survived half a dozen confidence votes on the special rearmament budget in the course of the winter but it then disintegrated over the question of electoral reform. The reform act that was passed in May 1951 modified the system of proportional representation introduced in 1946. Thenceforward any party or alliance of parties that secured an absolute majority in any parliamentary constituency would be able to take all the seats in it. Proportional representation would be confined to cases where no such majority obtained.

This reform was, of course, designed to inhibit any migration to the Gaullist and Communist extremes. But in the June elections these parties still got 120 and 100 seats respectively as against a total of 290 for the old Third Force and 110 for the remainder. Like the Communists, the Gaullists opposed the Schuman and Pleven Plans. Unlike them, they supported the decision to authorize, for the first time since the formal separation of Church and State, state subsidies to Catholic schools. The Socialists left the new government that René Pleven had formed on this issue and this resulted, ultimately, in its downfall. For most of 1952 France was governed by a conservative coalition under Antoine Pinay that drew its support from the band of the political spectrum between the middle of the MRP and the middle of the RPF. Communist prestige fell as a result of the temporary lurch to militancy made in accordance with advice brought back from Moscow that spring by the party veteran Francois Billoux. One estimate suggests that party membership fell from 750,000 to 420,000 between 1949 and the middle of 1953.

Shortly before the Italian elections of June 1953 the 1948 proportional representation system was modified with respect to the Lower House. But this did not prevent gains by both the Left and the Right wing extremes. The Communists and the Nenni Socialists were able to capitalize on a prevailing mood of impatience and so increase their total share of the Lower House poll from 31% to 35%. Meanwhile, the Monarchists and other Right Wing groups, drawing benefit from the influence of land-owners hostile to the land reform of 1950, increased theirs from 5% to 13%. The Christian Democrats lost over 40 seats in the Lower House and so Signor de Gasperi became unable to re-form the four-party coalition that he had been leading.

*Chapter VII*
# CHINA AND JAPAN

(i) *China goes Communist*

HEAVY weapons had been used comparatively little in China and so, at the end of the war, her economic position appeared relatively strong. Distribution had become chaotic but the physical production potential was not greatly impaired. In Manchuria, indeed, output was generally above 1937 levels. Also, thanks to the billion dollar aid programme, a large foreign exchange reserve had been accumulated. Falling prices associated with the sale of hoarded goods reflected public optimism about the post-war prospects.

Time was to prove, however, that Chiang Kai-shek's Nationalist *régime* based then on Chungking could not be reconciled with Mao Tse-tung's Communist one located at Yenan. The former had an army of some 200 divisions which included nearly 2,000,000 men with rifles; one fifth of the divisions were in the crack Central Army which was largely American trained and equipped. The Communists boasted an army of 1,000,000 regulars and 2,000,000 militiamen but many of the regulars lacked shoulder arms and only a fraction of the militia was useful for anything but porterage. Over half of the regulars were in North China and over a third in the centre. Mao claimed that the land he controlled had a population of 100,000,000.

Great Power recognition of Chiang's administration as the National government of China placed upon it the triple responsibilities of accepting locally the Japanese surrender, setting economic recovery in motion and transforming itself into a broad coalition. All this was beyond it. Chiang himself remained as incorruptible as they come, but most of his relations and officials were soaked in the native tradition of warlordism and bureaucratic peculation. The Sixth National Congress of the Kuomintang, which met in May 1945, passed resolutions in favour of the abolition of KMT cells inside the army and the schools and in favour of other parties being allowed to organize. But in doing so it reflected the personal authority and political skills of Chiang rather than any progressive idealism on the part of the great mass of delegates. Vested interests would have precluded basic economic and social reform even had Chiang had any clear ideas about this. It was significant that, in the course of 1945, T. V. Soong, leader of one of the 'four big families', became both Prime Minister and Chairman of the Supreme Economic Council.

On August 14th, 1945, a treaty was signed with the USSR which seemed to ensure Russian co-operation in Manchuria and elsewhere. That same day MacArthur authorized Chiang to receive the Japanese surrender in the China theatre; American planes and ships had been made ready to transport his troops for this purpose. But these events did not daunt the Communists. Their army commander Chu Teh cast brutal scorn on the recent Nationalist war effort as he rejected a Chungking instruction to stand fast. Immediately he had done so, he ordered his men to go out and disarm all the Japanese they could find. Wild enthusiasm was affected by the Communists over the Sino-Soviet treaty which was described as heralding a new dawn for all Asia. Only on August 26th did Mao accept an invitation to Chungking issued a fortnight previously.

His joint communiqué with Chiang, released on October 10th, seemed to indicate a large measure of agreement. A constitution was to be framed as soon as possible and, in the meantime, Chiang was to appoint an advisory council of 40, of whom not more than half were to come from his party. A three to two majority in this council was to be sufficient to override any Presidential veto. The Communists had agreed that they should contribute 20 rather than 48 divisions to a 100-division national army. But several problems had not been resolved. Among them were the exact mode of integration of the two armies and the future of the various local Soviets.

By now hostilities had broken out as Nationalist troops, aided by a few Japanese and ex-puppet units, made some endeavour to reassert Kuomintang authority. Attempts to reach Tatung and Kalgan failed but the Communists were cleared from much of the Lower Yangste. Concurrently, however, about 100,000 lightly armed Red Chinese soldiers infiltrated into rural Manchuria and appropriated many of the 500,000 small arms and 2,700 artillery pieces owned by the Japanese Kwantung army.

The United States had been reluctant to help Chiang deploy into Manchuria because it would encourage civil war and would involve an extension of his forces that was too great from the military point of view. But early in October 53,000 American Marines went ashore to occupy in strength a strategic enclave that embraced Peking and Tientsin, an enclave that was to be maintained for a year. A month later strong Nationalist forces moved into Manchuria from behind the Great Wall. Meanwhile 300,000 Soviet troops retained control of most of the big towns and the Chinese Communists of much of the countryside.

In December General Marshall, acting in the capacity of President Truman's representative, began his twelve month endeavour to arrange a peace. He joined with Chou En-lai and the Nationalist Chang Chih-chung to form a Committee of Three. Early in the new year this committee

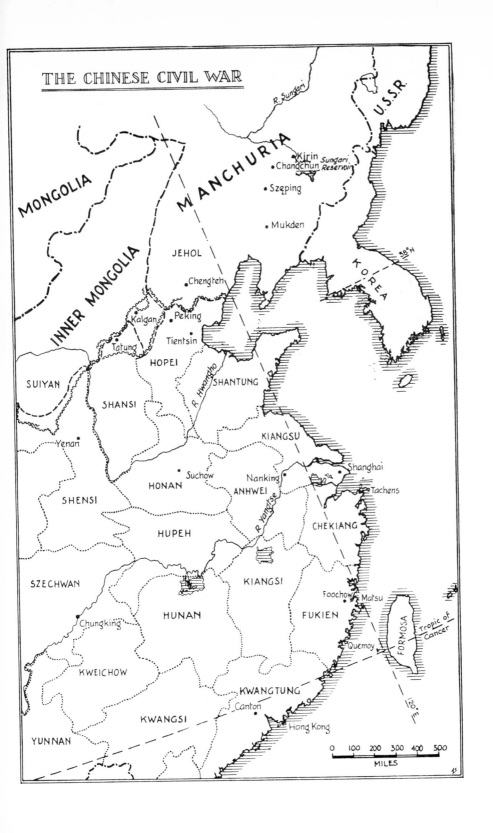

THE CHINESE CIVIL WAR

arranged a cease-fire and this was enforced over much of North China by tripartite truce teams. A Political Consultative Conference was then convened at which all important parties were represented, and this agreed to summon a National Assembly within four months to approve a constitution based on the 1936 draft.

This was a truce that never came to Manchuria. Russian troops finally withdrew during the spring and their places were taken by a quarter of a million Nationalists—chiefly from the Central Army. Yet, because Nationalist troops of all ranks looted without compunction and also because no proposals were made to meet the strong local desire for partial autonomy, the Communists continued to strengthen their rural power and influence. But Chiang, still believing that the time was ripe for an unqualified victory in Manchuria, prevaricated for weeks before admitting truce teams and, having done so, he made their work impossible. Nationalist artillery helped thwart desperate Communist attempts to retain Szeping and Changchun and in early June the Sungari was crossed. Concurrently, however, many places in the South of the province fell back into Communist hands, some of their garrisons showing an ominous lack of martial qualities when faced with moderate odds. Fighting now became extensive again in China Proper. Sixty thousand Communist troops were all but encircled in Hupeh and Honan.

Believing himself to hold a decisive military advantage, Chiang resisted a Communist demand that a cease-fire precede any peace negotiations. However, after some persuasion by Marshall, he agreed to a fifteen-day truce. But, despite an extension to the 30th of the month, this yielded no settlement; this was because, in the absence of any political *quid pro quo*, the Communists refused to withdraw on the scale required of them.

Hopes of a compromise now dwindled to vanishing point. Inside the Kuomintang the forces of illiberalism waxed strong. Anti-American demonstrations were organized, secret police activity was greatly extended, and, worst of all, two leaders of the radical intellectual Democratic League were assassinated. Meanwhile the Nationalist military machine embarked on what was virtually total war. By the autumn it had driven an important part of what was now styled the People's Liberation Army from the mouth of the Yangste into the hills of Shantung and it had, in addition, seized Tatung, Chengteh, and Kalgan. Much of this progress was of dubious strategic value because it was made against an opponent all too willing to trade land for combat casualties; its real importance lay in the fact that, since the Communists demanded as a condition of any cease-fire a return to the January positions, it made the prospects of peace with mutual honour ever less bright. They vanished entirely when the Nationalists unilaterally convened a national assembly in November, 1946. Almost immediately Chou En-lai abandoned for good his assigned role of Communist representative at the new Nationalist capital of Nanking and several weeks later General Marshall left for the United States.

By this time the Nationalists had much weakened their own position by a series of administrative errors. To begin with they drastically over-valued their own *fapi*—as the standard unit of currency was called—paper money in terms of the notes they redeemed from the former Japanese occupied areas. They made this error, late in 1945, by taking cognizance of a Shanghai black market rate that had become unnaturally high thanks to the brief flush of post-war optimism and to a temporary dearth of *fapi* in the newly liberated areas. Once it was officially over-valued the *fapi* flooded into these parts causing immediate inflation within them, and, outside them, a *fapi* shortage that could only be met by fresh printing. Soon the government was printing notes to correct deficits in its own budgets caused by rising prices, an incorrigibly bad tax collection system and defence appropriations that sometimes came to three-quarters of the available revenue. Thus began an inflationary spiral which during the first three years of external peace forced up the Shanghai price indices by about one third each month. The big bureaucratic families grew yet richer on this spiral but the rest of the population languished in it. Draconian restrictions on imports and on flights of capital abroad were occasionally announced but were never properly enforced and in the absence of appropriate controls the internal inflation caused dramatic diminutions in the reserves of foreign currency.

Defence planning was equally clumsy. Graduates from Chiang's old academy of Whampoa were largely protected from the post-war axe and were given preferential treatment where promotion was concerned. As a result many of the 200,000 army officers dismissed and, indeed, many of those retained became disaffected. Symbolically enough, a Whampoa man became Chief of the Supreme Staff in the reorganized high command of 1946 and it was his privilege of direct access to Chiang that undermined the civilian control that the new structure was supposed to ensure. In theory the reorganization should have produced greater functional efficiency as well but, coinciding as it did with the outbreak of general hostilities, it merely magnified confusion.

Acute symptoms of the incipient disintegration of Nationalist China appeared first in its most developed provinces—Formosa and Manchuria. Thousands of people died in a savage Formosan revolt against a reactionary and brutal governor early in 1947. Meanwhile probes by Communist columns of at least divisional strength, which were supported by a few ex-Japanese tanks, were made across the frozen Sungari. By June the Nationalist garrisons at Changchun and Kirin were isolated and a large Communist artillery train was in use against Szeping. Heavy Nationalist reinforcements were then sent to Manchuria and so began the policy of absolute military commitment to that province which ultimately was to prove so disastrous. The situation was temporarily stabilized but the tactical initiative there and everywhere else had passed into Communist hands.

On the Nationalist home front the deterioration was even more marked. Only about one elector in every two hundred bothered to vote in the

National Assembly elections held that November, and the elections themselves were highly irregular. Yet the Assembly thus created rejected Chiang's nominee for Vice-President and chose instead Li Tsung-jen—a leader of the radical Kwangsi faction. Within a few weeks Li had decided to leave Nanking and go to Peking to live under the protection of his old friend General Fu Tso-yi. Fu was an exceptionally able and progressive officer, and Chiang had recently felt obliged to appoint him as Commander in the North.

In the summer of 1948 a new gold yuan currency was introduced in order to halt the forty-fold rise in prices that had occurred since the previous year. To support it a rigid system of price controls was instituted. For these measures to become effective nationally it was essential that they did so in Shanghai, which remained the country's commercial capital. Chiang's son, 'Tiger' Chiang Ching-kuo, was appointed to take charge of this megalopolis, which was now characterized by rice riots and the deaths of thousands of untended refugees. He managed well until he tried to take action against an agent of the mighty Tu Yu-shan—gangster, dope-pedlar and philanthropist. Many years ago Tu, as an Elder in the Green Shirts secret society, had met a young novitiate called Chiang Kai-shek, and Tu now used this link to secure for his agent a nominal punishment. Next his mother stopped 'Tiger' Chiang from checking the black market operations of the Yangtse Development Corporation which was controlled by her brother-in-law. By October the 'Tiger' had resigned and raging inflation set in again. Still the old Chiang spoke out against 'manipulationists'.

A rough military parity between the two sides appears to have existed in June 1948. The Nationalist air force of 400 modern combat aircraft was to see little active service and so can be discounted. On the ground each side had, according to Nanking, rather over two million troops, some one million rifles, and two thousand guns. But the balance of power, even as measured in these crude inventory terms, moved decisively in favour of Mao over the next nine months. In the last quarter of the year the Nationalists lost half a million men in a vast battle of movement around Suchow and almost as many again as Manchuria surrendered. In January 1949 the North China army, which for months had been freely passing arms to the supposed enemy, capitulated; this enabled a North China People's Government to be established in Peking.

Faced now with catastrophe at the front, a disintegration of his higher command and a crescendo of criticism from the legislature, Chiang temporarily handed over the Presidency to Li Tsung-jen who was now prominent in the ever-growing peace party. Li tried to negotiate with Mao on the latter's proposals for a progressive coalition, but he had no base to bargain from. His physical inability to disband the secret police or even to enforce orders for the release of political prisoners convinced the Communists that all his liberalism was phoney. Formal peace talks were delayed until most of the members of Li's executive returned to Nanking from Canton whence they had gone against his wishes. Two days after the talks collapsed in April a strong Communist column effortlessly crossed the Lower Yangtse—an obstacle which, had it been loyally defended, might have cost them a million lives. Hopes that the Communist military machine would be corrupted or confused by the big Yangtse cities were not realized. Instead it bore down remorselessly on a disaffected South. Early in December Chiang rejoined the rump of the Kuomintang and led it to Formosa. Li Tsung-jen fled to the United States.

## (ii) *A Revolution Consolidated*

In July 1949 Mao announced that thenceforward China would lean towards the USSR. That he was earnest in this intent was shown by his long sojourn in Moscow the following winter. Out of this came treaties that provided for regular foreign policy discussions between the two countries, for the establishment of three joint stock companies, and for the Soviet loan to China of the modest but useful sum of $300,000,000. The loan bore a 1% rate of interest, and was expendable over five years and re-payable within fifteen.

It was not until after the new international orientation of China had been confirmed by her involvement in the Korean War that the regime's domestic programme became uncompromisingly Communist. Harassment of foreign firms began immediately but Mao at first sought to enlist the support of the broad mass of Chinese businessmen in his campaign against the landlords and certain privileged monopolies. As part and parcel of this apparently non-doctrinaire approach to the task of reconstruction, schools and religious foundations were promised protection. So were national minorities. The Political Consultative Conference created in June 1949 was described as the sovereign elective body of an alliance of all urban and rural popular forces.

One of the Conference's chief duties was the appointment of the Central People's Government Council. Mao was its chairman but, of his six vice-chairmen, three were non-Communist. They included the head of the Revolutionary Committee of the Kuomintang, the head of the Democratic League and the widow of Sun Yat-sen. The council chose Chou En-lai to be the first Prime Minister and Foreign Secretary but only half of the other twenty ministers were members of the Communist Party. Among them, however, were the men responsible for the Interior and for Public Security.

Late in 1952 Peking claimed that two million 'bandits' had been eliminated since the take-over. But most of these must have been landlords or rich peasants who had tried to obstruct land reform. Systematic resistance by organized guerrilla bands was not on this scale. The Peking authorities later admitted that 400,000 armed men were at large in June

1950 but claimed that their number was halved in the course of that summer. Little help was afforded them from Formosa, then or subsequently. The loss of Hainan that April and the arrival in the Formosa Straits in June of an American naval squadron that was under orders to block attacks from either direction circumscribed the Kuomintang considerably. It was, in any case, preoccupied with rebuilding its shattered army and crushing dissension among the local civilians. Some amphibious raids were launched, however, and Nationalist remnants in North-East Burma made a few sorties. But Peking knew well how to turn these puny efforts to her own psychological advantage.

Perhaps the greatest initial triumph on the home front was the curbing of inflation. Urban prices trebled in the first ten weeks of 1950 but by the year's end had almost returned to their previous value. The turning point came in March with the introduction of a uniform currency, the imposition of much heavier but more rational taxes and the commencement of the compulsory sale of Victory Bonds. The state and private stockpiling that followed the outbreak of the Korean War caused some further price fluctuations but 1951 proved to be a year of mild deflation.

'Korea' cost China many lives and enforced delays in her investment programme but there is little doubt that her leaders were right when they claimed that its net result was an acceleration of its social and economic transformation. Vast supplies of Russian arms made the Chinese army and air force more up-to-date. The appropriation of £200,000,000 of British investments and of other foreign investments worth about as much again eased the country's international payments position. Most important of all, however, was the wonderful opportunity afforded by the war for coercion and indoctrination. During the first half of 1951 hundreds of thousands of mass accusation meetings took place, and many of them culminated in public executions with on-the-spot press or wireless coverage. With this effort went the development of a new specialized network of propagandists inside the Communist Party and the New Democratic Youth Corps. Each of these organizations boasted a membership in excess of five million and within two years over half of them had been formally enrolled as propagandists. By 1952 both propaganda and administrative action were being directed towards corruption in the government service and the alleged malpractices of private business. Something approaching a million firms had to pay a total of over a billion dollars following convictions for bribery, espionage and the like. Yet another way in which the Korean war facilitated the consolidation of Communist China was that it made it easier than might otherwise have been the case to establish a military presence in Tibet. This was because Delhi was too anxious to do what it could about peace in Korea to worry unduly about the potential threat along the Himalayas.

Propaganda dividends abroad were sought through the subversion of European prisoners of war. Though this endeavour was often characterized by severe and prolonged physical torture and mental cruelty it achieved indifferent results. Brutal maltreatment of the 200 Turkish regular troops captured did not result in one spiritual conquest. More than 7,000 American soldiers and airmen were made prisoners and over a third of these died in captivity. Only twenty declined to be repatriated and only sixteen of the mass who did return were subsequently found guilty of gross misconduct.

A great search was made inside the POW camps and elsewhere for 'evidence' that the United States Air Force had disseminated dangerous bacteria over Korea and Manchuria. Russia and North Korea joined China in this germ warfare propaganda which reached its peak in 1952. Certain scientists from the West lent their authority to huge reports published by Communist-sponsored agencies. Neither the World Health Organization nor the International Red Cross was allowed to investigate.

By the time the Korean War ended China had become a strongly totalitarian society and her economy had started to assume a classical Marxist pattern. Under the land reform scheme launched in June 1950, some 120,000,000 acres of arable had been confiscated from about 3,000,000 churches, shrines and 'feudal' landlords and distributed among the peasants. The first state farms and collectives had been formed. Manufacturing industry was mostly in public hands. The time was ripe for the launching of the initial Five-Year Plan.

## (iii) *Japan*

In August 1945 Japan was an economic and spiritual void. Into this void came the Supreme Allied Commander, General MacArthur, plus an administration comprised chiefly of senior staff officers from the Pacific War and earnest young 'New Deal' graduates. Neither group was well acquainted with the Japanese culture or language. Both had energy and vision. Initial contacts with the conquered people were not easy to make but in this respect the Supreme Command Allied Powers (SCAP) derived much advantage from Imperial goodwill. The Emperor urged his statesmen to collaborate and, meanwhile, he destroyed his own mystique by making frequent public appearances as a pedestrian in a pin-stripe rather than occasional ones as a Field Marshal on a white charger.

A Japanese official committee was appointed to draw up a draft of a new constitution but its approach to the problem was markedly cautious. Its members felt, to quote their chairman, that 'some of the roses of the West when cultivated in Japan are apt to lose their fragrance'. SCAP discarded their draft in favour of one of its own and had this steered through the Diet, with large supporting votes and few amendments, late in 1946. Thenceforward the Emperor has been a mere constitutional monarch effectively dependent upon two elective chambers. General Elections for the all-important Lower House must take place at least every fourth year; half the Upper House retires every three years. Most of the Cabinet must have seats in the Diet; all of them must be civilians. A constitutional amendment requires a two-thirds majority in both houses and in a popular referendum. Embodied in this constitution is an elaborate declaration of human rights and an article that renounces forever warlike preparations.

Some 5,000 men were eventually convicted in the war-crime trials that began early in 1946 but these were dwarfed in immediate importance by the purges initiated later that year. They excluded from public and commercial life some 200,000 people who were felt to have made a significant contribution to the Japanese war effort. Society was deprived in this way of very many leaders but this did not deter SCAP from introducing functional democracy. Within three years the Land Reform Act of 1946 reduced from 46% to 8% the proportion of the arable that was rented. Other measures strengthened the bargaining power of the industrial workers and democratized local government. Soon the Ministry of Education lost its monopoly of textbook production and was made to devolve much of its administrative power. The Economic Decentralization Act of 1947 sought to eliminate the *zaibatsu* industrial combines.

A heavy poll in the General Election of 1946 made the Liberals the biggest single party in the Lower House—the House of Representatives. But then the Liberal leader, Johiro Hatoyama, fell a victim to the purge and so Shigeru Yoshida, the sixth alternative to be canvassed, became head of the new Liberal-dominated coalition. Economic discontent induced SCAP to order another election the following year and this gave rise to a Socialist-cum-Democrat coalition. Within eighteen months this had been broken up by factionalism and soon afterwards Yoshida stepped back into the breach to snatch six years of power.

Yoshida matched his part. He was tactless, condescending, awkward, irritable and remote, but he could strike well the attitudes needed to offset his political dependence upon SCAP. As Ambassador in London he had acquired some of the outward signs of an English patrician—cigars, traditional etiquette, a disdain for pedants and a Rolls-Royce. Who could have been a better foil for the SCAP men from the Eastern Universities and the Pacific Theatre of War?

All the major political controversies of the second Yoshida era were products of the Cold War. On January 6th, 1948, the United States Secretary of the Army enunciated a new policy of building Japan up to be a bulwark of freedom. Doubts about the wisdom of permitting unrestrained industrial expansion were cast aside, and economic growth and internal stability became the sole tests of SCAP policy. The break up of the *zaibatsus* was discontinued and foreign trade restrictions considerably eased. Strikes in government offices became illegal and all nationwide strikes were proscribed by SCAP. Early the following year reparations were suspended, a National Police Reserve was created, and a coast guard was formed. In 1950 the NPR received the formal authorization of SCAP.

Monetary circulation was severely curtailed in the spring of 1949 to halt the tenfold price inflation of the previous two years. Acute industrial unrest developed as half a million men became idle and this unrest found expression in numerous strike actions. Nearly 1,000 Communists had been released from prison in 1945 and many of them acquired positions of prominence within the new trade union movement then being created. Now, it seemed, was the 'Party's' time of opportunity. China was going Red. The January election had placed thirty-five of its supporters in the House of Representatives. National membership had doubled to 90,000 in twelve months.

The opportunity was wasted through arrogance and impatience. Violent demonstrations and lethal railway sabotage alienated the uncommitted. So did the hopelessly brainwashed condition of the first prisoners of war to return from Russia. So did a Soviet assertion that all prisoners had been repatriated, which was made at a time when Tokyo calculated that 320,000 remained. So did abject party acceptance of a Cominform stricture for alleged lack of militancy. Such episodes prepared the climate for official measures of restraint. Communist newsprint allocations were cut in 1949. Warrants for the arrest of several Communist leaders were issued in July 1950. Meanwhile, the employment situation began to improve in certain parts of the economy as a result of the increase in foreign military expenditure that was occasioned by the outbreak of war in Korea.

Enthusiasm for the peace treaty[1] was qualified by widespread dislike of the security agreement with the United States that came into force on the same April day in 1952. Under it the USA was free to deploy troops throughout Japan for regional defence and obligated to help the government keep civil order if so required. The treaty was exclusive and could only be ended by mutual consent. A related arrangement gave the United States full jurisdiction over all the American troops in Japan and all the American civilians attached to them.

Unarmed neutrality had become a strong aspiration—especially among the young, and so support was readily forthcoming for Communist demonstrations against these measures. Hundreds of policemen were injured on May Day alone. But with industrial production already at 125% of the pre-war maximum the masses were losing all interest in Marxian remedies for life's various ills. The real threat to Yoshida's survival now came from within his own ranks. Hatoyama was among the 180,000 purgees restored to full freedom in 1950 and 1951, which was awkward for Yoshida who in 1946 had agreed that Hatoyama could have the Liberal leadership back as soon as he became available. Now Yoshida contended that Hatoyama's health made the power transfer impracticable.

[1] See page 686.

This question caused a Liberal split and by the middle of 1953 the Yoshida faction was running a minority government in uneasy alliance with the Reform Party.[1]

[1] The Reform Party is the name that the Democratic Party had by then assumed. At the time of its formation in 1945, it had, in fact, called itself the Progressive Party. Early in 1947, whilst in the process of absorbing the Co-operative Party, it had re-named itself the Democratic Party. The name 'Reform Party' was adopted early in 1952.

# Chapter VIII
## SOUTHERN ASIA

### (i) *A Sub-Continent Divides*

A COMPLETE polarization of the Indian political scene was revealed by the elections held in the autumn of 1945. The Moslem League won all the thirty Moslem reserved seats in the Central Assembly and Congress the vast majority of the remainder. The League had campaigned for the creation of an independent Islamic state to be called Pakistan. Congress called for extensive provincial autonomy within a federal system.

That winter some of the leaders of the Indian National Army—a force of about 20,000 men enlisted by the Japanese from among the Indian troops they took prisoner—were brought to trial for treason. Congress formed a Defence Committee to plead their case and Pandit Nehru himself contended that 'they are a fine body of young men ... and their dominating motive was love for India's freedom'. The defendants were convicted but, after pressure from Gandhi, Nehru, and others, their sentences were suspended. Perhaps this promoted a belief that the military code was something that could be broken without dishonour. A series of minor disturbances broke out in navy and air force establishments and they culminated in a politically inspired naval mutiny at Bombay in February 1946. Disaffection within the armed forces helped bring morale in the civilian government services close to breaking point and so put a considerable additional premium on early independence.

Three British Cabinet Ministers arrived in Delhi in March and, after some preliminary talks, suggested that the country should be divided into a group of predominantly Hindu provinces and a group of predominantly Moslem ones and that the provinces should be free to deal, either individually or at group level, with all matters other than defence, foreign affairs and communications, which they said, should be an All-Union responsibility. Both the League and Congress showed interest in this scheme but they differed in the interpretations they wished to place on it. Congress said the provincial groupings must be optional; the League said compulsory. Congress wanted the Union to have direct taxation powers;

665

the League did not. A speech by Nehru on July 10th highlighted these differences. Just over a fortnight later the League withdrew its tentative support for the scheme and called for 'Direct Action' to establish an independent Pakistan.

Another subject of controversy was the composition of the interim Government. The first British proposal was that it should be composed chiefly of Congress leaders of Hindu extraction and of League members. But Congress, which had consistently claimed to be an intercommunal party, could not accept the thesis that it should nominate no non-Hindus. Eventually the Viceroy asked Nehru to form a multicommunal government; this he did on September 2nd.

By now communal violence had broken out. Four thousand people died in Calcutta in the middle of August in riots that had obviously been encouraged by the local League leaders. Soon the trouble extended to rural Bengal and to Bihar and the United Provinces. Mohammed Ali Jinnah led a group of League representatives into the interim Government in October partly in order to try to lessen this tension. But this only led to further administrative paralysis.

A conference in London in December 1946 was followed by a new British policy statement. By conceding the principle of compulsory provincial groupings and making it clear that no major region would be compelled to accept the constitution against its will, the statement encouraged those who called for Pakistan. Two months later the British Prime Minister committed his government to independence not later than June 1948. He indicated that partition might be necessary if a full constituent assembly had not decided its future by then. He thereby strengthened the League's interest in boycotting the constituent assembly that had been convened after the London conference.

Dr Ambedkar, leader of the Hindu Untouchables, had long supported Jinnah in his claim for Pakistan. And most of the chief Congress spokesmen became reconciled to the idea in the spring of 1947. They felt that passive resistance would only erupt into bloodshed in the current atmosphere of embitterment, and that Mahatma Gandhi's alternative suggestion of restoring Moslem confidence by leaving them to run the interim Government was not worth pursuing. They felt, also, that Pakistan would be too unstable to last long. Yet another factor that influenced them was the pressure for the partition of the Punjab and Bengal from the Sikh and Hindu communities there. Communal violence, instigated chiefly by Moslems, had by now broken out in the Punjab.

Lord Mountbatten replaced Lord Wavell as Viceroy in March 1947. He quickly became convinced that almost immediate independence was essential and of this he persuaded London. And so the Indian Independence Act was rushed through Parliament in July. It provided for the creation, on August 15th, of two new Dominions—India and Pakistan. The princely states were left free to choose their own destiny but, on July 25th, the Viceroy pointedly advised them to accede to one or the

other of the Dominions, making their choice in the light of their geographical positions and the communal balance of their peoples.

The personal efforts of Mahatma Gandhi resulted in Bengal being
affected by less communal violence after independence than had been
feared. But in the Punjab what has been called 'the pendulum of communal frenzy' began to oscillate wildly. Many Sikhs and some Hindus
butchered Moslems in the East Punjab. So vengeance was extracted from
the Sikhs in the West Punjab, among them the farmers of the canal lands
of Lahore. The canal farmers marched down to Delhi and into Uttar
Pradesh in well disciplined and well armed bodies, cutting down fleeing
Moslems as they did so. Several thousand murders took place in Delhi
itself but the tide of bloodshed was stemmed by the firm administration of
Uttar Pradesh. There Hindu police showed no compunction about firing
on Hindu rioters as the need arose. Gradually the violence subsided
everywhere as the refugee movements were completed and as the monsoon
came to an end. Gandhi's assassination by a Hindu fanatic caused so
widespread a revulsion against communal savagery as to prevent a recurrence in 1948. But by then half a million people had been killed and
twelve million had fled over the borders. Serious riots occurred again in
West and East Bengal in 1950.

Sardar Patel, Nehru's Deputy Prime Minister until his death in 1950,
was a man of conservative temperament and resolute will. His most
important contribution to the progress of the new India was to persuade
almost all the 240 princely states that lay in or around her boundaries to
accede to her without delay. Only Junagadh and Hyderabad declined to
do so. Junagadh was a small state in the Kathiawar peninsula with a six-
to-one Hindu majority. When its Moslem ruler tried to accede to Pakistan
the Indian army marched in and held a plebiscite to reverse the decision.
The Nizam of Hyderabad, another Moslem in charge of a predominately
Hindu state, hoped that, with a quarter of a million regular soldiers and
auxiliaries, he could preserve some measure of independence. But his
domains were invaded in September 1948 and resistance collapsed within
four days.

Kashmir, the ancestral home of Pandit Nehru, posed a problem of a
different and less tractable kind. Some three-quarters of its people were
Moslem, its main communication routes led out to West Pakistan, and it
lay astride some of the most important head waters of the Indus—a river
upon which West Pakistan completely relied. But before independence
the Hindu Maharaja had distributed thousands of rifles to his Hindu
subjects in Jammu and these were soon used to terrorize the local Moslems.
October 1947 saw an invasion by 2,000 tribesmen—Pandit Nehru at first
thought 50,000—who advanced from the North-West Frontier into
Kashmir, acting with the knowledge and approval of at least some members
of the Pakistan government. As they drew close to Srinagar, the Maharaja
acceded to India and so obtained an airlift of Indian troops. The Indian
army was able to secure Srinagar, thanks, in part, to the delay the tribesmen

incurred by looting the Baramula convent, but hopes that it would regain all Kashmir come the springtime were dashed by the progressively deeper involvement of Pakistan regular troops. At the end of 1948 the United Nations, helped by contacts between the British commanders of the two regular armies involved, negotiated an armistice. But it proved impossible to reach a permanent settlement. India was now anxious to postpone indefinitely the decision by plebiscite she had promised in late 1947.

Her change of attitude stemmed in part from growing doubts about the viability of Pakistan. These doubts were not baseless. The five million refugees who had fled in 1947 included a high proportion of the country's big merchants, bankers, doctors, technicians and academicians. Jinnah, who had become the first Governor-General, died in 1948. Liaquat Ali Khan, a Prime Minister of high character and ability, was assassinated in 1951. Khwaja Nazimuddin, his successor, was arbitrarily dismissed during the economic and political crisis of 1953. National elections could not be held because no constitution had been framed. Local and provincial elections demonstrated that the factious cliques of landlords that now dominated the Moslem League had obtained absolute supremacy in West Pakistan. In the Eastern province the League wielded much less power, but this contrast merely served to emphasize the division of the country.

The Gandhian principle of a pyramid of power stretching up from the village councils was not implemented in the quasi-federal Indian constitution of 1950. The character of this constitution is wholly Western and, indeed, 250 of its original articles were taken directly from the 1935 Government of India Act. Defence, communications, currency and banking are among the subjects dealt with at union level. Education, public health and irrigation, for example, are handled at State level. The Union and State governments share powers and responsibilities in respect of certain other matters, such as economic and social planning and the amendment of criminal law.

Nehru swept Congress to victory in the 1951–2 elections. His party got 45% of the votes for, and 75% of the seats in, the House of the People, the lower chamber of the Union parliament. The runners-up, the Communists, got only 3·3% of the votes and 4·8% of the seats. Disorderly behaviour caused voting to be adjourned at only seven of the 133,000 polling stations. India had shown that universal suffrage could operate against a background of 83% illiteracy.

A National Planning Commission was established in March 1950 to co-ordinate, by advice and prescript and through subventions, the economic development of the States. The next year saw the initiation of the first Five-Year Plan. It saw, also, the first constitutional amendment. This placed beyond the purview of the courts acts passed by individual states to authorize the abolition of the Zamindar system. The Zamindars were those who exercised an hereditary right to collect the government's land tax and make a margin of profit in the process. In 1947 this class held sway over half the land in the country. By 1956 it had almost ceased to exist.

Nehru immediately brought foreign policy under his personal control and soon gave it a characteristic stamp. Shortly before independence an Asian Relations conference was held in Delhi and in 1949 delegates from fourteen countries met there to condemn Dutch policy in Indonesia. India accepted that the North was the agent of aggression in Korea but argued that that war had several root causes, one of them being Communist China's continued absence from the Security Council. India was reluctant to see the United Nations invoke military sanctions and she only sent an ambulance unit to Korea herself. She was, moreover, utterly opposed to the United Nations crossing the 38th Parallel. But this did not stop the American Congress from authorizing the free shipment to India of two million tons of grain early in 1951. Neither did it stop Peking from accusing Delhi of helping the imperialists to subvert Tibet. These accusations coincided with the entry into Tibet of the Chinese army in the autumn of 1950.

## (ii) From Burma to New Guinea

The leading political movement in post-war Burma was the Anti-Fascist People's Freedom League led by Aung San. At first it included the Burmese Communist Party but towards the end of 1946 this organization left the League because of its policy of negotiating, as opposed to simply seizing, independence. Shortly before this, however, a fissure had taken place inside the BCP. The so-called 'Red Flag' group, which was led chiefly by wartime resistance men, decamped to the Irrawaddy delta to recommence guerrilla activity. The less radical White Flag rump contested the election of the spring of 1947 but secured only seven of the 210 elective seats. Nearly all the remainder were won by the League and its allies, who were thriving on the prospect of independence within the year.

But violence was now disintegrating the Burmese body politic. Aung San and six members of his administration were murdered by gunmen in July; and the impact of this vicious blow was compounded by the situation that soon faced the AFPFL. Just after the assumption of independence in January 1948, there was a wave of militant strikes. In March the White Flags entered the jungle. Within the year the Karen community and much of the army also were in revolt. So was part of the People's Volunteer Organization—the League's paramilitary force. But conflict between the several insurgent groups—as witness, for example, PVO atrocities against the Karens—enabled the AFPFL government, now led by U Nu, to carry on. By 1951 it had stabilized the military situation and in the general election of the following year it won 180 seats.

A tenth of the six million people in Malaya in 1947 were Indians and a slight majority of the remainder were Chinese. From the Chinese community came nearly all the rebels of 1948 and the great mass of their sympathizers. A large majority of the security forces, on the other hand, were of Malayan extraction. Thus, the revolt can be regarded as symptomatic of Chinese resentment at their underprivileged political position. In 1945 the promise had been held out of a constitution that would give real scope for democratic centralized government, but the constitution actually imposed on the federation early in 1948 left important powers in the hands of the rulers of local states; all of these were conservative Malays. Political weakness appeared the more alarming against the background of economic distress. Along the jungle margins lived over half a million Chinese 'squatters'; this group was made up of people who had turned to subsistence agriculture during the war and their economic and legal position was now precarious. Meanwhile the numerous Chinese urban poor suffered much hardship through food shortages and inflation.

Shortly before the new constitution became effective a 'palace revolution' within the Malayan Communist Party secured the leadership for Chin Peng—a talented twenty-five-year-old who had received a British decoration for his armed resistance to the Japanese. Soon he and his party moved into the jungle to begin a campaign of violence. The authorities declared a State of Emergency as early as June 1948 but, in practical terms, their initial reaction was not as energetic as it might have been. Not until Sir Harold Briggs became Director of Operations in 1950 was a comprehensive pacification plan adopted and only when Sir Gerald Templer became both Director of Operations and High Commissioner in 1951 was this plan vigorously enforced. Its essence was the use of 40,000 British and Commonwealth troops, 70,000 police, and 250,000 part-time Home Guardsmen to isolate the six or seven thousand hard-core guerrillas. Its key feature was the resettlement of the 600,000 squatters in 500 'new villages'. Within these villages, in most of which, one may note, amenities were very good, populations could be carefully controlled. The proof of the Briggs Plan's effectiveness was a drop in the number of terrorist incidents from 2,500 in 1951 to 320 in 1953.

The Filipino People's Anti-Japanese Army (the Hukbalahap) had its roots among the debt-ridden peasantry of central Luzon. At the end of the war it suspended its campaign of guerrilla war but, having received little recognition or reward for its services, it held on to some caches of arms and kept itself in being as a veterans' association. As such it entered a Democratic Alliance and helped it contest the elections that were held on the achieving of independence in 1946. In the prevailing atmosphere of corruption the Alliance did badly and so certain Huk groups resorted to violent action against the big landlords. Guerrilla warfare was intensified after a collapse of truce talks in 1948. The campaign made progress against callous and inept security forces and early in 1950 the Huks announced the start of a general offensive that was to secure victory within two years. But that September the Ministry of Defence passed into the hands of

Ramon Magsaysay, an upright and efficient liberal. By 1953 Huk activity had declined substantially.

Ahmed Sukarno, head of the Japanese-sponsored wartime administration,[1] proclaimed Indonesia an independent republic prior to the arrival of British troops in September 1945. In the government reconstruction of that November Sukarno became President and a Socialist, Dr Sjahrir, his Prime Minister. The Dutch were reluctant to negotiate with what they regarded as an administration of traitors and by their obduracy encouraged Indonesian extremists to resist physically the landing of their troops. By the end of the year these extremists had also become involved in combat against the British.

The British withdrew at the end of 1946, an agreement having then been signed between the Dutch and the Indonesian Republic. The Republic was to contain what one may regard as the pivotal islands of Java, Sumatra and Madura and it was to be part of an Indonesian Union under the Netherlands crown. Defence, external affairs and certain financial matters were to remain in Dutch hands. But there was deadlock over the detailed constitutional arrangements and this, plus dissatisfaction over the apparent inability of the Republicans to check lawlessness within their own territory, impelled the Dutch to resume hostilities in the summer of 1947. Just before this happened Sjahrir was succeeded as Premier by the more Left Wing Socialist, Sjarifoeddin.

Sjarifoeddin was replaced by the conservative Mohammed Hatta early in 1948 and became the leader of a pro-Soviet People's Democratic Front. The Front opposed a fresh agreement negotiated through a Security Council committee which provided for a series of plebiscites to determine how each island should be related to a United States of Indonesia. Local Communists, acting apparently on their own initiative, staged a revolt at Madiun in September; three months later Dutch troops began another 'police action'. But, after further United Nations pressure, peace talks were resumed in 1949 and that December all the territory of the former Dutch East Indies except New Guinea was transferred to a federal United States of Indonesia. The following August the federal structure was replaced by a unitary one. A dominion-type relationship with the Netherlands was preserved until 1954 but its practical importance was small.

## (iii) *To Dien Bien Phu*

Early in 1945 the Japanese had induced Bao Dai, the Emperor of Annam, to declare his country independent under their protection. But when they surrendered he abdicated in favour of Ho Chi-minh—leader of the League

---

He had, of c ourse, been active as a radical nationalist ever since the 1920s.

671

for the Independence of Vietnam or, to use the abbreviated vernacular, the Vietminh. This league, which had been formed in 1941, had some 50,000 members, about a tenth of whom were avowed Communists. Part of the Vietminh had conducted a desultory guerrilla campaign during the closing stages of the war. Many American arms and advisers were dropped to support this token effort.

Whilst Chinese Nationalists marched into the North of Vietnam, British and French troops landed in the South. French troops clashed with Vietminh around Saigon that autumn and in the New Year bombarded parts of Haiphong. But in March it was agreed that 15,000 French troops would join 10,000 Vietnamese in keeping order in Tongking and that Annam and Tongking, and perhaps Cochin China, would be united within an Indo-Chinese Federation and the French Union. Soon afterwards the last of the British and Chinese contingents withdrew.

The truce was short-lived. The Vietminh were using Japanese and Chinese instructors and supplies to bring their number of trained riflemen up to 40,000. This and their acts of terrorism against rival nationalists aroused a French distrust of their intentions which a token disbandment of the Communist Party did little to assuage. For his part Ho Chi-minh was infuriated by a French High Command decision to make Cochin China, where the Vietminh were still weak, independent of Annam and Tongking. He resented also the French refusal to negotiate about the federal framework, the status of minorities and the retention of bases. Fighting flared up again in November and within a few weeks the Vietminh had gone over to a general offensive.[1]

The next three years were ones of steady Vietminh progress within the context of an ever deepening conflict. The French failure lay essentially in their inability to conjure up an alternative nationalist movement that was tough enough to withstand terrorism, flexible enough to make a tolerable settlement, and authentic enough to command general allegiance. After many months of negotiation Bao Dai was induced to return from 'the fleshpots of Hong Kong' in 1949 to take charge of a new Vietnamese state that was to be autonomous within the French Union.[2] Cochin China was included in it and it was given the right to establish its own standing army and to maintain diplomatic missions in a few specified places. How little the masses were impressed by this initiative is illustrated by the fact that only 1,200 people, many of whom were resident Europeans, bothered to vote in the Cochin China regional election of March 1949.

By then the Vietminh field forces had doubled in size despite repeated French attempts to eliminate them by means of ambitious mechanized and airborne envelopments. At first the Vietminh could only obtain extra

---

[1] The relations between Ho Chi-minh and the French until this stage had been, in fact, curiously ambivalent. Ho Chi-minh had wanted the French in Tongking because of his fear of the Chinese occupation force. The French found Ho easier to deal with than some of the conservative nationalists.

[2] Bao Dai contends that his time in Hong Kong was, in fact, one of privation!

INDO - CHINA

TONGKING

CHINESE
MAINLAND

Phong Saly
Dien Bien Phu
Nam Tha
Sam Neua
Luang Prabang
Plaine des Jarres
Xieng Khouang
N
VIETNAM
Red River
HANOI
Haiphong

GULF OF
TONGKING

HAINAN

Vinh

VIENTIANE

Udon Tham

THAILAND

L A O S
Savannakhet
Mekong
Muang Ubon
Pakse

Dong Hoi

A N N A M

Da Nang

Quang Ngai

S
VIETNAM
Gui Nhon

Ban Me Thuot

Nha Trang

BANGKOK

CAMBODIA

PNOMPENH

SAIGON

GULF OF
SIAM

COCHIN CHINA

0   50   100   150   200
MILES

arms by capturing them or smuggling them through Thailand but they acquired an important additional source with the arrival of Chinese Communist troops on the Northern frontier in 1949. A large part of the French Union army was switched North to try to seal off the border zone but was to prove too weak to do so. The political Left in France had become hostile to the Indo-China involvement and so had helped to ensure the retention of a law that precluded the dispatch of conscripts overseas. As a result the total size of the French Union army in that theatre was still only 130,000.

In 1949 the Vietminh announced a *levée en masse*. A shortage of competent staff officers and inadequate control of territory prevented the measure being immediately effective but its introduction showed nevertheless the way in which the balance of power was tilting. Most commentators believe that Vo Nguyen Giap, the Vietminh army commander, was premature in his claim that a transition from guerrilla to co-ordinated mobile warfare took place in 1947. But by the beginning of 1950 it obviously had occurred, at least in the Red River basin. In the course of that year the Vietminh received formal recognition from the Communist bloc and the following spring its own Communist Party was reformed.

Between his appointment as army commander in December 1950 and his death in January 1952, General de Lattre de Tassigny gave a display of energy and genius that seemed for a while to arrest the trend. His policy of reducing the number of scattered garrisons in order to provide men for offensive mobile columns worked so well as to make Giap admit, in a broadcast in October 1951, that reversion to simple guerrilla warfare might be necessary. But from the time de Tassigny died the French position crumbled. On November 18th, 1951, the Chinese announced the completion of a railway line to the frontier and it is thought that, within the next two years, their shipment of supplies to the rebels accelerated from 50 tons a month to 500. American aid helped the security forces expand to 325,000 by 1953—180,000 in the Expeditionary Force, about 100,000 in the Vietnamese army, and perhaps 40,000 native auxiliaries in the remote interior—but this mass was insufficient to contain 150,000 Vietminh regulars in a country in which it was often possible to infiltrate battalion perimeters that were only a mile or two in circumference. By 1953 over a third of all the villages in Vietnam were under firm Vietminh control and only half the remainder were securely in French hands. Early that year the Vietminh widened the war with a large scale invasion of Laos and so the French High Command was ordered to provide a covering force for this newly sovereign Associated State. The place the force chose to operate from was Dien Bien Phu.

# Chapter IX
## THE MIDDLE EAST AND AFRICA

### (i) *The Middle East*

HALF-WAY through 1946 Russia began to display a deep official interest in the Mediterranean. An abortive attempt to become a trustee of Libya was followed by a suggestion to Turkey that the Black Sea Powers should revise the Montreux Convention in order to restrict further the entry into the Black Sea of warships from other states and make provision for joint Turko-Soviet defence of the Dardanelles. Overtures ceased with the negative Turkish note of October 18th, but, lest pressure was renewed, an American military mission was established in Istanbul in the spring of 1947. At about the same time the United States began to station large warships in the Mediterranean continuously.

Turkey was admitted to NATO, despite Scandinavian hostility, in 1952. By this time she had begun an important experiment with constitutional democracy. The 1950 general election, which had been the first ever to take place under impartial conditions, had resulted in a heavy defeat of Atatürk's old movement—the Republican People's Party—at the hands of the Democrats, the opposition group that had been permitted to form in 1945. Adnan Menderes now became Premier and Ismet Inönü retired from the Presidency to lead the Republican opposition.

The Left Wing Tudeh Party grew strong in North-West Persia during the wartime years of Soviet occupation. Some insurgent activity occurred at the end of the war, and then in November 1945 the Democrats, as the local Tudeh supporters styled themselves, rose in force and declared Azerbaijan to be autonomous within the Persian state. Tabriz, its capital, fell to the insurgents on December 16th, after the Red Army had blocked Persian Army attempts to reinforce the provincial garrison. But the insurgent position was fatally undermined by the Soviet announcement, made five days after a Teheran protest to the Security Council on March 19th, of an early Red Army withdrawal. An agreement was soon signed that provided for the absorption of the rebel units into the national army and the gendarmerie and for a measure of Azerbaijani autonomy. Mean-

675

while some Tudeh members were brought into the Persian cabinet though they did not remain long.

Britain, as the trustee for the Palestine mandate sought to keep Jewish immigration below 2,000 a month. Her aim was to preserve a communal balance and so facilitate the emergence of a two-nation state. But, coming as it did in the wake of the Nazi pogroms, this policy was one that Zionists found intolerable. Whilst desperately overladen tramp steamers tried to run the Royal Navy's blockade of the Palestine coast, the Jewish guerrilla campaign inside the country steadily mounted in intensity. Haganah, the Jewish national army, sought to restrain the brutal fanaticism of the few thousand zealots in the Irgun Zvai Leumi and the Stern Gang but was itself responsible for many acts of violence. Terrorists killed 150 people in the course of 1947; 30 of them were Jews possessed of the spirit of compromise and 90 of them were members of the security forces. By then 100,000 British troops were acting in support of the civil power.

In the spring of 1946 an official Anglo-American study commission urged the early admission of 100,000 Jewish refugees but argued against any attempt to partition Palestine. But these recommendations, taken together, suited neither the Jewish Agency nor the Arab League and they were, in fact, disowned by the United States government that autumn. During the winter the British sounded the opinions of interested parties once again and then, in February 1947, advanced fresh proposals. The gist of these was that legal immigration should treble and that Palestine should be organized for some years into semi-autonomous zones pending agreement on a democratic constitution. After these proposals had been rejected, Britain referred the matter to the United Nations. After the General Assembly passed, in November 1947, a resolution in favour of partition, Britain disclaimed all further responsibility and indicated that she would completely withdraw by May 15th, 1948. As that day approached, Palestine slid into a state of open war.

Haganah's 10,000 riflemen and four tanks beat encircling Arab armies possessing 90,000 men and 200 tanks. Part of the explanation lies in the respite it gained from the first United Nations truce, which ran from June 11th to July 18th. Most of it lay in the apathy and poor co-ordination of the Arab contingents. Thus, four Iraqi brigades crossed the Palestine border on May 15th and rapidly reached a point only ten miles from the middle of the Israeli coastline. But there they stopped and waited and from there they fell back. The Egyptian record was, in general, little better. At the height of the fighting the Engineer Corps was pulled out of the line to build a rest house for King Farouk.

1949 witnessed the inevitable series of armistices between individual Arab states and the new state of Israel. By the beginning of that year, over 80% of the 850,000 Palestinian Arabs had fled from their homes and 750,000 Jews were in what had been Palestine as against 550,000 in 1945. In May 1950 the three leading Western powers said that they would resist any major violation of the new Arab-Israeli frontier from either side. Thus Israel was left with an area a quarter as large again as that envisaged for her in the United Nations partition plan of 1947.

The Palestine War was one of the climacterics of Arab history. The reaction against the humiliation that had been experienced was first clearly visible in the Syrian army coups of 1949. But it was Egypt—culturally and commercially the most advanced Arab state—that was to experience the biggest social upheaval. Fear of such an upheaval can be invoked to explain the behaviour of the conservative nationalist Wafd Party that returned to power in 1950. The Wafd revived demands that the British leave the Canal Zone and that Egypt be united with the Sudan. It also rejected an American suggestion that Egypt join a regional defence pact. But the new reformist brand of nationalism was not easily to be diverted from social questions by external bogies and, indeed, the post-Korean collapse of cotton prices in 1951 heightened its conviction that the Arab world would only find real strength and unity through social reform. The anti-British riots that broke out in Cairo in January 1952 developed into a random proletarian offensive against all manifestations of wealth. One of the first acts of the young officers who seized power from Farouk in July was to redistribute the land from certain large estates. Only a low rate of compensation was paid.

Middle Eastern oil production much more than doubled between 1946 and 1950. Saudi Arabia experienced the most dramatic expansion and this explains why, in 1950, she became the first state in the area to extract a 50:50 agreement out of a foreign oil company working a local concession. Such agreements generally stipulate that half the distributed profits[1] made by a company from an oilfield will be given to the state in whose territory the oilfield lies. But it was Iraq that best demonstrated how oil revenues might be purposively applied. A Development Board was set up in Baghdad in 1950 that was soon using 70% of the oil revenues on water control and other aspects of economic development.

A parliamentary commission headed by Dr Mussadiq recommended, in February 1951, that the assets of the Anglo-Iranian Oil Company—a firm in which the British government had a controlling interest—should be expropriated. For some years dissatisfaction had been growing in Persia with the Anglo-Iranian policy of limiting distributed profits. This policy had been adopted at the request of the British government in order to support endeavours to keep wage demands in Britain low. But what this meant for Persia was that they were drawing $1·5 worth of government revenue for every ton of oil produced in 1950 whereas Saudi Arabia, for example, was getting almost three times that.

A peaceful settlement seemed possible until early 1951 for by then negotiations on a 50:50 royalty agreement and on special compensation for the years of low dividends had made some progress. But there was another factor in the equation—Mussadiq and the other big landowners

[1] The profits were reckoned as being the difference between a notional (or 'posted') selling price and the local production cost.

who controlled Parliament. These men were natural xenophobes and had, in any case, a special interest in diverting the thoughts of radicals from issues like land reform. They also dearly wished to crush General Razmara, recently made Premier on the personal decision of the Shah, as he was determined to reduce corruption and to promote social reform. Against Razmara and against Anglo-Iranian, they made common cause with the Tudeh Party in 1951. The assassination of the general, the seizure of the oil assets, and the accession to the Premiership of Mussadiq occurred in quick succession. By the end of 1952 Mussadiq had formally assumed dictatorial powers. But with the oil industry at a standstill, his dictatorship was profoundly unstable.

## (ii) *Africa South of the Sahara*

Though Black Africa had felt the direct impact of World War II less than other major regions, well over one hundred thousand of its men had served in the armies of the belligerents and some had fought overseas. By this and other influences, notably the rivalry between de Gaulle and Vichy France, political development was stimulated. A new generation of radical African leaders was much in evidence at the sixth and last Pan-African Congress, which was held in Manchester in 1945. Resolutions were decisively passed in favour of colonial freedom and against exploitation by 'monopolistic' extractive industries and through discriminatory land laws. The Portuguese and Spanish territories remained apparently unaffected by the rising tide of African aspiration that this Congress symbolized but thenceforward Britain and France felt obliged to adjust their policies continually to take account of it.

Gold Coast discontent, fanned by the swollen shoot disease that ravaged the cocoa crop, erupted into violence with the Accra riots of February 1948. Late in 1949 Dr Kwame Nkrumah, a gifted orator and organizer who had imbibed a diluted Leninist philosophy during his years as a student and a teacher in the West, formed the Convention People's Party and began to call for 'positive action' to obtain immediate self-government. Soon afterwards a new constitution was brought in; this stipulated that nearly all the seats in the legislature were to be filled by two-stage elections based on adult suffrage, and that the Council of Ministers was to be, subject to imperial reserve powers, responsible to that body. After the 1951 elections Nkrumah emerged from a term in prison for breach of Emergency Regulations and became the first Gold Coast Premier.

All but ten of the 146 representatives that were on Nigeria's Central Legislative Council in 1953 had been chosen by one or other of the three regional assemblies. The legislature had, in its turn, chosen most of the members of the Central Executive. Further East, however, evolution has

678

been less rapid. Only a quarter of the Legislative Council of Uganda and only a seventh of that of Northern Rhodesia was then composed of representatives of the African community and these had, in fact, been nominated by the respective British colonial governors. The selection for the Kenya Legislative Council was exceptionally complex but it involved less than half of the fifty-two members being chosen by direct election and none of those directly elected was African. Only 3% of those on the common electoral roll of Southern Rhodesia were non-Europeans.

Hopes for the peaceful evolution of British East Africa were dimmed by the rising, in 1952, of the Mau Mau, a secret society that operated within the land-hungry Kikuyu tribe of Kenya. Within two years over 3,000 people had been killed in the fighting, mostly by the security forces. The Mau Mau dedicated itself, at oath-taking ceremonies of extreme obscenity, to the elimination of all traces of Western influence.

Until 1940 Senegal had been the only French colony in West and Equatorial Africa that sent deputies to France and was also the only one that could boast any kind of territorial assembly. But in 1946 all the colonies were authorized to elect deputies to the French National Assembly and, what was almost as important, to elect assemblies that would enjoy, among other things, considerable financial competence. But two electoral rolls were maintained everywhere except in Senegal—one for local citizens and another, with much smaller constituencies, for those from Metropolitan France. At first the local franchise was restricted but in 1951 it was extended to include most men and many women. Grand Councils, to be chosen by the territorial assemblies, were created in 1946, for West and Equatorial Africa respectively. They, too, wielded considerable financial power.

Every effort was made by France to strengthen the economic and cultural links she had forged with her African dependencies. Public investment by the metropolitan country became proportionately heavier in French West Africa, for example, than in British. Between 1946 and 1956 the European community in the former increased from 32,000 to 90,000. Many of its members had found posts as teachers, for French was the only medium of instruction used in the schools. One consequence of this was a narrow educational base. Around 7% of the total populations of the Gold Coast and West and East Nigeria were attending school in 1953; in French West Africa the proportion was but a quarter of that.

The 1946 constitution provided for the participation of France and all her colonies and protectorates in two advisory bodies—a High Council and an Assembly of the French Union. But the High Council did not meet at all until 1951 and then only French and Indo-Chinese delegations were present. The larger and more representative Assembly did start to meet at intervals in 1947 but its influence was slight. Such political pressure as 'Overseas France' did bring to bear on Paris was exercised through the deputies it elected to the National Assembly. Their number rose from

20 in 1946 to 83 in 1951. The total number of deputies was just over 600 in each year.

The Afrikaner dominated Nationalist Party was victorious in the 1948 elections in the Union of South Africa. Soon they began to sharpen and extend the pattern of white dominance and to give it theoretical backing by means of the doctrine of *Apartheid*, i.e. separating the communities, both territorially and otherwise, as far as possible, and promoting the development of all of them, under white supervision and in accordance with their respective cultures and traditions. The Suppression of Communism Act gave the government general authority to stop any 'promotion of disturbances or disorder' intended to effect 'any political, industrial, social, or economic change'. The Group Areas Act consolidated the residential segregation of Africans from Europeans and made sharper that of Asians from Europeans. One result was closer co-operation between the African National Congress and the South African Indian Congress on measures of passive resistance.

Defenders of racialism within the Union stressed that in, for example, 1952 the African money income per head in the Union was almost four times as high as that in Kenya. And they pointed out that expenditure on the education of each African child was four times the Kenyan level and eight times the Nigerian one. This was why 11% of the African population (or 41% of those of school age) were then at school. But progress in these and other material aspects always strengthens the case for gradual political and social integration. This was acknowledged in the legislative bodies of the Rhodesias and Nyasaland when they came together to form the Central African Federation in 1953. But their professed goal of inter-racial partnership was too far out of line with some contemporary realities and also too imprecise to assuage African hostility to this federation.

# Chapter X
## THE WESTERN HEMISPHERE

### (i) *American Politics Before Korea*

It is sometimes asserted that the United States went isolationist for a while after World War II. Evidence in support of this view is seen in the sudden cancellation of Lend Lease immediately after the Japanese surrender and the rapid and large reduction in the size of the American armed forces. However, reversion to isolationism would have involved a systematic disentanglement from foreign commitments and, in particular, effective dissociation from the United Nations Organization. The truth would seem to be that loyalty to UNO was the one established theme in American diplomacy during the first year of peace. How great this loyalty was is shown by the scale of the American participation in the United Nations Relief and Rehabilitation Administration. Other aspects of policy were left ill-defined precisely because of a conviction that power politics and real United Nations authority were mutually exclusive. At Fulton, Missouri, in March 1946 Winston Churchill spoke of an Iron Curtain having descended across Europe and of the Communists seeking the fruits of war though perhaps not war itself. From Secretary of State Byrnes came the comment that the United States wished to back the United Nations rather than Britain against Russia or Russia against Britain. As late as early 1947 Senator Vandenburg, by then Chairman of the Foreign Relations Committee, got the Graeco–Turkish Aid Bill amended so as to ensure that aid would cease if and when United Nations assistance rendered it superfluous.

American policy towards the Chinese remained confused right up to the time of their involvement in Korea. Fervent lip-service was being paid to the doctrine of non-interference. Meanwhile aid to the tune of one and a half billion dollars was passed to Chiang through UNRRA[1] and other agencies; among the military items were about 500 warplanes. Through this aid, political pressure was brought to bear to seek for non-military solutions, to hold elections and to promote liberals within the administration. Neither the aid nor the pressures altered the final outcome of

[1] See Chapter XXIII.

war; all that they did was to burden the Truman administration with responsibility for the melancholy course of events. Chinese Communists were enabled to depict their struggle in simple patriotic terms; American Republicans became free to blame the Democrats for Chiang's eviction. Intellectual integrity and a deep regard for George Marshall inhibited Arthur Vandenburg from making his comments too caustic but even he argued that Russia's being invited to declare war .on Japan was a root cause of the disaster. Other Republicans deplored, then and subsequently, the phasing out of American aid in 1948 and 1949.

By the end of 1946 American policy in Europe was hardening into one of Communist containment. The administration decided that the deepening division of Europe made further support for UNRRA futile. On September 6th, Mr Byrnes announced in Stuttgart that American troops would stay in Germany as long as they were required. Adverse official and Congressional comment about developments in Eastern Europe became progressively more frequent. The United States Air Force and the Royal Air Force began some joint planning. Then, in February 1947, President Truman enunciated with reference to Greece and Turkey the doctrine that 'totalitarian *régimes* imposed on free peoples by direct or indirect aggression' were a threat to general peace. Henceforward all local difficulties bar Palestine were seen as aspects of the Russian problem.

The most remarkable early manifestation of the heavier commitment to Europe was, of course, the Marshall Plan. Though Senator Taft fiercely contended that 'People do not completely collapse, they go on living anyway', the Economic Co-operation Administration Bill experienced little modification as it passed the Senate by 69 votes to 17 and the House by 329 votes to 74. Written into the Act was an expectation of European economic integration and this objective was, indeed, near to the heart of Paul Hoffman—the first ECA administrator. Early in 1947 Congress, encouraged by such Republican leaders as Arthur Vandenberg, Thomas Dewey, and John Foster Dulles, as well as by their Democratic counterparts, passed resolutions in favour of European federalism. Two years later Allen Dulles, J. W. Fulbright and others sponsored a Committee for a United Europe which soon raised a lot of money to send to the European Movement. Ferocious Congressional criticism of Britain's disinclination to join the Schuman Plan was further proof of the way in which European unity had become an American interest. By then Dean Acheson and Averell Harriman were advancing what has since become known as the 'twin pillars' concept of an Atlantic Community based on a United Europe and on North America.

Truman's moderately radical economic philosophy led him into frequent collisions with Congress. As early as September 1945 Republicans and Southern Democrats combined to wreck his 22–point domestic reconstruction programme and the following year they made him remove wartime price controls from food. At the mid-term elections the Republicans gained full control of Congress and were thus enabled to weaken rent control and to reduce taxes further. Their contention was that inflation occurred because production lagged badly behind a soaring post-war demand. Production was, they claimed, held back by price controls and by high and very progressive taxation which combined to discourage honest businessmen and to sustain a buoyant black market. Mr Truman replied that the inflation would have got entirely out of hand without the remaining controls and without his having achieved, despite a distinct lack of co-operation from the legislature, some modest budget surpluses. His State of the Union messages regularly included demands for more adequate price and rent controls and for higher company taxation, and during his 1948 Presidential campaign he lambasted the retiring Eightieth Congress for its inertia which was an outcome, he said, of its subservience to lobbyists.

The first half of 1946 witnessed some large and bitter wage strikes and in May a desperate President sought the provision of emergency powers to issue injunctions for the deferment of strikes, to withhold seniority rights from strikers and to draft into the armed forces men who remained on strike in establishments the army took over. A panicky House of Representatives passed the relevant Bill by 306 votes to 13 but, led by Vandenberg and Taft, the Senators pruned it severely. This gave the President an opportunity to veto the final version on the grounds of its ineffectiveness. For this he was more than grateful, for his original proposal had aroused the bitter opposition of organized labour.

During the next twelve months little strike action occurred because production was rising fast enough for most employers to concede freely large wage increases. Yet 1947 was the year that Congress chose in which to pass the Taft–Hartley Act. Thenceforward between 60 and 140 days notice were required of any strike or lock-out, and demarcation and sympathy strikes were banned along with strikes by federal employees. Other provisions included were to the effect that unions could not use their funds politically and that they had to file affidavits stating that all their officials were non-Communist. The House overrode the Presidential veto by 331 to 83 and the Senate by 68 to 25.

1947 had been a more comfortable year for Harry Truman than 1946 but he remained about the only American who thought he would secure re-election. In the autumn of 1946 he had been obliged to dismiss Henry Wallace, his Secretary of Commerce, after a speech in which he said that collaboration with the USSR should be the basic theme of United States foreign policy. In 1948 Wallace took over a million votes from Truman as leader of a new Progressive Party that stood against conscription and the Marshall Plan and for studied indifference to the affairs of Eastern Europe. Another renegade Democrat—Governor Thurmond of South Carolina—deprived Truman of a further million votes by campaigning on a State's Rights ticket. The President had, of course, become closely identified with the cause of Negro civil rights. He had tried to preserve in some form the wartime Fair Employment Practices Committee and, against considerable opposition, especially from the navy, had enforced integration within the armed forces.

Good strategy and an increasingly strong personality enabled Truman to lead the Democrats to victory in the Congressional as well as the Presidential elections. His own chief opponent, Thomas Dewey, tried to keep election fever low by speaking in vague and general terms about little in particular. Meanwhile, Truman himself heavily punctuated a dramatic railway tour with 'whistle stop' speeches that were informal in style and aggressive in substance and delivery. Immediately after the respective party conventions he had recalled Congress so that he could challenge them to pass several moderate reform measures. Out of their failure to do so he gleaned a lot of ammunition. He swept the Middle West by condemning Republican reluctance to accept rigid farm price supports. He consolidated his hold on the white industrial trade unionists by calling for Taft-Hartley repeal. He mobilized a good Negro vote by campaigning for civil rights. He drew dividends throughout the country from the international isolationism of the Republican Right. Dewey was beaten by two million votes.

During this time the campaign against subversion was getting under way. In 1947 a government Loyalty Board was set up to scrutinize Federal civil servants. In 1949 heavy fines and longish terms of imprisonment were imposed on certain Communist leaders following their conviction on charges of plotting to overthrow the government by force; most of the evidence against them had come from Communist apostates and from FBI agents who had penetrated Leftist cells. There was in that same year one episode which illustrated the danger latent in any purification drive. Senator Hickenlooper of Iowa, a strident Right Winger, levelled charges of negligence, though not disloyalty, against David Lilienthal, the then Chairman of the Atomic Energy Committee and a former head of the Tennessee Valley Authority—the most dramatic of the New Deal projects. The Republicans on the Joint Committee on Atomic Energy rallied behind Hickenlooper but were outvoted. The able and dedicated Lilienthal nevertheless resigned.

## (ii) *The United States during the Korean War*

The outbreak of the Korean War coincided approximately with Senator Vandenburg's withdrawal from public life on grounds of health. The juxtaposition gave a unique opportunity to what may be called the Pacific Firsters within the Republican Party. Many of these men, such as, for example, ex-President Hoover, and Senators Dirksen, Knowland and Taft, came from the Middle West or the Pacific Coast and they tended to resent what they saw as the control of their party and country by the Ivy League and Wall Street. Their natural conservatism found its current expression not so much in domestic 'bread-and-butter' issues as in international and ideological ones. They placed more emphasis than the Democrats and the Eastern Republicans on the importance of the Pacific and on the deterrent and punitive effect of air and seapower; they placed less on the need to keep wars limited and on the value of multilateral alliances and of the commitment of American ground troops to Europe. Early in 1951 nearly a quarter of the Senate voted against the dispatch of four American army divisions to Germany. This may be taken as some rough measure of the relative strength of the 'Pacific First' bloc.

Its hero was, of course, General MacArthur. Here was a more than life-size personality whose innate vanity, parochialism and perfectionism had been accentuated by nearly ten years of supreme authority in war and peace. No sooner had he taken up his appointment as United Nations Commander in Korea than he was quarrelling with his own government over Formosa. Early in 1950 the Democratic administration had overridden military advice and Republican protests and firmly dissociated itself from Chiang Kai-shek's future career. As late as September the President sought to preserve the letter, if not the spirit, of that policy by insisting that the use of the Seventh Fleet to separate the combatants in the Formosa Straits in no way implied long term support for the Nationalists. But by that time MacArthur had come back from Taipeh full of praise of the 'indomitable' Chiang and had publicly committed himself to the view that he should be regarded as a great military asset.

Talks between the President and the General at Wake Island in October 1950 were, apparently, quite harmonious, but MacArthur's haughty demeanour, both during and after them, left few grounds for expecting that this harmony would be preserved. The final crisis broke as the United Nations forces fell back in the spring of 1951. MacArthur began openly to question the wisdom of keeping the war limited even if his troops proved able to stay in Korea and in March he sent a letter along these lines to Joseph Martin—then the Republican Minority Leader in the House of Representatives. Martin read out this letter on the floor of the House and within a few days MacArthur was sacked. He flew quickly home and, on a Republican initiative, was invited to address a joint session of Congress. This he did with so fine a blend of dignity and emotion that he came across to Herbert Hoover, for example, as the 'reincarnation of St Paul'. The following day he went to New York to be welcomed by a crowd nearly twice as large as that which had greeted Eisenhower in 1945 and a ticker tape barrage nearly twice as heavy as the one Lindberg attracted in 1927. But during the summer feelings subsided as armistice talks began in Korea and as a Senate enquiry demonstrated how difficult it had become to evolve any satisfactory strategy for the conduct of war. One particular point that the enquiry established was that the United States Air Force had not yet the strength to maintain an adequate deterrent posture against

Russia and, at the same time, carry out the bombardment of China advocated, at least on occasions, by MacArthur.

One aspect of the intensification of the Cold War in the Far East that aroused little controversy within the United States was the Japanese Peace Treaty, which was signed by 48 nations in San Francisco in September 1951. This treaty, which restored Japan's independence whilst formally depriving her of all imperial possessions, was largely the product of the energy and skill of a Republican special adviser to the State Department —John Foster Dulles. By agreeing not to invite the Chinese Nationalists to the treaty conference, he persuaded Britain to join the United States in the formulation of treaty proposals. Australia and New Zealand were induced to sign the treaty by the promise of a mutual security pact.

Espionage and subversion—the internal Cold War threat—became major issues in 1950 with the trials of the Rosenbergs and of Alger Hiss and Senator Joseph McCarthy's accusations against the State Department. Julius and Ethel Rosenberg were sentenced to death in March 1951 for sending to the USSR, in 1945, details of the first atomic bomb. Several appeals followed but they were executed in June 1953. There was much genuine unease about the severity of the sentence. There was also an international Communist propaganda blitz that was designed, among other things, to depict the whole trial as an attempt to frame two Jews. As the blitz was generated so was a great wave of anti-Semitism within the Soviet bloc.

Alger Hiss had been a prominent New Deal intellectual and a member of the State Department team at Yalta. In 1948 he was mentioned to the House Un-American Activities Committee as having trafficked in official documents whilst a clandestine member of the Communist Party before the War. Spurred on by an energetic young Congressman called Richard Nixon, the Committee followed this point up. Eventually Hiss was indicted for perjury and, in January 1950, was found guilty on a retrial. As soon as the verdict was announced, Dean Acheson, who earlier had testified to the integrity of Hiss, announced that he would stand by him. He thereby drew much fire towards himself in the bitter public debate that followed.

But it was Joseph McCarthy who became the centre of the biggest controversy. This Senator had had an indifferent political career up to 1950 and, in fact, in 1949 had been censured by the Board of Bar Commissioners for unprofessional conduct. Thus he had come to be desperately in need of a distinctive and favourable image, and so to meet it he conjured up the issue of Communists in the State Department. He learnt of a letter that the then Secretary of State Byrnes had written in July 1946 in which he said that a screening committee had recommended against the permanent employment of 284 State Department officials and that 79 of these had already been dismissed. This vague and obsolete piece of information was the sole basis for the claim made on February 9th that he had a list of 205 Communists in the State Department. On the 10th he said he had the names of 57 Communist card holders in the State Department—the figure 57 being related, apparently, to a House Appropriations Committee report of 1948. Shortly afterwards he presented orally to the Senate a list of 81 State Department officials whom he personally regarded as Communists. This presentation was sublime rubbish. Some of the 'cases' were duplicates; not all were still in the Federal service; many were perfectly loyal. Small wonder that he was branded by the President six weeks later as the Kremlin's greatest asset.

In July the Senate accepted the report of the Tydings sub-committee which dismissed McCarthy's accusations as 'the most nefarious campaign of half-truth and untruth in the history of the Republic'. How then did McCarthy survive politically as long as he did? Much of the explanation lies in the fact that the public, the press, and the rank and file of Congress had been numbed and confused by the Hiss affair and by the state of the Cold War. In this new atmosphere the Republican leadership came reluctantly to acknowledge that McCarthy might have electoral value. Dramatic evidence of this was seen in the support he gave to the candidate who unexpectedly defeated Senator Tydings in the November elections.

Many of the 134 investigations Congress carried out in 1951 were concerned with corruption within the public service; one such probe led to the dismissal of an Assistant Attorney-General. Most of the blame for this state of affairs fell on the ruling Democrats and 'Communism and Corruption' became a standard taunt in the 1952 election. Richard Nixon, now Republican candidate for the Vice-Presidency, plugged away steadily at the 'scandal a day' administration. One major attempt was made to query his own use of funds but this he beat down with devastating aplomb.

Taft hoped to win the Republican nomination through his control of the party machine, but he found that he could not withstand the ground-swell that rose in support of Dwight D. Eisenhower—a man in whom military distinction and limitless charm were combined with an endearing awkwardness where politics were concerned. Eisenhower's public career had been made in Europe, so he was, as one might say, an Easterner by adoption. But his platform was designed to command the general approval of all Republican activists. Federal expenditure was to be cut and federal planning powers curtailed. The South Korean army was to be expanded and the Soviet satellites were to be liberated by methods short of war. A pledge he made late in the campaign to go to Korea if elected received massive and highly professional publicity.

The war-weary electorate were attracted by the hope of new and simple initiatives in foreign policy. They tended to be repelled by Democrat pride in a domestic prosperity that had risen concurrently with the casualty totals in Korea. The intellectual lucidity of Adlai Stevenson, the Democrat's Presidential nominee, was too moderate and too remote to suit the public mood. Also, Stevenson made the blunder of trying partly to dissociate himself from the Truman *régime* in Washington. This proved to be a fiercely partisan campaign in which the premiums on solidarity were high. In the event, the Republicans got control of the executive and obtained a slender majority in Congress.

The new administration quickly scrapped most of the price and allocation controls that still survived from those imposed at the start of the Korean War. A bold new drive for peace in Korea was soon initiated. Meanwhile, the naval restraints on Nationalist operations against the Chinese mainland were removed. Other policy changes were more subtle. Eisenhower's first Cabinet was a middle-of-the-road one and only included one supporter of Senator Taft. The Senator himself became Senate Majority Leader but he had by then only a few months to live.


## (iii) *Latin America*


1948 was a year of counter-revolution in several of the Latin American republics. The socialist Democratic Action party had come to power in Venezuela in 1945 with the aid of a group of revolutionary young officers. Now it was to be deposed in a military counter-coup. The Chilean Communist Party was outlawed as a sequel to its involvement in the coal miners' strike of the previous autumn. Meanwhile, a military junta seized power in Peru and suppressed not only the Communists but also the *Alianza Popular Revolucionar Americana* party, which had gained a majority in the 1945 election through its demands for land reform and Indian advancement.

A trend to conservatism was thus begun. Getulio Vargas had abandoned his dictatorship in Brazil in 1945 to permit a return to democracy; in 1950 the Brazilian people, weary of price inflation and political confusion, voted him back to the Presidency. Between 1948 and the coup of 1953 Colombia had to endure an official Right Wing terror and the guerrilla resistance to it. Bolivia provided the only conspicuous example of the reverse process at work. The radical *Movimiento Nacional Revolucionar* party seized power again in 1952 and forthwith nationalized the tin-mines, a sector of the economy long characterized by the severe exploitation of a predominantly Indian labour force.

Colonel Perón retained throughout this period the hold he had obtained on Argentina in the 1946 elections. His rule, which was based on the political and industrial organization of the urban working class, soon became highly dictatorial. The courts and the press were ruthlessly controlled and a network of informers was set to discipline the public. Emphasis was placed on national progress through urban expansion, military modernization, and the use of the wartime reserves of foreign currency to purchase foreign assets. One estimate is that agricultural and pastoral real output fell by 50% between 1946 and 1952.

The United States continued to display, through diplomatic action and economic and military aid, the active interest in hemispheric defence she had developed during the war years; this resulted in the Inter-American Treaty of Reciprocal Assistance being signed in Rio in 1947 and in the Organization of American States being established at Bogotá in 1948. So where, as in Guatemala, established commercial interest reinforced considerations of grand strategy she was acutely sensitive to any indigenous Leftist tendencies. From 1944 Guatemala had been ruled by President Arévalo, a vague and indecisive radical, whose hegemony had been punctuated by a score of revolts. But in 1950 he was displaced by the more militant Colonel Arbenz. Soon Communist influence inside the government and the labour movement increased sharply, and in 1953 a quarter of a million acres of land reserved by the United Fruit Company—an American concern—were confiscated. So the Caribbean was brought to the brink of a major Cold War conflict.

## Chapter XI
## KOREA

### (i) *The Pre-Invasion Years*

BEFORE and during World War II Korean exiles kept a provisional government going in Nationalist China, whilst inside the country a resistance movement was maintained. Whereas the provisional government was predominantly Right Wing the internal resistance was under Left Wing control. On August 10th, 1945, in accordance with the Potsdam Agreements, Soviet troops began to move down to the latitude of 38[1] N. Meanwhile the local Left Wing militants proclaimed the establishment of a People's Republic in Korea and the Russians recognized this as a caretaker *régime* within their zone of occupation. Behind the network of provisional people's committees stood, in addition to the Red Army, 100,000 Korean militiamen who had been equipped with light arms taken from the Japanese. Above them operated the People's Interim Committee which was run by 35-year-old Kim Il Sung. Like several of his principal colleagues Kim had spent the war in Russia and he returned as a Red Army major. There were, in addition, some North Korean Communists who had spent the war with the Chinese in Yenan.

During 1946 about half of North Korea's 5,000,000 acres of farmland were given to some 750,000 former tenant families. The land in question had been confiscated from various sources. All ex-enemy holdings were seized as were those of 'traitors' and idle rentiers. No landowning family and no religious foundation was allowed to keep above twelve acres. Though this redistribution was accompanied by the imposition of a 25% tax on produce and by a heavy compulsory levy for collective purchases of equipment and fertilizers, it must have been most welcome to the peasant masses. Few assets of any other kind were nationalized apart from some previously held by alleged collaborationists and by Japanese commercial interests.

That summer all pro-Marxist elements were fused into a Korean

---

[1] To be quite precise, the decision that the boundary should exactly coincide with the 38th Parallel was taken by the US government on August 15th.

National Democratic Front ready for the local elections in November. By the use of its propaganda monopoly, plus such direct coercive techniques as ration manipulation and land deed revocation, the KNDF got 99·6% of the electorate to the polls and collected 97% of their votes for itself. The new committees thus formed elected a convention which, after ritualistic confirmation of the 1946 reforms, transmuted itself, in February 1947, into a People's Assembly. Kim Il Sung headed the new cabinet, thus confirming the ascendancy of the 'Muscovite' group over the 'Yenan' group.

Early in 1948 the People's Militia was reorganized as a field army. The following September Kim Il Sung announced the creation of the Korean Democratic People's Republic. At the end of the year Moscow claimed that the Red Army had been entirely withdrawn. But it was perhaps significant that its former commander had stayed behind to become the first Soviet Ambassador.

The American field force under Lieutenant-General Hodge began disembarkation in South Korea on September 9th, 1945. The General set aside the pretentious People's Republic and established direct military rule. An initial decision to keep on for a while the 70,000 Japanese administrators was quickly reversed in response to a surge of protest. Within one year Koreans had started to displace Americans from executive posts and within two only 3,000 United States citizens remained in civil administration. However, all important orders still required American countersignatures.

Partition on the 38th Parallel especially handicapped the South. South Korea comprised only 43% of the area but in it lived, in 1945, 64% of the 25,000,000 Koreans. By 1950 it held another 4,000,000 people—half of them refugees from the North. Over half the electric power had come from the North, but manufacturing was concentrated in the South. In the absence of power sources, export markets and Japanese managers, industrial output slumped by 80%.

These social and economic circumstances were not conducive to the growth of constitutional democracy. They favoured rather a migration to political extremes. Reunification was another issue that tended to polarize attitudes. Everybody wanted it but only on their own terms. In December Byrnes and Molotov agreed upon the establishment of a US–Soviet Joint Commission that would seek to create a provisional administration and to work out a trusteeship system to last for a transitional five years. By this act they inadvertently knocked some shape into the conservative wing of South Korean politics. An Anti-trusteeship Committee was formed which gave some order and purpose to what had been pure chaos.

Sixty-nine year old Synghman Rhee started now to emerge as the dominant Rightist. Twenty-five years in exile taken up with tireless and often lonely struggle had made this champion of Korean aspirations far better known to Americans than any of his fellows. Not unnaturally, then, he was made Chairman of the Representative Democratic Council set up to advise the authorities in 1946. But this Council was not a success. The

People's Republic could not be asked to participate because in certain outlying districts it was still trying to behave as if it were the government. Yet several reliable Western journalists were at that time reporting that it was the 'Republic' that enjoyed majority support. Certain leading liberals were invited to join the Council but declined. Therefore, that body became simply a focus for overt Right Wing propaganda against the Joint Commission. The Soviet representatives on the Joint Commission were not willing to interview any Koreans who were prepared to say openly that trusteeship was a bad thing. For their part the radical Right of South Korea were happy to instigate riots in order to sabotage Commission meetings in Seoul. On May 8th, 1946, the Commission adjourned *sine die*. So far nothing had been accomplished.

But the spirit of moderation was not yet dead in South Korea. That October a Coalition Committee was set up under the joint chairmanship of Kimm Kiusic, a leading conservative, and Lynh Woonhyung—a former head of the People's Republic. The Committee drew up a programme for land reform and other measures, and it was informally consulted by the authorities on a number of current problems. But the extreme Left staged strikes and violent riots to coincide with its deliberations. In Taegu alone 50 civilians and as many police were killed. By the year's end 500 people had been convicted for insurrectionary activity. A few were eventually executed.

Meanwhile half of an Interim Legislative Assembly was being elected in four stages. The other half was to be appointed by the military commander. Indirect elections, as was concurrently being demonstrated North of the border, were especially susceptible to manipulation. In some localities only the opinion of village headmen was sought. In many the 30,000 strong armed police force was used for intimidation; over half its officers had served the Japanese. Naïve public acceptance of lavish conservative land reform promises also helps explain why only two Leftist candidates were successful. To help correct this imbalance General Hodge nominated men of the moderate Left for over half of the 45 non-elective seats. But the end product was not a chamber capable of reasoned and constructive deliberation. Appeals from General Hodge to leave matters like trusteeship alone and concentrate on immediate practical issues were ignored. The Right were hellbent on early autonomy for South Korea and in December 1946 the ever obstinate Synghman Rhee had gone to Washington to lobby for this. His action compelled General Hodge to deny publicly that such autonomy was now a goal of United States policy.

In June 1947 a revived Joint Commission invited representative groups from both Koreas to apply to be consulted on reunification. Because of double counting the aggregate paper strength of those who did so from the South was 38,000,000 adults and of those from the North 14,000,000. The USSR then demanded that 75% of the 400 South Korean groups be ignored. They apparently sought to eliminate Right Wing opinion and also to secure for North Korea parity of bargaining power.

Now the Americans despaired of the Joint Commission and so lifted the ban on demonstrations against its continued existence. This extra degree of freedom was used to initiate a 'White Terror'. Back in March nearly 3,000 arrests had been made after an abortive General Strike. Thenceforward pretexts were deemed irrelevant. Lynh Woonhyung was murdered in July within easy view of a Seoul police box. A police officer was detailed to assassinate Chang Duksoo—head of a pro-Joint Commission faction inside the conservative Korean Independence Party. He did so on December 2nd. American hopes that a new middle-of-the-road Democratic Independence Party would become a stabilizing force were not fulfilled. In the prevailing atmosphere of hate moderate men looked small.

That November the UN General Assembly passed by 43 votes to nil an American resolution calling for a Temporary Commission on Korea to supervise elections for a national assembly. The Soviet Union still argued that Korean opinion should be informally sampled first and, alternatively, that all foreign troops should withdraw and leave the Koreans somehow to resolve things for themselves. The UN Temporary Commission was never allowed into North Korea and the Ukrainian SSR declined to fill the place it had been allotted on it. The members eventually came from Australia, Canada, China, El Salvador, France, India, the Philippines and Syria.

Early in 1948 the Interim Committee of the General Assembly recommended that elections soon be held in South Korea alone. Left Wing groups were hostile to the idea and so was the Korean Independence Party, but, by a small majority, the Temporary Commission decided to go ahead. Despite a boycott by leaders of the Left and Centre, 72% of all adults voted and UNTCOK was able to describe the ballot as a valid expression of the public will. Synghman Rhee's Society for the Rapid Realization of Independence won 55 of the 198 assembly seats and so Rhee became temporary chairman and, as such, free to appoint the committee that was to draft the new constitution. Strong executive powers were vested in the President under this constitution and he could readily strengthen them himself by order and decree. The new Republic of Korea, under President Rhee, hurried into existence on August 15th.

The first months were inauspicious. The cabinet chosen virtually consisted of the pure milk of reaction. General Lee, who had organized a militant anti-Communist movement of 1,000,000 youth, was made Prime Minister and Minister of Defence. The Minister of Education was a graduate of the Nazi philosophy school at Mannheim. The Foreign Minister was Chang Taik Sang—a former head of Seoul police—but soon he fell victim to Rhee's fear of able subordinates. Another early resignation was that of the sole progressive—the Minister of Agriculture. He had been too eager to introduce general land reform as a follow-on to the redistribution of 700,000 ex-Japanese acres carried out in March 1948. Such an act was passed in 1949 but only because Assembly back-benchers heavily overrode two Presidential vetoes.

In October 1948 a large rebellion broke out in the Yosu district. Twenty thousand people were convicted and many executed in the course of its suppression. The winter brought many more arrests, a political purge of schoolteachers, and the closure of seven newspapers for 'agitating the public mind'. An invasion scare was manufactured to justify all this. On June 26th, 1949, Kim Koo was murdered. He was head of the Korean Independence Party and an old rival of Rhee's from the days of exile. United States pressure compelled Rhee to hold the elections due in May 1950. As a result, his support in the Assembly fell from 56 to 12.

Back in 1947 General MacArthur and the Pentagon had discounted the strategic importance of Korea. During 1949 the US garrison of two divisions was completely withdrawn. Just before independence the creation of a 50,000–man ROK army began but it never received from the United States any tanks or effective anti-tank weapons. This was because Rhee and his colleagues continually speculated in public about a liberation of the 'lost territories'. Then, as subsequently, they justified their pretensions by claiming that in December 1948 the UN had acknowledged them to be the lawful government throughout Korea. All the General Assembly resolution had said, however, was that the Republic had been legitimately established in South Korea'

Guerrilla activity died down but slowly during 1949; border clashes, sparked off mainly by North Koreans, grew more severe and frequent. Then, on January 12th, 1950, Dean Acheson publicly excluded Korea and Formosa from the American defence perimeter and said that they must rely upon themselves and upon the UN. Repatriation of Korean volunteers in the Chinese Liberation Army began within a few weeks. A fifth Korean infantry division was activated on March 1st and a sixth on April 4th. Meanwhile the crack Chinese 4th Field Army returned from the South to its home bases in Manchuria. In March Radio Pyongyang announced a voluntary saving scheme for arms procurement. By June its broadcasts were full of new reunification proposals. On the 19th of that month the Republic of Korea warned the Security Council of a build-up on its border. Nobody took much notice. American intelligence was satisfied that North Korea intended no invasion that summer.

## (ii) *The Year of Mobile War*

Communist spokesmen have always blamed South Korea for the heavy fighting that broke out along the 38th Parallel at dawn on June 25th. But their attribution of guilt cannot be reconciled with several of the established facts. Some of the earliest clashes occurred in the Western sector that had, from the South Korean standpoint, highly inconvenient geography. Two hours after daybreak amphibious assault troops landed quite deep in South Korea. Right at the start the Communists committed well over 100 T–34 tanks and 150 Yak and Ilyushin warplanes and to all these Russian-built machines their opponents had no antidotes. Both sides could muster about 100,000 soldiers but the North's advantage in weaponry was supreme.

Twenty-nine hours after aggression commenced the Security Council asked all UN members to act to secure a cease-fire and the restoration of conquered territory. Late on June 27th (Eastern Standard Time) it resolved that the UN should furnish the Republic of Korea enough armed assistance to check the aggression. Earlier that day President Truman had ordered United States planes and ships to screen Formosa and to bombard Communist forces to defend Pusan. On the 29th he authorized air and naval operations North of the parallel and the commitment of ground troops South of it. Disembarkation of the 24th Infantry Division began the following day and within a week this formation had seen action. Four thousand of its men ferociously defended Taejon throughout the third week of July and so enabled other United Nations forces to form the Pusan box'—a rectangular defence zone that was delimited in part by the Naktong river and which had Waegwan as its north-western extremity. At this stage the conquest of South Korea was still a distinct possibility. A bit more dash might have taken a Communist column advancing along the South coast through to Pusan before the 'box' was consolidated. Throughout August and early September the United Nations Command, in which were included the remaining South Korean divisions, sustained a desperate mobile defence of the 'box'. But United Nations air superiority was now absolute and with each day UN ground strength grew. Five hundred tanks arrived in August and the number of American soldiers committed rose from 45,000 to 65,000. Meanwhile, the first British troops appeared. By September 8th Pusan was secure.

The liberation of South Korea began a week later with the Inchon amphibious landing. General MacArthur, then the Supreme Commander, took what he spoke of as a 5,000 to 1 chance when, against all professional advice, he dispatched the 10th Corps across the forty-foot tides, extensive mudflats and strong seawalls of that port. But the gamble came off and twelve days later it stood triumphant among the bloodied remains of Seoul. Outflanked and under heavy pressure from the 8th Army inside the 'box' the North Korean army disintegrated. Within six weeks the prisoner of war total had reached 135,000 and 240 T-34s had been found abandoned. Never again did that army fight at more than corps strength.

Whilst the reoccupation of Seoul was in progress Communist China started to utter grim warnings. The Chairman of the World Peace Salvation Society told a youth rally held in Peking on the 24th that practical help should be given to 'the Korean people', and the next day the Chief of Staff told the Indian Ambassador, K. M. Pannikar, that despite the atomic bomb the Chinese would resist an advance to the Yalu. When South Korean troops crossed the border on October 1st 'spontaneous' demonstrations broke out in China, and Chou En-lai told Pannikar afterwards that there would be war if Americans did likewise. Six days later 1st Cavalry crossed and other units soon followed. Tenth Corps went ashore at Wonsan on the 25th after a tiny minesweeping flotilla had slaved for a fortnight to clear some of the 3,000 sea-mines laid there that August under Soviet supervision. Ten days previously Chinese 'volunteers' had started to swarm into Korea.

Encouraged by Central Intelligence Agency and other advice that the Chinese would not intervene, MacArthur was pressing North to the Yalu which he regarded as easily the most tenable defensive line within reach. Political and military leaders in Washington and in London were in very general agreement that an advance to the 'waist' of North Korea would improve the opportunities for Korean reunification, but few viewed with relish the idea of total occupation. However, no firm restraints were placed on the Supreme Commander. Late in October the 6th Korean Division was driven back by the Chinese just after one of its platoons had reached the Yalu. At that stage China had dispatched 150,000 troops across the river—three times as many as UN intelligence thought.

Steadily the United Nations army over-extended itself. As 10th Corps moved North on an impossibly wide front it retained practically no physical or wireless contact with the 8th Army to its left. The morale and hence the efficiency of poorly clad troops fell as they were struck by winter winds of unexpected bitterness. Then on the 26th of November the Chinese People's Volunteers tore a huge gap in the UN centre with a savage onslaught against the 2nd Korean corps. Two days later the US 25th Infantry Division and the Turkish brigade were ambushed whilst withdrawing down a long defile. They were hammered mercilessly. Over on the East coast the 1st Marine Division began the heroic fighting withdrawal from the Chongjin that led to the smooth seaborne evacuation from Hungnam of the 1st Marines and of the other 10th Corps elements.

Ruthless disengagement averted immediate disaster but at every level from New York to North Korea United Nations morale collapsed. That the Chinese military shared the view of their American counterparts that evacuation of the whole peninsula might well become inevitable, was shown by Chou En-lai's scornful rejection, on December 22nd, of a General Assembly cease fire proposal. That such a deduction was unwarranted was soon shown by General Ridgway who, a few days later, assumed command of an 8th Army that henceforward included 10th Corps. He prepared the army for the full exploitation of its superior firepower on the comparatively compact front that it was establishing through Osan and Wonju. In March the United Nations retrieved Seoul and held it against renewed onslaught in April and early May. The United Nations counter-offensive that followed then threw the Chinese into some confusion and 17,000 prisoners were taken. Pyongyang was seized but not retained because the aim now was to create a situation conducive to bargaining. After Lester Pearson and Dean Acheson had publicly indicated

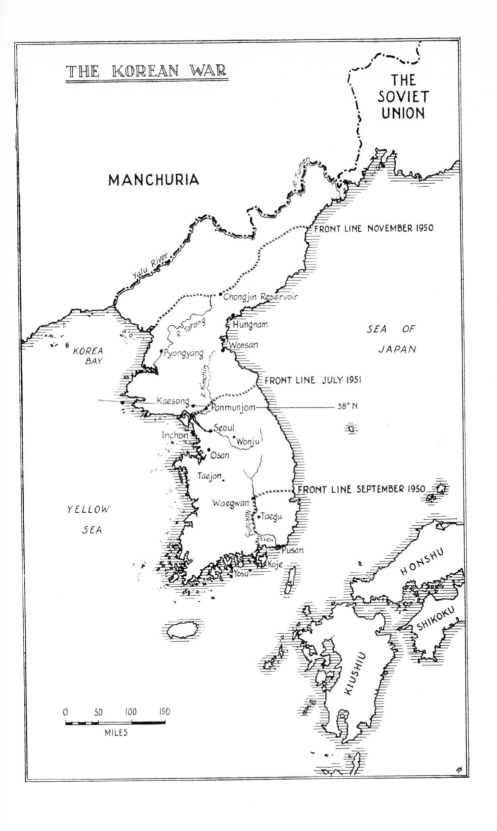

THE KOREAN WAR

THE SOVIET UNION

MANCHURIA

R. Tumen

FRONT LINE NOVEMBER 1950

Yalu River

Chongjin Reservoir

R. Tatong

Hungnam

Wonsan

SEA OF JAPAN

KOREA BAY

Pyongyang

R. Kimchin

FRONT LINE JULY 1951

Kaesong

Panmunjom

38° N

Seoul

Inchon

Wonju

Osan

Taejon

FRONT LINE SEPTEMBER 1950

Waegwan

YELLOW

Naktong River

Taegu

SEA

Pusan

Koje

HONSHU

Yosu

SHIKOKU

KIUSHIU

0    50   100   150

MILES

that an outright military verdict was no longer sought, cautious informal overtures were made in New York. Eventually both Malik and Gromyko stated that a cease-fire was feasible and so in a broadcast on June 30th General Ridgway[1] made a formal proposal. Eight days later military negotiations began.


## (iii) *The Long Haul to Peace*


Negotiations dragged on, first at Kaesong and then at Panmunjom, for a full two years. During this time the front line altered little. Both sides took swift advantage of the comparative lull to construct fortifications in depth. By Christmas the Communists had created a defence zone fourteen miles deep that made them militarily much more secure than ever they had been in June. Battles of prestige, such as the bitter one for Pork Chop Hill shortly before the armistice, sometimes grew to considerable proportions but most actions were confined to company or battalion level. Before talks began the Communists suffered some 1,200,000 battle casualties, the South Koreans 170,000 and other UN contingents 85,000. For the last two years the respective figures were 450,000 and 100,000 and 70,000. By 1953 1,200,000 troops were in Korea with the Communist field army and 720,000 with the United Nations Command.

The United Nations air and naval offensive continued throughout the war. Naval task forces blocked coastal supply routes, supplied guerrillas, and evacuated refugees. The air effort was at first directed chiefly towards effecting the complete isolation of the enemy front line. When it became clear that the ability of fighter bombers to cut transport links was being seriously reduced by anti-aircraft fire and by mass human porterage the emphasis was switched to general economic targets. Attacks on irrigation dams commenced in the autumn of 1952 and were renewed at the peak of the rice-growing season the following May. Soviet-built Manchurian based MIG-15 jet fighters tried to prevent raids on targets near the Yalu but much superior electronic equipment helped the F-86 *Sabres* to secure a 13 to 1 advantage in dogfights with the MIGs. All in all some 3,000 planes were lost by each side in the course of the war; many of those from the UN side fell to small arms fire.

Why did the Communists not speedily conclude an armistice rather than endure constant attrition? Part of the explanation can probably be found in their resentment at the United Nations success in preserving South Korea. A wish to use external tension to promote cohesion of the new China may have been another influence. More concrete ones were the

[1] He had by then succeeded General MacArthur as the United Nations Commander-in-Chief in Korea and the United States Commander-in-Chief in the Far East. See p. 685.

major differences of principle and interest that quickly arose in respect of the cease-fire terms.

It took six months to agree that the combatants would be separated by a demilitarized zone 4,000 yards wide and that its axis would follow the line of final contact. At first the Communists had stuck out for an axis along the 38th Parallel which would have given their opponents 1,500 square miles less territory as well as a less defensible frontier. Eventually, however, they gave way on this point.

This Communist concession was soon followed by two more. The Communists accepted the principle that foreign garrisons could remain and that their troops could be rotated at a rate of up to 1,000 men per day. In addition they ceased to insist that there should be a Soviet delegate on the neutral commission that was to supervise the armistice. Meanwhile the United Nations dropped a demand for a ban on airfield construction.

Late in 1952, however, the talks almost died out over the question of whether prisoners of war should be forcibly repatriated in disregard of the Geneva principles. How important this issue was a United Nations survey carried out in July had revealed. This had shown that 68% of the 20,000 Chinese prisoners and 32% of the 112,000 Koreans did not want to go home. The Communists argued, of course, that all such evidence was spurious and that the men concerned were wanted for impressment into the service of Synghman Rhee and Chiang Kai-shek. Wireless links with the over-large and too thinly guarded compounds were used to trigger off violent riots in support of this thesis. After 75 prisoners had been killed in a battle at Koje in February, *Pravda* commented that whereas Dachau was a death camp 'Koje is a whole island of death'. On the same December day that China rejected an Indian-sponsored General Assembly resolution in favour of voluntary repatriation, 82 rioters were killed at Pongnam camp.

Negotiations revived with an exchange of sick and wounded in the spring of 1953. A Communist proposal of early May was based on the voluntary principle but made no clear provision for those who elected to stay. But on the 25th the United Nations made the counter-proposal from which was derived Article 3 of the Armistice Agreement. This article said that agents from their own countries could work for three months trying to influence those men who declined to return immediately. Then the post-war political conference would have a month in which to decide the fate of those who still remained. Should its deliberations be inconclusive Chinese prisoners would be released in a neutral country and Koreans either in a neutral country or else in Korea itself. Agreement was reached along these lines on June 8th.

Agreement on Article 3 brought peace without reunification and without obligatory Chinese withdrawal, too close for Synghman Rhee's comfort and so, by unilateral action, he released 22,000 anti-Communist prisoners. Eisenhower reacted quickly. His personal emissary extracted a written pledge from Rhee that, in return for lavish economic aid and a military alliance, he would observe an armistice. At Panmunjom the word was passed that the United Nations would stand aside if Rhee marched North. The talks went forward and the truce was signed in July.

The South Korean army had fought well under the United Nations but logistic dependence and a dearth of heavy equipment would have precluded it from fighting alone. But by July 1953 Rhee was little given to cool appreciations of reality. The domestic history of his republic at war both demonstrates and explains this. War generated an enormous black market and a twenty-fold monetary inflation. Guerrilla activity received a substantial boost when a complete North Korean division infiltrated through the Central Mountains to within twenty miles of Taegu three months before the Kaesong talks. Faced with such problems Rhee became fanatically impatient of Assembly criticism of mass executions of villagers and other illegal behaviour. He sought to cripple the legislature by making it bicameral and by transferring to the populace its right to elect the President. For months the Assembly declined to amend the constitution although many of its members were arrested and some court-martialled and although martial law was imposed in Pusan and a severe censorship throughout the country. But in mid-1952 after it had been blockaded in the parliament building for 48 hours, the Assembly capitulated. Rhee was subsequently re-elected by five million votes to two million.

Communist willingness to compromise was probably increased by the use of a nuclear threat. The removal of the naval restraints on Chinese Nationalist action can be seen as reflecting Eisenhower's conviction that the threat of an extension of the Korean War beyond the peninsula had to be used to discourage further obduracy. He felt also that to extend the war without nuclear weapons would involve far too many Allied casualties. The implication of all this was rendered the graver by a Joint Chiefs of Staff report that the number and quality of the nuclear warheads in hand was such that it would only be economic to use them against rearward strategic targets. No formal decision was taken but several staff appreciations were made along these lines and from February onwards hints were dropped in Delhi, the Formosa Straits and Panmunjom that this was so. The visit to Delhi that Mr Dulles paid in late May was not made the occasion of any intimation to Pandit Nehru but it is almost certain that some Indian officials were then advised of American intentions. As soon as the armistice was signed sixteen of those states that had assisted in the United Nations military effort jointly declared that the war theatre would inevitably be enlarged if hostilities were renewed.

# SECTION TWO    FROM PANMUNJOM TO VENUS

*Chapter XII*
## RUSSIA SINCE STALIN

MALENKOV became Chairman of the Soviet Council of Ministers on Stalin's death and so ushered in a period of relatively liberal government under a 'collective leadership', consisting of the leading members of the Praesidium of the Communist Party of the Soviet Union—the body that had recently replaced the Politburo as its senior executive institution. Within weeks widespread amnesties had been declared and the charges against the Jewish doctors denounced as being false and based largely upon confessions improperly obtained. By the end of 1953 the omnipotence of the secret police had been undermined by the trial and execution of Laurentia Beria himself. He was convicted of, among other things, working for British Intelligence in the Caucasus after 1917 and of subsequently helping foreign spies and rightist *emigrés*. Foreign observers noted how strangely relaxed and gay the 'collective leaders' became with the removal of Stalin and Beria—the Soviet Union's two most formidable bosses.

But by that winter signs of a rivalry between Malenkov and Kruschev, who had now succeeded him as the First Secretary of the Communist Party of the Soviet Union, could be perceived. Malenkov was, in a sense, the representative of the managers and technocrats—men who were often party members but usually for reasons of expediency rather than deep conviction. He felt that, particularly since the USSR now had a thermo-nuclear deterrent against modern war which, if it ever did occur, would mean 'the destruction of world civilization',[1] the time had come to lay a little more stress on consumer goods at the expense of heavy industry. Such a modification of the then current Five Year Plan was announced in the Supreme Soviet in August 1953. Two months later a joint government and party order called for thousands of new eating houses by 1956.

Mr Kruschev, on the other hand, was more concerned with the 'virgin lands'. In the New Year he announced that grain production would have to rise by a third within a few seasons and that this would necessitate boosting the ploughed acreage by over 25,000,000 acres in the 'frontier lands' of Kazakhstan, Siberia, the Volga basin and Transcaucasia. The Praesidium reaction to all this was cool. Mikoyan and Bulganin were, it would seem, unenthusiastic. Kaganovich was hostile and Molotov more

[1] A phrase he used on March 12th, 1954.

701

so. Malenkov felt the intensive margins of agriculture to be more worthy of attention than the extensive ones.

Kruschev's subsequent recovery of prestige was no doubt aided by the interests that had forced Malenkov to retract quickly the suggestion that even the USSR was liable to virtual annihilation in the event of thermo-nuclear attack. Perhaps it was associated also with the official reaction against the alarmingly rapid 'thaw' that had taken place in the realms of literature and art. But it dates essentially from the sharpening of the controversy about consumer goods that took place in the autumn of 1954. Though *Izvestia*, the government paper, adhered to the Malenkov line for a while, *Pravda*, the party one, argued constantly against it. Molotov was influenced against Malenkov by this campaign. So were most of the generals. But still the Chairman was loth to budge. Extra pressure was applied in the form of a somewhat sinister trial. This resulted in V. S. Abakumov, a former Minister of State Security, being shot for helping to organize the major purge that had taken place in Leningrad in 1949. Since in 1957 Malenkov was openly, and probably justly, accused of complicity in the Leningrad Affair, it is likely that various insinuations were made at the time of the Abakumov trial. On February 8th, 1955, he resigned his government post, confessing, as he did so, his lack of experience and the importance of heavy industry. Marshal Bulganin succeeded him.

The duumvirate of 'Mr B and Mr K' came thus to dominate the Soviet scene for a while. By their joint tours of Eastern Europe and Southern Asia in 1955, by their participation in the Geneva Four Power Summit Conference of that year, and by their visit to Britain in 1956, they came to symbolize a new 'Geneva Spirit' of flexibility and reconciliation in Great Power relationships which was matched by the 'Bandung' mood in Afro-Asia.[1] But this spirit was expressed also in the more formal aspects of Soviet diplomacy. The dissolution of the Cominform was staged to coincide exactly with the arrival of the Soviet leaders in Britain. And the previous May the USSR made certain concessions to the Western position on General and Complete Disarmament. That same month she joined in the signature of the Austrian Peace Treaty, abandoning certain long-standing claims in order to do so—and also, of course, abandoning her military encirclement of Hungary. Almost simultaneously she joined with her East European allies in signing the Warsaw Pact, which provided for the establishment of a joint high command. But perhaps that pact should be regarded as having been an institutional consolidation intended to make possible continuing flexibility in other respects; shortly afterwards a cut of *c.* 700,000 in the size of the Soviet armed forces was announced.

Neither the 'Geneva Spirit' nor the duumvirate was destined for longevity. The former was crushed at Hungary and Suez and the latter was fatally undermined by an increasing manifestation of talent and

[1] A major conference of Afro-Asian states was held at Bandung in Indonesia in 1955.

energy by Mr Kruschev. Among his many attributes were an intense pride in his humble origins, a love of conviviality and of argument, a capacity for appearing excitingly indiscreet, a gift for explaining complex programmes in simple homespun language laced with a wealth of old Russian proverbs, and, above all, a mind that combined a deep sense of political tactics with a passionate faith in the glorious future facing Soviet Communism. Schemes as bold as that for the 'virgin lands', or the one to grow more maize which soon followed it, gave him the scope he longed for.

Early in 1956 the official antipathy towards the ghost of Stalin suddenly deepened and this proved to herald a merciless indictment of him by Kruschev in a 'secret speech' made before a closed session of the 20th Congress of the CPSU on February 25th. Stalin was castigated as a tyrannical usurper who was personally responsible for purges in which thousands of honest Communists had perished, often after enduring barbaric tortures. He had, said Kruschev, ignored warnings of the coming Nazi invasion and had, through his sublime incompetence, helped to cause Russia's early defeats. He had also, among many other things, distorted history and ideology and isolated himself behind a vast web of bureaucracy. And in an open speech to the same congress Kruschev launched another famous theme by supporting a recent contention in *Kommunist*, a theoretical journal, that 'war was not fatally inevitable' because 'capitalism' could be overthrown by economic and peaceful competition within a framework of 'peaceful co-existence'.

These initiatives were taken despite the fact that his own position within the Praesidium remained far from impregnable. Molotov had been isolated and humiliated in the course of the rapprochement with Tito that took place in 1955 and that June, during Tito's trip to Moscow, was to be dismissed from his post as Minister of Foreign Affairs. But the denigration of him and of some of the other Praesidium members that was implicit in the 'secret speech' was, of necessity, cautious and qualified, and, indeed, the structure of the speech suggested that more than one pen had shaped the final draft. Rapid publication in Washington meant that knowledge of its contents spread far quicker than could have been intended. The severe riots that broke out in Tiflis were some measure of the traumatic effect this had even within the USSR.

Kruschev's star now started to wane again. Molotov and Kaganovich accompanied him and Mikoyan to Warsaw in October 1956 in the course of the attempt to discourage, partly by a subtle threat of armed intervention, Gomulka's election as First Secretary. Shortly afterwards Molotov was accorded potentially extensive powers in respect of economic administration and cultural discipline. Meanwhile, certain of Kruschev's 'errors' were emphasized at a plenum of the Central Committee of the CPSU whilst his apparent success with the 'virgin lands' was systematically played down. But the next plenum, held early in 1957, marks the beginning of his great surge to victory under the banner of 'democratic centralism'. Party endorsement was given to his thesis that 200,000 industrial establishments

703

and 100,000 construction sites couldn't be controlled from Moscow and that the thirty or so All-Union production ministries should be replaced by a hundred or more regional economic councils, *sovnarkhozy* as they came to be known. One effect of this would obviously be to enhance Kruschev's importance as the head of the Communist Party machine which remained, of course, as centralized as ever. A law was passed by the Supreme Soviet on May 8 that required the reorganization to be complete by July 1st. No other member of the Party Praesidium spoke in its support.

An official announcement made on July 4th condemned the 'Anti-Party Group of Malenkov, Molotov and Kaganovich' for stubborn adherence to a 'sectarian and dogmatic approach'. And it was revealed that they had been expelled from the government and the Praesidium. Soon afterwards Malenkov was put in charge of a remote power station and Molotov made the Ambassador to Outer Mongolia. Then Marshal Zhukov was condemned for 'Bonapartism' and replaced as Minister of Defence by Marshal Malinovsky. Zhukov had been a stalwart, and perhaps crucial, opponent of the 'Anti-Party Group' but his unique influence throughout the armed forces and his anxiety to channel the political control of the army exclusively through himself made him too dangerous to retain. Bulganin was replaced as Chairman by Kruschev early in 1958. Three years later Stalin's body was transferred from the Red Square mausoleum to a lesser place of honour at the foot of the Kremlin Wall.

Kruschev dedicated himself to the reshaping of the USSR in accordance with his own social and ideological outlook. A system of part-time vocational training was introduced in 1958 in place of the last two years of compulsory secondary education. Both this and the drive to ensure that would-be graduates got practical experience of labouring conditions were partly intended to smash the cult of intellectualism that seemed to Mr Kruschev to favour the entrenchment of a new and almost hereditary managerial *élite*. Rules introduced within the nine million strong Communist Party in 1961 required that between a quarter and a half of the members of any elective committee at any given time should be, on account of the excessive length of their previous service, ineligible for renomination. This move was intended to militate against the real danger that the CPSU would become a moribund middle-aged pressure group. Only 21% of the delegates to the 21st Congress in 1959 had joined the party since 1946.

Propaganda was intensified against the scores of thousands of religious houses that still functioned and was sustained against corruption, violent crime, adolescent delinquency—markedly on the increase in the USSR as it was almost everywhere else—and alcoholism. Some of these '*bourgeois* survivals' were felt to require more direct forms of pressure as well. A People's Militia and Comradely Courts were established in 1959; two years later the authority of the latter was formalized and, in many cases, extended to permit them to despatch to forced labour any found guilty of idleness or what was called 'immoral' behaviour. The death penalty was meanwhile made a permissible sentence for such crimes as large scale 'speculation', forgery or embezzlement, when these were committed by males.

Writers were regarded by Mr Kruschev as his 'ideological artillery'. From this unsolicited responsibility stemmed a requirement for conformity. The most famous of the many who denied this obligation was Boris Pasternak. His novel *Dr Zhivago* earned him the Nobel award after its publication in Italy but his acceptance of this honour was withdrawn after he had been expelled from the Writers' Union and threatened with exile. The virulent campaign that was launched against him ceased after he had appealed by letter to Mr Kruschev but in December 1960 his close friend Olga Ivinskaya was sentenced by a secret court for currency offences. And she was not released from jail until just after Kruschev's fall from power. But a significant example of the kind of radicalism that was becoming permissible was provided by the publication in 1962 of a novel called *One Day in the Life of Ivan Denisovich*. The labour camp that is so vividly depicted belonged to the Stalinist era but it might have been expected that, since some camps still existed, the strictures it delivered would not have been officially welcome.

Jews tended to be victimized in the campaign against economic crimes. Northern Kazakhstan, which had become an important 'Virgin Soil Territory', was separated from the rest of that state in 1960 and Russian made the official language within it. But, in general, national minorities were faring much better. A decree of early 1957 restored the autonomy of the deported groups—the Balkars, Chechens, Ingushi, Kalmyks and Karachai—and made provision for their return home.

The impression made by Sputnik was such as to make possible the practice by the Russians of bold and tough-minded diplomacy between 1957 and 1962. Certain other factors persuaded the Soviet leaders that this was an option that should be taken up. One was the constant debilitation of the German Democratic Republic by the steady flow of refugees out through West Berlin—the rate averaging a 1,000 a day just before 'the wall' was erected in 1961 and the total since 1949 having reached almost three million. Free elections in the GDR might have checked the movement but might also have led to a withdrawal of Soviet troops and so to a weakening of the cohesiveness of East Europe. No strategic catastrophe could have stemmed from this for, as mankind moved into the intercontinental age, the military importance of all such intermediate zones progressively diminished. But acute emotional discomfort would have been involved in this sphere of influence dissolving just as the one in China was collapsing. So Russia was prepared to consider reducing her own power in Central Europe only if this was associated with the denial to West Germany of tactical nuclear weapons and with, perhaps, her being separated in some measure from her allies in the European Economic Community and NATO.

In October 1957, just as NATO was preparing to implement a new tactical nuclear strategy, Adam Rapacki, the Polish Foreign Minister, presented to the UN General Assembly a proposal for a nuclear free zone that would consist of Poland, Czechoslovakia and the two Germanies. Soviet support for this idea was immediate and sustained and was soon to be related to a renewed emphasis on the part of the USSR on the need to solve the political problem of Germany. This should be done, it said, by Western recognition of the Oder-Neisse border, by the establishment of confederal links between Pankow[1] and Bonn, and by altering the status of what Mr Kruschev called the 'cancerous tumour' of West Berlin. What was generally envisaged was that West Berlin should become a 'free city' with all four occupation powers, and perhaps the UN also, having token detachments of troops there. East Berlin would, under a peace treaty, become simply part of East Germany.

The campaign for this solution reached a dramatic climax in 1961 with the announcement, on June 15th, that the USSR would, if necessary, sign a unilateral peace treaty with the Democratic Republic by December 31st and so, among other things, oblige the Western powers to work directly with it in order to maintain the access routes to West Berlin. Three weeks later heavy increases in Soviet defence expenditure were announced. A Warsaw Pact conference in Moscow ended on August 5th and on the 13th West Berlin found itself being enclosed by 'the wall', a wire and concrete circumvallation that served to hold back all but the most daring of those who might have fled. At the end of the month the USSR broke the voluntary moratorium on nuclear testing in the atmosphere that the nuclear nations had operated since 1958 and within nine weeks she had conducted fifty explosions above the earth's surface including one equivalent to 60,000,000 tons of TNT. But in mid-October Mr Kruschev announced that there would, in fact, be no separate treaty that year.

Soviet defence expenditure continued to display a bias—which was hard to justify so far on in the thermonuclear era—in favour of attack submarines, anti-aircraft systems, tanks and other traditional means of war. The bias obviously arose out of a wish on the part of an influential military bureaucracy to retain extensive responsibilities, a desire of the more puritan of the Marxists to maintain a martial atmosphere, and a widespread disregard of concepts like marginal utility and relative cost effectiveness. Its effect was to induce a slow rate of procurement for intercontinental rockets. This effect was reinforced by the Soviet practice, from 1961, of investing a good proportion of her rocket resources in an Intermediate Range Ballistic Missile force located within her own borders and targeted on Western Europe.

Accurate location of the larger Soviet missile sites by means of space reconnaissance began in the autumn of 1961 and in June 1962 Robert McNamara, the US Secretary of Defence, pointed out, in a speech at Ann Arbor in Michigan, that this breakthrough, together with a growing American superiority in intercontinental weapons, enabled the USA to

[1] Part of East Berlin.

present her chief rival with the option of fighting any war in terms of military targets alone. No doubt this speech was intended to remind the West Germans and others that, since its implementation need not imply national suicide for the United States, her nuclear guarantee to Europe remained credible. Very probably the Russians felt his remarks to be aimed at them rather than Bonn and accordingly resorted to the only means they had of quickly increasing the number of missiles they had trained on the Western hemisphere.

Neither the skill with which the Cuban crisis was resolved nor the *détente* that followed was sufficient to convince some Soviet military and political leaders that their country had not been humiliated as a result of a characteristic display of impetuosity on the part of Nikita Kruschev. Recent policies of cultural relaxation, the provision of more consumer goods, and increased party control over economic administration had to be halted or reversed that winter. Meanwhile both the party and the government became more conciliatory towards China and towards her only firm ally, Albania. But, in a new climate of impatience, these switches tended to be seen as further proof of Kruschev's inherent unpredictability. Besides, they did nothing to eliminate some of the most important causes for dissatisfaction. Agricultural output was consistently disappointing, except on the private plots, with the result that limited reserves of gold had had to be squandered on grain from Canada, America and Australia.[1] The Council for Mutual Economic Assistance—an institution which was used to co-ordinate the economic policies of the USSR and Eastern Europe and which had originated, in fact, back in 1949—was achieving only moderate success in its efforts to promote growth through the special concentration of each Communist nation on those lines of production for which it was best suited. Splits and vacillations had come to characterize Communist parties in many lands as a result of the tension between Moscow and Peking. The military hierarchy was ostentatiously cool in its reception of the partial test ban treaty. Early in 1964 rumours started to circulate in Moscow and elsewhere that Kruschev was soon to resign.

---

[1] Russia sold £200,000,000 of gold between January 1963 and April 1964.

# Chapter XIII
## NATIONAL ROADS TO COMMUNISM?

THE general improvement in relations between Yugoslavia and the Soviet Bloc that followed Stalin's death was reflected in a rapid decrease in the number of frontier 'incidents'. This improvement marked the cautious beginning of the sustained Soviet diplomatic offensive that culminated in the visit to Belgrade in 1955 of Bulganin and Kruschev, a visit in the course of which they put the whole blame for the 1948 rupture squarely on Beria's shoulders. The offensive was aided by the friction that preceded the Trieste 'provisional' settlement of 1954—a settlement that gave Yugoslavia part of Zone A as well as the whole of Zone B but which left Trieste itself as a customs-free port in Italian hands. It was helped, too, by the way in which, despite the restrained initial behaviour of both the governments concerned, the Cyprus question rapidly eroded all goodwill between Greece and Turkey; this ensured that Yugoslavia's diplomacy was not unduly constrained by her having signed a trilateral pact with those two countries in August 1954. But the result was not a Yugoslav return to the Soviet camp. The treatment Tito had received from Stalin[1] had convinced him of the wisdom of remaining a 'positive neutralist'. His visit to India and Burma in the winter of 1954–5 reflected his determination to play that role.

Russia's desire to impress Yugoslavia favourably did not develop sufficiently fast to inhibit her armed intervention in the affairs of East Germany in June 1953. Some 200,000 refugees had fled to West Germany in the first five months of that year—approximately the same number as in the whole of 1952. Conflicting advice from Moscow led to rapid changes of policy in respect of liberalization; these culminated in the announcement of June 12th that heralded several important reforms but which left unmodified a new plan for higher output 'norms' in the building trade. Within four days the labourers on the Berlin building sites had stopped work and within the next twenty-four hours public demonstrations and sympathetic strikes had broken out in scores of cities throughout the zone. On the 17th Soviet troops and tanks appeared on the streets in many places and early the following morning they fired on the crowds in Berlin. By the time the rising had been crushed, several hundred people had been killed.

[1] See Chapter IV Section ii.

The spokesmen for the Soviet bloc all said that everything had been the fault of American-sponsored 'Fascist provocateurs'.

A trend towards emancipation then began, however, though always it proceeded within narrow and arbitrary limits. Amnesties were granted in several countries in 1953. Most of the joint companies that the various governments had established on a bi-national basis with the USSR had been abolished by 1956, the only important exceptions being the uranium firms in Rumania, Bulgaria and East Germany. More emphasis was given to consumer goods, at least until the fall of Malenkov. And during the Malenkov period less stress was placed on collectivized agriculture; thus in Hungary and Poland (both countries in which about two thirds of the arable had, in any case, remained in private hands) and in Czechoslovakia the collectivized sector was reduced. However, Hungary reverted to a policy of steady collectivization late in 1955 though Poland did not. Agricultural organization had long since ceased to be a live issue in the USSR itself and so Soviet guidance in respect of it was neither exact nor mandatory.

That the spirit of Stalinism was far from dead was shown by acts such as the execution in 1954 of Lucretiu Pátràscanu, the Rumanian theoretician who had been arrested for deviationism. The old Stalinist faction regained power in Hungary in 1955 when Imre Nagy was replaced as premier by András Hegedüs, a youthful and rather obscure figure. Hegedüs was a loyal follower of Matyas Rákosi—the old Comintern veteran who had lost the premiership to Nagy in 1953 but who had remained First Secretary of the Hungarian Communist Party. But although Rákosi now speedily re-imposed a Stalinist economic philosophy he no longer sought to suppress so ruthlessly freedom of speech and conscience. Scapegoats were found for the Rajk execution,[1] an action which was now acknowledged to have been wrong. Cardinal Mindszenty's form of internment was made less harsh. Dissentient intellectuals were treated with comparative mildness.

Edward Ochab, who became First Secretary of the Polish Communist Party in March 1956, was another example of an old Stalinist who was prepared to adapt himself to a changing situation. His policy of controlled liberalization was one which would have been difficult to achieve in Poland at the best of times and which had become virtually impossible in the wake of Kruschev's 20th Congress speech—the full text of which was released by the US State Department on June 4th. Later that month a demonstration at Poznan in favour of better wages developed into a massive patriotic and anti-Communist rally, and then into a gun battle against the authorities in which hundreds of casualties were inflicted. Soon afterwards Bulganin came to Poland and described the episode as a plot by 'international reaction' to exploit 'national peculiarities' in order to 'restore capitalism'. He thus flatly contradicted the thesis that Ochab had already enunciated which was that the revolt had social and economic origins and that it was 'erroneous to concentrate attention . . . on the

[1] See Chapter IV Section i.

ICELAND

SWEDEN

NORWAY

Oslo

SCOTLAND

IRELAND

NORTH
SEA

Dublin

BALTIC SEA

ATLANTIC

OCEAN

BRITAIN

DENMARK

London

NETH.

Berlin

Poznań

Brussels

BELGIUM

Warsaw

Paris

Bonn

GERMANY

POLAND

FRANCE

Prague

CZECHOSLOVAKIA

PORTUGAL

SWITZERLAND

Vienna

Madrid

AUSTRIA

Budapest

SPAIN

Trieste

HUNGARY

ITALY

YUGOSLAVIA

RUMAN

Belgrade

Rome

Sofia

BULGA

MOROCCO

ALBANIA

Corfu

GREECE

ALGERIA

Tunis

Athens

TUNISIA

MEDITERRANEAN

CRETE

SEA

0   100  200  300  400  500
MILES

LIBYA

# AROUND THE IRON CURTAIN

ARCTIC OCEAN

FINLAND

ESTONIA

LATVIA

HIA

WHITE RUSSIA

UKRAINE

Leningrad

Moscow

Kiev

Kharkov

hares

BLACK SEA

UNION OF SOVIET SOCIALIST REPUBLICS

ARAL SEA

CASPIAN SEA

GEORGIA

Tbilisi

AZERBAIJAN

ARMENIA

Ankara

TURKEY

AFGHANISTAN

Teheran

Nicosia

CYPRUS

SYRIA

LEBANON

Haifa

Tel Aviv

Alexandria

ISRAEL

Amman

Jerusalem

IRAQ

Baghdad

PERSIA (IRAN)

Cairo

JORDAN

KUWAIT

EGYPT

SAUDI ARABIA

PERSIAN GULF

machinations of provocateurs and imperialist agents'. But none of those arrested for participation in the rising was charged with acting as foreign agents and few of them were committed to prison. And so these events accelerated Poland's shift to a position from which she upheld the Soviet alliance but pursued, as Gomulka said, her own 'national road to Communism'. Gomulka's official rehabilitation, which had been confirmed on April 6th, marked the commencement of this shift; his election as Communist First Secretary on October 19th, with Ochab's backing, marked the culmination of it.

The Soviet leaders, acting on the request of Marshal Tito, summoned Rakosi to Moscow in July 1956; on his return he confessed subscribing to such errors as the cult of personality and gave up the First Secretaryship of the Hungarian Communist Party. In early October Imre Nagy was readmitted to the Communist Party and the bodies of Rajk and his colleagues were given grand state funerals. But these gestures effected no abatement of the tide of radical and patriotic protest—the tide gained strength, in fact, in the atmosphere of economic crisis produced by a bad harvest failure. Here also the protests largely assumed the form of public rallies and these culminated in the mass demonstration held in Budapest on October 23rd. Leaflets circulated in the course of it urged solidarity with Poland, neutralism, the end of collectivization and the establishment, in all its aspects, of the rule of law. Part of the Red Army garrison, which had been heavily reinforced over the previous few days, was used against some of the demonstrators, but the general Soviet policy proved to be, at that time, one of appeasement. Imre Nagy was permitted to become the Prime Minister of a broad coalition and János Kádár, who was believed to be one of his political friends, became First Secretary of the Communist Party. And on October 30th the Red Army began to evacuate Budapest.

Almost immediately afterwards, however, the Kremlin conducted its great *volte face*. Thousands of Soviet tanks and many support troops were ordered into Hungary in order to curb the revolutionary movement. Moscow's interest in doing this stemmed from the fear that unless the policy of making concessions was halted there would be soon nothing left of its sphere of interest in Eastern Europe. Its resolve to arrest the trend may have been strengthened by the temporary disruption of the Western alliance caused by the Anglo-French ultimatum to Egypt.

Nagy reacted to the Soviet concentration of force by broadcasting an announcement of Hungary's withdrawal from the Warsaw Pact, but this gesture was countered by Kádár's arbitrary formation, under Red Army protection, of a rival and pro-Soviet government. Early on November 4th, at Kádár's nominal request, the Russian troops began a ruthless police action. Resistance was fierce but short in Budapest; in some rural areas it dragged on for weeks. The published official estimate of the death roll was over 25,000. Refugees flocked out and by the end of the year 150,000 had reached foreign soil. Nagy was not among them. He was abducted when

712

leaving the Yugoslav Embassy under a guarantee of safe conduct and in a Hungarian government vehicle. His execution followed in 1958.

Western inaction during the suppression of the Hungarian reform movement meant that, thenceforward, the forces of radicalism in Eastern Europe acted with marked circumspection. Their fear of provoking renewed Soviet intervention was, it would seem, increased by the military and economic breakthrough that was apparently revealed by Sputnik. So the principle of alliance with the USSR never again came under overt attack and domestic policies continued, in general, to be modelled on Soviet precedents. Collectivization of agriculture went ahead almost everywhere, for example, despite the fact that private enterprise produced manifestly superior results. The proportion of the arable that was under private control in particular countries ranged between 35% and 80% in 1954; in 1963 it was well below 20% in every case bar two. The exceptions were East Germany and, of course, Poland. One of Gomulka's early decisions was to permit the dissolution of nearly all the Polish collective farms; the result was that, although collectivization nominally remained an official objective, 87% of the arable was still in private hands in 1963. East Germany had long retained a large sector of co-operatives, each of which was comprised of a group of loosely connected private farms, but many of these were transformed into full collectives after the food crisis of 1962.

Soon Gomulka came to stand out among the leaders of the smaller Warsaw Pact countries as being a man who conformed relatively closely to the anti-dogmatic Kruschev model. Eventually Kádár did so as well. But neither felt able to free himself completely from association with Stalinist personalities or identification with neo-Stalinist policies. Toleration, in fact, reached its zenith as a principle of Polish government as early as December 1956, with the achievement of a 'concordat' between State and Church. This provided for, among other things, optional religious instruction in government schools, the cancellation of clerical appointments previously made by the government and the establishment of bishoprics in the western territories. The following month Cardinal Wyszynski, whom Gomulka had released from internment, gave conditional moral support to the government by asking all Catholics to vote in the forthcoming single-list elections. But within a few months relations started to deteriorate again. Restrictions were placed on religious teaching in schools and Roman Catholic churches became subject to heavy taxation. By 1963 many church schools had been closed, religious instruction had virtually stopped in government schools and restraints had been placed on extra-mural instruction. Cardinal Wyszynski, addressing a gathering of half a million Polish pilgrims in 1962, spoke of war being vindictively waged against the Church. A bitter public debate subsequently broke out between him and Gomulka about who best represented the non-belligerent attitudes extolled by, for example, Pope John XXIII. By now Gomulka was committed to what he called 'ideological mobilization' and this was directed not only against clerics but also against the large and outspoken body of secular dissent. That this kind of official pressure was not incompatible with some flexibility in respect of affairs of business was shown by continued government acceptance of a large and variegated sector of small private firms and also by the application of the principles of free competition to certain nationalized firms.

Vigorous purges were conducted in many departments of Hungarian national life between 1956 and 1958 and many people were detained for suspected subversion. Interference in Church affairs was renewed, meanwhile, and this culminated, in 1959, in the Roman Catholics being obliged to have the government endorse all ecclesiastical appointments. A formal promise was made in 1957 that peasants would not be forced to enter collectives. Yet both 1959 and 1960 saw strong government pressure being exerted in favour of collectivization with the result that the percentage of the arable so held rose from 13 to 60. But thenceforward Kádár's rule became more relaxed. Most of the political prisoners were released. The value as leaders in society of many non-party members was explicitly acknowledged. Many travel visas were issued and up to half a million foreign tourists were received each year. But these concessions to liberal opinion in regard to internal matters were not matched by any in the field of international affairs. Hungary's foreign policy continued to be an almost exact copy of that of the Soviet Union.

Elsewhere relaxation was slow and limited. Rumania stayed under the control of the tough and doctrinaire Gheorghiu-Dej and so changed little. Unrest broke out among the Hungarian minority in 1956 but was handled with despatch. The most significant reform in Rumania came in 1963 when tuition in the Russian language was made optional in the schools. In that same year Rumania displayed strong hostility to Soviet proposals for the closer integration of the European Communist states through the Council for Mutual Economic Assistance and she also made various overtures to China and Albania.

Vulko Chervenkov, Bulgaria's Stalinist Premier, was dismissed in 1956 for engaging in the 'cult of personality' but within twelve months he rejoined the government and thenceforward that country was governed largely in accordance with Stalinist precepts. After the widespread amalgamations of 1959 the average size of Bulgarian collectives became 10,000 acres.

Early 1956 saw much Czech intellectual and student activity in favour of the end of radio-jamming, a free press, the right of foreign travel and other basic freedoms. But because, in the opinion of some Western commentators, of their memory of Munich, the Czechoslovakians were inert during the Hungarian revolt. Hostility towards the *régime's* principles and its practices persisted, of course, particularly in the Catholic stronghold of Slovakia, but it was kept under control by frequent, and often harsh, sentences for espionage and sabotage and by a sustained offensive against religion. Not until 1962 was the big Stalin monument in Prague dismantled and not until 1963 were some victims of the Slansky trial rehabilitated and Archbishop Beran released. East Germany remained effectively in the charge of the two firm Stalinists, Otto Grotewohl and Walter Ulbricht. No doubt their replacement by national Communists was deemed by Moscow an experiment too dangerous to embark upon.

The local cold war between Yugoslavia and the other European Communist powers was renewed in the middle of 1956 and it deepened after the Hungarian revolt. Tito publicly gave vent to the opinion that, while the second Soviet intervention in Hungary was an evil necessary to the preservation of peace, the first had been in no way justifiable; *Pravda*'s reply, made on November 23rd, openly accused Yugoslavia of fomenting trouble through interference in Hungary's internal affairs. And, despite repeated attempts by Tito to limit both the scope and the intensity of the disagreement, relations were bad throughout 1957 and 1958. Zhukov's dismissal induced Tito to use lumbago as an excuse not to attend the Fortieth Anniversary celebrations. Later Kruschev called Yugoslavia the Communist 'Trojan Horse' and a $175,000,000 Soviet industrial credit was postponed indefinitely. Sofia and Tirana began a fierce but unsuccessful propaganda campaign against alleged Yugoslav maltreatment of the Albanian and Macedonian minorities.

Tito's response to these pressures was to cultivate political and commercial links with those governments who claimed to be aligned neither with the USA nor the USSR. Thenceforward he travelled extensively in Afro-Asia and Yugoslavia became responsible for such work as the training and equipment of the new Sudanese navy and the construction of the Ghanaian naval base. Tito's warning against the small nations 'being tutored by the big', delivered after Kruschev's trip to the USA, reflected Belgrade's interest in some kind of 'third force' that might counterbalance the superpowers. Efforts to mobilize such a group to deal with the international consequences of the 1958 Iraq revolution bore little fruit, but in September 1961 a Conference of Non-Aligned Nations was held in Belgrade. The tone of this conference was somewhat to the 'Left'. The FLN was there to speak for Algeria; Cuba was the only representative from the New World. Among the men from other states were Nasser, Nkrumah and Sukarno.

Annoyance at the way the conference equally divided responsibility for nuclear test resumption led the United States to suspend her aid to Yugoslavia that November. A few months before a major trade agreement had been signed by Yugoslavia and the USSR, and relations between Belgrade and all the Warsaw Pact states improved noticeably in 1962 and 1963. But Tito continued both to preach and to practise policies of non-alignment.

Yugoslavia did not let the difficulties involved in being a neutralist in a position so close to Central Europe unduly inhibit her economic and social development. From 1953 she registered an average national economic growth rate superior to any in Europe bar Federal Germany's. Her mineral output rose spectacularly; she began to build merchant ships of over

20,000 tons displacement. Her proportion of illiterates dropped from 25% to 5% between 1953 and 1961. That such gains did not automatically lead to a free society was shown by the continued persecution of Milovan Djilas, a distinguished former member of the Yugoslav Politburo, for his inconveniently candid strictures against both Stalinists and Titoists. But the Yugoslav road to Marxist socialism was, in several important ways, refreshingly different. Private peasant holdings, loosely linked through co-operatives, remained, as in Poland, dominant. And some 200,000 people about three-quarters of them from the manual grades, were, by 1961, in the non-agricultural Workers' Councils, about 700,000 having served as council members at some time during the 1950s. And the councils appeared often able to take real decisions on matters such as marketing and industrial and social investment. But anti-social behaviour within the new managerial class, to which Djilas had drawn attention, continued. Tax evasion and the misuse of collective property were among the malpractices attacked by Marshal Tito in his May Day speech of 1962.

*Chapter XIV*
# INTERDEPENDENCE IN WESTERN EUROPE

IN a speech in Paris on December 14th, 1953, John Foster Dulles warned that unless the European Defence Community were established, the United States might have to consider 'an agonizing reappraisal' of its commitment to Europe. Eight months later the French National Assembly rejected the plan by 319 votes to 264. The MRP was very solidly for it; the Communists very solidly against. Every other party was divided on the matter. So was the Mendès-France government.

A crisis of some magnitude now faced the Western alliance. NATO needed extra men and those Germany could best provide. But France had become unwilling to contribute to an international army with German units in it and so it seemed most unlikely that she would stay in an alliance that contained an independent German force. And without France NATO would be weaker, both militarily and politically.

But acute though this dilemma appeared, it was not unresolved for long. Earlier that summer French and Dutch ministers, anticipating the collapse of the EDC, had begun to impress upon a reluctant British government the need for some special British link with Western Europe to offset German influence. They thereby paved the way for a London Conference that on October 3rd agreed that the Brussels Treaty relationship should be expanded into a Western European Union that would include Germany and Italy and that would have authority to supervise certain of the armaments of its members and, in particular, to ensure that the Federal Republic kept a pledge not to manufacture nuclear, bacteriological or chemical weapons on its own territory. Britain committed herself to keep four army divisions and a tactical air force on the continent.[1] The occupation *régime* in Germany was ended meanwhile and she was admitted to NATO. From 1958 her armed forces, like those of several other allies, began to acquire tactical weapons armed with American nuclear warheads; in her case, as in the others, the warheads remained in American custody. By 1962 NATO had amassed twenty-four divisions in the Central Area, nine of which were German; it therefore felt ready to implement the Forward Strategy agreed in 1950.

Thenceforward French fears of Germany diminished. France acquiesced

[1] These agreements were formalized in Paris later that month.

in the absorption of the Saar by the Federal Republic in 1957, insisting only that no economic harm was thereby caused to herself. So a new atmosphere began to be generated and optimism revived among those who longed to see Western Europe become more united. In the summer of 1955 the Foreign Ministers of the European Coal and Steel Community met at Messina and chose one of their number—Henri Spaak of Belgium, a dedicated European—to supervise what proved to be a brilliant and enthusiastic team of experts that was being assembled to study the development of a common market and of a multi-national nuclear energy authority. Treaties establishing the European Economic Community and Euratom were signed in Rome on March 25th, 1957, and they came into force on January 1st, 1958.

Under the relevant Rome Treaty, all restrictions on trade between EEC members were to be removed by the 1970s and, indeed, before 1964 tariffs were to be reduced by an average of a third and all permanent quotas abolished. A common external tariff was to be established and its level was not to be above that of the average of the several national tariffs that it would replace. Farmers would be guaranteed, principally by the operation of that tariff, minimum prices for their major products. All unfair trading practices—such as cartels—were progressively to be abolished. Social policies were to be 'harmonized', largely in order to eliminate artificial differences in labour costs; financial policies were to be harmonized, chiefly with a view to reducing the need for unilateral restrictive actions to ease balance of payment crises. Obstacles to the free movement of capital and labour were to be removed. And, in order to minimize the hardship that so much economic change would entail, an Investment Bank was to be created to assist the redevelopment of the more backward parts of the Community and a Social Fund to retrain those who became redundant. A Development Bank was also to be set up to provide capital funds for the colonies of member countries and those former colonies that had preserved some kind of formal association; and the associated territories were to have (at least for a five year experimental period) the same access to the markets of the 'Six' as if they were full members. All major policy issues arising out of this programme were to be resolved by a Council of Ministers.

The preamble to the treaty stated that the signatories wished 'other peoples of Europe who share their ideals to join in their efforts' but Henri Spaak insisted that each member state must have a right to block new entries. This provision was made to allay the fears of many socialists that Spain and Portugal would join and of men like Konrad Adenauer that the Community would lose its sense of identity if it became too large.

Euratom was brought into existence so as to promote the joint development of nuclear energy for peaceful purposes. And in this case, too, overall control was exercised by a Council of Ministers. American support for the 'Europe of the Six' was early shown by her arranging to provide nuclear fuel for Euratom. This support grew as the USA came to feel herself harder pressed by Soviet technology and by the challenge of Afro-Asia.

Britain sent an observer to Messina but it was to be some years before she showed much awareness of how magical an appeal 'Europe' was coming to have for many on the continent. Two months after the Rome Treaty was signed Reginald Maudling, then Paymaster-General, was made responsible for sponsoring a European Free Trade Area within which there would be no internal tariffs on industrial products—a project which she had already had cleared by an Organization for European Economic Co-operation committee as being one possible way of bridging the gap between the Community and the rest of OEEC. But London's unwillingness, largely because of the system of Commonwealth trading preferences, to accept a common external tariff or to negotiate a comprehensive agreement for agriculture, was poorly thought of in Paris and in Bonn. And British attempts to play off the French against the Germans rebounded badly. France finally killed the idea in November 1958.

Four months later experts from Norway, Sweden, Denmark, Austria, Switzerland, Portugal and Britain met to examine the possibility of a free trade area confined to their countries. Out of their deliberations evolved a convention for a European Free Trade Association which was initialled in Stockholm in November, 1959; it provided for the creation of an industrial free trade zone, without a common external tariff, by 1970.

By August 1963 EFTA had undertaken to complete its programme of tariff removals before 1967 whilst EEC had already reduced duties by 60%. No doubt these moves had led to greater international specialization in respect of some products and greater competition in respect of others and so helped economic growth. However the exact results are hard to assess because they took place against a general background of expansion. Italian industrial production, for example, rose at an annual average of almost 9% between 1954 and 1961 and meanwhile her balance of payments position became a good deal more healthy. In such achievements could be seen a triumph for the philosophy of the mixed economy. The Italian government co-ordinated all major investment particularly so as to promote light engineering, automobiles, chemicals and other industries with encouraging export prospects. Much of the money needed to mine the newly discovered natural gas deposits and to use the gas thus obtained was provided by a State holding company. Much government capital and planning effort went into building dams and other public works in the South and this encouraged Northern manufacturers to invest in that region and so prevent a worsening of the imbalance between it and the North. And, of course, foreign tourists assisted this national resurgence in a variety of ways. Over nine million came in 1960, seven times the total for 1948.

But material improvement did not ensure political stability. The Christian Democrats never enjoyed an absolute majority in the Lower House and so were often obliged to enter into coalitions with the smaller parties of the Centre. But this necessitated concessions being made to moderate opinion on matters such as legislation concerning farm tenancy and these annoyed the more conservative of the Christian Democrats—the *concentrazione* as they were known. Another destabilizing feature was the increasing interest in mutual co-operation shown by many men of the centre on the one hand and many members of the Nenni socialist party on the other. Kruschev's denunciations of Stalinism helped promote this interest. Eventually, in 1962, it led to the formation by Amintore Fanfani, a Left Wing Christian Democrat, of an administration that—in exchange for pledges to nationalize electricity, develop regional government, and adopt other 'progressive' measures—was to enjoy the parliamentary support of the Nenni group. And Pietro Nenni, plus several of his colleagues, actually entered the new coalition formed by Aldo Moro after the election of 1963.

Though their party membership—which had exceeded 2,000,000 in 1951—had declined in recent years, the Communist share of the poll rose above 25% in 1963. Their skill on television had enabled them to harness the tide of social radicalism that was rising in the expanding Northern cities and to channel some of the resentment that radicals felt at Pietro Nenni's compromise.

The Trieste problem was resolved in 1954 by the incorporation of most of Zone A into Italy and of the rest of the Free Territory into Yugoslavia. However, Italian military and political attention continued to be focused on the North-East frontier because of a campaign that was launched by German-speaking irridentists in the South Tyrol. Italian diplomacy was not vigorous on the wider world issues and Italy tended to play a smaller role within the Western alliance than her economic progress might have led one to expect. The strength of her Communist movement partly accounts for this. So does the failure of any outstanding leader to emerge to replace de Gasperi who died in 1954. Geography also contributes to the explanation for Italy continued to be regarded, and to regard herself, as essentially a Mediterranean nation. She was, for example, left within NATO's Southern European Command—apparently in order to avoid too brittle a confrontation within it between the Greeks and the Turks—and so was excluded from the much more important Central European area.

Some hope that France might have a reasonable period of political stability was generated by the formation of the government of Pierre Mendès-France in June 1954. Although its members were drawn mainly from the ranks of the Radicals and the Social Republicans—as the Gaullists had been called since the General's formal withdrawal from politics in 1953—it enjoyed the conditional support of the Socialists. Soon Mendès-France and his ministers were displaying their skill and energy by good management of the economy and of the crises concerning Tunisia, Indo-China and European defence. But their rule ended in the New Year when they lost a vote of confidence on their handling of the Algerian revolt. The appointment of Jacques Soustelle—a leftist Social Republican —as temporary governor-general and the despatch of heavy troop reinforcements had caused misgivings among some of their supporters.

A general election was held twelve months later which led to the formation of a new coalition under a Socialist, Guy Mollet. At first it drew political strength from the fact that no alternative alliance of forces could be envisaged that was likely to be united in its attitude towards Algeria and the Middle East. But eventually in May 1957, it fell in the face of resentment at extra taxation and rising prices—both of which stemmed largely from the nation's military burdens. But by then it had lasted sixteen months, a record for post-war France.

That autumn France had no government for five weeks and from the middle of April, 1958—a time of exceptionally bitter fighting in Algeria— it again lacked one for a month. On May 14th, shortly after the FLN had announced the execution—for reprisal purposes—of three French soldiers, Pierre Pflimlin, who was known to favour negotiations, was sworn in as Premier. All this was more than the European settlers or much of the army could stand. A wave of demonstrations—in which the Moslems played some part—swept Algeria from the 13th and a large number of Committees of Public Safety were formed both there and in Corsica, where rebel paratroops landed on the 24th. Jacques Soustelle flew out and joined the executive of the Algiers Committee.

Pflimlin resigned on 28th and shortly afterwards President Coty asked General de Gaulle to form a government. For weeks his name had been canvassed by the Social Republicans, by the rebellious 'colonels' and the settlers, who assumed that he would favour the permanent integration of Algeria with France, and by many of the moderates in Parliament, who saw in him the only person who could maintain national unity and so preserve the rule of law.

De Gaulle expressed a readiness to 'assume the powers of the republic' as early as May 15th but he studiedly remained aloof from all plots and factions. When he accepted office he did so only on condition that he would have decree powers for six months and that, towards the end of the time, he would submit a new constitution to a popular referendum. The constitution of the Fifth Republic was duly submitted—and approved by 79% of the metropolitan voters and 95% of those abroad—on September 28th. It made ministerial office incompatible with assembly membership, made ministers less dependent on assembly support and gave them considerable influence over the legislative process. And the President was accorded extensive reserve powers over both the executive and the legislature. De Gaulle became President on December 21st.

A currency devaluation helped the new *régime* generally to sustain the economic momentum that France had built up in the recent past. And steps were taken to ensure that a greater proportion of the national product was directed towards regions other than the North and East and that private capital formation received less emphasis by comparison with houses, hospitals, and schools. Meanwhile France disengaged herself from North Africa and began to repair the damage that a grim struggle had inflicted on her unity and morale. Her recovery was helped enormously by the large and noble personality of de Gaulle himself and by the wide base of his political support. It was assisted also by the reintroduction of single member constituencies with two ballots; the effect of this was to cripple the small parties and de Gaulle's chief opponents—the Communists.

De Gaulle's chief foreign policy ambition was that the Common Market should become an informal political bloc led by France. He saw it as remaining within a Western alliance but as pursuing, individually or collectively, certain independent lines of policy, confident in the knowledge that the independent strategic deterrent of France could ensure it against nuclear blackmail. Work on this deterrent had been in progress for some years before de Gaulle's return to power—despite the hostility displayed towards it by such statesmen as Edgar Faure and Guy Mollet—and by 1963 the first *Mirage IV* supersonic bombers had been built and plans for some missiles and submarines laid. Two hundred and fifteen deputies supported a censure motion in respect of this programme that was debated in December, 1960.

The new Europe must, thought de Gaulle, be built around a Franco-German *entente*. Close links with Adenauer were cultivated from 1958, a policy which culminated in the Treaty of Collaboration of 1963; this envisaged extensive and continuing consultation on defence and other topics. And during his spectacular tour of Germany the previous autumn de Gaulle had seemed to imply that a joint strategic force should be the eventual aim. 'Everything suggests to us,' he said, 'that we must build this Franco-German union. It is true of both France and Germany that they never achieved anything great . . . without the military element having played an eminent part in it.'

Adenauer's rapport with de Gaulle is at first sight hard to relate to the enthusiam for the American connection he had evinced a decade earlier. But the strength of that enthusiasm can be explained in terms of his personal regard for Dulles and his awareness that Europe was still weak. The ardent old-world Catholic from the Rhineland had always had private doubts about the desirability of dependence on the USA. And in 1956 he publicly emphasized the dangers involved in the USA and the USSR having a permanent nuclear duopoly. But he never satisfied himself that a viable alternative was in view; both he and Franz-Joseph Strauss, his Defence Minister, were trying in 1960 to persuade the French not to push ahead too fast with a national *force de dissuasion* lest it encourage the USA to retire from Europe.

The Berlin Foreign Ministers' conference of early 1954 reached a complete deadlock on the question of German reunification. Molotov proposed that the two German legislatures should co-operate on equal terms to create a provisional government that would prepare free and secret all-German elections. His three Western colleagues insisted, however, that there should be free all-German elections, preferably under United Nations supervision, to elect an assembly that would adopt a constitution, choose a government and sign a peace treaty. By doing so they accurately reflected general Bundestag opinion as expressed, for example, in a resolution passed almost unanimously in June, 1953. But in stressing that a united Germany must be left free to join NATO the Foreign Ministers, and the Federal government, went further than the Social Democrats in Bonn. Their leader, Herr Ollenhauer, said that it had to be accepted that after reunification Germany would be non-aligned. The Social Democratic Party (the SPD) pressed also for rearmament to be postponed until the possibilities of unification had been more fully explored. But the Bundestag approved the proposed accession to NATO by 314 votes to 157 early in 1955. Later that year Adenauer visited Moscow and relations with the USSR were 'normalized'.

Over the next few years there was some debate about what the relationship should be between reunification and the various proposals for military disengagement in Central Europe. In May 1957 Eisenhower joined in the speculation about a thinning out of the forces on each side of the Iron Curtain; the State Department had subsequently to assure the Federal government that no disengagement would be allowed to occur except after a properly conducted reunification. But in March 1959 the SPD called for the demilitarization of Central Europe as a preliminary to reunification. By this move it gave expression to the anxiety many young Germans then felt about involvement in a tactical nuclear strategy.

German economic policy remained in some respects very traditionalist during these years. Price stability and the balancing of budgets were considered of great importance; little deliberate planning for full employment took place until some time after the 1958 recession. On the other hand subsidies and tax concessions were freely used to boost particular lines of production. Public saving—other than that by nationalized industry—financed nearly a third of German gross investment in the early 1960s; the proportion in Britain was about one tenth. The percentage of the British gross national product absorbed in taxation fell from 32·5 in 1950 to 27·6 in 1960; the corresponding German figure rose from 30·3 to 33·9. Some months before the general election of 1957 the national insurance scheme was greatly extended.

The SPD was handicapped both by the onset of prosperity and by the continuation of the Cold War. But its strength in the Bundestag slowly rose and this, plus gains by the Free Democrats, meant that in 1961 the CDU/CSU axis lost the overall majority that it had held virtually since 1953. The modest SPD advance in 1961 was largely due to the impact made in the battle for the chancellorship by Willy Brandt, the Mayor of West Berlin. He had accepted nomination only on condition that the SPD at last committed itself firmly to NATO.

1962 saw a hardening of opposing attitudes on foreign policy within the CDU/CSU coalition. The USA had ostentatiously taken military precautions during the Berlin crisis of 1961 whereas France had remained nonchalant. Yet after the crisis had been resolved spokesmen for the Right of the CDU and for the CSU began to question more openly whether the transatlantic nexus was worth preserving in its present form. Strauss reasonably argued that excessive American anxiety to see NATO conventional forces strengthened undermined the authority of the nuclear deterrent. The growth of American airlift capacity that was then taking place was unfairly interpreted by some as being the precursor to a partial withdrawal of American ground forces from Germany. The same people disliked the partial test ban because it was launched by a concert of the thermonuclear powers and because it involved a kind of *de facto* recognition of Eastern Germany. Ludwig Erhard, the Economics Minister, did not share these doubts to the same extent as Adenauer and this, together with some personal antipathy, explains why Adenauer was reluctant to have Erhard succeed him as Chancellor. When he did so in October, 1963, Adenauer, then in his 88th year, retained the CDU party chairmanship.

President Kennedy tried in several ways to meet, or to anticipate, the fears of impending desertion. The Trade Expansion Act of 1962, which provided for a lowering of tariffs between the USA and the EEC, was designed partly to consolidate the Atlantic community. The plan for a NATO Multilateral Fleet of mixed manned *Polaris* ships put forward at Nassau in December, 1962, was to be one of the ways in which strategic forces would be welded inseparably. Many Germans on the Left and in the Centre became enthusiastic about the MLF as something that might satisfy their aspirations completely. Some members of the German Right welcomed it as a possible first step towards a European deterrent. To de Gaulle it was anathema.

*Chapter XV*
# THE EMERGENCE OF THE EAST

## (i) *China*

THE Chinese Communist authorities estimated that their output of physical goods rose by 45% during the Five-Year Plan of 1953–7, and most Western authorities regard this as only a mild exaggeration. Industry was said to have expanded by an average annual rate of 15% and agriculture by 4%. Meanwhile, nearly all the factories were nationalized and nearly all the farms brought into co-operatives.

To help sustain this national effort a martial atmosphere was preserved. Three to five year general conscription was introduced in February 1955, a few weeks after the seizure of the Nationalist island of Yikiang and the bombardment that led to the evacuation of the Tachens. In the course of that year nearly a quarter of the central government budget was devoted to defence. Shortly before the conscription decree, preventive arrest of political suspects was formally introduced. The arrest of the liberal writer Hu Feng soon afterwards heralded the onset of a new wave of revolutionary vigilance in the intellectual field.

Credit terms were arranged for only a fifth of the two billion dollars worth of Soviet aid received by April 1956—all the rest had to be paid for immediately in cash and kind. In any case, the aid China was then giving to other Asian countries was of a comparable monetary value. Soviet aid was of especial importance, however, in that it came largely in the form of skilled technicians and specialized machinery. Scores of investment projects benefited including the new railway line to Sinkiang and the bridge at Wuhan—the first ever over the lower Yangste. By 1955 well over 80% of China's imports were coming from the USSR and almost all of them consisted of building materials or machinery.

From these close commercial ties stemmed a common Sino-Soviet approach to international affairs. So the new Muscovite diplomacy of the first Stalin era was paralleled in Peking. Contained in the Sino-Indian treaty of 1954 were five new principles of co-existence. These principles, which for a year or two were heavily stressed in both Delhi and Peking, included respect for territorial integrity, non-aggression, non-interference in each other's internal affairs, equality and mutual benefit, and peaceful co-existence. Early in the next year Chou En-lai was at the Bandung conference where he played a leading and conciliatory role. Thus, it was there that he made the suggestion, which was taken up that August, that China should have informal talks directly with America on the areas of disagreement between them. The Asian aid programme referred to above was, of course, another aspect of this policy of positive co-existence. At about this time Tibet was designated an autonomous region within the Chinese People's Republic; meanwhile, the Indian government relinquished control of the postal service that it had been operating in that province.

Though there is little evidence that the USSR was able to influence China's internal policy directly, one cannot but notice how the marked liberalization of the intellectual atmosphere which had begun in China late in 1955 accelerated after Kruschev's denunciation of Stalin at the 20th Congress. Within a few months Mao had urged his followers to 'Let a hundred flowers bloom and a hundred thoughts contend' and the Minister of Public Security had announced an end to the arbitrary arrests, forced confessions, and unjust sentences of recent years. Incessant originality of thought was officially required of all intellectuals during the ensuing few weeks.

But soon the government became uneasy, though the unease was caused not so much by the criticism directed against it by the liberal intelligentsia —which was rarely very startling or provocative—as by the support that criticism received from young students educated under the Communist *régime*. Other causes for concern were the increasingly open expressions of local nationalism in Sinkiang, and the growth of a violent resistance movement among the Kham and the Amdo in Tibet. Mao made a speech in February 1957 that recognized the need to tolerate constructive criticism but which ominously described 'revisionism' as a greater menace than 'doctrinairism'. Chou En-lai's fierce attack on leading members of the Democratic League at the yearly session of the National Congress was symptomatic of the wave of official intolerance that characterized that summer. Now the 'Hundred Flowers' episode was officially described as having been a device to encourage weeds to expose themselves.

It was the second session of the 8th Congress of the Chinese Communist Party, which met in May 1958, that adopted the remarkably ambitious programme for immediate economic expansion that was entitled the Great Leap Forward. The 750,000 rural co-operatives were amalgamated in average groups of 30 into a more highly organized type of collective farms known as communes. These were heralded as a short cut to pure Communism and, more particularly, as a means of bringing the economies of large-scale production to the countryside. Their introduction coincided with a fantastic drive to double 'steel' output within the year by having low quality ingots turned out on hundreds of thousands of back-yard furnaces. Parallel to the commune system ran a People's Militia into which scores of millions of men and women were inducted. Very few firearms were issued to the militia but it served to strengthen internal security and to provide labour gangs to work on roads and irrigation schemes.

Peking took a very firm line against Belgrade in the row that began at about the same time as the Great Leap Forward over the Yugoslav contention that the Communist Party of the Soviet Union need be accorded no special ideological primacy. But by this time strains were beginning to develop between Moscow and Peking. The Russians had given the communes a cool reception, perhaps through resentment of the proposition that somebody else had lighted upon a short cut to paradise that had eluded them for forty-one years. No doubt the Chinese were irritated by this apparent lack of revolutionary ardour and this irritation must have been enhanced by the Soviet disinclination to exploit what the Chinese saw as the immediate and decisive military advantage produced by the launching of Sputnik. This, said Mao, meant that the East Wind was prevailing over the West Wind; this, said the *People's Daily*, meant that the strategic superiority of the anti-imperialist bloc had reached unprecedented heights and that international affairs had now reached a major turning point. Sputnik was the name given to the first pilot commune. This surge of Chinese confidence only proved, in fact, that the Russians had briefed them very inadequately on the realities of the thermonuclear balance.

China was less restrained than Russia in her attitude towards the Iraqi revolution of 1958 and the Anglo-American landings in the Lebanon and Jordan. The former clearly wanted the latter to put troops into Iraq to protect the revolutionary *régime* against any further moves by the Anglo-American forces.

Some differences of emphasis may also have existed with regard to the Formosa Straits crisis of that summer. The ambassadorial talks in Warsaw between the Chinese and the Americans, which had begun in 1955, were suspended in December 1957 and soon afterwards the Chinese began to strengthen their military installations opposite Quemoy and Matsu. Fifty thousand shells were fired at those islands in the initial bombardment of August 23rd and about ten times that number in the course of the next six weeks. Within four days of the revival of hostilities President Eisenhower had publicly announced that he felt that the importance of the off-shore islands had recently increased because of a reinforcement of their Nationalist garrison. Three days later the USSR announced that she would regard any attack on China as one upon herself.

No direct amphibious assault against either Quemoy or Matsu could possibly have succeeded. Their combined ration strength of 80,000 gave them a density of soldiers on, or under, the ground about ten times as great as, say, that which the Japanese had achieved on the island fortress of Okinawa in 1945. But the garrisons could have been starved out, over a period of several months, by the bombardment of their supply beaches. The Americans decided to forestall this possibility in September by

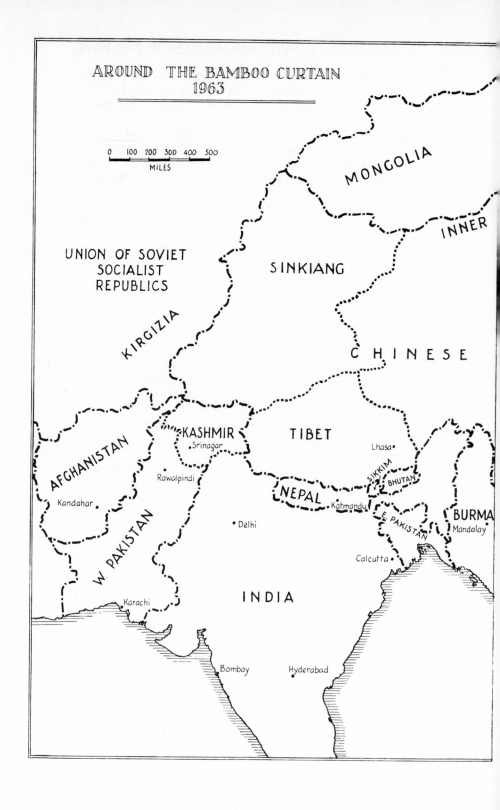

AROUND THE BAMBOO CURTAIN
1963

0   100  200  300  400  500
MILES

UNION OF SOVIET
SOCIALIST
REPUBLICS

MONGOLIA

INNER

SINKIANG

KIRGIZIA

C H I N E S E

TIBET

AFGHANISTAN

KASHMIR
•Srinagar

Lhasa•

SIKKIM

BHUTAN

NEPAL

Kandahar •

Rawalpindi•

Katmandu•

E. PAKISTAN

BURMA
Mandalay•

•Delhi

W. PAKISTAN

Calcutta •

Karachi•

INDIA

Bombay•

Hyderabad•

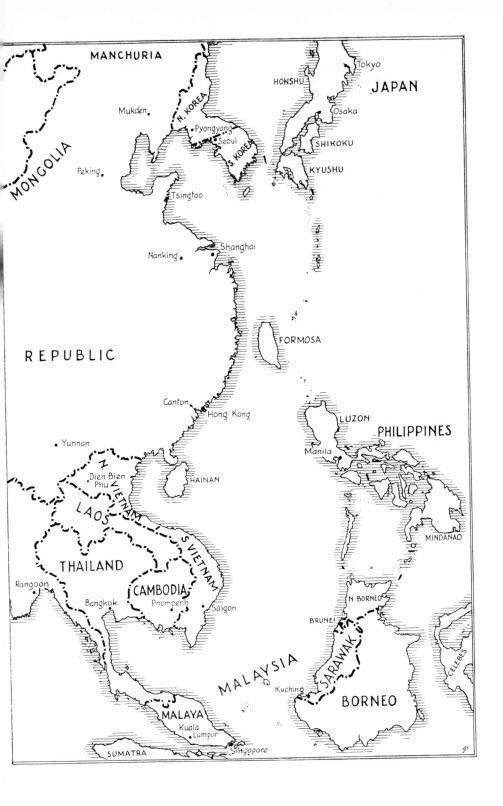

MANCHURIA

MONGOLIA

HONSHU

JAPAN

Tokyo

Mukden

N. KOREA

Pyongyang

Seoul

S. KOREA

Osaka

SHIKOKU

KYUSHU

Peking

Tsingtao

Nanking

Shanghai

REPUBLIC

FORMOSA

Canton

Hong Kong

LUZON

PHILIPPINES

Manila

Yunnan

Dien Bien
Phu

N VIETNAM

HAINAN

LAOS

S VIETNAM

MINDANAO

THAILAND

CAMBODIA

Rangoon

Bangkok

Pnompenh

Saigon

N BORNEO

BRUNEI

SARAWAK

MALAYSIA

Kuching

BORNEO

CELEBES

MALAYA

Kuala
Lumpur

SUMATRA

Singapore

starting to escort Nationalist convoys to the edge of the territorial waters around the offshore islands. Meanwhile, ambassadorial talks were resumed in Warsaw at the instigation of Chou En-lai.

Some commentators assumed at the time that the Soviet Union was putting pressure on China to maintain an atmosphere of tension in the Formosa Straits. They reasoned that the Soviet Union must have expected to profit from testing the degree of American involvement with Chiang Kai-shek. And, of course, the open criticism levelled at the end of September by both President Eisenhower and Mr Dulles of the extent of the Nationalist build up on Quemoy and Matsu does show that the administration in Washington felt more than somewhat uneasy about its commitments to the Kuomintang. But it is perhaps significant that Mr Kruschev's very strongly worded note to Washington in support of Peking was delivered only after the Chinese had come to the Warsaw conference table on September 15th. It would appear reasonable on general grounds to suppose that Russia was more conscious than China of the dangers implicit in too bold a confrontation.

It was around this time that China commenced development of an atomic bomb. Perhaps this decision should be seen as a manifestation of the fresh wave of pessimism that swept over her official circles in the autumn of 1958. By now the Great Leap Forward was admitted to be running into severe difficulties and the possibility of widespread civil disturbances aided and abetted from Formosa could not have been absent from the thoughts of those in power. Air battles over the Formosan Straits in September had demonstrated the superiority of Nationalist military equipment and, although a few weeks later Mr Dulles had got Chiang to renounce violence as the 'principal' means of returning to the mainland, he had conceded that it might be used in support of some large scale spontaneous uprising.

By now tens of thousands of East Tibetan rebels were engaged in a fierce fighting retreat towards Lhasa and so were engulfing the Brahma-putra valley in bitter conflict. Early in March 1959 the citizens of Lhasa restrained the Dalai Lama from accepting a suspect invitation to visit the Chinese military headquarters and so shortly afterwards the capital was shelled and stormed. The Dalai and some 10,000 of his followers withdrew to India. On their arrival they asserted that about 10,000 of their fellow Tibetans had been killed in the Battle of Lhasa and perhaps 90,000 since the revolt began.

The Chinese press then began a vigorous propaganda offensive against alleged Indian collusion with the Tibetan rebels. In reality, however, the Delhi government was anxious that the Tibetan affair should not become a Great Power crisis. It used its influence to help discourage the Dalai from seeking to invoke immediately international aid. Fairly general guerrilla warfare continued inside Tibet throughout 1960 but by then world interest had waned. Sino-Indian hostility had been kept alive, however, by the armed clash that occurred in Ladakh in the autumn of 1959.

*Tass* issued a statement on September 10th, 1959, that explicitly dissociated the USSR from China's policies in the Himalayas. At the end of the month Mr Kruschev visited Peking to warn his hosts that 'We must not test the strength of the Imperialists'. His reception was bleak and no *communiqué* was issued. Obviously the Chinese had at last decided that the material advantages of Soviet aid and protection were outweighed by the emotional satisfactions of forthright independence. Soviet criticism of the communes had by then become open and Moscow was clearly regarding 'neutralist and bourgeois' Delhi at least as sympathetically as she was Peking. China has since claimed that it was at this time that Russia withdrew an offer to help her manufacture an atomic bomb which had been made in 1957.

In the first half of 1960 the quarrel appeared to crystallize for a while into a neat ideological debate about the implications of modern weapons. Chinese spokesmen denied a Soviet contention that war could be totally eliminated from the earth even before the defeat of capitalism, and asserted instead that not even a nuclear war could destroy the socialist camp. All Soviet technicians and all their blueprints were abruptly withdrawn from China after the Bucharest Communist conference of July 1960, and what has been called the 'New Cold War' began in earnest. For some time China named Yugoslavia when clearly alluding to Russia, and Russia used Albania as the proxy for China,[1] but by 1963 this quixotic convention had been cast aside. China condemned Soviet policies during the Cuban rocket crisis as being compounded of adventurism and appeasement. She then refused to sign the partial test ban and accused the USSR of having sought ever since 1960 to subvert Sinkiang province. By now it was obvious to everybody that the conflict was in reality not one about theory, but one caused by differences in national interests and attitudes.

Grain production was officially claimed to be 250,000,000 tons in 1958. This claim was probably several tens of millions of tons too high and, in any case, it represented an advance of less than a half over the 185,000,000 tons claimed in 1957, whereas a two-fold expansion had been planned. Besides, the modest gain that was made was achieved only through the adoption of measures that disturbed the ecological balance and so left the Chinese rural economy pathetically vulnerable to natural calamity. Campaigns were launched against grain-eating birds; it was claimed that the massacre of sparrows alone passed the billion mark. Crop planting densities were doubled. Forests were slaughtered to provide charcoal. So when between 1959 and 1961 China was struck by the worst sequence of droughts and floods in perhaps a century grain output fell by at least a third. Not until about 1965 did it regain its 1957 level. Bread and rice rations became very tight in the big cities during these lean years, and it

---

[1] Stalinism continued to flourish in the primitive environment of Albania. It drew added strength from a nationalistic dislike and fear of the 'revisionists' of Yugoslavia. As the split between Moscow and Peking deepened so Tirana drew closer to Peking. Moscow broke off relations with her during 1961.

is much to the credit of the authorities that so little evidence emerged of price inflation or of a black market. Scarce foreign exchange had to be expended on the purchase of 15,000,000 tons of grain from such non-Communist countries as Canada and Australia. Meanwhile debt repayments to the Soviet Union had to be kept up. As the *People's Daily* was later to remark, this was a grim time for the Russians to choose for the withdrawal of 1,400 experts and the cancellation of 600 specific aid agreements.

China's industrial recovery from these many blows was remarkably fast. Construction of such heavy capital items as oil refineries went on; so did work on the atomic bomb, though it remains something of a mystery how China got round the technical and financial problems involved in the construction and operation of the gaseous diffusion plant from which, it seems, she got her enriched uranium. Over ten thousand individual items were on display at the Chinese commercial exhibition in Tokyo early in 1964.

A personality cult of Mao Tse-tung on the mainland has been matched by one of Chiang Kai-shek on Formosa. In this case the cult is part of the official ideology of counter-revolution; as Chiang said in his order of the day of October 10th, 1963: 'To us recovery of the mainland is a sacred mission to end Communist aggression in Asia and to remove the danger of nuclear war'. Because of this preoccupation children born to the Chinese *emigrés* are registered as belonging to the province from which their parents came, and Confucianism and Mandarin Chinese is taught in every high school. Between 1961 and 1963 heavy defence surtaxes were levied in the hope that the economic misfortunes of the mainland might create new opportunities.

All this has had a stultifying effect on Formosa. No elections for the National Assembly and Legislature are ever held because, it is argued, 'most of the country' is in Communist hands. Yet elections have been held for the provincial assembly that controls in reality exactly the same area. But the native Formosans, who still constitute over 80% of the population, are not allowed to form their own communal parties even for these provincial contests. This means that their feelings of local nationalism, which have been accentuated by the privileged position of the Kuomintang Chinese in the government service and elsewhere, can find few outlets for articulate expression. Formosan living standards rose at an average rate of 2% per year during the 1950s but this by no means created an atmosphere of contentment.

## (ii) *Japan*

Japan appears to have been the leader of the world investment boom of the 1950s. By the middle of the decade she was ploughing back about a third of her gross national product and so was enabling it to expand at an annual rate of 7%. That she was able to keep her investment ratio so high is, at first sight, surprising. She remained highly susceptible to balance of payment crises and, in dealing with them, relied heavily on holding back domestic expansion by means of credit restriction. However, her manufacturing sector was largely composed of small firms that were capable of altering their policies quickly and radically in response to government pressures. Therefore, when, as in 1953, 1957 and 1962, deflation was resorted to, there was no need for it to be unduly drastic or long lived.

With quantitative expansion goes structural change and so the Japanese economy came to project a very different image from what it did before the war. From 1955 she was the world's chief builder of ships. She did pioneer work in fields such as giant tanker construction and microelectronics. Her cameras, watches, and optical instruments gained extensive world markets thanks to their progressive improvement in quality. Between 1937 and 1960 steel and chemical outputs quadrupled; textiles, on the other hand, barely recovered their previous position.

But Japan, for all her industrial and commercial energy, found it hard to rebuild her export trade. Not until 1959 did its volume, measured in real terms, regain the 1937 level. Part of the trouble was that Japan was not admitted to the General Agreement on Tariffs and Trade until 1955 and that even then fourteen GATT members waived their commitments in respect of her. Part of it was the drastic trade reorientation enforced by post-war changes. Even in the peak year of 1957 not more than 2% of her trade was with China, whereas before 1937 a quarter of it was. The United States had now become Japan's dominant trading partner.

Many teachers and other intellectual groups kept alive a militant radicalism that was mildly Marxist, strongly Sinophil, and bitterly anti-American. In general, however, the comparative affluence of town and countryside succoured the forces of political conservatism. What did not seem to wax with prosperity was any great faith in the current way of life. Indeed, some have interpreted the striving for wealth as a mindless urge to sublimate all the doubts occasioned by unprecedented defeat in war. They have pointed out that certain aspects of the Westernization that went hand-in-hand with economic change have been manifestly neurotic. A moral confusion was reflected in the formation of many new religious groups and in a cult of violence that has helped produce the high incidence of crime and the spasms of rioting in the streets and in the Diet. Chief among the new sects was the Soka Gakkai; this was led by Buddhist zealots who sought to extend its power by all available methods, including forcible conversion and political activity. Late in 1964 it claimed a membership of 13,000,000.

An event occurred early in 1954 which evoked more popular revulsion than anything since Hiroshima. The fishing vessel *Fukuryu Maru* was showered with a strange dust whilst going about her lawful occasions. After her return to harbour some of her crew contracted radiation sickness and it transpired that the dust had come from a thermonuclear test at

733

Bikini; by that time her cargo of tuna fish had been widely distributed. American reluctance to accept full responsibility and, in particular, her tardiness in acknowledging that the boat was outside the pre-announced danger zone exacerbated the resulting tension.

That November Premier Yoshida completed a tour of Western countries that had been widely interpreted at home as indicating too firm a diplomatic alignment. A week later the Hatoyama Liberals combined with the Progressives to form a new Democratic Party and before the end of the year Hatoyama had succeeded Yoshida as Prime Minister.

In the elections of February 1955 the Democrats won 185 seats and the Liberals 112. The Socialists, who had been split into two parties since 1951, registered with their total of 156 seats a total gain of 21. Later that year both the conservatives and the socialists were reunited. The latter had agreed to commit themselves to the nationalization of key industries and a neutralist foreign policy.

Soon negotiations began with the USSR on the restoration of normal relations. They made slow progress until, early in 1956, the USSR used her twelve mile territorial water limit to oblige Japan to agree to a fisheries convention that would only come into force with the re-establishment of diplomatic links. This was provided for under an agreement ratified on December 12th and that same day Russia withdrew her opposition to Japanese entry to the United Nations. But she had not returned any of the Kurile islands. Neither had she accepted the Japanese claim that she had still to return 11,000 prisoners of war.

Just before the election of May 1958 China severed all the close cultural and commercial relations she had lately been cultivating with Japan. She did this largely as a protest against a Tokyo statement, made under strong pressure from Taipeh, that official endorsement of a recent commercial treaty in no way implied recognition of Peking. But the Left was able to reap little electoral advantage from this setback. The Socialists gained but eight seats; the Communists fielded 100 candidates only to lose one of the two seats they already held. The Liberal-Democrat government, now led by Nobusuke Kishi, was left with 287 parliamentary seats.

The Left gave rather more impressive displays of its strength in its blocking of a government proposal made later that year to increase police powers of arrest and detention and in its resistance to revision of the 1952 Mutual Security Treaty with the United States and of the associated Administrative Agreement. The government sought, in 1959, a revision that would preclude the American garrison being used for internal security, give Japan a say in any deployment of that garrison overseas, remove certain special privileges it enjoyed and eliminate the Japanese contribution to its upkeep; most of these objectives were effectively realized in the new treaty and agreement signed in June 1960. Meanwhile, however, the Socialists, encouraged by a Soviet contention that any revision would be but a prelude to Japan becoming a nuclear rocket base, had launched a general political offensive against the whole principle of a military nexus with the United States. Shortly before the treaty was signed President Eisenhower cancelled an impending visit to Japan because of repeated anti-American demonstrations; shortly after the signature Mr Kishi was replaced as Prime Minister and leader of the Liberal Democrats by Mr Ikeda. The Liberal-Democrats made some modest gains in the election of that autumn and almost held their own in the one of 1963, but how sensitive the public remained to the nuclear issue was shown by the prolonged intergovernmental discussions in 1963 about whether nuclear-driven but conventionally-armed American submarines might visit Japanese harbours.

## (iii) *The Two Koreas*

1953 saw the Communist front still firmly in control of North Korea. Soon after the armistice agreement at Panmunjom it began to use this control to impose a rate of industrialization substantially greater than that achieved in the South, and further to remodel agriculture along Marxist-Maoist lines. Thus at the end of 1958 a programme to form bigger 'co-operative farms' analogous to the Chinese communes was announced.

As economic recovery proceeded, the country came ever more firmly under the control of Kim Il Sung. Most of the leaders of the South Korean Communists in exile had been shot as American spies by 1956. Later came a purge of those Communists who had fought alongside Mao in the Yenan campaigns.

Kim Il Sung sought effective autonomy by playing off Russia against China. Only Russian military assistance was accepted but China provided a third of the economic aid received in the first decade of peace. De-stalinization was little stressed in North Korea lest it undermine the cult of the personality of Kim Il Sung. Pyongyang tended to side with Peking over Yugoslavia, Cuba and the Sino-Indian border. Some argue that Moscow has welcomed or even encouraged this independence because it has enabled her to contact China through North Korea. Mr Kosygin's visit to that country in the middle of the Vietnam crisis of February 1965 could be cited in support of that contention.

Synghman Rhee prepared for the South Korean constituency elections of May 1954 with the usual round of purges. The Liberal Party, which had been created in 1951 to furnish him with his own political machine, sought a mandate for unspecified constitutional reforms. However, despite much electoral malpractice they won only half the 200 seats in a 97% poll. But within a month recounts had secured for them another 25.

All the reforms the Liberal leaders had in mind were designed to strengthen the institutional power of Synghman Rhee. Thus, the premiership was to be abolished so that the President became direct head of the executive and that executive was no longer to be responsible to the legislature. In September 1954 assembly opposition to these proposals was broken by a brazen display of jerrymandering. Meanwhile, Rhee sought to maintain a sense of impending crisis by extravagant demands for preventive war on China. He was firmly snubbed in this regard by the United States, which in the course of that summer announced the withdrawal of six of the eight divisions in her garrison.

The virulence of the overt opposition was again shown in 1956 when Dr John Chang defeated Rhee's nominee for the Vice-Presidency and when the President's own vote slumped. So in 1960 bribery, official and semi-official violence, and vote forgery were used on an unprecedented scale to ensure Rhee's survival and Chang's defeat. Widespread riots broke out as soon as the results were announced and, meanwhile, Washington began to press hard for a change in the *status quo*. Rhee resigned from the post of President in April and within a few months Chang had become premier. But he was evicted the next year by an army junta. Two years later the junta, faced with internal discontent and American pressure, allowed a return to parliamentary rule.

# Chapter XVI
# A ZONE OF INSTABILITY

## (i) *The Geneva Settlement and its Breakdown*

LATE in 1953 East and West began to discuss informally a reduction of tension in the Far East. Then, at the Berlin Foreign Ministers' meeting, Mr Molotov suggested that there should be a conference of all interested nations, including China. A British resolution adopted by the Ministers on February 18th called for such a conference to begin in Geneva on April 26th. Representatives of the Vietminh, Vietnam, Laos and Cambodia were to be able to participate in its discussions on Indo-China.

Six weeks before the conference started 50,000 Vietminh soldiers began an assault against the 9,000 men of the French Union garrison at Dien Bien Phu. Two major French errors soon became apparent. One was to underestimate the ability of the Vietminh to concentrate in that terrain massed artillery imported from China. The other was a failure to anticipate their skill at camouflaging and protecting guns set on forward slopes close to the garrison perimeter. Gunfire prevented any use of the French airstrip after the end of March. Early on May 8th the garrison ended its frenzied resistance and its survivors entered a captivity that was harsh even by Vietminh standards.

The deterioration of the French position at Dien Bien Phu, and in the Red River delta, led during April to a sudden abandonment of the previous Washington view that France could win without direct American intervention. Mr Dulles, in particular, came to favour publicly warning China before Geneva that she would incur aerial reprisal by France's allies if her aid to the Vietminh did not cease. By the middle of the month, however, he was advocating merely an air strike against the Vietminh storage areas at Dien Bien Phu and, if the conference collapsed, air or ground intervention against other Vietminh positions. But Britain declined to support any immediate military action or to make any commitments about the future. She was also anxious to postpone detailed public discussion of any new regional security pact.

At the first plenary session on Indo-China the Communists conceded that their Free Laos and Free Cambodia movements could not be accorded independent representation. But despite this auspicious start the conference ground on so slowly, and with so few informal contacts between delegates, that in the middle of June President Eisenhower suggested the American delegation bring things to a close. Shortly afterwards, however, Pierre Mendès-France restored the sense of urgency by committing himself, in his investiture speech, to peace in Indo-China by July 20th. The next day the conference agreed to establish military sub-committees to examine the mechanics of a cease-fire in Laos and Cambodia. Such a study had already been initiated in respect of Vietnam. The main delegations then adjourned until these committees were ready to report.

They reassembled in the middle of July and on the 21st of the month the armistice agreements, which roughly corresponded to a draft suggested to France by Britain and the United States three weeks earlier, were signed by the commanders of the French Union forces and the Vietminh. International Control Commissions staffed, at Chou En-lai's suggestion, by India, Canada and Poland were to be set up to supervise the truce. Among the most important immediate tasks of the Vietnam Commission was that of moving 100,000 Vietminh supporters north and 600,000 Catholics and 250,000 other anti-Communists south; this was in consequence of a provisional division of the country at the 17th parallel. Elections were to be held in Laos and Cambodia in 1955 and in Vietnam by July 1956. No military build-ups were permitted nor, with the exception of two French posts in Laos, were any foreign bases to be established. All delegations, except the United States and non-Communist Vietnam, orally pledged themselves to unify Vietnam through free elections. In a separate statement the United States promised not to disturb the settlement. No accord was reached on Korea.

The Vietminh at Geneva had much contact with the Chinese but little with the Russians. But soon Ho Chi-minh led the new state of North Vietnam into a position of neutrality between Russia and China. Traditional Vietnamese distrust of Chinese overlordship was reinforced by the practical considerations that a small state bargains best if it remains in the overlap between two spheres of influence, and that the further economic reconstruction proceeded, the more important it would become to draw upon some of Russia's accumulated skills. The army commander, Vo Nguyen Giap, seemed especially anxious that his men should be able to reap the benefits of Soviet professionalism.

Russia supplied North Vietnam with a large consignment of Burmese rice in 1955 but most of the aid received in the first four years of peace came from China. It included, for example, many advisers on land reform and the establishment of rural mutual aid teams. But through her identification with the North Vietnamese agricultural programme, Peking drew upon herself popular resentment at its shortcomings. Hanoi's brief emulation of the 'One Hundred Flowers' campaign in 1956 swiftly revealed how strong the resentment was. And that autumn, as troops were being deployed in force against the peasants of Nghe An province, several leading pro-Chinese officials were dismissed. However, the 'Chinese' faction partially re-established itself late in 1957 and it helped organize the collectivization of over 80% of the peasants during the following three years. But Vietnam did not try to imitate China's experiment with communes and she started to receive most of her aid from Russia and Eastern Europe. When the Sino-Soviet dispute developed, Vietnam gave China only qualified support.

The new constitution of 1960 strengthened the position of President Ho Chi-minh and so helped him hold his *régime* at this delicate point of international balance. Its introduction was made the occasion for North Vietnam's first general election; though less than a quarter of the seats were actively contested, over 98% of the electorate is said to have voted. Characteristic Marxist disdain for the countryside could be seen in the arrangements made for the over-representation of the towns.

' In accordance with the Geneva agreements the Left Wing Pathet Lao forces withdrew to the two most northerly Laotian provinces—Phong Saly and Sam Neua—pending their reabsorption into national politics. Some armed clashes in 1955 were followed by tortuous negotiations that eventually produced a settlement in November 1957. This provided for the admission of the Pathet Lao into the government, and for its providing two battalions for the national army and half the officials for the northern provinces. But non-Communist political groups became alarmed when the Pathet Lao—known for electoral purposes as the Neo Lao Haskat—won over half the extra seats created for the supplementary election of May 1958. That August Phoui Sananikone formed a new government that did not contain the Pathet Lao. He then compelled the International Control Commission to continue an adjournment indefinitely on the grounds that its work was complete.

One Pathet Lao battalion (both of which were by then in semi-custody), fled east in the summer of 1959 and desultory fighting continued for some months afterwards. Elections were held again early in 1960 but the failure of the Pathet Lao to gain even a single seat seemed to serve as proof of its contention that the election was rigged. That August, Vientiane was seized by a young American-trained paratroop captain called Kong Lee and he put a neutralist, ex-Premier Prince Souvanna Phouma, in power. The southern town of Savannakhet then became the centre of a Right Wing resistance movement led by Boum Oum, the titular prince of Champassac, and by the former Defence Minister, General Phoumi. Their large though ramshackle army recaptured Vientiane, after subjecting it to a quite excessive bombardment, but in the meantime the Neutralists and the Pathet Lao took over the key airstrips and dropping zones in the Plaine des Jarres. A Soviet airlift, which had started when Kong Lee was in possession of Vientiane, was now stepped up and North Vietnamese instructors were brought in as well as equipment.

Peace negotiations began after a Right Wing offensive broke down early in 1961. President Kennedy spoke in favour of a neutral Laos in March and in May the International Control Commission was reinstated in order to supervise a cease-fire. A fourteen nation peace conference then began at Geneva.

Further hostilities in the spring of 1962 culminated in the flight of 3,000 Rightist troops from the positions they had taken up, against American military advice, at Nam Tha. But in July the Geneva Conference approved the proposed reduction and integration of the several Laotian armies and the recent formation of a broad coalition with Souvanna Phouma as Premier and Phoumi and Souphannouvong as his deputies. But this government neither worked as one body nor imposed its will across the land. Most of the mountainous East and North remained under independent Pathet Lao control throughout 1963. It was through these districts that men and supplies flowed from North Vietnam to the insurgents in South Vietnam.

Ngo Dinh-diem was appointed the first Prime Minister of South Vietnam by Bao Dai—the playboy Emperor—but in the well staged referendum of October 1955 he obtained a mandate to establish a republic with himself as president. He denied that he was bound by the Geneva Agreements and said that the character of the *régime* in the North made talk of free elections unreal.

Diem was yet another of those who saw the art of government as consisting of the enforcement of arbitrary and personal rule within a framework of constitutional democracy. He frequently by-passed the law courts and the National Assembly and set up many local detention centres. Many of his repressive measures ante-dated the subversion they had ostensibly been designed to combat. Others, such as the 'morality laws' of 1962 and the campaign against the Buddhists in 1963, were irrelevant to it. Rice production nearly doubled between 1955 and 1959 but little effort was made to grapple with the more fundamental question of land tenure. Less than a fifth of the acreage owned by the few thousand large landlords had been redistributed by 1961. Bitter resentment had been caused in the immediate post-war period by attempts to use troops to collect up to eight years rent arrears—i.e. the equivalent of four years' harvest—legally due to absentee landlords.

The Vietcong—the post-war successor within the South of the Vietminh —began in 1957 to assassinate systematically village elders, headmen and local officials. Four hundred and seventy were killed in that year. By 1959 the annual total was 1,600 and in 1960 4,000. What hope remained of rural progress was snuffed out by this insurgent terror.

A National Front for the Liberation of South Vietnam was formed in Hanoi late in 1960. Ten months earlier the Vietcong had launched their first full scale attack on a regular army regiment. Two months earlier Vietminh troops had been in action within the borders of the South. A year and a half later the Indian and Canadian members of the International Control Commission reported that the entry through Laos of men and materials from North Vietnam was in serious violation of the 1954 truce. After the death of Diem in the army coup of November 1963 this input markedly rose. Between late 1961 and early 1964 the Vietcong regular field force trebled to 30,000 men. The strength of the United States military mission with the government forces had risen to 11,000 by late 1961 and 16,000 by late 1963.

As the scale of the conflict grew, the balance of advantage shifted towards the Vietcong. Government lists of troops killed and missing rose from 5,700 for 1962 to 9,000 for 1963. At the same time the estimate of Vietcong killed or captured dropped from 26,000 to 21,000. An official American survey completed early in 1963 found that the Vietcong were then able to run an adequate tax collection system in 37 out of the 40 provinces. Perhaps a quarter of the South Vietnamese population of 14,000,000 was by then firmly under Vietcong control.

## (ii) *From the Mekong to New Guinea*

Australia, New Zealand, Britain, France, the United States, Pakistan, Thailand and the Philippines formed the South-East Asia Treaty Organization in September 1954; India, Burma, Ceylon and Indonesia had declined to join. The treaty covered all the Asian and Pacific territory of its members south of 21° 30′ N[1] and, under a separate protocol, responsibility was also assumed for the 'Designated States' of Cambodia, Laos and South Vietnam. Its purpose was to check armed attack and subversion and to provide for the co-operative strengthening of free institutions and national economies. Many SEATO naval and military manoeuvres have been carried out but no network of commands has been set up, nor any national forces permanently assigned. Perhaps the treaty's most important result has been that its Asian members have become magnets for United States military and economic assistance. Her aid to them quadrupled between 1954 and 1957, and by 1962 Thailand, the Philippines and the Designated States were drawing an annual total of $670 million. For Burma,[2] Malaya and Indonesia the figure was $94 million.

Popular dislike of the local Chinese, a relative absence of land hunger and a vast web of official informers have enabled the Thai authorities to keep systematic subversion in check. But the elections Field Marshal Pibul Songgram allowed at last, in 1957, ten years after his seizure of power, were held in a way which provoked considerable spontaneous unrest. General Sarit, the Defence Minister, was called in to restore order and so became

---

[1] It therefore just excluded Hongkong.

[2] U Nu was in power in Burma until 1958 and again from 1960 till 1962. In 1960 and again in 1962 he was obliged to give way to a Revolutionary Council headed by General Ne Win.

able much to enhance his prestige within the army. He used this to force Pibul out and, after attempting to restore parliamentary government, himself assumed autocratic powers towards the end of 1958. So things remained until his death five years later.

Ramón Magsaysay resigned his post as Filipino Minister of Defence in 1953 in order to fight for the Presidency. After his election by a wide margin, he strove vigorously to fulfil his mandate for agrarian reform, economic development and governmental integrity. He also continued the armed struggle against subversion and in 1954 was rewarded with the capture of the Huk leader. But after the President had been killed in an air crash in 1957 his Nationalist administration lost its reforming impetus. Some revival of Huk activity took place over the next few years.

Preparation for Indonesia's first, and long heralded, national election went slowly forward in 1954 against a background of banditry and general discontent. The poll was, in fact, held late in 1955 and the result was a qualified success for the PNI—the Java-based socialist Indonesian Nationalist Party that marched still behind the banner of President Sukarno although he was now supposed to be an apolitical head of state. PNI got the most votes but *Masjoemi*—the moderately conservative Islamic movement—won as many seats despite the fact that the elections did not embrace most of the outer islands, where the stand of *Masjoemi* against unduly centralized government was especially popular. Both *Nahdatul Ulama*—a militantly anti-Western orthodox Islamic group that was strong among the Javanese peasantry—and the Communists did better than expected. Each party got between six and eight and a half million votes.

Sukarno wished the Communists to enter the new government but was opposed by *Masjoemi* and by Mohammed Hatta, the widely esteemed Vice-President. In the event a PNI-*Masjoemi* coalition was formed under the rather Left Wing PNI ex-Premier, Ali Sastroamidjojo.

This coalition rapidly became unstable. Hatta's resignation late in 1956 symbolized the unease that all moderates and conservatives felt at the dissolution of the Union with the Netherlands and at the repudiation of the debt to the Dutch. This unease was increased by President Sukarno's declaration of early 1957 in favour of a 'guided democracy' in which he would rule with advice from an advisory council on which social organizations would be represented as well as political parties. And political antagonisms within the army were aggravated by a continuing dispute as to whether the service should be modelled mainly on 'European' lines or on revolutionary militia ones.

Serious army revolts broke out in Sumatra, Borneo and the Celebes during the winter of 1956–57. Something like peace was restored by negotiation the following autumn but was shattered almost immediately by the backlash from a refusal by the United Nations General Assembly to press for a renewal of bilateral talks on the longstanding Indonesian claim to Dutch New Guinea.[1] Soldiers and trade unionists seized many Dutch

[1] Or West Irian, as it was often called.

assets and the expulsion of the 50,000 Dutch residents began. Since Dutchmen owned the inter-island shipping service and ran the export industries on which the outer islands so heavily depended the economic consequences were especially disastrous outside Java. Armed resistance began afresh in Sumatra and the Celebes early in 1958. This was encouraged by American intelligence.

But Sukarno was able to turn the revolutionary situation to his advantage. Though 20,000 rebels refused to surrender until 1961 the impetus of their movement was broken within a few months by the consummate professionalism of the Army Chief of Staff, Colonel Nasution. Sukarno was thus left free to purge the heavily implicated *Masjoemi* and then, in 1960, to dissolve it formally. 1960 was also the year of the formation of a People's Consultative Congress, which was intended by Sukarno to serve as the advisory council in his 'guided democracy'. He filled 110 places within it with politicians chosen in roughly equal proportion from the PNI, *Nahdatul Ulama* and the Communists. The other 86 appointees were from the armed forces and the police and from worker and peasant organizations. In 1961 and 1962 agreements were made for the supply of Soviet arms.

By the time Sir Gerald Templer left Malaya in 1954 the Communist insurrection was well under control; in 1960 the emergency was officially ended. Independence was given to Malaya in 1957 on the basis of a federal constitution that preserved for the Malay community certain of its traditional advantages. Islam remained an established religion and Malay became the sole alternative to English as an official language. One result of linguistic provision has been that schools have been unable to get grants-in-aid unless they are prepared to teach in Malay. Discontent on this score has often been in evidence among the Chinese element within Tungku Abdul Rahman's multi-communal Alliance party but this has not prevented the Alliance from preserving an absolutely dominant position in Parliament.

In May 1961 the Tungku unexpectedly declared himself in favour of a federal union of Malaya, Singapore and the British territories in Borneo. Such a Malaysian federation came into being in August 1963 but its early months were troubled ones. Indonesia, who laid geographic claim to all Borneo, and the Philippines, who laid historical claim to Sabah, broke off relations with Malaysia after a team of United Nations investigators had reported that the peoples of Sabah and Sarawak had joined the federation freely. The Sultanate of Brunei decided not to come in partly because an armed rising in 1962 had illustrated how powerful Indonesian-sponsored subversion had become. By the end of 1963 Malaysian Borneo was frequently being entered by Indonesian armed patrols.

## Chapter XVII
## SOUTH FROM THE HIMALAYAS

(i) *India Under Stress*

By the Avadi resolution of 1955 Congress committed itself to the creation of a socialistic society based on the public ownership of key industries, the redistribution of wealth and economic growth. Implementation of these Fabian principles had by then, of course, already started. Under the first two five-year plans, which ended in 1961, some fifteen billion dollars of public and ten billion dollars of private money were invested. The plans boosted the national income by rather more than 40% and so, although the simultaneous rise in population was 22% and although perhaps a quarter of the added income was used for extra investment, some improvement of living standards was recorded. General industrial production doubled whilst for certain basic items, such as machine tools and sulphuric acid, the expansion rate was considerably higher. Literacy rose from 17 to 24%.

Agriculture benefited from the public investment which made the acreage of irrigated land half as large again but it benefited even more from various institutional changes in the country. Official limitation of interest rates for moneylending has helped, despite much evasion, to contain a primary source of petty tyranny. Two hundred State land reform acts have meant that eventually only a tenth of the cultivated land was left in private estates of more than thirty acres. Land reform was accelerated by the amendment of the Union constitution to allow States to set a ceiling on individual land ownership and to prevent the law courts from determining the amounts of compensation. But private landlords were often replaced by State ones, for the tenants concerned usually had little real chance, under the conditions laid down, of purchasing the plots they worked. Rent control has been introduced with the aim of reducing average rents from over 50% of the crop value to between 20 and 25%; consequently rents have dropped appreciably in most areas despite widespread evasion. The Gandhian tradition of change through moral suasion has been kept alive by Vinobe Bhave, who in 1951 founded the land-gifts movement. Only four million acres, about 1% of the cultivable area, was donated by landlords in the first decade of this movement but Bhave and his followers helped make the climate of opinion more conducive to other methods of redistribution.

On Gandhi's birthday in 1952 the Community Development programme began—a programme which Nehru claimed was changing the face of rural India. Each group of about 100 villages was placed under a Project Officer responsible for co-ordinating all the major services—agricultural, veterinary, educational, co-operative and so on—and for involving village councils in local planning as heavily as possible. Most of India's farmland had been covered by the project by 1960 and the average improvement in productivity that resulted may have been 10%. But government reports in 1957 and 1958 suggested that the richer villages and the richer individuals, being able to offer more security on loans and being able to exert more influence, tended to fare best under the scheme.

Hindu society was still stabilized and paralysed by caste and by family but in each case the framework had loosened a little. Custom will lag behind law, but the fact that it was made a criminal offence to deny an Untouchable access to a public well or eating place is important. Widows, wives and daughters all had their positions strengthened by a new Hindu marriage code. Its enactment, after years of delay, represented a victory for Nehru over the reactionary wing of Congress.

Such economic and social advances are normally associated with the greater political integration of the nation in question but in India it was regional rather than national bonds that were strengthened. Many of the younger politicians came from lower down the caste and class structure than did, say, Nehru and so were more provincial and less sub-continental in language and outlook.

Language is the key to regional strength. There are in India, in addition to hundreds of tribal tongues, two major language groups. One derives from Sanskrit and has as its chief members Hindi, Bengali, Gujrati and Marathi. The other, which is supreme south of the River Tabti, is Dravidian and includes, in particular, Kannada, Telugu, Malayalam and Tamil. Hindi is neither homogeneous nor particularly rich in literary forms but its primacy in the nodal and densely populated valley of the Upper Ganges led to its adoption as a national language along with English in 1950. The constitution stipulated that Hindi should entirely replace English in 1965 and that, in the meantime, the Union government was to do all it could to promote Hindi. But in 1963 legislation was passed for the indefinite retention of English as an associate language. Over 80% of the speeches in the Lok Sabha were still in English rather than Hindi and almost all the written and spoken business of the central government was still conducted in English.

Both the leaders of Congress and the spokesmen for the professions had previously failed to acknowledge how great were the technical difficulties of transition. A further consideration was that, in the Dravidian area in particular, English was regarded as a buffer that could check the

745

advance of Hindi whilst the regional languages were being built up. Out of the new regional consciousness arose a pressure for monolingual States. For some years the Union government refused to make concessions but in October 1953, less than a year after the death through fasting of a prominent Telugu leader, the separate state of Andhra was formed to coincide as closely as possible with the predominantly Telugu speaking area of Madras. Within months Nehru had agreed also to form a Reorganization Commission that was to advise on the redrawing of boundaries along linguistic lines. Many of its proposals were included in the reforms of 1956; these dramatically altered India's political geography, particularly in the South. Hyderabad, for example, ceased to exist and the total number of States fell from 26 to 14.

But linguistic troubles continued. Maharashtrian resentment at inclusion in Bombay, which had resulted in serious riots in the State capital early in 1956, obliged the government to divide Bombay into the new States of Maharashtra and Gujarat in 1960. Agitation in favour of a Sikh State caused many thousands to be arrested in Delhi and the Punjab that year and the following. Assam was also a centre of linguistic disturbance at that time. In 1963 the Dravida Munnetra Kazhagam, a virulent southern separatist group with a fascistic ritual, held a quarter of the seats in the legislative assembly of Madras.

Congress lost ground as a result of these regional tensions and a generalized discontent with its rather corrupt and somewhat lethargic hegemony. Between 1954 and 1958 its membership fell from eight million to four and early in 1958 a tired and depressed Nehru talked openly of resignation. But for all its faults and inner conflicts Congress remained absolutely supreme in Union politics. In 1963 it held 359 of the 496 seats in the Lok Sabha. Thirty-three were held by Communists, twelve by Socialists, and most of the remainder by Hindu conservative groups.

The Communists had become the official opposition in the Lok Sabha as a result of the 1957 General Election. That same year they were able to form a government in Kerala—the only Communist State government India has so far had. But bitter hostility to the *régime* was generated by the officially condoned terror campaign against non-Communists and, within the large Roman Catholic minority, by the plan to nationalize the schools. Mass civil disobedience began in 1959 and so the Union government took over the administration. In fresh State elections in 1960 the Communists got but a quarter of the seats.

1955 marked the zenith of India's policy of promoting an Afro-Asian 'area of peace' between the two Cold War camps. This was the year of the Bandung Conference and of excellent relations between Delhi and both Moscow and Peking. No permanent organization was established at Bandung and no comparable conference of that kind was held until the one in Belgrade in 1961.[1] The authentic Afro-Asian movement was effectively

[1] The Cairo Conference of 1957 was much more under Communist influence, Soviet delegates being present as well as Chinese.

destroyed by the separate evolution of pan-Africanism and by the growth of Sino-Indian rivalry in the Himalayas.

The instability in Eastern Tibet[1] gave the Chinese a strategic interest in building a road through the Indian province of Ladakh so as to connect Sinkiang with Lhasa. Work on this road started in 1955 and to begin with India acquiesced in this encroachment within an ill-defined border area. But in 1957 she protested against a Chinese visit to Fort Khurnak and two years later there was a bitter exchange of notes about a border clash in which nine Indian policemen had been killed.

The next year the Chinese infiltrated some troops as part of their policy of keeping alive a claim to the North-East Frontier Agency, a claim derived from the Chinese failure ever to ratify the decision of the Simla Conference of 1913 to accept the McMahon Line as the northern border of the NEFA and so of India. The seriousness of this challenge was enhanced by the fact that for some years up to 40,000 Indian troops had been trying to quell a revolt in support of complete Nagaland independence. An agreement was signed in 1960 with the Naga People's Convention—a government sponsored group of moderates—for the creation of a Naga State within the Union. But the rebels fought on.

Sino-Indian tension mounted rapidly during 1962 until in October Nehru announced that the army had been ordered to rid India of the intruders. This was attempted by the infiltration of patrols between the Chinese outposts; these induced the Chinese to launch heavy counter-attacks which, despite some desperate Indian resistance, carried them to the limit of their boundary claims in Ladakh and to positions in the NEFA well south of Bomdila. At least a fifth of the quarter of a million troops the Chinese had in Tibet became involved in the fighting. Elements of three or four Indian divisions were engaged but the Indian troops within the battle zone were usually outnumbered several times over. In early December the Chinese terminated the campaign by a withdrawal to their 1959 positions. They therefore remained in control of their strategic highway in Ladakh. Some 7,000 Indian troops had been taken prisoner by then.

For some years India's press and parliament had been following closely the events in the Himalayas. But the concept of China as the mortal enemy was, none the less, novel. Few Indians, Nehru being an exception, had evinced much concern about the fact that China, for all her miscalculations and misadventures, appeared to have kept up a higher farming output per head of population[2] and had industrialized herself at a much faster rate than India. Many, Nehru being an example, had realized that China would have the cultural strength to modify Marxism and had all too glibly assumed that this would mean that she would render it more tolerant and pragmatic. Indian academicians had tended to devote little close study to the Chinese revolution. Defence expenditure had been held at about 2%

[1] See page 726.
[2] Commentators tended to forget that this had generally been the case in pre-war days as well.

of the national income and most of it had been oriented towards Pakistan and much towards the open sea.

The reactions to the heavy Chinese attacks was all the sharper for the previous indifference, words like 'betrayal' and 'Pearl Harbor' being freely used. Defence expenditure jumped from £378,000,000 in 1962–3 to £650,000,000 in 1963–4; the army, in particular, expanded as six new mountain divisions began to be formed. By late 1963 both the USSR and the USA had sent or promised over $100,000,000 of military aid and Australian, British and American planes had flown in an Indian air defence exercise. The narrow patriotism of Hindu communalists had strengthened, particularly in the towns; and a frontier agreement between Pakistan and China had reinforced this trend. Congress had had, meanwhile, some very bad election results and in August six Congress ministers had felt obliged to resign from the Union government in order to devote themselves to strengthening their party machine.

## (ii) *Pakistan and Kashmir*

The Pakistan political balance was rudely shaken by the East Bengal Assembly elections of 1954. Nine of the 270 seats went to the Moslem League; three-quarters of the rest went to an opposition United Front that campaigned for the acceptance of Bengali as an official language alongside Urdu and for more provincial autonomy. But later that year, after communal rioting had broken out, the assembly was suspended by the governor. Hindu emigration continued.

A corresponding decline of the Moslem League in the west wing of Pakistan, which was welded into one province in 1955, was reflected in the formation of the secular conservative Republican party in 1956 and in the marked progress in West Pakistan of the National Awami Party—a neutralist group that was formed in 1957. But neither the proliferation of parties nor the long awaited promulgation of a constitution in 1956 revitalized the political scene. The Communist Party had been made illegal and none of the other Left Wing parties enjoyed much popular support. Politics, in the absence of any articulate radicalism, became more and more a matter of factional manoeuvres sustained by corruption. Early in October 1958 the President, Major-General Iskander Mirza, suspended the constitution. At the end of the month full powers were assumed by General, later Field Marshal, Ayub Khan, the commander-in-chief of the army. He left soldiers and retired officials in charge of most of the major departments of government. But civilians were well represented on the advisory commissions that were set up to help guide the administration. The commission that reported on education in 1959 found that the profession was rent by factiousness and riddled with cynicism, lethargy opportunism and suspicion. As much had become true of most of the other public services.

Most army officers came from West Pakistan but by two early measures the new *régime* demonstrated that this did not oblige it to serve the vested interests of that province. The movement of the seat of government from the commercial capital of Karachi to Rawalpindi made it less subject to undesirable influences. Meanwhile, land reform eroded some of their powers; the 6,000 leading western landowners, who owned an average of 1,500 acres apiece, had a third of their land redistributed to 150,000 peasants. Compensation rates were generally low.

Ayub Khan spoke of having the country 'organized like the army' but what he introduced was not military autocracy but a functional alliance between the army and the rural lower middle classes. Its institutional expression was the Basic Democracy pyramid established in 1959. Some 8,000 local councils—known as *Union panchayats*—were established. Five people were elected to each council; they nominated five more. Some of the members of the superior sub-district, district and divisional councils were chosen by and from the *panchayats;* others were government officials. The elective *panchayat* members became in 1960 an electoral college for the purpose of passing a vote of confidence in Ayub Khan. He was endorsed by 95% of these voters.

The same electoral college, operating under a new constitution that had largely been formulated by Ayub Khan himself, chose new national and provincial assemblies in 1962. One feature of these assemblies was that no member of a government was allowed to sit in them. Soon Ayub Khan, acting in response to public criticism, introduced an ordinance to change this but, in 1963, this unilateral initiative was ruled *ultra vires* by the High Court at Dacca. The rule of law still prevailed in Pakistan.

The 1962 constitution was related to Islamic precepts more explicitly than its predecessor of 1956. Thus it required a research institute and an advisory council to be set up to tender advice on the reconstruction of the law and of society along Islamic lines. Late in 1963 Ayub Khan himself became the president of a reconstituted Moslem League. But this apparent commitment may well mean little. Nowhere in Pakistan is religious fundamentalism weaker than it is in the ranks of the armed forces.

A joint statement in August 1953 by the governments of India and Pakistan reaffirmed that Kashmir's future should be settled through a 'fair and impartial plebiscite'. But in his letter of the following March Pandit Nehru argued that the recent decision by Pakistan to accept military aid from the United States had changed the whole context of the dispute. The Kashmir Constituent Assembly—the descendant in Indian-held Kashmir of the popular assembly created in 1939—decided in 1956 to integrate the province with India. Delhi remained committed to the principal of local self-determination but said that complete withdrawal of the Pakistan army must precede any plebiscite. An offer by the United States in 1962 to mediate was rejected by India. Nehru indicated that no agreement would be possible as long as Pakistan kept referring the matter to the Security Council. The deadlock over Kashmir stands in contrast to the agreement in 1959 over the division of the waters from the main Indus tributaries—a problem that had threatened to prove just as intractable.

*Chapter XVIII*
# FROM THE CASPIAN TO THE NILE

ON August 16th, 1953, after an unsuccessful attempt by his Imperial Guard to replace Dr Mussadiq with General Zahedi, the Shah of Persia went into exile. He returned a few days later, however, after the army, aided by royalist demonstrations that American agents had done something to encourage, had proved able to seize Teheran and install Zahedi in the premiership. Within a year Mussadiq had been sentenced to three years solitary confinement and scores of Tudeh suspects had been arrested.

American emergency aid, which Mussadiq had been refused that May, was quickly forthcoming for the new *régime*. During the summer of 1954 an oil settlement was reached that took account of, among other things, the growing American interest in Persian security and Persia's need for American help in rebuilding her export trade. A total of eight companies formed an international consortium to produce oil and to sell it; about 50% of the capital was thenceforward British and 40% American. Compensation for the partial transfer of its capital assets was paid to British Petroleum—the name by which Anglo-Iranian was now to be known—by the other members of the new consortium. And the consortium agreed that 50% of its profits within Persia should go to the Persian government.

When the 1945 to 1963 period is considered as a whole, the part played in the Cold War by the Middle East appears less prominent than that played either by Europe or by the Far East. But between 1955 and 1958 the region was the principal arena of the struggle. This seems to have been due in large part to the desire of the West, and of John Foster Dulles in particular, to surround the USSR with a cordon of interlocking alliances. Turkey, already a member of NATO, and Pakistan, already a member of SEATO, were made to serve as linch-pins. Negotiations about the supply of American military aid to Pakistan had begun by the autumn of 1953 and in April 1954 Turkey and Pakistan signed a treaty of military and non-military collaboration which was intended as the forerunner of a regional framework. Within nineteen months it had in fact been succeeded by the Baghdad Pact of which Iraq, Persia, and Britain were also signatories. Iraq had joined despite strong pressure from Egypt. Jordan had not despite strong pressure from Britain.

Russia's first post-war loan to a non-Communist nation was the one she made early in 1954 to Afghanistan—a country that, ever since 1947, had been clamouring for the secession of the Pathan parts of Pakistan. Various other overtures were made to Kabul during the next two years but by 1956 it was Cairo that had become the obvious focus of the Soviet counter-offensive in the Middle East. Concentration on Cairo meant winning the friendship, however conditional, of Colonel Nasser—the dynamic young son of a post office clerk who had recently become Egypt's Prime Minister and so the undisputed head of her revolution. Nasser's policy was one of secularism and nationalism at home and neutralism abroad. He continued the repression of the local Communists and he crushed the Moslem Brotherhood—the large and semi-secret movement of Islamic conservative nationalists that was by then the only viable threat to the free officers. He obtained, subject to certain rights of re-entry, British evacuation from the canal zone. Initially he sought American defence aid but was told that this would be limited, in order to preserve the arms balance against Israel, and its despatch would probably depend upon Egypt gearing herself to Western arrangements for regional defence. So in September 1955 an arms deal was signed with Czechoslovakia.

Negotiations over the financing of the Aswan High Dam contributed heavily to the dramatic collapse of good relations between Egypt and the West. Generous though vague offers of long term aid made by Russia late in 1955 were well timed to coincide with increasing Western unease about the viability of the project[1] and with Egyptian resentment at America's unwillingness to commit aid years in advance. The Zionist and cotton lobbies in the United States vigorously opposed the scheme and their arguments drew strength from the Arab guerrilla offensive against Israel, the exclusion of Israeli shipping from the Suez Canal and Egypt's precipitate recognition of Communist China. In the middle of July 1956 first America and then Britain cancelled their provisional offer of Aswan aid and so, since the USSR now publicly refused to commit herself in this regard, Colonel Nasser felt obliged to take action that would, at least in appearance, meet his need for extra capital. So, in a vitriolic speech delivered on July 26th, he announced the seizure of the Suez Canal Company. Some compensation was promised.

Nearly a third of the ships that passed through the canal were British and nearly half the company's shares belonged to the British government. France was also involved commercially and she had been incensed by Nasser's helping the FLN in Algeria. So France and Britain led the Western opposition to nationalization, contending that the riparian state could not be allowed sole control of the canal. Most of Egypt's sterling and franc assets were frozen and the United States was induced to join the two European powers in inviting twenty-four nations to a conference in London. A majority at the conference, to which Greece and, of course, Egypt had refused to send representatives, supported a proposal tabled by Mr Dulles for international operation by a Suez Canal Board. But

[1]See Chapter XXIII, Section i.

Ceylon, India, Indonesia and the USSR backed the Egyptian demand that, though she should become answerable to the United Nations on matters of general principle, she must remain free to operate the waterway herself. In September the three leading Western powers sought to establish a Suez Canal Users' Association that would employ pilots, co-ordinate traffic and collect dues. This failed to materialize.

Israel was by now convinced that an armoured counterblow was the only way of checking a sustained Arab guerrilla campaign and realized that the delivery of such a blow would be unwise without some guarantee of Western air protection. So she had begun staff discussions with the French and to accept *Mystère* fighters from them. But, as her sympathetic initial reaction to the act of nationalization had shown, she was loth to become a committed member of some anti-Arab alliance. And Britain for her part was anxious not to become too obviously associated with Israel; yet she wanted an excuse for intervention more substantial than mere nationalization. France's concern was to reconcile the complex interests of her two partners.

Her intrigue reached its culmination in a secret conference held at Sèvres on October 23rd—a fortnight before the American Presidential elections and two days after a pro-Nasser swing in the Jordan elections had heralded the formation of a joint command with Egypt and Syria. Christian Pineau and Selwyn Lloyd, the French and British Foreign Ministers, and Ben Gurion, the Israeli Prime Minister, were among those who attended. Pineau has said that all the major moves made in the subsequent ten days were planned and co-ordinated there.

More or less secret Israeli mobilization began on the 25th and three days later, as French naval units in the Western Mediterranean were putting to sea, several French *Mystère* squadrons landed in Israel. The next day the Israelis struck, supported by the French air force planes and a French cruiser, and on the 30th Britain and France sent an ultimatum to Egypt and Israel which demanded that each of them pull back ten miles from the canal to allow an Anglo-French amphibious task force to take up positions in the buffer zone thus created. Allied raids on Egyptian aerodromes began ninety minutes after Cairo's rejection of this ultimatum. As they continued so did the slow approach of the task force to Port Said.

There is little doubt that the Anglo-French assault was essential to the Israeli success. The Egyptian brigades in the Sinai had been deployed on the assumption that mobile army reserves from the Nile delta, acting with strong air support, would be able to destroy the Israeli envelopment of their right flank that was correctly anticipated. But the Anglo-French air offensive precluded any attempt to gain aerial control of the Sinai and the seaborne threat obliged the army command to keep many men and over 200 tanks west of the canal. Even as things were some stiff resistance was offered to the Israeli advance and had this been rather more general and sustained that advance might have collapsed ignominiously. The 5,000 vehicles in the Israeli column were so unsuited to the rough desert tracks

753

that 2,000 broke down beyond immediate repair during the five days it took to conquer the Sinai.

Early on November 5th French and British paratroops dropped near Port Said and the next day amphibious forces came ashore. Some units were twenty-five miles beyond Port Said at dawn on the 7th and local allied military opinion was that Suez could have been reached within two days. The War Office in London said five would be needed and noted that the Egyptians had, in any case, made ready for a prolonged guerrilla resistance. But the real extent of the Allied military advantage will never be known for by then a cease fire had come into force. Some would claim that a prime reason for this was Marshal Bulganin's threat, made on the night of the 5th, to retaliate on behalf of Egypt with strategic rockets. His notes were not sent, however, until it had become virtually certain that the threat would never have to be implemented. The key fact was that world opinion moved overwhelmingly against Britain and France. One consequence was a flight of capital from London that was so fast that, had it continued, it would have made a devaluation of the pound inevitable within a few days. Another was that the United Nations exercised strong moral pressure; it also, by quickly assembling a peace-keeping force for dispatch to the area, provided the two Western nations with the chance to withdraw without suffering intolerable humiliation.

Britain's image as a liberally minded nation and as a swift and ubiquitous military power suffered severe damage at Suez and thenceforward her active military role in the Middle East was almost entirely confined to the Arabian peninsula, an area in which she had operated for well over a century and which remained predominantly 'feudal' and tribal in atmosphere. Between 1957 and 1959 small contingents of British troops and local levies successfully checked Saudi indirect aggression against Muscat and Oman by means of a series of limited operations that required at all levels of command an almost surgical degree of precision and finesse. In 1961 Britain made a heavy but somewhat laborious deployment to Kuwait in response to a rather casual Iraqi threat to annex that tiny sheikdom, which by then was yielding a third of the total Middle Eastern oil output and which had so far shared hardly any of her wealth with other Arab states. By the end of 1963 some of the Yemeni workers in Aden were spearheading a campaign of sporadic violence aimed at reversing the colony's inclusion in a new federation that otherwise consisted of the British-protected sheikdoms of South Arabia. The campaign was, of course, strongly supported by the Yemeni republican movement, which had been struggling to impose its control on that country since 1962. Forty thousand Egyptian troops and many planes were aiding this endeavour.

The USA sought to fill the vacuum that was left by Suez. January 5th, 1957, saw the public formulation of what was known as the Eisenhower Doctrine. This said that America would help, on request, any nation or group of nations in the Middle East to 'resist overt armed aggression from any country controlled by international Communism'. Shortly afterwards

Mr Dulles emphasized that the doctrine did not provide for the overthrow of any government by force.

The doctrine was applied twice. Each time the aim was to prevent incumbent *régimes* from being undermined by pressures applied below the threshold of overt aggression. After King Hussein of Jordan had introduced martial law in April 1957 in order to contain a leftist threat, the United States, despite some official misgivings in Amman, openly prepared for naval and military intervention in support of him. The following summer President Chamoun of the Lebanon, himself a Maronite Christian, appealed for American help against Sunni Moslem rebels who were trying to organize his dismissal. Fifteen thousand American troops came ashore and formed a security area that embraced Beirut; then General Chehab, another Maronite but one more acceptable to all factions, was made President elect. From then on traditional sectarian attitudes and privileges counted for rather less in Lebanese political life. And the only major threat to the stability of the state was the Ba'athist[1] attempt at a coup at the end of 1961; 6,000 arrests were made after its collapse.

Chamoun's request for help came hard upon a Bastille Day army revolution in Baghdad. In this revolution lay an eloquent demonstration of the power of anti-Western sentiment in the post-Suez years, even in a nation that was booming economically. For Iraq's annual revenue from oil imports was to rise from $14,000,000 to $270,000,000 during the 1950s and, thanks to policies initiated by the Nuri-es-Said administration, much of this expanding income was being directed to long-term development. Yet Said and the leading members of the Hashemite Royal Family were butchered by the rebels and Brigadier Kassem, a vain and unstable fanatic, installed as Premier.

A reign of terror was soon begun in order to confirm Kassem in the position of 'sole leader'. The pro-Muscovite Communists were denied first high office and then legal status but their energy and ruthlessness was exploited both in demonstrations and in the people's courts. Brutal war was soon waged against the Kurds in the north. Iraq demonstrated her adoption of a neutral posture in the Cold War by leaving the Baghdad Pact—which therefore had to rename itself the Central Treaty Organization—and subsequently she received much Soviet military and economic aid. Some Western aid was accepted also but, despite this, an attempt was made to appropriate the oilfields. Neither progress nor security stemmed from policies so drastic and conflicting. A Ba'athist *régime* came temporarily to power with Kassem's assassination early in 1963.

The traditional antagonism between Baghdad and Cairo was soon shown to have survived the revolution of July 14th and so to have ensured the indefinite postponement of the creation of a single Arab state. That the economic, cultural and political obstacles to the realization of this aim remained insuperable seems obvious in retrospect. Yet the quest for Arab unity had been, and continued to be, a constant inspiration to young

[1] See below.

nationalists in all Arab countries. A crucial though ambivalent factor in this quest was the Ba'ath Socialist Party, the organization that had been formed by the amalgamation, in 1953, of the Arab Socialist Party and Michel Aflaq's Ba'ath (Resurrection) Party and which commanded especial support along the 'fertile crescent' that extends from Beirut to south of Mosul. The Ba'athists disliked the cult of Nasser's personality and distrusted his particular brand of authoritarian socialism and these feelings, plus a strong sense of their own exclusiveness, could have been expected to make them unwilling to seek any unity that was under Cairo's auspices. Yet in 1958 the Syrian Ba'athists, acting to forestall a presumed Communist challenge, persuaded Nasser to fuse Egypt and Syria to form the United Arab Republic. What this nexus in fact entailed was a growing control of Syria from Cairo. Syrian military and business circles became increasingly exasperated with this state of affairs and so in 1961 Syria withdrew from the UAR. Hatred between Nasser and what he called the 'Fascist, Nazi' Ba'athist *régime* in Damascus destroyed the slender hope that was raised in 1963 of a federa llink between Egypt, Syria and Iraq.

The Persian and Turkish people maintained throughout the decade a slow and erratic progress. Between early 1962 and late 1963 Persia carried through the first stage of a subsidized programme of land redistribution which was designed to break the absolute grip that a class of largely absentee landlords retained on the life of most villages. Perhaps a sixth of the total arable land was redistributed to over a quarter of a million families during this time and thousands of co-operatives were set up in an attempt to make the new and enlarged smallholdings viable. An army coup in Turkey in 1960 removed the illiberal Democratic *régime* that had ruled since 1950 and prepared the way for its replacement by the Republican People's Party led by Atatürk's old disciple, Ismet Inönü. Turkey's chief concern in foreign policy had been to prevent Enosis—the unification of Greece and Cyprus for which the Greek Cypriot leaders had hoped. The London Agreements of 1960, through which Cyprus became independent, ruled out Enosis and provided special guarantees for those Cypriots who were of Turkish origin. But the Greek Cypriots, led by President Makarios, pressed hard for a re-negotiation of these agreements; this led to a serious outbreak of communal violence in the course of 1936.

## Chapter XIX
## PAN-AFRICA?

### (i) *Algérie Algérienne*

FRANCE was persuaded by defeat in Indo-China to try a new approach in North Africa. Tunisia was offered internal autonomy in July 1954. Sixteen months later the French released from detention the popular Sidi Mohammed ben-Yussef and reinstated him as Sultan of Morocco. Both his country and Tunisia were fully independent by the end of 1956.

Algeria was a harder problem to solve. A tenth of the population was of European extraction and this group retained, under the 1947 statute, important political privileges. Though the Algerian Assembly was empowered to legislate on most internal matters, its value as an instrument for improving the Moslem position was severely limited by the disproportionate power of the European vote within it and by the Governor-General's qualified veto. Also, official interference with the elections had, both in 1948 and 1951, worked to the disadvantage of militant Moslem elements. And there was no evidence that the policy of assimilation to which Paris had long subscribed would ever be pursued with vigour by the authorities on the spot in the absence of effective pressure from below. Less than 1% of the higher civil servants of Algeria were Moslem in 1956.

Out of the Moslem sense of frustration arose the spirit of Algerian nationalism. In the summer of 1954 a small group of young militants, whose outlook had been strongly influenced by the course of an unsuccessful rising at Sétif nine years before, formed the *Front de Libération Nationale* and that November they launched a rebellion. Within two years 20,000 guerrillas, who were receiving military supplies and other assistance from Tunisia and Egypt, were tying down 400,000 French Union troops. Soon an electrified barrage known as the Morice Line was brought into operation to hamper movement to and from Tunisia and, meanwhile, General Massu's paratroopers, using electric shock and other tortures, consolidated the French hold on Algiers. But these gains were offset by the spread of FLN terrorism among the 400,000 Algerians working in France.

Many Frenchmen were too certain that economic links bound Algeria irrevocably to France, too complacent about the progress of assimilation, and too eager to account for the apparent support for the FLN in terms of intimidation. So successive French governments, operating in this climate of complacency and for ever concerned with their own political survival, lagged continually behind the needs of the hour. Not until 1958 was a common electoral role offered and even then the proposal was made without prior consultation with any Moslem representatives. It was, moreover, linked to a plan for regional devolution which looked, to some eyes, suspiciously like a plot to isolate the coastal towns and the oilfields of the Sahara.

Life was made yet more difficult for the ministers in Paris by the independent attitude of their subordinates across the Mediterranean. Premier Mollet was given no forewarning of the plot, hatched in November 1956, whereby several FLN leaders were kidnapped by the diversion of a plane flying from Tunis to Rabat. The air force raid against the Tunisian village of Sakhiet Sidi Youssef was executed in open defiance of standing orders. Torture was never officially condoned by Paris.

A climax came when, in 1958, Algeria served as the main base for the military revolt that culminated in de Gaulle's return. Much of the officers corps had become convinced that political meddling and a general lack of ruthlessness had caused the struggle against Communism to be lost in Indo-China. Now they felt that struggle had been resumed in Algeria—the traditional 'North-West Frontier' of the army of France. A totalitarian challenge could only be countered, they contended, by authoritarian and totalitarian methods.

During the first year and a half in office de Gaulle concentrated on improving the possibilities of compromise. At first he felt obliged to leave full civil authority in the hands of the army commander but when General Salan was succeeded in that post by General Challe the civilian chain of command was made independent again. The Constantine Plan was launched which provided for an increased expenditure on economic and social development that was to be financed over five years by means of a fund worth 2,000 billion old francs. A concomitant of it was a rapid increase of the proportion of Moslems in positions of official responsibility. And within de Gaulle's first year as president over 1,000 politically un-reliable French Army officers were transferred from Algeria.

In September, 1959, de Gaulle proposed that, within four years of peace, the Algerian people should choose by referenda between complete independence, close integration with France, and some kind of federal link. The bulk of metropolitan opinion backed this initiative and even the FLN provisional government displayed a cautious interest. But the threat of compromise spurred the extreme Right to thoughts and acts of violence. A section of it attempted a revolt in Algiers in the New Year and several prominent men used the witness box at the subsequent trial to express their political approval of the defendants. Among them were Marshal Juin, Generals Weygand and Massu and Messrs Bidault and Soustelle.

But by no means all the verbal attacks on official policy came from the advocates of *Algérie française*. Over 100 intellectuals signed a manifesto that asserted the right of soldiers to refuse to fight in North Africa. Both laymen and clerics levelled vehement protests against the continuing use of torture. Many of the Moslems of Algiers demonstrated openly in support of the FLN during a Presidential visit in December, 1960.

Referenda held in France and in Algeria early in 1961 showed large majorities in support of the principle of self-determination. With this mandate behind it the French government began to negotiate openly with the FLN in May.[1] Integration had by now been abandoned and the FLN was told the choice would lie between complete secession and some kind of independence-with-association. The talks broke down completely in July but were resumed the following March; by then de Gaulle had conceded one of the main points of dispute by stating that the Sahara undoubtedly belonged to Algeria. Agreements were soon reached on a Franco-Algerian association that involved France giving extensive economic assistance in exchange for some military facilities and guarantees for the European minority. Ninety-one per cent of the voters in France and 99·75% of those in Algeria endorsed the agreements in referenda. Many acts of violence were, in fact, committed against the Europeans in Algeria and well over 600,000 of them left in the course of 1962.

The remarkable readiness of most Frenchmen to accept this settlement stemmed in large part from their revulsion against the *Organization de l'Armée Secrète* and the other Rightist terror groups that became so prominent in 1961. That spring Generals Salan and Challe had tried to lead another revolt from Algiers. After that terrorism became more widespread on both sides of the Mediterranean. Assassination plots were laid against de Gaulle; racist mobs lynched Moslems in Algeria; everywhere the plastic bomb became the symbol of *Algérie française*. For a few months the future of the Fifth Republic seemed to hang in the balance. But General Salan, who had apparently become the OAS leader, was caught and sent to prison early in 1962 and after this, and the actual achievement of Algerian independence, the challenge waned. Georges Bidault renounced politics as he went into exile in April 1963 and shortly afterwards a two year old state of emergency was abolished in France.

## (ii) *Self-Determination in the Tropics*

Constitutional progress in French tropical Africa accelerated from 1956 and in 1958 de Gaulle staged a referendum in which each state decided its own future. Somaliland chose to remain an Overseas Territory. Guinea opted for immediate independence—despite the consequent loss of French

---

[1] The two sides made a previous, but very brief, attempt to negotiate at Melun. This was in June 1960.

technical and financial aid. The rest, together with Madagascar, became Member States of the French Community; this was a status which involved a guaranteed prospect of further political evolution towards the ultimate goal of complete independence. In 1960 they all, in fact, acceded to full sovereignty, the French Constitution being amended to allow them to remain within the Community if they so wished. Six were still members in early 1964. By now, however, membership had come to mean very little.

The Mau Mau rebellion in Kenya—which had necessitated the deployment of up to 15,000 troops—was finally brought under control in 1956. Thenceforward both British East and British West Africa marched remarkably peacefully towards independence. The chief problem in the Gold Coast lay in meeting the demands from the Ashantis in the North for guarantees against domination from Accra; Nkrumah's Convention People's Party had secured 57% of the overall vote in the 1956 elections but only 43% in Ashanti. So included in the constitution for the proposed unitary and independent state of Ghana were several regional assemblies whose consent—as expressed by a two thirds majority—was necessary for certain types of constitutional change. The Gold Coast became Ghana in March, 1957.

Nigeria settled for the federal solution as the best way to contain the threat of internal tension—a threat that had its main roots in tribal rivalry. The federal legislature and those for the three regions were bicameral; among the powers concentrated at regional level were those concerning the social services, local taxation, regional roads and development and native and customary courts. Nigeria became independent on these terms in 1960. Sierra Leone followed her in 1961 and the three states of East Africa, Kenya, Uganda and Tanganyika, between then and 1963. All six states retained their Commonwealth membership.

Richard Nixon's attendance at the Ghanaian independence celebrations marked the beginning of an era in which Ghana, by virtue of her early acquisition of sovereignty and the strong personality of Nkrumah, became the symbol of the New Africa for doubter and enthusiast alike. It was the doubter whose expectations were most accurately confirmed. Soon active members of the CPP had been systematically placed in many dignified and lucrative positions extending over a wide range of official and unofficial national organizations. Conspicuous among them were the regional and district commissioner posts, newly created to co-ordinate development and check anything that was regarded as subversive at local level. Within months of independence tribal and regional political parties were banned and soon a Preventive Detention Act was passed which enabled the government to detain for up to five years any opponent whose conduct it judged to be 'prejudicial to the maintenance of law and order'. When Ghana became a republic in 1960, President Nkrumah was accorded strong powers. A further constitutional amendment in January 1964—by which time the opposition could muster only 15 out of the 103 MPs— established the CPP as the sole national party; the amendment was

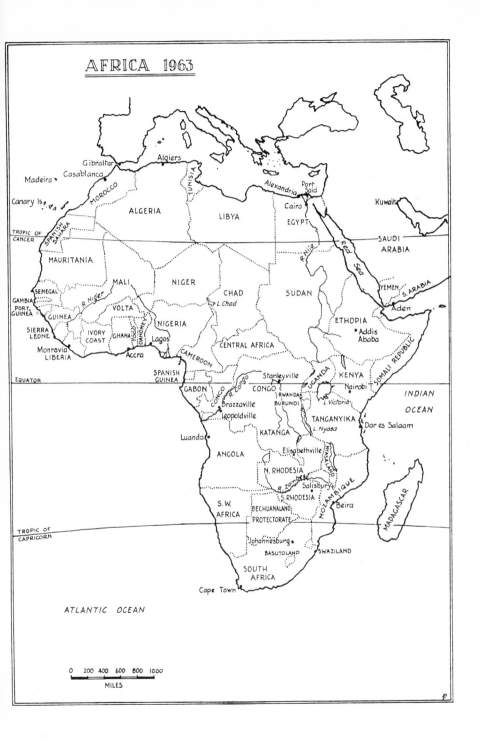

AFRICA 1963

approved by 99·9% of the voters in the subsequent referendum. And at this same time the domination of the judiciary by the executive was made complete.

Apologists would have found it easier to justify this highly totalitarian interpretation of 'African Socialism' if it had led to economic success. But it was far from clear that it did. Ghana's hard currency reserves fell from $600,000,000 in 1956 to $70,000,000 in 1964, a trend that scared off many foreign investors and seriously impeded the government's long term development plans. The progressive decline in world cocoa prices was partially responsible but so was official mismanagement. The heavy expenditure on the social services was admirable from many standpoints but not necessarily conducive to immediate economic progress; the considerable outlay on central government buildings and upon the more ostentatious kinds of public works may have done something to foster nationalism and undermine tribalism but it had little direct effect on production. The same was true of the defence budget which, measured as a percentage of the gross national product, became quite high, at least by Black African standards.

Nkrumah spoke of a need for the 'African personality' to make an impact on the world stage and it was to this end that he sponsored the Conference of Independent African States and the All-Africa People's Conference that were held in Accra in 1958. But the further progress of the Pan-African movement was impeded by the occurrence of ideological and territorial disputes—notably between Morocco and Mauritania, Morocco and Algeria, Ghana and Nigeria, and Ethiopia and Somaliland. Certain of the various tensions were reflected in the emergence of rival multi-national groupings. But at the Addis Ababa conference of July 1963 thirty of the thirty-two independent states came together to form the Organization of African Unity. Among the aims outlined in its charter was the eradication of 'all forms of colonialism from Africa'. Its chances of doing this entirely by direct action were clearly going to depend upon the willingness of its Arab members to provide military power and expertise.

Many Pan-African nationalists felt, as did many white supremacists, that a major battle in the struggle for Southern Africa had already been joined in the former Belgian Congo. The precipitate Belgian withdrawal from that ill-prepared colony in 1960 had left a situation that was ripe for catastrophe. The majority in the newly constituted parliament was led by Patrice Lumumba, who favoured the creation of a unitary state; the minority parties included the federalists under Kasavubu and a Leftist group led by Antoine Gizenga. Outside the several larger towns nationalism was very weak and tribalism strong.

Within four days of independence—which was on June 30th—the paramilitary *Force Publique* had mutinied against its Belgian officers. Many Africans and Europeans were assaulted in the rioting that ensued and so the Belgian army re-entered the Congo and occupied key centres. So on July 11th, the central government, acting upon Nkrumah's advice,

appealed to the United Nations against Belgian aggression. Tribal conflicts had broken out by then and the Katanga authorities were claiming,
with active encouragement from European business interests, that their
rich copper mining province was independent. Soon Katanga became, in
many parts of Africa, a byword for European intrigue.

## (iii) *Towards a Capricorn Alliance?*

In 1951 Portugal, reverting to a nineteenth century precedent, designated
her colonies Overseas Provinces. Subsequently a public works programme
was launched in Angola that helped to attract 100,000 extra settlers there
within a decade. But Portugal lacked the capital required to develop
amenities for the Africans at a comparable pace and she was reluctant to
encourage foreign investment lest it bring revolutionary ideas in its wake.
African secondary education emphasized technical skills; the humanities
were played down for fear they would produce a class of underemployed
intellectuals. Africans who attained citizenship sometimes achieved a
social and economic status above that of the poorer of the white settlers.
But the proportion that had reached the educational standards required
to do so was as low as 1% as late as 1950. Discontent among the underprivileged Angolan masses was held in check by stark brutality, by
collective punishments and by recourse to a web of informers.

Blessed also by the absence of a free opposition in Lisbon, this colonial
*régime* long went unchallenged. But an organized African nationalist
movement began to develop around 1957 and four years later several
thousand of its supporters launched a rebellion in Angola's Northern
provinces. A few months later all Angolan Africans were admitted
nominally to full citizenship and, ostensibly at least, routine forced labour
was abolished. The accent was not on reconciliation, however, but on
suppression. The military garrison was expanded to 25,000 white and
7,000 African troops and savage counter-attacks were launched by land
and from the air. The revolt continued to smoulder, nevertheless, throughout 1962 and 1963; meanwhile a good third of Portuguese Guinea slid
into rebel hands and some partisan activity began in Mozambique.
Eventually 40,000 troops were concentrated in Angola; 16,000 more were
in Mozambique and 7,500 in Guinea.

The British intended the Federation of Rhodesia and Nyasaland to lead
to the creation of a multi-racial society based on an expanding economy.
It failed because informed African opinion suspected it from the start, and
did so ever more intensely as it became ever more clear how reluctant the
Europeans were to dilute their own power. From 1958 only twelve of the
fifty-nine members in the Federal Assembly had to be Africans and
another three Europeans representing African interests. Qualifications

763

for the A roll, which was used to elect the 45 ordinary members, were such that less than 2,000 of the 100,000 electors on it were Africans in 1958. About 45,000 were eligible for inclusion on the B roll; they shared equally with the A roll members the ballot for half of the special African seats, occupants for the rest being chosen by the all-African district councils.[1] Only 700 Africans bothered to register as B roll voters for the 1958 elections. Only fifteen constituencies were fought at all in the election of 1962. Southern Rhodesia contained, in 1962, 220,000 Europeans and 3,710,000 Africans, Coloureds and Asians; Northern Rhodesia and Nyasaland contained 5,450,000 people, 80,000 of them European.

An Advisory Commission under Lord Monckton reported to the British government in 1960 on the working of the Federation. The report said that accelerating exports and greater creditworthiness showed that economically the Federation had been a good thing, but that the deepening African hostility to it, especially in the two Northern territories, could not be overcome 'without drastic and fundamental changes both in the structure of the association itself, and in the racial policies of Southern Rhodesia.' Among the changes recommended were a devolution of some powers to the three territories, a broader franchise and a much larger proportion—a majority of the Commissioners said 50%—of African seats in the federal assembly. And an acknowledgment of the constitutional right of any territory to secede was considered essential to the survival of the association. Stress was laid also on the need to end legalized discrimination within the territories themselves; reference was made in this connection to Southern Rhodesia's pass laws and to her Land Apportionment Act. Review conferences were subsequently held in London but they were inconclusive and the Federation broke up in 1963. Northern Rhodesia became the independent state of Zambia in 1964; Nyasaland became Malawi.

The Southern Rhodesian election of 1962 was fought under the 1961 constitution which provided for fifty constituencies and fifteen electoral districts. Seventy-five per cent of the ballot strength in the constituencies came from voters of the A roll; 75% of that in the districts came from voters on the B roll. To be eligible for the A roll one had to have an income of £720 p.a.; average African take home pay was of the order of £100. To be eligible for the B roll £120 p.a. and two years of secondary education were required; 3,300 Africans were in secondary school late in 1959.

Much arson and minor sabotage, which was obviously intensified by the high incidence of African unemployment, broke out that summer and led to the banning of Joshua Nkomo's Zimbabwe African People's Union two months before the poll. ZAPU's boycott of the election resulted in only 25% of the 10,000 B roll voters going to the ballot boxes. Victory went to the white dominated Rhodesia Front party which opposed

[1] These A and B roll qualifications were, in fact, identical to those used in the Southern Rhodesian election of 1962.

'forced integration' through legislative change. Winston Field then became Prime Minister and Ian Smith took over the Treasury.

ZAPU remained active but was weakened by the formation in 1963 of the breakaway Zimbabwe African National Union under the Reverend Ndabaningi Sithole. Meanwhile Winston Field's *régime* pushed through drastic legislation to check subversion, including some providing a mandatory death penalty for petrol bombing. By now some of its members were starting to contemplate seriously an eventual Unilateral Declaration of Independence. But one uncertain factor was that of how much active support, as opposed to mere sympathy, would come from Portugal and South Africa. Both these governments rested their claims to survival in Africa on historical continuity, and the preservation of existing sovereign rights.

## (iv) *Apartheid in Practice*

Two of the clauses in the 1909 South African constitution were 'entrenched'; this meant that a two-thirds overall majority in parliament was required for their removal. One of the clauses ensured equal status for the Afrikaans and English languages; the other provided for a qualified multiracial franchise and, although Africans had been excluded from its provisions in 1936, it still served to keep the Cape Coloured voters on the common electoral roll. The Nationalist Party strove to have the latter repealed and eventually succeeded in 1956. To do so it much enlarged both the Senate and the Appellate Division of the Supreme Court and, so many alleged, packed them with its political friends.

Grave though the related constitutional issues were, the partial disenfranchisement of the Cape Coloured people had less immediate effect than certain other *Apartheid* measures, such as the Bantu Education Act of 1953, which provided for close supervision by the Department of Native Affairs of all education of African children. Dr Verwoerd, the doctrinaire Nationalist Senator who became Prime Minister in 1958, said this was desirable because 'Good racial relations cannot exist when the education is under the control of people who create wrong expectations on the part of the Native himself.' Many other measures were promoted in the same spirit. For example, industrial legislation passed between 1953 and 1957 precluded Africans from striking or their being represented during disputes by fellow Africans; it also enabled the Ministry of Labour to determine the racial balance in most occupations. African attendance at churches located in European districts was made less easy by another statute. And two laws passed in 1959 provided for total segregation within the university system.

Restraint on the growth òf the African urban population was basic to the whole programme. A 1952 Act enabled the government to deport at

765

will from any district any tribal groups or individual Africans. It also limited, subject to certain exemptions, the unauthorized residence of any African in an urban or 'proclaimed' area to a maximum of three days. Exemptions were normally granted to any workers who had lived in the area for ten or fifteen years; they were also granted to their wives, minor sons and unmarried daughters. But great social distress was caused by this kind of legislation and by the government's reluctance to spend enough public money on the improvement of the overcrowded African townships. Crime and immorality flourished; tribal riots occurred in the Johannesburg area in 1957 and a communal one in some squalid outskirts of Durban in 1960. Failure to carry passes in urban areas led to 340,000 Africans being convicted in, for example, 1955. The total number of people convicted for some offence or other exceeded 1,500,000 in 1959.

Over 3,500,000 Africans lived in urban areas in 1963 as against 2,500,000 in 1948. This trend the Nationalists sought to reverse. A 1959 Statute deprived the Africans of parliamentary representation and made provision for a series of Bantustans—that is, tribal areas which, after a prolonged period of supervision, would achieve internal self-government. The first Bantustan assembly opened in the Transkei in 1963; 45 of its 109 members had been elected, the rest being chiefs approved of by the government.

The Bantustan controversy highlighted the differences in approach between the Afrikaners who dominated the Nationalist Party and the English speaking South Africans who controlled the United Party—the official opposition. The British element, which owned by far the greatest part of all the mining and industrial capital in the land, felt that *Apartheid* was certainly economically harmful and probably unworkable. The Afrikaners, based as they were on the countryside, felt a moral revulsion at the idea of South Africa's demography being shaped by the labour requirements of *laisser faire* big business. Stemming as they did from a close-knit community, and held together by the Dutch Reformed Church, the Broederbond secret society and a rich folk-memory, they pursued definite aims with energy and confidence. Those of British extraction, on the other hand, were generally sure of the value of the imperial connection but of little else. United Party spokesmen talked of gradual integration and communal balance with deliberate vagueness; still they failed to prevent serious revolts over racial policy among their supporters in parliament. At each general election the Nationalists' representation rose. And their political ascendancy was confirmed when, in 1960, the European electorate decided by 850,000 votes to 775,000 that South Africa should become a republic. From then on there was a rapid convergence of opinion between the Afrikaners and the British element. More intermarriage between those two communities assisted this trend.

Many Africans were numbered among the 150 or so people against whom proceedings were unsuccessfully taken in the Treason Trials that ground on in Johannesburg between 1956 and 1961. Shortly after the trials began 40,000 African commuters from Alexandra, a township ten miles outside Johannesburg, began a bus boycott in protest against a rise in fares. Three months of struggle brought success but whilst the campaign was in progress the government announced plans for a drastic reduction in Alexandra's size; by 1962 it had been ordained that it should be inhabited only by working adults, living alone.

March 1960 saw a big political offensive by the Africans; it was a tragic failure. Sixty-seven people were killed when police, acting, they claimed, after some provocation, directed heavy and continuous fire against a large crowd at Sharpeville. Nine days later 30,000 Africans marched into Cape Town but were induced to disperse by official promises that their representatives would have an opportunity to present their case – promises which were never kept. By then a State of Emergency was in force. Soon 1,700 people of all races had been detained and a ban placed on the African National Congress and on the Pan African Congress, a more militant breakaway movement.

Two African subversive organizations were in action by 1963 but they were achieving little. The security forces had greatly expanded by then and the arbitrary powers of the Minister of Justice had been greatly increased. Thus, by an act of 1963, which the United Party supported, he became able to place anybody in solitary confinement without trial for one or more periods of ninety days.

# Chapter XX
# LATIN AMERICA

By 1954 almost all the civilian branches of government in Guatemala had been penetrated by a small but energetic Communist Party aided by an all too efficient secret police. So the United States began to seek support from the Organization of American States (OAS)—an arrangement for consultation between the twenty-one American republics which had been set up in 1948.[1] The OAS did not condemn Guatemala outright but all its members except Mexico, the Argentine and Guatemala herself backed a United States resolution that described Communism as a threat to the independence of the Americas.

As violence rose in Guatemala, and as evidence accumulated of invasion preparations in neighbouring states, the Arbenz *régime* turned for military assistance to the Eastern bloc; in May it received from there a big load of arms on board a Swedish ship. Three weeks later Colonel Castillo Armas led 200 armed exiles in from Honduras and then a number of planes, at least some of which had been supplied by the US Central Intelligence Agency, bombed parts of Guatemala City. Neither the army nor the people offered much resistance and within a fortnight Jacopo Arbenz had become a refugee in the Mexican Embassy. Castillo Armas ruthlessly hunted down Communist suspects and then got his rule endorsed for an indefinite period by a 1,000 to 1 majority in an open ballot. He was killed in 1957.

The assassination of Armas was, in fact, part of a trend that persisted from about 1954 to 1961. In the former year military *putschistas*, who generally stood far to the political Right, held sway in twelve of the republics; by mid-1961 only General Alfredo Stroessner of Paraguay remained. The other countries where military dictators had been assassinated were Dominica, Nicaragua and Panama. They had been deposed in the Argentine, Colombia, Cuba, Ecuador, Haiti and Venezuela. Most of these men fell victim to a fresh wave of radicalism caused by falling world commodity prices. Balance of payments crises, aggravated by domestic nflation and by undue reliance on the export of one or two primary products, caused living standards to rise only slowly and so served to emphasize the structural weaknesses of these immature economies.

[1] See Chapter X, Section iii.

Dependence on the United States for over half the overall export market and for much public and private capital was a characteristic weakness. So was a marked grouping of the town dwellers into a few very large cities. Another was the great concentration of landownership; for, say, 3% of the population to hold 60% of the cultivated area was typical in 1960. Among such groups as the Andean Indians or the Negroid communities of North-East Brazil rural poverty was accentuated by social and cultural factors. Almost everywhere former peasants streamed into towns whose manufactures were not expanding fast enough to absorb them. The many Indian families that lived literally on top of the trash dumps of Lima symbolized the malaise of a continent.

The career of President Vargas of Brazil ended in tragedy in 1954. Inflation had led to foreign trade difficulties and labour unrest which, together with corruption within the President's family and elsewhere, had undermined the popularity of his government. So after an air force officer had been accidentally killed by a member of the President's bodyguard who was trying to murder an opposition journalist, a deputation of officers obliged Vargas to resign. Shortly afterwards he committed suicide.

Juscelino Kubitschek won the 1955 Presidential election in a contest against two opponents of more conservative views, one backed by the army and the other by business; about 40% of the electorate, which comprised all literate adults, voted for him. During his term of office, which was limited by statute to five years, the economy became stronger in several important respects. Strong feelings of economic nationalism persisted in Brazil but they had not, except in the case of the nationalized oil industry, precluded a large inflow of private capital from a variety of foreign sources. Brasilia, the new federal capital on the cool and grassy Goiás plateau, had been created out of nothing; at the time of its inauguration, in 1960, its population was 140,000.

Field Marshal Teixeira Lott, Kubitschek's Minister of War, was easily beaten in the 1960 Presidential election by Jânio Quadros, a moderate whose use of the broom as a symbol was intended as a reminder of his fine anti-corruption record in local politics. He began energetically, seeking to reform finance and land tenure and to build strong trade links with the Communist world. But, then, in August 1961, he suddenly resigned, frustrated by military and Congressional opposition to his reform programme.

President Perón's charismatic influence over, and understanding of, the Argentinian people were gravely diminished by the death, in 1952, of his wife Eva. Left in virtual isolation he soon came fatally to overestimate his ability to force through new and controversial economic and religious policies.

Much nationalist resentment was generated, particularly within the army, by the decision that Perón took in 1955 to let a foreign oil company, Standard Oil of California, prospect within the country. But what had already provoked yet more virulent opposition was the campaign he had launched against the Catholic Church at the end of the previous year. He imprisoned certain clergy, banned religious demonstrations in the streets, legalized divorce and prostitution, and, in the spring of 1955, sought to disestablish the Church of Rome. Two senior prelates were deported on June 15th and so the following day the Vatican excommunicated all who had joined in the persecution of its faith. Rome's initiative coincided with an abortive but sanguinary naval revolt and these events were soon followed by the sacking, by young *perónistas*, of some of the finest churches in Buenos Aires.

Perón then tried to alter course. He dismissed some of his more militant Cabinet Ministers, including those responsible for Education and the Interior, released various prisoners and offered political freedom 'within the limitations imposed by good manners, decency, and the need for appeasement'. But this approach was no more successful than the other at checking factionalism and violence and eventually, on September 16th, 1955, a General Lonardi led a revolt of the garrison in the Catholic stronghold of Cordoba. Others rallied quickly to his slogan of *Christus vincit* and within three days Perón had sought asylum on board a Paraguayan gunboat. Lonardi acted swiftly to purge *perónistas*, devalue the currency and cancel the Standard Oil contract. But he was regarded in some influential circles as politically too lenient and in others as too Catholic and so in November a military junta deposed him. After nearly three years of indecisive rule this junta arranged a general election. Perónist candidates were disallowed but Perón's followers were able to ensure the victory of Dr Arturo Frondizi, the scholarly leader of the *intransigente*, as the Left Wing of the Radicals were called.

His enemies were happy to depict Frondizi as an amoral opportunist but one can, in fact, see the hallmark of statesmanship in the way in which, through conciliation, skill and toughness, he built himself up as a focus of national unity. By the end of 1961 he had restored the *perónista* movement to something like its due place in the scheme of things. He seemed also to have placated the Catholics and to have kept the military influence on politics in check. Economic recovery had contributed to this success and a factor in the recovery had been Argentina's becoming virtually independent of oil imports which previously had occasioned a third of the total import bill. By his courageous decision, made in 1958, to grant certain kinds of concession to foreign companies, Frondizi made the required oil expansion possible.

Few if any Latin American states, apart from the Argentine, Uruguay and perhaps Chile, were as advanced as Cuba in 1953 in regard to such indices of progress as the scale of social services, the density of communications and the spread of consumer goods. Yet within the next six years Fidel Castro's '26th of July' movement was to come to power.

Many interrelated factors contributed towards this in some way surprising development. Cuba's prosperity was completely geared to her sugar exports and these had been decreasing in relation to those of her competitors and remained, moreover, heavily dependent upon an official American quota.

The percentage of American capital in sugar milling had diminished over the years. But American ownership of half the capital of the main railways and many of Havana's public utilities helped to sustain the fifty year old tradition of a revolution permanently frustrated by 'Yanqui' imperialism. Meanwhile, general revolutionary sentiment was kept buoyant by the all-pervasive atmosphere of stagnation. The nature of their occupation kept the sugar workers inactive half the year and, largely because of this, they were liable to chronic indebtedness. Massive bureaucracy and corruption stultified the sugar industry and every other one. Declining educational standards alienated the student community in particular. There were, moreover, no effective conservative elements in society other than those motivated purely by hope of easy profit. The Church lacked any coherent social attitude. The army did not feel proud to serve under Fulengio Batista, the dictator who had illegally resumed[1] power in 1952 and retained it by many acts of arbitrary brutality.

Fidel Castro led a fierce though unsuccessful attack on a government barracks on July 26th, 1953, but he did not lead his followers into the Sierra Maestra to fight as guerillas until November, 1956. Twelve months later the guerrillas were still only a few hundred in number and Batista remained in complete control of the lowlands. But his control was kept by mass arrests and tortures and, indeed, by thousands of murders. In March 1958 the United States, unlike Great Britain, stopped supplying him with arms. Two months later his large army conspicuously failed to press home a campaign of extermination against the rebels. The following New Year's Day Batista fled the country and Fidel Castro came to power committed to industrialization, land reform, educational expansion, the end of corruption, and free speech. Several of his leading colleagues had strong Marxist leanings but the Cuban Communist Party had declined to back his movement until the middle of the previous year.

Totalitarian tendencies quickly became apparent within the new *régime*. Hundreds were executed after purification trials and parliamentary elections were postponed indefinitely. But, meanwhile, land reform was started and, in the autmn of 1959, it was extended to some American-owned estates. In all cases compensation was in the form of long-dated bonds rather than in the form of the prompt, hard payments implicitly requested in a State Department note in June. That note marked the beginning of a swift deterioration in Havana-Washington relations. After some people had been hit by anti-aircraft shrapnel as a plane flew over Havana in October to distribute leaflets, Fidel Castro, by then Cuba's Premier, appeared on television to liken the incident to Pearl Harbor. By now a large flow of refugees to Florida had begun.

Early in 1960 the American government asked Congress for authority

[1] He had first seized power in 1934.

771

to alter sugar quotas if and when desired. Then Cuba decided to import Soviet oil. A few weeks later the United States began to give military training to Cuban exiles in conditions of semi-secrecy. The passage through Congress of the quota legislation in June was followed immediately by the Cuban nationalization of Shell and Esso because they had refused to process Soviet crude oil. A week later, on July 6th, President Eisenhower reduced the Cuban sugar quota. Continued sequestration of American commercial and business assets and the massive import of Soviet bloc arms were among the Cuban countermoves. In October the USA stopped the export to Cuba of almost all goods other than medical supplies and certain foodstuffs and on January 3rd, 1961, she severed diplomatic relations with her.

April 1961 brought the Bay of Pigs invasion, organized by a Revolutionary Council of Cuban exiles headed by José Miro Cardona, who had, significantly enough, been the first Prime Minister of the Castro *régime*. Inadequate air support and the failure of the Cuban masses to welcome them as liberators (despite predictions by American intelligence that they would) obliged the 1,500-strong invading force to surrender within a few days.

This triumph greatly strengthened Castro's internal position and accelerated his drive to reorganize the state along Marxist lines. Within a year he had decisively undermined the independent strength of the old Cuban Communist Party though he had retained the services of many of its members with whom, as the collective farm plan of August 1962 illustrated, he shared a variety of objectives. But none of this meant that his foreign policy had to become a mirror reflection of Moscow's. For one thing, of course, the international Marxist camp was by now divided against itself by the Sino-Soviet dispute. The outcome of the missile crisis intensified his determination to disregard this dispute and stay on good terms with both Moscow and Peking. He spent five weeks in the USSR in 1963 but did not sign the Test Ban.

The whole Western Hemisphere, apart from Canada, could be said to be involved in the trial of strength between Washington and Havana by the time Cuba was 'excluded' from the Organization of American States early in 1962. At first this involvement seemed likely to serve as a stimulus for development. In 1961 the United States government launched the Alliance for Progress; this programme, which was designed to eliminate hunger and illiteracy, provided for the receipt by Latin America over ten years of twenty billion dollars' worth of foreign aid and investment (including eleven from United States public funds). It also called for, among other things, widespread tax and land reform. But the hope that this offer initially aroused dwindled as conservative militarism resurged in many parts of the continent. Military coups intended to curb the Left took place in Ecuador and El Salvador in 1961 and Peru in 1962. Sweeping *perónista* gains in the Argentine elections of 1962 caused the military to arrest President Frondizi, suspend Congress and appoint a puppet caretaker government; elections were permitted in 1963 but *perónista* participation was forbidden.

The Brazilian military would not let the leftist Vice-President João Goulart succeed Quadros until, by constitutional amendment, many presidential powers had been transferred to a Prime Minister with a seat in parliament. But by early 1963 Goulart had appointed men sympathetic to him to several key military commands and so, helped by the active support of organized labour, became able to hold a referendum to reverse the constitutional changes.

## Chapter XXI
# THE UNITED STATES SINCE KOREA

SHORTLY before Christmas, 1953, Admiral Radford, then the Chairman of the Joint Chiefs of Staff, introduced the phrase 'The New Look'—a phrase that came generally to be used to describe a new approach to defence in the course of which greater priority would be given to nuclear weapons of both the strategic and the tactical variety. Army manpower declined by 50% over the next couple of years but that of the Air Force was slightly expanded. The B–52A *Stratofortress*—the first intercontinental bomber to be built to a post-war specification—began to fly in August 1954. A year later the development of the *Atlas* Intercontinental Ballistic Missile was made a crash programme. Design studies for *Polaris* commenced in 1956.

Some concern was evinced, especially abroad, when, in January 1954, John Foster Dulles, the Secretary of State, said that the United States was to base its defence primarily upon 'a great capacity to retaliate, instantly, by means and at places of our own choosing' and to place more reliance 'upon community deterrent power and less upon local defensive power'. The first part of this formulation was taken by some as implying that the United States had released herself from any obligation to consult her allies in time of crisis but Mr Dulles later declared that this was not so. The second part was in apparent conflict with the policy, which the Secretary of State himself was then so vigorously pursuing, of enclosing the Soviet bloc within a series of interlocking regional alliances and bilateral treaties. However, the interlocking of alliances invoked at least a mild threat of automatic escalation of any local conflict and, in any case, both the cordon of alliances and the doctrine of strategic response were expressions of an old Anglo-Saxon tradition about the nature of Russian power. For a century or more it had been argued that the armies of the Eurasian heartland were of overwhelming numerical strength and that they derived a great advantage from being able rapidly to deploy along interior lines of communication. Another manifestation of the persistence of this tradition was the frequent misinterpretation of the Western intelligence estimates that the USSR had a paper order of battle of 175 divisions. American and British politicians often spoke as if this meant that they constantly had 175 divisions at full war strength. Dwight D. Eisenhower and John F. Kennedy were among those guilty of this inexactitude.

Dulles was later to give three examples of occasions when the USA had been brought to 'the brink of war'. One was Korea in 1953; another was Indo-China in 1954; the third was Quemoy-Matsu in 1955. From 1953 these Nationalist-held 'offshore islands' had been used as springboards for occasional guerrilla raids against the Chinese mainland. Early in 1954 Chiang Kai-shek had pledged a 'holy war' to liberate the mainland 'in the not distant future'. Later that year sporadic air and artillery action had taken place and then in mid-January 1955 the Communists had seized the small island of Yikiang and had bombed the Tachens, a Nationalist-held island group that was too remote to be easily supplied or to serve any serious military purpose. Bombardments of Quemoy and Matsu began afresh and were matched by Nationalist raids on mainland ports, in one of which a British steamer was sunk. Meanwhile Chou En-lai declared that the 'liberation of Formosa' was a domestic affair which the United States must cease to obstruct. Soon afterwards a speech by Marshal Bulganin and some aerial activity over the Yellow Sea served to demonstrate Soviet support for Peking.

The crisis was stabilized by the United States naval evacuation of the Tachens, without Communist interference, early in February 1955. It was resolved by contacts between Dulles and Molotov in Geneva that May which were followed by a trip to Taipeh by Admiral Radford and Walter Robertson, an Assistant Secretary of State. But while this crisis lasted it posed acute dilemmas for the Eisenhower administration. America's explicit defence commitments extended only to Formosa and the Pescadores. However, Chiang Kai-shek had, through his militant advocacy of a 'forward policy', made it possible for his sympathizers to impress upon American leaders that the offshore islands were essential to the maintenance of these commitments for if they were sacrificed, Nationalist morale would collapse. So whilst Eisenhower deplored the call by Senator Knowland, the Republican majority leader, for an immediate naval blockade of the mainland, both he and Dulles felt obliged to prepare for the implementation of various additional measures of punishment or deterrence, including, perhaps, the use of tactical nuclear weapons, should the Communists intensify what was seen as a 'Nazi' pattern of provocation. Both also became persuaded that the offshore islands could only be abandoned as part of a settlement in which Peking renounced its claim to Formosa. And the President, in particular, attached importance to the part played in containment by the main defence perimeter of the Western Pacific—that is to say, Korea, Japan, Okinawa, and Formosa.

Healthily pragmatic as these attitudes no doubt seemed to those who evinced them, they attracted a lot of criticism. The British and Canadian governments openly expressed their doubts about the wisdom of any involvement in the offshore islands. So did several leading members of the Democratic Party.

During this crisis, relations between the United States and her major allies remained cordial, however. Such proved not to be the case during the Middle East one that broke in the course of the next year. The USA soon made it clear that she regarded the nationalization of the Suez Canal as a wrongful act and that she would try to promote an international solution to the issues raised. But she made it clear, too, that she was prepared to countenance, in pursuit of this aim, nothing more drastic than economic sanctions. To many British people, especially ones of Conservative persuasion, this appeared as the culmination of a Middle Eastern policy that had long been compounded of naïvety and humbug. No doubt this view was extreme but it was true, nevertheless, that the United States policy towards the Middle East was full of inconsistencies. One example of prevarication was provided when she sponsored the Baghdad Pact, declined to join it herself and then immediately associated herself in all its committee work through the despatch of observers. Clumsy and inconsistent American handling of the Aswan Dam negotiations appeared to have precipitated the Egyptian decision to nationalize the canal. Some weeks after that decision had been implemented Mr Dulles aggravated transatlantic resentments by laying oral emphasis on the special 'non-colonial' character of the American world posture.

But President Eisenhower and his colleagues were to excel themselves by the skill with which they demonstrated that their strong disapproval of the Anglo-French military action—of which, incidentally, they had received no advance notice—did not mean that the Western alliance had been ruptured. As early as October 31st, the President emphasized that the current difference of opinion with Britain and France 'in no way minimizes our friendship' for them. Later the USA condemned the Soviet rocket threat and took several steps to ease Britain out of the economic difficulties that her arbitrary initiative had produced. The President met each Prime Minister again in the spring of 1957.

In 1954 a group composed mainly of liberal Democrats introduced a bill designed to outlaw the Communist Party; it did not enjoy government backing but it passed through Congress virtually *nem con*. But the biggest headlines concerning counter-subversion were being made by Senator McCarthy. Early in March Senator Flanders, a fellow Republican, attacked him on the floor of the Senate and, almost simultaneously, Edward Murrow produced a critical television study of him. Late in April the Senate Permanent Sub-Committee on Investigations of Government Operations, of which McCarthy was now chairman, began to investigate an army charge that its chairman and its chief counsel, a certain Mr Cohn, had exercised improper pressure to get special treatment for a Private Schine, formerly one of its assistants. No agreed report was published but all members concurred with the view that Cohn had been unduly forceful in this regard. A month later, on September 27th, a Senate select committee reported that McCarthy had acted improperly in inciting government employees to hand over documents, in ridiculing and abusing his fellow senators, in refusing to assist in a committee investigation of his financial activities and in his manner of treatment of a certain witness.

Some of these misdemeanours merited, it was felt, formal censure. A censure motion was, in fact, passed by the upper house on December 2nd by 67 votes to 22, Senator Knowland being among the twenty-two Republican dissentients. So ended 'the McCarthy era'—an era characterized by an illiberalism that ran contrary to some of America's best traditions. That McCarthy and men like him were taken so seriously by so many for so long was partly due to the fear and confusion engendered by the peculiarly sinister and mysterious nature of the challenge being presented by Stalinist Russia.

The mid-term elections of 1954 gave the control of both houses back to the Democrats and this advantage they retained in 1956. But in 1956 President Eisenhower, fighting his second duel with Adlai Stevenson, increased his personal vote from 55% to 58% of the electorate. Suez and Hungary contributed to the scale of the victory but more permanent factors ensured it. One was 'Ike's' enormous personal popularity. The other was prosperity. A technological revolution had begun, evidence of which was to be seen in the steady expansion in the proportion of industrial funds that were being devoted to applied research, the numerical dominance that 'white collar' workers were achieving over 'blue collar' ones, and the demographic explosion of California—the state where many of the newer industries were strongest. National electricity consumption, a good index of ease and comfort at work and in the home, rose 71% between 1954 and 1960. Consumer credit scales soared.[1] The number of passenger cars in service rose from 48,000,000 to 62,000,000, and the number of television sets from 27,000,000 to 53,000,000. Gaps in the spread of good roads, playgrounds, schools and mental hospitals reflected an unhealthy contrast between private affluence and 'public squalor' but, on the other hand, college and university expenditure had doubled during the years in question.

But this did not mean that the 'American Dream' had become true for each and every citizen. To define as 'poverty' an income of $4,000 p.a. for a family of four would seem odd to many non-Americans but within the context of high induced wants and limited government welfare it made sense. And by such definitions upwards of 30,000,000 remained poor. Some were so primarily because they lived in remote areas that had become too dependent on marginal farms and declining industries. Some were so mainly because they were old or disabled or fatherless. Many were so mainly because they were coloured. America's 22,000,000 Negroes had a mean living standard of but half the national average. Their divorce rate was twice the norm; their illegitimacy rate several times more. Their life expectation was several years shorter. The Supreme Court ruled unanimously in 1954 that 'separate educational facilities are inherently unequal, and so in conflict with the 14th Amendment. Yet by 1963 only 1% of the Negro pupils in the states of the old Confederacy were in unsegregated

[1] 11% of take-home pay was pledged against credit sales in 1960 against 7% in 1941.

schools. A concentration of Negro communities in the decaying centres of old Northern cities both reflected and perpetuated economic and social underprivilege. Unmarried mothers gave birth to 43% of all the babies that were born in Harlem in 1964.

One novel, and rather disturbing, feature of the fifties was a developing balance of payments problem. The USA had emerged from World War II in an apparently impregnable trading position and by late 1957 her government had utilized it to distribute to various other countries economic aid worth $40,000,000,000;[1] another $22,000,000,000 had been given in the form of military aid. There was, in addition, extensive local expenditure by the numerous military garrisons abroad and a large net outflow of private capital especially to Canada and Western Europe. Many nations came thus to accumulate dollars and to do so whilst the USA's own reserves of gold slowly declined. But for some years this situation provoked little searching of either official or academic souls. Dollar surpluses abroad were rightly seen as facilitating multilateral trade and the aid and investment programmes as facilitating growth and so, among other things, increasing the effective demand for American exports. Besides, aid was still felt to be central to the policy of containing the Soviet bloc. Well over half the grand total had gone to Europe, over a quarter to the Far East, and much of the rest to South-East Asia. Congress often pared appropriations but most of its members did not seek large reductions. Economic aid declined from $7,400,000,000 in the peak year of 1951 to $3,000,000,000 in 1963 but this was the result of European recovery and not of an American change of heart.

But as America's own economy thirsted for ever more raw material imports, as European manufacturers became more competitive within their own continent and elsewhere, the balance of trade surplus upon which all this generosity rested became less certain. Indeed 1959 hardly showed a surplus at all. Meanwhile, more and richer tourists went abroad. The results were that the balance of payments deficit shot up to $4,000,000,000 in 1959 and that in the three years ending in 1960 the value of the United States Treasury gold reserve at Fort Knox fell by a quarter to eighteen billion dollars as a result of people abroad deciding to cash dollar receipts.

But what appeared more alarming to many than shifts in the economic balance of power within the 'free world' was the apparent Russian ascendancy in military and civilian science and technology. By announcing the appointment of a special scientific assistant almost immediately after the orbiting of *Sputnik I* President Eisenhower communicated his own apprehension to the public at large. Further evidence of official unease soon appeared in the form of the excessive publicity given first to the presumed projection beyond the atmosphere of some tiny aluminium pellets and to the preparations to launch a 'grapefruit size' *Vanguard* satellite which, in

[1] Much of this aid was, of course, channelled through multi-national institutions.

the event, exploded on its launching pad. Some people linked these misfortunes with the apparent predilection of the President for golf and so generated the legend that only the Russians were proving to be professionals in science and politics. And the legend was encouraged by gloomy prognoses about an impending 'missile gap'. These derived from the fallacious premise that because the USSR had perfected a certain weapons system she would be willing and able to mass produce it. They were, therefore, the exact counterpart of the intercontinental bomber gap that had lured Congress into voting extra Air Force appropriations back in 1956.

Unease about the foreign affairs outlook was one factor that conditioned the forthcoming Presidential contest. Another was a measure of shame and anger about the manifest incompetence of top level American diplomacy. A visit to the USSR by Vice-President Nixon, arranged shortly before the retirement of Mr Dulles on account of failing health, was the prelude to a visit to the USA by Mr Kruschev in the autumn of 1959. Two days before the Soviet leader's arrival his scientists scored the first ever direct hit on the moon and so his tour was in the nature of a triumphal progress. American leaders had long feared that such contacts would serve merely to provide propaganda opportunities and to underemphasize the importance of such specific matters of dispute as West Berlin. Their fears seemed to have been realized.

Worse was to follow. A 'summit' conference, to be attended by Presidents Eisenhower and de Gaulle, Mr Macmillan and Mr Kruschev, was scheduled to start in Paris on May 16th, 1960. But ten days before that the Russians, who had recently brought an improved ground-to-air missile into service, reported that they had shot down an American intruder. A Washington denial that any deliberate violations of Russian airspace had ever occurred was swiftly countered by a Soviet statement that the pilot of the Lockheed U-2 in question had been captured alive and well after being shot down near Sverdlovsk. Then Mr Kruschev saw President Eisenhower at the preliminary meeting of the proposed 'summit' and asked him to apologize for the spy flights, punish those involved and promise never to allow any more. When the President declined he staged some angry press conferences and then aborted the 'summit' by storming back to Moscow. Later came the cancellation of the President's visit to Japan.[1]

Forty-three year old John Kennedy's electoral victory over Richard Nixon was in part the outcome of his ability to communicate his vision of a 'New Frontier' on which the USA might regain her lost prestige and self-esteem; this communication involved, among other things, being able to relate national needs to personal circumstances. The call for a high and sustained growth rate had significance to voters affected by the odd combination of falling employment and continuing inflation that seemed to characterize 1960; the call for increased federal aid to schools made a big impact in the new suburban areas. His success derived also from his

[1] See Chapter XV, Section ii.

articulate frankness about such awkward national issues as Quemoy-Matsu and delicate personal ones as his Roman Catholicism. Qualities such as that stood him in good stead in the television debates with his opponent.

But his final lead of 0·15% was only secured by his success in re-capturing some of that fraction of the Negro vote that the Democrats had lost in 1956; this factor was probably decisive in states as far apart as Illinois and South Carolina. Both parties were for civil rights but the Democrats made the case more strongly, calling for 'equal access . . . in all areas of community life including voting booths . . . housing and public facilities'. This demand, plus Kennedy's personal handling of the issue, mobilized much of the resurgent mood of Negro radicalism that for some months past had been reflected in numerous 'sit-ins' at segregated lunch counters.

The new President's energies in the field of diplomacy were especially directed to an attempt to consolidate the Atlantic alliance around the 'twin pillars' of a united Europe—by which was meant the Common Market with Britain inside it—and the United States. Thus in a speech at Philadelphia on July 4th, 1962, he declared that the USA looked forward to a 'declaration of interdependence' along those lines. But perhaps the two most melodramatic episodes were those concerned with Cuba. The 'Bay of Pigs' was one;[1] the missile crisis the other.

A Lockheed U–2 that overflew the island on October 14th, 1962, brought back evidence that ground-to-ground missiles were being installed and that *Ilyushin*–28 light bombers were being added to Fidel Castro's inventory of aircraft. Surveillance was increased and special military dispositions made and then, on October 22nd, a Presidential broadcast revealed that an American naval blockade was to begin shortly to check this build-up and to secure the removal, under United Nations auspices, of the 'offensive' weapons already installed. The right was reserved to resort to tougher measures if necessary and a warning was given that if one Soviet nuclear missile was fired at any target in the Western Hemisphere it would induce a full retaliatory counterblow against the USSR herself.

Twenty-five Soviet ships were approaching Cuba. However, at what was in some cases almost literally the last moment they all altered course except for one tanker which was screened and then allowed through. Moscow Radio informed the world that the entire crew had voiced their determination to defy the 'piratical' blockade.

Trilateral negotiations by telegram between Mr Kruschev, President Kennedy and U Thant later led to an agreement on the supervised withdrawal of the weapons in question and to an assurance by the United States that she would not conduct hostilities against Cuba. On November 21st the blockade was lifted and so what was perhaps the most dramatic conflict the nuclear era had yet witnessed came peacefully to a close. American supremacy in terms of strategic nuclear forces and in terms of an ability to wage limited war in the Caribbean made compliance with the

[1] See Chapter XX.

modest objectives of the United States a rational course of action. American diplomacy was such as to ensure that reason did prevail in the Kremlin rather than blind fury. No retaliatory pressure was put on West Berlin. An oblique Soviet threat to invade Turkey if Cuba was invaded had never to be put to the test.

President Kennedy brought many academic advisers into, or near to, his administration and this helped give it an exciting flavour of visionary pragmatism. Intellectual guidance was most articulate, and perhaps most pertinent, in the field of economics and this was one in which the government had an exceptionally impressive record. In spite of a wave of business nervousness in 1962—to which the President contributed by compelling the United States Steel Corporation to rescind an 'inflationary' price increase—the three years together represent one of the biggest phases of economic resurgence in the country's history. Initial recovery was helped by a large increase of expenditure on defence and aerospace activities, an increase that considerably strengthened both general and limited war forces, enabled the President to establish a manned lunar landing by 1970 as 'a major national commitment', and ensured that the *Mariner* probe was placed in the vicinity of Venus late in 1962. Then in his last summer in office President Kennedy introduced a proposal for a ten billion dollar tax cut, although neither a budget surplus nor a reduction in federal expenditure nor a national recession were in prospect at the time. It was, among other things, some measure of how far his own economic education had proceeded in a mere thirty months.

The elections to the 87th Congress in 1960 preserved the Democratic majorities but they strengthened the influence of conservative elements, and, as usual, this influence was especially strong within the committees, the work of which could greatly affect the speed and course of any legislative programme. Medical care for the aged and the long term financing of foreign aid were among the proposals from the executive that were blocked; other plans were modified. Faced with this balance of power, which was little different in the 88th Congress elected in 1962, the President decided not to press immediately for a large legislative extension of civil rights. But on June 19th, 1963, he sent down a major bill designed, he said, to 'enable the legislature to catch up with the judicial and executive branches'. On November 21st a report on a compromise bill was submitted by the House Judiciary Committee to the House Rules Committee and so early enactment seemed possible. But the following day the President was murdered.

## (i) *Britain in Search of a Role*

THE Labour government formed by Clement Attlee in 1945 pushed through a massive programme of economic and social change. Railways, canals, docks, coal mines, the gas and electricity services, and the central bank were brought wholly under public ownership, and civil aviation and long distance road haulage largely so; and a start was made with the implementation of a plan to nationalize over 100 firms in the iron and steel industry. A commission was appointed to check malpractice by private monopolies. Structural unemployment was relieved by applying more vigorously the principle of coaxing or steering new factories to areas of work shortage. Another act preserved the wartime system of guaranteed farm prices. Several Development Corporations were established, each being required to direct and finance the construction of a new town close to, but not too close to, an existing conurbation. A Town and Country Planning Act was passed that instituted a levy for the development of land by building and that co-ordinated and extended the controls intended to ensure that private building schemes were not incongruous in aesthetic, social or economic terms. Existing government schemes for insurance against sickness, unemployment and old age were consolidated and extended; a free National Health Service was set up. The extension of the 'Welfare State' in these and other directions automatically involved a considerable downward redistribution of income but the effect was magnified by making tax schedules more 'progressive'. In 1938 the 500,000 highest paid citizens earned 17% of the nation's total personal income after tax; in 1949 the percentage was 10. The government's supporters claimed that all this constituted a well balanced exercise in pragmatic socialism and so created the conditions for national recovery; its opponents claimed that much of it was wrong in principle and ill timed in relation to the country's parlous economic situation.

Nobody could deny, of course, that the economic situation was parlous. Britain had suffered less from direct war damage than many combatants and she had as a legacy from the war years an extensive system of economic controls—an asset rated highly by her new government. But she had financed a mammoth war effort largely by allowing non-strategic industries to decline sharply and by piling up huge liabilities abroad. Her export trade in 1945 was, in real terms, 45% of the pre-war level whereas 200% was the level deemed essential to maintain national solvency in the new world situation. Her readily available reserves of gold and foreign currency were valued at £600,000,000, a figure similar to that for 1937; those liabilities that she might be called upon to meet at short notice—the sterling balances as they were called—were £3,700,000,000, i.e. eight times as much as before.

In December 1945 the British and American governments agreed that Britain's Lend Lease obligations should be virtually cancelled and that America should loan to Britain, at 2% interest, $3,750,000,000, which was to be paid back over about fifty years from 1952; soon afterwards Canada gave a credit of $1,250,000,000. The American loan was offered after the British had—very reluctantly—given an undertaking that sterling would be made freely convertible into other currencies twelve months after the loan became available, a condition which represented a very strict interpretation of the philosophy of free multilateral payments enunciated at the Bretton Woods international conference in 1944. Parliament and Congress approved the loan agreement but there was strong and bipartisan opposition in both legislatures.

Sterling was duly made convertible on July 15th, 1947; on August 20th, when but $400,000,000 of the loan was left and gold and dollars were leaving the national account at the rate of $35,000,000 a day, convertibility was suspended. During the next economic crisis, which came in 1949, the exchange value of the pound was lowered to $2·80 from $4·03—a rate which had been set to cover wartime imports and which was inappropriately high for an increasingly competitive peacetime environment. The payments crisis which occasioned the devaluation was caused by the American recession; this had reduced her imports from Europe by a third in the first half of the year.

There was a £300,000,000 trading surplus in 1950 but this gave way to an even larger deficit in 1951. For this the Korean War was to blame. By early 1951 several taxes had increased and the country had committed itself to spend £4,700,000,000 on defence within three years;[1] already this burden was making its impact on, for example, engineering exports. And the balance of payments was being subjected to even more direct strains in the form of stockpiling, high world commodity prices and the collapse of wage restraint at home. To Britain's difficulties were added those of the rest of the sterling area—the group of countries, corresponding roughly to the old British Empire, the economies of which are aligned to the pound and which then tended to pool their dollar reserves. Some of them were hit badly by the slump in commodity prices that followed the initial 'Korean' boom. Thus the price of Merino 64s on the London wool market rose

[1] In 1952 this was stretched to four years.

from 140 pence a pound in June 1950 to 320 pence in March 1951 and then fell to 120 pence that September.[1]

Inflation, continuing shortages, the Persian oil crisis and the resignation of three Labour ministers—Aneurin Bevan, John Freeman and Harold Wilson—who felt that the rearmament schedule was too steep, undermined a Labour government that was already showing many signs of physical and mental exhaustion. So the Conservatives were returned to office in the election of October 1951 with Winston Churchill as their Prime Minister. Anthony Eden succeeded him in 1955 and was himself replaced by Harold Macmillan in 1957. Four general elections took place in the decade after 1949. Each time the Conservative party improved its parliamentary position.

The Tory retention of power was in spite of the fact that their husbandry yielded only a slow and irregular national growth rate. For the poor economic performance of these years several explanations can be advanced. Britain's reserves-to-liabilities ratio slowly improved, as was shown by a final move to full convertibility in 1958, but it remained uncomfortably low. This meant that she could rarely accept the sharp rise in imports that tend to be associated with the first phases of vigorous expansions. And her responsibilities as the provider of a major international currency inhibited her from further devaluations. High external military expenditure— £140,000,000 net in 1952 and £215,000,000 in 1960—was another source of strain and so was the traditional obligation to export capital to the sterling area.

But it is clear that until the nineteen-sixties the British public were more impressed by the fact that their own living standards were reaching the highest points ever than by the fact that other people's were perhaps rising faster. The slogan 'You've never had it so good', which had been coined by Mr Macmillan, made a great impact in the weeks of glorious sunshine that preceded the general election of 1959. For what had changed for many was not just a standard but a style of living. Rationing ended in 1954; the number of private cars doubled between 1951 and 1959; personal savings, measured in real terms, quadrupled.

But the 1955 and 1959 election results must be regarded as being in part a positive vote of no confidence in the Labour Party. For several years after the ministerial resignations of 1951, Aneurin Bevan and his many supporters felt obliged to challenge their party's leadership repeatedly on a variety of issues from West German rearmament to free spectacles under the National Health Service. An image of rampant disunity was thereby created. Claims that the disputes were in the nature of healthy controversies was belied by the ludicrously low level of cross-voting that occurred between the two factions.

Harold Wilson's dissociation from the opposition of his fellow Bevanites to the formation of SEATO helped promote a decrease in factional strife after 1954 but Labour had then to reckon with the growing contrast

[1] $1 = 86 pence; £1 = 240 pence.

between many of its traditional postures and the new style of life mentioned above. Its inherent puritan bias, its record of austerity in office, and its close links with the blue collar trade unions made it seem rather alien to white collar workers from the new housing areas. So did its repeated insistence on the virtues of centralized public ownership. That this insistence was the product of a doctrinal reflex rather than a thought-out attitude was suggested by the fact that no two of the lists of major industries successively approved for nationalization were the same.

Labour was racked by fresh dissension after its 1959 defeat and these focused even more than before on the personality of Hugh Gaitskell—the party leader since 1955. He failed to persuade his party to amend its constitution to exclude as an aim the full nationalization of 'the means of production, distribution, and exchange'. But he persuaded the 1961 party conference to reverse the previous year's decision to plump for 'unilateral nuclear disarmament'. And a few months before his rather sudden death early in 1963 he secured a wide measure of party support for a policy of entering the European Common Market only if the interests of the Commonwealth, EFTA and British agriculture were fully protected and if it was clear that no foreign policy ties were involved.

On July 31st, 1961, Mr Macmillan told the House of Commons that Britain would join the Common Market 'if satisfactory arrangements can be made to meet the special needs of the United Kingdom, of the Commonwealth, and of the European Free Trade Association'. Wide support for this initiative was forthcoming on the continent, de Gaulle himself saying in September that 'The Six have always wanted other countries, and particularly Britain, to join the Common Market, accept its obligations, and reap its benefits.' In June 1962 he was visited by Macmillan at Chateau de Champs, and was greatly impressed by the strength of the British Prime Minister's desire to lead his country 'into Europe'. But it appears that no examination was then made of the possibility of Anglo-French nuclear collaboration within the framework of the Common Market. The pride and vagueness inherent in both men may have been partly responsible for the omission at that time of so crucial a topic. What was probably more decisive, however, was their fear of disturbing too soon their fragile harmony.

Events were soon to show just how fragile this harmony was. Hard British bargaining on the future entry to European markets of temperate zone foodstuffs from the Commonwealth and on the arrangements for agricultural protection revived de Gaulle's doubts about the correctness of her basic attitude. The crystallization of Labour's reservations about EEC appeared the more serious in the light of its excellent prospects of regaining power. The intensifying American quest for 'interdependence' made it clear that she wanted Britain 'inside Europe' in order to restrain its separate evolution. And growing rumours of an impending cancellation of the American air-launched missile *Skybolt* made it likely that Britain would ask the USA if an option she had taken on *Polaris* might be urgently brought forward.[1] This was because *Skybolt* had been intended not only for the USAF's B-52 intercontinental bombers but also for the 'V-Bombers'—the strategic deterrent that the Royal Air Force had been operating since 1955.

Matters were clinched when de Gaulle was visited by Macmillan at Rambouillet in December 1962. This time the question of military nuclear collaboration did come up, and when it did so Macmillan confirmed that the British government expected *Skybolt* to be cancelled and said that it felt the best alternative to be *Polaris*.

But, although this information was itself sufficient to ensure that de Gaulle would block Britain's entry into the EEC, the brusqueness of his subsequent public declaration of this intent owed much to the precise form of the defence agreement that Macmillan made with Kennedy at Nassau on December 21st. This agreement envisaged the supply of *Polaris* missiles for installation on all the ballistic submarines that Britain and France might build and the placing of all these vessels under direct NATO control. It also provided for the formation within NATO of the Multilateral Force—a proposed fleet of *Polaris*-firing surface ships, each of which was to be 'mixed-manned', i.e. manned by crews drawn from several nationalities. What would be involved, therefore, was a closer and more formal integration of NATO and an undermining of the special nuclear status of Britain and of France.

These proposals were, of course, quite unacceptable to de Gaulle and their bi-national presentation caused him added offence. The whole affair was too reminiscent of the British refusal to join the EDC, of her securing complete exemption from Western European Union arms control arrangements, of her privileged access to American nuclear data, and other devices by means of which she maintained an illusion of splendid isolation. At his press conference of January 14, 1963, de Gaulle denounced Britain as a country whose equivocation and whose apparently special links with the USA, EFTA and the Commonwealth would ruin the EEC were she to enter it.

Dean Acheson had observed, a fortnight before Rambouillet, that 'Great Britain has lost an empire and has yet to find a role.' The search for a role became an agonizing one in the course of 1963—conducted as it was in the wake of the collapse of the EEC talks and amid mounting evidence of negligence and incompetence on the part of the government. An ailing Mr Macmillan resigned in October and was replaced by Sir Alec Douglas-Home—a cavalier aristocrat from rural Scotland. His political task was to prepare for electoral battle with Labour's new leader, Harold Wilson—a man whose roots lay in the dour toughmindedness of the industrial middle class of Yorkshire.

---

[1] In 1960 Eisenhower had agreed that *Polaris* would be supplied to Britain, on request, from 1970.

## (ii) *The Old White Dominions*

Canada's retention of a strong sense of nationhood, despite the fact that half her population lived within 100 miles of her long southern border, derived in no small measure from the existence of Quebec—the province whose core was composed of 4,500,000 French speaking Roman Catholics. And with the displacement, in 1960, by an energetic Liberal administration of the corrupt and negative Union Nationale one, which had governed the province for many years, Quebec politics and cultural life became distinctly more vital. But this resurgence coincided with the rise of a separatist movement—a movement that hoped to capitalize particularly on urban middle class resentment at the way in which French had come to be regarded as a second class language throughout much of the Dominion. But the separatists lacked unity and good leadership and were rather predisposed to violence. For these reasons they failed to attract more than a tiny minority of the Quebecan public.

Canada was more exercised than most countries by the question of what her place in the world was to be. Recurrent friction with the United States over economic matters was one of the factors that generated this concern. Major specific instances were provided by American tardiness in starting her share of the work on the St Lawrence Seaway and Canadian delays over the Columbia River development treaty. Lesser ones included discrimination against Canadian farm and mineral exports. The hold on Canadian industry that American corporations appeared to have was another source of unease. So, one might add, was the progressive integration, from 1951, of Canadian and American air defence.

But Canada offset this economic and strategic involvement by playing the political role of an interpreter between the USA and Europe and between the West and Afro-Asia. She was an enthusiastic member of NATO right from the start but she often called for greater emphasis on its non-military aspects. She played an active part in international peacekeeping in the Sinai desert, Indo-China, the Lebanon and the Congo. She openly criticized British policy at Suez and several aspects of the foreign policy of the Eisenhower administration. She declined to use her nuclear experience to develop her own nuclear warheads.

But just how circumscribed the areas of choice were became clear during John Diefenbaker's Progressive Conservative administration. Diefenbaker was able to break the Liberal twenty year hold on office in 1957 largely because he benefited from a surge of anti-Americanism. Yet one of the first acts of his government was to agree to the establishment of a joint North American Air Defence Command. Little was subsequently done to realize the hope that Mr Diefenbaker expressed that 15% of Canada's exports might be diverted to Britain. In 1959 the Canadian *Arrow* fighter aircraft was cancelled in favour of, among other things, the

787

American *Bomarc*, a ground-to-air missile that could not be satisfactorily deployed without American nuclear warheads. For years no such warheads were issued because the two countries failed to agree on their control. In 1961 the Liberal Party argued that such warheads should not be used in Canadian airspace. Yet it accepted them on its return to office in 1963.

A Liberal and Country Party alliance, led by Mr Robert Menzies, drove Australia's Labour government from office late in 1949. Bitter antagonism had been aroused in some quarters by a federal attempt to nationalize all the private banks. Also industrial unrest had been widespread and it had culminated, in the winter before the election, in a seven week national coal strike. The government met this challenge with remarkable toughness but, coinciding as it did with the Communist triumph in China, the episode served to strengthen greatly popular distrust of the Left.

Menzies had obtained a mandate to have the Communist Party outlawed but his subsequent endeavour to do this was frustrated in 1951 first by a High Court ruling and then by a referendum. The debate over domestic Communism then subsided only to be revived in 1954 by the defection of Vladimir Petrov, the Third Secretary at the Soviet Embassy. A Royal Commission was set up to investigate his assertion that he had been part of a spy ring and it found that he had. Dr Herbert Evatt, leader of the Labour Party since 1951, criticized the way the affair had been handled and, adducing as evidence some correspondence he had had with Mr Molotov, claimed that Petrov and others had forged documents in order to embarrass the Labour Party. For some time past his attitude towards Communism had caused restiveness among Labour's Catholic Action group in Victoria and now this erupted into open rebellion. 1955 therefore witnessed the disintegration of the Labour administration in Victoria and the formation of a Labour splinter group at federal level.

In New Zealand also industrial militancy contributed to the fall of a Labour Government in 1949. Labour regained power with a parliamentary majority of one in 1957 but lost it again in 1960. Neither in these two elections nor in the one of 1963 were great political issues at stake. A feeling that it was 'time for a change' contributed to the defeat of the National Party in 1957 and resentment at Labour's extensive import controls helped bring about its return in 1960.

The fall of Singapore in 1942 had served for all Australasians as a dramatic demonstration of their own vulnerability. So after the war they sought to provide themselves with guarantees stronger and more enduring than a general expectation of British naval support. Australia spent much money on the economically rather unprofitable development of her exposed and under-populated Northern Territory. In 1951 the two countries signed the Pacific Security Treaty with the United States. And they came to collaborate closely with Britain in the defence of Malaya and Malaysia. In 1963 Australia formally agreed to the establishment on her western coast of a communications centre for American ballistic submarines. Arthur Calwell, Labour's leader since 1960, urged 'no annihilation without representation' and demanded that the use of the base be made completely subject to a bi-national control arrangement.

## (iii) *The Wider Commonwealth*

Practically all the independent states that, within the twentieth century, had formed part of Britain or her Empire were still in the Commonwealth in 1963; the only exceptions were Ireland, Burma and South Africa. But although, or perhaps because, the Commonwealth remained so large, it became a good deal less cohesive. For one thing, partly because of a decline of the sterling area as an economic club, intra-Commonwealth trade became relatively less important. Thus only 4% of the £3,500,000,000 increase in imports that was registered by the rest of the Commonwealth between 1953 and 1962 was provided by British exporters. A vast web of commercial and professional links remained but a comprehensive and systematic examination of them would probably have revealed a general centripetal tendency. Over much of the Commonwealth English held its own as the language of business and government but the exclusiveness of this bond was reduced by greater world activity by the United States and by other nations becoming more familiar with the Anglo-Saxon tongue.

What was true of commerce and culture was generally true of government also. Commonwealth countries came to rely less on Britain for military aid and, as they did so, often turned to foreign countries rather than their fellow Commonwealth members. But the members of Commonwealth Africa constituted an exception; they were operating about 20 bi-national aid programmes with Commonwealth countries in the middle of 1964 and only 17 with foreign ones. And foreign journalists remarked on the close collaboration between Commonwealth contingents—'the whisky and Sandhurst set'—in the course of the Congo operation.

Intra-Commonwealth diplomacy gradually lost some of its distinctive flavour. The status of High Commissioners came more to resemble that of Ambassadors. The proportion of direct official contacts, as opposed to those arranged through standard diplomatic channels, decreased. The exchange of confidences became relatively less frequent as well as more selective. But one unique link that survived with little modification was the Commonwealth Prime Ministers' conference in London; between 1955 and 1963 this met six times.

By 1963 the Commonwealth had twenty members and there was a 1,000-fold range in area and population between the smallest, Zanzibar, and the largest, India. Its assumption of this new pattern was essentially due to the 1949 ruling that India could, as a republic, remain within the association. This was a precedent that was not without its critics, notably

Field Marshal Smuts who realized that it would serve as a useful lever for the Nationalist republicans in his native South Africa.

Commonwealth evolution was punctuated by other climacterics. Internal affairs had come to be regarded as ineligible for discussion at the Prime Ministers' conferences but when, in 1961, South Africa applied for readmission on becoming a republic, *apartheid* was, with Dr Verwoerd's reluctant consent, made a subject of debate. John Diefenbaker was among the many heads of state who contended that *apartheid* was an anomaly unacceptable in a multi-racial association; Robert Menzies was the only one who publicly disagreed with this. The outcome was that South Africa withdrew her application.

Most of the other member governments undoubtedly felt Commonwealth links to have been strengthened by South Africa's departure. But Britain was soon to weaken this feeling by her application to join the EEC, even though she committed herself to securing EEC safeguards for Commonwealth trade. It was widely assumed, particularly in Australia and New Zealand, that Britain had turned finally towards Europe and away from the Open Sea. But this was too simple and too hasty an assessment. Thus Harold Wilson's election as leader of the British Labour Party in 1963 was followed by a renewed Labour emphasis, especially in defence terms, on the East of Suez role.

A significant example of Commonwealth political co-operation was provided by the Geneva settlement of 1954. Anthony Eden displayed a concern about the consequences for Malayan stability and intra-Commonwealth relations of a worsening of the Indo-China situation and, in contrast with his subsequent behaviour over Suez, kept in close touch with the Asian Commonwealth and with the Dominions. He laid emphasis on British respect for Commonwealth viewpoints when objecting to aspects of American policy and he persuaded Mr Dulles not to deprive India of an opportunity to join the proposed regional security pact. But he also devoted time to, for example, describing to Pandit Nehru early in 1954 the Franco-American fears that an immedite cease-fire would facilitate Vietminh subversion and to dissuading India from being too outspoken in her condemnation of SEATO. The nature of the Commonwealth as, to quote from a speech Lester Pearson made as early as 1949, 'a bridge between the East and the West', gives it the potential to play a conciliatory role in similar situations in the future. The same could apply in respect of disarmament initiatives; the declaration on this subject in the 1961 Prime Minister's communiqué was an encouraging omen. Relevant here is the marked disinclination of the Commonwealth countries, all of which are imbued with the British traditions of pragmatism and compromise, to adopt rigid ideological attitudes.

## Chapter XXIII
# THE UNITED NATIONS

### (i) *The Framework Evolves*

THE United Nations Charter became effective on October 24th, 1945; that was the date by which it had been ratified by the five Great Powers and by a majority of the other signatories. The most important of the institutions it authorized were the Security Council, the General Assembly and the Secretariat. But significant also was the provision it made for bringing within the orbit of the UN various 'special agencies', some of which had already been created. Thus extensive work was done in the first year or two of peace by the United Nations Relief and Rehabilitation Administration. In 1946, however, the United States—from whence a high proportion of UNRRA's resources had come—announced itself unable, in view of the current decline in international harmony, to allow the continuation of multilateral aid in this form. Some of UNRRA's work was taken over by the United Nations International Children's Emergency Fund, which even by 1953 had vaccinated 23,000,000 children against tuberculosis, cured 3,000,000 of yaws and protected 12,000,000 against malaria.

Other special agencies include the International Labour Organization, the UN Educational, Scientific and Cultural Organization, the World Health Organization and the Food and Agriculture Organization. FAO, for example, which had a gross income close to $30,000,000 in 1961 has acted as a clearing house for information and has provided many field officers to advise on matters such as food storage, fish farming and pest control. Some of the Communist countries did not belong in 1963; some countries that were not UN members—e.g. West Germany—did. FAO became affiliated to the UN by an agreement that was approved by the General Assembly.

No Communist country apart from Yugoslavia was a member of either the International Monetary Fund or the International Bank at the end of 1963.[1] But both these agencies have made a useful though modest contribution to the economic progress of the rest of the world. The IMF, the

[1] Cuba was not a member of the Bank and was about to leave the IMF.

authorization of which became effective in December, 1945, has operated a system of cash reserves that members can draw upon to meet temporary balance of payments deficits; on December 31st, 1963, it held $3,200,000,000 worth of gold and $12,000,000,000 worth of national currencies.

The International Bank for Reconstruction and Development, or the World Bank as it was more often called, had by that date made 370 loans worth $7,500,000,000 in seventy countries. The loans were made primarily to enable countries to meet the foreign expenditure on basic development projects. And the IMF generally declined to make any firm offer of a loan until strong evidence was forthcoming that the project in question was viable. The withdrawal, in the summer of 1956, of the tentative offer of aid for the Aswan Dam became inevitable once the USA and the United Kingdom had cancelled their individual offers to Egypt. The withdrawal was preceded, however, by several expressions of doubt by IBRD officials as to whether the Egyptian government could honour its own financial commitments in respect of Aswan.

The Korean War was unique among the military and political operations of the United Nations in respect of both scale and character. In character because of the degree to which it obliged the UN temporarily to take sides in the Cold War. In scale because of the volume and duration of the effort required and the number of countries that contributed to it. Fourteen nations eventually sent ground troops to Korea and the total strength of the UN service personnel in the theatre, other than Americans and South Koreans, was in the region of 50,000. The force on duty by the first Christmas included Australian, British, Filipino, French, Netherlands, Thai and Turkish infantry, Indian and Swedish medical units and a South African air squadron.

Untypical though the Korean War proved to be in relation to the future pattern of events, it influenced that pattern a great deal. Large General Assembly majorities named China an aggressor in February 1951, and that May called for embargoes on shipments to her of arms, petrol and other strategic materials. Ever afterwards there was a solid body of UN opinion, led by the United States, that remained resolutely opposed to the Communist Chinese replacing the Nationalists in the General Assembly and on the Security Council. Communist pressure in favour of this change was renewed in the autumn of 1963 but the General Assembly voted against it by 57 votes to 41; there were 12 abstentions. Yet the USA herself had indicated in January 1950 that she would accept the Chinese People's Republic onto the Security Council if seven of the eleven members voted in favour of inviting her. Trygve Lie, the Norwegian who was then Secretary General, began to canvass energetically for the support required and his endeavours might well have borne fruit but for the Korean outbreak.

It was only the temporary absence from the Security Council of the Soviet delegate, Jacob Malik—ostensibly in protest against China's continued exclusion—that enabled the Security Council to act effectively at the start of the Korean War. United States apprehension lest such a conjuncture should never recur led to her introduction of the 'Uniting for Peace' proposals that were passed by the General Assembly on November 3rd, 1950—the only formal opposition coming from the Soviet bloc. The resolutions in question ensured that in future war situations emergency sessions of the General Assembly could be called by seven Security Council members if effective Council action had been blocked by one of the permanent members exercising its power of veto. The value of this prerogative was thereby diminished. It was not, however, eliminated. It remained important, for example, as a way of excluding unwelcome applicants from UN membership. Between 1945 and 1963 the USSR used the veto approximately 100 times. In 1961, for instance, she blocked a resolution deploring the Indian invasion of the Portuguese territory of Goa.

The Congo was the scene of the second largest, and, as things turned out, the second most controversial of the operations that the UN undertook. A resolution was passed by the Security Council on July 14th, 1960, that authorized the Secretary-General 'to provide . . . military assistance . . . until, with the technical assistance of the United Nations, the national security forces might be able, in the opinion of the government, to meet fully their tasks'; the voting was eight to nil with Britain, China and France abstaining because of reservations regarding a paragraph that asked Belgium to withdraw its troops. Within four days the United Nations had 3,500 troops in the Congo and within two months 19,000. But a force of this size was only assembled so quickly by much recourse to improvisation. Wheeled transport long remained in short supply—a serious matter in a territory that was all but a million square miles in extent. Several of the Afro-Asian contingents arrived short of wireless sets; many of the European ones lacked tropical clothing and tentage. Many of the units involved were flown into the Congo by the USAF and the RAF; neither Britain nor the USA nor any of the permanent members of the Security Council sent any ground troops, however.

Relations between the United Nations and Patrice Lumumba, the Congolese Premier, became bad during August because the UN felt that it had no mandate to enforce the submission of President Tshombe's breakaway *régime* in Katanga. Since a *gendarmerie* was then being built up under Belgian officers in Katanga the central government stood little chance of imposing its will unaided. Tension rose and as it did so the USSR concentrated more and more on the direct support of Lumumba. On September 6th the *Organisation des Nations Unies au Congo* closed Leopoldville airport to prevent the USSR from moving Lumumbist reinforcements to South Kasai where fighting was in progress against a movement seeking to establish, with Katangan armed assistance, a separate mining state in that Baluba tribal area; at the same time Radio Leopoldville was temporarily closed down by ONUC. These two moves

793

almost precipitated the withdrawal of the Guinea, Ghana and United Arab Republic contingents because their governments felt that it helped President Kasavubu—the constitutional head of the Congo republic—in attempts he was then making to oust Premier Lumumba.

The Security Council met on September 14th after Colonel Mobutu—the army Chief of Staff—had arrested Lumumba. After the USSR had vetoed a Tunisian-Ceylonese motion supporting ONUC in its aim of restoring order, an emergency session of the General Assembly was convened under the 'Uniting For Peace' procedure. On the 20th it carried by 70 votes to nil a resolution urging Dag Hammarskjöld, as Secretary-General, 'to continue to take vigorous action' to seek peaceful solutions of the Congo's internal conflicts, and urging also that all military aid be channelled through the UN. The Soviet bloc, France and South Africa abstained.

Lumumba was transferred, at Kasavubu's request, to Elizabethville—the Katangan capital—early in 1961; shortly afterwards he was murdered, probably on Tshombe's instructions. In February the Security Council gave ONUC a mandate to disarm foreign intruders, meaning especially the hundreds of mercenaries—mainly French and Belgian—in Katanga; many of them were disarmed in the course of an operation that August. Meanwhile Kasavubu came to work more closely with Antoine Gizenga—the leader of a powerful Lumumbist breakaway movement based on Stanleyville—with a view to imposing upon Tshombe a form of Congo unity tighter than the confederation he hoped for. A major reason why Tshombe sought a loose relationship was that he did not want too high a proportion of Katanga's mining revenues to be spent outside that province.

Hammarskjöld was killed on a flight to see Tshombe in September 1961 and so it was U Thant, working then in the capacity of Acting Secretary-General, who put forward a new federal proposal in the following August. Tshombe, like the other parties concerned, seemed to accept the scheme in principle but he did little to implement it and continued instead to rebuild his mercenary army. In late December the United Nations moved in strength against the mercenary and gendarmerie positions; meanwhile Katanga was threatened with UN economic sanctions. Resistance soon collapsed and early in 1963 Tshombe agreed to end the secession.

The Congo affair focused the unease several of the larger and more powerful nations felt about the concept of world affairs being ordered by an organization that consisted of over 100 nation states. Kruschev himself launched an attack on Hammarskjöld in the General Assembly in 1960; at the same time he proposed the *troika*. Under this scheme the Secretariat would have had not one chief executive but three—one representing the Soviet bloc, one the West and one the non-aligned group. But the virulence of the Afro-Asian opposition effectively killed this cumbersome project.

A symptom of wider uncertainties about the desirability of international peacekeeping arrangements in an age of revolutions was to be found in the UN's accumulation of financial deficits. Fifty-two out of the 99 members were in arrears in respect of their subscription to the main budget at the end of 1961. The special account for the United Nations Emergency Force that had been screening the Sinai Desert ever since Suez was being under-subscribed by about a third; only 19 members had paid by then the full annual contribution due from them for the Congo operation. No Soviet bloc state was subscribing to UNEF or to ONUC; France and Belgium were among the countries not subscribing to ONUC. The International Court of Justice advised in 1962 that UNEF and ONUC expenditures should be paid for by all member states. The USSR was among those who disregarded this judgment.

## (ii) *Towards a Peaceful World?*

Various institutions were established within the framework of the United Nations to promote partial or complete disarmament. The Soviet Union joined Canada, Britain and the United States in sponsoring the Atomic Energy Commission that the General Assembly set up in 1946. That summer Mr Baruch presented to the AEC an American plan for an International Atomic Development Authority for the management of all nuclear projects of potential military importance and for the control and licensing of the rest. He said that once such an authority had been properly established the United States would dismantle her own nuclear stockpile —a stockpile that was then very small. But Mr Gromyko of the USSR insisted that all nuclear weapons be outlawed before the authority became effective, that it should have powers not of control but only of limited inspection, and that no sanctions for violation should be imposed without full Security Council consent. Little was done to resolve these differences between 1947 and 1952 when both the AEC and a parallel Commission for Conventional Armaments—which had been formed in 1947—were replaced by a new Disarmament Commission.

Both disarmament and arms control figured prominently in the diplomatic controversies of the 1950s and several aspects of both were exhaustively examined by the Eighteen Nation Disarmament Conference which held sessions in Geneva, under the auspices of the United Nations, from 1962. But nearly all the schemes put forward strongly reflected the special strategic interests of their originators. The USSR was invariably most anxious to enhance the advantage it gained from being able to operate on interior lines of communication; a general elimination of foreign bases was seen as a means to this end. She was also loth to sacrifice her 'intelligence' lead and eager to reduce or make irrelevant the Western nuclear preponderance. Western policies naturally revealed an opposite bias.

The world political climate remained such that such attempts as were made to harmonize conflicting approaches to disarmament never came to fruition. But arms control fared just a little better. The International Geophysical Year revived an old interest in the demilitarization of the Antarctic and this became the subject of a twelve nation agreement in December 1959. Four years later the General Assembly voted unanimously against the placing of nuclear weapons in orbit; this was a gesture that probably had symbolic value although no provision could be made for inspection and although, conversely, little benefit would have been reaped by any violation. This ban on space weapons was followed almost immediately by a more important measure—the signature by the three thermonuclear states of a treaty precluding nuclear tests in the atmosphere the oceans and outer space. Other nations were invited to accede to it and virtually all bar France and China did so. Each of these countries was by then engaged in the construction of a gaseous diffusion plant from which to obtain trigger material for hydrogen bombs. These might be hard to test underground.

None of the above measures involved any serious hurt to the pride or self-interest of any major nation and this limited their worth as portents. Such grounds for optimism about the arms race as existed were based not so much on such concrete steps as had been taken to halt it as in the gradual spread, at least within government and academic circles, of the realization that trite theories of deterrence and containment could provide no final answers. A total of twelve Pugwash Conferences, in which scientists from the Communist world discussed disarmament and related topics with those from elsewhere, were held between early 1957 and early 1964. An Arms Control and Disarmament Agency was established by the Kennedy administration in 1961. And the panache of President Kennedy himself gave intellectualism and internationalism a wider appeal than they had enjoyed for a long time.

A new mood was fostered also by an increasing awareness of the approach of a stable strategic deadlock between the USA and the USSR, a deadlock that would rest on large numbers of ICBMs. Both countries had brought anti-missile missiles to an advanced stage of development, and indeed the USSR had begun a token deployment, but neither seemed at all likely to become able to shoot down a worthwhile proportion of the other's intercontinental rockets. An absolute weapon had at last been created in the form of the ICBM.

In other respects the outlook was less reassuring. Prognoses of a race war between the 'white' and 'coloured' peoples could be convincingly challenged on the grounds that the world pattern of tension and conflict remained infinitely complex. But still the possibility existed that eventually, perhaps as a result of their economic progress falling further and further behind their ever rising expectations, the non-white communities would start to form more of a common front. This danger was connected with that of nuclear proliferation. By December 1963 China was only ten months off her first nuclear explosion. India's vigorous programme for the civil application of nuclear power had provided her with the opportunity of making fission bombs, should she so decide, at less than two years notice. Statesmen and writers had often argued that modern science has magnified both the perils and the opportunities with which mankind is faced. Of no year had this been more true than it was of 1963.

# EPILOGUE 1964–66

No doubt future historians will tend to discuss the sixties as if they were a single entity very much as the historians of today incline to generalize about the twenties and the thirties. But the portion of this decade that has now elapsed has been far too eventful to lend itself to any broad interpretation. The salient characteristic of the New Frontier movement in the United States was its sense of impending, but avertible peril. Sometimes that sense seems to have been appropriate only to a brief phase which, thanks to the evolution of military techniques, has now receded into a remote past; at other times it seems as apposite as ever. Sometimes the Cuban crisis looks like becoming the classic illustration of the proposition that history does not repeat itself; at other times that pattern of conflict looks as though it is about to reappear around Berlin or Hanoi. The past pulsates before our eyes because the present is so turbulent.

To appreciate how fast things change one has only to consider the fate of some of those who were star international figures, say, late in 1963. Konrad Adenauer, Ben Bella, Nikita Kruschev, Harold Macmillan, Pandit Nehru, Kwame Nkrumah and Ahmed Sukarno are among those whose direct influence has, for one reason or another, ended or diminished. Their successors have been men with markedly different aptitudes and policies, a fact which helps us to evaluate the fallen stars of 1963 and the episodes with which they were associated. A thorough and precise understanding of particular recent situations must await the publication and scrutiny of additional source material. Few really balanced and perceptive assessments of the broader aspects of the first nuclear decades are likely to appear for many years to come. But we can see already some of the more direct results of events that occurred only several years ago. The importance of, say, the Franco-German treaty of 1963 can perhaps be gauged. We can begin to comprehend the extent of the change that came over the British political scene in the course of that same year.

These considerations apply already up to 1963 but only to a limited extent beyond it. There is, in addition, the purely practical problem that the material that deals with the last eighteen months remains as yet too diffuse and disorganized to be handled with acceptable ease and confidence. Herein lies a valid case for taking the main narrative through 1963 but not beyond it. An invalid argument, though one which seemed substantial

798

when this book was first conceived, is that 1963 could prove a turning point in human affairs. 1964 will be at least as entitled to that accolade and, indeed, 1965 and 1966 will have claims as well.

1964 was a year in which important developments took place in most of the key centres of power and in all the areas of open conflict. France became yet more determined to play a role independent of the United States and demonstrated this determination in several ways. She recognized Communist China and her President followed a visit to Mexico with an extended tour of other parts of Latin America. During this tour he laid emphasis on the value of the cultural links between all Latin countries and referred to a need for some kind of 'Third Force' between Washington and Moscow. The French call for the neutralization of Vietnam, Laos and Cambodia was a related theme.

Pandit Nehru died in May and was replaced as India's Prime Minister by Lal Bahadur Shastri. But this led to little alteration in the general pitch of India's foreign policy. Her heavy condemnation of the nuclear test that China carried out in October was a reaction that was very much in line with the Nehru tradition.

Nikita Kruschev was censured by the Central Committee of the Communist Party of the Soviet Union on October 14th and he resigned immediately, ostensibly on health grounds. His successor as First Secretary to the Party was Leonid Breshnev, a 57 year old Ukrainian who was a former engineer. Aleksei Kosygin, a 60 year old native of Leningrad, took over the job of Chairman of the Council of Ministers. The removal from the scene of the ebullient Mr Kruschev provoked many expressions of surprise and disapproval in the ranks of world Communism.

No comparable reaction was to be observed among America's major allies to Lyndon Johnson's defeat of Barry Goldwater, by an unprecedented margin, in the 1964 Presidential election. Senator Goldwater's search for, as he put it, a choice rather than an echo led him into a militant conservatism, which was epitomized by his famous assertion that 'Extremism in the defence of liberty is no vice. Moderation in the pursuit of justice is no virtue.' This was a philosophy which was to be applied both at home and abroad. President Johnson's platform, on the other hand, was built around the more optimistic vision of what he called 'The Great Society'—that is to say, one great in moral and aesthetic terms as well as in material ones. He saw the 1964 Civil Rights Act as one step in that direction. Its aim was the final elimination of discrimination based on colour in respect of the franchise, the use of such buildings as petrol stations, restaurants, and hotels, the use of public amenities of all kinds and recruitment by medium and large firms. It sought to achieve this aim by prescript and by an extension of the machinery for reducing racial tension and curbing racialist behaviour. Senator Goldwater disliked the idea of the federal government taking upon itself so much of the responsibility for Negro advancement.

The Labour Party won the British general election of October 1964 by the exceptionally narrow margin of three parliamentary seats. The mandate upon which it was elected was one of basic adaptation to the needs and opportunities of the age of science and technology. Very soon, however, attention had to be concentrated not on long term structural reform but on preventing immediate economic collapse. The new government had inherited a remarkably large balance of payments deficit and the difficulties this created were accentuated by a serious run on sterling in November. Heavy borrowings from foreign banks and the rather traditional financial techniques of dear money and credit restriction were the principal methods adopted to bring the situation under control.

The most distinctive foreign policy initiative that Labour took during its early weeks in office was to launch the concept of an Atlantic Nuclear Force as an alternative to a NATO Multilateral Fleet. The ANF was to be composed of the British *Polaris* submarines and V-Bombers, some American *Polaris* submarines, a French contribution if possible and a small mixed-manned element.

The United Nations sent a peacekeeping force to Cyprus in March and this presence helped the UN to keep the incidence of communal violence down and prevent the situation leading to war between Greece and Turkey. The risk of such a war was always considerable and it became acute in August when Turkish warplanes came to the aid of some Turkish villages in the north-west of the island that were coming under Greek Cypriot attack.

Heavy fighting continued, meanwhile, across the length and breadth of South Vietnam and on August 5th, after some American destroyers had been fired on in international waters by North Vietnamese torpedo boats, American aircraft attacked coastal installations in North Vietnam. A civil war between Republicans, operating with the support of large Egyptian regular forces, and Royalists continued throughout most of the year in the Yemen and this struggle overlapped with a campaign of terrorism being waged by Arab nationalists within the Federation of South Arabia. Malaysia was another federation that was coming under pressure. But though many armed Indonesians were infiltrated into it they failed to effect its collapse.

Some of these areas of conflict became less dangerous in 1965. Cyprus became relatively quiescent. A truce was signed in the Yemen. Malaysia suffered the secession of Singapore, which became an independent state within the Commonwealth, but obviously stood to gain from the course of events in Indonesia where the Communist party was ruthlessly repressed in the aftermath of an attempted coup at the end of September, an event for which the Communist party was judged at least partly responsible. But the Vietnam situation became more grave and there were, in addition, serious hostilities between India and Pakistan and a rebellion, albeit a bloodless one, by Rhodesia.

Routine air attacks on communications in North Vietnam began in February in retaliation for a big increase in the infiltration of men and supplies through Laos and by sea into South Vietnam. Soviet ground-to-air missile batteries were soon moved into North Vietnam by way of reply but clashes between them and American or South Vietnamese aircraft were infrequent because the batteries were deployed principally in defence of Hanoi and Haiphong which, perhaps in accordance with some tacit agreement between the Americans and the Russians, were not then being attacked. Bitter ground fighting developed in the South as the Vietcong guerrillas tried to take decisive advantage of the limitations the summer monsoon placed on mechanized movement; this aim they failed to realize largely because the American force level in South Vietnam was continually raised. It rose, in fact, from 25,000 men to well over 150,000 in the course of the year; meanwhile, the estimated 'hard core' strength of the Vietcong increased from 35,000 to 75,000. Both sides observed a truce over Christmas and the air attacks on the North were not resumed for several weeks afterwards. The USA used those weeks to conduct a world-wide diplomatic offensive in favour of constructive peace talks. This failed.

Fighting between India and Pakistan broke out in the Rann of Kutch in April but a cease fire agreement covering that district was signed on June 30th. A few weeks later, however, infiltrators from Pakistan began to foment serious disturbances in the Indian-held part of Kashmir. Towards the end of August units of the Indian Army crossed the Kashmir cease-fire line in the course of security operations. Their doing so provoked a strong counter-attack by Pakistani regular units and soon this threatened the main Indian line of communication through Jammu. So on September 6th the Indian Army in the Punjab advanced towards Lahore, in order to create a diversion. Much air and some naval warfare developed mean-while and on the 17th China delivered an ultimatum about India's allegedly provocative military constructions in Sikkim. But on the 22nd a cease-fire was arranged and early in 1966 President Ayub Khan and Mr Shastri—each of whom had been a moderating influence through-out—met at Tashkent in Soviet Central Asia to try to arrange a settlement.

Ian Smith, who had become Prime Minister of Rhodesia as a result of the Cabinet crisis of April 1964, made a 'Unilateral Declaration of Independence' on behalf of his country in November 1965. He did so because weeks of intense discussions between his government and the British had failed to produce agreement about the conditions under which independence could be granted. The main point at issue was that of what rate of progress towards 'majority rule'—i.e. universal suffrage for all races—should be guaranteed by the independence constitution.

Britain began to impose economic sanctions from the moment UDI was declared and many other countries followed her example. Harold Wilson consistently maintained that sanctions would be able to force Ian Smith to return to the conference table but many people in Black Africa, and some in Britain, doubted the efficacy of economic war and deplored Mr Wilson's reluctance to use military force for the purpose.

The confrontations between Rawalpindi and Delhi and between

Salisbury and London weakened the bonds of Commonwealth and so did the failure of the attempt to launch a Commonwealth Peace Mission to end the war in Vietnam. Awareness of this was to be detected in the revival of Britain's political interest in Europe. Edward Heath—the man who, as President of the Board of Trade, had led Britain's delegation at Brussels during the negotiations on her proposed entry into the Common Market which collapsed in 1963—had become leader of the Conservatives in July 1965 and soon he started to commit his party to 'joining Europe' more openly than ever before. The Labour government still had considerable reservations about the Treaty of Rome but its willingness to strengthen certain links with Europe was reflected in the arrangements made for closer aeronautical collaboration with France.

President de Gaulle made his hostility to supranational institutions in general and to NATO in particular abundantly clear in 1965. French spokesmen used the deadlock that developed over agricultural policy in June as an occasion to call into question the whole concept of rapid and thorough economic integration as envisaged in the Rome Treaty. They also made it clear that they regarded this controversy as essentially an aspect of a fundamental debate about the future evolution of Western Europe. France continued her reassertion of independence at the NATO level also; in October NATO was described by her Foreign Minister as 'a cumbrous and costly organization that tends to dilute France's responsibility'. De Gaulle was elected to serve as President for a further seven years in December but on a smaller share of the first ballot than most people had expected.

Several hundred people were killed or seriously injured in the riots that took place in the Negro quarter of Los Angeles in August but the attention of the American government was focused on external affairs for most of 1965. It was not, however, the affairs of Europe that caused the most acute concern but those of Asia and the Caribbean. The dominant preoccupations were the interrelated ones of Vietnam and the containment of China but the Dominican Republic was an important one too. On April 30th a large force of American soldiers and marines started to land there in order to protect American lives and property and to ensure that a Communist-dominated *régime* did not result from the civil war that had broken out the previous week; later they were joined by contingents from certain other OAS members. This was an operation that raised some basic issues about the aims and methods of foreign policy.

China became very isolated in the course of the year. Russia's sponsoring of the Tashkent conference represented, in geopolitical terms, her heading China off in the race for influence within the Indian sub-continent. Events in Indonesia shaped to China's disadvantage; so, in some respects, did those in Vietnam. Another setback for Peking was the postponement and eventual cancellation of the Afro-Asian summit that was to have been held in Algiers; this development was partly the result of the deposition of Ben Bella in a military coup in June.

China's reaction to adversity was not to solicit the friendship of the USSR; it was to make her impatience with Soviet caution more manifest than ever. But just as China's intransigence can be presumed to have stemmed largely from an urge to compensate for a persisting weakness in terms of the most modern weapons so Russia's caution can be seen as reflecting the fact that she no longer felt a need to be adventurist. Solid fuelled strategic missiles mounted on mobile launchers were paraded in Moscow in May 1965 so as to demonstrate to the rest of the world that the era of American superiority in terms of thermonuclear war was drawing swiftly to a close. That the USSR was still capable of being utterly intransigent when she so wished was shown by her stubborn refusal to sign any nuclear non-proliferation treaty that left any scope for the creation of an Atlantic Nuclear Force in which Federal Germany had any kind of share in the actual or potential control over strategic weapons.

In the course of 1966 settlements were reached in respect of two long-standing international conflicts. The death through heart failure of Mr Shastri brought his Tashkent meeting with President Ayub Khan to a tragic close; but, just before Mr Shastri died, the two statesmen signed an agreement whereby India and Pakistan renounced the use of force to solve their differences. Six months later representatives of Malaysia and Indonesia signed an agreement at Bangkok which ended formally the latter's attempt to disintegrate the former by means of 'confrontation'.

The *détente* between Kuala Lumpur and Djakarta was not an unqualified blessing for it helped accelerate the worsening of relations between 'K.L.' and Singapore. It constituted, nevertheless, an important contribution to Asian stability. Elsewhere on the continent, however, the signs were less auspicious. China was plunged into turmoil by a 'cultural revolution' against all things *'bourgeois'* which was launched by young 'Red Guard' supporters of Mao Tse-tung at a Peking rally in August. Resistance to all the exhortation and intimidation this involved eventually became strong and so by the end of the year China seemed on the verge of disintegration, even the loyalty of the People's Liberation Army being in some doubt.

For some weeks during the spring South Vietnam was again rent by factional stresses additional to those produced by the Viet Cong. This time Buddhism, regionalism and military 'warlordism' combined to produce menacing disturbances in and around the Northern cities of Da Nang and Hué. But the political situation stabilized later. Meanwhile, the military situation remained a virtual stalemate but one that was maintained at a higher level of violence than before. The most publicized indices of the rise in intensity of the conflict were, of course, those measuring the growth of the American commitment. The number of American servicemen 'in country' rose to 375,000 during 1966; and from August onwards bombing of the North was extended to the Hanoi area in an attempt to make active support of the Viet Cong less easy for, and less attractive to, the North Vietnamese. But the United States remained most anxious to avoid a diplomatic or military showdown with the USSR as a result of the Vietnam war. She was, moreover, very successful at doing so. This was probably because the Soviet Union was too preoccupied with the diverse aspirations of her various Communist neighbours to feel able to pursue very dynamic policies in the world at large.

A sudden and sharp intensification of another old conflict—that between the Arab States and Israel—occurred in the closing weeks of the year. It happened when Israeli forces, reacting to infiltration by Arab guerrillas moving in through Jordan from Syria, launched a reprisal raid against a Jordanian village. Jordan's manifest inability to retaliate in kind generated renewed pressures in Cairo and elsewhere for King Hussein's overthrow and so the episode stimulated further the struggle that was developing in and around the Arabian peninsula between the revolutionaries led, in effect, by President Nasser and the more conservative elements led by King Faisal of Saudi Arabia. The rather desultory fighting that continued in Yemen and South Arabia was a key of this struggle.

Almost identical notes delivered by France on March 11th to every other sigtnatory of the Atlantic Treaty of 1949 announced her decision to conduct a unilateral withdrawal from all of NATO's military framework. This decision was, she suggested, in line with the strategic realities of the present day and was 'in no way incompatible with her membership in the Alliance nor with her participation, should the need arise in military operations at the side of her allies'. France, it transpired, would have been willing to have NATO's political headquarters stay in Paris but the other allies, spurred on by Britain and the USA, decided that, for operational and other reasons, it would be better if it joined the main military headquarters (Supreme Headquarters Allied Powers Europe) in a move to the Brussels area. The last meeting that NATO Council was ever to hold in Paris, which took place in December, showed, nevertheless, that a desire for close relations with France remained strong among NATO members. Herr Willi Brandt, for example spoke of the need to put substance into the Franco-German treaty of 1963. He was addressing the council as the Foreign Minister of the tripartite coalition that Dr Kiesinger, the new *Bundeschancellor*, had formed in Germany, following the fall of the Erhard administration. The balance of forces within this coalition reflected, in several ways, the progress that 'Europeanism' was making in Bonn at the expense of 'Atlanticism'. So, in some respects, did a small but significant revival of right wing extremism in the Federal Republic.

Britain's reaction to the French withdrawal from NATO is indicative of the emphasis her Labour government was still placing, at the beginning of 1966, on the traditional British 'special relationship' with the United States. Later in the year, on the other hand, London concentrated more wholeheartedly on the cultivation of fresh links with Europe. Two factors played a particularly important part in producing a switch of priorities that was real though seldom admitted. The lesser of them was the Bangkok settlement and the withdrawal of British forces from Borneo that this entailed; for that withdrawal meant that, since Britain had no intention of sending any troops to Vietnam, she could no longer claim any special influence over American policy in the Far East on the grounds that she was making an active contribution to the security of the area. Yet more important, however, as a formative influence on British policy, was the acute crisis the pound sterling went through on the international money market in July 1966. For this was a severe setback to Britain's hopes for rapid and sustained economic growth and so to those of maintaining some kind of major and distinctive world role.

South African refusal to co-operate fully in the operation of an oil embargo fatally undermined Britain's attempt to restore constitutional rule in Rhodesia by means of economic warfare. Therefore, in December, after the cabinet in Salisbury had refused to accept as a basis for fuller negotiations a 'working document' drawn up by Mr Ian Smith and Mr Harold Wilson at a meeting held on board a British cruiser, Britain persuaded the Security Council to make various economic sanctions, including oil, mandatory against Rhodesia for UN members. This action was, moreover, taken only a few weeks after the General Assembly had voted to end the South African mandate over South-West Africa. Thus the credibility of the United Nations as an effective law-enforcing body had become one of the factors at stake in the resolution of the essentially racial conflicts of Southern Africa.

The assumption by the UN of such wide responsibilities might have engendered more enthusiasm than, in fact, it did if the organization had been flourishing in other respects. But the deadlock over the initiation and control of peacekeeping operations was unresolved; and progress in the field of disarmament proved, in 1966, to be especially disappointing. The one positive gain that was registered in the latter respect was the sponsorship by the UN General Assembly of a general treaty banning nuclear warheads from space; and this was a singularly hollow victory because the contents of space vehicles are practically uninspectable and there are, in any case, few if any rational reasons for including in those contents nuclear bombs! Much more substantial would have been the signature of a nuclear non-proliferation treaty and the prospects for this tended, if anything, to become less bright. For the most conspicuous trend that emerged in the debates on this subject at the Eighteen Nation Disarmament Conference at Geneva was an increasing determination on the part of the potential nuclear Powers not to foreclose the nuclear option unless the existing nuclear nations committed themselves at least to the stabilization of their military nuclear programmes. So it was especially unfortunate that the Russians began that summer to extend considerably their deployment of anti-missile missiles. In order to make this possible, they followed the Americans in announcing a substantial increase in defence expenditure. Meanwhile, the growing menace of global poverty was highlighted by the acute grain shortages that afflicted such countries as China, Egypt and India. Such was the spirit of 1966.

# SELECT BIBLIOGRAPHY

Allen, G. C., *Japan's Economic Recovery*, Oxford University Press, London, 1958.

*The Annual Register of World Events*, Longmans, Green and Co., Ltd., London.

Ball, Margaret, *NATO and the European Union Movement*, Stevens and Sons, Ltd., London, 1959.

Beaton, Leonard, and Maddox, John, *The Spread of Nuclear Weapons*, Frederick A. Praeger, Inc., New York, 1962.

Behr, Edward, *The Algerian Problem*, Hodder and Stoughton, Ltd., London, 1961.

Beloff, Max, *The United States and The Unity of Europe*, The Brookings Institution, Washington, D.C., 1963.

Black, Cyril E., and Thornton, T. P., *Communism and Revolution*, Princeton University Press, Princeton, N. J., 1964.

Boyd, Andrew, *The United Nations: Piety, Myth and Truth* (rev. ed.), Penguin Books, Inc., New York, 1963.

Brecher, Michael, *Nehru: A Political Biography*, Oxford University Press, New York, 1959.

Brodie, Bernard, *Strategy in the Missile Age*, Princeton University Press, Princeton, N. J., 1959.

Buchan, Alastair, *China and the Peace of Asia*, Frederick A. Praeger, Inc., New York, 1965.

Butwell, Richard, *South East Asia: Today and Tomorrow*, Frederick A. Praeger, Inc., New York, 1961.

Carter, Gwendolen M., *The Politics of Inequality*, Frederick A. Praeger, Inc., New York, 1958.

Conquest, Robert, *Power and Policy in the USSR*, St. Martins Press, New York, 1961.

Dallin, David J., *Soviet Foreign Policy After Stalin*, J. B. Lippincott and Co., Philadelphia, Pa., 1961.

Dedijer, Vladimir, *Tito Speaks*, Weidenfeld and Nicholson, Ltd., London, 1953.

Djilas, Milovan, *The New Class*, Frederick A. Praeger, Inc., New York, 1957.

Eden, Anthony, *Memoirs: Full Circle*, ill., Houghton-Mifflin Co., Boston, Mass., 1960.

Eisenhower, Dwight D., *Mandate for Change*, New American Library, Inc., New York, 1963.

Fall, Bernard, *Street Without Joy* (rev. ed.), Stackpole Books, Harrisburg, Pa., 1966.

Fischer-Galati, Stephen (ed.), *Eastern Europe in the Sixties*, Frederick A. Praeger, Inc., New York, 1964.

Fryer, D. W., *World Economic Development*, McGraw-Hill Book Co., New York, 1965.

Galbraith, J. K., *The Affluent Society*, Houghton-Mifflin Co., Boston, Mass., 1958.

Goodspeed, Stephen S., *The Nature and Functions of International Organization*, Oxford University Press, New York, 1959.

Grindod, Muriel, *Italy*, Oxford University Press, New York, 1964.

Grosser, Alfred, *The Federal Republic of Germany: A Concise History* (trans.), Frederick A. Praeger, Inc., New York, 1964.

Hatch, John, *A History of Post-War Africa*, Frederick A. Praeger, Inc., New York, 1965.

Honey, P. J., *Communism in North Vietnam*, Massachusetts Institute of Technology Press, Cambridge, Mass., 1963.

Hoskyns, Catherine, *The Congo Since Independence*, Oxford University Press, London, 1965.

Inkeles, Alex (ed.), *Soviet Society: A Book of Readings*, Houghton-Mifflin, Boston, Mass., 1961.

Kaufmann, William, *The McNamara Strategy*, Harper and Row, New York, 1964.

Kennedy, J. F., *The Strategy of Peace*, Harper and Row, New York, 1960.

Kolarz, Walter, *Religion in the Soviet Union*, St. Martins Press. Inc., New York, 1962.

Leakey, L. S. B., *Defeating Mau Mau*, Methuen and Co., Ltd., London, 1954.

Legum, Colin, *Pan-Africanism*, Frederick A. Praeger, Inc., New York, 1965.

Lieuwen, Edwin (ed.), *Generals vs. Presidents: Neo-Militarism in Latin America*, Frederick A. Praeger, Inc., New York, 1964.

Lomax, Louis, *The Negro Revolt*, Harper and Row, New York, 1962.

Luard, Evan (ed.), *The Cold War*, Frederick A. Praeger, Inc., New York, 1964.

Mancoll, Mark (ed.), *Formosa Today*, Frederick A. Praeger, Inc., New York, 1963.

Nettl, Peter, *The Eastern Zone and Soviet Policy in Germany*, Oxford University Press, London, 1951.

O'Brien, Conor Cruise, *To Katanga and Back*, Grosset and Dunlap, Inc., New York, 1966.

Palmer, A. W., *Yugoslavia*, Oxford University Press, New York, 1964.

Partner, Peter, *A Short Political Guide to the Arab World*, Frederick A. Praeger, Inc., New York, 1960.

Patterson, George, *Peking vs. Delhi*, Frederick A. Praeger, Inc., New York, 1964.

Rees, David, *Korea—The Limited War*, St. Martins Press, New York, 1964.

Robertson, Terence, *Crisis: The Inside Story of the Suez Conspiracy*, Atheneum Publishers, New York, 1965.

Seton-Watson, Hugh, *The East European Revolution*, Frederick A. Praeger, Inc., New York, 1956.

——, *Neither War Nor Peace*, Frederick A. Praeger, Inc., New York, 1960.

Shonfield, Andrew, *Modern Capitalism*, Oxford University Press, New York, 1965.

Solzhenitsyn, Alexander, *One Day in the Life of Ivan Denisovich*, E. P. Dutton Co., New York, 1963.

Sorenson, Theodore, *Kennedy*, Harper and Row, New York, 1965.

Tew, Brian, *International Monetary Cooperation*, Hillary House Publishers, New York, 1965.

Tinker, Hugh, *India and Pakistan*, Frederick A. Praeger, Inc., New York, 1966.

Truman, Harry, *Memoirs*, Vol. II, *Years of Trial and Hope*, Doubleday and Co., Inc., New York, 1958.

Warriner, Doreen, *Land Reform and Development in the Middle East*, Oxford University Press, New York, 1962.

Werth, Alexander, *De Gaulle, A Political Biography*, Simon and Schuster, New York, 1966.

White, Theodore, *The Making of a President 1960*, Atheneum Publishers, New York, 1961.

Wildes, Harry Emerson, *Typhoon in Tokyo*, Allen and Unwin, Ltd., London, 1954.

Williams, Francis, *A Prime Minister Remembers*, William Heinemann, Ltd., London, 1961.

Williams, P. M., *The Politics of Post-War France*, Longmans, Green and Co., Ltd., London, 1954.

Windsor, Philip, *City on Leave*, Chatto and Windus, Ltd., London, 1962.

Wolfe, Thomas, *Soviet Strategy at the Crossroads*, Harvard University Press, Cambridge, Mass., 1964.

Woodman, Dorothy, *The Republic of Indonesia*, The Cresset Press, London, 1955.

Zinkin, Maurice, *Development for Free Asia*, Oxford University Press, New York, 1963.

# STATISTICAL TABLES

Note: These statistical tables have been compiled, unless otherwise noted, from the figures given in the League of Nations *International Statistical Yearbooks* (Economic and Financial Section, Geneva, 1927 to 1945) and the United Nations *Statistical Yearbooks* (Statistical Office of the United Nations, Department of Economic and Social Affairs, New York, 1949 to 1964).

Some of the individual figures are estimates made on the basis of the best available information and therefore must be used with caution. Taken together, however, they present a reasonably accurate and reliable picture of trends of production, consumption and income.

The sign '...' indicates that the figure for that year is either unavailable or negligible.

## POPULATION

### In thousands, 1900–1962

| | 1900 | 1913 | 1920 | 1925 | 1929 | 1933 | 1937 | 1946 | 1948 | 1952 | 1958 | 1962 |
|---|---|---|---|---|---|---|---|---|---|---|---|---|
| Egypt | ... | 12,144 | ... | 14,055 | 14,500 | 15,210 | 16,008 | 18,835 | 19,528 | 21,421 | 24,666 | 27,285 |
| Congo | ... | 15,000 | ... | 15,000 (est.) | 10,000 | 10,000 | 10,154 | 10,622 | 10,885 | 11,763 | 14,254 | 15,617 |
| Rhodesia | ... | 1,620 | 1,883 | 2,015 | 2,400 | 2,602 | 2,781 | 3,456 | 3,554 | 6,676 | 6,450 | 7,265 |
| S. Africa | ... | 6,323 | ... | 7,525 | 8,000 | 8,430 | 9,805 | 11,420 | 11,890 | 11,912 | 15,035 | 16,640 |
| Canada | 5,250 | 7,500 | ... | 9,400 | 10,000 | 10,760 | 11,339 | 12,307 | 13,227 | 14,430 | 17,120 | 18,600 |
| USA | 89,000 | 96,512 | ... | 116,257 | 123,000 | 126,000 | 128,961 | 141,235 | 146,571 | 156,981 | 174,882 | 186,591 |
| Mexico | ... | 15,550 | 14,235 | 15,000 | 16,000 | 17,600 | 18,737 | 22,779 | 23,876 | 26,922 | 32,895 | 37,233 |
| Argentina | 4,090 | 7,875 | ... | 10,087 | 11,000 | 12,030 | 13,490 | 15,912 | 16,420 | 18,056 | 20,060 | 21,418 |
| Brazil | ... | 25,000 | 30,636 | 32,500 | 41,000 | 44,900 | 38,687 | 46,650 | 48,350 | 54,477 | 65,740 | 75,271 |
| China | 303,000 (est.) | 441,900 | ... | 448,231 | 452,791 | 450,000 | 452,460 | 455,592 | 463,493 | ... | 646,530 | ... |
| Taiwan | ... | ... | ... | ... | ... | ... | ... | ... | ... | 8,000 | 9,851 | 11,327 |
| India | 287,000 (1891) (est.) | 320,000 | 318,000 | 325,000 | 352,370 | 363,100 | 379,778 | 329,828 | 342,120 | 367,000 | 410,686 | 449,381 |
| Pakistan | ... | ... | ... | ... | ... | ... | ... | 72,587 | 73,321 | ... | 88,762 | 96,558 |
| Indonesia | ... | 48,000 | 49,351 | 53,230 | 61,000 | 63,500 | 67,938 | 72,290 | 72,000 | 78,163 | 89,441 | 97,765 |
| Iran | 7,000 (est.) | 9,000 | ... | 9,000 | 9,000 | ... | 16,200 | 17,000 | 17,000 | 19,559 | 19,677 | 21,277 |
| Japan | 43,200 | 53,363 | ... | 59,737 | 64,700 | 67,500 | 70,040 | 75,300 | 80,171 | 85,500 | 91,540 | 94,930 |
| Turkey | ... | 19,574 | ... | 13,139 | 14,000 | 15,200 | 16,725 | 19,040 | 19,500 | 21,983 | 26,247 | 29,059 |
| France | 38,900 | 37,790 | 39,000 | 40,610 | 41,230 | 41,900 | 41,200 | 40,600 | 41,100 | 42,600 | 44,789 | 46,998 |
| W. Germany | 56,000 | 66,978 | 60,894 | 63,166 | 64,739 | 65,350 | 57,600 | 47,657 | 48,850 | 50,642 | 54,283 | 56,947 |
| E. Germany | ... | ... | ... | ... | ... | ... | ... | 18,657 | 18,500 | 18,779 | 17,355 | 17,102 |
| Italy | 32,347 | 35,598 | 37,766 | 39,113 | 40,459 | 42,217 | 42,650 | 44,994 | 45,706 | 46,865 | 49,041 | 50,170 |
| Poland | (7,960) | (10,145) | 26,746 | 29,847 | 31,084 | 33,024 | 34,359 | 23,930 | 23,970 | ... | 28,770 | 30,324 |
| Spain | 18,566 | 20,299 | 21,286 | 22,170 | 23,075 | 24,242 | 25,043 | 27,246 | 27,761 | 28,306 | 29,798 | 30,817 |
| Sweden | 5,136 | 5,639 | 5,875 | 6,044 | 6,112 | 6,212 | 6,276 | 6,719 | 6,883 | 7,125 | 7,409 | 7,562 |
| UK | 41,155 | 45,789 | 43,552 | 45,202 | 45,875 | 46,610 | 47,289 | 49,185 | 50,065 | 50,429 | 51,842 | 53,441 |
| Australia | 4,500 | 4,872 | ... | 5,992 | 6,200 | 6,657 | 6,836 | 7,466 | 7,710 | 8,649 | 9,842 | 10,705 |
| N. Zealand | ... | 1,147 | ... | 1,415 | 1,450 | 1,546 | 1,587 | 1,761 | 1,840 | 1,995 | 2,282 | 2,485 |
| USSR | 129,000 (1897) | 161,200 | ... | 141,000 | 161,000 | 168,000 | 170,000 | 193,000 | ... | ... | 206,850 | 221,465 |

# IRON ORE (CONTENTS) PRODUCTION

### In thousand metric tons, 1913–1962

| Country | 1913 | 1920 | 1929 | 1933 | 1937 | 1939 | 1946 | 1948 | 1954 | 1958 | 1962 |
|---|---|---|---|---|---|---|---|---|---|---|---|
| Egypt | 20 | 78 | 50 | ··· | ··· | ··· | ··· | ··· | ··· | ··· | ··· |
| Congo | ··· | 80 | ··· | ··· | ··· | ··· | ··· | ··· | ··· | 89 | 230 |
| Rhodesia | ··· | ··· | 7 | 25 | 7 | 4 | ··· | 15 | 35 | 84 | 384 |
| S. Africa | ··· | 2 | 38 | 170 | 295 | 312 | 656 | 699 | 1,186 | 1,416 | 2,772 |
| Canada | 279 | 117 | 123 | ··· | 850 | 874 | 773 | 1,456 | 3,673 | 7,847 | 13,920 |
| USA | 62,975[1] | 68,889[1] | 37,226 | 8,918 | 36,991 | 26,423 | 36,154 | 50,891 | 39,952 | 36,572 | 39,672 |
| Mexico | ··· | ··· | ··· | 50 | 90 | 111 | 171 | 227 | 314 | 581 | 1,091 |
| Argentina | ··· | ··· | 30 | 9[3] | 126[3] | 363[3] | ··· | 17 | 30 | 29 | 60[2] |
| Brazil | 440[1] | 1,489[1] | 971 | 540 | 240 | 297 | 396 | 1,069 | 2,088 | 3,526 | 6,652[2] |
| China | ··· | ··· | ··· | 779 | ··· | ··· | 12 | ··· | ··· | ··· | ··· |
| India | ··· | ··· | 1,545 | 170 | 1,870 | 1,930 | 1,565 | 1,483 | 2,675 | 3,739 | 8,137 |
| Pakistan | ··· | ··· | ··· | ··· | ··· | ··· | ··· | ··· | ··· | 3 | 30 |
| Iran | ··· | ··· | ··· | ··· | ··· | ··· | ··· | ··· | ··· | 149 | ··· |
| Japan | 153[1] | 315[1] | 88 | ··· | 293 | 429 | 282 | 297 | 900 | 1,146 | 2,023 |
| Turkey | ··· | ··· | ··· | ··· | ··· | 155 | 73 | 121 | 301 | 609 | 457 |
| France | 43,054[1] | 13,921[1] | 16,231 | 9,678 | 11,520 | 10,161 | 5,021 | 7,555 | 14,240 | 19,320 | 21,553 |
| W. Germany | 7,309[1] | 6,299[1] | 2,089 | 828 | 2,759 | 3,928 | 1,024 | 1,793 | 3,140 | 4,132 | 3,900 |
| E. Germany | ··· | ··· | ··· | ··· | ··· | ··· | ··· | ··· | 419 | 395 | 493 |
| Italy | 603[1] | 390[1] | 360 | 264 | 502 | 468 | 73 | 280 | 559 | 650 | 565 |
| Poland | ··· | 184[1] | 217 | 54 | 268 | 600 | 143 | 224 | 536 | 581 | 682 |
| Spain | 10,789[1] | 5,480[1] | 3,070 | 853 | 596 | 1,148 | 750 | 767 | 1,370 | 2,466 | 2,889 |
| Sweden | 7,476[1] | 4,519[1] | 6,874 | 1,685 | 9,136 | 8,360 | 4,308 | 8,205 | 9,285 | 11,027 | 13,333 |
| UK | 16,254[1] | 12,811[1] | 4,028 | 2,274 | 4,333 | 4,417 | 3,574 | 3,990 | 4,369 | 4,008 | 4,191 |
| USSR | 10,300[1] | 160[1] | 7,849[1] | 7,200 | 14,600 | 14,000 | ··· | 16,231 | 37,321 | 51,513 | 74,298 |
| Australia | 176[1] | 615[1] | 572 | 490 | 1,255 | 1,727 | 1,229 | 1,356 | 2,300 | 2,580 | 3,175 |
| N. Zealand | ··· | 4 | 4 | 3·3 | 0·3 | 0·6 | 3·4 | ··· | 1 | 1 | 1 |

(India and Pakistan figures are bracketed together — combined — for the earlier years; W. Germany and E. Germany figures are bracketed together — combined — for the earlier years.)

NOTE: The figures generally refer to the iron content of marketable ores mined. The data are sometimes only rough estimates obtained by applying a fixed percentage to the figures for production of crude ores.

[1] Ore production, not iron content.
[2] 1961 production.
[3] Exports only.

## COAL PRODUCTION

### In thousand metric tons, 1900–1962

| | 1900 | 1913 | 1920 | 1929 | 1933 | 1937 | 1939 | 1946 | 1948 | 1954 | 1958 | 1962 |
|---|---|---|---|---|---|---|---|---|---|---|---|---|
| Congo | ... | ... | ... | 114 | ... | 36 | 27 | 102 | 117 | 379 | 294 | 76 |
| Rhodesia | ... | 221 | 525 | 1,037 | 484 | 1,029 | 1,118 | 1,613 | 1,696 | 2,748 | 3,535 | 2,826 |
| S. Africa | ... | 8,205 | 10,942 | 13,018 | 10,714 | 15,491 | 16,890 | 23,602 | 24,017 | 29,315 | 37,085 | 41,275 |
| Canada | ... | 13,426 | 12,021 | 12,273 | 9,954 | 13,411 | 13,364 | 14,776 | 15,296 | 11,609 | 8,558 | 7,283 |
| USA | 244,000 | 517,060 | 597,169 | 552,309 | 347,608 | 448,303 | 402,156 | 536,837 | 592,911 | 379,154 | 389,355 | 395,552 |
| Mexico | ... | 890 | 715 | 1,054 | 647 | 1,242 | 877 | 893 | 613 | 1,314 | 1,476 | 1,107 |
| Argentina | ... | ... | ... | ... | ... | ... | 0.5 | 3.1 | 17.5 | 33 | 136 | 211 |
| Brazil | ... | 26 | 302 | 348 | 646 | 763 | 1,047 | 1,897 | 2,025 | 2,055 | 2,240 | 2,448 |
| China | ... | 13,779 | 20,670 | 18,030 | ... | 36,469 | 37,527 | 13,890 | 32,430 | 83,660 | 270,200 | ... |
| Taiwan | ... | ... | ... | ... | ... | ... | ... | 1,000 | 1,650 | 2,118 | 3,181 | 4,554 |
| India | ... | 16,468 | 18,250 | 22,721 | 20,107 | 25,438 | 28,215 | 30,187 | 30,607 | 37,471 | 46,056 | 61,370 |
| Pakistan | ... | ... | ... | ... | ... | ... | ... | ... | 245 | 563 | 607 | 990 |
| Indonesia | ... | 568 | 1,096 | 1,832 | 1,035 | 1,373 | 1,781 | 157 | 540 | 900 | 603 | 471 |
| Iran | ... | ... | ... | ... | ... | ... | 75 | 150 | 150 | 252 | 194 | 158 |
| Japan | ... | 21,316 | 29,245 | 34,258 | 32,524 | 45,258 | 52,409 | 20,368 | 33,726 | 42,718 | 49,674 | 54,399 |
| Turkey | ... | 843 | 700 | 1,421 | 1,860 | 2,307 | 2,696 | 3,831 | 4,023 | 3,690 | 4,075 | 3,893 |
| France | 33,400 | 40,016 | 24,303 | 53,780 | 46,887 | 44,346 | 49,147 | 47,155 | 43,291 | 54,405 | 57,721 | 52,359 |
| W. Germany | 149,000 | 190,109 | 107,525 | 163,441 | 109,905 | 171,124 | 174,698 | 53,940 | 99,814 | 145,758 | 150,005 | 141,999 |
| E. Germany | ... | ... | ... | ... | ... | ... | ... | ... | 2,848 | 2,648 | 2,903 | 2,575 |
| Saar | ... | ... | ... | 13,579 | 10,561 | 13,365 | 13,258 | 12,566 | ... | ... | ... | ... |
| Italy | 0.5 | 1 | 152 | 223 | 324 | 1,272 | 2,024 | 1,167 | 972 | 1,074 | 724 | 692 |
| Poland | ... | ... | 30,702 | 46,236 | 27,356 | 36,218 | 46,000 | 47,288 | 70,262 | 91,619 | 94,981 | 109,604 |
| Spain | ... | 4,016 | 5,421 | 7,108 | 5,999 | 2,084 | 6,606 | 10,759 | 10,423 | 12,398 | 14,445 | 13,880 |
| Sweden | ... | 364 | 440 | 395 | 349 | 460 | 444 | 488 | 374 | 267 | 319 | 139 |
| UK | 228,000 | 292,043 | 233,216 | 262,045 | 210,430 | 244,251 | 235,050 | 193,132 | 212,806 | 227,686 | ... | ... |
| Australia | ... | 12,614 | 13,011 | 10,532 | 9,238 | 12,268 | 13,752 | 12,977 | 15,020 | 20,080 | 20,770 | 24,874 |
| N. Zealand | ... | 1,182 | 939 | 1,389 | 857 | 986 | 1,061 | 974 | 968 | 827 | 850 | 711 |
| USSR | 16,200 | 36,011 | 7,775 | 41,668 | 76,205 | 127,968 | 145,000 | ... | 150,012 | 243,681 | 353,030 | 386,437 |

NOTE: The figures relate to anthracite and bituminous coal but exclude lignite and brown coal.

## PETROLEUM PRODUCTION

In millions of barrels, 1913–1920; in thousand metric tons, 1920–1962

| | 1913 | 1920 | 1929 | 1933 | 1937 | 1939 | 1946 | 1948 | 1954 | 1958 | 1962 |
|---|---|---|---|---|---|---|---|---|---|---|---|
| Egypt | 0·1 | 0·1 | 272 | 238 | 171 | 666 | 1,282 | 2,092 | 2,278 | 3,184 | 4,671 |
| Congo (Brazzaville) | … | … | … | … | … | … | … | … | … | … | 123 |
| S. Africa | … | … | … | … | … | … | … | 40 | 34 | 24 | … |
| Canada | 0·2 | 0·2 | 137 | 142 | 308 | 974 | 929 | 1,660 | 12,984 | 22,365 | 32,975 |
| USA | 248·4 | 442·9 | 138,104 | 122,536 | 177,661 | 170,941 | 237,526 | 273,007 | 312,846 | 330,955 | 361,658 |
| Mexico | 25·7 | 157·1 | 6,700 | 4,870 | 6,733 | 6,100 | 7,038 | 8,372 | 11,967 | 13,380 | 16,000 |
| Argentina | 0·1 | 1·7 | 1,365 | 1,951 | 2,238 | 2,655 | 2,965 | 3,323 | 4,231 | 5,102 | 14,404 |
| Brazil | … | … | … | … | … | … | … | 19 | 130 | 2,473 | 4,365 |
| China | … | … | … | 10·6 | 8·5 | 0·4 | 66·6 | 122 | 789 | 2,264 | 2 |
| Taiwan | … | … | … | … | … | … | … | 3 | 5 | 203 | … |
| India | 7·9 | 8·4 | 219 | 224 | 297 | 320 | 301 | 249 | 269 | 203 | 1,025 |
| Pakistan | … | … | … | … | … | … | … | 65 | 260 | 302 | 446 |
| Indonesia | 11·2 | 17·5 | 5,239 | 5,535 | 7,662 | 7,949 | 302 | 4,376 | 10,775 | 16,274 | 22,784 |
| Iran | 1·9 | 12·2 | 5,549 | 7,200 | 10,330 | 9,737 | 19,497 | 25,270 | 3,000 | 40,903 | 65,320 |
| Japan | 1·9 | 3·2 | … | … | 351 | 332 | 191 | 159 | 58 | 367 | 760 |
| Turkey | … | … | … | … | … | … | … | 3 | … | 329 | 595 |
| France | 0·4 | 0·4 | 75 | 79·2 | 70·5 | 70·5 | 51·7 | 70 | 526 | 1,387 | 2,370 |
| W. Germany | 0·5 | 0·2 | 103 | 238 | 451 | 741 | 649 | 635 | 2,666 | 4,432 | 6,776 |
| E. Germany | … | … | … | … | … | … | … | 9 | … | … | … |
| Italy | … | … | 6 | 26·5 | 14·4 | 12 | 10·8 | … | 72 | 1,546 | 1,808 |
| Poland | (7·8) | 5·6 | 675 | 551 | 501 | 500 | 117 | 140 | 184 | 175 | 202 |
| Spain | … | … | … | … | … | … | … | 1 | … | 72 | … |
| Sweden | … | … | … | … | … | … | … | 36 | 84 | 94 | 128 |
| UK | … | … | … | … | … | 3·7 | 56·4 | 156 | 161 | 146 | … |
| USSR | 62·8 | 25·4 | 14,477 | 21,489 | 30,500 | 29,530 | … | 29,249 | 59,281 | 113,216 | 186,242 |

NOTE: The figures refer to crude petroleum including shale oil but excluding natural gasoline.

## GRAIN PRODUCTION

Wheat unless otherwise stated; figures in thousand metric tons, 1910–1962

| | 1910–13 | 1920–24 | 1929 | 1933 | 1937 | 1948 | 1954 | 1958 | 1962 |
|---|---|---|---|---|---|---|---|---|---|
| Egypt | 93 | 977 | 1,230 | 1,087 | 1,235 | 1,089[2] | 1,729 | 1,412 | 1,605 |
| Congo[1] | 272 | 186 | 355 | 318 | ... | 324[2] | 322 | 320 | ... |
| Rhodesia[1] | 52 | 100 | 192 | 104 | 148 | 212[2] | 306 | 449 | 516 |
| S. Africa | 171 | 185 | 289 | 272 | 276 | 535 | 578 | 616 | 698 |
| Canada | 5,365 | 9,253 | 8,288 | 7,672 | 4,905 | 10,515 | 9,035 | 10,834 | 15,392 |
| USA | 18,782 | 16,107 | 22,115 | 15,029 | 23,784 | 35,749 | 26,777 | 39,665 | 29,735 |
| Mexico[1] | 300 | 2,232 | 1,468 | 1,907 | 1,635 | ... | 4,488 | 5,277 | 6,015 |
| Argentina | 4,002 | 5,345 | 4,424 | 7,787 | 5,650 | 5,200 | 7,690 | 6,720 | 5,020 |
| Brazil[1] | ... | ... | 4,484 | 5,292 | 5,560 | 5,449 | 6,690 | 7,787 | ... |
| China | ... | ... | 21,300 | 21,000 | 17,320 | 21,695[2] | 23,350 | 28,950 | ... |
| Taiwan | 41 | 23 | ... | ... | ... | 13[2] | 15 | 40 | 42 |
| India | 9,575 | 9,427 | 8,728 | 9,604 | 9,971 | ... | 8,014 | 7,997 | 11,807 |
| Pakistan | 1,547 | 1,450 | 2,002 | 1,930 | 1,984 | ... | 3,669 | 3,587 | 4,129 |
| Indonesia[1] | 643 | 726 | ... | ... | ... | ... | 2,721 | 2,634 | 3,202 |
| Iran | ... | ... | ... | ... | ... | ... | 2,100 | 2,700 | 2,700 |
| Japan | ... | ... | 830 | 1,051 | 1,372 | ... | 1,516 | 1,281 | 1,630 |
| Turkey | 3,822 | ... | 2,718 | 2,617 | 3,694 | 4,867 | 5,010 | 8,671 | 8,581 |
| France | 8,862 | 7,405 | 9,178 | 9,861 | 7,017 | 7,634 | 10,566 | 9,601 | 14,054 |
| W. Germany | 3,765 | 2,493 | 3,349 | 5,604 | 4,467 | 1,953 | 2,914 | 3,720 | 4,591 |
| E. Germany | | | | | | 941 | 1,081 | 1,363 | 1,315 |
| Italy | 4,989 | 4,849 | 7,079 | 7,923 | 8,064 | 6,155 | 7,283 | 9,815 | 9,521 |
| Poland[3] | (509) | 4,996 | 7,009 | 7,073 | 7,253 | 6,304 | 5,844 | 7,329 | 6,703 |
| Spain | 3,550 | 3,745 | 4,197 | 3,762 | ... | 2,432 | 4,798 | 4,550 | 4,820 |
| Sweden | 220 | 273 | 517 | 795 | ... | ... | 1,021 | 598 | 890 |
| UK | 1,587 | 1,952 | 1,354 | 1,700 | 1,533 | ... | 2,828 | 2,755 | 3,689 |
| USSR | 20,660 | 9,200 | 18,877 | 27,727 | 30,830[4] | 32,750[2] | 42,399 | 76,568 | 70,600 |
| Australia | 2,463 | 3,667 | 3,453 | 4,826 | 5,096 | 5,190 | 4,589 | 5,854 | 8,353 |
| N. Zealand | 188 | 192 | 197 | 231 | 156 | ... | 112 | 164 | 251 |

[1] Maize.
[2] 1948–52 average.
[3] Rye.
[4] 1935–6.

STEEL PRODUCTION

In thousand metric tons, 1900–1962

| | 1900 | 1913 | 1920 | 1929 | 1933 | 1937 | 1939 | 1946 | 1948 | 1954 | 1958 | 1962 |
|---|---|---|---|---|---|---|---|---|---|---|---|---|
| Rhodesia | .. | .. | .. | 39 | 9 | .. | .. | 7 | 9 | 33 | 60 | .. |
| S. Africa | .. | .. | .. | .. | .. | 284 | 368 | 516 | 596 | 1,431 | 1,832 | 2,634 |
| Canada | .. | 1,060 | 1,118 | 1,400 | 417 | 1,425 | 1,407 | 2,111 | 2,903 | 2,898 | 3,955 | 6,508 |
| USA | 10,000 | 31,803 | 42,809 | 57,339 | 23,605 | 51,380 | 47,898 | 60,421 | 80,413 | 80,115 | 77,342 | 89,202 |
| Mexico | .. | .. | .. | 124 | 54 | 16 | 77 | 239 | 270 | 454 | 988 | 1,851 |
| Argentina | .. | .. | .. | .. | .. | .. | .. | .. | 122 | 186 | 244 | 644 |
| Brazil | .. | 43 | 52 | 27 | 30 | 76 | 114 | 343 | 483 | 1,148 | 1,360 | 2,200 |
| China | .. | .. | .. | .. | .. | 427 | 485 | .. | 4 | 2,225 | 11,080 | 12,000 |
| Taiwan | .. | .. | .. | 20 | .. | .. | .. | .. | .. | 25 | 107 | 182 |
| India | .. | 63 | 158 | 584 | 709 | 930 | 1,066 | 1,314 | 1,277 | 1,712 | 1,842 | 5,112 |
| Pakistan | .. | .. | .. | .. | .. | .. | .. | .. | 2 | 10 | 10 | 7 |
| Japan | .. | 240 | 811 | 2,294 | 3,198 | 5,801 | 6,696 | 564 | 1,715 | 7,750 | 12,118 | 27,546 |
| Turkey | .. | .. | .. | .. | .. | .. | .. | 80 | 102 | 169 | 160 | 242 |
| France | 1,565 | 6,973 | 3,050 | 9,717 | 6,577 | 7,920 | 7,944 | 4,408 | 7,236 | 10,627 | 14,616 | 17,240 |
| Saar | .. | .. | .. | .. | 1,676 | 2,350 | 2,030 | 291 | 1,228 | .. | .. | .. |
| W. Germany | 6,461 | 12,236 | 7,798 | 16,245 | 7,617 | 19,849 | 23,633 | 2,555 | 6,790 | 20,628 | 26,265 | 32,563 |
| E. Germany | .. | .. | .. | .. | .. | .. | .. | .. | .. | 2,330 | 3,043 | 3,622 |
| Italy | 135 | 934 | 774 | 2,122 | 1,771 | 2,099 | 2,283 | 1,153 | 2,125 | 4,207 | 6,271 | 7,490 |
| Poland | .. | .. | 972 | 1,377 | 833 | 1,441 | 1,000 | 1,219 | 1,955 | 3,949 | 5,663 | 7,684 |
| Spain | 122 | 242 | 250 | 694 | 506 | .. | .. | 641 | 624 | 1,102 | 1,560 | 2,196 |
| Sweden | 300 | 750 | 498 | .. | 630 | 1,106 | 1,152 | 1,203 | 1,276 | 1,861 | 2,431 | 3,595 |
| UK | 5,500 | 7,787 | 9,213 | 9,791 | 7,137 | 13,192 | 13,434 | 12,899 | 15,116 | 18,817 | 19,879 | 20,820 |
| Australia | .. | 14 | 219 | 440 | 399 | 1,108 | 1,213 | 1,107 | 1,245 | 2,246 | 3,183 | 4,234 |
| USSR | 1,600 | 4,212 | 163 | 5,003 | 6,889 | 17,730 | 18,796 | .. | 18,639 | 41,434 | 54,920 | 76,300 |

SOURCE: As stated in the introduction; also Ingvar Svennilson, *Growth and Stagnation in the European Economy*, UN Economic Commission for Europe, Geneva, 1954, p. 260 for 1900 figures.

NOTE: The figures refer, as far as possible, to the total production of crude steel, both ingot and steel for castings.

## STEEL CONSUMPTION

Apparent consumption expressed in terms of crude steel in thousand metric tons, 1900–1962

| | 1900 | 1913 | 1922 | 1929 | 1933 | 1937 | 1952 | 1954 | 1958 | 1962 |
|---|---|---|---|---|---|---|---|---|---|---|
| Egypt | | | | | | 191 | 159 | 275 | 231 | 474 |
| Congo[2] | | | | | | 41 | 253 | 196 | 188 | 66 |
| Rhodesia | | | | | | 52 | 182 | 190 | 236 | 211 |
| S. Africa | | | | | | 941 | 1,736 | 1,751 | 2,154 | 2,376 |
| Canada | | | | | | 1,702 | 5,125 | 4,778 | 6,165 | 6,419 |
| USA | | | | | | 40,999 | 81,337 | 93,260 | 91,206 | 91,058 |
| Mexico | | | | | | 326 | 978 | 820 | 1,332 | 1,890 |
| Argentina | | | | | | 846 | 859 | 1,448 | 1,629 | 1,546 |
| Brazil | | | | | | 430 | 1,241 | 1,522 | 1,781 | 2,852 |
| China | | | | | | | 1,049 | 2,823 | 6,290 | 15,240 |
| Taiwan | | | | | | | | 118 | 136 | 330 |
| India | | | | | | 1,504 | 1,849 | 2,276 | 3,616 | 6,437 |
| Pakistan | | | | | | | | 245 | 329 | 637 |
| Indonesia | | | | | | 224 | 218 | 256 | 268 | 246 |
| Iran | | | | | | 126 | 43 | 162 | 336 | 353 |
| Japan | | | | | | 5,590 | 5,308 | 6,808 | 10,954 | 23,011 |
| Turkey | | | | | | 164 | 381 | 456 | 319 | 560 |
| France | 2,520[1] | 4,750[1] | 3,995 | 7,290 | 4,692 | 5,451 | 10,616 | 9,478 | 13,458 | 14,923 |
| W. Germany | 6,650[1] | 11,900[1] | 9,853 | 11,846 | 5,931 | 14,851 | 14,640 | 17,507 | 20,918 | 27,804 |
| E. Germany | | | | | | | | | | 6,611 |
| Italy | | 1,150[1] | 1,118 | 2,505 | 1,891 | 2,280 | 3,994 | 4,865 | 6,259 | 11,938 |
| Poland | | | 984 | 1,248 | 492 | 1,110 | | 3,906 | 5,009 | 7,197 |
| Spain | | 500[1] | 585 | 1,285 | 555 | 170 | | 1,214 | 1,644 | 2,809 |
| Sweden | 350[1] | 560[1] | 420 | 936 | 824 | 1,367 | 2,513 | 2,591 | 2,937 | 4,005 |
| UK | 4,580[1] | 6,270[1] | 3,023 | 7,450 | 5,531 | 10,921 | 16,006 | 17,139 | 18,637 | 17,731 |
| USSR | | | | | | 17,523 | 35,100 | | 49,908 | 73,981 |
| Australia | | | | | | 1,221 | 2,201 | 2,616 | 2,855 | 3,572 |
| N. Zealand | | | | | | 212 | 413 | 352 | 390 | 476 |

SOURCE: As stated in the introduction; also Svennilson, *op.cit.* pp. 276-9 for European figures
to 1933.

[1] Apparent consumption, not corrected for indirect trade.
[2] Leopoldville.

## CEMENT PRODUCTION

### In thousand metric tons, 1900–1962

| | 1913 | 1920 | 1929 | 1933 | 1937 | 1939 | 1946 | 1948 | 1952 | 1954 | 1958 | 1962 |
|---|---|---|---|---|---|---|---|---|---|---|---|---|
| Egypt | ... | ... | 180 | 288 | 323 | 368 | 588 | 768 | 947 | 1,237 | 1,511 | 2,232 |
| Congo (Leopoldville) | ... | ... | 60 | 11 | 25·5 | 35·1 | 81·5 | 127 | 240 | 346 | 393 | 162 |
| Rhodesia | ... | ... | ... | 21·5 | 52·9 | 58·5 | 66·4 | 71 | ... | 397 | 796 | 400 |
| S. Africa | ... | ... | ... | 310 | 840 | 949 | 1,180 | 1,308 | 2,021 | 2,162 | 2,722 | 2,658 |
| Canada | ... | ... | 1,945 | 477 | 979 | 910 | 1,835 | 2,221 | 2,913 | 3,592 | 5,730 | 6,207 |
| USA | 15,707 | 17,059 | 29,481 | 10,912 | 20,138 | 21,212 | 28,102 | 35,210 | 42,350 | 46,433 | 54,830 | 58,937 |
| Mexico | ... | ... | 225 | 514 | 345 | 410 | 738 | 833 | 1,757 | 1,783 | 2,539 | 3,352 |
| Argentina | ... | ... | 350 | 226 | 1,060 | 1,130 | 1,154 | 1,265 | 1,545 | 1,683 | 2,471 | 2,945 |
| Brazil | ... | ... | 96 | ... | 571 | 698 | 826 | 1,265 | 1,616 | 1,683 | 3,790 | 5,039 |
| China | ... | ... | ... | ... | ... | ... | ... | 660 | ... | 4,600 | 1,300 | 9,000 |
| Taiwan | ... | ... | 185 | 143 | 146 | 225 | 97 | 236 | 447 | 536 | 1,015 | 1,841 |
| India ⎱ | 377 | 567 | 570 | 653 | 1,142 | 1,748 | 2,068 | 1,578 | 3,594 | 4,468 | 6,186 | 8,587 |
| Pakistan | ... | ... | ... | ... | ... | ... | } | 329 | 539 | 682 | 1,089 | 1,395 |
| Indonesia | ... | ... | ... | 74 | ... | 170 | ... | 38 | ... | 147 | 299 | 511 |
| Iran | ... | ... | ... | ... | ... | ... | ... | 53 | ... | 65 | 410 | 745 |
| Japan | ... | 1,500 | 4,274 | 4,318 | 6,104 | 6,199 | 929 | 1,859 | 7,118 | 10,675 | 14,985 | 28,787 |
| Turkey | ... | ... | 65 | 143 | 226 | 284 | 325 | 336 | 459 | 703 | 1,517 | 2,323 |
| France | 1,930 | 2,550 | 5,787 | 5,221 | 4,285 | 3,600 | 3,859 | 5,830 | 8,830 | 9,557 | 13,629 | 16,852 |
| W. Germany ⎱ | 6,833 | ... | 7,039 | 3,820 | 12,605 | 14,540 | 2,328 | 5,580 | 12,886 | 15,984 | 19,737 | 28,593 |
| E. Germany | ... | ... | ... | ... | ... | ... | } | ... | ... | 2,635 | 3,558 | 5,432 |
| Italy | 1,365 | 1,050 | 3,497 | 3,554 | 4,258 | 6,112 | 2,019 | 3,211 | 6,652 | 8,776 | 12,838 | 20,157 |
| Poland | (660) | 231 | 1,008 | 411 | 1,289 | 1,500 | 1,399 | 1,824 | 2,457 | 3,403 | 5,058 | 7,544 |
| Spain | 511 | 480 | 1,820 | 1,407 | ... | 1,194 | 1,835 | 1,803 | ... | 3,323 | 4,817 | 6,788 |
| Sweden | 390 | 281 | 570 | 403 | 876 | 1,185 | 1,462 | 1,486 | 2,116 | 2,465 | 2,510 | 3,054 |
| UK | 2,923 | 2,333 | 4,776 | 4,471 | 7,361 | 8,344 | 6,679 | 8,657 | 11,316 | 12,152 | 11,854 | 14,253 |
| USSR | ... | ... | 2,367 | 2,710 | ... | ... | ... | 6,455 | ... | 18,992 | 33,308 | 57,328 |
| Australia | ... | ... | 720 | 326 | 732 | 882 | 735 | 1,029 | 1,257 | 1,727 | 2,456 | 2,935 |
| N. Zealand | ... | ... | ... | 98 | 176 | 233 | 230 | 238 | 263 | 323 | 561 | 631 |

SOURCE: As stated in the introduction; also Svennilson, *op. cit.*, pp. 282–3 for 1900–13 figures.
NOTE: The figures cover, as far as possible, all hydraulic cements used for construction.

## CEMENT CONSUMPTION

Apparent consumption in thousand metric tons, 1913–1950

| | 1913 | 1920 | 1929 | 1933 | 1939 | 1946 | 1950 |
|---|---|---|---|---|---|---|---|
| UK | 2,273 | 1,745 | 3,935 | 4,354 | 7,837 | 5,526 | 8,160 |
| Germany[1] | 5,924 | 2,200 | 6,257 | 3,714 | 14,215 | 2,673 | 9,770 |
| France | 1,652 | 1,885 | 5,720 | 4,764 | 3,228 | 3,894 | 6,589 |
| Italy | 1,332 | 1,053 | 3,482 | 3,463 | 4,605 | 2,078 | 4,850 |
| Sweden | 265 | 218 | 469 | 367 | 1,182 | 1,579 | 1,689 |
| Poland | (590) | 191 | 925 | 409 | 1,500 | 1,025 | 2,262 |
| Spain | 581 | 458 | 1,991 | 1,405 | 1,158 | 1,773 | 2,047 |

SOURCE: Svennilson, *op.cit.*, pp. 284–5.

[1] From 1946, West Germany and Saar only.

## MERCHANT SHIPPING

### Fleets in thousands gross registered tons, 1913–1962

| | 1913 | 1921 | 1929 | 1933 | 1937 | 1939 | 1948 | 1952 | 1958 | 1962 |
|---|---|---|---|---|---|---|---|---|---|---|
| Egypt | ... | ... | ... | 46·6 | 68·5 | ... | 82 | 92·8 | 129 | 237 |
| S. Africa | ... | ... | ... | 523[1] | 537[1] | 629[1] | 456[1] | 414[1] | 194 | 233 |
| Canada | ... | 1,134 | 1,335 | 1,331 | 1,257 | 1,223 | 2,007 | 1,692 | 1,516 | 1,704 |
| USA | 5,429 | 17,026 | 14,376 | 12,563 | 11,788 | 11,362 | 29,165 | 27,245 | 25,590 | 23,273 |
| Mexico | ... | ... | 54 | 40 | 33·5 | 30·4 | 114 | 160 | 162 | 201 |
| Argentina | 215 | 167 | 297 | 318 | 293 | 291 | 683 | 1,034 | 1,029 | 1,262 |
| Brazil | 329 | 499 | 561 | 489 | 473 | 485 | 706 | 794 | 911 | 1,204 |
| China | 87 | 163 | 319 | 400 | 600 | 258 | 809 | 614 | 540 | 522 |
| Taiwan | ... | ... | ... | ... | ... | ... | ... | ... | ... | 486 |
| India | ... | 197 | 199 | 187 | 221 | 238 | 315 | 477 | 674 | 1,013 |
| Pakistan | ... | ... | ... | ... | ... | ... | ... | 142 | 128 | 313 |
| Indonesia | ... | ... | ... | ... | ... | ... | ... | ... | 119 | 335 |
| Japan | 1,500 | 3,355 | 4,186 | 4,258 | 4,475 | 5,630 | 1,024 | 2,787 | 5,465 | 8,870 |
| Turkey | 157 | ... | 172 | 188 | 195 | 224 | 241 | 444 | 596 | 729 |
| France | 2,201 | 3,652 | 3,378 | 3,470 | 2,844 | 2,934 | 2,786 | 3,638 | 4,338 | 5,162 |
| W. Germany | 5,082 | 717 | 4,093 | 3,888 | 3,928 | 4,483 | 428 | 1,398 | 4,056 | 4,924 |
| E. Germany | ... | ... | ... | ... | ... | ... | ... | ... | 21 | 315 |
| Italy | 1,522 | 2,651 | ... | 3,285 | 3,174 | 3,425 | 2,100 | 3,289 | 4,900 | 5,412 |
| Poland | ... | ... | 50 | 67·1 | 93·2 | 121·6 | 180 | 278·6 | 458 | 867 |
| Spain | 841 | 1,116 | 1,161 | 1,218 | 1,044 | 902 | 1,147 | 1,216 | 1,607 | 1,995 |
| Sweden | 1,047 | ... | 1,510 | 1,658 | 1,494 | 1,577 | 1,973 | 2,332 | 3,303 | 4,167 |
| UK | 18,696 | 19,572 | 20,166 | 18,592 | 17,436 | 17,891 | 18,025 | 18,624 | 20,286 | 21,658 |
| USSR | 974 | 413 | 440 | 843 | 1,258 | 1,316 | 2,097 | ... | 2,966 | 4,684 |
| Australia | ... | 694 | 678 | 642 | 657 | 495 | 524 | 559 | 631 | 574 |
| N. Zealand | ... | ... | ... | ... | ... | 175 | 184 | 232 | 256 | 241 |

NOTE: The figures relate to merchant shipping registered in each country on July 30th of the year stated. Gross registered tons equal 100 cubic feet or 2·83 cubic metres. Only vessels of 100 gross tons and more are included.

[1] All British colonies in South Africa.

## SUMMARY OF BALANCE OF PAYMENTS

From 1929 to 1938 in millions of old US gold dollars
From 1946 to 1962 in millions of currency units

| | 1929 | 1933 | 1938 | 1946 | 1948 | 1954 | 1958 | 1962 |
|---|---|---|---|---|---|---|---|---|
| Egypt (E£) | … | … | … | 11·2 | 3·9 | -0·2 | -6·2 | -4·0 |
| N. and S. Rhodesia (R £) | … | … | … | 23·6 | … | -1·6 | 5·8 | 4·7 |
| S. Africa (SA £) | -73·6 | 62·8 | -26·2[4] | … | … | 76 | 12 | 24 |
| Congo (Belgian Congo F) | … | … | … | … | 92 | … | … | … |
| USA (US $) | 95 | -31 | -300 | 156 | 1,152[1] | -147 | 488[1] | -1,025[1] |
| Canada (C $) | -27·7 | -7·7 | 14·5 | 4 | 0[1] | 167[1] | 0[1] | 0[1] |
| Mexico (US $) | … | … | … | 82 | 6·8 | -98·6 | -70 | -267 |
| Argentina (US $) | 3·3 | -2·8 | -72·8 | -22 | 186·6 | -98·5 | 1·1 | -6·6 |
| Brazil (US $) | … | … | … | … | 14 | 15 | -161 | -68 |
| China | … | … | 74·9[5] | 39 | … | … | … | … |
| Taiwan (US $) | -22·8 | -58·8 | … | … | … | -0·4 | 6·1 | -1·7 |
| India (Rupee) | -62·6 | 16·6 | -54 | 45 | -604 | -45 | -215 | -89 |
| Pakistan (Rupee) | … | … | … | … | 6·3 | 22·8 | -25·8 | -49·8 |
| Indonesia (US $) | -34·6[2] | 3·6[2] | -39·7[2] | -49[2] | -9 | … | -9 | -41 |
| Iran (US $) | … | … | … | -469[7] | 10·2 | -59 | 13·9 | 9 |
| Japan (US $) | -17·7 | -36·1 | -23·8[5] | -20 | 26·9 | 17·7 | 71·6 | 5·7 |
| Turkey (US $) | -39·7 | 9·1 | … | -134·8 (M £T) | 17·6 | 10·3 | -30·8 | -4·5 |
| France (US $) | 0 | 0 | … | -5 | -6·9 | 39·5 | -16·4 | 53·8[3] |
| W. Germany (DM) | | | … | … | … | 416 | 400 | 400 |
| E. Germany | … | … | … | … | … | … | … | … |
| Italy (US $) | -1·0 | -5·5 | -4·5[4] | -101 | -3·2 | -35·7 | 37·0 | -792·4 |
| Poland (US $) | … | … | … | -15 | … | … | … | … |
| Spain (US $) | -45·3 | -38·9[6] | -12·5 | … | … | 11·6 | -15·2 | 79·3 |
| Sweden (Kronor) | … | -4·3 | … | 19 | 374 | -69 | 464 | 339 |
| UK (£) | -57·7 | -40 | -30·9 | 68 | 48·9 | -27 | 43 | 115 |
| Australia (A £) | 33·1 | -47·4 | 7·7 | 12 | … | -19·3 | 34·5 | 197 |
| N. Zealand (NZ £) | … | … | … | … | … | -8·3 | -4·7 | 4·95 |

NOTE: No sign indicates a credit and a minus sign indicates a debit.

[1] Excluding military end-items and service donated which amounted to in millions of US $:

| | Canada | USA |
|---|---|---|
| 1961 | 35 | 1,539 |
| 1958 | 148 | 2,281 |
| 1954 | 284 | 3,161 |
| 1948 | … | 300 |

[2] Million Indonesian guldens.
[3] In 1961.
[4] In 1937.
[5] In 1936.
[6] In 1932.
[7] In million rials.

## VALUE OF IMPORTS AND EXPORTS

In million US dollars, 1929–1948

| | 1929 | 1933 | 1937 | 1939 | 1946 | 1948 |
|---|---|---|---|---|---|---|
| Congo | ... | 19·4 | 41·4 | 33·5 | 77·9 | 190·8 |
| | | 31·2 | 74·1 | 46·8 | 126·4 | 237·5 |
| Egypt | 454 | 150 | 193 | 155 | 330 | 663 |
| | 431 | 161 | 200 | 152 | 285 | 591 |
| N. Rhodesia[1] | 29·9 | 11·1 | 20·0 | 20·6 | 32·7 | 64·8 |
| | 7·6 | 21·0 | 59·3 | 45·6 | 53·1 | 114·7 |
| S. Rhodesia | 72·3 | 25·6 | 41·9 | 40·0 | 83·2 | 176·4 |
| | 50·7 | 15·5 | 31·2 | 25·8 | 68·3 | 106·3 |
| S. Africa | 676 | 272 | 506 | 404 | 859 | 1,420 |
| | 422 | 141 | 208 | 151 | 385 | 540 |
| Canada | 2,200 | 488 | 811 | 723 | 1,838 | 2,630 |
| | 1,995 | 645 | 1,012 | 901 | 2,241 | 3,103 |
| USA | 7,557 | 1,996 | 3,176 | 2,403 | 4,966 | 7,197 |
| | 9,015 | 2,228 | 3,361 | 3,192 | 9,776 | 12,663 |
| Mexico | 306 | 89 | 170 | 121 | 542 | 581 |
| | 482 | 121 | 219 | 150 | 316 | 465 |
| Argentina | 1,388 | 378 | 482 | 353 | 588 | ... |
| | 1,537 | 470 | 758 | 466 | 1,168 | ... |
| Brazil | 714 | 232 | 331 | 262 | 674 | 1,134 |
| | 781 | 291 | 350 | 305 | 942 | 1,173 |
| China | 1,254 | 495 | 280 | 158 | 561 | ... |
| | 761 | 245 | 363 | 122 | 148 | ... |
| India | 1,626 | 488 | 677 | 560 | 1,077 | 1,561 |
| | 2,001 | 654 | 717 | 701 | 960 | 1,274 |
| Iran[2] | 130·2 | 55·5 | 85·4 | 58·6 | 119·1 | ... |
| | 225·4 | 124·0 | 159·3 | 140·6 | 303·0 | ... |
| Dutch E. Indies | 784 | 226 | 280 | 258 | 106 | 428 |
| | 1,009 | 333 | 550 | 418 | 58 | 392 |
| Japan | 2,142 | 837 | 1,363 | 1,073 | 305 | 683 |
| | 2,030 | 794 | 1,200 | 1,317 | 103 | 259 |
| Turkey | 210·6 | 59·7 | 90·5 | 92·8 | 113·5 | 275 |
| | 126·3 | 76·9 | 109·5 | 99·5 | 209·0 | 196·8 |

## VALUE OF IMPORTS AND EXPORTS—*continued*

### In million US Dollars, 1929–1948

| | 1929 | 1933 | 1937 | 1939 | 1946 | 1948 |
|---|---|---|---|---|---|---|
| France | 3,867 | 1,891 | 1,703 | 1,119 | 1,965 | 3,347 |
| | 3,337 | 1,229 | 960 | 807 | 854 | 2,012 |
| W. Germany ⎫ | | | | | 712 | 1,581 |
| ⎬ | 5,441 | 1,712 | 2,205 | 2,440 | 227 | 706 |
| ⎪ | 5,448 | 1,979 | 2,384 | 2,266 | | |
| E. Germany ⎭ | | | | | ... | ... |
| | | | | | ... | ... |
| Italy | 1,898 | 656 | 735 | 542 | ... | 1,499 |
| | 1,316 | 528 | 550 | 569 | ... | 1,068 |
| Poland | 593 | 157 | 239 | 145[3] | 144 | 510 |
| | 535 | 183 | 227 | 148 | 127 | 528 |
| Spain | 894 | 273 | ... | 112[3] | 302 | 470 |
| | 691 | 220 | ... | 78 | 266 | 361 |
| Sweden | 810 | 320 | 542 | 602 | 879 | 1,130 |
| | 823 | 313 | 511 | 454 | 708 | 1,107 |
| UK | 10,128 | 3,838 | 5,185 | 3,783 | 5,267 | 8,381 |
| | 6,989 | 2,366 | 2,999 | 2,198 | 3,894 | 6,841 |
| USSR[1] | 767 | 303 | 256 | ... | ... | ... |
| | 805 | 431 | 329 | ... | ... | ... |
| Australia | 1,062 | 298 | 408 | 426 | 568 | 1,082 |
| | 1,130 | 450 | 583 | 461 | 637 | 1,316 |
| N. Zealand | 399 | 117 | 224 | 179 | 231 | 448 |
| | 446 | 180 | 258 | 203 | 321 | 505 |

SOURCE: *UN Statistical Yearbook*, 1948

NOTE: The top figure gives the value of imports; the bottom figure the value of exports.
All figures are expressed in US dollars of the gold content fixed on January 31st, 1934.

[1] Excluding silver.
[2] Including petroleum.
[3] 7 months.

ESTIMATES OF NATIONAL INCOME

1929–1962

| | 1929 | 1933 | 1937 | 1939 | 1946 | 1954 | 1958 | 1962 |
|---|---|---|---|---|---|---|---|---|
| Egypt, million E £ | ... | ... | ... | ... | ... | 869·4 | 1,187·8 | ... |
| Congo (Leopoldville), million francs | ... | ... | ... | ... | ... | 44,560 | 48,050 | ... |
| Rhodesia, million £ | 14 | 11·1 | 19·2 | 28·2 | 47·7 | 310·2 | 409 | 491·4 |
| S. Africa[2], million rand | 257 | 278 | 375 | 434 | 690 | 3,039 | 3,715 | 4,601[1] |
| Canada, million C $ | 4,789 | 2,452 | 4,062 | 4,373 | 9,821 | 19,002 | 24,986 | 30,509 |
| USA, 1000 million $ | 87·3 | 39·6 | 73·6 | 72·5 | 180·28 | 300·3 | 364·7 | 450·3 |
| Mexico, 1000 million pesos | 2·8 | 2·7 | 4·9 | 5·7 | 24·1 | 64·4 | 114·7 | 160·5 |
| Argentina, 1000 million pesos | ... | ... | 9·3 | 29·3 | 120·3 | 106·3 | 271·2 | 905·6 |
| Brazil, 1000 million cruzeiros | ... | ... | ... | ... | ... | 451·2 | 1,046·2 | ... |
| China, 1000 million yuan | ... | ... | ... | ... | ... | 74 | 125 | ... |
| Taiwan, million NT $ | ... | ... | ... | ... | ... | 18,807 | 32,827 | 58,731 |
| India, 1000 million rupees | ... | ... | ... | ... | 87·3 | 96·1 | 126 | 140·3[1] |
| Pakistan, million rupees | ... | ... | ... | ... | ... | 20,116 | 21,379 | 24,069[1] |
| Indonesia[3] 1000 million rupiahs | 4,971 | 2,070 | 2,768 | 2,933 | 2,123·6 | 91·8 | 174·2 | ... |
| Japan, 1000 million yen | ... | ... | 16·8 | ... | ... | 5,984 | 8,359 | 15,421 |
| Turkey, million Liras | ... | ... | 1,606[4] | ... | ... | 14,785 | 33,873 | 52,603 |
| France, 1000 million NF | 0·25 | 0·2 | 0·28 | ... | 26 | 122·3 | 188·6 | 270·6 |
| W. Germany, 1000 million DM | 72·3 | 44 | 71·5 | 87·2 | ... | 121·1 | 180·1 | 273·2 |
| E. Germany, million DM | ... | ... | ... | ... | ... | ... | 64,899 | 79,547 |
| Italy, 1000 million Lire | ... | ... | 131[4] | ... | ... | 9,931 | 13,468 | 19,393 |
| Poland, 1000 million zlotys | ... | ... | ... | ... | ... | ... | 321·3 | 426·1 |
| Spain, 1000 million pesetas | ... | ... | ... | ... | ... | 292·8 | 498·6 | 670·6 |
| Sweden, million kronor | 8,220 | 6,840 | 10,274 | ... | 21,790 | 38,891 | 50,466 | 66,669 |
| UK, million £ | 4,178 | 3,728 | 4,616 | 5,482 | 8,662 | 14,447 | 18,427 | 22,631 |
| USSR[5], 1000 million new roubles | 28,900 | 48,500 | 96,300 | 128,300[6] | ... | 84 | 126 | 166 |
| Australia, million A £ | 726 | 622 | 832 | 861 | 1,388 | 3,997 | 4,924 | 6,251 |
| N. Zealand, million NZ £ | ... | 101·3 | 173·3 | 210·1 | 365·9 | 802 | 962 | 1,240 |

(In the original, braces link the W. Germany and E. Germany rows for 1929 and 1954, indicating combined figures.)

NOTE: National income is the sum of the incomes accruing within a year to the factors of production supplied by the normal residents of a country, before deduction of direct taxes, and equals the sum of compensation of employees, income from unincorporated enterprises, rent, interest and dividends accruing to households, savings of corporations, direct taxes on corporations and general government income from property and entrepreneurship.

1 In 1961.    2 Until 1946 in million SA £.    3 Until 1939 in million guilders.
4 In 1938.    5 Until 1940 in million roubles.    6 In 1940.

# FOREIGN INVESTMENTS IN THE UNITED STATES

In millions US dollars, according to various estimates, 1897–1919

| | 1897 | 1908[1] | 1914 | 1919 |
|---|---|---|---|---|
| Great Britain | 2,500 | 3,500 | 4,250 | 1,595 |
| Germany | 200 | 1,000 | 950 | 550 |
| The Netherlands | 240 | 750 | 635 | 410 |
| France | 50 | 500 | 410 | 130 |
| Canada | … | … | 275 | 315 |
| Belgium | 20 | … | … | … |
| Austria-Hungary | … | … | 150 | 112 |
| Switzerland | 75 | … | | |
| Others | … | 250 | 420 | 250 |
| Floating Loans | … | 400 | 110 | 324 |
| Total | 3,395 | 6,400 | 7,200 | 3,686 |
| Gross American Investment Abroad | 685 | 2,525 | 3,514 | 6,956 |
| Net Foreign Investment | +2,710 | +3,875 | +3,576 | −2,971 |
| Net American Investment Abroad | −2,710 | −3,875 | −3,576 | +2,971 |
| American Government Loans | | | | 9,591 |
| Total American Overseas Investment | | | | 12,562 |

SOURCE: Cleona Lewis and Karl T. Schlottebeck, *America's Stake in International Investments*, (Washington, D.C., 1938)

[1] This estimate, by Sir George Paish, probably exaggerates the level of investment of Germany, France and the Netherlands by contrast with the more careful calculations of 1914 which are based on the statistics of dollar investments prepared by Allied governments and the American Custodian of Enemy Property in 1919.

# INDEX

# INDEX

# INDEX

Benin state, 101
Bennett, R. B., 427, 480
Benois, Aleksandr, 200
ben-Yussef, Sidi Mohammed, 757
Benz, Karl, 31
Beran, Archbishop, 634, 715
Berchtold, Count, 207
Berg, Alban, 202
Bergson, Henri, 198, 200, 203
Beria, Laurentia, 630, 701
Berlin
    Baghdad railway project, see Baghdad
      Railway
    Congresses of, 1878 and 1885, 38,
      40, 62, 97, 101, 117
    Post World War II—
      airlift, the, 645
      crisis 1961, 724
      Foreign Ministers' conference
        1954, 722, 737
      Kommandatura, four-power, 642,
        644, 645, 646
      rising 1952, 708
      'Wall, the', 705, 706
Bermuda, 547
Bernstein, Edouard, 51
Betancourt, Ròmulo, 479
Bethlen, Stephen, 341, 342
Bethmann-Hollweg, Chancellor, 152,
    167, 227, 243
Bevan, Aneurin, 784
Bevin, Ernest, 325, 395, 517, 538
Bezobrazov, Tsarist officer, 131, 132,
    133
Bhave, Vinobe, 744
Bianchi, Michele, 336
Bidault, Georges, 647, 648, 758, 759
Bikini atoll, 734
*Bilaim*, Zionist group, 56
Billoux, François, 652
*Bismarck*, battleship, 556
Bismarck, Otto von, 37, 38, 40, 48, 58
    European policies, 117, 121–3
Bismarck Islands, 580
Björko Treaty 1905, 142
Björnson, Bjornstjerne, 147
Black Hand secret society, 189, 206,
    208, 213
Blanchard, General Georges, 539
*Blaue Reiter* school, 199, 202, 265
Blériot, Louis, 31
Blücher, Marshal Vassili, 379, 413, 455
Blum, Léon, 440, 441, 497, 649
Blyden, E. W., 106
Bock, Field Marshal von, 531, 559, 560
Boer War, see South Africa

Bolivia, 391, 479, 688
    Catavi massacre, 478
    Gran Chaco war, 478
Bolsheviks, see under Russia, Tsarist,
    and USSR
*Bomarc* missile, 788
Bonar Law, see Law, Bonar
Bonomi, Ivanoe, 334, 336, 582
Borah, William E., 392
Borden, Sir Robert, 70, 375, 388
Boris III, King, of Bulgaria, 316
Bormann, Martin, 601
Borneo, 742
    Indonesian infiltration into, 743, 804
Borodin, Alexander, 22
Borodin, Michael, 379, 407, 408, 413
Bosanquet, Bernard, 203
Boselli, Paolo, 233
Bosnia Herzegovina, 207
    Archduke's murder 1914, 206–7
    crisis 1908–9, 155–6, 158, 159, 160
Botha, Louis, 73
Boum, Oum, 739
Bourguiba, Habib, 492
Boxer rebellion, see under China
Bradley, General Omar, 593, 597
Brandeis, Louis, 193
Brandt, Willy, 723, 804
Braque, Georges, 199
Brauchitsch, Field Marshal von, 560
Brazil, 61, 99, 100, 108, 194, 389,
    391, 470, 473, 474–6, 688, 769,
    773
    Brasilia, creation of, 769
    economic dependence on US, 475
    fascism in, 474–5
    Volta Redondo steel works, 475
    World War II contributions, 564
Breshnev, Leonid, 799
*Breslau*, German cruiser, 220
Brest-Litovsk, treaty of, 251, 252
    253–4, 256, 303
Breton, André, 265
Briand, Aristide, 141, 150, 159, 227,
    242, 307, 308, 329, 391, 392, 440,
    441
Briggs, Sir Harold, 670
Britain, battle of, 295
British Broadcasting Corporation,
    394–5, 592
British Guiana, 67
British Petroleum (Anglo-Iranian Oil
    Company), 751
British South Africa Company, 34
Brooke, Rupert, 200, 216
Brown, Sir Arthur Whitten, 294

# INDEX

# INDEX

# INDEX

# INDEX

Nagasaki, atom bombing of, 607
Nagy, Ferenc, 635
Nagy, Imre, 709, 712, 713
Nahas Pasha, 369
Napoleon Bonaparte, 29, 62
Napoleon III (Louis Napoleon), 36
Nassau agreement 1962, 724, 786
Nasser, Colonel Gamal Abdel, 715, 752–4, 756, 804
    Suez War and, 753
Nasution, Colonel, 743
Natal colony, 74
National Association for the Advancement of Coloured People, 107
National Recovery Act (US), 466–7
Nationalism, emergence of, in Europe, 39–41; in Far East, 78 (see also individual countries)
NATO (North Atlantic Treaty Organization), 650, 651, 675, 705, 720, 751
    Atlantic Nuclear Force, 800, 803
    Brussels Treaty, 717
    French attitude to, 802, 804
    Multilateral Fleet proposals, 724, 786, 800
    West Germany, admission to, 717, 723, 724
Nazimuddin, Khwaja, 668
Ne Win, General, 741
Negrin, Juan, 499
Nehru, Jawaharlal, 283, 487, 655, 666, 667, 668–9, 700, 745, 746, 747, 749, 790, 798, 799
Nehru, Motilal, 377
Nejd, the, 26, 182, 236, 370
Nenni, Pietro, 649, 652, 720
Netherlands, the, 42, 47, 317
    colonial empire, 23, 24, 94, 108, 113, 114, 486
        administrative policies in, 94–5, 95–6, 110–11, 487
        Indonesian Republic established, 671
        Japanese conquests in, 567
        West Irian (New Guinea) crisis, 742–3
    Depression, Great, effects of, 435
    World War I neutrality, 216
    World War II, 536, 538–9, 547, 561, 564
    Lend-Lease aid, 565
Neuilly, treaty of (1919), 309
Neurath, Constantin von, 529
New Deals, see under Roosevelt, Franklin Delano

New Guinea, 304, 375, 567, 580, 671, 742–3
New Ireland, 304
New Zealand, 26, 167
    defence policy, post-1945, 788
    Depression, Great, effects of, 428
    early development of, 26, 74–5, 76–7
    exclusion of Orientals, 74, 76, 77
    inter-war years, 375–6, 489–90
    Japan, fear of, 75, 77, 174–5, 375
    Maori people, 74, 76, 78, 93, 105, 111–12, 376
    World War I
        contribution to, 77, 225
        mandate awards, 304, 375
    World War II, 490, 549
Newfoundland, 547, 560
    incorporated into Canada, 480
Ngo Dinh Diem, 740, 741
Nicaragua, 195, 388, 470–1, 768
Nicholas II, Tsar, 119, 133, 139, 140, 156, 186, 206, 210, 213, 245, 246
    'Fundamental Laws' of, 139–40
    October Manifesto, 139
Nicholas, Grand Duke, 231, 235
Nicholas, King, of Montenegro, 356
Nicholas, Prince, of Rumania, 353
Nielsen, Danish composer, 202
Nietzsche, Friedrich, 59, 200, 203, 337
Nigeria, 104, 678, 679, 762
    independence granted, 760
    Royal Nigeria Company, 34
Nijinsky, Vaslav, 202
Nine-Power Treaty (on China), 415
Nitti, Francesco, 334
Nivelle, General, 230, 241, 242
Nixon, Richard, 624, 687, 760, 779
Nkomo, Joshua, 764
Nkrumah, 281, 492, 678, 715, 798
    President of Ghana, 760, 762
Nobel, Alfred, 44
    Nobel Peace Prize, 56
Nolde Emil, 198
Nomura, Admiral Kichisaburo, 561
Non-aligned Nations, Conference of, 1961, 715
Norris, Frank, 66
Northern Securities case (US), 129
Norway, 38, 431, 435
    break-up of union with Sweden, 146–8, 153
    EFTA, membership of, 719
    World War II, 535, 536
Noske, Gustav, 344, 345
Nouvelle Revue Française (Gide), 201
Nova Scotia, linguistic anomaly in, 71

# INDEX

THE WORLD IN 1965